"This book is destined to become the standard work on Biblical eschatology. It is a very balanced and scholarly treatment from a devout evangelical who is committed to the inspired word of god."

EDGAR F. SANDERS
Director Biblical Research Institute

"The most exhaustive work I know of on the subject of predictive prophecy and its fulfillment. It will be the standard work on the subject for years to come and should be in the libraries of clergymen, theological seminaries, and institutions of higher learning."

HAROLD LINDSELL
Editor
Christianity Today

"It is a major work of unusual scope. Although the viewpoint of the author is obvious, he does not overemphasize it, but indicates different methods of interpretation and possible alternative conclusions in controversial passages. In my opinion, the greatest value of this work is its correlation of all possible predictive prophecy into one sequence of presentation, so that other interpreters can gain a better perspective on the total subject."

MERRIL C. TENNEY
Professor of Bible and Theology
Wheaton College

". . . A helpful reference book in any pastor's library."

M. A. LUNN
Department of Publications
Church of the Nazarene

"The material is presented in a manner serviceable to the general public no less than to scholars. Its usefulness is not limited to those of a particular eschatological bent."

CARL F. H. HENRY
Eastern Baptist Theological Seminary

Encyclopedia of Biblical Prophecy

ENCYCLOPEDIA

OF BIBLICAL

PROPHECY

The Complete Guide to Scriptural

Predictions and Their Fulfillment

J. BARTON PAYNE

WIPF & STOCK · Eugene, Oregon

Grateful acknowledgment is made to the following publishers for permission to reprint from copyrighted material: THE LOCKMAN FOUNDATION: *The New American Standard Bible and New Testament,* Copyright © 1960, 1962, 1963, 1968, 1971 The Lockman Foundation; ABINGDON PRESS: *The Interpreter's Bible*; John Bright, *The Kingdom of God*; BAKER BOOK HOUSE: Louis Berkhof, *Principles of Biblical Interpretation*; J. Barton Payne, *Outline of Hebrew History*; Bernard Ramm, *Protestant Biblical Interpretation*; WM. B. EERDMANS PUBLISHING CO.: *The New International Commentary*; H. L. Ellison, *Ezekiel: The Man and His Message*; J. Barton Payne, *The Imminent Appearing of Christ*; Geerhardus Vos, *Biblical Theology*; A. J. HOLMAN COMPANY: *The Biblical Expositor*; JOHN KNOX PRESS: Claus Westermann (ed.), *Essays on Old Testament Hermeneutics*; NAZARENE PUBLISHING HOUSE: *Beacon Bible Commentary*, Copyright 1964 Beacon Hill Press of Kansas City; ZONDERVAN PUBLISHING HOUSE: J. Barton Payne, *The Theology of the Older Testament,* Copyright © 1962 Zondervan Publishing House; J. Dwight Pentecost, *Things to Come,* Copyright 1958 Dunham Publishing Company; Merrill F. Unger, *Zechariah,* Copyright © 1963 Zondervan Publishing House.

Wipf and Stock Publishers
199 W 8th Ave, Suite 3
Eugene, OR 97401

Encyclopedia of Biblical Prophecy
The Complete Guide to Scriptural Predictions and Their Fulfillment
By Payne, J. Barton
Copyright © 1973 by Payne, J. Barton All rights reserved.

Hardcover ISBN-13: 978-1-7252-8674-0

Publication date 9/3/2020
Previously published by Harper & Row, 1973

This edition is a scanned facsimile of the original edition published in 1973.

Preface

We live in an uncertain world. Men of today are casting about eagerly, and
almost pathetically, in search of meaningfulness. For while we have amassed
knowledge, we seem to have missed truth. Indeed, apart from God and from
His revealed words that constitute the Bible,[1] mankind and life and time
do seem to be essentially purposeless. Yet the Lord of grace, who once sent
His Son Jesus Christ to redeem the world (John 3:16), will some day send
Him again to lead this world into its intended goal of glorifying God
(Rom. 11:36). This is the hope which pervades the whole of Scripture,
both Old and New; for even "the Old Testament foreshadowing [of Christ]
is far more than a matter of isolated and detailed predictions; it is something organic to Israel's faith itself."[2]

Evangelical Christianity has consistently recognized that the Bible is
mankind's only valid source of truth in respect to God and to the future.
Scholars in this tradition have therefore devoted themselves to the exposition of the Holy Book and through the years have produced thorough
commentaries on its various portions. It is not the purpose of the present
survey to replace the more detailed exegetical studies; and throughout the
pages that follow, footnoted references are made to these works, primarily
to those which are more readily available in English, for the reader's
further guidance. But there still remains an urgent need within Christian
literature for a synthesis of God's "precious and magnificent promises"
(II Pet 1:4, NAS). Currently there exist a number of books, some on
specialized prophetic themes, and others on introductory matters of prophetic interpretation; but perhaps simply because of the vast bulk of the
revelational matter that is involved, no truly comprehensive study has as

1. See below, p. 6.
2. John Bright, *The Kingdom of God,* p. 212.

yet been undertaken. As a representative of the former type of book, J. Dwight Pentecost's *Things to Come* states of its own, by no means inconsiderable content, "There has been little attempt to synthesize the whole field of prophecy . . . and there is a great need for a synthetic study and presentation of Biblical prophecy";[3] or, as a representative of the latter type, Robert B. Girdlestone's *Grammar of Prophecy* confesses about itself, "No attempt is made to give a complete interpretation of prophecy."[4] The author can thus do no more than repeat Girdlestone's quotation from Bacon's *Advancement of Learning,* in which he notes the need, even at his day, for a study in which "every prophecy of the Scripture be sorted with the event fulfilling the same throughout the ages of the world, both for the better confirmation of faith, and for the better illumination of the Church touching those parts of prophecies which are yet unfulfilled. . . . This is a work which I find deficient; but it is to be done with wisdom, sobriety, and reverence, or not at all."[5]

It is my hope that the following study will be of assistance to Christian believers, in providing the perspective that is to be gained through synthesis and the advantages of having before one a comprehensive picture. For those who are not commited to the full authority of Scripture and might wish, personally, to accept somewhat less than the whole of the Bible's content—e.g. in those areas that are of a yet future fulfillment—it is hoped that this volume may assist in presenting at least what the Biblical teachings appear to be. For the amillennialist, who visualizes no future Messianic kingdom on earth, it is hoped that those passages designated, "Fulfillment: period 16 (= the millennium)," may be incorporated into other periods of accomplishment without detriment to the study as a whole. For dispensationalists, who would find more predictive material (especially in reference to the "tribulation" period), whether through a more elaborate typology or through the addition of yet future ideas to those predictions that have now already been fulfilled (by theories of a "double sense" or of "compenetration"), it is hoped that what follows may provide a solid point of departure, at least, for such further study.

Passages from the Bible are normally quoted from the American Standard Version of the Old Testament and from the New American Standard Version of the New Testament (La Habra, Calif.: The Foundation Press, 1960), except that in the former the personal name of God, Jehovah, has been replaced by the more original reading, Yahweh, and the pronouns of deity have been capitalized into conformity with the NAS usage.

Finally, I express my appreciation to all who have contributed to the project that follows: to the Alumni Association of Wheaton College, Illinois, for the 1969–1970 faculty research award, and to the College's

3. P. viii.
4. P. 109.
5. Pickering, ed., p. 119.

Graduate School of Theology and Board of Trustees, for the year's leave of absence from the classroom, which have made possible the completion of the *Encyclopedia;* to the administration and faculty of the San Francisco Conservative Baptist Theological Seminary, for receiving me into their graduate program during this year and particularly to the following professors, Dr. Charles A. Hauser, Jr., Dr. Bernard E. Northrup, and Dr. H. LaVern Schafer, for their generous guidance and suggestions in the fields, respectively, of hermeneutics, Old Testament, and New Testament; and to the gracious assistance of the libraries and librarians of the theological schools in the San Francisco Bay area and of the Bethany Bible College and University of California at Santa Cruz.

J. BARTON PAYNE

St. Louis, Missouri

Contents

BIBLIOGRAPHY 683

INDEXES 693

Tables

How to Use This Encyclopedia

To find the discussion of a particular verse of Biblical prediction:
The prophetic Scriptures are listed according to their 66 books, in the order by which they occur in the English Bible.
Under each book, the verses are listed under their particular prophecy, according to the order of its appearance.
In case a verse is not the first revelation of a given prophecy, or in case of other difficulty in finding it, Index 1, at the end of this volume, lists all the predictive verses of the Bible, indicating by paragraph number where each is discussed.
If a verse is not listed in Index 1, it has not been felt to be predictive; but Index 2 lists those passages that are most frequently mistaken for predictions, with the pages where these are explained.

To find and to study the discussion of a prophetic subject in one book:
Predictions are listed according to the order of the verse in which they are first described.
The method by which each prophecy is analyzed is explained in the prefatory note to the predictions, on pages 147–150
To bring together in this way all the verses on one subject in a given book is one of the best approaches for gaining perspective; for example, all the verses about Jesus' statement, "This generation will not pass away until all these things take place," are listed under Matthew 10:23b, or about His disclosures on the rapture of the church, under Luke 17:33b.

To investigate a single topic of prophecy:
Index 3 has the alphabetic listing of subjects.
It will refer both to the pages of discussion in the introductory sections, on the principles for interpreting Biblical predictions, and to Summary A, just before the indexes, on the chronological listing of prophecies according to their fulfillment, which catalogs all the Biblical books

that contain revelations on a particular prophecy.

From Summary A, one may then check the numbered listing of this prophecy under each book.

Major topics—prophecies about Christ, about the various ancient nations, and about predictions that are made through types—are listed separately in Summaries B, C, and D.

To understand the principles by which to interpret the Biblical predictions:
The topics of the introductory sections, on method, are outlined in the Table of Contents.

A summary of basic principles, together with the pages where each is presented, comes at the end of the introductory sections, on page 143.

To see the overall prophetic outline of a book:
An introduction that is prefixed to each particular book gives its structure, key verse, and basic statistics.

To appreciate the amount and distribution of Biblical prediction:
A Statistical Appendix at the end of this volume, just before the Bibliography, tabulates the numbers of separate predictions and predictive verses in each book, with their literary forms and percentages out of the whole.

The conclusion to this Appendix lists individual statistics of particular interest.

To grasp the order of the events prophesied in the Bible:
Summary A lists all the predictions of Scripture, both those that have already been accomplished and those that are still to be accomplished, in the order of their fulfillment.

It is divided into 18 periods of historical achievement: Nos. 1–13 are past, No. 14 is present, and Nos. 15–18 are future.

To find brief definitions of prophetic terminology and chronological periods:
The following pages of this preface summarize the meanings that are associated in this volume with particular words, with page references to their further discussion.

They contain a key for the practical pronunciation of Hebrew and Greek words, as these are represented in the volume.

They also present an outline of key Biblical dates and of the chronological periods as used in this study.

Definitions of Terms Relating to Prediction, as Employed in This Study

Allegorization	See Mystical interpretation.
Allegory	The expansion of a series of metaphors into a narrative (see below, p. 19).
Analogy	A historical or Biblical parallel used for determining the meaning or fulfillment of a given passage (p. 47).
Cycle	A progressive series of predictions that is paralleled by a corresponding block of matter in the same book (p. 130).
Developmental fulfillment	Progressive accomplishments for a comprehensive or generalized prophecy (p. 135).
Figurative sense	The intended meaning when one thing is said under the form or figure of another (p. 17).
Inferred prophecy	A prediction whose existence or content is not expressly stated (p. 41).
Literal sense	Narrowly, the primary meaning of words; or more broadly, the customary, socially acknowledged designation of language for the time in which used p. (16).
Metaphor	A declaration of identity, based upon a point of similarity (p. 19).
Metonymy	The interchange of one noun for another because of some inherent relationship between the two (p. 19).
Multiple sense	Additional interpretation(s) placed upon a passage beyond its originally intended meaning (p. 121).
Mystical interpretation	The assignment of a meaning to Scripture other than that originally intended by the Author (p. 43).
Normal interpretation	The assignment to Scripture of its original, divinely intended meaning (p. 43).

Parable

A simile expanded into a narrative, yet still conveying only one central truth (p. 19).

Poetic sense

Truth that is somewhat above and beyond a statement's literal, historical assertion (p. 18).

Prediction

The announcement of future events beyond human power to discern, or at least beyond current awareness (p. 8).

Progressive
prediction

The occurrence of a series of separate forecasts that together exhibit a chronological sequence in fulfillment (p. 129).

Prophecy

Broadly, the message of a prophet (p. 4); more narrowly, a synonym for prediction (p. 9).

Prophet

A spokesman of God's special revelation (p. 4).

Simile

A declaration of correspondence (p. 19).

Single fulfillment

The assignment to a specific prediction of but one legitimate accomplishment (p. 126).

Symbol

An object or event that connotes some matter of timeless significance (p. 21).

Symbol, predictive

A material (nonverbal) medium of communication that prefigures a situation that is yet future and not presently existing (p. 21).

Telescoping

The leaping of a prophecy from a near to a far horizon without notice of intervening matter (p. 137).

Type

A predictive symbol of truth to be accomplished in the work of Jesus Christ, but which also possesses an independent historical reality so as to communicate this same fundamental truth to its immediate contemporaries (p. 21).

Key Dates in Biblical Chronology

While legitimate differences of opinion still exist over the precise dates for certain events of Biblical history, evidences from astronomy, archaeology, and secular history have made its basic outline increasingly clear. Variations in datings, particularly within the Old Testament, now stem primarily from a reluctance on the part of some critical writers to accept the Scriptural testimony at its face value; and among conservative scholars such pivotal dates as 930 B.C. for the division of the Hebrew kingdom or 1446 for the exodus are accepted with little difference if any. The following list corresponds closely to the proposals of my article, "Chronology of the OT," in Merrill C. Tenney, ed., *The Pictorial Encyclopedia of the Bible* (Grand Rapids: Zondervan, 1973), and, for the NT, to those of Jack Finegan, *Handbook of Biblical Chronology* (Princeton University Press, 1964). Its dates provide the chronological framework for the study that follows.

Terah	2263–2058 B.C.	Samuel's victory	1063
Abraham	2133–1958	Saul's accession	1043
His entrance into Canaan	2058	David's accession (in Judah)	1010
Isaac	2033–1853	Solomon's accession	970
Jacob	1973–1826	Division of the kingdom	930
His descent into Egypt	1843	Jehu's slaying the kings	
Joseph	1882–1772	north and south	841
Moses	1527–1406	The fall of Samaria	722
The exodus	1446	Josiah's reform	622
Reentrance into Canaan	1406	Jerusalem's fall to Babylon	586
Division of the land	1400	Cyrus' decree for the return	538
Ehud's victory	1315	Ezra's return	458
Deborah and Barak's victory	1215	Nehemiah's refortification	444
Gideon's victory	1169	Alexander's capture of Judah	332

Antiochus III's capture of Judah 198
Antiochus IV's abomination 168
Judas Maccabeus' cleansing 165
Hasmonean independence 143
Pompey's capture of Judah 63
Herod the Great 37–4 B.C.
Jesus' birth 5 B.C.
Jesus' ministry A.D. 26–30
Paul's conversion 33

Council of Jerusalem 49
Deaths of Paul and Peter 64
Jewish War 66–70
Jerusalem's fall to Rome 70
Division of Rome, east and west 395
Rome burned 410
Fall of western Roman empire 476
Fall of eastern Roman empire 1453

Periods of Prophetic Fulfillment, as Used in This Study[1]

Period	Date of Beginning[2]	Biblical Books
1. Primeval-patri-archal	2133 B.C. (patri-arch Abraham)	Genesis, Job
2. Egyptian	1843	Exodus 1–12:36
3. Wilderness	1446	Exodus 12:37–Deuteronomy
4. Conquest	1406	Joshua
5. Judges	1382	Judges–I Samuel 10:23
6. United Kingdom	1043	I Samuel 10:24–I Kings 11 (I Chron–II Chron 9), Psalms–Song of Solomon
7. Divided Kingdom	930	I Kings 12–II Kings (II Chron 10–36), Isaiah–Lamentations, Hosea–Zephaniah
8. Exilic	586	Ezekiel, Daniel
9. Persian	538	Ezra–Esther, Haggai–Malachi
10. Greek	332	———(predicted in Daniel, etc.)
11. Maccabean	168	———(predicted in Daniel, etc.)
12. Roman	65	———(predicted in Daniel, etc.)
13. Life of Christ	5 B.C.	Matthew–John
14. Church	A.D. 30	Acts–Revelation
15. Christ's Second Coming	?	(predicted in Revelation, etc.)
16. Millennium	?	(predicted in Revelation, etc.)
17. Final Judgment	after the 1,000 years	(predicted in Revelation, etc.)
18. New Jerusalem	after the 1,000 years	(predicted in Revelation, etc.)

---

1. Elaborated below, on pp. 93–110.
2. See preceding list.

Abbreviations

AB   The Anchor Bible
ANET J. B. Pritchard, ed., *Ancient Near Eastern Texts Relating to the OT*
ASV   American Standard Version
BA   *The Biblical Archaeologist*
BASOR *Bulletin of the American Schools of Oriental Research*
BBC   *Beacon Bible Commentary*
BH   R. Kittel, ed., *Biblia Hebraica*, 3d and subsequent editions
BS   *Bibliotheca Sacra*
CAH   *The Cambridge Ancient History*
Camb The Cambridge Bible for Schools and Colleges
CBQ   *The Catholic Biblical Quarterly*
Cent The Century Bible
ETS B *Evangelical Theological Society, Bulletin* (1958–68)
ETS J ————, *Journal* (1969 on)
ETS P ————, Annual *Papers* (1952–56)
ExGkT *Expositor's Greek Testament*
GK   E. Kautzsch (trans. by Cowley), *Gesenius' Hebrew Grammar*
HDB   J. Hastings, ed., *Dictionary of the Bible*
IB   The Interpreter's Bible
ICC   *The International Critical Commentary*
IDB   *The Interpreter's Dictionary of The Bible*

ISBE *The International Standard Bible Encyclopedia*
JB   The Jerusalem Bible
JBL   *Journal of Biblical Literature*
Jos, Ant Josephus, *Antiquities*
KB   L. Koehler and W. Baumgartner, *Lexicon in Veteris Testamenti Libros*
KD   C. F. Keil and F. Delitzsch, *Biblical Commentary on the OT*
KJV   King James Version
LXX   Septuagint
MT   Masoretic Text
NAS   New American Standard Bible
NBC   F. Davidson, ed., *The New Bible Commentary*
NIC   *The New International Commentary*
NT   New Testament
OT   Old Testament
PTR   *The Princeton Theological Review*
RSV   Revised Standard Version
TDNT G. Kittel, ed., *Theological Dictionary of the NT*
WC   *The Westminster Commentary*
WTJ   *The Westminster Theological Journal*

OTHER ABBREVIATIONS

ch(s).	chapter(s)	p., pp.	page(s)
consec.	consecutive	per.	period
ed.	edition or editor	perf.	perfect
f., ff.	following	plu.	plural
fem.	feminine	prep.	preposition
fig.	figurative	pt.	participle
Gk.	Greek	rev.	revision or revised
Heb.	Hebrew	sim	similar
impf.	imperfect	sym.	symbolical
lit.	literally	sing.	singular
masc.	masculine	typ.	typical
mg	margin	v., vv.	verse(s)
MS(S)	manuscript(s)	vol(s).	volume(s)

Guide to Pronunciation of the Biblical Languages

Hebrew, Aramaic, and Greek words, as they appear in this study, are transliterated in such a way as most closely, and yet most simply, to represent their English phonetic equivalents. For their listing, see Index 4. Attention is directed to the following symbols:

a	the *a* in mat	ai	might
ā	father	dh	the *th* in this
e	met	g	get
ē	mate	s	sit
i	mit	th	thin
ī	machine	' (between consonants): a reduced vowel, as the *a* in barometer, "b'rometer"	
o	ought		
ō	mote	' (between vowels): a break, as between the two *o*'s in cooperate, "co'operate"	
u	put		
ū	rule		

All Hebrew words are accented on the last syllable, unless otherwise noted, as *qáyis*.

INTRODUCTION:
THE INTERPRETATION
OF BIBLICAL PREDICTION

PREFATORY NOTE

The modern reader's understanding of Biblical prophecy will be affected, and often determined, by the interpretive principles with which he approaches his subject. The following sections seek therefore to reduce the present-day confusion in prophetic interpretation by furnishing an introductory methodology through which the predictive portions of Scripture may be identified and understood in a consistent manner; for as Girdlestone long ago observed, "The neglect of the study of prophetic method is one secret of the great variety of opinions amongst students of prophecy."[1]

1. *The Grammar of Prophecy*, p. vi.

The Nature of Prediction

A. The Prophetic Movement in Israel

1. THE REVELATORY EXPERIENCE. Scripture recognizes prophecy as a "medium of divine communication."[2] As seen from a more general perspective, Israel possessed three basic classes of human media for revelations from God, each with its own particular function. As expressed in Jeremiah 18:18, "The law shall not perish from the priest, nor counsel from the wise, nor the word [or *vision*, Ezek 7:26] from the prophet."[3] That is, while the wise, Israel's compilers of proverbial wisdom, were inspired to communicate principles for the direction of life, and while the Levitical priests, informed by Yahweh's law book, were equipped for the restoration of those who had fallen short of the divine standards, it was the prophet who occupied that central position of revealing God's will, His specific "word" for men, reproving their sin against His "counsel" and guiding them repentantly to seek His "law" from the priest.

The most utilized Hebrew noun for prophet, *nāvī*, remains uncertain in etymology but seems to come from the root meaning "to announce."[4] Biblical usage confirms the concept of the prophet as *an announcer*: for example, when God sent Moses to Egypt He explained, "See, I have made thee as God to Pharaoh, and Aaron thy brother shall be thy *prophet*: thou shalt speak all that I command thee, and Aaron thy brother *shall speak*

2. Alfred Edersheim, *Prophecy and History in Relation to the Messiah*, pp. 122, 126.
3. See J. B. Payne, *Theology of the Older Testament*, p. 45.
4. KB, p. 588, though cf. G. Vos, *Biblical Theology, Old and New Testaments*, pp. 209–210. Others prefer to take this root in its passive sense: not so much "one who calls," emphasizing the prophetic activity, as "one who is called," emphasizing God's previous raising up of the prophet. Guillaume's conclusion is that "the *nāvī* is one who is in the state of announcing a message which has been given to him, the passive recipient," *Prophecy and Divination among the Hebrews and Other Semites*, pp. 112–113.

unto Pharaoh" (Ex 7:1–2). To this, then, corresponds the basic meaning of the Greek word *profḗtēs, one who speaks forth* in behalf of another; in classic culture, one who interprets the will of some deity.[5] The apostle Peter thus insists, "No prophecy was ever made by an act of human will, but men moved by the Holy Spirit spoke from God" (II Pet 1:21). A prophet may therefore be defined as a *a spokesman of God's special revelation*; and prophecy, in its broadest sense, as simply *the message of a prophet.*

The noun *nāvī* appears first in Scripture at Genesis 20:7 (cf. Ps 105:15)[6] in reference to Abraham, where it signifies a man who knows God (Gen 18:18), though not as yet one who also functions as an official teacher. Regular prophecy arose with Moses (Dt 18:18, Hos 12:13; cf. Num 11:25, 12:2) and became more organized under Samuel (I Sam 10:5, 19:20). In David's times the sanctuary singers were those "who prophesied in giving thanks and praising Yahweh" (I Chron 25:3; see vv. 1 and 5). But whether among these, or among the reforming prophets of the 9th century B.C. (e.g. Elijah), or among the writing prophets that commenced in the 8th, the *nāvī* was a man who ministered the word of God to his contemporaries. Prophecy is thus preeminently historical: revealed organically to the consciousness of the prophet, mediated through an ancient Near Eastern culutre, and spoken in terms of its day and with forms and purposes that were suited to actual situations.[7]

Yet Biblical prophecy goes beyond all this and can only be misunderstood if restricted to the capacities of the ancient human consciousness.[8] Israel's

5. TDNT, VI:784, citing Aeschylus, *Eumenides*, 19.

6. Though prophecy itself appears as early as Enoch, Lamech, and Noah; cf. Jude 14, Gen 5:29, 9:25.

7. See below, p. 18 on form, for example, or pp. 118–119 on fulfillment.

8. Contrast C. A. Briggs, "The prophets cannot transcend the psychological and physical features of human nature," *Messianic Prophecy*, p. 55. Thus also Riehm takes issue with Hengstenberg's distinguishing between the "sense the prophets attach to their own utterances and what God intended in these utterances"; Riehm insists: "The contents of a prophecy can include only the sense in which at the time of its utterance . . . the prophets themselves intended to be understood by their contemporaries," *Messianic Prophecy*, pp. 6–7, 19. Others would propose that while individual prophetic situations that are cited within Scripture may occasionally transcend the capacities of the speakers concerned (e.g. that of Caiphas, below, or of Lamech, see p. 158, Genesis, fn. 21), still, the Scriptural writings themselves must be restricted in the meanings assigned them to what was the conscious, historical understanding of their human writers; cf. Walter C. Kaiser, Jr., "The Eschatological Hermeneutics of Epangelicalism (Promise Theology)," ETSJ, 13 (1970), 92, 96. The goal that lies behind this proposal is the commendable one of inhibiting any introduction of allegorized interpretations, that is, of "reading in" to the text matters that are not there; see below, pp. 43 ff. But apart from the dubious validity of seeking to distinguish between the consciousness of quoted prophetic speakers and the consciousness of the final writers of the Biblical books, there remain connected with this approach two other major problems: (1) of Scripture's affirmations concerning the uncertainties of its writers; and (2) of its concrete examples of predictions where God's originally intended meaning (as declared elsewhere in Scripture) seems on the face of it to have been unlikely of contemporaneous comprehension. For the former, answer is given that verses such as the above-cited I Pet 1:10–11 and Dan 12:8 may indicate prophetic ignorance only over the *time* of fulfillment and not over

prophets searched diligently, attempting to fathom their own predictions (I Pet 1:10–11); and, upon occasion, they were compelled to confess ignorance over their own visions (Dan 8:27, Zech 4:13) or words (Dan 12:8). Rarely, they might even have been unaware that they *were* speaking prophecy. When Abraham, for example, sought to allay the suspicions of his son Isaac by suggesting, "God will provide for Himself a lamb for the burnt offering" (Gen 22:8), when apparently he had nothing other in mind than Isaac himself as the sacrifice, he spoke far better than he knew; compare the case of Caiphas in John 11:49–52. Prophecy is transcendent as well as historical; and what its contemporaries may have thought must remain secondary to what God's inspiration may determinatively reveal as His primary intention.[9]

---

the *meaning* of the predictions (cf. ibid., pp. 94–95); but while I Peter may be so interpreted (e.g. as in ASV, though contrast NAS or KJV), Daniel states that its writer did not understand "the issue of these things" (12:8): not just the length of the enigmatic "time, times, and a half" of v. 7, but what should be the "outcome" (JB) of these things, "i.e. the revelation of ch. 11," E. J. Young, *The Prophecy of Daniel*, p. 260. To the prophet, "the words were shut up" (v. 9); and it would be only later that "they that are wise shall understand" (v. 10). For the latter, answer has been attempted that the contemporaneously understood meanings may really be satisfactory. On the one hand, the capacities of a man like David must not be underestimated: in writing the 16th Psalm, for example, "because he was a prophet, and knew that God had sworn to him with an oath to seat one of his descendants upon his throne, he looked ahead and spoke of the resurrection of Christ" (Acts 2:30–31). Yet on the other hand, when Willis J. Beecher argues that one's criterion for content should be, "What did this mean to an intelligent, devout, uninspired Israelite of the time to which it belongs?" (*The Prophets and the Promise*, p. 14), he is in essence surrendering those supernaturalistic, divinely intended meanings that Scripture elsewhere asserts for the passages concerned. He grants in respect to certain Messianic prophecies, for example, that as first spoken there was "no hint of referring to a coming person who is to appear some centuries in the future" (p. 403); and, however appealing it may be for present modes of thinking to limit the phenomena of prophecy to "events that are not, under this definition, miraculous" (p. 406), he must then make his peace with the later (NT) portions of Scripture that do assign to them miraculous, Messianic meanings. In actuality, Beecher must have recourse to what is essentially a theory of double meanings, even though he would seek to justify the process by asserting that both the OT and the NT senses reflect one underlying promise of blessing, claiming, "with the promise they are on common ground" (p. 403); yet see below pp. 135–136.

9. Raymond E. Brown adduces the term *sensus plenior*, which he defines as "the deeper meaning intended by God but not clearly intended by the human author, that is seen to exist in the words of Scripture when they are studied in the light of further revelation or of development in the understanding of revelation," in "Hermeneutics," *The Jerome Bible Commentary*, II:616. Berkhof states rather sharply, "There is no truth in the assertion that the intent of the secondary authors, determined by the grammatico-historical method, always . . . represents in all its fulness the meaning of the Holy Spirit," *Principles of Biblical Interpretation*, p. 60; cf. John Bright's emphasis upon "the theology that informs the text." *The Authority of the OT*, pp. 143–144, 170–171. Such "informing," lest it degenerate into allegorization, must be limited to those instances in which God Himself expressly declares the nature of His original intent via later Biblical passages; see below, pp. 74 ff. As Berkhof, for example, notes, "Sometimes NT writers furnish explicit and striking explanations of OT passages, and reveal depths that might easily have escaped the interpreter," op. cit., p. 138.

The OT has two other major terms for prophet: *hōzé*, and *rō'é*, both meaning "one who sees," a "seer" (I Sam 9:9). As contrasted with the divine proclamation to men that is connoted by *nāvī*, these latter nouns emphasize God's mode of revelation to the prophet. They underline, furthermore, the pictorial nature of much of prophetic revelation, whether given by dreams, for the less mature (e.g. Gen 37:5–10, Jd 7:13–15, and see especially Dan 2:1, 4:5, or by visions, which constitute God's more normal mode of revelation to His prophets, awake and conscious (Ezek 7:26; compare Isa 1:1 and contrast Jer 23:27, 32). Their "seeing," in turn, goes far to account for such prophetic phenomena as the use of figurative language, their telescoped chronological perspectives, and for what Oehler describes as prophetic "intuition."[10] Yet many of God's revelations seem also to have been verbal, whether spoken audibly or by some more mental mode (Jer 30:2).[11]

2. THE INSPIRED WRITING. Both OT and NT teach that the inscripturated language of the prophets possesses an authority equivalent to that of the words of God Himself. In Isaiah 34:16, for example, the prophet seemingly refers to his own writing as "the book of Yahweh"; and in II Peter 1:20–21 the apostle's denial to prophecy of "private interpretation" relates contextually to its origin, as inspired, rather than to subsequent usage or application by its readers.[12] A final OT prophet could look back both upon "the law, and the words which Yahweh had sent by His Spirit by the former [preexilic] prophets" and find them equally authoritative (Zech 7:12). Even so, the modern reader who would enter into a sympathetic understanding of Biblical prophecy is called upon, by Christ Himself, for vital faith in Scripture as the word of God written and therefore inerrant in its autographs (Lk 24:25, 44).[13]

3. HOLINESS, AS THE GOAL OF PROPHECY. Scripture teaches that history is holy: not simply because its events embody the decrees of the holy God, "who works all things after the counsel of His will" (Eph 1:11), but because its entire course has been designed for the achievement of holiness. Mankind possessed an original holiness, in conformity to the perfections of deity (cf. Eph 4:23–24, Col 3:10); and, though this was lost at the fall, God in His grace promised restoration to His people through His older covenant or testament, that Israel might become a "holy nation" (Ex 19:5–6). History's goal of attaining such holy conformity to its Lord is expressed, on the one hand, personally, in the testamentary promise that

10. *Theology of the OT*, p. 488; see below, pp. 17, 137.
11. Vos, op. cit., pp. 230–248.
12. See. P. Fairbairn, *The Interpretation of Prophecy*, Appendix G, pp. 507–508.
13. See J. B. Payne, "Apeitheo: Current Resistance to Biblical Inerrancy," Bul. ETS, 10 (1967), 3–14; cf. *Theology of the Older Testament*, ch. IV, and pp. 505–519.

dominates the pages of Scripture from beginning to end: "I will be their God, and they shall be My people" (Gen 17:7, Rev 21:3; cf. Gen 3:15). Correspondingly, "The prophet may be said to be the incarnation of the idea of the covenant: his was the most close and confidential relation to God."[14] It may be expressed, on the other hand, in terms of sovereignty: "The one pervading and impelling idea of the OT is the royal reign of God on earth. . . . This Messianic idea is the sole *raison d'être* of the OT viewed as revelation."[15] In either event, the goal of prophecy consists of the holiness of God, as it is yet to be experienced within history.

As John Bright therefore insists, history must have a future, a "destination";[16] and to this future, prophecy finds itself linked in two major ways.[17] First, prophecy demonstrates that holiness is to be made available through its source in Jesus Christ, "the One of whom Moses, in the Law, and the Prophets wrote" (John 1:45). The prophetic movement in Israel "predicted the sufferings of Christ and the glories to follow" (I Pet 1:11); indeed, "the testimony of Jesus[18] is the spirit of prophecy" (Rev 19:10). The Lord Jesus is mankind's only hope for righteousness, sanctification, and redemption" (I Cor 1:30); and so "in Him alone prophecy finds its proper explanation and its adequate result."[19] Even from the viewpoint of language, "To say that Jesus is the Christ means that He is the Messiah promised and predicted in the OT."[20] Second, the prophets demonstrate that holiness can be effectuated or made operative in the lives of their contemporaries by appeals to the future. All now recognize that the "message was given to influence the present action";[21] but, both by promise and by threat, "It was the underlying view of the future which gave meaning and emphasis to their admonitions about the present."[22] Terry thus divides the specific predictions of the OT into two groups: some inculcate present holiness through "an impersonal portraiture of a coming kingdom of power and righteousness, in which humanity attains its highest good"; but others consist of "the announcement of a person, the Anointed One, with whom all the triumph and glory are connected"; and he styles both as Messianic.[23]

In summary, whether holiness be considered in respect to its source or in respect to its effectuation, Jesus Christ remains the heart of prophecy.

14. E. A. Edghill, *An Enquiry into the Evidential Value of Prophecy*, p. 315.
15. Edersheim, op. cit., pp. 48, 135.
16. *The Kingdom of God*, p. 30.
17. See A. B. Davidson, *OT Prophecy*, p. 12.
18. Objective genitive, "about Jesus," H. B. Swete, *The Apocalypse of St. John*, p. 249.
19. Fairbairn, op. cit., p. 33. For a listing of prophecies with personal reference to Christ, cf. Summary C, pp. 665–670.
20. Edersheim, op. cit., p. xii.
21. A. Berkeley Mickelsen, *Interpreting the Bible*, p. 287.
22. Edersheim, op. cit., p. 38; cf. his entire ch. 5, on "the moral element in OT prophecy."
23. *Biblical Hermeneutics*, p. 237.

In Him "all the hope of Israel has found its fulfillment and become present fact."[24] Kirkpatrick cautions: "Appeal must be made, not to the predictive elements of prophecy only, but to the work of the prophets as a whole. . . . We find in Christ, not only the fulfillment of the predictions of the prophets, but the consummation and realization of the whole of their teaching."[25]

Edghill affirms that Jesus "takes prophecy as a whole and claims to fulfill it all. . . . In Him alone prophecy as a spiritual and historical phenomenon finds its reasonable explanation. In Him alone its teachings attain to completion: in Him its ideals are carried into the sphere of actual life."[26]

B. *The Status of Prediction Within Prophecy*

While it therefore becomes clear that foretelling is not to be treated as synonymous with the essence of Biblical prophecy, still, the very fact that the prophets find their focal point in Jesus Christ and His holiness does, as indicated above, elevate the future into a place of prominence in prophetic thinking; and this, in turn, provides the occasion for predictive utterance.

1. PREDICTION DEFINED. A prediction is an "announcement, more or less specific, of the future";[27] it is "a miracle of knowledge, a declaration or representation of something future, beyond the power of human sagacity to discern or to calculate."[28] At times it thus seems also to include matters which may, indeed, already have occurred but of which the parties concerned could not otherwise have become aware until a later date—an example is I Samuel 9:20 (cf. 10:22), with its statement about the return of Saul's asses. Oracles of this type would be predictive in the sense of announcing, "You will find that. . . ."

The making of forecasts, thus defined, is an activity in which, so to speak, any man might seek to engage; but since God alone possesses the requisite knowledge of the future (Isa 44:6–8; cf. I Cor 1:25), it is only He who can really "declare the things which are to come hereafter" (Isa 41:23). In the pagan culture of ancient Greece this unique association of God with foretelling led to a specialization of the term *profétēs*, out of its general connotation of a spokesman for deity, into that more specific concept of

24. Bright, *Kingdom*, pp. 18, 215, though not thereby excluding those hopes that are fulfilled in Christ at His *second* advent.
25. *The Doctrine of the Prophets*, p. 11.
26. Op. cit., p. 447.
27. Fairbairn, op. cit., p. 18.
28. Thomas H. Horne, *An Introduction to the Critical Study and Knowledge of the Holy Scriptures*, I:119; cf. W. J. Beecher's inclusion within the prophetic task of "the disclosing of secrets," along with the foretelling of what is specifically future, op. cit., pp. 106–107.

one who makes predictions, "one who speaks in advance";[29] and, in modern parlance "prophet" is similarly employed, e.g. a "weather prophet." Supernaturalistic predicting, however, remains a solely divine activity; and for the Christian, who accepts the authority of Jesus, including His commitment to the Bible as the unparalleled word of God, the prophecies of Scripture "must necessarily be divine," and these alone.[30] They are seen as the only legitimate forecasts of the future that God has authorized. The Biblical prophets, in their advocacy of holiness, may thus further be defined as the "instruments of revealing God's will to men, specially by predicting future events, and, in particular, by foretelling the incarnation of the Lord Jesus Christ and the redemption effected by Him."[31]

2. SCRIPTURAL TESTIMONY. Examples of inspired prediction appear throughout the Biblical record and can by no means be restricted to those books that happen to be authored by specifically named prophets. The subjects of these forecasts are kaleidoscopic: "Nothing seems too great and nothing too small";[32] yet even the most ordinary possess the authority of divine revelation. Saul's servant could testify about the Lord's "seer" Samuel, "All that he saith cometh surely to pass" (I Sam 9:6; cf. v. 9); so why should they not ask him about the lost asses? And Samuel did tell them! (9:20, 10:16). Certain predictions border on the category of what might constitute merely plausible inferences; an example is I Kings 20:22, with its message that the Syrians would again attack Israel in the following year. But however simple, minute, or in themselves seemingly insignificant, they speak forth "always in connection with and subserviency to important transactions affecting the interests of God's people."[33]

With the diversity appears divine unity. For within Biblical prediction there exists an organic development, even as the entire prophetic movement takes its rise out of the progress of redemptive history. Berkhof observes: "Some of the most important prophecies are first couched in general terms, but in the course of God's progressive revelation increase in definiteness and particularity, as we note in those of a Messianic character. They remind one of the bud that gradually opens into a beautiful flower."[34] Terry cites an early, concrete example: "The oracle of Balaam touching Moab, Edom, Amalek, Kenites, Asshur, and the power from the side of Kittim (Num

29. TDNT, VI:784.
30. Horne, op. cit., I:120. Liberalism that insists upon its right to withhold commitment to Biblical prophecy exhibits a willingness to accord similar "status" to prophets of "the various religions of the world . . . guided by the divine Spirit," Briggs, op. cit., p. 3, but see also pp. 17–18, 42–43.
31. F. Meyrick, "Prophet," in Smith's Dictionary of the Bible, p. 2594; for "redemption," in its broadest aspect (see below, p. 24), may also include events that are yet future.
32. Girdlestone, op. cit., p. 9.
33. E. P. Barrows, Companion to the Bible, p. 608.
34. Principles of Biblical Interpretation, p. 149.

24:17–24), is the prophetic germ of many later oracles against these and similar enemies of the chosen people."[35]

Scriptural testimony does not limit itself to examples but moves onward into direct assertions concerning the theory of prediction: "The prophets who prophesied of the grace that would come . . . predicted glories to follow" (I Pet 1:11); and Jesus Himself stated, "Behold, I have told you in advance" (Mt 24:25), or again, "From now on I am telling you before it comes to pass, so that when it does occur, you may believe that I am He" (John 13:19). Then after His own departure, He would send the Holy Spirit, "and He will disclose to you what is to come" (16:13). Oehler argues, "When it is said in Isaiah 42:9, 'New things do I declare: before they spring forth I tell you of them,' the idea of pure prediction could hardly be more precisely expressed";[36] it is, in fact, one of Isaiah's dominant themes (see also Isa 37:26, 41:21–28, 43:9, 44:7–8, 45:22, 46:10, 48:3–8). Furthermore, from Scripture's viewpoint it is the predictions that prove the prophet (Jer 28:9); the actualization of punishment for the heathen, for example, or the rise of the Gentile church (see below, Zech., prophecy No. 4), would stand as proofs that the Angel of Yahweh had really spoken to Zechariah (2:9, 11), and the second temple, as finished by Zerubbabel, with foreign help, would prove that Yahweh Himself had sent both the prophet and the angel who interpreted these things to him (4:9, 6:15). Unfulfilled predictions, on the other hand, become proof of false prophecy (Dt 18:22);[37] and Micaiah could affirm, in connection with his forecast of Ahab's death at Ramoth-gilead, "If thou return at all in peace, Yahweh hath not spoken by me" (I K 22:28).[38] The Hebrew Scriptures seem indeed to be consistently oriented around predictive themes; critical scholars, such as Rowley, recognize that as far as the Bible itself is concerned the prophets "regarded the foretelling of the future as of the essence of their function," and Raymond Brown adds, "Whether modern scholars like it or not, prediction was the way the NT writers themselves related the testaments."[39]

3. OPPOSITION TO PREDICTION. But is the position of the Bible a tenable one? Skeptics have answered with an emphatic no:

> Justin Martyr, one of the early church fathers, wrote as follows: "There were among the Jews certain men who were prophets of God, through whom the prophetic spirit published beforehand things that were to come to pass ere

35. Op. cit., p. 317.
36. Op. cit., p. 487.
37. Guillaume suggests, "The ultimate explanation of the great place that the Hebrew prophets came to occupy is to be attributed . . . to the fact that their prophecies were fulfilled," op. cit., p. 108.
38. See subsec. 4 below, concerning the values of prediction, for further evidences of this sort.
39. H. H. Rowley, *The Relevance of Apocalyptic*, p. 34; Brown, op. cit., II:615.

ever they happened" (*Apologia*, CXXXI, I). This conception of the prophetic function was held for a long time by leading scholars of the Christian church and it still prevails among those who do not accept the methods and results of the movement known as Higher Criticism. But in spite of the fact that this view is a time-honored one and has many adherants at the present time, it is not supported by the most reliable information which we possess today concerning the character and work of the Hebrew prophets.[40]

The school of modern critical scholars represented in the symposium edited by Claus Westermann, *Essays on OT Hermeneutics* (1963), opposes the whole concept of a supernatural, verbalized prediction; and the older "modernism" has long asserted: "Prophecy is a declaration, a forthtelling, of the will of God—not a foretelling. Prediction is not in any sense an essential of prophecy, though it may intervene as an accident—whether it be a justifiable accident is another question."[41] Yet the so-called unjustifiable accident is one which has refused to be silenced; and this has led its opponents into a somewhat reconstructed attack, as follows:

The prophets were . . . explicit in their teaching about last things. They were constantly speaking to their contemporaries about events to take place at some future time. This does not imply that the prophet had any advance information about what would happen at any specific date. It means simply that he believed certain things would have to happen sometime in order to make possible the fulfillment of the divine purpose.[42]

Not far behind such criticism, however, lies a frankly anti-Biblical philosophy, which becomes apparent from an observation such as this: "[in] the NT books . . . it is implied that seers of centuries long past foresaw the NT developments. This kind of thing seems to the modern mind to border on the incredible."[43] What sentiments of this sort seem actually to reflect, however, is man's rationalistic antipathy to the supernatural. It makes the assumption that the course of earthly events just *is not* to be affected by spiritual forces from without, which means, in turn, that religion becomes essentially irrelevant to real life. As Meyrick long ago observed,

There is no question that if miracles are, either physically or morally, impossible, then prediction is impossible; and those passages which have been accounted predictive, must be explained away as being vague, as applying only to something in the writer's lifetime, or on some other hypothesis. This is only saying that belief in prediction is not compatible with the theory of atheism, or with the philosophy which rejects the overruling Providence of a personal God.[44]

40. Charles H. Patterson, *The Philosophy of the OT*, pp. 142–143.
41. R. H. Charles, *Critical Commentary on the Book of Daniel*, p. xxvi.
42. Patterson, op. cit., p. 528.
43. Gurdon C. Oxtoby, *Prediction and Fulfillment in the Bible*, p. 12; cf. "incredible visionary powers," p. 62.
44. Op. cit., p. 2597.

Reaction, however, has set in; and thought that is truly modern exhibits a swing back toward an acknowledgment of the centrality within Scriptural religion of predictive utterance. A Jewish scholar writes,

A prophet, simply stated, was someone deemed close to the Deity who through special revelation was able to predict the future. The remarkably elevated content of the literary prophecy of the Tanak [the OT] led scholars toward the end of the 19th century to minimize the element of prediction in prophecy. From that generation we have inherited the misleading epigram that the prophets were not "foretellers" but "forthtellers." In fact they were both.[45]

And a Protestant insists: "That the prophets were not merely preachers of righteousness, but foretellers of the future, is plain to every reader";[46] he goes on to quote A. S. Peake, "It is rather unfortunate that the reaction from the old-fashioned view that prophecy was in the main prediction has led to the prevalent belief that the prophets were scarcely concerned with the future at all. . . . For really the predictive element in prophecy was very prominent."[47] It remains true that "prophecy had always a present meaning and present lesson for those who heard it";[48] but, as indicated above, this fact by no means denies relevance to predictive activity for the achievement of prophecy's primary goal of holiness. So too in apostolic times,

The NT church had to live in tension between its confidence that the victory of the Kingdom of God had already been made actual in Christ, and its eager expectation of the victory which as yet no human eye could see. . . . The church could not escape that tension except by surrendering all hope for the future. And that the church could not do, for that would have been to give up its God and its Christ and to cut loose from that eschatological element which was indigenous to its gospel—as, indeed, it had been indigenous to Israel's faith since the beginning.[49]

4. VALUE OF PREDICTION. The importance of predictive prophecy, as thus asserted, for the people of God is evidenced at the outset by the bare fact of Biblical statistics. Commentators are accustomed to state that "fully one quarter of the Bible is prophecy";[50] and, while this estimate appears to

---

45. Samuel Sandmel, *The Hebrew Scriptures*, p. 48.
46. Rowley, loc. cit.
47. *The Servant of Yahweh*, p. 83. Guillaume devotes a chapter in *Prophecy and Divination* to "Prediction: Inseparable from Prophecy" and insists, "There is no prophet in the OT who was not a foreteller of the future. . . . When a prophet ceases to prophesy in this sense he ceases to be a prophet and becomes a preacher. . . . The power of predicting the future was regarded by the Hebrews as the distinguishing mark of prophetic activity," pp. 111–112.
48. Edersheim, op. cit., p. 37; cf. Fairbairn, *The Typology of Scripture*, I:126, "It is true that the prophet was God's messenger, in an especial sense, to the men of his own age; and as such usually delivered messages, which were called forth by what had actually occurred, and took from this its impress. But he was not necessarily tied to that."
49. Bright, *Kingdom*, p. 239.
50. Charles Feinberg, *Premillennialism or Amillennialism?* p. 3.

be a generalization, it is still approximately correct. As tabulated below,[51] out of the OT's 23,210 verses, 6,641 contain predictive material, or 28½ percent. Out of the NT's 7,914 verses, 1,711 contain predictive material, or 21½ percent. So for the entire Bible's 31,124 verses, 8,352 contain predictive material, or 27 per cent of the whole.

In reference to specific values, the fact of predictive prophecy brings, first of all, glory to God; for each prediction testifies to its Author's wisdom and sovereignty over the future. As Isaiah spoke forth to the Israelites of his day, "Who hath declared it from the beginning, that we may say, He is right?" (41:26). Predictions point up His powers, as contrasted with those of any conceivable rivals; as the Lord went on to speak through His prophet, "Before it came to pass I showed it thee, lest thou shouldest say, Mine idol hath done them" (48:5). The modern skeptic sometimes seeks to disparage the Biblical predictions by emphasizing NT "fulfillments" as divergently superior to the prophetic intent of the OT, asserting, for example, that "to glorify prediction rather than fulfillment is . . . to miss the significance of the Christian gospel."[52] But while no one should minimize the glories of the gospel, remarks such as this seem to have missed the significance of prophecy. When Joshua spoke out in faith and foretold the miracle of the cutting off of the waters of the Jordan (Josh 3:13), he assured his people, "Hereby ye shall know that the living God is among you" (v. 10); and to this end the prediction itself contributed, just as did the subsequent miracle.

The above incident serves also to exhibit some of the values of these predictions for their original proclaimers: the accomplishment of the miracle *and* its forecast combined to magnify Joshua in the eyes of Israel (4:14), just as Yahweh had foretold it would (3:7). When the patriarch Joseph repeated the prediction of his people's return from Egypt to Canaan (Gen 50:24–25), his words showed forth the faith of the speaker (Heb 11:22); compare also the case of David as he expressed his confidence in the face of Goliath (I Sam 17:37). The vindication, through accomplished prediction, of the prophet Zechariah has already been noted;[53] and God's Spirit spoke similarly for Ezekiel: "When this cometh to pass (behold, it cometh), then shall they know that a prophet hath been among them" (Ezek 33:33).

In a highly specialized manner, the fulfillment of short-range predictions —for example, the rending of Jeroboam's altar (I K 13:3)—sometimes served to validate other, longer-ranged ones—i.e., the coming of Josiah (v. 2), still some 308 years distant.[54] Compare the briefer compass of Luke

51. See Statistical Appendix.
52. Oxtoby, op. cit., p. 119.
53. See above, p. 10.
54. Concerning Jer 44:29–30 and its prediction of the death of Pharaoh Hophra, the notes of the Jerusalem Bible explain: "Jeremiah makes this short-term prophecy, offering its fulfillment as a sign, cf. 28:17ff, commending his prediction of a more distant event, namely, invasion by Nebuchadnezzar in 568–567," p. 1321, though

1:13, 20–22, in which an immediate fulfillment in regard to the dumbness of Zacharias confirmed the message of the birth of his son John some nine months later; or, II Kings 20:8–10, in which an immediate fulfillment for the predicted backward motion of a shadow validated the prediction of Hezekiah's recovery from sickness that was to occur in just three days. Luke, furthermore, explains that the angel's short-range prediction came to Zacharias ". . . because you did not believe" the more distant one (1:20). Horne states, for the entirety of inscripturated prophecy: "It was calculated to serve as an evidence of the divine origin of Scripture,"[55] though its value in this regard seems to have been more true for its ancient readers than for its modern.[56]

The Biblical prophecies possessed no small measure of value for their original listening audiences. Some were designed to grant them assurance or comfort; for example, the foretelling in Exodus 3:12 of the Hebrew's impending worship on Sinai served as an immediate "token" to Moses of the reality of his commission from God and to reassure his doubts (v. 11); the three detailed predictions of I Samuel 10:2–7, with fulfillments on that very same day, availed as "signs" to Saul (v. 8) that he really was God's choice for king over Israel; and the Lord's forecasts of blessing and of safe conduct back to Canaan in Genesis 28:15, 20–21, were twice claimed by Jacob when he was about to meet his brother Esau (32:9, 12)—he was reminding Yahweh, as it were, of His promised protection. Fairbairn speaks also of the Lord's threats against the ungodly as matters of disguised comfort for the righteous.[57]

As indicated above,[58] a major value for Biblical prediction lay in its power to motivate its hearers toward holiness. As the apostle Peter said, "We have the prophetic word made more sure [by Christ], to which you do well to pay attention" (II Pet 1:19). Some of the prophecies were aids to faith: Jesus said, "Now I have told you before it comes to pass, that when it comes to pass, you may believe" (John 14:29); and David forecast his victory over Goliath "that all the earth may know that there is a God in Israel" (I Sam 17:46; cf. v. 47)—its truth was proclaimed by his prophecy as well as by his deed that followed. Some were aids to devotion and ritual observance: the fulfillment of Nahum's predictions against Nineveh was designed to promote the keeping of feasts and the performance of vows (Nah 1:15). Some, if not most, were aids to moral living. Both the promises of divine blessing and the threats of impending judgment constituted urgent motivations to ethical conduct. As Girdlestone quipped, "The object of prophecy was not to excite surprise but to stimulate enter-

---

in this case the former incident was still 19 years away, while the latter followed it by only a little over a year; see below, under Jer., prophecy No. 81.

55. Op. cit., I:122.
56. See below, pp. 15–16.
57. *Interpretation*, pp. 44–47.
58. See p. 7.

prise";[59] and as Peter tells us in Scripture, "Since all these things are to be . . . what sort of people ought you to be in holy conduct and godliness" (II Pet 3:11). The attempt, correspondingly, has been made in the volume that follows to point up a number of these moral goals to prediction; but even where it has not, their existence may be assumed to lie close to the surface. The most climactic revelation of all begins with the preachment, "Blessed is he who reads and those who hear the words of this prophecy, *and heed the things which are written in it*" (Rev 1:3).

Far from fading away with the passage of time, the value of the Bible's predictions in all the above categories grows ever greater as their accomplishments unfold. "It was undoubtedly God's intention that His method of procedure toward the church in her state of [OT] minority, not only should minister what was needed for her own immediate instruction and improvement, but should also furnish materials of edification and comfort for believers to the end of time."[60] The one exception might appear to be in the area of apologetic evidence for the inspiration of Scripture. A century and a half ago T. H. Horne felt it possible to assert: "The book which contains these predictions is stamped with the seal of heaven: a rich vein of evidence runs through the volume of the OT; the Bible is true; infidelity is confounded for ever; and we may address its patrons in the language of Saint Paul, 'Behold, ye despisers, and wonder, and perish!' "[61]—to which those who are committed to Christ would not hesitate to add an Amen! Today, however, history has removed modern man from his direct observation of many of the prophetical fulfillments *as subsequent to* their forecasting; and naturalism and skepticism have substituted for him a multitude of explanatory, antisupernaturalistic alternatives. E. A. Edghill, for example, has addressed a thick volume to *An Enquiry into the Evidential Value of Prophecy,* especially in light of his own general commitment to the methodology and results of higher criticism; and he has been able to come up with only this cautiously worded conclusion about OT prediction: "It made easier the acceptance of the doctrine of the Incarnation,"[62] though not actually anticipating it. "Prophecy *prepared the way* [italics mine] for the true appreciation of the character of the personal Messiah whose advent it predicted";[63] and again, "The fulfillment of prophecy we *claim* to find in Jesus Christ. In His person . . . all that was written concerning Him received its complete accomplishment, not indeed always in the letter, but invariably in the spirit. . . . We therefore will wait in hope for its more complete accomplishment"[64]—sentiments which are hardly likely to convince the suspicious. Kirkpatrick's work on prophecy now cautions, "It is

---

59. Op. cit., p. 12.
60. Fairbairn, *Typology*, I:49.
61. Op. cit., I:126; and compare Fairbairn, *Interpretation*: on pp. 230–233 he claims a greater weight to Messianic predictions than modern criticism would grant.
62. P. 577.
63. Ibid., p. 583.
64. Ibid., pp. 591–592, 609.

more properly addressed to believers for the support of their faith than to unbelievers for the removal of their doubts."[65] There are, in fact, certain points at which explanations for the predictions are frankly difficult to discover (e.g. Ezek 26:12, 29:11, or 29:19–20). The Christian, as he follows the example of his Master, cannot question the ultimate veracity of the word;[66] but in his dialogue with others "the argument of fulfilled prophecy" for the doctrine of inspiration sometimes turns out to be more of an embarrassment than a "proof." In such cases it is to be hoped that the following study may assist in alleviating the problems. There remain, moreover, far more numerous examples in which *The Wonders of Prophecy*[67] continue to shine forth (e.g. Isa 53:9–10, Dan 9:26, or Zech 11:12) and over which one may reaffirm Horne's comprehensive definition of prophetic values: "The use and intent of prophecy, then, was to raise expectation, and to soothe the mind with hope—to maintain the faith of a particular providence, and the assurance of the Redeemer promised, and particularly to attest the divine inspiration of the Scriptures."[68]

C. *Predictive Forms*

1. SPOKEN. Most of the prophetic revelations of Scripture assume verbalized forms. The most common among these, in turn, is that of (a) the ORACLE, which is here understood in its simplest category, as a literally expressed, prosaic declaration, even though it may be presented in the balanced structures of poetic parallelism. An example of an oracle which is so elementary that it borders almost upon the predictable appears in the divine revelation to Moses (Ex 7:15), "Get thee unto Pharaoh in the morning; lo, he goeth out unto the water." The verbalization is here unquestionably literalistic, for it utilizes only the primary meanings of the words concerned. A step further along is Ramm's definition, that "the customary, socially acknowledged designation of a word is its literal meaning";[69] for when a given word combines into a phrase, or is employed in a particular context, its socially acknowledged meaning may become removed from its more primary connotation. Exodus 7:3 thus predicts, "And I will harden Pharaoh's heart," in which *harden* and *heart* have advanced into secondary concepts, but ones that are still literal in the sense of being the "customary, socially acknowledged" meanings which their contemporary audience would naturally associate with them in such a verbal setting.

Terry puts forward a general rule that "words should be understood in

65. Op. cit., p. 11.
66. See above, p. 6.
67. A title by John Urquhart.
68. Op. cit., I:122.
69. *Protestant Biblical Interpretation*, rev. ed., p. 90.

their literal sense unless literal interpretation involves a manifest contradiction or absurdity." His criterion, confessedly, leaves considerable leeway for subjective sensitivity. Terry himself grants that this principle, "when reduced to practice, becomes simply an appeal to every man's rational judgment"; and men differ to no small degree as to what may seem "absurd" and improbable. He therefore appeals more specifically to total context: "Reference must be had to the general character and style of the particular book, to the plan and purpose of the author, and to the context and scope of the particular passage in question."[70] In the expression, for example, "I will return the *sh'vūth, captivity,* of My people," *sh'vūth* seems primarily to signify *the imprisonment of debt;* and to "bring it back" for someone is to "turn one's fortune to the good."[71] This secondary, or derived, meaning is what appears to be intended, e.g. in Job 42:10 or Psalm 14:7. Yet it is the further fact of Israel's historical "captivity" or exile that seems to be suggested in Hosea 6:11 and Psalm 126:1, 4; and in Amos 9:14 it is hard to tell which idea is meant, though context might again suggest the "good fortune" interpretation.

Biblical prophecy contains (b) FIGURES as well as straightforward oracles. In contrast with its literal sense, a statement may be designated as figurative when "one thing is said under the form or figure of another thing."[72] Terry invokes a more technical title and proposes, "When a word is employed in another than its primary meaning, or applied to some object different from that to which it is appropriate in common usage, it is called a trope,"[73] meaning, literally, a *turn* in language.

The presence of figurative language in the Bible is usually self-evident, as demonstrated by the nature of the subject[74]—e.g. that "two nations" are in Rebekah's womb (Gen 25:23)—or, as stated above, by the nature of the context, e.g. that the "lampstand" of Ephesus would be removed (Rev 2:5; see 1:20).[75] Terry then accounts for its presence as follows: "The fundamental reason for the figurative style, which is so prominent a characteristic of prophecy, must be sought in the mode of revelation by vision";[76] cf. Hosea 12:10, "I have multiplied visions, and by the ministry of the prophets have I used similitudes."

70. Op. cit., p. 159.
71. KB, p. 940.
72. Barrows, op. cit., p. 546.
73. Op. cit., p. 157.
74. Cf. Fairbairn, *Hermeneutical Manual,* p. 138, "When anything is said which, if taken according to the letter, would be at variance with the essential nature of the subject spoken of, the language must be tropical" = metaphorical.
75. Cf. Barrows, op. cit., pp. 547–549; or Joseph Angus, *The Bible Handbook, an Introduction to the Study of Sacred Scripture;* rev. by Samuel G. Green, pp. 221–222.
76. Op. cit., p. 320; cf. Fairbairn, *Interpretation,* pp. 109–125 and 140–142, though cf. also Davidson's caution, op. cit., pp. 160–161: much of revelation was not visionary.

Figurative usage may be said to begin with a prophet's recourse to poetic forms. The Canaanitish literature which preceded the coming of the nation of Israel into Palestine had been marked by the employment of parallel stichoi, or lines; and when God's time arrived for the production of Hebrew prophecy it too is found to exhibit metrical arrangements and consistent repetitions both in thought and in the choice of words. Poetic usage also affects its feelings and modes of expression, for "the prophet was often both a poet and orator."[77]

A given phrase may be classified as poetic if it represents matters in a way somewhat above or beyond their prosiac history, if it idealizes them.[78] Poetic phraseology may thus take the form of embellishment, or hyperbole, in which more is said than is literally meant.[79] Isaiah 32:14, for example, speaks of the overwhelming character of Sennacherib's attack on Jerusalem in 701 b.c. by proclaiming, "The hill and the watch-tower shall be dens for ever." Leupold, accordingly, calls attention to "the relative use of the term 'forever' in this context";[80] and Girdlestone quotes the same passage, adding, "We know that the continuance of the desolation here implied will come to an end, for the very next verse points to Restitution—'*Until* the Spirit be poured upon us.' "[81] In similar fashion Jeremiah 25:9 anticipates "desolations of *ōlām*," *perpetual* desolations, at the hands of Nebuchadrezzar but then two verses later limits Judah's exilic period to 70 years, after which would come a return of the Hebrews to Canaan (29:10).[82] Poetic phraseology, such as Obadiah's that Jacob is to "devour" Edom, is self-explanatory and, where v. 18 of his prophecy is discussed, is passed by without comment. Occasionally, however, where the prophet's elevated discourse becomes so marked, or so subject to possible misunderstanding—as for example when God spoke through Zephaniah (1:2–3), referring apparently to Nebuchadrezzar's attack in 586, and threatened, "I will consume all things" from the land, even "the birds and the fishes"—an explanatory note on the poetry is introduced into the treatment of the passage.

Expositors differ as to the extent of the poetic language of Biblical prophecy. Girdlestone appears to have gone too far when he generalizes: "Its language at first sight looks extremely exaggerated. It is in truth thor-

---

77. W. J. Farley, *The Progress of Prophecy*, p. 25.

78. Fairbairn, *Interpretation*, Part I, V:III is devoted to the subject of "Poetical Elevation," pp. 126–138.

79. Bullinger, in his exhaustive analysis of figurative usage in Scripture, limits his discussion of hyperbole to an early section on "figures involving addition," without listing it under "figures involving change," whether of individual words (such as metonymy) or of their intended application (as metaphor): *Figures of Speech used in the Bible, Explained and Illustrated*, pp. 423–428.

80. *Exposition of Isaiah*, I:503.

81. Op. cit., p. 14; see also p. 116, below, and under Isa 29:18.

82. Compare Jer 31:12–14, that in the postexilic days, "they shall not sorrow any more at all."

oughly oriental."[83] Fairbairn speaks rather of "the regulated use" of poetry in prediction and cautions:

Prophecy was too directly and energetically practical in its aim to admit so much of a poetical nature, as might be proper in a sacred ode or song; and a comparison of such portions of Scripture with those which are more strictly prophetical, of the last chapter of Habakkuk, for example, with the two preceding chapters in the same book, will show at once, in how subdued a form the poetical spirit usually works in the prophetical portions, as compared with the others.

Yet even he concludes that prophecy "stands more nearly allied to the poetical than to any other species of composition which we can name. . . . It was in vision that the prophet received the revelations given to him, and in uttering them he naturally spoke as in an ecstatic or elevated frame of mind."[84]

Figurative language of a more advanced nature may produce definite shifts in the meanings of words. Metonymy identifies the interchange of one noun for another because of an inherent relationship between the two. Ephraim, for example, may represent the northern kingdom of Israel. A pervasive sort of prophetic metonymy occurs early in Scripture in the patriarchal blessings, in which these heroes of Genesis speak repeatedly of the later tribes and nations that will be descendant from them in terms of their individual children at the time: see 9:25–27; 25:23; 27:28–29, 39–40 (but also the more informal 28:3–4), 48:15–20; and above all, 49:2–27; cf. the chapter's introduction (v. 1), "that I may tell you that which shall befall you in the latter days."

Further figures are those which affect the application or intended meaning of Biblical language in its larger groups of words. A simile is a declaration of correspondence, as in Zechariah 12:8, "The house of David shall be as God, as the Angel of Yahweh"—they would not of course actually become divine; but they would cease to be its opposite, namely feeble. If a simile is then expanded into a formal narrative it becomes a parable— still, however, with but one central teaching rather than a complex of truths.[85] Christ's parables were often explained by the Lord Himself.

A metaphor is a direct declaration of identity, based upon some point of similarity. The prediction of Genesis 49:27 thus states, "Benjamin is a wolf," meaning, clearly, that the Benjamites would become *like* a wolf, though this is not overtly stated. If a metaphor, in turn, is expanded so that a series of metaphors are combined into one composition, the result is an allegory, a narrative that "speaks other" ideas, that provides different or secondary meanings from those actually expressed, e.g. the story of Israel

83. Op. cit., p. 13.
84. *Interpretation*, pp. 128–129.
85. George E. Ladd, *Jesus and the Kingdom*, p. 215.

as "a vine out of Egypt" in Psalm 80. The intended subject of an allegory may be identified, as in Psalm 23, where the Lord Yahweh is signified by "the shepherd," or it may not, as in Luke 19:12, on "the pounds," in which the fact that the nobleman going away to receive a kingdom means Christ is never expressly stated. Several of our Lord's narratives that are often classified as parables are really sustained metaphors, and therefore constitute allegories, e.g. the above "parable of the pounds" for which the actual title *pārābolē,* appears (though cf. Lk 4:21, Heb 9:9, 11:19, on the broad usage of this noun). In the prophetic analyses that make up the body of the work that follows, the more obvious metonymies, similes, and metaphors are left without specific identification, for example, under Joel 2:31, that "the moon shall be turned into blood," meaning that it will assume a color like blood. But those which seem less clear and about which question might arise are distinguished by the cautioning word "figurative" (abbreviated, "fig.") as in Joel 2:11, where Yahweh's "army" stands as a figure for a locust swarm, or in 3:16, where His "roaring" identifies divine judgment (cf. Zeph 2:11b).

Two of the most common sources for the Biblical figures are: the world of life and nature, as in Psalm 23 above, and the world of the previous history of Israel.[86] For the latter, Biblical prediction not infrequently makes use of phrases drawn from a specific historical situation to suggest its figurative language for similar but yet future events. In Micah 1:3–4, for example, Yahweh's coming in judgment and the mountains "melting" is based on the events of Sinai (cf. Jd 5:5 [ASVmg], Ps 97:5), which became figures for His activity, at this point, to punish Israel in 722 B.C. Barrows states it as a principle that "this primitive history of Israel furnishes for the prophets who lived in later ages a rich treasury of images which it would be absurd to interpret in a literal way."[87] Thus Hosea and Ezekiel could anticipate the Assyrian and Babylonian exiles as another "wilderness" experience (Hos 2:14, discussed under 1:11c, and Ezek 20:35, under 6:8).[88] But such a methodology is one which should be invoked only with strong contextual justification.[89]

Just as in the case of poetic language, opinions differ as to the extent of the Bible's employment of figures in reference to its larger word-groups. Girdlestone would again propose that "it is always more or less figurative."[90] But Feinberg seems to have greater statistical support when he insists that it is not generally or pervasively so;[91] for the following study demonstrates

86. Fairbairn, *Interpretation*, pp. 142–171.
87. Op. cit., p. 624.
88. Per Fairbairn, *Interpretation*, p. 165.
89. See Barrows' own cautions, below, under the limits of valid prediction, p. 44, and the discerning of fulfillments, p. 83.
90. Op. cit., p. 48.
91. Op. cit., p. 17; cf. Davidson, op. cit., p. 160, and compare the listings under each of the Biblical books below.

a proportion of only 9½ percent figurative (see below, pp. 674–675, 681). In any event, the affirmation by Barrows is well stated, that the Scripture's "figurative language is no less certain and truthful than its plain and literal declarations."[92] The tropes and figures that occur within divine revelation thus exercise a double function: on the one hand, to lend forcefulness, by making a striking effect upon their recipients; and on the other, to provide clarification, by emphasizing the truths of God to a degree that sometimes becomes possible only by figurative analogies.

2. ACTED. Predictive revelations may be granted in the form of prophecies that are acted out, that are pictorial in nature rather than verbal. In correspondence to the forthrightly spoken *oracle* stands (a) the acted SYMBOL. The general concept of symbol is that of a material object or event that connotes some matter of timeless significance. More specifically, however, a predictive symbol is herein defined as a material (nonverbal) medium of communication that prefigures a situation that is yet future, not one that is presently existing. It consists of an object lesson that draws its sole meaning from the thing predicted. A type, on the other hand (see part b, below), stands in correspondence to the verbalized *figure,* in that it is a predictive symbol or prefiguration that is presented through an independently existing historical reality, just as a figure of speech conveys a second thought that grows out of its accepted common usage. That is to say, the type possesses another, separate existence among its immediate contemporaries, even while communicating its developed, God-given truth about the future.[93]

Both of these acted forms, but particularly the simple predictive symbol, had the following definite purpose to fulfill: the prophet "uses the acted sign as an example and a proof that a certain action will take place. . . . What is of fundamental importance is the belief in the power of the prophet's signs—a power not his own, but a power given to him by Yahweh."[94] Jeremiah, though frequently classified as the most spiritual of the prophets, had regular recourse to enacted, concrete predictions of this sort (see 13:1, 19:1, 27:2, 28:10, 43:9, 51:63); and Ezekiel became the greatest exponent of all for symbolic proclamation. Yet symbolism tended to appear early in the course of redemptive history; and typology in particular is customarily found centuries in advance of the Bible's verbalized expressions of the revelatory propositions that it conveyed. By NT times almost all prophecy had come to assume the form of abstract verbalization[95] (though cf. Lk 22:30 on a yet typical value to the Lord's Supper).

An acted-out or pictorial form of inspired prediction is found to charac-

92. Op. cit., p. 557.
93. See Fairbairn, *Typology,* I: 67.
94. Guillaume, op. cit., pp. 170, 174.
95. Davidson, op. cit., pp. 13–14.

terize not only certain eventual, public presentations that were made by the prophets, but also those prior modes of revelation by which God first communicated to His servants. Visions might, upon occasion, have been purely worldless symbols (Rev 12:1–6)(?), though the divine Spirit almost always brought them into focus by means of accompanying messages (e.g. Zech 1:8–6:8); dreams, however, were seldom verbalized and consisted rather of acted scenes, which the recipient could do no more than describe.[96] Scripture confirms that the dreams which it portrays were both inspired and significantly predictive: e.g. concerning "the dream of Pharaoh: . . . what God is about to do He hath declared unto Pharaoh" (Gen 41:25; cf. v. 28). The king's particular dream, moreover, came in a double experience, ". . . because the thing is established by God, and God will shortly bring it to pass" (v. 32).

For the most part, Scripture explains its own predictive symbols, often through accompanying verbalizations (e.g. Rev 17:9–12). Sometimes illumination is accomplished simply through the name of the object, e.g. Genesis 2:9, Scripture's earliest: "the tree of life." Of a more recondite nature is Amos 8:1, the prophet's vision of "a basket of *summer fruit*," Heb. *qáyis*: presumably intending a name play with the noun *qēs*, "end," and signifying Israel's ripeness for its "end" in judgment. Sometimes explanation is to be derived from contextual indications, e.g. Zechariah 3:9, the symbolical "stone, set before [the priest] Joshua": probably a sign of the completion of the temple (cf. 4:8), appearing as it does in the historical context of Joshua's efforts toward its reconstruction (4:14; cf. Hag 1:14); see below, Zech., prophecy No. 1. Certain of the dreams of Scripture may be self-explanatory, for example, Joseph's, on the eleven sheaves bowing down to his sheaf (Gen 37:7): compare his brothers' immediate grasp of the implication of his rule over them (v. 8). Other dreams may be delayed in their explanation, until the appearance of "a man in whom the Spirit of God is" (41:38); but if they are genuine forecasts from above, God can and does give the interpretation (40:8; 41:16, 39).

In the body of the study that follows, prophecies that consist of non-verbal symbols are identified as "symbolical" (abbreviated "Sym.") in each case, e.g. the four carpenter-smiths of Zechariah 1:20–21, or the Man with the line for measuring Jerusalem (2:1). But such verbalized predictions as may occur within symbolical visions are not so distinguished, e.g. in 1:16a, "My house shall be built," or in 2:5, "I will be the glory in the midst of her."

(b) The TYPE consists of an action—not to be confused with a verbal message[97]—that represents and conveys a teaching of double import: its truth was a reality to its contemporaries, and yet it had accomplishment in the future work of Jesus Christ. The justification for typology derives from the fundamental unity that exists within God's plan of salvation in general

---

96. See Barrows, op. cit., p. 555.
97. Angus and Green, op. cit., p. 221; W. J. Beecher, op. cit., p. 127.

and within His redemptive testament in particular (Heb 9:15, 11:40). The NT affirms that the OT ceremonial was "a symbol for the time then present, according to which sacrifices are offered which cannot make the worshiper perfect, since they relate only to . . . regulations imposed until a time of reformation," when Christ should come (9:9–10). As Fairbairn has stated it, "The realities of the Gospel . . . are the ultimate objects which were contemplated by the mind of God, when planning the economy of His successive dispensations."[98] Indeed, Fairbairn's emphasis upon the Gospel, far from minimizing the significance of the older forms, is actually what gives them their meaning. Otherwise the OT's rituals at their best would be arbitrary and at worst would smack of outright magic. The types were designed from their very inception to be shadows (Heb 10:1), ineffectual in themselves (vv. 4, 11), but inherently descriptive of the accomplishments of Christ (v. 12; cf. 9:28). Correspondence extends even to details: that no bone of the Passover lamb should be broken (Ex 12:46; cf. John 19:46) or that the sin offering should be burned outside the camp (Lev 4:12; cf. Heb 13:12).[99]

The word *túpos*, "type," comes from the root *túptō*, "to strike," and means literally a "blow." But it occurs in the NT with a wide range of meanings: from a *mark* or *imprint* (John 20:25), to a *pattern* (Acts 7:44) or an *example* (II Thess 3:9), down to a specifically objective foreshadowing, such as Adam's existence as a *type* of Christ (Rom 5:14). Its Biblical usage remains therefore insufficient for one to formulate a definition for *túpos* in its exact, predictive sense.[100] From the NT's concrete examples, however, and particularly from the context of *túpos* in passages such as Hebrews 8:5, a type may be defined as "a divine enactment of future redemption."[101]

From this definition, four corollaries appear: (i) A type must have a divine origin; for Hebrews 8:5 stresses the fact of the tabernacle's holy place being a "copy," a result of God-given direction. Even as Yahweh was the One who decreed the ultimate redemption of mankind in Christ, and He alone, so only God could enunciate a type that would be predictive of that event, and He alone. For those, therefore, who do not believe in a God who reveals genuinely miraculous predictions the whole concept of typology becomes, correspondingly, impossible. As Lampe has observed concerning the

98. Fairbairn, *Typology*, I:47. So also the modern writer B. W. Anderson, *Israel's Prophetic Heritage*, p. 177, speaks of "the dramatic unity of Scripture . . . that events of the OT, seen from the angle of Christian faith, foreshadow and point beyond to the decisive event of God's revelation in Jesus Christ."

99. Fairbairn hesitates at this point (ibid., I:166): "The occasional outward coincidences between our Lord's personal history and things in God's earlier dispensations were the *signs* of a typical relationship rather than that relationship itself,—a likeness merely on the surface, which give indication of a deeper and more essential agreement," all of which is true; but still the OT situation *was* designed to be directly prophetic of Calvary.

100. Cf. ibid., I:42–46, on the inadequacy of Scripture to furnish proof in this regard: the same applies also to the other NT nouns used to designate types: *ántitupos*, "antitype"; *skĩá*, "shadow"; and *hupódeigmá*, "copy."

101. See Payne, *Theology*, pp. 357–360.

higher criticism of the Bible during the past two centuries, "The most definite and conclusive result of all this critical investigation was the breaking down of the old conception of the unity of Scripture and the consequent discrediting of the typological and prophetical exegesis familiar to so many generations of Christians."[102] It is true that in an attempt to recover some measure of divine reality in reference to both the Old and New Testaments a number of recent critical writers have emphasized what they have denominated as "typological exegesis."[103] Yet Lampe himself acknowledges that much of what the NT identifies as typical cannot, under the critical presuppositions, be accepted as the real intent of the OT at all;[104] and von Rad assures his readers, "This renewed recognition of types in the OT is no peddling of secret lore, no digging up of miracles, but is simply correspondent to the belief that the same God who revealed himself in Christ has also left his footprints in the history of the OT covenant people."[105] Stanley Gundry thus rightly questions the reality of the movement's stress upon "types": "But what meaning can such terms have in a system of interpretation that repudiates predictive prophecy and verbal inspiration?"[106] Little appeal to the advocates of this approach can therefore be made in this book.

(ii) A type must be redemptive; for 8:5 relates types to "the heavenly things" that God had in store for His own. Redemption, be it noted, is here understood in its broad sense, extending downward even into the Messiah's eschatological kingdom. The Feast of Tabernacles, for example, may thus be said to be typically predictive, though its foreshadowing of His as yet future ingathering of the nations (cf. Zech 14:16). This second feature of typology follows directly from the first; for all of God's revelation to mankind, from Genesis 3:15 and on, is directed to the goal of human restoration, whether that revelation be spoken (John 20:31, Rom 15:4) or acted (Eccl 3:14, Heb 1:14). Since reconciliation to God, moreover, requires a response and elicits worship, this redemptive quality that characterizes the known Biblical types furnishes typology with an important general qualification, namely, "All that was really typical . . . stood related to a religious worship."[107] Just so, the individual human types of the OT, such as Melchizedek, or even Adam, drew their prospective significance by the manner in which they illustrated man's way of approach to God through Jesus Christ. The fact that Biblical typology concerns Israel's ritual is well expressed by L. Alexander's detailed definition, which is one of the best: "Types are

102. *Essays on Typology*, p. 17.
103. Cf. certain of the articles in Claus Westermann, ed., *Essays on OT Hermeneutics* (1963), as W. Eichrodt, "Is Typological Exegesis an Appropriate Method?" who answers yes, in "an ancillary position," p. 245, or H. W. Wolff, who goes further and insists that "the typological approach is indispensable," "The Hermeneutics of the OT," p. 181.
104. Op. cit., pp. 15, 18, 23, 34.
105. *OT Theology*, II:36.
106. "Typology as a Means of Interpretation," ETSJ, 12 (1969), 240.
107. Fairbairn, *Typology*, I:189.

symbolical institutes expressly appointed by God to prefigure to those among whom they were set up certain great transactions in connection with that plan of redemption which, in the fulness of time, was to be unfolded to mankind."[108]

(iii) A type must be a pictorial enactment; for Hebrews 8:5 goes on to emphasize the tabernacle as an objective thing that Moses "erected." Types, in other words, must have existed, from the time of their enunciation, as prophecies of redemption that were symbolically acted out.

(iv) A type must have a future reference; for the same verse in Hebrews thus speaks of the type as a "shadow." Furthermore, since men throughout the ages have been saved upon the same basis, a given rite must have symbolized in its OT anticipation the same general teaching that it now typifies to the saints of the NT. The preparatory stage would, necessarily, have had to have been "of more obvious meaning, and of more easy comprehension than the ultimate and final."[109] When God's wrath, for example, brought death upon Israel by fiery serpents, the salvation that the Israelites gained by looking in faith at the brazen serpent on the pole (Num 21:9) served as a type of the final salvation from God's wrath that is gained, though less obviously, by looking in faith at Christ lifted up on the cross (John 3:14). Simultaneously, however, this pictorialness of typology makes the acted prophecy, in the last analysis, more obscure and difficult to interpret than the spoken prophecy: "Prophecy . . . naturally possesses something of the directness . . . of historical description. But types, having a significance or moral import of their own, apart from anything prospective, must, in their prophetical aspect, be somewhat less transparent, and possess more of a complicated character."[110]

A question, then, that naturally arises concerns the extent to which this anticipatory character was actually appreciated by the OT saints; and to it three kinds of answers may be made.[111] (i) As symbolical of Israel's sanctification to God, the ceremonial of the types seems to have been well understood by its contemporaries. In fact, as long as the ceremonial was accepted by Israel as a sign of sincere commitment to God and of the nation's reliance upon His redemption, then whether or not they understood the antitype of which its rites were typical, or even the fact that the rites *were* typical, becomes a matter of relatively minor importance.

(ii) As symbolical, moreover, of the general substitutionary way of salvation, the Mosaic types had a meaning that could hardly have escaped even the most obtuse. Berkhof affirms: "The sacrifices that were brought spoke of the forgiveness of sin on the basis of the atoning blood of Christ, and the

108. From his *Connection and Harmony of the Old and New Testaments*, 1841; as quoted in Fairbairn, *Typology*, I:25.
109. Fairbairn, *Typology*, I:51, though he carries this too far and sometimes ends up with the OT saints finding meanings that are not the same as the general truth taught in the NT.
110. Ibid., I:106.
111. Cf. Payne, *Theology*, pp. 351–352.

oft-repeated washings symbolized the purifying influence of the Holy Spirit. . . . The following passages prove that the Israelites had some conceptions of the spiritual significance of their rites and ceremonies . . . ,"[112] and he then lists, among other references, Psalm 51:7, "Purify me with hyssop, and I shall be clean: wash me, and I shall be whiter than snow." Their understanding of such a verse must have been not simply that blood sprinkled from hyssop related somehow to the forgiveness of sins, but that this ritual performance symbolized an action of justification that God Himself would yet carry out for His people.

(iii) As symbolical, therefore, of the redemptive program of God which He had devised in His heavenly eternity, the OT types came to be appreciated by at least some of their contemporaries. Moses and his associates are stated to have understood that their construction of the tabernacle would have to follow, precisely, the revealed heavenly pattern (Ex 25:40). God was providing acted predictions of Calvary when He revealed the ceremonial law.

A survey of Biblical types indicates that they might consist of a person, as Adam; an event, as Israel's crossing of the Red Sea; a thing, as the temple; an institution, as the sabbath; or a ceremonial, as the release of the scapegoat.[113] Some types are to be classified as complex, in that they possess several features, each purposely designed to be prophetic; Melchizedek and the Passover service are cases in point. Yet the types themselves preserved unity, being expressive of one central spiritual process.[114] The Biblical prophecies that exist in the form of types are marked as such in the discussions that follow, e.g., "Joel 1:9a (typ.): the meal offering; see Lev 2:1." On the Scriptural limitations to typology, see Section II-D, below.

The existence of the above-listed predictive forms constitutes one of today's chief handicaps to the interpretation of Biblical prophecy, which would otherwise require little in the way of a special hermeneutic. Terry therefore observes, "A thorough interpretation of the prophetic portions of the holy Scriptures is largely dependent upon a mastery of the principles and laws of figurative language, and of types and symbols,"[115] especially so, for example, in the apocalyptic portions.[116] The following two sections, accordingly, do not attempt to achieve a thorough treatment of Biblical hermeneutics; but they do seek to answer two major questions: of determining what portions of Scripture really are predictive and, if they are predictive, of what events. They concern, in other words, the limits of true prediction and the nature of fulfillment.

112. Op. cit., p. 135.
113. C. I. Scofield, *Reference Bible*, p. 4; cf. Summary D, below, pp. 671–672.
114. Cf. Fairbairn, *Typology*, I:156.
115. Op. cit., p. 313; cf. his subsequent call for a special prophetic hermeneutic: it is the "figure and symbol" that "demand great care on the part of him who would understand and interpret," p. 315.
116. See below, p. 86.

The Identification of
Predictions

The complexity of the task that faces a man who would achieve consistency in his methodology for dealing with the predictions of Scripture must not be underestimated. Ramm has cautioned that "in a real sense the most difficult problem in hermeneutics is the interpretation of prophecy, and the interpretation of it has divided both theologians and interpreters into warring camps."[1] The first part of this hermeneutical task consists in establishing precisely which of the various Biblical materials are properly to be included within one's study. As a result, much of the section that follows is necessarily negative: it is concerned with the setting of consistent limits by which to exclude from each of the four predictive forms that have been defined in I-C above any passages that do *not* appear to constitute valid forecasts of the future. See also Index 2, below, which is a selection of passages that are not considered to be properly predictive. For Mickelsen admonishes: "Read nothing into prophecy that is not there. It is just as dangerous to put more on the map than God put there as it is to remove any part of that which he did unfold."[2]

A. *Limitations on Oracles*[3]

1. TEXTUAL MISREPRESENTATION. The process of excluding spurious material from the study of prophecy begins with a recognition of the limits

---

1. *Protestant Biblical Interpretation* (1950 ed.), p. 155.
2. *Interpreting the Bible*, p. 294.
3. While some of the principles and illustrations that follow may apply also to figurative predictions, or even to enacted prophecies, their discussion is introduced at this point as fundamentally qualifying the simple "oracle" form.

27

of the authentic Biblical text, delivered by the hands of God's authoritative prophets and apostles, for which inspiration is claimed.[4] The prediction, for example, which has been attributed to Christ, of a so-called immunity for believers from the results of snake handling or of drinking poison occurs in one of the nonauthentic additions to the Gospel of Mark (16:18); and while the forecast of our Lord's death that He made in connection with His breaking of the bread at the Last Supper forms a valid part of the record in Matthew and Mark, one must note that it is bracketed as a "later addition" to the text of Luke 22:19b–20 in the Aland Greek Testament.[5] Similarly open to question is the concluding word of Luke 13:35a. Even the NAS reads, "Behold, your house is left to you *desolate*"; but it margins the adjective "desolate" as a gloss that has been supplied because of later MSS. This verse is not actually predicting desolations at all, e.g. such as occurred during the events of A.D. 70; but it simply states that Jerusalem "is being left to you. . . . You have it entirely to yourselves to possess and protect, for God no longer dwells in it."[6]

An allied form of misrepresentation concerns those instances in which a prediction comes into being not because of supplementation occurring in late MSS but because of mistranslation into English of what is in itself authentic text. The KJV of II Thessalonians 3:5, for example, reads, "The Lord direct your hearts into the love of God, and into the patient waiting for Christ." The Greek text, however, has no word for "waiting"; compare the rendering of ASV or NAS, ". . . direct your hearts . . . into the steadfastness of Christ." No expectation of the second advent is really involved in this verse.[7] In Hosea 11:12 both the KJV and the ASV proclaim, "Judah yet ruleth with God," which might suggest the Lord's future Messianic kingdom; but a more correct rendering appears in the ASVmg, "Judah is yet unsteadfast with God," which shows that this verse too is quite nonpredictive. Hosea 4:16 reads in most versions, "Now the Lord will feed them as a lamb in a large place," which might again seem to foretell blessing. The context, however, is threatening. Keil therefore understands this *wide area* as a place where the lamb becomes a prey of wild beasts, so that the prophet would here be anticipating "banishment and dispersion among the nations."[8] But since the *wide field* seems to have good connotations, the phrase is better rendered as a question: "Will Yahweh feed them as a lamb in a wide place?" The answer then is no; Israel possesses no such prediction! The familiar KJV rendering of Revelation 10:6, that "time" shall be no more, has an appearance of looking forward into eternity itself; but the noun *khrónos*, as used at this point, means basically "delay" (ASV, NAS);

4. See above, p. 6.
5. See below, Statistical Appendix, p. 675.
6. ICC, *Luke*, p. 352.
7. Cf. J. B. Payne, *The Imminent Appearing of Christ*, p. 93.
8. *Minor Prophets*, I:83.

the angel is simply saying that the events of the next verse are to follow without further postponement. Occasionally, pseudo-prediction may even develop out of today's misunderstanding of the King James English: John 15:27, for example, "Ye also shall bear witness," is not a prediction at all, but rather an older imperative usage.[9]

2. LINGUISTIC ALTERNATIVES. No human language is without its ambiguities; and the following paragraphs describe certain categories in which the words of Scripture might conceivably be understood as predictions of the future but in which they probably should not be or, at least, are sufficiently doubtful as to render their employment inadvisable. (a) Past alternatives to the future. The Hebrew OT normally distinguishes past action by using verbs in the "perfect" (completed) aspect, as opposed to the "imperfect" (incompleted) aspect. Yet when verbs in the perfect appear with a prefixed conjunction, designated "waw consecutive," they are to be rendered as equivalent to the imperfect. Such conversion, however, is not always the case: the same prefixed particle, now designated "waw conjunctive," may also introduce the simple perfect. To illustrate the ambiguity that results, Joshua 1:13 quotes Moses' words to the two and one-half eastern tribes; and it is rendered by the ASV, ". . . and Yahweh will give you this [Transjordanian] land." But (God) through Moses had already assigned them their territory; so the conjunction prefixed in w'nāthan, is better taken as a waw conjunctive, rather than as a consecutive, and translated with KJV and the Jerusalem Bible, "He has given you this land." So in Jeremiah 51:20–23, where ASV translates, "Thou [Babylon] art My battle-axe . . . and with thee *will* I break in pieces the nations," the Jerusalem Bible, Laetsch, and others read what is really a more satisfactory past tense for the second verb, and also for what follows.[10]

9. ICC, *John*, II:500, disputes even its meaning as a command, proposing " 'Ye also bear witness,' a statement of fact, not an imperative."
10. Cf. II Sam 7:9–11a (= I Chron 17:8–10a). 7:9a reads, "I have cut off all thine [David's] enemies"; and KD, *Samuel*, p. 343, then renders what follows: "and so *made* thee a great name . . . and *created* a place for My people Israel, and *planted* them, so that they *dwell* [perfect rendered as a present] in their place, and do not tremble [imperfect, see (b), below] any more (before their oppressors); and the sons of wickedness do not oppress [imperfect] them any further, as at the beginning, and from the day when I appointed judges over My people Israel: and I *create* thee [ASVmg, "have caused thee to"] rest from all thine enemies." A waw consecutive form with the perfect follows in 11b, "Moreover, Yahweh *telleth* thee. . . ." For Yahweh *had given* him rest from all his enemies round about" (7:1); and he already had a great name, since the conquest of I Sam 8 must precede this statement of rest from all enemies in 7:11a (the "after this" of 8:1, in other words, must be like that of 10:1, which describes—in 10:16–19—events already stated in 8:3–5, where he "got him a name," 8:13). The imperfects in II Sam 7:10b might seem really to reach into the future: they "shall be moved no more, nor shall the children of wickedness afflict them any more." But in II K 21:7–8 a qualification is attached to this promise: "if only they will observe to do according to all that I have commanded them"; and, unhappily, they did not.

On the other hand, perfect forms in a predictive context often imply an emphatic future, styled "prophetic perfect." For example, Samuel's spirit could say to Saul (I Sam 28:17), "Yahweh hath rent the kingdom out of thy hand, and given it to thy neighbor, even to David." In point of fact, though David had been anointed for some time previously, Saul still ruled the land. But in Samuel's mind *and message* the divine rending was as good as done; it was already accomplished "this day" (v. 18) as far as God was concerned. Oehler explains it thus: "The matter of revelation being given to the prophets in the form of intuition, the future appeared to them as immediately present . . . compare, e.g. Isa 9:1,5."[11] But this argument too, the phenomenon of the prophetic perfect, must not be invoked indiscriminately. The KJV apparently assumes that the perfect of Micah 6:13 is to be treated as anticipatory and reads, "Therefore also *will* I make thee sick in smiting thee."[12] But the rendering of the ASV, "Therefore I also *have* smitten thee with a grievous wound," seems preferable—cf. the idea of repentance as to be brought about by calamities already suffered which is taught in Amos 4:6–11.[13] So too in the NT, the Greek verbs of Mark 1:15 (Mt 3:2) stand in the perfect tense: "The kingdom of God is at hand, *éngiken, has come near* . . . the time is [lit., *has been*] fulfilled." Bright insists that interpreters recognize their precise force: "What all the ages had desired to see now is here—in this Jesus (Luke 10:23–24)";[14] cf. Luke 11:20. "Not that it would one day begin, or that it was about to begin: he declared that it had, in truth, already begun; the Servant is here and has begun his work,"[15] though the kingdom was not to be without future elements as well.[16]

(b) Present alternatives to the future. In the Hebrew OT the "imperfect" aspect represents incomplete action but does not thereby constitute a true "tense": its contextual surroundings must the rather determine, in any given case, whether the incomplete activity is immediately present or still future. In respect to David's words in II Samuel 22:44 (= Ps 18:43) the ASV opts for the latter, by rendering: "A people whom I have not known *shall serve* me"; but Delitzsch prefers the former and suggests, "People that I knew not *serve* me," and refers to Toi of Hamath (II Sam 8:10) as an

11. *Theology of the OT*, p. 488. Barnes, writing in the Camb. *Hag-Mal*, seems to have missed this point, that future things may be spoken of as present or past, when he judges the substance of Zech 11 to be "a vivid reminiscence of a past judgment" (p. 82), e.g. v. 8, "I cut off three shepherds in one month," which he refers to Jehoiakim, Jehoiachin, and Zedekiah (p. 83).

12. In this vein Keil, *Minor Prophets*, I:501, suggests, "The perfect expresses the certainty of the future," which is a possibility; but it appears less likely.

13. So in reference to Hab 3:3–15 S. R. Driver (Cent, *Minor Prophets*, II:85–86) comments, "In the description past tenses predominate . . . the future, in accordance with a frequent usage of the prophets . . . being vividly imagined as past, and described accordingly"; but see below, p. 438.

14. *The Kingdom of God*, p. 197, with documentation.

15. Ibid., p. 198.

16. Ibid., p. 238. On fulfillment in reference to the kingdom, see below, pp. 97, 134.

example;[17] cf. the Jerusalem Bible, "A people I did not know are now my servants."[18] The present, as an alternative to the future, occurs frequently in Isaiah 40 ff.[19] The ASV may indeed translate 40:10–11, "The Lord Yahweh will come [impf.] as a mighty one, and His arm will rule [pt.] for Him: behold, His reward is [no verb] with Him"; but these clauses could be better rendered, ". . . comes . . . rules . . . and is [as currently in the RSV]," referring to Hezekiah's deliverance in 701 B.C. from Sennacherib; cf. vv. 15–17, 23–24.[20]

Just as was true of the perfect, so also the incompleted aspects of Biblical language may be used to express a dramatic future. In the OT this phenomenon occurs particularly with the interjection *hinnē*, "behold," followed by a participle.[21] While Exodus 4:14, for example, might have been taken as no more than an observation made to Moses—"Behold, Aaron cometh forth to meet thee"—in point of fact it was only later that God came and ordered Aaron to start out (v. 27); so v. 14, in consequence, does constitute a true prediction. But again, discrimination becomes necessary in deciding just where the application of this principle is not simply possible, but is really desirable. The NT may provide the following illustrations. John 3:34 says, "He [Jesus] whom God has sent speaks the words of God, for He gives [Greek present] the Spirit without measure." Could this be an anticipation of our Lord's bestowal of the Holy Spirit at Pentecost, which John the Baptist had already predicted in 1:33? Parallelism might seem to favor such an approach, the *He* of the second clause being the same as the *He* (Jesus) of this first. But the following verse suggests that the giving is an action done by God the Father, directed to the Son,[22] so that the present tense should remain as a true present and not be considered a prediction. Again, Colossians 3:6 (NAS) says, "On account of these things [a list of

17. *Samuel*, p. 482.
18. Or Jer 2:27, "In time of trouble they will say . . ."; but KD, *Jer*, I:68, "they say," contemporary (because of the Scythian raids?), not predictive. So in Jd 5:11 the Heb. impf. may be future or simply present: "There *shall* they rehearse the righteous acts of Yahweh," ASV; but, "There they extol Yahweh's blessings," JB. Similarly in I Sam 25:28b, ASV, "Evil shall not be found in thee [David] all thy days"; but in actuality the king sinned later in life, badly: cf. II Sam 12, Ps 51. JB therefore renders, "In all your life there is no wickedness to be found in you"; for David did plead at least general innocence at this point; cf. in the preceding ch., 24:11. It might be noted that KD, *Sam*, p. 244, translates the subject of 25:28 as "misfortune" (which did eventuate, II Sam 15) and then renders the clause in question, ". . . may it not be found . . ."; cf. 26:24 (though the negative is here *lō*, rather than the more normal *al*, plus the impf.-jussive). Driver explains this last form as "chosen with the view of generalizing the statement as much as possible, so as to allow it to include a possible future—'*is not to be* found in thee,' etc." *Notes on the Hebrew Text and the Topography of the Books of Samuel*, p. 201.
19. Cf. my analysis of 51:17–52:12, WTJ, 30 (1968), 187.
20. Note also 41:2–3, 25, or 46:11; see WTJ, 29 (1967), 51–52, 56, 184, and the listing in 30 (1968), 195.
21. Or even an adjective, as in Isa 7:14, "Behold a virgin *shall conceive*," lit., ". . . a virgin, pregnant."
22. Camb, *John*, p. 104.

sins] the wrath of God *will come, érkhetai*," present; but for the same form in Ephesians 5:6, the NAS translates, "Because of these things the wrath of God *comes* upon the sons of disobedience." The latter expresses a generalization rather than a prediction and is more probably the correct rendering.[23] A crux of interpretation appears in Luke 17:21, "The kingdom of God is [Gk. present] in your midst," NAS, ASVmg, or, ". . . within you," ASV, NASmg. The former reading presents a greater number of Biblical parallels and appears more likely in this context, as addressed to the Pharisees. But *is* the kingdom among them, so that they have no need to look for it; or *will* it be among them, suddenly? The parallel of Mark 1:15[24] again suggests the present, in which the King had appeared, and not a prediction of the future.

(c) The potential, as an alternative to the future. At certain points the Semitic "imperfect" aspect may represent not only a present, or a future, but also a subjunctive or jussive (indirect imperative). In Judges 5:24 the ASV's declaration "Blessed shall be Jael . . ." thus appears in the Jerusalem Bible as "Blessed be Jael"; and for the Aramaic of Daniel 6:16, while the ASV may translate, "Thy God will deliver thee," Keil invokes context (cf. v. 20) and insists, "Darius could not have had this confidence," and renders the clause more effectively as a nonpredictive jussive, "May God deliver thee,"[25] thus expressing a somewhat feeble hope.[26] Again, the ASV text for Daniel 3:17 reads, "God will deliver us out of thy hand, O king." But the ASVmg, more correctly, translates, "If our God be able to deliver us, He will deliver us out of thy hand. . . ." The latter, by indicating the conditional context, shows that the three friends of Daniel were not assured of deliverance and, correspondingly, were not predicting it. Even where a potential situation reflects a more definite assurance on the part of the speaker, the future that is involved need neither be distant future nor constitute a specific Biblical prediction. The words of the apostle Paul in II Corinthians 13:4, "We are weak in Him, yet we shall live with Him because of the power of God directed toward you," are thus explained by Hodge as follows: "The life of which Paul speaks was the state in which he manifested apostolic power [to be displayed on his forthcoming visit to Corinth, v. 2]. There is no reference to the future or eternal life."[27] Context is the best key for clarifying ambiguities.

3. GENERALIZATION. An extensive body of Biblical material that has a tendency to be confused with predictive prophecy, and which sometimes does actually overlap it, is that of Scripture's indefinite, or at least nonparticular-

---

23. See below, p. 35, note 40.
24. See p. 30, above.
25. *Daniel*, p. 215.
26. See below, p. 41.
27. *An Exposition on the Second Epistle to the Corinthians*, p. 304.

ized, anticipations. Malachi 3:17, for example, states that those who fear God shall be His own possession. This is a generalization. But it becomes definite when the latter half of this verse adds that it will be on the day of God's making up His special treasure, on the day of God's final judgment, that they will become His own possession in a particular way, by being spared from the condemnation of the rest of humanity; and the thought is now transformed into a specific prediction. Seen from another aspect, generalizations may become predictive, if they describe a situation which will be true in the future, but which was not applicable during the period of the speaker; e.g. Jeremiah 31:31–34, on God's future, newer testament.[28] Exodus 15:26 thus generalizes, "If thou wilt do that which is right . . . I will put none of the diseases upon thee, which I have put upon the Egyptians." Yet Exodus 23:25, which is similar, introduces the factor of time, which renders it truly prophetic: it looks forward to an era of Israel's occupation of Canaan (v. 23), *and* of their obedience to God (v. 25)—"Ye shall serve Yahweh your God . . . and I will take sickness away from the midst of thee," words which must hence be applied to Yahweh's specifically future Messianic kingdom.

Nonpredictive generalizations may be distributed among categories such as the following: (a) Statements of principle. Examples like the following are typical of the Bible's assertions of timeless truth or principle: Amos 5:9, God brings sudden destruction on the strong; Habakkuk 3:17–19, when facing trouble in general, the prophet trusts God, and "He will make me to walk upon my high places"; Zechariah 1:3, God will turn to men as they turn to Him; Malachi 2:12, "Yahweh will cut off the man that doeth this [practices divorce]"; Mark 4:24, "By your standard of measure it shall be measured to you"; or James 1:5, "If any of you lacks wisdom, let him ask of God, who gives to all men generously, and it will be given to him."[29] The generalized character of certain other verses in the Bible may be less obvious; but the following would likewise appear to be simple statements of principle: Isaiah 27:8, "In measure, when Thou sendest them away, Thou dost contend with them," meaning: "Whenever God's chastisements fall upon His people, they are in careful measure."[30] Obadiah 15a, "The day of Yahweh [such time as He may choose for acts of intervention[31]] is near upon all the nations"; and it is from this statement of general truth, then,

28. Gen 2:24, however, on a man's leaving his father and mother to cleave to his wife, should not be counted as a prediction; for while some of its elements were nonexistent at the time when Adam first made his statements (v. 23) it did, shortly thereafter, become descriptive of the general situation that was to arise.

29. Other examples, not truly predictive, but stating principles of timeless validity, would be: Gen 12:3a, God's blessing of those who bless Abraham; Hos 13:11, that God gives and takes away kings; Mic 7:7–10, ". . . I will bear the indignation of Yahweh . . . until He execute judgment for me"; Mal 3:10, tithe, and receive a blessing.

30. BBC, IV:117.

31. See below, p. 132.

that the prophet goes on in 15b to reveal a specific prediction concerning the desolation of Edom.[32]

Special cases that illustrate Scripture's statements of principle appear either in the OT or in the NT's quotations of words from the OT. Isaiah 28:16, for example, had stated, "Behold, I lay in Zion a stone . . . he that believeth shall not be in haste." This verse is then used in the NT to describe the function of Christ as a foundation stone (Rom 9:33, 10:11, I Pet 2:6).[33] But in Isaiah these words constitute but a generalized statement of God's providing sound teaching for His own followers, as opposed to the false-hoods upon which the wicked were relying (Isa 28:15). Luke 16:31 is the conclusion of Jesus' description of the rich man and Lazarus: "If they do not listen to Moses and the Prophets, neither will they be persuaded if someone rises from the dead." Commentators may observe, "This was most remarkably exemplified in the results which followed the raising of another Lazarus (John 12:10) and the resurrection of our Lord Himself (Mt 28:11–13)."[34] But exemplification is not to be equated with direct predic-tion by Jesus, "as foretelling his own resurrection and its failure to persuade the Jews. This cannot be the intention because the risen Jesus never ap-peared to any but his own disciples as his chosen witnesses. The proposition is general as it stands."[35] I Corinthians 5:12 announces, "Those who are outside, God judges." NASmg suggests as an alternate translation, He "will judge"; but *The Expositor's Greek Testament* opts for the former and cautions, "Paul is not anticipating the Last Judgment, but laying down the principle that God is the world's judge."[36]

(b) Statements of process. Another of the Bible's types of generalization concerns not so much theoretical principles as practical happenings. The vision of Zechariah 5:3–4 thus depicts how sinners, represented by those

---

32. Cf. Obad 12–14, eight negative commands, to the effect: "Rejoice not over Judah in the day of their destruction." But these imperatives do not appear to be uttered in anticipation of some such day's coming. Keil, *Minor Prophets*, I:363, suggests, "Obadiah has not any particular conquest in his mind . . . he rises from the particular historical event [just past] to the idea which it embodied," i.e. a gen-eralization. Or the force of the entire passage may be assigned to the past, and "Obadiah's intense feeling throws the description of Edom's behavior into the form of imperatives," ICC, p. 27.

33. Cf. H. C. Leupold, *Exposition of Isaiah*, I:442–444.

34. Camb, *Luke*, p. 271.

35. Lenski, *Luke*, p. 861.

36. II:813. Cf. Rom 3:4, which includes an explanation, ". . . that Thou mightest be justified . . . when Thou art judged." The point of reference is not God's judging at the final judgment, as in Rom 2, but "that Thy rectitude, under all circumstances, might be seen and acknowledged," Charles Hodge, *Commentary on the Epistle to the Romans*, p. 72. So also in I Tim 5:24, "The sins of some men are quite evident, going before them to judgment; for others, their sins follow after"; NBC, p. 1072: i.e., some men are pursued later by the after effects of their sins, which in due course find them out." Even those who maintain some reference to the final judg-ment grant that this v. refers "primarily to Timothy's judgment," ICC, *Pastoral Epistles*, p. 64; cf. v. 25.

who steal and swear falsely, are continually being punished (Heb., a Qal pt.). Its sequel, the vision of vv. 6–11,[37] then goes on to note that such people may be expected to go back to their place in Shinar, Babylon, and so concentrate in the area of worldly power.[38] Similar instances appear in the NT record of Christ's discourse with Nathanael, John 1:50–51: "You shall see greater things than these: you shall see the heaven opened, and the angels of God ascending and descending upon the Son of Man." The Lord was describing a general historical process: "From this point onwards Christ's Messianic work of linking earth to heaven, and re-establishing free intercourse between man and God, goes on."[39] So also in 2:4 Jesus states, "My hour has not yet come," not, apparently, intending any specific event, such as His death, but more generally, "His hour for 'manifesting forth His glory' (v. 11) as the Messiah by working miracles";[40] cf. vv. 7–11 that follow.

Statements of historical processes, presently going on, may be conjoined to other revelations that are truly predictive oracles. In Habakkuk 1, for example, v. 12 predicts that the Chaldeans are about to correct Israel, as they did with a vengeance in 586 B.C. But v. 13, which follows, is not predictive, as it describes how they devour men more righteous than themselves. Thus the remainder of the chapter, through v. 17, illustrates what they are already doing (as in v. 7) and not what they will do (as the prediction of their further marching that appears in v. 6). Yet just as in the case of statements of principle that may go on to introduce more truly predictive matters, so if a given statement of process comes to foresee the introduction of some new situation, one not presently existent, then this too serves a legitimately prophetic purpose; e.g. Genesis 2:17, on the predicted entrance of death into human history.[41]

37. Cf. how v. 6, "their" appearance, refers back to the sinners of vv. 3–4.

38. So in I Sam 8:11–18, Samuel outlines the sorts of things that a king would do. Saul is later seen to have precisely "fulfilled" one of these items of royal process (14:52), that of drafting mighty men for his armed forces (per 8:11); but Samuel's words seem hardly to have been intended as a specific prediction. Again, Job 31:14 reads, "What shall I do when God riseth up?" not in final judgment, as in 19:29, but more in a kind of providential intervention, "God's rising up from his apparent inactivity and indifference to what it taking place in the world," ICC, II:224. Similarly E. J. Young, *The Prophecy of Daniel*, p. 258, paraphrases Dan 12:4 (cf. v. 10), on the anticipated reactions of men to Daniel's prophecy, as a process: his book "contains the truth as to the future. Many shall go to and fro in search of knowledge, but they shall not find it."

39. Camb, *John*, p. 82.

40. Ibid., p. 84. So Rom 1:18 states, "The wrath of God is revealed from heaven against all ungodliness." Ch. 2:2–3 goes on, indeed, to speak of the final judgment; but ch. 1 is stressing God's judgment as already active (v. 24), and the revelation of His wrath appears "equally as His righteousness is revealed (see v. 17)," in the gospel (NBC, p. 943). Eph 5:6 seems similarly to speak of this continuous historical process: "The wrath of God comes upon the sons of disobedience."

41. Yet God's statement to Adam in 3:19, "unto dust shalt thou return," was uttered after Adam's fall and loss of freedom from death. It might indeed be con-

A major aspect of the Bible's nonpredictive statements of continuous process concerns this whole area of life after death and of heavenly immortality. Heaven as the abode of God is in itself of course eternal and not subject to foretelling, as if it were a thing yet to be realized in the future. The fulfillment of all actual predictions, on the other hand, must possess relationship to some identifiable point in history. Yet the picture in Revelation 15:3 of saints that are singing in heaven remains essentially timeless; it is not related to the course of history and is therefore not predictive. In contrast, the anticipation that was stated by Christ of Satan's attempted war in heaven and of his being cast down from it (John 12:31) is prophetic, since these latter events are associated with His own historical death and victorious ascension. Yet our Lord's wonderful promise, "If I go and prepare a place for you, I will come again, and receive you to Myself; that where I am, there ye may be also" (John 14:3), is not so much a prophecy as an assurance that He hereby grants to each believer as he faces his own individual participation in the general process of death.[42]

So also a number of the Bible's statements about the future kingdom of God may relate solely to spiritual salvation as a timeless and hence nonpredictive fact of heaven; e.g. I Corinthians 6:9–10, "The unrighteous . . . [classes specified] shall not inherit the kingdom of God" (cf. vv. 11, 13),[43] or Philippians 1:19, where Paul knew that the present sufferings would "turn out for my deliverance," NASmg, *salvation,* "the heavenly issue of the whole process in glory,"[44] or 3:14, "the prize of the upward call of God," namely, "the heavenly reward."[45] So in II Timothy 4:18 he affirms, "The Lord will deliver me from every evil deed, and will bring me safely to His heavenly kingdom." Similarly in the OT, Ezekiel's question (18:31, 33:11), "Why will ye die, O house of Israel?" does not appear to be a specific threat of the exile, as if that event were to befall only the wicked within Israel (cf. 21:3). Rather, " 'Death' is used to denote the complete destruction with which transgressors are threatened by the law."[46]

---

sidered predictive of his specific death, 930 years later; but this verse appears rather as a statement of the whole historic process of death for the human race, of which Adam served as the representative (or, some would prefer to say, "seminal" or "realistic") head. Such physical disintegration had by this time become a current reality, and 3:19 should not apparently be considered as a specific prediction.

42. Note that He had just spoken of His own going away, and of His disciples following Him in death (13:36–37); and when He was questioned about His statement in 14:3, He explained it by saying that He was "the life" (v. 6). The immediate context therefore suggests nothing about His visible second advent but rather uses "I come" in a different sense (cf. its spiritual usage in v. 18); cf. Payne, *Imminent Appearing,* p. 74. Marcus Dods has observed, "The promise is fulfilled in the death of the Christian, and it has changed the aspect of death. The personal second coming of Christ is not a frequent theme in this Gospel," *ExGkT,* I:822.

43. Cf. Gal 5:21, over which IB, X:565, notes the possibility of broad application, either to heaven or earth; or Eph 5:5.

44. Camb, *Phil,* p. 51.

45. ICC, p. 110.

46. Even Isa 56:1, 5, may have reference to the believers' heavenly status: "My salvation is near to come . . . I will give them an everlasting name."

Correspondingly, many references in the NT to the Christian's heavenly reward are more properly viewed as a part of the generalized process of future life than as specific predictions. Examples might include the following: Luke 6:35, "Love your enemies and do good, and your reward will be great": this reward seems to correspond to that of Matthew 5:12—"for your reward in heaven is great"—and not to involve a prediction of God's later (final) judgment[47] but simply "the greater glory that shall be ours in heaven."[48] II Corinthians 4:17: afflictions "produce for us an eternal weight of glory," apparently not a Pauline forecast of concrete historical fulfillments on earth but an anticipation of "the inconceivable excellence and blessedness of heaven."[49] James 1:12: "He will receive a crown of life," not in a specific eschatological bestowal, as in II Timothy 4:8, I Peter 5:4; but *of life* is best taken as an epegetical genitive, *the crown which is life*, as in Revelation 2:10—"the blessed life of eternity constitutes the crown."[50]

Some Scriptural passages of this sort are difficult to categorize but still seem more generalized and processlike than specifically predictive, e.g., Revelation 3:5, "He who overcomes shall be clothed in white garments [in heaven after death, cf. 6:11], and I will confess his name before My Father and before His angels." Compare II Timothy 2:12b, "If we deny Him, He also will deny us" (followed by v. 13, "If we are faithless, He remains faithful," a statement of principle);[51] 12b thus apparently depicts a continuous process of denial "before the eternal angel world,"[52] and not a

47. Though cf. H. Alford, *The Greek Testament*, I:34.

48. Lenski, *Mt*, p. 197.

49. Hodge, *II Cor*, p. 104. So in Col 3:24, the apostle enjoins industriousness upon slaves, "knowing that from the Lord you will receive the reward of the inheritance," namely, "the (heavenly) inheritance, appositional genitive," Lenski, *Col*, p. 184, cf. 4:1, "inasmuch as slaves could not be inheritors of an earthly possession," ICC, *Eph-Col*, p. 295. Or in II Tim 2:11 he states, "If we died with Him [in baptism, cf. Rom 6:4], we shall also live with Him," "in heaven forever," Lenski, op. cit., p. 794; so ExGkT, IV:163, refers to newness of life now, but "the prominent notion here is of the life to come." Heb 10:34-35 states, "You accepted joyfully the seizure of your property, knowing that you have for yourselves a better possession and an abiding one . . . a great reward": "This is the 'reward' of which Jesus spoke in Lk 6:23, 'Your reward is great in heaven,'" NIC, pp. 270-271, though Heb 10:36 speaks also of obtaining a promise at the Lord's Parousia (*q.v*).

50. ICC, *James*, p. 152. In the figurative phraseology of Rev 2:17, the overcomer is to receive "hidden manna [cf. Ex 16:33, Heb 9:4, on manna inside the ark, which was now thought of as if in heaven, Rev 11:19] and . . . a new name written on a white stone which no one knows but he who receives it"; probably "manna in the next life following his liberation from death . . . and possibly a kind of amulet with the secret name of Jesus, which the martyr has not denied, engraved on it . . . to insure a blessed immortality," IB, XII:387. Alternatively, since the *name* seems distinguished from the *My new name* [of Christ, 3:12], it may be a name for the believer signifying his "new status . . . the overcomer's right to enter the kingdom of God in a character all his own, molded by the grace of God in him," NBC, p. 1173. In either event, the reference is to heaven.

51. Cf. Mt 10:32-33, Lk 12:9-10 (treated as predictive in the body of this work, but of another matter, namely Christ's ascension into heaven and appearing before His Father, which is a more specific item of anticipation to be adduced from these verses).

52. Lenski, *Lk*, p. 673.

particularized prophecy. One might state, in summary, that the Bible's anticipations of the resurrection and of final judgment are predictions of events, but that those of immortality are generalizations and more concerned with a continuous process.

(c) Generalized reporting. A final group of passages that resist classification among the specific predictions of Scripture are certain indefinite Biblical citations of previous prophetic revelations. As a rule, in this book such reports of earlier prophecies are considered to be repetitions of the original predictions. For example, the earlier prophecies that Israel was to receive an inheritance in the land of Canaan (Gen 12:7, Ex 3:8) are subsequently requoted in both OT and NT (Ps 105:11, Acts 7:5). Yet sometimes the later reports may become so generalized that the original predictions can no longer be identified, and such reports are therefore incapable of proper classification; e.g. within Peter's preaching, such comprehensive statements as Acts 3:24, "All the prophets who have spoken, from Samuel and his successors onward, announced these days" (cf. v. 18); in Paul, an allusion to "the gospel which He promised beforehand through His prophets in the holy Scriptures" (Rom 1:1-2; cf. Eph 3:6; or Heb 11:39, "what was promised"); or this more specific but still not identifiable prophetic announcement in Stephen's speech, as he described Israel's treatment of the prophets, "They killed those who had previously announced the coming of the Righteous One" (Acts 7:52; cf. 13:27, 29). Such reports or recordings are so general as to forbid their association with some particular prophecy that they might be said to reflect. Yet Acts 13:23, on Jesus' coming from the offspring of David "according to promise," does progress sufficiently beyond generalized reporting to be included in the study of Scriptural prophecy, as a restatement of II Samuel 7:13b; and it is so counted below (listed under Acts 2: 30).

4. INTENTION. Girdlestone insists, "Prophecy does not work out its own fulfillment, but stands as a witness until after the event has taken place."[53] This sort of a limiting factor, moreover, necessarily excludes from the category of genuine foretelling all predictions that merely reflect the desires or intentions of their original speakers. Isaiah's prayer (II K 20:11) for the backward motion of a shadow should not therefore be considered as a prediction; and when the shadow did actually move backward it acted out of response to another aspect of nonpredictive intention, namely the command of Yahweh. The prophecy that was involved occurred in v. 9, when Isaiah spoke out in faith and proclaimed, "This shall be a sign unto thee . . . the shadow. . . ." The words likewise of Haggai 2:19 limit themselves to Yahweh's immediate intention: "From this day I will bless you," specifically, with crops; the prophecy works out its own fulfillment and thus should not be considered predictive. Yahweh speaks similarly in Zechariah 8:10-13,

53. *The Grammar of Prophecy*, p. 1.

"Before these days there was no hire or peace. But now . . . the ground shall give her increase . . . and ye shall be a blessing." His intent was one of prompt execution; for v. 15 continues, "So again have I thought in these days to do well unto Jerusalem."

On the other hand, even a matter of immediate fulfillment may constitute a true prediction as long as its accomplishment does not lie within the province of the speaker, e.g. Jonah's prophetic words, "Cast me into the sea, and it shall be calm"; but contrast Christ's cursing of the barren fig tree (Mk 11:14): this latter action lay within our Lord's power, and He proceeded to do it. In the case of the manna, Exodus 16:4—"I will rain bread from heaven for you"—reflects God's immediate nonpredictive intention; but when Moses repeated these same words to the people (vv. 6–8), then, from his lips, it became a prediction. Compare Daniel's confident affirmation that he would show Nebuchadrezzar the interpretation of the king's dream (Dan 2:16; cf. vv. 24–25) *before* God had yet revealed its meaning to him.

Scripture contains several categories of "intentions" which need to be distinguished from its predictions. These include the following: (a) Threats. At the inception of redemptive history God's word came to the serpent, "Upon thy belly shalt thou go" (Gen 3:14); but this threat is descriptive of God's intention at the moment and is not a prophecy. Compare Hosea 4:9–10, that sexual promiscuity is not to bring about Israel's increase (cf. 2:9–10); Hosea 12:14, blood-guiltiness is to remain upon Ephraim; or Amos 8:11–13, there will eventuate a thirst for the hearing of the words of Yahweh: that is, God threatens to desist from further guidance of the Israelite nation.[54]

(b) Commands are not predictions—cf. Genesis 1:3, "Let there be light" —unless context suggests some later accomplishment—cf. v. 26, "Let them have dominion," a goal for humanity that has been achieved only in Jesus Christ[55]—or unless the command goes beyond the power of the human speaker; cf. Joshua, commanding the sunlight to be prolonged (Josh 10:12–13). Zechariah 8:19, on the other hand, despite its somewhat imperative cast, did not turn out to be predictive: the prophet's oracle amounted to a directive in answer to the people's question in 7:3 and proclaimed, "The fasts shall be joy and gladness." Barnes states, "Probably the prophet intends his promise in its literal sense."[56] But the Jews preferred to maintain their fasts[57] and thus never attained to the blessing proffered through Zechariah. His words therefore fall into the category of a conditional prophecy that was not accomplished.[58]

A special type of command-by-way-of-choice appears in Exodus 8:9.

54. Cf. Keil, *Minor Prophets*, I:319.
55. See below, p. 155, and cf. Isa 56:7, "My house shall be called ["should be called," BBC, IV:239] a house of prayer for all people."
56. Camb, *Hag-Mal*, p. 68.
57. Cf. Keil, op. cit., II:306, 319.
58. See below, pp. 62–63, 67 (note 42).

Moses there extended to Pharaoh an opportunity to choose a time for the ending of Egypt's second plague. In verse 10a Pharaoh said, "Tomorrow"; and, 10b, Moses agreed and achieved a miraculous answer by praying to God (vv. 12–13). But Pharaoh's word hardly constitutes a prediction: his choice and also Moses' prayer need furnish no more than two differing examples of intentions expressed by men that were not inherently descriptive of the future.

The Bible's commands are sometimes difficult to distinguish from its predictions. OT phraseology, particularly with the waw consecutive, may shade off from a predictive into an imperative sense without change in form; e.g. Exodus 3:18, "And they shall hearken to thy voice [predictive]: and thou shalt come, thou and the elders of Israel, unto the king of Egypt, and ye shall say unto him [command]. . . ." Yet the words of v. 22—"and ye shall despoil the Egyptians"—though conceivably only imperative, do appear from the surrounding context to be an actual forecast. Numbers 33:52, on the other hand, starts with a command, "Ye shall drive out all the inhabitants of the land and destroy their images," and then shifts in v. 53 to prediction, "Ye shall take possession of the land and dwell therein, for unto you have I given it."[59] NT phraseology occasionally evidences a similar sort of fluctuation; e.g. the three verbs in the future tense that appear in Luke 1:31. The first two are predictive, but the third has more of an imperative force; cf. the NAS rendering, "You *will* conceive, *and bear* a son, and you *shall* name Him Jesus" (cf. a similar situation in Mt 1:21). Yet earlier in the same chapter, a parallel statement related to the naming of John the Baptist does appear to be prophetic, "Elizabeth *will* bear you a son, and you *will* give him the name John" (1:13, *q.v.*).

(c) Resolution, as found among men, constitutes but another form of intention, specifically, one that is not to be confused with prediction. For example, Micah 4:1–4, with its prophecy of God's future kingdom, in which the nations will not "learn war any more," is followed in v. 5, first with a cautioning statement about the peoples' walking "every one in the name of his god,"[60] and second, with the prophet's own affirmation, "We will walk in the name of Yahweh our God for ever." As a resolution, it was commendable; but had it been an inspired prediction, the conduct of Micah's generation and also of those that followed would have had to have far exceeded the known attainments of the nation of Judah. Yet God's resolution, in Genesis 6:7, to destroy creation by the flood was both valid and also truly predictive, since it was revealed 120 years in advance (v. 3); compare His resolve expressed in 7:4, which likewise forecast the future, though by this time only seven days prior to the achievement.

A particular form of intention that must be carefully distinguished from predictive prophecy is that of the purpose clause. Exodus 3:10, for example,

59. See the Jerusalem Bible.
60. See below, p. 428.

expressed God's choice of Moses, "that thou mayest bring forth My people out of Egypt." But Moses objected (v. 11); his leadership was therefore not as yet a matter of determined prophecy, though it did become so in v. 12.

In similar fashion, (d) the promises contained in Scripture depend for their validity as prophecy upon the situation and upon the speaker; even the promises of God must possess a future eventuation and fulfillment if they are to be considered as specifically predictive. For example, His words of comfort that were declared after the flood—"seedtime and harvest, and cold and heat, and summer and winter, and day and night shall not cease" (Gen 8:22b)—describe the preservation of an order that was then already established; they do not foretell a further eventuation. Contrast the implications for a future cataclysm inherent in the words of 8:22a, "While the earth remaineth. . . ."[61]

(e) Hopes consist of normal anticipations, not of supernatural predictions: cf. the women's expectations of Obed for Naomi, as expressed in Ruth 4:15, "He shall be a nourisher of thine old age." In Exodus 32:30 Moses gave utterance to a lofty hope: "Peradventure I shall make atonement for your sin"; but he was not sure. This was not prophecy (cf. I Sam 6:5). Yet the Bible's divinely directed blessings, as Jacob's in Genesis 49, or curses, as Joshua's on the refortifying of Jericho (Josh 6:26), were inspired, were predictive, and were eventually fulfilled.

5. INFERRED PROPHECIES. A final question over the limits of Scriptural oracles concerns the possible inclusion of prophecies whose existence or exact content is not expressly stated but must be inferred. An example of relative certainty, even though not recorded in the book of the man concerned, appears in II Kings 14:25, which speaks of a national expansion by Jeroboam II, "according to the word of Yahweh which He spake by Jonah the prophet." Less obvious is II Kings 6:31, in which King Jehoram of Israel (852–841) threatened the life of Elisha because of the seriousness of a siege being suffered by Samaria. "No doubt Elisha had promised help from Yahweh and thus encouraged resistance."[62] But this conclusion would have remained an inference of considerable doubt had the passage stood by itself; it would hardly have been included in the study that follows. Yet in v. 33 Jehoram says, "Why should I wait for Yahweh any longer?" It thus appears that Elisha must have told him to wait. Did the prophet enforce this revelation with a promise of deliverance? Likelihood is great, and these words are therefore discussed below; see II Kings, prophecy No. 16.

61. See below, p. 159. W. J. Beecher seeks to class most predictions, and even the entire interrelationship between the Testaments, under the category of promise; but in so doing he seems to press the NT references to "promise" beyond reasonable limits, *The Prophets and the Promise*, especially ch. 8.
62. JB, p. 461.

B. *Limitations on Predictive Figures*

1. LEGITIMATE FIGURES, BUT NONPREDICTIVE. The identification of prophetic subjects within those portions of the Bible that utilize figurative language must commence with the recognition that not all figures are predictive. Just as in the case of Scripture's more literally phrased "oracles," so limits must be set to the intended significance of its figures; and as Mickelsen cautions, "The well-balanced interpreter has objective reasons for both literal and figurative meanings."[63] A striking verbal picture may lend color and force to a prophetic anticipation;[64] the idea, as a result, becomes more effectively communicated, e.g. in Micah 4:12–13, that Yahweh has gathered Judah's enemies "as sheaves to the threshing floor: arise and thresh, O daughter of Zion. . . ." Yet figures may also obscure the modern reader's understanding of the revelation, so that the unwary interpreter may be led to discover predictions where none were actually intended. For example, in Daniel 10:1 "a thing was revealed" to the prophet, "even a great warfare." But the latter expression does not appear to be predictive of the wars that are described in the following chapter (11:2 ff.); more probably it depicts the struggle that Daniel was to experience within himself in receiving the revelation (cf. 10:8–11, 16–18).[65]

Similes and metaphors require a close regard to their total context for the identification of possible prophetic meaning. Micah, for example, states, "I am as the grape gleanings of the vintage: there is no cluster to eat" (7:1). His simile might suggest exemption from a general deportation; but Horton cautions, "It does not refer to exile or political downfall. The city is crowded and rich; but when the good have disappeared . . . the population is mere prickly stubble."[66] When a simile becomes expanded into a parable, the interpreter must still limit his quest for prophetic meaning to that one basic idea that the story intended.[67] Unless the symbolism of sustained metaphors (= allegory) is clearly present, it invites methodological disaster to make a parable "go on all fours": e.g. in our Lord's story of the mustard seed, to make the birds of the air that nest in the branches of the eventual mustard tree (Mk 4:32) prophetic of anything other than the future growth of the kingdom.[68] This alone is the point of the parable.

2. ILLEGITIMATE FIGURES: ALLEGORIZATION. More extreme is the error of introducing figurative predictive meanings into contexts where the very presence of figures appears to be dubious. The fact of the existence of

63. Op. cit., p. 305.
64. See above, p. 21.
65. Young, op. cit., p. 224.
66. Cent, *Minor Prophets*, I:264.
67. See above, p. 19.
68. Cf. Feinberg's insistence that the birds foreshadow "mere professors and not really children of the kingdom," *Premillennialism or Amillennialism?* p. 70.

legitimate figures within Scripture provides no carte blanche for an allegorized method of interpretation. A primary canon is that figurative meanings must be limited to those which the Biblical authors themselves (or, Author Himself) intended to be so understood.[69] "If an interpreter declares that a certain expression is figurative, he must have . . . compelling grounds . . . from an objective study of all factors."[70]

The examples of valid Biblical prediction that have been so far adduced have all sought to represent "normal" interpretation, namely, that method by which one attempts to assign to Scripture its original, divinely intended meaning. A given passage may be either literal or figurative in its form, but normal interpretation seeks for whatever might have been those socially intelligible denotations which God willed for the passage to designate at the time in which He had it written.[71] Allegorization,[72] on the other hand, represents a usage of language in other than its customary, socially acknowledged meanings: it is the assignment of ideas to Scripture on the assumption that God's word may now convey a second or different meaning from that originally intended by the author(s).[73] As criticized by its opponents, "Allegorism invented the interpretation for the sake of the truth which it wished to teach";[74] and Fairbairn has been insistent upon its differentiation from legitimate Christian typology: "The typical is not properly a different or higher sense, but a different or higher application of the same sense,"[75] since it symbolized to its contemporaries the same truth whose fulfillment it typified for the future.[76]

For precision's sake, one must distinguish the allegorizing method from the literary form of allegory.[77] The existence, that is, of allegories within Scripture, of stories that were deliberately designed to carry a series of

69. See above, p. 17.
70. Mickelsen, op. cit., p. 304.
71. Cf. the somewhat similar definition of Ramm for the literal meaning of individual words; above, p. 16.
72. Ramm, op. cit., rev. ed., pp. 220–225, discusses at length the present-day confusion over terminology for these contrasted methods of interpretation. The antonyms "normal-allegorized" are herein preferred to "literal-figurative" (since these constitute but two subdivisions within the broader category of normal interpretation) and to "material-spiritual" (since a normal interpretation need be no less spiritual, and a forced interpretation may yet be materially oriented). Similar observations are made by Roy L. Aldrich in BS, 112 (1955), 53–54, and by E. R. Craven in Lange's commentary on Revelation, p. 98, though with a preference for the term "normal-mystical." Yet the qualifier "mystical" might seem to imply an undue antipathy to objectivity. Pentecost favors "grammatico-historical vs. allegorical," *Things to Come*, p. 4. Yet the latter term likewise has drawbacks, in that "allegory" possesses a more restricted connotation and identifies a legitimate literary form, the meanings of which are truly those that were intended by the author.
73. Fairbairn complains that the original is used "to convey some meaning of a quite diverse and higher kind," *The Typology of Scripture*, 1:2.
74. A. Edersheim, *Prophecy and History in Relation to the Messiah*, p. 167.
75. Op. cit., I:3.
76. See above, pp. 22–23, 25.
77. Cf. Pentecost, op. cit., pp. 7–8.

sustained second meanings, must not be confused with the interpretive process of allegorizing, by which an account is interpreted as if possessing a second meaning distinct from that originally intended. Biblical allegories are to be found in some number and have been discussed above;[78] allegorization, however, occurs but once in Scripture,[79] in Galatians 4:21–31, in Paul's use of the lives of young Ishmael and Isaac to depict the bondage of Judaism as contrasted with the freedom of Christianity. The apostle, moreover, specifically identifies his method as allegorical (v. 24); he makes no claim that the applications he draws for his Galatian readers are those that were intended by the original text of Genesis; and his particular allegorizations (e.g. in vv. 25 or 29–30) are not discussed in the following study, as if constituting real prophecies—except as references to other, legitimate predictions may happen to be included within them (e.g. that Isaac's birth had been a matter of promise, v. 28).

Commentators of the modern period have come increasingly to recognize the import of the literal (normal) intent of God's prophets. Davidson is emphatic: "This I consider the first principle in prophetic interpretation—to read the prophet literally—to assume that the literal meaning is *his* meaning—that he is moving among realities, not symbols, among concrete things like peoples, not among abstractions like *our* Church, world, etc."[80] Barrows wisely cautions that "a favorite expedient with those who deny the supernatural character of revelation is to explain the miraculous transactions recorded in the Bible as figurative or mythical."[81] It rests upon today's interpreter to strive to transport himself out of current naturalistic thinking into thought patterns of Scripture before assuming, for example, that a predicted eschatological drying up of a great river (Rev 16:12) could not be historically intended (cf. Josh 3:16–17). As Davidson states, "Prophecy is poetical, but it is not allegorical. . . . When the prophets speak of natural objects . . . they do not mean human things by them. When Joel speaks of locusts, he means these creatures. When he speaks of the sun, the moon, and the stars, he means these bodies."[82] The Biblical supernaturalist must also be on his guard, lest he permit his particular theological presuppositions to draw him aside into allegorized departures from the actual revelations of Scripture, even when these concern such possibly unpalatable matters as a glorification of warfare or a reimposition of annual pilgrimages. Oehler explains, "Generally speaking, the prophets mean just what they say. As

78. Pp. 19–20.
79. Cf. Farrar's caution: "Allegory, though once used by St. Paul by way of passing illustration, is unknown to the other apostles, and is never sanctioned by Christ," *History of Interpretation*, p. 217.
80. *OT Prophecy*, p. 167, though he goes on to qualify these words, to the effect that *fulfillment* need not be literal; cf. Ramm, op. cit., 1950 ed., p.161, quoting him, and see below, pp. 81, 83.
81. *Companion to the Bible*, p. 549.
82. Op. cit., p. 171.

they understand it, the Holy Land and Jerusalem are to be the centers of the glorified kingdom of God, and restored Israel is to be at the head of the nations."[83] Ramm lays down this standard: "Interpret prophecy literally unless the evidence is such that a spiritual interpretation is mandatory, e.g., where the passage is poetic or symbolic or apocalyptic in literary form, or where the NT evidence demands a spiritual interpretation."[84]

The real question, then, focuses upon whether the NT ever permits or requires such "spiritual" types of interpretation, that one might be tempted to view them as divine authorizations for procedures that would otherwise have been shunned as being allegorized. One must recognize that the "spiritualizer" of today is as opposed as any to the introduction of illegitimate allegorization. Allis, for example, stigmatizes the latter as a method "to empty words of their plain and obvious meaning, to read out of them what is clearly intended by them."[85] As stated earlier, in this work's initial definition of prophecy,[86] the true intent of Scripture must be that which God has designed, since He is its primary author; it is not that which might, mistakenly, have been inferred by His servants the prophets, its secondary authors. Wyngaarden thus defines spiritualization not as a form of allegorization that is imposed upon Scripture from without but as "any special import, or broadened meaning, or figurative usage, or richer implication that *the Holy Spirit gives* [italics mine] to any item, with a view toward realizing the fulfillment of the typical, OT kingdom, in the antitypical, NT kingdom, as identified with the church."[87] He then decides for "the spiritualization of the entire typical kingdom, including Israel, Zion, and the Promised Land."[88]

But while "Zion" may be used figuratively for the church, in reference to those who stand either regenerated on earth (Ps 87:5–6) or perfected in heaven (Heb 12:22–23), such instances are demonstrated by their contexts;[89] and they do not validate his conclusion that Zion may legitimately be allegorized elsewhere when its denotation is local and the context requires its literal meaning, e.g. Matthew 21:5, on the daughters of *Zion* during Palm Sunday.[90] This problem comes to the fore in reference to the divine kingdom: for it may connote God's spiritual rule in a man's heart, either

---

83. Op. cit., p. 491.
84. Op. cit. (1950), p. 172, but that apocalyptic form, ipso facto, requires "spiritual interpretation" appears open to question; see below, pp. 85–89.
85. *Prophecy and the Church*, p. 18.
86. See above, p. 4 and elaborated below, p. 73–75.
87. *The Future of the Kingdom in Prophecy and Fulfillment*, p. 86.
88. Ibid., p. 8.
89. Cf. Rev 11:8, making such usage explicit: "the great city, which mystically is called Sodom and Egypt, where also the Lord was crucified."
90. In a sense this is what Wyngaarden himself says, when he makes a rule for determining a given prophecy's "spiritual" interpretation the question: "Does it fit into the organic unity represented by the church?" (p. 176). It is only his feeling for what "fits in" that produces what are in fact his broad allegorizations.

in the OT (Ps 74:12, "God is my King, working salvation in the midst of the earth") or in the NT church age (Col 1:13, God "transferred us to the kingdom of His well-beloved Son"),[91] without thereby denying the more literal kingdom elsewhere, particularly in the OT's and the NT's age to come (cf. Dan 7:13–14 [quoted by Christ in Mk 14:62], Mt 19:28, Acts 1:6). Especially significant is the expansion of the inclusiveness of the idea of Israel, so that Isaiah 19:25 can speak of "Egypt, My people," or Ephesians 2:19 can speak of the breaking down of the middle wall of partition and of Gentile converts as "fellow citizens," without thereby minimizing the literality of the future kingdom or of the genuine participation that the church, as true Israel, is yet to have in it (e.g. Rev 2:26–27). One therefore concludes that the NT's "spiritualization" is primarily a matter of augmentation rather than of replacement: when Israel's cities are treated as cities, even when crowded with pilgrims from all backgrounds, they mean those very cities; and when its nation acts like a nation, though bursting with an expanded citizenry, it means that nation. Ramm's principle is found to hold good, that one must "interpret prophecy literally" unless the evidence drawn from any clarifications which have been inspired by God Himself vouchsafe an augmented inclusiveness as part of the original divine intent.

The implications of deviation from a "normal" methodology for understanding Scripture are serious ones. The result, indeed, of allegorized interpretation is to destroy the value of prophecy. Edghill comments: "A spiritualizing exegesis which is obviously opposed to the original sense of the prophet's words . . . surrenders the whole case for the value of prophecy. . . . If Edom and Babylon are to be allegorically interpreted, the value of the message lies not in the original prophecy, but in the sense which another dispensation has taught to put upon their words."[92] Whether to allow "another dispensation" to revoke the meaning of the prophetic message is the question that underlies the positions represented in today's millennial controversy. Scholars of every persuasion grant that the "root of their differences lies in the method of Biblical interpretation."[93] By holding to literal meanings, the present writer feels compelled to accept the validity of millennialism, as opposed to what he can only designate as the allegorized conclusions of amillennialism. Yet this methodological sword is double-edged; for the normal reading of Scripture may find itself opposed to current millennial interpretations as well. Compare Berry's criticism of dispensationalism for its "great freedom in allegorizing, especially in the form of

---

91. Cf. Acts 28:31, or Mt 21:43, where the kingdom of God is taken away from the Jews and "given to a nation producing the fruit of it"—though some might refer this to a yet future kingdom, and to a later generation of Jews.
92. *An Enquiry into the Evidential Value of Prophecy*, pp. 90–91.
93. Allis, op. cit., p. 17; Feinberg, op. cit., p. 32; and quoted by Ramm, op. cit. (1950), p. 156, as "axiomatic."

types,"[94] which may, in turn, be imported into the eschatological formulations of Scripture. Isaiah 29:3, for example, threatens Jerusalem with the advance of Sennacherib: "I will lay siege against thee with posted troops." The notes of the Scofield Bible then comment, "The near view is of Sennacherib's invasion; the far view is that of the final gathering of the Gentile hosts against Jerusalem at the end of the great tribulation, when a still greater deliverance will be wrought";[95] but such an approach must be set down as allegorized and lacking in hermeneutical justification.

C. Limitations on Predictive Symbols

Sound interpretation must recognize the limits which apply to those prophecies of Scripture that assume an acted-out form, as well as to those that are spoken. Just as in the case, moreover, of the Bible's figures, so in regard to its symbols, those that are genuinely predictive must be distinguished from passages which lack either a prophetic bearing upon the future or, more basically, a valid symbolic character of any sort.

1. LEGITIMATE SYMBOLS, BUT NONPREDICTIVE. The commentary of Psalm 95:11 on Numbers 14:23, 29–35, indicates that the physical death of the disbelieving Israelites whose bodies fell in the wilderness of Sinai symbolized a corresponding loss of divine favor toward them. They thus serve as a warning to those of any period who falter in their faith; they constitute a picture of human failure to obtain salvation and to enter heaven (Heb 3:6–4:11). Yet while Numbers 14:35 may legitimately be understood as symbolical, the wilderness Israelites are not described in Scripture as having been originally designed to predict any specific later group of people; they are but "examples for us," demonstrations of the principle "that we should not crave evil things" (I Cor 10:6). In corresponding fashion Moses may be said to have been a symbol of the prophetic ideal (Dt 34:10) but without thereby becoming a predictive symbol: through his words he foretold Christ (18:15), but in his objective person he does not appear to point forward as an acted-out prediction.[96] David, in turn, may be understood to have symbolized Israel's kingship, and particularly his own Davidic dynasty (I K 12:16). His name is thus used for the Messiah (Ezek 34:23, Hos

94. "There is much forced and arbitrary interpretation," *Premillennialism and OT Prediction*, pp. 4, 8. Yet dispensationalism does recognize the literal meaning that underlies its allegorizations, which is more than can be said for Berry's amillennialism.
95. P. 737. Truly Messianic material does, however, appear later in the Isaianic context, e.g. 32:1 or 34:1.
96. Vs. Fairbairn, op. cit., I:74.

3:5); but, again, it is David's words in the Messianic psalms rather than the Davidic person that in fact predicted Jesus.[97]

Similarly, among the OT prophets, a symbolical happening need not necessarily have been a prediction of the future. In one of Ezekiel's enacted, God-given visions concerning Jerusalem (8:3, 10:1), "The glory of Yahweh went forth from over the threshold of the house . . . and mounted up from the earth" (10:18–19); it "went up from the midst of the city and stood upon the mountain [Olivet] which is upon the east" (11:23). This experience of the prophet might have been predictive of a future departure of the glory cloud, Shekinah; but it could be simply descriptive of what happened at this point in 592 B.C.: "a sign that both temple and city had ceased to be the seats of the gracious presence of the Lord. . . . The glory of God remained [on Olivet] to execute the subsequent judgment upon Jerusalem."[98] The vision, in other words, may correspond not to an anticipated, but to a simultaneous, reality. The sabbath institution, insofar as it serves as a symbol of heavenly rest, provides a final OT illustration; for this aspect of it is not specifically predictive. The sabbath existed as symbolical from the date of its hallowing by God (Gen 2:3), even before heaven had been revealed as man's destiny; and it continues thus timelessly symbolical on into the NT era (Heb 4:9–11; cf. v. 14). Only when considered as a type of rest in Christ (Mt 11:28) may the sabbath be assigned a truly predictive value.

In the NT, symbolic prophecy concentrates in John's Revelation; yet not all that appears in the Apocalypse is thereby rendered predictive. For example, in Revelation 5:1, "I saw a book written, sealed up with seven seals." In v. 9 Christ is then said to be "worthy to break its seals; for Thou didst purchase for God with Thy blood men from every nation"; v. 5, He has thus "overcome so as to open the book." Some interpret this scroll as "the book of destiny or doom for the earth and its unrighteous inhabitants, a prophecy of the calamities that are soon to be inflicted upon them,"[99] as in ch. 6, which is revealed in connection with the opening of the seals. Yet the content of the book seems to be associated with Christ's redemption; "and we are told, 20:12, of the opening of a very important Book, the Book of Life; and that Book belongs to the Lamb that was slain, 13:8, 21:27. Is not then this book the same as that?"[100] Such an understanding is supported by the number of the saved, from all nations, as compared with the crowded writing upon the scroll. But if then the scroll represents the totality of the redeemed, its symbolism would not be primarily of a predictive character.

---

97. Elijah too falls short of being an acted prediction of John the Baptist, even though the latter possessed his same spirit and power; see Mal 4:5.
98. KD, *Ezek*, I:154.
99. IB, XII:405; cf. the possible connection between Rev 5:7 and 6:1.
100. Camb, pp. 34–35.

Again, Revelation 4:4 visualizes 24 elders in white garments, with crowns on their heads. The details suggest symbolism, but in what way? Two questions are really involved. (a) What do they symbolize? A strong case can be made out that the elders represent angels and not humans.[101] But since elders appear generally as representatives of people (cf. Num 11:16–17), and since the 12 patriarchs plus 12 apostles do receive stress elsewhere in Revelation (21:12–14), it seems likely that the elders represent the church of God, the Israel of both the OT and the NT, many of whom (although not all, cf. John himself) were then with the patriarchs in heaven; cf. the white garments of the deceased saints in 3:5, 6:11. (b) But what is the period involved? Dispensational interpreters often propose a time following Christ's coming for His church, and the crowns would then indicate the completion of a judgment in connection with His return (II Cor 5:10). The fact that they "cast their crowns before the throne" (Rev 4:10) would indicate that they had just received them and that therefore the rapture and resurrection must have come at 4:1 in Revelation's chronology.[102] Actually, however, it is questionable whether the symbolism is intended to portray matters yet future to the time of John's original vision. In the immediate context (2:10) crowns symbolize heaven's glory, the reward beyond the grave for those "faithful unto death" (so James 1:12, and cf. Heb 12:23 on the perfection attained by the blessed dead).[103]

The symbolism of ch. 13 possesses the advantage of interpretation in ch. 17. The beast out of the sea (13:1) is explained in 17:3, 16, as supporting and yet surviving the ancient Roman empire, the woman of 17:3, which makes martyrs (v. 6), sits on seven hills (v. 9), has universal rule (v. 15), and is "the great city" (v. 18); so the beast would seem to equal

101. Cf. G. H. Lang, *The Revelation of Jesus Christ*, pp. 124–136: their activity in interpretation (7:13–17) is a task elsewhere committed to angels (cf. 10:8, 17:1); and when they speak of the human saints they use the third person, "they," not "we," as if the latter were a group distinct from themselves (5:10, ASV). The crowns too are not inappropriate (Col 1:16). Cf. Payne, *Imminent Appearing*, p. 79.

102. E. Schuyler English, *Re-thinking the Rapture*, p. 97; cf. Lang's extended argument, op. cit., pp. 109–123, for a futuristic interpretation of the whole of chs. 4–5, based upon Christ's "standing" (5:6) by the throne, but evaluated in Payne, op. cit., p. 171.

103. So too in the earlier sections of the 2nd cycle of Rev (chs. 12–22), ch. 12 presents a series of symbols for matters either past or contemporaneous to its original audience: v. 1, a woman clothed with the sun and moon and having a crown of 12 stars (Israel, Gen 37:9); vv. 2, 5, the woman giving birth to a Son who is to rule all nations with a rod of iron (Jesus, the Messiah, 19:15, Ps 2:9); and vv. 3–4, her being opposed by a dragon (Satan, as stated in v. 9). But v. 5, the Son is caught up to heaven (Christ's ascension, past); vv. 7–12a, the dragon is cast out of heaven (see John 12:31); vv. 6, 14–16, the woman is yet nourished by God for 3½ years, the latter half of Daniel's 70th week (?), during which the gospel is confirmed to the Jews, until the church's scattering upon Stephen's martyrdom (see Dan 9:27a); and vv. 12b–13, the dragon's persecution both of the woman and of "the rest of her offspring, who hold the testimony of Jesus" (the church; cf. Rev 2:13).

world political power in general (13:2). Its seven heads are seven kings (17:10), who came to be involved in blasphemous emperor worship and Christian persecution (13:4–8). Five of the kings had fallen—presumably the emperors Caesar, Augustus, Tiberius, Caligula, and Claudius—the sixth was then reigning, namely Nero (A.D. 54–68)[104] or, if one begins counting with Augustus, Galba (68–69); and there was another who "has not yet come."[105] 13:3, the head (or the beast itself, vv. 12, 14; cf. 17:8) with the fatal wound, "as if it had been slain" but was healed, seems to portray the beast's survival of the blow inflicted by the incarnation of Christ's kingdom into history.[106] Thus in 13:11–17 the beast out of the earth, though not identified in ch. 17, would seem to represent the native religions of the land, in their support of Roman emperor worship.[107] Of the various symbols only the "seventh head" would then appear to be truly predictive. Yet by failing to recognize the cyclic character of Revelation (with chs. 12 ff. reverting to John's own time), interpreters have sought, with dubious justification, to find in these symbolic figures "great actors of the tribulation time."[108]

2. ILLEGITIMATE SYMBOLS: OBJECTS THAT ARE NOT REPRESENTATIVE OF FURTHER TRUTHS. The number of nonverbal matters taken from the Bible that have been forced into unjustifiable utilization as predictive symbols is legion. The following are but a few such, drawn from the opening chapters of Scripture. Genesis 1:1 states that God created heaven and earth. Yahweh's subsequent revelation (8:22) suggests that the earth, thus created, was not to remain forever; it seems therefore to constitute a foregleam of the message of Revelation 21:1 about a new heaven and a new earth.[109] Fairbairn, however, building upon this verbal prophecy,[110] goes

104. Cf. the cryptic number of the beast, 666 (13:17–18): this might be the sum of the numerical equivalents either of the Heb. letters in "Caesar Nero" or, more probably, of the Gk. letters in "Latin"; H. B. Swete, *The Apocalypse of St. John*, pp. 175–176.

105. Identifications vary, depending generally on the date one otherwise assigns for the writing of Rev; see below, p. 592, or Camb, pp. 105–106, for a summarization.

106. Cf. P. Minear, "The Wounded Beast," JBL, 72 (1953), 93–101.

107. Particularly in animating images (13:15) and in requiring the bodily "mark of the beast" for commercial activity (vv. 16–17); see Swete, op. cit., pp. 171–173, for ancienct parallels.

108. John F. Walvvord, *The Revelation of Jesus Christ*, p. 187.

109. See below, p. 608; cf. Fairbairn, op. cit., "In addition to the evidences of design in nature, which show a specific direction toward a final cause . . . there have been brought to light evidences . . . of a striking unity of plan," I:77. "There is found in the person and kingdom of Christ a grand archetypal idea toward which . . . the divine plan was working," I:79.

110. Combined also with a recognition of the legitimately active-predictive character of Adam as a type of Christ: "The work of creation in Adam carried in its very constitution the signs and indications of better things to come for man . . . a destiny was in the purpose and decrees of the Almighty (which no one will dispute)," ibid., pp. 95–96.

on to assert a corresponding but questionable form of nonverbal prediction: "The creation itself was of such a kind as to proclaim its own relative imperfection, and at the same time, by means of certain higher elements interwoven with it, to give promise of a state in which such imperfection should be done away."[111] Imaginative interpreters can thus discover in the goodness of the garden of Eden (Gen 2:8–9) predictive symbols of the New Jerusalem, whether sorrowless (Rev 21:4), undefiled (21:27), curseless (22:3), or even lacking in night (22:5); and in the river of Eden, with its four great headwaters (Gen 2:10–14), predictions of the fountain of life (Rev 21:6), the river of life (22:1), or simply water of life in general (22:17). But Eden's streams were real Mesopotamian rivers, and the products of Eden were designed to be "pleasant to the sight and good for food"; however much John's Revelation may have been influenced by the data of Genesis, it yet remains to be established that the objective features of Genesis were originally intended to be symbolical of anything at all, let alone to be treated as acted predictions of Revelation 21–22.

D. *Limitations on Types*

1. FROM THE NATURE OF TYPOLOGY. By making use of the previous proposed definition for a type, as being that which is "a divine enactment of future redemption,"[112] one is provided with a basis, similarly fourfold, for setting limits to this final form of Biblical prediction. (a) Since a type must be *divine* in its origin, all typical "discoveries" by human interpreters remain in the category of allegorizations, if they cannot be shown to have been a part of God's original intention. It is on this basis that Bishop Marsh enunciated his famous dictum: "There is no other rule by which we can distinguish a real from a pretended type, than that of Scripture itself . . . expressly declared by Christ or by His apostles to have been designed as prefigurations of persons or things relating to the NT."[113] This Marshian position is reflected by the Scofield warning, "Nothing may be dogmatically asserted to be a type without explicit NT authority; and all types not so authenticated must be recognized as having the authority of analogy, or spiritual congruity, merely."[114] In any event, this feature of divine origin requires that the most basic grouping within typology consist of those figures that are expalined elsewhere in Scripture.

111. Ibid. But he concedes, "The Lord Himself, at the close of creation, pronounced it all very good"; and it appears open to question whether incompleteness necessarily connotes imperfection, so as to require something truly perfect yet to appear.
112. See above, p. 23; and Payne, *Theology of the Older Testament*, pp. 357–360.
113. From his Lectures, as quoted by Fairbairn, op. cit., I:19.
114. Op. cit., p. 100.

(b) Yet the *redemptive* character of typology opens the way for broader identifications. There exist a number of matters in the Bible that are clearly parts of redemptive contexts and that occupy, in parallel with other *known* types, a significant place in the ceremonial worship of Israel. Such items may then, by analogy, be recognized as genuine types, even though they may never be given explicit elucidation elsewhere in Scripture. One of these, for example, would be the double crown that the prophet Zechariah placed upon the head of Joshua the high priest and that was subsequently "laid up for a memorial in the temple of Yahweh" (Zech 6:15); it served as an acted prediction of Christ's future twofold office of priest and king.[115] Most evangelical scholars therefore feel that Marsh, by limiting types to those matters that are expressly declared to be so by the NT, went too far in his generally laudable attempt to prevent uncontrolled typology. Fairbairn, for example, criticizes the Marshian view: "Were men accustomed . . . to regard the inspired records of both covenants as having for their leading object 'the testimony of Jesus,' they would know how much they were losers by such an undue contraction of the typical element in OT Scripture."[116] He notes that the divine intent for a given type may be deduced as well as stated: "No one holds the necessity of inspiration to explain each particular prophecy, and decide even with certainty on its fulfillment; and why should it be reckoned indispensable in the closely related subject of types?"[117]

(c) That the Biblical types were *enacted* prophecies, representing to Israel the same basic salvation that was later accomplished by Christ, produces what is perhaps the most important single principle in the delimiting of typology, namely, that a given item must be symbolical to its contemporaries before it can be considered typical for the future. Vos thus compares symbol and type:

> They are in reality the same things, only different in this respect that they come first on a lower stage of development in redemption, and then again, in a later period, on a higher stage. Thus what is symbolical with regard to the already existing edition of the fact or truth becomes typical, prophetic, of the later, final edition of that same fact or truth. From this it will be perceived that a type can never be a type independently of its being first a symbol.[118]

Far too many commentators have exhausted themselves over theories about the typical significance in respect to Christ of, say, the details of the life of Joseph. To his contemporaries, if Joseph were considered symbolical at all, it would have been in respect to just one thing: the power of God's providence. This basic, Biblical truth must not be obscured by futile speculations over the "meaning," e.g., of his Gentile wife in respect to the church.

---

115. See below, under Zech., prophecy No. 13.
116. Op. cit., I:20.
117. Ibid., I:21.
118. *Biblical Theology, Old and New Testaments*, p. 162.

Even concerning certain ceremonial matters, such as the colors that were used in the hangings of the tabernacle, the modern interpreter simply does not know whether they are types or not.

(d) Types possess a *future* reference. If the full meaning, therefore, of a given matter appears to be limited to its immediate context, then that matter should not be treated as if it were typical. The Scofield Bible, for example, after stating its previously quoted Marsh-like definition of typology, goes on to discover typical meanings in even the utilitarian hooks and boards of the tabernacle, sometimes several mutually exclusive meanings for the same items.[119] Allis thus accuses Scofield's followers of letting allegorization in at the back door, as it were.[120] Pentecost defends this sort of practice, saying, "The Scriptural use of *types* does not give sanction to the allegorical method of interpretation:"[121] But his answer seems to beg the question by leaving undefined what constitutes a type in the first place. Excesses tend to bring into disrepute the whole field of typology, together with the valid explanations of inspired types, which are so necessary for the understanding of the OT.

2. FROM THE VARIETIES OF TYPES. Further limitations that help to identify authentic typology arise out of certain ways in which the five major kinds of Biblical types[122] relate themselves to the above-stated definition. (a) Because of the general connection between typology and the redemptive ceremonialism of the OT, relatively few *individuals* warrant designation as types. The persons that are often proposed, other than Adam and Melchizedek,[123] do not appear to be inherently redemptive in respect to mankind and should not, in consequence, be considered typical.[124]

(b) While some Biblical *events* are clearly predictive, e.g. Noah's rescue from the flood through the medium of the ark—it depicts salvation as related to baptism[125]—others are not so clear. Fairbairn admits that "the historical types . . . wanted for the most part something of the necessary correspondence with the antitypes: the one did not occupy under the Old the same relative place that the other did under the New."[126] Indeed, most OT events "appear ostensibly connected with the theatre of an earthly

---

119. E. g. in reference to the boards of the tabernacle; cf. op. cit., pp. 103, 105.
120. Op. cit., p. 21; see above, p. 47.
121. Op. cit., p. 9.
122. See above, p. 26.
123. See above, p. 24.
124. In reference to the person of Isaac, at the time of his intended sacrifice by his father Abraham, the NAS of Heb 11:19 reads that he "received him back from the dead as a type." But its margin more accurately renders the Gk. *en pārābōlē,* as "figuratively speaking." So while Isaac's restoration (Gen 22:13) served as a symbol, acted out, of resurrection, it was still not predictive; nor should Isaac be considered as a divinely devised type of Christ's resurrection on Easter.
125. See below, under Gen., prophecy No. 13.
126. Op. cit., I:69.

existence, and with respect to seen and temporal results; while in the later [NT] it is the higher field of grace and the interests of a spiritual and immortal existence that come directly into view."[127] In other words, at numerous points OT events were not symbols, irrespective of what may later have been associated with them in the NT; e.g. Ishmael's being driven from the home of Abraham did not symbolize the divine disfavor (contrast Gen 21:13, 20!) that is spoken of in connection with it in Galatians 4:30. Such events could not, therefore, have been in themselves acted predictions of the later issues, though their employment for illustrative purposes remains always possible. But at other points their earthly limitation may be only ostensible: in the case of the ark's riding out the flood there *was* a real spiritual salvation experienced and symbolized, and it predicts the corresponding NT redemption. An entire category of event sometimes claimed to be typical is that of the Biblical miracle, and particularly the mighty acts of Jesus. Fairbairn asserts: "Every miracle He performed was a type in history; for, on the outward and visible field of nature, it revealed the divine power He was going to manifest, and the work He came to achieve in the higher field of grace."[128] Actually, however, our Lord's miracles provide little that may be seen as directly predictive. Some suggest no real symbolic prediction of the future, e.g. the coin found in the fish's mouth. Some may have been predictive, but the record remains noncommittal as to what, e.g. the water turned into wine. Some may find hints of explanation, e.g. the great draft of fish, intimating that His disciples were to become fishers of men (?); but even this would be more of a generalization than of a specific prediction.

(c) The identification of the typology of an object or *thing* may be guided in part by the principle of the necessary unity in concept as to the matter symbolized, in both the OT and the NT. Fairbairn's negative limitation is therefore valid, that forbidden or sinful things cannot be types.[129] Just as in the case of events, the utilization of a given OT object as an illustration by the NT does not in itself render that OT object into something that must have been designedly typical. Concerning Exodus 34:33–35, on the veil that Moses wore over the glory that was reflected by his face, II Corinthians 3:13 simply states, "We are not *as* Moses"; and v. 14 adds, "Until this very day at the reading of the old covenant the same veil remains unlifted" despite its removal by Christ, by which the apostle indicates a

127. Ibid., I:64. So Gen 3:21 speaks of God's making coats of skins for Adam and Eve. Such action truly symbolizes His care, as He clothed them; but it does not seem to have constituted a type, specifically, as if it taught animal sacrifice, typifying Christ's loss of life.

128. Ibid., I:70. Similarly, in the OT, Moses' striking the rock at Kadesh twice, and bringing forth life-giving water (Num 20:8–11), is often discussed as a type of Christ's redemptive death, but with doubtful validity. Contrast the genuine typology that appears in Exodus 17:6; see below, Ex., prophecy No. 42.

129. Ibid., I:141.

degree of correspondence between the OT and his own NT situation: not that Moses had been thereby predicting Christ's termination of the OT dispensation.[130]

(d) In reference to the *institutions* of Israel, where typology is legitimately involved it must be remembered that the institution makes the type, and not later words about it. So the historical occurrence of the manna was a type (see under Ex 16:4); but in this book subsequent verbal allusion to it is not counted as predictive.[131]

(e) As stated previously, Israel's *ceremonial* worship is legitimately and consistently typical.[132] Exception arises principally within the extensive OT laws concerning cleanness, e.g. on animals to be avoided in eating (Lev 11 or on leprosy (ch. 14). Their explanation appears to be primarily hygienic.[133] Even when symbolism may be involved—e.g. the law on avoiding garments composed of mixed materials, to symbolize separation and holiness (?), 19:19—these ordinances still indicate no typology of future redemption. So the procedure in respect to birth-uncleanness limits its symbolism to the matter of sin (12:1–2), though the sacrificial ceremonies for its removal do typify Christ (vv. 3–4, 6–8).

3. FROM THE PROGRESS OF HISTORY. Typology possesses a relationship to the time factor within history. At the very opening of Scripture, it might be asked whether L. Alexander's definition of typology in reference to God's "plan of redemption"[134] rules out the possibility of types prior to Adam's fall. The answer, however, seems to be in the negative because, even before this event, man had been placed into a probationary situation; and the Edenic reward of probation, i.e. life, corresponds to that promised by redemption.[135] Fairbairn thus properly observes, "In the Scriptural form of representation, the original work continues to occupy the position of the proper ideal: all things return, in a manner, whence they came . . . paradise restored."[136]

Yet the progress of history may bring many of the aspects of typology to

130. In similar fashion the object that is Jerusalem served legitimately as a symbol of David's greatness and of a "kingdom of God" (II Sam 5:6–10, I Chron 11:4–9), but without necessarily intending to portray the Lord's final kingdom. Rev 21:2, 10, in speaking of the "New Jeruslem," simply builds on the former idea.
131. Unless discussing its typology, as John 6:32–33.
132. See above, p. 24.
133. See Payne, *Theology*, pp. 369–372, as opposed to Vos, op. cit., 190.
134. See above, p. 25.
135. Fairbairn thus goes too far when he asserts, "Typology . . . should confine itself to God's work in grace, and should move simply in the sphere of 'the regeneration,'" op. cit., I:98.
136. It must, however, again be cautioned that not *all* in Eden was typical of better things in the future. For example, rather than speaking of creation without the curse as being a type of the Messianic kingdom one may better speak of the millennium as being a restoration to what had been fully present at the first.

an end. Typical institutions or ceremonies continue predictive only so long as legitimately observed. Passover-keeping, for example, should no longer be considered as predictively symbolical after its last official observance, in A.D. 30 when Christ converted it into the Lord's Supper. But the Jewish temple received its fulfillment and therefore lost its future significance with Christ's incarnation.[137] The various testaments, or covenants, continue to be typical of the death of Christ with each mention in, or citation from, the OT and on up to the Last Supper in the NT; for they all continued in force: Abraham's did not repeal the Noachian, nor did Sinai the Abrahamic (Gal 3:17). But the other three basic varieties of typology—persons, things, and events —are predictive only in themselves, not in subsequent recollections of them. Adam, for example, is not to be regarded as typical at every mention of his name, or even in all the events of his lifetime, but only in his acts that were representative for mankind.

137. In the study that follows, its mention is thus not counted as typically predictive beyond this point.

The Identification of Fulfillment

One aspect of current skeptical thinking about prophecy has been its disparagement of (OT) prediction, combined with a more affirmative emphasis upon (NT) fulfillment.[1] Yet paradoxically, one also discovers a depreciation of the idea of fulfillment in favor of Scripture's original, predictive design; e.g.: "The foretelling of the future in prophecy has always a spiritual purpose, which is liable to be lost, if we concentrate on fulfillment."[2] Actually, both criticisms are expressive of one and the same underlying attitude of doubt, namely, that what the OT prophets said should correspond to what the NT history in fact became. Rudolf Bultmann thus follows the earlier strictures of the 19th century *Heilsgeschichte* theologian J. C. K. Hofmann in stating, "It is not the words of the OT that are really prophecy, but the history of Israel. . . . Prophecy is not the prediction of coming events for the realization of which we have to wait. Prophecy is rather history itself, insofar as this is a movement leading to a goal . . . ,"[3] and the most that many in the movement of modern "Biblical" theology are willing to affirm is that the OT possesses an "openness toward the NT."[4] Oxtoby, for example, divides predictions into those for fulfillment in the immediate future and those for the end of the age. Of the former, he questions the possibility of even an intended fulfillment: "Sometimes a prophet filled in the details for the sake of vividness, perhaps without expecting these further elements actually to occur." Of the latter, their fulfillment suffers its death

1. See above, p. 13.
2. H. L. Ellison, *Ezekiel: The Man and His Message*, p. 105.
3. "Prophecy and Fulfillment," in Claus Westermann, ed., *Essays on OT Hermeneutic*, pp. 55–56.
4. W. Eichrodt, following Karl Elliger, "Is Typological Exegesis an Appropriate Method?" in ibid., p. 243.

by qualifications: "Though the imagery is usually specific, their formulations must be considered representative rather than actual . . . they represent what *must* be [Italics his] rather than what shall be."[5] Under either category, the very concept of definite fulfillment may be ruled out as illegitimate.

That such has not been the case throughout the history of the church hardly requires documentation.[6] But while it is not the place of the present study to reproduce Canon Farrar's *History of Interpretation* (1886) or the more detailed, recent study of Seventh-Day Adventist LeRoy E. Froom, *The Prophetic Faith of Our Fathers* (4 vols., 1945), one should identify at the outset, in addition to liberal skepticism, at least three major historical positions that other interpreters are now assuming toward the subject of prophetic fulfillment.[7] (1) First in time is the system of classical (pre)-millennialism, which has antecedents in the earliest patristic writers. They emphasized the literal fulfillment of the OT prophecies—particularly those of an earthly kingdom, i.e. the millennium of Revelation 20—to be fulfilled in the Christian church, as the Israel of God. Patristic premillennialism is represented by such current works as my *Imminent Appearing of Christ,* which holds to the potentially immediate return of the Messiah to establish His earthly kingdom, or George E. Ladd's *The Blessed Hope,* which does not. (2) At the start of the 5th century Augustine's *City of God* initiated the school of amillennialism, which would limit the achievement of the OT's prophetic hopes and the fulfillment of Revelation 20:1–6 to spiritual categories within the church. As Angus and Green explain,

> Many are content to rest in general interpretations without seeking for literal and particular fulfillments. Giving great weight to the facts that the distinction between Jew and Gentile is formally abolished and that our dispensation is spiritual, thinking, moreover, that the descriptions in prophecy, if taken literally, would lead to a belief in the restoration of Judaism . . . they conclude with a spiritual interpretation of the whole.[8]

Amillennialism has been the predominant position of Lutheran and Reformed Protestantism; cf. Martin Wyngaarden's *The Future of the Kingdom in Prophecy and Fulfillment,* or O. T. Allis', *Prophecy and the Church.*

5. *Prediction and Fulfillment in the Bible,* pp. 84, 86, 93; cf. A. B. Davidson, *OT Prophecy,* p. 178: "It is rarely safe to ask, to what historical event does the prophet here refer? because he may have no such reference. It is safe to assume that he has some general thought which he is uttering. This is both safe and fair, because the cases in which the prophets utter general principles preponderate greatly over the cases in which they directly predict future contingencies. . . . Who knows whether he [the prophet] was thinking of any historical event? He is predicting things, not individual historical events."

6. E.g. see above, p. 11.

7. The position of 19th-century postmillennialism, as represented for example in the writings of P. Fairbairn, *The Interpretation of Prophecy* (though dating back to Daniel Whitby in 1706), is here dismissed as no longer a current option, though cf. L. Boettner, *The Millennium,* 1957.

8. *The Bible Handbook,* p. 247.

(3) With the rise of the Plymouth Brethren movement under J. N. Darby in the 1820's, dispensational premillennialism has attained a wide following among modern evangelicals.[9] It is distinguished by its insistence that the OT prophecies are to receive their literal fulfillment in the restored polity of Israel after the flesh, rather than in the church.[10] Among its major presentations are J. Dwight Pentecost's *Things to Come* and C. C. Ryrie's *Dispensationalism Today,* and its popularization through the notes of the Scofield Reference Bible.

A. *The Necessity of Fulfillment*

While these three branches of contemporary evangelicalism may differ as to the *form* of prophetic fulfillment, they stand united upon its *reality* as inspired of God. As stated years ago by von Orelli, "In distinction from human ideals and hopes, which may be genuine and noble without being realized, prophecy is spurious and a product of human ingenuity unless it is fulfilled."[11] Whether achieved by intent—as apparently by Christ in His triumphal entry (Mt 21:3–4)—or by the most extraordinary of coincidences—as by Judas in his casting thirty pieces of silver to a potter (27:7–10)—every inspired prophecy does come to pass. The one apparent exception would concern those few predictions that are quoted, historically, within the pages of Scripture but which the Biblical writers themselves would remove from the classification of valid prophecy (see subsec. 2, below).

1. VALID PREDICTIONS. Within the category of inspired revelations about the future, Scripture yet distinguishes between those prophecies whose fulfillment is unconditional and inalterable and those equally divine forecasts whose accomplishment might still be affected or even obviated by the responses of their listening audiences. (a) Unconditional prophecies. Scripture is explicit that the Lord carries out what He has promised. A spoken assurance may accompany God's initial revelation: "I, Yahweh, have spoken, surely this will I do unto all this evil congregation . . ." (Num 14:35); compare the confidence with which His human intermediary may conclude a Biblical book: "Thou wilt perform the truth which Thou hast sworn unto our fathers" (Mi 7:20). Again, the assurance may be stated in retrospect, by either Yahweh or His witnesses: "My words, which I com-

9. For surveys illuminating the rise and character of modern dispensationalism, see Chas. C. Ryrie, *Dispensationalism Today,* or Ladd, op. cit., pp. 19–60, and Payne, op. cit., pp. 11–42.
10. See further, pp. 107–108, below.
11. *The OT Prophecy of the Consummation of God's Kingdom,* p. 50.

manded My servants the prophets, did they not overtake your fathers? . . . As Yahweh thought to do unto us, so hath He dealt with us" (Zech 1:6). Where kings of Judah, for example, might raise a question, God was willing to provide supernatural signs by way of further confirmation, whether coming in the form of a miracle (Isa 39:7-8, the shadow going backward, to assure Hezekiah) or in the form of another prophecy (7:13-14, the Messiah's birth, to threaten Ahaz). Negatively speaking, an eventuation of non-fulfillment constituted sure proof that a given prediction had been the work of presumptive men and not of Israel's God: "If the thing follow not . . . Yahweh hath not spoken: the prophet hath spoken presumptuously" (Dt 18:22). On the positive level, one may conclude, with Scripture, that a valid prophecy which has not yet been fulfilled must receive eventual, historical fulfillment in the future.

Disbelief in respect to prophetic fulfillment is no new phenomenon; it commenced contemporaneously with the revelatory situations. To most of the Hebrews, the forecast by Moses that on the next day God would furnish food in the wilderness for more than 600,000 men was incredible (Num 11:21-22); contrast the assurance God granted to this greatest among the OT prophets: "Is Yahweh's hand waxed short? Now shalt thou see whether My word will come to pass unto thee or not" (v. 23). It is little wonder, therefore, that modern writers should exhibit a similar skepticism toward particular predictions appearing within God's word. John Bright has said of Daniel 7:13, for example, "The heavens did not open to reveal the Son of Man coming in the clouds to receive the Kingdom from the Ancient of Days. Furthermore, they never would."[12] H. H. Rowley asserts bluntly, "The writers of these [apocalyptic] books were mistaken in their hopes of imminent deliverance; their interpreters who believed the consummation was imminent in their day have proved mistaken; and they who bring the same principles and the same hopes afresh to the prophecies will prove equally mistaken."[13] Bright explains, "We cannot think like ancients . . . that we should express our faith in exactly the terms that were so natural and meaningful to the early church," specifically in their "eager expectation for the return of the Lord."[14] Berry represents old-school liberalism when

12. *The Kingdom of God,* p. 192. He does believe in a future kingdom of peace and of moral world order, to be achieved through commitment to the rule of God, p. 95, by which he means that men are to "submit to a universal and just moral law," p. 250. More explicitly, "Saving faith is that a man cast himself on God made visible in Christ. . . . He recognizes his Lord and turns his back on all false notions," p. 258.
13. *The Relevance of Apocalyptic,* p. 158: cf. Payne, op. cit., p. 29.
14. Op. cit., pp. 245, 238. But this is no trifle concerning "exact terms." If he really holds "that the Christ of the church's gospel corresponds in all essentials to the Jesus of history," p. 189, and that "we are to stand before the NT church and receive correction," p. 260, then his skepticism appears inconsistent, to say the least; cf. his dilemma over Jesus' words, that "likely . . . contributed" to their belief in His second coming, p. 238.

he generalizes over the prophecies, "They were based upon conditions and ideas then prevailing. Most of them have not been fulfilled. Those that have not been fulfilled never will be and never can be. . . . These predictions give no information for the time yet future." Similar tendencies appear also in Bright's more recent suggestion that "the Christian faith summons us to believe nothing that contradicts reason";[15] yet it is possible that God may transcend human wisdom.

Two questions remain, however, for students who are committed to the necessity of prophetic fulfillment. One concerns the extent of its detailed accomplishment. A. B. Davidson expresses this caution: "We must not assume that none of its details and no part of the form will have to be fulfilled";[16] and he provdies concrete illustration from the forecast of Zech 9:9: "In that prophecy of Zechariah regarding the coming of the King to Zion, it would be unwise to say that only the idea of Christ's humility and peaceful rule is predicted in the . . . riding upon an ass . . . now that history shows it to have been actually verified . . . [as] a real element of the prediction."[17] In contrast, however, Terry pleads for "not literal but substantial fulfillment of the great ideas of prophecy";[18] and Riehm goes further still and insists, "We do not suppose the Spirit to have in some exceptional way concretely envisaged to the prophets certain individual historical facts of the NT fulfillment. . . . Revelation refuses to be magical."[19] Correspondingly, some have argued in respect to this same verse in Zechariah that "the prophecy would have been as truly and really fulfilled if the triumphant procession of Palm Sunday had never taken place. That single incident in the life of our Lord was not the point which the prophet had in view."[20] Terry then proceeds to deprecate such detailed OT prophecy as Samuel's prediction about Saul's lost asses: "Its method borders closely on the popular conceptions of fortune-telling." But, like it or not, miraculous precision in fulfillment is what the OT teaches about its own prophecies; and the same hermeneutical approach is inculcated through the way Zechariah is understood by the NT as well.

A second question concerns the matter of delayed fulfillment. Scripture itself recognizes the problem; e.g. Habakkuk 2:3, "The vision is yet for the appointed time, and it hasteth toward the end and shall not lie: though it tarry, wait for it; because it will surely come, it will not delay." The apparent tension between "tarrying" and yet "not delaying" resolves itself through recognition that the latter term signifies "to fail," or to be late in the sense of materializing beyond God's appointed time. Rowley has thus confused

15. *Premillennialism and OT Prediction*, pp. 33–34; Bright, op. cit., p. 272, and see above, p. 11.
16. Op. cit., p. 184.
17. Ibid., p. 186; cf. p. 193.
18. *Biblical Hermeneutics*, p. 337.
19. Or supernatural (?), see above, p. 11; *Messianic Prophecy*, pp. 310 and 142.
20. Terry, loc. cit., referring to C. H. H. Wright on Zechariah.

human impatience or misunderstanding over the "tarrying" divine word with an inherently fallacious revelation, when he accuses certain OT prophets of an open admission of nonfulfillment: "The prophecies were not always fulfilled, indeed; and we know that Jeremiah found the non-fulfillment of his prophecies a serious problem, and roundly accused God of letting him down (Jer 20:7 ff.)."[21] But context makes it clear that the oracles in question concerned "violence and spoil," v. 8, specifically, as a part of the Babylonian captivity, v. 6; and full accomplishment was merely a matter of time. Within the space of Jeremiah's next 19 chapters, the prophet was granted comprehensive vindication; cf. the later addition to his volume (51:64b) of ch. 52 as a historical testimonial to his prophetic veracity. Furthermore, this matter of delay in fulfillment contribtued to the attainment of the moral goal of Biblical prediction.[22] As Zimmerli summariges it,

> The messenger's word always sets up a tension-laden interval between the message and the occurrence of that which is announced. This time interval which is granted in the sending of the messenger is then properly understood by the listener when he understands it as a time in which it will be possible for him to bend himself to the will of the one who sends the message.[23]

Far from constituting a nonfulfillment, such tarrying plays its own major part in the total effectuation of divine providence.

(b) Conditional prophecies. Within the category of valid God-given predictions, Scripture distinguishes a special class of revelations whose accomplishment is made contingent upon the fulfillment by men of certain conditions, which are equally God-given. That is to say, God is no changeless, impersonal force but reacts rather, in a living way, to the responses that are made by human persons. In Exodus 9:15, for example, His own words document the reality of divine change, since they foretell what He might have done, but did not because of one man's intercession: "For now I had put forth My hand, and smitten thee [Moses] and thy people with pestilence, and thou hadst been cut off from the earth; but . . . ." (cf. II K 20:1–5). It is not that God's standards, His decrees, or His nature are changeable; it is, in fact, the very immutability of the character of deity which necessitates the application of differing aspects of His fixed principles, in accordance with such changes as may be exhibited by fickle men. Prophecy in particular has been designed by God for moral ends, so as to motivate men into conformity with divine holiness.[24] Should men, therefore, seek to take advantage of its holy assurances, toward nonmoral ends (e.g. as in Jer 7:4, 8–10, or Mi 3:11), change becomes then not only possible but inevitable. God accordingly rebuked the priestly house of Eli, seemingly

---

21. Op. cit., p. 35.
22. See above, p. 7.
23. "Promise and Fulfillment," in C. Westermann, ed., *Essays on OT Hermeneutics,* p. 101.
24. See above, pp. 6–7, 14–15.

complacent in its corruption, "I said indeed that thy house should walk before Me for ever; but now . . . be it far from Me; them that honor Me I will honor, and they that despise Me shall be lightly esteemed" (I Sam 2:30).

Contingency is set forth as a principle in Jeremiah 18:7–10:

> At what instant I shall speak concerning a nation . . . to destroy it; if that nation, concerning which I have spoken, turn from their evil, I will repent of the evil that I thought to do unto them. And [correspondingly] at what instant I shall speak concerning a nation . . . to build it; if they do that which is evil in My sight, that they obey not my voice, then I will repent of the good, wherewith I said I would benefit them.

This theory is then illustrated in practice by the following excerpt from one of Jeremiah's later sermons: "Yahweh sent me to prophesy against this city all the words that ye have heard. Now therefore, amend your ways and obey the voice of Yahweh your God; and Yahweh will repent Him of the evil that He hath pronounced against you," 26:12–13.[25] The concept of conditional prophecy is further confirmed by those of his oracles in which alternative results are laid out before men, depending upon their response to stated conditions; cf. 38:17–18 or 42:10–17,[26] or Romans 11:22, "To you, God's kindness, if you continue in His kindness; otherwise you also will be cut off."

Application of the conditional principle is necessarily restricted. On the basis of what may be observed from the above, Berkhof appears justified when he defines two requirements that must be met if a given prophecy is to be considered conditional: (1) it must be of near application; and (2) it must possess elements that are capable of satisfaction by the prophet's contemporaries.[27] Jonah's famous oracle of doom, "Yet forty days and Nineveh shall be overthrown" (3:4), meets both of these prerequisites: its realization was imminent; and its relationship to its hearers is explicit, even though its precise conditionality remains unexpressed. The very reason for the prophecy lay in the wickedness of the city (1:2); and the Ninevites' reaction was one of prayer to God and of turning from their evil way (3:8). The result was that God did not execute the evil that He had planned and predicted (3:10). Ethan's equally significant revelation, however, to David —"My testament will I not break, nor alter the thing that is come out of

---

25. Cf. the message of his younger contemporary, Ezekiel, "When I say to the righteous, that he shall surely live; if he trust to his righteousness, and commit iniquity, none of his righteous deeds shall be remembered; but in his iniquity that he hath committed, therein shall he die. Again, when I say unto the wicked, Thou shalt surely die; if he turn from his sin, and do that which is lawful and right . . . he shall surely live, he shall not die," 33:13–15.

26. Or Jer 17:24–26 (cf. 22:4): "If ye hearken unto Me, to hallow the sabbath day . . . then shall there enter in by the gates of this city kings sitting on the throne of David . . . and they shall come bringing sacrifices." V. 27, "But if ye will not, then will I kindle a fire in the gate of Jerusalem." The latter is what eventuated.

27. *Principles of Biblical Interpretation*, p. 150.

My mouth," Ps 89:34—does not fit into these requirements: its fulfillment was neither proximate nor dependent upon the king's response. The Lord's promise to David thus remains firm in its forecast of God's testamentary redemption in Christ Jesus.

A guideline for conditionality appears also through one's consideration of the group addressed. Girdlestone, for example, allows for the modification of prediction "in the case of any specified person or generation" but not in respect to "the gracious counsel of God towards the children of men as a whole";[28] and he goes on to quote Romans 11:29, "The gifts and the calling of God are irrevocable." He explains, "These irreversible promises do not depend on man's goodness, but on God's."[29] Of a similar nature are God's statements of condemnation *concerning* foreign powers—not statements *to* them, such as Jonah's to Nineveh—for they express the settled purposes of the Lord.[30] In reference to the future that God has promised for His own people, Peters affirms, "The Kingdom itself pertains to the Divine Purpose, is the subject of sacred covenants, is confirmed by solemn oath, is to be the result or end designed in the redemptive process, and therefore cannot, will not fail. The inheritors of the kingdom, however, are conditioned—a certain number known only to God."[31] This emphasizes that it is not the promises that are conditional, but only the parties or perhaps the chronological periods involved. Pentecost thus seems to have gone too far when he insists, "Prophecies based on unchanging covenants cannot admit the addition of any condition."[32]

The Abrahamic testament, for example, was specifically conditional in its application to the individuals concerned, as opposed to the unconditioned grace that marked the revelation of the Noachian. Anyone who refused the rite of circumcision thereby broke the Abrahamic testament and was cut off from God's people, Gen 17:14. In reference, again, to the land of Canaan, God's promise as such was unconditional: its conquest by Joshua was accomplished in dependence upon testamental rights (Neh 9:8); its partial repossession by Nehemiah was made possible because of God's keeping His testament (vv. 32, 36); and the occupation of its capital, Jerusalem, by God's elect church both during the millennium and throughout the eternity of the new heavens and the new earth is guaranteed by His prophetic word (Rev 20:9, 21:2). But history demonstrates how Israel also lost the land—first in 586 B.C., for despising the word of Yahweh's prophets (II Chron 36:16), and again in A.D. 70, for rejecting and crucifying God's Son (Mt 21:41). Genesis 18:19 specifies that only as Abraham's children do justice and judgment will the Lord bring upon them what He has spoken.

---

28. *The Grammar of Prophecy*, p. 29.
29. Ibid.; cf. Fairbairn, *The Interpretation of Prophecy*, pp. 63–64.
30. Fairbairn, op. cit., p. 69.
31. *The Theocratic Kingdom*, I:176.
32. *Things to come*, p. 49.

In other words, the participation of individuals and groups in the promise *is* conditional.[33] Analogy, moreover, would suggest that claims of modern Zionists to the possession of Palestine be studied in the same light; cf. Ezek 21:27.[34]

The chief problem that is raised by the presence of contingencies among the predictions of Scripture is the danger of improper application of the principle in regard to particular passages or types of passages. Girdlestone, for example, invokes a condition to explain Genesis 2:17, "In the day that thou eatest thereof thou shalt surely die." He assumes that some compensating factor must have been present in man, since "Adam did not actually die when he ate the forbidden fruit"[35] (though death did enter the world at this time, Rom 5:12; further, see Gen. prophecy No. 4, below, and its note 14). Confessedly, God's threat at this juncture was conditional; but the condition was that of Adam's obedience in respect to eating the fruit. The whole point of the passage is that Adam, having failed to meet the stated condition, must surely suffer the consequences. Again, there appears in Joel 2:26b the sweeping promise, ". . . and My people shall never be put to shame." 2:26a had been speaking of Judah's contemporaneous recovery from an ancient locust plague; and one is tempted to assume that even as Judah's repentance of vv. 15–17 had brought the plague itself to an end, v. 18,[36] so some later relapse on their part must have terminated their potentially eternal security. Yet the same promise of endless protection reappears in 2:27 and 3:17; and Joel seems to have been led from the idea of God's immediate blessing of 2:26a into that of His eschatological promise in 2:26b; cf. v. 27a, "and ye shall know that I am in the midst of Israel."

Most serious is the appeal to conditionality, as employed occasionally by amillennialists such as Albertus Pieters, who asserts that the prophecies concerning Yahweh's future earthly kingdom have now lapsed, because of the failures on the part of God's people to meet His prerequisite conditions.[37] His approach, however, fails to recognize G. N. H. Peters' distinction between unconditional promises and conditional participation in these promises; for in itself the millennium was neither of near attainment nor of such a quality as to be affectable by the ancient Hebrews. H. L. Ellison has gone so far as to maintain that

except where a promise is confirmed by God's oath (Gen 22:16, Ps 105:9) we are safe in concluding that every statement of God about the future has some element of the conditional. . . . If we could grasp this clearly it would

33. Cf. G. H. Lang, "God's Covenants Are Conditional," *Evangelical Quarterly*, XXXII (1958), 86–97.
34. J. B. Payne, *Theology of the Older Testament*, pp. 98–99. Their status following Christ's return, should they once again meet God's testamentary conditions (see Rom 11:26–27), is of course another matter.
35. Op. cit., p. 28.
36. "Then was Yahweh jealous for His land and had pity on His people," ASV.
37. *The Seed of Abraham*, pp. 125–127, 137.

clear away much false exegesis on prophetic Scripture. We would feel under
no compulsion to explain away the obvious . . . many promises that are con-
veniently relegated to the Millennium will be seen to refer to the time of
the prophet.

Yet he seems to give away his own case when he adds, "No difficulty will
be found in recognizing minor contraditions and development in the message
of any particular prophet."[38] That is, if when he denies prophetic fulfillments
by having recourse to the principle of contingency he still finds himself at
odds with the truthfulness of the prophets themselves, it would appear better
to hold fast to the prophecies and to limit conditionality to those relatively
few passages where its presence is clearly justified.

Scripture provides illuminating instances both of conditions that men
achieved and of conditions that they missed. Among the former are various
threats that people *avoided* through the exercise of obedience and of dis-
cretion. David, for example, inquired of Yahweh whether Saul would come
against him at Keilah (I Sam 23:11) and, if he did, whether the men of
Keilah would deliver him up to the jealous king (v. 12). When God answered both queries in the affirmative, David took warning and departed;
and Saul did not come down against the town.[39] So Amos' first two visions
of woe (7:1–6) led to his own intercession with God; and the Lord revealed, "It shall not be" (yet contrast v. 8). Revelation 2:16b is directed
against those at Pergamum who hold the teachings of the Nicolaitans: "I
will come, and I will make war against them," that is, unless the church
repents, v. 16a, which it presumably did, since these heretics seem to have
been but a minority (v. 15, and compare v. 6). Cf. vv. 22–23, which present
parallel threats against the followers of a false prophetess, "Jezebel," at
Thyatira.[40] Of similar nature are the results, either good or bad, that men

38. *Ezekiel: the Man and his Message*, pp. 103–104.

39. An instance of avoided threat, that also involves textual criticism, is that of
the word of the man of God to King Amaziah in II Chron 25:8, "If thou wilt go
[against Edom] . . . God will cast thee down before the enemy." Amaziah did in
fact go against Edom and, far from being cast down, won a notable victory, vv.
11–12. It therefore appears best to emend the first clause of v. 8, with the Jerusalem
Bible, "If they [not Amaziah himself, but a large group of mercenaries from N.
Israel] come, God will cast. . . ." This employment of mercenaries was the thing
that the man of God was opposing, v. 7. So when the king did not let them come, then
the prophecy ceased to apply, and he was not cast down.

40. Cf. the well-known oracle of Rev 3:16, to the church at Laodicea: "Because
you are lukewarm, and neither hot nor cold, I will spit you out of My mouth." But
the English, *I will* represents *méllō*, "I am likely to [note: such a sense may appear
questionable in the NT; but in any event]: the word does not necessarily imply that
the intention is final, and v. 19 shows that it is not," Camb, *Rev*, p. 27. Swete in
fact adds, "The needed discipline came at length under Marcus Aurelius, when
Sagaris, the bishop of Laodicea was martyred. . . . By a whole hearted devotion to
the Master, the Laodicean church would arrive at a better mind, and be no longer
'tepid' but 'fervent in spirit.'" *The Apocalypse of St. John*, p. 63. Their repentance
may indeed have developed much earlier, in response to John's appeal, rather than
after the century of delay suggested by Swete.

find that they can *achieve*, as they meet Scripture's prescribed conditions. Malachi 3:17, for one, identifies certain men who are spared from condemnation and counted as God's special treasure. The basis for this prophecy lay in Malachi's observations concerning those who tempted God and thought they had escaped (v. 15). In reaction, some of the more righteous feared and served God (vv. 16, 18); and the result was both immediate, by their incorporation into God's book of remembrance (v. 16), and final, in the promised relationship of 3:17. Amos 5:6, for another, admonishes the men of Samaria, "Ye turn justice to wormwood . . . seek Yahweh . . . lest He break out like fire . . . in Beth-el." But they kept on in their wickedness and so, one might say, met the condition for doom, just as Amos had anticipated in the preceding verse, foreseeing, "Beth-el shall come to nought."

Among the Bible's passages that illumine conditionality are a latter group that include numerous examples of blessings lost because of conditions unmet. In I Kings 3:14 the Lord advised Solomon, "If thou wilt walk in My ways, as thy father David did walk, then I will lengthen thy days." But in the parallel verse of II Chronicles 1:12 this option is not represented; and Keil explains, "The conditional promise, 'long life' (I K 3:14), is omitted, because Solomon did not fulfill the condition, and the promise was not fulfilled."[41] Ezekiel 43 spoke of a temple that the prophet's hearers were to rebuild in Israel (v. 11), and he beheld in a vision that "the glory of Yahweh filled the house" (vv. 1–7; cf. 44:2, 4). Yet this theophany did not historically occur at the rebuilding of the temple; and the explanation appears to lie in 43:9, "Now let them put away their whoredom . . . *and* I will dwell in the midst of them forever": no general conversion, no glory cloud! Finally Malachi 3:11–12 foretells a blessed land, marked by an end of (locust) plagues or of crop failures. But there was a reason that lay behind Judah's current setbacks and need for this word: v. 8, they had been withholding their tithes from God. Malachi pleads, v. 10, that they bring forward the tithes so as to receive God's blessing. The results correspond: according to v. 9, they had been cursed for their impiety before; and this curse presumably continued unalleviated thereafter, while the blessings of vv. 11–12 remained unrealized.[42]

Even when a given prophecy receives its stated accomplishment, factors of contingency may play a part, either in the time or in the manner of its attainment. On the one hand, the phenomenon of delayed fulfillment, as noted in part (a) above, may be conditioned by matters of human response. Huldah the prophetess, for example, confirmed the fate of Jerusalem according to the curses of the Deuteronomic law (II K 22:16–17) but then

41. KD, *Chron*, p. 306.
42. Cf. Zech 8:16, 18–19: "Execute the judgment of truth . . . and the word of Yahweh came unto me, saying, The fasts shall be joy and gladnness and cheerful feasts; therefore love the truth and peace."

communicated an altered schedule of timing from God to King Josiah: "Because thou didst humble thyself before Yahweh, when thou heardest what I spake against this place . . . and hast wept before Me; I also have heard thee, saith Yahweh. Therefore, behold, thou shalt be gathered to thy grave in peace, neither shall thine eyes see all the evil which I will bring upon this place," vv. 19–20. On the other hand, a phenomenon of modification may enter into a given prediction's manner of accomplishment, even while the prophecy itself is being literally fulfilled. The patriarch Jacob had prophesied that the tribes descending from Simeon and Levi would be scattered in Israel, and they both were (see Gen 49:7, below). But intervening acts of faithfuness on the part of the Levites transformed their mode of scattering into one of leadership, as contrasted with the absorption suffered by Simeon.[43]

Particular instances of modification present acknowledged difficulties in interpretation. Concerning the prophet Micah's threat that Zion should be plowed as a field (3:12), men a century later, in Jeremiah's day, asked, "Did not Hezekiah fear and entreat the favor of Yahweh," who "repented of the evil which He had pronounced against them?" (Jer 26:19). But while this earlier king's repentance might conceivably have obviated what should then be judged to have been conditional prophecy on the part of Micah, this case too may perhaps be better understood, like Josiah's, as one of postponement rather than of abrogation; cf. Jeremiah's reiteration of Micah's prediction (Jer 7:14) and history's eventual execution of the threat (52:13–27).

A concluding caution to be noted is that the presence of contingent elements in a passage need not inevitably imply the presence of specific prophecy. A statement of principle may exhibit an attached condition and still be nothing other than a timeless generalization. It becomes true, that is, whenever the given condition may happen to be fulfilled; but it does not thereby become predictive.[44] An example would be Haggai 1:8, "Build this house . . . and I will be glorified, saith Yahweh." Or again, statements of immediate intention—which should not be considered as strictly prophetic[45]—may, simultaneously, be contingent; cf. in this same verse, "Build the house, and I will take pleasure in it." Yahweh is, as it were, simply anticipating what would be His own appropriate reaction.

2. INVALID PREDICTIONS. The principle of the necessary fulfillment of the forecasts of Scripture finds exception in a limited number of prophecies which are quoted in the Bible, not as a matter of revelation but simply as a matter of historical record. They are not to be considered as valid prophecies, and they are not so treated in the study that follows. They stem not

43. See Fairbairn, op. cit., pp. 76–78.
44. See above, pp. 32–38.
45. See above, pp. 38–41.

from the writers of the Biblical books, but from certain of the actors who happen to be quoted within these books and about whom the context warns us that they are not to be accepted as approved speakers. They may be considered under three classifications.

(a) The existence of false prophets—of men who laid specific claim to divine revelations when they had not in fact received such—is testified to in both testaments: Dt 18:20–22, Neh 6:12; Mt 7:15, Acts 13:6. In the century that followed the division of the Hebrew kingdom (930 B.C.), three major categories of false prophets appear. There were Jezebel's outrightly pagan prophets, who served Baal and Asherah (I K 18:19); there were the hypocritical charlatans of Ahab's court (22:6–7), prophets for pay, a disgrace to the name of the Lord (Mi 3:11; cf. Amos 7:12); and there were sincere prophets, who were well-meaning but still revelationless, and hence might prove mistaken (I K 13:11–18).[46] It is not that such men were thwarting the will of Yahweh, for their activities lay within the scope of God's ultimate decree. When Jeremiah, for example, exclaimed, "Ah, Lord Yahweh! surely Thou hast greatly deceived this people, saying, Ye shall have peace" (4:10; cf. 6:14, 8:11, 14:13, 23:17), he seems to have been referring to God's utilization for His own ends of the false prophets;[47] cf. the case of the court prophets of Ahab, predicting his victory at Ramoth-gilead, I K 22:6, 11–12. But this does not relieve them of their own responsibility or of their personal, sinful motivations (in contrast with Yahweh's righteous motivation, vv. 20–22); compare how they were questioned by Jehoshaphat even at the time (v. 7) and condemned by Micaiah for their lying spirit (v. 23). Correspondingly, when Micaiah mimicked their prophecy, v. 15, his words were immediately recognized by Ahab as a mockery, v. 16.

Chapters 23 to 29 in Jeremiah document in particular the running conflict experienced by this great servant of God during the closing years of the Judean monarchy. He contended with the false prophets in general, who "teach vanity; they speak a vision of their own heart, and not out of the mouth of Yahweh. . . . If they had stood in My counsel, then had they turned My people from their evil way" (23:16, 22); with the temple prophets of Jerusalem, who sought to slay Jeremiah for his preaching (26:8); with the Judean prophets who opposed subservience to Babylon and predicted a prompt return of the temple vessels that had been seized by Nebuchadrezzar in 597 (27:14–16); with Hananiah, who dramatically broke off the yoke from Jeremiah's neck, by which the latter had been symbolizing Judah's necessary submission to Babylon (28:1–11); cf. Jeremiah's response against this false prophet, including a threat of death within the year—which came about (vv. 12–17); with Ahab and Zedekiah in Babylon, whom he threatened with execution by Nebuchadrezzar, that

46. Payne, *Theology*, p.56.
47. T. Laetsch, *Bible Commentary, Jeremiah*, p.69.

they should be "roasted in the fire" (29:21–23); and with their colleague Shemaiah, who even dispatched letters from Babylon back to Jerusalem, seeking to have Jeremiah imprisoned for his prophecy of the 70-year-long exile (vv. 24–32).

(b) A second class of Scripturally disapproved and hence invalid speakers would consist of those ordinary men who chose to identify their own faulty conclusions with that groundwork of revelations concerning which they may have become familiar. An example is the statement by David's men who were hidden with him in the cave of En-gedi, when Saul came alone into this same cave: "Behold, the day of which Yahweh said unto thee, I will deliver thine enemy into thy hand, and thou shalt do to him as it shall seem good unto thee," I Sam 24:4. In truth, no such oracle is otherwise known. The man may actually have deduced it from Saul's seemingly providential fall into their power.[48] But David subsequently regretted even such minor symbolic actions as he then took against Saul, v. 5; and he specifically repudiated his men's statement, v. 6. Compare also the previous words of David's more noble friend Jonathan: "The hand of Saul my father shall not find thee; and thou shalt be king over Israel, and I shall be next unto thee," 23:17. The second of these predictions was indeed true: 20:13 implies that Jonathan had become aware of David's divine designation to the throne; and later in 23:17 he states that Saul too had come to this conviction, for the news of David's anointing must have got out (cf. 24:20). The first prediction was true also, by inference from God's choice of David. But the third was not: it was only a wish by Jonathan, truly expressed, but not a matter of divine revelation.

(c) A final, limited group of invalid predictions are those which arise from the lips of recognized prophets or apostles—who were not always above censure; cf. Paul's condemnation of Peter in Gal 2:11–14—where context indicates that they were speaking by opinion rather than by revelation. In Acts 27, for example, Paul advised the men on board the ship of Alexandria, "I perceive that the voyage will certainly be attended with damage and great loss, not only of the ship, but also of our lives," v. 10. Commentators express their belief that the apostle's phrase "I perceive" is "here used of the result of experience and observation, not of revelation, cf. 17:22, 19:26, 21:20";[49] for in point of fact, though the ship was lost, all hands were saved alive, 27:44. Compare Paul's own later words in vv. 21–22, "Men, you ought to have followed my advice and not to have set sail from Crete, and incurred this damage and loss. Yet now I urge you to keep up your courage, for there shall be no loss of life among you, but only of the ship"; and this last statement *is* specifically claimed to have come by divine communication, vv. 23–24.

Again, in Acts 20:25 Paul addresses the Ephesian elders: "I know that

48. KD, *Sam*, p. 235.
49. ExGkT, II:520.

you all, among whom I went about preaching, will see my face no more"; cf. v. 38. F. F. Bruce asks, about the alternative possibilities, "Does this mean that not all, but only some, would see him again; or that none of them would do so?" In light of v. 38, Bruce favors the latter, assuming that the statement simply reflects Paul's opinion at the time; for he grants, "The Pastoral epistles imply, though they do not explicitly assert, a later visit to Ephesus (cf. I Tim 1:3, II Tim 1:15 ff.)."[50] Such a visit is suggested by Philemon 22, I Timothy 4:13, and II Timothy 4:13, 20, as well. So Lenski explains, "The emphatic egó, 'I for my part know,' helps to indicate[51] that Paul is expressing only his own conviction.[52] . . . He differentiates most clearly between what the Holy Spirit actually testified to him (v. 23 [see below, under 20:22]) and what he himself felt he knew in addition to that testimony."[53]

B. Methodology for Ascertaining Fulfillment

1. CONTEXT. In discussing the attainment of the Bible's predictions, as one moves onward from the fact, from the "what" of necessary fulfillment, to the method, to the "how" of proper procedure for determining an intended accomplishment, the most basic principle to recall is that which F. E. Marsh entitles "the law of association or context."[54] That is to say, the Scripture writer himself may go on to define the nature of the fulfillment of a given prophecy within his own immediately surrounding declarations. His subsequent definition may be explicit, e.g. in Exodus 7:13, that "Pharaoh hearkened not unto them, as Yahweh had spoken"; cf. the preceding predictions in 4:21 or 7:3. Or in Numbers 26:64–65, "Among these there was not a man of them that were numbered at Sinai. For Yahweh had said of them, They shall surely die in the wilderness"; cf. the preceding predictions in 14:29, 32–33. Again, his definition may be inferential, e.g. in Exodus 7:15, that on the following morning Pharaoh would go out unto the water. This precise act is not thereafter described; but the following context, v. 20, does speak about "the waters that were in the river, in the sight of Pharaoh," and, v. 23, about how the king then "turned and went into his house," which leaves the fact of his prior "going out unto the water" beyond legitimate doubt. It is the existence of such obvious demonstrations

---

50. *The Acts of the Apostles*, pp. 379–380.
51. The pronoun is not in itself determinative—for the same form occurs in v. 29, which is of legitimately predictive character, *q.v.*—but it may here indicate contrast with the specific revelation two verses earlier, in v. 23.
52. Cf. WC, p. 390, "He had a conviction . . . not literally correct."
53. *The Interpretation of Acts*, p. 844; cf. Alford's detailed exposition of the force of the verb "know," as used by Paul, *The Greek Testament*, II:211–212.
54. *The Structural Principles of the Bible*, p. 230.

that belies the contention of E. J. Carnell that "prophecy is *not* self-inter-preting."[55] Carnell proceeds to adduce the instance of Malachi 4:5, as non-self-interpreting in reference to John the Baptist. But such a case appears to be the exception rather than the rule. Ordinarily, context is the guide to meaning, provided only, as he himself goes on to explain, that prophecy "is not to have its full sense made out" in this way.[56]

The method of appealing to context may provide explicit assistance, either as to the manner or as to the time of fulfillment. The former is par-ticularly relevant in one's approach to figurative prediction. Thus Isaiah 55:12, that the trees should clap their hands, is explained in reference to the peace of God's people; in Micah 4:4, the promise that "they shall sit every man under his vine and under his fig-tree" is similarly defined both by the words that precede, "Nation shall not lift up sword against nation," and by the words that follow, "and none shall make them afraid"; and in Zechariah 3:10 the application of this same figure to Messianic scenes becomes apparent from the thought of the preceding verse, "I will remove the iniquity of that land in one day." The latter type of assistance, concern-ing time, may be either absolute or relative. Context may, on the one hand, furnish an exact statement of date. For example, Zechariah 8:12–13 speaks of a situation of prosperity and of blessing which might suggest the millen-nium; but both what goes before and what follows after this oracle point to a more contemporary time of fulfillment: v. 11, "But *now* I will not be . . . as in the former days"; and v. 15, "So again have I thought *in these days* to do well unto Jerusalem." The prophet explains his own meaning. Scrip-ture's more relative sort of guidance to times of fulfillment may, on the other hand, be illustrated by Isaiah's Immanuel prophecy, 7:14, when two verses later the prophet adds that "before the child shall know how to refuse the evil and choose the good," the land would be forsaken of its kings. The latter event had been assigned a limit of 65 years (see below, under Isa 7:8b); but precisely how much "before" Immanuel this forsaking, in turn, would be is not stated, only that the appearance of the Messianic child (cf. 9:6) would be later, relative to it.

2. ANALOGY. A valid methodology for ascertaining the fulfillment of the forecasts found in Scripture must progress beyond the immediate contexts of the prophetic writers who may have been involved in their initial revela-tion and go on into a comparison of the analogous sources of legitimate illumination. Angus and Green insist, "It is a golden rule, that each of the predictions of Scripture must be compared with others on the same topic, and with history, both profane and inspired."[57] As Edersheim has put it, "Prophecy can only be fully understood from the standpoint of fulfillment

---

55. *The Case for Orthodox Theology*, p. 54.
56. See p. 4 above, and its note 8.
57. Op. cit., p. 246.

. . . first the historical, then the exegetical argument."⁵⁸ This means that for the OT one's method of interpretation must embrace three major aspects: the analogy of Israel's other prophetic revelations on the subject at hand, so as to interpret in terms of the rest of the OT; the analogy of truth, insofar as this may have been preserved also in ancient secular writings, to interpret, that is, in terms of known history; and above all the analogy of Christ and the apostles, to interpret in terms of the NT and its clarifications about fulfillments.

(a) The rest of the OT. The necessity for invoking the analogy of other inspired declarations out of the history of the Hebrews appears from Conrad von Orelli's observation that a "characteristic feature of prophecy is the partial nature of the individual prophetic utterances. One picture must be supplemented by the others, in order not to be misunderstood."⁵⁹ He adds: "Prophecies need to be combined, that they may supplement each other" against "one-sided representations."⁶⁰ F. E. Marsh summarizes this principle under his "law of interpretation or reference"; stated concisely, "The best interpreter of the Bible is the Bible itself."⁶¹ Thus when the 7th-century prophet Zephaniah foresees a day of the universal worship of the Lord, "every one from his place" (2:11), and when the 6th-century prophet Zechariah predicts that "many peoples and strong nations shall come to seek Yahweh" (8:22), their oracles ought to be understood in the light of the 8th-century prophet Isaiah, whom they had doubtless studied, especially ch. 2:2–4, on how all nations would finally flow to Jerusalem, so that the fulfillment of all three is to be sought in the Messiah's yet future millennium and not in His present church. Attention is here directed to Summary A, at the conclusion of the study,⁶² in which are listed in their order of chronological fulfillment all the Biblical prophecies on each particular topic.

(b) History. Horne has stated: "The event is the best interpreter of a prediction."⁶³ The methodology that he proposes follows, necessarily, from the principle of the analogy of truth, namely, that the Lord who inspires prophecy is the same God who ordains the course of history, which He therefore had perfectly in mind in even His earliest forecasts. This hermeneutic of historical analogy demands, moreover, the fullest possible knowledge of history, of names, and of other cultural references on the part of the serious interpreter.⁶⁴ Particularly for Scripture's verbalized prophecies that assume figurative forms—including much of its symbolical

---

58. *Prophecy and History in Relation to the Messiah*, pp. 111, 113.
59. ISBE, IV:2465.
60. *OT Prophecy of the Consummation*, p. 32.
61. Op. cit., p. 237; cf. p. 253; the Reformation principle of the *analogia Scripturae.*
62. See below, pp. 631–659.
63. *An Introduction to the Critical Study and Knowledge of the Holy Scriptures*, p. 388; cf. Girdlestone, op. cit., p. 172, "History is the best commentary on prophecy."
64. B. Ramm, *Protestant Biblical Interpretation* (1950), pp. 163–164.

apocalyptic writing; see part 3(c), below—or for its acted prophecies, with their symbolic object lessons, one's procedure must always be, first, to discover the meaning of the symbol in the culture of the writer; second, to check later history for a possible development in its meaning; and third, to ascertain such final explanation as may be found in the NT.[65] On the ways in which historical environments, together with their corresponding cultural patterns, are subject to change, so that, for example, the terminology employed for instruments of warfare must be reinterpreted into their "equivalents" for whatever may be the historical period that is being predicted, see below under part 3(a).

(c) The NT. Edersheim states emphatically that for a divinely informed methodology in prophetic interpretation "we take our best guidance from the NT";[66] and he proceeds to quote John 12:16, "These things His disciples did not understand at the first; but when Jesus was glorified, then they remembered that these things were written of Him." Compare also Luke 24:25–27, which makes it clear that only in the light of Christ's suffering and subsequent resurrection was it possible for even His closest followers ot understand "the things in Moses and all the prophets concerning Himself." The basis of legitimacy for invoking the NT in one's determination of prophetic fulfillments lies in commitment to the unity of the Scripture. Some commentators, it is true, hesitate to submit individual judgments to the control of NT revelation. But if the same God guided the inscripturation of both testaments, then He must possess the right to explain to us in the one what He meant in the other. Such a concept of unity within the word also embraces doctrine, along with fulfillment; or, as Fairbairn observes, "Moses and Christ, when closely examined and viewed as to the more fundamental parts of their respective systems, are found to teach in perfect harmony with each other. The law and the prophets of the OT, and the gospels and epistles of the new, exhibit but different phases of the same wondrous scheme of grace."[67]

In its specific application, the principle of the NT analogy may be found sometimes to add to, or sometimes to clarify (but never to subtract from or to deny), certain features of God's older revelations. Haggai 2:6, for example, had predicted that Yahweh would "shake the heavens and the earth. . . ." Hebrews 12:26 then quotes Haggai, and 12:27 explains that this "denotes the removal of those things which can be shaken." Especially does the NT analogy bring out the work of Christ, when the OT may simply have foreseen divine activity in general; for at a number of points,

---

65. Ibid., p. 173.
66. Op. cit., p. 113.
67. Robert C. Dentan, for example, proposes the abandonment of the Reformation principle of the analogy of Scripture, suggesting that only so may one construct "Biblical Theology in the modern sense," *Preface to OT Theology*, p. 6; Fairbairn, *The Typology of Scripture*, I:172.

as Girdlestone observes, "the attributes and functions of Jehovah may legitimately be regarded as realized and embodied in the Only-begotten Son."[68] Furthermore, it is the NT commentary which exercises the final control in the discovery of the Lord's specific intention in His older forecasts. It is the analogy which enables one to distinguish between the probable (limited) understandings of the human secondary authors of the OT and the full meaning that God originally intended,[69] without in the process lapsing into subjective and allegorized interpretations;[70] cf. the justifiable concern in this regard expressed by Walter C. Kaiser.[71] Actually, when all is said and done, the instances of such NT elucidation are relatively few; and where it is not to be had, one must necessarily restrict himself to the methodology of historico-critical OT interpretation or, in the words of W. J. Beecher, to "what it meant to an intelligent Israelite of the time to which it belongs."[72]

The standard of NT analogy possesses further applicability that goes beyond precise points of exegesis. Meyrick lays it down as a rule of prophetic analysis: "Interpret according to the principles which may be deduced from examples of prophecies interpreted in the NT."[73] When the NT thus asserts the necessity of death, depicted by the shedding of blood, for the establishment of the Sinaitic testament (Heb 9:18–20), one is legitimately advised to seek out the corresponding elements in God's earlier Abrahamic (Gen 15:10–18), Noachian (8:20–21), or even Edenic (3:15) testamentary revelations. Still more broadly, the NT's commitment to the truthfulness of God's word demands an interpretation of prophetic fulfillments that will be harmonious with the Lord's truth as understood elsewhere. Yet just as in the case of specific applications, this methodology must not thereby be elevated into the status of a comprehensive or exclusive principle, as seems to have been suggested by Carnell's previously mentioned approach to the OT: "Prophecy is not to be its own interpreter." Carnell then significantly qualifies his own words: "It is part of the character of the Scripture prophecies not to be so framed as to be *fully* [italics mine] understood before the event. . . . It is not to have its *full* [same] sense made out (like that of any other kind of composition) by the study . . . of each prophecy itself, but it is to be interpreted by the event that fulfills it."[74] For if the ideas deduced from the concrete examples of the NT's treatment of the Old are made all-determinative, the OT must

68. Op. cit., p. 85.
69. See above, p. 5.
70. See above, pp. 43–45.
71. "The Eschatological Hermeneutics of Epangelicalism (Promise Theology)," ETS J, 13 (1970), 94.
72. *The Prophets and the Promise*, p. 14.
73. *Smith's Dictionary of the Bible*, p. 2600.
74. Op. cit., pp. 54–55. In particular cases, however, he may still have unduly limited prophecy's self-understandability.

then soon forfeit its right to speak for itself, even in areas not touched upon by the later revelation.

If the failing of liberalism lies in a disregard of the analogy of the NT, the failing of evangelicalism lies in an uncriticalness toward its limitations. The NT uses the OT in several different ways: it quotes from it not only to designate the accomplishment of its predictions, but also to prove, to explain, or to illustrate a variety of its propositions.[75] The purposes of apostolic citations from the OT may range from that of affirming the fulfillment of detailed prophecies down to mere allusions about similar happenings or to the reuse of familiar phrases.[76] Sometimes even the phraseology may not be the same, and the analogy is reduced to one that concerns only the vague resemblance of idea. A number of the Psalms, for example, received their accomplishment in David and should not be styled Messianic because of the appearance of some similar thoughts in the NT. Thus Psalm 18:43 states, "A people whom I have not known shall serve me," a concept that might appear similar to that of Ephesians 2:11–12 but which refers only to David's foreign conquests; or Psalm 24:7 exclaims, "Lift up your heads, O ye gates . . . and the King of glory shall come in," a statement perhaps suggestive of our Lord's triumphal entry but which probably refers to David's bringing of the ark into Jerusalem in II Samuel 6.[77] Others are those psalms which show a similarity to certain OT passages that *are* noted by the NT analogy as having Messianic fulfillment, but which are not themselves to be so classified, e.g. Psalm 34:20, "He keepeth all his bones, not one of them is broken": it is apparently not predictive of Christ's crucifixion; for John 19:36 seems better related to the known typology of the Passover in Exodus 12:46.[78]

Where the fact of direct citation can be established, still the case may be one simply of words reused because of some appropriateness to the NT situation, but without regard to the original context. With Psalm 31:5, for example, compare Luke 23:46, "Father, into Thy hands I commend My spirit," where our Lord does not claim that His own death was the subject intended by David the psalmist.[79] If the NT should provide a measure of explanation, along with a given quotation, then one must never fail to take into consideration the precise formula under which the OT material is introduced into the New. The NT formula may, on the one hand, establish a Messianic intent in God's original revelation. Thus when the psalmist

75. Ramm, op. cit., pp. 165–166.
76. T. H. Horne, op. cit., I:101.
77. Cf. also Pss 21:4 or 61:7, perhaps similar in idea to Heb 7:24, but not really anticipatory of the NT situation.
78. Similarly, Ps 97:7 might seem related to Heb 1:6; but the latter is more probably a citation of Dt 32:43, LXX, *q.v.*
79. In this same regard, cf. Ps 42:5, 11, with Mt 26:38, or Ps 38:11 or 88:8 with Lk 23:49; and see J. B. Payne, "So-called Dual Fulfillment in Messianic Psalms," ETS P (1953), 63, 71.

forecasts, ". . . and Thy years shall have no end" (102:25–27), the Christian believer may be sure that its reference is to Christ, since its quotation in Hebrews 1:10–12 is introduced by the explanation, "But of the Son He says . . ." (v. 8); or when David records, ". . . Lo, I am come: in the roll of the book it is written of Me, I delight to do Thy will" (Ps 40:6–8), we may have confidence that he is speaking on behalf of our Lord, for its quotation in Hebrews 10:5–7 is introduced by the clarifying words, "Therefore when He comes into the world, He says . . ." (v. 5). Yet on the other hand, when Psalm 8:2 is quoted in Matthew 21:16 it is introduced by the mere question, "Have you never read, 'Out of the mouth of babes Thou hast prepared praise . . .'?"; when Psalm 44:22 is quoted in Romans 8:36, the apostle prefaces it by saying only, "Just as it is written, 'For Thy sake we are being put to death all day long . . .'"; and when Psalm 116:10 is quoted in II Corinthians 4:13, he explains, "But having the same spirit of faith, according to what is written, 'I believed, therefore I spoke,' therefore also we speak. . . ." In these latter three cases the OT is claimed to furnish no more than general affirmations, which are shown by the NT's formulas of citation to have been appropriate for later reemployment, but without thereby having to have been all along intentionally predictive of that reemployment. In a slightly different vein, Exodus 3:6 is quoted by Christ in Matthew 22:31–32 as follows: "But regarding the resurrection of the dead, have you not read that which was spoken to you by God, saying, 'I am the God of Abraham, Isaac, and Jacob'? God is not the God of the dead but of the living." Our Lord here deduces the necessity of human resurrection from the fact of men's relationship to God. But His teaching is an insight, an application, drawn from a passage that was not originally a prophecy.

One formula of citation that has a particular bearing upon the matter of maintaining proper limits to evangelicalism's employment of the principle of NT analogy is the phrase, *hína plērōthé*, "that it might be fulfilled," and its parallel expressions. Appearing particularly in Matthew, but also in John and other of the NT writings, this formula may indicate the precise, intended accomplishment of an OT prediction, e.g. in Matthew 12:17–21, on Christ as the Servant of Yahweh, predicted in Isaiah 42:1–4, or in John 12:38, on His fulfilling of Isaiah 53:1. Yet it may also denote a loose relationship of illustration to elucidate some principle, or of similarity in words or ideas to an OT affirmation that may not in itself have been predictive at all, e.g. in James 2:21–23, on the confirmation of Abraham's faith "when he offered up Isaac his son on the altar [Gen 22]," to which James adds, "and the Scripture was fulfilled, *eplērōthē*, which says, 'Abraham believed God, and it was reckoned to him for righteousness' [Gen 15:6]." Again, in John 18:9, Jesus interceded for His disciples at the time of His final arrest, "that the word might be fulfilled, *hína plērōthé*, which He spoke, 'Of those whom Thou hast given Me I lost not one.'" But this action of His was just an added illustration for the affirmation of protection for those whom God had given Him, which He had already stated in the previous chapter; for as Westcott observes, "His words, 17:12, were spoken of the past,"[80] even when first uttered. W. J. Farley therefore concludes that at some points the phrase "indicates little more than analogy and correspondence beween two events which, in themselves, had nothing to do with each other."[81]

Specifically, one must guard against an unwarranted claiming that certain OT verses have to be considered Messianic because of their citation in the NT under this formula. Matthew 13:14–15, for example, comments on the failure of the multitudes to comprehend Jesus' parables, adding, "And in their case the prophecy of Isaiah is being fulfilled, which says, 'You will keep on hearing, but will not understand.' " Isaiah 6:9, however, had not been predictive (though it *was* prophecy, in the broad sense) when first spoken; and Christ appears simply to have made an application of its truth to His own times. A few verses later, Matthew 13:35 quotes the words of the chief musician Asaph from Psalm 78:2, in which he laid claim to speak in the *māshāl*, or "wisdom-saying" form,[82] and states that it is paralleled by Christ's method of teaching through narrative-similes, "so that what was spoken through the prophet might be fulfilled, saying, 'I will open my mouth in parables; I will utter things hidden.' " Oxtoby therefore defines the NT concept of fulfillment as "correspondence of an event with a prior announcement . . . [but] in some cases it means very little more than a correspondence in phraseology . . . no actual correspondence is intended."[83]

Similar examples occur in the quotation of Psalm 41:9 by John 13:18, "that the Scripture may be fulfilled, 'He who eats my bread has lifted up his heel against me,' " and of Psalm 69:4 and 21 by John 15:25, 19:28, the former of which reads, "that the word may be fulfilled, 'They hated me without a cause.' " But in none of these citations was the passage that is quoted from the OT of a predictive nature—they were simply descriptive of contemporary events in the career of David; and the Bible's claim of relationship between the two testaments thus necessarily limits itself to certain resemblances in verbal forms, which gained fulfillment, as the NT

80. *The Gospel According to St. John*, p. 253.
81. *The Progress of Prophecy*, pp. 302–303.
82. Oxtoby, op. cit., p. 43.
83. Ibid., pp. 67–68. This in itself is not without significance, when applied, for example, to Isa 7:14. The bare fact that as the verse is quoted in Mt 1:23 it is introduced by the formula—"This took place that what was spoken by the Lord through the prophet *might be fulfilled*, saying . . ." (v. 22)—could thereby prove little as far as the original intent of Isaiah was concerned. But when one recognizes that Matthew's contextual stress rests upon the virgin birth of Christ, as conceived in the womb of Mary by the Holy Spirit (vv. 18, 20), then the fact of "correspondence in phraseology" requires the presence of the term "virgin" in Isaiah as well. And since the Isaianic context is predictive, and since no one pretends that any such virgin birth actually occurred in the prophet's own time (see below, under Isa 7:13), then the reference must indeed be Messianic, unless, of course, God's Spirit Himself could be said to have intentionally foretold two different births by the one phrase; see below, pp. 124–126.

often uses this word, in the sense of a new application to the career of Jesus. On the other hand when Psalms 69:25 and 109:8 are quoted in Acts 1:16–20, under the formula, "the Scripture had to be fulfilled," the apostle suggests a real and necessary connection between OT revelation and the NT event, "which the Holy Spirit foretold by the mouth of David concerning Judas . . . for it is written in the book of Psalms, 'Let his homestead be made desolate.' " Whether therefore the formula *hína plērōthé* has the indefinite meaning or is actually claiming a true prophetic fulfillment must be detemined in each case by the nature of the OT passage that is being quoted and by the evidence of the New.

The former method—that of using OT phrases to illustrate what are essentially distinct NT teachings—may be clarified by observing other instances in the apostolic revelation, where the formula "that it might be fulfilled" is *not* invoked. Psalm 118:22, which refers to Israel (?) as a rejected stone, is used in the NT to describe Jesus Christ, with these formulaic explanations: "Did ye never read in the Scriptures . . . ?" (Mt 21:42); or, Jesus "is the stone which . . ." (Acts 4:11); or again, "This precious value is, for those who disbelieve, 'the stone which . . .' " (I Pet 2:7). Again, Psalm 68:18, referring to Yahweh's past triumphs, is used in the NT to describe the grace given to the church, with the explanation, "Therefore it says, 'When He ascended on high . . . He gave gifts to men' " (Eph 4:7–8), claiming a parallel between the present and the past, but not necessarily claiming the present to have been predicted by that past. Even certain of the statements that are genuinely predictive may be reused in the NT to illustrate truths other than those belonging to them. Thus Joel 2:32a (*q.v.,* prophecy No. 10) seems to speak of the rapture of the church so as to escape the outpouring of the wrath of God at the return of Christ, when it says, "Whosoever shall call on the name of Yahweh shall be delivered." But this verse is used by both Peter, in Acts 2:21, and Paul, in Romans 10:13, to illustrate that all who call on Christ are saved, now. But neither claim that in this particular verse Joel was originally referring to their own apostolic church age (though, conceivably, he *might* have been, had Christ in fact come and established His Messianic kingdom at that point).

The failure to appreciate this distinction has led a number of modern critical writers into such sweeping condemnations as the following, by Bultmann, who speaks of "the impossibility of the NT and the traditional understanding . . . [that] prophecy is the forecasting of future happenings, and [that] fulfillment is the occurrence of what has been forecast." He excoriates the NT's methodology by claiming: "In accordance with the traditional view, prophecy becomes understandable from the fulfillment, in the sudden coming to light of a secret meaning of words which in their context had originally meant something quite different. . . . In all these cases the writers in the NT do not gain new knowledge from the OT texts, but read from or into them what they already know."[84] Yet his censures seem to arise from a failure to appreciate just what the apostolic writers are trying to do, and to distinguish what the true limits to evangelicalism's appeal to the NT analogy really are. Within its Biblically determined bounds, the principle of analogy remains basic for ascertaining prophetic fulfillment. It has been summarized by Meyrick, when he states: "In respect to things past, interpret by the apparent meaning, checked by reference to events; in respect to things future, interpret by the apparent meaning, checked by reference to the analogy of the faith."[85]

3. LITERARY FORM. A proper methodology for approaching the subject of the fulfillment of Biblical prediction must recognize certain issues that are raised by each of the four major prophetic "forms," as defined in Section I[86] and as clarified in respect to their limits in Section II above.[87] Even (a), the forthrightly verbalized oracle, raises a question, by reason of its very prosaic down-to-earthness. For owing to the fundamentally historical character of divine revelation,[88] "The prophet spoke of future glory in terms of his own society and experience."[89] This appears particularly in the prophetic terminology that is used for matters such as the means of transportation or the instruments of war. Micah 5:6, for example, states that the armies of the Messiah will waste the land of Assyria "with the sword." Other weapons would obviously be more appropriate, should the action occur today. But should its accomplishment be subject to an even longer postponement, then one can only speculate as to the form that the Messianic artillery will actually take. Mickelsen thus speaks of fulfillment by "equivalents";[90] indeed, OT prophecy could hardly have been intelligible to Micah's original audience without some such terminological updating having to arise in respect to its later hearers. The reality, moreover, of this hermeneutical need for cultural appreciation lays special demands upon the modern expositor, for conscientious attention to the lives and times of the prophets. Failure in this regard can result only in fanciful exegesis, for example in the discovery by certain early-20th-century Jehovah's Witnesses of predictions of steam locomotive transportation and other traffic problems[91] in Nahum's forecast of the fall of Nineveh (612 B.C.), e.g. "The chariots rage in the streets; they rush to and fro in the broad ways: the appearance of them is like torches;

84. "Prophecy and Fulfillment," in Claus Westermann, ed., *Essays on OT Hermeneutics*, pp. 50, 53.
85. *Smith's Dictionary of the Bible*, p. 2600.
86. See above, pp. 16–26.
87. See pp. 27–56.
88. See above, p. 4.
89. Ramm, op. cit., p. 157; cf. A. B. Davidson, op. cit., p. 188, that the prophet "expressed truths for the instruction of the people of God of his own day in terms of the conditions of the world in that day."
90. *Interpreting the Bible*, p. 296.
91. J. F. Rutherford, *The Harp of God*, pp. 233–234.

they run like the lightnings[!]" (2:4). The important fact to maintain—at least in the still unfulfilled Micah passage—is that whatever be the particular weapons, there *will* be a conflict, at the time and place identified, and with the results that are indicated. As Davidson cautions, "Still the truth of the prophecy will no doubt be realized."[92]

Yet the undeniable need for cultural reinterpretation has led some to a disparagement of basic teachings that are found within the prophetic message. The same A. B. Davidson who contends for the realization of prophecy thus finds himself unwilling to concede a place for Assyria in Biblical eschatology; and he goes on to speculate: "When Micah speaks of the Messiah . . . he conceives Him as coming in the conditions of the kingdom of God then existing . . . [but] that form may require some modification in interpretation . . . very different from his conception of it."[93] He grants that the "Scriptures represented the Assyrian as existing in the time of the Messiah"; but he concludes, "We must distinguish between the general idea and the particular form, not now likely to be realized."[94] If one then asks what effect this has on the inspired truthfulness of the Scriptures, Davidson is forced to confess, "It makes them share in the imperfection of the dispensation to which they belonged";[95] and from here it takes only a minor move to reach the position of Riehm, who states flatly that "the OT imagery . . . is not of the substance of revelation."[96] Yet can one draw the line even here? The NT, along with the Old, speaks of eschatological military campaigns in this same area east of the Euphrates River (Rev 16:12). It would appear best to recognize that while the particular people, the Sargonid dynasty of the 8th- and 7th-century B.C. Assyrians, may come to an end, the land still remains;[97] and it is the land which will experience precisely these events which Scripture forecasts in its regard.

(b) Figures. It is but a short step from the cultural adaptation which characterizes the nontropical[98] language of the Biblical oracles to the consciously figurative phraseology of its more poetically conceived predictive verbalizations. In fact, even during the OT period it is probable that such eschatological forecasts as Micah promised, that "they shall sit every man under his vine and under his fig tree" (4:4), were already being understood in a sense somewhat beyond that of the small farmer. At the outset one must recognize the presence of poetic hyperbole in the fulfillment of certain of the predictions. Zechariah 7:14, for example, refers to the earlier prophecy, "I will scatter them among all the nations they have not known."

92. Op. cit., p. 169.
93. Ibid., pp. 164, 166.
94. Ibid., pp. 187–188; cf. Edward Riehm, *Messianic Prophecy*, p. 225. But Davidson still expresses a feeling of caution in this regard, op. cit., p. 194.
95. Ibid., p. 169; cf. p. 333.
96. Op. cit., pp. 231–232.
97. Cf. Davidson, op. cit., p. 476, for opposition to such distinction.
98. See above, p. 16.

But the intended thought must be not that the Jewish captives were to be scattered among literally *all the nations,* but simply *all over* the nations; for this verse is retrospective, and its latter part testifies to the prophecy's now past accomplishment—"Thus the land was desolate." That is, at the time when Zechariah wrote, he was aware that the Jewish dispersion was not yet, at least, literally universal; he must therefore knowingly have been employing a poetic figure.

This instance of hyperbole leads one into those more definitely figurative examples from Scripture in which words actually shift their meaning;[99] and it suggests the first of what may be considered as five major methods for ascertaining the fulfillment of the Bible's prophetic tropes:[100] namely, *declaration by the author.* The prediction of Hosea 8:13, 9:3, 6, thus says, "Ephraim shall return to Egypt." In 9:3 Hosea adds, "and they shall eat unclean food in Assyria." But does this latter clause then explain what is meant by Israel's figurative "returning to Egypt" (synonymous parallelism), or does it add literally a second place of exile (progressive parallelism)? The answer must be the former, not simply because history knows of no escape by the northern tribes to Egypt, but even more because the author himself goes on to say explicitly, "They shall not return into the land of Egypt, but Assyria shall be their king," 11:5.[101]

Second, if there appears to be a real choice between literal and figurative fulfillment, *context* may favor one or the other. Zechariah 9:14, for example, declares, "Yahweh shall be seen over them, and His arrow shall go forth as the lightning." The latter simile might suggest Christ's second advent (cf. Lk 17:24) and thus a literal "seeing" of deity, even if of the Son rather than of Yahweh the Father. Yet the "them" of v. 14 is defined in v. 13 as the Jews experiencing their victory over the (Seleucid) Greeks, after their return from Babylonian exile, v. 12; and what was therefore to be "seen" (figuratively) would be divine providence at work through Judas Maccabeus. Similarly, Amos 8:8–10 speaks of the land trembling, and rising and sinking, and of the sun being darkened; cf. the phenomena at Christ's return, Revelation 6:12. But the surrounding context is that of God's punishment upon His sinful kingdom of Ephraim in 722 B.C. (vv. 4–7, 10), thus figuratively described.[102]

99. See above, p. 19.
100. For the first two of these, compare the methodology for ascertaining fulfillment in general as described above under Part A, Context, pp. 71–72; and for the next two, Part B, Analogy, pp. 72–80. For the fifth, see above, p. 18, on the figurative form as a whole.
101. So Fairbairn, *Typology,* I:112–113, and most others, but Cheyne, Camb, *Hosea,* p. 91, prefers to see a contradiction in Hosea's own thinking.
102. A more complex example is that of Zech 6:12–13. It concerns (1), v. 12a, God's word to the prophet, "Speak unto Joshua the high priest," on whose head symbolic crowns are to be placed (v. 11). It goes on (2), v. 12b, to describe "the Branch [who] shall grow up out of His place," referring to the life of Christ during His first advent. It concludes (3), v. 13b, by predicting that "He shall rule upon

Third, an awareness of *historical background* may suggest that a given term in a predictive section may be utilized simply in reflection of a parallel situation in the past, and hence in a figurative sense. Hosea 2:15, for example, appeals to that past "day when Israel came up out of the land of Egypt." When therefore the verse just preceding forecasts, "I will bring her into the wilderness," one's historical understanding would indicate not a literal return of Ephraim to the Sinaitic deserts (cf. above, on 8:13, 9:3, 6),[103] but rather a figurative allusion to the exile, as performing a correspondingly disciplinary function. The appearance of a term historically may thus suggest the use of that same term prophetically, primarily to illustrate parallelism, with the latter usage being tropical.[104] Caution must, however, be advised concerning such appeals to the figurative, particularly in reference to descriptions that arise out of the OT's cultural background. Barrows insists, "It would be wrong to press it as of universal and exclusive application.[105] Where no reasons to the contrary exist, the literal interpretation, as the most natural and obvious, deserves the preference."[106]

Fourth, *the analogy of Scripture,* and especially of the NT, may decide for a figurative interpretation. An example already cited is that of Malachi's prediction in 4:5 of the coming of Elijah as a forerunner to Christ,[107] which received an at least not completely literal fulfillment in John the Baptist. Yet to revert to Barrows' caution against pressing the principle of figurative meanings derived from a word's historical background into one of universal or exclusive application, one must emphasize the illegitimacy of forcing from the principle of NT analogy any methodology of comprehensive "spiritualization." A. B. Davidson seems to have fallen into an unwarranted procedure of reinterpreting prophecies, based simply upon the time of their

His throne," that is, Christ in His millennial kingdom. But between (2) and (3) appears the twice-repeated assertion, vv. 12c, 13a, "He shall build the temple." Does it go with (2), figuratively, for the 1st-century church, as in Eph 2:21-22? Or with (3), literally, for a millennial temple? Actually, it fits best with (1) Joshua, because in the Zechariah context the only temple found is the one in the time of this priest, vv. 14-15, being then very literally built by Joshua; cf. 4:9, 14. Confessedly, the subject of vv. 12c, 13a, would more naturally be the Branch of 12b, though see below, under 1:16a.

103. P. 82.

104. Again, Ezekiel calls attention to how God once brought Israel into the wilderness, 20:10. When he then goes on to predict, "I will bring you into the wilderness of the peoples," v. 35, historical analogy again suggests a figurative description of exilic chastening. So Fairbairn, *Typology,* I:113.

105. This, after he had just explained away the coming of the nations to Jerusalem (Isa 2:2 and Zech 14:16) as a figure for their conversion!

106. *Companion to the Bible,* p. 628. Of the Jewish nation he therefore notes, the "very explicit prophecies of their captivity and dispersion for their sins, and their subsequent restoration upon repentance . . . seem to warrant the expectation of a literal fulfillment hereafter of the promise made to Abraham that his seed should inherit the land of Cannan for ever," p. 629.

107. See above, p. 72, and also below, under Mal. prophecy No. 9 and Mt., prophecy No. 8 (with note 15).

accomplishment. He states that if predictions are fulfilled in the OT period they are to be interpreted literally; but if they refer to NT times, then "we shall probably have to strip off from them the OT form, which arose from the dispensation and time when the prophet lived, and look for their fulfillment in a way corresponding to the spirit of the NT dispensation and the altered conditions of the world."[108] His approach, however, confuses legitimate cultural interpretation[109] with the problem of determining figurative meaning, which must depend upon the exegesis of each prophecy individually, lest it degenerate into allegorization.[110]

Fifth, even when such objective criteria as the above four are perhaps lacking, the element which, for lack of a more precise title, may be styled one's *general understanding* may show that a term's usage is figurative. Malachi 1:11 thus foretells—without further clarification—a day when Yahweh's "name shall be great among the Gentiles; and in every place incense shall be offered unto My name, and a pure offering." This situation does not appear to be millennial, because the Gentiles are here directly contrasted with an ancient God-rejecting Israel, vv. 10 and 12 (both before and after v. 13). Yet in OT days (and presumably also in millennial days) pure offerings could not be presented "in every place," but only at Jerusalem. General understanding would therefore suggest that the "incense" connotes, figuratively, prayer and other forms of acceptable worship by Gentiles during the NT church age. Again, there are five points in the OT prophets where the ruler of the Messianic age is identified, not as a descendant or Branch of David (cf. Jer 23:5, Rev 22:16), but simply as "David": Isaiah 55:4 (cf. v. 3), Jeremiah 30:9, Ezekiel 34:23-24, 37:24-25, and Hosea 3:5, i.e., Ezekiel 34:23, "I will set up one shepherd over them, David"; cf. I Kings 12:16, where "David" has come to mean the royal line *established by* the son of Jesse. Yet some dispensationalists would go so far as to claim a reinstatement of "the historical David, who comes into regency over Palestine by resurrection at the second advent of Christ";[111] such reasoning would, however, seem to represent a misunderstanding of a natural metaphor.

(c) Symbols. In contrast with the normal verbalisms, that have been discussed in (a) and (b) above, those prophecies that assume an acted-out form—whether by physical performance, as in the case of objejct

108. Op cit., p. 192.
109. See above, p. 73.
110. See above, pp. 42-47. What seems in fact to have conditioned Davidson's thinking is Ramm's observation that "if prophecy be taken literally, then the premillennial interpretation is mandatory," op. cit., p. 168.
111. Pentecost, op. cit., p. 500; cf. pp. 501, 524. He argues that in these five passages "Jehovah is distinguished from David. If David referred to Christ, no distinction could be made." But this appears to be a pointless objection in the light of Ps 110:1 etc. His further argument, that the allusions in Ezek 40-46 to a prince who presents sacrifices for himself cannot refer to Christ, assumes both that this prince must be David and that the setting is millennial, neither of which assumptions seems to be necessary; see below, in the introduction to Ezekiel.

lessons, or through mental perception, as in dreams—are marked by a relatively infrequent occurrence in Scripture.[112] The one great exception are the Biblical books or portions of books that are designated by the title "apocalyptic." The type of historical background that nurtured the revelatory form of the apocalypse was one of material and spiritual distress. While interpreters differ as to the exact limits of such writing (depending largely upon their particular definition of apocalyptic), the canonical apocalypses would appear to commence with Joel (in 735 B.C.?),[113] when Judah was facing a locust plague of overwhelming proportions. They move on through "the little apocalypse" of Isaiah 24–27, datable to the Assyrian danger of 711 B.C. and of the years that followed (cf. 20:1); they include the exilic writings of the latter part of Ezekiel and, preeminently, of Daniel, together with the visions of Zechariah's later ministry, chs. 9–14, when Greece began to threaten Persia (ca. 490; cf. 9:13); and they extend on into certain NT revelations: Christ's apocalyptic discourse (Mt 24–25, Mk 13, Lk 21), portions of Pauline material in I and II Thessalonians, and above all John's Book of the Revelation, often called "The Apocalypse." Numerous examples of noninspired apocalyptic appear as well, during both the intertestamental and the post-testamental ages, when God's people, either Jewish or Christian, faced crises due to Hellenistic or Roman oppression.

For this literature there has arisen in recent thinking, particularly within liberal circles, the demand for a distinctive methodology in ascertaining its intended fulfillments, one that is sharply set apart from the procedures that are recognized as appropriate for prophetic interpretation elsewhere. Rowley, for example, observes, "An earlier generation emphasized the predictive element in prophecy, and the relation between prophecy and apocalyptic, in which the predictive element is particularly prominent, appeared beyond question. In modern times . . . the link with the apocalyptists has seemed less close."[114] Charles H. Patterson fairly well illustrates the present critical consensus when he says, "It seemed reasonable enough that the very few writings of this [apocalyptic] order which belong to the canonical books should be interpreted in accordance with the same principles that were used in connection with the prophetic writings. But this practice is no longer followed by competent OT scholars."[115]

Certain features, it is true, are granted to be characteristic of apocalyptic in common with prophecy. Both are revelatory, claiming equivalency to God's own words; both are predictive, cf. the very root meaning of *āpokālúptō*, "to uncover, to disclose," especially of the "day of Yahweh";[116] both proclaim a judgment on that day against the pagans; both offer hope

112. See below, Statistical Appendix.
113. See below, introduction to Joel.
114. *The Relevance of Apocalyptic*, p. 13.
115. *The Philosophy of the OT*, p. 411.
116. See below, pp. 131–133.

for the vindication of God's righteous remnant and of their blessedness in His kingdom of peace; and both are concerned more with the redemption of society than of individuals. Rowley thus comments on that fact that "apocalyptic is commonly confused with the eschatology of apocalyptic"[117] and concludes that eschatology as such is no criterion for distinguishing this literature: "We must beware of making the contrast too sharp or too absolute, or of forgetting that in the prophets there are passages with a definitely apocalyptic flavor."[118]

Yet when one examines the major examples of Biblical apocalyptic, especially Daniel and Revelation, there do appear to be certain distinguishable features that mark off these writings, both in respect to form and in respect to content. For the former, (i) with the exception of Christ's apocalyptic discourse, their original presentation seems to have assumed a written rather than an oral form; contrast the usual "preaching" method of the OT prophets.[119] (ii) The apocalypses, correspondingly, tend to be more continuous and to exhibit parallel cycles of predictions,[120] rather than to consist of separate, brief oracles. (iii) Their composition is usually in prose, with but a few poetic snatches.[121] (iv) Most obviously, among these formal differences, they contain more symbolism, especially of animals and other living forms.

Normally these symbols are provided with interpretation; e.g. in Revelation 17:10, "The seven heads are seven mountains, on which the woman sits."[122] Yet on occasion the symbolical happenings of apocalyptic may be recorded without elucidation. Meanings may then sometimes be inferred from the context, e.g. that the bowman on the white horse of Revelation 6:2 represents an aggressive militarism—a fulfillment that is suggested by its comparison with the other three horsemen of the Apocalypse, which follow. Sometimes, however, the meaning is less clear, e.g. that the unwritten messages of the seven thunders in 10:3–4 may have covered ground similar to that of the seven trumpets of God's wrath, chs. 8–9 preceding, or of the seven outpoured bowls, ch. 16 following.[123] Indeed, support for this inference is insufficient to justify its inclusion among the known prophetic fulfillments of Scripture.

Interrelationships are particularly significant for an understanding of apocalyptic: "It is noticeable that the successive writers freely appropriate both the language and symbols of their predecessors . . . Isaiah imitates some passages of Joel; Ezekiel draws from both; Zechariah makes much

117. Op. cit., p. 23.
118. Ibid., p. 36.
119. Though perhaps not so for Isa 40–66?
120. See below, p. 130.
121. Rowley, op. cit., p. 14.
122. For convenient lists of the apocalyptic symbols, see M. C. Tenney, *Interpreting Revelation*, pp. 186–193; E. R. Craven, in Lange's *Commentary on the Holy Scriptures, Revelation*, pp. 1–41; or Henry Cowles, *The Revelation of John*, p. 39.
123. Cf. ExGkT, V:412.

use of Daniel and Ezekiel; and there is scarcely a figure or symbol employed in John's apocalypse which is not appropriated from the OT books."[124] In practice then, one may conclude relative to the four above-listed features of apocalyptic form that the first two, on its written composition, suggest the need for one's close attention to the device of literary repetition; the third reduces the hermeneutical problem in dealing with poetry; but the fourth adds to one's task in interpreting symbols.

In respect to its content, most of the special features that are claimed for the apocalyptic literature arise out of its general background of serious distress.[125] (i) Its basic purpose becomes one of comfort and encouragement; cf. Revelation 14:12, in contrast with the rigorous condemnations of prophecy; cf. Hosea 4:1 (but note also Isa 40:1). (ii) Since human help may seem to be in vain, apocalyptic lays stress on divine sovereignty and determinism; cf. Daniel 4:35. Rowley thus speaks of the "lasting validity" of its "belief that lies behind all this that God is in control of history. . . . They did not believe that God was indifferent to the world He had made; nor did they think He was impotent to take a hand in its course";[126] cf. the very title of his well-known study, *The Relevance of Apocalyptic*. (iii) It exhibits a greater dualism: of angels and of the Messiah contending against Satan and the Antichrist. (iv) There is less subject matter on immediate moral reform, though one must not fail to note, e.g., the confessions of Daniel 9:4–19 or the exhortations of Revelation 2–3 (note also the minimal moral emphasis in the prophecies of Isa 40–55 or of Nahum). (v) Apocalyptic possesses a universal orientation, proportionate to the world unrest that marks off its background; cf. Revelation 20:8. (vi) It exhibits a division of time into periods, e.g. the successive empires of Daniel 2 and 7 or the "seventy weeks" of 9:24–27. (vii) It stresses divine intervention by cataclysm; hope, that is, lies in an invasion from the heavenly world.[127] (viii) There is lesser mention of judgment upon God's people, as compared, e.g., with Amos 5:18, in prophecy (yet cf. a similar lack in the prophecy of Obadiah).

These differences, however, are primarily matters of degree. One con-

---

124. M. S. Terry, *Biblical Hermeneutics*, p. 340.
125. See J. B. Payne, *Theology*, p. 61.
126. Op. cit., pp. 151–152. Yet he feels called upon to confess that the apocalyptic writer's approach to God's sovereignty over history was a misguided one, pp. 156–157: "He was living in an evil age, and believed it to be the final fling of evil. . . . It is easy for us to see that they were mistaken, and that their prophecies were unfulfilled"; cf. above, p. 60. Indeed, the only concrete value with which Rowley seems finally to be left is that "by their very suffering their little lives are linked to the eternal will and purpose of God," which appears as both unrealistic and as pragmatically hopeless.
127. "Speaking generally, the prophets foretold the future that should arise out of the present, while the apocalyptists foretold the future that should break into the present," ibid., p. 35. But this is "generally" speaking. In point of fact, there appears to be an identity in belief in the distant, cataclysmic future; it is just that the apocalyptist had less interest in applying himself to the nearer, natural progress of current events.

cludes that (iv) and (viii) are negative and thus irrelevant to interpretation; (vi) provides important chronological data for grasping the sweep of Biblical prediction; and the rest simply give a greater stress to matters that are already found within prophecy. The supernaturalistic climax to human history that characterizes apocalyptic is an essential element in the prophetic world view as well. Similarly, the inspired apocalypses exhibit a degree of present optimism and a prophetic ethic that stands in marked contrast to the disappearance of these elements from post-canonical Jewish apocalyptic. The difference between true prophecy and true apocalyptic is thus essentially one of emphasis. Moreover, even this difference serves to bring out a fullness to the revelation of the kingdom of God, which, as taught by Jesus, possesses both a present reality and a future consummation.[128]

In addition to the above-listed features of apocalyptic, valid in the extent to which they appear applicable, liberalism has insisted upon a series of more questionable distinctions between prophecy and apocalypse. These do constitute legitimate criticisms of the noncanonical apocalypses, but they seem hardly to do justice to the inspired revelations of Scripture. They again concern both the form and the content of the literature. Formal features include the matter of pseudonymity: that the name of Daniel, for example, was falsely attached to a much later book, at least according to critical theory.[129] John's revelation, however, presents a plausible statement of authorship, as do all the rest of the Biblical apocalypses, if their own testimony, that is, be allowed to stand. A corresponding accusation is that of esoteric character: that an ancient authorship was supported by tales of the book's having been hidden from the public.[130] The apocalyptic form is also said to be marked by artificial claims to inspiration, by assertions of pseudo-ecstasy in the receipt of visions, and by a tendency to "play with numbers."[131]

Among the distinctions applied by liberal writers to the subject matter of apocalyptic, one of the most common is the charge of pessimism in respect to history. In point of fact, however, it is only that "the apocalyptists had little faith in the present to beget the future. This is why they are so

128. Cf. G. E. Ladd, "Why Not Prophetic-apocalyptic?" JBL, 76 (1957), 192–200.

129. "The prophets spoke from the standpoint of the present, while from the time of the issue of the Book of Daniel it became a characteristic of the apocalyptists that they threw themselves back into the past, under an assumed name, and put in the guise of prophecy things that were past in their own day as the prelude to their unfolding of the grand dénouement of history which they believed to be imminent," Rowley, op. cit., p. 36.

130. So, in I Enoch 1:2, II Enoch 33:10, or II Esdras 12:37. It is true that Daniel, an inspired writer, also speaks of a present sealing up of his writing, 8:26, 12:4, 9; but then so too does the nonapocalyptic Isa 8:16. Cf., on the other hand, the express repudiation of concealment in Rev 22:10, cf. 1:3.

131. Following J. Lindblom, "Die Jesaja-Apokalypse (Jes. 24–27)," *Lunds Universitets Arsskrift*, N.F., Avd. 1 (1938), Bd. XXXIV:3, quoted by Rowley, op. cit., p. 23, who adds, rather significantly, "Some of these are rather the accidents than the essence of apocalyptic."

often, and so unfairly, called pessimists," explains Rowley.[132] One may, that is, concede his own inability to "bring in the kingdom" and yet still follow Christ in faithful service and be solidly optimistic about God's eschatology. Again, they are criticized for believing that history must culminate in a crisis in their own day.[133] Yet writers such as Daniel were well aware of the distance of the scene they were painting, Daniel 12:4, 9.[134] John's Apocalypse does speak in relative terms of Christ's coming as "soon," 1:3, 22:20; and Paul's use of the pronoun "we" in I Thessalonians 4:15 demonstrates the apostle's belief in the imminence of his Lord's Parousia, meaning that it *could* have been in his day. But then, compare the similar hope that pervades the whole of prophecy: "Yet once, it is a little while, and I will . . ." (Hag 2:6). Finally there is alleged an apocalyptic addiction to mythology, and especially to dualistic Zoroastrian influences manifested in legends of spirits fighting with dragons, etc.[135] Such claims, however, reflect antipathy against what the Scriptural apocalypses teach, in an unmistakably straightforward manner, about the archangel Michael, Satan, and other angelic spirits (cf. Dan 12:1, 10:20–21, 8:21).[136] Basically, one may conclude with Terry that "the hermeneutical principles to be observed in the interpretation of apocalyptics are, in the main, the same as those which apply to all predictive prophecy."[137]

(d) Types. Concerning those enacted prophecies which possessed a simultaneous, contemporary significance in their own right,[138] Pieter Verhoef has aptly observed: "It will always remain a very difficult problem to define precisely the exact content of the typological material in the Bible."[139] Yet to some degree at least, a methodology for ascertaining its intended fulfillment can be derived, both from its contemporaneous reality and from its predictive design. On the one hand, the very fact that the Biblical types served as meaningful symbols among those to whom they were first revealed leads directly into Fairbairn's initial principle for their interpretation: "We must always, in the first instance, be careful to make ourselves acquainted with the truths or ideas exhibited in the types, con-

132. "They did not believe in the power of the evil present to bring in the longed-for tomorrow. But that was not because they were pessimists, but because they were realists. They would have had no use for our modern myth of progress and they certainly would not have accepted the widespread modern idea of moral and spiritual evolution," ibid., p. 163.
133. Ibid., p. 36.
134. Critics, it is true, would put Daniel itself late in Maccabean times; but still, the stated chronology of 9:24–27 brings the fulfillment into Roman days, at the least.
135. Cf. Rowley, op. cit., p. 40.
136. Cf. the more evangelically oriented, but equally invalid distinctions argued by H. L. Ellison, *Ezekiel*, pp. 104–105.
137. Op. cit., p. 340.
138. As types are defined above, pp. 22–26.
139. "The Relationship Between the Old and the New Testaments," in J. B. Payne, ed., *New Perspectives on the OT*, p. 286.

sidered merely as providential transactions or religious institutions."[140] For as has been stated previously,[141] the Mosaic institutions symbolized to the OT saints the same general teachings that they now typify to the New. Furthermore, just as spoken prophecies possess a single intended meaning, to be determined by careful exegesis,[142] so Fairbairn insists that the fulfillment of the Biblical types ought likewise to be restricted to the one radical meaning which belongs properly to each typical feature.[143]

On the other hand, the prospective character of inspired types, the fact that from their inception they were designed to anticipate the Person and work of Jesus Christ, points to the use of further divine revelation for determining their precise fulfillments. Specifically, just as the fourfold definition of Scriptural types as "divine enactments of future redemption" provides a key for the delimitation of Biblical typology,[144] so too the elements of this definition establish criteria for deciding about its fulfillments. That is, even as the *divine* responsibility for types establishes the fact that their strongest examples must be those that are cited elsewhere in Scripture, so too the evidence of Biblical analogy, where it exists, enables the interpreter to affirm, "I know that they are types, and I also know what they mean," e.g. that the tabernacle, on the basis of John 1:14 (Gk.), must be a foreshadowing of Christ's incarnation.[145]

Second, even as the *redemptive* character of types makes possible their identification, even when not granted explicit elucidation elsewhere in the word, so the expositor of such instances becomes capable of discussing their fulfillments but should also be careful to say, "I know they are types, but I am not sure what they mean." For example, the double crown of the post-exilic high priest Joshua must be typical—it is directly associated with the redemptive counsel of peace that is to be achieved by the Messianic Branch, Zechariah 6:13. But the crowning of Joshua is never mentioned again in divine revelation; and while its fulfillment seems to lie in Christ's united office of priest and king, Keil's suggestion of His united Person remains as a possible alternative interpretation.[146]

Third, even as the *enacted* quality of types makes possible the limitation of some potentially typical objects to the category of merely contemporane-

---

140. *Typology*, I:150.
141. See above, p. 25.
142. See below, pp. 123–126.
143. Op. cit., I:154; and see above, p. 26. Generally there appears one such feature per type, e.g. the laver, indicative of cleansing from impurity, though upon occasion several distinct features may be found within the more complex institutions of Scripture, e.g. the lamb used in the Passover service: with its basic significance of substitutionary atonement, but also pointing forward to the spotless character of Christ, and to the preservation at Calvary of His bones from being broken; see below under Ex 12:3, 5, and 8, respectively.
144. See above, p. ???.
145. Cf. Payne, *Theology*, pp. 357–360.
146. See below, under Zech 6:11, note 33.

ous (nonpredictive) symbols, so also, in reference to these same objects, the cautious student must confess, "I do not know whether they are types or not,"[147] and remain silent over the subject of their fulfillment; e.g. the fact that the robe of Aaron's ephod was "all of blue" (Ex 28:31) has purposely not been discussed below.

Fourth, even as the necessity for a *future* point of reference served to eliminate from consideration as typical all such matters as possessed only an immediate, nonsymbolic, utilitarian function, so likewise the Bible-centered exegete should be the person to state flatly, "I know they are not types," and to emphasize that purported "fulfillments" represent human applications and not divine meanings. The fathers of the early church, for example, achieved little for the cause of trinitarianism by invoking as evidence the three stories of Noah's ark!

C. *Periods of Fulfillment*

1. ORGANIZATION IN RESPECT TO THE FULFILLMENTS OF BIBLICAL PREDICTION. In reference to their historical accomplishment, prophecies as a whole may be divided into those that relate to the near future and those that relate to a more distant scene. Throughout its course Scripture exhibits instances of the former; and these are usually self-understood, provided that one admits the reality of truly predictive revelation. Barrows provides the description that they "are all specific in their character and have a single exhaustive fulfillment."[148] For example, the very first nonsymbolic prophecies to appear in Scripture—concerning Adam's death for eating the forbidden fruit, Genesis 2:17, Noah's "comforting" preservation of life, 5:29, and the deluge with its worldwide destruction, 6:3—received direct accomplishment, respectively, in Genesis 3:19, 8:18, and 7:21. But it is left up to the interpreter to organize these many discrete fulfillments into a comprehensive and Biblically meaningful totality.

Prophecies of the latter type, with a more distant fulfillment, "give, as a rule, only general views relating to the conflicts of God's people and their final triumph. Where minute incidents are introduced (Ps 22:18, Zech 9:9) it is apparently for the purpose of identifying to future generations the Messiah as their main subject."[149] Further, and probably because of the pictorial, visionary mode of much of prophecy, the long range of time ahead is less frequently "linked to definite historical epochs:[150] commonly the description of the future is presented in a kind of continuity . . . carried

147. See above, p. 53.
148. Op. cit., p. 607; and see below, pp. 123–126.
149. Ibid., p. 609.
150. The burden of pt. 1, ch. 5, in Fairbairn's *Interpretation*, pp. 171–181.

onward to its proper consummation."[151] This is what Horne denominates as "the chain of prophecy,"[152] a merely relative succession of events, even for such detailed matters as Daniel's visions of the four world empires (chs. 2, 7). Here again it must be the interpreter, operating from the vantage point of his awareness of the analogies both of history and of Scripture, who designates those particular periods to which the predictions of God's word are then to be assigned.

But while all such activity must inevitably remain open to criticism for its subjectivity, still the value for comprehensive correlation renders necessary the erection of some classification of predictions according to the periods of their fulfillments. This is required not only for perspective but also for basic harmonization. As Oehler states,

> Since the matter of prophecy presents itself to view as a multitude of individual facts, it may sometimes appear as though single predictions contradicted each other, when they are in fact only those parts into which the ideas revealed have been separated, mutually completing each other, e.g. the representation of the Messiah . . . on the one side a successful ruler, on the other the servant who atones for sins by undergoing death. . . . The two characteristics of the Messianic age are even united . . . [and Oehler cites the revelations of Micah 5, but this is] merely external juxtaposition.[153]

Since testimony concerning Christ is the spirit of prophecy,[154] the focal points of Biblical prediction are to be found in the two comings of the Messiah, periods 13 and 15 in the study that follows. But for those extensive lapses of time that occurred before His first advent and that will occur after His second advent, a more detailed subdivision appears to be advisable. Horne, for example, advocates a major unit on prophecies relating to the Jewish nation, which he subdivides into ten sections from 1, Abraham, to 10, "Hosea's prediction of the present state of the Jews."[155] I would propose twelve periods of prophetic fulfillment to extend from the OT prophecies with attainments that begin in primeval times, down to the NT era; two more periods for Christ's two advents, separated by the period of the present-day church (No. 14); and a final three periods that are to arise after His second coming. Chronological year dates[156] are assigned for the fourteen periods that extend up to the present; but for those times that are yet future it is not for man to know the "day or the hour" (Mk 13:32), and identification must therefore be restricted to Scripture's own relativistic designations, e.g. the period of God's final judgment.

151. Ibid., p. 174.
152. Op. cit., I:122.
153. *Theology of the OT*, p. 490.
154. See above, p. 7.
155. Op. cit., pp. 122–124.
156. See above, p. xix.

2. A CHRONOLOGICAL OUTLINE. A proposed sequence that is based upon the books of the Bible commences, period 1, with the Primeval-Patriarchal era (to 1843 B.C.), which involves the fulfillment of 25 separate Biblical predictions.[157] The two epochs that are here combined concern, first, God's dealings with the primeval world as a whole (Gen 1–11:26) and, second, His self-disclosures to the four generations of His particularly chosen patriarchs: Abraham, Isaac, Jacob, and Joseph (Gen 11:27 onward, from Abraham's birth in 2133 B.C.). Their combination is a plausible one, not simply because of the minimal amount of predictive fulfillment that occurred during the former epoch (6 prophecies in all, involving only 12 vv.), but more basically because the era that results corresponds to that period of time which is covered by the Book of Genesis. Historically, it may be said to terminate with Israel's descent into Egypt at the above-noted date of 1843, though the predicted death of Jacob, which occurred 17 years later in 1826, is also included below, so that the era may embrace this last prophetic fulfillment to appear in Genesis.

Period 2, Egyptian (1843–1446), 25 predictions. This era covers the four centuries of Israel's prophesied sojourn in Egypt (Gen 15:13),[158] as described in Exodus 1–12:36. I assume that Moses composed the books of the Pentateuch in order, and in such a way that Genesis would already have been in existence at the time of the nation's exodus,[159] perhaps even before Moses' return to rescue his people from Egypt. This very goal may indeed have been a cause for the book's inscripturation; see Gen 15:13–16, 46:4, 50:24–25. In any event, the historical descriptions that appear in Genesis are taken to indicate fulfillments that were achieved during the Egyptian period, e.g. the forecasts of the nations that should develop from Ishmael, 17:20 etc., whose reality is afterward described in 25:16.

Period 3, Wilderness (1446–1406), 16 predictions. Exactly 40 years elapse from the time of Israel's departure from Egypt (Ex 12:37) up to the entrance into the promised land (Josh 5:10); cf. the foretelling of this precise time span in Numbers 14:34 (listed under 14:22). The era embraces, then, those fulfillments that occurred following Exodus 12:37, throughout the remaining portions of the Pentateuch.

Period 4, Conquest (1406–1382), 27 predictions. This fourth era is held to include the actual six years of military campaigning by which Israel gained possession of Canaan (cf. Josh 14:10), plus also that succeeding epoch of the closing years of Joshua's life and "all the days of the elders that outlived Joshua" (24:31). It thus includes the distribution of the land among the tribes and those other fulfillments that are related in the Book of Joshua.

157. For their tabulation, see Summary A, below, p. 631, and so for each of the 18 periods.
158. Which see, for the detailed chronological calculation.
159. See below, p. 155; cf. the reference to "the book" in Ex 17:14, ASVmg.

Period 5, Judges (1382–1043), 25 predictions. This incorporates the times of the Book of Judges but also of the administrations of Eli and Samuel, as described in I Samuel 1–7, and down to the establishment of the Hebrew monarchy. While dated technically from the commencement of the first (or Mesopotamian) oppression, this period is still defined so as to include the opening prediction of Judges (1:2), which concerns Judah's tribal success, though actually this event may have occurred at any point following the death of Joshua in about 1390.

Period 6, United Kingdom (1043–970), 32 predictions. The precise point of inception for the kingdom of Israel is taken as being not Saul's private anointing by Samuel at Ramah (I Sam 10:1) but his public anointing at Mizpah, 10:24. The last prophetic fulfillment to be included under period 5, of the judges, is therefore God's oracle that Saul would be found hidden among the baggage at Mizpah, v. 22. The era lasts down to the death of Solomon in 930, through I Kings 11 (= II Chron 9).

Period 7, Divided Kingdom (930–586), in which the number of fulfillments rises sharply to a figure of 139. This is the most extensive total to be found in Scripture, surpassing even period 13, the climactic era of the life of Christ. Such an amount is due not simply to the span of years, which approaches four centuries, but also to the frequency of the prophecies that are recorded in the Bible's historical books which found fulfillment during this period, namely those of I–II Kings and II Chronicles, which amount to some 74 in number. Elijah and Elisha were together responsible for a major block of predictions that were fulfilled in the latter 9th and early 8th centuries. In addition there are those further oracles that begin in the latter part of the 8th century, coming from the books of the preexilic prophets—Isaiah and Hosea through Zephaniah—plus even those predictions of Jeremiah and of the exilic prophet Ezekiel that received their fulfillments prior to the fall of Jerusalem in 586.

Period 8, Exilic (586–538), 29 predictions. Through Jeremiah God had predicted a 70-year captivity for Judah, which does correspond to the historical time lapse from the first deportation, involving Daniel and his friends, in 605 to the eventual return of the Jews under Zerubbabel in 537 and his re-laying of the temple foundation in 536.[160] Yet the limits of the exile may for practical purposes be set from the destruction of Jerusalem and from the third and greatest of the four Jewish deportations, in 586, down to the decree of Cyrus in 538, which authorized the nation's return and with which II Chronicles ends and the Book of Ezra commences.

Period 9, Persian (538–332), 31 predictions. After the interlude of the exile, God's redemptive program for His people came once again to center in the land of Israel. The Hebrews who returned to Palestine consisted

160. See J. B. Payne, "Chronology of the OT," in M. C. Tenney, ed., *The Pictorial Encyclopedia of the Bible.*

primarily of the tribes of Benjamin and Judah, Ezra 1:5, 4:1, hence the very name "Jew." Yet even in Josiah's day there had occurred a measure of restoration for N. Israel, II Chronicles 34:6 (see below, under 30:9), Nah 2:2; and under the Persian overlords representatives of both "the house of Jacob" (Obad 18 = Judah) and "the house of Joseph" (that is, some of the ten tribes) returned to the land. Obadiah 20 mentions ex-captives of Israel as well as of Jerusalem (cf. Ezek 16:53–58, Lk 2:36); and Zechariah 8:13 addresses both groups as present in the postexilic capital; cf. his references to "all the tribes," 9:1, or to Ephraim and Zion as jointly opposing the Greeks, 9:10. W. E. Barnes concludes, therefore, "Zechariah does not regard the ten tribes as 'lost.' "[161] With the composition of Nehemiah's autobiography early in the reign of Darius II of Persia, from 423 B.C. on (Neh 12:22, cf. 13:6), and with the corresponding close of the OT canon, the history of revelation entered its "400 silent years," devoid of authentic new prophecies until the onset of the NT period, No. 13.

Period 10, Greek (332–168), 25 predictions. While Alexander the Great's decisive victory over Darius III of Persia near Arbela did not occur until 331, Palestine came under Greek control following his capture of Tyre and Gaza during the preceding year. Prophecy as such was known to have ceased (I Macc 4:46, 9:27, 14:41), but the fulfillment of oracles that had been revealed at earlier dates continued.

Period II, Maccabean (168–63), 14 predictions. Some of the forecasts of the Book of Daniel were directed toward the Jewish conflict against Antiochus IV at the opening of this period, from the setting up of his "abomination" upon the altar of the Jerusalem temple in 168 down to the time of its cleansing by Judas the Maccabee in 165 (cf. chs. 8 or 11, through v. 39). This phenomenon, however, by no means reduces Daniel to the status of a pseudonymous product of the Maccabean age, since the book carries on with equally significant predictions that were fulfilled in the Roman era (ch. 9) or that are yet to be fulfilled in future ages (chs. 7, 12). Jewish expansion later in this same 2nd century, under the Hasmonean descendants of the Maccabean family, brought about a number of fulfillments for OT prophecies that related to various peoples who surrounded Judah.

Period 12, Roman (63–5 B.C.), 7 predictions. This twelfth era stands as a distinct political period within Hebrew history, namely, that of the Romans and, during its latter four decades,[162] of their local administrator, King Herod. Yet by this point in time most of the longer-ranged OT predictions had either received their accomplishment or were awaiting the two advents of the Messiah, so that it is able to claim a total of only the seven sporadic forecasts indicated above.

161. Camb, *Hag-Mal*, p. 67.
162. For while Roman sway over Palestine was actually to continue on for centuries to come, this period has been limited to fulfillments occurring prior to the NT.

Period 13, Life of Christ (5 B.C.–A.D. 30),[163] 127 predictions. The 1st-century career of Jesus constitutes the heart of God's plan of salvation and is also one of the two main focuses for Biblical prophecy, Acts 3:24. This is true not only theologically and historically, as He shed His blood on behalf of the many, in order to establish the divine testament (Mk 14:25) which had been foretold by the Scriptures from Genesis 3:15 onward; but it is true statistically as well. For upon this 13th period converge all of the OT's prophecies of redemption and of the Messiah's first advent, all of the Biblical types (with the exception of only ten, plus parts of two others),[164] and all of the predictions having near-future fulfillment (prior to Pentecost) that are found in the four Gospels. It was during the ministry of Jesus that the OT concept of the remnant[165] became concentrated into the Person of our Lord[166] and then expanded again into that group of His followers who formed the nucleus of an ever-growing Christian community. Corresponding distinctions that had once been foretold by the prophet Zechariah thus began to appear within the flock of Israel: from Zechariah 13:7, "the little ones in the flock" are identified with those believers whom Christ regathered after His resurrection (Mt 26:31–32, Mk 14:27–28); cf. Zechariah 11:7, 11, on "the poor of the flock," who wait for God and recognize that the Jewish nation is falling from God's protective favor, v. 10 (cf. Acts 3:23). It is in reference to this concept of changing communities under God that the Gospels proclaim the "kingdom" as having come in Jesus Christ.[167] Feinberg explains, "The very kingdom that had been promised to Israel was now at hand in the Person of the King."[168] Yet controversy has arisen over Feinberg's understanding of the historical realization of the promise, as indicated by the fact that the above quotation occurs in his chapter entitled "The Kingdom Offered, Rejected, and Postponed." By the promised kingdom, he means the "essentially worldly kingdom," namely, that "millennium and kingdom are exactly the same ideas."[169] The Lord's Prayer and the Sermon on the Mount, for example, are thus not designed for church use but for the millennium.[170] But as antagonism against the Master began

---

163. Assuming these to be proper chronological limits for the life of Jesus, from His conception to His ascension into glory; cf. J. Finegan, *Handbook of Biblical Chronology*, pp. 248, 294, 296. 5 B.C. would likewise include those predictions that were fulfilled in John the Baptist's birth 6 months prior to Christ's.

164. See Summary D, below, pp. 671–672; cf. p. 680.

165. Cf. below, as discussed under Isa 6:13b or 7:3.

166. Cf. below, under Isa 42:1a.

167. See above, p. 30.

168. *Premillennialism or Amillennialism?* p. 62.

169. Ibid., pp. 63, 107.

170. The Scofield Bible sought to distinguish between "the kingdom of heaven" as outward and millennial (as at these points in Mt 5) and "the kingdom of God" as more inward and universal, p. 1003; cf. Feinberg, op. cit., pp. 163–164. But more recent dispensationalist scholars conclude that "such a categorical distinction does not seem to be supported by Scriptural usage," Pentecost, op. cit., pp. 433–434;

to develop within the Jewish community, he views Jesus as "turning from the purpose first outlined in His coming" to a differing goal of filling individual needs, commencing at Matthew 11:28 and displaying itself most clearly in the parables of Matthew 13.[171] George Ladd would appear, however, to have demonstrated that Christ's proclamation of the kingdom of God, or kingdom of heaven, stands normally equivalent in the Gospels to His preaching of salvation and eternal life, as in Matthew 19:23–24; cf. v. 16.[172] He grants that the Jews expected the earthly Davidic kingdom (as in John 6:15), but he insists that Jesus,

did not offer them the sort of kingdom they wanted. . . . Before the coming of the earthly phase of the kingdom, there must come another manifestation of the kingdom in saving power. The cross must precede the crown. . . . The very fact that he did not come as the glorious King, but as the humble Savior . . . proves that his offer of the kingdom was not the outward, earthly kingdom, but one which corresponded to the form in which the King himself came to men.[173]

Yet on the assumption that the purpose of Christ's first coming was for spiritual redemption and not for a setting up of the millennium (Rom 8:3), does the Lord's simple announcement, "The kingdom of God is at hand" (Mk 1:15), render him liable to a charge of deceptive reinterpretation of the OT hope? The answer must be no: first, because the OT had taught about a humble phase of the kingdom (Zech 9:9) as well as a glorious one (v. 10) and had predicted a Messianic prince who should suffer and die (Dan 9:26, Isa 49:7, 53:12, Zech 12:10; cf. Lk 24:26, John 3:14) before He should conquer; and second, because Christ consistently proclaimed His immediate kingdom in the spiritual terms of repentance, belief, regeneration, and eternal life (Mk 1:15, John 3:3,15), and not of political power or conquest (John 6:15, 18:36).

Period 14, Church (A.D. 30, to the second advent of Christ), 88 predictions. The prophetic period within which we now live may be said to have begun, chronologically, with the ascension of Jesus into heaven on May 18, A.D. 30 (Acts 1:3, 9).[174] Theologically, however, it is to be considered as the "church age," namely, that era which is characterized by the replacement of the typical OT economy of redemption with the economy of salvation by faith based directly upon Christ as our Savior that is expressed through the sacraments of the church. This would move its inception back some seven additional weeks to the symbolical rending of the veil of the

---

cf. John F. Walvoord, BS, 110 (1953), 5–6, and the noncommital approach of Alva J. McClain, *The Greatness of the Kingdom*, p. 19. See below, p. 134, as well.

171. Feinberg, op. cit., p. 66.

172. *Crucial Questions About the Kingdom of God*, ch. 5.

173. Ibid., pp. 113, 117.

174. Cf. Finegan's probable dating of our Lord's crucifixion to April 7, A.D. 30, op. cit., p. 296.

temple at Christ's death (Mt 27:51) and to the conversion of Passover into the communion service and His revelation of the testament in His blood at the Last Supper the evening before (26:28). In this period are fulfilled those predictions of the near future that occur within the pages of Acts and of the NT epistles, plus also those longer-range church prophecies of the Gospels that are accomplished in advance of Christ's Parousia.

Within evangelicalism, however, one of today's two major controversies relative to prophetic fulfillments concerns the forecasts of the church age. The legitimacy of assigning a place to this 14th period within the perspective of those Biblical predictions that had been revealed prior to it is now widely questioned among dispensational interpreters. Pentecost writes, "The existence of this present age, which was to interrupt God's established program with Israel, was a mystery (Mt 13:11)." He cites Colossians 1:26–27 on "the mystery which had been hidden from past the ages and generations, but has now been manifested to His saints . . . this mystery, which is Christ in you, the hope of glory," and concludes: "In this passage the apostle Paul calls the divine program developed in the church a *mystery*, something which was not formerly revealed, and therefore unknown."[175]

Yet to me, dispensationalism's denial to the church of a place in OT prophecy appears open to serious doubt. Apart from the NT's claims that such major church events as the inauguration of the newer testament or the experience of Pentecost were the fulfillment of OT predictions (see Heb 8:8 and Acts 2:16, under 1:4),[176] there arises, on the one hand, the definition of the term "mystery" and, on the other, the precise matters to which this term is applied in the NT. The noun *mustērion*, connotes not something weird, as in the modern usage, or esoteric in the sense of special knowledge available only for the duly initiated, as in the ancient mystery religions, but, in both the OT and the NT, the hidden counsel of God that has at some time, not necessarily the present, come to be revealed. So Romans 16:25–26 speaks of "the mystery which has been kept secret for long ages past but now is manifested, *and by the Scriptures of the prophets*[177] . . . has been made known to all the nations."[178] A mystery need

---

175. Op. cit., pp. 134–135. Compare L. S. Chafer's assertion: "The sum total of all the mysteries in the NT represents that entire body of added truth found in the NT which was unrevealed in the OT," *Systematic Theology*, IV:76.

176. Dispensationalism's effort to explain such passages as simply analogous to the "real" fulfillments in the yet future millennium stand self-condemned; cf. C. C. Ryrie, *The Basis of the Premillennial Faith*, pp. 117–118, or Pentecost, op. cit., p. 470, with Payne, *Theology*, pp. 76–78.

177. "The new method of salvation, although apart from law, was witnessed to by the Law and the Prophets," ICC, *Romans*, p. 436, so that the "now" of Rom 16:26 involves an OT manifestation as well. On the reality of *mustēriā*, in the OT, note the appearance of this very term for the "secrets" in Dan 2:18, etc., LXX.

178. "It is a divine purpose which God has kept hidden from man. At last, however, in the course of His redemptive plan, God reveals this purpose, and by the Scriptures of the prophets makes it known to all men," Ladd, *The Gospel of the Kingdom*, p. 52.

not, therefore, have been entirely unknown or unappreciated in previous times. As Paul states in Ephesians 3:3–6, "By revelation there was made known to me the mystery . . . which in other generations was not made known to the sons of men, *as* it has now been revealed to His holy apostles . . . to be specific, that the Gentiles are fellow heirs."[179]

When it comes then to identifying precisely what it is that is defined by the NT term "mystery," it seems important to observe that the revelation, even of previously hidden elements in a given doctrine—e.g. the exact relationship of the Gentiles to the church-body of Christ, Colossians 1:26–27—does not thereby divorce the doctrine as a whole from prior revelation; cf., relative to God's plan for the Gentiles, Isaiah 19:23–25, or the verses that are listed below under 24:16a and 44:5.[180] It would thus seem improper to move onward from the phrase in Matthew 13:11, Mark 4:11, citing "the mysteries of the kingdom of heaven," to a denial of a place within prophecy for this present age. "The mystery of the kingdom which is revealed to the disciples is Jesus Himself as Messiah."[181] As elaborated by Ladd, "The mystery is that this Kingdom of God has now come to work among men, but in an unexpected way . . . the Kingdom is now here with persuasion rather than power. . . . God has entered into history in the person of Christ to work among men . . . humbly, unobtrusively."[182]

A closely related question then concerns the relationship between Christianity and Judaism, between the people of the church and the people of the synagogue, in this 14th period. During the church age, prophetic ful-

179. Pentecost suggests at length that the "as" clause "is explaining, not limiting, the mystery there set forth," op. cit., pp. 136–137; but other exegetes seem to agree that "Hebrew prophecy had not been silent respecting the divine secret (cf. Isa 56:5)," NIC, *Eph, Col*, p. 72, only that "this doctrine was not formerly revealed so fully or so clearly as under the Gospel," Chas. Hodge, *A Commentary on the Epistle to the Ephesians*, p. 163. In Col 1:26–27, on the other hand, the mystery of Christ's being "in" the believing Gentiles does seem to have been originally revealed in NT times (even though the saints of OT Israel actually were *in Christ*, John 14:6, Eph 2:12, and cf. I Cor 15:18 with the OT quote in v. 54).

180. The NT, e.g., adds to the OT doctrine of the resurrection the "mystery" element that some believers will experience the resurrection without having to pass through the experience of death (I Cor 15:51); but it then goes on to equate the total resurrection doctrine with the OT hope (v. 54; cf. Isa 25:8). In the same fashion, as a supplement to Israel's ancient anticipation of a gathering together to meet their Redeemer (Isa 27:13, Zech 10:10), the NT adds the new element of the bodily rapture of the saints to meet Christ in the air (I Thess 4:17); but an attempt to distinguish this rapture hope from that of the OT (as in Walvoord, *The Rapture Question*, p. 36) runs afoul, both of the progressively supplemental character of revelation in general and of the elsewhere-indicated equation of these two aspects of the blessed hope in particular (II Thess 2:1, Mt 24:31), Payne, *The Imminent Appearing of Christ*, pp. 126–127.

181. TDNT, IV:819.

182. *The Gospel of the Kingdom*, pp. 55, 64. Further, "The kingdom which is to come finally in apocalyptic power has in fact entered the world in advance in a hidden form to work secretly within and among men," *Jesus and the Kingdom: The Eschatology of Biblical Realism*, p. 221.

fillments concerning unconverted Jews do appear, corresponding to Zechariah's predictions of the main body of the flock of Israel as scattered, as being two-thirds cut off, and with its survivors "brought into the fire," 13:7–9. The apostle Paul speaks of Israel after the flesh, I Corinthians 10:18; but he adds that they are no longer truly Israel in the sense of being God's people, Romans 9:6. They are cut off theologically as well as politically, Romans 11:17. The OT had predicted a time when God would designate the Jews as "driven away, and that which I have afflicted," Micah 4:6–7, "My dispersed," Zephaniah 3:10; and the NT church could speak even of "a synagogue of Satan," Rev. 2:9, 3:9. The NT, moreover, quotes words of Jesus about coming "times of the Gentiles" (Lk 21:24). These would seem to commence with the Roman siege and capture of Jerusalem in A.D. 70, about which Jesus was then warning His disciples: "When you see Jerusalem surrounded by armies . . . flee to the mountains" (vv. 20–22). These "times," then, would still appear to be going on today because, even though the Israeli army captured the Old City of Jerusalem in 1967, the present policy is as little receptive of Christ and is as "Gentile" in the NT sense (see Rom 2:28, Phil 3:2) as was the preceding Arab rule.

The church, on the other hand, represents the culmination of Hebrew history: it constitutes the fulfillment of the predicted new testament to be made "with the house of Israel and with the house of Judah" (Jer 31:31, Heb 8:8, 10:17-19). The phenomena are as follows: The ministry of Jesus was directed toward Israel and Judah (Mt 10:6). Elect Jews did receive the gospel and became those who made up His church (18:17), thus continuing as God's people (Rom 11:5). Faithless Jews, on the other hand, ceased to be true members of God's household (Eph 2:19), and were broken off from the "tree" of Israel (Rom 11:17; cf. 9:6). But then the church expanded; and, just as in the case of proselytes down through the preceding centuries, Gentiles continued to be engrafted into Israel (vv. 17, 19). They became joint citizens in Israel and heirs under the testament (Eph 2:12–13; cf. Rom 2:29, Gal 3:29, Phil 3:3), "the Israel of God" (Gal 6:16).[188] It is true that at certain points in the NT "Israel" is applied to the unbelieving portion of the Jewish nation, particularly with reference to their conversion at the Lord's second coming (Rom 11:25–27). But far from indicating a future distinction, Scripture guarantees that the standing of the believing Gentiles is to continue without change (v. 22); it is the converted Jews, rather, who join the church and who will thus be reengrafted into Israel (vv. 23–24);[184] "and thus all Israel [though once

183. Taking the *kai*, as "*even* upon the Israel of God." To render it *and*, as if a distinct group of Hebrew-Christians were contemplated, would oppose the thrust of the epistle as a whole. That distinction has now come to an end within God's people; cf. Ramm, op. cit. (1956 ed.), pp. 244–245.

184. A similar OT witness appears in Mi 5:3, "The remnant of His brethren shall return to Israel." Christ's brethren must include Gentiles, joining Israel; but *the remnant* signifies Jews, those who escape from the troubles to come upon Israel (5:1, 3a) before His birth.

TABLE 1

Development of Israel in Romans 11

| B.C. | Christ's First Coming | Conversion of Cornelius | Christ's Second Coming | Millennium |

The Saved

The Saved

Only Jews

"God's people" (Rom 11:1)

"A remnant according to God's gracious choice" (Rom 11:5) (still only Jews)

"Branches broken off" (Rom 11:17-21)

"Branches grafted in" (Rom 11:17, 19)

"Fellow-citizens of the household of God" (Eph 2:19)

Former Gentiles "continue in His kindness" (Rom 11:22)

"Branches grafted again into their own olive tree" (Rom 11:23-24)

"Thus all Israel will be saved" (Rom 11:25-26)

"A spirit of stupor" (Rom 11:8)

"Now the fall and diminishing of them is the riches of the Gentiles" (Rom 11:12, KJV)

"The severity of God . . . because of unbelief" (Rom 11:23-23)

(Apostate Jews)

Gentiles

"Aliens from the commonwealth of Israel" = "having no hope and without God in the world" (Eph 2:12, KJV)

"Wild olive" (Rom 11:17)

The Lost

Lost

obdurate] will be saved" (v. 26).[185] So in the final New Jerusalem, "the bride, the wife of the Lamb" (Rev. 21:9), is marked by "the names of the twelve tribes of the children of Israel" (v. 12), which serves to underscore, as Fairbairn observes, "the unbroken continuity of the church, and the essential oneness of her relation to the promises of God."[186] The course of development is shown in Table 1.

The church age terminates in a time of trouble known as the great tribulation. Revelation 7:14 is the one point in Scripture at which the precise term "the great tribulation" appears.[187] This passage has an eschatological setting and elaborates upon the conditions that will set the stage for the manifestation of "the presence of Him who sits on the throne . . . [when] the great day of [God's] wrath has come," 6:16–17.[188] Thus Matthew 24:29 also speaks of natural catastrophes and of the coming of the Son of man as "immediately after the tribulation," here consisting of false prophets who attempt to lead men astray (vv. 23–28). The Revelation passage goes on to speak of multitudes of faithful saints who stand as martyrs in heaven, 7:9; but this too must occur before the onset of the natural phenomena and of the Lord's visible advent; for the saints of Revelation are never identified as killed by the catastrophes that fall upon nature (cf. 9:4, 16:2) but only by the persecutions of men (11:7, 16:6, 20:4).[189] Furthermore, it is the Lord's coming that permanently terminates such matyrdoms; for when the faithful witness the signs in nature, they are told, "Lift up your heads, because your redemption is drawing near" (Lk 21:28). Apart from Matthew 24:29 (Mk 13:24) and Revelation 7:14, the noun *thlĭpsis*, "tribulation," is not used in the NT in reference to its final manifestation but only to tribulation in general, e.g. in John 16:33, "In the world you have tribulation, but take courage; I have overcome the world." Relevant passages must therefore be identified by their context: that of persecution immediately preceding the glorious appearing of Christ.

In the OT, Daniel 12:1 states, "There shall be a time of trouble [LXX, *thlĭpsis*], such as never was since there was a nation even to that same time: and at that time thy people shall be delivered," as v. 2 goes on to say, ac-

185. Payne, *Theology*, p. 76.
186. *Interpretation*, p. 52; cf. pp. 51–53.
187. Rev. 2:10 had spoken of a limited period of "tribulation," and 3:10 had alluded to what is probably the same sort of event as "the hour of trial." Both, however, refer to churches in the ancient Roman province of Asia and are best understood as warnings about 1st-century persecutions only; see these vv. as discussed below, Rev., prophecies No. 5 and No. 11.
188. Ch. 7 thus goes back in time to depict how God's saints are "sealed" to protect them from the catastrophes in nature, v. 3, that ch. 6 had first revealed as heralding His coming, 6:12–14. For Christians who live through these elements of God's wrath will not be harmed by it, I Thess 5:4, 9 (1:10 seems to refer not to this but to present deliverance from the threat of hell; see Payne, *Imminent Appearing*, pp. 74–75).
189. The bulk of Revelation is often assigned to the tribulation period, when actually it speaks of this final time of persecution only in 6:9–11, 7:14, 11:7–10, and 16:6.

complished by means of the resurrection which accompanies the Messiah's advent. By the same token, passages containing predictions about the eschatological Antichrist, such as Daniel 7:20–21, 24–25, 11:40–45, and II Thessalonians 2:3–11, may be accepted as legitimate references to the great tribulation, since this leader exists as the church's final persecutor and is himself slain at the appearance of the Messiah (II Thess 2:8; cf. Dan 11:45). But these passages do not constitute an extensive body of material.[190] The tribulation is a brief, specialized antecedent to Christ's return.[191] Its duration is nowhere clearly stated in Scripture. Some dispensationalist writers grant that the troubles of the last days make their appearance gradually, even before what is technically designated the great tribulation,[192] and that when this period does come its beginning is hard to fix exactly.[193] The "times" in Daniel's "time and times and half a time" of persecution by the Antichrist (7:25, 12:7) could consist of anywhere from three and a half days to seven and a half decades; and it seems best simply to say that the tribulation will be known to be over when the Lord is seen coming in glory. It is the advent of Christ that provokes the ultimate opposition of the Antichrist (Rev 19:10) and reveals him for what he truly is. He has of course been manifested in the world prior to the day of the Lord (II Thess 2:2–3); but his final revelation is associated with the glorious appearing of the Son of God, who shall bring to naught both him and all that for which he stands (v. 8). Whether or not the Antichrist is yet revealed on earth no one can, or should try to, say;[194] but when Christ does come in glory, then all shall be made plain. It is for this latter revelation that the church daily prays.

Period 15, Christ's Second Coming (the "wrath of God" through Armageddon), 52 predictions. Modern theology is marked by a revival of thought

190. The much-discussed passages of Daniel's 70th week (9:24–27) and the Lord's quotation of his "abomination of desolation" (Mt 24:4–22) seem by now to possess preterist significance only and to extend in their application no further than A.D. 70; see below under Dan., prophecy No. 34 and Mt., prophecy No. 28. Josephus' descriptions of the frightful wrath suffered by the Jews at the hands of Titus explain why the tribulation of Mt 24:21 could well have been, in its own way, of unrepeatable magnitude. Yet Pentecost, in *Things to Come*, devotes more than 140 pp. to the events of the great tribulation, more than to either Christ's second advent or the millennial kingdom.

191. It has been understood, in its classical interpretation, as a potentially present antecedent to the Parousia. It is the possible contemporaneity of this period, indeed, that guarantees the hope of the imminence of our Lord's appearing; cf. Payne, *Imminent Appearing*, p. 114.

192. René Pache, *The Return of Jesus Christ*, p. 117.

193. Leon J. Wood, *Is the Rapture Next?* p. 32.

194. Paul's Thessalonian context suggests that while the impersonal power of lawlessness was already at work, v. 7, the Antichrist's personal coming was a sign which had as yet remained unfulfilled up to the point of his writing. To insist, however, that it is yet unfulfilled today would imply an identity in world conditions that fails to take seriously the specifically anti-Christian character of much of modern society; Payne, *Imminent Appearing*, p. 120.

on our Lord's second advent.[195] Actually, "the blessed hope" (Titus 2:13) pervades the apostolic writings, and its initial revelation goes back to David in the 6th period (I Chron 16:33, Ps 96:12–13), as stated in terms of God the Father: "Sing before Yahweh, for He cometh. . . ." Edghill explains,

> It is the belief that Jehovah Himself would come to Zion to reign in her midst. . . . [But in Ezek 34:22–24] the work of Jehovah and His servant David are so similar as to be practically indistinguishable. . . . Here then were two ideas, the advent of Jehovah and the reign of the Messianic king, unreconciled yet not irreconcilable. . . . Even in the OT we find some progress toward their reconciliation. Thus Malachi predicts . . . [that] when Jehovah does come He will come as the Angel of the covenant (3:1) . . . who, if identical with Jehovah Himself, is yet in a sense to be distinguished from Him, and may be legitimately compared to the house of David (Zech 12:8).[196]

The period of Christ's second advent, along with that of His incarnation, forms one of the two primary loci for the whole pattern of predictive fulfillment; and evangelical interpreters of all schools join in affirming with the Apostles' Creed that Jesus Christ the Son ascended into heaven, "from whence He shall come. . . ."

As a 15th prophetic era it is here taken to extend from the great earthquake and the darkening of the heavenly bodies that herald His return (Mt 24:29, Rev 6:12; "the great day of God's wrath," v. 16), through His appearing on the clouds (Mt 24:30, Rev 1:8), His raising of the dead saints, and His rapturing of those yet alive, to be with Himself (Mt 24:31, I Thess 4:17), and His descent to the Mount of Olives (Zech 14:4, Acts 1:11), down to His achievement of victory over the Antichrist and his various allies, first at Jerusalem (Joel 2:12–14, Zech 14:1–3) and finally at Armageddon (Dan 11:45, Rev 16:16), in a series of campaigns lasting for perhaps five months (9:5–10).

During this period the human followers of the Messiah are normally assumed to consist of God's saved people, the church. For those events which occur after the conversion of the Jews at Christ's appearing (Zech 12:10), then Israel after the flesh should also be included within the church constituency. Exceptions appear in Micah 4:7 and Zephaniah 3:13, where the Lord's eschatological people are described as a "remnant," those who come back to Him after having been previously driven out (Mi 4:6). It is noteworthy, however, that in both cases the following verses (Mi 4:8, Zeph 3:14) drop the opprobrious titles and the subject becomes simply the

195. One writer affirms, "It seems to me eminently reasonable to believe that if the Kingdom of God is ever to be realized on earth, Christ will have the manifestly supreme place in it," Rowley, op. cit., p. 148; and see Payne, *Imminent Appearing*, p. 5, though also its cautioning qualifications.

196. *An Enquiry into the Evidential Value of Prophecy*, pp. 236–237, 240, 244. The phrase "My Servant David" is properly assumed to represent David's descendant, as in I K 12:16.

"daughter of Zion and Jerusalem," so that the whole of God's people is again contemplated, that is, the full church. As Keil concludes, "We must not restrict the description of salvation . . . to the people of Israel who are lineally descended from Abraham, and to the remnant of them; but must also regard the Gentiles converted to the living God through Christ as included among them."[197] Prophetic forecasts that refer distinctly to Israel aftei the flesh and that find their fulfillment subsequent to the rise of the Christian church are relatively infrequent in Scripture. On the basis, however, of those exceptional portions where they do occur (e.g. the last 6 chs. of Zech), "Israel" may, in summary, be said to signify the people of the synagogue (not of the church) under the following conditions: (a) when dealt with in a way specifically distinguished from God's dealings with the Gentiles, as in Zechariah 9:10a; (b) when possessing Palestine prior to the Parousia, as in 13:8; (c) when scattered in punishment, as in 11:16; (d) when indicted as disbelieving before the Lord's second coming, as in 12:11–14; (e) when not raptured to be with Christ at His appearing, as in 12:10; (f) when described as being then converted to Him, as in 13:1; cf. Rom 11:26–27; and (g) when brought back to Palestine and the Messiah by means other than the rapture, as in 14:5a; cf. Isa 14:2a (see under 11:11), Zeph 3:10. Conversely, Israel means the believing church: (a) when specifically called Gentile, as in 9:10b; (b) when noted as increasing, subsequent to the times of redemption, as in 10:8; (c) when sown in foreign lands and favored by God, as in 10:9; (d) when identified as believing prior to His appearing, as in 11:11; (e) when gathered to be with Christ at His Parousia, as in 10:10;[198] and of course (f) in all references to the kingdom when Israel after the flesh becomes reengrafted into the true Israel, as in 12:5.[199]

Period 16, Millennium (the 1,000 years of Satan's binding, from Rev 20:2 to 20:7), 46 predictions. It is in reference to this era of the Messiah's future, earthly kingdom that modern evangelicalism's second great controversy over prophetic fulfillment has arisen. Revelation 20 undoubtedly *says* that there will be a 1,000-year period between the first resurrection (of the saved) and the general resurrection (at the final judgment), vv. 5–6, 12, during which Satan is no longer to deceive the nations of the earth, vv. 3, 8. Equally obvious is the earthward orientation of OT eschatology, where Zechariah, for example, foretells that after Christ has raptured the church He will "bring them into the land of Gilead and Lebanon" (10:10); and

197. *Minor Prophets*, II:164.
198. So in Zech 12:7, the house of David and the inhabitants of Jerusalem are noted as delivered subsequently to the "tents of Judah." Since the former belong to Israel after the flesh, converted at the appearing of Christ, v. 10, the latter, which are to be delivered first, would seem to correspond to the raptured church; see below, Zech 12:7 (under 8:7) and 12:5.
199. Payne, "The Church and Zionism in the Predictive Cycles of Zechariah 9–14," ETS P (1956), 65.

Isaiah proceeds to locate the marriage supper of the Lamb "in this mountain," namely, Mount Zion (25:6–7; cf. 24:23 and I Cor 15:51–54). Yet those who would interpret these predictions figuratively find, instead, a series of symbols that picture the spiritual church and the life in heaven. An exclusively figurative interpretation of the earthly elements found in the prophecies of the eschatological kingdom thus leads one to a correspondingly amillennial position: the second coming of Christ (per. 15) will immediately usher in the final judgment and New Jerusalem (pers. 17–18) with no intervening millennium (per. 16). In support of a figurative hermeneutical approach, E. J. Young has contended:

> Since the revelation granted to the prophets was less clear than that given to Moses [Num 12:6–8]; indeed, since it contained elements of obscurity, we must take these facts into consideration when interpreting prophecy. We must therefore abandon once and for all the erroneous and non-Scriptural rule of "literal if possible." The prophetic language belonged to the Mosaic economy and hence, was typical. Only in the light of the NT fulfillment can it properly be interpreted.[200]

But while recognizing both the elements of obscurity that appear within the prophetic oracles[201] and the basic function that prophecy executes as supplementary to the law,[202] I cannot but question whether these facts justify amillennialism's typical, and indeed exclusively typical, application of the earthly predictions of the OT to today's spiritual church. In the first place, the very use of the term "typical" seems improper. For Biblical typology concerns contemporaneously existing objects and actions that were, at the same time, symbolic of the future; but it does not apply to verbal statements.[203] The typical nature of some of the Mosaic *institutions* does not, therefore, automatically limit the Mosiac *predictions* to a figurative fulfillment. Indeed, if the foregoing study of principles for prophetic interpretation has achieved a measure of hermeneutical consistency, it has demonstrated that the millennial predictions may not be dismissed as conditional[204] and that forecasts, for example, of a first resurrection may not be transmuted into a cryptogram for conversion in this life or for the spirit's survival in heaven—especially when its prediction is followed in the same context by that of another (and literal) resurrection!—without lapsing from exegesis into allegorization.[205]

In the second place, when the light of NT interpretation is brought to bear upon the matter of the OT's prophetic fulfillment, the apostolic analogy is *not* found to support the claim that the earthly situations therein predicted

---

200. *My Servants the Prophets*, p. 215.
201. See below, pp. 140–142.
202. See pp. 6–7 above, on the relationship of the prophets to the older testament.
203. See below, p. 125.
204. See above, pp. 62–68 (esp. pp. 65–66).
205. See above, pp. 42–47 (esp. 46), pp. 83–84.

are assigned only a spiritualized accomplishment.[206] As Ramm has cautiously summarized the evidence, "Sometimes it [the OT] is cited as being *literally fulfilled* . . . sometimes the NT cites the OT *in an expanded . . . sense.* . . . An extreme literalism or an extreme typological approach is equally contrary to the method by which the NT interprets the Old."[207] Furthermore, once the legitimacy of any literal interpretation be granted, an objective exegesis would seem to forbid the exclusion of a clear, literal meaning and the substitution of a figurative interpretation, unless there be actual justification for each such instance. Ramm gots on to reason, "In keeping with the system of hermeneutics . . . we make the literal the control over the typological. Therefore, *interpret prophecy literally unless the implicit or explicit teaching of the NT suggests typological interpretation.*"[208] This being so, and if prophecy is really infallible, then the fact of a necessary fulfillment for its predictions of an earthly Messianic kingdom renders the millennial concept inescapable.[209]

Ultimately, the most satisfactory method of interpretation appears to lie in a synthesis that combines, wherever possible, the belief in a literal future accomplishment with the conviction of its universal applicability to the spiritual people of God. One may thereby maintain both the reality of the coming kingdom of Israel upon earth and, at the same time, the confidence that its saved citizenry will consist of our own NT church. The amillennialist who hesitates over the one and the dispensational premillennialist who hesitates over the other seem equally to be subject to criticism.[210]

Concerning the character of this 16th, or millennial, era of prophetic fulfillment, it is important to assign full weight to its spiritual as well as to its material features. The following, highly varied list of prophetic topics, for example, which find their accomplishment in this period have been com-

206. See above, pp. 61, 72, 83.
207. Op. cit., (1956 ed.), pp. 243, 247. His analysis is: "The amillennialist makes the greatest divorce between the form and the fulfillment of prophecy and that is why the more literal-minded postmillennarians and premillennarians are restive with it. The dispensationalists judge that the distinction between the form and the idea of prophecy is spurious [an extreme criticism, indeed, in the light of his following statement], and therefore they look for the fulfillment of prophecy to be *very similar* [italics mine] to the precise form in which it was given in the OT." He concludes, "*Some change in the form of fulfillment* must be expected," p. 241.
208. Ibid., p. 247.
209. When Vos was faced with the problem of the nonfulfillment and, for an amillennialist as himself, the seeming impossibility of any future fulfillment of a number of Biblical prophecies which speak directly of events upon this earth, he conceded, "The adoption of premillennialism would greatly limit the field of the impossible in this respect," *Biblical Theology,* p. 232. Indeed, there arise a number of points in Scripture in which prophecies of judgment, literally fulfilled, are balanced contextually by prophecies of restoration that would seem to necessitate a correspondingly literal fulfillment. God spoke through Jeremiah, for example, saying, "Like as I have brought all this great evil upon this people, so will I bring upon them all the good that I have promised them," 32:42, and cf. 31:28.
210. Payne, *Theology,* p. 490.

piled from the Book of Isaiah in the order of their occurrence: millennial geography, discussed below under Isa., prophecy No. 7; a millennial temple, under No. 8; a heart-felt seeking for God, No. 9; divine teaching, No. 10; the Messianic rule, No. 11; millennial peace, No. 12, prosperity, No. 14, and holiness, No. 15; the presence of the Shekinah, or glory cloud, No. 16; Jewish sanctification, No. 31; Messianic concern for the lowly, No. 35; a curseless world, No. 43; Jewish reassemblage, No. 44; millennial joy and peace, No. 46; and so on. As George N. H. Peters concludes, "While a purely naturalistic Kingdom, without spirituality, is unscriptural, so likewise an entire spiritual kingdom, without the sanctified union of the material or natural, is utterly opposed to the Word of God."[211] Thus in the significant passage of Isaiah 49, where Messianic prophecy reaches its climax in the equation of Christ with the divine testament, the ultimate relevance of our Lord's redemption is viewed as affecting the physical earth: "I will give Thee for a testament of the people, to raise up the land, to make them inherit the desolate heritages," v. 8.

The human subjects that are concerned in the fulfillments of the Bible's millennial predictions consist of those living at the time of Christ's return, plus the saved dead, who participate in the first resurrection. Dispensational writers tend at times unduly to limit both of these groups. The living may be restricted to the saved, on the assumption that "all sinners will be cut off before the institution of the Kingdom."[212] Such a conclusion, however, hangs dependent upon the dubious assignment of Matthew 25:41 and certain other statements of judgment to the beginning of the millennium (see next period). Those who believed in Christ prior to His appearing are then, according to some, totally restricted from the future earthly kingdom. Pentecost argues, "Those who would place resurrected individuals on the earth to undergo the rigors of the King's reign miss the purpose of God in the millennial age";[213] but one wonders if he himself may not have missed something of the desirability of the millennium or of the Christian's hope of "ever being with the Lord," I Thessalonians 4:17—who is noticeably on earth, Isaiah 9:7, 11:4, 16:5, 32:1, etc. The millennial church is described as "living and reigning with Him," Revelation 20:7; and if an individual member is indeed foreseen to be wielding "authority over the nations; and he shall rule them with a rod of iron . . . as I also have received authority from My Father," 2:26–27, it would appear difficult to divorce such action from life on earth. Amillennialists, on the other hand, sometimes argue against the applicability to the millennium of passages such as the above-cited I Thessalonians 4:17 because of their allusions to eternity, to the saints *ever* being with the Lord. Robert Culver, however, clarifies the real possibility of an

211. Op. cit., III:460.
212. Pentecost, op. cit., p. 504.
213. Ibid., p. 538. Yet in fairness, one must note that other dispensationalists would consider his statement extreme.

overlap between the limited period of the 1,000 years and the everlasting kingship of Christ, the two of which possess a simultaneous point of origin (though the latter continues on without termination); and he concludes, "The Bible places the future millennium within the future kingdom . . . at the beginning of it."[214]

Period 17, Final Judgment (from the postmillennial release of Satan to the departure of the godless into the lake of fire), 14 predictions. A sequence of forecasted events which constitute a distinct era of fulfillment are cataloged in the latter portion of Revelation 20: the final, Satanically inspired revolt of Gog and Magog (vv. 7–9),[215] the ultimate condemnation of their demonic instigator (v. 10), the passing away of the present universe (v. 11), the final judgment itself, with the accompanying general resurrection (vv. 12–13), and God's concluding disposition of all those who are involved in it (vv. 14–15). The chief topic of present-day discussion in regard to this period concerns its inclusiveness of the judgments of God. In a providential sense, Yahweh's judgments over mankind may appear as continuous, throughout all historical periods, e.g. in Psalms 7:8, 50:4–6, or 75:7 (which are thus not really predictive at all). In an administrative sense, His judgments over the earth characterize the entire millennium, e.g. Psalm 72:12–14, Isaiah 2:4, 11:3–4. Yet in the specifically judicial "courtroom" sense of sentencing men to their ultimate destiny, God's activity seems to me to be Scripturally identifiable with this one, 17th period. A form of individual reward cannot, of course, be disassociated from men's very participation in the first resurrection at the outset of the Messianic kingdom, but the same fact seems correspondingly true of their reception into heaven at death (II Tim 4:18). Within some dispensational circles it has become customary to assign certain of the Bible's judicial passages to a series of specific points located near the commencement of the millennium, such as that of the judgment seat of Christ in II Corinthians 5:10 (see below, under II Cor., prophecy No. 1), "the judgment of the Gentile nations"—though these are actually described as individuals, and without ethnic distinction—in Matthew 25:31–45 (see under Mt., No. 68), or even what is apparently nothing other than the exilic judgment of Israel in Ezekiel 20:34–38. Writers of such persuasion object that the final judgment of Revelation 20:11–15 is not to be considered applicable to the church, either because Christians can no longer be subject to condemnation or because only the dead are mentioned. But the very point of the reference in vv. 12 and 15 to "the book of life" is to demonstrate that only those who are apart from Christ are condemned (v. 15), while the remainder of mankind which

214. *Daniel and the Latter Days*, p. 41.
215. The ultimate demonstration of human depravity: rebellion after centuries of life in the very kingdom of God. Yet the very fact of His irresistible sway, plus perhaps the presence of resurrected lives in daily contact with their own more limited bodily existence, may contribute to this final act of self-determination.

is present, that is, the saved, are on the contrary justified and then rewarded according to their works (vv. 12–13). Further, while the dead are particularly singled out, as indicative of the absolute inclusiveness of the final judgment, this does not thereby deny the presence of others, particularly in light of the Bible's regular uniting into one great assize of the eternal recompensing of both the saved and the lost together (cf. Dan 12:2–3, Mt 25:46, John 5:28–29—the first and last of these references also bring together the two resurrections, but for the separation of which a stronger case is to be made out; see the conclusion to Sec. D, below).

Period 18, New Jerusalem (from its appearance in Rev 21:1–2 and thence onward without end), 15 predictions. Also within this era are to be included the corresponding fulfillments of prophecies concerning the destiny of the lost within the lake of fire. Pentecost, it may be noted, presents an elaborate hypothesis of an earlier role for the eternal city, when at the commencement of the millennium it is said to be "transferred from heaven to a position over the earth. . . . This dwelling place remains in the air, to cast its light . . . onto the earth so that 'the nations of them which are saved shall walk in the light of it: and the kings of the earth do bring their glory and honor unto it' (Rev 21:24)."[216] Yet according to the sequence of Revelation, the New Jerusalem does not seem to put in its appearance until after period 17 and the final judgment of chapter 20. On the basis for distinguishing its era in passages appearing in the OT, particularly in Isaiah, see sec. 3(d), below.

3. CRITERIA FOR RELATING PREDICTIONS TO THEIR PROPER PERIODS OF FULFILLMENT. Without seeking to establish separate principles for determining the assignment of the Bible's prophecies to each of the above-outlined eighteen periods, one may yet recognize four major areas within which the questions most frequently arise about deciding among alternative possibilties of fulfillment: namely, within OT, NT, future (millennial), and final times. (a) Indications of OT times. Even within a single OT period, there may appear certain diverse epochs for the conceivable accomplishment of given forecasts. In period 7, on the divided kingdoms, for example, considerable similarity exists between the Assyrian campaigns against Judah —including a deportation to Mesopotamia which may have exceeded all others in the history of that small nation (II K 18:13)[217]—and the Baby-

---

216. Op. cit., p. 577.
217. When Sennacherib boasted of carrying captive some 200,150 from Judah, quite possibly an exaggerated figure, but still far greater than what is recorded for Nebuchadrezzar's deportations 100 years later, II K 24:14, in his 8th year, and 25:11, in his 19th (the specific number is not given for this later and greatest Babylonian captivity; but, by the analogy of Jer. 52:28–29, which tells of certain preliminary deportations during Nebuchadrezzar's 7th and 18th years, still suggests many less in 586 than in 701).

lonian campaigns a century thereafter. Isaiah and Micah include extensive predictions about the sequence of both events, which may be contrasted as follows:

701 B.C.	Isaiah	Micah	586 B.C.	Isaiah	Micah
Towns taken	5:29, 10:6	1:9	Jerusalem taken		
			only here	27:10	3:12
A vindication			God vindicated,	1:28	2:4
of God,	29:19–20	3:4	idols finally		
images defiled	30:22	3:7	removed	2:18	5:13
Distress and			A full end, the		
breaking	5:30, 28:13	1:11	land emptied	6:11, 24:1	5:11, 7:8
			Babylonian		
Assyrian captivity	36:1	1:16, 2:10	captivity	39:6–9	5:10
Men humbled	5:15	2:3	The king perishes	7:16b	4:9

Care is necessarily demanded in the distinguishing of fulfillments, both in passages where the historical situation is designated—e.g. Assyria, in Isaiah 10:5, 52:4; or Babylonia, in 39:6, 43:14—and especially in those passages where it must be inferred from context—e.g. the Assyria of 701 in 5:26, or in 40:1: "Comfort ye My people" (cf. 39:8 and 33:6); or the Babylonia of 586 in 5:5, or in 52:11: "Depart ye, touch no unclean thing" (cf. 51:14 and 48:20).[218]

A basic key for the identification of fulfillments achieved during OT times lies in the tendency of the preexilic Israelites toward the worship of idols (even as suggested by some of the above references from Isa and Mi), and from which the exile *did* generally succeed in purging them (Ezek 14:11, Dan 3:18).[219] Isaiah 30:22 and 31:7, on Judah's anticipated defiling of their graven images, probably refers, therefore, to the contemporary reforms of Hezekiah; and when Ezekiel 36:26 speaks of the "new heart and new spirit" that Yahweh will give them, this seems likewise to designate the prophet's contemporary exilic community, for the gift was to occur as a part of their being cleansed from idolatry (vv. 25, 29).[220] Because of the characteristic "uncleanness that destroyeth" (Mi 2:10b), it appears that the command of Micah 2:10a, "Arise and depart, for this land is not your resting place," must refer to the calamity of 586. So then in v. 12, God's promise, "I will surely gather the remnant of Israel," must correspondingly refer back to the remnant indicated in v. 10 and thus have a postexilic fulfillment.

Their sin led to a destruction that is still datable to OT times, and not to the final destruction of heaven and earth which precedes God's judgment

218. See below, under the introduction to Isaiah.
219. Though cf. even postexilic Zech 13:2.
220. Cf. Isaiah's prediction of the devastations by Sennacherib, 32:9–14 and 19, "until the Spirit be poured upon us from on high," v. 12.

and the advent of the New Jerusalem (cf. Rev 20:11). So when Zephaniah 1:18 imposes the curse of God's fire that will consume *kol hā-ā́res,* this term may mean simply *all the land,* of Judah, not *all the earth;* for vv. 16–17 involve the more limited siege and deaths of 586. Similar references to the fall merely of the *land* of Judah may thus be understood for vv. 2–3 as well; cf. vv. 4–6 (and so also in Isa 24:1, 4; cf. vv. 2, 5). The much-quoted phrase "the time of Jacob's trouble" (Jer 30:7) could just as well relate to their woes at the advance of Nebuchadrezzar (vv. 5–6; cf. 22:23) as to the woes preceding the return of the Messiah (vv. 8–9). Yet while the word of Isaiah 1:25, "I will purge away thy dross," stands in a context of pre-exilic paganism, v. 27, still ch. 4:4 refers to the time in which Yahweh "shall have purged the blood of Jerusalem" in a context of eschatological glory.[221]

Another area in which one may distinguish B.C. fulfillments from those of later times concerns God's promised acts of favor. In Deuteronomy 7:13 the blessings of multiplied people and of products could be millennial; but they seem to find adequate fulfillment in Israel's united kingdom (per. 6), in accordance with their entrance into Canaan in 6:3. Yet a similar verse in Exodus 23:25 is assigned a millennial accomplishment (per. 16) because of its simultaneous forecast of God's removal of sickness and all barrenness (vv. 25–26). In Deuteronomy 7, however, the transition to the Messianic millennium seems to occur only at the beginning of the next verse (14). Just as in the matter of the curses, so too with the blessings, the Hebrew noun *hā-ā́res,* creates a difficulty in interpretation. In Psalm 37:9, 11, etc. (cf. 25:13), one should probably read with the ASV, "But the meek shall inherit the land," that is, Palestine, immediately (cf. 37:3), not with the KJV, "inherit the earth," as if in millennial times. The same thought applies to our Lord's quotation of these verses in Matthew 5:5 and the meek's being rewarded "in this life . . . not the millennial earth."[222]

Particularly to be distinguished are the promises of Israel's return from exile in 537 (per. 9) and of the nation's regathering at the return of Christ (per. 15). When Zechariah 2:7 specifically names a return as being composed of those who dwell "with the daughter of Babylon," this forecast would seem to be postexilic. Zechariah 1:17 might at first appear to be more millennial in character: "My cities shall yet overflow with prosperity, and Yahweh shall yet comfort Zion and shall yet choose Jerusalem." Here, however, it is the surrounding context which suggests Zerubbabel's rebuilding of the temple in the 6th century B.C. (v. 16; cf. 4:7–10); and despite initial reverses (Hag 1:6, 9–11; 2:16–17), Judah did succeed in regaining land and goods under the Persians and the Ptolemaic Greeks (2:19). Ezekiel 34:11–22 or 36:22–37:23 may sometimes speak of the return from

---

221. Commentaries frequently neglect to explicate these distinctions in fulfillment, and Isaiah himself might not have been able to define those periods of accomplishment that were not to be found impinging upon his own day.

222. Lenski, *The Interpretation of Mt,* pp. 188–189.

exile in poetic language, e.g., "The land that was desolate is become like the garden of Eden," 36:35 (or 34:14, 22); but the meaning is that "ruined cities are fortified and inhabited." The respective positions of these prophecies, standing between sections on Judah's exilic punishment (Ezek 34:1–10 and 36:16–21) and on the presumably first coming of Jesus the Good Shepherd (34:23 and 37:24) again suggest an OT fulfillment.[223]

(b) Indications of NT times. A special aspect of Jewish restoration that moves beyond Zerubbabel and into an A.D. dating is that of Israel's predicted "increase."[224] Jeremiah 3:16 associates it with a loss of concern for the ark of the covenant, namely at the passing away of the ceremony-oriented Mosaic dispensation, at the death of Christ (cf. Mt 26:28, 27:51);[225] and Jeremiah 23:3b and 30:19–20 locate it in contexts between the postexilic return (23:3a and 30:18) and the future kingdom of the Messiah (23:4–6 and 30:21), which would suggest that increase which is identifiable with the expansion of the church (per. 14) among Gentiles as well as Jews.[226] Similarly, when Zechariah 2:11 foresees a day when many nations (but not all) will be joined to the Lord "and shall be My people," it implies a fulfillment in NT (not millennial) times.[227] Again, when prophecy speaks of a scattering of Israel, but in a context of blessing and not of penalty—as in Zechariah 10:9, "I will sow them among the peoples"—its reference too would appear to be to Israel in the NT church and not to Israel in the OT exile.[228]

Context constitutes a major guide for the ascertaining of fulfillments in NT times, whether the oracles in question refer to "Israel after the flesh" or to "the Israel of God." Concerning the former, Micah 4:6 is a case in point. The following context speaks of a remnant ruled by God in Zion, which indicates a millennial accomplishment. The group, therefore, out of which that remnant is taken must be the Jews of the present age, identified as "her that is driven out, and her that I have afflicted" (v. 6), and not those of the

223. See below, under D-3, on predictive cycles, and under the introduction to Ezekiel.
224. Increased population may, of course, concern the B.C. restoration of period 9, as might be the case in Mi 2:12's speaking of the reassembled remnant of Israel making "great noise by reason of the multitude of men."
225. Of similar import would appear to be the prediction of Mal 1:11 on the offering "in every place" of pure sacrifices by Gentiles. As noted above, p. 84, these must be figurative, since literal offerings could not be legitimate anywhere outside of Jerusalem. The time for fulfillment would most naturally arise during the church age, not simply because of the Gentile obedience that characterizes this period, but also because this is preeminently the time of their spiritualized sacrifice, while temple ceremonial stands in abeyance; cf. Rom 15:16.
226. Payne, Theology, pp. 475–478.
227. Though even in the millennium, loyalty is predicted as being to some degree imperfect; cf. the "many nations" of Zech 8:22; and when 14:16–19 foretells that "all the nations . . . and all the families of the earth" are to keep the Feast of Tabernacles, the possibility of disobedience is also envisioned.
228. See also p. 104, on the parallel question of distinguishing the church from Judaism.

Babylonian exile.[229] Concerning the latter, Zechariah 10:8 provides an illustration of slightly earlier date but still of NT fulfillment. The preceding context had spoken of exile (v. 2) and then of Maccabean victories (vv. 3–7), yet the following context (v. 9) relates to the present dispersion of the church (cf. Acts 8:1, 4; 11:19) in blessing (as noted above). So when the intervening verse (Zech 10:8) foresees an increase among the redeemed, church augmentation, as at Pentecost, Acts 2:41, comes naturally to mind.

(c) Indications of future, millennial times. A factor that was crucial during the days of our Lord's incarnate ministry, and which has yet to be considered, is that of distinguishing the Bible's prophecies of Christ's first and second comings (cf. John 12:34). Yet the perspective that the church has acquired through His death and resurrection now provides a major means of clarification (v. 16). The analogy of NT Scripture has already located most of the predictions at either one advent or the other, and the analogy of history has demonstrated certain prophecies as having been accomplished and others as not—and hence *to be achieved* at His return. Beyond such analogous evidence, one's assignments of fulfillment may be based upon the person or upon the work of Jesus. In reference to the former, a humility of person characterized His first coming (Isa 42:2, 50:6); but attributes of glory will distinguish His second (49:7, 53:12a), as *addīr ūmōshēl*, Jeremiah 30:21, as a *"mighty* (approaching magnificent)"[230] *and* a *ruling* one. The work of Christ, His kingdom of "salvation," in its broadest sense, characterizes both of His comings; but His work of redemption from the internal guilt of sin marks off the first (as in Dan 9:24, Zech 3:9); and from sin's external forces, the second (Dan 2:44b, 7:13–14). As the NT summarizes, "So Christ, having been offered once to bear the sins of many, shall appear a second time, not to bear sin, to those who eagerly await Him, for salvation" (Heb 9:28).

A basis for distinguishing between those to whom He comes, whether to the church, in its rapture (per. 15), or to the Jews, in their regathering (per. 16), is to be found in Scripture's teaching that the latter are to be brought back by other people (Isa 14:2, 49:22) and by the use of standard means, e.g. a highway, 11:16, 35:8. The church, in contrast, experiences its rapture by the direct act of God. It may be identified by such supernatural elements as the sounding of His great trumpet (Isa 27:12–13, Mt 24:31, I Thess 4:16; "the last trumpet," I Cor 15:52)—cf. His (figurative) "roaring like a lion" (Hos 11:10)—or as the comparison of the movement of His people with the course of birds through the heavens (Hos 11:11; cf. I Thess 4:17).

229. Zeph 3:10 speaks likewise of the nations bringing the Jews back to Palestine, which must be millennial. So when those brought back are identified as "My dispersed" (and this cannot here designate the church, because it refers to a group that has not been raptured at Christ's return), this phrase too points to Jews in the present age; and so also vv. 18–20.

230. KB, p. 11.

Predictions of the Messiah's millennial kingdom may be distinguished from forecasts about His present reign in the church (e.g. Rom 5:21) by factors that are similar to those employed in reference to His two comings; methodologically, in fact, it appears highly inconsistent on the part of amillennialists to accept His return as literal, coming with the clouds just as prophesied, but then to question His rule as being equally literal upon the earth. Geographical allusions, indicating the localized presence of Jesus Christ, form a basic key to the identification of millennial prophecies. When Zechariah 8:22, for instance, speaks of many nations seeking the Lord, one might think of them in the church age, as in Zechariah 2:11; but the nations in ch. 8 "come to seek Yahweh in Jerusalem." Again, Micah 2:13 foresees the Messiah in His coming as "their king, passing on before them." But His "passing" brings Him within a city, and He regathers His people in order to lead them through an earthly gate; so Micah would here seem to be referring to the rapture of the church to the hills of Palestine. From the same passage appears a further factor, that of cataclysm. The Messianic king carries the predicted title of "the Breaker," and His followers too "break forth and press on to the gate." So while it was a spiritual kingdom that was *set up* in the days of Rome, Daniel 2:44a (cf. Acts 8:12, I Pet 2:9), its cataclysmic description as "breaking in pieces and consuming all these [other] kingdoms," v. 44b, seems less appropriate to the present body of Christ than to that future church, when "the kingdom of the world has become the kingdom of our Lord and of His Christ" (Rev 11:15).

A series of distinctive millennial characteristics revolves about the city of Jerusalem, and the ancient Mount Zion in particular. "Yahweh will utter His voice from Jerusalem and . . . dwell in Zion My holy mountain," Joel 3:16–17; cf. Romans 11:26, on the Deliverer's coming from Zion. Zechariah 8:3 must likewise refer to the Jerusalem of the day of the Messiah's second advent; for it lauds it as "the city of truth," which has never yet been its condition up to the present. References within prophecies to a future temple and its accompanying memorial sacrifices[231] show that their fulfillment must be millennial, e.g. in Malachi 3:3–4, which follows chronologically upon Christ's Parousia, v. 2.[232] Surrounding the city, the land of Israel will be marked by exceptional fertility. Amos 9:14, on the vineyards and gardens of regathered Israel, could refer simply to period 9's postexilic restoration; but v. 13, preceding, requires a millennial understanding, since this fertility will be truly phenomenal. Similarly, Zechariah 8:4 speaks of a greatly increased span for human life, which shows in turn that God's predicted coming to Jerusalem in v. 3 is not the event of His first but of

---

231. See above, p. 108. Christ has indeed made the atonement for sin once and for all, Heb 7:27, 9:12, 10:10; yet the church's present communion service in remembrance of Him will be subject to replacement upon His return (I Cor 11:25–26), and Isa 60:6–7 does lay emphasis on sacrifices of thanksgiving and praise.

232. One's rule, as elsewhere, is to take the meaning as literal, unless solid contextual reason appears to the contrary, as in 1:11; see note 225, above.

His second advent. But there still exists a limit, an approaching termination to the life *span* (cf. Ex 23:26, Isa 65:20), so that this data may not be assigned to the ultimate New Jerusalem—see (d) below.

A final distinguishing feature of the millennium is its permanence: "I will plant them upon their land; and they shall be *lō . . . ōdh, no more* plucked up," Amos 9:15. This Hebrew phrase, or its positively stated equivalent, *adh-ōlām, unto perpetuity,* "for ever," constitutes a regular clue[233] to the period of the future Messianic kingdom; e.g., "The fool shall *no more* be called noble" (Isa 32:5; cf. Jer 30:8); for, as already observed, the millennium does constitute the first segment of eternity.[234]

(d) Indications of final times. The millennium terminates with a destruction of heaven and earth as then constituted. It is true that the heavens are said to "split apart" or "open" at Christ's premillennial coming, Revelation 6:14, 19:11; but following Gog's postmillennial revolt, "earth and heaven fled away, and no place was found for them," 20:11. To this latter event must therefore be referred Isaiah 34:4 and also Haggai 2:6–7a, 21–23, for Hebrews 12:26–27 explains the latter as "the removing of those things which can be shaken."[235] To the period of the final judgment are then to be assigned all references to the divine sentencing of men to their ultimate destiny.[236]

Yet the characteristics of the millennium have been found to possess an eternal validity, so that they are carried over bodily into the Bible's description of the new, final earth. It is then well nigh impossible in the contexts of the OT to distinguish the two, except at those points where the analogy of Revelation 21–22 makes it possible to discern certain features, as pertaining in particular to the final state of restoration. The only exception to this carryover is that such aspects of the first stage of the eternal kingdom as may have been due to the presence of the unregenerate will, per force, reach their termination. After the final resurrection, for example, there

---

233. With occasional exceptions: cf. Isa 32:14, which declares in reference to Sennacherib's attack on Jerusalem, "The hill and the watch-tower shall be for dens for ever" (See above, p. 18). So in v. 17 the prophet predicts, "The work of righteousness shall be peace [in 701 B.C.]; and the effect of righteousness, quietness and confidence for ever." J. A. Alexander, *Commentary on the Prophecies of Isaiah,* II:5, proposes, "The phrase *adh ōlām,* not being limited in this case as it is in v. 14 must be taken in its widest sense." But "tranquility of mind and permanent security" (Adam Clarke, ad loc.) may still be true for the individual, so that 701 seems again to be the proper time of fulfillment. See also Jer 32:12b–14, that "they shall not sorrow any more," on its postexilic accomplishment.

234. See above, p. 108.

235. Zeph 3:8b might seem similar: "All the earth shall be devoured in the fire of God's jealousy." But this appears rather to be a figurative description of Armageddon, v. 8a. Even if this were not the case, the scorching of men with fire does appear in the 4th bowl of God's wrath, Rev 16:8, just before Christ's return; and in Zeph 3:20 the regathering of Israel is associated with the burning, "at that time," which is thus not postmillennial.

236. See above, pp. 109–110.

will be no more death; "and the Lord Yahweh will wipe away tears from off all faces" (Isa 25:8; contrast 65:20 during the millennium). The fundamental feature of the final restoration lies in the unique presence of God with His own.[237] Predictions of the Messianic times that involve a sacramental sanctuary must therefore find their fulfillment in the future earthly kingdom rather than in the final New Jerusalem, because John said of the latter, "I saw no temple in it; for the Lord God, the Almighty, and the Lamb are its temple" (Rev 21:22). Indeed, "There shall no longer be any night; and they shall not have need of the light of the sun, because the Lord God shall illumine them; and they shall reign forever and ever" (22:5).

4. THE ORDER OF PREFERABILITY WHEN DECIDING BETWEEN ALTERNANATIVE POSSIBILITIES FOR PERIODS OF FULFILLMENT. Despite the presence of the various criteria that have been listed in the preceding section for the assignment of predictions to their divinely intended times of accomplishment,[238] instances still remain in which diverse, and yet acceptable, historical fulfillments are found to vie with one another for acceptance. By way of illustration, Isaiah 13:11 states that Yahweh "will punish the world for their evil . . . and I will cause the arrogance of the proud to cease." The context of the chapter speaks of Babylon (vv. 1, 19), which, according to the criterion of the passage's use of this very name (as noted above, p. 112), would suggest its accomplishment at the close of the exile (per. 8) and at the collapse of the Babylonian land before Persia. Yet the context of the surrounding paragraph concerns a darkening of the sun because of the wrath of Yahweh (vv. 10, 13), which, according to the criterion of cataclysm (as noted above, p. 115), would suggest its fulfillment at the return of Christ (per. 15). It happens that in this case of Isaiah 13:11 the word for "the world" is not the ambiguous noun éres, "earth" or "land," but a term that is almost always universal, tēvēl, "the continents,"[239] so that the alternative of cosmic, eschatological wrath is the one to be chosen. Methodologically, one may select six basic types of evidence for deciding upon alternative dates of fulfillment. They are here listed in an order of their descending importance and are illustrated from the relatively uncomplicated predictions found in the historical Books of Kings.

(i) Statements of identification appearing in the immediate context. In I Kings 11:31, for example, the prophet Ahijah gave to Jeroboam ten pieces of a rent mantle, symbolizing that he would receive the rule over ten of the tribes of Israel; and then in the course of this very event, which is

237. Payne, *Theology*, p. 503.
238. And indeed, sometimes because of these very criteria, when two or more may seem to apply to a single oracle.
239. KB, p. 1018.

described in the following chapter, 12:15 specifies that it was "brought about to establish the word which Yahweh spake by Ahijah."

(ii) Statements of identification drawn from other places in Scripture. In I Kings 5:5 Solomon explains his construction of the temple as being what "Yahweh spake unto David my father, saying, 'Thy son, whom I will set upon thy throne, shall build the house for My name.'" Provided only that one grants the inspiration of this passage in Kings, it settles automatically any question about the fulfillment of II Samuel 7:13a, which it quotes. God, that is, serves as His own best interpreter for His earlier predictions; and this analogy of Scripture must, for the believer, take precedence over all criteria that are listed hereafter.

(iii) Identifiable factors arising from content. In I Kings 9:7 Yahweh forecasts, "I will cut off Israel out of the land which I have given them; and this house, which I have hallowed for My name, will I cast out of My sight." The analogy of history, with its known exile of Judah and with its record of Nebuchadrezzar's burning of the Solomonic temple in August of 586 B.C., can leave little doubt about the fulfillment in this case.[240]

(iv) Contextual uniformity. The same passage of 9:7 goes on to predict: "Israel shall be a byword among all peoples." Presumably this oracle refers to the same calamity of 586 that had been spoken of just before, and to nothing else. Yet uniformity of context may not be a totally reliable guide, should other factors suggest the presence of phenomena such as progressive prediction or prophetic telescoping.[241]

(v) Preferability of nearest fulfillment. In II Kings 21:12 Yahweh warned Manasseh, "Behold, I bring such evil upon Jerusalem and Judah that whosoever heareth it, both his ears shall tingle." The fulfillment is not stated (so as to invoke methods i or ii); a precisely identifiable element such as the burning of the temple (as in iii) is lacking; and the idea commences fresh in the context (eliminating method iv). But in light of the normal relevance of prophecy to its own times,[242] one would tend to expect a fairly contemporaneous fulfillment. In this particular instance, the piety of Manasseh's grandson Josiah did succeed in postponing the threatened doom until after Josiah's death in 609 (22:20); but 23 years later all was indeed swept away.

(vi) Similarity in language. A century before Manasseh, according to

---

240. Yet the value of such allusions may be limited by indefiniteness, either of the point of reference or of the prophet's relationship to it. Two highly debatable examples concern Jeremiah's references to "proclaiming the covenant" (11:6) and to the "evil out of the north" (1:15, etc.). By the former did he mean the ancient Sinaitic testament or Josiah's immediate reformation of 622, and by the latter did he refer to the Scythians or to the Babylonians? And if he intended the Scythians, did he then relate the prophecy in 6:22–23 to them as captors or as the mere terrors which historical analogy suggests? Cf. J. B. Payne, "The Arrangement of Jeremiah's Prophecies," ETS B, 7 (1964), 122.

241. See sections D-3 and D-5 below.

242. See above, p. 4.

II Kings 11:17 in the ASV, "Jehoiada made a covenant between Yahweh and the king [Joash] and the people, that they should be Yahweh's people." In point of fact the term here used for covenant or testament is definite, *hab-b'rīth*, "the covenant," which suggests a renewal of the well-known Sinaitic testament.[243] The promise that they should be Yahweh's people likewise recalls the language of Exodus 19:5 and suggests a reaffirmation of the typical truth of the blood of the testament and of its pointing forward to the newer testament of Jesus Christ (see under Gen 15:10, below). Yet similarity in language may be subject to modification by the factors previously listed: context may demonstrate, for example, that "the horn, a little one," of Daniel 7:8 need not be identical with the "little horn" of 8:9; and terms such as "the day of Yahweh" may have an extended range of meanings.[244]

A number of additional qualifications concern the fifth of the above-listed methods or principles. The standard of "earliest possible fulfillment" is based on the fundamental definition of a prophet as "a spokesman of God's special revelation"[245] and hence as a preacher to his contemporaries. Terry therefore explains, "Prophecy deals mainly with the persons and events of the times in which it was first uttered. The prophet was a power of God, a living messenger to kings and peoples. He voiced God's message for the time."[246] Edersheim correspondingly concludes, "Prediction would, with rare exceptions, be a sign of immediate judgment or deliverance."[247] This leads in turn to what might be called the policy of "conservative interpretation." That is, if there is uncertainty over fulfillment, it is usually best to choose the least spectacular accomplishment and the one closest to hand. The interpreter will then less easily become guilty of reading fancies into Scripture. The "conservative" process starts indeed with an assumption that many passages may even possess a wholly past, nonpredictive meaning.[248]

But it is significant that the above-quoted statements of Terry and Eder-

---

243. For historical confirmation of this sort of procedure, see below, in the introduction to Deuteronomy.
244. See below, under section D-2.
245. See above, p. 4.
246. Op. cit., p. 326.
247. *Prophecy and History in Relation to the Messiah*, pp. 146–147.
248. See Section II, above. Isa 22:1–14, for example, on the "tumultuous city," despite the objection of Young, NIC, *Isa*, II:88, may be no more than descriptive. "The period is probably that of Sennacherib: what is described is the revelry to which the city gave itself up when the Assyrian king in 701 B.C. raised the siege, or blockade, of Jerusalem," ICC *Isa*, I:364; cf. II K 19:8. Leupold also, *Isa*, I:344, questions how much is predictive: there is "the usual style of Hebrew narrative relating a past event." So in vv. 3–4, the expressions, "All thy rulers fled away together . . . labor not to comfort me for the destruction," relate to the past. Leupold, however, adds, "Yet we feel that the pattern is broken in vv. 5–7. Then with v. 8 the text goes back to the narrative of the past." But even this section, in the ASV, is simply present, v. 5, and past, vv. 6–7, e.g. in the last named, "The horsemen set themselves in array at the gate"; cf. W. Fitch in NBC, p. 579, "But this *had* not sent them back to their God."

sheim speak only of prophecy as being "mainly" of immediate fulfillment; there are, and there must be, those "exceptions" which reach forward into the distant future.[249] To insist upon an exclusively near fulfillment, as liberalism *does*,[250] necessarily denies such miracles of word as the anticipations of Josiah and Cyrus, by name, in I Kings 13:2 and Isaiah 44:28–45:1; it converts Daniel's detailed "predictions" of the Seleucid Greek kings (11:5–39) into a Maccabean forgery; and it rules out truly Messianic prophecy altogether.

Furthermore, a stress on the principle of nearest possible fulfillment should always entail a corresponding stress on the full adequacy of the particular, close-at-hand accomplishment. Von Orelli insists, "A prophecy can only be regarded as fulfilled when the whole body of truth included in it has attained living realization."[251] Thus when Genesis 27:40 foresees Edom's shaking off of Israel's yoke, this cannot be associated with the Edomite king Hadad's presence as an adversary to Solomon (I K 11:14); for Solomon continued to receive his regular tribute (4:21; cf. 16:25). Under Jehoshaphat, a Hebrew deputy ruled Edom (22:47); and only with his son is Edom's independence for the first time recorded (II K 8:20); see the discussion under Genesis 25:23b.

Finally, the concept of near fulfillment and of the prophets' obvious interest in their own times must not be allowed to usurp the precedence over principles (i) and (ii) above, namely, over the verdict of Scripture itself. Fairbairn cautions: "We must be guided, not so much by any knowledge possessed, or supposed to be possessed, by the ancient worshippers concerning their prospective fulfillment, as from the light furnished by their realization in the great facts and revelations of the gospel."[252] A major example is that of the older testament as a whole: the shed blood was intended to signify a testamentary disposition (Heb 9:16–18), even on Sinai, though the Hebrews may not have realized this at the time.[253] A number of the early prophecies were probably misunderstood altogether. When Judges 4:9, for example, predicted, "Yahweh will sell Sisera into the hand of a woman," most would then have thought of Deborah, the leader and judge, who spoke the words; but its fulfillment came about through Jael, vv. 17–22. Antisupernaturalism may disguise its skepticism under appeals to the superior relevancy of near fulfillments. R. F. Horton thus spoke sharply against the interpretation of Micah 5:1 by E. B. Pusey, who understood it in reference to Roman attack upon Jerusalem, and said:

To Pusey and the old commentators all things were possible: inspiration was a divine freak, freed from all historical or psychological conditions. We are

249. Cf. Fairbairn's warning in this regard, p. 12 above, note 48.
250. See above, Section I, B-3, and below, III, D-5.
251. *Prophecy of Consummation*, p. 55.
252. *Typology*, I:145.
253. Payne, *Theology*, pp. 82–87.

bound to keep within more sober interpretation. . . . We may reasonably think that he foresaw the pre-exilic fall of Jerusalem . . . but to have foreseen the Roman siege hundreds of years later . . . could have served no spiritual purpose then.[254]

Yet in its own context Micah's verse does stand between a prediction of the Babylonian exile and restoration (4:10), followed by what appears to be one on the Maccabean triumphs (vv. 12–13), and a forecast of the incarnation of Christ, which is confirmed by the NT (5:2). Further, if warnings about divine chastisements upon Jerusalem through the Roman general Pompey in 63 B.C. and the Caesars' puppet king Herod in the decades that were to follow were held to be incapable of providing spiritual lessons for Micah's contemporaries, one wonders what value the prophet's word of the birth of the Ruler at Bethlehem (5:2) might have had for them either.

D. *Single Fulfillment*

In stressing as they did the principle of the *analogia Scripturae*, the leaders of the Protestant Reformation were acting under the conviction that "the true and full sense of any Scripture is not manifold but one."[255] Calvin, for example, would tolerate no deviation into esoteric allegorizations, such as had marked (and marred) medieval Catholic exegesis; he insisted, "The true meaning [singular] of Scripture is the natural and obvious meaning, by which we ought resolutely to abide."[256] But that this issue has still a contemporary interest and importance is indicated by Ramm's statement that "one of the most persistent hermeneutical sins is to put two interpretations on one passage of Scripture, breaking the force of the literal meaning and obscuring the word of God."[257] One might cite, for instance, Erich Sauer's claim (1952) about holy writ: "Everything is historically conditioned and yet at the same time interpenetrated with eternity. All is at once . . . temporal and super-temporal. . . . They [the prophets] speak of the return from Babylon and simultaneously promise the gathering of Israel at the still future kingdom."[258]

1. THE PROBLEM OF MULTIPLE SENSE. The terminology that is employed to identify the above-illustrated phenomenon shows considerable

254. Cent, *Minor Prophets*, I:250.
255. Westminster Confession of Faith, I:9.
256. On Gal 4:22.
257. Op. cit. (1950 ed.), p. 87. For representative statements on the question of double fulfillment, cf. (pro) John Davison, *Discourses on Prophecy*, p. 196; (pro, via the path of types), Fairbairn, *Typology*, bk. 1, ch. 5; and (con) Terry, op. cit., pp. 383–389.
258. *The Dawn of World Redemption*, p. 145.

variety. Willis J. Beecher lists a series of designations that are frequently introduced—some indicate that the NT gives a new sense: e.g., double meaning, double reference, manifold fulfillment, or antitypical fulfillment; others indicate that the NT, in some way, reflects unexpressed thoughts that are said to underlie the OT forms: e.g., generic prophecy, or representation of the promise (which is his own preference). Yet concerning these alleged categories, Beecher himself grants that "some are of a pretty desperate character"; and it would appear the part of honesty to recognize all of them as describing, in essence, that what the NT is presenting is simply "accommodated or allegorical interpretation."[259]

Two modern movements have in particular been characterized by an appeal to the hermeneutic of double sense. On the one hand stands liberalism, with its overall denial of authentic prediction. Yet in the attempt of its stepchild, neoorthodoxy, to preserve a measure of relevance for the prophetic text, a number of scholars have recently invoked a distinction regarding Scripture between "what it meant," as originally given, and "what it means," i.e. that supposedly more valid circle of thought which today's interpreters find they may adduce from it.[260] A variation on this theme has been urged by that branch of Roman Catholic expositors who agree with the conclusions of liberalism's exegesis of the OT but who still feel bound (by church tradition) to maintain something of the NT's understanding of prophecy as well. Cuthbert Lattey, for example, inclines toward a correlation of Proverbs 30:19 *and* 20 with Isaiah 7:14 and toward an admission that the Isaianic noun which is usually rendered "virgin" might even signify an adulteress.[261] Furthermore, he hesitates to treat the prophecy in a non-literal fashion or to take refuge in typology.[262] He therefore adduces a principle of "compenetration," meaning that the oracle "was not uttered *primarily* with reference to things at that time."[263] By means of this distinction he is able to accept the critical approach to Isaiah 7 but at the same time to maintain a traditional Roman approach to Matthew 1.

On the other hand stands dispensationalism, with its presupposition that the church cannot be predicted within the OT writings.[264] But one gains the feeling that its advocates are wrestling with an unabated need to preserve the relevance of its pages for today's ordinary readers.[265] This, plus the movement's absorbing interest with eschatological events, has resulted in

---

259. *The Prophets and the Promise*, p. 404.
260. Cf. K. Stendahl, "Biblical Theology," IDB, I:418–432; and see above, p. 24.
261. "The Emmanuel Prophecy: Isaias 7:14," CBQ, 8–9 (1946–47).
262. 9 (1947), 151.
263. 8 (1946), 370.
264. See above, p. 98.
265. Pentecost, for example, op. cit., pp. 46–47, describes at length "the law of double reference," by which he may mean simply a combining of two successive events in one prophetic context (as below, sec. 5, "telescoping"); but he speaks also of "double meaning" within a single prophecy. Cf. note 277, below, or Scofield's discovery of detailed points on the life of Christ in even the boards and the hooks of the tabernacle, Reference Bible, pp. 103, 105.

such excess in the allegation of double or multiple senses that Berry, after providing documentation,[266] has harshly accused the position of "a practically complete neglect of historical background." He asserts, though far too sweepingly, "They give the impression of being honest in purpose but of having no conception of what real interpretation is."[267]

The problem of multiple sense comes to the fore at points of either real or apparent[268] claim on the part of the NT to exhibit the fulfillment of OT predictions. The approach of many hermeneutical manuals, though differing in details of definition, is to propose two alternatives. Fairbairn elaborates as follows:

> The opinion contended for, on the one side, has been, that the predictions contain a double sense—the one primary and the other secondary, or the one literal and the other mystical; while, on the other side, it has been maintained that the predictions have but one meaning, and when applied in NT Scriptures, in a way not accordant with that meaning, it is held to be simple accommodation of the words.[269]

This latter view dominated the older liberal scholarship, being required by its commitment to evolutionary antisupernaturalism.[270] Fairbairn, who on the basis of NT analogy insists that the passages in question must be truly predictive of Messianic times, naturally rejects such a view: "The single sense contended for has thus too often differed from the real sense, and many portions have been stript of the evangelical import."[271] But one should rightly ask whether dual fulfillment, or double sense, is the only alternative to "one meaning, with the NT not accordant with that meaning." There would seem to remain another possibility, namely, "one meaning with the NT accordant with, and specifically expressing, that meaning."[272]

Three basic reasons appear for maintaining the concept of one (NT) meaning as opposed to that of the so-called dual fulfillment. (a) The first arises from the very nature of hermeneutics. John Owen, the 17th century Puritan, long ago laid down the dictum, "If the Scripture has more than one meaning, it has no meaning at all;"[273] and most of the more recent writers have agreed that dual fulfillment is incompatible with objective

266. E.g., its finding forecasts of the eschatological campaigns of the Antichrist in Hab 1 or Dan 8 or 9.
267. *Premillennialism and OT Prediction*, pp. 6–12.
268. Pentecost, op. cit., p. 11, thus speaks of Jer 31:15, on "Rachel weeping for her children," as having a "partial fulfillment in Mt 2:17–18," though Jeremiah's oracle would seem to have no necessary connection with it; see below, p. 129, and introduction to Matthew.
269. *Typology*, I:13.
270. See below, introduction to Psalms, notes 6 and 23.
271. Op. cit., I:136.
272. Clinton Lockhart, in his *Messianic Message of the OT,* has worked out in some detail these, not two, but three alternative approaches for certain passages.
273. In Terry, op. cit., p. 493; cf. Berkhof, *Principles*, p. 58, "It is absolutely foreign to the character of language that a word should have two, three, or even more significations in the same connection. If this were not so, all communication among men would be utterly impossible."

interpretation. Ramm says, "What a passage really means is one thing. If it meant many things, hermeneutics would be indeterminate."[274] Fairbairn himself observes that such an approach causes uncertainty of application and makes the meaning too general for practical employment.[275]

Yet Fairbairn and others have attempted to substitute a modified variety of dual fulfillment, based on the forms of Hebrew prophecy. The presence, however, within Scripture of figurative language hardly serves as a justification for the concept of multiple meaning. As R. T. Chafer has pointedly remarked, "The literal sense of the words employed in a figure of speech is not to be taken as the meaning of the figure, but rather the sense intended by the use of the figure. In all such cases, therefore, there is but one meaning. In such cases the literal is not the sense."[276] Most common is an appeal to the fact of typology. As Sauer puts it, "A typical prophecy . . . has a double fulfillment. . . . It is fulfilled by the appearance of the type . . . and is completely fulfilled when this type also is fulfilled in the Messianic development. . . . In this sense prophecy concerning the Israelitish kingdom is frequently at the same time a prediction relating to the period of the church."[277]

But the typical approach fails on at least two grounds. First, many of the alleged Biblical passages do not satisfy the above-worked-out definition of types.[278] In Psalm 40, for example, concerning Christ's words to Yahweh, "I delight to do Thy will," O. S. Stearns says flatly, "The Psalmist was a type of Christ."[279] But a type must have a unified symbolism for all ages; yet if David delighted to do God's will, that in itself had no contemporary symbolical significance. Further, a type must be specifically defined so as distinctively to represent that matter which still lies in the future; but as

274. Op. cit. (1950 ed.), p. 88. So Terry, op. cit., p. 413, "The moment we admit the principle that portions of Scripture contain an occult or double sense we introduce an element of uncertainty in the sacred volume, and unsettle all scientific interpretation"; and Berkhof, op. cit., p. 57, "Scripture has but a single sense, and is therefore susceptible to a scientific and logical investigation. . . . To accept a manifold sense . . . makes any science of hermeneutics impossible, and opens wide the door for all kinds of arbitrary interpretations."

275. *Typology*, I:135.

276. *The Science of Biblical Hermeneutics*, pp. 80–81.

277. Op. cit., pp. 146–147; he concludes, "Spiritualizing . . . one should do and not leave the other undone." Cf. Fairbairn, *Typology*, I:109, "David bore typical relations to Christ. . . . What had formerly taken place in the experience of the type must substantially renew itself again in the experience of the great antitype," or Barrows, op. cit., pp. 618–622, on the argument for typical words (not just historically objective types).

278. See especially pp. 51–56.

279. *A Syllabus of the Messianic Passages in the OT*, p. 295. So Fairbairn, *Typology*, I:123–124, claims, "What took place in him [David] was at once the beginning and the image of what . . . was to be accomplished." Yet elsewhere on these same pp. he is forced to grant, "It is impossible by any fair interpretation of the language to understand the description of another than Christ"; see below, introduction to Psalms, note 22, and the discussion under Ps 40:6c.

Stearns himself admits, if David be typical in Psalm 40, then the term "type" may be applied "to any sufferer who thus yielded freely to the divine will."[280] Again, a type must be divinely purposed; but there appears to be no Biblical evidence that God intended David's obedience as a type of Christ. A second ground, and more serious, arises because this approach takes typology, which concerns objects and actions that are symbolic of the future, and forces it to apply to verbal statements, which is a quite different matter. Terry pinpointed this logical fallacy, still so widely held:

> As many persons and events of the OT were types of greater ones to come, so the language respecting them is supposed to be capable of a double sense. The second psalm has been supposed to refer both to David and to Christ, and Isa 7:14–16, to a child born of a virgin who lived in the time of the prophet, and also to the Messiah. . . . But it should be seen that in the case of types the language of Scripture has no double sense. The types themselves are such because they prefigure things to come, and this fact must be kept distinct from question of the sense of language used in any particular passage.[281]

(b) One finds a second reason for single, unified meaning in the evidence from the NT. As Lockhart described the decisive attitude of Acts 2:29–31 toward Psalm 16, "The apostle Peter argues that David could not refer to himself, for he died and saw corruption, but that he was a prophet, and foresaw that Jesus should be raised without corruption. . . . It seems not easy to mistake the apostle's meaning."[282] Terry thus concludes:

> The words of Scripture were intended to have one definite sense, and our first object should be to discover that sense and adhere rigidly to it. . . . We reject as unsound and misleading the theory that such Messianic psalms . . . have a double sense, and refer first to David or some other ruler, and secondly to Christ.[283]

In fact, from reading the NT, it is safe to say that one would never suspect the possibility of dual fulfillment.

(c) The third reason for single fulfillment is the evidence from the OT contexts. Fairbairn, for example, grants that his principle of multiple sense not infrequently fails to work out in the concrete cases where its presence is attempted to be shown.[284] Terry says flatly, "The language of Psalm 2 is not applicable to David or Solomon, or any other earthly ruler. . . . Isa 7:14 was fulfilled in the birth of Jesus Christ (Mt 1:22), and no expositor has ever been able to prove a previous fulfillment";[285] see below for a more detailed analysis of that area within which the concept of dual fulfillment is generally felt, if anywhere, to be the most necessary, namely in that of the

280. Loc. cit.
281. Op. cit., p. 384; and see above, pp. 22 and 106.
282. Op. cit., pp. 123–124.
283. Op. cit., pp. 384–385.
284. *Typology*, I:135.
285. Op. cit., p. 384.

Messianic psalms.[286] As has been stated by Berkhof, concerning the psalms that "give utterances of the suffering and triumphant Messiah . . . the deeper sense of the Bible does not constitute a second sense. It is in all cases . . . the proper sense of Scripture."[287]

2. COROLLARIES OF SINGLE FULFILLMENT. The standard of a single, nonmultiple sense in Biblical prediction leads one into related conclusions in respect to both the meaning and the usage of the prophecies of Scripture. On the one hand, the fact of but one legitimate accomplishment for each forecast promotes the possibility of diverse meanings when the same phrase may occur in more than one passage, particularly when approached upon the principle of a uniform period of fulfillment within each single context (see iv, in sec. B–4, above). That is, if the whole of Joel 2:18–26a is descriptive of Judah's recovery from an 8th-century locust plague, then the *mōrē*, (not "former rain," but) *teacher for righteousness, v.* 23, must also refer to some contemporary religious instructor of that nation, presumably Joel himself (see under Joel, prophecy No. 6, note 11), and not to the later leader of the Dead Sea sect at Qumran, or to Jesus the prophetic teacher from Galilee[288]—whether considered by way of intended fulfillment or by theories of double reference—even though in *other* contexts the phrase "teacher" may have Messianic connotations (Isa 2:3, John 3:2). So also in Obadiah,[289] just as the Jewish possession of the mount of Esau in v. 19a is Maccabean in its fulfillment, so too, presumably, are the Philistine, Samaritan, and Gileadite conquests in v. 19b; they stand accomplished without, for example, further (allegorized) reference to the expansion of the church. In Zechariah 2:11 (cf. v. 9), at the conclusion of a series of predictions, there occurs the expression, "And thou shalt know that the Lord of hosts hath sent Me unto thee." Verses 8–11 are all in the first person, of an angel speaking to the prophet, probably the divine Angel of Yahweh (2:3; cf. 1:11–12). Then in Zech 4:9 (cf. 6:15) comes the same phrase except for the number of the final pronoun—"unto you," plural—so that Keil claims that all four passages must be Messianic, referring to the Angel.[290] But the first-person speaker in chs. 4 and 6 seems to be Zechariah himself, and one must conclude that here again there are diverse meanings for identical words.

Certain of the Bible's set phrases have tended to encourage misunder-

286. See below, introduction to Psalms, and Payne, "So-called Dual Fulfillment in Messianic Psalms," ETS P (1953), 63–65.
287. Op. cit., pp. 59–60.
288. See E. B. Pusey, *Minor Prophets*, I:190, though modern conservatives are hesitant so to commit themselves; cf. NBC, in loc.
289. And cf. Zech 9:5—Ashkelon's not being inhabited would seem to apply to the same period as that in which the Philistines see the fall of Tyre, in 332 B.C., v. 4, though this desolation cannot be specifically proved for Ashkelon at this point.
290. *Minor Prophets*, II:248.

standing when subjected to a uniformity in meaning (cf. also sec. 3–c, below), either through a rigid assignment to the same period for accomplishment irrespective of context or, when diverse contexts are recognized, through added theories of a double sense, with the design that the reader may still end up with a uniform kind of fulfillment. Both Jeremiah 22:20 and 30:14 refer to "all thy [Zion's] lovers." But in the former instance these are destroyed, indicating Judah's leaders; and the passage is specifically predicting Jehoiachin's captivity in 597 B.C. (see under 13:19). In the latter instance Zion's lovers are the nations in alliance with her,[291] who forget her, specifically Egypt in 586. Similarly, both Zechariah 8:12 and 9:17 refer to the agricultural products of grain and wine; but the former depicts Judah's prosperity following the rebuilding of the temple in 515 B.C. (per. 9), and the latter describes her prosperity following the Maccabean victory of 165 (period 11). Of a corresponding nature are Ezekiel's references to "branches, yielding fruit"; but in 36:8 the fulfillment is postexilic (per. 9 again) and in 34:27, millennial (period 16). Particularly well known is the picture of every man sitting "under his vine and under his fig tree." In I Kings 4:25 (cf. I Macc 14:12) it denotes contemporary peace and prosperity; but in Micah 4:4 and Zechariah 3:10,[292] the millennium.

The possibility of diverse meanings extends beyond phrases into the related matter of the concepts that they represent. Girdlestone's *Grammar of Prophecy* contains, for example, a section on the idea "The Lord cometh"[293] which concludes that the expression indicates a range of "various visitations and actions of God. . . . In some passages the time referred to is already past; in others it appears to be still future, e.g. the second coming of Christ." Thus in Psalm 50:3, the teaching that "our God cometh and doth not keep silence" concerns matters of His immediate admonition to the saints, v. 7;[294] and in Matthew 10:23 (*q.v.*) the concept which is forecast by "the coming of the Son of Man" seems to be that of God's visitation upon the Jews through the Romans in A.D. 70. But Psalm 96:13 speaks of God's coming for the Messianic rule of the earth. An idea conveyed through a more figurative expression relates to the Lord's "roaring from Zion." Originally, in Amos 1:2, this depicted Yahweh's punishments that should come upon Israel. But these words are quoted in Joel 3:16a in

291. JB, pp. 1298, 1300.
292. Keil here exhibits an undue stress upon uniformity of context (principle iv, above) by associating Zech 3:10 with v. 9b, preceding, on Christ's atonement: "By the wiping away of all guilt and iniquity . . . all the discontent and all the misery which flow from sin will be swept away, and a state of blessed peace will ensue for the purified church of God," op. cit., II:262. But by so doing he disregards the parallelism in the Zecharian cycles between 3:10 and 6:13 (the principle of contextual indication of meaning, with its priority of iii, above; and cf. pp. 130 and 448 below).
293. Pp. 56–57.
294. V. 6, indeed, is already past: lit., "The heavens have declared [waw consec. with the impf.] His righteousness."

reference to God's defense of the church at His return, while Hosea 11:10 uses this figure to identify His specific summoning call for the church's rapture.

These last examples suggest the special care with which the interpreter must be on guard against insisting upon a uniformity in the meaning of the Bible's symbols. It is obvious that the "lion" may represent power that is either good (Yahweh, Hos 11:10, and the Messiah, Rev 5:5) or evil (Satan, I Pet 5:8, and the Antichristian beast, Rev 13:2). Yet commentators have become involved in exegetical incongruities by insisting, e.g., that leaven must uniformly represent an increase that is evil.[295] The figure of "bringing back the captivity" seems originally to have connoted the release of a man from an imprisonment for debt, and hence to convey the general idea of a restoration of fortune (see under Joel 2:32b, 3:1). Prophecies employing this figure may then refer to the Persian restoration of the Jews from exile, so that they may eventually occupy the Philistine plain (Zeph 2:7), or to their millennial regathering (3:20); compare the idea of the coming of the church with Christ to Palestine, in the first cited passage, in Joel 2:32–3:1. Again, the figurative term of "the corner" indicates a leader who sustains a government (Jd 20:2 [ASV, "chiefs"], I Sam 14:38 [same], Isa 19:13). The expression may then be applied to Yahweh's teaching, Isaiah 28:16, or to Israel itself, Ps 118:22;[296] but at other points it appears best to limit the significance of "the corner" to its earlier meaning of human leadership among the Hebrews, e.g. in Zechariah 10:4 specifically to that of Judas Maccabeus, as an anticipated deliverer.

But while the principle of single fulfillment may restrict a given phrase to but one originally intended meaning in each context and thus produce a diversity of potentialities for the same phrase at different points, it still, on the other hand, leaves open the possibility of a wide usage for prophecy by way of subsequent application. The above-noted references in Psalms and Isaiah to "the corner" are applied to Christ in the NT (Mt 21:42, Acts 4:11, I Pet 2:7, and Rom 9:33, 10:11, I Pet 2:6, respectively), as a period which exhibits *similar* situations, though not the ones described in the OT. As Terry explains, "The sense in every case is direct and simple; the applications and illustrations are many."[297]

The NT epistles thus repeatedly quote OT prophecies, though not in reference to their actual fulfillments; for example, II Corinthians 6:16 cites Leviticus 26:11 (on God's presence with His people in the yet future testament of peace), 6:17 cites Isaiah 52:11 (on Israel's departure from unclean Babylon), and 6:18 freely renders Hosea 1:10 (on the inclusion of Gentiles in the family of God), all to illustrate the Christians' present enjoyment of the presence of God and our need to maintain separation from the uncleanness of the world, though only the last, Hosea 1:10, had

---

295. C. Feinberg, *Premillennialism or Amillennialism?* p. 71.
296. See above, pp. 34, 79.
297. Op. cit., p. 385.

this originally in mind. Terry therefore makes it clear that, "We may readily admit that the Scriptures are capable of manifold practical *applications*; otherwise they would not be so useful for doctrine, correction, and instruction in righteousness (II Tim 3:16),"[298] though he remains firm in his insistence upon single fulfillment for Biblical prophecy.

3. PROGRESSIVE PREDICTION. Although the individual prophecies of Scripture are best understood each in terms of its one intended accomplishment, there may appear within a broad Biblical context a series of separate forecasts that together exhibit a pattern of chronological progress in fulfillment, the whole of which may be identified as a progressive prediction. At the simplest, a single predictive verse may possess two parts, for example in one of the opening disclosures by Yahweh to Hosea: "Yet a little while and I will avenge the blood of Jezreel upon the house of Jehu," 1:4a, fulfilled in the murder of the last of Jehu's dynasty in 752 B.C., "and [I] will cause the kingdom of the house of Israel to cease," 1:4b, executed 30 years later, at the fall of Samaria to Assyria in 722. Somewhat more developed is the six-verse sequence that is found in Zechariah 2:6–11a. This passage commences with a word about the return of the Jews from Babylon, a process which was then already in progress (vv. 6–7); but it moves on to predict: the divine punishments that would fall upon the ancient predatory nations, especially Judah's contemporary Persian master (vv. 8–9); the coming of God in Christ to dwell in the midst of His people (v. 10);[299] and the subsequent growth of the church (v. 11a).

Upon this sort of a basis, the Bible's progressive predictions may then be traced out into truly complex patterns, either of repetition or of specification. For the former, Jeremiah 31:2–30 exhibits a phenomenon of alternative predictive thoughts. Following an introduction, vv. 2–3, in which Israel's forthcoming exile is illustrated by the parallel of the people's former wilderness experience, the passage then prophesies both:

| the exile, and | 7 | 10–11 | 15 | 18–20 | 22 | 28a |
| the return, in vv: 4–6 | 8–9 | 12–14 | 16–17 | 21 | 23–27 | 28b, |

to which vv. 29–30 form a practical conclusion, recognizing individual responsibility as operative throughout the process. For the latter,

Micah 4:9–5:4, and
v. 9   the fall of Jerusalem, 586
10a   Babylonian exile
10b   Persian restoration, 538
11–13 Maccabean victories
5:1   the fall of Jerusalem to
        Pompey in 63 B.C.
2–3a   the birth of Christ
3b   conversion of the Gentiles
4   the Messiah's millennial rule

Jeremiah 3:6–18, shows a detailing in sequence:
v. 6–10 Judah's preexilic sin (nonpredictive)
11–14   the return to Zion
15   the presence of good postexilic leaders
16   increase in the spiritual church
17   God's throne in Zion
18   The regathering of the nation of Israel

298. Ibid., p. 383.
299. And see also vv. 5b and 11b–13, before and after.

With lesser symmetry in its pattern—as is often true, because of the practical purposes of Biblical prophecy—but still manifesting a specific chronological progress, is Micah 6:14–7:17:[300]

6:14–15	the plundering of 8th-century Judah by Assyria
6:16, 7:4, 8a	its desolation in 586 by Babylon
	(ethical observations are inserted by Micah in 7:1–3 and 5–7)
7:8b–9, 11a	the rebuilding of Jerusalem and its walls, by Nehemiah, 444
	(a minor retrogression on the fall of Babylon in v. 10)
11b–12	Gentile incorporation into Israel the church
13	the desolation of Israel the nation by Rome in A.D. 70
15–17	Gentile nations submit to Christ in the millennium

Another feature that is common within Biblical prophecy is that of repeated teaching by the means of major blocks of predictive matter, e.g. the series of four great visions revealed to the prophet Daniel (chs. 7, 8, 9, and 10–12), in elaboration upon the dream that he interpreted earlier in his career (ch. 2). When such major repetition is then combined with a parallel progressiveness in each part, the result is cyclic prophecy. This characteristic may be exhibited on a reduced scale in the two cycles of Jeremiah, ch. 30. Verses 1–3 form an introduction, on Israel's restoration. Then follow two (or three?) progressive predictions in:

	vv. 4–9,	and vv.	10–22:
Exilic fear	4–7a	10a	12–15
Judah saved from exile, 538 B.C.	7b	10b–11a	17–19
Babylon broken	8a	11b	16
Eschatological Judah, no more to be oppressed	8b		20
David raised up as millennial ruler	9		21a
but also as ransoming (NT) priest (anticipating ch. 31)[301]			21b–22;

and a conclusion, vv. 23–24, returns to Judah's immediate anticipation of exile, under the figure of a tempest of Yahweh's wrath that is bursting forth upon the head of the wicked.

The phenomenon of cyclic prophecy is particularly characteristic of the continuous and consciously literary prose of Biblical apocalyptic.[302] Predictive cycles appear with the greatest consistency in Zechariah and Revelation, the climactic apocalypses of the OT and NT respectively; but they

---

300. From the liberal standpoint Horton, Cent, *Minor Prophets*, I:268, questions the very possibility of predictions with accomplishments at the later points in such a sequence: "It is one thing, by ignoring time and distance of events, to find 'fulfillments' of obscure prophecies in the long range of history, and quite another to trace out the meaning of the prophet's oracles, as they appeared to him. The former method has its uses and is justified by the manner in which the NT quotes from the Old; but the latter method is the only one which sober exegesis can attempt."

301. For those sections of ch. 31 which lie outside its main, repetitive body (see above, p. 129) carry on with the Messianic themes of ch. 30: in vv. 1, 31–34, Christ's priestly work at His 1st coming; and in vv. 35–40, His kingly work at His 2nd.

302. See above, p. 86.

also evidence themselves in Isaiah and Ezekiel,[303] and in other among the more predictive of the Bible's prophecies.[304] The latter, and most clearly apocalyptic, portion of Zechariah, for example, commences with a compressed cycle in 9:1–10:

> vv. 1–5 Alexander the Great's campaign of 332 B.C.
> 6 subsequent Philistine decline
> 7–8 Maccabean successes
> 9 the incarnation of Christ as the king, in His humility
> 10a the fall of Jerusalem, A.D. 70
> 10b church preaching of the gospel
> 10c the millennial reign of Christ the king, in His glory

But as Barnes notes in respect to v. 13 that follows, "The prophet turns back to portray events which must precede the coming of Zion's King, announced already in v. 9";[305] and the remaining sections of the prophecy fall into three definite cycles—9:11–ch. 10, 11–13:6, and 13:7–ch. 14—each of which elaborates different aspects to the basic outline of 9:1–10.[306]

The concept of progressiveness within a series of predictions may further be applied to one of the previously noted corollaries to the idea of single fulfillment—namely the first such, that of possibly diverse meanings for one phrase if it appears in different contexts.[307] When so applied, this concept produces an important principle for the understanding of Biblical prophecy: that of the progressive significance of certain of the terms that identify the times of fulfillment for Scriptural predictions. The OT phrase which is most comprehensive in its denotation of God's progressive intervention into human history, that is, of "the time of the manifestation of some special attribute or purpose of God,"[308] is *yōm Yahwe,* "the day of the Lord." Its first specific Biblical citation appears in the mouths of certain of the contemporaries of Amos, about 760 B.C. These Israelites, confident of their position as members of God's elect people, were eager for the "day" to put in its appearance, that they might inherit the earthly blessings foretold by Moses and others. They may have had in mind such an occurrence as "the 'day' of Midian" (Isa 9:4) half a millennium previously, when God had granted Israel a great victory and rich plunder from her Midianite enemies (Jd 7:25–8:21). Amos, however, preached that because of their sin they had forfeited their standing; and "the day" could involve them only in judgment, not blessing. The prophet therefore cried out words of doom: "Woe unto you that desire the day of Yahweh! Wherefore would ye have

303. See below, in the introductions to the respective books.
304. E.g. in Hos 1–3; see below, introduction to Hosea and Table 10.
305. Camb, *Hag-Mal,* p. 76.
306. See below, introduction to Zechariah and Table 11.
307. See above, pp. 126–128.
308. Girdlestone, op. cit., p. 55.

the day of Yahweh? It is darkness and not light!" (Amos 5:18; cf. Joel 1:15, 2:1). Isaiah too proclaimed: "The loftiness of man shall be bowed down, and the haughtiness of men shall be brought low; and Yahweh alone shall be exalted in that day" (Isa 2:17, cf. 3:18). The classic statement of this woeful aspect to the day of Yahweh comes to expression in Zephaniah's presentiments of impending distress and desolation, 1:15, "That day is a day of wrath."

Yet Zephaniah concludes his prophecy by reaffirming the ultimate truth of the older, popular optimism in reference to the day of the Lord: "Yahweh thy God is in the midst of thee, a mighty one who will save; He will rejoice over thee with joy" (3:17).[309] This same pattern, moreover, appears consistently in the other prophets, even in Amos (cf. 9:14). As Isaiah assured his people against the threats of the Assyrian, "And the light of Israel [God] will be for a fire, and it will burn and devour his thorns and his briers in one day" (10:17). This particular prediction seems then to have been fulfilled in the heavenly sent destruction of Sennacherib's host in 701 B.C. (37:36).

The "day" is thus characterized by an observable accomplishment of the general aims of divine redemption. It refers to that point in history at which the sovereign God lays bare His holy arm on the behalf of His testament and of its heirs, but without necessary reference either to miraculousness or to a particular point in chronology. As Pusey asserts, it is "any day in which He avengeth sin, any day of judgment, in the course of His providence or at the end."[310] The title *yōm Yahwe* can thus apply to almost all of the progressive stages of the OT's prophetic fulfillments. In Joel 1:15, 2:1, 11, the day of Yahweh consists of a contemporary locust plague, datable to about 735 B.C. Amos' day of darkness came at Assyria's exile of Ephraim in 722. In Zephaniah 1:7, it relates to the destruction of Jerusalem in 586; and in Isaiah 13:7, it concerns the capture of Babylon by the Medes and Persians in 539. Its point of specification thus advances down through the entire course of history and reaches its climax in passages such as Joel 3:14 and Zechariah 14:1–4 on Christ's second coming and His victory of Armageddon or Malachi 4:1, where the phrase, "Behold, the day cometh," refers to God's final judgment at the end of the world. The "day," moreover, may entail either a blessing or a curse. It may concern God's elect people Israel, or it may apply to the nations of the pagan world. It may produce effects that are cataclysmic and cosmic, or it may come to pass in a way that is quietly providential and localized. The one feature common to all of these passages is this: the day of Yahweh does concern the action of God in human history for the progressive accomplishment of His redemptive testament. Perhaps the most adequate, inclusive definition

---

309. See below, introduction to Zechariah and especially the brief chart on Zephaniah's use of "the day of Yahweh."
310. *The Minor Prophets*, I:170.

for the day of Yahweh is Vos's martially phrased suggestion: "The day monopolized by Jehovah as His day of victory."[311] By extension, the same concept of progressiveness in meaning that is found in the *yōm Yahwe* may apply to Scripture's abbreviated phrases: "in that day," or simply, "the day of. . . ." Isaiah, for example, when enabled to foresee tragedy for his immediate contemporaries, predicted, "It is a day of treading down, from the Lord, Yahweh of hosts" (22:5); and Micah spoke to Jerusalem of "the day of thy watchmen" (7:14), i.e., the day which the prophets had foretold, here meaning 586 B.C. Similarly, in N. Israel, Amos' expression, "Behold, the days come," might relate to the times of his own preexilic audience (8:11, per. 7); but it might also identify those of the millennium (9:13, per. 16). Of the phrase "In that day . . . ," S. R. Driver says, "The expression is a common one in the prophets, especially Isaiah, who use it for the purpose of introducing fresh traits in their pictures of the future."[312] In Zephaniah 3:11 it dates Israel's final conversion to the time of Christ's appearing; but in Micah 5:10–11, after the prophet had talked of the millennium in vv. 4–9, he suddenly goes back to 586 B.C., saying, "In that day . . . I will cut off the cities of thy land." For by "prophetic telescoping"[313] he saw it all at once, because even 586 was still 150 years ahead of Micah. So 7:11 informs Jerusalem of "a day for building thy walls [444 B.C.; but the prophet continues]; in that day shall the decree be removed." Yet v. 12 shows that *the decree* relates to the middle wall of partition, the removal of which will permit Gentiles to share in the Jewish church (A.D. 30 ff.). Finally, in Malachi 3:17 "the day," when God makes up His special treasure, refers to the final judgment.

Three, more particularized, phrases yet possess this same relativistic and progressive character. Two of them, which occur in Habakkuk 2:3, tell how the prophet's vision is for "the appointed time" and how it hasteth toward "the end." Both predict the fall of Babylon in 539, vv. 6–13; but v. 14 advances also to that time when "the earth shall be filled with the knowledge of Yahweh, as the waters cover the sea," quoting Isaiah 11:9 on the curseless situation in God's yet future Messianic kingdom (cf. "the end" as used in Dan 11:40, for a time just before this, or in I Cor 15:24, 1,000 years later). A third phrase is "the latter days" and its related expressions. Girdlestone states, "The last days are the latter or later days as compared with the present, and we must not restrict them to one fixed point."[314] He proceeds to give examples, starting with Genesis 49 and

---

311. Op. cit., p. 313; cf. Edmond Jacob, *Theology of the OT*, p. 319. Vos subsequently expressed preference for the idea of "the contrast between darkness and light [purging and conversion]," though both of these elements may be adequately subsumed under the above cited concept of "victory," Payne, *Theology*, pp. 464–465.
312. Camb, *Joel and Amos*, p. 226.
313. See below, sec. 5.
314. Op. cit., p. 54. Cf. W. J. Beecher, op. cit., p. 305, "There is nothing in the phrase itself to indicate whether the latter time to which it refers is proximate or remote or eschatological."

ending with John 6:39–54, on the resurrection of the righteous. Oehler observes, "In Genesis 49:1, where the expression first occurs, it refers to the time of the settlement of the tribes in the promised land."[315] Yet 49:10 does go on to speak of the Messiah's coming forth from the tribe of Judah; and Culver then generalizes, in his volume entitled *Daniel and the Latter Days*: "Whenever the scope of an OT prophecy is measured by these words . . . the times of the yet future establishment of the Messiah's kingdom on earth . . . are always within the scope of that prophecy."[316] Yet an examination of the OT passages where the phrase occurs yields evidence against the necessity for a consistent application to yet future periods. The predictions, for example, in Deuteronomy 4:30 and 31:29 were accomplished in the captivity of 586 B.C. and the subsequent fall of Babylon and postexilic restoration (32:36a, 40–43); they need have no reference to a great tribulation yet in store for modern Zionists.

The NT phrase that most frequently identifies various, progressive times for the fulfillment of its prophecies is that of the interchangeable expressions "kingdom of God" and "kingdom of heaven,"[317] together with their equivalents. Their application may be to the contemporaneous rule of Christ, Matthew 4:17 (= Mk 1:15), Acts 8:12—in Matthew 12:28 Jesus thus says, "But if I cast out demons by the Spirit of God, then the kingdom of God has come upon you"; and again, Luke 17:21, "The kingdom of God is in your midst."[318] Yet the "kingdom" may be used in a generalized way for life after death (II Tim 4:18 or Mt 5:12, cf. v. 10). It may concern the future earthly kingdom, which is not "to appear immediately" (Lk 19:11), whether as begun by the Messianic marriage feast (Mt 8:11), or as terminated by the final judgment (13:41). It may even identify the Christians' entering into the New Jerusalem after this judgment (7:21, cf. v. 23), into "the kingdom of their Father" (13:43; cf. Dan 12:3). Each instance must be decided by its own context, not by the mention of the term "kingdom."

4. DEVELOPMENTAL FULFILLMENT. The title "progressive prediction," as used in the preceding section, identifies the occurrence within one prophetic context of a connected series of prophecies with sequential periods of fulfillment. This concept is, however, to be distinguished from two other, related phenomena of Biblical prophecy: that of developmental accomplishment, which applies the principle of progressive fulfillment to a single comprehensive or generalized prophecy (this section), and that of prophetic telescoping, which describes those progressive predictions that exhibit chronological gaps in their fulfillment (sec. 5, following). Con-

---

315. Op. cit., p. 489.
316. P. 107.
317. See above, p. 96, note 170.
318. See above, p. 30.

cerning the former, Scripture occasionally demonstrates that when a prophecy possesses sufficient latitude there may occur a progressive completion in its fulfillment. Genesis 3:15, for example, speaks in quite general terms of the bruising of Satan's head, the fulfillment of which began at Christ's death and ascension (John 12:31–32, Rev 12:5, 10), is continued in the church (Rom 16:20), and will eventuate in his being cast both into the abyss (Rev 20:3) and, eventually, into the lake of fire (v. 10). Later in this same book, Genesis 17:4 foresees Abraham as the father of a multitude of nations. Genesis 25:16 then speaks of twelve princes of Ishmael, born during Abraham's lifetime, and from whom twelve nations later developed; Jacob's twelve tribes of Israel and Esau's Edomites came into being through his son Isaac, only after Abraham's death (29:31 ff., 36:8 ff.); at a later date the Samaritan nation at least claimed his ancestry, through "our father Jacob" (John 4:12) and Galatians 3:29 asserts his fatherhood over the Gentile Christians among the nations. W. J. Beecher thus speaks of "cumulative fulfillment,"[319] through which "a promise may continue being fulfilled through future period after period."[320]

Yet developmental fulfillment is to be distinguished from what Barrows, for instance, entitles "progressive fulfillment," but which refers in reality to certain reapplications[321] of a prophecy which happens to demonstrate a general principle. Barrows cites as an example Isaiah 6:9–13,

"Hear ye indeed, but understand not," with the threatened desolation that should follow. This prophecy had a true fulfillment [its only intended fulfillment, indeed] in the Babylonian captivity. . . . But [Barrows goes on to assert] the same prophecy had a more awful fulfillment in the generation of Jews who rejected our Lord and were destroyed by the armies of Rome (Mt 13:14–15, John 12:39–41, Acts 28:25–27, Rom 11:8, etc.), and its fulfillment is yet in progress.[322]

But when Paul, e.g., introduces this Isaianic passage in Acts 28, he uses the following introductory words, "The Holy Spirit rightly spoke through Isaiah to your fathers, saying, 'You will keep on hearing but not understand . . .'"; and he seems to appeal to it more as an illustration out of the past than as a prophecy being currently fulfilled.[323]

Above all, this principle of developmental fulfillment is to be distinguished from the use to which Beecher proceeds to put it, saying, "Most of the prophetic predictions are of this type,"[324] on the basis of which he then lapses into what is nothing more or less than dual meanings. A char-

319. Op. cit., p. 376.
320. Ibid., p. 129.
321. See above, pp. 128–129.
322. Op. cit., pp. 622–623.
323. The formula of citation in Matthew, "The prophecy of Isaiah is being fulfilled, which says . . . ," is but another example of the use of the verb (*ānā*) *plēróō*, to denote a mere correspondence, not the Isaianic intent; see above, p. 77–79.
324. Op. cit., p. 130.

acteristic instance is his approach to Psalm 22: "The prophet had primarily in mind some typical man or personified people of his own time, the representative of the promise for that generation."[325] To adduce his previously mentioned theory of "cumulative fulfillment" in such cases smacks of a subterfuge for disguising a belief in two different senses, one in the OT, and one as later claimed for this passage in the NT. Yet a legitimate developmental fulfillment concerns but a single object, whether Satan or Abraham's producing of nations. Actually, cases of true developmental fulfillment are rare in Scripture. Apart from the above-mentioned promises of Genesis 3:15, on Satan's being bruised, and 17:4, on nations coming from Abraham, there appear to be only seven other valid instances in Scripture: Genesis 9:25, on Canaan's becoming a servant; 12:7a, on Israel's being given Canaan; 25:23a, on Esau (Edom) serving Jacob; Leviticus 3:1, on the peace offerings as a type, of communion; 25:8, on the Year of Jubilee as a type, of release; Isaiah 11:1, on the Messiah as a *nēser* (branch, and Nazarene); Zechariah 13:7c, on the "sheep" being scattered after Christ's death. Even the passage about the world's being blessed in Abraham (Gen 12:3)—which Beecher asserts to be Scripture's fundamental promise, whose developing "fulfillment" is said to permeate and explain all other major Biblical predictions—seems in fact to have had but one intended accomplishment, in the outreach of the gospel to the Gentiles (see under Gen, prophecy No. 19).

A unique phenomenon is discussed below under Isaiah, prophecy No. 8: here the prophet predicts a ritualistic type (the future millennial temple), which will itself serve as an objective forecast of the unimpaired fellowship of God with His people in the ultimate New Jerusalem.

Finally, developmental fulfillment must be limited to those instances of genuinely expanding prophetic attainment, such as the above cases from Genesis 3:15 and 17:4. Matters of mere repetition have been covered by the principle stated in sec. C–4, above,[326] through one's resting upon the first adequate fulfillment. In the study that follows, the fact, for example, that Edom would shake off Israel's yoke (Gen 27:40) might have been noted as having attained historical accomplishment upon various occasions —e.g. after Amaziah's humiliation by N. Israel in 790 B.C. (discussed under Gen prophecy No. 50)—but the Edomites' original, effective revolt occurred half a century earlier, soon after the achieving of independence by Mesha of Moab to their north, II K 8:20, 22.[327] No further fulfillment was therefore necessary, and in the body of the following study such nondevelopmental repetitions pass without further mention.

325. Cf. his handling of the Messianic Branch in Zech 6, as "fulfilled in Zerubbabel," yet "ready for whatever completer fulfillment Yahaweh [*sic*] might have in store," p. 342; or his understanding of the prophecy in Ps 110, "It is an idea rather than a conception of fact," p. 348.

326. Pp. 118–119.

327. See above, p. 120.

5. PROPHETIC TELESCOPING. If an expanding prophetic attainment was what distinguished the progressiveness of developmental fulfillment, then, in contrast, it is a contracting horizon and an incompleteness in matters progressively predicted that characterizes what Vos entitled the "foreshortening of the beyond-prospect,"[328] but what many call simply "prophetic telescoping." That is to say, Biblical prophecy may leap from one prominent peak in predictive topography to another, without notice of the valley between, which may involve no inconsiderable lapse in chronology. Jeremiah 30:8, for example,[329] speaks of the breaking of Judah's Babylonian yoke; but this in turn suggests that more permanent (millennial) security when "strangers shall no more make him [Jacob] their bondmen." Edersheim cautions,

It is an entire misunderstanding to regard such prophecies as not applying to the Messianic future, because they occur in the midst of references to contemporary events. As the rapt prophet gazes upon those hills and valleys around him they seem to grow into gigantic mountains . . . while here and there the golden light lies on some special height . . . which applies exclusively to that Messianic Kingdom.[330]

It is partially because of this phenomenon that critical writers have been led to charge the prophets with erroneous hopes for a divine salvation that would have solely near-at-hand fulfillments, and to deny the miracle of long-range prediction altogether. A. B. Davidson thus seeks to restrict prophecy to matters that were consistently immediate in their intended accomplishment: "As one in the darkness thinks he hears the approach of an evil which he dreads, these prophets, when the sound of Jehovah's goings was more distinctly heard than usual, deemed that what they heard was the warning of His coming to shake terribly the earth. . . . His final appearance was closely connected with these manifestations."[331] But the primary author of Scripture, let it be affirmed, is God, who is not "in the dark," but who knows the end from the beginning. It would be fairer to postulate that the visionary experience, through which the prophets so often received their revelations from the Lord, may sometimes have been pictorial to the extent of merely by-passing such logical categories as chronology, whether near *or* distant.[332] Particularly concerning time, "The fulfillment is wider than either the hearers, or perhaps the speakers of it, had perceived";[333] compare Sec. IA1, above.[334]

"Telescoping" springs from the very nature of the prophetic task in

328. Op. cit., p. 311.
329. See above, p. 130, as charted.
330. Op. cit., pp. 127–128.
331. Op. cit., p. 380; and see above, p. 120.
332. See above, p. 6.
333. Edersheim, op. cit., p. 37.
334. Pp. 4–5, and notes 8 and 9.

proclaiming holiness, as found both in Christ and in society, both in the future and in the present.[335] Correspondingly, "The prophet must speak prophetically, yet intelligibly to his own contemporaries."[336] Yet the details of certain more distant developments lay beyond the grasp of the original hearers. F. E. Marsh thus speaks of "the law of variation" in respect to times of fulfillment, which he illustrates from Ezekiel 26.[337] In vv. 1–11 this passage speaks of the siege of Tyre by Nebuchadrezzar, 585–573 B.C., the "he" of vv. 8–11; but most of the remainder of the chapter has reference to Tyre's ultimate destruction in 332 by the troops of Alexander, the indefinite "they" from v. 12 onward. Such a shift in pronouns underscores the previous conclusion that while the prophets may, upon occasion, have seen all of Israel's future blessing as a united thing, God on the other hand did not, and He therefore saw to it that criteria for distinctions were written into the inspired text. Zechariah 8, for example, expatiates upon the promises for God's people; but: vv. 1–8 are millennial, on complete holiness and lengthened life spans "in those days" (v. 6); vv. 9–19 are postexilic, on material provisions and spiritual truth "in these days" (v. 9); and vv. 20–23 are again millennial, on Gentiles seeking the God of Israel in Jerusalem "in those days" (v. 23).

Scripture exhibits gradations in the degree of its prophetic telescoping. The phenomenon may be said to begin with certain near-at-hand predictions in which time sequences are passed by without stress. Amos 7:9, for instance, disregards the progressive development that is observable in Hosea 1:4[338] and reverses the two chronological elements, when it says that the sanctuaries of Israel are to be laid waste *and* the house of Jeroboam slain. More characteristically, the "foreshortening of the beyond-prospect" involves a forward leap directly from a given point in prophecy to the future kingdom of God's Messiah. In Habakkuk 2:13–14, the point of departure is the immediate threat of Babylon, from whose fall (v. 13) the prophet presses straight on to the millennium (v. 14). In Micah 2:12–13 the contextual point is that of the return of Judah's exiles from Babylonia in 538 (v. 12), which was then still two centuries ahead, but from which Micah advances to the return (i.e. the rapture) of Israel at Christ's second coming (v. 13). Obadiah 21 looks forward, first to Israel's judging Edom (in Maccabean times), and second to the kingdom's being the Lord's (millennial); cf. Dan 11:39–40. The prophets apparently viewed it all as one great redemptive act.

Not infrequently OT prophecy may point to Christ's first coming, which it proceeds to telescope into His second coming. In Malachi 3:1, "My messenger [John the Baptist, Mk 1:2, Mt 11:10] prepares the way before Me"; and so the Angel of the testament (Christ) comes to the temple, all in NT times (cf. Hag 2:9). But then Malachi 3:2–3 immediately asks, "Who

335. See above, p. 7.
336. Edersheim, op. cit., p. 129.
337. Op. cit., p. 255.
338. See above, p. 129.

can abide the [fearful, second] day of His coming," when the sons of Levi are purged so as to make offerings in righteousness, though sacrifice can be resumed only in the millennium. Perhaps the most classic instance of the telescoping of Christ's two advents is to be found in Isaiah 61:1–2, which is used by F. E. Marsh to illustrate what he calls "the secret of the significant break."[339] Here, at the synagogue in Nazareth, Christ quoted the passage as fulfilled in Himself (Lk 4:18–21); but He stopped after the words, ". . . to proclaim the favorable year of the Lord," without adding the next phrase, "and the day of vengeance of our God," which applies only to His second coming. Critical analysts, such as Oxtoby, deny this break and assume that the entire passage must have been used, even though it is not quoted, so as (in a general sort of way) "to reassure his hearers of divine favor." But as far as the original prophecy is concerned, Oxtoby must then say, *about it all,* "The prophet did not have Nazareth in mind"; and he can justify its use only because "under new circumstances . . . a new appropriateness had been sensed."[340] This theory of reinterpretation is not needed, however. The parts of Isaiah that our Lord quoted fit His first coming and the parts He omitted do not, but concern His second.

Yet OT prophecy does not invariably telescope Christ's two advents, nor is the church age any more of an interruption or "great parenthesis"[341] within OT prediction than are the longer telescoped periods that have been identified above. The prophetic surveys of Daniel 2, Zechariah 11, or Revelation 17 carry straight through the post-NT division of the Roman empire and the fall of its respective branches in A.D. 476 and 1453, and on to the Parousia of Christ. The sin of interpreters throughout the history of the Christian church has rather been that of assuming that their own point in time must be directly connected with our Lord's return. Evangelicals will disagree with Rowley's criticism of the Biblical apocalyptists but must recognize the validity of his basic contention: "Men, wth an exaggerated perspective of their own day, precisely like that of the apocalyptists, have believed that the prophecies had their own day in mind. . . . Where for more than two thousand years a hope has proved illusory, we should beware of embracing it afresh."[342] Our Christ *could* indeed come today, and prophecies of the last time such as II Timothy 3:1–7 or Revelation 6:11 *suggest* the present; but there remains the equal possibility of a telescoped interval between current conditions and the eschatological tribulation.

A final point of departure for both OT and NT telescoping is that of the earlier elements of the Messiah's future kingdom, as compared with certain later ones, and the millennium's coming between. Prophecies such as Daniel 12:2 or John 5:28–29 may bring together as one both the premillennial and the postmillennial phases of humanity's resurrection, and in Matthew

339. Op. cit., p. 360.
340. Op. cit., pp. 39–40.
341. Per dispensationalism, cf. Pentecost, op. cit., pp. 136–137.
342. Op. cit., pp. 157–158.

25:31–32 the final judgment may be directly linked to the Parousia of Christ. Such verses, however, do not disprove millennialism. The omission of data that are spelled out in other passages constitutes the essence of prophetic telescoping. The data may be factual. Zechariah 14:1–2, for example, speaks of nations fighting against Jerusalem. The occasion or reason in not here given, though this may be assumed to have been precipitated by Christ's appearance in the clouds, which had caused the conversion of the Jewish inhabitants of Jerusalem in 12:10; cf. the prediction of Christ's fighting against these nations in 14:3 immediately thereafter. Or the data may be chronological. The key to it all is whether the progressive revelation of later Scriptures requires an actual time separation. Revelation 20:4–6, 12–13, is thus clear on the fact of two resurrections, separated by the 1,000 years; and 19:19–21, 20:7–9, on two battles, one against the Antichrist-beast before the millennium and the other against Gog and Magog after it. But no such separation in history is explicated for the various aspects of the final judgment, or for a rapture before the tribulation as opposed to the first resurrection after it; so these latter factors of fulfillment are not to be separated by purportedly telescoped intervals of time.

E. *Limitations in the Comprehension of Fulfillments*

A primary purpose in prophetic exegesis should be to avoid as far as possible personal idiosyncrasies and to maintain objective standards of interpretation, such as are summarized at the close of this section. Nevertheless some uncertainties seem inevitably to remain; e.g. for Matthew 16:28, as discussed below under Matthew prophecy No. 28, a specific fulfillment is only "tentatively adopted."

1. LIMITATIONS DUE TO THE ORIGINAL RECORD. Some measure of ambiguity takes its rise from the very limitations within language. Girdlestone thus concedes, "Sacred truths can only come to us through the medium of human faculties, and largely through human terminology. . . . The Biblical words are as so many illustrations, pointing to something better, though in themselves inadequate to convey the whole truth."[343] For one's grasp of the totality of truth is no necessary corollary to his belief in inerrancy: a revelation may be partial, but still absolutely true, insofar as it does communicate. Then within Biblical prophecy in particular there exists what might be called an intentional indefiniteness. Meyrick has developed a thesis of Hengstenberg's, declaring, "God never forces men to believe, but there is such a union of definiteness and vagueness in the prophecies as to enable those who are willing to discover the truth, while the willfully blind

343. Op. cit., p. 53.

are not forcibly constrained to see it."[344] It has become an accepted adjunct to prophetic studies to criticize Bishop Butler's oft-quoted statement, "Prophecy is nothing but the history of events before they come to pass."[345] Yet Fairbairn adds in caution, "Prophecy approximates more nearly to the manner of history at one time than another, varying considerably in this respect, according to the circumstances in which it was given."[346]

In two special respects, however, prophetic writing does present difficulties for the comprehension of its fulfillments. On the one hand, a few predictions seem designedly enigmatic, particularly in reference to the identification of objects or situations, e.g. the precise civil disorders predicted for Egypt in Isaiah 19:2, or the personality of "the cruel lord" to whom they will be given over in v. 4. Commentators go to considerable lengths to survey the "many guesses" that have been attempted.[347] Isaiah may himself have been unaware of their exact specification;[348] but it is still incumbent upon the modern interpreter, in the light of history, to seek to determine what fulfillment is most likely.[349] There was a fulfillment! And such ambiguities may be progressively clarified.[350] The identification of "the lawless one" in II Thessalonians 2:3 or of the meaning of "the number of the beast: 666" in Revelation 13:18 seems purposely to have been left vague by the apostles, perhaps for their own protection at the time, but perhaps also for the admonition of Christians of later times, who were not to feel excused from the possibility of accomplishment in their days.

On the other hand, the original prophetic records remain limited in communication because of their incomplete nature. Riehm observes: "Prophecy succeeds in apprehending only individual, fragmentary elements of the saving purpose of God."[351] When it predicts an event in history, it seldom elaborates upon either its antecedent causes or its subsequent effects; and limitations seem inevitably involved in prophecy's "many portions and many ways," according to Hebrews 1:1. Riehm concludes that the "OT picture of the Messiah falls strikingly short of the NT God-Man. . . . The actual execution of God's saving purpose in Christ goes far beyond the contents of Messianic prophecy."[352] Even the NT Gospels, while conveying all that is necessary for belief on Christ and in finding eternal life in His name (John

344. Op. cit., p. 2596.
345. *Analogy*, II:vii, quoted in Edghill, op. cit., p. xvii, or Fairbairn, *Interpretation*, p. 84; cf. Mickelsen's opposition to the idea of prophecy as "history written before hand," op. cit., p. 289.
346. *Interpretation*, p. 109. See above, pp. 18–19, 20–21, on the degree of poetic or figurative language to be found in prophecy.
347. ICC, *Isa*, I:321, or NIC, *Isa*, II:19.
348. Cf. NIC, II:16.
349. As in NIC, II:18–19.
350. Mickelsen, op. cit., p. 292.
351. Op. cit., p. 271; cf. p. 294, on the above-mentioned telescoping of the twofold Messianic coming.
352. Ibid., pp. 271, 296, and illustrated on pp. 281–288; cf. A. F. Kirkpatrick's insistence that "the fulfillment is greater than the prophecy," *The Doctrine of the Prophets*, p. 17.

20:31), do not present the entire picture of His career; for "there are also many other things which Jesus did, which if they were written in detail, I suppose that even the world itself would not contain the books which were written" (21:25).

2. LIMITATIONS DUE TO THE MODERN INTERPRETER. Further problems for the comprehension of prophecy arise out of the gaps in today's knowledge of the past, so that for some of the predictions that were accomplished in ancient times one must admit, "No known fulfillment." Exodus 34:24, for example, made the forecast that after Israel's entrance into Canaan, when God's people should go up to the central sanctuary to keep the three annual feasts,[353] the men of the surrounding nations would not seek their lands. On the basis of God's other miracles at this time, one may assume that they did leave them alone; but there is no specific evidence. Believers in Christ assume—though it is similarly unverifiable—the fulfillment of the Lord's promise to the dying thief that he would, on that day, be with Him in paradise (Lk 23:43). A more prosaic instance is that of Isaiah 21:13–17 on an Assyrian campaign against the desert tribes of Kedar, for which sufficient facts are simply not available. The prophet had predicted that "within a year, all the glory of Kedar shall fail" (v. 16); and while the dating was clear enough at the time of its utterance, such is no longer the case.

Finally, even with increasing linguistic understanding and historical knowledge, there remains the fallibility of the human interpreter and of the value judgments that he must necessarily make. The most cautious expositors will thus exhibit divergent interpretations for difficult passages, e.g. on the identity of "the terrible ones" in Isaiah 29:20, whether Judean or Assyrian.[354] Fairbairn long ago cautioned in respect to typology, "Even on the supposition that some progress has now been made in laying such a [more solid and stable] foundation, we cannot hold out the prospect that no room shall be left for dubiety, and that all may be reduced to a kind of dogmatical precision and certainty."[355] At such points the interpreter must guard against claiming finality for his own particular comprehension of fulfillments—and in this regard I would make no claim to be an exception.[356]

353. This oracle should not be relegated to the category of timeless generalization; for the verse preceding speaks specifically of God's casting out the Canaanites before Israel and of His enlarging of their borders. So presumably this promise of protection relates similarly to the precise period of the conquest.
354. In the parallelism: "The terrible one is brought to nought,
        And the scoffer ceaseth,"
the first line could refer, synonymously, simply to the ruthless among the Judean people, BBC, IV:128; cf. IB, V:327. But the use of *ārīsīm*, "terrible ones," for the overpowering Assyrians in v. 5 might suggest a similar connotation, and hence progressive parallelism, here; so J. R. Dummelow, ed., presumes "the foe without" as opposed to those "within," *A Commentary on the Holy Bible*, p. 435.
355. *Typology*, I:140–141.
356. Cf. Payne, "The Effect of Sennacherib's Destruction in Isaianic Prophecy," *WTJ*, 34 (1971), p. 38.

A Summary of Basic Principles for the Interpretation of Prophecy: 22 Characteristics

		See above, p.:	Illustrations from the mid-years of Isaiah, 711–701 B.C.
The NATURE of Biblical prediction is:			
1. Historical	Prophecy arises out of real situations	4	32:9
2. Transcendent	God's guiding inspiration surpasses human capacities.	5	24:22
3. Moral	Prediction relates closely to contemporaneous preaching.	7	32:6–15
4. Evangelistic	Prophecy motivates men toward commitment to God.	14	31:6–7
5. Predictive	Foretelling occupies a major place in it.[357]	10, 13	Most of chs. 24–35
6. Messianic	Prophecy attains its goal in Jesus.	7	35:4
The FORM is:			
7. Literal	Most prophecy is straightforward in its declaration.	16	30:22
8. Poetic	Exalted feeling may produce Oriental hyperbole.	18	32:14
9. Figurative	Context may demonstrate some language as intentionally nonliteral.	43	30:26
10. Symbolical	A prediction may be acted as well as spoken.	21	20:2
11. Typical	An event may symbolize to its contemporaries a truth later achieved by Christ.	52	36:7
The FULFILLMENT is:			
12. Necessary	Prophecy is inspired and therefore, when noncontingent, must be fulfilled.	60	30:19, 44:26
13. Contingent	Fulfillment may be modified, provided it is near at hand and subject to conditions affectable by its contemporaries.	62–68	38:1
14. Analogous	Other Scriptures are determinative for interpretation.	72–80	25:8 = I Cor 15:54
15. Preferably near	The closest adequate fulfillment is the best.[358]	118–119	Most of chs. 28–34
16. Simple	The meaning of Scripture is not manifold but one.	121–126	29:3
17. Progressive	One context may yet advance through a series of predictions.	129–131	29:14–18

357. Ibid., p. 35.
358. Ibid., p. 37.

18. Similar	Prophecies may show resemblance without being equivalent.	119	32:15 = Acts 2:4
19. Telescoped	Prophecy may advance directly from a near to a far horizon.	137–140	31:9–32:1
20. Cyclic	Major blocks within a book may reach parallel climaxes.	130–131	24–27, 34–35
21. Eventual	If a prophecy has not yet been fulfilled, it shall be.	60	32:5
22. Occasionally ambiguous	Prophecies vary in perspicuity.	140–142	32:5

THE BIBLICAL
PREDICTIONS

PREFATORY NOTE

The following study provides a listing, together with suggested analyses and identifications of fulfillment, for all Biblical predictions, as defined in the preceding introductory sections. The need for such comprehensive synthesis is indicated by Ramm's observation concerning modern evangelical disagreements over prophecy: "The greatest single factor causing such a diversity of interpretation within the circle of orthodoxy is the vast amount of material to organize and harmonize."[1] Cyclopedic organization for the predictions has been attempted by an arrangement that follows the sequence of the 66 books of the Bible in their standard canonical order. In a concluding summarization they are then briefly restated in chronological order according to fulfillment.[2] It is actually 62 of the volumes of Scripture that are concerned, since both Ruth and the Song of Solomon in the OT and Philemon and III John in the NT seem devoid of predictive material.[3] To each book has been prefixed a brief introduction, giving the historical setting and basic organization in reference to the predictions therein contained; for as Girdlestone observes, "In dealing with the Books the question of their date has to be considered, for they have to be studied in connection with the history of the times in which they were written."[4]

Prophecies that repeat themselves within a single book are combined into

1. *Protestant Biblical Interpretation* (1950 ed.), p. 156.
2. See below, Summary A, pp. 631–659 ff.
3. Not that Messianic teachings and other predictions have not been sought for in these books: some have even assigned to Ruth basic identification as a "piece of Messianic literature . . . refreshing in its Messianism . . . the book must be understood as Messianic," J. A. Huffman, *The Messianic Hope in Both Testaments*, pp. 50–51. But this result is achieved only by the allegorized methodology of understanding Boaz and Ruth as types of Christ (the bridegroom-Redeemer) and of the church (the bride) respectively; see pp. 51, 53, above. A similarly forced approach mars the history of the interpretation of the Song of Solomon. Paul's words in Philemon 22—"Prepare me a lodging, for I hope that through your prayers I shall be given to you"—seem to be, not so much a firm prediction of his release from his first Roman imprisonment, as a particularly optimistic hope; see above, p. 41 sec. 4 (e).
4. *The Grammar of Prophecy*, p. 105.

147

one discussion, e.g. God's promise of the land of Canaan, as revealed to the various patriarchs of Genesis (12:7, 26:3, 28:4, 48:4, etc.; see under Gen. prophecy No. 24). But this applies only within the book concerned. Yahweh's predictions of the fall of Samaria that appear in Hosea and Amos, though of parallel scope and though revealed at about the same time and place, are listed separately under these two distinct prophetic volumes. When the same prophecy happens to be recorded in two (or more) Biblical books, having been incorporated into one later than the other—as in Chronicles, for example, when compared with Samuel or Kings, or as in the synoptic Gospels—then the later instance still receives a listing, though without discussion except for a cross reference to the earlier citation; see Appendix, pp. 676–679 below, on major groups of prophecies that are recorded in more than one book. The total predictive revelation of God on a given subject is listed in the concluding Summaries.[5] Even in two works by the same author, e.g. when the Genesis promise of Canaan reappears in the second book of Moses (Ex 3:8), or when the fall of Samaria is prophesied in both I Kings (14:15) and II Kings (17:23), the differing historical periods involved, together with our need of a practical and consistent method of organization, have dictated separate discussions. The particular prophecies are then numbered consecutively according to the order of the appearance of their first citation in a given book. Where applicable,[6] the designations figurative (abbreviated, fig.), symbolical (sym.), or typical (typ.) are added to the list of references on the basis of the character of the historical revelation.

The Bible's predictive verses are each designated according to their primary subject. Leviticus 9:24, for example, describes as its primary topic God's acceptance of a burnt offering. Now in so doing, it makes a passing reference to the fact that the offering was resting "upon the altar." But both the altar and its sacrifice were types, or acted predictions, of the same atonement that would some day be made by Jesus Christ; and the verse is listed only in respect to its more primary concern, namely, the offering. Yet earlier, in Leviticus 8:11, the interest of Moses does focus upon the altar and its sacred anointing, so that this latter verse is assigned in its subject to the typical value of the altar. Similarly, in Leviticus 23:26–32, Israel's annual (and typical) Day of Atonement constitutes the primary subject. Verses 28, 30, and 31 go on to legislate, "And ye shall do no manner of work in that same day, for it is a day to make atonement for you." Verse 32 then explains, "It shall be unto you a sabbath of solemn rest"; but this passage is still listed under "Day of Atonement" and not under the more secondary idea of "sabbath." In 23:24–25, however, concerning the Feast

---

5. With special sections devoted to the nations neighboring upon Israel that are most frequently mentioned in prophecy (Summary B), to predictions making personal reference to Christ (Summary C), and to the Biblical types (Summary D).

6. See above, pp. 20, 22, 26.

of Trumpets—which seems to have had no typical or predictive value of its own—similar references to the sabbath *are* included as typically prophetic and listed under Leviticus prediction 23, on the sabbath as a type of rest in Christ.

It so happens that Leviticus 8:11, cited above in reference to the altar, concludes with an added note, ". . . and [Moses also anointed] the laver and its base to sanctify them." Here then was a distinct matter of typology; and its reference is listed separately under "laver" and printed Lev *8:11b* —the italics indicate that this concluding line forms but a minor portion of the verse and is therefore not to be counted in the adding up of verses that are devoted to the idea of the laver. Occasionally a verse may be found almost equally divided, as Lev *9:2a*, on sin offering, and 9:2b, on burnt offering. But in the totaling up of figures, this reference has been assigned to the latter—note that "9:2b" is *not* printed in italics. The basis of choice lies in the merely mechanical matter of length: for there is a slightly longer statement concerning the burnt offering, as being "without blemish." Subjective decisions have now and then had to be made in these regards, but consistency has been maintained as far as possible. Nothing is omitted; and only the particular designation of topic for a verse, or perhaps for a portion of a verse, is really involved. In the numerical totals[7] one verse is never counted more than once.

As a sample listing, the 9th distinct prediction that God revealed through the prophecy of Zephaniah appears written as follows:

9. Zeph *2:11b*; 3:8, *19a* (1 v., fig.): "for Yahweh will famish the gods of the earth," that is, defeating their national armies . . . [discussion follows]. Fulfillment (per. 15): the battle of Armageddon, as in Num 24:17c, here adduced to substantiate God's more immediate activity against the peoples of Transjordan (Zeph 2:9, Nos. 7–8, above).

It is to be noted that Zephaniah's prediction of this eschatological conflict of Yahweh receives some mention in Zeph *2:11b* and *3:19a* but that it constitutes the dominant subject only of 3:8; the total for the topic therefore amounts to but 1 verse in this book. Its fulfillment occurs in what is designated period 15, that is, in the time surrounding the second coming of Jesus Christ.[8] The same divine victory had been prophesied initially by Balaam in Numbers 24:17c; and to prevent unnecessary duplication in describing the fulfillment, cross reference is simply made to this earlier passage.

There exist other categories of information, whose discussion would doubtless be of interest and profit, which could be ferreted out on the basis of the list of predictive prophecies that follows. While their systematic coverage has not been attempted in the present survey, these categories might include such matters as the form of revelation—whether spoken by

7. See below, Summary A, pp. 631–659; Statistical Appendix, pp. 674–675.
8. See above, pp. xxi, 103–105.

God or by angels, or in a dream or in the sermon of a prophet—and the nature of the party to whom spoken.

In the OT, the text followed is generally that of the Masoretic Hebrew and Aramaic. Emendation has been limited to those cases for which unusually compelling reasons appear; e.g. II Samuel 24:13, where the predicted *seven* years of famine should read, with the Greek, *three* years, as evidenced by context and by the parallel passage of I Chronicles 21:12; or Genesis 49:10, the famous "Shiloh" prophecy, *q.v.* In the NT, the authenticity of passages is accepted in accordance with the apparatus of the Aland Greek Testament.[9]

9. See introductory discussion above, p. 28.

THE
OLD TESTAMENT

GENESIS

The opening book of God's Bible sets a pattern for predictive prophecy, from which this phenomenon then develops throughout the remaining portions of both Old and New Testaments. Just as in other major aspects of Scriptural study—for example, the history of salvation or the development of Biblical theology—it is in the Book of Genesis that the Lord sets the stage: establishing the primary issues or questions and providing, in at least an initial way, His own wonderful answers to man's basic needs. Terry makes a point of the "organic relations of prophecy"; and it is in Genesis, as the divine seed plot for later growth, that this characteristic becomes most apparent. He explains, "Prophecies are first presented in broad and bold outline, and subsequently expanded"; in particular he emphasizes Genesis 3:15 as "a brief but far-reaching announcement of the long conflict between good and evil. . . . It may be said that all other prophecies of the Christ and the kingdom of God are comprehended in the protevangelium as in a germ."[1] Similar affirmation could be made for the various aspects of the typical position of Adam in respect to Christ (see below, Nos. 1 and 5).

The predictions of Genesis are less directly connected with the circumstances of the book's composition than are those of the four remaining volumes of the Pentateuch, for the author of Genesis was contemporaneous with none of the happenings that are described in his book. He lived, indeed, some three centuries after its last recorded event—the death of Joseph in approximately 1772 B.C.—and he seems personally to have been involved in none of the various predictions. Even the types of Genesis 1–2 concern what appear to have been matters of common knowledge to our first parents; e.g. in 1:26, man's status of dominion over creation (which anticipates the Messiah's eventual triumph), or in 2:3, God's resting on the sabbath (anticipating our rest in Christ.)[2] The writer of Genesis simply records with

1. *Biblical Hermeneutics*, p. 316.
2. It remains theoretically possible that only Moses (not Adam) may have been the first hearer of the revelation of God's hallowing the sabbath; but cf. Vos's assertion, "It is certain that the week of seven days was known before the time of Moses . . . Ezek 20:12, Neh 9:14 mean no more than that the institution in its specific OT form dates from the time of Moses," *Biblical Theology, Old and New Testaments*, p. 155.

inspired accuracy the prophecies that were current among the Hebrews long before his own time.

Neither Genesis itself nor the subsequent writings of Scripture make any direct statements about the authorship of this book. Stylistic similarities do bind Genesis to the remainder of the Pentateuch and suggest a common origin for the whole. Declarations, moreover, made by Christ, such as Luke 16:29, 31, in which He subsumes all of OT Scripture under the title "Moses and the Prophets," suggest His belief in Mosaic responsibility for the first five volumes of the Bible. See below, under the introduction to Exodus, for greater detail.[3] It seems clear, however, that in writing Genesis Moses must have availed himself of previously existing sources, whether literary or oral, for example, genealogical registers, such as "the book of the generations of Adam" (5:1),[4] or poems, such as the Blessing of Jacob (49:2–27). The patriarch Joseph, whose life and personal contacts span three-fourths of the subject matter of Genesis, constitutes a likely point of origin for these source data.[5]

Modern criticism, it is true, is united in its opposition to the concept of true Mosaicity for the Pentateuch. Yet even though not directly related to the prophecies, OT introduction does impinge upon the present study, primarily because of its bearing on the authenticity of the Genesis predictions as these are presented in Scripture. Genesis 49, for example, miraculously forecasts certain aspects of the settlement in Canaan made by the twelve tribes that were to descend from Jacob's sons. Moses, moreover, comes prior to Israel's entrance into Canaan and could therefore have had no *natural* knowledge of the modes of settlement. But it is the same antisupernaturalism which denies a Mosaic authorship to Genesis as, by very definition, impossible that must all the more deny the reality of such predictions as proceeding from the lips of the patriarch Jacob himself. Those with a concern for the validity of the prophetic content of Scripture do therefore have a stake in the arguments concerning its literary origins.

The specific date of composition for Genesis is sometimes held to be dependent upon previous inscripturation for the bulk of Exodus–Numbers, with "the first book of Moses" being written later, as a conscious introduction to the whole.[6] Yet from Exodus 17:16, the existence of "the book"[7] may be implied as early as this incident in the opening months of Israel's wilderness period (1446–1406 B.C.). Without question, Genesis has the

3. For answers to criticisms against the Mosaic authorship of Genesis, particularly as based on the so-called post-Mosaica of the book (e.g. 12:6, 14:14, 36:31, 40:15), reference may be had to standard evangelical commentaries and introductions, e.g. John H. Raven's *OT Introduction,* pp. 99–107.

4. Though without committing oneself, however, to theories of the *tōl'dhōth,* "generations," as source documents composed, e.g. by Adam himself and by his immediate successors, as claimed by Peter Wiseman, *New Discoveries in Babylon.*

5. Attention, for example, has been called to his (inscribed?) coffin, 50:26.

6. H. C. Leupold, *Exposition of Genesis,* p. 8.

7. See below, p. 174.

marks of having been written to preserve the record of God's immediate purpose to restore Israel to Canaan (cf. Gen 15:13 14, 46:3–4), as well as that of His overarching purpose in history to redeem lost mankind (3:15, 12:3). So Moses may well have composed this his first volume for the edification of the people either prior to or during the course of his 1447–1446 campaign before Pharaoh to deliver his fellow Hebrews from Egypt. The book falls naturally into two major sections, which may be outlined as follows: I. Primeval history, from creation to Abraham (Gen 1–11:26), man's plight as a fallen and increasingly sinful creature; II. Patriarchal history, from the birth of Abraham in 2133 B.C. to the death of his great-grandson Joseph in 1772 (Gen 11:27–ch. 50),[8] God's choice of the family of this one man, to be the seed plot for His chosen people and for the eventual incarnation of His Son as the redeemer of men: Abraham (11:27–25:10), and the three succeeding generations of Isaac (15:11–ch. 27), Jacob (28–36), and Joseph (37–50).

Predictions begin to appear in Genesis from its very start: eight occur in the first three chapters, even before mankind's expulsion from Eden. As might have been expected at this early point,[9] half occur in the concretely enacted form of types. To the patriarchs, God's prophecies appear characteristically in the form of direct revelations from the deity. Some, however, take on variety as acted symbols: upon occasion, in reference to children and to their future significance (as in 25:26 or 48:14), or again, as the visualized symbols of dreams (as in 37:7–9 or 40:9–19). By the time of the completion of Genesis, more than a third of the book's forecasts—28, to be specific—are found to have assumed a figurative form, owing primarily to their appearance in the poetic style of the blessings through which the patriarchs foretold particular outcomes for their descendants.

Predictions are involved in 212 out of the book's 1,533 verses, which amounts to some 14% of the whole. Yet these embrace 77 distinct prophecies, more than for any other narrative portion of the OT. It exceeds the sum even for most of the overtly prophetic books of the Bible, e.g. the 66 of Ezekiel or the 56 of Revelation; and it is surpassed in count only by the major prophecies of Isaiah and Jeremiah, the detailed apocalyptic of Zechariah, and, in the NT, by the total of 81 prophecies that appear in the Gospel of Matthew.

1. Gen 1:26, 28 (2 vv., typ.): "Let man have dominion . . . over all the earth." The idea is repeated in Ps 8:3–8; but in fact this ideal was not attained by Adam and his race: Heb 2:8, "But now we do not yet see all things subjected to him." Fulfillment (per. 13): Adam's potential of

---

8. See above in front matter, Key Dates in Biblical Chronology, and J. B. Payne, "Chronology of the OT," in M. C. Tenney, ed., *The Pictorial Encyclopedia of the Bible.*
9. See above, p. 21.

dominion the rather anticipates Christ's victory at His ascension: "But we do see . . . Jesus, because of the suffering of death crowned with glory and honor" (Heb 2:9). See also p. 50, above, note 110.

2. Gen 2:3 (1 v., typ.): God "hallowed the seventh day." Fulfillment (per. 13): Christ's ministry, which would give rest; see below under Ex prophecy No. 41.

3. Gen 2:9; 3:22, 24 (3 vv., typ.): the tree of life. To its contemporaries the tree was a sacramental symbol of life,[10] associated with the possibility of man's living forever (3:22). Even its central position in the garden (2:9) may be indicative of the central place of the truth it symbolized. The tree, moreover, did not lose its power through humanity's fall; it prophesies a life yet to be attained in the future;[11] cf. Scripture's more straightforward prediction of this same phenomenon in Rev 2:7, 22:14. Fulfillment (per. 18): mankind's perfected life in the New Jerusalem (Rev 22:2).

4. Gen 2:17 (1 v.): in the days of Adam's eating fruit from the tree of the knowledge of good and evil, he should "surely die." Adam did sin by eating (3:6); and as a result (fulfillment, per. 1), he together with the whole human race became subject to death (3:19);[12] witness the repeated refrain in Gen 5, ". . . and he died." Scripture defines the precise time of fulfillment as "the day that thou eatest thereof." This should not be understood only as a form of spiritual death (as, e.g., in Rom 7:9 or I Tim 5:6),[13] since the context concerns what was to become man's "normal" physical death (Gen 3:19); nor was it but a conditional threat that may not have been fulfilled.[14]

5. Gen 3:6, 17-19 (4 vv., typ.): Adam "is a type of Him who was to come" (Rom 5:14). Fulfillment (per. 13): Christ's death and resurrection for the justification of men. Ver. 6: as Adam had one evil act, so Christ was to perform one great deed of righteousness (Rom 5:18); and vv. 17-19, when Adam was cursed in his position of headship for humanity, he prefigured Christ, procuring men "justification of life" by free grace (Rom 5:12, 14-19); "The last Adam became a life-giving spirit" (I Cor 15:45). Fairbairn comments: "A fallen head could give birth only to a fallen off-

10. For it did serve as a medium through which God willed that life should be conveyed. This stands in contrast to the concept of magic, which would seek to compel the supernatural into actions contrary to its will.

11. Vos, op. cit., pp. 38-39. Contrast the tree of the knowledge of good and evil (2:9b, 17a), which was an instrument of contemporaneous probation, but which was not typical of future hope.

12. Ibid., p. 47.

13. Though Adam did suffer a real separation from God by being driven from His presence in the garden, 3:23, 24.

14. It was clearly not a threat of immediate intention; see above, p. 39. Vos's explanation, moreover, of "the inevitable eventuation" of death, ibid., p. 49, seems to correspond insufficiently to the words "in that *day*." Most likely appears Keil's suggestion, *Pentateuch*, I:105-106, that on the day of man's eating, the germ of death entered him—though not death itself—so that he came under its power and became mortal (Rom 5:12a).

spring—so the righteousness of Heaven had decreed; and the prospect of rising again to the possession of immortal life and blessing [cf. No. 6, on Gen 3:15, that follows] seemed, by its very announcement, to call for the institution of another head, unfallen and yet human, through whom the prospect might be realized."[15]

6. Gen 3:15a (1 v., fig.): "I will put enmity . . . between thy seed [the serpent's] and her seed [Eve's]," though in the process ". . . . thou shalt bruise His heel." This significant verse is rightly called the "proto-evangel,"[16] for the fact that enmity would be put between man and the tempter indicates his corresponding reconciliation with God. Gen 3:15 is also described as the "Edenic testament," or covenant; for even though it does not contain the actual term *b'rīth*, the testamentary situation is neces-sarily assumed, both because of the presence of all its major features and because of the development of all subsequent redemptive *b'rīths* from it.[17] The most basic feature of God's covenants, that of "the death of the testa-tor" (Heb 9:16), appears in rudimentary, pictorial form through the figure of the bruising of the heel of the seed of the woman.[18] Fulfillment (per. 13) is in Jesus, who suffered on our behalf that He might reconcile us to God.

7. Gen *3:15b*: the Messianic instrument through whom the victory will arise springs from humanity. Scripture is as yet ambiguous as to whether it is even a single person that is intended. *Zérah*, "seed," may be taken either as a collective (as in 22:17) or as a singular: "It [He *or* they] shall crush thy head, and thou shalt bruise its [His *or* their] heel." Context does imply that since the serpent is to have a representative leader—"thy head"—so also should the seed of the woman; but this is not spelled out.[19] Yet the wording of Gen 3:15 was providentially designed by the Holy Spirit as simple, but at the same time true and congruous with its future fulfillment (per. 13) in the one person of Christ. It is this potentiality of individualistic reference that constitutes the point of Gal 3:16, with its explanation that the

15. *The Typology of Scripture*, I:203.
16. See above, p. 153.
17. E.g., the antecedent bestowal of benefits by God, in a historical prologue (Gen 2:8), the stipulations (2:15), and the resultant blessings and curses; Luis Alonso-Schökel, "Sapiential and Covenant Themes in Genesis 2–3," D. McCarthy and Wm. Callen, eds., *Modern Biblical Themes*, p. 55; cf. his insistence that it foreshadows God's later dealings wtih Israel as a nation, p. 56. Compare my chart, *Theology of the Older Testament*, pp. 92–93; and see further under 15:10, No. 30, below.
18. The Heb. text makes it clear that the seed who wins the victory is not the woman (or, particularly, the virgin Mary, as suggested by Roman Catholic inter-preters; cf. P. Heinisch, *Theology of the OT*, pp. 338–339). Even the fact that it is the seed of the woman (Eve) as opposed to that of the man (Adam) seems to possess little theological significance: the thought is expressed in this way simply because it is the woman who bears the children. The phrase "seed of woman" can hardly be said to imply the virgin birth (cf. 24:60).
19. Vos, op. cit., p. 55, "We are not warranted in seeking an exclusively per-sonal reference to the Messiah here."

promise was directed not toward "seeds," as many, but toward "seed," one, which is Christ.

8. Gen *3:15c* (fig.): the head of the serpent to be "bruised" (= crushed). Behind the snake as tempter, moreover, lay the equally real, but spiritual, evil personality of Satan. This latter fact is primarily a matter of NT rather than contemporary revelation (Rom 16:20), though it is also indicated in the Genesis context, not simply by the snake's ability to speak, but by the very relationship it was assuming with mankind. Man, as the bearer of God's image, was to hold dominion over all the lower forms of life (1:28); but here came a beast that assumed a position of full equality with man. Satan is indeed "the great dragon, the old serpent" (Rev 12:9).[20] The fulfillment of this prophecy is marked by successive stages; see above, p. 135. Per. 13: Christ rendered Satan powerless, broke the fear of death in which he held mankind (Heb 2:14–15), and by His passion, and particularly at His ascension, cast him down from heaven (John 12:31, Rev 12:9–10); in per. 14, the church crushes him under foot (Rom 16:20); in per. 16, the millennium, Satan will be bound (Rev 20:1–3); and, after its expiration, in per. 17, he will be cast into the lake of fire (v. 10).

9. Gen 4:4; 8:20–21; 22:2–3, 6–7, 10, 13; 31:54; 46:1 (11 vv., typ.): sacrifice, as a type fulfilled (per. 13) in the death of Christ; see under Lev. No. 2. The blood of animals could not take away sins (Heb 10:4, 11), but Christ "offered one sacrifice for sins for all time" (10:12; cf. 9:12). When God therefore accepted, for example, Abel's sacrifice, it must have been as a type, "a shadow of the good things to come" (10:1; cf. 8:5). Cain's offering was not such a type and was not accepted.

10. Gen 5:29 (1 v.): Lamech called his son's name Noah, "saying, This same shall comfort us, *nahēm*, in our work . . . because of the ground which Yahweh hath cursed." Fulfillment appears to lie in the comfort afforded by Noah (per. 1) against God's curse upon man's sin, commencing with toil (3:17) but climaxing in destruction by the flood, from which Noah did rescue the representatives of both man and beast (6:8, 18–22; 7:1–3, 24; 8:1, 18).[21]

11. Gen 6:3, 7, 13, 17; 7:4 (5 vv.): "My spirit [of life] shall not dwell in man for ever . . . his days shall be 120 years" (cf. ASVmg to 6:3);[22] for He would destroy mankind by a deluge, and specifically, by the time of

---

20. The underlying presence of Satan is further borne out by the nature of the subsequent curse; compare Rom 8:21 with Isa 65:25, Payne, op. cit., pp. 216, 291–292.

21. Leupold, op. cit., pp. 245–246, "By the spirit of prophecy Lamech, like other godly patriarchs, sensed that in an unusual way this one would bring comfort to the troubled race. This he did by preserving the small godly remnant in the ark. This unusual form of comfort Lamech may never have dreamed of. Yet his prophecy is a valid one," the fourth to be fulfilled in all of Scripture (cf. No. 4, above, No. 11, that follows, and also Jude No. 6). See above, p. 4, note 8.

22. See Vos, op. cit., pp. 61–62, and Payne, op. cit., p. 207.

7:4, "in yet seven days" (cf. v. 10). Fulfillment (per. 1): the flood of Noah.

12. Gen 6:18 (1 v.): God to establish His testament with Noah. Fulfillment (per. 1): He did, in 9:9–17.

13. Gen 7:23; 8:1, 4, 16–19 (7 vv., typ.): the ark, bearing its living cargo "safely through the water," received its typical fulfillment (per. 14), in Christian salvation through the rite of baptism (I Pet 3:20–21). In parallel to the flood waters washing away the wrong, and to the ark preserving the saved souls, so baptism is specifically called the *antítupov,* "antitype," of this event (v. 21).

14. Gen 8:22 (1 v.): "While the earth remaineth . . . day and night shall not cease." These words suggest a period for the earth's duration, but one which may some day end; cf. the promise of 9:11, 15, that it will never again be destroyed *by a flood of water*—but perhaps by fire (II Pet 3:6–7)? Fulfillment (per. 17): at the final judgment (Rev 20:11), when earth, and heaven too, are to flee away from before God's great white throne; see Ps 102:26a.

15. Gen 9:4 (1 v., typ.): prohibition against eating blood, anticipating fulfillment (per. 13) in Christ's death; see Lev. No. 20.

16. Gen 9:8–17 (10 vv., typ.): the Noachian *b'rīth,* "testament." Fulfillment (per. 13): Christ's testamentary death, see further under 15:10, No. 30, below. The demise of the testator had been depicted in the preceding sacrifices, 8:20–21; and the basic promise of reconciliation with God comes out in His guarantee to preserve that redemptive seed (9:9), by whom the serpent would yet be crushed (cf. 3:15).[23]

17. Gen 9:25, *26b, 27b* (1 v., fig.): Canaan to be a servant to his brothers. Fulfillment (pers. 4–6, 12, from the conquest, continuing down through Israel's united kingdom, and into Roman times): in Abraham's day, punishment had not yet been meted out to the Canaanites (15:16); but it *was* accomplished by a series of later Semites (9:26): by Joshua (Josh 9:21, 23, 27), by the Hebrew tribes during the days of the judges (Jd 1:28, 30, 33, 35), and by David and Solomon (I Chron 22:2, II Chron 2:17–18). The last major aspect of fulfillment occurred in the fall of Phoenician Carthage, 146 B.C., and of the remaining Canaanites, 63 B.C., to the Japhethite (Gen 9:27) Romans.

18. Gen 9:26a (1 v., fig.): Yahweh's title, "the God of Shem." Fulfillment (pers. 1, 13): from patriarchal times and onward, God has been especially associated with the Semitic peoples, represented in figure by their ancestor Shem. This became true, above all, in reference to Abram (e.g. No. 22 or 30, below); cf. Scripture's later phrase, "Yahweh, the God of Abraham" (28:13); and it suggests Christ's eventual descent from the Semitic branch of humanity.

23. See Payne, op. cit., pp. 93–94.

19. Gen 9:27a, 12:3, *18:18b, 28:14c* (2 vv., fig.): Japheth to "dwell in the tents of Shem." This phrase does not here connote conquest (as in Ps 78:55) but rather a sharing in spiritual blessings (as in 84:10, 120:5); otherwise Noah's blessing would have been turned into a curse upon Shem. Then to Abram, and later to Jacob, God promised, 12:3, "In thee shall all the families of the earth be blessed." The *niph'al* verb, *w'nivr'khū,* could carry the reflexive force of "bless themselves" (RSV). This is indeed the meaning of the distinctive *hithpa'el* stem in 22:18 (see No. 47, below). But the *niph'al* at this point would seem to stand in contrast to it. Further, the inspired NT quotes 12:3 as having the passive meaning (Gal 3:8), which suggests that the one Holy Spirit intended to convey this same meaning, namely, "be blessed," in Genesis.[24] Fulfillment (per. 14): for this same Galatians quotation applies 12:3 to the universal Christian church, "those who are of faith" (Gal 3:7, 9); cf. Paul's commissioning to the Gentiles (Acts 9:15) and the subsequent opening up of the life of faith to Cornelius and the rest (Acts 10:34–35, Eph 2:13, 19).

20. Gen 12:1 (1 v.): God's promise to show Abram the land (of Canaan, 11:31). Fulfillment (per. 1): Abram did thereafter arrive in Canaan (12:5), and God specifically directed him to "lift up his eyes" unto all the land (13:14–15).

21. Gen 12:2a; 13:16; 15:5; *17:2b;* 18:18a; 21:12; 22:17b; 24:60a; 26:*4a,* 24; 28:3; 32:12; 35:11; 46:3; 48:4a (13 vv.): a great nation to come from Abram. Specifically, it is Isaac's seed that is to become the nation (21:12; cf. v. 13). Concerning its numerical increase God promised, "I will make thy seed as the dust of the earth" (13:16), "as the sand of the sea" (to Jacob, 32:12), as the stars (15:5). Rebekah is addressed as "the mother of thousands of ten-thousands" (24:60): and Jacob is to be "a company, *qāhāl,* of peoples" (28:3, 35:11; cf. 48:4).[25] Fulfillment (per. 2): in Egypt the Abrahamic seed became a great nation (Dt 26:5; cf. Gen 48:4). Ex 1:7 records, "The children of Israel were fruitful and increased abundantly, and multiplied." By the time of Num 23:10 an outsider (Balaam) could exclaim, "Who can count the dust of Jacob, or number the fourth part of Israel"; and in Deuteronomy Moses stated, "Ye are this day as the stars of heaven for multitude" (1:10; cf. 10:22).[26]

22. Gen *12:2b, 22:17a*: God to bless Abram. Leupold explains, "A man is blessed when due to the gracious working of God all goes well with him (cf. 39:5); the things that he undertakes thrive; and true success crowns all his endeavors."[27] Fulfillment (per. 1): Soon thereafter Yahweh gave to Abram riches from Egypt (13:2, 5) and a victory in war, for which

---

24. See ibid., p. 189.
25. "The officially convened assembly of the twelve tribes," W. J. Beecher, *The Prophets and the Promise,* p. 198.
26. Yet cf. also No. 45, below.
27. Op. cit., p. 412.

Melchizedek blessed him (14:19). His status is specifically defined as blessed in 24:1; cf. v. 35.

23. Gen *12:2c*: Abram's name to become great. Fulfillment (per. 1): already in his own time this patriarch became famous: Abimelech of Gerar acknowledged that God was with Abram (21:22); the Hittites at Hebron called him a "prince of God among us" (23:6); and his fame has increased henceforward.

24. Gen 12: 7a; 13:15, 17; 15:7, 19–20; 17:8a; *24:7a*; 26:3, *4b*; 28:4, 6, 13; 35:12; *48:4b* (12 vv.): God to give the land of Canaan to Abraham's seed. It would be given "for ever" (13:15; cf. Dt 4:40), as an "everlasting possession" (Gen 17:8, 48:4). The promise is specifically referred to as fulfilled in Josh 21:43–44, cf. 11:16 (per. 4); and its repossession by the Israel of God is a major aspect of millennial times (per. 16).

25. Gen 12:*7b*–8; 13:4, 18; 22:9; 26:25; 33:20; 35:1, 3, 7 (9 vv., typ.): the altar, as a God-given place of sacrifice and communion. Fulfillment (per. 13), in Christ as the place of true offering; see Ex 27:1.

26. Gen 14:18a (1 v., typ.): Melchizedek, as "without genealogy" (Heb 7:3). It is not that this king had no genealogy (cf. the parallel phrases in Heb, "without father, without mother"); it means, rather, Melchizedek, "whose genealogy is not traced from them [Levites]" (Heb 7:6). That is, Genesis identifies him simply as "king of Salem," specifically lacking in priestly relationship. Fulfillment (per. 13): he was a type of Christ's non-Levitical genealogy from the tribe of Judah (Heb 7:13–14).

27. Gen *14:18b* (typ.): Melchizedek, as priest—"and he was priest of God Most High." Fulfillment (per. 13): Melchizedek typified Christ in His priesthood. As the former's name meant *king of righteousness* (Heb 7:2), so Christ has made righteousness available for men (Phil 3:9); and as his title as ruler of (Jeru)salem meant king of *peace* (Heb 7:2), so Christ has brought peace to men's hearts through His canceling of sin (Phil 4:7). The coming of Christ in such a position meant that the replaced, Levitical priesthood could not be perfect (Heb 7:11), nor could the law, which also was to be changed (v. 12), by Christ's "bringing in of a better hope" (v. 19).

28. Gen 14:19–20 (2 vv., typ.): Melchizedek, in his greatness. For this king both blessed Abram and collected tithes from him (Heb 7:6–7); thus the later Levites, "so to speak . . . paid him tithes also" (vv. 9–10). Fulfillment (per. 13), in the corresponding greatness of Christ (v. 4).

29. Gen 15:4; 17:*16a*, 19a, *21b*; 18:10, 14 (4 vv.). Abram to have a son, through Sarah (17:16), one year after his 99th year, which was 2034 B.C. (17:21; 18:10, 14). Fulfillment (per. 1): the birth of Isaac in 2033. B.C. (21:2).

30. Gen 15:10–11, 17–*18a*; 17:2–*4a*, 7, *8b*–9 (7 vv., typ.): the Abrahamic testament. In this revelation appears the very heart of Biblical prediction. That which had been presented in rudimentary form in the Edenic testament of 3:15 (No. 6 above) and first designated by the Heb. term

b'rīth in the Noachian testament of 9:8 (No. 16), is here portrayed in its redemptive fullness. The monergistic divine grace and the eternity of the testament, as well as its bequest of reconciliation with God, appear together in Gen 17:7. Here for the first known time in history were spoken the words which constitute the classic expression of the testamental promise: "And I will establish My testament between Me and thee and thy seed after thee in their generations for an everlasting testament, to be a God unto thee, and to thy seed after thee" (cf. Ex 6:7, Hos 2:23, Jer 31:33, Rev 21:3).[28] The necessity of a death for the ultimate effectuation of the testament is brought out by the atoning blood that was shed in the accompanying sacrifices (15:9, 10). It is shown even more strikingly in the confirmatory sign of God's self-maledictory oath (v. 17).[29] For in the legal practice of the ancient Near East, when the parties to a covenant passed between the sections of dismembered carcasses that were subject to destruction by scavenger animals, this rite served as a dramatic pledge of the part of those who were entering into the bond of the *b'rīth* that such should be done to them if they violated its stipulations (cf. Jer 34:18–20).[30] But at this point it was not Abram but only the flaming torch which symbolized the presence of God, God alone, that passed between the pieces. As Gen 15:17–18 demonstrates, God committed Himself to the threat of self-dismemberment, so as to make a testament with Abram. Fulfillment (per. 13): the violent execution of the Son of God, the necessary death of the testator, that "those who have been called may receive the promise of the eternal inheritance" (Heb 9:15–16).[31]

31. Gen 15:13, *46:4a* (1 v.): Israel to sojourn in another land for 400 years, there to serve and to be afflicted. Fulfillment (per. 2): the time of the Hebrews in Egypt, by round number. Exodus 12:40 specifies 430 years in which the "children of Israel dwelt in Egypt *and in the land of Canaan*" (LXX). Since they were to live in Canaan for 33 years,[32] the precise time of their sojourn in Egypt would have been 397 years, or from 1843 to 1446 B.C.

32. Gen 15:14a (1 v.): "That nation whom they shall serve, will I judge." Fulfillment (per. 2): God's 10 plagues upon Egypt (Ex 7:14–12:29).

33. Gen *15:14b:* Israel's subsequent departure from Egypt. Fulfillment (per. 2): the exodus (Ex 12:41). This prophecy falls, significantly, in a testamentary context (Gen 15:10–11, 18; see No. 30, above); and in Ex 2:24 God is specifically stated to have based its fulfillment upon His remembering of the testament.

---

28. The testament also included secondary, confirmatory elements (cf. Nos. 21, 24, above and Nos. 37, 45, below), such as God's promise of the land (15:18) and of numerous seed (17:2).
29. Vos, op. cit., p. 100; cf. John Murray, *The Covenant of Grace*, pp. 16–17.
30. IB, V:1058.
31. Cf. Payne, op. cit., pp. 80, 82, 97.
32. Cf. Joseph's age of 39 when they came to Egypt (Gen 41:46–47; 45:6) and of 6 when the group first entered Canaan (30:25; 31:41).

34. Gen *15:14c:* and they shall come out "with great substance." Fulfillment (per. 2): the property that the Hebrews carried out of Egypt (Ex 11:2–3, 12:35–36; cf. also the prediction in 3:22).

35. Gen 15:15 (1 v.): Abram to die in peace, in a good old age. Fulfillment: (per. 1): he was 175 at his death in 1958 B.C. (25:7), specifically "in a good old age" (v. 8).

36. Gen 15:16, *46:4b,* 48:21, 50:24–25 (4 vv.): Israel's return to Canaan, "in the fourth generation" (15:16). Joseph underscored the prophecy by ordering his own bones to be carried up to Canaan (50:24–25; as they were, Ex 13:19, Josh 24:32). Heb 11:22 explains that this act was one of faith. Jacob's prior orders for burial in Canaan (Gen 47:30, 49:29–30) are sometimes so interpreted too;[33] but this is not stated, only that he wished to be buried with his fathers. The term "fourth generation" cannot denote the technical concept of a generation of about 30 years— actually there were at least ten generations spent in Egypt (I Chron 7:25–27) during the 400 years of Gen 15:13 (No. 31, above). It rather denotes lifetimes,[34] some of which still surpassed 100 years at this time. Fulfillment (per. 4): Israel reentered its own land, crossing the Jordan in the spring of 1406 B.C. (Josh 3:16–17).

37. Gen 15:18b (1 v.): the God-given boundaries of the promised land. Abram's seed would possess from the *nāhār,* "river" of Egypt, i.e., the Nile,[35] to the Euphrates. Fulfillment (per. 6): this was achieved in Solomon's day, to the "border" of Egypt, I K 4:21.

38. Gen 16:10; 17:20; 21:13, 18 (4 vv.): Hagar's seed, the Ishmaelites, to multiply into a nation, with 12 princes (17:20). Fulfillment (per. 2): 12 sons of Ishmael are listed in 25:13–15; and by the time of Moses' writing of Genesis they had developed into as many Arabian nations, v. 16. In the days of Gideon, 1169 B.C., they constituted serious opponents to Israel (Jd 8:24); and in I Chron 5:10, 19–20 (under Saul, 1043–1010) and in Ps 83:6 (probably the invasion sung about by Jahaziel the Asaphite in II Chron 20:14–17, 853 B.C.) these Hagarites[36] continued to be serious enemies. The Arabs of today trace their descent from Ishmael.

39. Gen 16:11 (1 v.): Hagar to bear a son. Fulfillment (per. 1): Ishmael, born in 2057 (v. 15).

40. Gen 16:12 (1 v., fig.): Ishmael to be nomadic, "a wild ass among men," with his hand against others. Fulfillment (per. 1): Hagar was driven from Abram's home (21:14), so that Ishmael grew up in the wilderness (vv. 20–21). "He abode over against his brethren," 25:18.

41. Gen 17:4b–6, 15, 16b (5 vv.): Abraham to be "the father of a

33. Leupold, op. cit., p. 1140.
34. So. W. F. Albright, BASOR, 163 (1961), 50; or K. A. Kitchen, *Ancient Orient and the OT,* p. 54.
35. Y. Aharoni, *The Land of the Bible,* p. 59, not the *naḥal,* "brook," Wadi el Arish.
36. ICC, *Chron,* p. 120.

multitude of nations": kings are to come from him (v. 6),[37] and some also from Sarah (v. 16). His name, correspondingly (v. 5), was changed to *av-rāhām,* "father of a multitude"[38]; cf. the Arabic noun *ruhâm,* "multitude."[39] Some of the earlier aspects of fulfillment (per. 2) are: the 6 sons of Keturah, including Midian (25:2–4); the 12 princes of Ishmael (vv. 13–16); and the 2 nations born from Rebekah, Edom and Israel (v. 23). Edom in particular had kings before Israel did (36:31–39), the eighth ruling at the time of Moses' writing Genesis (perhaps the predecessor of the king mentioned in Num 20:14). Later, in the church age (per. 14), Christian nations become an engrafted seed of Abraham as well (Gal 3:14, 29; cf. Rom 11:17). See above, p. 135.

42. Gen 17:10–14, 23–27; 21:4; 34:14–17, 22–24 (18 vv., typ.[40]): circumcision. This initiatory rite served as a sign and seal of the testament, 17:11, 13; God in fact declared them practically equivalent: "This is My testament . . ." (v. 10). Circumcision symbolized the removal of unfitness, and particularly that of the natural life. When Moses therefore referred to his "uncircumcised lips" (Ex 6:12) he was signifying poor native speaking ability. To speak of an "uncircumcised heart" (Jer 4:4) was to picture a soul that was covered with its natural wickedness. In contrast, then, "to circumcise" meant to remove one's sin (Dt 10:16) and "to love Yahweh thy God with all thy heart and with all thy soul that thou mayest live" (30:6). Circumcision thus becomes the earliest Biblical symbol of regeneration (Lev 26:41). It was "a seal of the righteousness of faith" (Rom 4:11).[41] But this comes only through Christ; so it pointed typically to its fulfillment (per. 13) in the true "circumcision of Christ: a circumcision made without hands, in the removal of the body of the flesh" (Col 2:11–12).[42]

37. Beecher, loc. cit., argues that v. 6, "I will make nations of thee," is to be understood, in parallel with 28:3, 35:11, or 48:4 (see under No. 21, 12:2a), as "Israel, which would exist in the form of an assembly of nations." Yet he himself interprets 17:4–5 as referring to a plurality of nations, pp. 200–201; and it seems improper to mark off v. 6 as having a different point of reference.

38. The name also of Abram's wife was changed (v. 15), from Sarai to Sarah. Its meaning, "princess," remains the same, -ai being simply a more archaic fem. ending than -ah, GK, p. 224. But the very fact that it was God who changed it gives divine validation to the concept of "princess," for the future.

39. KB, p. 8, versus AB, p. 124.

40. "Circumcision was symbolic of a spiritual reality, and it pointed beyond itself to the time of its spiritual accomplishment," A. Edersheim, *Prophecy and History in Relation to the Messiah,* p. 168.

41. Some commentators have denied to circumcision its individualistic application and have looked upon it as a sign of mere external incorporation into the nation of Israel; cf. Oehler, *Theology of the OT,* pp. 193–194. Confessedly, membership in the elect community was involved in the idea of circumcision. But its chief contextual point of relationship is with God's redemptive testament and the fundamental, associated divine promise that Yahweh would be their God (Gen 17:7).

42. See Payne, op. cit., pp. 391–394.

43. Gen 17:*19b,* 21a (1 v.): God to establish His testament with Isaac, for his seed. Fulfillment (per. 1): He did, 26:3, 24.

44. Gen 22:8 (1 v.): "God will provide for Himself the lamb for a burnt offering." Leupold states, "In the light of what follows, Abraham's answer is well-nigh prophetic."[43] For at the time, Abraham the human speaker seems only to have been thinking of Isaac himself as the sacrifice. Fulfillment (per. 1): in the ram that was caught by its horns in a thicket (v. 13). The patriarch then provides an immediate commentary by his phrase, "Jehovah-jireh," *yir'e,* Yahweh *will see,* in the sense of "look out for, choose" (as in 41:33, "Let Pharaoh look out a man").

45. Gen *22:17c, 24:60b,* 27:29a, 28:14a (2 vv.): Abraham's seed to possess the gate of its enemies (22:17; cf. 24:60). In similar fashion Jacob was later told that peoples and nations would bow down to him, i.e. to his descendants (27:29); and, "Thou shalt spread abroad to the E, W, N, and S" (28:14). Fulfillment (per. 6):[44] in the conquests of David, which II Samuel 8 specifies as directed to the W (v. 1), E (v. 2), N (v. 3), and S (vv. 13–14); cf. the tribute paid to Solomon (I K 10:25).

46. Gen *22:18a, 26:4c, 28:14b:* in these passages the blessing that is to come upon all the nations of the earth is for the first time associated with the *seed,* respectively, of Abraham, Isaac, and Jacob. Contrast No. 19, above, where it is rather Abraham and Jacob themselves who are involved. Fulfillment (per. 13): the coming of Jesus the Messiah as a descendant of the specific family of Abraham, within the general group of the Semitic people (No. 18, above). Scripture does not yet, however, reveal that the Messiah would necessarily be one individual (No. 67, below); and Christ was careful to say that Abraham saw His day (though perhaps not His person, John 8:56).

47. Gen 22:18b, to Abraham, 26:4d, to Isaac (2 vv.): "In thy seed shall all the nations of the earth bless themselves" (ASVmg),[45] that is, they shall seek this family's seed as the means for invoking blessings on themselves. Fulfillment: there is today in Christ a blessing for every man, but all the nations do not yet seek Him. It is in the future Messianic kingdom

43. Op. cit., p. 626. See also p. 5, above.

44. In period 2, in Egypt, Israel is specifically noted as "multiplied and mighty" (Ex 1:7, 9, 20), a great and populous nation (Dt 26: 5); see No. 21, above. Yet Dt 6:3 suggests a still future development, corresponding to these vv. of No. 47: "that ye may increase mightily, as Yahweh the God of thy fathers hath promised unto thee"; cf. 13:17.

45. The rendering "bless themselves" for the *hithpa'el* verb (cf. No. 19 above), *w'hithbār'khū,* might suggest no greater thought than that of the usage of the verb in Gen 48:20, where the meaning is explained, "God make thee as. . . ." This would imply merely their looking to the seed of Abraham as a standard of comparison for invoking blessings on themselves. Better, however, is the analogy of Jer 4:2, where the identical *hithpa'el* form appears and stands in parallel with "and in Him [God] shall they glory," meaning, seek Him as the means for invoking blessings on themselves; cf. Oehler, op. cit., p. 62.

(per. 16) that the Gentiles will come asking for Him (not at this point for the seed of Israel as a whole), Isa 11:10.[46]

48. Gen 24:7b, 40 (2 vv.): God "will send His angel before thee, and thou shalt take a wife for my son." Could Abraham's word about *taking a wife* be no more than a command from the patriarch to his servant? The possibility of the girl's being unwilling to follow the servant is noted in v. 8. But vv. 40–41 indicate Abraham's further confidence that the angel of Yahweh would prosper him in his mission, even though the family, subsequently, might withhold consent. Fulfillment (per. 1): Rebekah obtained (vv. 48–51, 56), 1993 B.C. (25:20).

49. Gen 25:23a (1 v., fig.): "Two nations are in thy womb." Fulfillment (per. 2): Rebekah, through her twin sons, did produce two separate nations—of Esau, the Edomites (36:1–9), and of Jacob, Israel, which became a nation while in Egypt, Dt 26:5 (see No. 21, above).

50. Gen *25:23b*; *27:29b*, 37a, *40b* (1 v., fig.): ". . . and the elder shall serve the younger . . . thou shalt serve thy brother." Fulfillment: Israel, represented in figure by its ancestor, Rebekah's younger son Jacob, did become stronger than Edom, descended from the elder son Esau, and eventually mastered that people. Per. 6: I Sam 14:47, Saul "put them to the worse"; but it was David who conquered Edom (II Sam 8:14, Ps 60 title, I K 11:15–16), about 1000 B.C., though the Edomite Hadad became an adversary to his son Solomon (I K 11:14). Per. 7: 150 years later, however, under Judah's ruler Jehoshaphat (869–848), Edom had no king, only a deputy from Judah (22:47). The land revolted from Hebrew control in the days of his son Jehoram (848–841) and set up a king (II K 8:20, 22), only to be reconquered by Amaziah, soon after his accession in 796 (14:7, 10). Yet after Amaziah's humiliation before N. Israel in 790, Edom seems to have made good its revolt and is described as, in turn, attacking Judah under Ahaz in 735 (II Chron 28:17). Per. 11: the Edomites were defeated by Judas Maccabeus in 164 (I Macc 5:3, 65). But "this doom was ultimately fulfilled when the Idumaeans (the Grecianized name for this people) were conquered by the Jews under John Hyrcanus [135–105] and ceased to have a separate national existence";[47] for this latter monarch had them forcibly circumcised and incorporated into Israel.[48]

51. Gen 25:26 (1 v., sym.): Jacob's grasping the heel of his twin brother Esau at their birth. Fulfillment (per. 1): Jacob later cheated Esau out of his birthright (25:31–34) and then stole their father Isaac's blessing (27:10–29). As Esau then cried to Isaac, "He hath supplanted me these two times" (v. 36).

---

46. The quotation of this verse as a passive in Acts 3:25 suggests that the Holy Spirit was at this point combining the ideas of two different verses: the Messianic character of Gen 22:18, "the seed," and the universally bestowed blessing of 12:3 (No. 19 above). The latter fact, however, was not contained in the OT revelation of 22:18; cf. Vos, op. cit., p. 91.

47. IB, VI:863.

48. Jos, *Ant*, XIII, 9, 1; XV, 7, 9; *Wars*, IV, 5, 5.

52. Gen 27:28, 33, *37b* (2 vv., fig.): "God give thee of the dew of heaven," of grain and wine. Fulfillment (per. 4): Jacob's descendants did, in Canaan, receive of God just such a fertile land, Dt 11:14.

53. Gen 27:39 (1 v.): "Behold, far from [JB; not "of," ASV][49] the fatness of the earth shall be thy dwelling." Fulfillment (per. 1): Esau and his descendants settled in Edom, 36:7–8, away from the fertile land of Israel.

54. Gen 27:40 (1 v., fig.): Esau—a figure for Edom—to live by the sword, and someday shake off Israel's yoke (see No. 50, above). Fulfillment (per. 7): in the days of Jehoram of Judah, shortly after the successful revolt of Mesha of Moab to their north; see under 25:23 (No. 50).

55. Gen 28:15, 20, 21; 32:9, *12a* (4 vv.): God to bring Jacob back to Canaan in safety. This oracle was specifically claimed by Jacob, when about to face Esau on his return, 32:9, 12. Fulfillment (per. 1): God did bring him back, 20 years later, in 1876 B.C. (33:18); cf. 35:3, in which Jacob cited the Lord's former revelation.

56. Gen 37:7–10 (4 vv., sym.): Joseph's two dreams—he is to rise in status, and his brothers and parents are to do him obeisance. Fulfilled (per. 1), with his brothers' repeated bowing down: 42:6; 43:26, 28; 44:14. 42:9 explains that Joseph remembered his earlier dreams. His father apparently did not literally so act;[50] but 45:11 and 47:12 note that Joseph provided for him and so became, in fact, his superior. Cf. Jacob's respectful address to Joseph: "If now I have found favor in thy sight, put, I pray thee. . . ."[51]

57. Gen 40:9–11 (3 vv., sym.), Pharaoh's butler's dream: a vine with three branches, and the butler squeezes out its fruit and serves the cup to Pharaoh. Joseph interpreted, vv. 12–13: restoration for the butler in three days. Fulfillment (per. 1): at the time and in the manner interpreted, vv. 20–21; cf. 41:13.

58. Gen 40:16–17 (2 vv., sym.), Pharaoh's baker's dream: three baskets of bread on his head, but birds ate some of the bread that was for Pharaoh. Joseph interpreted, vv. 18–19:[52] in three days the baker was to be hanged and the birds were to eat his flesh. Fulfillment (per. 1), exactly as inter-

---

49. Isaac's prophecies to Jacob (v. 28, No. 53) and to Esau (v. 39, here) are similar; but in the former the Heb. prep. *min*, "from," is partative, "God give thee *a portion* from the fatness," while in the latter the "from" is separative, "Dwell *away from* the fatness," a purposeful play on words, J. B. Payne, *An Outline of Hebrew History*, pp. 43–44.

50. AB, p. 537 speaks of 47:31, "And Israel bowed himself . . .," as "a gesture of mute appreciation on the part of a . . . man on the point of death"; but Leupold, op. cit., p. 1141, counters with the alternative suggestion "that Jacob 'bowed down in prayer,' thanking God that He had granted him satisfaction."

51. "Respect for one who occupies an eminent and responsible position," ibid., pp. 1139–1140.

52. Vv. 13a (No. 57) and 19a (here) are practically identical; but in the former, the "lifting up of the head" is figurative, for restoration, and in the latter literal, for hanging, cf. the stress in vv. 16–17 upon the head of the baker.

preted: on the third day (vv. 20, 22), two years before the beginning of the period of plenty in 1852 B.C. (41:1).

59. Gen 41:1–7, 17–24; 45:6, 11 (17 vv., sym.), Pharaoh's dreams (recounted by Pharaoh in 41:17–24 with greater detail): seven fat cows eaten by seven lean ones, and seven thick ears of grain eaten by seven blasted ones. Interpreted by Joseph, vv. 26–31, 34–36, the same situation being depicted by both: seven good years, followed by seven years of famine. In specific reference to v. 21, on the cows—"when they had eaten them up, it could not be known that they had eaten them; but they were still ill-favored, as at the beginning"—Joseph pointed out, vv. 30–31, that "all the plenty shall be forgotten . . . by reason of the famine which followeth." Fulfillment (per. 1). It happened: seven years of plenty, 1852–1845 B.C., followed by famine, 1845–1838 (41:47–48, 53–57; 47:13, 20).[53]

60. Gen 46:4c (1 v.), to Jacob: "Joseph shall put his hand upon thine eyes." The purpose was to close them, as a last duty to the dead.[54] Fulfillment (per. 1): at Jacob's death, in Egypt, 1826 B.C. (49:33); Joseph's performance of that specific act may be assumed from 50:1 (cf. vv. 2–14).

61. Gen 48:14, 17–18, 19a, *20b* (4 vv., sym.): the future superiority of Ephraim over Manasseh, as shown by Jacob's laying his *right* hand on Ephraim. Verbal explanation follows in v. 19: Manasseh's "younger brother shall be greater than he," and in v. 20 Jacob mentions Ephraim and Manasseh in that order. In the census of 1445, the tribe of Ephraim led that of Manasseh, 40,000 to 32,000 (Num 1:32–35); but by 1406 Ephraim had fallen behind, 32,000 to 52,000 (26:28–37). Ephraim became prominent from the time of Joshua, one of its greatest representatives (13:8), and acted high-handedly under the judges (Jd 8:1–2, 12:1–6). Fulfillment, however, came into focus at the division of the Hebrew kingdom in 930 (per. 7). Jeroboam, who received the rule in Israel, was an Ephraimite (I K 11:26); and the northern state continued to be essentially the kingdom of Ephraim (II Chron 25:7, 10; Isa 7:2–9, 17).

62. Gen 48:16, *19b*–20a; 49:22, 25–26 (5 vv., fig.): Ephraim and Manasseh (a figure for the descendants), to "grow into a multitude in the land" (48:16) and to constitute a standard for invoked blessings (v. 20; cf. note 45, above).[55] The tribes that spring from Joseph are to be like a fruitful bough (49:22), with blessings of the womb (v. 25).[56] Fulfillment

---

53. History does not record this particular famine; but for a similar, 7-year famine in the IIIrd Dynasty, 2600 B.C., see G. A. Barton, *Archaeology and the Bible*, pp. 368–369.

54. Leupold, op. cit., p. 1108.

55. In v. 19, the phrase, *m'lō-haggōyīm*, suggests not so much that Ephraim is to be "a multitude of nations" as *the fullness of the nations*, "a real multitude of people," ibid., p. 1156.

56. A play on words with *efráyim*, Ephraim, lit. "doubly fruitful"; cf. 41:52 and KB, p. 777.

(per. 4): these two tribal units were allocated the central areas of Canaan (Josh 16–17), "the children of Joseph" coming second in the distribution (16:1), immediately after Judah (ch. 15). Their growth receives testimony from the following remark to Joshua: "Why hast thou given me but one lot and one part for an inheritance, seeing I am a great people, for as much as hitherto Yahweh hath blessed me?" (17:14). "And Joshua spake unto the house of Joseph, even to Ephraim and to Manasseh, saying, Thou art a great people and hast great power; thou shalt not have one lot only: but the hill country shall be thine" (vv. 17–18), probably indicating the wooded land of v. 15, beyond the earlier borders of Ephraim.[57]

63. Gen 49:4 (1 v., fig.): "Boiling over as water," Reuben is not to have the preeminence in Israel. I Chron 5:1–2 states that the birthright was transferred to Joseph. The cause lay in Reuben's incest with Bilhah (35:22); and the tribe of Reuben, as a result (per. 4), came to be isolated in the southern sector of Transjordan (Josh 13:15–23; cf. 22:24–25). On this "metonymy," from individual to tribe, see above, p. 19. It did prosper later, in the reign of Saul, 1043–1010 (I Chron 5:10), but was generally among the first to be encroached upon and was carried captive by Tiglath-pileser III of Assyria in 733 (vv. 6, 26).

64. Gen 49:7 (1 v., fig.): Simeon and Levi to be scattered in Israel. The cause lay in their violence and treachery against Shechem, 34:25–29; even when they were censured by Jacob (v. 30), they remained belligerent (v. 31). Simeon, as a result, fell from 59,000 in 1445 B.C. (Num 1:23) to 22,000 in 1406 (26:14) and is omitted in Moses' blessings on the tribes in Dt 33. Their predicted scattering was fulfilled (per. 4) when they were assigned no tribal land of their own by Joshua but had to exist as a subgroup within the borders of Judah (Josh 19:1–9; cf. Jd 1:3). Some of the Simeonites later scattered northward, so as to be included in the ten northern tribes, as opposed to Benjamin and Judah in the south (II Chron 15:9, 34:6), or even to areas outside Canaan (I Chron 4:38–43). At the assignment of lands, Levi also was scattered, among the 48 Levitical cities of Josh 21:1–42. But this was now an honor, and for the teaching of the other tribes (Dt 33:10): their curse, though still fulfilled (per. 4), had been converted to a blessing by Levi's faithfulness while in the wilderness (vv. 8–9; cf. Ex 32:28).

65. Gen 49:8 (1 v., fig.): Judah, a figure for the tribe that would descend from him, to be praised[58] and bowed down to by his brothers. Fulfillment: I Chronicles 5:2 explains that Judah prevailed over his brethren and that the national leader came from him, especially (per. 6) in David, as made king in II Samuel 5:1–4, 1003 B.C.

66. Gen 49:9 (1 v., fig.): Judah to be a lion, in victory over his enemies;

57. KD, I:185.
58. A play on words between *yōdhūkhā*, "shall praise thee," and *y'hūdhā, Judah,* lit., "praised"; cf. 29:35.

cf. v. 8b. Fulfillment (per. 6): David was chosen, in part for the success with which he had so far led the troops of Israel (II Sam 5:2); and he went on to win many more victories (ch. 8).

67. Gen 49:10a (1 v., fig.): the scepter to remain in Judah "until[59] *shīlō*, come; and unto Him. . . ." *Shīlō* cannot refer to the city of Shiloh (ASV text), for that town was destroyed before Judah ever rose to power (Jer 7:14); the following clause, moreover, indicates a person. As a noun or adjective from the root *shālā*, "to be at ease," *shīlō* might suggest a "peaceful one" or "rest-giver," as a term for the Messiah; but this view lacks Scriptural confirmation and arose, indeed, only within the last century. *Shīlō* seems best rendered as in the LXX, which divided the term into three elements: "*she*, whom"; *l'*, "to"; and *ō*, "Him." The thought expressed is thus, "whom, to Him (it is)"; or, "to whom it is." The sentence then reads, "The scepter shall not depart from Judah until the One come whose it is" (cf. ASVmg). The same Hebrew syntax is repeated in the confirmatory Messianic prophecy of Ezek 21:27. Gen 49:10a becomes therefore the first Biblical prophecy in which the deliverance, which had been mankind's anticipation from 3:15 onward, is explicitly said to come about through one individual (see No. 7 and 46, above). The NT accordingly can speak of "Him of whom Moses wrote in the Law," John 1:45, 5:46. Fulfillment (per. 13): the birth of Jesus within this royal tribe (Heb 7:14), so that upon Judah Messianic prophecy is henceforward concentrated (cf. Mt 2:5–6).[60]

68. Gen *49:10b* (fig.): "and unto Him shall the obedience[61] of the peoples be." Fulfillment (per. 16): this situation must pertain to Christ's second advent, with a kingship of political reality; for it is one in which the peoples obey Him. So too Ezek 21:27 (see No. 67, above) connects His coming with the ending of the overthrow of the sovereignty of Judah; and Rev 5:5 describes His redemptive victory by saying, "the Lion" (see No. 66, above) that is from the tribe of Judah has overcome. Gen 49:10b thus becomes the initial prophecy of the future kingdom of God on earth.

69. Gen 49:11–12 (2 vv., fig.): Judah to prosper, with wine and milk. So many will be his grapes that he can afford to hitch donkeys to the vines; and his garments are splashed from the grape treading. Fulfillment (per. 4): Judah's territory (Josh 15) included Hebron, where the spies sent by Moses found grapes of outstanding quality (Num 13:22–24).

70. Gen 49:13 (1 v., fig.): Zebulun to dwell "*l'hōf*, toward the sea-shore," with "his side *'al*, toward Sidon." The mention of Sidon rather than Tyre was to be expected in Jacob's time, since Sidon was the older city, though Tyre would be closer geographically. Fulfillment (per. 4): Zebulun's border did not, in fact, extend down the Esdraelon Valley to the coast,

59. Nor need it depart thereafter; cf. the inclusive use of *until* in 26:13, 28:15.
60. Payne, *Theology*, pp. 259–260.
61. KB, p. 397; KJV's "gathering" lacks support.

which was allocated to Asher, but only *toward* it, though the commerce of the ships did flow through Zebulun (Josh 19:10–16).

71. Gen 49:14–15 (2 vv., fig.): Issachar, like a bony[62] donkey lying down between a pair of saddle bags,[63] to toil and serve. Fulfillment (per. 4): Issachar's territory in fertile Esdraelon, E of Zebulun (Josh 19:17–23), though Manasseh to the S came to control some of its cities (17:11).

72. Gen 49:16–17 (2 vv., fig.): Dan to judge[64] his people, like any other tribe of Israel;[65] and may he even be like a dangerous snake. God foresaw a time when there would be need to encourage Dan about attaining full tribal status; for the Danites were badly pushed back from their coastal lands W of Benjamin and Ephraim after the death of Joshua (Jd 1:34). Fulfillment (per. 5): yet soon thereafter[66] the Danites fell violently on Laish in the far N (18:1, 27–28); and Dan produced the 11th-century judge, the dangerous Samson, 13:2, 25.

73. Gen 49:19 (1 v., fig.): "Gad, a troop shall press upon him";[67] but he shall press back. Fulfillment (per. 5): located in central Gilead (Josh 13:24–28), Gad was particularly open to attack from the eastern desert and from Ammon, Jd 11:12, Jer 49:1. But it could and did strike back, Jd 11: 32–33.[68]

74. Gen 49:20 (1 v., fig.): Asher, in a figure for his descendants, to produce fine food. Fulfillment (per. 4): located on the coast, N of Carmel (Josh 19:24–31), the men of Asher possessed a rich land. Deut 33:24 describes Asher poetically as "dipping his foot in oil" from the olives.

75. Gen 49:21 (1 v., fig.): Naphtali is like a deer let loose, producing branched antlers.[69] The figure may indicate swiftly moving warriors, as in II Sam 22:34, I Chron 12:8, Ps 18:33. Fulfillment (per. 5): probably the marshaling of Naphtali from the N, and their rapid move across mountainous terrain to Tabor, under the Naphtalite Barak (Jd 4:6, 10; 5:15).

76. Gen 49:23–24 (2 vv., fig.): the Joseph tribes, though attacked, to keep strong. The basis for their hope would lie in God, "from there where the Shepherd, the Stone of Israel, is," v. 24; cf. II Sam 22:32b.[70] Fulfillment (per. 4): during the conquest, Ephraim and Manasseh had to face the iron chariots of the Canaanites (Josh 17:16); but Joshua encouraged his people against them, v. 18; cf Jd 1:22–25, 35.

77. Gen 49:27 (1 v., fig.): Benjamin to devour like a wolf. Fulfillment

---

62. Ibid., p. 194.
63. AB, p. 367; KB, p. 580.
64. A play on words: Dan mean *judge;* cf. 30:6.
65. AB, loc. cit.
66. For this event is recorded in Josh 19:47, written about 1375 B.C.
67. Another play on words: *gādh g'dhūdh y'ghūdhennū.*
68. Note also I Chron 5:18–22, which probably belongs to the same time as v. 10, namely that of Saul, ICC, *Chron,* p. 124, though KD, p. 109, asserts, "certainly at a later time," which the text does not give, but at least before 733.
69. KB, pp. 64, 1006; not "giving goodly words."
70. Leupold, op. cit., p. 1195.

(per. 5): an apparent anticipation of the violence of Israel's second judge, Ehud of Benjamin (Jd 3:15–23, 26–29), or of the whole tribe (19:22–20:25). The expression could apply to Saul's expansion, I Sam 14:47–48, or to certain violent Benjamites under David, I Chron 12:2, 16–18; but the earliest fulfillment is the most likely.[71]

71. See above, p. 118.

EXODUS

For the remaining four books of the Pentateuch—Exodus through Deuteronomy—most of the prophetic matter was revealed historically through the person of Moses. Genesis had concluded with the family of the patriarch Jacob (= Israel) descending into Egypt in 1843 B.C. and with his son Joseph's death there in 1772. The opening chapter of Exodus then rapidly surveys the succeeding centuries, during which Yahweh magnified this single patriarchal clan into a nation exceeding 2 million souls (Ex 1:7, 12:37); but the remainder of the book centers on Moses and his leadership of oppressed Israel in the "exodus" out of the land of the pharaohs. The predictions that it contains commence with the Lord's call to Moses early in 1447 B.C. (2:24 ff.), at a point when he was already in his eightieth year (7:7); and they continue on into its closing chapter, which is to be dated in the spring of 1445, some two seasons later (40:17).

According to the Biblical evidence, Moses was not only the mediator of the Pentateuchal prophecies but also their recorder, so that Exodus–Deuteronomy are frequently subtitled "the second through fifth books of Moses." More precisely, Scripture defines three levels of Mosaicity within these books. (1) Parts written down by Moses:

Ex 3:6 (E),[1] per Lk 20:37	Lev 18:5 (H), per Rom 10:5 ASV
Ex 17:8–13 (E), as stated in v. 14	Num 33:3–49 (P), cf. v. 2
Ex 20:22–ch. 23 (E), cf. 24:4	Dt 5–30 (D), cf. 31:9
Ex 34:10–26 (J), cf. v. 27	Dt 32:1–43 (D), cf. 31:22

These embrace approximately 32 out of the 187 chapters of the Pentateuch. But this first level may well include considerably more material, where the work of his immediate hand simply has not happened to be recorded within the OT text; compare the case of Lev 18:5, above. (2) Parts composed by Moses, though not necessarily written down by him, as Dt 1:6–4:40

1. Representing the "source documents" as these have been assigned by the Welhausen school of criticism: J = the Jahwist, ca. 850 B.C.; E, the Elohist, 750; D, the Deuteronomist, 622; and H, the Holiness code, which is included in P, the Priestly source, 444.

or 33:2–29. These include all his quoted statements and, for practical purposes, remain equivalent to the previous level. (3) Parts historically authentic and springing from the Mosaic period, which seem to include the remainder of the Pentateuch, e.g. Dt 1:1–5, 4:41–49, or ch. 34, on Moses' death; compare the threats of 4:2 and 12:32 against anyone's making post-Mosaic additions to the content of the text.[2] This position is reinforced by the rest of the Bible (cf. Josh 1:8, I K 2:3). II Chronicles 34:14, for example, speaks of "the book of the law of Yahweh, [lit.:] by the hand of Moses" (ASVmg); and references by our Lord to "the book of Moses" (Mk 12:26, Lk 24:44) indicate His own belief in a Mosaic superintendence over the Pentateuch as a whole.[3]

Since the days of Julius Wellhausen a century ago, higher criticism has been unanimous in its rejection of this evidence and in its substituting of a theory that the Pentateuch must be composed of various strata, interwoven by redactors so as to form the present five books. On stylistic and theological grounds the school of Wellhausen identified a series of anonymous source documents, often discovering several within a given chapter or even a single verse and dating them anywhere from 600 to 1,000 years after the time of Moses (see note 1 above). Yet it appears significant that the Pentateuchal portions that are stated to have been written by Moses, as listed above, come from all the various "documents," each supposedly with its own style! Much has been written in recent years of the outmoded nature of Wellhausen's evolutionary approach to the history of Hebrew religion.[4] But his theory of an essentially post-Mosaic Pentateuch continues to hold the field in contemporary liberal scholarship.[5] Critical views of this sort, however, undercut the whole concept of Biblical prediction: they convert the "prophecies," such as Ex 23:27 on the success of the Israelites' conquest of Canaan or 23:29 on their gradual expulsion of the Canaanites, into what becomes but a thinly disguised form of historical description. Note also Christ's words in John 5:46–47.

The Book of Exodus appears then to have been written, by Moses, as something of a journal during the two brief years that concern all but its opening chapters. It was presumably added, as it was composed, to that part of the Pentateuch which already existed (primarily Genesis); note, e.g., Yahweh's words to Moses concerning the Amalekite war (17:14),

2. Redaction is therefore to be limited to the *form* of the text, e.g. in keeping the language or the script up to date; cf. R. Laird Harris, "On a Possible Revision of the Biblical Text During the Monarchy," ETSP (1953), 18–24.

3. Cf. the recognition by Arthur Weiser of Christ's teaching in this regard, *The OT:Its Formation and Development*, p. 72.

4. Cf. H. F. Hahn, *The OT in Modern Research*, pp. 33–34, or N. H. Ridderbos in C. F. H. Henry, ed., *Revelation and the Bible*, pp. 338–340.

5. R. K. Harrison, *Introduction to the OT*, pp. 512–513; cf. Wm. F. Albright's recognition of a source underlying JE, composed during the period of the judges, but his final date for J itself is even later than that proposed by Wellhausen (*From the Stone Age to Christianity*, p. 250).

"Write this for a memorial in *the* book" (ASVmg).[6] The historical narrative of Exodus falls into two distinct parts: I. Israel in Egypt (period 2 of predictive fulfillment), the nation's oppression and deliverance, 1–12:36; II. Israel's opening year in the wilderness (per. 3), 1446–1445 B.C.—first, their journeys up until arrival at Mount Sinai in the third month of the exodus, 12:36–ch. 18; and second, Israel's stay at Sinai, chs. 19–40. This stay includes (a) the nation's adoption as God's "peculiar [= specially possessed] people" under the Sinaitic testament, ch. 19 (cf. 5, as the high point of the entire book); (b) the revelation of two legal codes that should regulate her life as the redeemed people of God, chs. 20–24 (the basic principles of the Decalogue, 20:3–17, and then the representative legislation of the Book of the Testament, 20:23–ch. 23); and finally (c) the construction of the tabernacle, as a visible demonstration of the dwelling of Yahweh in the midst of His adopted nation, chs. 25–40 (including both His instructions as given on the Mount, 25–31, and then, with much verbal duplication, their subsequent execution by Moses, 35–40).

The predictive material of Exodus corresponds largely to the above outline: most of the prophecies in the earlier sections take the form of spoken oracles; but those from ch. 25 onward are almost entirely typical in form, consisting of objective phenomena related to the tabernacle. When to these are added, out of the earlier chapters, such major elements of OT typology as the Passover service (12:3) or Israel's sabbath observance (16:23), it becomes apparent why Exodus ranks second only to Leviticus in its revelation of the forms and meanings of the Biblical types. 387 out of the book's 487 predictive verses, or 80%, concern typology. Viewed then as a whole, the 487 verses that involve prophecy convey 69 distinct predictions, and they occupy 40% out of the 1,213-verse total that makes up the Book of Exodus.

1. Ex 2:24; 6:*4a*, 5 (2 vv. typ.): the Abrahamic testament. Fulfillment (per. 13): as in Gen. prophecy No. 30.

2. Ex *3:8a*, *17a*; 6:6a, *7b*; 7:4b, *5c* (2 vv.): Israel to be delivered from Egypt. Fulfillment (per. 2): Ex 12:41, 51; 13:18; as in Gen. No. 33.

3. Ex 3:8b, 17b; *6:8a*; *12:25a*; 13:5a, 11a, 19; 15:13, 17; 23:*20b*, 23b; *33:14b* (8 vv.): God's promise to bring Israel back to Canaan, to "the mountain of Thine inheritance, the place which Thou hast made for Thee to dwell in, the sanctuary, *miqdāsh,* which Thy hands have established" (13:17); cf. v. 13, "Thy holy habitation, *n'wē qodhshékhā.*" Concerning this last phrase, commentators have explained: "The holy habitation of God was Canaan (Ps 78:54), which had been consecrated as a sacred abode for Jehovah in the midst of His people by the revelations made to

---

6. Though cf. E. J. Young's caution against overstressing the definite article, *An Introduction to the OT,* p. 45.

the patriarchs there, and especially by the appearance of God at Bethel (Gen 28:16 ff., 31:13, 35:7)."⁷ Psalm 78:54 reads, "He brought them to His holy border, *g'vūl qodhshō*"; and 83:12 thereafter designates the land as "the habitation [ASVmg, 'pastures'] of God," from the root *nāwe*, as in Ex 15:13. Concerning v. 17, however, it has been proposed⁸ that Moses' inspired utterance relates not to the land in its entirety but to the sanctuary at Jerusalem: first David's tent and then Solomon's temple.⁹ Yet Lange cautions, "It seems one-sided to refer the prophecy directly to the definite locality of the sanctuary on Moriah";¹⁰ and from Dt 3:25 (and also Ps 78:54) it would appear that Moses' reference to "that mountain" (paralleling the phrase in Ex 15:17) might apply to the Canaanitish "hill-country" (ASVmg) as a whole. So Auberlen concludes: "In spirit Moses already saw the people brought to *Canaan,* which Jehovah had described, in the promise given to the fathers and repeated to him, as His own dwelling place where He would abide in the midst of His people in holy separation [cf. the use of *miqdāsh,* in Num 18:29 for the 'hallowed part'] from the nations of the world."¹¹ Fulfillment (per. 4): Joshua 3:16–17; as in Genesis No. 36.

4. Ex *3:8c, 17c; 13:5b:* Israel to inherit "a good land and a large, a land flowing with milk and honey." Fulfillment (per. 4): as in Gen No. 52.

5. Ex *3:12a*; 4:12, 15–16; 11:8 (4 vv.): that God would empower Moses and Aaron for speaking and leading Israel out of Egypt; cf. Moses' own later assurance in 11:8. Fulfillment (per. 2): they did so lead, 12:31; cf. 11:3, on the greatness of Moses in the sight of the Egyptians.

6. Ex 3:12b (1 v.): Israel to serve God on Sinai. Fulfillment (per. 3): they did, 19:17. On the purpose of this prophecy, see above, p. 14.

7. Ex 3:18a, 4:8 (2 vv.): Israel to be obedient to Moses. Fulfillment (per. 2): they were, 4:31.

8. Ex *3:18b*; 5:3, 8, 17; 8:8, 25–29; 23:18; 32:8; 34:25a (12 vv., typical): sacrifice. Fulfillment (per. 13): as in Lev. No. 2.

9. Ex 3:19; 4:21, *23a*; 7:3–*4a*; 9:30; 11:9 (5 vv.): Pharaoh to refuse Moses' request for Israel's release. Behind it would lie God's hardening of the pharaoh's heart, 4:21. Fulfillment (per. 2): he refused, 5:2; God hard-

7. KD, *Pentateuch,* II:54.
8. So, ibid., II:55–56, for v. 17.
9. The issue is complicated by liberalism's charge of *vaticinium post eventum,* namely, of pseudo-prophecy, actually composed after the event "predicted"; for if the Exodus reference were indeed to a Jerusalem temple, it would have anticipated this structure by almost 500 years, the genuineness of which antisupernaturalism simply could not admit. But while Moses' prediction of such a sanctuary remains quite possible for the believing mind, the question remains whether this is indeed the intended fulfillment, or simply the occupation of the *land* some 40 years beyond Ex 15 under Joshua.
10. II:54, though he does then make reference to the tabernacle's early location at Shiloh (Josh 18:1); cf. Dummelow, *A Commentary on the Holy Bible,* p. 62, "The fixed abode of the ark is meant here, perhaps Shiloh its first resting place."
11. Recognized by quotation in KD, II:56.

ened him, 9:12, 10:20, 27, 11:10. 7:13 and 8:15 cite, indeed, the previous prophecy.

10. Ex 3:20a; *6:6b; 7:4c, 5b;* 9:14 (2 vv.): God to smite down Egypt, with miraculous interventions. Fulfillment (per. 2): the ten plagues, as in Gen 15:14a. More specifically, when 9:14 reads, "I will this time send all My plagues upon thy heart," this must refer to the last three, which yet remained.[12]

11: Ex *3:20b,* 6:1, 11:1b (2 vv.): Pharaoh to release the Israelites— to drive them, indeed, from his land (6:1, 11:1). Fulfillment (per. 2): so it was, 12:31–32.

12. Ex 3:21–22 (2 vv.): Israel is not to depart empty from Egypt but is to ask jewels, raiment, etc. (not "borrow," KJV), and so despoil the Egyptians. Fulfillment (per. 2): so it was, 11:3, 12:35–36; as in Gen 15:14c.

13. Ex 4:14 (1 v.): Aaron to meet Moses returning to Egypt, with joy. Fulfillment (per. 2): he did, v. 27.

14. Ex 4:23b; 11:*1a,* 4–7; 12:12–13, 23, *27b* (8 vv.): the 10th plague, God's slaying of the firstborn of Pharaoh and of all Egypt (though not of Israel, 11:17, 12:3, 23). Fulfillment (per. 2): it came to pass, 12:29.

15. Ex 4:25–26; 12:*44b,* 48 (3 vv., typ.): circumcision. Fulfillment (per. 13), as in Gen. No. 42.

16. Ex 6:4b, 8b; 12:25b; *13:5c, 11b;* 20:12; *32:13b;* 33:1 (5 vv.): God's covenanted promise to grant Israel the land of Canaan. Fulfillment (per. 4), as in Gen. No. 24.

17. Ex 6:7a (1 v.): God's testament to be granted to Israel. Fulfillment (per. 3): at Mount Sinai, 19:5.

18. Ex 7:5a, *7:17a* (1 v.): the Egyptians, including also the pharaoh (v. 17), to recognize Yahweh, as a result of Israel's exodus; cf. 8:10, a similar, though here nonpredictive, goal on the part of Moses. Fulfillment (per. 2): so it came about, 8:19, 10:7; cf. Pharaoh's recognition in 8:8, 9:27, 10:16–17, 12:31.

19. Ex 7:15 (1 v.): Pharaoh to go out to the water the following morning (cf. No. 22, below). Fulfillment (per. 2) may be inferred from v. 20; for while it does not describe his "going out," it does state that the water was "in the sight of Pharaoh" and then, v. 23, that he turned and went into his house.

20. Ex 7:17b–19 (3 vv.): the 1st plague upon Egypt, God's turning the waters into blood.[13] The prediction was contained in Yahweh's instructions

---

12. "From the plural, *'strokes,'* it is evident that this threat referred not only to the seventh plague, viz. the hail, but to all the other [remaining] plagues," ibid., I:490.

13. This change may refer primarily to coloring matter, Joel 2:31, cf. II K 3:22; for it could be filtered out, Ex 7:24. But the speed of the change, with its universality and deadliness, remains miraculous.

to Moses concerning what he was to say to Pharaoh, and which Moses did carry out, v. 20. Fulfillment (per. 2): the plague came, vv. 20–21.

21. Ex 8:2–4 (3 vv.): the 2nd plague, frogs. Fulfillment (per. 2): v. 6.

22. Ex 8:20 (1 v.): a later prediction of the same nature as No. 19 above, on Pharaoh's going out to the water. Fulfillment (per. 2), again by inference.

23. Ex 8:21–23 (3 vv.): the 4th plague, flies; but not on Goshen. Fulfillment (per. 2), v. 24. The exemption of Goshen is not here specified; but it may be assumed, for "Yahweh did so." This seems especially probable in light of the subsequent distinctions that *are* recorded, for the 5th (9:6–7), 7th (9:26), and 9th (10:23) plagues.

24. Ex 9:3–5 (3 vv.): the 5th plague, murrain on the cattle of Egypt, except for Israel's, and foretold to come about on the following day. Fulfillment (per 2): it was so, vv. 6–7.

25. Ex 9:9 (1 v.): the 6th plague, boils on man and beast. Fulfillment (per. 2): vv. 10–11.

26. Ex 9:18–19 (2 vv.): the 7th plague, hail; but not on Goshen. Fulfillment (per. 2): vv. 23–26.

27. Ex 9:29 (1 v.): Moses' prediction of the ceasing of the hail. Fulfillment (per. 2): it stopped, v. 33.

28. Ex 10:4–6 (3 vv.): the 8th plague, locusts. Fulfillment (per. 2): vv. 13–15.

29. Ex 10:25a; 18:12a; *20:24c*; *24:5b*; 29:22, 24–28, 31–34; 32:6b (13 vv., typical): peace offerings, in contrast to burnt offerings. Fulfillment (pers. 13 and 16), as in Lev. No. 5.

30. Ex *10:25b*; *18:12b*; 20:24b; 24:5a; 29:15–18, 28–39, 41–*42a*; *32:6a*; *40:29b* (9 vv., typ.): burnt offerings. Fulfillment (per. 13), as in Lev. No. 3.

31. Ex 12:3–4, 6–7, 10–11, 14, 21–22, 24, 26–28, 42–45, 47, 49–50; 13:13–16; 34:20, *25b* (25 vv., typ.): Passover. This term had a fourfold connotation. (1) Passover was an event, of the year 1446 B.C.: the death angel struck, but "passed over" Israel, 12:27. (2) It was a ceremony, more than simply a heavy feast to prepare Israel for the exodus that commenced the following morning, vv. 31–33. The unleavened bread (12:8, 15–20; 13:3, 6–10) pointed to the purity of the believers (cf. I Cor 5:8) but indicated primarily the hastiness of their departure from Egypt (Ex 12:34, Dt 16:3); and the bitter herbs (Ex 12:8) were suggestive of the bitterness of their preceding bondage (1:14). Items of this sort[14] are symbols, but not yet of a predictive variety;[15] there is no indication that God intended them to be types foreshadowing Jesus Christ. The most significant part of the Passover ceremony, however, consisted of slaying the Paschal lamb and marking the doorways with its blood (12:6–7); for this was a token of

14. See also J. B. Payne, *Theology of the Older Testament*, p. 402.
15. See above, pp. 47–48.

Israel's preservation (v. 13) through redemptive substitution (13:13). *All* the firstborn in the land of Egypt had been doomed to death (11:5); but Israel's eating of the lamb became "the sustenance of a new, a ransomed life,"[16] 12:8, 13:15; cf. John 6:53–57. (3) The Passover was perpetuated as an annual feast (Ex 12:14). Israel's firstborn children, that is, continued perpetually to be God's; and they stood in unabated need of divine redemption (Ex 13:2, Num 3:13), because of the fact of sin (cf. this stress in Ex 13:15): "Henceforth these first-born . . . lived, in a sense, out of death . . . in holy consecration to the Lord . . . as an act of redemption, saving them from guilt."[17] (4) The Passover eventuates in typology; it served as a medium for Israel's anticipatory faith. Fulfillment (per. 13): Christ, the believer's Passover, sacrificed for us (I Cor 5:7) on the very afternoon that history's last legitimate Paschal lambs were being prepared, John 13:1, 18:28. The Passover was also *specifically* predictive in two regards, as follows.

32. Ex 12:5 (1 v., typ.): that the Passover lamb must be "without blemish." Fulfillment (per. 13): the sinlessness of Christ, I Pet 1:18–19.

33. Ex 12:8–9, 46 (3 vv., typ.): that the lamb must be maintained whole, without a bone being broken (cf. Num 9:12). Fairbairn explains, "The lamb must be preserved entire, and roasted, so that it might not be served up to them in a mutilated form, nor have part of its substance wasted by being boiled in water." Fulfillment (per. 13): the body of Christ, "dealt with as a sacred thing and preserved free from violence,"[18] John 19:33, 36.

34. Ex 14:3–4, 13–14, 17–18 (6 vv.): Pharaoh to pursue Israel, and yet fail. Fulfillment (per. 3): this occurred, vv. 5–9, 23–28, 30–31.

35. Ex 14:16 (1 v.): Israel to pass through the Red Sea on dry ground. Fulfillment (per. 3): they did, vv. 22, 29.

36. Ex 14:19–20 (2 vv., typ.): the cloud of God's presence, shielding Israel at the Red Sea. "By the cloud passing over and resting between them and the Egyptians, and afterwards by their passing under its protection through the Red Sea in safety, they were baptized into Moses; for thus the line of demarcation was drawn between their old vassalage and the new state and prosperity on which, under Moses, they had entered."[19] Their new status, moreover, was not simply one of freedom but also of salvation, of reconciliation with God (19:4). Fulfillment (per. 14): Christian baptism; see I Cor 10:1–2.

37. Ex 14:22 (1 v., typ.): Israel's crossing through the Red Sea. Fair-

16. P. Fairbairn, *The Typology of Scripture*, II:387; cf. the contextual stress upon the redeemed community, 12:3–4, 21 (see I Cor 10:17), celebrating in their homes, 12:22, 46.

17. Ibid., II:45.

18. Ibid., II:387.

19. Ibid., I:368. Fairbairn adds, "Christ and the gospel were there; for all that was then given and done linked itself by a spiritual bond with the better things to come."

bairn elaborates upon the contemporaneous symbolism of this event, upon which basis the NT is enabled to posit a further typology: "The passage of the Israelites through the Red Sea, under the guidance and direction of Moses, Paul represents as a sort of baptism to him; because it . . . sealed the death of Israel to the bondage of Pharaoh . . . and their expectation of the inheritance promised them by Moses."[20] Fulfillment (per. 14): baptism, as in No. 36, above.

38. Ex 15:14–16 (3 vv., fig.): Moses' anticipation of the trembling and the "melting away" of the people of Canaan and of the lands surrounding it, when they should learn of Israel's crossing the Red Sea. Fulfillment (per. 3): these very phrases became descriptive of the dismay of the Canaanites at Jericho, Josh 2:9, 11, 24.

39. Ex 16:4–5, 13–22, 31–35 (17 vv. typ.): manna, Israel's "bread from heaven," 16:4; cf. Num 11:6–9, Ps 78:24. Its source was God; and its result, life; see John 6:35. "Paul calls it 'the spiritual meat' (I Cor 10:3). . . . Such meat being God's special provision for a redeemed people . . . contained a pledge that He who consulted so graciously for the life of the body, would prove Himself equally ready to administer to the necessities of the soul, as He did in a measure even then, and does now more fully in Christ."[21] Fulfillment (per. 13): the incarnation of Jesus Christ, "the bread which comes down out of heaven," John 6:33; cf. Rev. 2:17.

40. Ex 16:6–8, 12 (4 vv.): Moses' prediction that Israel would see the glory of God, with provision of quail and manna. Fulfillment (per. 3): all came about, the glory (v. 10), the quail (v. 13a), and the manna (vv. 13b–14).

41. Ex 16:23–30, 20:8–11, 23:12, 31:12–17, 34:21, 35:1–3 (23 vv., typ.): sabbath. In Exodus 31:13 the sabbath is stated to be a sign, "that ye may know that I am Yahweh who sanctifieth you." V. 16, moreover, designates it "a perpetual *b'rīth*," thus closely identifying it with God's redemptive testament.[22] Fulfillment (per. 13): Christ's sanctifying ministry, which would give rest, Mt 11:28–30; cf. Gen 2:3. The sabbath was a shadow of good things to come;[23] but "the substance belongs to Christ," Col 2:16–17.[24]

20. Ibid., II:65.
21. Ibid., II:60. Fairbairn, however, goes too far in finding typical significance in matters such as the plentifulness of the manna for all, its availability around the camp, its need for daily gathering, etc., II:61–62.
22. Cf. Payne, op. cit., p. 396. This function of testamentary sanctification seems to have been that of the 7 special "convocation sabbaths" of Lev 23 also (listed under Lev 19:3, below; cf. ibid., p. 400); but such concepts are not evident for the new moons (Num 10:10, 28:11) or for the sabbatic years (Lev 25:1–7), so that these latter are not subsequently discussed as predictive.
23. The sabbaths as observed by Judaism after the inception of Christ's ministry are thus omitted from further predictive consideration; see above, p. 56.
24. The sabbath served also as a symbol of heaven, Heb 4:9–11; see above, p. 135. But this is hardly predictive: for from Adam onward all the OT saints were

42. Ex 17:6 (1 v., typ.): the water that flowed out when Moses struck "the rock in Horeb," specifically, at Rephidim.[25] Fulfillment (per. 13): Christ, who gives His life that men may receive "living water" (John 4:11), "springing up to eternal life" (v. 14). He could thus proclaim, "Come to Me" and drink (7:35, 37). His sacrifice, moreover, availed for the OT saints as well (Heb 9:15, 11:40); and Fairbairn explains, "The rock typically so represented Christ . . . that in drinking of the water which flowed from it, they at the same time received Christ. [It was] in the nature of a sacrament, and answered to our spiritually eating and drinking of Christ in the Supper."[26] As stated in I Cor 10:4, "They were drinking from a spiritual rock that followed them, and the rock was Christ." It is not that a rock literally followed them to Kadesh (Num 20:8–11),[27] according to rabbinic legend, but that "the waters flowing from it pursued for a time the same course [as the Hebrews]. The region of Sinai is elevated . . . the ground slopes from the base to a considerable distance all around, so that the water would naturally flow with the Israelites."[28] The life-giving quality is the one and only feature of the rock that is Scripturally indicated as being typical, not the accompanying details, such as its being smitten.[29] Even in respect to the preservation of life afforded by its water, "the great mass" of Israel probably did not get "the faintest glimpse of Christ" in it; cf. the NT's further statement, of criticism, in I Cor 10:5. Yet still, "Such as really were children of faith . . . could apprehend that what God was now doing to them . . . He did as a sign and pledge that such provision as He had made for the lower necessities of their nature, He must assuredly have made, and would in His own time fully disclose, for the higher."[30]

43. Ex 17:14, 16 (2 vv.): that God would have continuing war with Amalek until He had blotted it out. Fulfillment (per. 7): when a group from Simeon smote the last recorded remnant of the Amalekites, in the days of Hezekiah, I Chron 4:39–43.

---

taken to glory immediately upon death (Ps 73:24; cf. 49:15, and Payne, op. cit., ch. 30); cf. the continued observance of sabbath in the New Jerusalem, Isa 66:23.

25. Probably in the Wadi Refayid, IDB, IV:36. Rephidim is said to be "at the mount of God" (18:5), for it was only one day's march from Sinai (19:1–2); KD, *Pentateuch*, II:75–76.

26. Op. cit., II:65; cf. the manna in ch. 16, No. 39 above, and the crossing of the Red Sea, typifying baptism, No. 36 and 37.

27. The rock in Kadesh is a different one and appears to carry no typical value; see above, p. 54.

28. Ibid., II:64. He cites in support: Ps 78:20, "The waters gushed out and the streams overflowed"; 105:41, "They ran in the dry places like a river"; and Isa 48:21.

29. Fairbairn states with some bluntness, "The smiting of the rock by Moses with the rod could not suggest the idea of anything like violence done to it. . . . Moses was the mediator between God and the people . . . while the smiting of Christ, which is commonly held to correspond with this . . . is nothing more than a specious accommodation of the language," ibid., II:67–68.

30. Ibid., II:66.

44. Ex 17:15; 20:*24a,* 25–26; 21:14; 24:4, *6b;* 32:5, misc. references to altars, but especially 27:1–8; 30:28a; 31:9a; 35:16; 38:1–7, 30b; 39:39; 40:6, 10, 29a, *33b,* on the tabernacle's brazen altar (29 vv., typ.):[31] the altar, *mizbeah,* "place of slaughter." Fulfillment (per. 13): the death of Christ. There is no way to God except as one moves by the altar, Heb 9:22.

45. Ex 19:5–6; 24:6–8; 34:*10a,* 27–28 (7 vv., typ.): the Sinaitic testament, by which Israel became the chosen people, adopted by Yahweh for His "own possession" (19:5). In particular, the nation became united with Him by the sprinkling of blood (24:8): part on the altar, directed to God, but the other part on the people, so that they came literally under the blood. Fulfillment (per. 13): the death of Christ the testator for the salvation of His people; see especially His explanation at the Last Supper, "This is My blood of the testament" (Mt 26:28), and the commentary in Heb 9:18–22, that the OT saints too were being cleansed by the blood of Christ.

46. Ex 23:16, 34:22 (2 vv., typ.): the Feast of Ingathering, or Tabernacles. This harvest festival is the one OT feast that is singled out for observance (and fulfillment) in the eschatological context of the testament of peace (per. 16). Oehler notes: "The admission of this festival into Zechariah's prophecy of Messianic times (14:16) is undoubtedly founded on the kindred thought, that the keeping of the Feast of Tabernacles is an expression on the part of the nations of their thankfulness for the termination of their wanderings, by their reception into the peaceful kingdom of the Messiah."[32]

47. Ex 23:20–*23a;* 32:34; 33:*2a,* 14a, 16–17 (7 vv.): the Angel of Yahweh to guide and guard Israel in the wilderness. This "Angel of the Lord" possessed the qualities of deity and yet is a Person distinct from Yahweh; the OT thus seems to describe preincarnate appearances of Christ (Gen 16:7–13, Ex 3:2–6, and so on to Mal 3:1).[33] Ex 33:14–15 therefore speaks of Yahweh's "presence," *panékha,* lit., "Thy face," as identical with the Angel;[34] and in v. 16 Moses prays simply "that Thou goest with us." Fulfillment, per. 3; for Num 20:16 looks back upon the phenomenon of the Angel as accomplished. So in Jd. 2:1–2 the Angel of Yahweh appeared again to Israel, stating that He had brought them out of Egypt and into the land of Canaan (cf. Josh 5:13–15).

48. Ex 23:*23c,* 27–28, *31b;* 33:2b; 34:10b–11, *24a* (5 vv.): God to

---

31. The material of the Hebrew altar seemed to possess no specially typical meaning. It could be specified as "an altar of earth" (20:24), perhaps symbolizing a repudiation of human skill or depicting human unworthiness, or of unhewn stones (v. 25)—which still probably lined the brazen altar—and thus not profaned by human effort. But such symbolism is not indicated as having a further, predictive connotation.
32. *Theology of the OT,* p. 351.
33. Payne, op. cit., pp. 167–170.
34. KD, II:152, 234.

overthrow, to drive out, and to cut off the Canaanites before Israel. "I will send the hornet before thee" (23:28), a figure for the fear of God, Josh 24:12:[35] and in the process He would perform unparalleled marvels (34: 10). Fulfillment (per. 4): not a man of their enemies stood before them, Josh 21:44, cf. 11:16–20.[36]

49. Ex *23:25a:* the future blessing upon Israel in her land, especially an abundance of water, and the bread that results from it. Fulfillment (per. 16): compare Amos 9:13–14, with its millennial prosperity, and the as yet unrealized character of No. 50–52, following.

50. Ex 23:25b (1 v.): sickness to be taken away. Fulfillment not yet realized, but only in per. 16: millennial health, "the glorious prospect before Israel, if the people remain true to the Lord."[37]

51. Ex 23:26a (1 v.): no more barrenness or miscarriages.[38] Fulfillment (per. 16): millennial fruitfulness of the human population.[39]

52. Ex *23:26b:* "The number of thy days I will fulfill"; that is, they will "not be liable to a premature death."[40] Fulfillment (per. 16): men's attainment to full lifetimes during the future Messianic kingdom (cf. Zech 8:4).

53. Ex 23:29–30 (2 vv.): Israel's gradual conquest of Canaan, "little by little." Fulfillment (per. 5): as their eventual occupation of the land so developed, Jd 1:19–36.

54. Ex 23:31a, *34:24b* (1 v.): an enlargement of Israel's territories, once the Canaanites should be cast out. The borders of the land are predicted to extend from the Red Sea to the Euphrates (23:31). Fulfillment (per. 6): under Solomon, as in Gen. No. 37.

55. Ex 25:8–9; 26:1–30, 36–37; 27:9–19, *21a;* 29:4, 42b–46; 30:24, 26a, 29, 36; 31:7a; 34:26; 35:11, 15, 17–18, 21a; 36:1, 3–4, 6, 8–34, 37–38; 38:9–21, 24–28, *30a,* 31; 39:32–34, 38, 40; 40:1–2, 5, 8–9, 17–19, 22a, 24, 26a, 28, 33–38 (136 vv., typ): the tabernacle, signifying God's presence with men (25:8). "I will dwell among the children of Israel and will be their God" (29:45). This truth was especially depicted by the figures of the angelic cherubim on the mercy seat of the ark in the holy of

---

35. KD, II:153–154. John Garstang developed a theory on the hornet, as symbolizing the presence of Egypt and of its troops in Canaan during the period of the judges, *The Foundations of Bible History: Joshua-Judges,* pp. 112–115. But while his reconstruction appears likely, with slight modifications (see Payne, *An Outline of Hebrew History,* pp. 79–80, 81–83), the hornet is better understood as above.

36. Yet in this same context are stated conditional elements: that much would depend on their obedience, Ex 23:22; cf. vv. 25, 32; compare Moses' intimations of national noncompliance, v. 33.

37. C. F. H. Henry, ed., *The Biblical Expositor,* I:110.

38. J. P. Lange, ed., *Commentary on the Holy Scriptures,* II:98.

39. Not primarily of cattle: the ASV, "cast her young," is misleading as a rendering for *shākhal, pi'el,* "bereave of children, suffer abortion," KB, p. 969.

40. KD, II:153.

holies, 25:18–22, and on the curtains, 26:1, 31. The tabernacle thus served as a sacrament, as the visible sign and seal of the reality of Yahweh's testamentary promise to be present as Israel's God and of the fact that He and sinners were now truly reconciled. To this the very names of the tabernacle bear witness: *mishkān*, God's active "dwelling" with His own (25: 9mg); *ōhel mō'ēdh*, the "tent of meeting," where God met with Moses (29: 42–4); or, the "house of Yahweh," the place, that is, of His localized appearance (34:26).[41]

At the time of God's revelation of the tabernacle, Moses was cautioned that its construction must conform to the meaningful pattern which was made known to him on the mount (Sinai, Ex 25:9, 40; Heb 8:5). "The outer tabernacle . . . which is a symbol" (Heb 9:8–9) was "a mere copy" (v. 24). Behind it there lay as a pattern "the true tabernacle, which the Lord pitched, not men" (8:2) in "heaven itself" (9:24). Yet the heavenly abode of God was not a predictive matter,[42] so in this regard the tabernacle would not have been a type of the future. Its typical function lay rather in its foreshadowing of the incarnation of Jesus Christ. Here (per. 13) God fulfilled His eternal, heavenly plan of redemption by "communicating" His own being, when "the Word became flesh and dwelt, *eskēnōsen*, lit., *tabernacled*, among us," John 1:14. Jesus could thus speak of His body as "this temple," 2:19. It is true that the NT describes other, subsequent forms of God's tabernacling, or "templing," with men: e.g. in the church (I Cor 6:19, Eph 2:20–22) or in the New Jerusalem (Rev 21:3, where there is no sanctuary building, "for the Lord God and the Lamb are its temple," v. 22); but the features that the NT elaborates concerning the tabernacle (see below, No. 56–67) all apply to Christ's incarnate ministry, and it appears best to restrict the prophetic meaning of the "dwelling" to this one, earliest period of adequate fulfillment.[43]

Before the completion of the wilderness sanctuary, there had been erected a preliminary structure, with the same name as the tabernacle, "the tent of meeting" (Ex 33:7); but this earlier construction appears to have been more of a personal tent of Moses: the presence of God in the pillar of cloud was not permanently there, and it does not seem to have had the typical value of the subsequent tabernacle. Yet the permanent temple buildings which eventually replaced the movable tabernacle of Moses, once Israel had settled in Canaan, perpetuated its same general form and function and so continued to serve as God-inspired types of Christ (cf. I Chron 28:12, 19).

Moreover, even as Moses had been cautioned to observe every aspect of the heavenly pattern (25:9), so too the individual pieces of tabernacle furniture and the activities that were associated with them were designed to convey meaningful truths, arising out of the basic fact of the presence of

41. See also Payne, *Theology*, pp. 361–362.
42. See above, p. 36.
43. See above, p. 118.

God with men; see the predictions that follow, through No. 67. Yet the teaching values for some of the furnishings seem to have been adequately achieved by their contemporaneous symbolism, without reference to predictive typology.[44] Thus, within the holy place, the golden altar of incense (30:1–9) symbolized prayer (Ps 141:2; Lk 1:10; Rev 5:8, 8:3–4) without necessarily typifying the future intercessory work of the ascended Christ;[45] the table of showbread (lit., "bread of presence," because of its position "before Me always," Ex 25:30) depicted in essence the presentation to God of the products of Israel, and perhaps also their good deeds; and the lampstand (vv. 31–39) represented the people of God in their "shining" for Him (cf. Zech 4:6–7, 14, where this same object symbolized the ministries of Zerubbabel and Joshua), without intending a reference, for example, to Christ's future status as the light of the world (John 8:12). As Fairbairn summarizes it,

> The ground of most of the erroneous interpretations on the furniture and services of the Holy Place, lay in understanding all directly and peculiarly of Christ. And this, again, arose from not perceiving that the Tabernacle was intended to symbolize what concerned the people in their relation to God, not less than what concerned God in His relation to them. . . . It is better to consider the things belonging to the Holy Place as having immediate respect to the calling and services of Christ's people.[46]

Other matters relative to the tabernacle demand even greater care in interpretation. Fairbairn himself points to Moses' final anointing of the sanctuary (40:9–11) as a type of Christ's being filled with the Spirit (John 3:34).[47] Confessedly, the tabernacle was designed with Christ in mind, and its effectiveness depended on His work of reconciliation. But the act of its anointing is adequately explained as a symbol of the Spirit's activity of sanctification in OT days (cf. I Sam 16:13–14). Finally, there are numerous aspects to the tabernacle that may not have been symbolical in any regard and could not, as a result, be legitimately applied to the subject of typology at all.[48] That the shaping of the most holy place as a 15-foot cube was "a symbol of perfection"[49] seems open to question; compare Fairbairn's caution, "Some things may have been ordered as they were from convenience, others from necessity, others again from the general effect they

---

44. E.g. the fact that only the Levitical priests were allowed to enter the sacred tent "spoke of imperfection," Fairbairn, op. cit., II:256, 328; but this would still be in symbol for the present, and not in type for the future.

45. As *is* taught, for example, in Rom 8:34. The most that may perhaps be claimed would concern the position of this altar of incense, as lying between the brazen altar of sacrifice and the most holy place of God's presence, indicating that "acceptable prayer must have its foundation in . . . that work of propitiation which He has accomplished," ibid., II:317.

46. Ibid., II:327.

47. Ibid., II:219.

48. See above, p. 52.

49. Ibid., II:254.

were fitted to produce, rather than from any peculiar significance in other respects."[50] He then specifies as among the nonsymbolic features of the tabernacle its materials,[51] its general structure,[52] and its appearance.[53] All such matters were simply "the best and fittest of their several kinds"[54] and were designed "for glory and for beauty" (Ex 28:2, on the tabernacle; cf. I Chron 22:5, on the temple).

56. Ex 25:10–16, 21b, *22b*; *30:6b*, *26b*; *31:7b*; 35:12a; 37:1–5; 39:35a; 40:3a, 5, 20, *21a* (18 vv., typ.): the ark of Yahweh. The central object of the entire tabernacle complex was the ark, over which the cloud of God's presence came particularly to rest, 25:12, 40:34. It was named "the ark of His testament" (Rev 11:19, KJV; cf. Num 10:33), a phrase that is explained by its description in II Chron 6:11 as "the ark wherein is the testament of Yahweh"—the two tables of the Decalogue, which contained the stipulations of the testament, thus representing the whole of God's testamentary arrangement for human redemption. On the mercy seat, which formed its cover, see No. 57, below; its other features appear to represent mere utility or ornament.[55] Fulfillment (per. 13): Christ, the presence of God Himself, executing the testament for man's salvation, Mt 26:28.

57. Ex 25:17–21a; 22a; 26:34; 30:6c; *31:7c;* 35:12b; 37:6–9; *39:35b; 40:20b* (11 vv., typ.): the mercy seat, *kappóreth*, lit., the "atoning cover" of the ark. Yet this golden plate may be treated as an object distinct from the ark itself, Lev 16:2; cf. I Chron 28:11's designation of the temple as "the house of the mercy-seat" (ASVmg). Explanation for the theological function of the mercy seat may be derived from its position, as intervening between the divine glory cloud that was above the ark and the stone tablets of the Decalogue that were within it. As noted by Fairbairn, "The tables of the covenant contained God's testimony [Ex 25:16, 21–22]. . . . It became a testimony against them on account of sin. . . . A covering was therefore needed for them between it on the one hand, and God on the other —but an atonement-covering . . . a propitiatory, a place on which the holy eye of God may ever see the blood of reconciliation."[56] Fulfillment (per. 13): the atonement of Jesus Christ. For the translation of *kappóreth* into Greek is *hilāstḗrion*, "propitiatory," which is then employed in Rom 3:25

50. Ibid., II:205; cf. 211.
51. E.g. the ram skins, "for the purpose of protection from the elements," ibid., II:210.
52. E.g. the frames, sockets, ropes, etc., so it might be portable, ibid., II:209–211.
53. E.g. the colors, as of the ram skins dyed red, "for ornament," not "red for guilt," ibid., II:208–209.
54. Ibid., II:207.
55. E.g. "the border of gold around the top . . . it had in common with the table of show-bread and the altar of incense; so that it could not have been meant to denote anything connected with the peculiar design of the ark, and in each of the articles, indeed, it seems merely to have been added for the purpose of forming a suitable and becoming ornament," ibid., II:328.
56. Ibid., II:329–330.

as follows: "God has set forth Jesus Christ as a *hilāstḗrion,* an *atoning cover,* through faith in His blood."[57]

58. Ex 26:31–33; 35; 27:21b; *30:6a; 35:12c;* 36:35–36; *38:27b; 39: 34b;* 40:*3b,* 21b, *22b, 26b* (8 vv., typ.): the veil of the tabernacle. This curtain formed the division between the most holy place, representing God's presence in heaven (Heb 9:24), and the outer room of Israel's immediate life and service, beyond which the way in to God stood in need of being laid open (v. 8). Fulfillment (per. 13): the dividing curtain constituted a prediction of the incarnation of Christ, of His flesh (10:20), which veiled off His deity during His life and ministry (cf. Phil 2:7). But with the tearing of His body on the cross (John 19:18, 34) the veil was rent (Mt 27:51) and became the new and living way by which men may enter into heaven and the presence of God (Heb 10:19–20).

59. Ex 28:1; 30:30; 40:13b, 15 (4 vv., typ.): Israel's Levitical priests, specifically in their function of offering sacrifices, so as to effectuate atonement with God, Heb 8:3.[58] The OT priests, however, "serve as a copy and shadow of the heavenly things," v. 5; ultimate perfection was not attained through them, 7:11. Fulfillment (per. 13): the atoning death of Christ, in the execution of which He becomes the better, the permanent high priest, 5:10, 8:22–28; and cf. Gen 14:18b, above, on the priestly work of Melchizedek.

60. Ex 28:2–5, 39–43; 29:5, 8–9, 29; 31:10; 35:19, *21b;* 39:1, 27–29, 41; 40:*13a,* 14 (21 vv., typ.): priestly garments. They were composed of *badh,* "linen," and *būs,* a "fine white valuable web, byssus"[59]—cool and clean, "holy garments" (Ex 29:29, Lev 16:4); cf. Rev 19:8. Fulfillment (per. 13): the priestly purity of Christ; see Heb 4:15, 7:26.

61. Ex 28:36–38, 29:6, 39:30–31 (6 vv., typ.): the inscribed miter plate of the high priest, "holy to Yahweh."[60] Israel's priests were to be holy (Lev 21:8), and Aaron in particular "shall bear the iniquity of the holy things" (Ex 28:38); see below under Lev 1:2, sacrificial procedure, part 5. Fulfillment (per. 13): the holiness of Christ, Lk 1:35, I Pet 1:19; and see No. 60, on priestly purity, preceding.

62. Ex 29:10–14, 36–37 (7 vv., typ.): sin offering. Fulfillment (per. 13): an in Lev. No. 6.

63. Ex 29:19–21, 33, 35 (5 vv., typ.): consecration of the priests.

---

57. Payne, *Theology,* p. 380.
58. Israel's priests did have other, nonatoning functions, such as exhibiting a personal example of piety, of teaching the people, or of inquiring for oracles; but these activities were not designedly predictive (typical). Only such passages therefore as relate the nation's priests directly to sacrifice and to atonement are included in the listings that follow; others, such as Lev 10:8–11, are not.
59. KB, p. 114.
60. Other items of the high-priestly vestments—such as the breastplate, with its flashing stones (= the urim and thummim? See Payne, *Theology,* p. 48); the ephod on which it was suspended, with its onyx shoulder stones; and on down to the bells on the hem of the robe (28:6–35)—evidence contemporaneous (OT) symbolic values only, not typical.

Aaron and his sons were "hallowed" (v. 21), sprinkled with the blood of the ram of consecration. In particular, the blood was placed on their right ear (perhaps symbolizing their need to hear God's word), on their thumb (to offer sacrifices, etc.), and on their great toe (to tread God's courts and to walk as an example, Dt 33:9). In all this, their consecration anticipated (per. 13) Christ's holy dedication (John 17:8, Heb 2:17, 7:26, I John 2:6) to His work of atonement; cf. Ex 29:33.

64. Ex 29:23, 40; *40:29c* (2 vv., typ.): meal offering. Fulfillment (per. 13): as in Lev. No. 4.

65. Ex 30:10 (1 v., typ.): the day of atonement, in which blood was placed on the incense altar. Fulfillment (per. 13): as in Lev. No. 19.

66. Ex 30:11–16 (6 vv., typ.): atonement money. Each Israelite was to contribute one-half shekel to the sanctuary, "a ranson for his soul unto Yahweh . . . that there be no plague among them" (v. 12); it was "atonement money . . . to make atonement for your souls" (v. 16). Fulfillment (per. 13): true atonement could be achieved only in Christ's death, Acts 13:39, Rom 5:11.

67. Ex 30:17–21, *28b; 31:9b;* 38:8; 40:7, 11–12, 30–32 (12 vv., typ.): the laver of the tabernacle. It was designed for washings, outer exhibitions of consecration on the part of the priests; for the clean hands were to suggest innocence (Ps 26:6) and to accompany a pure heart (24:4). Num 8:7 thus speaks of "water of expiation"; cf. a similar stress on cleanness through the priests' linen garments, No. 60, above. Under Solomon the Mosaic laver was replaced with a much larger molten "sea," with portable lavers on wheeled bases (I K 7:23–39); but these still had this same function. Fulfillment (per. 13): the "washings" were but temporary anticipations of Christ, the truly pure one who was to come, Heb 10:9–10.

68. Ex 32:13a (1 v.): that the patriarchs' seed was to multiply as the stars. Fulfillment (per. 2): as in Gen. No. 21.

69. Ex 34:24c (1 v.): that no one should covet the Israelites' lands when they would be participating in the three annual pilgrimage feasts that God had ordained. Fulfillment: context favors per. 4, the conquest (see v. 24a, under No. 48, above); but there is no recorded instance of the actual fulfillment.

LEVITICUS

The place of Leviticus in the OT corresponds somewhat to that of Romans in the New, for both embody a generally systematic presentation of God's way of salvation. Moses' second book, Exodus, had stressed Yahweh's adoption of Israel as His own people (Ex 19:5); and its latter half had recorded their erection of the tabernacle, the visible demonstration of His dwelling in their midst (25:8, 40:33–34; cf. Lev 1:1). Now, in the early spring of 1445 B.C., God's people were ready not simply for a Levitical handbook on the use of this tabernacle, but for a comprehensive written revelation on the nature of that testamentary redemption of which they had become currently the inheritors. In essence the third book of Moses consists then of divine legislation, which may be summed up in its teaching on "holiness" (Lev 11:44–45; 20:7–8, 26).

Leviticus 20:26 distinguishes two aspects to the life that is holy: (a) God's holiness, in providing a living way of access to Himself; and (b) men's holiness, in responding to divine grace through activities that reflect the will of their Lord. These same two aspects characterize the respective halves of the Book of Leviticus. Chapters 1–16 depict the only way to God: through sacrifice (1–7), priesthood (8–10), cleanness (11–5), and the ultimate accomplishment of reconciliation through atonement (16). Chapters 17–27 then exhibit a pattern for the committed life: with a ceremonial standard of reverence for blood (17), a moral standard of conduct (18–22) —including in 19:18 one of the greatest commandments of all, love for one's neighbor as oneself—a devotional standard for regular worship (23–25; plus an appendix on vows, (27), and a concluding appeal by Moses to his people (26).[1]

The exhortations of this last section are enforced by a series of threats and promises that render it strongly predictive in nature. The more narrative portions of Leviticus, which are restricted to chs. 8–10 and 24:10–23, contain little which might be considered prophetic, as is true also of chs. 11–15 on cleanness.[2] But the main body of the book comprises the highest concentration of typical prophecies to be found anywhere in Scripture. Specifically, Leviticus contains 37 distinct prophecies; and out of the book's 859 verses, 506, or 59%, involve predictions in some form or another. But by actual count, 462 of the 506 concern types, which is the highest percentage (91%) for any major portion of the Bible.[3]

The revelations and the events of Leviticus cover no more than one month, in March/April, 1445 B.C. (compare Ex 40:17 and Num 10:11). Most of the book must have been written down, as soon as each section was revealed to God's servant (cf. 4:1, 6:1, 6:8), though Moses' completion of the volume as a whole[4] could not have occurred before the Day of Atonement, which was celebrated in the fall of that year, as recorded in 16:34b.

1. Cf. J. B. Payne, "Leviticus," in C. F. H. Henry, ed., *The Biblical Expositor*, I:118–150.
2. See above, p. 55.
3. See below, p. 674, the final column of the Statistical Appendix. The higher percentage figure for Ezra and Nehemiah is due simply to their limited predictive nature all together.
4. See above, in the introduction to Exodus. Iiberal Scholars, however, generally assign the bulk of Leviticus to the "H" or "P" documents, and so to the latest "strata" of the Pentateuch, about 1,000 years later than Moses.

1. Lev 1:1; 8:3–4, 10; 9:5, 23; 10:9; 14:11, 23; 15:31; *16:2a;* 19:30b; 20:3; *24:3b; 26:2b;* 27:25 (13 vv., typ.): the tabernacle. Fulfillment (per. 13): as in Ex prophecy No. 55.

2. Lev 1:2; 7:37–38; 17:1–9; 19:26; 22:24–28; 23:*8a,* 25b, 37; 24:9; *26:31b;* 27:9, 11 (23 vv., typ.): sacrifice. God's redemptive testament was made by sacrifice (Ps 50:5); it was made effectual by the death of the testator (see Gen 3:15a or 15:10, above). On the specific, typical predictions that Leviticus associates with its five major varieties of different OT offerings, see below, No. 3–7; but the general teaching that characterizes all its sacrifice is that of atonement. The verb *kappēr,* "to atone," suggests the "covering over" of human guilt through the interposition of a *kōfer,* "ransom" (see Ex 21:30, 30:12, Lev 16:30; and Ex prediction No. 57, above, on the *kappōreth,* or "mercy seat"). Atonement diverts the plague that would otherwise fall upon man should God "see through" to the sinner (Num 8:19, Ex 32:30; cf. Prov 16:14).[5]

The placating, or propitiating, of divine wrath is particularly demonstrated in the OT through the five chief stages of its sacrificial procedure.[6] (1) The selection of the sacrifice. To serve as an adequate ransom the victim itself must be perfect, without defects, Lev 22:17–25. This was true for each of the offerings that employed animals: the burnt, 1:3, 10; peace, 3:1; sin, 4:3, and trespass, 5:15. For the meal offering there could be no leaven, which was suggestive of corruption (Mt 16:6, I Cor 5:6–8, Gal 5:9), or honey, for "what is peculiarly pleasing to the flesh is distasteful to God."[7] But "the salt of the testament" was required (Lev 2:13) as a symbol of incorruption and preservation (Mt 5:13). In the selection of a sacrifice even such factors as unusual size or a victim's having "anything lacking in his parts" or being *qālūt,* "stunted" or "with shortened tail"[8] (Lev 22:23), would restrict its use to free-will offerings; it could not be used for fulfilling a vow. On the typical accomplishment of this first step in the sacrificial procedure, see especially under the whole burnt offering, No. 3, following.

(2) The laying of the hands of the offerer upon the animal's head; cf. 16:21, "Confess over him all the iniquities of the children of Israel . . . and put them upon the head of the goat." The sacrifice thus became a proxy for the sinner (cf. Num 27:18–21) and took his place (cf. 8:18–19) as the sin-bearer, specifically in the burnt, Lev 1:4, peace, 3:2, and sin offerings, 4:4.[9]

5. J. B. Payne, *Theology of the Older Testament,* pp. 249–250, 378–379.

6. On other theories of sacrifice, with varying degrees of validity, see ibid., pp. 382–383.

7. P. Fairbairn, *The Typology of Scripture,* II:312.

8. KB, p. 839.

9. The procedure recorded in Dt 21:1–9, for the case of an unexplained murder, does not appear to constitute a sacrifice. The elders of the nearest town washed their hands over a heifer, whose neck had been broken, v. 4. "They were personally cleared from the guilt, but the guilt itself was not atoned . . . and, accordingly, none of the usual sacrificial terms are applied to the transaction with the heifer," Fairbairn, op. cit., II:354.

All pointed toward the time when Christ should be made sin for us, II Cor 5:21.

(3) The slaying of the burnt, 1:5, peace, 3:2, and sin offerings, 4:4. The death of the sacrifice substituted for that of the sinner; the animal received the punishment in place of the man (Num 6:11; cf. Lev 19:20–21). Fairbairn has explained, "The victim became symbolically a personation of sin, and hence must forthwith bear the penalty of sin—death. When this was done, the offerer was himself free alike from sin and from its penalty."[10] The particular symbol of the surrendered life was its blood (Gen 9:4; and see below, No. 17), "given to you upon the altar to make atonement for your souls: for it is the blood that maketh atonement by reason of the life," Lev 17:11.[11] It is true that these bloody ministrations were incapable in themselves of atoning for sins; but they stood as types of Christ's once-for-all sacrifice (see below, fulfillment).[12] As an apostle later stated, "He Himself bore our sins in His body on the cross," I Pet 2:24.

(4) The committal of the sacrifice to God, by sprinkling of blood and by burning; so for the burnt offering, 1:5, 8–9, meal, 2:2, peace, 3:2, 5, and sin offerings, 4:5–10. The blood (life) constituted the atoning ransom, 17:11; it was the price paid to God that anticipated the work of Christ, who "offered Himself without blemish to God," for the cleansing of His people, Heb 9:14. Fairbairn justifies its acceptability to God as follows:

That the blood had already paid, in death, the penalty of sin, and was no longer laden with guilt and pollution . . . God could with perfect consistence receive it as a pure and spotless thing, the very image of His own holiness, upon His table or altar. In being received there, however, it still represented the blood or soul of the offerer . . . reestablished. Hence also the peculiar force of the expression in I Peter 1:2, "unto," not only obedience, but also "sprinkling of the blood of Jesus," unto the participation of His risen, divine, heavenly life, replete with the blessedness of God.[13]

The meal offering emphasized this procedural step of committal through its employment of oil and incense, Lev 2:1, 16, presumably indicating the presentation to God by means of the grace of the Spirit (cf. I Sam 16:13–14, Ps 141:2). On the typical significance of the burning of certain sacrifices "without the camp," see under the sin offering, No. 6, below.

10. Ibid., II:275.
11. Lev 5:11–13 does permit in this one instance a substitution of flour, for the poor. Heb. 9:22 thus states, with care, that "according to the Law, one may almost say, all things are cleansed with blood," though it hastens to add, since even the flour was given as a substitute for life blood, that ultimately "without shedding of blood [Christ's] there is no forgiveness."
12. Payne, *Theology,* p. 384.
13. Op. cit., II:275–276; contrast the view of Oehler, who reduces the whole idea of sacrifice to one of expiation, the making of reparation, through symbolic self-surrender, in which the sacrifice never does "bear sin," *Theology of the OT,* pp. 279–280, rather than of propitiation, the placating of the wrath of God through the infliction of a penalty.

(5) The demonstration of restored fellowship. At the ceremonial ratification of the Sinaitic testament, for example, half the blood of the offerings was scattered on the altar; but the remaining half was gathered into basins and literally sprinkled out over the people, Ex 24:6, 8. As Moses explained, "Behold the blood of the testament, which Yahweh hath made with you." Most frequently this final stage of procedure was portrayed by a meal of communion, v. 11; see below under No. 5, as a particular characteristic of the peace offerings. Even with the sin offerings, though some were burned outside the camp, others were eaten by the priests: "It is most holy [not unclean], and He hath given it you to bear the iniquity of the congregation, to make atonement for them before Yahweh," Lev 10:17; cf. 6:25, 29. This does not mean that the priest thereby incurred iniquity. Rather, "The eating could only be intended to give a symbolical representation of the completeness of the reconciliation—to show by their incorporation with the sacrifice, how entirely through it the guilt had been removed."[14] In the instance of the first burnt offering at the tabernacle, the reality of restored fellowship was confirmed by fire coming forth from Yahweh and consuming the sacrifice, Lev 9:24; cf. Jd 6:19–21.

Fulfillment (per 13): the blood of animals could never take away sins (Heb 10:4, 11), but Christ "offered one sacrifice for sins for all time" (v. 12; cf. 9:12). It was this which constituted the OT sacrifices a "sweet savor" to God, literally a *rêah nîhôah,* a "smell that placates." The expression, though anthropomorphic, signified God's satisfaction in respect to the offerings and the propitiation of His divine wrath, as He graciously accepted these sacrificial tokens of the ultimate redemptive work of Christ. Of the following five major varieties of OT sacrifice, the first three are often grouped together as "sweet savor" offerings; cf. Lev 1:9 (burnt), 2:2 (meal), and 3:5 (peace). This does not mean, however, that the other two varieties were not placating (cf. 4:31), but simply, as W. G. Moorehead points out, that the latter were concerned more expressly with the "guilt" of particular sins.[15]

3. Lev 1:3–17; 6:8–13; 7:8; 8:18–21; 9:2b, 3b, 7b, 12–14, 16, 22b, 24; 12:6a, 8a; 14:20a, 22b, 31b; 15:15b, 30b; 16:3b, 5b, 24b; 22:17–20; 23:12, 18a (41 vv., typ.): burnt offering. The distinctive element in this, the first of the Mosaic "sweet savor" offerings (1:9, 13, 17), was God's command to "burn the whole" on the altar, 1:9, 13. Its name in Hebrew was the *ōlā,* what "goes up," in smoke. To the OT worshipers this symbolized a full and lasting surrender to God. It was a *kālīl,* "wholly burnt" (6:22), a *tāmīdh,* "continual" burnt offering (Ex 29:38, 42; cf. Lev 6:9, 12–

14. Fairbairn, op. cit., II:295.
15. *Studies in the Mosaic Institutions,* p. 132. By the same token, the "sweet savor" offerings are not to be denied a primary relevance in respect to men's guilt, a fact which their very identification as *placating* makes clear. For a summarization of other methods of classifying the Mosaic sacrifices, see J. J. Reeve, "Sacrifice in the OT," ISBE, IV:2641.

13). Correspondingly, it typified (as fulfilled in per. 13) Christ's entire self-surrender (Ps 40:8, Lk 2:49); cf. Mt 26:39, "not as I will, but as Thou wilt." The perfection of the OT sacrifices anticipated the coming of Christ as "holy, innocent, undefiled, separated from sinners" (Heb 7:26), as "a lamb unblemished and spotless" (I Pet 1:19).

4. Lev 2:1–16; 6:14–23; 7:9–10; 8:26; 9:*4b,* 17; 10:12–13; 14:10, *20b, 21b, 31c;* 23:13–14, *18b* (35 vv., typ.): meal offering.[16] This offering did not involve the presentation of flesh; it consists of ceral products, though it always appears in company with other offerings of blood; cf. 23:18, burnt offerings "with their meal offerings." Scripture employs the same term, *minhā,* for purely human tribute (II Sam 8:2, 6); so it symbolizes the consecration of one's life and property to the Lord, e.g. the "first fruits" of Lev 2:14. While not in itself an offering of atonement, it expresses grateful devotion for the atoning work that God would yet accomplish for His own. In a similar way, the typology of the meal offering is to be distinguished from that of the burnt offering. The latter depicted Christ's complete obedience in his penal suffering and substitutionary death. But the meal offering typifies His living obedience through a life of dedicated righteousness in satisfying the demands of the moral law (Mt. 3:15).[17] The comparative symbolism and typology of these, as well as of the other three major OT sacrifices, is shown in Table 2.

5. Lev 3:1–17; 7:11–36; 8:25, 27–29, 31–32; 9:4a, 18–22; 10:14–15; 19:5–8; 22:21–23, 29–33; 23:19b–20 (71 vv., typ.): peace offerings. The *sh'lāmīm,* relate particularly to the *shālōm,* "peace," of reconciliation with God that atonement produces.[18] This reestablished communion is shown by the worshipers' eating, in the presence of God, the animals that were sacrificed, 7:15–16. An exception appears in certain fat parts that were burned, so as to be the Lord's, 3:3–4, 17.[19] In the peace offering there is typified the peace with God that Jesus gained on Calvary (per. 13) and the communion of the saints "in Christ" (Col 1:27). This third sacrifice, accordingly, constitutes a close parallel to the Lord's Supper (John 6:51, I Cor 10:16); and it points forward still to that blessed final communion (per. 16) when we shall sit down together in the kingdom of heaven (Ps 22:29, Lk 14:15, Rev 19:6–10).

6. Lev 4–5:13; 6:24–30; 8:2, 14–17; 9:1–*2a, 3a,* 6–7a, 8–11, 15; 10:16–20; 12:6b–7, 8b; 14:19, 22a, 30–31a, 32; 15:14–15a, 29–30a; 16:3a, 5a, 6–9, 11, 25, 27–28; *23:19a* (95 vv., typ.): sin offering. After the

16. In the old English of KJV, "meat [*food,* not flesh] offering"; actually the *minhā* was the one offering *not* composed of meat.

17. Moorehead, op. cit., pp. 153–154.

18. Subvarieties of peace offerings covered several differing matters of immediate symbolism, e.g. when offered out of thanksgiving, 7:12, or to fulfill a vow, v. 16.

19. The requirement of eating the meat before the third day, 7:15–18, seems to have had a pragmatic basis: to guard the holy flesh against desecration or spoilage, KD, *Pentateuch,* II:325.

TABLE 2[20]
The Old Testament Offerings

Name	Translation	Major References	Distinctiveness	Symbolism	Typology
"Sweet Savor" Offerings					
Ōlā	Burnt offering	Lev 1, 6:8-13	Wholly burned on the altar (Lev 1:9)	1. Placating the wrath of God by substituting a victim in death (Gen 8:20, Lev 1:4) 2. Complete consecration (cf. Lev 6:13, a continual offering)	1. Christ's vicarious death for the redemption of sinners (II Cor 5:21) 2. His entire self-surrender (Ps 40:8; cf. Lk 2:49, Mt 26:39)
Minḥā	Meal offering	Lev 2, 6:14-23	Nonbloody products, accompanying other bloody offerings (Lev 2:1, cf. 23:18)	Consecration of one's life and substance (Lev 2:14)	His righteous fulfilling of the law (Mt 3:15)
Sh'lāmīn	Peace offering	Lev 3, 7:11-34	Most parts eaten before God by the sacrificer (Lev 7:15)	1. Placating God's wrath (as above; cf. Lev 3:2) 2. A thanksgiving meal of reconciliation with God (Lev 7:12)	1. Vicarious redemption (as above) 2. Communion in Christ, now (John 6:51) and in the future kingdom (Rev 19:6-10)
Guilt Offerings					
Ḥaṭṭāth	Sin offering	Lev 4-5:13, 6:24-30	For a specific sin (Lev 5:1-4) Some victims' bodies burned outside the camp (Lev 4:12)	1. Placating God's wrath (as above; cf. 4:4) 2. Confession (5:5), with the transference of the guilt to the animal (4:21)	1. Vicarious redemption (as above) 2. Christ's suffering "without the camp" (Heb 13:12), the passive bearing of the penalties of men's sins (Isa 53:6)
Āshām	Trespass offering	Lev 5:14-6:7; 7:1-10	Same as the ḥaṭṭāth, plus repayment to the wronged party (Lev 5:15)	1. Placating God's wrath (as above; cf. 5:18) 2. Confession with transferred guilt (as above, 7:7) 3. Social restitution for wrong (5:16)	1-2. Same as above (Isa 53:10), plus: 3. His active redressing of every legal claim of God (Gal 4:4)

20. Payne, *Theology*, p. 526, or *Biblical Expositor*, I:129.

three "sweet savor" offerings come the latter two of the Mosaic sacrifices, the "guilt" offerings. The Hebrew term for the first of these is *hattāth,* which carries the basic meaning of "sin" and, by development, "purification from sin" (Num 8:7, 19:9) but, specifically, "sin offering," the fourth Mosaic sacrifice. It was designed to propitiate the Most High because of a concrete sin that the man concerned had committed.[21] To emphasize the transference of his sin to the sacrificial animal and the removal of the guilt of that sin, it was required that the carcasses of some of the guilt offerings be taken outside the camp and burned, 4:12, 21; 6:30; 9:11; 16:27 (cf. Ex 29:14; Num 19:3, 7); and while the blood could be considered holy, Lev 6:27, and presented to God on the altar, the sin that had been transferred to these offerings still caused the pots in which they had been boiled to be smashed, or the metal ones scoured, v. 28. So Christ (per. 13) suffered outside the city of Jerusalem, reproached and bearing the penalty of men's sins (Heb 13:11-12, Isa 53:6).

7. Lev 5:14–6:7; 7:1–7; 14:12–18, 21a, 24–29; 19:21–22 (37 vv., typ.): trespass offering. *Āshām,* may mean simply "guilt"; but it also designates the "trespass offering." This sacrifice is included under the sin offering in much of the Biblical discussion, 7:7; but it involves the added fact of repayment to the wronged human party, 5:15, 6:4–5; cf. I Sam 6:3. Fulfillment (per. 13): Christ became Himself a propitiating sin offering, but Isa 53:10 also describes Him as a trespass offering. For our Lord made atonement, not only by His passive obedience in bearing men's sin, but also by His active obedience in making compensation for us to God. As Moorehead states, "Both are fulfilled in the Lord Jesus Christ, who bore the penalty due to sin [the sin offering] and redressed every claim of God upon the sinner [the trespass offering]."[22]

8. Lev 8:1, 5, 22–24, 30, 33–36 (19 vv., typ.): consecration of the priests. Fulfillment (per. 13): as in Ex 29:19. In specific correspondence to Christ's holiness, the priests were required to be without physical blemish, 21:16–24.

9. Lev 8:6, *11b; 16:4b, 24a* (1 v., typ.): the laver, and priestly washing. Fulfillment (per. 13): as in Ex. No. 67.

10. Lev 8:7, 13; 16:4a, 23 (4 vv., typ.): garments of the priests. Fulfillment (per. 13): as in Ex. No. 60.

11. Lev 8:9 (1. v., typ.): the high priest's miter plate. Fulfillment (per. 13): as in Ex No. 61.

12. Lev 8:11a (1 v., typ.): the altar of burnt offering. Fulfillment (per. 13): as in Ex. No. 44.

21. Both the sin and the trespass offerings included atonement for unintentional violations, 4:2, 5:15. But these guilt offerings were not limited to such sins of ignorance, or even to those sins which were simply unpremeditated, 5:1, 4 (cf. 6:2–3, 19:20), unless the sinning party continued in unrepentance (Num 15:30, I Sam 3:14).

22. Op. cit., p. 171.

13. Lev 12:3–4 (2 vv., typ.): circumcision. The cleansing accomplished through circumcision is also apparently the basis for the lesser time of the mother's impurity at the birth of a male, v. 4, than at the birth of a female, v. 5. Fulfillment (per. 13): as in Gen. No. 42.

14. Lev 14:4–7, 49–53 (9 vv., typ.): cleansing of a leper. Even as this dread disease could be associated with sin (cf. Dt 24:9), so the rites performed in the rare case of a person's recovery from it included typical elements that portrayed divine forgiveness. In addition to various sacrifices, Lev 14:10–32, Moses prescribed the slaying of a bird and the setting free of another which had been dipped in the blood of the former one. Fulfillment (per. 13): Christ's blood, which frees from sin, I John 1:7.

15. Lev *16:2b, 12b, 15b;* 24:3a (1 v., typ.): the tabernacle veil. Fulfillment (per. 13): as in Ex. No. 58.

16. Lev 16:2c, *13b, 14b, 15c* (1 v., typ.): the mercy seat. Fulfillment (per. 13): as in Ex. No. 57.

17. Lev *16:2d* (typ.): the ark of the testament. Fulfillment (per. 13): as in Ex. No. 56.

18. Lev 16:10, 20–22, 26 (5 vv., typ.): the scapegoat. This goat that "escapes" was designated *for Azazel,* v. 10, a personality who appears in opposition to Yahweh, v. 8,[23] and is presumably Satan (cf. the demonic status of Azazel in I Enoch 8:1, 10:4, etc.). The goat's purpose is to make atonement, Lev 16:10, but not as a sacrifice—for in contrast with the other goat that was employed in the Day of Atonement service (see No. 19, following) it is not called a sin offering, nor is it slain. It is simply an instrument for carrying the sins that had been confessed over its head (v. 21) back to their demonic author in the wilderness (cf. Mt 12:43, Rev 18:2 and also 17:3).[24] Fulfillment (per. 13): Christ's atoning death, which overcomes Satan and breaks his hold upon men (I John 3:8, Heb 2:15–16).

19. Lev 16:12–19, 29–34; 23:26–32 (21 vv., typ.): the Day of Atonement. This day, Heb., "Yom Kippur," was a sabbath, 16:31, marked by national self-abasement, vv. 29, 31. Climactically, "Three times on the Day of Atonement the high priest passed the veil and stood before the awful presence of the ark":[25] (1) with incense, as an acted prayer for mercy "that he die not," v. 13; (2) with blood from the bull of the sin offering for himself and his priestly household, to be sprinkled on the mercy seat, vv. 6, 11, 14; and (3) with the blood of the goat of the sin offering for the people, v. 15, to make atonement for the tabernacle, v. 16, the altar, vv. 18–20, and the people themselves, vv. 24, 30. Yet the very repetition of this ceremony every year, plus the threefold activity on each occasion, portrayed the inherent weakness of the Levitical system (Heb 10:3, 7:27; contrast 9:12); but it

23. The parallelism suggests that *azāzēl,* is therefore probably not, as in KJV, and even the ASVmg, a common noun, meaning "removal" or "the scapegoat."
24. See Payne, *Theology,* pp. 292–293, 407–408.
25. Moorehead, op. cit., p. 191.

TABLE 3[26]
The Old Testament Sacred Times

	Moral Obligation		Historic Symbolism		Spiritual and Sacramental Symbolism		Typology	
	OT	Present Form	OT	Pres.	OT	Present Form	OT	Present Form
Sabbath (weekly, and 7 convocation)	Rest (Ex 23:12; cf. creation, 20:11)	Rest (Sunday, changeless moral duty Rom 13:10)	Israel's rest from Egypt (Dt 5:15)	—	God's sanctifying of Israel (Ex 31:13)	Sunday preaching and sacraments (Acts 20:7)	Rest in Christ (Mt 11:28) Heavenly rest (Isa 66:23)	Sunday, worship of Christ (Rev 1:10) Sunday, type of heaven (Heb 4:11)
New Moons	—	—	—	—	God to remember Israel (Num 10:10)	Regular intercessory prayer (?)	—	—
Sabbatic Year	Charity (Ex 23:11, Dt 15:2)	Relief offerings (Gal 2:10)	—	—	God's control of land (Lev 25:2)	Stewardship of property (?)	—	—
Year of Jubilee	Liberty and property rights (Lev 25:10)	Individual rights under God (?)	—	—	Same (Lev 25:23)	Same	Eschatological blessing in both advents (Lk 4:17-21 and Isa 61: 2-7)	Lord's Supper, type of future kingdom (I Cor 11:26)
Passover	—(it was exclusivistic; Ex 12:43-44)	—	The exodus (Ex 12:14)	—	Redemption (Ex 13:15) in common (12:22)	Lord's Supper, sacramental communion (I Cor 10:16)	Christ's substitutionary' death (I Cor 5:7)	Lord's Supper, memorial of past atonement (I Cor 11:24)

			Hasty departure (12:34)	Unleavened purity (Ex 23:18)	Sincerity and truth (I Cor 5:8)	—	Lord's Supper, type of future kingdom (I Cor 11:26)
			—	First sheaf is God's (Lev 23:11)	Church offerings (?)	—	—
Pentecost	Social sharing (Dt 16:11)	Christian compassion (?)	—	Loaves dedicated to God (Lev 23:17)	Grace at meals (?)	—	—
Tabernacles	Same (Dt 16:14)	Same	Wilderness camping (Lev 23:43)	Harvest is from God (Lev 23:39)	Thanksgiving (?)	Eschatological ingathering (Zech 14:16)	—
Trumpets	—	—	Former New Year? (Ex 12:2, 23:16)	Same as New Moon (Lev 23:24)	New Year's (?)	—	—
Day of Atonement	Humble confession (Lv 16:28)	Times of penitence (?)	—	Cleansing from sin (Lev 16:30)	Baptism (Acts 22:16)	Christ's redemption (Heb 9:12)	Good Friday and Easter Services (?)

26. Payne, *Theology*, pp. 524-525, or *Biblical Expositor*, I:146-147.

typified Christ's fully atoning death (per. 13; 9:12, 28) and His "entering within the veil" (6:19–20) to present this act of satisfaction before the presence of God in heaven itself (9:24).

20. Lev 17:10–14 (5 vv., typ.): the prohibition against eating blood. The creature's blood symbolized its life (Dt 12:23), and it was to be used for making atonement (Lev 17:10). Fulfillment (per. 13): in Christ's death; for only through His blood sacrifice can men come to God, Heb 9:22–26.

21. Lev 18:3; 20:22, 24; *23:10a;* 25:2, 38 (5 vv.): the Lord's bringing of Israel to Canaan. Fulfillment (per. 4): as in Gen. No. 36.

22. Lev 18:24–25, 28; 20:23 (4 vv.): God to destroy the Canaanites. Fulfillment (per. 4): as in Ex. No. 48.

23. Lev 19:3, *30a;* 23:3, 7, 8b, 15–16, 21, 24–*25a*, 38; 24:8; 26:2a (11 vv., typ.): sabbath. Fulfillment (per. 13): as in Ex. No. 41.

24. Lev 21:1–24; 23:10b–11 (26 vv., typ.): priests. Fulfillment (per. 13): Christ's atonement, as in Ex. No. 59; cf. the repeated references to their sacrificial activity and typical holiness, Lev 21:6–8.

25. Lev 23:5 (1 v., typ.): Passover. Fulfillment (per 13): as in Ex. No. 31.

26. Lev 23:33–36, 39–43 (9 vv., typ.): the Feast of Tabernacles. Fulfillment (per. 16): as in Ex. No. 46. The comparative symbolism and typology of this and of the other Mosaic "sacred times" are shown in Table 3.

27. Lev 25:8–17, 27–28, 30–31, 33, 40–41, 50–52, 54; 27:17–18, 21–24 (27 vv., typ.): the Year of Jubilee. The freeing of servants and the return of properties on this 50th year (25:10; cf. Ezek 46:17) were a type of deliverance, both individually (Isa 61:1–2a; cf. Lk 4:18–21) at Christ's first coming (per. 13), now fulfilled, and cosmically (Isa 61:2b–7) at His second (per. 16), as yet unfulfilled.

28. Lev 26:5, 10 (2 vv.): millennial plenty. This concluding section in Leviticus (see introduction, above) consists of Mosaic threats and promises, which commence in 26:4 with Yahweh's generalized intention to send the rains in their season if Israel will walk in His statutes. But with v. 5 the divine promises attain such lengths, e.g. that "the vintage shall reach unto the sowing time," that their adequate fulfillment can be assigned only to per. 16, as in Ex. No. 49.

29. Lev 26:6–8 (3 vv.): millennial peace. Fulfillment (per. 16): including an end to war, vv. 6–8, and the removal of evil beasts, v. 6.

30. Lev 26:9a (1 v.): the multiplication of Israel's population. Fulfillment (per. 16): as in Ex. No. 51.

31. Lev 26:9b, 11–12 (2 vv.): the Testament of Peace. The term *b'rīth* is here for the first time invoked in reference to God's future Messianic kingdom. Yahweh's tabernacle will be among His people, who will be accepted by God, v. 11. V. 12 enunciates the standard testamentary

promise, "I will be your God, and ye shall be My people." Fulfillment (per. 16): see Ezek. No. 45.

32. Lev 26:15, *44b,* 45b (2 vv., typ.): the Sinaitic testament. Fulfillment (per. 13): as in Ex. No. 45.

33. Lev 26:16–32 (17 vv.): Israel's punishment. If they break God's *b'rīth,* v. 15, then Israel must suffer "the vengeance of the testament," v. 25. Fulfillment (per. 7): this includes terror—sickness and famine before the enemy, v. 16—that progresses through four augmentations, vv. 18, 21, 23, 27, and climaxes in the land's desolation, v. 32, in 586 B.C.

34. Lev 26:33–35, 41, 43 (5 vv.): further punishment. The land of Palestine is to "enjoy its sabbaths" of desolate rest, vv. 33b–35, while Israel (fulfillment in per. 8) shall be scattered in exile, II K 25:11–12.

35. Lev 26:36–39 (4 vv.): Israel to be fearful and perish or pine away in their exile. Fulfillment (per. 8): as documented in Ps 137, Jer 29:21–22.

36. Lev 26:42a (1 v., typ.): the Abrahamic testament. Fulfillment (per. 13): as in Gen. No. 30.

37. Lev 26:*42b,* 44a, *45a* (1 v.): that God would remember His testament with Israel. Fulfillment (per. 8): since He is their God (cf. No. 28, above), He will not "abhor them to destroy them utterly" in their exile, v. 44. Furthermore, He will "remember the land," v. 42, which may even suggest restoration.

NUMBERS

The content of the Book of Numbers may be divided into four sections, corresponding to the historical subdivisions of Israel's 40-year sojourn in the great wilderness east of Egypt (prophetic period 3),[1] 1446–1406 B.C.: I. Numbers 1–10:10, at Sinai, up to Israel's departure in the 2nd month of 1445 (10:11), in the 2nd year after the exodus; II. 10:11–ch. 14, from Sinai to the nation's failure at Kadesh, in the middle of that same year (cf. 13:20); III. 15–20:13, the 38 years of wilderness wandering (Dt 2:14), until midsummer, 1407 (Num 33:38; cf. 20:24); IV. 20:14–ch. 36, from Kadesh to the Plains of Moab, on the eastern bank of the Jordan, early in 1406 (Dt 1:3). Numbers is thus basically historical in nature, like Genesis, rather than legal and discursive, like Exodus in its latter half, Leviticus, and Deuteronomy. It is, moreover, largely a record of Israel's failures, which may be summed up by the words in 32:23, "Be sure your sins will find you out."

1. Except for the time at the beginning of this period, which was involved in the nation's journey out of Egypt in the spring of 1446 (= Ex 1–18) and in the majority of its year-long stay at Mount Sinai (= Ex 19–40 and Lev), and for the time at the end, during its final two months on the Plains of Moab (= Dt).

Yet interspersed among the narratives are various legal materials, either as supplementary to the priestly codes revealed at Mount Sinai (Num 5–6, 9:1–14, 10:1-10; cf. also 15, 18–19) or as prefatory to Moses' major Deuteronomic legislation on the Plains of Moab (28–30). These contain a considerable amount of prediction in the form of Biblical typology, continuing the pattern set by Exodus and Leviticus in this regard. Indeed, 86% of the prophetic data in Numbers concerns types, which comes close to the figure for Leviticus and actually exceeds the 80% for Exodus, though very little of what appears in Numbers belongs to types that are newly revealed.[2] The oracular prophecies of the fourth book of Moses center in ch. 14, with its revelations stemming from the report of the spies at Kadesh, and in chs. 23–24, with the oracles of Balaam.

The Book of Numbers contains 1,288 verses, of which 458, or 36%, concern a total of 50 separate predictions. The volume itself seems to have been developed in the manner of a journal, composed by Moses as the factual course of events unfolded; cf. 33:2 on his chronicle of Israel's journeyings.[3] It terminates one month before his own death in February or March of 1406 (cf. Dt 34:8).

1. Num 1:1, 50–51, 53; 2:2, 17; 3:7–8, 23, 25–26a, 28–29, 32, 35–38, 47, 50; 4:1–4, 15, 16b–49; 6:13; 7:1a, 2–9, 85, 89a; 8:9, 19, 22–26; 9:15–23; 10:3, 11, 17, 21; 11:16, 24, 26; 12:4–5, 10; 14:10; 16:9, 18–19, 42–43, 50; 17:4, 7–8, 13; 18:2–4, 6, 21–23, 31; 20:6; 27:2; 31:6, 30, 47, 54 (122 vv., typ.): tabernacle. Fulfillment (per. 13): as in Ex prophecy No. 55.

2. Num 3:1–6, 10; 5:16–17; 18:1, 5, 7–19; 25:10–11 (26 vv., typ.): priests. Fulfillment (per. 13): as in Ex No. 59.

3. Num *3:26b, 31b*; 4:13–14; 7:*1b*, 10–11, 84, *88b;* 16:38–39, 46–47 (9 vv., typ.): the altar of burnt offering. Fulfillment (per. 13): as in Ex No. 44.

4. Num 3:31a; 4:*5b*–6; 7:*89c*; 10:33, 35–36; 14:44 (6 vv., typ.): the ark of the testament. Fulfillment (per. 13): as in Ex No. 56.

5. Num *3:31c*, 4:5a, *18:7b* (1 v., typ.): the tabernacle veil. Fulfillment (per. 13): as in Ex No. 58.

6. Num *4:16a*; 5:15, 18, 25–26; 6:15, 17b, 19b; 7:13, 19, 25, 31, 37, 43, 49, 55, 61, 67, 73, 79, *87b*; *8:8b*; 15:4–7, 9–14, *24c*; 28:5, 7, *8b*, 9b, *10b*, 12–13a, 14a, 20–21, 28–29; 29:3–4, 9–10, 14–15, 18, 21, 24, 27, 30, 33, 37 (52 vv., typ.): meal offering. Fulfillment (per. 13): as in Lev. No. 4.

7. Num 5:8, 6:12 (2 vv., typ.): trespass offering. Fulfillment (per. 13): as in Lev. No. 7.

---

2. Only three such appear below: No. 27, on the red heifer; No. 30, on the brazen serpent; and No. 43, on the Levitical testament.
3. See above, the introduction to Exodus.

8. Num 5:9; 6:*14c, 17a,* 18–*19a,* 20; 7:17, 23, 29, 35, 41, 47, 53, 59, 65, 71, 77, 83, 88a; *10:10b* (16 vv., typ.): peace offering. Fulfillment (pers. 13 and 16): as in Lev. No. 5.

9. Num 6:10–11a, *14b,* 16a; 7:16, 22, 28, 34, 40, 46, 52, 58, 64, 70, 76, 82, *87c*; 8:8c, 12a; 15:22–29, 28:15, 22, 30; 29:5, 11, 16, 19, 22, 25, 28, 31, 34, 38 (38 vv., typ.): sin offering. Fulfillment (per. 13): as in Lev No. 6.

10. Num 6:*11b,* 14a, *16b*; 7:15, 21, 27, 33, 39, 45, 51, 57, 63, 69, 75, 81, 87a; *8:8a, 12b*; 10:10a; *15:24b,* 23:1–6, 14–15, 17, 29–30; 28:1–4, 6, 8a, *9a,* 10a, 11, *13b, 14b,* 19, 23, 27; 29:2, 8, 13, 17, 20, 23, 26, 29, 32, 36 (47 vv., typ.): burnt offering. Fulfillment (per. 13): as in Lev No. 3.

11. Num 6:21; *8:21b*; 15:1–3, 8; 22:40; 28:24, 31; 29:6, 39 (10 vv., typ.): sacrifice, in general. 22:40 concerns offerings by the pagan king Balak; but, as has been observed, "They were offered unquestionably not to the Moabitish idols, from which Balak expected no help, but to Jehovah, whom Balak wished to draw away, in connection with Balaam, from His own people (Israel), that he might secure His favor to the Moabites."[4] Fulfillment (per. 13): as in Lev 1:2.

12. Num *7:89b* (typ.): the mercy seat. Fulfillment (per. 13): as in Ex. No. 57.

13. Num 8:5–7, 15, 20–21a (6 vv., typ.): priestly cleansing, by washing. Fulfillment (per. 13): as in Ex. No. 67, on the laver.

14. Num 9:1–11, 13–14; 28:16; 33:3 (15 vv., typ.): Passover. Fulfillment (per. 13): as in Ex. No. 31.

15. Num 9:12 (1 v., typ.): no bone of the Paschal lamb to be broken. Fulfillment (per. 13): as in Ex. No. 33.

16. Num 10:29; 11:12; 14:16, 40; *15:2b*; 27:12; 32:7; *33:53b* (6 vv.): Canaan to be granted to Israel. Fulfillment (per. 4): as in Gen No. 24.

17. Num 11:6–9 (4 vv., typ.): manna. Fulfillment (per 13): as in Ex. No. 39.

18. Num 11:18–23 (6 vv.): flesh to be provided for Israel to eat. It was to come the next day, v. 18, and last a month, v. 19. Moses expressed incredulity, vv. 21–22; but God reassured him, v. 23. Fulfillment (per. 3): quail were brought in by "a wind of Yahweh," both the next day and the following, for Israel to gather, vv. 31–32. Accomplishment of the exact duration of one month is not stated; but the point of the quail's miraculous quantity, v. 31, was "to give them flesh for a whole month."[5]

19. Num 14:22–23, 28–*30a,* 32–35; 32:11 (9 vv.): Israel not to see Canaan but to face death for 40 years in the wilderness, one year for each day of the spying out of the land, 14:34. Specifically, this pertained to those who were 20 years old and over. Fulfillment (per. 3): by the end of

4. KD, *Pentateuch,* III:175.
5. KD, III:73.

the wanderings, not a man of these was left, 26:64–65 (citing the previous prediction), 32:13, Dt 2:14–16.

20. Num 14:24, *30c, 32:12a* (1 v.): spoken to Caleb, that God would bring him into Canaan and that his seed would have a possession in it. He would be given land on which his feet had trodden, Dt 1:36. Fulfillment began in Num 14:38, when he and Joshua were not slain along with the ten faithless spies; cf. 26:65. But the promise came to pass in Josh 14:6–15 (per. 4), where Caleb made direct reference to the original prophecy: "Yahweh hath kept me alive, as He spake," v. 10.

21. Num 14:30b, 31; 15:18; 33:53a (4 vv.): Israel to reenter Canaan and settle there. Fulfillment (per. 4): as in Gen. No. 36.

22. Num *14:30d*, 32:12b (1 v.): Joshua to enter Canaan, to dwell there: cf. God's similar word to Caleb in 14:24 (No. 20, above). Fulfillment (per. 4): Josh 3:17, his entrance, and 19:49–50, his dwelling in his inheritance, where he was later buried, 24:30.

23. Num 14:43 (1 v.): Moses' prediction at Kadesh that Israel would fall by the sword of the Amalekites and Canaanites because of their disobedience. Fulfillment (per. 3): the groups that Moses had named "smote them and beat them down, even unto Hormah," v. 45.

24. Num 15:32–36; 28:18, 25–26; 29:1 (9 vv., typ.): sabbath. Fulfillment (per. 13): as in Ex. No. 41.

25. Num 16:5–7 (3 vv.): Moses' forecast that on the next day Yahweh would show Korah and his 250 followers those whom He had really chosen to be His ministers. Fulfillment (per. 3): Korah was swallowed up by the ground, v. 32; and the 250 were devoured by fire from Yahweh, v. 35.

26. Num 16:30 (1 v.): Dathan and Abiram, with their families, to go down alive into hell, as the earth would open. Fulfillment (per. 3): this occurred, just as Moses finished speaking, vv. 31–32.

27. Num 19:1–22, 31:23 (23 vv., typ.): the ashes of a red heifer,[6] a special sin offering (19:9). When mixed with water, the resulting "water for impurity" (vv. 13, 20–21) was to be used for sprinkling, in the ritual purification of those who had contacted a dead body. The underlying thought is that death arises because of sin; hence the sin offering (vv. 9, 17). Fulfillment (per. 13): "For if the blood and goats and bulls and the ashes of a heifer sprinkling those who have been defiled, sanctify for the cleansing of the flesh, how much more will the blood of Christ . . . cleanse your conscience," Heb 9:13–14.

28. Num 20:*26a*, 28 (1 v., typ.): priestly garments. Fulfillment (per. 13): as in Ex. No. 60.

29. Num 20:26b (1 v.): Aaron to die on Mount Hor. Fulfillment (per. 3): it was so, v. 28.

---

6. Why the heifer was required to be red is uncertain, perhaps because of its use in purifying the (red) human body; or the color may not have had a particular meaning in itself; cf. P. Fairbairn, *The Typology of Scripture*, II:359.

30. Num 21:8–9 (2 vv., typ.): "Yahweh said unto Moses, Make thee a fiery serpent, and set it upon a standard: and every one that is [snake-] bitten, when he seeth it, shall live" (v. 8). So Moses made a brazen serpent; and when any man looked on it, he was saved (v. 9). Yet ultimately all life is in Christ, John 1:3–4. Furthermore, this event "was in itself so extraordinary and peculiar, so unlike God's usual methods of dealing in providence . . . it seems to be without any adequate reason . . . until it is viewed as a dispensation specially designed to prepare the way for the higher and better things of the gospel."[7] Fulfillment (per. 13): "As Moses lifted up the serpent in the wilderness, even so must the Son of Man be lifted up [on Calvary's cross]; that whoever believes may in Him have eternal life," John 3:14–15.

31. Num 21:34 (1 v.): that God would deliver Og into Moses' hand, just as He had his fellow king Sihon. Fulfillment (per. 3): v. 35, He did.

32. Num 23:24, 24:8–9 (3 vv., fig.): Balaam's oracles that Israel would win victories, like a lion. Fulfillment (per. 6): as in Gen 49:9, in the triumphs of David, though the seer here transfers to all Israel, under David their king, what had there been limited to Judah: rising up like a lion or lioness from prey.

33. Num 24:7a (1 v., fig.): "Water shall flow from his buckets," indicating Israel's abundance. Fulfillment (per. 4): as in Gen. No. 52; cf. Dt 8:7, that their forthcoming settlement in Canaan would be in a land of brooks.

34. Num 24:7b, 17a (1 v.): Israel to be exalted as a kingdom. It was not simply that Yahweh was their king, as in 23:21, but that they were to have a human monarch. This truth had been implied, indeed, in the forecast of Gen 49:8, 10, that the rule over Israel would come to reside in Judah; but it is here for the first time that the presence of a king is explicitly stated. Fulfillment (per. 6): in the anointing of Saul, I Sam 10:1, 24, 11:15, which inaugurated the kingdom, but especially in that of David, over all Israel, II Sam 5:3.

35. Num 24:14, 17b (1 v.): Balaam's revelation to Balak of Moab about what Israel "shall do to thy people in the latter days . . . [to] smite through the corners of Moab." Fulfillment (per. 6): by David, II Sam 8:2.

36. Num 24:17c: Balaam's oracle, "I see Him, but not now; I behold Him, but not nigh: there shall come forth a star out of Jacob . . . and shall break down all the sons of tumult," Heb., shēth, "defiance."[8] This goes beyond David's victories (see No. 32 and 34–35, above) and finds complete fulfillment (per. 15) only in the Messiah's triumph, with its ensuing world domination, at Armageddon, Rev 16:16, 19:19–21.

37. Num 24:18 (1 v.): "Seir also shall be a possession . . . while Israel doeth valiantly." Fulfillment (per. 6): as in Gen. No. 50, and particularly

7. Ibid., I:66.
8. KB, p. 1014.

in its first stage of accomplishment, under David, since this is the stress in the present context; see No. 35, above.

38. Num 24:19 (1 v.): "One out of Jacob . . . shall destroy the remnant of the city," referring back to the Edomites in v. 18 (No. 37, preceding). "City," at this point, "is employed in a collected and general sense, as in Ps 72:16. Out of every city in which there is a remnant of Edom, it shall be destroyed,"[9] Fulfillment (per. 11): as in Gen. No. 50, 3rd stage— Idumaea's incorporation into Judah by John Hyrcanus.

39. Num 24:20 (1 v.): Amalek to come to destruction. Fulfillment (per. 7): as in Ex. No. 43.

40. Num 24:22 (1 v.): the Kenites to be wasted until carried captive by Assyria. Fulfillment (per. 7) is inferential; but since some of the Kenites are known to have settled in N. Israel (Jd 4:11) they would probably have been carried off with the Galilean Israelites by Tiglath-pileser III in 733 B.C. (II K 15:29).

41. Num 24:23–24a (2 vv., fig.): "Ships shall come from the coast of Kittim [Cyprus], and they shall afflict Asshur, and shall afflict Eber." The power from the Mediterranean to the west is not named, but as this prophecy is elaborated in Dan 11:30 it can refer only to Rome. *Asshur* stands then in figure for the Mesopotamian powers of a later date; cf. Ezra 6:22, where "the king of Assyria" in fact designates Persia. *Eber,* the ancestor of Abram the Hebrew but also of a number of other related peoples (cf. Gen 10:21, 25), "represented the western Semites,"[10] Syrians as well as Jews. Fulfillment (per. 12): Rome's deposing of Antiochus XIII, last monarch of Syria, and its absorption of the Near East, following Pompey's successes of 63 B.C.

42. Num *24:24b* (fig.): the ships of Kittim (see No. 41, preceding) also to come to destruction. Fulfillment (per. 14): the ultimate fall of Rome, dated technically to A.D. 476, and the deposition of Romulus Augustus the Little as the last of its emperors.

43. Num 25:12–13 (2 vv., typ.): the word of Yahweh to Aaron's grandson Phinehas, for his suppression of Israel's apostasy at Baal-peor, "Behold, I give unto him My testament of peace: and it shall be unto him, and to his seed after him, the testament of an everlasting priesthood; because he was jealous for his God, and made atonement for the children of Israel." Beyond this basic bestowal of the priestly office and the corresponding gift of reconciliation with God for this limited group of Levites, the Levitical testament exhibits a broader redemptive significance: the turning away of divine wrath through an eternally established priesthood (cf. v. 11), and the turning away of men from their iniquity through the teaching ministry of this same office (see Mal 2:6). In truth, the atoning work of the Levitical priests became ultimately effective because it anticipated (per.

9. KD, III:195.
10. Ibid., III:199.

13) Christ's testamentary work of divine propitiation (Heb 7:11, 19).[11]
44. Num 27:13, 31:2 (2 vv.): prediction of the death of Moses, follow-ing his viewing of Canaan. Fulfillment (per. 3): in Dt 34:5, after God had shown him the promised land.
45. Num 29:7 (1 v., typ.): the Day of Atonement. Fulfillment (per. 13): as in Lev. No. 19.
46. Num 29:12, 35 (2 vv., typ.): the Feast of Tabernacles. Fulfillment (per. 16): as in Ex. No. 46.
47. Num 33:55 (1 v.): Israel to suffer under such of the Canaanites as they might fail initially to drive out. Fulfillment (per. 5): so it came about, Jd 2:23, cf. 1:34; see especially during the days of Jabin, king of Canaan (4:2–3), 1236–1216 B.C.
48. Num 33:56 (1 v.): Israel finally to be expelled as exiles from the land, just as God was planning in Moses' time in reference to the Canaanites. Fulfillment (per. 8): as in Lev. No. 34.
49. Num 34:1–12 (12 vv.): the borders of Israel's possession in Canaan, as anticipated through Moses just prior to the conquests: from the Brook of Egypt (the Wadi el-Arish), through Kadesh-barnea, the Dead Sea, and the Jordan, as far as Lebo-hamath in the north. This was a less extensive territory than that which had been predicted in Gen 15:18 or Ex 23:31 and corresponded only to what would actually be distributed by lot for the 9½ western tribes, Num 34:13. Fulfillment (per. 4): the distribution of Canaan among the tribes, Josh 13–19, as performed by Joshua and Eleazar the priest (Josh 14:1–2, 19:51). Even the land allotted was not fully occupied in the days of Joshua (13:1–6), though it was considerably ex-ceeded under David and Solomon; see Gen prediction No. 37, above.
50. Num 36:4 (1 v., typ.): the Year of Jubilee. Fulfillment (pers. 13 and 16): as in Lev. No. 21.

11. J. B. Payne, *Theology of the Older Testament*, pp. 102–103.

DEUTERONOMY

The Book of Deuteronomy constitutes a distinct literary unit within the Pentateuch, since it records a "covenant renewal," in the six-part pattern of the suzerainty treaties of the 2nd-millennium B.C. Hittites. These parts are: 1. Preamble (Dt 1:1–5); 2. Historical prologue (1:6–4:49); 3. Stipula-tions (5–26); 4. Curses and blessings of ratification (27–30); 5. Enlisting of witnesses (31:19–22, 31:28–32:45); and 6. Succession arrangements (32:46–34:12, plus elements out of 31), including directions for the dis-position and public reading of the text (31:9–13, 24–27; cf. ch. 27).[1] The

1. J. B. Payne, *New Perspectives on the Old Testament*, pp. 242–243.

final section, on succession arrangements, appears particularly significant in defining the nature of Yahweh's redemptive *b'rīth*. That is, within the various possible covenantal categories, God's promise assumes the special form of a last will or testament; for as Meredith Kline summarized it, "From the viewpoint of the subject people a treaty guaranteeing the suzerain's dynastic succession is an expression of their covenantal relation to their overlord; but from the viewpoint of the royal son(s) of the suzerain, the arrangement is testamentary . . . it is not in force while the testator lives."[2] Hence, when the Deuteronomic covenant-mediator Moses faces death and passes his privileges on to Joshua, he depicts God (in Christ) bequeathing the inheritance of divine reconciliation to His adopted sons, the people of Israel (cf. Heb 9:15–18). The message of Deuteronomy may therefore be epitomized under these two key verses, descriptive of the renewed *b'rīth*: "Hear, O Israel, Yahweh *our* God [testamentary reconciliation] is one Yahweh," Dt 6:4; "and thou shalt love Yahweh thy God [the testamental stipulation] with all thy heart and with all thy soul . . . ," v. 5, words which Jesus defined as the greatest of all the commandments (Mt 22:36–38).[3]

The classification of Deuteronomy as a record of *b'rīth* renewal serves also to reinforce the Bible's teaching on this volume's historical origin as "the fifth book of Moses."[4] K. A. Kitchen insists that it "*must* be classed with the late-second-millennium covenants"[5] and sharply criticizes D. J. McCarthy for "making the astonishing assumption[6] that the casual combination of [later, Wellhausenist] sources should just happen to produce a direct correspondence with a covenant-form half a millennium obsolete!"[7] Specifically, the Book of Deuteronomy claims for itself to consist of two speeches (1:6–4:40, and chs. 5–26), with supplements (27–30) and two songs (32:1–43 and 33:2–29), delivered by Moses on the eastern bank of the Jordan in the 11th month of the 40th year of the exodus (1:3), or in January/February, 1406 B.C. As compared with the more technical character of Leviticus, these messages of Deuteronomy, the "second law," were popular in scope, being addressed to "all Israel" (1:1, 5:1, 29:2, 31:1),[8] to guide them in their impending settlement in the new land of Canaan. Moses claimed a further responsibility for the personal inscripturation of at least the first song (31:22) and presumably the latter of the speeches; for 31:9, 24, describe Moses' "writing the words of this law in a book," and it is the latter half of the second speech (chs. 12–26) that contains most of the actual laws of Deuteronomy.[9]

2. "Dynastic Covenant," WTJ, 23 (1960), 13.
3. Cf. also vv. 39–40 and the introduction to Leviticus, above.
4. See above, under the introduction to Exodus.
5. *Ancient Orient and OT*, p. 99.
6. *Treaty and Covenant*, p. 154.
7. Op. cit., p. 101.
8. Or to its representatives (27:1).
9. Cf. R. K. Harrison, *Introduction to the OT*, pp. 635–636.

The predictive revelations of this volume occur with the greatest frequency in the testamentary historical prologue, which is Moses' first address (1:6–4:40), in the more generalized exhortations in the first half of his second address (chs. 5–11), in certain of his supplementary messages (especially chs. 28 and 30), and in the prophetic blessing upon the 12 tribes that makes up his second song (33:2–29). The fifth book of Moses contains the first examples in Scripture of the emphatic repetition of certain major predictions, e.g. No. 1, God's promise to Israel of the land of Canaan, repeated 45 times in 43 whole verses, starting in 1:8, or No. 13, His threat of Israel's final collapse, repeated 18 times in 68 whole verses, starting in 4:26. Statistics indicate a total of 58 distinct prophecies within Deuteronomy. These occupy 344 out of its 959 verses, or 36%, which is the same figure arrived at for Numbers. A series of typical prophecies appears particularly within the ceremonial laws of chs. 12–26, while the figurative form characterizes many of the Mosaic blessings in ch. 33—cf. the corresponding phenomenon in Jacob's similar but earlier blessing in Gen 49.

1. Dt 1:8, 20–21, 25; 3:20; 4:1, 40; 5:16, 31; 6:10–11, 18, 23; *7:13b*; 8:*1b*, 10; 9:23; 10:11; 11:9, 21, 31; 12:1, 9; 15:4, 7; 16:20; 17:14a; 18:9; 19:2, 8, 14; 20:16; 21:1, 23; 24:4; 25:15; 26:1, *3b*, 9, 15; 27:2–3; *28:52b*; 30:20; 31:20a, *21b*; 32:49; 34:4 (43 vv.): God's promise of the land of Canaan for Israel. Fulfillment (per. 4): as in Gen. prophecy No. 24.

2. Dt 1:35 (1 v.): that no Israelite of the exodus generation should see Canaan. Fulfillment (per. 3): as in Num. No. 19.

3. Dt 1:36 (1 v.): Caleb's being excepted from this curse—Caleb is to see Canaan and receive the land upon which his feet have trodden. Fulfillment (per. 4): as in Num. No. 20.

4. Dt *1:38a*, Joshua too exempted from the curse against entering Canaan, Fulfillment (per. 4): as in Num. No. 22.

5. Dt 1:38b; 3:28; 31:*3b,* 7–8, 23 (5 vv.): that Joshua would cause Israel to inherit Canaan. Fulfillment (per. 4): so it was; see especially Josh 18:4–5.

6. Dt 1:39; *4:22b*; 5:33; 6:1; *7:1a*; 8:7–9; 11:8, 10, 29; 32:13–14 (11 v.): God's promise to bring Israel into Canaan.[10] Fulfillment (per. 4): as in Gen. No. 36.

7. Dt 2:24, 31 (2 vv.): an allusion by Moses, in retrospect, to a previously unrecorded prophecy of God, to give over Sihon of Heshbon to Israel. Compare the parallel prediction concerning Og of Bashan, which had been recorded in Num 21:34; cf. No. 9, below. Fulfillment (per. 3): it was so, Dt 2:30, 33–36, 3:6, 8, 12.

8. Dt 2:25, 11:25 (2 vv.): that God would place a terror of Israel upon all people, as they should hear of God's protection over His nation up to

10. 32:13–14 looks back upon this as if it were already accomplished.

this point. Fulfillment (per. 3): as in Ex. No. 38. The immediate context in Dt concerns Sihon; this very reaction is documented in the next period, at Jericho (Josh 2:9, 11, 24).

9. Dt 3:2 (1 v.): Og delivered up to Israel. Fulfillment (per. 3): as in Num. No. 31; cf. Dt 3:3–12.

10. Dt 3:21–22; 4:38; 6:19; 7:1b–2, 19–20, 23–24; 9:1–6; 11:23; 12:2, 10, 29–30; 18:12, 14; 19:1; 25:19; 31:3a, 4–6; 33:27 (30 vv.): that Yahweh would overpower the Canaanite kingdoms and drive out their peoples before Israel. The result would be rest and safety for the Hebrews (12:10, 25:19). Fulfillment (per. 4): as in Ex. No. 48.

11. Dt 4:13, 23; 5:2–3; 9:9, 11, 15; 17:2; 29:1, 9–15, 21; 33:9 (18 vv., typ.): the Sinaitic testament. The activity recorded in 29:1 suggests an official supplementation: "These are the words of the testament which Yahweh commanded Moses to make with the children of Israel in the land of Moab, besides the testament which He made with them in Horeb." Pentecost thus proposes a distinct testamentary revelation, which he entitles the "Palestinian Covenant."[11] But v. 25 later identifies it as "the testament of Yahweh, the God of their fathers, which He made with them when He brought them forth out of the land of Egypt." Since the framework of the entire Book of Deuteronomy appears to be following a Hittite-like treaty of suzerainty renewal,[12] these verses in ch. 29 are best understood in reference to the ceremony by which Israel reaffirmed their obligations and privileges under the Sinaitic testament. Fulfillment (per. 13): as in Ex. No. 45.

12. Dt 4:22a; 31:14a, *16a*; 32:50 (3 vv.): that Moses would die in Transjordan without entering Canaan. Fulfillment (per. 3): as in Num. No. 44.

13. Dt 4:26; 6:15; 7:4b; 8:19–20; 11:17; 28:15–35, 38–40, 42–63; 29:22–24, 27–28a; 30:18; 31:17–18, 21a, *29b*; 32:*21b*–26, 30, 35, *36b* (68 vv.): Israel to perish from its promised land of Canaan. These prophecies include certain more general matters, such as poverty (28:17–18, 43–44), pestilence and disease (vv. 21–22, 27, 59–61), drought (vv. 23–24), and other calamities (vv. 38–40, 42), but they especially foresee Israel's military defeat (vv. 25–26, 29, 34, 48). The final campaign is noted in detail: the coming of the hostile nation from afar, with a foreign language, 28:49,[13] the terrible sieges throughout the land, 28:52–57, and failure in battle such that one enemy would chase 1,000 Jews, 32:30. Fulfillment (per. 7): as in Lev. No. 33.

14. Dt 4:27; 28:36a, 41, 64a; *29:28b* (4 vv.): Israel to be scattered among the nations and to be few in number. Fulfillment (per. 8): as in Lev. No. 34.

15. Dt 4:28; *28:36c, 64b* (1 v.): Israel to lapse into idolatry while in

---

11. *Things to Come*, ch. 6.
12. See above, introduction to Deuteronomy.
13. Hence 32:21, "a foolish nation"?

exile. Fulfillment (per. 8): it was so, Ezek 14:1–7; see Dan 3 for a climactic illustration of this danger.

16. Dt 4:29–30, 30:1–2 (4 vv.): Israel to seek God in the exile, and to find Him. Fulfillment (per. 8): an example is the way in which Daniel sought God (Dan 9:3); cf. the assurance of divine favor subsequently granted to him (v. 23).

17. Dt 4:31; 7:9, 12; 8:18 (4 vv., typ.): the Abrahamic testament; for this testamentary transaction with "thy fathers" is expressly distinguished from the Sinaitic in 5:3 (see No. 11, above). Fulfillment (per. 13): as in Gen. No. 30.

18. Dt 5:12–15, 16:8 (5 vv., typ.): sabbath. Fulfillment (per. 13): as in Ex. No. 41.

19. Dt 6:3, 7:13a, 8:1a, 12:20, 13:17, 15:6, 30:16 (7 vv.): Israel to increase, so as to possess enlarged borders (12:20) and to rule over many nations (15:6). Fulfillment (per. 6):[14] as in Gen. No. 45.

20. Dt 7:4a; 29:26; 31:16b, 20b, 29a; 32:15–21a,[15] 32–33, 37–38 (14 vv.): that intermarriage with the Canaanites would turn Israel to other gods. 32:32 stated in figure that "their vine" would become even like that of Sodom and Gomorrah. Fulfillment (per. 5): it was so, Jd 3:6; cf. 2:11–13.

21. Dt 7:14; 28:4, 11 (3 vv.): no millennial barrenness. Fulfillment (per. 16): as in Ex. No. 51.

22. Dt 7:15 (1 v.): no millennial sickness. Fulfillment (per. 16): as in Ex. No. 50.

23. Dt 7:22 (1 v.): a gradual driving out of the Canaanites. Fulfillment (per. 5): as in Ex. No. 53.

24. Dt 10:1–3, 5, 8; 31:9, 25–26 (8 vv., typ.): the ark of the testament. Fulfillment (per. 13): as in Ex. No. 56.

25. Dt 11:24 (1 v.): the anticipated borders of Canaan, extending to the Euphrates. Fulfillment (per 6): as in Gen. No. 37.

26. Dt 12:5, 11a, 14a, 18, 21, 26; 14:23–26; 15:20; 16:2b, 6a, 7b, 11, 15b, 16a; 17:8, 10; 18:6; 26:2; 31:11, 33:19a (18 vv.): that God would choose a place for His habitation, "to cause His name to dwell there" (12:11). The only suggestion as to location appears in 33:19, "They shall call the peoples unto the mountain," for sacrifice. Fulfillment (per. 6): in the revelation to David of Mount Moriah as "the house of Yahweh God," I Chron 22:1; cf. II Chron 6:6.

27. Dt 12:6a, 11b, 13, 14b, 27a; 27:6b; 33:11b (2 vv., typ.): burnt offerings. Fulfillment (per. 13): as in Lev. No. 3.

28. Dt 12:6b–7, 11c, 17, 27b; 27:7 (5 vv., typ.): peace offerings. Fulfillment (per. 13 and 16): as in Lev. No. 5.

14. On the assignment of 7:13 to this (united kingdom) period rather than to millennial times, see above, p. 112.
15. Looking back on it as if accomplished.

29. Dt 12:16, 23–25; 15:23 (5 vv., typ.): no eating of blood. Fulfillment (per. 13): as in Lev. No. 20.

30. Dt 15:21, 17:1, *33:19b* (2 vv., typ.): sacrifice. Fulfillment (per. 13): as in Lev. No. 2.

31. Dt 16:1–2a, 4, 6b–*7a* (4 vv., typ.): Passover. Fulfillment (per. 13): as in Ex. No. 31.

32. Dt 16:13–15, *16b*; 31:10 (4 vv., typ.): Feast of Tabernacles. Fulfillment (per. 16): as in Ex. No. 46.

33. Dt 17:*14b*–20; *28:36b* (6 vv.): that Israel would some day set a king over them. Fulfillment (per. 6): as in Num. No. 34, when they first accepted Saul, I Sam 10:24.

34. Dt 18:1–5; 26:3a, 4 (7 vv., typ.): priests. Fulfillment (per. 13): as in Ex. No. 59.

35. Dt 18:15, 18–19 (3 vv.): that God would raise up a Prophet, from among Israel, like Moses, and give Him words to speak. The object of this prediction must, on the one hand, have possessed a contemporaneous relevance, since Israel was to have recourse to Him, rather than to the spiritists of the Canaanites, vv. 14–15. Yet He must, on the other hand, have had a continuing existence, coextensive with Israel's abiding in the promised land, v. 9; cf. vv. 19–21. The NT, in Acts 3:20–24, cf. 7:37, states that the prediction was fulfilled (per. 13) in the prophetic ministry of Jesus Christ; compare John 3:34, that "He whom God has sent speaks the words of God." For the reference to OT times, E. J. Young proposes that the subject of the Mosaic forecast might be either "an ideal person, in whom are comprehended all true prophets," or "the Spirit of Christ, in all the true prophets."[16] The latter appears preferable, in the light of I Pet 1:11, which reveals that it was the Spirit of Christ that was operative within God's earlier servants.

36. Dt 23:18; 31:*14b*–15 (2 vv., typ.): the tabernacle or "tent of meeting"; cf. 23:18, "the house of God." Fulfillment (per. 13): as in Ex. No. 55.

37. Dt 26:19; 28:1–3, 9–10, 13 (7 vv.): that Israel is to be "high above all nations," praised and honored. Fulfillment (per. 16): the preeminent status of Israel in the future Messianic kingdom; see especially the references listed under Isa. No. 51.

38. Dt 27:5–6a (2 vv., typ.): the altar. Fulfillment (per. 13): as in Ex. No. 44.

39. Dt 28:5–6, 8, 12; 30:9 (5 vv.): millennial plenty. Fulfillment (per. 16): as in Ex. No. 49.

40. Dt 28:7, 30:7 (2 vv.): millennial victory over enemies; Israel's foes are to inherit the very curses threatened against God's people in Dt (30:7). Fulfillment (per. 15): Armageddon, as in Num. No. 36.

---

16. *My Servants the Prophets*, p. 35.

41. Dt 28:65–67 (3 vv.): no ease from fear, while in the exile. Fulfillment (per. 8): as in Lev. No. 35.

42. Dt 28:68 (1 v.): a Jewish flight to Egypt, in ships, accompanied by the Jews' selling themselves for bondmen. Fulfillment (per. 8): probably a reference to the flight of the group which took Jeremiah to Egypt (Jer 43–44), though others would refer to a selling of Jewish slaves into Egypt by Titus, A.D. 70.[17]

43. Dt 30:3–5a, 32:36a (4 vv.): that God would return Israel to its own land after the exile. As 32:36 states, He will "judge His people," favorably (see next line). Fulfillment (per. 9): recorded in Ezra 1–2.

44. Dt 30:5b–6 (1 v.): Israel after the exile to be more numerous than in preexilic days, with circumcised hearts, so as to love Yahweh their God. The Israel of the postexilic return was not more numerous; but fulfillment may be found (per. 14) as the Gentiles are engrafted into the church, as in Gen. No. 19 and No. 41 (2nd stage). Blessings under the future Messianic kingdom then follow in Dt 30:7–9.

45. Dt 30:8 (1 v.): millennial obedience; God's people will "do all His commandments." This is not yet the case, but it will be then (per. 16 fulfillment); cf. I John 3:2.

46. Dt 32:40–43 (4 vv., fig.): God will make His arrows "drunk with blood," as He punishes the enemies who have exiled His people. Fulfillment (per. 8): the fall of Babylon in 539 B.C.; cf. Dan 5:30–31.

47. Dt 32:43a: on the basis of a pre-Christian Heb. MS. of Dt discovered at Qumran,[18] the traditional Masoretic text of the first line of this verse— "Rejoice, O ye nations, with His people"—may now be expanded into an approximation of the LXX:[19]

> Rejoice, ye heavens along with him,
>   And let the sons of God worship him;
> Rejoice, O ye nations, with His people,
>   And let all the angels of God ascribe might to him.

This presumably continues from v. 42 the quotation of Yahweh in the first person that began in v. 37,[20] though in 43b Moses himself concludes the poem by speaking of God in the third person—"For He will avenge the blood of His servants"—predicting the eventual fall of Israel's captor, Babylon (see No. 46, preceding). It is the LXX of 43a, moreover, that is quoted in Heb 1:6 in reference to Christ, "And let all the angels of God

17. KD, *Pentateuch*, III:445–446.
18. P. W. Skehan, BASOR, 136 (1954), 12–15.
19. F. M. Cross, The Ancient Library of Qumran, p. 135, would limit his reconstructed proto-MT (and presumably original Heb.) to, "Ascribe might to him, O sons of God," though he recognizes that the proto-Qumran text must also have included, "And bow down to Him, all ye divine ones," which he assumes to have been added from Ps 97:7, p. 136.
20. F. F. Bruce considers v. 43a also as spoken about Yahweh, rather than as forming a part of His oracle, NIC, *Heb*, p. 16.

worship Him."[21] As to the Person who is the object of this angelic worship in Deuteronomy, "The Messianic application is natural in the passage, for there Jehovah is the speaker; and if the *him* is applied to the ideal Israel, the ideal Israel or 'upright man' was the type of the Messiah";[22] cf. Ps 8:3 on Christ as the only true Adam, or Isa 42:1a on Christ as the only true servant Israel. Fulfillment (per. 13): the worship of Christ by angels, at His first advent (see Lk 2:13–14);[23] for Hebrews assigns this quotation to the time "when He brings the firstborn into the world," 1:6.

48. Dt 33:6 (1 v.): Reuben to diminish in numbers, per ASVmg. Fulfillment (per. 7): generally, after the days of Saul; see under Gen. No. 63.

49. Dt 33:7 (1 v.): Judah to come back victorious from battles. The phrase "and bring him back unto his people" has been variously interpreted; but it probably refers to triumphant returns after fighting.[24] Fulfillment (per. 6): David's victories, as in Gen. No. 66.

50. Dt 33:10–11 (2 vv.): Levi to minister in the sanctuary, despite all enemies that may rise up against him. Fulfillment (per. 16): so, even down into the millennial kingdom, Isa 66:21, Jer 33:18.

51. Dt 33:12 (1 v., fig.): Benjamin to be so closely associated with Yahweh that he "dwelleth between His shoulders," like a son carried on his father's back (cf. I Sam 17:6). Fulfillment (per. 9): this tribe of Benjamin is distinguished, along with Judah, by its returning in greater numbers from the exile, Ezra 1:5, 4:1, and therefore enjoying the corresponding divine favor that followed.

52. Dt 33:13–17 (5 vv., fig.): the Joseph tribes, of Ephraim and Manasseh (v. 17), to be blessed by nature (cf. Gen 49:22) and by God with "the precious things of heaven . . . and of earth" and with military power (Dt 33:17) so as to "push the peoples" with their horns (like a wild ox), even to "the ends of the earth." Fulfillment (per. 7), climaxing in the reigns of Jehoash and Jeroboam II in Ephraim, II K 13:25, 14:25.

53. Dt 33:18, 19c (2 vv., fig.): Zebulun and Issachar are to "suck the abundance of the seas and of the sand," and so be able to offer grateful sacrifices to God. Fulfillment (per. 4): compare the prosperity indicated under Gen. Nos. 70 and 71.

54. Dt 33:20–21 (2 vv., fig.): Gad, fierce like a lion, to march at ("to," ASV mg) the head of the tribes, to "execute the righteousness of Yahweh." Fulfillment (per. 4): they kept their obligation to march out "before their brethren" at the conquest, Josh 1:14, 4:12, just as promised in Num 32:17, 21, 32. Gad apparently led in the original request of the 2½ tribes for settlement beyond the Jordan, Num 32:2, 6.

21. This quotation is sometimes referred to Ps 97:7, but with less likelihood, both because of the differences in wording and because of the nonpredictive character of the Psalm, in which the object of worship is Yahweh Himself.

22. Camb, *Heb*, p. 63.

23. Because of the association with angels, Camb, ibid., would prefer Christ's second advent.

24. KD, III:501.

55. Dt 33:22 (1 v., fig.): Dan to leap out like a lion of Bashan. Fulfillment (per. 5): as in Gen. No. 72.

56. Dt 33:23 (1 v., fig.): Naphtali to possess the Sea (ASVmg) and south.[25] Fulfillment (per. 4): they received Galilee,[26] and a little area south of it, Josh 19:32–39.

57. Dt 33:24–25 (2 vv., fig.): Asher to "dip his foot in oil," i.e., to be secure and prosperous. Fulfillment (per. 4): as in Gen. No. 74.

58. Dt 33:29 (1 v.): the Canaanites to be rendered subservient to Israel. Fulfillment (per. 4): as in Gen. No. 17.

25. Or perhaps omit this last phrase, with the ancient versions.
26. Though the Heb. *yām*, "sea," generally indicates the Mediterranean.

JOSHUA

Scripture opens with the Pentateuch, the five books of Moses; but following it chronologically is Joshua, which forms the opening volume of the second division of the canon of the OT. This latter is identified topically in the English Bible as "historical books" (Joshua–Esther); yet according to the nomenclature of the Hebrew OT these constitute "Former Prophets,"[1] as distinguished from the "Latter Prophets," which extend from Isaiah through Malachi. Their designation seems to be due not only to the authorship of Joshua and the books that follow it by men who were prophets, but more basically because of the truly prophetic character of their contents. "Prophecy" is here used in its broader sense of inspired teaching;[2] for while all thirteen of these books, with the exception of Ruth,[3] do contain predictive material, the more significant fact is that each presents a distinctive message from God. That is to say, they do not record the history of Israel simply to preserve factual details out of the millennium that extended from the death of Moses in 1406 down to the reign of Darius II of Persia in 423 B.C. (Neh 12:22). Primarily they were written to set forth the major religious truths that derive from the events that each one chronicles. The heart of Joshua, for example, lies in the concept of prophetic fulfillment, that Yahweh's work in history is true to His previously revealed promises: "There failed not aught of any good thing which Yahweh had spoken unto the house of Israel; all came to pass," 21:45.

The Book of Joshua falls into three distinct units that cover the main events of Israel's occupation of the promised land (prophetic period 4):

1. Accepting as originally historical the canonical arrangement described by Josephus, who included among the Former Prophets all of the historical books and limited his third division to the four books of poetry, *Against Apion*, I:8, Psalms through Song of Solomon; see below, under Chronicles and Job.
2. See above, p. 4.
3. See above, p. 147.

I. the entering into Canaan by Israel in 1406 B.C. and its military conquest, chs. 1–12; II. the division of the land, datable to the year 1400 (14:10; cf. Num 10:11, 13:5), after six years of fighting, chs. 13–22; and III. two farewell addresses of Joshua, shortly before his death in approximately 1390, chs. 23–24. Predictive matter is scattered throughout parts I and III, particularly in ch. 1, as Joshua assumed leadership over the Hebrews, and in ch. 23, his first message of farewell. Certain typical prophecies occur, particularly in 5:2–12, concerning the ceremonies that followed Israel's crossing of the Jordan, and in 8:30–35, concerning the rites of testamentary renewal on Mount Ebal. All in all, there appear 27 different predictions, occurring in 89 out of the book's 658 verses (= 12%).

Just as in the case of Judges, Ruth, Samuel, and Kings that follow it, in the Book of Joshua the volume is *about* the one named in its title rather than *by* him.[4] Moses' successor did, it is true, inscripturate certain matters which he added to the already existing Pentateuchal "book of the law of God" (Josh 24:26). These must indeed have made up some of the sources for the volume which later bore his name.[5] But this very section goes on to record the deaths both of Joshua and of the other leaders who survived him, vv. 29, 31, 33. The book, however, appears to have been composed by one of Joshua's contemporaries who participated in the events described (6:25)—cf. the "we" in 5:1, or the "your" in 15:4—perhaps by Phinehas the grandson of Aaron.[6] As a result, it could not have originated very long after 1375 B.C.[7]

1. Josh 1:2–3, *11b*, 15; 2:9, 24; 18:3 (6 vv.): Canaan promised to Israel; specifically, "every place that the sole of your foot shall tread upon," as God's previous promises to Moses are cited (1:3). Fulfillment (per. 4): as in Gen. prophecy No. 24.

2. Josh 1:4 (1 v.): prediction of the ultimate border of Israel's land, to reach to the Euphrates; cf. certain more detailed geographical specifications in 13:2–6. Fulfillment (per. 6): as in Gen. No. 37.

3. Josh 1:5, 3:10, 13:6 (3 vv.): Israel's victory in Canaan, "not a man

---

4. Contrast the case of the later histories of Ezra or Nehemiah, below.
5. Cf. such other sources as "the book of the *yāshār*" ("upright"), cited in 10:13.
6. Gleason L. Archer, *A Survey of OT Introduction*, p. 252.
7. The older liberalism sought to find in Joshua a continuation of Wellhausen's J, E, and D documents (chs. 1–12, 23–24) and P (chs. 13–22). It thus treated Joshua together with the Mosaic books as a "Hexateuch," and so dated the whole to about 400 B.C., in postexilic times. More recently Martin Noth (1948) and others such as John Bright have supposed that Joshua formed the second part of a four-volume "Deuteronomic history," extending from Dt on into Jd and Kings, and written during the exile, IB, II:541–546. Both of these views, however, do not accord with the Bible's own testimony. The undeniably Deuteronomic tone, e.g. of Josh 23:6–11, is most naturally to be explained as a direct result of the personal and written influence of the "Deuteronomist" Moses upon his faithful lieutenant Joshua; cf. E. J. Young, "The Alleged Secondary Deuteronomic Passages in the Book of Judges," *The Evangelical Quarterly*, 25 (1953), 142–157.

to stand before Joshua." Fulfillment (per. 4): it was so, 11:16, as in Ex. No. 48.

4. Josh 1:6, 8–9 (3 vv.): the personal triumph of Joshua, in causing the people to inherit the land, 1:6, to "have success," v. 8, and to experience God's presence with him, v. 9. Fulfillment (per. 4): thus it was, 11:23, as in Dt 1:38b.

5. Josh :11a; 3:5, 7, 13b (4 vv.): Israel to cross the Jordan.[8] In ch. 3 Joshua assured his people, "Tomorrow Yahweh will do wonders among you," v. 5; and he spoke out in faith, prophesying that "when the soles of the feet of the priests . . . shall rest in the waters of the Jordan, the waters of the Jordan shall be cut off, even the waters that come down from above; and they shall stand in one heap," v. 13. Fulfillment (per. 4): it was even so, at Adam, vv. 16–17. God had also foretold that it would mean a beginning to His magnifying of Joshua, v. 7, which *was* one of the results, 4:14.

6. Josh 3:3–4, 6, 8, 11, *13a*, 14–15, 17; 4:5, 7, 9–11, 16, 18; 6:*4a*, 6–9, 11–13; 7:6; 8:33 (24 vv., typ.): the ark of the testament. Fulfillment (per. 13): as in Ex. No. 56.

7. Josh 5:2–9 (8 vv., typ.): circumcision. Fulfillment (per. 13): as in Gen. No. 42.

8. Josh 5:10 (1 v., typ.): Passover. Fulfillment (per. 13): as in Ex. No. 31.

9. Josh 5:12 (1 v., typ.): manna. Fulfillment (per. 13): as in Ex. No. 39.

10. Josh 6:2–5, 16 (5 vv.): Jericho and its king to be given up to Joshua; and its wall to fall flat, on the 7th day. Fulfillment (per. 4): it was so, 6:20–21, 12:9.

11. Josh 6:24, 9:23, 18:1, 19:51, *22:19a* (4 vv., typ.): the tabernacle, or "house of Yahweh." Fulfillment (per. 13): as in Ex. No. 55.

12. Josh 6:26 (1 v.): a curse upon the one who should refortify[9] Jericho: "with the loss of his first-born shall he lay the foundation thereof, and with the loss of his youngest son shall he set up the gates of it." Hiel literally fulfilled this curse, under Ahab, 874–853 (per. 7), I K 16:34, perhaps because of his knowledge of this very curse and because of paganized superstition.[10]

13. Josh 7:11, 15; *23:16a*; 24:25 (3 vv., typ.): the Sinaitic testament. The last verse states that "Joshua made a testament"; but, "This conclusion of a covenant was really a solemn renewal of the covenant made at Sinai, like that which took place under Moses in the steppes of Moab,"[11]

---

8. They were to prepare, so as to be able to cross in 3 days, 1:11. Actually the spies were delayed 3 days, 2:22, so that it was the following day, plus 3 more after that (3:1–2), when they crossed; cf. KD, *Josh*, pp. 31–32.

9. The prophecy thus relates to more than a simple reoccupation of the site or to limited rebuilding, KD, pp. 73–74.

10. Cf. IB, III:144, on the possibility of Canaanitish "foundation sacrifices."

11. KD, pp. 232–233.

Dt 29:1 (see under Dt 4:13, above). Fulfillment (per. 13): as in Ex. No. 45.

14. Josh 8:1–2, 7 (3 vv.): Ai and its king to be given up to Joshua. Fulfillment (per. 4): they were, vv. 19, 22–29; 12:9.

15. Josh 8:30–31a; 9:27a; 22:19b, 23a, 26a, 28a, 29a (8 vv., typ.): altar. Fulfillment (per. 13): as in Ex. No. 44.

16. Josh *8:31b*; *22:23b, 26b, 27a, 28b, 29b* (typ.): burnt offerings. Fulfillment (per. 13): as in Lev. No. 3.

17. Josh *8:31c*; 22:*23d, 26c,* 27b, *28c, 29d* (1 v., typ.): peace offerings. Fulfillment (per. 13 and 16): as in Lev. No. 5.

18. Josh *9:27b:* that God would some day "choose a place" for His sanctuary. Fulfillment (per. 6): as in Dt. No. 26, Mount Moriah.

19. Josh 10:8, 19 (2 vv.): that the confederacy of southern Canaanites, headed by Jerusalem, would be delivered up to Joshua. Fulfillment (per. 4): it was, vv. 10–11, 16–23, 26–42.

20. Josh 10:12 (1 v., fig.): "Sun, stand thou still [lit., be silent] upon Gibeon; and thou, Moon, in the valley of Aijalon." Though phrased as a command, this statement lay beyond the province of Joshua's own powers; uttered "before the children of Israel," it served as an actual prophecy.[12] Fulfillment (per. 4): the sun "hasted not to go down about a whole day."[13]

21. Josh 10:24–25 (2 vv., sym.): Joshua's having his commanders place their feet on the necks of the five captured kings of the Jerusalem confederacy. He explained, "Thus shall Yahweh do to all your enemies," v. 25. Fulfillment (per. 4): as in Gen. No. 17, on the coming subservience of the Canaanites.

22. Josh 11:6 (1 v.): the Hazor confederacy of northern Canaan to be delivered up to Joshua. Fulfillment (per. 4): it was, vv. 8, 12.

23. Josh 13:14 (1 v., typ.): sacrifice. Fulfillment (per. 13): as in Lev. No. 2.

24. Josh 17:18, 23:5 (2 vv.): Ephraim and Manasseh to drive out the Canaanites from their enlarged territory; cf. Joshua's similar promise for the rest of the tribes as well, in 23:5. Fulfillment (per. 6): as in Gen. No. 17 (3rd stage). Its final achievement by David is confirmed by archaeological testimony.[14]

25. Josh *22:23c, 29c* (typ.): meal offerings. Fulfillment (per. 13): as in Lev. No. 4.

26. Josh 23:13a (1 v.): the nations that remained in Canaan to be a snare and a scourge to Israel.[15] Fulfillment (per. 5): as in Num. No. 48.

27. Josh 23:*13b*, 15, 16b; 24:20 (3 vv.): Israel finally to be destroyed out of Canaan. Fulfillment (per. 7): as in Lev. No. 33.

12. See above, p. 39.
13. On various modern attempts to circumvent the physical miracle of prolonged daylight that is here asserted, see J. B. Payne, ETS B, 3 (1960), 95.
14. Cf. W. F. Albright, *From the Stone Age to Christianity*, p. 291.
15. Joshua's threat was contingent, v. 12; but Israel "met" the conditions by failing in just the ways described.

JUDGES

Scattered throughout the 21 chapters of Judges appear 20 predictions that God revealed during the course of this 5th period in the history of Israel. These were the days when the Hebrews were ruled by the "judges," charismatic leaders more military than judicial, whom Yahweh would raise up for the deliverance of His people. The time involved was more than three centuries, from the opening foreign oppression of Israel in about 1382 to the death of Samson, the 12th judge, following 1070.[1] Politically the scene was marked by alternating eras of oppression and of deliverance, which appear to be correlated, respectively, with providentially designed times of international anarchy or of the exercise of Egyptian or Hittite "police" control, at least until 1175 B.C.[2] Theologically, however, owing to its prophetic viewpoint,[3] the Book of Judges reveals the divine philosophy of history which underlay the observable ups and downs of Israel's political cycles. It teaches that sin was the cause of the nation's times of servitude (Jd 2:13–14), that repentance preceded God's gracious interventions for their restoration (v. 16), and that human depravity repeatedly asserted itself, so that succeeding generations proved worse than their fathers (v. 19). Explanatory of man's inability when left to his own resources is the key expression and refrain of Judges, "In those days there was no king in Israel: every man did that which was right in his own eyes," 17:6, 21:25.

The Book of Judges seems therefore to have been composed by its prophetic author some time *after* the establishment of a king over Israel in 1043 B.C., though the statement of 1:21 requires a date prior to David's rise over all Israel and his expulsion of the Jebusites from Jerusalem in 1003. Authorship by Samuel (cf. his known writing activity in I Sam 10:25 and I Chron 29:29) at a point prior to Saul's rejection and the prophet's turning to anoint David in about 1025 B.C. would be a plausible suggestion.[4] In addition to its primary history of Israel's first 12 judges (chs. 3–16), his book contains an introduction that sets the historical stage by defining the nation's condition at the close of the conquest (chs. 1–2) and an appendix containing two detailed illustrations of Israel's depravity

1. The 5th historic period (of the judges) includes also the some 20 years of Samuel's judgeship, up to I Sam 8.
2. See J. B. Payne, "Israel, History of," in M. C. Tenney, ed., *The Zondervan Pictorial Dictionary of the Bible*, pp. 390–391.
3. See above, introduction to Joshua.
4. Cf. E. J. Young's quoting of the Talmudic tradition in this regard, *An Introduction to the OT*, pp. 179–180, which also claims, with probability, Samuel's inscripturation of Ruth; though this would seem to date *after* his anointing of David (cf. Ruth 4:22) and to present a brighter side to the premonarchial period. Liberal criticism would bring Judges down to a considerably later date and place it among certain other Deuteronomic writings of the late 7th century B.C. and subject to a final (priestly) editing in postexilic days; see R. K. Harrison, *Introduction to the OT*, p. 684.

(chs. 17–21), even in the days preceding its first judge (cf. 20:28 and the reference to the events of 18:27–29 as early as Josh 19:47). The predictive revelations involve 41 of the book's 618 verses, or a low 7%. Yet this corresponds to the observation later made in I Sam 3:1, "The word of Yahweh was rare [ASVmg] in those days; there was no frequent vision."

1. Jd 1:2 (1 v.): Judah to gain possession of their tribal lands. Fulfillment (period 5): they did, vv. 4, 8–10, 17–19.

2. Jd 2:1, 20 (2 vv., typ.): the Sinaitic testament. Fulfillment (per. 13): as in Ex. prophecy No. 45.

3. Jd 2:3, 21 (2 vv.): that God would no longer drive out the Canaanites, but that they should become a snare and a grief to Israel. Fulfillment (per. 5): as in Num. No. 47, and quoting the words of Josh 23:13. The corresponding historical fact is expressly stated in Jd 2:23.

4. Jd 2:5 (1 v., typ.): sacrifice. Fulfillment (per. 13): as in Lev. No. 2.

5. Jd 3:28 (1 v.): Eglon's Moabite forces to be delivered up to Israel. Fulfillment (per. 5): they were, vv. 29–30.

6. Jd 4:7, 14 (2 vv.): that on this stated day (v. 14), Jabin's Canaanite army under Sisera would fall by the river Kishon. Fulfillment (per. 5): it did, vv. 15, 23–24.

7. Jd 4:9 (1 v.): Sisera himself to be delivered up, not to Barak, but to a woman. Fulfillment (per. 5): he was, vv. 17–22, though not to Deborah, who had uttered the prophecy, but to Jael.

8. Jd 6:16; 7:7, 9, 15; 8:7, 9 (6 vv.): that God would be with Gideon, so that he would "smite the Midianites as one man." Victory would be achieved through his mere 300 men (7:7), and Gideon would capture the two enemy kings (8:7). Fulfillment (per. 5): as a result of panic caused by the 300 (7:21–22), two Midianite chieftains were captured and executed (v. 26); and 8:10–12 states in summary that 120,000 of the enemy were slain, while 8:21 details the way in which Gideon finally slew the two kings.

9. Jd 6:24, *26a, 28b* (1 v., typ.): altar. Fulfillment (per. 13): as in Ex 17:15.

10. Jd 6:25–28; 11:31; 13:16, 19–20, 23a; 20:26a; 21:4a (11 vv., typ.): burnt offering. Fulfillment (per. 13): as in Lev. No. 3.

11. Jd 7:13–14 (2 vv., sym.): the Midianite soldier's dream, of a loaf of barley bread that tumbled into the camp of Midian and overturned a tent. It was interpreted by his associate (v. 14) as depicting the sword of Gideon. Fulfillment (per. 5): vv. 21–22, the ensuing panic and fighting against one another that overthrew the enemy.

12. Jd 9:15, 20 (2 vv., fig.): the predictive curse in Jotham's fable, "Let fire come out of the bramble and devour the cedars of Lebanon." He explained it in v. 20: that Abimelech and the men of Shechem might devour each other. Fulfillment (per. 5): after three years came treachery, vv. 22–23 (detailed in vv. 26–49), with many deaths for the men of Shechem, vv.

40, 43–45, 49. Abimelech's own destruction followed, vv. 53–54, with an express citation of Jotham's original curse, v. 57.

13. Jd 13:3, *5a*, 7–8 (3 vv.): Manoah's wife to bear a son. Fulfillment (per. 5): her child was Samson, v. 24.

14. Jd 13:5b (1 v.): Samson to "begin to save Israel out of the hand of the Philistines." Fulfillment (per. 5): 15:20, 16:31, he judged Israel for 20 years and worked spectacular feats but accomplished no final deliverance.

15. Jd *13:19b, 23b* (typ.): meal offerings. Fulfillment (per. 13): as in Lev. No. 4.

16. Jd 18:6, 10 (2 vv.): success predicted for the Danites, "Go in peace: before Yahweh is the way wherein ye go." This they rightly interpreted as meaning that God had given over Laish to them (v. 10). Fulfillment (per. 5): as in Gen. No. 72; they indeed got Dan-Laish, Jd 18:27–29.

17. Jd 18:31 (1 v., typ.): the "house of God" at Shiloh. Fulfillment (per. 13): as in Ex. No. 55.

18. Jd *20:26b, 21:4b* (typ.): peace offerings. Fulfillment (pers. 13 and 16): as in Lev. No. 5.

19. Jd 20:27 (1 v., typ.): the ark of the testament. Fulfillment (per. 13): as in Ex. No. 56.

20. Jd 20:28 (1 v.): Benjamin to be delivered up to the united tribes of Israel, on the next day (cf. Gen 49:27 on the predicted violent character of Benjamin). Fulfillment (per. 5): it was overpowered and almost wiped out, vv. 35–37, 42–44, 46, 48.

I SAMUEL

I and II Samuel were one book in the Hebrew; its division into two parts occurred first in the Greek Septuagint version of the Old Testament. The prophetic author of Samuel remains unidentified, though from his reference to "kings of Judah" in I Samuel 27:6 it appears that he must have lived and written after the separation of Ephraim in the N. from Judah in the S., which followed the death of Solomon in 930 B.C. Yet the detailed descriptions that appear in reference to some of the last events in II Samuel, e.g. 17:17–21 or 18:19–30, suggest composition by one of those who had participated in them, perhaps the young man Ahimaaz, a son of Zadok the high priest.[1]

The subject matter of I Samuel concerns two major eras, both of which belong to the century that preceded Ahimaaz: I. the birth, youth, and 20-year judgeship (1063–1043, I Sam 7:2?) of Samuel, chs. 1–7, which

---

1. Cf. R. H. Pfeiffer, *Introduction to the OT*, pp. 356–358.

marks the close of the period of the judges (the 5th in Israel's history); and II. the 33-year reign (1043–1010, Acts 21:22, cf. II Sam 2:11) of Saul, chs. 8–31, which opens the nation's 6th historical period, that of the united kingdom. The writer must therefore have availed himself of older source materials for these eras. He would have found some in the works of Samuel (I Sam 10:25); cf. also his citation of the Book of the yāshār, "Upright," in II Sam 1:18. That the volume which he produced carries the name of Samuel must have been due to the latter's role as a determinative figure for the events that are described, and not due to his composition of the book; for Samuel's own death is recorded as early as I Sam 25:1.

The purpose of Ahimaaz—or of whoever the writer of I Samuel may have been—was to evaluate the establishment of a human kingship over Israel. This institution came into being on the one hand as a result of a gracious act by God for the more effective development of His people (9:16), but on the other as a result of Israel's sinful desire for comformity to the pagans (8:8, 20).[2] The overall key to the book is thus to be found in Samuel's prediction of the way in which his people would, in Saul, reap the due reward of their deeds: "And ye shall cry out because of your king whom ye shall have chosen, and Yahweh will not answer you in that day," 8:18.

The 31 predictions of I Samuel are distributed throughout the course of the narrative. The majority concern events of more or less proximate fulfillment, in the days of Eli, Samuel, Saul, and David. Their presentation involves 124 verses, or 15% of the 810 verses that make up the full book.

1. I Sam 1:3–4, 21, 25; 2:19; 9:12–13; 15:15, 21, 22c; 16:2–3, 5; 20:6, 29; 26:19 (16 vv., typ.): sacrifice. Fulfillment (per. 13): as in Lev. prophecy No. 2.

2. I Sam 1:7, 9, 24; 2:22; 3:3a, 15 (6 vv., typ.): the house of Yahweh at Shiloh, designated a "temple," 1:9. It is identical in function with the earlier tabernacle, for it is still called "the tent of meeting," 2:22. Fulfillment (per. 13): as in Ex. No. 55.

3. I Sam 2:10a: "Yahweh will judge the ends of the earth." The preceding verse, 2:9, had generalized over the Lord's retributive activity; but here, "Hannah's prayer rises up to a prophetic glance at the consummation of the kingdom of God."[3] Since the next line goes on to speak of the Messiah (No. 4, following), her prediction is presumably directed toward the latter's return rather than toward Yahweh's final judgment. Fulfillment (per. 15): as in Num. No. 36, Armageddon, considered as a judgment; cf. the identification in Rev 19:19 of God's enemies with "the kings of the earth."

2. Cf. J. B. Payne, An Outline of Hebrew History, pp. 92–93, and, "Saul and the Changing Will of God," BS, 129 (1972), 321–325. Contrast the liberal theory of interwoven pro-kingdom and anti-kingdom sources, dated respectively to Ahamaaz and to ca. 600 B.C., Pfeiffer, op. cit., p. 362.

3. KD, Sam, pp. 33–34.

4. I Sam 2:10b (1 v.): Hannah's forecast that Yahweh "will give strength unto His king, and exalt the horn of His anointed," Heb. *m'shīhō*, His Messiah. When the preceding line (No. 3, above) speaks of divine judgment upon the ends of the earth, it carries the prophecy beyond the achievements of God's earlier anointed one, David. Fulfillment: the Lord's empowering of Christ for His Messianic rule (per. 16), as in Gen. No. 68; cf. the assurance of Rev 11:15 that the kingdom of the world will become His.

5. I Sam 2:11–17, 28–30 (10 vv., typ.): priests, specifically as officiating at sacrifice, 2:13. Fulfillment (per. 13): as in Ex. No. 59.

6. I Sam 2:31, *32b*–34; 3:11–14 (7 vv.): Eli's house to be punished. This would include premature deaths, 2:31–32, and particularly the loss of Eli's sons Hophni and Phinehas in one day, v. 34. Their iniquities could never be expiated, 3:14. Fulfillment (per. 5): 4:11 reports their deaths; v. 18, that of Eli himself; and v. 21, that of Phinehas' wife.

7. I Sam 2:32a (1 v.): the Lord's allusion to "the affliction of My habitation," despite His general blessings of wealth on Israel. Fulfillment (per. 5): the actual destruction of the temple at Shiloh is not mentioned in I Sam 4 in the chronicle of Israel's defeat. It is later, however, in Jer 7:12; and the reality of the Philistine devastation of Shiloh, datable to about 1080 B.C., has received archaeological confirmation.

8. I Sam *2:33a,* 7:17, 14:35 (2 vv., typ.): the altar. Fulfillment (per. 13): as in Ex. No. 44.

9. I Sam 2:35–36 (2 vv.): Eli's line to be replaced by "a faithful priest," to whom the branch of Eli would come begging. Solomon's final driving out of Abiathar (per. 6) in favor of Zadok, I K 2:26–27, is specifically cited as occurring in fulfillment of the prophecy "concerning the house of Eli in Shiloh" (v. 27).

10. I Sam *3:3b;* 4:3–6, 11, 13, 17–19, 21–22; 5:1–4, 7–11; 6:1–3, 8–11, 13, 15a, 18–19, 21; 7:1–2; 14:18 (35 vv., typ.): the ark of the testament. Fulfillment (per. 13): as in Ex. No. 56.

11. I Sam 6:14, *15b;* 7:9–10; *10:8a;* 13:9a, 10, 12; *15:22a* (6 vv., typ.): burnt offerings. Fulfillment (per. 13): as in Lev No. 3.

12. I Sam *6:15c,* 10:8b, 11:15, *13:9b, 15:22b* (2 vv., typ.): peace offerings. Fulfillment (pers. 13 and 16): as in Lev. No. 5.

13. I Sam 7:3 (1 v.): a forthcoming deliverance for Israel from the Philistines. Fulfillment (per. 5): under Samuel, vv. 10–11, 13–14, about 1063 B.C.

14. I Sam 9:16a (1 v.): that God would send Saul to Samuel on the following day. Samuel, in faith, made preparations for his appearance at the appointed time, vv. 23–24: "He had foreseen his coming in a supernatural way."[4] Fulfillment (per. 5): Saul did arrive on the next day, vv. 15, 18.

15. I Sam *9:16b:* Saul to save Israel from the Philistines. Fulfillment

4. Ibid., p. 93.

(per. 6): by his victory at Michmash, 14:20–23, 31, plus later successes as well, v. 47.

16. I Sam 9:20, 10:16 (2 vv.): Kish's asses found; see above p. 9. Fulfillment (per. 5): the finding is not specifically confirmed; but from Samuel's further prediction of the precise way in which this eventuation would be communicated to Saul (10:2; see No. 17, following) and from Saul's own matter-of-fact reporting about the prophecy (v. 16), its accomplishment may be safely assumed.

17. I Sam 10:2–7 (6 vv.): what Saul would meet after leaving Samuel— v. 2, two men by Rachel's sepulcher, telling of Kish's shift in concern over the lost asses; vv. 3–4, three men by the oak of Tabor, carrying various objects, who would give Saul two loaves of bread; and vv. 5–6, a band of prophets, with musical instruments, by the hill of God. God's Spirit would then come upon Saul so that he would prophesy too (cf. v. 10). Fulfillment (per. 5): "All those signs came to pass that day," v. 9.

18. I Sam 10:22 (1 v.): God's oracle at Mizpah as to where they would discover Saul, "He hath hid himself among the baggage." Fulfillment (per. 5): they did find him there, v. 23.

19. I Sam 12:17 (1 v.): God to send thunder and rain, at Samuel's request, and during the wheat harvest, which would be most unusual that late in spring. Fulfillment (per. 6): it happened on the same day, v. 18, as a warning to both the ruler and his subjects in the newly established Hebrew kingdom about faithfulness to God, vv. 14–16.

20. I Sam 12:25, *25:29b*, 28:19 (2 vv.): that both Israel and its king, Saul, would be consumed if they did wickedly—and they did! Abigail foretold in a figure how God would "sling out" the life of David's enemies, 25:29b (cf. v. 29a, No. 30, below); and the spirit of Samuel later specified that Yahweh would deliver the army of Israel into the power of the Philistines on the next day and that Saul and his sons would be "with Samuel," 28:19, namely, dead. Fulfillment (per. 6): at the battle of Mount Gilboa, 1010 B.C., Saul died and the people of Israel either fled or were slain, 31:1, 6.

21. I Sam 13:14, 15:28, 23:17b, 24:20, 25:30–31, 28:17 (7 vv.): Samuel's oracle that Saul's kingdom was not to continue but that Yahweh would appoint another leader (David). God would bestow it upon "a neighbor of thine, that is better than thou," 15:28. This forecast was later affirmed by Jonathan, 23:17a, and even by Saul himself, 24:20. Fulfillment (per. 6): David finally replaced Saul's son Ish-bosheth, II Sam 4:7, 5:1–3; cf. Gen 49:8 on how the sovereignty over Israel would come to rest in Judah.

22. I Sam 14:10 (1 v., sym.): the Philistine garrison before Michmash to be delivered up to Jonathan, if they should tell him to come up to them. Fulfillment (per. 6): they did say to come up, v. 12; and Jonathan, relying on this token, overpowered them, vv. 13–14.

23. I Sam 14:32–34 (3 vv., typ.): against eating blood. Fulfillment (per. 13): as in Lev No. 20.

24. I Sam 14:41–42 (2 vv., sym.): the casting of lots, showing that Jonathan was the one who had violated Saul's interdict against consuming food. Fulfillment (per. 6): as the lot had anticipated, Jonathan went on to confess his violation, v. 43.

25. I Sam 17:36–37, 46 (3 vv.): that Yahweh would deliver David from Goliath, and Goliath be smitten. Fulfillment (per. 6): it was so, vv. 49–51.

26. I Sam 22:18 (1 v., typ.): the priests' linen garments. Fulfillment (per. 13): as in Ex. No. 60.

27. I Sam 23:4 (1 v.): God's oracle that the Philistines at Keilah would be delivered up to David. Fulfillment (per. 6): as in the next verse.

28. I Sam *23:17a,* 25:29a (1 v.): promises that David would not be found by Saul but is to be "bound in the bundle of life with Yahweh thy God." Abigail here employs the figure of guarding valuable items by binding them in a bundle, which is especially meaningful in the light of her preceding context, where she spoke of those "risen up to pursue thee," namely, Saul, 24:2, 26:2. Fulfillment (per. 6): David never was caught by the jealous king, 27:4.

29. I Sam 25:26 (1 v.): a prophetic curse, "Let thine [David's] enemies be as Nabal." Fulfillment (per. 6): Nabal's collapse and death, vv. 37–38, "sharing his tragic end as foreseen by Abigail."[5]

30. I Sam 25:28 (1 v.): Abigail's prediction, "Yahweh will certainly make my lord [David] a sure house." The following therefore constitutes, if anything, an understatement: "She gives such clear and distinct expression to her firm belief in the divine election of David as king of Israel, that her words almost amount to prophecy" (!).[6] Fulfillment (per. 13): the eternal status of Jesus, of the house of David, as in II Sam 7:13b.

31. I Sam 30:8 (1 v.): David to overtake the Amalekites who had raided Ziklag, and to recover all that they had taken. Fulfillment (per. 6): this came about, vv. 17–19.

5. *The Jerusalem Bible,* p. 377.
6. KD, p. 244.

II SAMUEL

The two books of Samuel have a common origin—in Ahimaaz, or some comparably prophetic writer, soon after 930 B.C. in Judah.[1] II Samuel is, however, distinctive in its content, as it takes up the thread of Israel's

1. See above, introduction to I Samuel.

history after the collapse of Saul's government (I Sam 31 and II Sam 1:1–4) and moves on to present and discuss the powerful reign of David, 1010–970 B.C. The book falls into four sections: I. David's 7½-year rule over the tribe of Judah alone, chs. 1–4; II. his accession to the throne of all Israel in 1003 and his subsequent success in establishing a Hebrew empire from the Nile to the Euphrates, chs. 5–10; III. the period of David's personal failures and the disorders that resulted, approximately 995 to 978; and IV. David's final years, included in an appendix that involves incidents from various points in his career, chs. 21–24.[2] A number of the prophecies of II Samuel were later taken up into I Chronicles, this being indicated in each case by parentheses, e.g. "II Sam 5:2 (I Chron 11:2)."

The overall intent of II Samuel is to define God's purpose in raising up David and in granting him the Davidic testament. This *b'rīth* served to establish his throne over God's people forever, 7:16. The kingdom of David thus constituted a milestone in the attainment of Yahweh's previous promises; but it was more: it was a stepping-stone to the ultimate kingdom of God's Son, the Messiah, v. 14. The 22 predictions of the book accordingly find their greatest concentration in ch. 7, on the prophet Nathan's testamentary revelation to David, and in ch. 23:1–7, on the king's own last words, as he reflected over the Messianic prospect that lay in store for Israel and thence, in its wider implications, for the entire world. Prediction engages the attention of 68 of the 695 verses of II Samuel, which amounts to but 10%.

1. II Sam 3:10, 5:2 (I Chron 11:2) (2 vv.) retrospective allusions to the previous predictions of the transfer of the kingdom of Israel from Saul to David. Fulfillment (per. 6): as in I Sam prophecy No. 21.

2. II Sam 3:18; 5:19, 24 (I Chron 14:10, 15) (3 vv.): that David would save Israel from the Philistines, along with all other enemies as well. Compare God's similar promises to Samuel and to Saul concerning the Philistines two generations and one generation earlier, respectively, I Sam 7:3 and 9:16b. II Sam 5:19 and 24 constitute specific promises for David's victories at Baal-perazim and Rephaim. Fulfillment (per. 6): 5:20, 26; 8:1, over the Philistines; cf. 7:1, 8:14, over all others.

3. II Sam 3:29, 39 (2 vv.): David's curse, "Let the blood of Abner fall on the house of Joab, and upon all his father's house." Fulfillment (per. 6): information about the "father's house" is lacking; but Joab is known to have paid for his crimes with his life; see I K 2:31–34, where extended reference is made to the king's curse.

4. II Sam 6:2–*17a* (I Chron 13:6–14, 15:25–*16:1a*); 7:2 (1 Chron 17:1); 11:11; 15:24–25, 29 (20 vv. typ.): the ark of the testament. Fulfillment (per. 13): as in Ex. No. 56.

---

2. See J. B. Payne, *An Outline of Hebrew History*, pp. 100–110.

5. II Sam *6:13b* (I Chron *15:26b*), 15:12 (1 v., typ.): sacrifice. Fulfillment (per. 13): as in Lev. No. 2.

6. II Sam 6:17b (I Chron 16:1b), 7:5–7 (I Chron 17:5–6), 12:20 (5 vv., typ.): the tabernacle, and other similar sanctuaries—e.g., the tent that David pitched for the ark in Jerusalem (6:17) is subsequently called "the house of Yahweh" (12:20), for God's presence was there. Fulfillment (per. 13): as in Ex. No. 55.

7. II Sam *6:17c*, 18a; 24:22, 24, *25b* (I Chron 16:*1c*, 2a; 21:23a, 24, *26b*) (3 vv., typ.): burnt offerings. Fulfillment (per. 13): as in Lev. No. 3.

8. II Sam *6:17d, 18b; 24:25c* (I Chron *16:1d, 2b; 21:26c*) (typ.: peace offerings. Fulfillment (pers. 13 and 16): as in Lev. No. 5.

9. II Sam 7:11–12 (I Chron 17:10–11) (2 vv.) "Yahweh will make thee [David] a house [dynasty] . . . I will set up thy seed after thee and establish his kingdom." Fulfillment (per. 6): Solomon succeeded his father; and he specifically cited this prophecy as having been thereby accomplished, I K 8:20.

10. II Sam *7:13a* (I Chron *17:12a, 22:10a,* 28:6a): Solomon to build the temple. Fulfillment (per. 6): he did, I K 7:51.

11. II Sam 7:13b, 15–16, 19, 25–30 (I Chron 17:12b [= 22:10c, 28:7], 13b–14, 17, 23–27); 22:51; *23:5a, c* (11 vv.): "I will establish the throne of his [Solomon's] kingdom for ever."[3] 7:15 states that the Lord's *hésedh,* His steadfast *loyalty* to His own promises, would not depart from him, as it did from Saul; and 22:51 speaks of His *hésedh* "to David's seed, for evermore." By the time then that Solomon had a son, he could say that God "made me a house, as He promised," I K 2:24. The poetic clause from David's "last words" (II Sam 23:5) should therefore read interrogatively, with the ASVmg: "For is not my house so with God?"—possessing the everlasting Davidic testament, as stated in the next line (see No. 19, below).[4] Keil and Delitzsch observe: "The posterity of David could only last for ever by running out in a person who lives for ever, i.e. by culminating in the Messiah, who lives for ever, and of whose kingdom there is no end."[5] For when 23:5c says that the house of David will *yasmíah,* cause a *sémah,* "shoot" or "branch," to shoot forth, this noun constitutes a title of the Messianic Branch out of Jesse; cf. Jer 23:5, Zech 6:12. Fulfillment (per. 13): in the Person of Jesus Christ, the royal and eternal son of David. His title of King was proclaimed on Palm Sunday (Mt 21:4–5) and was established by His resurrection and exaltation to heaven that followed. Peter at Pentecost could thus speak in the past tense,

3. God's statement in I Chron 17:14, that "I will settle Him in My house," seemingly employs *house* in parallel with *My kingdom,* in the next line, thus referring to Solomon's establishment as ruler over the people of Israel, ICC, *Chron,* p. 228.
4. On this reading, cf. E. A. Edghill, *An Enquiry into the Evidential Value of Prophecy,* p. 206.
5. *Samuel,* p. 347.

saying God "has made Him Lord," Acts 2:36; cf. his assertion in vv. 30–31 that David knew "that God had sworn an oath to seat one of his descendants upon his throne" and that he associated this with Christ and His resurrection.[6]

12. II Sam *7:14a* (I Chron *17:13a, 22:10b, 28:6b*): God's word concerning the eternal son of David (No. 11, preceding), "I will be His Father, and He shall be My Son." Since v. 14b reverts in its subject to Solomon (see No. 13, following), the question has been raised whether 14a might not be related to him as well, especially in the light of I Chron 22:10 and 28:6 (later quotations of this same prophecy), where Solomon is outrightly named. Keil and Delitzsch are willing to go this far: "Sonship includes the government of the world. This not only applied to Christ but also to the seed of David generally, so far as they truly attained to the relation of children of God."[7] Correspondingly Solomon is known to have ruled as far as the river Euphrates, at least at the start of his reign. But there was the condition attached, ". . . *if* he be constant to do My commandments," I Chron 28:7, which was an ideal that Solomon did not fulfill, so that the goal of universal government remained unfulfilled as well. To this extent II Samuel's concept of "sonship" would be like Isaiah's concept of "the Servant" (see under Isa 42:1a), as an ideal that was actualized only in Christ. Keil and Delitzsch thus conclude that the prophecy of II Sam 7:14a "is first fully realized in Jesus Christ [per. 13], the only-begotten Son of the heavenly Father. . . . The Father loveth the Son, and hath given all things into His hand (John 3:35)";[8] and this, it should be noted, goes beyond the sonship of achieved human power into the Sonship of begotten divine essence.

13. II Sam 7:14b (1 v.): David's seed to be "chastened with the rod of men." Fulfillment, coming in the very next reign (per. 6), namely, that of Solomon: I K 11:14, 23, 26–27.

14. II Sam 7:24 (I Chron 17:22) (1 v.): "Thou didst establish Thy people Israel to be a people unto Thee for ever." Fulfillment (per. 18): in the New Jerusalem,[9] where according to the concluding prophecy of the Revelation (before its epilogue), 22:5, "They shall reign forever and ever."

15. II Sam 11:4 (1 v., typ.): sin offering. For Bath-sheba is here said to be "purified from her uncleanness"; and Lev 15:29–30 had specified this offering, "to make atonement for her for the issue of her uncleanness." Fulfillment (per. 13): as in Lev. No. 6.

6. Christ's kingdom, then, *could* here be equated with His position of sitting on the right hand of Yahweh (Acts 2:34), per M. J. Wyngaarden, *The Future of the Kingdom in Prophecy and Fulfillment*, pp. 160, 171, though the actualization of His rule seems to relate more to that future time when His enemies shall be made the footstool of His feet (v. 35, *q.v.*), just as in I Cor 15:25.

7. Op. cit., p. 349.

8. Ibid., pp. 348–349.

9. This should not exclude its application to the prejudgment Messianic kingdom (per. 16) as well, since this latter constitutes the first stage of "for ever"; see above, pp. 108–109.

16. II Sam 12:10–12 (3 vv.): that because of David's crimes over Bathsheba, the sword, arising out of David's own family, would no more depart from his house. This would include a public humbling of David's wives, as compared with the king's secret sin with the wife of Uriah. Fulfillment begins in the next ch. (per. 6): Amnon's crime and death; then Absalom's revolt, involving his humbling of the concubines of David (16:22), and this son's resultant destruction, chs. 14–19; and, even beyond David's death, the plot and eventual execution of Adonijah, I K 1–2.

17. II Sam 12:14 (1 v.): the death of the child conceived by David's crime with Bath-sheba. Fulfillment (per. 6): as occurring in vv. 15, 18.

18. II Sam 23:3–4 (2 vv., fig.): among David's "last words," that "There shall be One that ruleth over men righteously, in the fear of God [ASVmg]. He shall be as the light of the morning. . . ." The ASV text presents a possible alternate rendering, of a generalized nature, "One that ruleth . . . shall be as the light. . . ." But in this context it is more natural to understand "a prophetic declaration uttered by David at the close of his life and by divine inspiration, concerning the true King of the kingdom of God."[10] Fulfillment (per. 16): the righteous and beneficent rule of the Messiah; cf. God's previous prediction of His reign in I Sam 2:10b.

19. II Sam 23:5b (1 v., typ.): the Davidic testament. The king's "last words" continue, "He hath made with me an everlasting b'rīth"; cf. 7:13b, No. 11, above, on the concept of eternity. It brings about David's own "salvation"; and it is of God: for the next phrase is "kol-héfes, not 'all my desire' but 'all the good pleasure' of God expressed in that covenant."[11] It is to be effectuated by the Messianic ruler, 23:3–4, No. 18, preceding; and the last line of the verse must therefore be rendered interrogatively (as was its opening line; cf No. 11, above): "for will He not cause it to put forth a shoot?"[12] —the Messianic Branch. Fulfillment (per. 13): in the testamentary death of Jesus; see God's previous revelations of the b'rīth, as discussed, e.g., under the Abrahamic testament, Gen. No. 30.

20. II Sam 23:6–7 (2 vv., fig.): "The ungodly shall be all of them as thorns: they shall be utterly burned with fire in their place." Fulfillment (per. 18): the ultimate destiny of the lost, in hell; cf. Mt 13:30 (listed under Mt. prophecy No. 10, Rev 20:15 (under Rev. No. 7).

21. II Sam 24:11–14 (I Chron 21:9–13) (4 vv.): a divinely given choice for David to choose between three penalties: three years of famine,[13] three months of military defeat, or three days of pestilence. David's relative preference for the last may be inferred from v. 14 (I Chron 21:13). Fulfillment (per. 6): it was so, v. 15.

22. II Sam 24:18, 21, 25a (I Chron 21:18, 22, 26a) (3 vv.), typical: the altar. Fulfillment (per. 13): as in Ex. No. 44.

10. KD, p. 485.
11. Ibid., p. 489.
12. Cf. Payne, Theology of the Older Testament, p. 261, and Edghill, loc. cit.
13. Following the text of Chron and the LXX[B] of Sam.

I KINGS

I and II Kings continue the record of the history of Israel, from Solomon to the exile. Like the books of Samuel they form but one volume in the Hebrew Bible; but unlike Samuel, with its unity in composition, the Book of I Kings seems to have had an origin distinct from that of at least the closing chapters of II Kings.[1] For the earlier parts of Kings provide no historical allusions to the four stages of Judah's exile to Babylon, which began with the captivity of Daniel and his royal friends in 605 B.C.[2] On the contrary, the writer of I Kings lived under conditions in Judah as they existed prior to the destruction of the temple and to the exile of the land, 8:8, 9:21, 12:19 (cf. II K 8:22, 16:6)[3] For more precise dating, the book's prophetic author seems consistently to have been writing from the perspective of Josiah's great reform in 622 B.C. against the paganized "high places" of Judah, 15:14, 22:43,[4] but prior to this king's calamitous fall in 609. II Kings 23:25a may thus have constituted his concluding word, when he wrote, "And like unto him was there no king before him, that turned to Yahweh with all his heart and with all his soul . . . according to all the law of Moses." S. R. Driver long ago noted certain resemblances in style between these sections of Kings and the prophecies of Jeremiah.[5] In the light, moreover, of Jeremiah's seeming participation in at least the initial stages of Josiah's campaign of reform (Jer 11:1–8), this great prophet of Judah may indeed have been the author of the book (cf. his later composition of laments over Josiah, II Chron 35:25). Written sources were, in any event, employed in the writing, especially the compilations of the court records, or chronicles (lit., "the matters of the days"), of the Hebrew kingdoms: 14:19, 29, 15:7, 31, etc.; cf. 11:41.

The prophetic message[6] of I Kings could be summed up in one of its opening quotations: "Keep the charge of Yahweh thy God, to walk in His ways, to keep His commandments . . . according to that which is written in the law of Moses, that thou mayest prosper in all that thou doest," 2:3. The book then goes on to describe how first Solomon (970–930 B.C., chs. 1–11) and then his four successors in Judah (down to 848, chs. 12–23) either

1. See below, introduction to II Kings.
2. Verses that are sometimes proposed in this regard, such as 9:7–9 (cf. II K 20:17–18, 21:14, 22:19–20), are actually predictive and demand no post-605 or post-586 authorship, per R. H. Pfeiffer, *Introduction to the OT*, p. 312; cf. how he is refuted by S. R. Driver, *Introduction to the Literature of the OT*, p. 198.
3. The occurrence of this same phenomenon in II Chron 5:9, written after the exile, is explainable from its use of I K 8:8 as a quoted source.
4. Though note also Hezekiah's activity in this regard a century before, II K 18:4.
5. Op. cit., p. 203.
6. See above, introduction to Joshua.

did or did not reign in comformity to the will of Yahweh, with corresponding historical results. During the post-Solomonic period the collateral lines of kings in N. Israel proved uniformly evil in nature, as they walked in the way of their kingdom's founder, "Jeroboam the son of Nebat, who made Israel to sin" (15:26, 34; 16:19; etc.).

Most of the predictions recorded in I Kings were delivered by the various prophets that Yahweh sent to His people, e.g., those proclaimed by Elijah, in chs. 17–21. The book's opening chapters also contain a considerable amount of typical prophecy, revealed in connection with Solomon's construction of the temple. Predictive matter involves 189 of the book's 816 verses, or 23% of the whole. The number of separate prophecies comes to 44, with the last 30 all being fulfilled in the course of Israel's immediately contemporaneous historical period, her 7th—that of the divided kingdoms.

1. I K 1:39; 2:*28a*, 29a, 30; 3:1, 2b; 5:3, *5a* (II Chron 2:4a), 17–18; 6:1–10 (3:1–4), 12, 14–38 (3:5–13); 7:12, 21 (3:17), 45 (4:16), 48–51 (4:19–20, 22;5:1); 8:4b (5:5b), 6b (7b), 8 (9b), 10–13 (5:11, 13–14; 6:1–2), 16–18 (6:5–8), 20 (10), 27–30 (18–21), *31b* (*22b*), 33 (24), 35 (26), 38 (29), 42–44 (32–34), 48 (38), *63b* (*7:5b*), 64a (7a); 9:1 (7:11), 3 (16), 10 (8:1), 15, *25d* (16); 10:5 (9:4), 12 (11); *12:27b*; 14:26 (12:9), 28 (11); 15:15 (15:18), 18 (16:2) (84 vv., typ.): the tabernacle or temple. Fulfillment (per. 13): as in Ex. No. 55.

2. I K 1:50–51, 53; 2:28b, *29b*; *3:4b*; 8:22, 31a, 54, *64e*; 9:25c (II Chron 1:6a; 6:12, 22a; 7:7d; 8:12b); 18:30–32; *19:10b, 14b* (11 vv., typ.): an altar for burnt offering. Fulfillment (per. 13): as in Ex. No. 44.

3. I K 2:4; 8:25; 9:5 (II Chron 6:16; 7:18); 11:36b, 38–39 (6 vv.): on the eternity of David's line, "There shall not fail thee a man on the throne of Israel." Fulfillment (per. 13): as in II Sam. No. 11, Christ the eternal son of David—and of Solomon.

4. I K 2:26; 3:15a; *6:19b;* 8:1, 3–*4a*, 5a, *6a*, 7, *9a, 21a* (II Chron 5:2, 4–*5a*, 6a, *7a*, 8, *10a; 6:11a*) (6 vv., typ.): the ark of the testament. Fulfillment (per. 13): as in Ex. No. 56.

5. I K 3:*2a*, 3; 8:*5b*, 62 (II Chron *5:6b*, 7:4); 12:27a; 18:29, 35–36 (6 vv., typ.): sacrifice. Fulfillment (per. 13): as in Lev. No. 2.

6. I K 3:4a (II Chron *1:6c*), *15b*; *8:64b; 9:25a* (II Chron *7:7b; 8:12a*); 18:33, 38 (3 vv., typ.): burnt offerings. Fulfillment (per. 13): as in Lev. No. 3.

7. I K 3:12 (II Chron *1:12a*) (1 v.): that no one would ever arise as wise as Solomon was to be. Fulfillment (per. 6): 4:30–31, he became wiser than all other men; and, 5:12, "Yahweh gave Solomon wisdom, as He promised him"; cf. 10:23–24.

8. I K 3:13 (II Chron 1:12b) (1. v.): Solomon to be unexcelled by the other kings (including those after him, I Chron 1:12) in riches and in honor. Fulfillment (per. 6): it was so, I K 10:23; cf. vv. 7, 20.

9. I K *3:15c*; 8:63a, 64d (II Chron 7:5a, 7c); *9:25b* (2 vv., typ.): peace offerings. Fulfillment (pers. 13 and 16): as in Lev. No. 5.

10. I K 5:5b; 8:19 (II Chron 6:9) (2 vv.): Solomon to build the temple. Fulfillment (per. 6): as in II Sam 7:13a (prophecy No. 10), which is directly cited.

11. I K 7:23–26 (II Chron 4:2–5), 30, 38–40, 43–44 (II Chron 4:6a, 14–15) (10 vv., typ.): lavers, and "the sea." Fulfillment (per. 13): as in Ex. No. 67.

12. I K 8:2, 65 (II Chron 5:3; 7:8) (2 vv., typ.): the Feast of Tabernacles. Fulfillment (per. 16): as in Ex. No. 46.

13. I K 8:9b, 21b, 23 (II Chron 5:10b; 6:11b, 14); 11:11a; 19:10a, 14a, (6 vv., typ.): the Sinaitic testament. Fulfillment (per. 13): as in Ex. No. 45.

14. I K *8:64c* (II Chron *7:7e*) (typ.): meal offerings. Fulfillment (per. 13): as in Lev. No. 4.

15. I K 9:7a, 9 (II Chron 7:*20a,* 22) (2 vv.): Israel to be cut off from their land, and to become a byword. Fulfillment (per. 7): 586 B.C., as in Lev. No. 32.

16. I K 9:*7b*–8 (II Chron 7:20b–21) (1 v.): the Lord's threat against His temple, should idolatry arise in Israel: "This house will I cast out of My sight." Fulfillment (per. 7): II K 25:9, Nebuchadrezzar burned it.

17. I K 11:*11b*–13, 32, 34–*36a*, 37 (6 vv.): predictions about the division of Solomon's kingdom. Except for one tribe, vv. 13, 32, 36, it would be taken from Solomon's son, vv. 12, 34–35, and given to one of Solomon's servants, v. 11. Fulfillment (per. 7): all but Judah was indeed taken from Rehoboam and bestowed on Jeroboam, 12:16–17, 19–20.

18. I K 11:30–31 (2 vv., sym.): the robe of Ahijah was rent into 12 pieces, with 10 given to Jeroboam. Ahijah explained his act, v. 31: 10 of the Hebrew tribes would be awarded to Jeroboam. The fulfillment (per. 7) is expressly cited in 12:15—Rehoboam maintained his rule in Judah, 12:17, and Benjamin came under his control too, v. 21, II Chron 11:1, 12; but the remaining tribes went to Jeroboam, apparently including Simeon, which came to be associated with the North, II Chron 15:8, 24:6.

19. I K 13:2, 32 (2 vv.): a threatening prophecy directed against Jeroboam's altar, "A son shall be born unto the house of David, Josiah by name; and upon thee shall he sacrifice the priests of the high places . . . and men's bones shall they burn upon thee"; v. 32 provides confirmation. This all came about, 308 years later (still per. 7), II K 23:15–16, 20, with the fulfillment of the prophecy being noted, v. 17.

20. I K 13:3 (1 v.): that Jeroboam's altar would be rent and its ashes poured out. This event would constitute an immediate sign, to validate the long-range prophecy of v. 2 (No. 19, preceding).[7] Fulfillment (per. 7): it was so, v. 5.

---

7. See above, p. 13.

21. I K 13:22 (1 v.): concerning the prophet who ate at Beth-el, in disobedience to God, "Thy body shall not come into the sepulchres of thy fathers." Fulfillment (per. 7): a lion slew him on the road, v. 24; and he was buried in Beth-el, v. 30. The prophecy is cited, v. 26.

22. I K 14:5 (1 v.): that the wife of Jeroboam would come disguised to see Ahijah the prophet. Fulfillment (per. 7): she did, v. 6; and Ahijah greeted her by name and thus demonstrated that her feigning was discovered.

23. I K 14:10–11, 13–14 (4 vv.): the house of Jeroboam to be destroyed, "every man-child," and their corpses to lie unburied. This would be done by another king, raised up of God. Fulfillment (per. 7): Baasha slew Jeroboam's son Nadab, who had reigned only from 910 to 909 B.C., 15:27–28, along with all his house, v. 29 (where the prophecy is cited).

24. I K 14:12 (1 v.): Jeroboam's son Abijah to die when his wife would return to the city of Tirzah. Fulfillment (per. 7): it was so, v. 17; and the prophecy is cited, v. 18.

25. I K 14:15–16 (2 vv.): N. Israel to be "rooted up out of this land, and scattered beyond the River [Euphrates]" because of Jeroboam's sins. Fulfillment (per 7): their fall to Assyria, 722 B.C., II K 17:6–7, 22–23.

26. I K 16:3–4 (2 vv.): Baasha's house (the dynasty) to be swept away and their bodies left unburied. Fulfillment (per. 7): his son Elah reigned only two years, 886–885, before he was murdered by Zimri, v. 10, who "left him not a single man-child, neither of his kinsfolks, nor of his firends," v. 11; and the prophecy is cited, v. 13.

27. I K 17:1 (1 v.): Elijah's threat against Ahab, "There shall be no dew nor rain these [ensuing] years, but according to my word." Fulfillment (per. 7): famine, 18:2, 5; the rain came only "in the third year," v. 1, that is, of Elijah's stay in Zarephath; cf. 17:14. The full duration of the drought was 3 years and 6 months, Lk 4:25, James 5:17,[8] until Elijah's word came announcing rain (see No. 31, below).

28. I K 17:4 (1 v.): the ravens to feed Elijah.[9] Fulfillment (per. 7): they did, v. 6, every morning and evening, until the brook Cherith dried up.

29. I K 17:9 (1 v.): a widow in Zarephath to sustain Elijah. Fulfillment (per. 7): one did, v. 15.

30. I K 17:14 (1 v.): Elijah's assurance to this widow, "The jar of meal shall not waste, neither shall the cruse of oil fail, until the day that Yahweh sendeth rain upon the earth." Its fulfillment (per. 7) was miraculous, v. 16 —this was indeed "the word of Yahweh, which He spake by Elijah."

31. I K 18:1, 41 (2 vv.): that God would send moisture again, after the drought, "an abundance of rain," v. 41. Fulfillment (per. 7): a great rain came, v. 45.

32. I K 19:17a (1 v.): Hazael of Syria to slay widely in Israel; cf. the later elaboration of this prophecy in II K 8:11–12. Fulfillment (per. 7):

8. Cf. KD, *Kings*, pp. 240–241.
9. So KB, p. 733, who maintain the pointing 'ōrēv, not ʿrav, "Arabs," which would hardly have been as noteworthy a matter.

"Hazael smote them in all the borders of Israel," II K 10:32; cf. 13:22; "The king of Syria destroyed them and made them like the dust in threshing," 13:7, which refers to the acts both of Hazael and of his son Ben-hadad III, v. 3, up until 803 B.C.

33. I K *19:17b:* Jehu to slay those left by Hazael. Fulfillment (per. 7): especially his murders of 841 B.C., II K 9:24, 28, 33; 10:6–7, 11, 14, 17, 25.

34. I K *19:17c:* Elisha to slay those left by Jehu. Fulfillment (per. 7): actually, the major slaughters effectuated by Hazael and by Jehu were caused by Elisha's anointing of them both; see No. 32 and 33, preceding. He also directly brought about the deaths of others, II K 2:42, 5:27; 7:2, 19–20, though Ellison proposes a less direct form of fulfillment: "It was in this sense that Elisha was to slay those who had been spared by foreign enemy and domestic upheaval: by being the human embodiment of God's turning from the people as a whole, he was the most effective instrument of judgment on them."[10]

35. I K 20:13–14 (2 vv.): the army of Ben-hadad II of Syria to be delivered over to Ahab. An unnamed prophet specifically advised the king to utilize the young troops of the district governors and for Ahab to initiate the attack. Fulfillment (per. 7): Syria was routed, vv. 20–21, 957 B.C.[11]

36. I K 20:22 (1 v.): the prophet's warning to Ahab, "At the return of the year the king of Syria will come up against thee" again; see above, p. 9. Fulfillment (per. 7): he did, 856, vv. 26–27, in such force as to "fill the country."

37. I K 20:28 (1 v.): Ben-hadad to be delivered to Ahab for a second time. Fulfillment (per. 7): 100,000 Syrian footmen were slain in one day, v. 29; and the wall of Aphek fell on 27,000 more, v. 30.

38. I K 20:36 (1 v.): a lion to slay the man who disobeyed the prophet, after Ahab's second victory over Ben-hadad. Fulfillment (per. 7), in the same verse: "as soon as he was departed from him."

39. I K 20:42; 22:17, 20, 23, 28 (II Chron 18:16, 19, 22, 27) (5 vv.): to Ahab for having spared Ben-hadad, "Thy life shall go for his life, and thy people for his people," specifically, at Ramoth-gilead (22:20). Fulfillment (per. 7): three years after the first of these prophecies (22:1) Ahab lost his life fighting Ben-hadad II at Ramoth-gilead, v. 35; and Israel gave up the battle, v. 36, and later suffered greatly under the Syrians, No. 32 above, and II K 13:7.

40. I K 21:19 (1 v.): Elijah's condemnation of Ahab, "In the place where dogs licked the blood of Naboth shall dogs lick thy blood, even thine." But to some extent this was a conditional prophecy: upon Ahab's repentance, God (through Elijah) relented, v. 29, at least in respect to the place. Dogs at Samaria did, however, lick Ahab's blood in 853 (22:38,

10. *The Prophets of Israel*, p. 45.
11. Cf. 20:22, 22:1, for this dating.

which cites this prophecy); and compare No. 43 below, on the deferring of fulfillment regarding place (per. 7) to Ahab's son (21:29).

41. I K 21:21–22, 24 (3 vv.): Ahab's house (dynasty) to be completely swept away, and their corpses to be abandoned without burial. Fulfillment (per. 7): executed by Jehu, II K 9:24, 10:7. He left "none remaining," 10:11, 17; the heads of Ahab's sons were left piled at the gate of Jezreel, v. °; and the prophecy is cited, vv. 10, 17.

42. I K 21:23 (1 v.): "The dogs shall eat Jezebel by the rampart of Jezreel. Fulfillment (per. 7): it was so, II K 9:35, where the prophecy is cited at length, vv. 36–37, quoting even more than had been recorded in I K 21, namely, "the body of Jezebel shall be as dung upon the face of the field. . . ."

43. I K 21:29 (1 v.): because of Ahab's repentance (see No. 40, above), the evil that Elijah had predicted was not to come about in this king's days, but in the days of his son. Fulfillment (per. 7): in 841 the punishment was carried out by Jehu upon Ahab's son Joram, II K 9–10. At the time, Jehu specifically recalled the curse of Elijah, that the penalty must be exacted in the very place of Ahab's crime against Naboth, II K 9:25–26.

44. I K 22:25 (II Chron 18:24) (1 v.): the prophet Micaiah's word to Zedekiah the son of Chenaanah, who had predicted victory for Ahab at Ramoth-gilead in 853, that when he should receive the reports of Ahab's actual disaster, "Thou shalt go into an inner chamber to hide thyself." The fulfillment (per. 7) is not stated in the record; but Zedekiah's falsehood *was* demonstrated by history; see No. 39 above. Keil suggests that it "was probably fulfilled at the close of the war, when Jezebel or the friends of Ahab made the pseudo-prophets suffer for the calamitous result."[12] Ellison has proposed that it was "probably during those grim years when Israel reeled beneath Syrian blows,"[13] in the half-century that followed.

12. *Kings*, p. 278.
13. Op. cit., p. 42.

II KINGS

II Kings completes the histories of the divided Hebrew kingdoms, from the death of Jehoshaphat in 848 to the exile, and specifically to ex-king Jehoiachin's release from his Babylonian imprisonment in 561 B.C. It continues to utilize the source materials (cited under I Kings) that were available through the court chronicles of the two kingdoms. It also incorporates certain matters directly from the prophetic writings. For instance, II Kings 16:5, on Ahaz, and 18:13–ch. 20, on Hezekiah, are taken from Isaiah 7:1 and chs. 36–39, respectively; cf. the explanation in II Chron 32:32. As a result, II Kings furnishes the first examples in Scripture of "reused" groups of prophecies that have come to be recorded in more than one book; see above, in the prefatory note to the Biblical predictions,[1] and below, in the summarization of such materials under the statistical Appendix.[2] They are followed in each case by a bracketed notation of the Isaianic source, to which reference should be made for the basic discussion, e.g. "II K 18:30 [see Isa 36:15]."

Much of II Kings was composed along with I Kings, presumably by Jeremiah or some similarly minded prophet, shortly after Josiah's great reform of 622 B.C.[3] Yet the completion of this work as it stands today could only have been achieved by an exilic prophet,[4] after 561 but seemingly before Babylon's fall to Persia in 539. For some mention must surely have been made of Cyrus' decree, which permitted the Jews to return to their own land (as in II Chron, see 36:22–23), had this momentous event occurred prior to the book's inscripturation. The Bible does not disclose the identity of this final editor of Kings, though some prophet in the approximate circumstances of Ezekiel seems to be required.[5]

The theme of II Kings may be expressed in its sobering evaluation of one of Judah's poorest monarchs, "Surely at the commandment of Yahweh came this upon Judah, to remove them out of His sight, for the sins of Manasseh, according to all that he did," 24:3; compare the similar judgment upon N. Israel in 17:15, "And they rejected His testament that He made with their fathers, and His testimonies which He testified unto them; and they followed vanity . . . and went after the nations that were round about them" (cf. Israel's original sin in seeking a king, I Sam 8:20). The book contains 50 separate prophecies, distributed throughout 144 of its 719 verses, which thus amount to 20% of the total. A number that are found in the earlier part of the volume arose out of the career of the prophet Elisha. The majority received their fulfillment during the course of the contemporaneous, divided-kingdom period (per. 7), though a number of

---

1. P. 148.
2. P. 676.
3. See above, on the circumstances of origin for I Kings, in the introduction to that book.
4. Cf. his supplement to Jeremiah's praise of Josiah in II K 23:25a, which necessarily assumes the termination of Judah's line of kings: "Neither after him arose there any like him," v. 25b.
5. This concept of dual authorship, in which the "Jeremiah" block of material is succeeded at II K 25:23b (plus the final figure of Josiah's reign, in 22:1) by a block of "Ezekiel" supplement, is to be distinguished from the view of liberal writers who use the idea of dual authorship as a basis for distinguishing parallel strata that run through the whole book, and with conflicting teachings (e.g. in respect to the legitimacy of the pre-Solomonic high places; cf. Pfeiffer's treatment of I K 3:3 and 3:4 in this regard, *Introduction to the OT*, p. 377), against which evangelical interpreters rightly object (e.g., E. J. Young, *An Introduction to the OT*, p. 201; yet note Archer's recognition of the legitimacy of dual authorship, *A Survey of OT Introduction*, p. 277).

typical matters that foreshadowed the life of Christ (per. 13) appear as well, especially in chs. 11 and 16, on the actions of Joash and/or Ahaz in reference to the temple and its rites.

1. II Kings 1:4, 6.16 (3 vv.): Ahaziah, king of Israel, not to recover from his fall. Fulfillment (per. 7): he died, 852 B.C., v. 17, which cites the prophecy.

2. II K 2:3, 5, 9 (3 vv.): Yahweh to take away Elijah from Elisha on that same day. Fulfillment (per. 7): his ascension that day into heaven, in a whirlwind, v. 11.

3. II K 2:10 (1 v.): a double portion of Elijah's spirit[6] to be given to Elisha, "if thou see me when I am taken from thee." Fulfillment (per. 7): Elisha did see this, v. 12; and then in v. 15 it was recognized that the spirit of Elijah had come to rest on Elisha.

4. II K 3:17 (1 v.): Elisha's encouragement to Jehoram of Israel and Jehoshaphat of Judah, facing drought while attacking Moab via the wilderness of Edom: the "valley shall be filled with water, and ye shall drink." Fulfillment (per. 7): v. 20, "There came water by the way of Edom, and the country was filled with water," probably by a flash flood. The two monarchs who are named require a dating for this event between 852 and 848 B.C.

5. II K 3:18–19 (2 vv.): Moab to be delivered up to the coalition of Israel and Judah, its fortified cities to be smitten, and its land devastated. Fulfillment (per. 7): thus it was, vv. 24–25.

6. II K 3:20, 16:12, 17:36 (3 vv., typ.): sacrifice. Fulfillment (per. 13): as in Lev., prophecy No. 2.

7. II K 4:16 (1 v.): the Shunammite woman to have a son, at the same season the following year. Fulfillment (per. 7): it was so, v. 17, and at the stated time.

8. II K 4:23; 11:5 (II Chron 23:4), 7a, 9 (23:8); 16:18a (5 vv., typ.): sabbath. Fulfillment (per. 13): as in Ex. No. 41.

9. II K 4:43 (1 v.): that a small amount of food would supply 100 of Elisha's people: "They shall eat, and shall leave thereof." Fulfillment (per. 7): there occurred a miraculous "multiplication of loaves,"[7] v. 44, "according to the word of Yahweh."

10. II K 5:3, 8, 10 (3 vv.): Naaman the Syrian to recover from leprosy; v. 8, "He shall know that there is a prophet in Israel." Fulfillment (per. 7): he did become clean, v. 14, by dipping seven times in the Jordan according to the word of Elisha.

6. On the "double portion," cf. ASVmg: "That is, the portion of the first born. See Dt 21:17." Elisha's wish was apparently that he might be the equivalent of Elijah's first-born son, as opposed to the lesser status of others of "the sons of the prophets."

7. JB, p. 459; and cf. Mt 14:16–21, 15:32–38.

11. II K 5:17a; 16:*13a*, 15a (2 vv., typ.): burnt offerings. Fulfillment (per. 13): as in Lev. No. 3.

12. II K *5:17b*; 16:13c, *15c* (1 v., typ.): peace offerings. Fulfillment (pers. 13 and 16): as in Lev. No. 5.

13. II K 5:27 (1 v.): Elisha's sentence upon his servant Gehazi, who had sinned by greed, "The leprosy of Naaman shall cleave unto thee and unto thy seed for ever." Fulfillment (per. 7): Gehazi's descendants are not known; but this dread disease did forthwith strike Elisha's servant, v. 27,[8] and presumably was passed on to his family.

14. II K 6:6 (1 v.): Elisha's oracle to Jehoram of Israel, "Beware that thou pass not such a place; for thither the Syrians are coming down." Fulfillment (per. 7): v. 10, the warning saved Israel, "not once, nor twice," but repeatedly. Indeed, the fact of Elisha's prophecies was recognized even by the Syrians, v. 12.

15. II K 6:32 (1 v.): the biography of Elisha includes this record of a contact of the prophet with a messenger from King Jehoram: "Ere the messenger came to him, he said to the elders, See . . . when the messenger cometh . . . is not the sound of his master's feet behind him?" Fulfillment (per. 7): the messenger did come, 6:33; and Keil adds, "In v. 33 we have to supply from the context that the king followed close upon the messenger . . . for the subject is not the messenger but the king, as is evident from 7:2 and 17,"[9] the latter of which describes the previous incident with Elisha as the time "when the king came down to him."

16. II K 6:33 (1 v.): Jehoram's query to Elisha, "Why should I wait for Yahweh any longer?" His very question assumes that the prophet had predicted a deliverance for Samaria, then under Syrian siege. This might, in fact, have already been inferred from the king's threat against Elisha in v. 31.[10] Fulfillment (per. 7): Samaria was delivered, miraculously, 7:6–7.

17. II K 7:1 (1 v.): Elisha's assurance to besieged Samaria as it was facing a desperate food shortage, "Tomorrow about this time shall a measure of fine flour be sold for a shekel and two measures of barley for a shekel in the gate of Samaria," that is, at a greatly reduced price. Fulfillment (per. 7): it was so, vv. 16, 18, "according to the word of Yahweh," after He had caused the besieging Syrians to flee (see No. 16, preceding).

18. II K 7:2, 19 (2 vv.): Elisha's word to a captain, who had doubted his prophecy (No. 17, preceding) of the deliverance of besieged Samaria and of food being sold more cheaply: "Thou shalt see it with thine eyes, but shalt not eat thereof." Fulfillment (per. 7): vv. 17, 20, he was trampled upon in the gate, when the people rushed out to the food, and died "as the man of God had said."

8. The reference to Gehazi in 8:4–5 must pertain to some earlier point in time; KD, *Kings*, p. 333.

9. Ibid., pp. 329–330.

10. See above, p. 41.

19. II K 8:1 (1 v.): Elisha's prediction to the Shunammite woman that "Yahweh hath called for a famine; and it shall also come[11] upon the land seven years." The fulfillment (per. 7) is not specified but is to be assumed from context; for as a result, "the woman and her household sojourned in the land of the Philistines seven years."[12]

20. II K 8:10 (1 v.): Elisha's message for Hazael to relay to Ben-hadad II, the ailing Syrian king who had sent him: "Go, say, Thou shalt not recover; for Yahweh hath showed me that he shall surely die," ASVmg. Fulfillment (per. 7): this came about; for on the day following his report[13] Hazael murdered his sick master, v. 15, and seized the throne.

21. II K 8:11–12 (2 vv.): that Hazael would do evil to Israel: burning strongholds and slaying men, women, and children. Fulfillment (per. 7): as in the more general prophecy of I K 19:17a. Precisely these kinds of acts are noted as done to Israel by others, Hos 10:14; so they may well have been performed by Hazael also.

22. II K 8:13 (1 v.): Hazael to become king over Syria. Fulfillment (per. 7): the next day Hazael murdered Ben-hadad and became ruler, v. 15 (see No. 20, above), approx. 843 B.C.

23. II K 8:19 (1 v.): the line of David to be preserved always. Fulfillment (per. 13): through Jesus Christ, as in II Sam. No. 11.

24. II K 9:8–9 (2 vv.): the house of Ahab to be cut off. Fulfillment (per. 7): by Jehu, as in I K 21:21.

25. II K 9:10 (1 v.): that dogs would eat Jezebel in Jezreel. Fulfillment (per. 7): as in I K. No. 42.

26. II K 9:26 (1 v.): Ahab to be requited for his sin against Naboth, in the latter's very plot of land. Fulfillment (per. 7): as in I K 21:29 (with the geographical detail of v. 19), prophecies No. 40 and 43, above.

27. II K 10:30, 15:12 (2 vv.): to Jehu, "Thy sons of the fourth generation shall sit on the throne of Israel." Fulfillment (per. 7): the four generations following Jehu ran: Jehoahaz, Jehoash, Jeroboam II, and Zechariah (841–752 for the dynasty, which was the northern kingdom's longest); cf. 15:12, where the prophecy is repeated, as fulfilled.

28. II K 11:3–4, 7b, 10–11a, 13, 15, 18–19; 12:4–9, 10, 11–15, 16c, 18; 14:14; 15:35; 16:8, 14b, 18b; 18:15–16; 19:1, 14; 20:5b, 8b (see Isa 37:1, 14; 38:20, 22b); 21:4–5, 7; 22:3–6, 8–9; 23:2a, 4, 6–7, 11–12, 24; 24:13; 25:9, 13a, 16b (II Chron 22:12; 23:3, 5, 9–10a, 12, 14, 18a, 20; 24:4–8, 12–14a; 25:24; 27:3; 28:21; 33:4–5, 7; 34:8–11, 14–17, 30a;

11. This verb may be rendered as a perf. rather than as a pt.: ". . . and it also came upon the land . . . ," which reading *would* provide a definite word as to the fulfillment.
12. Before the events of ch. 5, presumably; see note 8, above.
13. Hazael's reply to Ben-hadad, v. 14, that Elisha had said he would recover, seems to have been a lie, preparing the way for his crime. The ASV text follows the Heb. *q're*, reading, "Say *unto him*, Thou shalt recover. . . ." But he really did not; cf. KD, pp. 334–335.

36:10, 18, 19) (Jer 52:13, *17a, 20b*) (46 vv., typ.): the temple. Fulfillment (per. 13): as in Ex. No. 55.

29. II K *11:11b* (II Chron *23:10b*); *12:9a*; 16:14a, *15d*; 18:22 (II Chron 32:12) [see Isa 36:7]; 23:9 (3 vv., typ.): the altar of burnt offering. Fulfillment (per. 13): as in Ex. No. 44.

30. II K 11:17 (II Chron 23:16); 17:15, 35, 38; 18:12; 23:*2b*–3 (II Chron 34:*30b*–31), *21b* (6 vv., typ.): the Sinaitic testament. The first reference states, "Jehoiada made the testament between Yahweh and the king and the people, that they should be Yahweh's people," which Keil defines as "simply a renewal of the covenant which the Lord had made with Israel through Moses."[14] Fulfillment (per. 13): as in Ex. No. 45.

31. II K 12:16a (1 v., typ.): trespass offering. Fulfillment (per. 13): as in Lev. No. 7.

32. II K *12:16b* (typ.): sin offering. Fulfillment (per. 13): as in Lev. No. 6.

33. II K 13:15–17 (3 vv., sym.): the shooting by King Jehoash of an arrow eastward; in v. 17, Elisha interpreted the act as the sign of an overwhelming victory against the Syrians at Aphek. Fulfillment (per. 7): v. 25 does not give details, but it explains that "Jehoash took again out of the hand of Ben-hadad [III] the cities which he had taken out of the hand of Jehoahaz his father" (814–798); see I K 19:17a, above.

34. II K 13:18–19 (2 vv., sym.): Jehoash's striking the ground with arrows; he did it three times. In v. 19 Elisha thus predicted that he would smite Syria on three occasions. Actually, Jehoash should have struck with the arrows five or six times, "then hadst thou smitten Syria till thou hadst consumed it." Fulfillment (per. 7): "Three times did Joash smite Benhadad" of Syria, v. 25.

35. II K 13:23 (1 v., typ.): the Abrahamic testament. Fulfillment (per. 13): as in Gen. No. 30.

36. II K 14:25 (1 v.) states that Jeroboam II's restoring of the border of Israel, from Lebo-hamath to the Dead Sea, occurred "according to the word of Yahweh, the God of Israel, which He spake by His servant Jonah the son of Amittai, the prophet"; cf. Jonah 1:1—though the prophecy here referred to is not recorded in II Kings, in Jonah, or elsewhere. Fulfillment (per. 7): under Jeroboam (793–753) the son of Jehoash, as stated in this verse.

37. II K *16:13b, 15b* (typ.): meal offerings. Fulfillment (per. 13): as in Lev. No. 4.

38. II K 16:17; 25:13b, 16a (Jer 52:17b, 20a) (3 vv., typ.): laver and "sea." Fulfillment (per. 13): as in Ex. No. 67.

39. II K 17:23 (1 v.): the divinely threatened fall of N. Israel, "as He spake by all His servants the prophets." Fulfillment (per. 7): the nation's removal by Assyria, as in I K. No. 25.

---

14. Ibid., p. 363.

40. II K 18:4 (1 v., typ.): the brazen serpent of Moses. Fulfillment (per. 13): as in Num. No. 30.

41. II K 18:30 (II Chron 32:11); 19:10, 21, 29–32, 34; 20:6b [see Isa 36:15 etc., listed under Isa. prophecy No. 37], (9 vv.): Jerusalem's protection from Sennacherib.

42. II K 19:7a, 28, 33 [see Isa 37:7a] (3 vv.): Sennacherib's return to Assyria.

43. II K *19:7b* [see Isa 37:7b]: Sennacherib's subsequent death.

44. II K 20:5a, *6a*, 8a [see Isa 38:5] (2 vv.): Hezekiah's healing.

45. II K 20:9–10 [see Isa 38:8] (2 vv.): a shadow to move backward.

46. II K 20:17–18 [see Isa 39:6, under 5:13a] (2 vv.): the Babylonian exile.

47. II K 20:19 [see Isa 39:8, under Isa. No. 81] (1 v.): Peace, following Sennacherib.

48. II K 21:12–14, 22:16–19 (II Chron 34:24–27), 23:27 (8 vv.): Jerusalem to be delivered up to its enemies, v. 14, just as was Samaria, v. 13a (see I K 14:15, above), and to be "wiped out like a dish," v. 13b. Fulfillment (per. 7): 586 B.C., as in Lev. No. 33 or I K. No. 15.

49. II K 22:20 (II Chron 34:28) (1 v.): Josiah to come to his grave before the predicted calamities (see No. 48, preceding) should fall upon Jerusalem. Fulfillment (per. 7): his death in 609, 23:29, four years prior to the Babylonian advance into Judah, 24:1.

50. II K 23:21–23 (II Chron 35:1, 6–9, 11, 13, 16a, 17–19))3 vv., typ.: Passover. Fulfillment (per. 13): as in Ex. No. 31.

I CHRONICLES

The three Biblical writings of I Chronicles, II Chronicles, and Ezra exhibit a basic unity. I and II Chronicles formed but a single book until their division into two in the Septuagint, for the sake of mere convenience. Ezra, moreover, closely parallels Chronicles: in viewpoint, emphasizing Jewish national privilege and the significance of the Jerusalem temple, along with its Levitical priesthood; in subject matter, not simply by Ezra's continuing the historical narrative of Chronicles but by having the same stress on genealogies and statistical records; and down even to its literary style and vocabulary. When the opening lines of Ezra (1:1–3a) are then found verbally to reproduce the closing verses of II Chronicles (36:22–23), the conclusion of both early rabbinic tradition and the modern findings of William F. Albright seems highly probable: that Ezra himself must be the Chronicler.[1] E. J. Young, it is true, argues against the theory that all three

1. JBL, 40 (1921), 119.

of the writings may once have existed as one volume:[2] since Ezra's severing from the rest would then stand devoid of explanation, and since Ezra's introduction seems to be dependent upon Chronicles, not vice versa,[3] the Book of Ezra appears to be a deliberate sequel. Yet Chronicles fits admirably into the known program of that priest for the revitalization of postexilic Judah (cf. Ezra 7:10)[4] upon his return there in 458 B.C.,[5] and Chronicles may well have been written by Ezra at about this time.

Corresponding to Ezra's concern over genealogical purity for his community (cf. 2:62, 7:1–5), I Chronicles open with 9 chapters of genealogy. These commence with Adam and with a number of tribal tabulations taken from Genesis, but they bring them down to a listing of the legitimate inhabitants of Jerusalem just prior to its captivity (I Chron 9:1–2).[6] I Chronicles 10 parallels the final chapter of I Samuel, on the death of Saul in 1010 B.C. The remainder of the book is then occupied with the career of David, from his accession over the entirety of Israel in 1003 down to his concluding year of 970. I Chronicles 11–29 is thus closely tied to II Samuel, including considerable duplication of material; cf. Ezra's explicit appeal to written sources composed by the prophetic contemporaries of David (29:29). For the discussion of the predictions that happen to be so repeated, cross referencing to II Samuel and also to certain of the Psalms is indicated below by brackets. This procedure, which first became applicable in II Kings because of its quotation of predictions drawn from the Book of Isaiah, must here be employed with greater frequency.[7]

Yet Ezra was, at the same time, selective in his inclusion of matters from II Samuel. In line with his purpose of encouraging his dispirited contemporaries (cf. Ezra 4:23, 9:1, 10:12–13), he omits from his reuse of the fourfold content of II Samuel[8] reference to those confessedly less stimulating first and third sections: on David's reign over Judah alone (1010–1003) and on the period of the king's later, personal failures (ca. 995–978).[9] On the other hand, he introduces certain tabulations as addi-

2. An Introduction to the OT, pp. 412–413.
3. Which might have been suggested by the present order of the books in the Hebrew canon; see below.
4. In this regard, see especially the writer's introduction to Chronicles in The Wycliffe Bible Commentary, pp. 367–368.
5. See below, the introduction to Ezra.
6. The latest data of Chronicles are, in fact, certain references to the governor Zerubbabel, who led in the postexilic return of 538–537 and in the temple rebuilding of 520–515, and two of his grandsons (3:21a), which would bring the dating to about 500 B.C. The remaining four (unrelated) names (3:21b) may refer to other sons of Josiah (cf. v. 15). When the LXX connects them and their descendants (vv. 22–24) with the line of Zerubbabel, it would reduce the book's possible date to at least 400, which would be too late for Ezra, or even for the final close of the OT canon for that matter; cf. Young, op. cit., p. 414.
7. Cf., similarly, in II Chron·a number of bracketed cross references to I–II Kings.
8. See above, introduction to II Samuel.
9. Though not seeking to deny their reality; cf. the implications of his praise for "the first ways of David," II Chron 17:3.

tions to Samuel (e.g., ch. 12) and provides greater detail on the Mosaic rituals, the ark, and the Davidic singers (chs. 13, 15–16), on preparations for the temple (22, 28–29), and on David's priestly organization (23–27).[10] A key verse for the mood of I Chronicles might thus be taken from David's words in 22:17–18, "Is not Yahweh your God with you? . . . Now set your heart and soul to seek after Yahweh . . . and bring the ark of the testament and the holy vessels of God into the house that is to be built to the name of Yahweh."[11]

According to rabbinic practice, Chronicles is placed, not among the historical books of the "Former Prophets,"[12] such as Samuel or Kings, but in the third division of the Hebrew canon, that of the "Writings." It stands, indeed, as the final volume of the entire OT and is separated from Ezra by the Book of Nehemiah. This sequence, however, seems to have come about as a result of later Jewish rearrangement of the canon for liturgical and other reasons.[13] The earlier testimony of Josephus catalogs Chronicles among the Former Prophets, just as do the LXX and today's English versions. Furthermore, even with the distinct priestly emphases of Ezra, "Chronicles has much material in it of obviously prophetic origin."[14] The two greatest concentrations of predictive subjects in I Chronicles thus appear in ch. 16, with its quotations from three of the earlier historico-prophetic psalms, which David employed at his establishment of the ark in Jerusalem, and in ch. 17, quoted from II Samuel 7, on the Davidic testament and its prophetic implications for the future.

The predictions of I Chronicles total 24, approximately that of II Samuel's 22; but their content, appropriate to Ezra's priestly interests, is 77% concerned with typology, as opposed to a 50% figure for the earlier book. These 24 forecasts then occupy 132 out of the 942 verses of I Chronicles, or about 14%.

1. I Chron 6:10, 31a, 32, 48; 9:10, 13, 19, 21, 23, 26–27, 29; 16:1b [see II Sam 6:17b], 39; 17:5–6 [see 7:5–7]; 21:29a; 22:1a, 2, 5–8, 11, 14, 19a; 23:4, 24, 26, 28, 32; 24:5, 19; 25:6; 26:12, 20; 28:2a, 3, 10–13, 21; 29:1–8, 16, 19 (53 vv., typ.): tabernacle and temple. Fulfillment (per. 13): as in Ex. prophecy No. 55.

2. I Chron *6:31b*; 13:3, 5, 6–14 [see II Sam. No. 4]; 15:1–3, 12–15, 23–24, 25–29 and *16:1a* [see II Sam]; 16:4, 6, 37; 17:1 [see II Sam]; *22:19b*; 28:2b, 18 (30 vv., typ.): the ark of the testament. Fulfillment (per. 13): as in Ex. No. 56.

10. On the historicity of these additions, see below, introduction to II Chronicles.
11. "By reminding the people of the glory of that which God has given them, he hopes to convince them that true weal and blessing will come only by obedience to the theocratic principles which God has established," Young, op. cit., p. 425.
12. See above, introduction to Joshua.
13. Cf. R. Laird Harris, *Inspiration and Canonicity of the Bible*, p. 143.
14. Ibid., p. 174.

3. I Chron 6:49; 16:40; 21:18, 22, 26a [see II Sam 24:18, 21, 25a], 29b; 22:1b (5 vv., typ.): altar of burnt offering. Fulfillment (per. 13): as in Ex 17:15.

4. I Chron 9:22, 23:31b (1 v., typ.): sabbath. Fulfillment (per. 13): as in Ex 16:23.

5. I Chron 11:2 [see II Sam 5:2, under II Sam. prophecy No. 1], 10; 12:23 (3 vv.): allusions to God's previous promise to turn the kingdom of Saul over to David; cf. the qualification stated in 12:23, "according to the word of Yahweh." Fulfillment (per. 6): as in I Sam. No. 21.

6. I Chron 14:10, 15 [see II Sam 5:19, 24, under II Sam. prophecy No. 2] (2 vv.): David's saving Israel.

7. I Chron 15:26b [see II Sam 6:13b]; 16:29 [see Ps 96:8, under Ps. prophecy No. 6], 21:28 (2 vv., typ.): sacrifice. Fulfillment (per. 13): as in Lev. No. 2.

8. I Chron 16:1c, 2a [see II Sam 6:17c, 18a]; 21:23a, 24, 26b [see II Sam]; and also 23:31a, 29:21b (4 vv., typ.): Burnt offerings.

9. I Chron 16:1d, 2b; 21:26c [see II Sam 6:17d etc.]; and also 29:21a (1 v., typ.): peace offerings.

10. I Chron 16:15–17 [see Ps 105:8–10] (3 vv., typ.): Abrahamic testament.

11. I Chron 16:18 [see Ps 105:11] (1 v.): Israel given Canaan.

12. I Chron 16:33a [see Ps 96:12] (1 v., fig.): joy at Christ's return.

13. I Chron 16:33b [see Ps 96:13b]: the second advent.

14. I Chron 16:33c [see Ps 96:13c, under 2:6]: the future Messianic kingdom.

15. I Chron 17:10–11 [see II Sam 7:11–12], 22:9a (2 vv.): Solomon's succession.

16. I Chron 17:12a, 22:10a, 28:6a [see II Sam 7:13a], 20 (2 vv.): David's assurance to Solomon, 28:20, of God's blessing upon his work of constructing the temple, "He will not forsake thee, until all the work for the service of the house of Yahweh be finished." Fulfillment (per. 6): as in II Sam. No. 10.

17. I Chron 17:12b, 13b–14, 17, 23–27; 22:10c; 28:7 [see II Sam 7:13b etc.], 4 (12 vv.): as David said in retrospect, "Yahweh chose me to be king over Israel for ever," 28:4. Fulfillment (per. 13): Jesus, the eternal son of David, as in II Sam. No. 11.

18. I Chron 17:13a, 22:10b, 28:6b [see II Sam 7:14a]: Jesus, the Son of God.

19. I Chron 17:22 [see II Sam 7:24] (1 v.): Israel to endure for ever.

20. I Chron 18:8 (1 v., typ.): the brazen sea. Fulfillment (per. 13): as in Ex. No. 67.

21. I Chron 21:9–13 [see II Sam 24:11–14], (5 vv.): one of three penalties to fall upon David.

22. I Chron *21:23b,* 23:29 (1 v., typ.): meal offering. Fulfillment (per. 13): as in Lev. No. 4.

23. I Chron 22:9b, 13 (2 vv.): Solomon to prosper (v. 13); cf. David's allusion to a previous divine prediction, not elsewhere recorded, about his son, "I will give him rest from all his enemies round about . . . I will give peace and quietness unto Israel in his days." This prediction was underlined by the name that David was commanded to bestow upon his son: "His name shall be Solomon," *peaceful.*[15] Fulfillment (per. 6): Solomon's prosperity, I K 4:24–25, 5:4; cf. the peace and power that he was already enjoying at this time, when David recalled the prophecy.

24. I Chron *28:11b* (typ.): the mercy seat, on the ark. Fulfillment (per. 13): as in Ex. No. 57.

15. And David did obey, in so naming him, II Sam 12:24.

II CHRONICLES

Both in the circumstances of its origin and in the priestly character of its prophetic viewpoint, II Chronicles is identical to I Chronicles, with which it actually formed but one book.[1] But in subject matter, II Chronicles takes up the thread of Israel's history with the reign of David's son Solomon, 970 B.C. (chs. 1–9), and proceeds subsequently to chronicle the course of events for Judah in the south, following the division of the kingdom in 930 (chs. 10–36). It contains concluding notes on the Babylonian exile, 586 (36:20–21), and on the return of the Jews to Palestine in 538/537 (vv. 22–23). II Chronicles thus closely parallels the earlier works of I and II Kings, which constitute one of its primary written sources[2]—for the predictions that appear in both, cross reference to the appropriate discussion in Kings is indicated by brackets. Yet II Chronicles also appeals to a number of prophetic writings that are no longer extant as additional sources for its information (e.g. 12:15, 13:22, 20:34, etc.).[3] Liberal critics of a former generation tended to disparage their value and, in effect, to dismiss the historicity of II Chronicles altogether, where it did not actually reproduce I–II Kings.[4] More recent study, however, such as W. F. Albright's vindica-

1. See above, introduction to I Chronicles.
2. The oft-repeated formula of II Chronicles, "Now the rest of the acts of ———, are they not written in the book of the kings of Judah and Israel" (16:11, 25:26, etc.), would appear, however, to refer to some lost court chronicle (see above, introduction to I Kings, for similar citations in I–II Kings) and not to the canonical Books of Kings, since 27:7, for example, appeals to it for further information of a sort that cannot be found within the text of the corresponding section of II Kings.
3. For their listing and discussion, see E. J. Young, *An Introduction to the OT*, pp. 416–417.
4. E.g. in R. H. Pfeiffer's *OT Introduction*, pp. 786, 789, 802, 805–806.

tion of the role of Judah's "singers," which is emphasized in Chronicles (but not in Kings),[5] has done much to restore confidence in its truthworthiness—which evangelicals have never doubted.[6]

At points, II Chronicles differs markedly in its subjects from the content of I–II Kings. Its author, presumably Ezra, omits the entire history of the northern kingdom of Israel, both as theologically unprofitable and as pragmatically irrelevant to Ezra's postexilic Judean community. Correspondingly, it omits the extensive sections in I Kings on the career of Elijah and in II Kings on that of Elisha. The number of its nontypical prophecies thus drops from 34 in I Kings and 36 in II Kings to a total of but 20. But at the same time, II Chronicles adds considerable data on those victories in battle by which Yahweh vindicated His people of Judah (e.g. in chs. 13, 14, 20, 25), on the major reforms carried out by the more godly among Judah's kings (e.g. 15:8–18, 17:7–9, chs. 29–31, 34–35:19), and on various liturgical and priestly matters. A key verse for summarizing the spirit of II Chronicles is the affirmation found in 13:10, "But as for us, Yahweh is our God, and we have not forsaken Him; and we have priests ministering unto Yahweh, the sons of Aaron, and the Levites in their work." Yet II Chronicles remains an essentially prophetic book,[7] pointing back at the fall of Judah, because "they mocked the messengers of God, and despised His words, and scoffed at His prophets, until the wrath of Yahweh arose against His people," 36:16.

Predictions occur in 268 out of II Chronicles' 822 verses, or in some 31% of the whole. Almost half of its forecasts—17 out of a total of 37—are concerned with matters of typology. Prediction No. 1, on the temple, which was erected by Solomon for Israel's immediate worship but which also foreshadowed the incarnation of Jesus Christ—God present with men—is referred to in fully 143 verses, so that it constitutes the third most extensive prediction to be found within the Bible.[8] The proportion of predictive verses that are typical amounts to 87%, noticeably above that of I–II Kings, which, even with all its similar data on the temple, averages out to a lower 61%.

1. II Chron 1:3, 4b, *5b, 6b,* 13; 2:1, 5–6, 9, 12; 3:15; 4:7–9, 11, 21; 7:*1c*–3; 20:8–9a, 28; 23:6–7, 19; 24:16, 18, 27; 26:16, 18, 21; 27:2; 28:24; 29:3–7, 15–18a, 20, *21b,* 25, *31b*; 30:*1a,* 8, *15c,* 19; 31:11, 13, 16; 33:15; 35:2, *3b,* 5, *8a*; 36:7, 14–15, 17, 23. Also 2:4a; 3:1–13, 17; 4:16, 19–20, 22; 5:1, 5b, 7b, 9b, 11, 13–14; 6:1–2, 5–8, 10, 18–21, *22b,* 24, 26, 29; 6:32–34, 38; 7:*5b,* 7a, 11, 16; 8:1, 16; 9:4, 11; 12:9, 11; 15:18; 16:2 [see I K 5:5a, etc. under I K. prophecy No. 1]; and 22:12;

5. Cf. R. K. Harrison, *Introduction to the OT*, pp. 1166–1167.
6. Cf. Young, op. cit., pp. 417–424.
7. See above, introduction to I Chronicles.
8. Cf. Jer No 1 and Ezek No 1, on the fall of Jerusalem in 586.

23:*3a*, 5, 9–10a, 12, 14, 18a, 20; 24:4–8, 12–14a; 25:24; 27:3; 28:21; 33:4–5, 7; 34:8–11, 14–17, 30a; 36:10, 18–19 [see II K 11:3, etc.] (143 vv., typ.): tabernacle and temple. Fulfillment (per 13): as in Ex. No. 55; for it is to be noted that the factor of eternity (which might suggest period 16 or 18, the millennial kingdom or the New Jerusalem), as this is expressed in 7:16; cf. 33:4, 7—"I have chosen this house, that My name may be there for ever"—is conditional: II K 21:7–8, II Chron 33:8, "if only they will observe to do all that I have commanded them." And Israel did not!

2. II Chron *1:4a, 5:9a,* 6:41a, 8:11, 35:3a. Then 5:2, 4–*5a,* 6a, *7a,* 8, 10a; *6:11a* [see I K 8:1 etc., under I K. No. 4] (8 vv., typ.): the ark of the testament. Fulfillment (per. 13): see Ex. No. 56.

3. II Chron 1:5a; 4:1; *5:12b; 7:9b;* 15:8; 29:*18b*–19, *21c*–22, *27b; 33:16a; 35:16c.* Then 1:6a; 6:12, 22a; *7:7d;* 8:12b [see I K 3:4b etc., under I K. No. 2]; *23:10b* [see II K 11:17]; 32:12 [see Isa 36:7 (II K 18:22)] (10 vv., typ.): altar of burnt offering. Fulfillment (per. 13): as in Ex. No. 44.

4. II Chron. *1:6c; 7:7b; 8:12* [see I K 3:4a etc.]; also *2:4b; 4:6b;* 7:1a; 13:11; *23:18b; 24:14b;* 29:*7b, 24b,* 27–28, *31c*–32, 34–*35a; 30:15b;* 31:*2b,* 3a; 35:12, 14, *16b* (9 vv., typ.): burnt offering. Fulfillment (per. 13): as in Lev. No. 3.

5. II Chron *1:12a* [see I K 3:12]: Solomon to be wise.

6. II Chron 1:12b [see I K 3:13] (1 v.): Solomon to be rich.

7. II Chron *2:4c; 8:13b;* 23:4, 8 [see II K 11:5, 9, under II K. No. 8]; *31:3b* (2 vv., typ.): sabbath. Fulfillment (per. 13): as in Ex. No. 41.

8. II Chron 3:14 (1 v., typ.): the veil to the most holy place. The corresponding section in I Kings (6:31–32) speaks of olive-wood doors; yet, "The curtain may very well have been suspended within the doors."[9] So the latter would neither duplicate the veil nor take over its typical (prophetic) function. Fulfillment (per. 13): as in Ex. No. 58.

9. II Chron 4:2–6a, 14–15 [see I K 7:23 etc.], 10 (8 vv., typ.): Lavers.

10. II Chron 5:3; 7:8 [see I K 8:2, 65], 9a; 8:13c (4 vv., typ.): Feast of Tabernacles.

11. II Chron *5:6b;* 7:4 [see I K 8:5b, 62, under I K. No. 5]; 7:12; *8:13a;* 11:16; 15:11; 29:29, 33; 30:24; 33:17 (8 vv., typ.): sacrifice. Fulfillment (per. 13): as in Lev. No. 2.

12. II Chron *5:10;* 6:11b, 14 [see I K 8:9b, 21b, 23]; 15:12; 23:16 [see II K 11:17]; 29:10; 34:*30b*–31 [see II K] 32 (7 vv., typ.): Sinaitic testament. Under Asa, when 15:12 states, "They entered into the testament," it does not specify which particular one; but this too was probably the Sinaitic. Fulfillment (per. 13): as in Ex. No. 45.

9. KD, *Kings,* p. 82.

13. II Chron 5:12a (1 v., typ.): priests' garments. Fulfillment (per. 13): as in Ex. No. 60.

14. II Chron 6:9 [see I K 8:19, under I K. No. 10] (1 v.): Solomon to build the temple.

15. II Chron 6:16, 7:18 [see I K 8:25, 9:5, under I K. No. 3], 13:5a, 21:7a, 23:3b, (5 vv.): the line of David to endure forever. Fulfillment (per. 13): Jesus Christ, David's eternal son, as in II Sam. No. 11.

16. II Chron 6:41b, 13:10, 30:16, 31:2a, 35:10 (4 vv., typ.): priests. Their typical foreshadowing of Christ's atoning death is apparent in the above verses; e.g. 13:10, sacrificing, or 30:16, sprinkling the blood; cf. 6:41, their being "clothed with salvation." Fulfillment (per. 13): as in Ex. No. 59.

17. II Chron 7:1b, 5a and 7c [see I K 8:63a and 64d, under I K. No. 9]; 29:31a, 35b; 30:22; 31:2c; 33:16b (4 vv., typ.): peace offerings. Fulfillment (pers. 13 and 16): as in Lev. No. 5.

18. II Chron 7:7e [see I K 8:64c], 29:35c (1 v., typ.): meal offerings.

19. II Chron 7:20a, 22 [see I K 9:7a, 9]; 34:24–27 [see II K 22:16–19, under II K. No. 48] (5 vv.): fall of Jerusalem, 586.

20. II Chron 7:20b–21 [see I K 9:7b–9] (2 vv.): the temple to be destroyed.

21. II Chron 9:8 (1 v.): God to establish Israel forever. Fulfillment (per. 18): as in II Sam. No. 14.

22. II Chron 13:5b, 21:7b (typ.): the Davidic testament. Fulfillment (per. 13): as in II Sam No. 19.

23. II Chron 15:2, 7[10] (2 vv.): the message from a prophet of God to king Asa, "If you seek Him, He will be found of you , . . your work shall be rewarded." Fulfillment (per. 7): Asa did seek God, v. 8; and God was with him, v. 9. "He was found of them: and Yahweh gave them rest round about," v. 15.

24. II Chron 16:9 (1 v.): to Asa, after he had restorted to an unworthy alliance with Damascus in order to drive back Baasha of Israel,[11] "From henceforth thou shalt have wars." Fulfillment (per. 7): no specific conflicts are noted subsequently; but warfare in general between Judah and Israel did continue throughout Baasha's reign, I K 15:16. Furthermore, Asa's calling in of Damascus eventuated in disaster for Judah, under Joash, after 835 B.C., II K 12:17–18, II Chron 24:23–24.

10. JB makes vv. 3–6 predictive as well: not, "They turned unto Jehovah . . . and he was found of them" (ASV), but "They will return to Yahweh . . . and he will let them find him," v. 4. This latter is a possibility; but a rendering into the general present seems sufficient; cf. KD, *Chron*, pp. 360–363.

11. The Heb. texts date this passage to the 36th year of Asa's reign, 16:1; cf. 15:19, or to 874 B.C. But Baasha died in 886; so some copiest's error seems to have arisen in the present MSS: either the 36th year should be that in reference to the division of the kingdom in 930 and the history of the separate monarchy of Judah (so E. R. Thiele, *The Mysterious Numbers of the Hebrew Kings*, p. 60); or the *36th* should be read as the *16th* (cf. the 15th, in 15:10), and so 894 B.C.

25. II Chron 18:16, 19, 22, 27 [see I K 22:17 etc., I K. No. 39] (4 vv.): Ahab's death.

26. II Chron 18:24 [see I K 22:25] (1 v.): Zedekiah to go into hiding.

27. II Chron 19:2, 37 (2 vv.): because of Jehoshaphat's having allied himself with Ahab and later with Ahaziah of Israel, "For this thing wrath is upon thee from before Yahweh . . . Yahweh hath destroyed thy works." Fulfillment (per. 7): after his dealings with Ahab, Jehoshaphat suffered the invasion of 20:1–13; and during the brief reign of Ahaziah (853–852), the loss of their joint fleet at Ezion-geber, v. 37.

28. II Chron 20:9b, 15–17, 20 (4 vv.): Jahaziel's prophecy to Jehoshaphat, when facing invasion (see No. 27, preceding), "The battle is God's. Tomorrow . . . stand ye still and see the salvation of Yahweh" (vv. 15–17). The king himself had earlier affirmed, "Thou wilt hear and save" (v. 8),[12] and went on to assure his people that they would prosper against the enemy (v. 20). Fulfillment (per. 7): the attackers destroyed each other, v. 23, and none escaped, v. 24.

29. II Chron 21:14 (1 v.): that Yahweh would smite the household and substance of King Jehoram of Judah because of his apostasy. Fulfillment (per. 7): God did so; v. 17, the Philistines carried away "all the substance that was found in the king's house, and his sons also, and his wives."

30. II Chron 21:15 (1 v.): Jehoram to suffer a serious disease of the bowels. Fulfillment (per. 7): fatal after two years, vv. 18–19.

31. II Chron 25:16 (1 v.): a prophet's word to King Amaziah for his engaging in idolatry, "God hath determined to destroy thee." Fulfillment (per. 7): because of his sin and because of God's decree, he was defeated in battle, vv. 20–22, and finally slain in a conspiracy, v. 27.

32. II Chron 29:21a, 23–24a (3 vv., typ.): sin offering. Fulfillment (per. 13): as in Lev. No. 6.

33. II Chron 30:1b–5, 15a, 17–18; then 35:1, 6–9, 11, 13, 16a, 17–19 [see II K 23:21] (19 vv., typ.): Passover. Fulfillment (per. 13): as in Ex. No. 31.

34. II Chron 30:6 (1 v.): Hezekiah's appeal to the survivors of N. Israel, "Turn again to Yahweh . . . that He may return to the remnant that are escaped of you out of the hand of the kings of Assyria." Some of the N. tribes mocked; but others did come to seek God, vv. 10–11. As a result (fulfillment), before Josiah's 18th year in 622 (per. 7), much of Israel, up to Naphtali in the far north, had become reincorporated into the kingdom of God's chosen people, 34:7–8.

35. II Chron 30:9 (1 v.): further, "if ye turn again unto Yahweh, your brethren and your children shall find compassion before them that led them

---

12. This is actually a quote from 6:28–30, where Solomon's prayer had been that God *might* hear. But when Yahweh accepted the temple by coming in His glory cloud to dwell in it, Jehoshaphat apparently felt justified to claim that what had originally been a hope had now become a prophecy.

captive, and shall come again into this land." Fulfillment (per. 9): resulting from faithfulness (cf. vv. 10–11, per No. 34, preceding), some from N. Israel were found sharing in the postexilic restoration of Judah (Ezra 6:17, 8:35; cf. Lk 2:38), as in Hos 2:15.

36. II Chron 32:11 [see Isa 36:15 (II K 18:30)] (1 v.): deliverance from Sennacherib.

37. II Chron 34:28 [see II K 22:20] (1 v.): Josiah's death before the fall of Jerusalem.

EZRA

Having already composed the Books of Chronicles for the encouragement of his postexilic Jewish community, Ezra the priest, the scribe, seems later to have taken in hand to complete the history of his theocratic people, from the issuance of the decree of Cyrus in 538 which authorized their return to Palestine, and with which II Chronicles had closed (36:22–23), down to his own activity in the year 458 (Ezra 7:7).[1] Evidence is lacking that the Book of Ezra, written shortly thereafter, ever formed an actual part of Chronicles, to which it serves rather as a sequel.[2] Nor should the scribe's volume be treated as merely the earlier half of the history that continues in Nehemiah; for though these two works are undeniably related in topic, and though they now stand combined in the Hebrew Bible, their origin appears to be that of separate compositions; cf. the otherwise inexplicable repetition in Nehemiah 7 of the register of returning Jews found in Ezra 2.[3] The theme of the book, as well as the life goal of its author, appears in 7:10, "Ezra had set his heart to seek the law of Yahweh, and to do it, and to teach in Israel statutes and judgments."

While Ezra 7–10 is autobiographical in nature (cf. the first-person pronouns that commence with 7:28) and concern Ezra's own leadership in a second return of the Jews to Palestine in 458, followed by his various acts to enforce the Mosaic law, the preceding six chapters must have been compiled from previously existing sources and relate to Zerubbabel's first major return in 437 and to the events that followed during the ensuing 22

1. On the much-discussed subject of the dating of Ezra, cf. J. Stafford Wright, *The Date of Ezra's Coming to Jerusalem*. The fact that the Book of Ezra does not mention Nehemiah, but that Nehemiah after his arrival at Jerusalem in 444 does refer to Ezra as his colleague (8:9, 12:36, and cf. 10:1 in a section of Nehemiah that liberal criticism has assigned to Ezra), seem to require that the "Artaxerxes" whose 7th year is cited in Ezra 7:7 must indeed be Artaxerxes I and the year 458.

2. See above, introduction to I Chronicles.

3. See also G. L. Archer, *A Survey of OT Introduction*, p. 396.

years in the latter part of that preceding century.[4] The pattern of prophecies in Ezra's volume is unique within Scripture, in that none of the predictions assume the form of verbal declarations but that all, without exception, are typical in character, foreshadowing the work of Christ through the active representation thereof in the institutions of Israel. These types number 10 and occupy 63 out of the book's 280 verses, or 23%.

1. Ezra 1:2 [see II Chron 36:23], 3–5, 7; 2:68; 3:6b, 8–12; 4:1, 3, 24; 5:2, 8, 13–17; 6:3–8, 12, 16–17a, 22; 7:15–16, 17d, 19–20, 23–24, 27; 8:25, 29–30, 33, 36; 9:9; 10:1, 6, 9 (46 vv., typ.): the temple. Fulfillment (per. 13): as in Ex. prophecy No. 55.

2. Ezra 2:69 (1 v., typ.): priests' garments. Fulfilment (per. 13): as in Ex. No. 60.

3. Ezra 3:2–3a, 7:17c (1 v., typ.): the altar of burnt offering. Fulfillment (per. 13): as in Ex. No. 44.

4. Ezra 3:3b, 4b, 5a, 6a; 6:9; 8:35a; 9:4–5 (7 vv., typ.): burnt offering. Fulfillment (per. 13): as in Lev. No. 3.

5. Ezra 3:4a (typ.): the Feast of Tabernacles. Fulfillment (per. 16): as in Ex. No. 46.

6. Ezra 3:5b; 4:2; 6:3b, 10, 17b; 7:17a (4 vv., typ.): sacrifice. Fulfillment (per. 13): as in Lev. No. 2.

7. Ezra 6:17c, 8:35b (1 v., typ.): sin offering. Fulfillment (per. 13): as in Lev. No. 6.

8. Ezra 6:19–20 (2 vv., typ.): Passover. Fulfillment (per. 13): as in Ex. No. 31.

9. Ezra 7:17b (typ.): meal offering. Fulfillment (per. 13): as in Lev. No. 4.

10. Ezra 10:19 (1 v., typ.): a sacrifice that is inferred to be the trespass offering, because it was offered for guilt in respect to marriage, when a compensation would be in order. Fulfillment (per. 13): as in Lev 5:14, prophecy No. 7, q.v.

NEHEMIAH

Chronologically, Nehemiah was the last book of the OT to be put into writing; for while individuals of a later date, such as Alexander the Great or Antiochus IV Epiphanes, may have been *predicted*, the mention of Darius II of Persia in Nehemiah 12:22, whose reign dates from 423 B.C., concerns

4. With the exception of 4:6, and 4:7–23 on an interdicted reconstruction of Jerusalem's walls in Ezra's own day. But both passages are included in ch. 4, along with the other instances of Samaritan opposition to the Jews.

the latest figure to be contemporaneously *described* in the OT. Though linked with Ezra in the Hebrew canon, the Book of Nehemiah was originally separate and is essentially autobiographical in nature; cf. the first-person pronouns in 1:1 and 13:31 (its opening and closing vv.) and in much of the material that intervenes. It chronicles the effect upon Palestine of Nehemiah, a Jew who had come to attain a high rank in the court of Persia. At the outset of his first governorship over Judea, from 444 to 432 (2:1, 13:6), his personal zeal for recovering the prosperity of his postexilic people led in particular to the reconstruction of the fortifications of Jerusalem. The thrust of the book may thus be summed up in his expression of satisfaction in 4:6. "So we built the wall . . . for the people had a mind to work." The interval before his second term as governor (13:6) is not stated but would not seem to require many years,[1] so that the book would probably have been written, and the canon of the OT brought to a close, soon after 423.[2]

Fourteen predictive matters come to expression in Nehemiah, involving 45 of its 406 verses, or 11% of the book. Only two of these, however (totaling 2 vv.), possess the form of predictive oracles; the remainder are acted rather than verbal and point forward to the work of Christ through the types that are so characteristic of the institutional worship of Israel. Statistically, this accounts for 96% of the book's prophetic content, which gives Nehemiah the second highest such figure for the entirety of Scripture. It stands next only to Ezra, with its 100% proportion of typical prophecy, and ahead even of the 91% of Leviticus—though actually the last-cited is a more meaningful figure: it is just that Nehemiah, to start with, contains so relatively few predictions.

1. Neh 1:5, 9:32 (2 vv., typ.): Nehemiah prayed to the God "that keepeth covenant," Heb., *hab-b'rîth, the b'rîth* (1:5), evidently the Sinaitic testament. Fulfillment (per. 13): as in Ex., prophecy No. 45.

2. Neh 1:9 (1 v.): a retrospective quotation from Dt 30:3–5, on the return from exile. Fulfillment (per. 9): as in Dt. No. 43.

3. Neh 2:20 (1 v.): the governor's assurance to his people, on rebuilding the walls of Jerusalem, "The God of heaven, He will prosper us." Fulfillment (per. 9): the walls were rebuilt, in 52 days, 4:6, 6:15.

4. Neh 4:2, 12:43 (2 vv., typ.): sacrifice. Fulfillment (per. 13): as in Lev. No. 2.

5. Neh 6:10–11; *8:16b*; 10:32, *33e, 34a,* 36–39; 11:11–12, 16, 22; 12:40; 13:4, 7, 9a, 11, 14 (17 vv., typ.): temple. Fulfillment (per. 13): as in Ex. No. 55.

1. See below, in the introduction to Malachi.
2. The allusions in the genealogies of 12:11, 22, to Jaddua, great-grandson to Eliashib, the current high priest, could simply refer to him as a youth, since the marriage of one of Eliashib's grandsons is recorded in 13:28, though R. K. Harrison would prefer to treat the references to Jaddua as a later gloss, *Introduction to the OT,* pp. 1155–1156.

6. Neh 7:70, 72 (2 vv., typ.): priests' garments, paralleling their mention in Ezra 2:69. Fulfillment (per. 13): as in Ex. No. 60.

7. Neh 8:14–18 (5 vv., typ.): the Feast of Tabernacles. Fulfillment (per. 16): as in Ex. No. 46.

8. Neh 9:8 (1 v., typ.): the Abrahamic testament. Fulfillment (per. 13): as in Gen. No. 30.

9. Neh 9:14; 10:31, *33c*; 13:15–22 (10 vv., typ.): sabbath. Fulfillment (per. 13): as in Ex. No. 41.

10. Neh *10:33a*; 13:5, *9b* (1 v., typ.): meal offering. Fulfillment (per. 13): as in Lev. No. 4.

11. Neh *10:33b* (typ.): burnt offering. Fulfillment (per. 13): as in Lev. No. 3.

12. Neh 10:33d (1 v., typ.): sin offering. Fulfillment (per. 13): as in Lev. No. 6.

13. Neh 10:34b (1 v., typ.): the altar. Fulfillment (per. 13): as in Ex. No. 44.

14. Neh 13:29 (1 v., typ.): the Levitical testament. Fulfillment (per. 13): as in Num, No. 43.

ESTHER

Next to the four books that contain no predictions at all,[1] Esther holds the distinction of being the least predictive volume contained in Scripture: in the course of its 10 chapters (167 vv.) it can boast of but one lone forecast, whose single verse thus constitutes .6% of the whole. The Book of Esther describes the career of the talented Jewess of this name, who rose to the rank of queen of Persia, as wife of Xerxes I, Ahasuerus (485–465 B.C.). Its last recorded date is 473 (3:7); but its introduction would suggest that it did not receive its present written form until afer the death of Xerxes, though while this king was still well known (1:1).[2] It may have been composed by a prophet among the associates of Mordecai, the cousin of Esther (cf. 2:7, 10:3).[3] The book's purpose is to record the historical basis for the Jewish feast of Purim (9:26–32, cf. 3:7), namely, the overthrow by Esther of a plot against the Jews by an official named Haman; cf. 4:14 as

1. Ruth, Song of Solomon, Philemon, and III John.
2. Presumably shortly after his death in 465, E. J. Young, *An Introduction to the OT*, p. 375.
3. The historicity of the book has been questioned by liberal critics, who would treat it as a nationalistic Hasmonean story of the later 2nd century B.C., e.g. R. H. Pfeiffer's *Introduction to the OT*, pp. 732, 737. Yet cf. its recent defense by J. Stafford Wright, "The Book of Esther as History," in J. B. Payne, ed., *New Perspectives on the OT*.

a key verse for the book. Near the commencement of Haman's downfall appears the following predictive utterance by his wise men and his wife, Zeresh.

1. Est 6:13 (1 v.): "If Mordecai, before whom thou hast begun to fall, be of the seed of the Jews [he was], thou shalt not prevail against him, but shalt surely fall before him."[4] Fulfillment (per. 9): Haman's being hanged on the very gallows that he had erected for the execution of Mordecai, 7:10.

4. Cf. Keil's reference to 6:13 as "this prediction," *Ezra-Est*, p. 362.

JOB

Like Habakkuk in the later OT and I Peter in the NT, Job deals with the question of theodicy, literally, "God's justice," and how this can be understood in the face of the evils that so pervade human life. By its content Job thus belongs, like Proverbs and Ecclesiastes, among the volumes of the OT's practical "wisdom literature"; cf. the relatively low amount of predictive matter, never more than 3%, in any of these works. Correspondingly, while standing on the dividing line between the historical books and the poetic books, Job is usually classified with the latter in the English Bible's arrangement. In the title role stands Job himself, overwhelmed by disasters that strike his property, his family, and finally his own flesh. From the prologue, today's reader perceives this to have been the work of Satan, permitted by Yahweh for the trial of Job's faith; but of these facts Job and his friends were *not* aware at the time. The body of the book thus consists of poetic dialogue between Job and his three "miserable comforters" (chs. 3–31), followed by the analysis of Elihu (chs. 32–37), who emphasizes the chastening value of suffering (e.g. 33:17–19), and finally by the appearance of God Himself (chs. 38–41), who provides, indeed, no theoretical solution to the problem of evil but rather challenges mankind to a practical knowledge of His own sovereign power and wisdom. Afterward, Job recognizes not a philosophical answer[1] but the Person of God Himself (40:4–5, 42:2–6). A key verse for the book, which is also a prediction, and which seems to express more than Job himself may have intended when he uttered it (see No. 9, below), is thus 23:10, "He knoweth the way that I take; when He hath tried me, I shall come forth as gold."

Job and his friends were not Hebrews,[2] but probably Edomites; compare

1. Though the book does contain a series of significant contributions to the question of theodicy; cf. J. B. Payne, *Theology of the Older Testament*, pp. 437–443.
2. Compare the foreign origin of the somewhat parallel wisdom chapters of Agur and Lemuel in Prov 30–31, and cf. I K 4:30.

1:1, on Job's location in Uz, with Lam 4:21, and the connection of Eliphaz the Temanite with the names of some of the early descendants of Esau in Edom, Gen 36:10–11. Their locale is therefore removed from the mainstream of the prophetic movement in Israel. The time of their action is also early, apparently antedating the Mosaic legislation and most of the historical prophets.[3] The book's predictions hence total but 10 and involve 22 of its 1,070 verses, which amounts to only 2%. Yet this volume of discourse over Job's dilemma does constitute inspired Scripture. From the fact of the frequent use of the divine name Yahweh in the prosaic, narrative Hebrew of the prologue, the superscriptions to the dialogue (cf. 38:1; 40:1, 3, 6), and the epilogue—but not in the quoted speeches of the book, with the exception of two instances by Job himself, 1:21, 12:9)—it would appear that the book's compiler must have been a Hebrew. Since, moreover, its distinctive teaching concerning Satan shows its effect in Israelitish thinking within a century after the time of Solomon (I K 22:19–22) but is not reflected earlier, it is possible that Solomon, the composer of the Bible's other wisdom books of Proverbs and Ecclesiastes, may also have been responsible for Job.[4]

Yet while it is the prologue and epilogue that discuss sacrifice, with its typical-prophetic significance, it is in the speeches of Job (at his high points of spiritual insight in chs. 14, 17, and 19) and of Elihu (ch. 33)[5]— but never of Job's three friends, with the exception of 25:2 (see No. 10, below)—that far-reaching aspects of God's design for history come this early to expression: aspects of human redemption, of resurrection, and of judgment for both the saved and the lost. It is therefore not simply because of the historical narrative but also because of the teaching that, according to the older arrangement of the Hebrew canon,[6] Job is appropriately included as the last of the eight books of the Former Prophets.[7]

1. Job 1:5, 42:8 (2 vv., typ.): sacrifice. The term used is ōlā, technically, "burnt offering"; see Lev 1:3. But because of the pre-Mosaic date of the life of Job (as noted above), and just as in Gen 4:4, 8:20, etc., it appears unwarranted to insist upon the specific typology that came later to be associated with this variety of offering. Fulfillment (period 13): as in Lev. prophecy No. 2.

2. Job 14:12a, 13–15 (4 vv.): "Man lieth down and riseth not: till the

---

3. E. J. Young, *An Introduction to the OT*, p. 341, "contemporary of the patriarchs" (per. 1, as in No. 9, below).

4. Ibid., p. 337.

5. On the full normativeness of the words of Elihu, as opposed to that of the three friends, or even of Job himself, see Payne, op. cit., pp. 337–338, and "Inspiration in the Words of Job" in John H. Skilton, ed., *The Law and the Prophets* (Philadelphia: Presbyterian and Reformed Pub. Co., 1973), ch. XXVI.

6. According to Josephus, as noted above, in the introduction to Joshua.

7. Josh, Jd–Ruth, Sam, Kings, Chron, Ezra–Neh, Est, Job.

heavens be no more, they shall not awake, nor be roused out of their sleep," 14:12. In the mind of Job, these phrases may have served simply as a pictorial way of saying that men do not rise from death[8]; but in their inspired wording they do correspond to God's later revelation of the resurrection, once the heavens are no more (cf. No. 3, following): as stated in Rev 20:11, "Earth and heaven fled away, and I saw the dead standing before the throne."[9] Job therefore continues, "Thou wouldest appoint me a set time. . . . I will wait [ASVmg] till my release shall come. Thou wouldest call, and I would answer Thee," vv. 13–15. A. B. Davidson comments, "The phantom, for he will not believe it to be quite a phantom, is too glorious to lose sight of, and he will, in spite of reason and experience, pursue it."[10] Fulfillment (per. 17): resurrection for the dead, here intimated for the first time in Scripture; see Dan. No. 56 12:2b), and also Job No. 7, below, for the resurrection of the righteous.

3. Job *14:12b*: ". . . till the heavens be no more" (see No. 2, preceding). Fulfillment (per. 17): their passing, as suggested in Gen. No. 14 and foreseen in Rev. No. 56 (20:11); see also Ps. No. 47 (102:26a).

4. Job 17:3; 33:23–30, 32 (10 vv.): Job's appeal to God, "Be surety for me with Thyself" (17:3). Commentators observe, "The thought already expressed in ch. 16:21[11] receives a still stronger expression here: God is conceived of as two persons, on the one side as a judge who treats Job as one deserving of punishment, on the other side as a bondsman who pledges himself for the innocence of the sufferer before the judge, and stands as it were as surety against the future."[12] Again: "This passionate longing for a heavenly Witness on his side strikingly points forward to the Christian thought of an 'advocate with the Father, Jesus Christ the righteous' (I John 2:1). Here faith is reaching out for a 'God for us.' "[13] The inspired Elihu later anticipates it this way, in ch. 33: v. 23, "If there be with Him an Angel, an interpreter, one among a thousand [Delitzsch, "One who soars above the thousands"[14]] to show unto a man his righteousness ["the way of salvation which he has to take to get free of sin and death,"[15] ASVmg]"; v. 24, "then God is gracious unto him, and saith, Deliver him from going down to the pit, I have found a ransom." 26, "He restoreth unto man his righteousness"; and the ransomed sinner exclaims, 28, "His hath redeemed my soul from going into the pit." Fulfillment (per. 13): Jesus, the second Person of the Trinity, the divine Angel of the Testament (see Mal

8. KD, *Job*, I:229–230.
9. Payne, op. cit., pp. 458–459.
10. The *Theology of the OT*, p. 483.
11. And also 16:19, "He that voucheth for me is on high." But these vv. are descriptive of the present, "even now," and reveal less of that predictive element which is suggested by Delitzsch's allusion to the future in his comment on 17:3.
12. KD, I:295.
13. NBC, p. 397.
14. KD, II:230.
15. Ibid.

3:1b), giving Himself as a ransom for many, Mt 20:28 (discussed under Mt. No. 2).

5. Job 19:25a, 27 (2 vv.): Job's afirmation, "I know that my Vindicator [ASVmg; Heb. *gō'ēl,* a kinsman who vindicates rights, as in Ruth 3:9, 12, or Lev 25:48–49] liveth, and at last He will stand up . . . [see also under No. 6, following]: whom I, even I shall see on my side." Fulfillment (per. 17): the justification of the righteous in God's final judgment, as in Rev 20:12b, 15b (Rev. prophecy No. 12); cf. Ps 1:6a.

6. Job *19:25b:* Job also predicted, "At last He will stand upon the dust";[16] that is, at the climax of history, and for the ressurrection of the righteous (see No. 7, following), there will be a coming of God to the soil in which Job's body lies buried. Fulfillment (per. 15): the second advent of Jesus Christ, as in Ps. prophecy No. 45.

7. Job 19:26 (1 v.): Job then talks of his body in its relation to God his Redeemer (see No. 5, and 6, above), when He will stand up "upon the dust," v. 25. His next line (v. 26a) might read, "And after my skin hath been thus destroyed. . . ." It appears more satisfactory, however, to render not as a noun, *ōrī,* "my skin," but as a verb, an infinitive, *ūrī,* "my awaking." The whole verse then reads, "And after my awaking [cf. 14:12 and Ps 17:15], though it [the dust] hath been thus destroyed, yet from my flesh shall I see God," ASVmg. The Heb. prep. *min,* "from," in 26b, could also signify "without my flesh" (ASV), indicating spiritual immortality rather than bodily resurrection; but the resurrection concept better accords with the previous "awaking" and with Job's thought about hope for his body that began in 14:12–17.[17] Fulfillment (per. 15): the resurrection of the righteous; see Isa. No. 76, and also No. 2, above.

8. Job 19:29 (1 v.): Job's warning to his heartless friends, "Wrathful are the punishments of the sword [ASVmg] . . . know there is a judgment." Fulfillment (per. 17): the Lord's final judgment of the wicked, as in Ps 1:5, Rev 20:12–15.

9. Job 23:10 (1 v., fig.): Job's assertion, "When He hath tried me, I shall come forth as gold." In his original utterance, Job seems to have meant that divine investigation would simply substantiate his own claims to freedom from guilt and deserved punishment, and to uprightness (vv. 3, 7).[18] Yet the words suggest also a deeper truth, of a man's being refined through his sufferings; cf. Elihu's revelations in 33:17, 29–30, 34:31–32, and even Eliphaz's, in 5:17. Fulfillment (per. 1): not just that Job was restored (cf. 42:10, 12, in the epilogue), and that he was acknowledged as having spoken

---

16. This phrase is better rendered with the ASVmg, "upon the dust," in accordance with 17:16, 20:11, 21:36, than with the ASV text, in reference to His standing "upon the earth," as in 41:33; for here in ch. 14 the contextual emphasis is on Job's body.

17. Cf. Payne, op. cit., p. 458.

18. Cf. JB, p. 745, "Let him test me in the crucible"!

what was right, at least more so than the three friends (v. 7),[19] but that by his very trials he learned humility (40:4, 42:6), and gained knowledge of God (42:5).

10. Job 25:2 (1 v.): a veiled allusion by Bildad to an instance of God's exercise of His power, "He maketh peace in His high places." Job 4:18, 15:15, had pointed to the fact of angelic sin; and Delitzsch correspondingly interprets 25:2 as "an actual restoration of the equilibrium that had been disturbed through self-will, by an act of mediation and the exercise of judicial authority on the part of God."[20] The historical fulfillment (per. 13) is clarified by the NT: at Christ's triumphant passion and subsequent ascension into glory, Satan was cast out from heaven, no more to accuse the saints, as in the days of Job; see John 12:31, Rev 12:8–10.

19. Payne, op. cit., p. 337, note.
20. II:46; cf. AB, *Job*, p. 164.

PSALMS

When Jesus told His disciples, "All things which are written about Me in the Law of Moses and the Prophets and the Psalms must be fulfilled" (Lk 24:44), He confirmed not simply the predictive character of the Psalter— including its Messianic statements, which specifically foretold His coming —but also its importance as representing, along with the Law and the Prophets, one of the three major divisions of the OT canon. For according to the most ancient description of the organized Hebrew Bible, that of Josephus in NT times, the third division of Israel's canon consisted of but four books,[1] "containing hymns to God and precepts for the conduct of human life."[2] In this poetic subdivision of the OT Scriptures, which came later to be identified as the "Writings," the Psalter thus holds first place, being followed by Proverbs, Ecclesiastes, and the Song of Solomon. Psalms is by far the largest of the four: its Hebrew text requires almost as many pages as does Jeremiah's (which is the longest in the Bible); and its total of 2,526 verses[3] is the greatest for any volume of Scripture. Furthermore, when one recalls that the Song of Solomon contains no predictive matter whatsoever and

1. As opposed to the 5 of the Pentateuch and the 13 of the Prophets: 8 historical "Former Prophets" (see above, under the introduction to Job, note 7) and 5 sermonic "Latter Prophets" (Isa, Jer–Lam, Ezek, Dan, and "the twelve"—the Minor Prophets).
2. *Against Apion*, I:8.
3. Including the ancient titles, which constitute a part of the inspired text according to all Heb. MSS and are assigned regular verse numbers (thus raising the numbering of the succeeding vv. in the body of many of the psalms by one or two digits over what appears in present-day English Bibles).

that the prophetic verses of the two wisdom books of Proverbs and Ecclesiastes do not exceed 3% of their whole,[4] with none of even this minimal amount being directly Messianic,[5] it is no wonder that our Lord limited His designation for the third division of the canon to the Book of Psalms. Here, by way of contrast, appear some 59 separate predictions; and their verses, while amounting to only 10% of the Psalter, still total 242. Of these, moreover, 101 are directly anticipatory of Jesus Christ, they occur in 13 different Messianic psalms (see Table 4), and they constitute the greatest single block of predictive matter concerning the Savior to be found anywhere in the OT.[6]

The historical origin of the Psalms, as indicated by their various titles[7] and concluding doxologies, is connected in large measure with the person of King David. The book itself assigns 73 of its 150 chapters to David,[8] and the NT repeatedly authenticates these ascriptions.[9] Five of the anonymously titled psalms are also recognized, by other Scriptures, as being of Davidic composition;[10] and a number more are probably his as well. The Psalter is organized into five books: Pss 1–41, 42–72, 73–89, 90–106, and 107–150. The last psalm, moreover, of each collection has been composed with a terminal doxology that seems to have been designed for the book as a whole: 41:13, 72:18–20, 89:52, 106:48, and the entire 150th Ps for Book V. It thus appears that the origins of these five concluding chapters provide the key for the compilation of their respective books. Ps 41 was written by David; and since the remaining psalms of Book I are also at-

4. See above, introduction to Job.

5. The closest approximations would consist of certain scattered references to ceremonial types (e.g. Prov. 7:14) or to the general concept of atonement (16:6).

6. Compare below, Summary C, pp. 665–670. This is disputed by liberal critics. T. K. Cheyne has claimed, "All these psalms are (let me say it again, for it concerns modern apologists to be frank) only Messianic in a sense which is psychologically justifiable. They are, as I have shown, neither typically nor in the ordinary sense prophetically Messianic, *The Origin and Religious Content of the Psalter*, p. 340. But while "the tendency of criticism is to deny . . . Messianic reference," it must then face the fact that "the evangelists and apostles held a view of the Psalter that cannot be defended, if . . . Christ is not contemplated in the Psalms," W. T. Davison, HDB, IV:160.

7. Liberal Biblical criicism consistently rejects the psalm titles as of little value, e.g. IB, IV:8. But such denial appears to spring from an evolutionary bias, which does not admit as genuinely Davidic the advanced spiritual conceptions that Scripture thus assigns to an era 1,000 years B.C. From the viewpoint of lower criticism, no reason exists for denying their authenticity within the text of the OT; and from that of higher criticism the analysis of R. D. Wilson, PTR, 24 (1926), 353–395, has demonstrated the compatibility of Davidic authorship with the content of each psalm attributed to him.

8. While the formulaic title "Psalm of David" has sometimes been interpreted to mean merely "of Davidic character" or "belonging to a collection entitled *David*," its usage indicates Davidic authorship; cf. Pss 7, 18, or Hab 3:1.

9. Pss 16 (Acts 2:25), 32 (Rom 4:6), 69 (Acts 1:16, Rom 11:9), 110 (Lk 20:43, Acts 2:34).

10. Pss 2 (Acts 4:25), 95 (Heb 4:7), and 96, 105, and 106 (underlying David's words in I Chron 16:8–36, though cf. HDB, IV:148).

tributed to him,[11] David himself must have brought together this first collection. He further composed Ps 106 (cf. I Chron 16:34–36), so that Book IV must likewise be traced to David's own hand, prior to his death in 970 B.C. King Solomon (d. 930), who was responsible for the doxology of 72:18–20, would seem to have been the historical compiler of Book II.[12] Book III, however, was completed and collected by unnamed Korahite singers soon after 586 B.C. (cf. 89:39–40, 44).[13] Finally, certain chapters of Book V came into being shortly after Israel's return from exile in 537 (cf. 107:1–3, 126:1–2). It then remained for a Spirit-led scribe to add his own inspired composition of Pss 146–150 as a grand hallelujah for the entire Psalter; cf. its closing thought, 150:6, as a key verse for the whole volume. Since this last writing occurred in 444 B.C. (147:13) at the time of Ezra's proclamation of the written law and reform of temple worship (Neh 8–10), it may well be that Ezra himself executed the final compilation of the book (cf. Ezra 7:10).[14]

Most significant among the poems of the Psalter, from the predictive viewpoint, are the 13 definitely Messianic psalms. This number is ascertained on the basis of unambiguous NT statement or, in the case of Ps 72, by clear OT reference to the ruler of the eternal Messianic kingdom (cf. vv. 6–8). It has not been permitted to include either those psalms which the NT may cite for the sake only of general teaching, illustration, or mere phraseology,[15] such as Ps 44:22, "For Thy sake we are killed all the day long" (quoted in Rom 8:36), or which the OT may identify simply in terms of Yahweh's theocratic rule, such as Ps 96:13, "For Yahweh cometh to judge the earth";[16] but it embraces only those compositions specifically intended to foretell the Person and work of Jesus. Of these 13 Messianic psalms, 8 are stated by Scripture to have been composed by David[17] and 4 others by those

---

11. Except for Ps 1, which constitutes the book's introduction; Ps 10, which combines with 9 to form one continuous acrostic; and Ps 33, which has no title.

12. His reference to "the prayers of David," 72:20, may be due to his father's having composed more than half the chs. that makes up Pss 42–72.

13. Though the body of Pss 88–89 was written by Solomon's Ezrahites who are named in their titles, the opening line of the title to Ps 88 seems to have been prefixed to both of these psalms—cf. the inappropriateness of the description "song [joyful]" to Ps 88 alone—and thus designates the sons of Korah as their ultimate compliers (cf. 89's terminal strophe, vv. 38–52, which they seem to have suffixed in the spirit of Ps 88).

14. J. B. Payne, "Psalms, the Book of," in M. C. Tenney, ed., *The Zondervan Pictorial Bible Dictionary*, pp. 694–696; cf. the conclusion of F. M. Cross that the evidence of the Dead Sea scrolls of Qumran establishes the Persian era as the latest possible point for inspired psalmody, *The Ancient Library of Qumran and Modern Biblical Studies*, p. 122.

15. See above, pp. 76–79.

16. Even though in such cases it is legitimate to recognize that Yahweh will, in fact, perform such rule through the Person of His Son the Messiah; see above, pp. 75, 104, and the actual analysis of this verse in terms of Christ, under prediction No. 45, below.

17. Pss 2, 8, 16, 22, 40, 69, 109, and 110.

associated with him during united kingdom times (per. 6).[18] This leaves only Ps 132, whose Messianic teaching consists of a brief restatement of Ps 89's anticipation of the everlasting duration of the Davidic dynasty.

The chief question about these psalms concerns then the relationship of David to their subject matter. Fairbairn asserts, "The description *must* have taken its form from the history and position of David, and should be read as from that point of view."[19] His approach, however, seems to allow insufficient recognition for the basicaly divine authorship of Scripture. As Berkhof cautions, "Scripture contains a great deal that does not find its explanation in history, nor in the secondary authors, but only in God as the *Auctor primarius*."[20] The appeal, moreover, that is not infrequently made to a theory of "double sense," one for the OT and another for the New, has been taken up in the introductory discussion[21] and has been found to be a precarious hermeneutic. Furthermore, the NT writers, in their citation of the Messianic psalms, would never leave the impression of the possibility of a meaning other than the NT one: Acts 1:16, for example, speaks of "the Scripture which the Holy Spirit spake before by the mouth of David concerning Judas"; compare the conviction expressed by Heb 7:17 concerning Christ and the intent of Ps 110:4, "It is witnessed of *Him*, 'Thou art a priest forever. . . .' " Finally, interpreters too frequently overlook the fact that contemporary OT events generally fail to correspond to the Messianic forecasts of the psalms. A. F. Kirkpatrick summarizes the situation:

> The king gave the inspired poets opportunity for dwelling on the promises and hopes connected with the Davidic kingdom. But successive princes of David's line failed to fulfill their high destiny. . . . The kingdom ceased to exist; yet it was felt that the divine promise could not fail, and hope was directed to the future. Men were led to see that the divine promise had not been frustrated but postponed, and to look for the coming One who should "fulfill" to the utmost that which had been spoken of Israel's king.[22]

Table 4 therefore lists in the last column some of the indications of an exclusively Messianic meaning that are drawn from the 13 psalms themselves, divided into three groups, based upon the person of the pronouns employed. Those in the third person are subject to the least misunderstanding, since David could easily have been capable of discussing the Messiah as someone "out there," who would yet arise, e.g. in the introduction and con-

18. 72, by Solomon, and 89, by the wise man Ethan; 102, anonymous, and 45, by the Korahite singers (whose history did not terminate with David), might confessedly be later, but their presence in Books IV and II of the Psalter necessarily limits their latest possible dates to David and to Solomon respectively.
19. *The Typology of Scripture*, I:377.
20. *Principles of Biblical Interpretation*, p. 134.
21. See above, Sec. III, Part C.
22. Camb, *Psalms*, I:lxxix; cf. Fairbairn, op. cit., I:124, "In Pss 2, 22, 45, 72, and 110 it is impossible by any fair interpretation of the language to understand the description of another than Christ."

TABLE 4
The Messianic Psalms

Psalm	Subject	Messianic vv.	NT Proof	OT Clue to Exclusively Messianic Meaning
A. Christ Spoken of in the Third Person				
8	Humiliation and glory	3-8	Heb 2:5-10; I Cor 15:27	v. 8, all things are under His feet, which cannot apply to mankind as a whole.
72	Rule	6-17	–	v. 5 is a transition to the future; 7, His reign is forever; 8, His territory universal; and 9-11, all worship Him.
89	Of David	3-4, 26, 28-29, 34-37	Acts 2:30	vv. 4, 29, 36-37, this seed of David is eternal.
109	Judas cursed	6-19	Acts 1:16-20	Adversaries (plu.) in vv. 4-5 shift in v. 6 to one preeminent betrayer. Plu. is resumed in v. 20.
132	Of David	12b	Acts 2:30	v.12, the seed is eternal.
B. Christ Addressed in the Second Person				
45	Throne forever	6-7	Heb 1:8-9	v.6, He is deity; yet, v. 7, not the Father.
102	Eternity	25-27	Heb 1:10-12	1-22 is addressed to Yahweh; v. 24, to El, a change in person. v. 28, Christ is man's hope for continuance.
110	Ascension and priesthood	All 7	Mt 22:43-45; Acts 2:33-35; Heb 1:13, 5:6-10, 6:20, 7-24	v. 1, He is David's Lord; v. 4, an eternal priest.
C. Christ Speaks in the First Person				
2	Kissing the Son	All 12	Acts 4:25-28, 13:33; Heb 1:5, 5:5	v. 7, the speaker is God's begotten Son; vv. 2, 12, an anointed one distinct from David; v. 8, possessing more.
16	Incorruption	10	Acts 2:24-31, 13:35-37	Not seeing corruption cannot apply to David.
22	Passion and brotherhood	All 31	Mt 27:35-46; John 19:23-25; Heb 2:12	v. 16, His pierced hands and feet, and v. 18, lots cast over His garments: not true of David.
40	Incarnation	6-8	Heb 10:5-10	Praises in vv. 1-5 and 9ff. are interrupted by a descriptive section. David did not always "delight to do God's will," v. 12; but Christ did, v. 8.
69	Judas cursed	25	Acts 1:16-20	The specific "desolate habitation" lies between generalizations in vv. 24 and 26, narrowed to Judas.

clusion to Ps 2, "Why do . . . the rulers take counsel against Yahweh's anointed? . . . Kiss the Son, lest He be angry" (vv. 1–2, 12). Those in which the Messiah is addressed in the second person may involve either statements that David himself is quoting—as in Ps 110, "Yahweh said to my [Messianic] Lord . . . 'Rule Thou in the midst of Thine enemies' (vv. 1–2)—or statements that the psalmist may utter directly to the Messiah, raising his eyes for a moment from an earthly to a heavenly horizon—as in Ps 45: Solomon's arrows may have been sharp (v. 5); but "Thy throne, O God [the divine Messiah], is for ever and ever [words which were apparently not addressed to Yahweh Himself, for the writer adds]: therefore God, Thy God, hath anointed Thee . . ." (vv. 6–7).

The last group, psalms in which Christ Himself speaks in the first person are the least obvious as to an exclusively Messianic intent. Berkhof, however, has offered the following general explanation:

> The lyrical poet . . . mounts to ever loftier heights, until he rests in God, in whom the life of humanity originates and who controls its joy and sorrow. . . . His song is, as it were, born of God. . . . [These poets] feel that they are united with Him who is the glorious Head of the church, who suffers for and with it, and is the author of its joy. This explains the fact that Christ is sometimes heard in the psalms, now singing a plaintive song, and anon raising up His voice in a psalm of victory.[23]

In the central part of Ps 2, for example, Christ speaks through His royal ancestor, "I will tell of the decree: Yahweh said unto Me, Thou art My Son" (v. 7); and in Ps 16 He affirms to Yahweh, "Thou wilt not leave My soul . . . to see corruption." Even Fairbairn concedes, "The plain import of the words seems to carry us directly to Christ, while it requires a certain strain to be put upon them before they can be properly applied to David."[24] One

---

23. Op. cit., p. 156. Cf. Sampey's answer to the problem that but certain vv. in a given psalm are Messianic: "Rationalistic critics insist that to apply part of a psalm to David and part to Christ introduces confusion. They contend that the language refers to the psalmist and to him alone, and that the application of certain vv. to our Lord Jesus is only by way of accommodation. This theory ignores the presence and activity of the Holy Spirit altogether; and when men talk of psychological impossibilities, they may be talking nonsense; for who of us can understand fully the psychological experience of men while receiving revelations from God? The real author of inspired prophecies is the Holy Spirit. His meaning is that which the reverent interpreter most delights to find. . . . We ought not to be surprised that we should be unable to explain fully the method of the Holy Spirit's activity in guiding the thought of prophets and psalmists in their predictions of the sufferings of Christ and the glories that should follow them," ISBE, IV:2493.

24. Op. cit., I:135; cf. Payne, "So-called Dual Fulfillment in Messianic Psalms," ETS P (1953), 63–66. Terry, *Biblical Hermeneutics*, pp. 399–400, explains, "The second psalm was composed in spiritual ecstasy. David became a seer and prophet. 'The Spirit of Jehovah spoke within him, and his word was upon his tongue' (II Sam 23:2). . . . He is lifted into visionary ecstasy, transcending all earthly royalty and power. He sees Jehovah enthroning his Anointed upon Zion, the mountain of his holiness. . . . Thus the second psalm is seen to be no mere historical ode, composed upon the royal inauguration of David or Solomon, or any other earthly

might still ask, however, how much the writer and the readers in David's day may have comprehended of the divine meaning; and Barrows replies,

How far the psalmist understood . . . his words is a question difficult to be determined. . . . Peter tells us that David, "being a prophet and knowing . . . that God would raise up Christ . . . he, seeing this before, spake of the resurrection of Christ"; whence we infer that in penning this [16th] psalm David was conscious of its higher application to Christ. . . . He had a deeper insight into the prophetic meaning of his words than many modern expositors are willing to admit. But however this may be, the Spirit of inspiration had in view the fulfillment of these psalms in Christ; and His intention, clearly revealed to us in NT, is our rule of interpretation.[25]

1. Ps 1:5–6; 9:7–8, 19–20 (6 vv.): "The wicked shall not stand [rise] in the judgment. . . . The way of the wicked shall perish" (1:5–6); "He will judge the world in righteousness" (9:8). In the latter passage the Heb. impf. aspect of the verb could—though with less likelihood—be rendered through an English present tense.[26] Yet Delitzsch appeals to the context and exegetes it: "This same God, who has just given proof that He lives and reigns [cf. 9:3–6, 15–16], *will* by and by judge the nations still more comprehensively. . . . It is the last judgment, of which all preceding judgments are pledges, that is intended. In later Psalms[27] this Davidic utterance concerning the future is repeated."[28] Fulfillment (per. 17): the condemnation of the wicked at the final judgment; cf. Rev 20:12–15.

2. Ps 2:1–3 (3 vv.): this passage is quoted in the NT, with explanation, as follows: "Why did the Gentiles rage? . . . The peoples, the kings of the earth, and the rulers . . . against the Lord and against His Christ. For truly in this city there were gathered together against Thy holy Servant Jesus, whom Thou didst anoint, both Herod and Pontius Pilate, along with the Gentiles and the peoples of Israel," Acts 4:25–27. Fulfillment (per. 13): the trial of Christ, Lk 23:1–25.

3. Ps 2:2b, 45:6–7 (2 vv.): reference to Jesus (see No. 2, above) as Yahweh's "anointed," 2:2. This title had been first revealed through Hannah, in connection with our Lord's future rule; see I Sam 2:10b. Here, however, occurs its initial application to the period of His first advent; cf. the later quotation of Ps 2 in Acts 4:27, as predictive of "Jesus whom Thou didst

---

prince. A greater than either David or Solomon arose in the psalmist's vision . . . the Son of Jehovah whom the kings of the earth are counselled to kiss. . . . It is only as the interpreter attains a vivid apprehension of the power of such ecstasy that he can properly perceive or explain the import of any Messianic prophecy."

25. *Companion to the Bible*, p. 622.

26. ICC or AB.

27. E.g. 96:13b, 98:9b (listed under 2:6, No. 5 below), though in these the context is one of joy in nature, which applies more naturally to Christ's second coming and earthly rule.

28. *Pss*, I:166.

anoint." Even so, vv. 6–7 of Ps 45, which are quoted in Heb 1:8–9 as words directed to Christ, address Him prophetically: "Thy throne, O God, is for ever. . . . Therefore God, Thy God, hath anointed Thee with the oil of gladness above Thy fellows." The Messiah's "fellows" may refer to the "many sons" (believers) whom He brings to glory, His "brethren" of Heb 2:10–11;[29] the Messiah's deity (45:6), and also His existence as the uniquely begotten Son of God (2:7, 12; cf. Acts 13:33, Heb 1:5, 5:5), are matters of major theological import, but they constitute eternal truths and are hence contemporaneous to David, rather than predictive, as he writes these psalms. Within Ps 45, the material preceding v. 6 concerns the wedding of a king, presumably Solomon; but vv. 6–7 then turn in their address from man to God[30]—the RSV rendering of the opening line, which would remove this distinction by reading, "Your *divine* throne endures . . .," is frankly illegitimate.[31] Retaining the Hebrew text, one must conclude with Clinton Lockhart, "It is evident that these expressions cannot reasonably apply to any of the Davidic kings,"[32] but only to Christ, the Son of God. Fulfillment (per. 13): the anointing of Jesus—the very terms *Messiah* (OT) and *Christ* (NT) are but the Hebrew and Greek forms of *anointed*—specifically, by God's Holy Spirit at His baptism, Acts 10:38.

4. Ps 2:4–5, 8–9, 12; 110:5–7 (8 vv., fig.): words directed to the Messiah, either by Yahweh, "I will give Thee the nations for Thine inheritance," 2:8, and, "Thou shalt break them with a rod of iron," v. 9, or by David, "The Lord at Thy right hand will strike through kings in the day of His wrath . . . He will fill the places with dead bodies. . . . He will drink of the brook in the way: therefore will He lift up the head," 110:5–7, a figure for maintaining His strength, as in the case of Samson in Jd 15:18–19. Delitzsch explains, "He will stand still only for a short time to refresh Himself, and in order then to fight afresh; He will unceasingly pursue His work of victory."[33] Fulfillment (per. 15): Christ's victory at Armageddon, as in Num. No. 36.

5. Ps 2:6; 22:28; *67:4b;* 72:9–11; 82:8; 89:21–25, 27; *96:13c* (I Chron *16:33c*); *98:9c*; 110:*1c*–2 (13 vv.): Yahweh's promise, in the prophetic perf., "I have set My king upon holy hill of Zion" (2:6). "For the kingdom is Yahweh's; and He is ruler over the nations" (22:28). The Messiah's enemies are to lick the dust, 72:9; Yahweh will "make Thine enemies Thy footstool," 110:1 (cf. I Cor 15:25). All nations are to bring Him tribute, Ps 72:10, and serve Him, v. 11. In Ps 89, vv. 19–20 are past, referring to David; but they "are followed by promissory futures from v.

29. F. F. Bruce, NIC, *Heb*, p. 21.
30. See above, p. 261.
31. Cf. R. L. Harris, *The Biblical Expositor*, II:55–56, or Payne, *Theology of the Older Testament*, p. 262.
32. *Messianic Message of the OT*, p. 115.
33. III:196.

22 onwards,"[34] to be fulfilled in the Davidic Messiah. Of v. 25, "I will set
. . . His right hand on the rivers," Delitzsch says, "What is promised is
world wide dominion, not merely dominion within the compass of II Chron
9:26 [the realm of David and Solomon], in which case it ought to have been
singular, the Euphrates."[35] So the words of v. 27b, "I also will make Him
. . . the highest of the kings of the earth," repeats the promise directed to the
nation of Israel in Dt 26:19, 28:1, but here made specific in the Messiah,
"in whom Israel's national glory realizes itself."[36] In the same vein 96:13
and 98:9 speak of God's "judging the world with righteousness and the
peoples with equity";[37] see under 67:4a (No. 31, below), on the character
of His reign. Fulfillment (per. 16): Christ's Messianic kingdom, following
Armageddon, as in Gen. No. 68; cf. I Sam. No. 4 (2:10b).

6. Ps 4:5; *27:6b;* 50:9, 13; 51:17; 54:6; 69:31; 96:8 (I Chron
16:29);[38] 118:27a; 119:108 (9 vv., typ.): sacrifice. Fulfillment (per. 13):
as in Lev. No. 2.

7. Ps 5:7; 9:11; 15:1; 20:2; 23:6; 24:3; 26:8; 27:4–6a; 30:title (v. 1,
Heb); 36:8; 42:4; 43:3; 46:4; 48:9; 52:8; 55:14; 61:4; 62:2; 65:4;
66:13a; 68:16, 24, 29; 69:9; 73:17; 74:3, 7; 76:2;[39] 78:60, 69; 79:1;
84:1–2, 4, 10; 92:13; 93:5; 100:4; 116:19; 118:26; 122:1, 9; 132:5, 7–
8a, 13–14; 134:1–2; 135:2, 21; 138:2 (52 vv., typ.): tabernacle or temple;
cf. the thought of 9:11, God "dwelleth in Zion." Fulfillment (per. 13): as in
Ex. No. 55. Other references in Ps to Yahweh's "holy temple" appear to
signify His abode in heaven, e.g. 11:4, 18:6, 29:9, 150:1, rather than an
earthly (typical) sanctuary.

8. Ps 8:3–8, 110:1b (7 vv.): "What is man, that Thou art mindful of
him? . . . Thou hast put all things under his feet" (8:4–6). These vv. are
quoted in Heb 2:6–9 of Christ's glorification: "We see Him, because of the
suffering of death, crowned with glory and honor." That is to say, the 8th
Ps puts into words what had been a typical enactment in Gen 1:26–28. Yet
Adam, and the human race in general, no longer fulfill such a position of
dominion; and since the fall "all things" are not subjected to him. Christ, in
contrast, is the only person who really achieves what man was meant to be:
He is "the last Adam," I Cor 15:45; and God has put all things in subjection
to Him, exalting Him to His own right hand, Ps 110:1. Fulfillment (per 13):
the ascension of Christ into glory; for Ps 110 is so quoted in Acts 2:34, cf.
Heb 1:13.

34. Ibid., III:39.
35. III:40.
36. Ibid.
37. Cf. the similar phraseology, but in the less joyful context of the final judgment
(per. 17), in 9:8 (listed under 1:5, No. 1 above).
38. The term at this point is *minhā,* technically, the "meal offering," but here used
more generally, as in Gen 4:4 and elsewhere.
39. But the ASV rendering of 77:13 as "in the sanctuary" is better read with
ASVmg as simply "in holiness."

9. Ps 16: title, 56–60: titles (in the Heb., v. 1 in each instance) (6 vv.): "Michtam of David." The noun *mikhtām*, seems to have the sense of "atoning";[40] cf. such allusions as the following in the bodies of the psalms concerned: "Thou wilt show me the path of life," 16:11; or, "Be merciful unto me, O God," 56:1, 57:1.[41] Fulfillment (per. 13): as in Job No. 4. True atonement is achieved only by Jesus, John 14:6.

10. Ps 16:9, 17:15, 22:29b (3 vv.): David's affirmation, "My flesh also shall dwell confidently" (16:9, ASVmg). Delitzsch explains, "He also hopes for his body that which he hopes for his spirit-life. He looks death calmly and triumphantly in the face. . . . It is impossible for the man who calls God his own . . . to fall into the hands of death."[42] Delitzsch, indeed, then limits this hope to the simple fact of not dying. But David did die, at least eventually; and J. A. Alexander accordingly insists, "This is applicable both to preservation from death and preservation in death, and may therefore without violence be understood of David . . . whose body is to rise again."[43] Similarly in 17:15 the king states, "I shall be satisfied, when I awake, with beholding Thy form." His hope must be viewed in contrast with the lot of the wicked, "whose portion is in this life" (v. 14, preceding); and his terminology of "waking up" suggests that it advances beyond the truth of spiritual immortality into that of a bodily awakening in resurrection, as in Job 19:26, Dan 12:2. As A. B. Davidson comments, "The passage seems to go further than even Ps 49.[44] and to refer to the awakening out of death, when God has brought in His perfect kingdom, which departed saints would live again to share."[45] Once again, in 22:29b, at the Messianic marriage feast (see v. 29a, No. 22, below), there shall appear not simply those who have survived upon earth; but also: "All they that go down to the dust shall bow before Him, even he that cannot keep his soul alive."[46] Fulfillment (per. 15): the resurrection of the righteous, as previously intimated in Job No. 7 (19:26).

11: Ps 16:10, *110:4b* (1 v.): David, speaking for the Messiah,[47] affirms,

40. According to S. Mowinckel, from the Assyrian; cf. IDB, III:378.
41. Cf. also 59:1, 60:1, or 58:11, "There is a God that judgeth in the earth."
42. I:227–228.
43. *The Psalms, Translated and Explained*, p. 68. V. 11, however, on the path of life that God would show David, does not seem to demand the idea of resurrection, though it is a definite statement of hope beyond death; cf. R. R. Dummelow, ed., *A Commentary on the Holy Bible*, p. 335, "The Psalmist's words contain an anticipation of the immortality which Christ has brought to light," and M. Dahood, AB, *Ps* I:91, thinks of it in terms of translation, "the same privilege accorded Enoch and Elijah."
44. In 49:14 the phrase, "The upright shall have dominion over them in the morning," may mean only "a new day dawning after death," NBC, p. 447.
45. *The Theology of the OT*, p. 466.
46. The pt. could mean: "those who are almost dead already with care and want," KD, I:326, and so simply the contrast between the prosperous and the poor. But Delitzsch cites Isa 25:6 as a parallel (*q.v.*); and this does concern victory over death through the first resurrection; see vv. 7–8.
47. See above, p. 261.

"Thou wilt not leave My soul to sheol [here = *the grave*, as in Job 17:13–14]; neither wilt Thou suffer Thy holy One to see corruption,"[48] 16:10. Then in 110:4 David addresses the Messiah: "Thou art a priest *for ever* after the manner [ASVmg] of Melchizedek." For Heb 7:3 speaks of Melchizedek as being "without end of life"; cf. v. 8, "it is witnessed that he lives on." But while the historical Melchizedek of the Biblical account (Gen 14) is *endless* only in the sense of having no required time of retirement from his term of priesthood, as did the Levites, and of having no recorded statement of death (though doubtless he did die), still this "indestructible life" (Heb 7:16) not simply proves that there is a better (NT) law than the Levitical, but it also points forward to a fulfillment (per. 13) in the resurrection of Christ.[49] Acts 2:25–31 and 13:35–37 make clear, moreover, that the prophecy of Ps 16 cannot refer to David, whose body did see corruption. Yet the fulfillment in Christ still becomes the basis for David's own hope in vv. 9, 11. As explained by Davidson, "The Messiah goes through that which the saint anticipates for himself, and causes it thus to be realized in the ordinary saint."[50]

12. Ps 20:3a, *40:6b*, 141:2 (2 vv., typ.): the Heb. term is, in each case, *minhā,* "meal offering"; cf. ASVmgs. Fulfillment (per. 13): as in Lev. No. 4.

13. Ps *20:3b*; *40:6d*; 50:8b; 51:*16b*, 19a; 66:13b–15 (5 vv., typ.): burnt offering. Fulfillment (per. 13): as in Lev. No. 3.

Psalm 22 is the one chapter in the Psalter in which the Messiah speaks forth the entire composition. Sampey declares, "Every sentence can be applied to Jesus without straining its meaning. If David took up his harp to sing of his own sorrows, the Spirit of God guided him to describe those of a greater."[51]

14. Ps 22:1–2 (2 vv.) thus reads, "My God, why hast Thou forsaken Me?" anticipating the utterance of these words by Jesus at His cruifixion, Mt 27:46.[52] Fulfillment (per. 13): Christ's necessary abandonment by the Father, during His suffering upon the cross of the penalty for men's sins; cf. II Cor 5:21.[53]

48. A proper rendering for the noun *sháhath*; see Harris, op. cit., II:59–60.
49. Melchizedek was also a symbol of Christ's preexistence, being simply "king of Salem" (Gen 14:18), without "beginning of days" (Heb 7:3); but this fact was not predictive, but rather descriptive of what Christ was at that time.
50. *OT Prophecy*, p. 344.
51. ISBE, IV:2492; and see above, pp. 261–262, on this "first person" form of Messianic prophecy.
52. Edghill comments, "In making that cry of despair His own, the Lord deliberately identified Himself with that ideal servant of Jehovah whose sufferings and final triumph form the subject of the Psalmist's theme," *An Enquiry into the Evidential Value of Prophecy*, p. 428.
53. Though this abandonment is probably to be identified with Christ's "descent into hell," as used by the Reformers, it terminated with His death and the Father's receiving of our Lord's spirit, Lk 23:46. It may also have begun with the agony in Gethsemane, 22:44.

15. Ps 22:6–8 (3 vv.): concerning Calvary, Mt 27:39 quotes Ps 22:7 as descriptive of those who were passing by, hurling abuse at Jesus and "wagging their heads"; and Mt. 27:43 records the derisive quotation of Ps 22:8 by the chief priests: "He trusts in God; let Him deliver Him now, if He takes pleasure in Him."[54] Fulfillment (per. 13): the mockery of Christ, as cited above.

16. Ps 22:10 (1 v.): "I was cast upon Thee from the womb; Thou art My God since My mother bare Me." Delitzsch observes, "Throughout the OT there is never any mention made of a human father to the Messiah, but always only of His mother."[55] Fulfillment (per. 13): Christ's holy youth; cf. Lk 2:20, "The grace of God was upon Him," or His own awareness, v. 49, "I had to be in My Father's house."

17. Ps 22:11–18 (8 vv., fig.): further descriptions by the Messiah, v. 15, "My tongue cleaveth to My jaws," as a figure for thirst, John 19:28; v. 16, "Evil-doers have enclosed Me; they pierced My hands and My feet,"[56] accomplished in John 19:18; v. 18, "They part My garments among them, and upon My vesture do they cast lots," quoted in John 19:24. Fulfillment (per. 13): Christ's sufferings on the cross. Farley grants, "It is a harder task to deny than to accept a direct relation between prediction and fulfillment in the case of such passages as Ps 22. . . ."[57]

18. Ps 22:19–21 (3 vv., fig.): "From the horns of the wild oxen Thou hast answered Me." Fulfillment (per. 13): God the Father did receive His spirit, Lk 23:46 (cf. note 53 on Ps 22:1, No. 14, above).

19. Ps 22:22–25 (4 vv.): v. 22 is quoted in Heb 2:11–12, on the relationship of Christ to His sanctified people, "He is not ashamed to call them brethren, saying, 'I will declare Thy name unto My brethren, in the midst of the church [NASmg; Gk, *ekklēsía*, "church"] will I sing Thy praise." Ps 22:25 adds, "I will pay My vows before them that fear Him." So after His resurrection Christ did fulfill this pledge from Ps 22 and honored the Father before the church (per. 14). He said, for example, "I am sending forth the promise of My Father upon you" (Lk 24:49); or, "As the Father hath sent Me, I also send you . . . receive the Holy Spirit" (John 20:21–22; cf. Acts 1:4–5). John 20:30 and Acts 1:3 speak of other signs and words at this time too, "the concerns of the kingdom of God" (Acts 1:3).

20. Ps 22:26 (1 v.): as a result of His passion, "The meek shall eat and be satisfied," Christ prophesied; "they shall praise Yahweh that seek after

54. Edghill continues, op. cit., pp. 308, 311, by noting a series of verbal parallels between Ps 22:6 and Isa 49:7, 51:7, 52:14, and 53:2–3, and concludes, "In Ps 22 we meet with the persecuted Servant . . . [in] language almost identical with that employed by the prophet. . . . Both alike prepare the way for the paradox of Christianity—Via crucis via lucis," by the way of the cross is the way of light.

55. I:314.

56. Cf. Kirkpatrick, Camb, *Ps*, I:119, exposing the later MT substitute reading, which is quoted in the ASVmg, ". . . have encompassed Me, like a lion, My hands and My feet."

57. *The Progress of Prophecy*, p. 303.

Him: let your heart live forever." Fulfillment (per. 14): the communion supper in the Christian church; for v. 26a had spoken of the *anāwīm*, "those who are outwardly and spiritually poor." Delitzsch then goes on to say,

Verse 26c is as it were the host's blessing upon his guests, "May this meal impart to you ever enduring refreshment. . . ." It relates to a spiritual enjoyment of spiritual and lasting results. How natural, then, is the thought of the sacramental eucharist, in which, having attained to the throne through the suffering of death, [Christ] makes us partakers of the fruits of His suffering![58]

21. Ps 22:27; 66:4; 67:7; 72:15; 86:9; 102:15, 21–22; 138:4–5 (10 vv.): as an eventual result, "All the ends of the earth shall remember [Calvary, Nos. 14–18, above] and turn unto Yahweh . . . and shall worship before Thee," 22:27 (66:4, 86:9); "They shall sing to Thy name," 66:4 (138:5), "shall fear the name of Yahweh," 102:15 (67:7), and "declare the name of Yahweh in Zion, when the peoples are gathered together to serve Yahweh," 102:21–22. Concerning the Lord's Messiah, "Men shall pray for Him continually and bless Him," 72:15. Fulfillment (per. 16): the universal seeking of God, in His future kingdom, as in Gen No. 47 (22:18b).

22. Ps *22:29a:* "All the fat ones of the earth shall eat and worship." The preceding context is that of the millennium, "All nations shall worship Thee, for the kingdom is Yahweh's," vv. 27–28 (see No. 5 and 21, above). The following phrase speaks of a category separate from *the fat ones,* namely, "he that cannot keep his soul alive," v. 29b, meaning the dead (see No. 10, above); so the *fat ones of the earth* must be those still living. Yet both together find the fulfillment of this passage in per. 15, at Christ's return, in the marriage supper of the Lamb (Rev 19:9), "the same great feast of which Isaiah, ch 25:6, prophesies."[59] It should thus not be related to per. 14, as if but a further description of the communion meal predicted in v. 26 (No. 20, above).

23. Ps 22:30–31, 102:18 (3 vv.): as a final result of Christ's passion, "A seed shall serve Him: it shall be told of the Lord unto the next generation," 22:30. "They [in turn] shall come and declare His righteousness unto a people that shall be born [so "three generations are distinctly mentioned"[60]], that He hath done it," 22:31, meaning the action of Calvary, vv. 1–21. Similarly, 102:18 declares concerning God's redemption of Zion, "This shall be written for the generation to come; and a people which shall be created shall praise Yah(weh)." Fulfillment (per. 14): missionary witnessing from generation to generation in the Christian church.[61] This

58. I:324.
59. Ibid., I:326.
60. Ibid., I:327.
61. Ibid., III:116, on 102:18, "A new, created people, the church of the future, shall praise God the Redeemer."

prophecy could, it is true, refer to missionary activity during the millennium. More probably, however, the immediately preceding mention of the dead saints, appearing at the Messianic feast in 22:29b, would suggest a divine explanation on how they came to be believers and so to be members of His church in the first place.

24. Ps 25:10, 14;[62] 44:17; 50:5, 16; 74:20; 78:10, 37; 103:18; 106:45; 111:5, 9; 132:12a (13 vv., typ.): the Sinaitic testament. 50:5 states, "My saints have made a testament with Me by sacrifice," lit., they "have cut [entered] My testament," thereby implying the *b'rīth* already established by God, through Moses.[63] Their procedure, by means of *sacrifice,* emphasizes the necessity of death, and hence the typical element of the *b'rīth,* foreshadowing the fulfillment (per. 13) through the sacrificial death of Christ, as in Ex. No. 45 (19:5).

25. Ps 26:6, 43:4, *51:19b,* 84:3, *118:27b* (3 vv., typ.): the sanctuary's altar of sacrifice. Fulfillment (per. 13): as in Ex. No. 44.

26. Ps *40:6a;* 50:*8a,* 14, 23; 51:16a; 56:12; 107:22; 116:17 (6 vv., typ.): peace offerings. Fulfillment (pers. 13 and 16): as in Lev. No. 5.

27. Ps 40:6c, 7–8 (3 vv.): the bulk of this psalm consists of confession by David, e.g. v. 12, "Mine iniquities have overtaken me, so that I am not able to look up" (cf. vv. 2, 17). Yet in its midst appear unhesitating affirmations of holiness: "Mine ears hast Thou opened [in obedience; see Isa 50:5].[64] . . . In the roll of the book it is written of Me: I delight to do Thy will," vv. 6–8. Davidson suggests, "Some things are said really and some ideally";[65] and when these three verses are repeated in Heb 10:5–7 they are identified as words of Christ. So vv. 6–8 are to be seen as an insert in what are otherwise David's testimonies. Concerning what had been written in the roll of the book about the Messiah, Ps 2:7–8 had referred to the eternal covenant of redemption between Yahweh and His Son, by which

---

62. David's word that to those who fear the Lord, "He will show them His testament" (25:14), is not further defined; and it could relate to the specifically Davidic *b'rīth.* Yet this generalized expression suggests, in itself, the well-known redemptive revelation on Sinai.

63. Cf. Payne, *Theology,* p. 80, note.

64. The quotation of this verse in Heb 10:5 follows the LXX in reading, "A body, *sōmā,* Thou hast prepared for me," which seemingly arose through scribal error for, "Ears, *ōtía*" (also, the preceding word ends in *s*). The NT thus accepts this rendering as an adequate representation of the thought; for though the term "body" is not found in the OT, it is not stressed in the New. Roger Nicole explains, "The writers of the NT could use the LXX, in spite of its occasional inaccuracy, and even quote passages which were somewhat inaccurately translated. They must never have profited by its errors, however; and we should not find any example of a deduction logically inferred from the LXX which cannot be maintained on the basis of the Heb. text. Heb 10:5–7 is not an exception to this principle. Although the word *sōmā* is found in the context (v. 10), this does not appear to be derived from the form in which Ps 40 has been quoted, and the reverse substitution of *ōtía* to *sōmā* in v. 5 would not impair the validity of the argument nor the appropriateness of the use of *sōmā* in v. 10." ETS P (1954), 47, 54.

65. *OT Prophecy,* p. 344.

Christ would receive the nations as an inheritance; but Ps 40, as developed in Heb 10:5–10, pinpoints the covenanted obedience to the time of His incarnation: "When He comes into the world, He says. . . ." Fulfillment (per. 13): the submission of Christ incarnate to the desires of His Father; for Jesus did delight to do the Father's will, John 4:34, 6:38, 17:4, as David too often did not.

28. Ps *40:6e* (typ.): sin offering. Fulfillment (per. 13): as in Lev 4:1.

29. Ps 47:9 (1 v.): divine sovereignty (cf. v. 8, preceding) is here illustrated prophetically, "The princes of the peoples are gathered together to be the people of the God of Abraham." Fulfillment (per. 16): widespread redemption and incorporation of aliens into Israel during the millennial kingdom—"In the mirror of the present event, the poet reads the great fact of the conversion of the peoples to Jahve which closes the history of the world";[66] cf. 87:4–6, No. 37, below, on a similar hope during the present church age as well.

30. Ps 48:8 (1 v.): concerning "the city of our God: God will establish it [Heb., *her,* the city] for ever." Fulfillment (per. 18): the New Jerusalem to be perpetual, Rev 21:25.

31. Ps 67:4a, 96:13d, 98:9d (3 vv.): "Thou wilt judge the peoples with equity" (67:4). Fulfillment (per. 16): as in II Sam No. 18 (23:3), the righteousness of the Messiah's future rule.

32. Ps 69:25 (1 v.): in the midst of a Davidic imprecation against those who have been cruelly persecuting the king (vv. 22–28), comes this more particular forecast: "Let their habitation be desolate; let none dwell in their tents," v. 25. The psalmist-monarch may not himself have been aware of the real import of this verse; but the NT identifies it as a God-given prophecy,[67] "which the Holy Spirit foretold by the mouth of David concerning Judas, who . . . acquired a field with the price of his wickedness; and falling headlong,[68] he burst open in the middle and all his bowels gushed out. . . . So that field was called, 'Field of Blood,' " Acts 1:16–19. Fulfillment (per. 13): the above-cited "desolation" of Judas and of the property he had caused to be acquired (cf. Mt 27:3–7).

33. Ps 72:5 (1 v.): "They shall fear Thee . . . throughout all generations." Fulfillment (per. 18): eternal reverence before God, Rev 22:5.

34. Ps 72:6–7, 16, *17b* (3 vv., fig.): v. 5 had stated, "They shall fear Thee [Yahweh] while the sun endureth" (see No. 33, preceding), and in this way makes a shift from the description of Solomon's reign, which appears in vv. 1–4,[69] to a preview of eternity. V. 6 thus foresees the Mes-

---

66. KD, II:100.

67. See above, p. 79; cf. the note of necessary relationship to its NT accomplishment, as sounded by the apostle in quoting this verse, "The Scripture had to be fulfilled . . .," Acts 1:16.

68. In the course of hanging himself, Mt 27:5.

69. C. Feinberg, *Premillennialism or Amillennialism?* p. 41, unnecessarily assigns these vv. to Christ too.

sianic king of the future and affirms, "He will come down like . . . showers that water the earth.[70] In His days shall the righteous flourish . . . in peace." Fulfillment (per. 16): prosperity, and abundance, v. 16, in the millennial kingdom, as in Ex. No. 49.

35. Ps 72:8 (1 v.): "He shall [lit., *let Him*] have dominion from sea to sea, and from the River [Euphrates] unto the ends of the earth."[71] The territories of the Messiah[72] are to take up where those of the psalm's author Solomon left off, I K 4:21. Fulfillment (per. 16): the extent of the Messianic kingdom, Rev 20:3, when the nations are no more deceived by Satan but receive Christ's rule.

36. Ps 72:12–14 (3 vv.): "He will deliver the needy when he crieth." Fulfillment (per. 16): Messiah's care for the poor.

37. Ps 72:17a; 102:*26b*, 27 (2 vv.): spoken *of* the Messiah, "His name shall endure for ever" (72:17); spoken *to* Him, "Thou shalt endure. . . . Thou art the same, and Thy years shall have no end" (102:26–27); cf. 89:4 etc. (No. 40, below), though these latter passages emphasize the everlastingness of Christ and His rule, from His incarnation (per. 13) onward. But the verses from Pss 72 and 102 fall into a context of eternity: e.g. 102:26a foresees heaven and earth perishing (No. 47, below; cf. Rev 20:11). 26b then goes on to speak of the Messiah, as is demonstrated by its quotation in Heb 1:10–12. Even in the psalm itself, it is to be noted that the identification of the One addressed shifts from Yahweh (6 times in vv. 15–22) to *Ēl,* "God" (in v. 24), the creator—which Christ was, John 1:3—though confessedly the psalmist may not himself have been aware of the Holy Spirit's intention at this point. Fulfillment (per 18): the eternity of the Messiah, Rev 22:3–5.

38. Ps 87:4–6 (3 vv.): after listing various nations (Egypt, Babylon, etc.) the Korahite singers prophesy, "Yea, of Zion it shall be said, This one and that one was born in her . . . Yahweh will count, when He writeth up[73] the peoples, This one was born there"; cf. Isa 4:3 and its reference to those "written unto life in Jerusalem." Delitzsch explains: "The nations will attain a right of citizenship in Zion (Eph 2:12) as in their second

70. The RSV rendering, "May he come down like rain," is here opposed to the Heb. impf. form (not jussive); cf. H. C. Leupold's criticism, in *Exposition of the Psalms,* p. 522.

71. Girdlestone, *The Grammar of Prophecy,* p. 50, would render, ". . . from the River to the ends of the land," meaning, "the literal boundaries of the promised land . . . the ends of the land being the south-west border of Palestine." But context speaks of kings and nations serving Him and seems to require the more universal understanding, as in NBC, p. 462.

72. For as Lockhart has observed, op. cit., p. 112, "At the very least, the poet is voicing the world's need for a ruler greater than any human king can be. His character should be more divine, his power more complete, and his period of rule more unrestricted, than is possible for any ruler of this world. No other than the Messiah could possibly realize this dream of royal excellence."

73. This action is not to be restricted to God's books at the final judgment, for "the book of the living (Isa 4:3) is one already existing from time immemorial," KD, III:20.

mother-city . . . they will experience a spiritual change which, regarded from the NT point of view, is the new birth out of water and the Spirit."[74] Fulfillment (per. 14): Gentile converts, now counted to be citizens of Israel, as in Gen. No. 19.

39. Ps 89:2, 28, 33–34, 39 (5 vv., typ.): the Davidic testament. Fulfillment (per. 13): as in II Sam. No. 19.

40. Ps 89:4, 29, 35–37; *132:12b* (5 vv.): God's promise concerning David, "His seed also will I make to endure for ever" (89:29). This forms a part of the content of the Davidic testament; cf. 89:3, 28, 34 (No. 39, preceding). 89:35, 49, 132:11 add that God had "sworn" it, a point emphasized by Acts 2:30, in pointing out the fulfillment (per. 13) in Christ the eternal son of David. The teaching had been first revealed in II Sam 7:13b (No. 11), which these passages are quoting; cf. 89:19. Cf. also Ps 72:17a (No. 37, above), which brings out this same everlastingness, though with particular reference to the future.

41. Ps 89:26 (1 v.): "He [the future David, the Messiah; cf. the notes on vv. 21–25, No. 5, above] shall cry unto Me, Thou art My Father, My God, and the rock of My salvation." V. 27 (see under No. 5) then adds, "I will also make Him My first-born, the highest of the kings of the earth." Fulfillment (per. 13): Jesus' being the Son of God, as in II Sam 7:14a (No. 12), which this psalm quotes (89:19). Christ had, of course, been the begotten Son of God from all eternity—Ps 2:7 is therefore not listed as a prediction—but He is here "made" first-born, as Delitzsch says, "with respect to the kings, i.e. above the kings, of the earth."[75] Compare Phil 2:9, on how "God highly exalted Him, and bestowed on Him the name which is above every name," and especially Rev 11:15.

42. Ps 89:30–32 (3 vv.): elaboration of II Sam 7:14, on a predicted chastening for Solomon. Fulfillment (per. 6): as in II Sam 7:14b (No. 13), which is here quoted (Ps 89:19).

43. Ps 95:11 (1 v.): a backward allusion to God's having sworn in His wrath that the wilderness generation of Israel "should not enter into My rest." David (Heb 4:7) here cites the words of Dt 12:9 about the denial to them of rest in the land of Canaan, which in turn confirms Moses' earlier prediction that that generation (per. 3) should not attain to it, Dt 1:35 (No. 2), Num 14:22 (No. 19, *q.v.*).

44. Ps 96:12–*13a* (I Chron 16:33a), 98:7–*9a* (3 vv., fig.): "Then shall all the trees of the wood sing for joy." Fulfillment (per. 15): cosmic gladness at the return of Christ (96:13b, No. 45, following); cf. Rom 8:20–21, on creation's hope for release from the curse (Gen 3:17–19), and Rev 19:7, on humanity's anticipation, "Let us rejoice and be glad, for the marriage of the Lamb has come."

45. Ps *96:13b* (I Chron *16:33b*), *98:9b:* creation is to rejoice before

74. Ibid., III:19.
75. Ibid., III:40.

Yahweh (No. 44, preceding), "for He cometh." When viewed under the interpretive principle that the functions predicted of Yahweh may be realized and embodied in Jesus,[76] these verses become, along with Job 19:25b, Scripture's first foregleam of the glorious second advent of Christ, the Messiah (fulfillment in per. 15); cf. Rev 14:14, 19:11, etc.

46. Ps 102:13, 16 (2 vv.): "Thou wilt arise and have mercy on Zion . . ." (v. 13). "For Yahweh hath built up Zion; He hath appeared in His glory" (v. 16). This hope is based on the prayers of the *arār*, "naked, stripped," v. 17. perhaps referring to David when he was forced to flee Jerusalem because of Absalom (II Sam 15:14), but the king and his men were still filled with concern for his desolate capital (v. 25; cf. Ps 102:14). The unnamed psalmist said, "It is time to have pity upon her" (102:13a); but the verb of the following clause—"Yea, the set time is come" (v. 13b) —may be a participle rather than perfect, and would so be read, ". . . the time is coming." For God's "appearing in glory" (cf. No. 45, preceding) was yet distant; cf. the stress on eternity in v. 12, "Thou, O Yahweh, wilt abide for ever." Fulfillment (per. 15): Christ's second coming, to establish Jerusalem; cf. Zech 12:8 (under Zech. No. 58).

47. Ps 102:26a (1 v., fig.): a contrast between the eternal God (see No. 37, above) and the earth and heaven that He has made, "They shall perish . . . as a vesture Thou shalt change them, and they shall be changed." Fulfillment (per. 17): the passing away of earth, or at least its transformation into the new earth, Rev 20:11 and 21:1 (cf. Heb 12:27), as in Gen 8:22 and Job 14:12b.

48. Ps 105:8–10 (I Chron 16:15–17) (3 vv., typ.): the Abrahamic testament. Fulfillment (per. 13): as in Gen No. 30.

49. Ps 105:11 (I Chron 16:18) (1 v.): the prophecy, in retrospect, of Israel's being given Canaan. Fulfillment (per. 4): as in Gen No. 24.

50. Ps 106:31 (1 v., typ.): the Levitical testament. Fulfillment (per. 13): as in Num No. 43 (25:12).

51. Ps 109:6–8a, 9–19 (13 vv.): an imprecation of David. Vss. 1–5, as well as those from 20 on, speak of David's enemies in the plural; but in vv. 6–19 there is a divinely directed shift to the singular, pointing to one epitome of evil, who receives imprecations of which no offender against a mere man would be worthy:[77] e.g. "When he is judged, let him come forth guilty; and his prayer be turned into sin" (v. 7); "let there be none to extend kindness to him" (v. 12); "let his days be few" (v. 8a); "let his children be vagabonds and beg" (v. 10); and "let his posterity be cut off" (v. 13); "because he persecuted . . . the broken in heart, to slay Him" (v. 16). The NT, in quoting Ps 109, makes it clear that whatever may have been in the mind of David as secondary (human) author of this Scripture, "the Holy Spirit foretold [these words] by the mouth of David concerning Judas,"

76. See above, p. 75.
77. Payne, "So-called Dual Fulfillment," p. 66.

Acts 1:16. Fulfillment (per. 13): the doom of Judas Iscariot, the "son of perdition" (John 17:12); cf. the desolation of his property as foreseen in Ps 69:25 (No. 32, above).

52. Ps 109:8b (1 v.): the line about Judas that is particularly quoted in the NT—"Let another take his office"; cf. Acts 1:20. Because of this prediction Peter affirmed, "It is therefore necessary that of the men who have accompanied us . . . one should become a witness with us," vv. 21–22. Fulfillment (per. 14): the transference to another of the apostolic office once held by Judas, vv. 23–26, though whether Matthias was the one whom God had actually selected for the 12th apostleship (v. 26), or whether Paul may have been the man (cf. I Cor 15:8–10), must be left open.

53. Ps *110:1a:* that David says of the Messiah (see No. 55, and note 79, below), "Yahweh saith unto *my Lord* . . .," implies the latter's deity; see Mt 22:44–45, etc. Fulfillment (per. 13): the divine nature of the Christ; cf. Zech 12:10d.

54. Ps 110:3 (1 v., fig.): David's prediction to the Messiah, "Thy people offer themselves willingly in the day of Thine army [ASVmg]. . . . Out of the womb of the morning Thou hast the dew of Thy youth." Concerning this figure Delitzsch suggests, "The host of young men is likened to the dew both on account of its vigorousness and its multitude . . . and on account of the silent concealment out of which it wondrously and suddenly comes to light."[78] Fulfillment (per. 15): the spirit of Christian youth who volunteer for the climactic campaign of Armageddon (Num 24:17c); cf. the 144,000 of Rev 7:4–8, 14:1–5, "who have not been defiled with women, for they are celibates, . . . who follow the Lamb wherever He goes" (14:4).

55. Ps 110:4a (1 v.): an oracle spoken to the Messiah,[79] "Yahweh hath sworn [cf. Heb 7:21–22] . . . Thou art a priest . . . after the manner [ASVmg] of Melchizedek"; see Gen 14:18b for this same prophecy, earlier revealed in the objective form of a type. Fulfillment (per. 13): Christ's non-Levitical priesthood, yet more perfect than what had been provided under the Aaronic priests, Heb 7:11.

56. Ps *110:6b:* "He will strike through the head over a wide land," ASVmg. Fulfillment (per. 15): our Lord's victory over the Antichrist at

78. III:191.

79. Concerning the One addressed, O. S. Stearns observes in his *Syllabus of the Messianic Passages in the OT*, p. 34, "How of David could it be said, 'Thou art a priest forever after the order of Melchizedek'? David never was and never could be. . . . Apply the Psalm to Abraham, or Hezekiah, or Zerubbabel . . . and the prophecy becomes ridiculous. In the Asmonean Dynasty we have priesthood donning royalty, but not royalty donning the priesthood, nor could it claim descent from Melchizedek. If the critics cannot verify the person thus limned by the Psalmist, as being in himself both King and Priest, may it not be that our Lord was truthful and minutely accurate when he confounded the scribes by asserting that the Messiah was both David's seed and David's Lord?" Cf. Barrows, op. cit., p. 620, to the same effect.

Armageddon; see No. 54 and 55, preceding. The *wide land* might refer to the battlefield, but more probably to the territories of the enemy leader; cf. Dan 7:8a and 11b, on the Antichrist.

57. Ps 132:8b (1 v., typ.): the ark of the testament. Fulfillment (per. 13): as in Ex. No. 56.

58. Ps 132:11, 17 (2 vv.): that David would have an heir upon his throne. Fulfillment (per. 6): Solomon, as in II Sam. No. 9 (7:11–12).

59. Ps 132:16 (1 v., typ.): "Her priests also will I clothe with salvation"; cf. I Chron 6:41b. Fulfillment (per. 13): the priests, types of Christ, as in Ex. No. 59.

PROVERBS

As a class, the volumes of OT wisdom literature—Proverbs and Ecclesiastes, with which may also be included Job[1]—are less occupied with forecasts of the future than are the books which are found in any other major category of Scripture. None exceeds 3% in prophetic content. Proverbs in particular, with its four prophecies, which involve only 7 out of its 915 total verses (or .8%), ranks second only to Esther (among the Biblical books that contain any predictions at all) as being the least prophetic volume in holy writ. Except, indeed, for its three prophecies that are typical in nature, Proverbs contains but a single, one-verse prediction: 16:6, with its reference to atonement, which even so only indirectly suggests the redemptive work of Christ.

The authorship, or at least the compilation,[2] of Proverbs 1–24 is attributed by Scripture itself to King Solomon (1:1 and 10:1, with 22:17 seemingly referring to the same author), whose reign over Israel may be dated from 970 to 930 B.C.; and while chs. 25–29 were "copied out" some three centuries later by the men of Hezekiah, these also are said to have had their individual beginnings in the wise son of David (25:1); cf. I K 4:32–34 on his fame as a writer of wisdom literature.[3] The purpose of the king's book is one of the most articulately stated in Scripture (cf. John 20:31 in the NT): "That thy trust may be in Yahweh, I have made known to thee this day . . . excellent things of counsels and knowledge, to make thee know the certainty of the words of truth" (22:19–21, a key passage for the Book of Proverbs). But this certainty is conveyed more through

1. See above, introduction to Job.
2. See below, the introduction to Ecclesiastes.
3. While the Solomonic composition for Prov 1–29 is regularly denied by the proponents of higher criticism, there appears to be no sound basis for departing from the explicit teaching of Scripture in regard to the book's authorship; cf. Gleason L. Archer, *A Survey of OT Introduction*, pp. 452–457.

King Solomon's discursive introduction on practical wisdom (chs. 1–9) and through the proverbial maxims that make up the body of the book (chs. 10–31) than through the threats and promises that characterize Biblical prediction. Chs. 1:20–33 and 8:22–36 describe Wisdom as such an objectively existing and divine Person that they effectively portray Christ, "the Wisdom of God" (I Cor 1:24); and compare 8:25–31 with John 1:1–3 and 8:35 with John 1:4.[4] But these passages too remain more contemporaneously descriptive than predictive. The literary maxims are grouped into four Solomonic collections: 10–22:16, 22:17–24:22, 24:23–34, and chs. 25–29. The concluding two chapters, 30–31, are inspired compositions by the otherwise unknown authors, Agur son of Jakeh and King Lemuel, who may have been Edomites or other, wise "sons of the east" (I K 4:30), similar in status to Job.[5]

1. Prov 7:14, 17:1 (2 vv., typ.): peace offerings. In 17:1, "a house full of *feasting,* with strife," the central noun is *zévah,* lit., "the sacrifices of strife,"ASVmg. Fulfillment (pers. 13 and 16): as in Lev. prophecy No. 5.

2. Prov 14:9 (1 v., typ.): trespass offering. Fulfillment (per. 13): as in Lev. No. 7.

3. Prov 15:8; 21:3, 27 (3 vv., typ.): sacrifice. Fulfillment (per. 13): as in Lev. No. 2.

4. Prov 16:6 (1 v.): "By mercy and truth iniquity is atoned for." Delitzsch explains: "The blood in the typical offering points to the objective ground of reconciliation. . . . The Scriptures also ascribe to good works a share in the expiation of sin in a wider sense—namely, as the proofs of thankful love."[6] Fulfillment (per. 13): the death of Christ, the basis of all true atonement, as in Job No. 4; cf. Mk 10:45, Rom 3:25.

4. Especially in light of the *lógos* doctrine of the Wisd of Sol 7:22; 8:3, 13; and 9:1. Cf. also Prov 30:4, "Who hath established all the ends of the earth? What is His name, *and what is His Son's name,* if thou knowest?" and see J. B. Payne, *Theology of the Older Testament,* pp. 170–172.

5. See above, introduction to Job.

6. *Prov,* I:338.

ECCLESIASTES

The "proverbs" which form much of the content of the Biblical books of wisdom literature (Job, Prov, Eccl) arose out of human life and are not so much matters of direct composition as of Spirit-directed compilation: "pondered, and sought out, and set in order" (Eccl 12:9). The person so responsible for the Book of Ecclesiastes was "the Preacher," Heb., *Qōhéleth* (1:1–2, 12; 12:8–10); and he *claimed* to be the wise and wealthy son of

David, king in Jerusalem (1:16, 2:4–9), words which are universally admitted to be an intentional identification of the writer with Solomon.[1] Furthermore, while some conservative scholars have labelled Ecclesiastes as pseudonymous and dated the book "about the time of Malachi,"[2] others have been deeply concerned to defend its Solomonic authenticity.[3]

But while the Song of Solomon was apparently composed early in that king's experience (cf. 3:11), and the Proverbs were compiled in stages throughout his career,[4] Ecclesiastes is marked as the product of his old age (12:1), written in reflection and in a measure of disillusionment, after Solomon's later suffering under sin and divine chastening (I K 11, cf. 9:6). He may have produced it shortly before his death in 970 B.C. Its key statement, "Vanity of vanities, saith the Preacher; all is vanity" (1:2, 12:8), expresses the futility of life apart from God. But though negative, this emphasis and the other themes of the book (which do contain positive aspects: cf. 3:14, chs. 10–11, or 12:13) are still truly inspired, "given from one Shepherd," 12:11, and are particularly relevant in these days of devotion to "vain" values and of disregard toward the God of judgment, v. 14.

The predictive burden of Ecclesiastes centers on this fact of Yahweh's final judgment (No. 1, below); for while the book has much more to say about life after death—e.g. ch. 9, on the hopeless fate of those whose hearts are evil, vv. 3–4, or on the impossibility of a "second chance" for further work and reward beyond the grave, vv. 5, 10—these facts are to be classified as *generalizations* and not as forecasts with specific accomplishments in earthly history, of the sort that make up the sequence of the Bible's fulfillments.[5] Ecclesiastes possesses then only two other prophecies, both of which are typical in form. This produces a total of but 7 predictive verses out of the 222 that make up the book, or about 3%.

1. Eccl 3:17–18, 11:9, 12:14 (4 vv.): "God will judge the righteous and the wicked; for there is a time there [= *with Him*[6]] for every purpose and for every work" (3:17). Delitzsch comments, "God will judge the innocent and the guilty; it shall be done some time, though not so soon as one might wish it . . . that He may permit the distinction between the good and the bad to become manifest."[7] "God will bring every work into judgment, with every hidden thing, whether it be good, or whether it be evil" (12:14). That is to say, "The author here [in the three passages listed

1. Cf. R. H. Pfeiffer, *Introduction to the OT*, pp. 729, 731.
2. E. J. Young, *An Introduction to the OT*, p. 369.
3. Especially Gleason L. Archer, *A Survey of OT Introduction*, pp. 462–470, and "The Linguistic Evidence for the Date of Ecclesiastes," ETS B, 12 (1969), 167–181.
4. See above, introduction to Proverbs.
5. See above, pp. 36–38.
6. KD, *Song and Eccl*, p. 266.
7. Ibid., pp. 266–267.

above] postulates a final judgment, which removes the contradiction of this present time, and which must thus be in the future."[8] Fulfillment (per. 17): the final judgment; cf. Rev 20:12–15.

2. Eccl *5:1a*, 8:10 (1 v., typ.): the temple. Fulfillment (per. 13): as in Ex prophecy No. 55.

3. Eccl 5:1b, 9:2 (2 vv., typ.): sacrifice. Fulfillment (per. 13): as in Lev. No. 2.

8. Ibid., p. 401.

ISAIAH

The division of the Hebrew canon that is known as the Latter Prophets commences with Isaiah. This identification is appropriate, not simply because of the dates involved—for these messengers of God, Isaiah through Malachi, did appear in the latter part of Hebrew history, from the mid-eighth century B.C. onward—but also because of the type of message therein presented. For while the Former Prophets, Joshua to Job,[1] mainly conveyed revelations from the past, as they interpreted the will of God from His activities which were observable in the history of His people, yet the "Latter" were inspired for preaching to the present, generally with an eye to the future, as they motivated their immediate hearers through prediction, and by interpreting the will of God from His words which foretold the Lord's purposes for His people.[2] The Bible's greatest blocks of predictive material are therefore to be found in the five volumes of the major prophets, Isaiah to Daniel, and particularly in the three longest: Isaiah, Jeremiah, and Ezekiel. Among these, Isaiah stands in third place, as far as the amount of verses that forecast the future is concerned—754 out of the 1,292 that make up the book, or 59%—but it ranks first, over all the other books of Scripture, in the number of its separate predictions, which total 111. Almost one-fourth of these, or 27, the highest figure for any book in the Bible, involve figurative language; but relatively few of the predictive verses concern types—only about 3%.

Isaiah has been described as the "princely prophet." He appears as a man of rank in 8th-century Jerusalem, possessing access to both high priests (Isa 8:2; cf. II K 16:10–16) and kings (Isa 7:3; 37:2, 21). His four decades of ministry touched on the reigns of four rulers in Judah (1:1): Uzziah (who died in 739), Jotham (d. 736), Ahaz (d. 726), and Hezekiah (d. 697).[3] He could only, however, have completed the book that bears

1. See above, introductions to Joshua and Job.
2. Cf. the basic definition of the OT prophet, pp. 6–8, above.
3. For a detailed discussion of the chronological problems of this period, see the writer's article, "The Relationship of the Reign of Ahaz to the Accession of Hezekiah," BS, 126 (1969), 40–52.

his name after the year 681 (see 37:38), by which time he may have been over eighty years old. His princely quality comes most to the fore in his concern over Israel's coming king, the Messiah. The Book of Isaiah is revealed as second only to Psalms in its quantity of prediction that is directly anticipatory of Jesus Christ, both as the royal son of David (22 vv.) and as the prophetic-priestly Servant of the Lord (37 vv.). For variety and for detail in Messianic prophecy—ranging from Christ's virgin birth (7:14) and childhood (9:6) in Nazareth (11:1), across His humble (42:2–3) and yet blessed ministry (61:1–2) in Galilee (9:1), through His vicarious death and resurrection (53:8–10) for the embodying of God's redemptive testament (49:8) and for a light to the Gentiles (42:6), and down to His triumphant return (35:4) and rule (16:5, 32:1)[4]—Isaiah is truly the greatest of the prophets. Yet his oracles possess always the practical application and immediate goal of drawing Israel into a deeper faith in God (7:9, 28:16, 30:15, 37:6, 43:10, 50:10): the key passage, indeed, for his entire volume might well be found in 26:3–4, "Thou wilt keep him in perfect peace, whose mind is stayed on Thee . . . Trust ye in Yahweh for ever; for in Yahweh is an everlasting rock."

The Book of Isaiah may be organized according to the reigns of the four monarchs under whom the prophet labored. (1) Messages under Uzziah, to 739 B.C., chs. 1–5. These consist of general prophecies, with chs. 2–5 emphasizing particular aspects of the great themes that are opened up in ch. 1: e.g., Israel's rebellion against her God (1:2) and the ensuing judgment (vv. 5, 7), survival for a remnant (v. 8), an appeal to faith and repentance (vv. 16–18), and the hope of restoration (vv. 19, 26).[5]

(2) Messages under Jotham's brief reign as sole monarch (cf. II K 15:5), to 736, ch. 6. Though often treated as the "call" of Isaiah,[6] the experience that this chapter recounts seems to have been conditioned by, and preceded by, the death of the good king Uzziah (6:1; cf. Isaiah's evident regard for him, as indicated by his composition of Uzziah's biography, II Chron 26:22), under whose rule Isaiah had already ministered for some time. It may thus be better considered as a recommissioning.[7]

(3) Messages under the weakling Ahaz, chs. 7–12, whose death in 726 B.C. apparently occurred in the same ancient calendar year as that of the Assyrian monarch Tiglath-pileser III (14:28–29). To this latter conqueror, Ahaz had deliberately submitted himself (II K 16:7–8) despite stern warnings from Isaiah (Isa 7:4–9, 17), and at such cost that his actual reign appears to have been terminated in 728, two years before his final demise.[8] It is, indeed, the shadow of Assyria that constitutes a persistent background to the remainder of Isaiah's prophecies.

4. See below, Summary C, pp. 665–670.
5. Cf. Gleason L. Archer, in C. F. H. Henry, ed., *The Biblical Expositor,* II:124.
6. E. J. Young, NIC, Isa, I:232–233; cf. *The Study of OT Theology Today,* p. 46.
7. J. A. Alexander, *Commentary on the Prophecies of Isaiah,* I:145.
8. Cf. Payne, loc. cit.

(4) Messages under Hezekiah, up to his death in 697, chs. 13–66. These oracles make up the bulk of the prophet's writing and may, in turn, be divided into three groups. (a) Words of warning against any attempted revolt from Assyrian domination, chs. 13–35, as Isaiah appealed to Hezekiah for trust in Yahweh, rather than in vain plots that sought aid from Egypt (20:6, 30:1–3; cf. 36:6, 37:9) or in frantic preparations of defense (22:9–11). His prophecies are organized into two major cycles, chs. 13–23 and chs. 28–33, each terminating with apocalyptic visions[9] of hope, chs. 24–27 and 34–35.[10] The first, eleven-chaptered group belongs basically to the period from 728 up to the advance of Sargon II of Assyria against the Philistine city of Ashdod in 711 (20:1; cf. 18:1)[11] and is composed of oracles directed against nine foreign nations[12] and against a foreign spirit which was appearing in Judah as well (ch. 22). Isaiah's "little apocalypse" consists then of a sweep through history that moves onward to God's eschatological kingdom and final judgment (ch. 24); and this is followed by elaborations on Yahweh's triumph over the wicked (25:1–5), on the hope of the righteous (25:6–12), and on their songs of victory through heaven's King (26–27). The second cycle carries on generally from 711 B.C. and down to the climactic advance of Sennacherib in 701.[13] The second cycle is one of the most involved, and least appreciated, sections in the whole of Isaiah; but it is composed essentially of alternating predictions of the advance of this Assyrian; of the destruction of his host at the hands not of men but of the Angel of Yahweh (31:8; cf. 37:36); and of the contemporary or short-range effect that God's miraculous deliverance would have upon Judah. Also interspersed are certain nonpredictive messages made up of the prophet's preaching against sin and his appeals for faith in God (see above, p. 34). These, together with two other predictive sections, one short-range (28:1–6) and one long-range (32:1–5)[14] are indicated in Table 5.[15] The second apocalyptic finale then also embraces a section on contemporary Edom (34:5–17), which amplifies the brief

9. See above, pp. 85–89.
10. KD, II:66–68, "These two chapters stand in precisely the same relation to chs. 28–33 as chs. 24–27 to chs. 13–23. In both instances the special prophecies connected with the history of the prophet's own times are followed by a comprehensive finale of an apocalyptic character. . . . We are transported directly into the midst of the last things."
11. An exception appears in 17:1–3, prior to the fall of Damascus to Assyria in 732.
12. See below, Summary B, pp. 660–664, on prophecies concerning the nations.
13. Though the opening passage, 28:1–6, must precede an earlier attack by the Assyrian Shalmaneser V. It predicts the fall of Samaria to this conqueror in 722 (vv. 1–4) and a subsequent repentance on the part of the Samarian remnant (vv. 5–6); see prophecies No. 27 and No. 55, below.
14. An eschatological prediction of the reign of the Messiah; see prophecies No. 15 and No. 38, below.
15. See Payne, "The Effect of Sennacherib's Anticipated Destruction in Isaianic Prophecy," WTJ, 34 (1971), 22–38.

TABLE 5
Prediction in Isaiah 28-33

	Isa 28:	29:	30:	31:	32:	33:
Prediction of:	(1-6)				(1-5)	
Sennacherib's advance	11-13, 17-29	1-4, 14	1-7, 13-14, 16b-17	1-3	9-14	7-9
The destruction of Sennacherib	–	5-8, 17	27-28, 30-33	4-5, 8-9	19	1-4, 10-12, 18-19, 23
Its effect on Judah	–	18-24	18-26, 29	7	15-18, 20	5-6, 13-14, 17, 20-22, 24
Preaching:						
Against sin	7-10, 14-15	9-13, 15-16	8-12, 16a	–	6-7	–
For faith and righteousness	16	–	15	6	8	15-16

notice which this nation had received as the seventh group in Isaih's preceding cycle (21:11–12).

(b) Words of encouragement (and censure), chs. 36–39, delivered to Hezekiah in connection with two historical narratives on the Assyrian threat. The opening pair of chapters describe the actual attack of Sennacherib in 701 B.C., during which Isaiah reversed his former counsel of submission to Assyria into a ringing declaration for resistance. Yet this paradox becomes understandable in the light of the prophet's fundamental appeal for faith in Yahweh: when the Assyrian "axe" turned from its God-given task of chastising Israel (10:5), treacherously broke its covenant with Hezekiah after his surrender (33:8; cf. II K 18:14–17), and blasphemously boasted itself against Him who had been wielding it (Isa 10:7–15; 36:7, 15, 8–20)—and when Hezekiah repented of his past intrigues and humbly sought the God of his fathers (37:1–4, 14–20)—then Isaiah could fearlessly proclaim the inviolability of Zion (vv. 6–7, 33–35).[16] Chs. 38–39 belong chronologically one decade prior to chs. 36–37 (see 38:6); they date presumably to the time of certain plots against Sargon of Assyria by Merodach-baladan (Marduk-pal-iddina) of Babylon in 712.[17] But prophetic reasoning underlies this unexpected arrangement: on the one hand, Isaiah's prediction of Babylonian exile in 39:7 becomes introductory to such passages as 43:5–6, 14, 44:28–45:5, which follow; and on the other hand Hezekiah's anticipation in 39:8 of peace

16. Payne, *Theology of the Older Testament*, pp 112–113.
17. 15 years before the termination of Hezekiah's 29-year reign in 697 (38:5), which apparently accounts for the date in the 14th year of this king that is prefixed to the whole section, in 36:1.

in his own time (cf. 33:6) is immediately introductory to Isaiah's sermons of comfort in 40:1–2 ff.[18]

(c) Words of consolation for Judah, after having been ravaged by Sennacherib previous to his retreat (cf. 36:1), chs. 40–66, which God's servant shared with Hezekiah and his people following 701 B.C. One of the most "assured results of modern criticism" is that these closing Isaianic chapters cannot constitute authentic oracles of the princely prophet but must stem rather from a so-called Deutero-Isaiah, or "the great unknown," some century and a half in the future. Because of its prediction, by name, of King Cyrus of Persia in 44:28 and 45:1, many critics see no alternative but to date this writing subsequent to 550 B.C. Yet the NT is explicit in its assignment of both halves of the book to the one man Isaiah, who "saw His [Christ's] glory and spoke of Him," John 12:37–41; and the arguments ordinary adduced from the OT in support of a Deutero-Isaiah appear to be essentially unsound. The purported Babylonian and exilic background for chs. 40–66[19] remains far from demonstrable. To be specific, the 527 verses that make up Isaiah's 27 concluding chapters may be divided between 185 vv. of theological teaching and 342 vv. of concrete illustration. The former exhibit a direct development out of the doctrines that were taught in the earlier chapters of the prophecy and that received a particular, historical stress both by King Hezekiah and by Isaiah during the crisis of 701: doctrines of monotheism (37:16, cf. 2:11) and of divine spirituality (37:19; cf. 2:8), omniscience (37:26; cf. 7:8) and omnipotence (37:26; cf. 10:6). These then constitute the recurrent theological themes of chs. 40–66; respectively, the uniqueness of Yahweh (40:18, 25 etc.), the futility of idols (40:19–20 etc.), prediction as an attribute only of deity (40:13–14 etc.), and Yahweh's sovereignty over history (40:15, 22 etc.). The concrete data of Isaiah's later chapters, moreover, are found to be remarkably un-Mesopotamian in character. Only 32 out of the 342 illustrative verses of 40–66 are found to concern the days of Cyrus and of Israel's return from its Babylonian captivity. But they may be compared with 37 vv. of illustration drawn from previous Hebrew history, with 115 vv. from the contemporary scene of Assyrian defeat (e.g. 40:2, 52:4), and with 158 vv. from events still in the (NT) future. Furthermore, 141 vv. from the last 27 chapters stand in direct opposition to the theory of Babylonian origin: they describe the cities of Judah as inhabited (40:9, 41:27, 61:3), the offering up of sacrifices upon the altar of the Jerusalem temple (43:23,

18. See Payne, "The Unity of Isaiah: Evidence from Chapters 36–39," ETS B, 6 (1963), 50–56.

19. E.g., C. T. Francisco, *Introducing the OT*, p. 118: "Both sides agree that the prophetical voice in chapters 40–66 speaks from the point of view of the Exile. Does this voice proceed from a flesh-and-blood prophet who himself has experienced the misfortunes of banishment from the homeland or from the eighth-century Isaiah as a work of imagination? The analogy of other prophecies would indicate that it is an actual prophet speaking to an audience of contemporaries."

62:6–9, 66:3), and a number of other related matters,[20] to such an extent that most truly modern critics now feel compelled to posit a Trito-Isaiah, in postexilic days, to account for these Palestinian phenomena. So in the study that follows, those few Babylonian items that do appear will be treated without apology as authentic predictions of the 8th-century Isaiah.

Among the prophecies of this last section that receive NT fulfillment, there are four that possess a particular, indeed an almost unique, significance. The opening verses contain Isaiah's announcement of John the Baptist, "the voice of one that crieth in the wilderness," as the Messianic forerunner, 40:3–5.

Two chapters later begins the first of Isaiah's five "Servant Songs," 42:1–7, 49:1–9, 50:4–9, 52:13–ch. 53, and 61:1–3,[21] compositions that make up the greatest single unit in all of Scripture on the Suffering Messiah and on His death as a vicariously atoning sacrifice for the justification of many. In contradistinction from Isaiah's usual definition of "the servant [in chs. 41–53; cf. 41:8, 44:1–2] or servants [in chs. 54–66; cf. 65:13–14] of Yahweh" as either the Israelite nation in its entirety or as some pious remnant taken from the larger body—but which is still collective in nature, e.g., that select group of Israel's prophetic messengers, 44:26—his five "songs" refer at only one point to the nation as God's servant (49:3). This passage then immediately notes the failure of the collective group to achieve the requisite purposes of the Lord's righteous servant (49:4; cf. 42:19, 43:22, 25) and proceeds to describe One individual who restores the rest and in whom the concept of the remnant is ultimately realized (49:5–6). Yet it is equally clear that no one person from Israel's history, whether past, present,[22] or immediately future, is able to satisfy such qualifications as the sinlessness, resurrected life, and eventual triumph that distinguish the Servant of Yahweh. A crucial question that yet remains to be answered concerns whether the Sufferer in Isaiah's five Servant Songs is to be identified with the Davidic Messiah. At the outset, both figures are seen to be characterized as divinely chosen and uniquely righteous (42:1, 6; cf. Ps 89:3–4, Isa 9:7, Jer 23:5). The Davidic Messiah is, moreover, described as a "witness to the peoples" (Isa 55:4), a function which is identical with that of the Servant, who is to be "a light to the Gentiles" (49:6). The Messianic king is also called a *nāghîdh*, "prince" (55:4), which is the

20. For a more complete analysis, see Payne, "Eighth Century Israelitish Background of Isaiah 40–66," WTJ, 30 (1968), 195–203.

21. The first 2 songs are often limited to 42:1–4 and 49:1–6, and the 5th is generally rejected entirely by liberal writers, as being the work of a separate author, the Trito-Isaiah; but cf. O. T. Allis, *The Unity of Isaiah*, p. 82, and H. H. Rowley, *The Servant of the Lord and Other Essays*, p. 6. L. H. Hough would include 50:10–11 in the 3rd song, ISBE, IV:2740.

22. Including the prophet himself, as in Acts 8:34; for note the "we" of the writer, which is contrasted with the Servant in 53:2–6, and also the inappropriateness of passages such as 42:1 when applied to Isaiah.

very term used by Daniel to describe the *priestly* Messiah (Dan 9:25–26). Again, the same Holy Spirit who is to rest upon the Davidic "Branch," so that He may decide with equity for the meek of the earth (Isa 11:1–4), rests upon the Servant, that He may bring forth justice to the Gentiles (42:1). The humiliation of the Messiah at His first coming (7:15; cf. Zech 9:9, 13:7) is closely paralleled by the unpretentiousness of the Servant (53:1, 42:3).[23] Most significant, however, is the final exaltation that is to be experienced by the righteous Sufferer: "Him whom man despiseth . . . a servant of rulers, kings shall see and arise; princes, and they shall worship" (49:7 and cf. v. 5); "kings shall shut their mouths because of Him" (52:15); and, "Therefore will I divide Him a portion with the great" (53:12).[24] Isaiah even says, in so many words, that the Servant is *anointed*, 61:1.[25] He and the Messiah must be one and the same. Zechariah correspondingly associates the Messianic Branch with the priestly function of removing men's iniquity (Zech 3:8–9); and he specifically equates the two offices in his phrase, "My Servant the Branch" (v. 8).[26] Christ Himself provides the final answer to this question by revealing His identity both as the Messiah (John 4:25–26, cf. 1:41) and as the Suffering Servant of Isa 53:12 (Lk 22:37; cf. Acts 8:35).[27] On the seven-staged development of our Lord's work as the Servant, see below under 42:1a.

Following the fourth and greatest of the Servant Songs, Isaiah moves forthwith into his presentation of a remarkable description of the church that results: enlarged in its outreach and more numerous in its offspring than Yahweh's spouse in the Israel of old, 54:1–9 (cf. Gal 4:27). The universalism, moreover, that had marked the prophet's thinking prior to 701 (as in 19:23–25) develops into a series of major predictions of Gentile incorporation into the spiritual Israel which is the church, 42:6, 44:5, 55:5, 65:1; cf. 56:3 (contemporaneous OT) and 60:3–4 (millennial).

Finally, near the conclusion of the book, come some of the OT's most significant foregleams of the ultimate New Jerusalem (54:9–13, 60:19–22, 65:17–19, 66:22; see under 24:23b), which is to appear after God's final judgment.

1. Isa 1:11a, 13a; *19:19a, 21a*; 43:24; 66:3 (4 vv., typ.): sacrifice. Fulfillment (per. 13): as in Lev. prophecy No. 2.

23. Cf. H. Ringgren, who identifies the Messiah and the Servant on this basis, *The Messiah in the OT*, pp. 65–67.
24. S. Mowinckel thus concludes: "The Servant displaces the king and himself becomes king," *He That Cometh*, p. 256.
25. Cf. the Qumran Isaiah-A reading of Isa 52:14, "I have anointed His visage more than any man." F. F. Bruce adds that Daniel's triumphant Son of man (7:13) seems to have been intentionally patterned on the Messianic Servant of Isaiah, *Biblical Exegesis in the Qumran Texts*, pp. 58, 91.
26. Zechariah further identifies the deity who is pierced (12:10) with the deity who will yet descend upon the Mount of Olives to reign (14:4).
27. Payne, *Theology*, pp. 279–280.

2. Isa *1:11b*, 43:23a, *56:7b* (1 v., typ.): burnt offering. Fulfillment (per. 13): as in Lev. No. 3.

3. Isa 1:12; 6:1; 8:18; 37:1, 14 and 38:20, *22b* (II K 19:1, 14 and *20:5b, 8b*); *44:28b*; 56:5, 7a; 62:9; 64:11;²⁸ 66:1, 6, *20c* (12 vv., typ.): temple. Fulfillment (per. 13): as in Ex. No. 55.

4. Isa *1:13b*; 56:2, *4a, 6a*; 58:13 (2 vv., typ.): sabbath. Fulfillment (per. 13): as in Ex. No. 41.

5. Isa 1:20, 24–25, 28–31; 2:10–21; 5:5–6, 9–10, 13b–17, 24; 6:11–13a; 7:16b; 8:14–15;²⁹ 10:22b–23; 24:1–12; 27:10–11 (51 vv., fig.): after describing what Judah has already suffered for her sins, 1:5–9,³⁰ Isaiah employs a series of figures to predict what shall yet be: "If ye refuse and rebel, ye shall be devoured with the sword [1:20] . . . shall burn and none shall quench [v. 31] . . . I will thoroughly purge away thy dross [v. 25]." He foretells that all that is proud and haughty is to be brought low, 2:12, including every fortified wall, v. 15, the great ships capable of going to Tarshish, v. 16, "and the idols shall utterly pass away," v. 18. Jerusalem and Judah are to suffer from famine and death, 5:13–14, and ultimately experience either occupation by aliens, 5:17, or uninhabited desolation, 5:9, 6:11, as Yahweh makes "a full end," 10:23—7:16, "The land . . . shall be forsaken of both her kings," N. Israel in 722 (see 7:8b, No. 22, below) and S. Judah in 586;³¹ 24:1, "Yahweh maketh the land [ASVmg]³² empty"; and 27:10, "The fortified city [Jerusalem: "formed" of God, but "a people of no understanding," v. 11; cf. 1:3–4] is solitary." Fulfillment (per. 7): as in Lev. No. 33, the destruction of Judah in 586 B.C., and not simply the attack of Sennacherib in 701 (No. 18, below); cf. the above-noted magnitude of the doom, which would include even Jerusalem.³³

28. But in 63:18, *miqdāsh* (cf. Num 18:29), seems to refer to the *Holy Land* (Zech 2:12, Ps 78:54) rather than to the specific *sanctuary*; cf. Payne, WTJ, 30 (1968), 192.

29. In 8:14, Yahweh's being a "stone of stumbling" to the two houses of Israel is repeated in Rom 9:33; cf. I Pet 2:8, as true of Christ in His day, "just as it is written" in Isaiah, but without thereby claiming this verse to have been intentionally predictive of Him.

30. NIC, I:53.

31. Following KJV, rather than ASV's reading, "the land whose two kings thou abhorrest shall be forsaken." For then the two rulers would be Rezin and Pekah (7:1, 8–9); but this: (1) presumes that v. 16 is designed to be of comfort to Ahaz, when the context is rather one of threat (vv. 13–15, 17–25); (2) forces *the land* (sing.) to refer unnaturally to Syria and N. Israel, cf. rather 8:14, "the two houses of Israel"; and (3) shifts the meaning of *qūs*, as found previously in this context (7:6), ASV, "and vex it," from KB's meaning II, Hiphil, "tear asunder," to KB I, "feel a loathing at," pp. 833–834. It would appear better to read with Henderson, "the land which thou *destroyest* [see 7:9b, No. 23, below] shall be forsaken of both its kings," quoted by Alexander, op. cit., I:174. Contrast NIC, I:293.

32. *hā-āres*, which ASV text renders as "the earth"; see above, pp. 112, 117. But compare the local, Israelitish tone of 24:5, "they have broken the covenant." Probably v. 4 also, "The world, *tēvēl*, languisheth," should be understood with Alexander, I:405, as a poetical description for Palestine.

33. See above, pp. 110–111.

6. Isa 1:26–27 (2 vv.): "I will restore thy [Jerusalem's, vv. 8, 21, 27] judges as at the first . . . afterward thou shalt be called a faithful town. Zion shall be redeemed with God's justice." Fulfillment (per. 9): the restoration of Jerusalem under such faithful leaders as Sheshbazzar and Zerubbabel, 538–515; Ezra 1:8, 11, 3:2–3, 5:2, 14–16. Postexilic times, "after the Babylonian captivity,"[34] are indicated, because the accomplishment is to follow the destruction of Judah's sinners, Isa 1:28, and to be marked by the cessation of the land's current idolatry, v. 29.[35]

7. Isa 2:2a (Mi 4:1a) (1 v.): "The mountain of Yahweh's house shall be established . . . above the hills"; cf. similar changes in topography that are foretold in Zech 14:4b and 10 (Zech. prophecies No. 70 and No. 75). So despite the various allegorizing interpretations that have been proposed by both liberals[36] and and conservatives[37] for this "exalting" of Zion, the Biblical teaching appears to be one of "miraculous geological changes."[38] Fulfillment "in the latter days" (per. 16): "physical changes,"[39] so that the temple area of Mount Moriah is elevated above its surroundings.

8. Isa *2:2b, 3b* (Mi *4:1b, 2b*); 60:7, 13 (2 vv., typ.): the presence of a "house of Yahweh" in the latter days (see No. 7, preceding), 2:2; "the house of My glory," 60:7, glorious in its cedar construction, v. 13. It has an altar, v. 7, where flocks are offered, for praise, v. 6. For defenders of the reality of this eschatological altar are careful to insist that "the millennial sacrifices *will have no relation to the question of expiation* [Italics theirs] . . . the sacrifices *will be memorial in character.*"[40] Fulfillment (per. 16): Jerusalem's millennial temple and system of sacrifice, a symbol of Christ's presence (see 4:5, No. 16, below), because the continuing existence of subdued but still unregenerate men will require a certain degree of sacramentalism, of outward signs and seals of truths that will be visible enough, but that will not have been wholly integrated into all of the elements of society.[41] Yet the millennial sanctuary will still be a type of that unimpaired fellowship with God in the templeless New Jerusalem, Rev 21:22; see above, p. 136.

9. Isa *2:2c*–3a (Mi 4:*1c*–2a); 11:10; 59:19a (3 vv., fig.): all nations are to "flow," like rivers, to God's house for instruction, declaring, "We will walk in His paths." Fulfillment (per. 16): a universal seeking for God's law, as in Gen. No. 47 (22:18b) and Ps. No. 21 (22:27).

10. Isa *2:3c* (Mi *4:2c*): the declaration of many peoples that from Mount Zion, and specifically out of Yahweh's temple (see No. 8, above),

---

34. H. C. Leupold, *Exposition of Isaiah*, I:71.
35. See above, p. 111.
36. ICC, *Mi*, p. 86.
37. KD, *Minor Prophets*, I:456; NIC, *Isa*, I:99–102.
38. IB, VI:922.
39. Camb, *Mi*, p. 35.
40. J. Dwight Pentecost, *Things to Come*, pp. 524–525; see above, pp. 108, 115.
41. Payne, *Theology*, p. 495.

"the God of Jacob . . . will teach us of His ways." Fulfillment (per. 16): universal teaching of divine truth in the future Messianic kingdom.

11. Isa 2:4a (Mi 4:3a); 9:7a; 25:3; 27:5; 45:23–24; 49:7b; 51:5b; 52:13, 15b; 53:12a; 55:4; 66:18 (11 vv.): on the Messiah's reign, "He will judge between the nations" (2:4); and there will be no end to the increase of His rule (9:7). The future representative of David (see above, p. 84) is to be "a witness to the peoples" (which associates Him with the mission of the Servant of Yahweh, cf. 43:10), but also "a leader and commander" to them (55:4); 25:3 foresees the time when "a strong people shall glorify Thee," cf. 27:5; and 49:7 proclaims, "Kings shall see and arise, and worship" the Lord's righteous Servant (cf. 51:5). Yahweh insists, "I will gather all nations and tongues; and they shall come, and see My glory" (66:18); and "unto Me every knee shall bow" (45:23). Fulfiillment (per 16): as in Gen. No. 68, God's millennial rule.

12. Isa 2:4b (Mi 4:3b); 9:5, 7b; 11:13; 14:3; 26:12; 54:14; 60:18 (7 vv., fig.): "They shall beat their swords into plowshares," 2:4; cf. a corresponding figure in 9:5, relating to the displacement of soldiers' garments. 11:13 foresees a sincere peace between Judah and Ephraim, so hostile in Isiaiah's own day (7:1); and 14:3 speaks of Judah's eschatological security, after her previous suffering under oppression. Fulfillment (per. 16): as in Lev. No. 29, millennial peace, when men "shall not learn war any more."

13. Isa 3:1–8, 16–26; 4:1 (20 vv.): "Yahweh of hosts doth take away from Jerusalem: bread, water, the mighty man . . . and I will give children to be their princes . . . and the people shall be oppressed, every one by another" (3:1–5), with a universal lack of food and clothing (vv. 6–7). Haughty women of the nobility are to be humiliated (v. 17) and the men slain (v. 25), so that many more women will be seeking marriage than there will be husbands available (4:1). Fulfillment (per. 7): the siege and collapse of Jerusalem in 597 B.C. and the captivity of its upper classes. As Leupold remarks, "Historically one is reminded of the course followed by Nebuchadnezzar, when, as II K 24:14 . . . reports, all qualified leadership was taken away from the city in the first deportation."[42] King Jehoiachin (age 18) was exiled; and though Zedekiah (then aged 21) was left on the throne, he was a weakling, Jer 38:5, 19—despite his good intentions, e.g. toward Jeremiah, v. 16, worthless counselors prevailed over him, v. 22.

14. Isa 4:2, 61:4, 62:3–7 (7 vv.): in 4:2 Isaiah predicted, "In that day [of the future Messianic kingdom; cf. vv. 3–6, No. 15–16, following] shall the branch of Yahweh be beautiful and glorious, and the fruit of the land shall be excellent." The *branch* at this point would not appear to be the Messiah, as in 11:1 (No. 39, below); but the parallelism of the second line favors a literal agricultural increase. In 61:4 the propet speaks, corre-

42. Op. cit., I:89.

spondingly, of eschatological times in which "they shall repair the waste cities"; and, in 62:4–5, "Thou shalt be called Hephzi-bah, *My delight* [is] *in her,* and thy land Beulah, *married*; for the land shall be married . . . thy sons shall marry thee." Zion, in other words, "may be said to be married to its sons who cherish and protect the land."[43] Fulfillment (per. 16): as in Ex. No. 49, millennial prosperity.

15. Isa 4:3–4, 32:*1b*–5 (6 vv.): in the Messianic kingdom, "he that remaineth in Jerusalem shall be called holy, even every one that is written among the living [ASVmg, *written unto life*]," 4:3. "Princes shall rule in justice. And a man [each one, not just the Messiah[44]] shall be . . . as the shade of a great rock in a weary land," 32:1–2. "The ears of them that hear shall hearken . . . and the tongue of the stammerers shall be ready to speak plainly [or, *advisedly*[45]]. The fool shall no more be called noble," vv. 3–5. Fulfillment (per. 16): as in Dt. No. 45, millennial holiness, for those written in God's book of life (Ex 32:32, Ps 69:28), when purged by God's "Spirit of justice and burning," Isa 4:4.

16. Isa 4:5–6 (2 vv.): "Yahweh will create over the whole habitation of mount Zion," not just over the temple, the pillar of cloud and fire, as in His OT tabernacle and temple; and also "a covering," for the specific protecting of the holy assemblies from heat and rain. Fulfillment (per. 16): the return of the glory cloud of God's presence,[46] the Shekinah, to the future city of Jerusalem, though still with "a canopy . . . over all the glory."[47] The latter is stated to be for shelter, but perhaps also for the withholding of His Person from more general view (cf. No. 8, above, on the need for millennial sacramentalism, and I K 8:10–13).

17. Isa *5:13a*, 24:13, 39:6–7 (II K 20:17–18), (3vv.): "My people are gone [= will go] into captivity" (5:13); they are to be "among the peoples, as gleanings" (24:13). Specifically, all the royal treasure of Judah is to be carried to Babylon; and Hezekiah's descendants are to be eunuchs [KB, p. 688, "court-officials"] in the palace of the king of Babylon" (39:6–7). Fulfillment (per. 8): as in Lev. No. 34 (26:33). Both the people and the treasures were so taken, Dan 1:2–3, II K 24:13–14; 25:9, 11, 13–15; and Dan 1:3 notes as being present in the palace "certain of the seed royal and of the nobles"; cf. II K 25:28–29 on the young king Jehoiachin's being eventually honored in the Babylonian court.

18. Isa 5:26–30; 7:17–18; 8:7–8; 10:5–6, 15; 28:11–13, 17–22; 29:1–3, 14–15; 30:1–5a, 13–14, 16–*17a*; 31:1–3; 41:26–27 (39 vv., fig.): God "will lift up an ensign to the nations from far . . . and they shall roar against them in that day like the roaring of the sea" (5:26–30).

43. BBC, IV:264; NIC, III:469.
44. See 9:7c, 32:1a (No. 35, below), on the righteousness of the Messiah's own reign.
45. BBC, IV:135.
46. Cf. its departure, in Ezek 10:18–19, 11:22–23.
47. NIC, I:186.

Leupold identifies the *nations* as Assyrians: "It is true that they are not mentioned by name in this passage. But in the light of 7:18 and especially 10:5 ff. it seems likely that no other enemy could be meant."[48] Two other figures occur in 7:18 and 8:7a, "Yahweh will hiss for . . . the bee that is in the land of Assyria," and "the Lord bringeth up upon them the waters of the River [Euphrates]," which are explained in 7:17, 20 and 8:7b as meaning the king of Assyria brought against Judah. Vv. 5 and 15 of chapter 10 further identify Assyria as God's "axe"; and 28:11 predicts that "by men of strange lips and with another tongue will He speak to this people," i.e. the contemporary Assyrian scourge, vv. 15, 18, and contrast 33:19, on the removal of these "fierce people, a people of deep speech that thou canst not comprehend." Judah is to be "broken and taken," 28:13, by "a decree of destruction upon the whole land" [ASVmg, not "earth"], v. 22. V. 2 of chapter 29 foresees concerning Jerusalem that "Ariel ['the hearth of God,' ASVmg] shall be unto Me as Ariel [burning]"; as explained in v. 3, the God-inspired enemy "will lay siege against thee with posted troops." Cf. 7:19 etc. (No. 29, below) on the resulting desolation. To those who were plotting with Egypt, Isaiah threatened, "Woe unto them that hide deep their counsel," 29:15; "refuge in the shadow of Egypt . . . shall be your confusion," 30:2–3, "a people that cannot profit them," v. 5a (cf. vv. 5b–6, No. 82, below).[49] Then, after all this had become a matter of the past, 41:26–27 seems to look back upon the one whom God had "raised up from the north," who even "called upon My name" (cf. 36:7); and Isaiah reminded his people, "Who hath declared it beforetime, that we may say, He is right?"[50] Fulfillment (per. 7): the advance of Sennacherib in 701, when Assyria was able to take captive all the fortified cities of Judah (36:1) and lay siege to Jerusalem (v. 2) and when Egypt proved to be a "bruised reed," just as predicted (v. 6).

19. Isa *6:13b*, 24:14–15 (2 vv.): after speaking of Judah's ultimate fall, vv. 11–13a (see under No. 5, above), Isaiah adds an encouragement, "As an oak, whose stock remaineth when felled, so the holy seed is the stock thereof" (6:13). Again, in an exilic context (see 24:13, under No. 17, above), he states, "Glorify ye Yahweh in the east, even the name of Yahweh, the God of Israel, in the coastlands" (24:14–15, ASVmg). Fulfillment (per. 8): the existence of a pious Jewish remnant in the exile.

20. Isa 7:3, 10:20–*22a*, 14:1a, 43:5–7, 48:20, 51:14, 52:11–12 (11 vv., sym.): Isaiah's having given his son the significant name "Shear-jashub," meaning "a remnant shall return," 7:3. The Jerusalem Bible explains, "i.e. will be converted to Yahweh and thus escape punishment."[51] So in ch. 10, after noting that only a remnant would be left of Sennacherib's

48. Op. cit., I:122.
49. See above, p. 280.
50. See Payne, WTJ, 30 (1967), 51–52.
51. P. 1153.

army, v. 19, the prophet continues: "The remnant of Israel . . . shall no more again lean upon him that smote them [Assyria, vv. 13–14], but shall lean upon Yahweh, the Holy One of Israel, in truth," v. 20. But this cannot refer to the very real revival following Sennacherib's defeat in 701 (see No. 81, below), since Israel did resubmit herself to Assyria under Manasseh. "A remnant of them shall return," v. 22a; but first must come the God-determined destruction of 586, v. 22b (see under No. 5, above). In ch. 14, after foreseeing the fall of Babylon just previously (No. 47, below),[52] Isaiah predicts, "Yahweh will set them in their own land," v. 1; and he later utters two imperatives in the name of the Lord: "Bring My sons from far," 43:6, and "Go ye forth from Babylon," 48:20. Fulfillment (per. 9): as in Dt. No. 43, the return of a chastened remnant from exile.

21. Isa 7:4, 7–8a, 9a; 8:1–4, 21–22; 9:11; 17:1–3 (14 vv.): Isaiah's prophetic description of Rezin of Damascus and Pekah of N. Israel, who were attacking Ahaz of Judah in 734 B.C. (cf. II K 16:5–6), as "tails of smoking firebrands," about to be extinguished, Isa 7:4. Their projected offensive "shall not stand," v. 7. "Damascus shall be a ruinous heap," 17:1.[53] Isa 8:1 describes a symbolic action of the prophet, when he publicly wrote upon a tablet, "For Maher-shalal-hash-baz," ASVmg, "The spoil speedeth, the prey hasteth." But while "the tablet is inscribed with a name that attaches to no one,"[54] the prophet later gives this name to a newly born son of his, to underline the predictions of what Assyria is to do (cf. 10:6). 8:21–22 foretells the distress and hunger to come upon the northern territories; for it is the area of the 3½ tribes of Galilee and Transjordan who fell to Assyria in the following year (II K 15:29) that is the subject of the next verse, 9:1. Finally 9:11 identifies the Assyrians in their attack against N. Israel as "the adversaries of Rezin," the Syrian monarch.[55] Fulfillment (per. 7): both of Ahaz's enemies were broken by Tiglath-pileser III, as validated by the Assyrian's own records: Israel in 733 (see further under 7:16b, No. 27, below), and Damascus in 732, but more drastically, for it ceased as an independent state altogether.

22. Isa 7:8b: in another prophecy datable to 734, Isaiah declared, "Within 65 years shall Ephraim be broken in pieces, so that it shall not be a people." Fulfillment (per. 7): this lapse of time brings one to 669, or precisely to the end of the reign of Esarhaddon of Assyria, who did bring in the foreign colonists who converted the former Samaria into "Samaritans," Ezra 4:2; cf. II K 17:24–40.

23. Isa 7:9b, 9:12 (1 v): Isaiah's counsel to Ahaz and his associates, when they were tempted to give up reliance on God and seek Assyrian aid against the local enemies, "If ye will not believe, surely ye shall not be

---

52. Cf. Leupold, op. cit., I:253.
53. Spoken before 732; see above, introduction to Isaiah, note 11.
54. ICC, I:144.
55. NIC, I:349–350.

established," 7:9. Ahaz, however, did not believe, vv. 12–13, and he called in the Assyrians, II K 16:7; "but it helped him not," II Chron 28:21 (despite the relief mentioned it II K 16:9). For Isaiah said, "The Syrians before and the Philistines behind shall devour Israel[56] with open mouth," 9:12. Fulfillment (per. 7): the series of calamities that came upon Ahaz, II Chron 28:5–21, including both Syrian, v. 5, and Philistine attack, v. 18. Even concerning his Assyrian "allies," so called, ". . . and Tiglath-pileser king of Assyria came unto him, and distressed him, but strengthened him not," v. 20. It appears significant that the 16-year reign of Ahaz was terminated in 728 B.C. (II K 17:1, 18:1); but not by his death, which did not occur until 2 years later, Isa 14:28–29, in the same calendar year in which Tiglath-pileser died.[57]

24. Isa 7:13–14a (2 vv.): "A virgin shall conceive, and bear a son, and shall call His name Immanuel." Terry speaks of this passage as "probably the most difficult of all the Messianic prophecies."[58] The standard interpretation proposed by liberal criticism is that Isaiah here refers to the son of a contemporary young woman, not a virgin, whose child will be named Immanuel, meaning that *God is* providentially *with us,* which would thus serve as a sign of the defeat of Judah's northern enemies (7:8). The non-Messianic interpretation, however, suffers under serious difficulties. On the one hand, the term *almā,* which the RSV here renders "young woman," is never used in the OT for a married woman, as this woman apparently was, and seems to connote a virgin (RSVmg) or at least "maiden" (Prov 30:19, RSV).[59] On the other hand, the coming of Immanuel is presented in a context of threat to Ahaz and not of encouragement; see from v. 13 on through to the conclusion of the chapter (see vv. 15, 16a, 19, Nos. 26, 27, 29, below, and vv. 16b, 17, Nos. 5, 18, above). The primary non-messianic argument is that for Isaiah's words to have had relevance for Ahaz they must have had an immediate fulfillment; but, while the relevance is true, the immediacy, as demonstrated by three major contextual factors, is false. (1) The kingship was to cease in both N. and S. Israel "before" Immanuel, v. 16; and while the former (but not the latter) did fall 12 years later, in 722, the prophet's only *stated* awareness was that Ephraim would be broken from being a people in 65 years, v. 8 (No. 22, above), which was hardly immediate. (2) Immanuel was to be a "sign," v. 14; and while signs in Isaianic usage need not be miraculous (cf. 8:18, discussed under Heb 2:12), when they were offered to kings they were (cf. 38:7–8), and this

56. *Israel* here denotes Judah (cf. II Chron 28:19), even as Isa 8:7–8 had been referring to the two Hebrew kingdoms. Furthermore, as Delitzsch notes, "The northern kingdom never suffered anything from the Philistines," I:258; contrast Judah's known suffering at their hands; cf. NIC, I:350.
57. See above, introduction to Isaiah and note 3.
58. *Biblical Hermeneutics,* p. 331.
59. Cf. NIC, I:287–289; Payne, *Theology,* p. 267; and, in detail, R. D. Wilson, "The Meaning of Alma (A.V. 'Virgin') in Isaiah 7:14," PTR, 24 (1926), esp. p. 316.

child's birth was to be particularly so (cf. 9:6, under No. 25, following). Those who advocate contemporaneous fulfillment confess: "To admit the possibility of an immediate application and still to insist on 'virgin' would put one in the awkward position of holding to a virgin birth in the time of Ahaz,"[60] which of course no one does; but this too was part of the "sign," as stressed also in the NT (Mt 1:20–23).[61] (3) The prophet's threat was addressed not simply to Ahaz but to the "house of David," v. 13 (though cf. v. 2); that is, the Messiah would replace once and for all the merely human kings of Ahaz's house and character.

Fulfillment (per. 13): the Messianic king, to be born of a virgin, i.e. Mary, Mt 1:25, Lk 1:34–35, and be God incarnate (see No. 25, following). Edghill thus summarizes, that the birth "is a sign to Ahaz of Isaiah's denunciation of gloom. . . . When face to face with the weak and faithless occupant of David's throne, he realized that he could put no hope in the present . . . [in the place of Ahaz] a child should arise who, after he had suffered a little, would be the more worthy to sit on David's seat and take the government upon his shoulder."[62] Immanuel did not, indeed, appear for more than seven centuries. But this time lapse need not diminish the contemporary relevance of Isaiah's warning. On the principle of "prophetic telescoping," the prophets in their forecasts not infrequently leaped over even millennia of intervening years.[63] Actually, moreover, a threat may serve as a valid force in motivating conduct, irrespective of the interval preceding its historical fulfillment, provided only that the contemporary audience does not know when this fulfillment is to take place. Even as the Lord's second coming should motivate our faithful conduct, no matter how distant it may in fact be (cf. I Thess 5:2–6), so Isa 7:14, on His miraculous first coming, was equally valid for motivating Ahaz, 730 years before Jesus' birth.[64]

25. Isa *7:14b*, 9:6 (1 v., sym.): the virgin would "call His name Immanuel," 7:14, as Mt 1:23 adds, "which translated means, 'God with us.'" Isa 9:6 then elaborates on this same Personage:[65] "Unto us a child is born . . . and His name shall be called Wonderful counsellor,[66] Mighty God, Everlasting Father, Prince of Peace." The first title, *péle*, indicates an *extraordinary thing* or *miracle*,[67] "a phenomenon lying altogether beyond

60. Dewey M. Beegle, "Virgin or Young Woman?" *Asbury Seminarian*, 8 (1954), 34.

61. This verse constitutes primary evidence on the futility of resorting to hermeneutical theories of "double meaning" or "multiple fulfillment"; see above, pp. 121–126. The *almā* of Isa 7:14 either was a virgin or was not and cannot simultaneously predict these two opposing meanings; see above, p. 78, note 85.

62. *An Enquiry into the Evidential Value of Prophecy*, pp. 379–382.

63. See above, pp. 137–140.

64. Payne, *Theology*, p. 269.

65. NIC, I:290, 331–332.

66. ASVmg; cf. NIC, I:332–333.

67. KB, p. 760.

human conception or natural occurrence."⁶⁸ Edghill explains, "The Hebrews looked upon such 'wonderful' ability as divine. It was God who is wonderful in counsel, *hiphlī ēsā*, Isa 28:29."⁶⁹ The second title, "Mighty God," as shown by the analogy of 10:21, is a clear indication of deity;⁷⁰ and He will be eternal in His fatherhood toward His people and in making peace. Fulfillment (per. 13): as in Ps. No. 53 (110:1a), the deity of the Messiah.

26. Isa 7:15, *53:2a* (1 v., fig.): concerning the Messianic child, "Butter and honey shall He eat, when He knoweth to refuse the evil and choose the good," 7:15. The "butter and honey" serve as figures for an oppressed land: natural rather than cultivated products; cf. vv. 22–23.⁷¹ Compare 53:2, on the Messianic Servant's growing up before Yahweh "as a root out of a dry ground." Fulfillment (per. 13): the moral growth of Jesus, learning to distinguish between good and evil (cf. Lk 2:40, 52), yet in a land that was afflicted—as it worked out historically, by the Romans—and no longer ruled by the dynasty of David. A. B. Davidson makes this summary: "The house of David, now unworthy, would be cut down to the roots; but out of the root of Jesse a branch would grow—Immanuel."⁷²

27. Isa *7:16a*; *8:14a*; 9:14–17; 10:3; 17:*3a*, 4–6, 9–11; 28:1–4 (15 vv.): before the coming of Immanuel, "the land shall be forsaken of its two kings," 7:16: N. Israel for the one; cf. v. 16b (under 1:20, No. 5, above) on S. Judah for the other. 8:14 foresees a heaven-sent "stumbling to both the houses of Israel"; and "Yahweh will cut off from Israel [specifically, N. Israel, v. 21] head and tail in one day," 9:14, namely, their leaders, and also their false prophets, as identified in v. 15. 28:1–2 speaks finally of "the fading flower" of the drunkards of Ephraim before a destroying storm. Fulfillment (per. 7): as in I K. No. 25, the fall of the northern kingdom to Assyria in 722.

28. Isa *7:18a* (fig.): "Yahweh will hiss for the fly of Egypt." Fulfillment (per. 7): though not as serious to Israel as "the bee of Assyria" (v. 18b, see under 5:26, No. 18, above), Shabaka of XXVth Dynasty Egypt did advance into Palestine, although defeated by the Assyrians at Raphia in 720 and at Eltekeh in 701.

29. Isa 7:19–25, 29:4, 30:17b, 32:9–14 (15 vv., fig.): when the Assyrian hosts attack (7:17–18, see No. 18, above), "The Lord will shave with a razor . . . the head and the hair" (v. 20); and the figure is explained, vv. 21–25, as meaning that in place of cultivated fields Judah will be reduced to "briars and thorns" and pasturing. They will be humbled to the dust, 29:4; "one thousand shall flee as the threat of one, till ye be left as an

68. KD, I:252.
69. Op. cit., p. 218.
70. Edghill hesitates over "any essential or metaphysical divinity," ibid., pp. 219–223, but cf. NIC, I:335–338.
71. NIC, I:298, but opposing Young's earlier view on pp. 291–292.
72. *OT Prophecy*, pp. 363–364.

ensign on a hill," 30:17, signifying, "a tiny remnant in a wide land devastated by war";[73] cf. 36:1, on how Sennacherib swept away all the fortified cities of Judah, except Jerusalem. 32:10 predicts: "After a year and days," ASVmg—Jerusalem Bible, "Within one year and a few days," which therefore dates the prophecy to early in 702 B.C.—"ye shall be troubled; the vintage shall fail"; and v. 14 adds, "The populous city shall be deserted . . . and the watch-tower shall be for dens for ever."[74] Fulfillment (per. 7): the desolation accomplished by Sennacherib in 701, so that Judah was reduced to the eating of "that which groweth of itself," 37:30, and so that she could be said to have "received of Yahweh's hand double for all her sins," 40:2.

30. Isa 8:9–10, 53:7–*8a* (3 vv.): the nations are challenged to "make an uproar"; but their counsels will fail, for "God is with us" (8:8–10). In Hebrew, this last phrase is the name of the Messiah, *Immanuel*, as in 7:14, 8:8. In the face of such raging by the nations, 53:7–8 describes Yahweh's Messianic Servant: "As a sheep that before its shearers is dumb, so He opened not His mouth. By oppression and judgment He was taken away"—quoted in Acts 8:33; cf. of Christ's silence at His trials before both Jews and Gentiles, Mt 26:63; 27:12, 14. Fulfillment (per. 13): as in Ps. prophecy No. 2 (2:1–3),[75] the trial of Christ.

31. Isa 8:17, 59:20b (2 vv.): "I will wait for Yahweh, who hideth His face from the house of Jacob, I will look for Him," 8:17, anticipating, that is, the time when He will no longer be so removed. Alexander says this about the "I" who is here talking:

Most writers make these the words of the Prophet [Isaiah]; but since he is addressed in the verse preceding, without any intimation of a change in speaker here, and since the next verse is quoted in Heb 2:13, as the words of the Messiah, it seems better to assume that throughout this passage the Messiah is the speaker. . . . For a time the import of God's promises shall be concealed from the majority [of the Jews, even as was true then, in 734 B.C., when the Messiah and His followers, including Isaiah, were "wonders" in Israel, 8:18], and during that interval the Messiah shall wait patiently until the set time has arrived.[76]

But when the time of fulfillment arrives, specifically, 59:20, when the Redeemer comes to Zion (per. 16, and so quoted in Rom 11:26), then the veil will be removed from Jewish hearts (II Cor 3:15–16, Rom 11:23): "and thus all Israel will be saved," Rom 11:26. But Isaiah makes it clear that the restoration at Christ's coming is "unto them that turn from trans-

---

73. BBC, IV:130; cf. NIC, II:353.
74. See above, pp. 18, 113, note 233, on the relative use of the term "for ever" in this context.
75. Here cited by Leupold, op. cit., I:171.
76. Op. cit., I:192, as also Young, NIC, I:315–316.

gression in Jacob," 59:20; see Zeph 3:11b on a corresponding removal of the haughty.

32. Isa 9:1–2 (2 vv., fig.): "The people that walked in darkness have seen a great light." The *people* are Galileans, like those of Naphtali, Zebulun, and Transjordan, who were taken captive in 733, 8:21–22 (the verses just preceding; see No. 21, above), II K 15:29. Fulfillment (per. 13): the spiritual enlightenment brought about by Christ's Galilean ministry, particularly through His dwelling at Capernaum, in reference to which this verse is so quoted in Mt 4:13–16.

33. Isa 9:3 (1 v.): "Thou hast multiplied the nation, Thou hast increased [ASV, over KJV] their joy" (cf. 12:1, etc., No. 46, below, on the future joy of God's people). Fulfillment (per. 16):[77] as in Ex. No. 51, millennial multiplication.

34. Isa 9:4; 11:14; *24:21b*; 25:1–2, 4–5, 10–12; 26:5–6, 11, 21b; 27:1, 4; *61:2b*; 64:2; 66:*14b*–17 (19 vv., fig.): Israel's future triumph revealed through a figure and a comparison, "The rod of his oppressor Thou hast broken as in the day of Midian," 9:4, which refers to a particularly famous deliverance (Jd 6–8). 61:2 thus speaks of "the day of vengeance of our God"; and 66:16, "For by fire will Yahweh execute judgment, and by His sword, upon all flesh; and the slain of Yahweh shall be many"; cf. 26:11, "Fire shall devour Thine adversaries," or 25:2, 5, "Thou hast made a fortified city a ruin [cf. 26:5–6] . . . the song of the terrible ones shall be brought low." As to the nature of the adversaries, 27:1 reads, "In that day Yahweh will punish Leviathan," the crocodile (Job 41); but while this figure had once represented Egypt oppressing Israel at the exodus (Ps 74:13–14), it now identifies "the inhabitants of the earth" in their iniquity (Isa 26:21, the v. just preceding). 11:14 specifies that in the course of the conflict Israel is to despoil the territories of Philistia, Edom, Moab (cf. 25:10–12), and Ammon. Fulfillment (per. 15): as in Num. No. 36, the battle of Armageddon, and God's corresponding deliverance for Israel.

35. Isa *9:7c*; 11:3, 5; 16:5; 32:1a; 42:4 (5 vv.): "A throne shall be established in *hésedh*, lit., *loyalty* to the standards of God; and One shall sit thereon in truth, in the tent of David, judging, and seeking justice and swift to do righteousness" (16:5), a point perhaps suggested by the breaking off of the Assyrian oppression against Judah, which had been predicted in 16:4b, just preceding (see under 10:12, No. 37, below). 32:1 announces, "Behold, a King shall reign in righteousness."[78] The latter thought develops out of Israel's anticipated conversion at Sennacherib's repulse in

---

77. If 9:3 be taken with vv. 1–2 (No. 32, preceding), this *increase* might suggest the 1st-century Gentile engrafting into the Israel that is the church, as in 54:1–8 etc. (see under 24:16a, No. 69, below), NIC, I:325–326; but its more direct connection appears to be with v. 4 (No. 34), and hence with Christ's second coming.
78. 32:17 is similar but appears to be more contemporaneous; see under 29:18.

701 (cf. 29:20–21, 30:20–21, under 29:18, No. 81, below); but this section goes beyond contemporaneous times when v. 5 predicts, "The fool shall no more be called noble . . ." (see under 4:3, No. 15, above). So Girdlestone claims a Messianic intent: "In Isaiah and his contemporaries the notable deliverance of Hezekiah and his people from the hand of Sennacherib is associated with a greater deliverance which was not accomplished until seven centuries later,"[79] or, for His righteous reign to become thus externally effective, an additional 19-plus centuries as well. God's Servant the Messiah will "set justice in the earth; and the isles shall wait for His law," 42:4. Fulfilment (per. 16): as in II Sam. No. 18, the righeousness of Christ's millennial reign: cf. 11:4a (No. 41, below) on His particular concern for the poor.

36. Isa 9:19–21 (3 vv., fig.): "They shall eat every man the flesh of his own arm: Manasseh, Ephraim; and Ephraim, Manasseh; and they together shall be against Judah." In explanation of this figure of cannibalism against one's own supporting tribesmen, Leupold proposes this fulfillment (per. 7): "Two brother tribes, Ephraim and Manasseh, begin to assail one another, as seems to have happened in the last days of the Northern Kingdom";[80] cf. Hoshea's conspiracy in 732 (II K 15:30) and the prophecies of Hos 7:3, 8:4. Furthermore, these tribes either had attacked Judah or were about to do so, II K 16:5.[81]

37. Isa 10:12, 16–19, 24–27, 33–34; 14:24–27; 16:4b; 17:12–14; 18:3–7; 29:5–8, 17, 20a; 30:27–28, 30–33; 31:4–5, 8–9; 32:19; 33:1–4, 10–12, 18–19, 23; 36:15 (II K 18:30, II Chron 32:11); 37:10, 22, 30–33, 35 (II K 19:10, 21, 29–32, 34); 38:6 (II K 20:6b) (59 vv., fig.): God will punish the "high looks" of the king of Assyria, 10:12, and "burn his thorns in one day," v. 17. In 18:3–5, all the inhabitants of the world are invited to see "the spreading branches He will take away"; and v. 7 adds that the Cushite (Ethiopian) rulers of Egypt's XXVth Dynasty will send Judah a present (cf. II Chron 32:23, and No. 81, below), for its later king Tirhakah was involved in Sennacherib's defeat (Isa 37:9).[82] 10:19 predicts, "The remnant shall be few, so that a child may write them"; and Delitzsch notes, "This really came to pass. Only a small remnant of the army that marched against Jerusalem ever escaped";[83] cf. their predicted route of march in vv. 28–32 (No. 38, following). Isaiah foresaw that "in an instant, suddenly," 29:5, "the multitude of all the nations that fight against Ariel [Jerusalem] shall be as a dream," v. 7, that is, "The sudden disappearance of Sennacherib's army is to be like the fading of a night-

79. The Grammar of Prophecy, p. 22.
80. Op cit., I:194; cf. NIC, I:355.
81. Cf. how Isa 9:12 appears to come before ch. 7, or 734 B.C.
82. Who was "about 20 or 21" at this time, K. A. Kitchen, Ancient Orient and OT, p. 83; cf. S. Gevirtz, Patterns in the Early Poetry of Israel, pp. 31–33.
83. I:272.

mare."[84] V. 17 adds, "Yet a very little while, and Lebanon shall be turned into a fruitful field, and the fruitful field shall be esteemed as a forest"; and Leupold explains, " 'Lebanon,' in the light of 10:34, would seem to be a type of the great Assyrian empire, again about to be reduced to a level of weakness,"[85] while Israel, on the other hand, would become more powerful. So 29:20 states, "The terrible one is brought to nought."[86] When 30:28 foresees a "sifting of the nations" (cf. 29:7, above, and also 33:3, 12), it should be recalled that other, subject nations were present with the Assyrian troops, 5:26, 22:6, 29:5. 30:31 goes on: "Through the voice of Yahweh shall the Assyrian be dismayed; with His rod He will smite him"; v. 33, "For a Topheth [a place for the burning of bodies in the Valley of Hinnom; cf. II K 16:3] is prepared for the king," and while Sennacherib himself did not die at Jerusalem, some of his soldiers may well have been cremated there.[87] Famous predictions appear in 31:8, "The Assyrian shall fall by the sword, not of man," and v. 5, "As birds hovering, so will Yahweh of hosts protect Jerusalem"; cf. 33:19, that henceforth "thou shalt not see the fierce people." King Hezekiah's assurance against Sennacherib was that "Yahweh will surely deliver us, and this city shall not be given into the hand of the king of Assyria," 36:15, and cf. 37:10 (quoted by the Assyrians). Isaiah then encouraged the king, informing him, "The virgin [i.e. inviolate] daughter of Zion hath laughed" Sennacherib to scorn, 37:22; "Ye shall eat this year that which groweth of itself, and in the second year that which springeth of the same; and in the third year sow ye and reap," v. 30, meaning that though the current year's crop had been destroyed and the sowing had been prevented for the next spring's harvest, yet after that would reappear the normal agricultural cycle, in peace. A remnant, vv. 31–32, would be saved from the calamity; and Sennacherib would not again even approach Jerusalem, v. 33. Fulfillment (per. 7): when 10:16 predicts, "among his fat ones leanness,"[88] Leupold comments, "This could have been what the angel of the Lord brought when he smote in the camp of the Assyrians in one night [cf. v. 17, "in one day"] 185,000 men (II K 19:35) . . . This may have been a swift striking bubonic plague that was used by the Lord."[89] But whatever the precise physical medium, this event ranks along with Israel's crossing of the Red Sea at the exodus

84. BBC, IV:126.

85. Op. cit., I:461; cf. 505–506.

86. "Most aptly thought of as foreign oppressors . . . either in isolated instances or even ultimately by way of total extinction," ibid., I:462. So some, as Alexander, op. cit., I:461, apply this thought to Messianic times; but the context of the earlier part of ch. 29 favors the immediate (cf. v. 17) Assyrian menace.

87. BBC, IV:132, though NIC, II:370–372, prefers a figurative understanding.

88. This need not refer to the later (and final) fall of Assyria in 612; for though v. 20 notes the return of Israel's remnant that trusts God (No. 20, above), this must be later in any event, some 75 years even after 612.

89. Op. cit., I:205; cf. the tale of Herodotus about mice overrunning the Assyrian camp, I:575.

as one of the two greatest deliverances that God's people ever experienced; and its anticipation makes up the longest single prophecy in the Book of Isaiah.

38. Isa 10:28–32 (5 vv.): Isaiah's forecast of the route of an invading Assyrian army, down Palestine's central ridge from the north: Michmash, Gibeah, Anathoth, and Nob, to the threatening of Jerusalem. Fulfillment (per. 7): according to Aharoni[90] this became the course of one of the two invading Assyrian armies in 701.

39. Isa 11:1 (1 v., fig.): "There shall come forth a shoot, *hōter*, out of the stalk, of Jesse, and a branch, *nēser*, out of his roots. . . ." This oracle introduces a noun—cf. the earlier verbal form, "to shoot forth a branch," in II Sam 23:5, listed under 7:13b—that is significant in two ways for the Messianic prophecy of the OT. Fulfillment (per. 13): as a first stage, it assigns the title of *Branch* (cf. Jer 23:5, Zech 6:12) to the Messianic scion of David who would be born in Bethlehem, as in II Sam 7:13b. As a second stage in a progressive fulfillment,[91] the noun *nēser* suggests His boyhood residence in *Nazareth*; for the name of this post-OT village seems to come from this same root, and to mean "sprout town," with connotations of being newly founded and lightly esteemed (John 1:46). Jesus, therefore, as a humble *sprout* appropriately came from lowly Nazareth, "that what was spoken through the prophets might be fulfilled, 'He shall be called a Nazarene,' " Mt 2:23.

40. Isa 11:2; *42:1b*; 51:4a, *5a*; 61:1–2a (4 vv.): in respect to the Messianic Branch, "The Spirit of Yahweh shall rest upon Him," in wisdom, might, and reverence for God. Then in 61:1 (cf. 51:4–5[92]) the Messianic Servant declares, "Yahweh hath anointed Me to preach glad tidings to the meek," a passage that Jesus quoted, through v. 2a, in Luke 4:18–21. 42:1 (quoted in Mt 12:18) speaks also of God's Spirit being placed upon Him, that He may "bring forth justice to the Gentiles." But this latter clause does not as yet describe either His millennial rule of righteousness, as in v. 4 (per. 16; see under prophecy No. 35, above), or His church's expansion to the Gentiles, as in v. 6b (per. 14; see under No. 69, below); it speaks rather of His personal anointing by the Spirit, to herald "true religion, as the rule and authority for life in all its relations."[93] Fulfillment (per. 13): Christ's endowment with the Spirit, John 3:34, at His first coming; for in repeating Isa 61 in Nazareth, He affirmed, "Today this Scripture has been fulfilled," Lk 4:21; see above, p. 139. This seems to be true, even for "the Spirit of might" (Isa 11:2); for "Jesus manifested it in His authority over demons, diseases, nature, and death."[94]

90. *The Macmillan Bible Atlas*, p. 99.
91. See above, pp. 134–136.
92. An "echo" of the Servant passages in chs. 42 and 49, IB, V:593.
93. KD, II:175. Young, however, associates 42:1 with v. 4. He thus feels that "something more than proclamation is here intended" and goes beyond Mt 12:18 to suggest the Servant's actual establishing of justice in the world, NIC, III:11.
94. BBC, IV:69.

41. Isa *11:4a:* He shall "decide with equity for the poor and the meek of the earth"; cf. vv. 3, 5 (under 9:7c, No. 35, above) on the Lord's righteous rule in general. Fulfillment (per. 16): as in Ps. prophecy No. 36 (72:12–14), Christ's concern, as future ruler, for the lowly.

42. Isa 11:4b (1 v.): "He shall smite the earth with the rod of His mouth; and with the breath of His lips shall He slay the wicked." Delitzsch comments, "The latter is not to be understood collectively, but as pointing forward prophetically to an eschatological person, in whom hostility towards Jehovah and His Anointed culminates most satanically."[95] He then correlates Ps 110:6 and the quotation of this Isaianic verse in II Thess 2.8. Fulfillment (per 15): as in Ps. prophecy No. 56, the slaying of the Antichrist.

43. Isa 11:6–9; 35:1–2a, *6b*–7; 55:10–13; 65:25 (12 vv.): "The wolf shall dwell with the lamb. . . . They shall not hurt nor destroy in all My holy mountain [= 65:25]; for the earth shall be full of the knowledge of Yahweh, as the waters cover the sea," 11:6, 9. "The desert shall blossom as the rose," 35:1; and there shall be "streams in the desert," v. 6, at the Lord's coming; cf. vv. 2b, 4 (see under 26:21a, No. 77, below). "Instead of the thorn shall come up the fir tree," 55:13. Fulfillment (per. 15): as in Ps 96:12, the joy in nature at Christ's return; cf. Rom 8:21. Yet Scripture seems to limit the curbed conduct of wild beasts to their relations with men and with the domesticated animals of mankind: they are prevented from destroying "in all My holy mountain," but elsewhere lions and wolves need be no less carnivorous than they seem to have been prior to or outside of Eden.[96]

44. Isa 11:11–12, 16; *14:2a*; 35:8–*10a*; 49:18–22; *51:11a*; *55:12a*; *60:9b*; 62:10; 66:20a (12 vv.): "The Lord will set His hand again the second time to recover the remnant of His people [the first time having been at their exodus from Egypt[97]] . . . and will assemble the outcasts of Israel from the four corners of the earth," 11:11–12, with eight areas of the ancient world being listed. V. 16 continues, "And there shall be a highway [so this must refer to Jews and not to the church, which will be raptured into the clouds to meet her Lord[98]] for the remnant of His people, that shall remain, from Assyria; like as there was for Israel in the day that he came up out of the land of Egypt"; cf. 35:10, "The ransomed of Yahweh shall return." Indeed, according to 49:19–20, the land is to be too narrow for its augmented inhabitants. 14:2a foresees that "the people [= 49:22] shall take and bring them to their place," in millennial times (cf. v. 2b); and 66:20 lists various conveyances, as horses, chariots, litters, or dromedaries. The imperative clauses of 62:10—which is also millennial in setting, vv. 4, 12—preserve a significant distinction: "Prepare ye the way of the people

95. KD, I:284.
96. Payne, *Theology*, p. 494.
97. Cf. ICC, I:225.
98. See above, pp. 105, 114.

[sing., the Jews]; lift up an ensign over [ASVmg] the peoples [plu., the Gentiles]," in whose lands the dispersed Hebrews reside. Fulfillment (per. 16): as in Hos. No. 6, the regathering of converted Jews, after Christ has set up His future kingdom.

45. Isa 11:15 (1 v.): "Yahweh will utterly destroy the tongue of the Egyptian sea [the Red Sea[99]]; and with His scorching wind will He wave His hand over the River [Euphrates, cf. v. 16], and will smite it into seven streams, and cause men to march over dryshod." Fulfillment (per. 15): the drying up of these bodies of water occurs here in preparation for a "second exodus," v. 16, that of God's millennial regathering of Israel (No. 44, preceding); but in later prophecy (cf. Rev. 16:12) this phenomenon appears separately, in anticipation of the battle of Armageddon, which is noted in v. 14 (see under 9:4, No. 34, above).[100]

46. Isa 12:1–6; 25:8b–9; 26:1–4; 27:2–3; 35:10b; 51:11b; 61:2c–3, 7; 66:13–14a (20 vv., fig.): Israel's future deliverance is depicted in terms of a water supply, "With joy shall ye draw water out of the wells of salvation. . . . Declare His doings among the peoples," 12:3–4. Again, "Yahweh will wipe away tears from off all faces; and the reproach of His people will He take away . . . we will be glad and rejoice in His salvation," 25:8; and, "Thou wilt keep him in perfect peace," 26:3. Then in 27:2–3 God's people are portrayed as "a vineyard of wine: sing ye unto it. I Yahweh am its keeper." Both 35:10 and 51:11 affirm that "sorrow and sighing shall flee away"; and, "Instead of dishonor, they shall rejoice in their portion," 61:7, with "everlasting joy," 51:11. Fulfillment (per. 16): joy and praise, as marking the future Messianic kingdom.

47. Isa 13:1–9, 14–18; 14:4–20; 21:1–10; 43:14; 46:1–2; 47:1–3, 5, 8–15 (56 vv.): God's declaration in respect to Babylon (13:1), "I have called My mighty men, for Mine anger" (v. 3), the Medes (v. 17). "Wail ye, for the day of Yahweh is at hand . . . to make the land a desolation, and to destroy the sinners thereof out of it" (vv. 6, 9). "Their infants also shall be dashed in pieces before their eyes" (v. 16). The description in v. 14, "They shall turn every man to his own people," is explained as follows: "There will be a frantic flight of the foreigner from Babylon."[101] 14:7 states that "the whole earth is . . . [to] break forth into singing" at the report of Babylon's fall; and v. 9, that "hell [the KJV's understanding is proper at this point] is moved to meet thee at thy coming." For v. 19 condemns

99. ICC, I:227.
100. Jeremiah's subsequent employment of this expression of the drying up of the Euphrates as a figure for the fall of Babylon (Jer 50:38) should not affect the literal understanding of Isaiah's prophecy at this point (cf. the "dryshod marching" of the men concerned), nor should it suggest reducing the reference in Rev 16:12 to a mere figure for a decrease in the resources of the "Babylon" of the Apocalypse, as advocated by Fairbairn, *The Interpretation of Prophecy*, pp. 523–524.
101. BBC, IV:74. Since v. 14 is tied to vv. 15–17 it must introduce a reversion to the discussion of Babylon, after the eschatological theme of vv. 10–13; see No. 48, following.

Babylon, "Thou art cast forth away from thy sepulchre," in unburied disgrace. In 21:1, Isaiah's phrase, "the wilderness of the sea," must refer to the Chaldean seaboard, because v. 9 proclaims, "Fallen, fallen is Babylon." See also 43:14, "I have sent to Babylon, and I will bring down all of them as fugitives"; 47:5, that Chaldea shall "no more be called, The mistress of kingdoms"; and the prophet's figurative use in 46:1–2 of the national deities for the people, "Bel and Nebo . . . are gone into captivity." Fulfillment (per. 8): as in Dt. No. 46, the fall of Babylon to the Medes and Persians, in 539 B.C. 21:2 also includes among the attackers Elam, particularly Anshan, which was by this time a part of Cyrus' Persia.[102]

48. Isa 13:10–13; 24:17–20; 26:20 (9 vv.): prediction of the heavenly bodies being darkened (13:10) and of earthquakes (v. 13), "And I will punish the world for their evil" (v. 11).[103] 24:20 says more pictorially, "The earth shall stagger like a drunken man . . . and the transgression thereof shall be heavy upon it." So 26:20 adds a word of God to Israel, "Come, my [Isaiah's] people . . . hide thyself for a little moment, until the indignation be overpast." The time is therefore of short duration, and it is interrupted by Christ's Parousia, v. 21 (see No. 77, below). Fulfillment (per. 15): the wrath of God, commencing with heavenly phenomena, as in Joel 2:30, but going further to predict divine punishments, falling upon the world for their iniquities: see above p. 117.

49. Isa 13:19–22, 14:21–23 (7 vv.) "And Babylon shall never be inhabited . . . neither shall the Arabian pitch tent there" (13:19–20); for, "Bedouins shrink in superstitious horror from camping on the sites of ruins."[104] Delitzsch comments, "The fulfillment did not take place so soon as the words of the prophecy might make it appear. . . . Yet at the time of Strabo (born 60 B.C. [= per. 12]) Babylon was a perfect desert."[105]

50. Isa *14:1b:* following Judah's restoration in 538 (v. 1a, see No. 20, above), "The sojourner shall join himself with them, and they shall cleave to the house of Jacob." Fulfillment (per. 9): the increase of proselytes in

102. NIC, II:61–62.
103. Leupold has an overly complicated explanation: "Thoughts of the final judgment blend in this description with thoughts of the immediate destruction of Babylon"; see No. 47, preceding. So he refers v. 12 to "few remnants of the once very populous Babylon," op. cit., I:244–245. But it is best to maintain a single, unified fulfillment for these vv.; see above, pp. 121–126. Alexander would then apply the whole to Babylon; even as in 13:9 (just before), *hā-ăres,* does seem to describe simply "the *land* (of Babylon)." But when concerning v. 11—"I will punish the world"—he goes on to presume that "*tēvēl,* is no doubt a poetical equivalent to *éres* [as in 24:4, see No. 5, above and note 32], and is here applied to the Babylonian empire, as embracing most of the known world," op. cit., I:275–276, he misses the dependence of Isaiah upon Joel 3:15 at this point and the universalism that is inserted within the localized oracle; see above, p. 117.
104. BBC, IV:74.
105. I:3004; cf. NIC, I:429, or IDB, I:335, "The inhabitants of Babylon moved to Seleucia and Babylon itself became deserted, so that at the beginning of the Christian era only a small group of astronomers and mathematicians still continued to live in the ancient city."

postexilic times; cf. the desire of some in this regard, as indicated in Ezra 4:2.

51. Isa 14:2b; 27:6; 45:14–17, 25; 49:23–26; 60:3–6, 8–12, 14–17; 61:5–6, 9–11; 62:1–2; 66:7–12 (37 vv.): "The house of Israel shall possess them [other peoples] in the land of Yahweh for servants . . . and they shall rule over their oppressors" (14:2). "Israel shall blossom and bud; and they shall fill the face of the world with fruit" (27:6), meaning "results of so striking a nature that the whole earth is abundantly blessed."[106] Yet from the viewpoint of the nations, this blessing need not be one of unmixed joy: "Egypt shall go after thee in chains and make supplication unto thee," 45:15; and, "Kings shall lick the dust of thy feet," 49:23. But in any event, "Nations shall come to thy light . . . they come to thee: thy sons shall come from far, and thy daughters shall be carried in the arms," 60:3–4. In context the *sons and daughters* seem here to designate the Gentiles;[107] cf. Ezek 16:61 (listed under v. 53b), or Isa 44:5, 49:12, etc. (No. 97, below), on the *present* status of the Gentiles. Because of these "children," then, "The wealth of the nations shall come to thee," 60:5, including gold and other precious things brought by ship, vv. 6, 9, 17. "Foreigners shall build up thy walls," v. 10, and "feed your flocks and be your plowmen," 61:5, with "their kings led captive. For that nation and kingdom that will not serve thee shall be utterly wasted," 60:11–12. V. 16 addresses Israel in a figure, "Thou shalt suck the milk of the nations"; and 61:6 adds, "Ye shall be named the priests of Yahweh." "All that see them shall acknowledge them," 61:9. Fulfillment (per. 16): as in Dt. No. 37, the privileged status and future world dominance of Israel in the Messianic kingdom. The gold and other gifts granted to the Jews by foreigners during postexilic times, such as those recorded in Ezra 6:8–9 or Zech 6:11 (see Hag 2:7b), simply do not constitute sufficiently adequate fulfillments.[108]

52. Isa 14:28–31 (4 vv., fig.): "Rejoice not, O Philistia, all of thee, because the rod that smote thee is broken; for out of the serpent's root shall come forth an adder, and his fruit shall be a fiery flying serpent. . . . I will kill thy root with famine . . . for there cometh a smoke out of the north." This *serpent* could hardly be a Judean ruler smiting Philistia (as Hezekiah, II K 18:8); for there was no succession of Hebrew smiters at this time, and Judah was not to Philistia's north but to its east. Fulfiillment (per. 7): as in Amos No. 4. The great Assyrian conqueror Tiglath-pileser III died late in 727 B.C., shortly before Ahaz in 726 (Isa 14:28). So the adder and serpent would be his sons and successors, Shalmaneser V (727–722) and Sargon II (722–705), the latter of whom smote Philistine Ashdod in his

106. Leupold, op. cit., I:424.
107. Payne, *Theology*, p. 477. 60:4 could, however, have an import similar to that of v. 9b (see under 11:11, No. 44, above), on the regathering of the Jews at Christ's return, KD, II:411.
108. See above, p. 120.

campaign of 711; cf. 20:1–6, in which the prophet insisted to Hezekiah against Judah's involvement.

53. Isa 15:1–9a; 16:1–4a, 7–12 (17 vv.): "Moab is laid waste" (15:1), and a number of Moabite cities are then named. "The abundance that they have laid up shall they carry away over the brook of the willows," v. 7, probably referring to their southern boundary, with Edom. Some interpreters would make this oracle a past lament; but the future tenses of the ASV seem to be needed in 15:6–7, 16:2, etc. Fulfillment (per. 7): Sargon II's campaign of 715 B.C., as in Amos No. 10.

54. Isa 15:9b, 16:14 (2 vv., fig.): "I will bring yet more upon Dimon, a lion upon them of Moab that escape, and upon the remnant of the land" (15:9). For in 16:13–14, Isaiah is declared to have supplemented his former oracle against Moab (No. 53, preceding). Specifically, "Within three years the glory of Moab shall be brought into contempt" (16:14). Fulfillment (per. 7): after the above-noted campaign of 715, "It would appear that in 713 Moab joined a coalition against Assyria headed by the city of Ashdod to the west. . . . This violation of the treaty may have brought on the prediction of 16:14,"[109] when Sargon advanced again in 711, destroying Ashdod (see No. 52, above) and those allied with it.

55. Isa 17:7–8, 28:5–6 (4 vv.): after predicting the 722 fall of Samaria, 17:4–6 (see No. 27, above), Isaiah foresaw, "In that day shall men look unto their Maker" (17:7) rather than to idols. He spoke further in 28:6 of their[110] new spirit of justice, and of strength for battle (cf. II Chron 31:21, 32:5–6). Fulfillment (per. 7): some "gleanings" of N. Israel (Isa 17:6) did accept Hezekiah's appeal to a more reformed faith, II Chron 30:11; cf. 34:9.

56. Isa 19:1–17 (17 vv., fig.): Isaiah's poetic announcement of a divine verdict, "The idols of Egypt shall tremble at His presence" (19:1); specifically, there will be civil war (v. 2), economic confusion (v. 10), and dread of God (v. 16), even from a mention of Yahweh or of His land, Judah (v. 17). V. 4 adds, "I will give over the Egyptians into the hand of a cruel lord." Guesses about the identity of this personage have ranged from the contemporary XXVth Dynasty rulers of Egypt down to Antiochus IV's invasions of that land in 170 and 168 B.C.[111] He was apparently a foreigner; and concerning fulfillment, it is "most natural to explain 19:4 as referring to the mad fury of Cambyses," the Persian conquerer of Egypt in 525 (per. 9).[112] The internal troubles could then refer to revolt against the XXVIth Dynasty pharaoh Hophra (killed in 567), cf. Jer 44:30, 40 years

109. Leupold, op. cit., I:274.
110. "The residue of His people" (28:5) may include Judah as well as the remnants of Ephraim (vv. 1–4).
111. See above, p. 141.
112. ICC, I:321. Young is less definite but favors "the rise of the Assyrian power. . . . It is a general picture of the political vicissitudes that are to come over Egypt," NIC, II:19.

earlier.[113] After Cambyses, would come the deceived pharaoh of Isa 19:11; for "the period between 404, when the Egyptians recovered their independence of the Persians, and 342 B.C. was filled with internal discord,"[114] the XXVIIIth to XXXth dynasties.

57. Isa 19:18–22 (5 vv.): "In that day there shall be five cities in the land of Egypt that speak the language of Canaan [that is, will be strongly Jewish], and swear to Yahweh of hosts; one shall be called the city of the sun.[115] . . . There shall be an altar to Yahweh in the midst of the land of Egypt. . . . and the Egyptians shall worship Yahweh with sacrifice and oblation" (vv. 18–19, 21). Fulfillment (per. 11): by Maccabean times Jewish communities were well established in Egypt. Delitzsch, moreover, has noted: "From the Grecian epoch . . . the extent to which Judaism spread among the natives was by no means small. . . . It was a victory on the part of the religion of Jehovah, that Egypt was covered with Jewish synagogues even in the age before Christ."[116] Specifically, when Onias IV, son of the murdered high priest Onias III, fled from Palestine, he erected a temple "like that in Jerusalem"[117] at Leontopolis in the nome (district) of Heliopolis (= "city of the sun"), NE of Memphis. Here at the apex of the Egyptian Delta, and so "in the midst of the land" (v. 19),[118] it survived from 160 B.C. to A.D. 73. When Isaiah therefore prophesied, "Yahweh will send them a savior, and a deliverer, and He will deliver them," v. 20, the particular reference may be to Onias and to the ruler, Ptolemy VII, who granted him the permission to build the temple.[119]

58. Isa 19:23–25 (3 vv., fig.]: "In that day there shall be a highway out of Egypt to Assyria." Vv. 23–24 go on to explain, "The Egyptians shall worship with the Assyrians. In that day shall Israel be a third with Egypt and Assyria." Charles Erdman insists, "No more remarkable missionary passage can be found in all the prophecies of the OT."[120] Fulfillment (per. 14): the equality of all nations in Jesus, Eph 2:14, 19 (cf. Isa 44:5, etc., No. 97, below), but particularly the conversion of Egypt to become a leading Christian country, as it was from the 3rd to the 7th centuries.

59. Isa 20:1–6 (6 vv., sym.): Isaiah's walking naked and barefoot; explained in v. 4, "So shall the king of Assyria lead away the captives of Egypt, and the exiles of Ethiopia." Fulfillment (per. 7): Assyrian attack against Egypt, climaxed in Ashurbanipal's sacking of Thebes in 663 B.C., which brought an end to the XXVth, Ethiopian dynasty; cf. Nah 3:8's retrospective reference to this event.

113. They could even denote the confusion before or after the preceding XXVth Dynasty, ICC, I:323.
114. Ibid.
115. ASVmg, and 15 Heb. MSS., with the Dead Sea Isaᵃ scroll.
116. I:366.
117. Jos, *Ant.*, XII:9, 7; cf. also NIC, II:49–50.
118. The Jewish temple at Elephantine in the 5th century B.C. had stood at the extreme S. end of Egypt, and it involved a more questionable theology as well.
119. Jos, *Ant.*, XIII:3, 1; for other alternatives see NIC, II:36–37.
120. *The Book of Isaiah, an Exposition*, p. 57.

60. Isa 21:11–12 (2 vv., fig.): concerning "Dumah. . . . Watchman, what of the night? . . . The morning cometh, and also the night." *Dūmā* means "silence," and it may be a play on words with "Edom," for the oracle concerns Edomite Seir. Its words suggest calamity.[121] Fulfillment (per. 7): as in Amos No. 8, continued suffering for the Edomites, probably at the hands of Assyria, in connection with Moab's revolt of 713 along with Philistine Ashdod, 15:9b, 16:14 (No. 54, above). For Sargon's annals record both Edom and Moab as having been contacted by Aziru of Ashdod "to alienate them from me."[122]

61. Isa 21:13–17 (5 vv., fig.): caravans in Arabia are to lodge in the "thickets" (v. 13, ASVmg), an expression that the prophet explains in v. 16, "For within a year all the glory of Kedar shall fail" and their mighty men be few. In regard to this prediction both the dating and the fulfillment (per. 7) are uncertain.[123] The reference is probably to the Assyrian campaign of 715; see 15:1 (No. 53, above) on Moab. Sargon's claim was that he "crushed the tribes of the Arabs . . . I deported their survivors,"[124] and Herodotus, 2, 141, speaks still of Sennacherib as "king of Arabians and Assyrians."

62. Isa 22:17–19 (3 vv., fig.): Yahweh will thrust the court functionary Shebna from his office over Hezekiah's palace and toss him "like a ball into a large country: there shalt thou die." Fulfillment (per. 7): by 701 Shebna was no longer "treasurer, over the house [palace]," but scribe (36:3, 37:2), having been replaced (as predicted in 22:21, No. 63, following) by Eliakim. Data is lacking on how the remainder of the prophecy was subsequently carried out in Shebna's exile; but he most likely suffered captivity to Assyria, cf. 36:1.

63. Isa 22:20–25 (6 vv., fig.): Isaiah's word to Eliakim son of Hilkiah —v. 21, he is to replace Shebna (see No. 62, preceding) over King Hezekiah's palace, with power (v. 22), "as a nail in a sure place" (v. 23), supporting other members of his household (v. 34); but then, v. 25, he is to be hewn down and his family retainers cut off.[125] Fulfillment (per. 7): Eliakim did receive the post over the royal establishment, 36:3, 37:2; but he remains otherwise unknown.

64. Isa 23:1–11 (11 vv.): Tyre to be laid waste, v. 1, and its strongholds to be destroyed, v. 11, presumably those on the Pheonician mainland, for the island of Tyre did not fall until Alexander's attack in 332. Sidon (see v. 12, No. 65, below) is twice mentioned in this oracle, but only in relation to Tyre: v. 2, that its merchants would be speechless over the report of Tyre's

---

121. ICC, I:357, "The seer replies that a change is coming, but whether with it any permanent relief is at present obscure to him. If his questioners care to do so, let them ask again another day."
122. Cf. ANET, p. 287.
123. See above, p. 142.
124. ANET, p. 286.
125. So the fact that he would bear the "key of David," v. 22 (cf. Rev 3:7), by no means makes Eliakim a type of Christ.

destruction—since the Sidonians were the people most closely connected with Tyre[126]—and that Sidon, as the older mother-city, should be ashamed when bereft of its Tyrian daughter.[127] Fulfillment (per. 7): as in Amos No. 7, perhaps Ashurbanipal's reduction of Tyre in 663 B.C.

65. Isa 23:12 (1 v.): "O oppressed Sidon: pass over to Kittim [Cyprus]; even there shalt thou have no rest." Fulfillment (per. 7): when Sennacherib advanced westward in 701, Luli king of Sidon fled to Cyprus, where he was murdered.

66. Isa 23:13–17 (5 vv.): a further oracle against Tyre, "The Chaldeans . . . set up their siege towers . . . they made it a ruin. . . . Tyre shall be forgotten seventy years . . . And it shall come to pass after the end of seventy years that Yahweh will visit Tyre, and she shall return to her hire." "The text is clear," says Delitzsch, that the Chaldeans are the destructive agents.[128] Fulfillment (per. 8): Nebuchadrezzar's 13-year siege of Tyre, 585–573. Though it gained only a qualified capitulation by the Phoenicians (cf. Ezek 29:17–18),[129] still, "The defeat of Tyre in 572 meant the end of Phoenician national life."[130] From 585 this brings one down to 515 for the 70 years.[131] J. A. Alexander explains:

That Tyre was a flourishing [commercial] city in the time of Alexander the Great is a matter of history. When it again became so is not. But since the fact is certain and the prophecy explicit, the most rational conclusion is that they chronologically coincide, or in other words, that Tyre did begin to recover from the effects of the Babylon conquest about seventy years after the catastrophe itself.[132]

67. Isa 23:18 (1 v.): Tyre's "merchandise shall be holiness to Yahweh . . . for them that dwell before Yahweh, to eat sufficiently." Leupold understands this to mean a "token of her better intentions by giving of her wealth to the Lord. Something of that spirit is indicated by Ezra 3:7 (cf. 1:4) when the city furnished materials for constructive work in Israel after the captivity,"[133] hence fulfillment (per. 9) in 536. That an actual conversion of Tyre is involved remains open to question; cf. Isa 23:17.[134]

126. Leupold, op. cit., I:362.
127. BBS, IV:99.
128. I:411; though NIC, II:135–136, is less certain.
129. KD, I:419–421.
130. IDB, IV:723.
131. Girdlestone, op. cit., p. 91, however, proposes, "Seventy may be a round number, in fact a generation."
132. Op. cit., I:401; cf. KD, I:414–415, "After the seventy years, that is to say, along with the commencement of the Persian rule." ICC, I:395, prefers a later date and relates the period to Tyre's eclipse by Alexandria, 332 on, with returning prosperity after the Seleucid victory over Ptolemaic Egypt in 198; but this amounts to more than 70 years.
133. Op. cit., I:370.
134. Though cf. NIC, II:140–142.

68. Isa 24:*5b*; 56:4b, 6b (2 vv., typ.): the Sinaitic testament. Fulfillment (per. 13): as in Ex 19:5 (Ex. No. 45).

69. Isa *24:16a*, 42:*6b*–7, *49:6b, 51:4b*, 54:1–8 (9 vv.): in the historical sweep of the apocalypse of ch. 24,[135] v. 15 has spoken of praise to God among the Jewish exiles (No. 19, above), and v. 17 moves into the yet future tribulation (see No. 70, next). In the interval stand these words, "From the uttermost part of the earth have we heard songs, Glory to the righteous" (v. 16); cf. 54:5, "The God of the whole earth shall He be called." Yahweh gives His Servant "for a light of the Gentiles," 42:6 (cf. 42:1b, under 11:2, No. 40, above), to which 49:6 adds, "that Thou mayest be My salvation unto the end of the earth." 42:7 gives the purpose: "to open the blind eyes, to bring them that sit in darkness out of the prison house." IB insists that this is "not to be taken as referring to liberation from exile but rather in a spiritual sense, a liberation of all the peoples from bondage. All of v. 7 is a development of *light to the nations*."[136] Earlier in ch. 54 Isaiah had employed a series of figures, beginning, "More are the children of the desolate than the children of the married wife" (v. 1). The prophet refers to the results of Christ's atonement in ch. 53, and the present oracle is quoted in Gal 4:26–27 as applying to the church. G Douglas Young explains, "Paul states that Isaiah is speaking by prophecy of the age in which we live; and he implies that Isaiah in that period sees the situation present to Paul's day, the present age."[137] Fulfillment (per. 14): as in Acts 1:8, the worldwide proclamation of the gospel in the Christian church; cf. Paul's quote of Isa 49:6 in Acts 13:46–47, when turning from the Jews to a Gentile audience.

70. Isa 24:16b (1 v.: "Woe is me! the treacherous have dealt treacherously"; for as Delitzsch describes the prophet, "He sees a dreadful, bloodthirsty people preying among both men and stores."[138] Fulfillment (per. 14): the tribulation that closes the present age, cf. Dan 7:21; for one should note the immediately following, eschatological wrath of God, vv. 17–20 (No. 48, above).

71. Isa 24:21a, 22a (2 vv.): "Yahweh will punish the host of the high ones on high . . . and they shall be gathered together as prisoners are gathered in the pit, and shall be shut up in the prison . . . many days." Fulfillment (per. 16): Satan and his demons—in contrast with the kings of the earth, v. 21b (see 9:4, No. 34, above)—shut up, per Rev 20:1–3, in the abyss, during the 1,000 years: cf. Gen 3:15c, 3rd stage. The *many days* of Isa 24:22 is, with Dan 7:12, the only OT indication of the actual, limited duration of the millennium.

135. See above, introduction to Isaiah.
136. V:469.
137. "OT Theology—A Method and a Conclusion," ETS (1955), 80. In his work *The Kingdom of God*, pp. 215–216, John Bright correspondingly develops the idea that if there is a true Messiah, He must have a kingdom; and hence, p. 226, appear the 12 apostles, in conformity to the concept of the 12 tribes of Israel.
138. I:431.

72. Isa *24:22b,* 34:1–3, 54:15–17 (6 vv.): a further word on Satan and his hosts (see No. 71, preceding), "and after many days shall they be visited," ASVmg, *punished.* From Isaiah's corresponding second cycle of apocalyptic prediction of the last times,[139] 34:2 reveals, "Yahweh hath indignation against all the nations." This oracle is even more comprehensive than Isaiah's earlier forecasts of the premillennial battle of Armageddon (No. 34, above); for it continues, "He hath utterly destroyed them"; cf. 54:15, "They may gather together against thee but shall fall." Both of these latter stand in postmillennial contexts (34:4, on the heavens departing, No. 73, following, and 54:9–13, on the New Jerusalem, No. 74). So fulfillment (per. 17): Satan's release from his prison, after the millennium, to bring about the battle of Gog, though those whom he deceives are destroyed and he himself is condemned to the eternal lake of fire, Rev 20:7–10; cf. Gen 3:15c, 4th stage.

73. Isa *24:23a,* 34:4, 51:6, *54:10a* (2 vv., fig.): a personification of nature, "Then the moon shall be confounded, and the sun ashamed" (24:23); and later come comparisons, "The heavens shall be rolled together as a scroll; and all their host shall fade away, as the leaf" (34:4). Fulfillment (per. 17): as in Gen. No. 14, the final passing away of heaven and earth, Rev 20:11, 21:1–3.

74. Isa 24:23b, 54:9–13, 60:19–22, 65:17–19, 66:22 (14 vv.): at the conclusion of his apocalyptic sweep through history in ch. 24 the prophet foretells that "Yahweh of hosts will reign in mount Zion, and before His elders[140] shall be glory" (v. 23); cf. Rev 22:4. Then follow four great predictions given near the close of Isaiah's ministry. In ch. 54 Jerusalem is assured, "My lovingkindness shall not depart from thee" (v. 10); "I will lay thy foundations with sapphires" (v. 11), which is cited in Rev 21:19; "and all thy children shall be taught of Yahweh" (v. 13).[141] Isa 60:19–22, "The sun shall be no more thy light . . . but thy God thy glory. The days of thy mourning shall be ended. Thy people shall be all righteous . . . the small one, a strong nation." Ch. 65: "I create new heavens and a new earth" (v. 17; cf. 66:22), "and there shall be heard in her no more the voice of weeping" (65:19). 66:22, "So shall your seed and your name remain." Fulfillment (per. 18): the final New Jerusalem of Rev 21:2; "and God Himself shall be among them," v. 3.

75. Isa 25:6 (1 v.): In this mountain [Zion] will Yahweh of hosts make unto all peoples a feast of fat things." Fulfillment (per. 15): as in Ps 22:29a (No. 22), the marriage supper of the Lamb.

76. Isa 25:7–*8a,* 26:19 (2 vv., fig.): "He will destroy in this mountain

139. See above, introduction to Isaiah, and especially note 10.
140. Possibly attendant angelic spirits, BBC, IV:109, but more likely the tribal (?) leaders of Israel, NIC, II:182–183; compare Rev. 4:4, as discussed above. p. 49.
141. Quoted in John 6:45 as applicable to the situation of Jesus, but this does not appear to be the Isaianic intent in the prediction; see above, p. 128.

. . . the veil that is spread over all nations." The figure is then explained, v. 8, "He hath swallowed up death forever." Cf. 26:19, "Thy dead shall live . . . the earth shall cast forth the dead [of Israel]." Fulfillment (per. 15): the first resurrection, of the righteous, because 25:8 is so quoted I Cor 15:54; cf. vv. 51–53.

77. Isa 26:21a, 35:2b–4, 59:19b–20a, 60:1–2, 62:11–12, 64:1 (7 vv.): "For behold, Yahweh cometh forth out of His place [heaven] to punish the earth" (26:21); "They shall see the glory of Yahweh. . . . Your God will come and save you" (35:2, 4); "The glory of Yahweh is risen upon thee" (60:1). Rom 11:26 quotes 59:20a on how "a Redeemer will come to Zion"; cf. v. 20b (under 8:17, No. 31, above) on the resultant conversion of the Jews. 62:11 is more impersonal, "Behold, thy salvation cometh"; but it continues, "Behold, His reward is with Him." Isaiah's final prediction in this regard takes the form of a prayer, 64:1, "Oh that Thou wouldest rend the heavens and come down, that the mountains might quake at Thy presence." Fulfillment (per. 15): as in Ps. prophecy No. 5, the Parousia of Jesus Christ; cf. Rev 1:7.

78. Isa 27:12, 13b (2 vv.): "Ye shall be gathered . . . a great trumpet shall be blown; and they shall come . . ." from the lands of their oppression "and worship Yahweh." Fulfillment (per. 15): the rapture of the church, as in Hos. No. 27. Contrast No 44, above, on the coming of the Jews by highways, 11:11–12, 16, or as aided by men, 14:2; but this is by the Lord's direct summons, as in I Thess 4:16–17.

79. Isa 27:13a: that the gathering of God's people to Himself (No. 78, preceding) is to be when "a great trumpet shall be blown." Fulfillment (per. 15): the last trumpet, I Cor 15:52, elaborating Hosea's more figurative reference to Yahweh's "roaring as a lion," 11:10.

80. Isa 27:13c, 49:8b: following upon its gathering to Christ at His return (No. 78, above), the church will "worship Yahweh in the holy mountain at Jerusalem" (27:13); He will cause them to inherit the land, currently desolate (49:8). Fulfillment (per. 15): as in Joel No. 11, the church's rapture to Palestine.

81. Isa 29:18–24; 30:18–26, 29; 31:7; 32:15–18, 20; 33:5–6, 13–14, 17, 20–22, 24; 39:8 (II K 20:19); 44:26–27 (35 vv.): a major series of prophecies, interspersed among predictions about Sennacherib's advance and subsequent annihilation (see No. 18 and 37, above), concerning the contemporary effects that this destruction would produce.[142] These commence with promises for Israel's vindication: "Jacob shall not now be ashamed . . . when he seeth his children [not destroyed by Sennacherib but] in the midst of him, they shall sanctify My name . . . and stand in awe of God," 29:22–23; and in v. 19, "The meek shall increase their joy in Yahweh." 33:17 predicts, "Thine eyes shall see the king in his beauty; they

142. See above, Table 5, and for greater detail, Payne, "The Effect of Sennacherib's Destruction," pp. 26–32.

shall behold a land that reacheth afar," i.e. Judah restored and Hezekiah, yet to appear in vindicated splendor, "glorified by the victory of his God,"[143] and no longer in robes of sackcloth, as at Sennacherib's advance (37:1).[144]

Conviction too would arise for the ungodly, and repentance for all: "The sinners in Zion are afraid; trembling hath seized the godless ones: Who among us can dwell with the devouring fire?" 33:14. 29:20–21 adds,[145] "The scoffer ceaseth and all they that watch for iniquity . . . and turn aside the just," meaning that "a wholesome reverence and fear has taken hold of them, a result not noted in II Kings 18 and 19, but a valuable supplement to this historical account."[146] Such conviction would come to the fore over matters religions as well as ethical: 30:22, "And ye shall defile thy graven images of silver . . . thou shalt cast them away as an unclean thing" (= 31:7).[147] More positively, 29:24 predicts, "They that err in spirit shall come to understanding." For when the convicted sinner asks in 33:14, "Who among us can dwell with the devouring fire?" Isaiah had a ready answer, vv. 15–16, "He that walketh righteously," and the prophet's specifications follow. 29:18 thus speaks of the deaf hearing the words of the book,[148] the idea being that "divine restoration brings true illumination."[149] Again, in 30:20, Isaiah foresaw: "Though the Lord give you the bread of adversity . . . yet shall not thy teachers be hidden any more, but thine eyes shall see thy teachers; and thine ears shall hear a word behind thee, saying, This is the way, walk ye in it"; compare how Hezekiah in 701 was to send his leading officials to seek God's word from Isaiah, 37:2. So also at the receipt of Sennacherib's threatening letter, after the withdrawal of the Rab-shakeh from Jerusalem, the king's immediate reaction was to go up to the house of Yahweh and implore divine guidance, v. 14. In ch. 32, Isaiah foretells

---

143. KD, II:63.

144. Cf. II Chron 32:22–23, "Thus Yahweh saved Hezekiah and the inhabitants of Jerusalem from the hand of Sennacherib . . . so that he was exalted in the sight of all nations from henceforth . . . and many brought gifts unto Yahweh to Jerusalem."

145. See above, p. 142.

146. Leupold, op. cit., I:517; cf. E. Riehm, *Messianic Prophecy*, p. 161. "Israel's deliverance from the yoke of Assyria is the beginning of a series of divine deeds of grace by which Israel is inwardly and outwardly prepared for, and made to participate in, the salvation destined for him."

147. Cf. Hezekiah's confession at the height of the 701 crisis, "Of a truth, Yahweh, the kings of Assyria have laid waste all the countries and have cast their gods into the fire: for they were no gods, but the work of men's hands," 37:18–19.

148. This expression "would seem to imply that the same book, which was hinted at in v. 11, is again under consideration, namely the book of the prophet . . . hearing will be utilized for the noblest conceivable purpose, hearing the message of God," Leupold, op. cit., I:461–462. KD, II:24, proposes simply, "Scripture words." The noun is anarthrous; and it could signify the understanding of any book (cf. JB, p. 1188) and, hence, even a removal of physical defects of hearing (!), Leupold, op. cit., I:461. Young, however, appears correct in claiming spiritual, rather than physical, deafness and in viewing the omission of the article as poetic, NIC, II:325–326.

149. BBC, IV:127.

desolation (that of 701, vv. 9–14) "until the Spirit be poured upon us from on high," v. 15 (cf. 44:3), while the rest of the verse carries on about the fall of Sennacherib. It would therefore seem to refer to this same repentance. V. 16 continues, "Then justice shall dwell in the wilderness, and righteousness shall abide in the fruitful field" (= 33:5]; and 33:6 predicts, "There shall be . . . wisdom and knowledge: the fear of Yahweh is thy treasure."

A final, immediate result of Sennacherib's defeat would be blessing, as foreseen in 30:18–19, "Blessed are all they that wait for Him. For the people shall dwell in Zion at Jerusalem; thou shalt weep no more; He will surely be gracious unto thee at the voice of thy cry." 44:26–27 thus speaks in retrospect of God's "confirming the prophetic word of His servant" that Jerusalem should be inhabited. 30:29 depicts the blessing, as it foretells, "Ye shall have a song as when a holy feast is kept, and gladness of heart"; cf. Isaiah's later direct appeal for song, 43:10–12. The most obvious blessing would be that of security: "And the work of righteousness shall be peace . . . and My people shall abide in safe dwellings and in quiet resting places," 32:17; and, "There shall be stability, *emūnā*, in thy times," 33:6. It was to this last oracle that Hezekiah seems to have referred in 39:8, "For there shall be peace and truth, *emeth*, in my days."[150] Isaiah went on to embody this hope in a series of beautiful comparisons: "How will Jerusalem look when Asshur has been dashed to pieces on the strong fortress?"[151] 33:20, "Look upon Zion, the city of our solemnities: thine eyes shall see a quiet habitation, a tent that shall not be removed, the stakes whereof shall never be plucked up, neither shall any of the cords thereof be broken"; the city, that is, will be like a tent that has no need to move. In Delitzsch's words, "Jerusalem stands there unconquered and inviolable."[152] Again, v. 21 states, "There Jerusalem will be with us, a place of broad rivers and streams, wherein shall go no galley with oars, neither shall gallant ship pass thereby," a picture of great tranquil waters, yet without hostile navies. Isaiah's intent must have been figurative; for these are terms appropriate to the lowland metropolis of Thebes or Babylon but manifestly unsuitable, in their literal sense, to the geography of Jerusalem, either present or millennial; cf. Joel 3:18b, Ezek 47:1b, Zech 14:4b, 8, 10. Furthermore, the truth that produces the figure consists in what God is about to do to Sennacherib, v. 22: "For Yahweh is our judge . . . He will save us"; v. 6, "with an abundance of salvation." But the anticipated blessedness can be quite down to earth as well: 30:23, "He will give the rain for thy seed [= 32:20] . . . and bread of the increase of the ground shall be plenteous. In that day shall thy cattle feed in large pastures." Cf. Isaiah's

150. Cf. II K 20:19, "Is it not so, if peace and truth shall be in my days?": meaning, KD, *Kings*, p. 468, "A lively affirmation." Such blessing can even be stated as a principle (nonpredictive): "And the effect of righteousness shall be quietness and confidence for ever," 32:17b.
151. KD, *Isa*, II:64.
152. Ibid.

promises in the very year 701 of recovery for the agricultural cycle, 37:30–31 (under No. 37, above). 30:25 states the prophet's assurance, "And there shall be upon every high hill brooks and streams of water, in the day of the great slaughter." Leupold explains, "The description is somewhat idealized, especially toward the end";[153] but it is still related to the Assyrian defeat. Thus v. 26 uses the loftiest of comparisons: "The light of the moon shall be as the light of the sun, and the light of the sun shall be sevenfold, as the light of seven days"; but Isaiah still dates this as occurring "in the day that Yahweh bindeth up the hurt of His people,"[154] and vv. 27–28, 30–33, go right on to anticipate the destruction of Sennacherib's host, "for through the voice of Yahweh shall the Assyrian be dismayed; with His rod will He smite him," v. 31.

Fulfillment (per. 7): the peaceful condition of Jerusalem that followed upon 701 B.C., 51:3. Sennacherib did not return, 37:37; and Judah retained her independence until the submission of Hezekiah's weak son Manasseh, 676. It would appear, moreover, that the event of 701 brought Hezekiah's earlier attempts at reform (II K 18:4, II Chron 29:3–31:1) into full fruition (see also No. 55, above).[155] In its aftermath, Isaiah was to become unrelenting in his mockery of Judah's once treasured idols (40:19–20; 41:6–7, 29; 42:17; 44:9–20; etc.); and in a more positive vein he was to announce, "Ye are My servant, saith Yahweh . . . that ye may know and believe Me," 43:10; "I have refined thee . . . in the furnace of affliction," 48:10.

82. Isa 30:*5b–7* (2 vv.): Isaiah's warning to Judah, "Egypt helpeth in vain." Fulfillment (per. 7): the forces of pharaoh Shabaka (XXVth Dynasty) were defeated by the Assyrians in SW Palestine at Eltekeh, 701, after which Sennacherib proceeded to advance on Jerusalem, cf. 31:1–3 (under 5:26, No. 18, above).

83. Isa 34:5–17 (13 vv., fig): Yahweh says, "My sword shall come down upon Edom" (v. 5);[156] "the land thereof shall become burning

---

153. Op. cit., I:478. Terry's standard hermeneutical principle holds good, that "words should be understood in their literal sense unless such literal interpretation involves a manifest contradiction or absurdity" (see above, p. 17). For at this point, "hyperbole marks the whole description. The pale light of the moon is to take on the brilliance of the sun, the light of one day of sunshine is to be the equivalent of an ordinary entire week of seven days. We can hardly rethink these thoughts without being reminded of an intense glare, which is certainly not what the prophet intends," Leupold, op. cit., I:479. Contrast Pentecost, *Things to Come*, p. 490, as he speaks of the millennium, proposing "This increased light probably is a major cause of the increased productivity of the earth."

154. Though Delitzsch, II:39, would relate it to "the glorification of nature . . . at the closing period of the world's history."

155. These reforms began in Hezekiah's first official year, or in 726/725; but Keil cautions that his activities, particularly in Israel (cf. II Chron 31:1), probably extend beyond this point, at least until after the fall of Samaria in 722, *Chron*, pp. 456–561.

156. The reference in 34:6 to the blood of the Edomites as shed by Yahweh's sword explains the metaphor of 63:1–6, which looks back on God's victory over

pitch . . . the smoke thereof shall go up for ever" (vv. 9–10). V. 8 presents the reason as being that of "recompense for the cause of Zion"; cf. the Edomite attacks of 735 on Judah (II Chron 28:17, as elaborated in Joel 3:19, Obad 10). Fulfillment (per 9): as in Obad No. 2, the destruction of Edom by the Nabatean Arabs, after their attempted rebuilding, Mal 1:4a. V. 4b thus speaks of Yahweh's "indignation for ever."

84. Isa 35:5–6a (2 vv.): "Then shall the lame man leap as a hart"; cf. similar recoveries for the blind, deaf, and dumb. Fulfillment (per. 16): as in Ex. No. 50, the healing of physical infirmities in the future Messianic kingdom.

85. Isa 36:7 (II K 18:22, II Chron 32:12); *56:7d* (1 v., typ.): the altar of burnt offering. Fulfillment (per. 13): as in Ex. No. 44.

86. Isa 37:7a, 29, 34 (II K 19:7a, 28, 33), (3 vv.): Sennacherib "shall hear tidings, and shall return to his own land" (v. 7); or, as God speaks to the king himself, in a figure, "I will put My hook in thy nose, and My bridle in thy lips, and I will turn thee back by the way which thou camest." Fulfillment (per. 7): Sennacherib's retreat in 701 B.C., v. 37. The *report* may have concerned the Ethiopian advance (v. 9), or Hezekiah's refusal to surrender, as demanded by Sennacherib's messengers (v. 9), or some word that came from Assyria.

87. Isa *37:7b* (II K *19:7b*): that Sennacherib would "fall by the sword in his own land." Fulfillment (per. 7): he was slain by two of his sons in 681, v. 32.

88. Isa 38:5; 7, 21–22 (II K 20:5a, *6a,* 8a) (4 vv.): Hezekiah to be healed of his boil, v. 21. On the third day, he was to go up to the temple, v. 22 (cf. II K 20:5); and he was to have 15 years added to his life, v. 5. Fulfillment (per. 7): he did recover, v. 9, as later elaborated in Hezekiah's psalm of gratitude, vv. 9, 17, 19–20. That he went up to the temple on the third day is not stated, though v. 20 does speak of his singing in the house of Yahweh; and, with the miracle of the shadow (No. 89, following), his actual appearing in the sanctuary on the day noted becomes a relatively minor assumption. On his length of life, this healing occurred in his 14th regnal year (36:1), so the additional 15 years would grant him a sum of 29, which became in fact the total for his reign (II K 18:2).

89. Isa 38:8 (II K 20:9–10) (1 v.): Isaiah's prediction that a certain shadow would "go back ten steps" for he had given Hezekiah the choice of this or of the shadow's advancing ten steps, and the king had asked for the harder sign, namely the retrogression. It happened forthwith, v. 8, as a sign for Hezekiah's somewhat more delayed cure, which was achieved on the third day (No. 88, preceding).

Sennacherib; compare 63:3, 6, with 22:5, on the treading down of Judah—see above, p. 119, note 248—cf. Payne, "Background of Isaiah 40–66," WTJ, 30 (1968), 191.

90. Isa 40:3–5 (3 vv., fig.): "The voice of one that crieth in the wilderness [ASVmg, in agreement with Mk 1:3], Prepare ye the way of Yahweh . . . the uneven shall be made level . . . and the glory of Yahweh shall be revealed." It is this hope, along with the fact that the Assyrian judgment of 701 has now become past, that justifies Isaiah's proclamation of comfort in vv. 1–2. Rose Price adds by way of interpretation: "The figure in v. 4 is drawn from the engineering operations of roadmakers for kings of the East. . . . Dishonesty must give way to sincerity, and pride of status must be given up. All this is involved in preparing a highway for our God through the desolation of society to the hearts of men."[157] The prophecy's fulfillment (per. 13):[158] is stated in all four Gospels—Mt 3:3, Mk 1:3, Lk 3:4–6 (citing the entire passage), and John 1:23—in John the Baptist as the forerunner of Christ, who is the glory of God, John 12:31.

91. Isa 42:1a; 49:1–2, 5–6a; 50:4–5; 53:1, 2b (9 vv.): "Behold, My Servant, whom I uphold; My chosen, in whom My soul delighteth" (42:1). This Person who can be identified only with God's Messiah, the son of David,[159] is foreseen as having a ministry that will develop through at least seven stages[160] (six, in addition to the above-listed verses), which may here be summarized as follows. 1. His servanthood commences with His birth through an ordinary human mother, 49:1, 5, His normal and humble growth, 53:2 (see No. 26, above), and His call to the work of a prophet, "to sustain with words him that is weary," 50:4, cf. 49:1–2.[161] He is Yahweh's "Servant, to bring Jacob again to Him," 49:5–6.[162] But though empowered by God's Spirit (No. 40, above), His ministry remains non-self-assertive (No. 92, following); and He meets with disbelief, 53:1. 2. His career becomes one of suffering and death (No. 99 and 101). 3. Though He is condemned as a criminal, yet by giving His life as a vicarious sacrifice He creates a spiritual "seed" who have been justified from their sins (No. 30 and 100). 4. He thus accomplishes God's purpose, is honorably buried with the rich, and rises again to prolong His days (No. 102 and 103). 5. He becomes a light also to the Gentiles, to the ends of the earth (No. 69 and 97). 6. He receives recognition, and power as ruler of the millennial world (No. 11, 34, 35, and 46), for the designation "servant" may be a title of honor (depending upon the rank of the master); cf. the status of Abraham, Moses, or even Nebuchadrezzar as "servants of Yahweh"

157. BBC, IV:164; cf. Young, NIC, III:30, "the sins of the nation."
158. Its fulfillment does not concern Judah's "return from Babylon, of which there is no mention in the text or context. . . . [That] the glory of God would be universally displayed [is] a promise too extensive to be fully verified in that event or period of history," Alexander, op. cit., II:95–96.
159. See above, introduction to Isaiah.
160. Payne, *Theology*, pp. 255–256.
161. Cf. AB, p. 104, on His powerful speech.
162. The Servant thus becomes the ultimate embodiment of the Isaianic concept of the remnant; see above, p. 96; and so the NT speaks of Christ's coming for "the lost sheep of the house of Israel," Mt 15:24; cf. John 1:11.

(Ps 105:6, Dt 34:5, Jer 25:9). 7. He constitutes in Himself the testament, God's redemptive program for human history (No. 93). Accomplishment for the first stage dates to Christ's incarnation (per. 13), during which "He emptied Himself, taking the form of a bond-servant" (Phil 2:7–8); cf. the citations of Isa 42:1 and 53:1 as fulfilled in Mt 12:18 and John 12:38. Both at His baptism (Mt 3:17) and at His transfiguration (17:5) He received divine testimony to the Father's "delight" in Him.

92. Isa 42:2–3 (2 vv.): Yahweh's Servant "will not lift up His voice in the street. A brused reed will He not break." Fulfillment (per. 13): the unpretentious ministry of Jesus; it is so quoted in Mt 12:17–21.

93. Isa 42:6a; 49:8a, 9a (3 vv.): God's word to the Servant, "I will give Thee for a testament of the people," 42:6. The forecast is repeated in 49:8–9, with the added statement of His goal: "to raise up the land [v. 8b, discussed under 27:13c, No. 80, above][163] . . . saying to them that are bound, Go forth; to them that are in darkness, Show yourselves." Von Orelli explains: "The Servant will be the instrument for again establishing, like Moses and Joshua, the holy nation." As the contextual references to the new testament and to the church's preaching to the Gentiles (42:6b–7, No. 69, above) indicate, the Servant's function at this point is one of "redeeming work . . . Instead of being able to bring salvation to the heathen world [cf. 49:6b–7, 9b–12, No. 69 and 97] the nation must itself first receive salvation. The first and greatest work of the Servant will be done on Israel–Judah, far from God and sunk in spiritual wretchedness."[164] Fulfillment (per. 13): Christ and the "day of salvation" (49:8) as achieved by the testament in His blood, Mt 26:28; cf. the quotation of v. 8 in II Cor 6:2. The testament, in other words, which divine revelation had so far considered as a legal disposition is here summed up as becoming a Person.[165] Christ is not only the everlasting Son of God who *establishes* the testament, but He is at the same time the priest who *officiates* at the death (Isa 52:15). He is also the Testator, the offering that *dies* (53:8); and He becomes Himself the living blessing of reconciliation; indeed, He *is* the inheritance that that is bestowed (49:6): "Thou art My salvation!"[166]

94. Isa *43:23b, 56:7c* (typ.): peace offerings. Fulfillment (pers. 13 and 16): as in Lev. No. 5.

95. Isa *43:23c* (ASVmg), *66:20b* (typ.): meal offerings; cf. the Anchor

---

163. See above, p. 108.
164. *The OT Prophecy of the Consummation of God's Kingdom*, p. 382.
165. Cf. the parallel found at Qumran, where, according to its own view, this Dead Sea community *is* the *b'rīth*, R. K. Harrison, *The Dead Sea Scrolls, an Introduction*, pp. 90 ff.
166. Payne, *Theology*, p. 113; cf. John Murray's description of the embodiment of the testament in the Messiah, *The Covenant of Grace*, pp. 24–25. Vos's statement, that through the Servant the testament will be realized, *Biblical Theology*, p. 277, is true; but it is inadequate, if full justice is to be done to the force of Isaiah's words.

Bible's rendering of "oblation" in 66:20 as "cereal offering." Fulfillment (per. 13): as in Lev. No. 4.

96. Isa 44:3–4 (2 vv., fig.): God's promise, "I will pour water upon him that is thirsty," which He then explains: "I will pour My Spirit upon thine offspring." The fulfillment of this prophecy is later than that of 32:15 (noted under No. 81, above), on the coming of God's Spirit in the post-Sennacherib revival of 701 (per. 7); and yet it is earlier than that of 59:21b (No. 106, below), on the millennial outpouring of the Spirit (per. 16). The Gentile engrafting that follows in the next verse (44:5, No. 97, below) suggests that 44:3–4 parallels Joel 2:28–29 in predicting Pentecost (per. 14).[167]

97. Isa 44:5, 49:9b–12, 55:5, 65:1 (6 vv.): Isaiah's vision of "foreigners, proselytes,"[168] being converted to the faith of Judah, "One shall call himself by the name of Jacob, and another shall . . . surname himself by the name of Israel," 44:5. Ch. 49 had spoken of Christ as the testament for Israel, vv. 8–9a (No. 93, above), but also as a light for the Gentiles, v. 6 (No. 69); vv. 9b–12 then express Isaiah's hope for an engrafting of this broader group: "These shall come from far," even from Sinim, v. 12, an area whose location is unknown.[169] They are compared with a flock being led, in terms suggestive of the exodus, vv. 9b–10, and on a prepared way, corresponding to that of 40:3–4, on the repentance preached by John the Baptist (No. 90, above), 49:11. NBC therefore concludes: "From the wide bounds of the wastes men and women will press into the kingdom of the Messiah."[170] After speaking of the Messiah in fulfillment of the Davidic testament (55:3–4, No. 104, below), Isaiah foresaw a missionary activity on the part of Israel, directed toward other peoples: "Thou shalt call a nation that thou knowest not, and a nation that knew not thee shall run unto thee," 55:5. God speaks in 65:1, "I am found of them that sought Me not . . . a nation that was not called by My name"; and the subject must once again be the Gentiles.[171] The Jerusalem Bible, together with most moderns, applies this verse to the Hebrews;[172] but Rom 10:20 explicitly refers it to non-Jews.[173] Fulfillment (per. 14): as in Gen. No. 19, the engrafting of

167. Alexander argues for more than a strict reference to Pentecost and favors "all the influences of the Holy Spirit," op cit., II:161.

168. IB, V:503.

169. KB, p. 656.

170. This conclusion follows chronologically from Christ's establishment of the new testament in vv. 8–9a. But, alternatively, it might denote the rapture of the church to Palestine, as in v. 8b (No. 80, above), or the millennial regathering of the Jews, that appears later in vv. 18–22 (No. 44), cf. Muilenburg's opposition to C. C. Torrey's identification of the subjects as Gentiles, IB, V:572.

171. So Alexander, op. cit., II:436–438.

172. P. 1245.

173. When Delitzsch, II:475, asserts, "We may assume that the apostle understood the Hebrew text . . . as relating to the calling of the Gentiles, without being therefore legally bound to adopt the same interpretation," he appears to be on dangerous ground; contrast Young, NIC, III:501.

Gentiles into the Israel that is the church; cf. 19:23–25 (No. 58, above), on the particular conversion of Egypt into full equality with Israel, in Christ. Girdlestone summarizes it by saying, "Isaiah points to the truth that the Gentiles would be associated with Israel in a special sense in the days of the Messiah. There would be a Jewish nucleus and Gentile adherents, or, as St. Paul puts it, an Israelite tree and Gentile grafts."[174]

98. Isa 44:28; 45:1–5, 13; 48:14–15 (9 vv.): Cyrus of Persia, prophesied by name, as punishing Babylon, 48:14 (cf. No. 47, above), and saying of the Jerusalem temple, "Thy foundation shall be laid," 44:28. Fulfillment (per. 9): Cyrus did appear, more than 150 years later; he captured Babylon in 539 and issued the decree that authorized the rebuilding of the temple, Ezra 1:2–4, in 538. The thought of Isa 45:1, that Yahweh would "subdue nations before him," was specifically repeated by the king, Ezra 1:2 (however sincerely); and the forecast of 45:13, "He shall let My exiles go free," found a similarly exact accomplishment in the final decree of Cyrus, Ezra 1:3.[175]

99. Isa 49:7a; 50:6–9; 52:14; 53:3, *4b, 9a, 12b* (7 vv.): Yahweh's Servant is "One whom the nation abhorreth, a servant of rulers," 49:7a (though subsequently to be exalted, v. 7b, see No. 11, above). Specifically, He suffers: from striking and spitting, 50:6 (cf. Mt 26:67, 27:30), though He remains steadfast in His hope in Yahweh, vv. 7, 9; from the marring of His visage, 52:14; and from being despised, as a man of sorrows, 53:3, being "numbered with the transgressors," v. 12, and being executed as a criminal and condemned to a grave with the wicked, v. 9a. Price comments: "Men assigned the Servant, not the burial of a saint, with reverence and honor, but that of an unjust oppressor for whom no man lamented,"[176] though His eventual grave *was* to become one of honor, v. 9b (see No. 103, below). Fulfillment (per. 13): the suffering, rejection, and death of Jesus Christ; see under Lk 2:34c and John 3:14. He specifically claimed to accomplish Isa 53:12 (Lk 22:37).

100. Isa *52:15a*; 53:5–6, 8b, 10a, 11b, *12c* (5 vv.): redemptive achievements of the Servant of Yahweh, "So shall He sprinkle many nations," 52:15, in atoning purification, cf. Heb 12:24.[177] "The chastisement of [i.e. "achieving"] our peace was upon Him, and with His stripes we are healed. . . . Yahweh hath laid on Him the iniquity of us all," 53:5–6. "As for His generation, who among them considered that He was cut off out of the land of the living for the transgression of My people, to whom the stroke was due?" v. 8, a passage that Acts 8:33–35 quotes in reference to

174. Op. cit., p. 119.
175. Cf. Payne, WTJ, 30 (1967), 55.
176. BBC, IV:226; cf. NIC, III:352–353, men "wanted to appoint" Him a grave with criminals, "however, He was with a rich man."
177. The reading of the ASVmg, "startle (many nations)," is less likely linguistically and poorer theologically; see E. J. Young, *Studies in Isaiah*, pp. 199–206.

Christ. In direct address to Yahweh, Isaiah predicts, "Thou shalt make His soul an *āshām, trespass-offering* [see Lev 5:14] for sin"; and this, in turn, attains redemption for the people, the "seed," whom He adopts as His heirs, Isa 53:10. Finally Yahweh speaks forth and declares, "By the knowledge of Himself shall My righteous Servant justify many; and He shall bear their iniquites" and make intercession for transgressors, vv. 11–12. Fulfillment (per. 13): Christ's death as an atoning sacrifice; cf. especially the parallel predictions in John, listed under 1:29.

101. Isa 53:4a (1 v.): Isaiah says of the Servant, "Surely He hath borne our griefs, *holī*, lit., *sicknesses*, and carried our sorrows." Fulfillment: the healing work of Christ during His earthly ministry (per. 13); cf. the detailed citation of the passage in Mt 8:16–17, "He healed all who were ill, in order that what was spoken through Isaiah the prophet might be fulfilled, saying, 'He Himself took our infirmities and carried our diseases.'"

102. Isa 53:9b (1 v.): the Servant was condemned to a death and to a grave with the wicked, v. 9a (discussed under No. 99, above), "*But* [read adversatively, it would prove to be] with a rich man in His death, *because* [ASVmg] He had done no violence. . . ." Fulfillment (per. 13): Christ's honored burial in the new tomb of Joseph of Arimathea, a wealthy man who had become a disciple of Jesus, Mt 27:57–60.

103. Isa *53:10b–11a:* a further result for the Servant, "He shall see His seed [cf. v. 10a, under No. 100, above]; He shall prolong His days." Edghill concludes, "Although his resurrection is not actually mentioned, it is necessarily implied in these words. . . . We may assert with confidence that the Servant is spoken of as dying, and rising again from the dead."[178] Fulfillment (per. 13): the resurrection of Christ; cf. 55:3 (No. 105, below), on "the sure mercies of David," which is quoted in Acts 13:34 as a basis for our Lord's rising from the tomb.

104. Isa *54:10c, 59:21a*, 61:8 (1 v.): God's promise to establish His testament of peace. It is designated by this technical name in 54:10, and described as everlasting in 61:8. Fulfillment (per. 16): as in Ezek 34:25, the divine *b'rīth* or charter for the Messiah's future kingdom.

105. Isa 55:3 (1 v., typ.): the Davidic testament, specifically, "an everlasting testament, even the sure mercies of David," whose achievement lay dependent on the coming of David's greater son, as "a witness to the peoples, [and] a leader" (v. 4; see No. 11, above). Fulfillment: what had been foreshadowed to David was accomplished in Christ (per. 13), as in II Sam. No. 19. The Isaianic passage is quoted in Acts 13:34, which relates the "sureness" of David's testament to the particular fact of Christ's resurrection.

106. Isa 59:21b (1 v.): after predicting the Messiah's second advent in v. 20 (see No. 77, above), God promises, "My Spirit that is upon thee

178. Op. cit., p. 307.

[Israel] and My words . . . shall not depart forever." Fulfillment (per. 16): the assured presence of the Holy Spirit in the future Messianic kingdom.

107. Isa 63:20–23 (4 vv.): "The child shall die a hundred years old" (v. 20). "They shall not plant, and another eat: for as the days of a tree shall be the days of My people . . . and their offspring shall be [ASVmg] with them" (vv. 22–23). Fulfillment (per. 16): an increased millennial life span, but still the bearing of children and eventual death for those not resurrected at Christ's coming (resurrection has so far been limited to the church, both dead and living; see No. 76, above).

108. Isa 66:19 (1 v.): "I will send such as escape of them [Gentiles, v. 18, presumably from the defeated armies at Armageddon] unto the nations . . . that have not heard My fame; and they shall declare My glory among the nations." Fulfillment (per. 16): a special, millennial missionary effort; cf. 2:3c (No. 10, above).

109. Isa 66:21 (1 v.): the Gentiles are to assist in the regathering of the Jews, v. 20 (see No. 44, above), "And of them also will I take for priests and for Levites, saith Yahweh." The *them* seems to refer to the same subject as appeared in the preceding verse, the Gentiles. "Having been incorporated [see No. 97, above] into the priestly congregation of Israel (ch. 61:6), [they] are not even excluded from the priestly and Levitical service of the sanctuary."[179] Isaiah's forecast might conceivably relate to the regathered Jews of v. 20, "But as what is here promised must be something extraordinary, and not self-evident, 'of them' must refer to the converted heathen, by whom the Israelites have been brought home"[180] (per. 16). Eph 2:14 obviates possible theological objections, "for the wall of separation has now been removed,"[181] between Jewish and non-Jewish believers in Christ.

110. Isa 66:23 (1 v.): in the new heaven and earth, "from one new moon to another, and from one sabbath to another, all flesh shall come to worship before Me, saith Yahweh." Fulfillment (per. 18): the keeping of these feasts, no longer as typical of the rest that Christ should some day bring (as in No. 4, above), but now as a memorial of His finished work.

111. Isa 66:24 (1 v., fig.): from the New Jerusalem of vv. 22–23, "They shall go forth and look upon the dead bodies of the men that have transgressed against Me: for their worm shall not die, neither shall their fire be quenched; and they shall be an abhorring unto all flesh." Fulfillment (per. 18): the second death, as in Rev 20:14–15; cf. Mk 9:47–48. If question should be raised about Isaiah's language, "How can they be the endless prey of worms and fire without disappearing from the sight of men? [Delitzsch replies:] The prophet precludes the possibility of our conceiving of the thing

179. KD, II:513; cf. also A. Edersheim, *Prophecy and History in Relation to the Messiah*, p. 176.
180. KD, loc. cit.
181. BBC, IV:295.

here set forth as realized in this present state. He is speaking of the future state, but in figures drawn from the present world: the eternal torment of the damned."[182]

182. II:516–517.

JEREMIAH

Although the prophecy of Jeremiah is divided into fewer chapters than either Psalms or Isaiah, it still forms the longest book of the Bible in its original Hebrew writing. It consists of the sermons, narratives, and personal reflections of Jeremiah, who was a member of the demoted clan of priests at the village of Anathoth, three miles north of Jerusalem (Jer 1:1; cf. I K 2:26). He ministered in Judah for more than four decades, from the 13th year of Josiah (= 627 B.C.) until after the collapse of the southern kingdom in 586 (Jer 1:2–3). The number of the subjects which he predicted amounts to 90, which ranks second only to Isaiah's 111. The total, moreover, of his verses that forecast things to come is 812, which surpasses that of Isaiah and attains almost to Ezekiel's climactic figure of 821. In fact, if one were to disregard Ezekiel's many allusions to ritualistic matters—which do prophesy Christ, but only by the way of objective types, which arise in history as enacted anticipations of His salvation—then Jeremiah would be found to have authored Scripture's largest block of verbal prediction. Out of his work's 1,364 verses, the 812 that foretell the future amount to 60%, a proportion almost identical to that which appears in Isaiah.

If Isaiah be considered Israel's "princely prophet," and the one most Messianic in his revelations, then Jeremiah would be distinguished as her "spiritual prophet," and the most personal of the nation's ministers. This is true, initially, because of what make up the "confessions" of Jeremiah,[1] by which the inner life of this prophet has become better known than that of any other figure in Scripture, with the possible exception of David as revealed in his psalms. But it is true, more basically, because of his grasp of man's spiritual standing before God. Jeremiah seems to have grown disillusioned as he saw the practical deficiencies in the external, typical religion that marked the whole period of the older testament (7:21–22). He looked forward to the day when even the ark would be unnecessary and unmissed from its place (3:16). Righteousness was the solution (7:23), but the heart of man is depraved and desperately wicked (17:9). There would have to come a personal, divine intervention, when God would betroth men to

1. 1:4–19; 10:23–24; 11:18–12:6; 15:10–21; 17:9–10, 14–18; 18:18–23; 20:7–18.

Himself so that they might know Him directly (cf. Hos 2:19–20). Through Jeremiah, then, Yahweh revealed the truth that serves as a key both to this book and to the whole of God's progressive dealings with mankind, as comprehended first in the OT and then in the NT: "Behold, the days come, saith Yahweh, that I will make a new testament with the house of Israel . . . I will put My law in their inward parts . . . and I will be their God, and they shall be My people . . . for I will forgive their iniquity, and their sin will I remember no more," 31:31–24;[2] cf. its fulfillment in Mt 26:28, Heb 8:6–13, 9:15.

In contrast to the generally chronological outlines of the other major prophets, the arrangement of the Book of Jeremiah is perhaps the most obscure in Scripture. Generally speaking, chs. 1–20[3] advance from 627 B.C. to the death of King Josiah in 609, while chs. 21–51 continue the history to 586. Within these latter chapters, 37–44 form a partial Jeremian biography during Judah's three final years, 588–586; and chs. 46–51 (see especially under 9:25–26f, 12:14a–17, and 25:12b–25) make up a section concerning the foreign nations, though most of it may once have stood after 25:13, where the LXX still preserves these chapters. Beyond this point, the chronological arrangement of Jeremiah's prophecies becomes more involved; see Table 6.

The inscripturation of Jeremiah proceeded through at least four known stages or editions. First, in the 4th year of Jehoiakim (605/604), God directed the prophet to write in a scroll, through dictation to his scribe Baruch, "all the words that I have spoken unto thee against Israel . . . and all the nations . . . even unto this day" (36:2). On the basis of the synthesis shown in Table 6, this first edition would seem to have included Jer 1–13:17,[4] 14–20, 22:1–19, 26, and 47, or approximately 22 chapters.[5]

The second edition, made in the 5th year of Jehoiakim and datable to the close of 604 B.C. (36:9, 22), embraced "all the former words that were in the first roll" (v. 28), plus "many like words" (v. 32). These latter would have included the prophecies communicated to Jeremiah during the preceding year—chs. 25, with 46, 48–51:58 (except 49:34–39), 36 itself, and 45—along with such other messages (possibly, his confessions, for example) as might have seemed suitable for motivating Judah to "present their supplication before Yahweh, and return everyone from his evil way" (36:7). Keil therefore writes, "We may say with perfect confidence that nothing of importance would be omitted from it,"[6] the total, that is, of the approximately 29 chapters, out of the book's eventual 52, that had been

2. J. B. Payne, *Theology of the Older Testament*, p. 115.
3. With the exception of 13:18–27.
4. Except for the later superscription in 1:3.
5. C. von Orelli, "Jeremiah," ISBE, III:1590. Possibly to be excluded are certain of his more comprehensive, noncondemnatory statements, such as the "confessions," see note 1, above.
6. KD, *Jer*, I:27.

TABLE 6
Chronological Arrangement of Jeremiah's Prophecies[7]

Date	Jeremiah	Criterion for Assignment[7]	Notes
I. Josiah (640-609 B.C.)			
627	1	#1, 1:2, and 25:3, 13th year of Josiah	Oct. 628-Oct. 627 B.C.
	2-6	#2, 5:16-17a, 6:22-24; #4, 3:6, under Josiah	Scythian raids, 628-626
627-622	7-10	#5, 7:18, 31, heaven-goddess; #6	Idolatry, pre-622
622	11:1-8	#2, 11:3, 6, Josiah's reform	Covenant, II K 23:2
620-609	11:9-13:17	#3, 11:10, post-622 disillusionment; #6	Josiah's reform cools, 11:9
	14-20	#5, 14:13, 20:7-8, false assurance	Still peacetime, 14:13
II. Jehoiakim (609-598)			
609-608	22:1-19	#2, 22:10; #4, v.18; #5, v.4, hopeful	Josiah dead, Jehoahaz exiled, and Jehoiakim king
	26	#4, 26:1, beginning of the reign	By Necho II after Carchemish
605	47	#2, 47:1, before Egypt smote Gaza	The 22 chapters to date
604	36:1-8	#1, 36:1, Baruch writes Jer's 1st ed.	4th of Jehoiakim-Oct. 605-4
	25	#1, 25:1, 1st of Nebuchadrezzar-Apr. 604-603	LXX has at 25:13
	46, 48-51 (except 49:34-9)	#2, 46:2, post-Carchemish, 605; #3	But before reading it, 36:9
	45	#1, 45:1, after Baruch's 1st writing, 4th year	2nd edition adds 8 chs. more
	36:9-22	#1, 36:9, 22, 5th year, 9th month-Dec. 604	Syrian foes, II K 24:2
600	35	#2, 35:11, danger; #4, 35:1, Jehoiakim	
III. Jehoiachin (Dec. 598-March 597)			
598-597	22:20-30	#4, 22:24, reign of Coniah	Coniah = Jehoiachin
	13:18-27	#2, 13:18, queen mother = 22:26	13:20 parallels 22:22

IV. Zedekiah (597-586)

597	23-24	#2, 24:1; #5, 23:2, same exile as 24	Soon after Jeconiah's carrying away,
	29-31[8]	#2, 29:2, same; #5-6, 30:3 follows	March 597
	49:34-39	#4, 49:34, beginning of the reign	Accession year, pre-Oct.
593	27-28	#1, 28:1; #4, 27:3, 12 (vs.27:1), Zedekiah: #5	LXX omits 27:1 (MT corrupt)
	51:59-64	#1, 51:59, 4th year of Zedekiah	Supplement, on Babylon
588	34:1-10	#2, 34:7, siege, Jan. 15, 588, on	Dated 39:1, 52:4
	21	#2, 21:4, siege; #3, Jeremiah still free	34:4-5 before 21:5
	34:11-22	#2, 34:22, Nebuchadrezzar leaves	Reenslavement, 34:10-11
	37	#2, 37:5, Nebuchadrezzar leaves; #3, 37:15, 21	Jeremiah's 1st imprisoned
587	32-33	#1, 32:1, 18th year of Nebuchadrezzar, Apr. 587-6	Jeremiah in prison, 32:2, 33:1
586	38	#3, 38:28, down to Jerusalem's fall	So near end of siege
	39:15-18	#3, 39:16, a response to Ebed-melech	Result of 38:7-13
	39:1-14	#1, 39:2, city fell July 19, 586	Cf. 52:5-7

V. Gedaliah and After (July 586 B.C. and on)

586	40-43:6	#1, 41:1, 7th month, Gedaliah dead	Month began Oct. 7
	43:7-ch. 44	#3, 43:7, cf. 42:7, 10 days later	In Egypt
Post-561	52	#2, 52:30, after 582; v. 31, after 561	52 not by Jeremiah, 51:64

7. Principles for establishing Jeremiah's sequence, in order of validity:

#1. Date expressly stated, specific to at least the year of the king.
#2. Historical allusion, to some other datable event.
#3. Logical relationship, prior or subsequent to other data found within Jer.
#4. Reference to a general period, within the reign of a given king.
#5. General tone, suggestive of a certain historical context.
#6. Successiveness in the text, least applicable in Jer of all the prophetic books, yet still legitimate within units of the Book, no other data conflicting.

For elaboration, see J. B. Payne, "The Arrangement of Jeremiah's Prophecies," ETSB, 7(1964), 120-125.

8. On the repetitive and cyclic character of chs. 30 and 31, see above, pp. 129-130.

so far revealed to the prophet. This second edition covered well over half of Jeremiah's ministry,[9] seems to have been generally chronological, and, unlike the first edition, which Jehoiakim had burned, survived to "form the basis of the collected edition of all Jeremiah's prophecies."[10]

A third edition would next have been produced, perhaps in stages (cf. 30:2, on "the book of consolation," chs. 30–31), but more plausibly at one later point, near the close of Jeremiah's ministry. Baruch might possibly have "collected and edited" the book;[11] but both the analogy of the known origin of the first and second editions and the force of the introductory statements that accompany Jeremiah's later chapters[12] forbid the usual critical conclusion of composition by,[13] rather than dictation to, Baruch. The very order in which the later prophecies now appear, with as much concern for topical as for chronological sequence, so suggests Jeremiah's own evangelistic purpose in respect to his people that Young concludes: "Even the arrangement of the prophecies may be due to the suggestion of Jeremiah, although actually carried out by Baruch."[14]

The present book, or fourth edition, if it may be so entitled, consists simply of the above, with the addition of a final, 52nd chapter, not by Jeremiah (51:64), but closely related to II K 24:18–ch. 25. Its function is apologetic, to furnish a historical vindication—gloomy as this is—to Jeremiah's four decades of unheeded warning. For while it is unfair to stigmatize this man of God as the "weeping prophet" (on the basis of verses such as 9:1 or 14:17), it remains correct that his life was marked by a persistent opposition on the part of his unrepentant countrymen (from 1:19 to 44:16) and that his message, though containing the ultimate hope of God's newer testament, was built around a conviction of contemporaneous doom for Jerusalem. This one thought (No. 1, below) occupies no fewer than 222 Jeremian verses and constitutes the most extensive single prophecy to be found in any book of the Bible.

1. Jer 1:13–16; 4:4, 11–14, 16–21, 27a; 5:29, 31; 6:1–8, 11–12, 15; 7:15, 19–20, 29, 32–34; 8:1–3, 10, 12–17; 9:1, 7, 9–15, 17–22, 26b; 10:17–22; 11:11–14, 16–17; 12:7–13, *14b*; 13:1–16; 14:10–12, 15–19; 15:1–3, 5–9, 12–13; 16:1–10, 16–18, 21; 17:3, *27b*; 18:11, 15–17; 19:1–13, 15; 20:3–4a, 5, 8, 10; 21:3–6, 8–10, 12–14; 22–5–8; 23:12, 15,

9. M. F. Unger, *Introductory Guide to the OT*, p. 325.
10. KD, I:26; so also von Orelli, loc. cit., and S. R. Driver, *The Book of the Prophet Jeremiah*, p. xlvii.
11. Unger, op. cit., p. 326.
12. E.g. 27:1, "In the beginning of the reign of [Zedekiah] . . . came this word unto Jeremiah from Yahweh, saying"; 42:4, "Then Jeremiah the prophet said unto them . . ."; cf. 21:1, 30:1, 42:9, 43:1, 10.
13. Cf. R. H. Pfeiffer, *Introduction to the OT*, p. 501.
14. *An Introduction to the OT*, p. 244; and cf. my more detailed analysis of the present arrangement of Jeremiah, "The Arrangement . . . ," pp. 125–128.

19–20, 33, 36, 39; 24:10; 25:9a, 11a, 18, *29a*; 26:6b, *9b*, 11–12a, 18a, 20; 27:13–15, 17; 29:15–*18a*; 30:12–15; 31:28a, 29–30; 32:3, 24, 28–32; 34:1–2, 17a, 18–20; 35:17; 36:3, 7, 29, 31; 38:3, 18a, *23c*; 39:15–16; 40:2; 45:4; 50:7 (222 vv., sym.): at the time when God called him to be a prophet, Jeremiah said, "I see a boiling caldron; and the face thereof is from the north" (1:13). Explanation for this symbol follows: "Out of the north evil shall break forth upon the inhabitants of the land" (v. 14); "the kingdoms of the north shall come against Jerusalem and against all the cities of Judah" (v. 15); cf. 6:1, 10:22 (cf. 13:20, on 597 B.C., under No. 34, below), 16:12, and 25:9. 4:4 ends with the divine warning, ". . . lest My wrath burn so that none can quench it"; cf. vv. 11–14; and this cannot refer to the contemporary Scythian raids (see No. 12, below), for it tells of chariots (v. 13), which these barbarians did not possess, and includes "the whole land" (vv. 20, 27). So 6:1, 6, speaks of siege against Jerusalem; cf. v. 12, "their houses shall be turned unto others" (= 8:10). 7:32 refers to the ravine below Jerusalem, "It shall no more be called The valley of the son of Hinnom, but The valley of Slaughter" (= 19:6). 8:2 predicts that the bones of the Judean kings are to be exposed; and 9:11 reads, "I will make Jerusalem heaps." Judah is to be "plucked up" from among her neighboring nations, 12:14.

Jer 13:1–11 employs a symbol: Judah is to be "marred" (v. 9) like a buried and rotten girdle (v. 7); vv. 12–14 present a figure, "I will dash them one against another" like those filled with wine; and 16:1–10, another symbol, that Jeremiah is to remain unmarried, for the people "shall die grievous deaths" (v. 4), and he is not to enter "into the house of mourning . . . for both great and small shall die" without burial or lamentation, or into the house of feasting, for the voice of mirth is to cease (vv. 5–9). Sword and famine are to come upon the land, 14:15; cf. II K 25:3. Judah is to be hunted out, even from the clefts of the rocks, 16:16. Because of their idolatry, Yahweh warns, "I will cause them to know My might," vv. 18–20; and "Fire shall devour the palaces of Jerusalem," 17:27b (= 22:5, 50:7).

19:1–13 contains the symbol of the potter's vessel, about which God told Jeremiah, "Break the bottle, and say unto them, Even so will I break this people and this city" (vv. 10–11). In a similarly symbolic vein the prophet renamed his persecutor, the high-ranking priest Pashhur, "Magormissabib," meaning "terror on every side" (20:3): a renewal in wording of Jeremiah's former Scythian prophecy (10:25, under No. 12, below); but now Babylon is for the first time named as God's destructive agent against Jerusalem (20:4) and as the "terror on every side" (v. 10).[15]

15. These words formed a part of the people's derisive mockery of Jeremiah: as they are paraphrased by Laetsch, *Bible Commentary, Jeremiah*, p. 177, "Terror round about? We do not see it! Let him bring it on if he can!" But what they were quoting was true.

21:4, datable to 588, becomes more explicit against Judah: "I will turn back the weapons of war that are in your hands, and I will gather the Chaldeans that besiege you . . . into the midst of this city." In v. 6 pestilence is forecast (= 24:10, 27:13) and in vv. 8–9, death (= 29:17, 34:17), unless one surrenders to the besiegers (= 38:2; cf. vv. 17, 20). V. 10 states, "This city shall be given into the hands of the king of Babylon [Nebuchadrezzar, 25:9], and he shall burn it with fire" (= 32:3, 34:2). 26:18 is a quotation of the prophet Micah's threat of more than a century before that Jerusalem should become heaps (Mi 3:12); and 31:28 quotes Jeremiah's original call, relating his commission to "pluck up and tear down" (1:10) to Jerusalem's fall in 586. 31:28 concerns the proverb of the sour grapes, which the prophet repudiated, teaching rather that "every one shall die for his own iniquity"; and ch. 32 specifically condemns the false prophets and priests of Judah.

Fulfillment (period 7): as in Lev. No. 33, the fall of Judah to Nebuchadrezzar, July, 586. In Jer 32:24, during the siege, the prophet had stated to Yahweh, "What Thou hast spoken is come to pass"; and in 40:2 a Babylonian officer alluded to Jeremiah's previous forecasts as now carried out.

2. Jer 1:18–19; 15:11, 19–21; 20:11, 13 (8 vv., fig.): God's initial assurance to His servant, "I have made thee this day a fortified city" (1:18); as explained in the next verse, "The whole land [Judah] shall fight against thee; but they shall not prevail against thee: for I am with thee, saith Yahweh, to deliver thee" (= 20:13). In 15:11 He adds, "I will cause the enemy to make supplication unto thee in the time of affliction" (= v. 19); and in 20:11 Jeremiah expresses his conviction that "My persecutors shall stumble . . . with an everlasting dishonor." Fulfillment (per. 7): Jeremiah was protected, especially just before and during the final fall of Jerusalem, 38:5–6, 11–13, 28; 39:11–14. The predicted supplication by the people to the prophet may be documented from 21:1–2; 37:3, 17; 38:14; 42:1–7.

3. Jer 2:16–17, 19, 36–37 (5 vv., fig.): after alluding to the fall of N. Israel a century before (vv. 14–15),[16] Jeremiah turns to Judah, "The children also of Memphis and Tahpanhes [Egyptian cities] have broken [lit., "shall pasture clean"[17]] the crown of thy head" (v. 16); "thine own wickedness shall correct thee" (v. 19). "From thence [Egypt] thou shalt go forth with thy hands upon thy head," in dismay (v. 37). Fulfillment (per. 7): Judah's defeat and King Josiah's death at Megiddo, 609, so that the nation became subject to Egypt, II K 23:29–35. The reference is not to the past; for the time is still that of Josiah's reign (1:2, 3:6), and the verbs are in the imperfect. Judah's previous appeals to Assyria, 2:18 (cf. II K 16:7), or to Egypt, v. 19—Sihor = the Nile—(cf. II K 18:21) had led only to the land's devastation (II K 18:13 and II Chron 28:21); and

16. BBC, IV:329.
17. Laetsch, op. cit., p. 39.

so now Josiah's intermeddling in world politics, v. 25 (cf. II Chron 35:20–22) would cost him dearly.[18]

4. Jer 3:11–14; 31:5–6, 8–*12a*, 16–17, 21 (13 vv.): an appeal to survivors of the northern kingdom, "Return, thou backsliding Israel . . . and I will take you, one of a city, and two of a clan [several cities], and I will bring you to Zion" (3:12, 14). So 31:5–6 speaks about people of the north, from the hills of Ephraim (cf. 50:19, under 31:12b, No. 67, below) and Samaria, coming to Zion; and vv. 8–9 specify, "A great company shall return hither," including pregnant women and crippled men, but "they shall not stumble." Cf. the joint prophecies of restoration for both N. and S. in 30:3, 31:27, 33:7, 50:5 (under No. 37). Fulfillment (per. 9): as in II Chron 30:9, the return to Palestine of some from N. Israel, along with those of Judah, in 538–537.

5. Jer 3:15 (1 v., fig.): at the restoration (No. 4, preceding), "I [Yahweh] will give you shepherds according to My heart, who shall feed you with understanding." Fulfillment (per. 9): the shepherd figure represents Judah's postexilic community leadership, as in Isa No. 6 (1:26).

6. Jer *3:16a, 23:3b*, 30:19b–20a (2 vv.): the prophet anticipates a time for God's people "when ye are multiplied and increased in the land" (3:16); and the Lord Himself promises, "I will glorify them, and they shall not be small . . . and their congregation shall be established before Me" (30:19–20). Fulfillment (per. 14): as in Gen. No. 19, the increase of the church through Gentile augmentation to Israel;[19] for Jer 3:16b (No. 7, following) goes on to speak of the termination of external worship in the new testament, and 23:3b stands chronologically between the postexilic return (v. 3a) and the future kingdom (vv. 4–6),[20] as does also 30:19–20, between v. 18, on the return, and v. 21, on the Messiah ruling in His future realm.[21]

7. Jer 3:16b; 30:22; 31:1, 31, 33–34; 32:40 (7 vv.): in days to come in Judah, "They shall say no more, The ark of the covenant of Yahweh . . . neither shall it be made any more." In 30:22 the Lord assures them that as a result of the Messiah's priestly mediation (v. 21c, No. 66, below), "Ye shall be My people, and I will be your God." There follows in ch. 31 what is perhaps the most significant prediction in all of Scripture:[22] v. 31, God foretells, "I will make a new testament with the house of Israel and the house of Judah"—for Christ's coming was to the Jews, Mt 15:24. This *b'rīth* is then characterized by four major features in Jer 31:33–34. (1) "I will put My law in their inward parts, in their heart"; cf. 32:40, "I will put My fear in their hearts." (2) Yahweh's promise to be their God, as

18. Ibid., and KD, I:76.
19. See above, p. 113.
20. See above, p. 113, on the sequence of this passage.
21. See above, p. 130, on this sequence.
22. See above, introduction to Jeremiah.

in 32:22 above—and, indeed, throughout Scripture, for this same fundamental promise of the testament appears from Genesis (17:7) to Revelation (21:3). (3) "They shall all know Me, from the least of them unto the greatest," which is Protestantism's affirmation of the priesthood of all believers. (4) "For I will forgive their iniquity, and their sin will I remember no more," in Christ. Similarly in ch. 32, vv. 38–39 had spoken of a spiritual conversion among the Jews of the exile, to fear Yahweh and to be His people (No. 68, below); but v. 40 then goes onto forecast, "And I will make an everlasting testament with them . . . that they may not depart from Me." Fulfillment (per. 14): "The new testament inaugurated at the last supper,"[23] as this passage is identified in Heb 8:6–13 (the longest single OT quotation to be found in the NT), 9:15, 10:16–19.[24]

23. J. Bright, *The Kingdom of God*, p. 229; see above, pp. 100–102.

24. Dispensational writers normally maintain that Heb 8–10 quotes Jeremiah's new testament as descriptive not of God's present relationship with the church but of His future relationship with the Jews. This claim, however, is difficult to support. C. C. Ryrie, for example, grants that the "better testament" of which Christ is the mediator, and which supersedes the older testament of Moses (Heb 8:6), refers to the church; but he would distinguish it from the "second testament," which is said to be the testament with the Jews, in the following verse, *The Basis of the Premillennial Faith*, pp. 120–121. The explanation that is put forward is that Jeremiah's quotation is introduced not, as might have been expected, to prove that the transcending of the older testament had been predicted by the prophet for accomplishment by means of the new testament of the church; Jeremiah's words are said rather to prove that since in the millennium there will be a superseding of the older testament by the new testament which will then be made with the nation of Israel, so now, by analogy, it is not impossible to think of a transcending of the old by the better testament of the church. Dispensationalism's interpretation suffers, at the outset, from the inherent unlikelihood of such unelaborated subtlety of thought. It results, moreover, in a weakened argument for the epistle. Its readers were being confronted with the temptation of lapsing back into Mosaic ceremonialism; and to explain that Jeremiah had predicted that in the millennium ceremonialism would be replaced by a more spiritual form of worship would hardly be as convincing as to quote the prophet to prove its replacement at the time then present. There appear also three major contextual objections to the distinctions that are drawn by dispensationalism. (1) Heb 8:13 records that it is by means of Jeremiah's new testament that God makes the first testament old. Yet the period of Moses' first testament was limited to the pre-Christian era (9:8). Furthermore, as Ryrie concedes, the passage "goes on to show in Heb 9 how the Christian order superseded the sacraments of the Mosaic covenant," ibid., p. 121 (v. 11). It follows, therefore, that the Christian order must itself be Jeremiah's new testament; cf. B. Ramm, *Protestant Biblical Interpretation* (1956 ed.), p. 256. (2) In 9:14 the purging of "your" (contemporary NT church) consciences is the equivalent to the forgiveness promised by the new testament in 8:12; and this forgiveness is accomplished through Christ's death as He mediates the new testament (v. 15). Since He *is* hardly mediating something that is to be set up only in millennial times, Ryrie confesses that the new testament of 9:15 was established by Christ's death, op. cit., p. 117; but since he feels he must maintain that the new testament of 8:12 is one that is distinct from that of the church, he is led to the conclusion that there must be two "new testaments" in Hebrews, the future one in ch. 8 and the present one in ch. 9, ibid. (3) Since Heb 10:16–17 again quotes Jeremiah's new testament, this also must be defined as the future new testament. Yet because of the remission of sins that will result from this "future" new testament, the writer says to the church, "Since *therefore*, brethren, *we* have confidence . . ." (v. 19)! The new testament is one, and it belongs to the church, Payne, *Theology*, pp. 76–78.

8. Jer *3:17a*, 31:38–39 (2 vv.): Jeremiah's prophecy moves onward[25] to a day when "they shall call Jerusalem the throne of Yahweh" (3:17). The city's limits will include the ancient borders of Jerusalem, from the tower of Hananel, north of the temple, to the hill Gareb, presumably the SW hill, which is modern (but not ancient) Zion.[26] Fulfillment (per. 16): as in Isa No. 16 (4:5), that the Messianic kingdom will center in God's presence in Jerusalem.

9. Jer 3:17b, 4:2, 16:19–20 (4 vv.): all nations will be gathered to Jerusalem "to the name of Yahweh" and will cease their evil ways (3:17), confessing the futility of idolatry (16:19–20); for "in Him the nations shall glory" (4:2). Fulfillment (per. 16): as in Gen. No. 47, Isa. No. 9, that all peoples will yet seek the Lord.

10. Jer 3:18–19a (2 vv.): that the houses of Judah and Israel together will come out of their diaspora (dispersion) to Palestine. Fulfillment (per. 16): as in Hos. No. 6, the millennial return of Jews to the land.[27]

11. Jer 3:*19b*–23, 31:40a (5 vv.): Jeremiah's forcast to the people of God in Palestine (including the returned Jews of No. 10, preceding), "Ye shall call Me, my Father, and shall no more turn away from following Me" (3:19). 3:22–23 then contains confessions by the redeemed, which "the prophet already hears in spirit."[28] Even the polluted valley of Hinnom is to become holy to Yahweh (31:40). Fulfillment (per. 16): the millennial holiness of God's Israel, as in Dt No. 45 (corresponding to that of the former pagans, in Jer 3:17, No. 9, above).

12. Jer 4:5–9, 29–31; 5:6–7, 9–18; 6:18–19, 22–26 (27 vv.): a warning, "Blow ye the trumpet in the *land*," but not primarily for *Jerusalem*, as though predicting the city's fall, in 586, which is the situation of 6:6 (No. 1, above); God's more immediate word is for Judah to "flee for safety, stay not; for I will bring evil from the north, and a great destruction" (4:5–6). "The heart of the king shall perish" (v. 19); and, adds the prophet, speaking figuratively, "a lion out of the forest shall slay them" (5:6). Prophesied details include: famine (v. 12)—for "they shall eat up thy harvest, flocks, and herds; they shall impoverish [ASVmg] thy fortified cities" (v. 17)— and flight into thickets, before horsemen and bowmen (4:29) with quivers (5:16), who are "murderers" (4:31) and cruel (6:23), before "a nation from far, mighty and ancient, whose language thou knowest not" (5:15). Jeremiah prophesied about Judah, "Take away her branches, but make not a full end," 5:10 (= v. 18);[29] for the invaders were soon to depart. Yet for the immediate future: "We have heard the report thereof: anguish hath taken hold of us. . . . Go not forth into the field; for the sword of the enemy

25. See above, p. 129.
26. Cf. J. Simons, *Jerusalem in the OT*, pp. 231–233.
27. In itself, this event could be postexilic, as proposed in BBC, IV:336; but because of the millennial context of v. 17, preceding, the accomplishment of these verses appears to be yet future.
28. KD, I:98–99.
29. Cf. the same promise in reference to 586, 4:27.

and terror are on every side [Heb., *māgōr-missābīb*, as in 20:3] . . . for the destroyer shall suddenly come upon us," 6:24–26. Fulfillment (per. 7): the known raids of barbaric Scythian horsemen, from the Russian plains north of the Caucasus, along the coast of Palestine, 628–626 B.C. The event corresponds to these chapters in time, since the year of Jeremiah's call was 627; and it would explain the mockery that Jeremiah faced (20:8, 10; cf. 6:25 and No. 1, above, note 15) when the barbarians later withdrew. While some of the prophet's first oracles found their fulfillment in Judah's ultimate fall to Babylon, "Other things are thought to be more relevant to the Scythians than to the Chaldeans."[30]

13. Jer 4:23–26, 28 (5 vv.): that the earth is to become waste, the heaven black, and the mountains to tremble "at the presence of Yahweh and before His fierce anger." Confessedly, this passage occurs in the center of predictions about the woes of 586 B.C. (No. 1, above); but "Jeremiah seems to see through, and beyond, the moment of Judah's destruction to a more distant scene . . . to the consummation",[31] cf. v. 27 (No. 1, and also No. 14, following), on the Babylonians, but looking ahead as well, for Yahweh would not make a *full* end. Fulfillment (per. 15): as in Isa. No. 48, the wrath of God.

14. Jer *4:27b*, 30:11c, 31:7, 46:28c (3 vv.): though the whole of Judah be devastated, "yet will I not make a full end," 4:27. The same thought appears in 30:11 and 46:28, with the addition, "but I will correct thee in measure." 31:7 refers to "Thy people, the *remnant* of Israel," in which Israel may possibly signify the northern kingdom.[32] Fulfillment (per. 8): as in Lev. No. 37 (26:42b), a preservation of the Hebrews in exile.[33]

15. Jer 5:19; 8:3, 18–19; 9:16; 13:17; *15:2b*, 4, 14; 16:13a; 17:4; *20:4b*; 24:9; 29:18b; 30:4–7a, 23–24; 31:15; *34:17b* (19 vv.): "Ye shall serve strangers in a land that is not yours" (5:19, 17:4), ". . . a land that is very far off" (8:19), "which thou knowest not" (15:14, 16:13). "Death shall be chosen rather than life by all the residue that remain in all the places whither I have driven them," 8:3. 20:4 is the first passage to specify that the captivity will be to Babylon, though 24:9 speaks more broadly, that King Zedekiah's exiles of 586, in contrast with the somewhat better treatment received by those of Jehoiachin in 597, are "to be a reproach, a taunt, and a curse, in all places where I shall drive them." 34:17, moreover, warns of their being "tossed to and fro among all the kingdoms of the earth." The prophet says, "We have heard a voice of trembling, of fear,

---

30. H. H. Rowley, *Men of God*, p. 153. He also suggests, "That there are some things in the oracles, which have been frequently called the 'Scythian Songs' . . . more relevant to the Chaldeans than to the Scythians is recognized; and that is why the oracles are believed to have been retouched," pp. 152–153, though evangelicals will insist upon the unity and early dating, believing that God intended these elements of the oracles for Babylon, from the start.

31. BBC, IV:343–344.

32. Ibid., IV:425.

33. Cf. KD, I:117.

and not of peace. . . . Alas! for that day is great, so that none is like it: it is even the time of Jacob's trouble" (30:5–7), until God "will break his yoke from off thy neck" (v. 8). In 31:15 he speaks figuratively of the nation's mother, "Rachel weeping for her children," until they "shall come again from the land of the enemy" (v. 16.).[34] Fulfillment (per. 8): "The time of Jacob's trouble (30:7) could be applied to the immediate situation [of 597 B.C., 29:2, and its deportation], though it has a much longer period in view—the whole period of the captivity,"[35] as in Lev 26:33. To this era corresponds the figure of the *yoke* (v. 8), which identifies the Babylonian rule in 27:2, 8, 28:14, and opposes the view of those who would apply 30:7 to a time of eschatological trouble.[36] Others would limit its application to the conclusion of the exile: "The days preceding the return shall be days of fear and agony, the death throes of the mighty Babylonian world empire. . . . For Babylon the great day will come, the like of which it had not experienced in all the centuries of its existence."[37] But the fearful party appears rather to be Judah, experiencing the unparalleled, Babylonian exile; cf. Ezek 5:9, "I will do in thee that which I have not done, and whereunto I will not do any more the like, because of thine abominations."

16. Jer 6:9 (1 v., fig.): Judah's (Babylonian) enemy "shall thoroughly glean the remnant of Israel as a vine: turn again thy hand as a grape gatherer." Laetsch comments, "We think of the repeated deportations and slayings of the Jews that had survived the long siege, Jer 52:24–20."[38] Fulfillment (per. 8): the continuing disasters that befell the remnant of Judah, down to 582 B.C. (52:30).

17. Jer 6:20a; 7:*21a*, 22a; *14:12a; 17:26a* (2 vv., typ.): burnt offerings. Fulfillment (per. 13): as in Lev. No. 3.

18. Jer *6:20b;* 7:21:b, *22b;* 17:26b; *33:11b* (2 vv., typ.): peace offerings. Fulfillment (pers. 13 and 16): as in Lev. No. 5.

19. Jer 7:2, 4, 10–12, 30; 11:15; 17:12, *26d;* 19:14; 20:1–2; 23:11; *24:1b;* 26:2, 7, *9c*–10; 27:16, 18, 21; 28:1, 3, 5–6; 29:26; 32:34; *33:11c;* 34:15; 35:2, 4; 36:5–6, 8, 10; *41:5b; 50:28b;* 51:11, 51; 52:13, *17a, 20b* [see II K 25:9, 13a, 16b, under 11:3] (34 vv., typ.): the temple, as in Ex. No. 55.

20. Jer 7:14; 26:3–*6a*, 9a, *12b, 18b* (5 vv.): God's forecast against the Jerusalem sanctuary, "I will do unto this house, as I did to Shiloh," 7:14; cf. I Sam 4:10–11, and the prediction of 2:32a. Jer 26:18 is a quotation of Mi 3:12, which made this same prediction more than a century earlier. Fulfillment (per. 7): as in I K. No. 16, the burning of the temple, in August, 586.

21. Jer 9:25–*26a*, 25:19–*20a*, 43:8–13, 46:13–26a (22 vv., sym.):

34. See above, p. 129; and on this verse's use in Mt 2:18, p. 477 below, cf. pp. 77–79.
35. NBC, p. 626.
36. As KD, II:5–6; and see above, p. 112.
37. Laetsch, op. cit., p. 240.
38. Ibid., p. 84.

that God would punish Egypt, "and all the mixed people" (25:20), still presumably referring to Egypt, as in Ex 12:38, Ezek 30:5. 43:8–9 describes Jeremiah's symbolic act, that he took large stones and concealed them at the entrance to the pharaoh's palace at Tahpanhes. Vv. 10–13 then follow with the explanation: "Nebuchadrezzar will spread his royal pavilion over them"; and he will smite the land of Egypt, take captives, burn temples, and break down the pillars, or obelisks, of "the house of the sun, probably *Heliopolis,* that is, *On,* see Gen 41:50" (ASVmg). In 46:26 God threatens the Egyptians and their leaders: "I will deliver them into the hand of Nebuchadrezzar king of Babylon" (cf. v. 13); and among the details are these: v. 16, the hired troops[39] are foreseen as saying, "Arise and let us go again to our own people"; v. 19, the city of Memphis is to become a desolation, without an inhabitant; and v. 25, the deity Amon of No (representing the people of his city, Thebes) is to be punished. Fulfillment (per. 8): "This successful expedition took place in 568–567, [when Egypt was] under the pharaoh Amasis."[40]

22. Jer *9:26c; 25:20b, 21a; 27:3a;* 49:14–16, 19–22 (7 vv.): Edom (= Uz, of 25:20; see Lam 4:21) is to be punished. God speaks of the future as past, "I have made thee small among the nations" (49:15). An invader, "whoso is chosen" by Yahweh, is to come up like a lion (v. 19) or like an eagle (v. 22). Fulfillment (per. 8): the attacker remains unnamed but is probably Nabunaid of Babylon, and the invasion, a part of his campaign of 552 against Tema; see Obad 1–4. The above-listed vv. are seemingly to be distinguished from Jer 12:17, 49:7–13, 17–18,[41] which speak of the ultimate expulsion of the Edomites from their land in about 500 B.C. (No. 32, below). For Jeremiah also envisages both their being attacked by Babylon, 12:14a (No. 29), and then their restoration from Babylonia, v. 15 (No. 30), prior to the permanent destruction of the land.

23. Jer *9:26d, 25:21c, 27:3c,* 49:2–5 (5 vv.): Ammon to be punished. 49:2, "Rabbah [the Ammonite capital] shall become a desolate heap"; v. 3, "for Malcam [= Milcom, their deity] shall go into captivity." Fulfillment (per. 8): Ammon's fall to Babylon in 582, as in Amos No. 9 (1:13–15), from which Jeremiah here quotes.

24. Jer *9:26e; 25:21b; 27:3b;* 48:1–10, 12–26, 28, 31–46[42] (42 vv.): Moab to be punished. In seeming reference to Nebuchadrezzar (cf. 27:6), 48:40 predicts, "He shall spread out his wings against Moab"; v. 8, "The

39. Herodotus, II, 152, 163, spoke of 30,000 Aegean mercenaries employed by Pharaoh Hophra (cf. 44:30).
40. JB, p. 1319; cf. ANET, p. 308.
41. Just as are Obad 1–4 from Obad 5–6, from which Jeremiah drew the wording of his own prophecies in 49:14–16 and 9–10 respectively. But since Obadiah dates more than a century before Jeremiah (see below, introduction to Obadiah), the fulfillment of Obad 1–4 seems to have been achieved long before Jeremiah's appearance and reuse of these vv. for his own times.
42. Jer 48 draws extensively upon Num 24:17, Isa 15–16, and Amos 2:1–3.

destroyer shall come upon every city"; v. 7, "and Chemosh [the national god, representing the people] shall go forth into captivity." Fulfillment (per. 8): Moab had been pro-Chaldean in 598 B.C. (II K 24:2); but they subsequently revolted from Babylon (cf. Jer 27:3), perhaps because of Nebuchadrezzar's exactions for his building programs.[43] Josephus asserts that the Babylonian king destroyed Moab, Ammon, and the neighboring peoples in 582–581;[44] and he must at least have deported the bulk of their populations,[45] for archaeology confirms that Transjordan was largely depopulated before the middle of the 6th century B.C.[46] Whatever Moabites returned after Babylon's overthrow in 539 (12:15, 48:47, Nos. 30 and 86, below) soon disappeared; see Zeph 2:9a.

25. Jer *9:26f*, 25:23–24, 49:28–33 (8 vv.): punishment upon "all that have the corners of their hair cut off, that dwell in the wilderness" (9:26), that is, the Arabian tribes (25:23, 49:32). 49:28–30 states that they are to be destroyed and have their property plundered by Nebuchadrezzar. Kedar is named; and Hazor, whose location is unknown, is to be "a desolation for ever." Fulfillment (per. 7): Wiseman comments on the quantity of Nebuchadrezzar's spoil taken from the Arab lands in early 598 B.C., quoting the cuneiform source: "He sent out his companies; and, scouring the desert, they took much plunder from the Arabs: their possessions, camels, and gods."[47]

26. Jer 11:1–4, 6–10; 14:21; 22:9; 31:32; 34:13; *50:5c* (13 vv., typ.): the Sinaitic testament. In 50:5, when the returning exiles are joining themselves to Yahweh "in an everlasting testament," the presumed reference is to a renewal of God's earlier redemptive arrangement.[48] Fulfillment (per. 13): as in Ex. No. 45 (19:5).

27. Jer 11:5 (1 v.): a quotation of God's former promise to give Canaan to Israel. Fulfillment (per. 4): as in Gen. No. 24 (12:7).

28. Jer 11:20–23 (4 vv.): death by sword and famine predicted for the men of Anathoth, because of their plots against the life of Jeremiah.[49]

---

43. A. H. Van Zyl, *The Moabites*, pp. 155–156.
44. *Ant*, X, 9, 7; Van Zyl, op. cit., p. 157. 581 is the more probable date, or even later, since in 582 the Moabites "remained neutral until Nebuchadrezzar's troops had all but disposed of their northern neighbor," Ammon (No. 23, above), and then actually provided assistance for Babylon, H. L. Ginsberg, "Judah and the Transjordan States from 734 to 582 B.C." *Alexander Marx Jubilee Volume*, p. 365.
45. HDB, III:412.
46. IDB, I:112.
47. *Chronicles of Chaldean Kings*, pp. 31–32, 71. Laetsch, op. cit., p. 350, refers to Berosus and to Arabian legends on the reality of such a raid; but their data remains uncertain.
48. BBC, IV:488; and see above, pp. 205–206, 208.
49. The prophet's preaching on behalf of Josiah's reformation (vv. 3–5 ?), may have antagonized the local priests to this extent, even though they were Jeremiah's kinsmen (1:1), because of the reform's insistence on priestly functioning only at the central sanctuary in Jerusalem, II K 23:5, 8–9, which directly affected their own livelihood at Anathoth.

The specific fulfillment is not recorded, but that it may have occurred during the time of Jerusalem's siege and famine in 586 appears likely, II K 25:3.

29. Jer 12:14a; 25:9b–10, 15–17, 27–28, 29b; 27:1–2, 4–7a, 8–11; 28:11–14; 30:16 (22 vv.): about the nations surrounding God's people, "All Mine evil neighbors, that touch the inheritance [of Israel] . . . I will pluck them up from off their land" (12:14); and they "shall go into captivity" (30:16). Concerning "all these nations round about [Judah]: I will utterly destroy them" (25:9); "and these nations shall serve the king of Babylon seventy years" (v. 11, uttered in 604 B.C.).[50] 27:7 specifies that they are to be subject to Nebuchadrezzar, to his son (Evil-merodach, II K 25:27, 562–560 B.C., or perhaps Nabunaid, as Nebuchadrezzar's next major successor), and to his grandson, Belshazzar (who seems to have been so considered; cf. Dan 5:11).[51] Should they refuse to serve Babylon (Jer 27:8), they would suffer exile (v. 10); but if they would submit, they might "remain in their own land" (v. 11). Fulfillment (per. 8): most of them attempted revolt and were punished with exile, just as were the Jews,[52] particularly those who had attacked Judah, 12:14, 30:16; cf. II K 24:2, on Syria, Ammon, and Moab.

30. Jer 12:15 (1 v.): a further divine oracle (see No. 29, above) on the nations around Judah, "I will have compassion on them and bring them again, every man to his land," namely Edom, and Israel's other neighbors (cf. Nos. 22–24). Fulfillment (per. 9): the return of the others, just as became true for Judah, from their exile in Babylonia after Cyrus of Persia had conquered it in 539.

31. Jer 12:16 (1 v.): the prophet continues, "If they will diligently learn the ways of My people . . . then shall they be built up in the midst of My people." Fulfillment (per. 11): the outstanding example is the incorporation of the Edomites (= NT Idumaeans), along with others (cf. the case of the Philistines in Zech 9:7), into Judah by the Hasmonean kings, as in Gen 25:23b (3rd stage).

32. Jer 12:17; 49:7–13, 17–18 (10 vv.): the completion of Edom's fall (cf. No. 22, above). 12:17, "But if they will not hear, I will pluck up that nation, destroying it, saith Yahweh."[53] 49:9–10, there are to be no gleanings;[54] v. 13, "all the cities of Bozrah [in Edom] shall be perpetual

---

50. 25:15 ff. includes "all the nations" to whom God would send Jeremiah; and the list that occurs in vv. 18–26 concerns primarily the local, surrounding enemies, though others appear as well, including Judah (v. 18), and Babylon herself (v. 26).

51. Both because of his position as a successor to Nebuchadrezzar and because his father, Nabunaid, had married a daughter of Nebuchadrezzar; cf. R. D. Wilson, *Studies in the Book of Daniel,* I:124.

52. IDB, I:112; cf. the list in Jer 27:2–3, on those who were plotting against Babylon at that time: Edom, Moab, Ammon, Tyre, and Sidon.

53. 12:17 includes the fate of other neighbors of Israel, whose destructions came to pass in similar ways; cf. 25:19–24 (No. 21, 23–25 above).

54. These vv. are based on Obad 5–6.

wastes"; and v. 18, "no man shall dwell there." Fulfillment (per. 9): as in Obad. No. 2, the cutting off of Edom by the Nabatean Arabs. On the forecast of 49:11, that their widows will seek Jewish protection, see Gen 25:23b on their migration into Idumaea (cf. No. 31, preceding).

33. Jer 13:18, 22:24–28 (6 vv.): Jeremiah is directed, "Say thou unto the king [Jehoiachin, 22:26] and to the queen-mother . . . the crown of your glory is come down" (13:18); they would be given into the hands of Nebuchadrezzar (22:25) to die in exile (vv. 26–27). Fulfillment (per. 7): the deposition of Jehoiachin in 597, II K 24:10–12, and his death in Babylon, 25:30; cf. Jer 13:19 (No. 36, following), on his captivity.

34. Jer 13:19–27, 22:20–23 (13 vv.): "Judah is carried away captive" (13:19),[55] under Jehoiachin (v. 18, No. 33, preceding). The prophet goes on to address Zion, God "shall set over thee those whom thou hast thyself taught to be friends to thee" (v. 21), i.e. the Babylonians, and perhaps other of those who joined in the attacks leading up to 597 B.C., as the Syrians, Moabites, etc., II K 24:2.[56] In 22:20–22 Jeremiah, by a poetic device, addresses the land: "All thy lovers are destroyed . . . and shall go into captivity." The *lovers* could be Judah's neighboring states, as in 30:14;[57] but at this point they stand in parallelism with "thy shepherds," namely, the leaders of Judah who were taken captive with Jehoiachin, II K 24:14.[58] Fulfillment (per. 7): as in Isa. No. 13, the deportation of 597, consisting of Judah's upper classes.

35. Jer *14:12b, 17:26c,* 41:5a (1 v., typ.): meal offering. Fulfillment (per. 13): as in Lev. No. 4.

36. Jer *16:13b:* v. 13a had foretold Judah's exile (see under No. 15, above); the passage continues, "and there shall ye serve other gods day and night." Fulfillment (per. 8): as in Dt. No. 15, the practice of paganism in the exile; similar idolatries characterized those who fled to Egypt as well, Jer 44:15–27.

37. Jer *16:14–15;* 23:3a, 7–8; 24:1–6; 29:10b–14, *22b;* 30:3, *7b*–8a, 10–*11a,* 17–18a; 31:23–24, 27, *28b;* 32:8–15, 36–37, 41–44; 33:7, *26b;* 46:27–*28a;* 50:*5a,* 8, *19a;* 51:*6a, 44b,* 50 (42 vv.): but after the exiles of 16:13 and 23:2 (No. 15 and 36, above), "I will bring them again into their land that I gave unto their fathers" (16:15); and this act of divine grace will surpass even the exodus as a matter of grateful recognition (16:14, 23:7).[59] 24:5–6 employs a comparison, in reference to the mem-

55. The following phrase, "wholly carried away captive" (which might suggest the general exile of 586), seems to mean only that the whole country surrendered in 597, including even "the cities of the south" (13:19), which made up "the part of the kingdom most remote for an enemy approaching from the north," KD, I:238.

56. Ibid., I:240.

57. Ibid., I:342–343.

58. See above, p. 127.

59. 23:7–8 follows a passage with Messianic fulfillment, but it corresponds to v. 3 and quotes 16:14.

bers of the 597 deportation with Jehoiachin: "Like these good figs, so will I regard the captives of Judah . . . for good. For I will bring them again to this land and plant them." In 30:7–8 God speaks more generally of Israel's being saved out of exile: "I will break his yoke [the rule of the Babylonian, 27:2, 8, 28:14] from off thy neck"; and 30:10–11 (= 46:27–28) repeats the thought,[60] adding, "I will save thee from afar, and thy seed from the land of their captivity; and Jacob shall return and be quiet and at ease, and none shall make him afraid" (= 32:37, they are "to dwell safely"),[61] in contrast to the fearful doom of the surrounding nations, 30:11b (cf. 25:29). 31:28b quotes the prophet's original, generalized call (1:10) on "building and planting," but here in special reference to the postexilic restoration.[62] In 32:8 Jeremiah's purchase of Hanamel's field served as a symbolical "word of Yahweh." It is explained in vv. 15, 43–44: "Houses and fields shall yet again be bought in this land"—though his act was one of personal sacrifice for the prophet, since this was the time of the final siege of Jerusalem, vv. 16, 24–25, 43, when land tenure meant little. In the book's final oracles, Jeremiah visualizes the state of the exiles themselves: 50:5, "They shall enquire concerning Zion with their faces thitherward." He informs them, "Flee out of the midst of Babylon," v. 8 (= 51:6, 45, 50); and God promises, figuratively, in respect to Bel, the god of Babylon: "I will bring forth out of his mouth that which he has swallowed up," 51:44 (cf. v. 34). Fulfillment (per. 9): Israel's return from exile, 538–537, as in Dt. No. 43.

38. Jer 17:21–22, 24, 27a (4 vv., typ.): sabbath. Fulfillment (per. 13): as in Ex. No. 41.

39. Jer 20:6 (1 v.): to Pashhur, a leading priest and chief officer of the temple, for his persecution of Jeremiah, "Thou, Pashhur, and all that dwell in thy house shall go into captivity; and thou shalt come to Babylon, and there thou shalt die." The accomplishment of this prophecy is not specifically documented, but it remains probable. Laetsch proposes that it was "fulfilled most likely at the deportation of Jehoiachin, 597 [per. 7, see No. 34, above], as shortly after this event Zephaniah is addressed as the chief supervisor of the Temple (ch. 29:25–26). It may have occurred in an earlier deportation mentioned in Dan 1:1–3, the third year of Jehoiakim."[63]

40. Jer 21:7; 23:1–2; 24:8a; 32:4–5; 34:3, 21; 37:17; 38:*18b*, 23b (10 vv.): "I will deliver Zedekiah king of Judah and his servants into the hand of Nebuchadrezzar . . . and he shall smite them with the edge of the sword," 21:7. The same group of leaders forms the subject of 23:1–2 (cf. 24:1) and makes up the "bad figs" of 24:8 (contrast the "good figs" of 24:1–6, noted under No. 37, above). 32:4–5 adds, "Zedekiah shall speak with Nebu-

---

60. See above, p. 130.
61. JB, p. 1300, "with no one to trouble him."
62. Cf. a similar phenomenon in v. 28a, under No. 1, above.
63. Op. cit., p. 175.

chadrezzar mouth to mouth [= 34:3] . . . and he shall bring Zedekiah to Babylon, and there shall he be until I visit him" (in death, see 34:4–5). Fulfillment (per. 7): Zedekiah was captured and carried northward to Nebuchadrezzar at Riblah, II K 25:6; his sons were slain before his eyes, and he was blinded (cf. Ezek 12:13) and sent as a prisoner to Babylon, II K 25:6.

41. Jer 22:10–12 (3 vv.): that King Jehoahaz (= Shallum), 609 B.C., is never to return to Judah but is to die in his Egyptian captivity. Fulfillment (per. 7.): it was so, II K 23:33–34.

42. Jer 22:18–19, *36:30b* (2 vv.): "Concerning Jehoiakim, king of Judah: they shall not lament for him . . . he shall be buried with the burial of an ass, drawn and cast forth beyond the gates of Jerusalem" (22:18–19); "his dead body shall be cast out" (36:30). The fulfillment (per. 7) of Jeremiah's prophecy has been widely questioned. This evil ruler died in December, 598; and, as Keil states, "There is no record of Jehoiakim's funeral or burial in II Kings 24. . . . [But] it is in the highest degree probable that Jehoiakim fell in battle against the Chaldean-Syrian armies before Jerusalem was besieged; also that he was left unburied outside of Jerusalem."[64]

43. Jer 22:29–30, 36:30a (3 vv.): "Concerning Jehoiakim: he shall have none to sit upon the throne of David" (36:30). Keil explains, "His son Jehoiachin ascended the throne. But this accession could not be called a sitting on the throne, a reign, inasmuch as he was immediately besieged in Jerusalem by Nebuchadrezzar, and compelled to surrender after three months, then go into exile to Babylon;"[65] cf. No. 33, above. Jeremiah went on, moreover, to prophesy of Jehoiachin, "Write this man childless" (22:30). Fulfillment (per. 7): though Jehoiachin had children,[66] I Chron 3:17–18 (Mt 1:12),[67] they were not "men, prospering, sitting upon the throne of David" (22:30): his only purely human, reigning successor, and Judah's last pre-Christian Davidic king, was his uncle Zedekiah, 597–586. From this situation arises the necessity of Christ's deity, to supersede Jeremiah's curse against Jehoiachin, even as it became crucial in His overcoming of the curse on Adam's seed in general; cf. Ezek 21:27, that there should be no more true crown in Judah until the coming of the Messiah.

64. I:341. The same possibility is granted by Oxtoby, *Prediction and Fulfillment in the Bible*, p. 82, even with his differing approach to Scripture; and he adds, "We simply do not have enough data to decide." For a summary of critical theories, see BBC, IV:400.

65. II:103.

66. As confirmed by archaeological "ration receipts," ANET, p. 308; cf. J. Finegan, *Light from the Ancient Past*, p. 226, and Wm. F. Albright, "King Jehoiachin in Exile," BA, 5 (1942).

67. And Lk 3:27 as well: for "Zerubbabel, the son of Shealtiel," was actually a son of Shealtiel's brother Pedaiah and a grandson of Jehoiachin. He was a nephew of Shealtiel, who may have died childless, so that Pedaiah married his widow (per Dt 25:5–10), cf. I Chron 3:17–19.

44. Jer 23:4, 33:25–26a (3 vv., fig.): in contrast with the evil officers who ruled under Zedekiah (34:1–2), God foretells, "I will set up shepherds over them, who shall feed them; and they shall fear no more" (23:4); "I will take of His [the Davidic Messiah's] seed [i.e. from all Christians; see 33:22a, No. 75, below] to be rulers over the seed of Abraham" (33:26). Laetsch adduces this parallel: "In Mt 19:28, Lk 22:28–30, the Lord gives special promises to His twelve apostles, who shall rule with Him."[68] Fulfillment (per. 16): millennial officers chosen from among the church, as in Mi. No. 33 (5:5b).[69]

45. Jer *23:5a;* 30:9, *21b;* 33:15a, 17, 19–20, *21b* (5 vv.): "I will raise unto David a righteous Branch," Heb. *sémah* (23:5). In Isa 4:2 this same noun had denoted literal plant growth in God's future kingdom, but the verbal root had appeared in II Sam 23:5 foretelling the Messiah as a branch out of the family of David; cf. Isa 11:1. Jer 30:9 thus states, "They shall serve Yahweh their God, and David their king, whom I will raise up unto them." This descendant[70] shall be of themselves and shall proceed from the midst of them," v. 21; but thenceforward He is to be eternal: "David shall never lack a man to sit upon the throne of Israel," 33:17 (cf. v. 21). Fulfillment (per. 13): the coming of Christ, from within the Hebrew nation, as the eternal son of David, as first predicted in II Sam 7:13b (prophecy No. 11).

46. Jer 23:5b, *33:15b* (1 v.): "He [the Branch, No. 45, preceding] shall reign as king, and shall execute justice and righteousness in the land" (23:5), in accordance with the precedent set by David himself, II Sam 8:15. Fulfillment (per. 16): as in II Sam. No. 18 (23:3), the righteousness of Christ's millennial rule; cf. Isa 11:3, under 9:7c.

47. Jer 23:6, *30:8b*, 33:16 (2 vv.): "In His [the Branch's] days shall Israel dwell safely; and this is His name whereby He shall be called, Yahweh, our righteousness" (23:6)—probably in contrast with the then reigning king, Zedekiah, whose name means *The righteousness of Yah*(weh), but whose life failed to measure up to his nomenclature. Jeremiah's point is not that the Messiah *is* Yahweh, but that through Him Yahweh will provide a righteousness, of deliverance; cf. the identical title for Jerusalem in 33:16. Thus, "Strangers shall no more make him [Jacob] their bondmen" (30:8).[71] Fulfillment (per. 16): as in Lev. No. 29, millennial peace and restraint of violence.

---

68. Op. cit., p. 272.
69. Keil suggests that the figure of the *shepherds* simply designates the Messiah, in the sense of 23:6 (No. 47, below); but compare the Micah passage.
70. As in I K 12:16—He is not David himself reincarnated; cf. 33:17, and p. 84, above.
71. 30:8b appears in Jeremiah, following Judah's postexilic deliverance from the Babylonian yoke, v. 8a (No. 37, above); but it moves onward in time to the nation's permanent release. Cf. the parallel in the second cycle of the chapter, v. 20b (No. 65, below); and see p. 130 above.

48. Jer 24:7, 32:38–39, 33:8 (4 vv.): after the return from exile, 24:1–6, 32:36–37, 33:7, (No. 37, above), "I will give them a heart to know Me: and they shall be My people, for they shall return unto Me with their whole heart" (24:7); "and I will cleanse them from all their iniquity" (33:8). Fulfillment (per. 9): postexilic regeneration, conversion, and reconciliation with God among the Jews, e.g., Ezra 1:5, 3:11.

49. Jer *24:8b*; 42:13–22; 44:7–8, 11–14, 26–29 (20 vv.): "I will give up . . . them that dwell in the land of Egypt" to a continuing exile and curse (24:8, datable to 597 B.C.). These earlier Jewish settlers along the Nile are "perhaps those who shared the captivity of Jehoahaz [No. 41, above], II K 23:34, or perhaps Israelite refugees in Egypt."[72] In connection with the further flight then of 586, which Jeremiah was compelled to accompany, the prophet threatened, "The sword, which ye fear [presumably Nebuchadrezzar's, 43:11], shall overtake you there in the land of Egypt, and the famine; and there ye shall die . . . and none of them shall escape . . . and ye shall see this place [Palestine] no more" (42:16–18; cf. 44:14). As he went on to explain, "They that escape the sword shall return out of the land of Egypt into the land of Judah few in number" (44:28).[73] In v. 26 God said, "My name shall no more be named in the mouth of any man of Judah in all the land of Egypt," meaning, "The living God will see to it that they will perform no more religious observance in His name";[74] in other words, they will be exterminated.[75] Fulfillment (per. 8): after Nebuchadrezzar's campaign of 568–567 (No. 21, above), the Jews living in Lower Egypt who escaped death were then, according to Josephus, deported to Babylon.[76]

50. Jer *25:11b–12a*; 29:*10a*, 28 (1 v.): in 604 B.C. (25:11–12) the prophet predicted a service for 70 years to the king of Babylon. He therefore counseled the exiles of 597 to make provision for permanent life in Babylon, 29:5–7. More generally, v. 28, "The captivity is long." Fulfillment (per. 8): the exile extended technically from the first deportation of Judah in 605 B.C. (Dan 1:1–4) to one of the following dates: 539, the Persian capture of Babylon; 538, the decree of Cyrus authorizing the return; 537, by the fall of which the first returnees had come to Palestine, Ezra 3:1–2; or 536, when the temple's reconstruction commenced, v. 8.

51. Jer. 25: 12b–14, *26c*; *27:7b*; 50:*1–3a*, 9–10, 14–16, 18, 21–32, 34–38, 41–46; 51:1–4, 6b, 8–14, 24, 27–28, 30–33, 44, 46–49, 52–56 (63 vv.): after the 70 years of domination by the Babylonians (Nos. 29 and 50, above), "Many nations and great kings [cf. 50:9, 41; including the same sort of barbaric Scythian horsemen that had terrified Judah; cf. 50:41–43

---

72. JB, p. 1293.
73. KD, II:166, ". . . more exactly stated that only a few individuals shall escape and return; thus no one shall remain behind in Egypt."
74. BBC, IV:468.
75. KD, loc. cit.
76. *Ant*, X, 9, 7, though his reliability has been questioned, IB, V:1095.

with 6:22–24, No. 12, above] shall make bondmen of them" (25:14).[77] "Tidings shall come one year, and after that in another year" (51:46), seemingly concerning the Persian advance under Cyrus. "Out of the north [= 50:41, 51:48] there cometh up a nation ["the kings of the Medes," 51:11] against her," 50:3. Ararat (Armenia) and other northern nations are to be allied with Cyrus and the Median power (51:27–28). The prophet commanded, v. 26, "Destroy her utterly," though this final removal came later (see 25:12c, No. 52, following); v. 28, men are to flee to escape out of the land (cf. v. 29); and v. 30, "all her men of war shall be brought to silence" (= 51:3). 50:15, Babylon's walls are to be thrown down (= 51:44), at a time, 50:24, when "Thou wast not aware." Fulfillment (per. 8): as in Dt. No. 46, the capture of Babylon in the autumn of 539; cf. the fall of the citadel to the invaders in the very night of the Chaldeans' careless feasting, Dan 5:30.

52. Jer *25:12c*; *30:11b*; *46:28b*; 50:3b, 11–13, 39–40; 51:25–26, 29, 34–43, 57–64 (27 vv.): "I will make the land of the Chaldeans desolate for ever" (25:12); God says further, to Judah, "I will make a full end of all the nations whither I have driven thee" (30:11, 46:28), and this applies in particular to Babylon. "None shall dwell therein" (50:3); it is to be "a desert" (v. 12), "a perpetual sleep" (51:39, 57). In 51:63 the prophet casts a scroll-book, weighted with a stone, into the Euphrates, meaning by this symbol, "Thus shall Babylon sink and shall not rise again." Fulfillment (per. 12): as in Isa. No. 49 (13:19), the eventual abandonment of the city's site.

53. Jer 25:20c, 47:2–7 (7 vv., fig.): that the Philistines, listed according to their four remaining cities (25:20), are to be punished. Jeremiah uttered the prochecy of ch. 47 "before Pharaoh smote Gaza" (v. 1), an event that fulfilled Zeph 2:4a (plus Jer 47:5a, No. 85, below) and that seems to date shortly after the battle of Carchemish in 605, when, according to Herodotus, Necho II took "Kadytis."[78] Yet except for 47:5a on Gaza, Jeremiah's prophecy apparently concerns a power whose home was in the north. In 47:2 he employs the figure of "waters rising up out of the north": as explained in v. 4, "Yahweh will destroy the Philistines," and he is referring to them as a group that is already a remnant (25:20, 47:4). Specifically, God will cut off from Philistia any possible help for the cities of Tyre and Sidon, which were to the north along the Mediterranean coast, v. 4; and His hostility appears to focus on Philistine Ashkelon, v. 7. Fulfillment (per. 7): after his victory at Carchemish on the Euphrates in 605, Nebuchadrezzar moved south after the retreating Egyptains and occupied the Philistine cities.[79] He attacked Ashkelon (which Jeremiah had singled out

77. In 25:26, 51:41, *Shishach* is a consonantal cipher for Babel, formed by exchanging the two *b's* (the 2nd letter of the Heb. alphabet) in BaBel for *sh's* (the 2nd from the last letter), and the *l* (12th letter) for *ch* (12th from the last). By a similar "atbash," *Leb-kamai* in 51:1 = *Casdim*, the *Chaldeans*.

78. *History*, II:159; cf. IB, V:1110.

79. D. J. Wiseman, op. cit., p. 28.

for attention in 47:7; cf. v. 5) in 604 and boasted that "He turned the city into a mound and heaps of ruins."[80] The Babylonian monarch thus "put out any remaining sparks of Philistine independence. He deported both rulers and people,"[81] though for the final disappearance of Philistine life, see Amos 1:8c, Zeph 2:4b.

54. Jer 25:22, 27:3d (2 vv.): that God's sword would be sent against "the kings of Tyre and Sidon and of the coast-land [ASVmg] which is beyond the sea," meaning, "their many colonies on the coasts of the Mediterranean."[82] Fulfillment (per. 8): submission by the Phoenicians to Nebuchadrezzar; cf. 27:6. Theirs, however, is the only group of people in the list of ch. 25 that is not elaborated upon later in Jeremiah, though the very fact stated in 47:3 (see v. 20c, No. 53, preceding) that the Philistines would not be able to come to their aid suggests the forthcoming siege of Tyre by Nebuchadrezzar, with its sword, famine, pestilence, and destruction, 27:8, just as predicted in Isa 23:13 and Ezek 26:1, *q.v.*

55. Jer 25:25–26a, 49:34–38 (7 vv.): punishment predicted for "all the kings of Zimri, Elam, and the Medes" and other "kings of the north" (25:25–26) who supported Nebuchadrezzar's western offensives (v. 9). In ch. 49 only Elam is named in the discussion; but Media became increasingly associated with the Elamites (cf. Isa 21:2), and Zimri may actually be an alternate designation for Elam.[83] In the chapter God says, "I will break the bow of Elam . . . and scatter them toward all winds . . . till I have consumed them" (vv. 35–37). Fulfillment (per. 9): the final breaking of Elam (per. 9) was preceded by the loss of various portions of this ancient land which lies to the east of Babylonia. Part of the province of Anshan seems to have been incorporated into Persia by Cyrus I, ca. 600 B.C.;[84] but "of the date or manner of the capture of Anshan . . . anticipated by Jeremiah . . . from the Elamites there is no direct record."[85] Attack on Elam by Nebuchadrezzar is difficult to verify;[86] and though the province of Gutium was seized by Cyrus II, the Great, prior to 539, *from Babylon*,[87] most of this territory appears to have lain outside Elam, and in Babylonia, in any event.[88] The Elamites were still actively threatening the old Chaldean city of Erech in 540; and Isaiah (21:2) had long before predicted their participation with Media in the final attack on Babylon in 539. But soon thereafter they, like the Medes, must have become forcibly assimilated into the empire of

---

80. Ibid., p. 69.
81. IDB, III:795.
82. Laetsch, op. cit., p. 212.
83. JB, p. 1295.
84. IDB, II:71.
85. CAH, IV:6.
86. Keil, II:260–262, denies any war by Nebuchadrezzar with Elam; and Wiseman, op. cit., p. 36, confirms this, unless a brief reference out of his 596–595 campaign record refers to Elam.
87. John Bright, *A History of Israel*, p. 341.
88. Y. Aharoni and M. Avi-Yonah, *The Macmillan Bible Atlas*, map 161, p. 104.

Cyrus; and so, "As early as 597 [49:34–39] Jeremiah was able to foresee the conquest of Elam by the Persians."[89]

56. Jer 25:26b, 29c–38; 45:5a (11 vv.): punishment upon "all the kingdoms of the world" (25:26); compare God's words in 45:5, "I will bring evil upon all flesh," or 25:29, "I will call for a sword upon all the inhabitants of the earth." Jeremiah goes on to predict in v. 31, "He will enter into judgment with all flesh"; and in v. 33, "The slain of Yahweh shall be from one end of the earth to the other." Vv. 34–35 foretell "dispersions" but "no way to flee." Fulfillment: the prophet's discussion of Yahweh's 6th-century B.C. judgments, 25:9–29a, leads him into the subject of the final battle of Gog and Magog. In its later and more elaborate revelation in Ezekiel 38–39, 38:17 indicates that the Lord had made prior disclosures about Gog: "Thou art he of whom I spake in old time by My servants the prophets of Israel, that prophesied those days for many years that I would bring thee against them." These verses then in Jeremiah appear as the likely reference points for Ezekiel's statement, since they advance beyond the more localized destruction of the Lord's enemies at the battle of Armageddon (per. 15, No. 65, below) into His world-embracing, post-millennial campaign against Gog and Magog (per. 17), as described in Rev 20:8–9.[90]

57. Jer 27:19; 52:17b, 20a [see II K 25:13b, 16a, under 16:17] (3 vv., typ.): the "sea," or laver. Fulfillment (per. 13): as in Ex. No. 67.

58. Jer 27:22a: that the temple vessels were to be carried to Babylon. Fulfillment (per. 7): it was so, II K 25:14–15.

59. Jer 27:22b (1 v.): when God should "visit them," the temple vessels would be restored to Jerusalem. Fulfillment (per. 9): as occurring in Ezra 1:7–11.

60. Jer 28:16 (1 v.): Jeremiah's threat against the false prophet Hananiah, "This year [593 B.C., v. 1] thou shalt die, because thou hast spoken rebellion against Yahweh." Fulfillment (per. 7): Hananiah died in September of that same year, v. 17: see above, p. 69.

61. Jer 29:21–22 (2 vv.): that the adulterous false prophets Ahab and Zedekiah, who were among the Jewish exiles in Babylon, would be publicly executed by Nebuchadrezzar, "roasted in the fire." No record exists of the accomplishment; but since the Hammurabi law code did prescribe burning for adulterers, its likelihood is great (per. 8).

62. Jer 29:32a (1 v.): God's word against an exiled false prophet, who was still opposing Jeremiah by means of letters, "I will punish Shemaiah and his seed: he shall not have a man to dwell among this people," that is, to share in the return from exile. Fulfillment (per. 8): no later record of Shemaiah exists, but the very absence of any reappearance for his family in postexilic Israel is in itself significant.

89. JB, p. 1329.
90. Pentecost, *Things to Come*, p. 504, uses these passages to advance a theory that "all sinners will be cut off *before* the institution of the Kingdom."

63. Jer *30:14a*, 37:7 (1 v., fig.): an oracle addressed to the nation of Judah, personified, "All thy lovers have forgotten thee; they seek thee not" (30:14). In more concrete terms the prophet later predicts, "Pharaoh's army, which is come forth to help you, shall return to Egypt into their own land" (37:7; cf. Ezek 17:17, spoken four years earlier). Fulfillment (per. 7): at her fall in 586 Judah was forsaken by the allied nations from whom she had anticipated help; cf. 27:3, 37:5–8. Pharaoh's particular desertion is demonstrated by Nebuchadrezzar's resumption of the siege of Jerusalem shortly after Jeremiah's utterance; cf. 34:22 (No. 77, below).

64. Jer *30:18b–19a*, 31:4 (1 v.): when Israel returns to Jerusalem, "the city shall be builded upon its own hill," accompanied by "thanksgiving and the voice of them that make merry." Fulfillment (per. 9): as in Mi. No. 37, in 444 B.C. Jerusalem's walls were reconstructed, Neh 6:15, and the city repopulated, 11:1, with attendant celebrations, 8:12, 12:27, 40, 43.

65. Jer *30:20b–21a*: the Messianic "ruler" (cf. vv. 9, 21b, under 23:5a, No. 45, above) shall "punish all that oppress" God's people. Fulfillment (per. 15): the battle of Armageddon, as in Num. No. 36.

66. Jer 30:21c (1 v.): God's words about the work of the future Messianic Branch, as rendered literally by Laetsch, "I will permit Him to approach, and He shall come near to Me. For who is He that will pledge His life to come near to Me?"[91] Fulfillment (per. 13): the atoning work of the Messiah, as a mediating priest, just as in Job 17:3 etc.; "He shall have priestly access to the Presence"[92] of God the Father.

67. Jer 31:12b–14, 25–26; 33:1–6, 9–13; 50:19b–20 (18 vv.): following the Jews' exile,[93] They shall come . . . unto the goodness of Yahweh: to the grain and to the new wine, and they shall not sorrow any more at all" (31:12). Yahweh explains in the next verse, "I will turn their mourning into joy [= 33:9, 11] and make them rejoice in their sorrow"; that is, they are to possess "unclouded joy as they forget all their former sorrow."[94] See also v. 25, "I have satiated the weary soul"; 33:3,6, "I will show thee great things: . . . health, peace, and truth"; or 50:19–20, "His soul shall be satisfied upon the hills of Ephraim . . . for I will pardon them whom I leave as a remnant." Fulfillment (per. 9): the goodness of God, as exhibited to the Jews who returned to their land in 538–537, but especially after their faithful performance of rebuilding the temple in 520–515; cf. Ezra 6:16, 22, and Haggai's revelation of (what had become by then) Yahweh's immediate intention of restoring prosperity—despite crop failures up to that point (Hag 1:6, 9; 2:16–17)—if they would truly seek God (2:19).[95]

68. Jer 31:18–20, 22; 50:4, 5b (6 vv.): in 31:18–19 the northern kingdom of Ephraim is depicted as speaking, in exile (v. 15), "I was

91. Op. cit., p. 242.
92. NBC, p. 626.
93. See above, p. 129.
94. KD, II:22.
95. See above, p. 38.

chastened . . . I repented, after I was instructed"; and in 50:4–5, "Israel and Judah together shall seek Yahweh their God. . . . saying, Come ye and join yourselves to Yahweh in an everlasting testament [the Sinaitic, see No. 26, above]," when they should take counsel about returning to Palestine (v. 5a; see No. 37, above). 31:22 forecasts, "A woman shall encompass a man": not Mary, but the "virgin of Israel," v. 21, in faith embracing Yahweh.[96] Fulfillment (per. 8): as in Dt. No. 16, exilic repentance.

69. Jer 31:35–37 (3 vv.): that Israel is not to "cease from being a nation before Me for ever." Fulfillment (per. 16): the millennial establishment of God's people as a permanent, political entity.

70. Jer *31:40b:* Jerusalem "shall not be thrown down any more for ever." Fulfillment (per. 18): as in Ps. prophey No. 30, the eternal status of Jerusalem.

71. Jer 32:6–7 (2 vv.): that Jeremiah's cousin Hanamel would come to him with an offer to sell a field in Anathoth. Fulfillment (per. 7): Hanamel did, v. 8, so that Jeremiah understood that his proposition was "the word of Yahweh" (see above, under No. 37).

72. Jer *33:18a, 21c, 22b*: references to "the priests, the Levites," in a context of future Messianic times; e.g. v. 22, "I will multiply the Levites that minister unto Me." Fulfillment (per. 16): the existence of many officiating Levites during the millennium; cf. Isa 66:21 on the incorporation of Gentiles into this rank and service. Such Levitical activity may, indeed, be one of the factors in the future increase of God's people as a whole (cf. v. 22a, No. 75, below).

73. Jer 33:18b (1 v.): "Neither shall the priests the Levites want a man before Me to offer . . . sacrifice continually." This passage cannot be limited in its application to the OT dispensation, for it stands in parallel with the eternity of the Messiah, vv. 21–22. Fulfillment (per. 16): Levitical sacrifice in the millennial temple, as in Isa No. 8 (2:2b). Since, however, Christ has once and for all made the atonement for man's sin (Heb 9:12, 28; 10:12), these observances cannot be atoning, but only "a thankful memorial to the finished work of Christ (cf. Heb 13:15)."[97]

74. Jer 33:21a (1 v., typ.): the Davidic testament. Fulfillment (per. 13): as in II Sam. No. 19.

75. Jer 33:22a (1 v.): in a context of service by millennial Levites (vv. 21c, 22b; No. 72, above), God promises, "I will multiply the seed of David My servant." Cf. Isa 53:10, on designating Christian believers as the "seed" of the Messiah; for all who receive the Savior become "children of God, heirs also, fellow-heirs with Christ," Rom 8:16–17, and are called His brethren," Heb 2:11. Fulfillment (per. 16): the multiplication of believers in Christ during the millennium. This is an event to be "realized by the reception of the heathen into the royal . . . privileges of the people of God."[98]

---

96. KD, II:28–31.
97. Payne, *Theology,* p. 496; and see above, p. 286.
98. KD, II:76.

76. Jer 34:4–5 (2 vv.): a personal word to King Zedekiah, "Thou shalt not die by the sword; thou shalt die in peace . . . and they shall lament thee." Fulfillment (per. 8): Zedekiah seems to have died, without violence, in prison, 39:7 (= II K 25:2). As Keil, moreover, observes, "His imprisonment would not necessarily be an obstacle in the way of an honorable burial after the fashion of his fathers";[99] cf. the privileges granted to Jehoiachin even before his death, 52:31–34 (= II K 25:27–30).

77. Jer 34:22, 37:8–10 (4 vv., with both passages datable to 588 B.C.): despite the diversion caused by an Egyptian advance (37:5), Nebuchadrezzar's army is to return to Jerusalem and destroy it. Fulfillment (per. 7): the Babylonians did return, at least by the next year, which was 587; cf. 37:21 with 32:1–2.

78. Jer 35:18–19 (2 vv.): because of the example set by the Rechabites' obedience, the Lord promised, "Jonadab the son of Rechab shall not lack a man to stand before Me [in worship, 7:10] for ever." Fulfillment: Rechabite priests existed during the NT era; "and in medieval and modern times (per. 14) travelers in Syria and Arabia have found tribes that claimed to be Rechabites and to follow the rules of Jonadab."[100]

79. Jer 38:21–23a (2 vv.): when Zedekiah's wives and children are to be brought out to a victorious Chaldean enemy, they will tell the misguided king, "Thy familiar friends have deceived [ASVmg] thee and have prevailed over thee." As Laetsch paraphrases the passage, the women would "ridicule his weak and vacillating policy in following his alleged friends who urged him on to a hopeless struggle."[101] The actual fulfillment (per. 7) of this oracle is unrecorded; but it is known that the Chaldeans seized Zedekiah's sons, 39:6, and they seem to have held the power over his daughters as well, 43:6.

80. Jer 39:17–18 (2 vv.): an oracle from God to Jeremiah's protector Ebed-melech, that at the fall of Jerusalem, "Thou shalt not be given into the hand of the men of whom thou art afraid [whether of the Babylonians, or of antagonistic Jewish princes] . . . but thy life shall be for a prey unto thee, because thou hast put thy trust in Me." He would escape with his life, even if with nothing more. The fulfillment (per. 7) is unknown; but it may be assumed, perhaps on the basis of the good treatment received by Jeremiah himself, 40:4–5.

81. Jer 44:30 (1 v.): as a pledge of the fulfillment of the other prophecies that involve the Egyptian kingdom of this period (cf. 42:13 and 43:8, No. 49 and 21, above), the Lord foretold, "I will give Pharaoh Hophra into the hand of his enemies that seek his life." Fulfillment (per. 8): Hophra was dethroned and executed by Amasis, who succeeded him in 569.[102]

---

99. Ibid., II:82.
100. IB, V:1062.
101. Op. cit., p. 297.
102. JB, p. 1321; according to Herodotus, II:161–162, 169, Hophra was strangled by an Egyptian mob. See above, p. 13, note 54.

82. Jer *45:5b:* a personal word of Yahweh to Jeremiah's scribe Baruch, "Thy life will I give unto thee for a prey in all places whither thou goest." Keil states, "It is intimated that he will be obliged to avoid destruction by flight, but will thereby save his life."[103] The precise fulfillment is unspecified; but Baruch is known to have been a member of the Jewish flight to Egypt in 586, 43:6–7.

83. Jer 46:5–6, 10–12 (5 vv.): while ch. 46 in its written form was composed in the fourth year of Jehoiakim, which commenced in October, 605 B.C., *after* the battle of Carchemish (v. 2) between the forces of Egypt and Babylon, the prophet's opening verses "view the scene on the eve of the battle";[104] and at this point Jeremiah says of the Egyptians, "In the north by the river Euphrates have they stumbled and fallen" (v. 6), though it is the hand of Yahweh that will direct the human forces, when "the sword shall drink its fill of their blood" (v. 10). Fulfillment (per. 7): Pharaoh Necho II's defeat before Nebuchadrezzar at Carchemish in 605, v. 2.

84. Jer *46:26b:* though Nebuchadrezzar invade Egypt (vv. 13–26a, No. 21, above), "Afterward it shall be inhabited, as in the days of old." Fulfillment (per. 8): Egyptian recovery after the Babylonian campaign of 568–567, as Amasis (see No. 81, above) continued on in his position as a pharaoh of the XXVIth Dynasty.

85. Jer *47:5a* (fig.): "Baldness is come upon Gaza." Fulfillment (per. 7): as in Zeph. No. 2; for unlike the other Philistine cities that Jeremiah threatened in ch. 47, who received their punishment at the hands of Nebuchadrezzar in 604 (see under Jer 25:20c, No. 53, above), Gaza is singled out in Jer 47:1 as having been smitten by a pharaoh, namely Necho II, a year earlier, in 605 B.C.

86. Jer 48:47 (1 v.): after God's oracle of doom upon Moab, vv. 1–46 (discussed under 9:26e, No. 24, above), the prophet adds, "Yet will I bring back the captivity[105] of Moab in the latter days." Fulfillment (per. 9): the Moabites shared, presumably, in the return of the various displaced peoples that resulted from Cyrus of Persia's taking control of Babylon in 539 (No. 30, above).[106] Ezra 9:1 and Neh 13:1, 23, mention Moabite women as wives of Israelites down to 425 B.C. But Moab's restoration must have been of limited duration (see No. 24, above); for in contrast with the various allusions to Ammon and Edom in I Macc (cf. No. 88, below), no further mention of Moab appears in any later source.[107]

87. Jer *49:2b:* because of the Ammonite occupation of Israelite territory in Transjordan (v. 1), Jeremiah foresees a future reversal in their respective

---

103. II:173.
104. BBC, IV:473; cf. IB, V:1106, which concludes that the poem of vv. 3–12 may have been "written either as prediction or in celebration of the victory."
105. On the term "captivity," see above, p. 17.
106. Though cf. the caution about present uncertainty in this regard, under No. 88, below.
107. Except in reference to its geographical area, in the eschatology of Dan 11:41.

positions: "Then shall Israel possess them that did possess him." Fulfillment (per. 11): as in Obad. No. 9, Maccabean Jewish expansion against Ammon.

88. Jer 49:6 (1 v.): just as in ch. 48, on Moab, in which restoration was to follow judgment (No. 86, above), so also in ch. 49, subsequent to the judgment of the Ammonites foretold in vv. 2–5 (No. 23, above), God promises, "Afterward I will bring back the captivity[108] of the children of Ammon. Fulfillment (per. 9): "How soon the Persians were able to restablish organized political activity in the land of Ammon is not known."[109] But by the Greek period, the Ammonite capital city of Rabbah was designated Philadelphia and became a leading city of the Decapolis, which "experienced a new prosperity."[110] probably under Ptolemy II, Philadelphus, 285–246 B.C.

89. Jer 49:23–27 (5 vv.): "Damascus is waxed feeble" (v. 24); "all the men of war shall be brought to silence" (v. 26). Fulfillment (per. 8): though the transfer in 605 from Egyptian to Chaldean domination "probably was effected without challenge,"[111] at a later point the city apparently "fell victim to Nebuchadrezzar's victorious army."[112]

90. Jer 49:39 (1 v.): God had foretold judgment upon the Elamites (No. 65, above); but, "In the latter days I will bring back the captivity of Elam." Acts 2:9 mentions Elamitic Jews as present at Pentecost; on the analogy, however, of Nos. 86 and 88, above, the fulfillment of this oracle would seem to belong earlier (per. 9). Leslie suggests as its accomplishment, "the change experienced by Elam when it had come under the power of the Persians."[113]

108. On the term "captivity," see above, p. 17.
109. IDB, I:113.
110. Elmer A. Leslie, *Jeremiah*, p. 168.
111. Ibid., p. 285.
112. Laetsch, op. cit., p. 348; at the same time he notes the lack of recorded historical validation for this particular disaster.
113. Op. cit., p. 209.

LAMENTATIONS

The text of Lamentations makes no claim in regard to its own authorship. The composer of the five poems (four of them acrostics) that constitute the chapters of the book does seem to have been an eyewitness of Jerusalem's fall to the armies of Babylon in 586 B.C. (see 2:12 or 4:10); he was, moreover, a man deeply moved by the sorrows of his people (1:16, 2:11), while at the same time recognizing that it was Judah's sin against her God which underlay her calamity (2:14, 4:13). In the oldest known arrangement of the Hebrew OT,[1] Lamentations appears, not with the four poetic books that make up the third division of its canon, but rather as forming one volume with Jeremiah, among the five Latter Prophets—which include Isaiah, and also Ezekiel, Daniel, and "the twelve" Minor Prophets—in its second, or prophetic, division. Jeremiah, indeed, is noted for his writing of other, earlier laments (II Chron 35:25); his literary style and phraseology, as evidenced by his great work of prophecy, find a number of close parallels in the Book of Lamentations;[2] the prophet was himself present in Jerusalem both during its final siege (Jer 38:20) and in the period that followed (39:14); and Jeremiah's feelings for his nation (cf. 9:1, 13:17) and his theological understanding of sin and judgment (5:31, 23:11–12) agree well with those exhibited by the poems of Lamentations. The long tradition of Jeremian authorship for this latter book would thus seem to be a correct one.[3]

The mournful theme of Lamentations is expressed in its opening lines, "How doth the city sit solitary, that was full of people!" (1:1); but a key verse that better defines the author's purpose for Judah appears two chapters later: "Let him put his mouth in the dust, if so be there may be hope" (3:29). Neither the cry of grief, however, nor the call for contrition directly concern prediction. The book contains only four prophecies: three by way of types, and one (4:20–21, No. 4 below) by way of verbal forecast, predicting that a catastrophe similar to Judah's lies in store for Edom. These account for no more than 8 out of the book's 154 verses, which amounts to a low 5%.

1. Lam 1:10; 2:1,[4] 6a, 7b, 20; 4:1 (6 vv., typ.): the temple. Fulfillment (per. 13): as in Ex. prophecy No. 55.

2. Lam 2:6b (typ.): sabbath. Fulfillment (per. 13): as in Ex. No. 41.

3. Lam 2:7a (typ.): altar. Fulfillment (per. 13): as in Ex. No. 44.

4. Lam 4:21–22 (2 vv., fig.): a prediction addressed to Edom, "The cup shall pass through unto thee also" (v. 21). In the next verse the prophet then explains the figure: God "will visit thine iniquity . . . [and] uncover thy sin." Fulfillment (per. 8): as in Jer. No. 22, the reduction of Edom by Nabunaid in 552 B.C. For this oracle concerns the same "cup" that was forced upon Judah, namely Babylonian punishment, rather than the final (Arabian) destruction that fell upon Edom a few decades later, as in Obad 5.

1. The 22-book listing of Josephus; see above, introduction to Joshua and note 1.
2. Cf. E. J. Young, *An Introduction to the OT*, pp. 363–364.
3. Though this is often denied; cf. R. H. Pfeiffer, *Introduction to the OT*, p. 723, who questions whether chs. 1 and 5, and especially ch. 3, with its deeper theological penetration, could stem authentically from the period of Jerusalem's fall.
4. The phrase "His footstool" could refer specifically to the ark, I Chron 28:2.

EZEKIEL

Third in the list of Israel's major prophets stands the exilic volume of Ezekiel. Though a dozen pages shorter than Jeremiah, its Hebrew text contains 821 verses of predictive matter, which constitute 65% of the book's 1,273-verse total. This comes to several more verses than are to be found for Jeremiah, it divides into 66 separate forecasts, and it forms the largest amount of predictive prophecy to appear in any one book of the Bible.

Like Jeremiah, who preceded him and exerted a strong influence on his ministry,[1] Ezekiel was a priest; but in 597 B.C., when 26 years of age,[2] he was carried captive to Babylon among the members of the second, or upper-class, deportation that accompanied the fallen monarch Jehoiachin (Ezek 1:3). In the 5th year of this exile, or in 593,[3] when Ezekiel reached 30 and would normally have commenced his priestly functioning at the sanctuary in Jerusalem (cf. Num 4:3), God called him to the prophetic office (Ezek 1:1-2). This holy summons occurred a decade after the exaltation of his fellow-servant Daniel, whose faithfulness and wisdom Ezekiel revered (14:14, 28:3). The last of his dated writings belongs to the 27th year (28:17), or 571, so that his preaching spanned a minimum period of 22 years. Next to the short prophecy of Haggai, Ezekiel's is the most closely dated book to be found in Scripture (cf. 8:1, 20:11, 26:1, etc.): its chronological unfolding is readily traceable, and its historical authenticity has remained essentially unquestioned, except by critics of the last 50 years.[4]

Perhaps because of a concern for priestly ritual, Ezekiel shows a deep involvement in religious symbolism. In contrast to the relatively minor place occupied by matters of typical prophecy among the other major prophets,[5] almost a quarter of Ezekiel's predictive matter (or 24%) consists of typology. His temperament was also such as to be attracted

---

1. Note, eg., the elaboration of Jeremiah's figure of the caldron (1:13-15) in Ezek 11:1-12, 24:3-14; of the two sisters (Jer 3:6-11) in 23:1-49; or the sour grapes (Jer 31:29-30) in 18:2-31.
2. Assuming that the "30th year" of 1:1 represents Ezekiel's age at the time of his call.
3. Calculating the calendar year as commencing in the spring; see E. R. Thiele, *The Mysterious Numbers of the Hebrew Kings*, p. 163.
4. Since Hölscher's analysis in 1924; cf. R. K. Harrison, *Introduction to the OT*, pp. 823-832. The prophet's interest in the affairs of Jerusalem (e.g. 3:4, 8:5-14, 11:10-13) have led some to place his earlier oracles in a Judean setting (cf. R. H. Pfeiffer, *Introduction to the OT*, p. 536), though Ezek 8:3 (cf. 3:11) makes it clear that his "rapture" to Jerusalem was a matter of visionary experience only; see E. J. Young, *My Servants the Prophets*, p. 187.
5. In Isa, Jer, and Dan, the proportion of their forecasts that take the form of enacted types amounts, respectively, to but 3%, 7%, and 4%.

to revelatory symbolism in general, to the extent that he has been charged even with psychological abnormality.[6] These remarkable, and almost bizarre, symbols lead directly, then, into the apocalyptic form of writing[7] that characterizes his later oracles (chs. 34–48). Ezekiel's heart-felt concern both over the sin of Judah prior to the fall of Jerusalem and over their yet future consolation after that date may be summed up by this key verse: "Cast away from you all your transgressions . . . and make you a new heart and a new spirit; for why will ye die, O house of Israel?" (18:31, cf. 33:11).

The Book of Ezekiel falls into three clearly marked divisions: I. Prophecies of doom against Jerusalem, chs. 1–24, which lead up to the city's fall in 586. Anticipation of this event (prediction No. 1, below) occupies 194 of the prophet's verses and constitutes the second most extensive prophecy in any book of Scripture; cf. Jeremiah, No. 1, on this same topic. Future forecasts begin only in ch. 4; but the portions that follow, through ch. 12, are marked by no fewer than 7 striking, symbolically enacted predictions. II. Prophecies concerning the pagan nations, chs. 25–32; cf. the existence of similar blocks of revelation, as appearing in Isa 13–23, Jer 46–51, or, on a smaller scale, in Zeph 2:4–15. Of the 7 nations that are introduced, Tyre (26–28:19) and Egypt (29–32) receive the most extensive treatment. III. Prophecies of hope for Jerusalem, revealed after 586. Most significant for a proper understanding at this point is the interpreter's recognition of the cyclic nature of the fulfillment of the prophet's carefully constructed apocalyptic revelations;[8] compare the inception of this phenomenon as observable in Isaiah[9] and its more elaborate development in the postexilic apocalyptic of Zechariah.[10] Ezekiel's major cycles are shown in Table 7.

Confusion can be the only result if the correspondences in matter and in times of fulfillment shown in Table 7 are disregarded. For example, of the some eight passages that Wyngaarden introduces to establish the self-contradictory position of millennialism, because of the "atoning implications of the millennial offering,"[11] all eight are drawn from Ezek 40–46, which concerns, in actuality, not millennial but ancient postexilic days.

1. Ezek 4:1–3, 7–11, 16–17; 5:1–2, 7–10, *11b*–17; 6:1–7, 11–14; ch. 7 (27 vv.); 8:18; 9:1–2, 5–10; 10:1–2; 11:7–9, 21; 12:14, 17–28; 13:10–16; 14:21; 15:1–8; 16:35–43, 52, 57–59a; 17:21; 19:14; 20:45–48; 21:1–17, 24, *29b*; 22:1–5, 13–14, 19–22, 30–31; 23:22–35, 45–49; 24:3–20, *21:b*–24 (194 vv., sym.): Ezekiel was instructed to make a model

6. See Harrison, op. cit., pp. 849–852.
7. See above, p. 86.
8. See above, pp. 86, 131.
9. See introduction to Isaiah.
10. See introduction to Zechariah and Table 11.
11. *The Future of the Kingdom in Prophecy and Fulfillment*, p. 73.

TABLE 7
Predictive Cycles in Ezekiel 33-48

Cycle 1 (chs. 33-34)	Cycle 2 (chs. 35-36:15)	Cycle 3 (36:16-39:22)	Cycle 4 (39:23-ch. 48)[12]
Palestine, past and contemporary (33-34:10, 16b-22)	The 6th-century desolation of Edom and other nations (35-36:7)	Israel's sin and exile (36:16-21)	Israel's sin and exile (39:23-24)
Postexilic Jewish restoration (34:11-16a)	The postexilic restoration (36:8-11)	The postexilic restoration (36:22-37:22a, 23)	Postexilic restoration (39:25-29) and temple rebuilding (40-46)[13]
Jesus the Good Shepherd (34:23-24)	—	David the Shepherd (37:22b, 24)	—
The millennial testament of peace (34:25-31)	Millennial security (36:12-15)	Testament of peace (37:25-28)	The millennial river and land (47-48)
—	—	Postmillennial Gog and Magog (38-39:22)	—

12. Since a new oracle, dated to 573 B.C., commences in 40:1, the material of 39:23-29 must form a literary conclusion to the preceding section, though from the viewpoint of Ezekiel's cyclic prophecy and its chronological fulfillment, the passage does mark a 4th presentation of the subjects described.

13. An exception might seem to appear in 43:2-7, 44:2, 4, on the return of God's glory cloud to the reconstructed sanctuary; but this accomplishment lay dependent upon a condition of Jewish sanctification, v. 9, which unhappily remained unfulfilled; see above, p. 67. For an outline of modern approaches to Ezek 40-46, see below under 5:11a.

of Jerusalem on a clay tile and to "lay siege against it" (4:1–2), while the presence of an iron pan between the prophet and the tile represented "a wall of iron" (v. 3), namely, an inescapable besieging force. As a supplementary symbol, 4:10–11, Ezekiel was to eat his food "by weight, 20 shekels a day [somewhat less than 10 ounces of meal] . . . and water by measure, the sixth part of a hin [less than a quart]." God's explanation follows in vv. 16–17, "I will break the staff of bread in Jerusalem . . . that they may want bread and water"; cf. 5:10, "The fathers shall eat the sons in the midst of thee." In 5:1–2, as another symbol, the prophet was ordered to shave his hair—the very shaving of one's head constituted a sign of mourning, Jer 41:5—and then to destroy this hair in three ways: part burned (cf. v. 4), part struck with the sword, and part scattered. As explained in v. 12, his action was indicative of the prospect awaiting the population of Jerusalem. 6:11 speaks directly of their deaths by sword, famine, and pestilence (cf. Jer 14:15, 21:6, under Jer 1:13), and 14:21, by wild beasts (which appear when a land becomes deserted, II K 17:25–26); but then, Judah's idolatry would be destroyed too, 6:3–4. In the prophet's vision of 10:2 came God's symbolic order to "scatter coals of fire over the city."

In 12:18, which is dated to 592, or only 6 years before the end, Yahweh commanded Ezekiel, "Eat thy bread with [symbolic] quaking" (cf. 21:6–7, on his "sighing"); and this was not for "times that are far off" (12:27), but "the days are at hand" (v. 23; cf. v. 28). 13:10–15 presents the figure of a whitewashed wall, which would fall, meaning that though the false prophets might gloss over Judah's failings with "visions of peace . . . [still] there is no peace" (v. 16, following Jer 8:11, 14:13). God is about to make the land desolate, like a vine cast into the fire (15:1–8, similar to Isa 5:1–7). 19:14 continues the figure of Israel as a vine, warning, "Fire has gone out of a rod [ASVmg] of its branches [referring to Zedekiah's rebellion aginst Nebuchadrezzar, 17:15–16]; it hath devoured its fruit"; and 20:47 foretells a burning for "the forest of the south," i.e. Jerusalem and the southern kingdom, as explained in 21:2, 4, which follow. Both the righteous and the wicked are to be cut off, v. 3; and Judah's scepter, "the rod that condemneth," shall be no more, vv. 13, 27, "in the time of the iniquity of the end," vv. 25, 29b. The kingdom shall be melted like silver in a furnace, 22:22.

By 591 B.C. (20:1) Ezekiel was spelling out certain details of the coming attack against Judah by the Babylonians and by their allied peoples, such as the Assyrians (23:23–24). Jerusalem is to "drink the cup" of Samaria (vv. 31–33), namely, to fall, just as did the Ephraimites. Finally, at the beginning of the year 588 (24:1), the prophet had recourse to a concluding pair of symbols: that of the boiling caldron (v. 3), with its rust, representing Judah's sin (v. 6), which must be consumed by burning (vv. 10–11); and that of Ezekiel's own lack of mourning at the death of his wife (v. 16), foreshadowing a similar lack of mourning rites among the Jews because of the depth of their disaster (vv. 22–24). Fulfillment (per. 7): the fall of Jerusalem in 586, as in Lev. prophecy. No. 33.

2. Ezek 4:4–6 (3 vv., sym.): God's directions to the prophet, "Lay the iniquity of the house of Israel upon thy left side . . . 390 days . . . and the iniquity of the house of Judah, 40 days, each day for a year." Fulfillment (per. 8): the dating of the exile, as caused by the Hebrews' iniquity, and its duration until the restoration. H. L. Ellison comments, "For Ezekiel the North, separated from God's sanctuary on Zion and from the Davidic king of God's choice, was in semi-exile from the time of the disruption: 390 years would reach 930–540":[14] and since Cyrus took Babylon in 539, this round figure is clearly sufficient.[15] He continues, "The last period was shared by both kingdoms . . . in round numbers [586 to 539 comes out actually to 47]. It is likely that the figure 40 was chosen as being . . . reminiscent of the 40 years in the wilderness";[16] and the total of the 390 plus the 40, or 430, might even have suggested the total preexodus period of 430 years, as stated in Ex 12:41 (discussed under Gen 15:13, above).

3. Ezek 4:12–15; 12:3–4, 7a, 8–11, 15; 14:22–23; 20:23; 22:15a (15 vv., sym.): Ezekiel's food (cf. 4:9–11, under No. 1, above) was to be baked over (v. 15—not mixed with!) a fuel composed of dung. V. 13 explains, "Even thus shall the children of Israel eat their bread unclean among the nations whither I will drive them," because foreign lands were counted as unclean, Amos 7:17, and this in turn meant that the food in them would be unclean, Hos 9:3. In 12:3–4, as a further object lesson, God instructed the prophet: "Prepare thee stuff for removing, and remove from thy place to another place in their sight . . . as when men go forth into exile." Explanation follows in v. 11, "So shall it be done unto them: they shall go into exile." 14:22–23 states directly, "A remnant shall be carried forth [from Judah]—and ye shall see their doings and be comforted," by recognizing, that is, the justice of God's punishment, v. 23. Fulfillment (per. 8): the exile, as in Lev. No. 34 (see also Dt 4:27, and the citation of these Pentateuchal predictions in Ezek 20:23).

4. Ezek 5:3–4, 12:16, 20:38, 22:15b–16 (5 vv., sym.): a little of Ezekiel's shaven hair (see 5:1–2, under No. 1, above) is to be bound up in his clothing; but "of these, again shalt thou take and cast them into the midst of the fire" (5:4). An additional, psychological penalty from God is suggested in 12:16, "But I will leave a few men of them . . . that they may declare all their abominations among the nations." In 20:38 the Lord goes further: "I will purge out from among you the rebels [cf. 22:15]; I will bring them forth out of the land where they sojourn [in exile], but

14. *Ezekiel: The Man and His Message*, p. 39.
15. The LXX of 4:5, 9, reads 190 rather than 390, presumably counting only until the fall of the N.: 930 to 722 = 188 years.
16. Op. cit., p. 34.

they shall not enter into the land of Israel." Keil explains that the *bringing forth* "is used here for clearing out by extermination, as the following clause shows."[17] Fulfillment (per. 8): as in Lev No. 35, the fact of continuing disaster for the exiled remnant of Judah; cf. the figure in 5:2, or a sword being drawn out after those who were to be scattered.

5. Ezek 5:11a; 8:6, 14, 16a; 9:3, *6c–7a*; 10:3–4, 18–19; 11:1; 23:38a, 39; 25:3; 40:5–37, 44–49; 41:1–21, 23–26; 42:1–12, 15–20; 43:4–8, 10–12; 44:1, 4–7a, 8–9; 45:1–5 (115 vv., typ.): Israel's temple. The reference in 23:38 to "My sanctuary" assumes added significance because of the symbolic name used for Judah in this chapter (v. 4), *Oholibah,* meaning "My tent, in her." Chs. 40–46 recount Ezekiel's visions of regathered Israel (40:2), and especially of the building that would be the house of God (v. 5), which was to stand in their capital city of Jerusalem (v. 2). The measurements of the house are given in 40:5–37, though the temple that the Jews finally succeeded in erecting, 520–515 B.C. (Ezra 5–6), fell markedly short of Ezekiel's requirements (cf. Hag 2:3, Zech 4:10). Five proposed interpretations dominate current discussion: that the prophet's words were (1) a prediction, for the past, and literal (the position of liberalism): it was simply a misjudgment on Ezekiel's part, "plans which he expected to be carried out."[18] Or, they could have been (2) injunction, for the past, and literal (an evangelical position): Ezekiel's command, though he refrains from stating it as a prediction; for the prophet's emphasis falls upon instructing the returnees "how to build it."[19] (3) A prediction of the present, and figurative (amillennial, or at least in accordance with that position): "a deliberately symbolic description of the worship of the Christian church,"[20] though this approach amounts to simple allegorization. (4) A prediction of the future, literal (some premillennialists): conceivably associated with the view of those who "look for a rebuilding of the temple at the second coming of Christ," though if the Messiah's temple of the future be identifiefid with the rites of literal blood atonement that characterize *Ezekiel's* structure, 43:20, then Beasley-Murray seems correct when he adds, "This view is challenged by the NT: the atonement of our Lord has nullified all [such] sacrifices for ever, Heb 10:18."[21] (5) A prediction of the future, but figurative (amillennial, or in accord with it): a picture of the new heavens and earth, after the final judgment, to the extent that its "essential truth will be embodied in the new age, under forms suitable

17. *Ezek,* I:283.
18. NBC, p. 663; so A. G. Hebert, *The OT from Within,* or Cent, *Ezek,* p. 287, "He expected it would be the duty of the priests to instruct the mass of the people on the actual subjects with which these chapters deal, 44:23."
19. NBC, loc, cit.
20. So Roehrs, in C. F. H. Henry, ed., *The Biblical Expositor,* II:258; cf. Beasley-Murray, NBC, loc. cit., "The heirs of the kingdom are no longer the Jewish nation but the Church, the New Israel in which the old Israel may find its true place."
21. NBC, loc. cit.

to the new [Christian] dispensation in Rev 21–22:5";[22] but cf. 21:22 on the absence of any temple in the New Jerusalem. In light of the objections to the latter three of the above proposals, a "past" interpretation deserves preference. Ezekiel himself, moreover, stated quite clearly, "Show the house to the house of Israel and let them measure the pattern . . . that they may keep all the ordinances thereof and do them" (Ezek 43:10–11), over which Ellison exclaims, "Can they possibly refer to any other time than the prophet's own?"[23] Furthermore, since the first proposal is incompatible with the character of Scripture, it appears best to view Ezek 40–46 as statements of obligation[24]—realizing that Ezekiel cannot be held responsible for the noncompliance of the next generation of his associates—and to limit the predictive value of these chapters to the usual, typical foreshadowing of Christ's incarnation by the historic sanctuaries of Israel (per. 13): as in Ex. No. 55.

6. Ezek 6:8–10; 20:33–37a, 39 (9 vv.): "Yet will I leave a remnant, when ye shall be scattered through the countries . . . that shall remember Me among the nations . . . and loathe themselves for the evils which they have committed"; and so Judah's calamity will not have been in vain (6:8–10). The verses in ch. 20 add, "I will bring you out from the peoples and gather you . . . with wrath poured out; and I will bring you into the wilderness of the peoples, and there will I enter into judgment with you . . . and I will bring you into the bond of the testament." Keil explains, "The gathering of Israel is not their restoration from the existing captivity . . . this leading out is an act of divine anger"; cf. 22:19–21, and 20:38 as noted under 5:3 (No. 4, above). It is "a spiritual severance from the heathen world, in order that they might not be absorbed into it";[25] cf. Ellison's remark, "There would be a testing in the wilderness—of the exile —and a judgment that would separate His true people from the idolators."[26] It parallels their disciplining after the exodus, v. 36, and results in a termination to Judah's idolatry, v. 39. Fulfillment (per. 8): exilic repentance, as in Dt. No. 16.[27]

7. Ezek 8:5, *16b*; *40:46b, 47b*; 41:22; 43:13–18a, 26 (9 vv., typ.): altar. Fulfillment (per. 13): as in Ex. No. 44.

8. Ezek 9:4, *5b*, 11 (2 vv., sym.): in one of Ezekiel's visions Yahweh commands, "Set a mark upon the foreheads of the men that sigh over all [Jerusalem's] abominations" (9:4); as explained two verses later, they were not to be slain with the others in the doomed city. Fulfillment (per.

22. Ibid., p. 664.
23. Op. cit., p. 142.
24. See above, pp. 39–40.
25. I:279–281.
26. Op. cit., p. 283; see above, p. 83, note 104. The thought may have arisen from Hos 12:9 (see under 4:19), though there the reference was more to punishment than to reformation.
27. Feinberg refers the matters of 20:33–39 to an eschatological judgment of the nation Israel, *Premillennialism or Amillennialism?* p. 192.

7): the protection of the godly at the fall of Jerusalem in 586. How this was accomplished in general remains unknown, though note Jeremiah's protection, for one, in Jer 39:11–12.

9. Ezek 11:10–12 (3 vv.): God's warning to Judah's self-confident leaders, "I will judge you in the border of Israel; this city shall not be your caldron" (= protection). Fulfillment (per. 7): it was literally so; for Zedekiah and his high officers were judged by Nebuchadrezzar at Libnah, in Syria to the north, II K 25:6–7, 18–21.

10. Ezek 11:13 (1 v., sym.): the prophet reports an incident in a vision, concerning one of the idolatrous leaders in Jerusalem, "When I prophesied, Peletiah died." Keil cautions, "The death of Peletiah was simply part of the vision." But the man seems to have died in fact as well; and Keil adds, "In all probability it was actually realized [per. 7] by the sudden death of this prince during or immediately after the publication of the vision,"[28] which dates to 592 B.C. (8:1).

11. Ezek 11:16 (1 v.): God's assurance to the exiles, especially to those of 597, "I will be a sanctuary for a little while [in light of the calamities noted in No. 4, above] in the countries where they are come." Fulfillment (per. 8): exilic protection, as in Lev. No. 37.

12. Ezek 11:17; 13:8–9; *16:53c, 55c*; *20:41b*–42; 28:25; 29:21; 34:11–13; 36:22–24; 37:1–14; 39:25, 27–28 (29 vv.): God's further promise, "I will assemble you out of the countries where ye have been scattered, and I will give you the land of Israel" (11:17); contrast the outlook for the false prophets (13:8–9), who "shall not enter into the land of Israel." In 29:21 He spoke figuratively, "In that day [after Nebuchadrezzar's attack on Egypt in 568–567, No. 41, below] will I cause a horn to bud unto Israel,[29] and I will give thee the opening of the mouth,"[30] an ending, that is, of "a silence induced by shame, cf. 16:63, and now to be broken by thanksgiving."[31] In this way God would sanctify His great name among the nations, 20:41, 36:23, where it had been disgraced by the exile of Israel, *His* people, 37:1–14 concerns one of Ezekiel's best-known symbolically prophetic visions, that of the valley filled with dry bones which reassembled and revived. Explanation is provided in vv. 11–13, "These bones are the whole house of Israel . . . I will open your graves," not in individual resurrection, but nationally, for "I will bring you into the land of Israel," thus terminating their exile in Babylon.[32] 39:28b goes on to state, "I will leave none of them any more there" among the nations who

---

28. I:148.

29. Not an individual, as Solomon (in Ps 132:11, 17), but national leadership in general, so as to reverse the calamity of Lam 2:3.

30. Not of Ezekiel personally, as in 24:25–27 (No. 32, below), since the latter was fulfilled before this prophecy—which is dated 571 (29:17)—was uttered, though 29:21 may be a reflection of the idea of ch. 24.

31. JB, p. 1387.

32. See above, Table 7.

took them captive. Such inclusiveness might suggest the total regathering of the Jews at Christ's second coming (see under Isa 11:11); but in this context it may simply denote the end of the captivity: compare 39:29a, which declares, "neither will I hide My face any more from them," not in a permanent restoration to the New Jerusalem (as in 37:25a, No. 50, below), but, more immediately, in the permanent end to the hiding of His face in the Babylonian exile, v. 23. Fulfillment (per. 9): the postexilic restoration of the Jews to Palestine, as in Dt. No. 43.

13. Ezek 11:18; 16:54a; 20:40–41a, 43–44; 36:25, *29a,* 31–33a; 37:23; 39:26 (12 vv.): upon Israel's return to Palestine (No. 12, preceding), "They shall come thither, and they shall take away all the detestable things thereof," 11:18 (= 37:23),[33] namely, "your idols," 36:25. 20:43 states, "There ye shall loathe yourselves for all your evils" (= 36:31); cf. 6:9, in No. 6, above, on a similar experience of repentance, even before the close of the exile. They will "bear their shame," 16:54, 39:26; and, more positively in 20:40, "There shall all Israel serve Me in the land; there will I accept them." Fulfillment (per. 9): Israel's final abandonment of idolatry, with a renewed dedication to God. For "the remnant that returned under Sheshbazzar, Zerubbabel, and Joshua had learnt certain aspects of Ezekiel's teaching well, and it was reinforced about a century later by the work of Ezra";[34] cf. Ezra 2:68, 3:2–5, 5:2.

14. Ezek 11:19–20; 36:26–28, *37:14a,* 39:29 (6 vv.): the basis for Israel's reform (No. 13, above) lies in the following acts of divine grace, "I will put a new spirit [lowercase] within you; and I will take the stony heart out of their flesh, and will give them a heart of flesh," 11:19 (= 36:26), "that they may walk in My statutes; and they shall be My people," 11:20. 36:27 adds, "I will put My Spirit [capital] within you" (= 37:14). Fulfillment (per. 9): the regeneration of postexilic Jews, as in Jer. No. 48 (24:7). For this portion of Ezek 36 *is* postexilic: note especially v. 18, on Judah's preexilic idolatry, followed in v. 25 by God's removal of this same, strictly B.C. problem—"I will sprinkle clean water upon you, and from all your idols will I cleanse you"; cf. v. 29 and p. 111, above. As Snaith insists: "Jeremiah and Ezekiel say that God will give men new hearts and will put His Spirit in them, not 'in a dim and distant future,' but in the days of return from exile and of the rebuilding of Jerusalem. This immediacy is quite clear from the contexts."[35]

15. Ezek 12:5–6, 7b, 12 (4 vv., sym.): God's directives to the prophet

33. 37:23 is placed between two references to the Messiah (vv. 22, 24); but it must still relate to the earlier restoration, in retrospect, as is shown by its reference to the idolatry of that time. See above, p. 111.

34. Ellison, op. cit., 83.

35. *The Distinctive Ideas of the OT,* p. 83. He adds, "If the suggestion of a far-distant future be made because it is thought that the references are apocalyptic, then we have a most extraordinary misapprehension. The crisis is near at hand. To suggest otherwise is a most amazing error."

for another symbolic action, "Dig thou through the wall in their sight, and carry out thereby . . . upon thy shoulder, in the dark; thou shalt cover thy face, that thou see not the land," vv. 5–6. Explanation follows in v. 12, "The prince that is among them shall bear upon his shoulder in the dark, and shall go forth: they shall dig through the wall; he shall cover his face [in sorrow]" (on his subsequent blinding, see v. 13, No. 16, following). Fulfillment (per. 7): Zedekiah's attempt to escape from Jerusalem at its collapse in 586 (II K 25:4b), "the literal occurrence of what is predicted here."[36] The "digging through" of the wall is not a forecast of the breach in Jerusalem's fortifications made by the Babylonians (v. 4a) but of one made by the Jews. II K 25:4b speaks only of flight through a gate; but Keil employs it in support of Ezekiel's predicted digging: "The expression, 'through the gate between the two walls,' renders this [statement by the prophet] very probable, whether the gate had been walled up during the siege, or it was necessary to break through the wall at one particular point to reach the gate."[37]

16. Ezek 12:13; 17:9–10, 15–16, 18–20; 21:25–26 (10 vv.): after the capture of Zedekiah (cf. No. 15, above), "I will bring him to Babylon; yet shall he not see it, though he shall die there" (12:13). Reference to this same event reappears in Ezekiel's allegory of the eagles and the vine, in which 17:9 states that the vine will "wither"; as explained in v. 16, Zedekiah is to die in the midst of Babylon. So also in 21:25–26, in respect to the "wicked one, the prince of Israel," the prophet warns, "Take off the crown." Fulfillment (per. 7): the fate of Zedekiah at the hands of Nebuchadrezzar, as in Jer. No. 40 (21:7). But Ezekiel adds the indication of his being blinded, II K 25:7. A previous prophecy (Ezek 12:12) had in fact prepared for this possibility by calling attention to Zedekiah's eyesight —"He shall not see the land with his eyes"—though *the land* in that case referred to Palestine, when he should flee Jerusalem in sorrow; see No. 15, above.[38]

17. Ezek 16:8, *59b*–60a, *61d*; *20:37b*; *44:7c* (2 vv., typ.): the Sinaitic testament. Fulfillment (per. 13): as in Ex. No. 45 (19:5).

18. Ezek 16:53a, 55a, *61c* (2 vv.): "I will turn again the captivity[39] of Sodom and her daughters . . . to their former estate," vv. 53, 55, along with the captivity of Judah and Samaria (see No. 12 and 19). V. 61 adds, "Thy younger sisters [= Sodom and its surroundings, v. 46] I will give unto thee for daughters" (cf. v. 61b, No. 19, following). Keil insists that Sodom is here not "a typical name denoting heathenism generally. . . . Verses 49–50 point undeniably to the real Sodom,"[40] as do also the

36. KD, I:160.
37. Ibid.
38. Ibid.
39. See above, p. 17.
40. I:128.

geographical directions in v. 46. But Keil then goes on to relate the passage to life everlasting, beyond this earth. A more literal fulfillment (per. 11) is to be found in the occupation of these Dead Sea areas by postexilic Jews: En-gedi, on the western shore, at the return in 538–537; but Sodom, at the southern end (?), not until the latter 2nd century B.C.[41]

19. Ezek 16:*53b, 54b, 55b*, 61b; 37:15–22a (9 vv.): Samaria's captivity to be returned, along with that of Judah, and even "comforted" by Judah's corresponding shame at this point, 16:53–55. In v. 61, God informs Judah, "I will give them ["thine elder sisters" = Samaria and its surroundings, v. 46] to thee for daughters, although [KD, JB] they were not of [Heb. *min,* lit., "from"] thy testament." 37:15–20 describes the prophet's symbolic action of uniting two sticks, labeled "Judah" and "Joseph." God explains in v. 22, " I will make them [Judah and Samaria] one nation upon the mountains of Israel." Fulfillment (per. 9): as in II Chron 30:9 or Jer 3:11, the participation of Hebrews from the 10 "lost tribes" in Israel's postexilic restoration. As Ellison observes, "Sufficient of the Northern tribes joined Judah under the divided monarchy and doubtless at the return from exile to make the modern Jew representative of 'all Israel' (Rom 11:26)."[42]

20. Ezek 16:*60b–61a*, 62–63 (2 vv.): "I will establish unto thee an everlasting testament. Then shalt thou remember thy ways and be ashamed . . . when I have forgiven thee all that thou hast done"; cf. Jer 31:34. Fulfillment (per. 14): the new testament of Jesus Christ, as in Jer. No. 7. For the above-listed verses stand at a point that is yet future to the postexilic return (v. 53c, No. 12, above) and to Judah's subsequent reconsecration (v. 54a, No. 13).

21. Ezek 17:17 (1 v.): as a factor against the revolt of Zedekiah from Nebuchadrezzar, the prophet warns, "Neither shall Pharaoh help him." Ezekiel's prediction was then repeated by Jeremiah, in 37:7, four years later; see under Jer 30:14a and 34:22. Fulfillment (per. 7): the pharaoh of Egypt did come up on Zedekiah's behalf, Jer 37:5; but he failed, cf. 37:21 with 32:1–2.

22. Ezek 17:22–*23a* (1 v., fig.): at the conclusion to his allegory of the eagles (see No. 16, above), Ezekiel portrays a divine act of grace, "I will take of the lofty top of the cedar, from the topmost of its young twigs a tender one; and I will plant it upon . . . the mountain of the height of Israel." The *top of the cedar,* v. 3, represents the Davidic family, while *the topmost of its young twigs,* v. 4, signifies Jehoiachin, carried into

41. Y. Aharoni and M. Avi-Jonah, *The Macmillan Bible Atlas;* compare map 171 (p. 109) and map 213 (p. 133.)
42. Op. cit., p. 132; cf. WC, pp. 201–202. Yet Ellison also asserts, with some inconsistency, "Nor can the small companies of Israel who doubtless joined Judah at the return from exile be considered in any sense a fulfillment. . . . We should, however, seriously consider another possibility, unfulfilled, or conditional prophecy. . . . It may be that Ezek 37:15–22 will never have a literal fulfillment."

Babylon, while the shoot *taken of* this latter suggests one of his descendants. Fulfillment (per. 9): the tender twig seems to represent Zerubbabel, in his role of leader at the return of the Jews from exile, Ezra 2:2, 3:2, etc.; for he was an offshoot (grandson) of Jehoiachin, I Chron 3:17, 19. Ellison prefers an accomplishment in the Messiah,[43] who does appear in v. 23b (No. 23, following); but Zerubbabel was the one who actually brought back the Jews to Mount Zion.

23. Ezek *17:23b*, 34:23-24, 37:*22b*, 24 (3 vv., fig.): the tender twig (Zerubbabel, No. 22, preceding) "shall bring forth boughs and bear fruit" (17:23). 34:23-24 then represents the Messianic hope under the name of an ancestor more remote than Zerubbabel of Jehoiachin:[44] "My servant David [see above, p. 84] shall feed them, and He shall be their shepherd and . . . be *nāsī, deputy, chief*[45] (= 37:25), among them." Some think of this as His being a politically ruling king.[46] The reference could indeed be millennial; but there is no specification of political kingship, and Christ *is* both the Good Shepherd (John 10:11) and a spiritual king (18:36), from the NT era onward. Ezek 37:24 adds that as a result of the Shepherd's presence, "They shall also walk in Mine ordinances."[47] Fulfillment (per. 13): the coming of Christ the Shepherd, as a descendant of David through Jehoiachin and Zerubbabel, Mt 1:12-13, Lk 3:27; cf. the Messianic nature of the following lines, vv. 23c-24 (No. 24, next).

24. Ezek 17:23c-24 (2 vv., fig.): Zerubbabel's descendant (No. 23, preceding) is to become "a goodly cedar: under it shall dwell all birds of every wing; in the shade of the branches thereof shall they dwell." Fulfillment (per. 14): the spread of the Christian gospel; cf. the similar figure of rest under the shade of branches in Mk 4:32.[48]

25. Ezek 20:12-13, 16, 20-21, 24; 22:8, 26; *23:38b*; 44:24; *45:17c*; 46:1, 3, *4b, 12c* (11 vv., typ.): the sabbath, "a sign that they might know that I am Yahweh that sanctifieth them" (20:12), and, "that I am your God" (v. 20). Fulfillment (per. 13): as in Ex. No. 41.

26. Ezek 21:18-23 (6 vv., sym.): Ezekiel is to portray roads from Babylon, leading against Ammon and Judah, and the king of Babylon casting lots "at the parting of the way" (v. 21), to determine which land to attack. The action ends with the divination that is for Jerusalem in Nebuchadrezzar's right hand, v. 22, indicative of his decision to attack

43. Ibid., p. 70.
44. See above, Jer., prophecy No. 45, note 70.
45. KB, p. 637.
46. Ellison, op. cit., p. 120.
47. Concerning the latter verses, Edghill concludes, from the very terminology, that Jesus "must have identified Himself with that good shepherd—the second David—of whom the prophet had foretold that he would yet arise to be the perfect representative to Israel of Jehovah's care and goodness," *An Enquiry into the Evidential Value of Prophecy*, p. 440.
48. The universality of Christ's political (millennial) kingship remains as an alternative possibility, cf. the figure of the spreading tree in Dan 4:11-12; but the nearer fulfillment deserves preference; see above, pp. 118-119.

the kingdom of Judah, even though the Jews may disbelieve it, v. 23. Fulfillment (per. 7): whether the Babylonian king ever actually conducted such a lottery is unknown, but the events which Ezekiel's action foreshadowed did materialize; and though the Ammonites had been plotting against Nebuchadrezzar (Jer 27:3), history witnesses to the postponement of his attack against them until four years after Judah's fall (see No. 28, below).

27. Ezek 21:27 (1 v.): concerning the crown of Judah (v. 26, see No. 16, above), Yahweh says, "I will overturn it: this also shall be no more, until He come whose right it is; and I will give it Him." Keil paraphrases God's word, about *this* which *shall be no more*, as meaning, "The existing state . . . and the monarchy, will I make into destruction."[49] But there is yet to come a restitution: "With the fall of Zedekiah the old order was to pass, never to be restored until the Messiah came"; for the phrase *He whose right it is* constitutes "the first extant interpretation of *Shiloh* in Genesis 49:10."[50] The latter verse (*q.v.*) should thus be read, "The sceptre shall not depart from Judah . . . until *Shiloh*, meaning, *He-whose-right-it-is*, comes." Fulfillment (per. 16): as in Gen. No. 68, Christ's being granted the rule of the earth, after His second coming.

28. Ezek 21:28–30 (3 vv.): against Ammon (cf. vv. 18–23, No. 26, above), "A sword is drawn for the slaughter," along with "the wicked that are deadly wounded" (meaning Judah, vv. 24–25; see No. 1 and 16, above), but now for the Ammonites in their land as well, v. 30. Fulfillment (per. 8): the fall of Ammon in 582, as in Amos No. 9 (1:13); cf. Jer 49:2–5, discussed under prophecy No. 23.

29. Ezek 21:31–32; 25:4–7, 10b (7 vv.): further threats against the Ammonites, "I will deliver thee into the hand of brutish men, skillful to destroy . . . thou shalt be no more remembered" (21:31–32). More precisely, "I will deliver thee to the children of the east for a possession" (25:4), i.e. to the Nabatean Arabs, who occupied their territory;[51] cf. v. 7, "I will cause thee to perish out of the countries: I will destroy thee." Fulfillment (per. 11): "By the 1st century B.C. Ammon had become part of the Nabatean kingdom";[52] cf. Jer 49:2b, on Jewish encroachment upon the Ammonites too.

30. Ezek 24:1–2 (2 vv.): God instructed Ezekiel, "Write thee the name of this day [Jan. 15, 588 B.C.]: the king of Babylon drew close to Jerusalem this selfsame day." Fulfillment (per. 7): it was so, II K 25:1. "The setting down and announcement of this date would constitute a public confirmation of his prophetic office, when news would filter through at a later date."[53]

49. I:304.
50. Ellison, op. cit., p. 86.
51. Ibid., p. 101.
52. IDB, I:113.
53. NBC, p. 657; cf. JB, p. 1389, "It will serve to verify the accuracy of his revelations."

31. Ezek 24:21a (1 v.): the temple to be destroyed. Fulfillment (per. 7): it was, as in I K. No. 16.

32. Ezek 24:25–27 (3 vv.): "at that day [= the general time]" of Jerusalem's destruction, when a refugee should come to Ezekiel with this word, the prophet would again be able to speak without his former restrictedness (3:26–27).[54] This was fulfilled (per. 7), 33:21–22, at the end of the year 586.[55]

33. Ezek 25:8–*10a*, 11 (3 vv.): "I will open the side of Moab . . . unto the children of the east." Fulfillment (per. 9): as in Zeph. No. 5, carried out in the later 6th century.

34. Ezek 25:12–14 (3 vv.):[56] against Edom, because of their crimes against Judah, v. 12: "I will lay My vengeance upon Edom by the hand of My people Israel." Fulfillment (per. 11): as in Gen 25:23b (3rd stage), Obad 18b. "This was fulfilled in the time of John Hyrcanus [ca. 120 B.C.[57]]; he conquered the Edomites and gave them the choice of Judaism or the sword."[58]

35. Ezek 25:15–17 (3 vv.): against the Philistines, "I will destroy the remnant of the sea coast." Accomplishment for this prophecy must arise later than for Jeremiah's Philistine oracles, which were both spoken and fulfilled in 605–604 B.C. (see under Jer 25:20c), since Ezekiel's 25th ch. dates after 586 (v. 3). Fulfillment (per. 11): as in Amos No. 6, the assimilation of the Philistine peoples into the Greeks, after 165 B.C., and their conquest by Simon, 148–146.

36. Ezek 26:1–4a, 6–11; 28:6–11, 16–19 (20 vv.): God's word against Tyre, "I will cause many nations to come up against thee," 26:3 (= 28:7), i.e., Nebuchadrezzar and his allies, 26:7—to strike down the surrounding towns in the field, v. 6; to set up siege works, v. 9; to breach the fortifications, and to slay people, v. 10. Ithobaal II, the king of Tyre, is to fall, 28:8. His pride is the cause of his being cast out of his island-mountain; but his privileges are compared with those of one of the cherubim, covering the ark in the Mount Zion temple, 28:16, or with those of Adam, in the perfection of Eden, vv. 13, 15. Fulfillment (per. 8): as in Isa. No. 66 (23:13), the 13-year siege of Tyre by Nebuchadrezzar, 585–573, though Ezek 29:18 goes on to note the latter's lack of plunder despite his arduous campaign.

37. Ezek 26:*4b*–5, 12–21; 27:1–2, 26–32, 34–36 (23 vv.): a further stage to the collapse of Tyre, "They [indefinite][59] shall make a spoil of thy

---

54. Cf. M. Greenberg, "On Ezekiel's Dumbness," JBL 77 (1958), 101–103.
55. 29:21 (see No. 12, above) is dated 571 and therefore cannot refer to this same "opening of the mouth."
56. The Edomites are also mentioned along with the Moabites in v. 8.
57. IDB, II:26.
58. Ellison, loc. cit.
59. See above, p. 138, on the evidence afforded by this passage for the interpretive principle of "prophetic telescoping."

riches" (26:12); "I will make thee a bare rock, built no more" (v. 14); and "The sound of thy harps shall be no more heard" (v. 13). The city is to be "not inhabited" (vv. 19–20); "Thou shalt never more have any being" (27:36), in her position, that is, as a ruling city, cf. John's parallel words about Rome in Rev 18:21–23. Fulfillment (per. 10): the fall of Tyre to Alexander in July, 332 B.C., by means of a causeway which he built out to the island in the course of 7 months of siege.[60] Though rebuilt in 314, Tyre sank to the status of a poor fishing village after its capture by the Arabs in A.D. 1291.

38. Ezek 28:20–24 (5 vv.): Phoenician Sidon to suffer pestilence and sword. Because this oracle is brief and is couched in general terms,[61] its fulfillment is not entirely clear. The reference may be to Sidon's revolt against Artaxerxes III of Persia in 345 (per. 9): as in Joel 3:4b.

39. Ezek 28:26; 34:14–16a; 36:8–11, 29b–30, *33b*–38 (15 vv.): after Israel's return to Palestine (28:25, No. 12, above), "They shall dwell securely therein: yea, they shall build houses and plant vineyards" (v. 26). In ch. 34 the prophet had recourse to a series of figures: v. 14, that God will feed His people with good pasture; v. 16, "I will bind up that which was broken." The reference must be to 538 B.C. and following; for the deliverance advances out of the troubles of 586 (compare v. 16 with v. 4), and Ezekiel resumes his discussion of contemporary matters in vv. 18–19. More literal are the expressions of 36:8, on the growth of fruit (= v. 30), and v. 10, on the multiplication of men (= v. 37) and the reinhabitation of cities (= v. 33). The thought must again be postexilic; for it contrasts with the desolation upon other, contemporaneous nations, v. 7. V. 35 invokes hyperbole when it says, "The land that was desolate is become like the garden of Eden"; but, as explained in the following lines, this means that "the ruined cities are fortified and inhabited"; see above, p. 113. Fulfillment (per. 9): as in Jer. No. 67, prosperity for the Jews of the restoration.

40. Ezek 29:1–6, 8–16; 30:1–9, 13–19; 31:18; 32:1–10, 12–21, 28, 31–32 (55 vv., fig.): God speaks against Egypt, under the figure of a great fish, "I will bring thee out of the midst of thy rivers," 29:4. As explained in vv. 8–10 (ASVmg), "I will bring a sword upon thee and will cut off from thee man and beast; and the land of Egypt shall be a desolation [= 30:17] . . . from Migdol [in the NE Delta, Ex 14:2, Num 33:7]

---

60. Wyngaarden, and others, would associate the predicted Greek destruction with that of the mainland city rather than that of the island. He asserts, "Alexander built to the island, using the stones of Old Tyre, its timbers and its dust, in the mounds of the ruins left by Nebuchadrezzar. Accomplishing the prophecy, he cast these materials into the waters," *The Future of the Kingdom in Prophecy and Fulfillment*, p. 16. But the mainland structures do not appear really to have formed "Old Tyre"; evidence favors the island's having been the original town; cf. HDB, IV:823.

61. KD, I:425.

to Syene [in the far S, at Aswan, by the 1st cataract = 30:6], even unto the border of Ethiopia." The time of Egypt's fall is designated as a "day of Yahweh," 30:3.[62] Further details include these: v. 9, "In that day messengers shall go forth from before Me in ships [refugees from Egypt, fleeing up the Nile] to make the Ethiopians afraid"; v. 13, Egypt shall have "no more prince"; and 31:18, "Pharaoh and all his multitude shall be brought down to hell, with them that are slain by the sword," just like the Assyrians before them, vv. 2–3 (cf. v. 10, No. 42, below). Their fall is illustrated in 32:17–32, which follows, and in the course of which the strong are pictured as rising up from the midst of hell in a welcome to them. 32:5 states, "I will lay thy flesh upon the mountains," and v. 7, "I shall extinguish thee." The figure then of heaven being darkened represents the amazement of the peoples over Egypt's collapse, vv. 9–10. V. 11 inserts a more immediate note, that the sword of the king of Babylon is to come upon the pharaoh (see 29:19, No. 41, following).[63] But the next verse again speaks more generally of the swords (plu.) of the terrible of the nations (the Medes and the Persians), so that "all the multitude thereof shall be destroyed" and Egypt shall be made desolate, v. 15.[64] Yahweh says, "Neither shall it be inhabited 40 years . . . and I will scatter the Egyptians among the nations," 29:11–12; and though they are to be regathered at the end of the 40 years, vv. 13–14, Egypt "shall be the basest of the kingdoms . . . they shall no more rule over the nations," v. 15. Fulfillment (per. 9): as in Isa. No 56. Redpath observes,

In 29:11 a very sweeping statement is made. The words mean that for that [40-year] period Egypt would lose its importance. . . . It is to be noticed that neither the name of the conqueror of Egypt nor that of his nation is mentioned in the prophecy. . . . [Yet] the first occupation by the Persians, which began under Cambyses, lasted close upon 40 years (525-487 B.C.); and many cruelties, from which the Egyptians suffered, are attributed to him by Herodotus.[65]

41. Ezek 29:19–20; 30:10–12, 20–26; 32:11[66] (13 vv.): God's more immediate threat, "I will give the land of Egypt unto Nebuchadrezzar king of Babylon, and he shall carry off her multitude and take her spoil"

62. See above, pp. 131–133.
63. Ellison exhibits no minor skepticism at this point: "Nebuchadrezzar will at the most have fulfilled the Tahpanhes prophecy of Jeremiah, but certainly neither the wider prophecy of Jer 43:11 ff. [on his smiting the land of Egypt; but why not?] nor Ezek 30:1–19 [on the multitude of Egypt to cease by the hand of Nebuchadrezzar, which is a legitimate statement; but it is significant that the Babylonian is not mentioned beyond v. 12]. Ezek 29:10–13 was not fulfilled either in the time of Nebuchadrezzar or later," op. cit., p. 102. Yet contrast Redpath, below.
64. These events did not eventuate under Nebuchadrezzar, who did not slay Pharaoh Amasis, even though he did defeat his army. Contrast 32:31–32.
65. WC, p. 159.
66. It is to be noted that the succeeding sections in Ezek 30 (i.e. v. 13) and 32 (i.e. v. 12) move on to Egypt's more complete overthrow by the Persians four decades later (No. 40, above).

(29:19), "and fill the land with the slain" (30:11). 30:21 predicts, in a figure, "I have broken the arm of Pharaoh . . . [v. 25] when I shall put My sword into the hand of the king of Babylon." Vv. 23 and 26 forecast, just as in the event of Egypt's final fall (29:12, No. 40 preceding), "I will scatter the Egyptians among the nations." Fulfillment (per. 8): the campaign of Nebuchadrezzar against Egypt in 568–567, as in Jer. No. 21 (9:25), though this Ezekiel passage dates to 571 (Ezek 29:17), only three years before the accomplishment.

42. Ezek 31:10–11 (2 vv.): a backward reference to Assyria (cf. v. 3), "Thus said Yahweh [in the past; for Assyria fell in 612, and this recollection is 25 years later, in 587, v. 1], I will deliver him into the hand of the mighty one of the nations; he shall surely deal with him." God's prophet then resumes his historical narrative: "I have driven him out . . . he went down to hell [sheol]," vv. 11, 15. Fulfillment (per. 7): as in Nah. No. 1, the fall of Nineveh to Cyaxares the Mede.

43. Ezek 33:27–29 (3 vv.): after the tragic events of 586 (v. 23), Ezekiel predicted that the remnant left in Judah after Gedaliah's death (II K 25:25–26) would fall by the sword, by wild beasts, and by pestilence. The land is to be left desolate. Fulfillment (per. 8): archaeology has confirmed that during the days of the exile the region was depopulated.[67]

44. Ezek 34:1–2, 7–10, *16b*–17, 20–22 (10 vv., fig.): "Woe unto the shepherds of Israel . . . I will cause them to cease from feeding the sheep." This prophecy constitutes an extension to the oracle against Judah's evil "shepherds" that is found in Jer 23:1–2 (listed under 21:7); but Ezekiel's message comes at a later time, after the fall of Judah (Ezek 33:21). Fulfillment (per. 8): the removal of Judah's civil rulers during exilic days. As Ellison notes, "For the time being, Jehovah Himself would be their king with no man as His representative (34:11–16)."[68]

45. Ezek 34:25, 27b–28, 30–31; 36:12–15;[69] 37:26a (10 vv.): Scripture's most complete revelation of God's "testament of peace," an "everlasting testament," 37:26. On the one hand, Ezekiel's *b'rīth* develops the four basic features of Jeremiah's new testament, Jer 31:33–34 (see under 3:16b), which would be:

Internal:	In Ezek, "They shall know that I am Yahweh," 34:27.
Reconciling:	"I will be their God and they shall be My people," 37:27 (=34:30).
Direct:	"I will put My sanctuary in the midst of them," 37:26.
Forgiving:	"I am Yahweh that sanctifieth Israel," 37:28.

67. John Bright, *A History of Israel*, p. 324.
68. Op. cit., p. 121.
69. Ezek 36:8–11 had been concerned with Judah's postexilic restoration, but the closing lines of the section suggest a transition, "and I will do better unto you than at your beginnings." Keil explains, II:104, "The promise was no doubt fulfilled in certain weak beginnings after the return of a portion of the people under Zerubbabel and Ezra; but the blessing, more especially in vv. 12–15, did not take place till long after"; cf. vv. 13–15, "Thou, land, shalt devour men no more . . . neither will I let thee hear any more the shame of the nations."

Yet on the other hand, the testament of peace goes beyond the heavenly new testament into the following parallel, but earthly, features as well:[70]

External: "I will cause evil beasts to cease out of the land," 34:25.
(Reconciliation with God remains constant, from Gen 17:7 to Rev 21:3.)
Visible: "My tabernacle shall be with them," 37:27.
Secure: "They shall no more be a prey to the nations . . . none shall make them afraid," 34:28.

Fulfillment (per. 16): the testament of peace as the "constitution" of the Messiah's future kingdom, as first suggested in Lev 26:9b, and then developed in Hos 2:18c.

46. Ezek 34:26–27a, 29 (2 vv.): in the future kingdom God promises, "I will cause the shower to come down in its season; there shall be showers of blessing" (v. 26), with resultant fruit on the trees (v. 27), and the land becoming "a plantation for renown" (v. 29). Fulfillment (per. 16): as in Ex. No. 49, millennial fertility and prosperity.

47. Ezek 35:1–15 (15 vv.): Seir (Edom) to be made a desolation, "I will lay thy cities waste" (v. 4), "a perpetual desolation, not inhabited" (v. 9). In 36:5, God's judgment against Edom is associated with His indignation against other nations as well (No. 48, following); so Ellison suggests, "Mt. Seir may indeed act as a symbol of the lot of all those who despise their birthright and set as the goal 'the lust of the flesh. . . .' [Yet] it is one thing to recognize the symbolic nature of so much prophetic promise, it is quite another to spiritualize it to mean something quite other than it could possibly have meant to the original hearers."[71] Fulfillment (per. 9): as in Obad. No. 2, the permanent expulsion of the Edomites from their land by the Nabateans, before 500 B.C.

48. Ezek 36:5–7 (3 vv.): because the nations surrounding Judah had boasted about taking over the former territories of the exiled Hebrews, God warns, "I have spoken against the residue of the nations and against all Edom" (cf. ch. 35, No. 47, preceding), v. 5; "The nations that are round about you shall bear their shame," v. 7. Fullfillment (per. 8): as in Jer. No. 29, their own servitude to Babylon, corresponding to Judah's.

49. Ezek 36:38a; 40:40–41, 43; 44:7b; 45:15a, 16; 46:21–24 (9 vv., typ.): sacrifice. Fulfillment (per. 13): as in Lev. No. 2.

50. Ezek 37:25a (1 v.): the people of the Messiah (v. 24) "shall dwell in the land for ever." Fulfillment (per. 18): as in II Sam No. 14 (7:24), the eternity of Israel.

51. Ezek 37:25b: along with His Messianic prophecy (No. 23, above), God includes a time factor, "David My servant shall be their prince for

70. J. B. Payne, *Theology of the Older Testament*, pp. 117, 479.
71. Op. cit., pp. 123, 130. He notes further, "The spiritualization of Scripture is seldom a spiritual process. It is normally the substitution of the expositor's own views for the teaching of Scripture."

ever." Fulfillment (per. 13): as in II Sam. No. 11, Christ the eternal son of David.

52. Ezek 37:*26b*–28; 47:1a; 48:8–9, *10b, 21b* (5 vv., typ.): God's promise, "I will set up My sanctuary in the midst of them for evermore" (37:26), "My tabernacle" (v. 27), God's "house," with an altar (47:1). It will be a means for leading the nations to a recognition of Yahweh (37:28). Fulfillment (per. 16): the millennial temple, as in Isa. No. 8 (2:2b). The theological truth that this building conveys by means of type continues on into the New Jerusalem, namely, that of God's tabernacling presence, Rev 21:3, though there will then be no more physical structure or temple, v. 22.

53. Ezek 38:1–23, 39:1–22 (45 vv.): prophecies of "Gog of the land of Magog, chief prince of Meshech and Tubal" (38:2 ASVmg, cf. 39:1). The location of Magog appears to lie north of the Black Sea (Gen 10:2), even as "the Mushki and the Tabali" are associated with the Armenian highlands to its southeast. Beasley-Murray observes, "Meshech and Tubal are always coupled together, in secular as well as Biblical writings; the reading of KJV and ASVmg is therefore preferable to that of ASV 'prince of Rosh, Meshech, and Tubal.' Their equation with Moscow and Tobolsk, and Rosh with Russia, is unsupportable."[72] Concerning Gog, the Lord says, "I will bring thee forth and all thine army"—comprising many peoples, which include Persia, Ethiopia, and areas "in the uttermost parts of the north" (38:4)—"upon the mountains of Israel" (38:8, 39:2), "to them that are at rest, that dwell securely . . . without walls" (38:11). Because of this last factor, Beasley-Murray states,   •

These two chapters are unique in OT prophecy in that they describe an uprising of foreign powers against the people of God after the commencement of the Messianic kingdom. The prophet has already predicted the coming blessedness of Israel (chs. 33–37); he now portrays the nation as long settled in their land and transformed into a prosperous community (38:8, 11, 12, 14). . . . Whereas he had said that Israel's restoration was "at hand" (36:8), he says that Gog shall be mustered after many days, in the latter years (38:8).[73]

Yet the Lord moves in action against Gog: "All the men that are upon the face of the earth shall shake at My presence, and the mountains shall be thrown down," 38:20. "Every man's sword shall be against his brother," v. 21; "and I will rain upon him and upon his hordes . . . great hailstones, fire and brimstone," v. 22. As a result, 39:9, "Israel shall go forth and make fires of the weapons seven years"; v. 11, "and I will give unto Gog a place for burial in Israel . . . The valley of Hamon-gog," meaning, *the multitude of Gog*; and, v. 12, "seven months shall Israel be burying them." Fulfillment (per. 17): earth's final, Satan-inspired revolt against Yahweh,

72. NBC, pp. 662–663.
73. Ibid., p. 662; cf. Ellison, op. cit., pp. 133–134.

postmillennial, according to Rev 20:8–9; compare also Jer 25:26b etc. with Ezek 38:17.

54. Ezek 40:38–39a, 42a; 43:*18b*, 23–24, 25b, 27a; *44:11b*; 45:*15c*, *17a*, 23a, *25b*; 46:2a, 4a, 6, 12a, 13, 15a (14 vv., typ.): burnt offering. Fulfillment (per. 13): as in Lev. No. 3.

55. Ezek *40:39b*; *42:13b*; 43:19–22, *25a*; 44:27, *29b*; 45:*17d*, 18–20, 22, *23b*, 25a; *46:20b* (10 vv., typ.): sin offering. Fulfillment (per. 13): as in Lev. No. 6.

56. Ezek *40:39c, 42:13c, 44:29c*, 46:20a (1 v., typ.): trespass offering. Fulfillment (per. 13): as in Lev. No. 7.

57. Ezek *40:42b*; *43:27b*; 44:3, *11c*; *45:15d, 17e*; *46:2b, 12b* (1 v., typ.): peace offering. Fulfillment (pers. 13 and 16): as in Lev. No. 5.

58. Ezek 42:13a; 44:29a; 45:13–14, *15b*, 17b, 24, *25c*; 46:5, 7, 11, 14, *15b, 20c* (10 vv., typ.): meal offering. Fulfillment (per. 13): as in Lev. No. 4.

59. Ezek 42:14, 44:17–19 (4 vv., typ.): priests' garments. Fulfillment (per. 13): as in Ex. No. 60.

60. Ezek 44:11a, 13–16; 46:19 (6 vv., typ.): priests. Fulfillment (per. 13): as in Ex. No. 59.

61. Ezek 45:21 (1 v., typ.): Passover. Fulfillment (per. 13): as in Ex. No. 31.

62. Ezek 47:*1b*–12 (11 vv.): Ezekiel is granted a vision (40:2) of a river, flowing east from the temple, and bordered with trees. Its purpose is then explained, 47:8–12: to "heal the waters" of the Dead Sea, so as to enable fishing; the trees are to produce food; and their leaves are for healing. Fulfillment (per. 16): as in Joel No. 22 (3:18b), a life-giving river coming from Jerusalem.

63. Ezek 47:13–21; 48:1–7, 10–14, 20–29 (31 vv.): a statement concerning the borders of millennial Israel: from Damascus, southward via the Jordan, to Kadesh-barnea, and west to the Mediterranean. In ch. 48, the land is divided into 12 E–W strips for the 12 tribes: 7 in the north; with a central section for the temple, the millennial city of Jerusalem, and the lands of the priests, the Levites, and the Ruler; and the remaining 5 strips to the south of this section. Fulfillment (per. 16): the oragnization of the land during Messiah's rule.

64. Ezek 47:22–23 (2 vv.): the land (No. 63, above) is to serve "for an inheritance unto you and to the strangers that sojourn among you . . . they shall have inheritance with you among the tribes of Israel. In what tribe the stranger sojourneth, there shall ye give him his inheritance." Fulfillment (per. 16): as in Ps. No. 29, the millennial incorporation of Gentiles among the tribes of Israel.

65. Ezek 48:15–19, 30–35a (11 vv.): a description of Jerusalem in the days of the future kingdom. If the units of measurement are cubits (1½ feet), the city will lie approximately 1¼ miles square (v. 16), surrounded

by a belt of meadows 125 yards wide (v. 17), and with agricultural lands 3 miles east and 3 miles west (vv. 18–19). Three gates appear on each of the city's four sides, named after the 12 tribes (vv. 30–34). Fulfillment (per. 16): the arrangement and measurements of millennial Jerusalem.

66. Ezek *48:35b:* "And the name of the city [see No. 65, preceding] shall be, Yahweh is there." Fulfillment (per. 16): as in Isa. No. 16 (4:5), the presence of God in the Messianic capital city.

DANIEL

The last, and shortest, of the four Major Prophets is Daniel.[1] It is also the one that contains the smallest percentage of predictive material: its 58 separate forecasts involve but 162 out of the book's 357 verses, or a modest 45%. Yet this proportion is due primarily to the historical narratives that appear in the first half of Daniel's 12 chapters: chs. 1, 3, and 6, for example, contain no verbal prophecies of the future whatsoever. The visions of chs. 7–12, on the other hand, are almost wholly predictive in nature. Ch. 7, together with its parallel in ch. 2, constitutes Scripture's most sweeping panorama of what was then future world history; and Daniel's predictions form one of the Bible's outstanding blocks of apocalyptic literature—along with Zechariah and Revelation. His writing, as a result, exhibits the highest proportion of symbolic prophecy to be found within the word of God, engaging slightly more than two-thirds of this book's prophetic content, even though Daniel's total number of symbolical predictions (20) is exceeded by Revelation's 24.[2]

Daniel the man was born into an unidentified family of Judean nobility at about the time of Josiah's reformation, which dates to 622 B.C. For this servant of the Lord was among the youthful hostages of the first Jewish deportation to Babylon, in the year 605 (Dan 1:1, 3),[3] when Nebuchadrezzar's own chronicles validate how he "conquered the whole area of Hatti [Syria and Palestine] and took away the heavy tribute of Hatti to Babylon" (cf. Dan 1:2).[4] After three years of special education in the learning of the Chaldeans (vv. 4–5), Daniel became an established "wise man" at

1. In the fourth century rabbinic leaders placed Daniel among the miscellaneous books that made up the third division of their canon, which they entitled the "Writings." Yet in the older arrangement attested by Josephus, Daniel did stand among the "Prophets," following the "Law" and preceding the four "Poets," Ps–Song of Sol; cf. Christ's designation of Daniel as a prophet, Mt 24:15.

2. See below, pp. 674–675, in the Statistical Appendix.

3. The 3rd year of King Jehoiakim, which is called his 4th (Jer 46:2) when 609–608 is not designated, according to the Babylonian system, as a separate "accession year."

4. D. J. Wiseman, *Chronicles of Chaldean Kings* (626–556), pp. 26, 29.

the Babylonian court (1:20, 2:13). More significantly, God gave him wisdom and "understanding in all visions and dreams" (1:17). Near the close of Nebuchadrezzar's 2nd official year (602 B.C.), Daniel's interpretation of a dream that the king had kept undisclosed brought about his promotion to the rank of chief among the wise men (2:48), a post which he held until the fall of Babylon, and on into the first year of Cyrus of Persia, in 538 (1:21, 6:28).[5] He was known and revered by his fellow prophet of the exile, Ezekiel (Ezek 14:14, 20; 28:3).[6] The last recorded event of his life was the receipt of a final major vision in 536 (Dan 10:1). Shortly thereafter, in his mid-eighties, he must have completed the book that bears his name; for note his use of first-person pronouns from 7:2 onward, the unity of the volume as a whole as evidenced by its style and content, and the allusion to "the book" in 12:4.[7]

The Book of Daniel was designed by the prophet to inspire the Jews of the Babylonian exile to a renewed confidence in God the Most High, 4:34–37; compare v. 34 as a key passage for the entire volume, "I praised and honored Him that liveth for ever and ever; for His dominion is an everlasting dominion, and His kingdom from generation to generation." By content, the book falls into the previously mentioned two parts: I. six narratives, chs. 1–6, each of which demonstrates the sovereign grace of God for those who will commit their way to Him; and II. four apocalyptic visions, chs. 7–12, predicting the course of world history under the hand of Yahweh. The prophet's pattern is established in ch. 7, with repetitions and special emphases appearing in the remaining chapters. Their scope is outlined in Table 8. Daniel 7 envisions the rise of four beasts, which are explained as representing successive kings (kingdoms, v. 23). Their description parallels that of the four parts of the image seen by Nebuchadrezzar in his dream, as recorded in ch. 2. The first empire must therefore be contemporary Babylon (2:38); and the fourth, Rome,[8] in which God's Messianic kingdom would be set up (v. 44). Between these two lie Persia and Greece. The vision further describes the disintegration of Rome into a ten-fold balance of power (2:42, 7:24; cf. Rev 17:12, 16), the eventual rise of the Antichrist for an indefinite period of "times" (Dan 7:8, 25),

5. Cf. J. B. Payne, "Daniel," in M. C. Tenney, ed., *The Zondervan Pictorial Bible Dictionary*, pp. 196–198.
6. Though recent criticism has attempted to relate these verses to a mythological Danel of Ugaritic legend; cf. E. J. Young, *The Prophecy of Daniel*, pp. 274–275.
7. See Young, *An Introduction to the OT*, pp. 380–382.
8. As indicated below, liberal writers consistently identify the 4th empire with the Greeks, eventuating in the persecutor, Antiochus Epiphanes. They must then assert that Daniel conceived of a fictitious Median empire existing as a separate kingdom between Babylon (1st empire) and Persia (3rd). But the passage most frequently adduced (5:31–6:1) speaks of a unified Medo-Persia (6:8, 12; cf. 5:28); and Daniel elsewhere identifies his 2nd empire as the dual kingdom of Media *and* Persia (7:5, cf. 8:3, 20) and his 3rd, as the fourfold Greek (7:6, 8:8, 22).

TABLE 8
Scope of the Apocalyptic Visions in Daniel 7-12[9]

Subject	Dan 7 (4 beasts)	Dan 8 (ram and he-goat)	Dan 9 (70 weeks)	Dan 10-12 (kings, north and south)
Date given	552 B.C.	550	538	536 B.C.

History content

(1) Babylon
539

(Cambyses 527)
(Ezra 458)

(2) Persia
331

(3) Greece
63 B.C.

(Maccabees

in 165 B.C.)

(4) Rome
A.D. 476

(Christ's 1st coming, A.D. 30)

Divided power
2nd coming
Millennium

9. Payne, "Daniel, Book of," in Tenney, op. cit., p. 198.

and his destruction when a "Son of man" comes with the clouds of heaven (7:13). This last figure symbolizes the saints of the Most High (v. 22), epitomized in Jesus Christ, the "last Adam" (Mk 14:62, I Cor 15:45). For though His kingdom was "set up" at His first coming, it will "consume [earth's pagan] kingdoms" at His glorious second advent (Dan 2:44) and millennial reign, the "season" of 7:12.

By language, two categories again appear within the Book of Daniel; for chs. 2:4b–7:28 are composed in the international tongue of Aramaic. But with ch. 8 the prophet resumes his use of Hebrew, probably because of the more restrictedly Jewish orientation of the remaining three visions. That of the ram and the he-goat depicts the coming victory of Greece (in 331 B.C.) over the amalgamated empire of Medo–Persia (8:20–21) and the subsequent persecution of Judah by Antiochus IV, Epiphanes (168–165 B.C.; 8:9–14, 23–26). Ch. 9, on the 70 weeks, then illuminates Christ's first coming 69 weeks of years (= 483 years) after the decree for Jerusalem's rebuilding, presumably to Ezra in 458 (Ezra 7:18, 25); cf. his results, as witnessed to in Ezra 4:12–16. With God-inspired accuracy, Daniel thus inaugurates the 70th of his weeks in A.D. 26, with the baptismal anointing of Christ (Dan 9:25; Lk 3:21–22, 4:18). In the midst of this week the Anointed One is to be cut off (Dan 9:26), but thereby making reconciliation for iniquity (v. 24) and causing OT sacrifice to cease (v. 27; see Mt 27:51, Heb 9:8–12). Yet for an additional 3½ years, God's redemptive testament will be confirmed to Israel (cf. Rev 12:6, 14), a few years subsequent to which Jerusalem will be rendered desolate (A.D. 70, Dan 9:26–27, Mt 24:15). Chs. 10–12, after elaborating on the succession of Persian and Greek rulers through Antiochus, then moves on to "the time of the end," foretelling the great tribulation caused by the Antichrist (Dan 11:40–12:1), the resurrections of the saved and the lost (12:2; cf. Rev 20:4–6, 12), and the final judgment (Dan 12:2).[10]

Modern Biblical criticism, however, overwhelmingly questions the authenticity of Daniel as a product of the 6th century B.C. When faced by such detailed predictions of the 3rd and 2nd centuries as fill Dan 11:5–39, these critics have no alternative but to bring down the writing of the "prophecy" to a time posterior to the events described, especially after the sacrilege of 168 as perpetrated by Antiochus (cf. the number of passages that predict it, as listed under 8:11, below). In light of the equally detailed predictions of the 1st Christian century, or later, in 2:41–44 or 9:24–27, the problem becomes even more pronounced. Since Daniel was extensively quoted (and misunderstood!) as early as 140 B.C. (Sibylline Oracles 3:381–400), or even 150 (I Enoch 14:18–22), or perhaps even earlier yet, by the sectarians at Qumran,[11] these critics have no recourse but to reinterpret these predictions of later events and to force them to apply to other happenings of more ancient times. The supposed coming of the Messianic kingdom, for example, or the accomplishment of the 70 weeks, must be understood in reference to the days of the early Maccabees (see note 8, above) rather than to those of Jesus, even though for the latter prediction this requires "surmising a chronological miscalculation on the part of the writer."[12] A dating of Daniel to the 2nd century B.C. is thus the result, fundamentally, of the presuppositions of skeptical criticism; and it stands opposed to the evidence and testimony.[13] It makes the book's

10. Skeptical writers do not recognize the distinctive emphases of the prophet's successive visions. Montgomery would even seek to enlist the aid of the hermeneutical principle of the Reformers, when he insists, "After any possible 'analogy of Scripture,' and indeed any possible interpretation of the book regarded as a unit, the atheistic and inhuman personage described in 11:21ff., who fully corresponds to the rule of Epiphanes [in vv. 40–45?], must be identified with the similar personage described in 8:24ff., a king in 'the latter time of the kingdom of Greece,' as specified in v. 21; and again with the little horn of the 4th beast of the 1st vision, 7:7 [the Antichrist]. In the vision of ch. 9, the prince that shall come, who 'shall destroy the city and the sanctuary,' v. 26 [Titus of Rome], is evidently the same personage. That is, all 4 visions of the second half of the book culminate in one and the same execrable tyrant. . . . He and his doings are the climax of the 'kingdom of Greece,' " ICC, p. 60.
11. Cf. R. K. Harrison, *Introduction to the OT*, p. 1118.
12. ICC, p. 393.
13. Payne, "Daniel, Book of," pp. 198–199; cf. such defenses of the authenticity of Daniel as K. A. Kitchen, *Notes on Some Problems in the Book of Daniel*, concerning its 6th-century Aramaic language, or E. M. Yamauchi, "The Greek Words of Daniel in the Light of 6th Century Greek Influence in the Near East," in Payne, ed., *New Perspectives on the OT*.

record of itself a deception; and it necessarily involves Jesus Christ—who believed that "Daniel the prophet" did predict Roman imperialism (Mt 24:15)—in a falsehood based on His presumed ignorance of Scripture.[14]

1. Dan 1:2; 5:2–3, 23; *8:11c, 13c;* 9:17; *11:31b* (5 vv., typ.): the temple. Fulfillment (period 13): as in Ex. prophecy No. 55.
2. Dan 2:16, 24–*28a* (5 vv.): Daniel's forecast that he would be able to tell Nebuchadrezzar the interpretation of the king's dream—though Daniel did not yet know it at this point (cf. v. 19). Fulfillment (per. 8): he did reveal the dream, vv. 29–45; and the king testified to his correctness, v. 47.
3. Dan 2:28b–32a, *39a;* 7:1–3, 5, 15–17; 8:1–4, 15–20 (22 vv., sym.): Nebuchadrezzar's dream of a great image, the upper part of which consisted of a head of gold and a breast and arms of silver, 2:32. The image is explained in vv. 28–29 as representing "what should come to pass hereafter . . . in the latter days." After Nebuchadrezzar's own kingdom (the head of gold, a nonpredictive symbol, v. 38), there "shall arise another kingdom inferior to thee" (v. 39). The image, with its various parts, is paralleled in ch. 7 by Daniel's own dream of four beasts coming up out of the sea. They are explained in the discussion that follows, 7:17, as denoting "four kings [the concrete idea of *kings* standing for the more abstract concept of *kingdoms*; cf. the interchange of these terms in 2:37–39], that shall arise out of the earth." The first beast (7:4), the lion, to whom a man's heart was given (cf. Nebuchadrezzar's heart experience, 4:16, 34), is thus the same king and kingdom of Babylon as was the head of gold in 2:32–38. So the second beast, like a bear "raised up on one side" (7:5), corresponds to the dual kingdom of the image's breast and two arms in 2:32, 39. Further, in 8:4, Daniel's vision of the conquering ram, before whom none could stand, serves to illuminate the concept of the "unbalanced" bear; for the ram "had two horns, and the two horns were high; but one was higher than the other, and the higher came up last," v. 3. Fulfillment (per. 9): "they are the kings of Media and Persia," v. 20, the joint kingdom that succeeded Babylon in 539 B.C.[15] Its inferi-

14. ICC, p. 62, admits, "The Jews under Rome found that [4th] Monarchy in their new mistress, witness Josephus; and this ruling Jewish interpretation was naturally carried over by the church with its vivid eschatological hopes . . . an interpretation followed by Jesus Himself in expecting the future setting up of the abomination of desolations."

15. Liberal criticism usually assigns the bear to Media only; see note 9, above. It recognizes that historically Babylon was succeeded by Persia and that this took place only after Cyrus had already incorporated Media into his realm. But it claims that the writer of Daniel *thought* Media succeeded Babylon—on the basis of 5:31, though this Darius was but one individual Mede, who seems to have been a subordinate of Cyrus; see J. C. Whitcomb, *Darius the Mede.* Yet on the data of 5:28, ICC, p. 263, says, "It is to be noted that the play of words gives 'Persia,' not 'Media,' despite the fact that in immediate sequence it is Darius the Mede who destroys the kingdom; the enigma is then based on the correct historical tradition of Cyrus' conquest."

ority to Babylonia may have reference to its lack of inner unity.[16] That the bear was raised up on one side, and that the ram's second horn was the higher, indicates the Persians as being later and yet greater than the Medes. When 7:5 says of the bear that "three ribs were between its teeth," the ribs may represent the conquered lands of Lydia, Babylon, and Egypt.[17]

4. Dan 2:*32b*, 39b; 7:6; 8:5–*8a*, 21; 11:3 (7 vv., sym.): another element to the image in Nebuchadrezzar's dream is "its belly and thighs of bronze," 2:32. V. 39 explains, "A third kingdom shall bear rule over all the earth." 7:6 speaks similarly of a third beast, a four-headed "leopard, which had upon its back four wings . . . and dominion [= 11:3] was given to it." Again, 8:5 describes how "a he-goat came from the west over the face of the whole earth." V. 7, it smote the ram (of Medo-Persia, No. 3, preceding), and, v. 8, "magnified himself exceedingly." Fulfillment (per. 10): universal rule, by the Macedonian empire of Alexander the Great;[18] for the worldwide authority that is predicted in 2:39 matches that of the goat in 8:5, and the four foldness of 7:6 matches the breaking of the goat's great horn in 8:8 (cf. 11:4; and see No. 23, below), and the goat, in turn, is specifically identified as Greece in 8:20. The same verse also designates the horn of the goat as its first king, Alexander, who struck down the Persian empire in 331 B.C.

5. Dan 2:*33a*, 40; 7:7a, 19, 23 (4 vv., sym.): the next element in the image about which Nebuchadrezzar dreamed consists of "its legs of iron," 2:33; as explained in v. 40, a fourth kingdom, strong as iron, "shall break in pieces and crush" all others. It is paralleled in 7:7 by the "fourth beast, terrible and powerful; and it had great iron teeth; it devoured; and it was diverse [= 7:23] from all the beasts that were before it"—so that its species is not even attempted to be named. Accomplishment (per. 12): as in Num 24:23, the Roman empire, "which shall devour the whole earth" (Dan 7:23). Liberalism insists, indeed, upon the fulfillment of this symbol in Antiochus IV and in the Maccabean opposition to him, 168–165 B.C. [19] But Judas and his brothers were not the Messiah;[20] and when Young advocates the Roman identification he explains, "This is the only position which interprets 2:44 correctly, a verse which distinctly states that the messianic kingdom will be erected in the days of the kingdoms already mentioned."[21]

16. KD, p. 106; Young, *Prophecy*, p. 74.
17. Young, *Prophecy*, p. 145.
18. Liberalism usually identifies the 3rd empire with Persia; see note 9, above. Keil is firm on the Greek identification but refers the four wings and heads of the leopard to Alexander's swiftness and sway in all directions, p. 227.
19. See note 10, above.
20. Liberalism argues that the writer of Daniel *hoped* for something of this nature and that "with the putting off of the fulfillment of the apocalyptic expectation of the comsummation of the kingdom of God, interpretation [as in the NT] simply proceeded to keep the prophecy up to date," ICC, p. 62, by turning to Rome.
21. NBC, p. 672.

6. Dan 2:33b, 41a, 43 (3 vv., sym.): a degeneration that appears later in the fourth section of Nebuchadrezzar's dream-image, namely, "its feet part of iron, and part of clay," v. 33. Verse 41 then reveals the situation that is taught by the mixture of the materials: "It shall be a divided kingdom"; cf. v. 42, "partly strong, and partly *t'vīrā,* fragile."²² Keil argues that the deterioration of the empire is "not because it separates into several kingdoms, for this is denoted by the duality of the feat, but [because it is] inwardly divided . . . [by] violent division arising from inner disharmony or discord";²³ cf. v. 43, "They shall mingle themselves with the seed of men, but they shall not cleave one to another." Fulfillment (per. 14): Rome's division into an eastern and a western empire in A.D. 395, which was but a manifestation of a serious internal weakening, e.g., "the mixing of different tribes brought together by external force in the kingdom."²⁴

7. Dan *2:34a, 44a* (sym.): as Nebuchadrezzar's dream continues, "A stone was cut out without hands," v. 34, the point being that "It is prepared, not by men, but by God."²⁵ Daniel interprets; v. 44: "In the days of those kings²⁶ shall the God of heaven set up a kingdom which shall never be destroyed." Fulfillment (per. 13): the beginnings of Christ's kingdom, during the Roman era;²⁷ cf. Mk 1:15, "the kingdom of God, lit., has come near."²⁸

8. Dan 2:34b–35a, *44c,* 45; 7:9b–10, *22a,* 26; 11:45a (7 vv., sym.): at the conclusion of Nebuchadrezzar's dream, the stone (Christ, 2:34a, No. 7 preceding) "smote the image upon its feet and brake them in pieces" (2:34b): Fairbairn appropriately cautions, "The moment of the brusing is not necessarily, or even probably, the moment of the formation of the stone; and a period seems to lie there of indefinite lengths—the period of the rise and progress of Christianity."²⁹ But eventually, as Daniel explains in v. 44, "It shall break in pieces and consume all these kingdoms." In corresponding fashion, the prophet's vision in ch. 7 tells how "One that was ancient of days did sit" in judgment; for His throne is fire, and it has

22. KB, p. 1135.
23. KD, p. 108.
24. Ibid., p. 109.
25. Young, *Prophecy,* p. 79.
26. Both Keil and Young quote Kliefoth's explanation, that "the latter [kingdoms] assumed the elements and constituent parts" of the former, KD, p. 108, Young, *Prophecy,* p. 70; for Christ's kingdom was actually to be set up "in the days of the *last* of the four," ibid., p. 78. Cf. Fairbairn, *The Interpretation of Prophecy,* p. 297, "The language is purposely indefinite. It does not indicate under which worldly dominion the kingdom represented by the stone should begin to develop itself—though, from the fourth worldly kingdom being mentioned the last in order, and being the one with which alone it appears coming into collision, the natural inference is that the commencement of the heavenly kingdom is to be assigned to the fourth form of the worldly one."
27. *The days of those kings* would hardly refer to "the latter stages of the fourth monarchy . . . this condition is not described as being distinguished by separate kings," Fairbairn, loc. cit.
28. See above, pp. 30, 96–97.
29. Fairbairn, op. cit., p. 298.

wheels as a chariot: "A fiery stream came forth from before Him; thousands of thousands ministered unto Him," vv. 9–10. The location of this conflict is, at least to some extent, finally revealed in 11:45, which says of the Antichrist (see No. 14 and 52, below), "And he shall plant the tents of his palace between the sea [Mediterranean] and the glorious holy mountain [Zion]," which is suggestive of the famous battlefield at the mountain pass of Megiddo; cf. II K 23:29–30, Rev 16:16. Fulfillment (per. 15): as in Num. No. 36, the battle of Armageddon, when Christ the rock smashes the feet, Dan 2:34, or more precisely "the toes of the feet," v. 42 (see No. 10, below), of the image. Ch. 7 thus emphasizes the transcendent majesty (white hair, white raiment) of God and of His armies, both angelic and human, moving in judgment (cf. the opening of the books, v. 10) against the Antichrist (cf. vv. 11 and 26, No. 15 and 17, below) to destroy his dominion.

9. Dan *2:35b;* 7:14a, 18a, 22b, 27a (4 vv., sym.): " . . . and the stone became a great mountain and filled the whole earth," 2:35. Even so, 7:14 says of the Son of man, "There was given Him dominion . . . that all peoples should serve Him." Fulfillment (per. 16): as in Gen. No. 68 (49:10b), the universal millennial kingdom of Christ. Daniel's explanation, 7:27, is that "the kingdoms under the whole heaven shall be given to the people of the saints of the Most High," under their Messiah (see v. 13, No. 19, below).

10. Dan *2:41b, 42; 7:7b, 20a, 24a* (1 v., sym.): in his interpretation of Nebuchadrezzar's dream, Daniel refers to "the toes of the feet" of the image; and according to 7:7, the beast with the iron teeth is characterized by ten horns, meaning, "a later phase of the [Roman] beast's existence."[30] Fulfillment (per. 14): the breaking up of the Roman empire into a balance of power, as developed in Rev 17:12, 16. For particular *toes* or *horns*, Young proposes "the kingdoms of modern Europe, for example. These kingdoms in one sense or another arise historically from the ancient Roman Empire." Yet he cautions that attempts to identify these kingdoms more precisely "is very precarious."[31]

11. Dan 2:44b; *7:14b, 18b, 27b* (1 v., sym.): the Messianic kingdom represented by the stone in Nebuchadrezzar's dream (2:44a; see No. 7 and 9, above) "shall stand forever . . . [and] never be destroyed" (44b). Fulfillment (per. 18): the everlasting dominion of the New Jerusalem, Rev 22:5—as opposed to the limited duration of the millennial states of Dan 7:12 (No. 18, below).

12. Dan 4:10–17, 20–26, 31–32 (17 vv., sym.): another inspired dream by Nebuchadrezzar, involving a great tree which is cut down. An angel then gives these instructions: "Nevertheless leave the stump," v. 15; and, "Let his heart be changed from a man's, and let a beast's heart be

30. Young, *Prophecy*, p. 148.
31. Ibid., pp. 149–150.

given unto him; and let seven times pass over him," v. 16. Daniel courageously interpreted this to the king: v. 22, the tree symbolizes Nebuchadrezzar himself, with his wide dominion; v. 25, "Thou shalt be driven from men and made to eat grass as oxen"; but v. 26, restoration will come about, after the king's recognition of the sovereignty of God. These points are also repeated by a voice from heaven, 12 months later, vv. 31–32. V. 33 then states, "The same hour was the thing fulfilled upon Nebuchadrezzar"; and v. 28 (cf. 5:20–21), "All this came upon the king," including the penitence and restoration, vv. 34, 36. Various suggestions have been made about a disease or an attack of insanity (e.g. lycanthropy, which involves illusions of being an animal), near the close of Nebuchadrezzar's reign (per. 8), 605–562 B.C.[32] Keil notes that the disability must have occurred after he had finished the major part of the building operations of which he became so proud, e.g. the world-famous hanging gardens of Babylon.[33] The duration of the *seven times* is uncertain. The unit of measure might be months, or seasons, or years,[34] though seven full years would be the more difficult to integrate into the known historical situation.[35]

13. Dan 5:5, 24–28 (6 vv., sym.): the miraculous writing by a man's hand on the wall of Belshazzar's palace of the consonantal text: "Mene, mene, tekel, upharsin." These words *could* simply indicate weights: "a maneh [weighing 60 shekels, Ezek 45:12; cf. Ezra 2:69], a maneh, a shekel, and a half-shekel." But the meaning of the terms, as interpreted by Daniel through the supplying of different vowels, is that of passive participles: "numbered [i.e. the kingdom of Babylon, brought to an end], numbered, weighed [i.e. the king, Belshazzar, found to be deficient], and divided [i.e. the kingdom, once again: dissolved]."[36] The last term involves, in fact, a double play on words: it is *divided*, and then given to the Medes and *Persians*. Fulfillment (per. 8): the fall of Babylon, 539, as in Dt. No. 46, for "in that night Belshazzar was slain," and the kingdom was given to Darius the Mede, representing Cyrus the Persian.

14. Dan 7:8a, 20b, 24b (3 vv., sym.): in Daniel's vision of the four beasts, and particularly concerning the ten "horns" that should succeed Rome (No. 10, above), "There came up among them another horn, a little one, before which three of the first horns were plucked up by the roots; and, behold, in this horn were eyes like the eyes of a man" (v. 8);[37] and it was "more stout than its fellows" (v. 20). In v. 24 Daniel explained that after the ten kings, "another shall arise . . . and he shall

---

32. Ibid., pp. 110–112. Cf. Harrison, op. cit., pp. 1118–1120, on the essential irrelevance of the legendary "Prayer of Nabonidus" from Qumran, in regard to the evaluation of Dan 4.
33. P. 138.
34. Young, *Prophecy*, p. 105.
35. Ibid., p. 111.
36. Ibid., p. 127.
37. Suggesting an individual man, not something superhuman, ibid., p. 148.

put down three kings." According to liberalism, this tyrant must be Antiochus IV, just as is true of the "little horn" in 8:9, 23 (No. 24, below).[38] The ASV, however, obscures the difference in terminology between 7:8 and 8:9; for the latter is a *horn mis-s'īrā,* "from the state of being little . . . meaning that from small beginnings the horn grew to great power,"[39] before this *Greek* ruler was "broken without hand" (8:25). Fulfillment (per. 14): the rise of the Antichrist, at the expense of other nations; cf. No. 10, above, on the uncertainty in attempting to identify these states. It would be precarious to deny that almost any modern tyrant *could* be the fulfillment of this symbol.

15. Dan *7:8b, 11a, 20c, 25a* (sym.): the little horn had "a mouth speaking great things," v. 8. As the prophet explained in v. 25, "He shall speak words against the Most High." Fulfillment (per. 14): blasphemies of the Antichrist; cf. II Thess 2:4.

16. Dan *7:9a*: at the coming of the Son of man (No. 19, below), "Thrones were placed." Since "this picture is clearly reflected in Rev 20:4," it is presumably the resurrected saints of Christ who occupy the thrones.[40] Fulfillment (per. 16): as in Dt. No. 37, the privileged status of power and rule for the saints, with the Messiah.

17. Dan 7:11b, *11:45b* (1 v., sym.): "The beast [see No. 14, above] was slain, and its body given to be burned with fire." Earlier in ch. 7 this beast had represented the 4th (Roman) empire; but, as Young states, "The kingdom fades into the background as far as significance is concerned, and all importance is given to its head";[41] cf. the interchange in Rev 17:11 between the even more universal beast of that passage and its last (8th) head, so that in 19:20 it is the now individualized "beast," with the false prophet who performed signs "in *his* presence," who is seized. Dan 11:45 states more generally that at the battle of Armageddon (see No. 8, above) the Antichrist "shall come to his end, and none shall help him." Fulfillment (per. 15): as in Ps. No. 56 (110:6b), the judgment of the Antichrist, but now thrown alive into the lake of fire (Rev 19:20).

18. Dan 7:12 (1 v., sym.): in reference to the nations that remain through the Messiah's second advent, Daniel reveals, "For the rest of the beasts [empires], their dominion was taken away; yet their lives were prolonged for a season and a time." Earthly political states thus continue through this period (the 16th). Fulfillment: the millennium, namely, a preliminary aspect with limited duration, to the Messiah's future, eternal

---

38. See note 10, above.
39. Ibid., p. 170. KB, p. 1274, concludes with the rendering "a little horn" in 8:9, but only by emending the Heb. text.
40. BBC, IV:654, a possibility allowed by Young, *Prophecy,* pp. 150–151, though he prefers to think of angels at this point.
41. *Prophecy,* p. 150.

kingdom, as suggested also by Isa 24:21a; cf. Gen 3:15c (3rd stage).

19. Dan 7:13 (1 v.): "There came with the clouds of heaven one like unto a son of man [human in form, as opposed to the preceding beasts], and they brought Him near before the ancient of days." Fulfillment (per. 15): as in Ps. prophecy No. 5, the second coming of the Messiah. Christ the Son of man specifically claimed Dan 7:13 as being descriptive of His own future advent, Mk 14:62.[42] The fact that later in ch. 7 Daniel connects the figure of the Son of man with the idea of the saints' possessing the kingdom, vv. 22, 27, does not thereby reduce the former to a mere symbol for the latter. By virtue of their position "in Christ" the saints do inherit the kingdom, v. 14 (cf. Lk 22:29–30); but only Jesus constitutes the true "remnant of Israel," the Servant of Yahweh, or the "last Adam";[43] and only the Messiah truly comes with the clouds.[44] Dan 7:13 does not depict the rapture of the saints, for the course of the Son of man is one of descent. Keil correctly observes: "If he who appears as a son of man with the clouds of heaven comes before the Ancient of days executing the judgment on the earth, it is manifest that he could only come from heaven to earth."[45]

20. Dan 7:21, *25b*; 12:1b (2 vv., sym.): the little horn "made war with the saints and prevailed against them." Fulfillment (per. 14): the great tribulation at the close of the present age,[46] owing to the Antichrist, "a time of trouble such as never was since there was a nation even to that time," 12:1; cf. Isa 24:16b.

21. Dan *7:25c:* the persecutor "shall think to change the times and the law." Fulfillment (per. 14): arrangements by the Antichrist, changing not simply the sacred calendar of Scripture or the laws of Moses (as was attempted by Antiochus Epiphanes), but also the seasons and fundamental conditions ordained by God for "the life and actions of men."[47]

22. Dan 7:25d, 12:5–7 (4 vv.): during the evil career of the little horn (No. 20 and 21, preceding), the saints "shall be given into his hand until a time, times, and half a time," 7:25 (= 12:7). In a similar vein 12:6 refers "to the end of these wonders," meaning, of the Antichrist's persecutions (11:40–12:1); and 12:7 predicts, "When they have made an end of breaking in pieces the power of the holy people, all these things shall be finished." Fulfillment (per. 14): the duration of the Antichrist's tribula-

---

42. H. H. Rowley, *The Re-discovery of the OT*, p. 268, uses these passages to demonstrate the equation of the concepts of the Son of man and of the Messiah in the mind of Christ.

43. See above, pp. 283–284, 371.

44. The dead saints do come with Him, being included in the accompanying *thousands* of v. 10; but in the context of Dan 7 the actual term "saints" is restricted in its usage to those who are still living and suffering from the Antichrist, on earth, v. 25.

45. P. 235.

46. See above, pp. 102–103.

47. KD, p. 242.

tion.[48] The noun "time" might signify a year, but it also might not (cf. 4:16, 23, under 4:10, No. 12, above); and "times" is not identified as a dual, as if to make a total of 3½ (though the parallel of Rev 12:14, cf. v. 6, might suggest this). The actual lapse in calendar time might be 3½ days—or 7½ decades—and no other statement in Scripture solves the question of the length of the great tribulation.[49] It would therefore appear best, with Young, to leave the period as simply "chronologically indefinite," though the three parts to the formula might indicate a lengthening (*time*>*times*), followed by a more abruptly terminating period (*times*> *half a time*), owing to God's intervention.[50]

23. Dan 8:8b, 22; 11:4 (3 vv., sym.): a further development concerning the he-goat (= Greece) and its great horn (Alexander, see No. 4, above), 8:8, "And when he was strong, the great horn was broken; and instead of it there came up four notable horns toward the four winds." The interpretation that was later granted to Daniel, v. 22, explains that "four kingdoms shall stand up out of the nation [left by Alexander], but not with his power"; and 11:4 adds, "for his kingdom shall be plucked up, even for others besides . . . his posterity."[51] Fulfillment (per. 10): after Alexander's death in 323 and the eventual fall of his leading general Antigonus in 301, the empire divided into some four major areas, controlled by Greek generals: Macedonia under Cassander, Asia Minor under Lysimachus, Syria and eastward under Seleucus, and Egypt under Ptolemy.[52]

24. Dan 8:9, 23b–*24a*; 11:21–*30a* (11 vv., sym.): out of one of the four divisions of Alexander's empire (No. 23, preceding), "a little horn [contrast the "horn, a little one," of 7:8a, No. 14, above] waxed exceeding great toward the south, east, and toward the glorious land," 8:9. As v. 23 explains, "In the latter time of their [the Greeks'] kingdom, a king of fierce countenance, and understanding dark sentences [i.e. deceitful] shall be mighty." Fulfillment (per. 10): the rise of Antiochus IV, Epiphanes, to the throne of Seleucid Syria, 175–164 B.C., and his military campaigns. Yet none of this would be "by his own power," 8:24. "He shall obtain the kingdom by flatteries," 11:21, usurping it from the son of his brother Seleucus IV, v. 20 (No. 50, below); and his initial successes against

---

48. Liberal writers seek a correlation with Antiochus' desecration of the Jerusalem temple, 168–165 (see note 10, above); but that defilement lasted for only 3 years and 10 days.

49. Dan 9:27, 2:11 and 12 (see Nos. 36, 31), and Rev 11:2 and 13:5 (see Rev. No. 31), 11:3 (see 11:11), and 12:6–14 (see p. 49, note 103) all refer to other matters.

50. *Prophecy*, p. 162.

51. A more correct statement than that of I Macc 1:6 (which is *not* prophecy, but historical narrative), which represents this division of the Greek empire among the Diadochi—the generals of Alexander who usurped the various parts of his realm—as if this were Alexander's wish.

52. As worked out by Havernick, Auberlin, etc.; BBC, IV:653.

Israel are to stem from God's providential will to chasten His people's transgression, 8:12c, 23a (No. 28, below). His specific aggression "toward the south" was accomplished against Ptolemy VII of Egypt (181–145), I Macc 1:16–19, who was "overwhelmed and broken," Dan 11:22, in 170–169. 11:26 predicts that "they that eat his dainties shall destroy him," for Ptolemy was defeated by treachery; but Egypt was not eliminated, for, v. 27, "Both kings shall speak lies at one table"—Antiochus and Ptolemy professed friendship. Yet, v. 29, the former "shall return into the south [Antiochus' second attack on Egypt, 168], but it shall not be in the latter time as it was in the former," i.e. with a Syrian victory; v. 30, "for ships of Kittim [Cyprus, to the west, the direction of Rome; cf. Num 24:24b] shall come against him," as the Roman ambassador, Popilius Laenas, would force his withdrawal from Egypt. His campaigning toward the east concerns Persia, as in I Macc 3:31, 37, 6:1–4, and that "toward the glorious land" concerns Palestine, I Macc 1:20–21, "the goodliest heritage of the nations" (Jer 3:19, ASVmg), lying between the east and the south. His action against "the prince of the testament," Dan 11:22, may be a forecast of the fate of Onias III, whom Antiochus deposed as high priest; and that "his heart shall be against the holy testament," v. 28, suggests his plundering of the Jerusalem temple at his first return from Egypt in 169, I Macc 1:21–28.

25. Dan 8:10, 24b–25a; 10:14, *20b*; 11:33b, 35 (6 vv., sym.): though the usurping horn's origin was "from the state of being little" (8:9, lit.; cf. No. 14, above), yet later on, "Some of the host of heaven, the stars, it cast down to the ground and trampled upon them," 8:10. V. 24 explains more prosaically, "He shall destroy the mighty ones and the holy people." More detail appears in ch. 11, which speaks of oppression, captivity, and martyrdom. This is introduced in 10:14 as revealing to Daniel "what shall befall thy people in the latter days"; and v. 20 says specifically, "Lo, the prince [guardian angel, or demon?] of Greece shall come," meaning that "the spirit of the Macedonian world-kingdom would arise and show great hostility" toward God's people.[53] Fulfillment (per. 10): as in Mi. No. 23 (4:11), persecution by Antiochus in his attempt to stamp out Judaism, 168–165 B.C. (No. 26, following); the same figure, of his grasping the stars, appears in the later narrative record of II Macc 9:10.

26. Dan 8:11–12; 11:30b–32a, 36–39; 12:11b (10 vv., sym.): the procedure of the persecuting "horn" (No. 24 and 25, preceding) is foretold, "It magnified itself, even to the Prince of the host; and it took away from Him the continual burnt offering, and the place of His sanctuary was cast down," 8:11 (= 11:31). The horn "shall prosper till the indignation be accomplished," 11:36. The 11th ch. adds these details as well: v. 30, "He shall return [after being checked in Egypt, 168; see No. 24, above]

53. KD, p. 423.

and have regard unto them that forsake the holy testament"; v. 31, "They shall set up the abomination that maketh desolate" (= 12:11), specifically, an altar to Zeus that was to be erected upon the Jerusalem temple's altar, I Macc 1:54; and v. 37 speaks of similar deeds against pagan practices, "He shall magnify himself [represented as Zeus] above every God." But, v. 38, his real trust is in might. Fulfillment (per. 10): Antiochus' profaning of the temple and forbidding the regular sacrifices, sabbath observances, etc., December, 168, to December, 165, I Macc 1:45–46, as he sought to unify his empire under Hellenistic culture; cf. II Macc 4:7–17. Montgomery comments on the prediction of his honoring "a god whom his fathers knew not" (Dan 11:38), noting:

> Apollo, the historic deity of the dynasty, disappeared almost entirely from the Seleucid coinage after the reign of Epiphanes, being replaced by Zeus. . . . Also, [by his opposition, v. 37, to] "the darling of women" . . . we think of some attempt of the king to control or suppress that lascivious cult, in line with his unification of religion. . . . This replacement of gods, so contrary to antique sentiment, may suffice to explain [the above references].[54]

27. Dan *8:11b, 12b, 13b; 11:31c; 12:11a* (typ.): burnt offering. Fulfillment (per. 13): as in Lev No. 3.

28. Dan *8:12c, 23a*: a revelation on God's purpose for allowing the pre-Maccabean persecution; Israel is "given over through transgression," v. 12, "when the transgressors are come to the full," v. 23. Fulfillment (per. 10): serious apostasy among Hellenizing Jews, just prior to the persecutions of Antiochus, I Macc 1:11–15.

29. Dan 8:13–14a, 26 (3 vv.): the duration of Antiochus' activity of profanation (see No. 26, above), "unto 2,300 evening-mornings," or about 6 years, 4 months. The profaning of the Jerusalem sanctuary extended precisely from the 15th of Chislev (Dec.), 168, to the 25th of the same month, 165, I Macc 1:54, 4:52. Some would relate this to half of the above period, or to 1,150 days. But even 1,150 (= 3 years, 2 months) is more than a month and a half too much; and furthermore the 2,300 figure gives no indication that it should be divided between the evenings and the mornings but simply indicates the total of day-and-night days, commencing with sunset; cf. the 40 days and 40 nights of Gen 7:4, 12. Fulfillment (per. 10): since the period terminates at the end of 165, it would seem to commence in mid-171, when Lysimachus, brother of the corrupt high priest Menelaus, made "the sanctuary [to be] trodden under foot" (Dan 8:13) through his stealing of the temple's sacred vessels, II Macc 4:39–42.

30. Dan *8:14b*: but "then shall the sanctuary be cleansed" (see No. 29, preceding). Fulfillment (per. 11): its cleansing by Judas Maccabeus, at the close of 165 B.C., I Macc 4:36–59.

31. Dan *8:25b; 12:11c–12* (1 v.): the ultimate fate of the persecuting horn, "He shall be broken without hand," i.e. not by the sword, but by

54. ICC, pp. 460–461.

an act of God (cf. Isa 31:8). Fulfillment (per. 11): the death of Antiochus in 164 B.C. beyond Babylon, by sickness, I Macc 6:9. This may also be the point of reference involved in the figure of Dan 12:11, that "from the time that the continual burnt offering shall be taken away . . . there shall be 1,290 days." From the onset of the Greek profanation of the temple in December, 168 (see No. 26 and 29), this period extends some 3 years, 6½ months, to mid-164, when the persecutor did die. Concerning the additional figure that is stated in v. 12, "Blessed is he that waiteth to the 1,335 days," Leupold speculates, "Assume that the first figure might have related to the death of the tyrant. Then happy would be the man who would live a month and a half more; for he would live, perhaps, to *hear* of the death of the tyrant, it being assumed that 45 days might be consumed till the news of his death in Persia had penetrated back to Judea."[55]

32. Dan 9:2 (1 v.): a quotation from Jeremiah on God's determination of a 70-year period (then primarily future) for the desolation of Jerusalem. Fulfillment (per. 8): Judah's total time of captivity from 605 to 537, as in Jer 25:11b, 29:10, which was just at this point, 538 (Dan 9:1), drawing to its close.

33. Dan 9:4; *11:22b, 28b, 30c, 32b* (1 v., typ.): the Sinaitic testament. Fulfillment (per. 13): as in Ex. No. 45 (19:5).

34. Dan *9:24a, 25c*: "Seventy weeks are decreed upon thy people . . . from the commandment to build Jerusalem unto Messiah [ASVmg] shall be seven weeks and sixty-two weeks." The term *shāvū'īm*, is not the usual (fem.) form for "weeks"[56] and would best be rendered as "heptads," meaning "units or periods of seven."[57] Keil seems properly to argue that since Jeremiah's 70 years were almost completed at this time in 538 B.C. (see 9:2, No. 32, above), Daniel's periods must extend further than Jeremiah's and denote 70 units of *seven* years each, or 490 years in all.[58] After 7, and then 62, of these "weeks" or heptads (= 483 years) is to come the fulfillment (per. 13) in the anointing of Jesus—the very title "Messiah" meaning *anointed* (No. 36, below). This anointing, in turn, occurred at His baptism (Acts 10:38), which may be dated to A.D. 26.[59] By counting 483 years before this event, one reaches 458 B.C. and the year of Ezra's return to Jerusalem; see v. 25 (No. 37, below).

Expositions of Daniel's prophecy of the 70 weeks (9:24–27) usually fall into one of four clearly distinguishable schools of interpretation, the point-by-point conclusions of which are listed in Table 9 for the sake of synthesis.

In reference to the commencement of the 70 weeks (the first point in Table 9 under 9:25), liberal writers may also take this date from Jeremiah's

---

55. *Exposition of Daniel*, p. 547, though he adds, "All guesswork."
56. In 10:2, where *shāvū'īm* does mean 7-day weeks, the term stands with a further qualification, lit., "weeks of days."
57. The basic definition of KB, p. 940.
58. Pp. 322–323, though cf. 338–339.
59. Jack Finegan, *Handbook of Biblical Chronology*, pp. 468–469.

TABLE 9
Interpretations of Daniel 9:24-27[60]

Subject	Liberal (Montgomery)	Traditional (Pusey)	Dispensational (Seiss)	Symbolical (Loupold)
9:24:Thy people	Israel past, p. 393	Israel and church past, p. 185	Israel past and future, p. 240	Israel and church past and future, p. 411
Weeks = periods of	7 years, 373	7 years, 186	7 X 360 days, Gaebelein, 140	Perfecting, 409
Make an end of sins and bring in righteousness	Maccabean utopian dreams, 375	Atonement on Calvary, 194	All promises to Israel fulfilled, 242	The new heaven and earth, 411
Anoint the most holy	Altar cleansed in 165 B.C., 375	Christ anointed by Holy Spirit, 196	Consecration of millennial Jews, 241	Consummation of God with man (Rev 21:3), 416
9:25:Command to rebuild Jerusalem	Jeremiah's word at Jerusalem's fall, 586 B.C., 392	Artaxerxes I's decree to Ezra, 458 B.C., 189	Artaxerxes I to Nehemiah, 444 B.C., 246	Cyrus' decree of return, 538 B.C., 418
End of 7 weeks	The return in 437 B.C., 379	Through the reforms of Nehemiah, 409 B.C., 191	Jerusalem's restoration, 396 B.C. (?), Gaebelein, 136	Christ's incarnation, 421
7 and 62 joined?	No, 392	Yes, 189	Yes, 242	No, 417
Anointed one	Jeshua, 379	Christ, anointed at baptism, 189	Christ, at His triumphal entry, 243	Christ, birth, 422
End of 62 weeks (total of 69)	171 B.C., 394	A.D., 26, 189	A.D. 30, 247	End of expansion of church, 424
9:26: "After" 62	Immediately after, 394	Later, midway in next 7 years, 201	Later, by 5 days, 248	Immediately after, 427
Messiah cut off	Onias III murdered, 381	Christ crucified, 198	Christ crucified, 249	Church progress ends, 427
Nothing for Him	Has no guilt, 381	Rejected by Jews, 197	Rejcted by Jews, 250	Has no influence, 427
Prince that shall come	Antiochus IV in 168 B.C., 383	Christ (see No. 35, below), or Titus in A.D. 70, 200	Titus in A.D. 70, 251	Antichrist in the future, 428

60. Cf. J. B. Payne, *Theology of the Older Testament*, pp. 520-522. The page numbers in each column refer respectively to: Liberal, J. A. Montgomery, ICC *Daniel*; Traditional, E. B. Pusey, *Daniel the Prophet*; Dispensational, J. A. Seiss, *Voices from Babylon*, with supplementation from A. C. Gaebelein, *The Prophet Daniel*; and Symbolical, H. C. Leupold, *Exposition of Daniel*.

TABLE 9 (Continued)

Subject	Liberal (Montgomery)	Traditional (Pusey)	Dispensational (Seiss)	Symbolical (Loupold)
Unto the end thereof shall be war	To His death in 164 B.C., 384	To its (Jerusalem's) fall in A.D. 70, 201	To its (Israel's) restoration 7 years before Christ's appearing, 250	To his death at Christ's appearing, 429
9:27: "And"; subsequent event?	No, v. 27 elaborates v. 26, 384	No, v. 27 elaborates v. 26, 192	Yes, different matters, 251	No, v. 27 elaborates v. 26, 431
Firm covenant	Antiochus allied with Hellenizers, 385	Christ's new testament with the saved, 193	Antichrist allied with regathered infidel Jews, 252	Antichrist enslaves the masses, 432
Beginning of 70th week	Follows 69th, 386	Follows 69th, 192	Parenthesis between 69 and 70, 251	Follows 69th, 428
In midst of week	For $3\frac{1}{2}$ years, 168-165 B.C., 386	After $3\frac{1}{2}$ years, in A.D. 30, 192	After $3\frac{1}{2}$ years, in middle of tribulation; and for its latter $\frac{1}{2}$, 252	After $\frac{1}{2}$ his period, 432; and for the latter $\frac{1}{2}$, 433
Sacrifice cease	Altar polluted, 386	OT system ended, 192	Altar polluted, 253	No church worship, 433
End of 70th week	Maccabean victory, 386	Stephen stoned, Jews reject new testament, Paul called, A.D. 33, 193	God's judgment, 251	God's judgment, 436
Upon the wing of abominations, a desolator	On a peak of the temple, Greek idolatry, 388	Against the temple with its Jewish sins, Titus; 199	On a peak of the temple, an idol, 253	By means of idolatry, Antichrist, 433
Until an end shall pour forth on a desolate (-tor)	Until Antiochus' death, 389	Until the end of desolate Jerusalem, 200	To the "consummation" and Antichrist's death, 255	Until his death, 436

original prophecy, in 604 B.C., so as to bring the termination closer to Maccabean times; but even this is still 50 years too many.[61] Dispensational writers usually begin with the decree granted to Nehemiah, in 444, so as to bring the date later, to Christ's triumphal entry; but such a point of departure takes it 10 years too far, so a shortened "prophetic year" of 360 days is sometimes introduced.[62] But while in early Israel the months seem to have had 30 days each (Gen 8:3–4, cf. 7:11; Num 20:29; and Dt 34:8, cf. 21:13), the total calendar was always kept oriented to the solar and agricultural year by adding 5 or 6 days at the end of a year or, at the latest, a 13th intercalated month after several years.[63] Leupold's attempt to apply (symbolically) the first 7 weeks to the period up to Jesus Christ, and the next 62 weeks on into the future, has been subject to wide criticism. Montgomery, for example, remarks, "However the 70 weeks are to be interpreted, whether historically, apocalyptically, or mystically, certain principles must be followed, if the writer meant anything sensible. The total 70 must be obtained in addition; [and] the denomination must remain the same: week cannot be a variable quantity, as now a septennium and now some other quantity of time."[64]

35. Dan 9:24b, 26a (1 v.): the divinely intended purpose of the 70 weeks is "to restrain[65] [ASVmg, Heb. kālā'] transgression, to seal up[66] sins [ASVmg, Heb. hātham, in the sense of reserve for punishment, Job 14:17], to make reconciliation for iniquity, to bring in everlasting righteousness, and to seal up vision and prophecy." Concerning this last point Young comments, "When Christ came, there was no further need of prophecy in the OT sense."[67] All these saving actions would be accomplished by the Messiah's being cut off, and having nothing, "after the 62 weeks," v. 26, and, as expressed in greater detail in v. 27, "in the midst of the last week." The central portion of v. 26 may well refer to this same climactic event, translating with the variant Hebrew and versional reading, ". . . and the city and the sanctuary shall be destroyed [see No. 38, below]

61. Montgomery, ICC, p. 383, grants, "To be sure, an objection may be made against our identification of the final week of the 70 with the period of Antiochus's tyranny, for the 62 weeks would then take us down some 65 years too far [counting from 586 B.C.]. We can meet this objection only by surmising a chronological miscalculation on the part of the writer."
62. More careful writers of this school recognize its unlikelihood and are content with general chronological correspondence; e.g. R. D. Culver, Daniel and the Latter Days, p. 145: "Even if [Robert] Anderson is wrong on some of the fine points of his thesis—if we accept the ordinary solar year and the usual date for the decree of Artaxerxes rather than the revised dates and the prophetic year of 360 days, the correspondence is too close to be accidental and is a remarkable confirmation."
63. Finegan, op. cit., p. 36
64. ICC, p. 391.
65. So KB, p. 436.
66. Ibid., p. 344.
67. Young, Prophecy, p. 200; cf. E. W. Hengstenberg, Christology of the OT, III:102–105.

along with the Prince that is to come," that is, Messiah the Prince, just as in v. 25.[68] Fulfillment (per. 13): Christ's atoning death, which has been calculated to have occurred on Apr. 7, A.D. 30,[69] 3½ years after His baptism (No. 34, preceding).

36. Dan 9:24c, 25b: an added goal of the 70 weeks, "to anoint the Most Holy." Fulfillment (per. 13): Christ's anointing by the Holy Spirit at His baptism (John 3:34; and see No. 34, above).[70] Liberalism would refer this phrase to the cleansing of the altar by Judas Maccabeus in 165 B.C. (see No. 30 above), [71] and others would refer it to a future consecration of the Jewish nation or of their temple; but Daniel's contextual stress is upon Jesus as "Messiah," meaning "the anointed one," vv. 25–26.

37. Dan 9:25a, 10:20a (2 vv.): that the 70 weeks are to commence with "the commandment to restore and to build Jerusalem . . . it shall be built again, with street and moat, even in troublous times," 9:25. This same rebuilding is suggested by 10:20. Here a "man," v. 5—but in fact, probably Christ; compare His description in v. 6 with Rev 1:13–15[72]— informed Daniel, "Now will I return to fight with the prince [guardian angel, or demon?] of Persia." Keil refers this struggle to the various "hindrances put by the spirit of Persia, hostile to Israel, in the way of their rebuilding the temple . . . and further, under Xerxes and Artaxerxes till the rebuilding of the walls of Jerusalem by Nehemiah."[73] Fulfillment (per. 9): the decree granted to Ezra in 458,[74] from which point onward Jerusalem's restoration did continue, despite setbacks. For opposition had to be faced by Nehemiah, both at his initial return to Judah in 444 to rebuild the walls and at his second governorship after 430; the "troublous times" seem, in fact, to have persisted throughout Daniel's first 7 heptads of years, or to about 409 B.C.

38. Dan 9:26b, 27b (2 vv.): that the city and sanctuary of Jerusalem— "thy holy city," v. 24; cf. 6:10—are to be made desolate by war; "upon

68. Pointing as yishshāhēth im rather than yashhīth am. Correspondingly, it appears questionable whether Dan 9:26 contains any reference to an Antichristian prince, Payne, The Imminent Appearing of Christ, p. 151.
69. Finegan, op. cit., pp. 468–469.
70. So Hengstenberg, op. cit., III:105–114, and Young, Prophecy, p. 201.
71. ICC, p. 375.
72. Payne, Theology, p. 169.
73. P. 423.
74. In the very year of Daniel's prophecy (538), Cyrus of Persia did issue an earlier decree which encouraged the return of the Jewish exiles to Palestine and authorized the rebuilding of the temple (Ezra 1:1–4; cf. Isa 44:28). But this decree of Cyrus did not mention the rebuilding of the city or its walls. Such restoration came to pass only in the following century, in the reign of Artaxerxes I (465–424), under Nehemiah in 444. There had been, however, under the same monarch, a previous attempt at restoring the walls, which had been thwarted by the Samaritans (Ezra 4:11, 12, 23). This original effort must have occurred under Ezra in 458, whose decree from Artaxerxes granted him just such extended powers (7:18, 25; 9:9); Payne, Theology, p. 277.

the wing of abominations shall come one that maketh desolate," 9:27. Young explains *the wing of abominations* as the pinnacle of the temple, considered to be an abomination, once Christ should terminate the system of OT sacrifice (see No. 39, below).[75] Then if the central phrase of v. 26 be rendered as "The people of the prince that shall come," the leader there referred to would be equivalent to the person who *maketh desolate* (v. 27); but see No. 35, above. Fulfillment (per. 14): as in Mi. No. 39, the destruction of Jerusalem by the Roman general Titus in A.D. 70.

39. Dan *9:27a*: "He shall confirm [KJV;[76] lit., "cause to prevail"] the testament with many for one week; and in the midst of the week He shall cause the sacrifice and the oblation to cease." A primary exegetical consideration is that of determining the subject of these words, whether the Messiah of v. 26 or the prince who leads the attacking people (if this be a proper reading in any event; see No. 35). Young, however, seems justified in insisting that "the subject is Messiah. . . . To construe 'prince' as subject does not appear to be the most natural reading, for the word occupies only a subordinate position in v. 26, where it is not even the subject of a sentence . . . Furthermore this entire passage is Messianic in nature, and the Messiah is the leading character, the great terminus ad quem of the 69 sevens. They lead up to Him, who is their goal."[77] Fulfillment (per. 13): as in Isa. No. 93 (42:6a), Christ's embodiment of the redemptive testament of God. As the Servant of Yahweh, He proclaimed the gospel to Israel during his 3½-year ministry (Isa 42:1–4, Mt 12:17–21), thus confirming to them the grace of the divine testament (Isa 42:6). Next, upon Calvary, He brought to a close the OT economy of redemption, rending the veil of the temple (Mt 27:51) and causing legitimate typical sacrifice once and for all to cease (Heb 9:12). The 490 years of Daniel's 70 weeks then conclude with the latter 3½ years of the final week, during which time the testament continued to be confirmed to Israel; cf. Acts 2:38. But this open message terminated with the stoning of Stephen; cf. 8:1, on the church being driven from Jerusalem.[78] The occasion, moreover, is datable to A.D. 33/34, the year to which Paul's conversion is to be assigned.[79] Dispensational writers commonly take Dan 9:27 as separated from, and subsequent to, v. 26 rather than as an explanation of it: and the subject who confirms the testament (or covenant) is held to be the prince of v. 26, meaning the Antichrist. Serious problems, however, beset such a reconstruction. To note but a few:[80] (1) it breaks up the sequence of the 70 weeks by introducing an interval before this last part; and, as Hengstenberg long ago cautioned, "The period of 70 hebdomads, or 490 years, is here predicted as one that will continue

75. *Prophecy*, p. 218.
76. Supported by ibid., pp. 208–209.
77. Ibid.
78. Payne, *The Imminent Appearing of Christ*, p. 149.
79. Finegan, op. cit., pp. 320–321.
80. See also Payne, *Imminent Appearing*, pp. 150–151.

uninterruptedly from its commencement to its close . . . what can be more evident than this? Exactly 70 weeks in all are to elapse; and how can anyone imagine that there is an interval between the 69 and the 1, when these together make up the 70?"[81] (2) it assumes an unprecedented covenant-making by the Antichrist, when Scripture contains no hint of any such covenant at all, let alone some earlier one that he could confirm at this point in Dan 9; and (3) it transforms a past prince of Rome into a future deputy of the devil, for as Young points out, "The emphasis of v. 26 is not upon a prince from a people, but upon the people who belong to the prince. . . . In other words, he must be their contemporary, alive when they are alive."[82]

40. Dan *11:2a*: "There shall stand up yet three kings in Persia." Fulfillment (per. 9): since Daniel was speaking under Cyrus II, the Great (10:1), the three succeeding him become Cambyses II (527–522), Smerdis (the pretender, 522), and Darius I, Hystaspis (522–485).

41. Dan 11:2b (1 v.): the rise and military campaign of a fourth king of Persia; for "through his riches he shall stir up all, against the realm of Greece." Fulfillment (per. 9): the famous Greco-Persian war of Xerxes, 480–479.

42. Dan 11:5 (1 v.): "The king of the south shall be strong"; but "one of his princes shall be strong above him," so as to gain "a great dominion." Fulfillment (per. 10): the *south* denotes Egypt, v. 8; so its initial Hellenistic king must be Ptolemy I (323–285). Yet Ptolemy's leading general, Seleucus I, Nicator, became an independent ruler in Babylon in 311 and moved on to conquer as far as the Indus during the next decade.

43. Dan 11:6 (1 v.): "The daughter [Berenice] of the king of the south [Ptolemy II, 285–246] shall come [in marriage, 252] to the king of the north [Antiochus II, 261–247], but neither shall stand." Fulfillment (per. 10): Antiochus' divorced wife, Laodice, murdered Berenice, Antiochus, and the son of the latter two.

44. Dan 11:7–8 (2 vv.): "But from her roots shall one enter into the fortress of the king of the north," plunder, and then "refrain some years." This was fulfilled (per. 10) by Berenice's brother Ptolemy III, 246–221.

45. Dan 11:9 (1 v.): "He [Seleucus II, 247–226] shall come into the realm of the king of the south, but he shall return into his own land"; for (per. 10) Ptolemy III defeated him, ca. 240 B.C.

46. Dan 11:10 (1 v.): "His sons [plu., Seleucus III, 226–223, and Antiochus III, the Great] shall war; and he [sing., Antiochus, 223–187] shall come on . . . to his [Ptolemy IV's, 221–203] fortress." The fulfill-

81. Op. cit., III:143.
82. *Prophecy*, pp. 211–212. As he proceeds to illustrate, "We cannot by any stretch of the imagination, legitimately call the army of George Washington the army of a general, and by that general have reference to Eisenhower. The armies of Washington are in no sense Eisenhower's armies. And the fact that Eisenhower was born in America many years after the time of Washington's armies does not in the least permit us to say that they are his armies."

ment (per. 10) consisted of attack by Antiochus, probably against Gaza, on the Egyptian border.

47. Dan 11:11–12 (2 vv.): "The king of the south [Ptolemy IV] . . . shall cast down tens of thousands, but he shall not prevail." Fulfillment (per. 10): he defeated Antiochus III at Raphia in 217 but failed to follow up his advantage.

48. Dan 11:13–17 (5 vv.): "The king of the north [Antiochus III] shall return with a greater army [202]. In those times shall many [e.g. Philip V of Macedon] stand up against the king of the south [the boy ruler, Ptolemy V, 203–181]." So also shall certain Jews, but "they shall fall," vv. 11–14. Fulfillment (per. 10): as in Zech 11:6, suffering for the land under the conflicting Greek kings. For Ptolemy's general Scopas retook Palestine in 200 and wasted Jerusalem. Daniel's prophecy continues, vv. 16–17, "The king of the north shall take a well-fortified city" —perhaps Gaza in 201; but the time sequence favors Sidon, where Scopas surrendered, 198, after his defeat at Paneas—"and he shall stand in the glorious land [Palestine]; and he shall give him [i.e. to Ptolemy] the daughter of women [Cleopatra, the daughter of Antiochus], but she shall not be for him": she turned against her father in favor of Ptolemy.

49. Dan 11:18–19 (2 vv.): "After this shall he [Antiochus III] turn his face unto the isles [Asia Minor]; but a captain [ASVmg; Lucius Scipio Asiaticus, representing Rome] shall cause the reproach offered by him to cease; and he shall stumble and fall." Fulfillment (per. 10): the Romans defeated Antiochus at Magnesia in 190, and he died in the course of an expedition 3 years thereafter.

50. Dan 11:20 (1 v.): "In his place, one [Seleucus IV, 187–175] shall cause an exactor to pass through the glory of the kingdom; but he shall be destroyed." Fulfillment (per. 10): the king attempted to rob the Jewish temple in Jerusalem, II Macc 3; and he was later assassinated.

51. Dan 11:*32c–33a*, 34 (1 v.): "The people that know their God shall be strong and do exploits and . . . instruct many [cf. I Macc 1:62, 2:42]. . . . They shall be helped with a little help, but many shall join themselves to them with flatteries." Fulfillment (per. 11): as in Mi. No. 24, the Maccabean resistance to the persecutions of Antiochus IV (vv. 30b–32b, No. 25 and 26, above), and specifically Judas' victories against great odds, I Macc 3–4.

52. Dan 11:40–44 (5 vv.): after a historical survey in 11:2–39, extending from 527 to 165 B.C. in its fulfillment,[83] Daniel's 4th great vision shifts at v. 40[84] to "the time of the end," signifying, "the end of the

83. See above, Table 8.
84. Leupold, op. cit., p. 510, would prefer to make this shift earlier, after v. 35; but there the term "end" seems simply to refer to the end of the Jewish persecution of 168–165. Vv. 36–39 harmonize with the career of Antiochus (see above, No. 26) and carry on from v. 35 with less break than occurs at v. 40; but cf. ICC, p. 464, which notes the inappropriateness of the material from v. 40 onward in respect to Antiochus.

present age or world."[85] At this point, "The king of the south shall contend with . . . the king of the north"; and the latter will retaliate: v. 40, invading countries ·by land and sea, and v. 41, entering "the glorious land" (= Palestine, v. 16). The lands of Edom, Moab, and the best portion of Ammon "shall be delivered out of his hand," perhaps through his sympathy for their own hostilities toward God and His people;[86] but, v. 42, "Egypt shall not escape." Yet according to v. 44, "Tidings out of the east and north shall trouble him," namely, out of Palestine (since he is now in Egypt), "and he shall go forth to destroy . . ."; cf. v. 45 (under No. 8, above), on the battle of Armageddon. Fulfillment (per. 15): Near Eastern campaigns by one who can only be the Antichrist (see No. 14, above), for they lead directly to the final battle of Armageddon and the other eschatological events of ch. 12 (No. 53–57, following). The king of the south who first opposes him is not further identified, except that previously in ch. 11 this term referred to Egypt (vv. 5, 8; and cf. v. 42), so that it presumably carries the same force here.

53. Dan *12:1a*: "Michael, the great prince, shall stand up for the children of thy people." Fulfillment (per. 14): the ministry of the archangel, in protecting the people of God during the great tribulation (v. 1b, No. 20, above).

54. Dan *12:1c*: in spite of the Antichrist's tribulation (v. 1b, No. 20, above), "at that time thy people shall be delivered, every one that shall be found written in the book." Fulfillment (per. 15): as in Hos. No. 27 (11:10), the rapture of believers—since the deliverance is related especially to those on the earth. They are among those written in the Lamb's book of life, Rev 20:12, 15; 21:27.

55. Dan 12:2a (1 v.): "Many of them that sleep in the dust of the earth shall awake, some [lit., "these"; contrast "the rest," in v. 2b, No. 56, following] to everlasting life." The partative force of the term "many" must not be neglected; for Young comments, "*Many*—we should expect the text to say all. In order to escape the difficulty, some expositors have taken the word many in the sense of all. However, this is forced and not natural."[87] For its elucidation, three major interpretations have been proposed, which may be plotted as follows:

Liberal (partial resurrection):	Evangelical amillennial (one resurrection):	Evangelical premillennial (two resurrections):
THE REST — NO RESURRECTION / SAVED / LOST — THE MANY	THE REST — ALSO RESURRECTED / SAVED / LOST — THE MANY	MANY / REST = OTHERS — LOST / SAVED — MANY = SOME

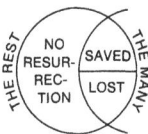

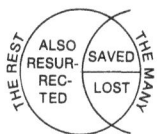

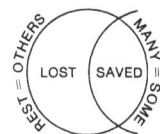

85. Young, *Prophecy*, p. 251.
86. Ibid., p. 252.
87. Ibid., p. 256.

Here liberal writers do not hold to the universality of future resurrection (John 5:28, Rev 20:12) and suggest but a partial rise for humanity: "Some only will be raised up: these, the righteous, and those, evidently the arch-sinners, to everlasting reproach. The rest are left in the shades."[88] Evangelicals of amillennial persuasion propose, "From the numbers of those who are asleep in the grave many, i.e. those who died during the tribulation, shall arise. Of these, some shall arise to life and some to reproach. The words, of course, do not exclude the general resurrection, but rather imply it."[89] But while "many" are indeed stated to be victims of the Antichrist, 11:44, the expression "many" as it appears in 12:2 is indefinite (no article), simply *many*, not *the* many of the previous chapter, to whom it gives no indication of referring. The amillennialist has also these problems: (1) Why should also the wicked among the tribulation dead be singled out for mention as rising? and (2) Does the resurrection of the tribulation dead really imply a total resurrection? If they are distinguished from among the rest of the dead, it would appear, as liberalism strongly contends, that the remainder should *not* rise. Evangelical millennialists accept the full partative force of the term *many* but equate it only with the first of the pronouns that follow, the *these* (ASV, *some* [1st occurrence]), meaning that those resurrected to life are the *many*. Fulfillment (per. 15): as in Isa. No. 76, the first resurrection; cf. Rev 20:5–6.

56. Dan *12:2b*: ". . . and some [lit., "these"] to shame and everlasting contempt." The millennial interpretation, which holds that this second group is *not* to be subsumed under the *many* of v. 2a, is brought into clear focus by the paraphrastic translation of S. P. Tregelles, "Many from among the sleepers of the dust of the earth shall awake; these shall be unto everlasting life; but those the rest of the sleepers, those who do not awake at this time, shall be unto shame and everlasting contempt."[90] Fulfillment (per. 17): as in Job No. 2, the general resurrection, including particularly the resurrection of the lost, Rev 20:14–15; contrast the first resurrection in v. 6.

57. Dan 12:3 (1 v.): "They that are wise and that turn many to righteousness shall shine as the stars for ever and ever." Fulfillment (per. 18): special reward in the New Jerusalem for those who are faithful to their Lord now.

58. Dan 12:13 (1 v.): a concluding, personal message to the prophet, "Thou shalt rest [in death], and shalt stand in thy lot at the end of the days." Fulfillment (per. 15): Daniel's own participation in the first resurrection, as stated in v. 2 (No. 55, above).

88. ICC, p. 471.
89. Young, *Prophecy*, loc. cit.
90. *Remarks on the Prophetic Visions in the Book of Daniel*, p. 162.

HOSEA

The last twelve books of the OT, in its present arrangement, are called the Minor Prophets: not because of their minor importance (which is in fact considerable), but because of their shorter length. Among the first six of these prophets (those dating to the 8th century B.C.), and particularly among the three that are associated with the northern kingdom of Israel—Hosea, Amos, and Jonah—the volume of Hosea stands in first place. This is not because it was necessarily the first in time but, as it seems, simply because it occupied the longest written scroll of the six. But its distinction rests also upon other grounds. Hosea covers the greatest period of time of any of the group: some 35 years, from about 760 B.C., in the prosperous days of Jeroboam II of Israel (who died in 753), down to about 725, when Hezekiah had assumed the rule in Judah (replacing Ahaz in 728); cf. Hos 1:1. But while Hosea apparently knew of Shalmaneser V of Assyria, whose accession took place in 727 B.C., 10:14, he remains silent about the historic fall of his nation to that same monarch in 722 (cf. II K 17:3–6). Preceding Israel's political demise, however, there had developed within the northern tribes a deep-seated moral and religious decay; see Hos 1:2 or 4:1–2. The thrust of Hosea's ministry was therefore a call to repentance and reform, 6:1; but it was based on the conviction of Yahweh's continuing love for His unworthy people, 11:1, 8, a conviction which sprang, in turn, from the prophet's experience within his own family circle. A key verse for the book thus arises from God's word to Hosea regarding his unfaithful wife, "Go again, love a woman beloved of her friend [her husband], and an adulteress, even as Yahweh loveth the children of Israel, though they turn to other gods," 3:1.

While the life of Hosea the son of Beeri remains unknown apart from his writing, the first three chapters of his prophecy do describe his wife and children and thereby provide information which richly illumines his inspired message. On the symbolic prophecies associated with the naming of the children, see below, predictions 1 and 2. Most significant is his continuing love for the undeserving wife Gomer. This very union of a prophet of God with a woman who had been, and continued to be, a public prostitute has scandalized superficial students and produced a whole series of exegetical vagaries. Pfeiffer says, "In spite of the obvious meaning of Hosea's words every conceivable interpretation of these two chapters has been offered. . . . Some critics cut the Gordian knot by regarding ch. 1 or ch. 3 as unhistorical, or considering either or both stories pure allegory."[1] Hosea 1:3, however, prohibits the vaporizing of these enacted events (even

1. *Introduction to the OT*, p. 567.

though they were symbolically prophetic) as mere figures of speech.[2] The idea that Hosea may have married Gomer in ignorance of her true character is ruled out by v. 2. Furthermore, "the assertion that 'woman of fornication' [v. 2] means 'proleptically' the bad woman she turned out to be some time after her marriage is pure sleight of hand."[3] Some again have proposed that Gomer may have been a harlot in spiritual matters only (i.e. was an idolator), just as was the northern kingdom as a whole;[4] but this hardly explains 2:2–4. Finally, there are those who would at least deny that Hosea ever took Gomer back (3:1) once he had put her away (2:2).[5] Yet ch. 3 can hardly refer to a different woman from the Gomer of ch. 1;[6] and the suggestion that chs. 1 and 3 concern but a single event that has been preserved in two accounts is refuted by its own advocates, who confess their assumption that the phrase "again" in 3:1 will have to be dismissed as the work of a later redactor.[7] The point is that God in His wisdom saw fit to overrule His usual standard that would have prohibited the marriage of His servant to an ungodly partner (Lev 21:7; cf. II Cor 6:14)—for the sake of revelation. The very enormity of Hosea's situation is what drives home the theme of God's undivorceable concern for the unworthy; for, "No other prophet comes nearer to the NT revelation of the love of God."[8] Hosea's prophecy is indeed the Gospel of John for the OT.

The book falls into two parts: I. Symbolical prophecies, based on the experiences of Hosea within his family, chs. 1–3; and II. Direct prophecies, applying the word of God to the two Hebrew nations, chs. 4–14. For while Hosea was primarily a prophet to northern Israel (1:4, 5:3, 6:4), he does include a number of references to Judah (1:11, 5:15, and see below, predictions 3, 17, and 22).[9] The opening three chapters exhibit a corresponding three cycles[10] of prophetic fulfillment, as shown in Table 10. The remaining chapters, 4–14, show less of a patterned organization and more of a repetition of themes that are representative of the prophet's sermons: themes of sin, of judgment—more than half of Hosea's predic-

2. As proposed by E. J. Young, *An Introduction to the OT*, p. 269.
3. Pfeiffer, op. cit., p. 568.
4. Ibid.
5. S. Sandmel, *The Hebrew Scriptures*, p. 76.
6. As proposed by Pfeiffer, op. cit., p. 569; yet contrast H. H. Rowley, *Men of God*, p. 84, or Sandmel, op. cit., p. 78, "Least of all should one suppose as many have, that Hosea experienced two successive divine injunctions to marry two different loose women."
7. C. Kuhl, *The Prophets of Israel*, p. 68.
8. H. L. Ellison, *Men Spake from God*, p. 36.
9. He recognizes even the higher place of Judah in the purposes of God, 5:15; cf. his dating by the Davidic monarchs in 1:1. Negative critics usually remove these references, as well as most of Hosea's prophecies of hope, as constituting non-authentic "interpolations of Judean editors," Pfeiffer, op. cit., pp. 566–567; but cf. Young, op. cit., p. 267.
10. See above, pp. 130–131.

TABLE 10
Predictive Cycles in Hosea 1-3[11]

	Hosea 1-2:1 *Extent of the kingdom*	Hosea 2:2-23 *Character of the kingdom*		Hosea 3 *Process of the kingdom*
Predeportation sin II K 15:8-12	1-4a Whoredom from God Vengeance on Jehu's dynasty	2 Whoredom to be put away	8 Gifts used for Baal	1 God loves Israel despite their other gods
Assyrian punishment II K 17:16-18	4b-9 Israel to cease Judah saved, 701 B.C.	3-5 Slay her with thirst	9-13 Her mirth to cease	
Exilic repentance Ezek 18:30-32		6-7 Her way hedged, so return to Husband	14-17 Baal taken away	
Present kingdom Rom 9:24-26	10 Numerous children Sons of God	The b'rith: 19-20 Thou shalt know God	23b-c Be My people	2-4 I bought her Israel kingless
Future kingdom Rom 11:25-27	1:11-2:1 Judah with Israel under One Head	18 Break the sword	21-23a Grain and wine	5 Israel return to David their king

11. J. B. Payne, ETSP (1954), 21.

tions (61 out of 111 verses) concentrate on the single subject of the fall of Samaria in 722 B.C., No. 2 below—and yet of restoration. For Hosea's latter chapters include such great forecasts as 6:1–3 (No. 18), on the Messiah's resurrection on the third day, or 11:10a, 13:14 (Nos. 27 and 28), on the believers' rapture and resurrection at His second coming. Hosea's 28 predictions involve 111 out of the book's 197 vv., and they make up 56% of the whole.

1. Hos 1:4a (1 v., sym.): God's word to the prophet, on the naming of his newborn son, "Call his name Jezreel"; and the explanation follows, "For yet a little while and I will avenge the blood of Jezreel upon the house of Jehu." The criticism is not directed against Jehu's extermination in Jezreel of the evil dynasty of Omri and Ahab that had preceded him, II K 9:24, 10:1–7, which had been carried out in the fulfillment of prophecy, 9:7, 25–26, and is spoken of with approval, 10:30, but against such bloodthirsty acts as are exhibited in 10:12–14. Fulfillment: the wiping out of the house of Jehu through the murder of Zechariah in 752 B.C., II K 15:10; cf. the more positive prediction of 10:13 (15:12).

2. Hos 1:4b–6; 2:3–4, 11–13; 4:3, 5–7, 14; 5:5a, 7–12a, 14a; 7:12–13, 16; 8:1–7, 14a; 9:7, 9, 11–14, 16; 10:2, 4–8, 10–11, 13–15; 11:6; 12:2, 11, 14; 13:1, 3, 7–9, 13, 15b–16 (61 vv., sym.): a further reason stated for the naming of Hosea's son Jezreel, "for . . . I will break the bow of Israel in the valley of Jezreel," 1:5, namely, in "the great plain in which all the great battles for the possession of the land have been fought. The brief historical account given in the books of Kings does not notice the place in which the Assyrians gained the decisive victory over Israel,"[12] but Jezreel remains likely. 1:6 describes a similarly symbolical prophecy, through the naming of the second child, "Lo-ruhamah," i.e. "not shown mercy" (= 2:4). In ch. 2, the thought moves, almost imperceptibly, from the fate of Hosea's faithless wife (v. 2) to that of the nation, with the following details on the latter's fall: v. 3, ". . . lest I make her a wilderness"; v. 11, to terminate her feasts; and vv. 12–13, to destroy the land's products, which had been perverted to the service of Baal; cf. 5:7, 9, that because of the sins at their new-moon feasts, "Ephraim shall become a desolation." In 4:5 God warns, "I will destroy thy mother," meaning the nation; since they have rejected the prophets and the Mosaic law, v. 6, the kingdom can no longer continue as His intermediating priest (cf. Ez 19:6).

7:12 states, "I will chastise them, as their congregation hath heard," referring to the already much repeated prophecies; but these further predictions then occur: 9:7, "the days of recompense are come"; 8:1, the destroyer advances like an eagle; 8:14, fire is to be sent on Ephraim's

12. KD, *Minor Prophets*, I:43.

cities, along with Judah's (see No. 17, below); 10:7, "her king is cut off" (= v. 15); and 7:16, her "princes shall fall by the sword" (= 9:16, 11:6) and become a derision, even into the land of Egypt. Behind all this lies the religious apostasy of the northern kingdom: the idolatrous "calf of Samaria [cf. I K 12:28–30] shall be broken in pieces," 8:6; and their other pagan objects of worship shall be destroyed, 10:2, and their altars become heaps, 12:11. Ch. 10 reveals the means for Israel's destruction: v. 10, "Peoples shall be gathered against them"; and the golden calf, v. 6, "shall be carried unto Assyria [cf. 11:5, under No. 16, below] for a present to King Jareb [itself a symbolic name, meaning "he contends"; cf. 5:13 ASVmg]." As it is summarized in ch. 13, "When he [Ephraim] offended in Baal, he died," v. 1, that is, "Samaria was given up to destruction (cf. Amos 2:2),"[13] afflicted with sorrows, v. 13, "dried up" in punishment, v. 15, and laid low by the sword, v. 16. Fulfillment (per. 7): as in I K. prophecy No. 25, the fall of Samaria in 722 B.C.

3. Hos 1:7 (1 v.): Judah to be saved "by Yahweh their God, not by bow nor by sword" (cf. Isa 31:8). Fulfillment (per. 7): the deliverance in 701 B.C. of the southern kingdom from Sennacherib and his Assyrian hosts; as in Isa. No. 37.

4. Hos 1:10; 2:*20b*, 23b (2 vv.): Gomer's younger son had been given the symbolic name of Lo-ammi (1:9), meaning that Israel had forfeited her status under the Sinaitic testament (Ex 19:5) and become "not My people;" but the Spirit of prophecy yet foresaw a restoration, when: "The children of Israel shall be as the sand of the sea; and in the place where it was said unto them, 'Ye are not My people,' it shall be said unto them, 'Ye are the sons of the living God,' " 1:10. For, "Thou shalt know Yahweh . . . and I will have mercy on her that had not obtained mercy [cf. 1:6, under No. 2, above]; and I will say to them that were not My people, 'Thou art My people,' " 2:20, 23. As Snaith comments, "This new Israel is clearly declared to be God's people. . . . He looks forward to a new beginning, a new Israel."[14] Fulfillment (per. 14): as in Gen. No. 19, the increase of Israel in the Christian church,[15] with its incorporated Gentile believers to become sons of the living God. Ironside objects, "Not to the Church do these words refer, but to literal Israel, who, upon the expiration of the now fast-concluding 'times of the Gentiles,' will be grafted in again into the olive tree of promise."[16] But these passages are quoted in Rom 9:24–26, with the explanation, "God called . . . even us, not from among Jews only, but also from among Gentiles; as He says also in Hosea. . . ."[17] A. B. Davidson thus emphasizes the comprehensiveness

13. Ibid., I:154, though IB, VI:705, prefers "death" in a spiritual sense.
14. *Mercy and Sacrifice*, pp. 58 and 50.
15. See above, p. 113.
16. *Notes on the Minor Prophets*, p. 25.
17. See Payne, "Hosea," pp. 13–14.

of the Pauline understanding, "The Gentiles are fellow heirs with Israel, and of the same body; but they do not thrust out Israel. Israel is still there and the Gentiles are merely grafted into its stock."[18]

5. Hos 1:11a, 2:1, 3:5 (3 vv.): 1:11 then emphasizes the particularly Jewish aspect of the restoration (cf. v. 10, No. 4, preceding), "Judah and Israel shall be gathered together, and they shall appoint themselves one head," "doubtless the Davidic king of 3:5";[19] and, 3:5 continues, they "shall come with fear unto Yahweh and to His goodness in the latter days." Pusey has suggested, "Both literal Judah and Israel were gathered into one in the one Church of Christ";[20] but Keil, who makes frequent reference to the church in OT prophecies, here insists, "This fulfillment falls within Messianic times, and hitherto has only been realized in very small beginnings, which furnish a pledge of their complete fulfillment in the last times when the hardening of Israel will cease and all Israel be converted to Christ."[21] V. 1 of chapter 2 thus states, "Say unto your brethren, Ammi . . . Ruhamah" (cf. 1:6, 9, No. 1 above); and it applies to the totality of Israel the same terms that 1:10 and 2:23 had found appropriate, in an earlier context, to the present, Gentile church (No. 4). Fulfillment (per. 15): as in Isa. No. 31, the conversion of all Jewish Israel to Christ, whom they will seek as their king; for even as Rom 9 confronts Ironside's neglect of the present kingdom in Hos 1:10, so Rom 11:25–26 confronts Pusey's neglect of the future kingdom in Hos 1:11. It is only at this time that "all Israel will be saved" (Rom 11:26).

6. Hos *1:11b, 2:23a*: after the Gentile engrafting. 1:10, and the Jewish acceptance of Christ, 1:11a, (No. 4 and 5, preceding), Israel and Judah "shall go up from the land," of their dispersion, 1:11b. The expression is reminiscent of their former departure from the land of Egypt.[22] Yahweh promises, "I will sow her [Israel] unto Me in the land" (2:23 ASVmg) that is theirs; and the verb "to sow" suggests a play on words with the noun "Jezreel," meaning "God sows"—see 2:21 (No. 13, below) and the conclusion to 1:11, ". . . for great shall be the day of Jezreel," when God brings back His people. Fulfillment (per. 16): the millennial return of Israel to Palestine, as subsequently elaborated in Isa 11:11 etc.

7. Hos 2:6–7, 14, 16–17; 5:15; *11:10a*; 14:4, *8a* (7 vv., fig.): after Samaria has collapsed in 722 B.C. (2:3, No. 2, above) and God has "hedged off" Israel from her old idolatrous ways, "Then shall she say, I will go and return to my first husband," 2:7. As noted long ago by Calvin,

---

18. *OT Prophecy*, pp. 491–492.
19. Camb, p. 46; so Snaith, op. cit., p. 50. The subject is not David himself (see above, p. 84, and Jer. prophecy No. 45 or Ezek. No. 23) but One of his dynasty. Camb, pp. 61–62, i.e. the Messianic king, ICC, p. 223.
20. *The Minor Prophets*, I:26.
21. Op. cit., I:45.
22. See above, pp. 20, 83.

"We may learn from this passage what true repentance is."[23] Yahweh Himself says, v. 14, "I will bring her into the wilderness and speak comfortably to her." The *wilderness* is a figure for trouble. But specifically, "It means the captivity . . . for this was in itself like living in a desert";[24] and the phrase appears to have arisen out of a comparison with "the day when she came up out of the land of Egypt," v. 15 (see note 22). G. A. Smith states, "The exile is described, with all plainness, under the figure of Israel's early wanderings in the wilderness."[25] In Hosea's later predictions, the prophet explains, "In their affliction they will seek Me earnestly," 5:15; "They shall walk after Yahweh," 11:10. The latter expression signifies "that walking in true obedience to the Lord which follows from conversion (Dt 13:5, I K 14:8)";[26] and it is based on God's mercy, to be shown to Israel in the exile, v. 9. In 14:4 God promises, "I will heal their backsliding," with the result, v. 8, that idolatry will come to an end. Fulfillment (per. 8): as in Dt. No. 16, the repentance of Israel while in exile. Keil notes, "The destruction of the might of the ten tribes and their expulsion into exile (cf. Hos 1:5) form the turning point through which the conversion of the rebellious to the Lord, and their reunion with Judah, are rendered possible."[27]

8. Hos *2:11b* (typ.): sabbath. Fulfillment (per. 13): as in Ex. No. 41.

9. Hos 2:15; 14:5-7, 8b (5 vv.): although He had taken away the products of Israel's land (2:9), God yet promises, "I will give her her vineyards from thence [from the exile, v. 14, No. 7, above], and the valley of Achor for a door of hope," 2:15. 14:5 speaks poetically, "I will be as the dew unto Israel; he shall be as the lily"; and v. 7 explains in slightly less figurative language, or at least in a changed figure, "They that dwell under his [Israel's] shadow shall return; they shall revive as the grain." This reference could be eschatological; but the surrounding contexts are of exilic repentance, v. 4, and of a turning from idols in ancient times, v. 8a (No. 7, above). God assures the captive Hebrews, v. 8b, "From Me is thy

23. *Commentary on the Twelve Minor Prophets*, I:89. Contrast the criticisms of liberalism: "It is not so much the expression of penitance, as of longing to escape the sense of misery," Camb, p. 50; or ICC, p. 237, "This is no genuine repentance, but only a desire for change, because change is expected to bring relief."
24. ICC, p. 239.
25. *The Book of the Twelve Minor Prophets*, I:247. But this figure must not be overworked, either as by Keil, who goes on to propose, "Canaan . . . is a type of the inheritance bestowed by the Lord upon His church," KD, I:60—for the anticipated deliverance of Hos 2 is connected with Israel's exilic cleansing from Baalism, v. 17—or as by Ironside, who pictures Israel "alone with Himself in the wilderness of the peoples (see Ezek 20:35), [when] He will plead with her. . . . In the Millennium . . . on the earth the restored wife of Jehovah will have her place in the land of Palestine. . . . Then will the words be fulfilled . . . I will take away the names of Baalim out of her mouth," op. cit., pp. 22–23.
26. KD, I:142.
27. Ibid., I:48.

fruit found"; that is, He is to be the source of their fruitfulness,[28] just as He would be of their conversion while in exile, v. 4. Fulfillment (per. 9): a return to Palestine for at least some of Hosea's people, the 10 northern tribes. Ellison may have overly minimized the numbers involved; but he demonstrates the prophecy's accomplishment when he observes, "God's purpose had to be finally fulfilled through the trickle of those who from time to time joined themselves to Judah under the monarchy (II Chron 11:13–16, 15:9, 30:11, 35:18) and those few who will have joined themselves to the returning exiles in the time of Cyrus."[29] Just as Achor had conveyed an unhappy memory (Josh 7:25–26) and yet played a part in Israel's past entrance into the promised land, so the exilic chastening (Hos 2:14, 16–17) would have a hopeful side and would open the way to restoration.[30] Girdlestone confirms the conclusion, and with a higher numerical calculation, saying, "This reunion and return is timed in Jeremiah 50:4 as contemporary with the downfall of Babylon. . . . It has been estimated that at least a quarter of those who returned from captivity were of the Ten Tribes. . . . They were thus included in 'the remnant of Jacob' at the time of the restoration."[31] So Zechariah, after the return, speaks regularly of Judah and Ephraim as being restored together, 9:10, 13; cf. Ezra 6:17, 8:35, Lk 2:36, Acts 26:7, and James 1:1.

10. Hos 2:*18a*, 19–20a (2 vv.): recognizing the inadequacies of God's earlier, Sinaitic testament with Israel (cf. 6:7, 8:1, No. 21, below), because of the contemporaneous apostasy of his people (2:8, 17), Hosea looked forward to a better time ahead when, as Yahweh said, "I *will* make a testament for them," 2:18. This future *b'rîth* was shown to have two aspects: an internal, "I will betroth thee unto Me in righteousness," v. 19, and an external, vv. 18, 21–22 (see No. 11–13, below); cf. the initial revelation of this latter element in Lev 26:9b. These aspects reached a more complete expression, respectively, in Jeremiah's new testament (see under Jer 3:16b), declared just prior to the exile, and in Ezekiel's testament of peace (see Ezek 34:25), revealed during it.[32] Meanwhile, however, Hosea particularly emphasized the *righteousness* that is to distinguish the former, the new testament. Snaith calls attention to

that new heart which God will implant in every man. . . . If the new covenant is going to stand the slightest chance of being even established, then God will have to give Israel those quantities of heart and mind which are essential. So we get Hos 2:19 with its talk of the betrothal gift which the bridegroom

28. Perhaps a wordplay on the noun *Ephraim* (as in 13:15), which means "doubly fruitful."

29. Op. cit., p. 166.

30. The exiles who returned after Cyrus' decree in 538 B.C. may even have entered the land by the old route through the Valley of Achor, Hos 2:15, though Achor may have symbolized the distress preceding restoration or perhaps serve as a figure for fertility; cf. Isa 65:10.

31. *The Grammar of Prophecy*, pp. 128, 130.

32. J. B. Payne, *Theology of the Older Testament*, pp. 113–114.

will give the bride: *sédheq, mishpāt, hésedh,* and *rahamīm* [righteousness, justice, loyalty, and mercies], i.e. a modelling of her conduct on what he knows to be the nature of God.[33]

Horton explains, "The language here is prepared for that doctrine of God's righteousness imparted to a sinner which Paul makes the pivot of his gospel."[34] Fulfillment (per. 14): the new testament of Jesus Christ, by which the church is betrothed to Him in righteousness; cf. II Cor 11:2, Eph 5:26–27.

11. Hos *2:18b*: that the future testament of peace (see No. 10, preceding) will include "the beasts of the field"; cf. Ezek 34:25. Fulfillment (per. 15): as in Ps. prophecy No. 44, the removal of the curse from nature at Christ's second coming; cf. Isa 11:6.

12. Hos 2:18c (1 v): "I will make a testament for them . . . and I will break the battle out of the land." Fulfillment (per. 16): as in Lev. No. 29, peace, in the Messiah's future kingdom.

13. Hos 2:21–22 (2 vv.): heaven and earth are to combine to produce grain, new wine, and oil; "and they shall answer, Jezreel," meaning, what *God sows,* cf. 1:11b (No. 6, above); compare the former, negative symbolism of Jezreel in 1:4 (No. 1 and 2, above). Ezekiel's testament of peace thus also speaks in some detail of the products of the soil that are yet to be (Ezek 34:26–27, 29). Fulfillment (per. 16): as in Ex 23:25a, millennial fertility; cf. Hos 2:18b (No. 11, above).

14. Hos 3:2 (1 v., typ.): of his faithless wife Gomer,[35] now reduced to slavery, but through whom Hosea depicts God's love for Israel (3:1), the prophet says, "So I bought her to me for 15 pieces of silver and a homer [= 10 ephahs, or bushels] and a half of barley," i.e. for a total price of 30 pieces of silver,[36] half the payment being in the despised commodity of barley (cf. Num 5:15).[37] Ultimate fulfillment (per. 13): the achievement of human reconciliation with God and of the saints' betrothal to Him, through "the purchase price paid at Calvary's cross";[38] cf. the direct, verbal prediction of this same event in Zech 11:12.

15. Hos 3:3–4 (2 vv., typ.): Hosea's instructions to Gomer, after his redeeming her from slavery (No. 14, preceding), "Thou shalt abide for me many days . . . thou shalt not be any man's wife: so will I also be toward thee," 3:3, meaning that the marriage relationship is not yet to be restored. God's explanation of the typical significance of the prophet's action appears

33. Op. cit., p. 85.
34. Cent, I:24; though in qualification, cf. Calvin, op. cit., I:113, "Some say that righteousness is what is conferred on us by God through gracious imputation . . . but here the prophet, I doubt not, intimates . . . truth and rectitude on both sides."
35. See above, introduction to Hosea.
36. ICC, p. 219, states, "The value of a slave is 30 shekels, the sum here named"; and so Camb, p. 59.
37. Cf. KD, I:68–69.
38. Ironside, op. cit., p. 29.

in v. 4: "For the children of Israel shall abide many days without king [= without a state] . . . and without sacrifice [= redemption], and without pillar and teraphim," signifying an absence of idolatry also.[39] Horton has suggested perhaps the most inclusive interpretation: "This foreshadows not only the exile, but the long subsequent career of Israel up to the time of Christ and even since."[40] Yet the exile seems hardly to be the period in view; for "the Jews took the teraphim with them into exile . . . (cf. Ezek 21:21),"[41] and Assyria and Babylonia abounded in images. Furthermore, for those who would repent (cf. 2:6, No 7, above), there did occur a return to the divine "husband" (vv. 7, 16). In the period then of the Persian and Maccabean restorations, and even under Roman rule, Israel again had days of both kings and priestly sacrifices. The fulfillment would thus appear to lie in per. 14, referring to the condition of most Jews during the church age; cf. Zeph 3:10b, Zech 13:8b. Pusey, for example, describes them as "free from idolatry, and in a state waiting for God, yet looking in vain for a Messias since they had not and would not receive Him who came unto them; praying to God; yet without sacrifice for sin; not owned by God, yet kept distinct and apart by His Providence, for a future yet to be revealed."[42] Such identification with "the long history of Jewry's dispersion"[43] is confirmed by two additional factors: (1) that the disciplinary period comes subsequent to the act of redemption—as Ironside has put it, "Though the purchase price was paid at Calvary's cross, Judah and Israel are wayward still, and the marriage covenant has not been renewed"[44]— and (2) that the condition of Hos 3:3–4 precedes Israel's millennial seeking of David their king, as foreseen in v. 5 (No. 5, above).[45]

16. Hos 4:19; 8:8, 13b; 9:3, 6, 15, 17; 11:5; 12:9 (9 vv., fig.): concerning his people Israel, Hosea exclaimed, "The wind hath wrapped her up in its wings," 4:19, meaning that Ephraim was about to find herself "swallowed up . . . among the nations," 8:8, driven from God's house (= His congregation; see under No. 25, below) in Palestine, and "wanderers among the nations," 9:15, 17. 9:3 employs a different type of figure: "They shall not dwell in Yahweh's land, but Ephraim shall return

---

39. Liberalism sees in this last reference a primitive, tacit approval of such idolatry; cf. Cheyne's remark, Camb, p. 60, "The worship of Jehovah in northern Israel presented features altogether alien to the orthodox worship of Jehovah according to the law, and . . . Hosea raises no protest against it." But Snaith (though assuming a writer later than Hosea) concludes, "The writer thinks that Israel will be well rid of . . . those heathen adjuncts to worship," op. cit., pp. 50–51.

40. Cent, I:26; so also Calvin, op. cit., I:129.

41. Camb, p. 61; as opposed to NBC, p. 684, "This finds its natural application in the punishment which befell Israel in her being deprived, during the time of exile, or her civil and religious institutions, both true and false."

42. Op. cit., I:43. Cf. Keil, I:71, "They continue for the most part to the present day without a monarchy, without Jehovah-worship, and without a priesthood."

43. Ellison, op. cit., p. 110.

44. Op. cit., pp. 29–30.

45. Payne, "Hosea," pp. 16–17.

to 'Egypt' [= a land of captivity and bondage]," meaning, in this verse, "They shall eat unclean food in Assyria." For the prophet goes on to explain his own metaphor, "They shall *not* return into the land of Egypt, but the Assyrian shall be their king," 11:5.[46] The period of Moses provides similar illumination for the Lord's forecast that is found in 12:9, "I am Yahweh thy God from the land of Egypt; I will yet again make thee to dwell in tents, as in the days of the solemn feast [specifically, of Tabernacles]." The idea here (cf. vv. 7, 11, 14) does not appear to be one of reformation or of restoration (as in 2:14)[47] so much as simply of punishment. Fulfillment (per. 7): the deportation in 722 B.C. of N. Israel to Assyria, II K 17:6, 18:11; cf. No. 23, below, and Num 24:22's prediction of a more specialized group 11 years earlier.

17. Hos 5:*5b*, 10, *12b, 14b; 8:14b* (1 v.): the kingdom of Judah to cease, even as will that of N. Israel (No. 2, above). The parallel with Ephraim's fall shows that these verses do not refer simply to Sennacherib's desolations in 701 (cf. No. 3, above). Fulfillment (per. 7): as in Lev. No. 33, Judah's fall to Babylon in 586.

18. Hos 6:1–3 (3 vv.): "Yahweh will heal us. . . . After two days will He revive us: on the third day He will raise us up, and we shall live before Him . . . He will come unto us as the rain that watereth the earth," these last words being a figure for blessing, as in Ps 72:6.[48] Concerning Hosea's prior anticipation, of being *raised up*, Kuhl proposes, "6:2 refers to the death and resurrection of heathen agricultural deities: Adonis and Tammuz."[49] But while many will reject his imputation of mythological superstitions to the content of Scripture, his thought yet carries this much validity: the *reviving* anticipated by Hosea and his faithful associates remained dependent upon a corresponding and prior work of God. Specifically, it is only because Christ lives that believers have the hope of living also (John 14:19; cf. the discussion under Ps 16:10). Fulfillment (per. 13): as in Isa. No. 103 (53:10b); as Pusey states, "The resurrection of Christ, and our resurrection in Him and in His resurrection, could not be more plainly foretold"; and he proceeds to elaborate on Hosea's exact prediction of the two days that were involved.[50] Hos 6:2 may thus be the point of reference for Paul's statement in I Cor 15:4, that Christ "was raised on the third day *according to the Scriptures*."[51]

19. Hos *6:6a* (typ.): peace offering. Fulfillment (pers. 13 and 16): as in Lev. No. 5.

46. See above, p. 83.
47. IB, V:701.
48. Though it there refers to Christ's second coming.
49. Op. cit., p. 72. He adds, "Nevertheless the reference is not to the resurrection but as in similar sayings in the Psalms quite generally to deliverance from trouble and sickness." Cf. the view of BBC, V:54, "The national revival [as in v. 11, No. 22, below, or 2:15, No. 9, above] is to take place in a short period of time."
50. Op. cit., I:63.
51. Payne, *Theology*, p. 276; so also T. H. Horne, *An Introduction to the Critical Knowledge and Study of the Holy Scriptures*, I:128.

20. Hos 6:6b (1 v., typ.): burnt offering. Fulfillment (per. 13): as in Lev. No. 3.

21. Hos. 6:7, *8:1b* (1 v., typ.): the Sinaitic testament. 6:7 compares Israel's present conduct under the Sinaitic revelation with Adam's (ASV) under the *b'rīth* of Gen 2, though this latter was still the original covenant of works and did not as yet typify Christ's death (as the Edenic testament of 3:15 would).[52] Fulfillment (per. 13): as in Ex. No. 45 (19:5).

22. Hos 6:11 (1 v): "Also, O Judah, there is a harvest appointed for thee, when I bring back the captivity[53] of My people." The *harvest* for Judah could be one of judgment,[54] paralleling God's condemnation of Ephraim in v. 10; but it would appear preferable to take v. 11, with its hopeful phraseology, as an abrupt reference to Judah's *un*likeness to Ephraim.[55] Fulfillment (per. 9): as in Dt. No. 43, Judah's return from exile (cf. No. 9, above, on Ephraim's).

23. Hos 8:10 (1 v.): a somewhat obscure divine oracle against the northern tribes, "Now will I gather them [perhaps into deportation centers, as preliminary to exile[56]]; and they begin to be diminished[57] by reason of the burden of the king of princes," i.e. Tiglath-pileser III, as then reigning in Assyria. Probable fulfillment (per. 7): the initial deportation to Assyria, in 733 B.C., of the 3½ tribes located in Galilee and Transjordan, II K 15:29; cf. No. 16, above, on the final deportation, for the remainder, in 722.

24. Hos *8:13a,* 9:4a (1 v., typ.):sacrifice. Fulfillment (per. 13): as in Lev. No. 2.

25. Hos *9:4b* (typ.): the temple. V. 8 would, however, seem to concern the false temple of Bethel[58] and so would not constitute a God-given type, while the phrase "house of Yahweh" in v. 15 signifies simply "the congregation of Jehovah (see 8:1)";[59] cf. No. 16, above. Fulfillment (per. 13): as in Ex 25:8.

26. Hos 11:8–9 (2 vv.): Yahweh asks, "How shall I give thee up, Ephraim? . . . I will not return to destroy Ephraim." Fulfillment (per. 8): as in Lev. No. 37, God's love, preventing Israel's destruction in the exile (v. 5).

---

52. Cf. Payne, *Theology*, pp. 92–96.
53. This expression may denote no more than recovery in general (see p. 17 above); but here it does seem to apply to Judah's literal restoration from exile.
54. KD, I:102–103. BH, p. 901, would read the passage in such a way as to make 6:11b part of 7:1, "When I would bring back the captivity, and when I would heal, then is iniquity uncovered," as in the RSV. But to have the same introductory preposition in 6:11b and 7:1 requires an unsupported emendation of the former.
55. NBC, p. 686.
56. ICC, p. 318.
57. The most probabzle rendering, KD, I:116; cf. ASVmg for alternative possibilities.
58. KD, I:123.
59. Ibid., I:127.

27. Hos 11:10b–11 (2 vv., fig.):[60] Yahweh shall "roar like a lion . . . and the children shall come trembling from the west . . . as a bird out of Egypt, and as a dove[61] out of the land of Assyria; and I will make them to dwell in their houses"; cf. Joel 2:32b, on their presence in Jerusalem. Keil explains, "The comparison to birds and doves expresses the swiftness with which they draw near, as doves fly to their dovecots."[62] Fulfillment (per. 15): the rapture of the church to meet Christ in the air at His second coming; cf. the correspondence of the figure of the Lord's *roaring* with the forecast of His shout and of the trumpet blast in I Thess 4:16.[63]

28. Hos 13:14–*15a* (1 v.): God's declaration concerning Israel, "I will redeem them from death . . . repentance shall be hid from Mine eyes." Kuhl says of God, "For Hosea, His redemptive power is able to deliver men thence," i.e. from the grave. Yet he adds, "But . . . it is impossible absolutely to determine whether this passage offers a threat or a promise."[64] Horton argues for the former: "The verse is a threat of implacable doom, 'Shall I ransom them from the hand of Sheol?' " with the answer being an emphatic No.[65] Or, alternatively, "Is it an unexpected flash of mercy? If so, the last part of the verse should be read in the light of Rom 11:29, where it is clear that 'repentance' means a change of mind on God's part; i.e. 'I will not change My mind about that.' "[66] A divine assurance of this latter sort is indicated by the positive note for Ephraim with which the next verse commences, "For[67] he will be fruitful among his brethren" (Hos 13:15)—seemingly a play on words with the noun "Ephraim," meaning "doubly fruitful" (cf. 14:8b, under No. 9, above); see Gen 41:52, 48:4, 49:22. Kuhl adds, "St. Paul, at least, rightly or wrongly, interprets this passage positively and, at the conclusion of his great resurrection chapter (I Cor 15:55), sounds it forth as a triumphal fanfare over the destruction of death,"[68] which settles the question for evangelicals. Fulfillment (per. 15): as in Isa. No. 76, the resurrection of the righteous dead; cf. the corresponding rapture of the living in No. 27, preceding.

60. This passage develops out of the thought of v. 10a, on Israel's coming to God in conversion during the exile (see under No. 7, above); and so Hosea proceeds to reveal another kind of coming, even though it involves a leap into the future.

61. This figure is later taken up by Isaiah, who asks in 60:8, "Who are these that fly as a cloud, and as the doves to their windows?" But Isaiah's is a picture of the ships of Tarshish, v. 9; so IB, V:702, visualizes how "the white-masted vessels converge on the city." The latter are to transport the converted Jewish diaspora, as well as silver and gold, to the Messiah in Jerusalem; but the figure in Hosea applies to people, not to ships, and applies more satisfactorily to the rapture.

62. KD, I:143.
63. See above, p. 114.
64. Op. cit., p. 71.
65. Cent, I:71.
66. NBC, p. 689.
67. KD, I:161–162.
68. Loc. cit.

JOEL

While Hosea prophesied to northern Israel, Joel son of Pethuel served as a minister of God to southern Judah (Joel 3:1, 6), especially to its capital city of Jerusalem (2:1, 15). But the events of his life are unknown, and the date of his ministry is a matter of inference. Indeed, Joel's message, together with the parallel prophecy of Obadiah, is the most difficult to assign to a historical situation of any in the Bible. As a result, while some scholars think of Joel as the oldest of the writing prophets and place him in the 9th century B.C.[1]—following losses to the Philistines and Edomites (cf. Joel 3:14, 19) by Jehoram (848–841 B.C.; II K 8:20–21, II Chron 21:16–17)[2]—others speak of Joel as the latest prophet to be named in the OT and date his book to the 4th century, considering it "one of the earliest of the apocalypses."[3] For those who accept the Isaianic authenticity of "the little apocalypse" (Isa 24–27) as traceable to about 711 B.C.,[4] dating for Joel[5] soon after the accession of Judah's weak King Ahaz to sole reign in 736, but before the Assyrian advance and initial deportation of northern Israel in 733,[6] becomes attractive. It accords with the Philistine and Edomite attacks of those days (II Chron 28:16–19) and with the apparent quotation of Obadiah (q.v.) by Joel 2:32.[7] A date in 735 would correspond, moreover, to Scripture's generally chronological arrangement of "the twelve" Minor Prophets: Hosea–Micah in the 8th century (with alternation between the north and south); Nahum–Zephaniah in the 7th; Haggai–Zechariah in the 6th; and Malachi in the 5th.

Joel's three brief chapters inaugurate Biblical apocalyptic as a form of revelation. Their theme is that of a locust plague, developed under two aspects, first of destruction (1–2:17) and then of restoration (2:18–ch. 3). Within the former aspect, ch. 1 describes the past, what occurred

---

1. "The oldest prophet whose oracles are preserved in literary form," C. von Orelli, *The OT Prophecy of the Consummation of God's Kingdom*, p. 221; cf. Merrill F. Unger, *Introductory Guide to the OT*, pp. 337–338; Gleason L. Archer, *A Survey of OT Introduction*, p. 292; see A. F. Kirkpatrick, *The Doctrine of the Prophets*, pp. 59–73.

2. The accession of Joash as a boy of seven in 835, under the high priest Jehoiada, II K 11:21, might thus explain the lack of reference to the king and the prominence of priests.

3. R. H. Pfeiffer, *Introduction to the OT*, p. 576; cf. Samuel Sandmel, *The Hebrew Scriptures*, p. 218. See above in the introductory discussion, on the nature of apocalyptic, pp. 85–89.

4. See Isa 20:1.

5. Compare John Davis' slightly earlier placement "after Hosea and before Amos," *A Dictionary of the Bible*, p. 382.

6. Joel makes no allusion to Assyria, or the even later Babylonian or Persian rulers of Palestine.

7. "Expressly quoted by Joel from Obad 17," IB, VI:754.

"before our eyes" (1:16). The Spirit cries out, "A nation has come up [Heb. perf.] upon My land, strong and without number; his teeth are the teeth of a lion," speaking in figures for the devouring locusts (v. 4).[8] Ch. 2:1–17 anticipates (with 1:15) another locust plague;[9] but this too passes, for 2:18 explains, "Then Yahweh had pity on His people."[10] A key verse for the entire book might indeed be 2:13, "Rend your heart, and not your garments, and turn unto Yahweh your God; for He is gracious . . . and repenteth Him of the evil." Within the latter aspect (2:18–ch. 3), the prophecy foresees a threefold restoration: in the immediate future, of what the locusts had eaten (2:18–27; see v. 25); in NT times, of spiritual blessings (2:28–29); and at Christ's return, of a corresponding restoration throughout the earth (2:30–ch. 3). Of Joel's 25 predictions, 20 thus concentrate in the latter part of his book. Prophecies occur in 50 of its 73 verses, which make up 68% of the whole.

1. Joel 1:9a, *13c*; 2:14 (2 vv., typ.): the meal offering. Fulfillment (per. 13): as in Lev. prophecy No. 4.
2. Joel 1:*9b*, *13d*, 14, 16; *3:18c* (2 vv., typ.): the temple. Fulfillment (per. 13): as in Ex. No. 55.
3. Joel 1:13a (1 v., typ.): priests, in the function of ministering at sacrifice. Fulfillment (per. 13), as in Ex. No. 59.
4. Joel *1:13b*; 2:17 (1 v., typ.): the altar. Fulfillment (per. 13): as in Ex. No. 44.
5. Joel 1:15; 2:1–11 (12 vv., fig.): "The day of Yahweh is at hand, and as destruction from the Almighty shall it come." It is then elaborated in ch. 2 as being "a day of darkness," caused by "a great people and strong," an event unparalleled, "even to the years of many generations" (v. 2); the metaphor of "Yahweh's army" (v. 11) is explained by similes: they are "*like* the noise of chariots, on the tops of the mountains do they leap" (v. 5); "they climb the wall *like* men of war" (v. 7). Fulfillment (per. 7): an impending, contemporaneous locust plague, 735 B.C., as identified in 2:25: "the locust and the caterpillar: My great army which I sent among you" (which looks back on the plague as now past). IB, VI:733 raises the possibility of eschatological armies as well as literal locusts but concludes, "It is true that some eschatological phrases are used of the judgments; but the locusts themselves in ch. 2 can still be interpreted as literal insects, pictured with vivid comparisons [note the

---

8. Compared also with fire, in 1:19–20, 2:3; see 2:5, "like the noise of fire that devoureth the stubble."
9. "Literal insects which are compared to an invading army and are sometimes described with poetic hyperbole," IB, VI:733; "the most natural and the most satisfying," as compared with interpretations that propose a typifying of human armies, Kirkpatrick, op. cit., pp. 50–51; cf. 54–56.
10. "The future tenses of the KJV are indefensible," NBC, p. 695; and KD, I:172.

term "like," above] and poetic exaggerations"; e.g., "Before them the heavens tremble; the sun and the moon are darkened" (v. 10). Such descriptions of the locust swarms, moreover, constitute the basis upon which Joel proceeded to develop the apocalyptic imagery of his eschatological passages that follow in 2:30–31 and 3:14–15.

6. Joel 2:19–26a (8 vv.): "I will remove far off from you the northern army and will drive it into a barren land, into the eastern sea and into the western sea; and its stench shall come up" (2:20). In its place, "He causeth to come down for you . . . the former rain [11] and the latter rain" (v. 23); "I will send you grain and new wine" (v. 19); "and ye shall eat in plenty and praise your God" (v. 26). Fulfillment (per. 7): contemporary deliverance from the invading locusts: see above, p. 126. Commentators cite how locusts came on Jerusalem from the north[12] in 1915 and were blown away into the Dead Sea (on other occasions into the Mediterranean on the west as well), "and the smell from decaying masses of insects was almost unbearable."[13]

7. Joel 2:*26b*–27; 3:*17b* (2 vv.): "My people shall never be put to shame, and ye shall know that I am in the midst of Israel." "Then shall Jerusalem be holy, and there shall no strangers pass through her any more," to "violate its sanctity."[14] Fulfillment (per. 16): the future Messianic kingdom, as in Lev. No. 29. God's immediate protection from the locusts leads on to the truth that "promised grace is guaranteed to the people for all ages,"[15] a security based on God's own presence.

8. Joel 2:28–29 (2 vv.): "It shall come to pass afterward [after the deliverance in Joel's day, vv. 19–26], that I will pour out My Spirit upon all flesh." Fulfillment (per. 14): in Acts 2:16 Peter quoted these words and identified the Pentecost experience as "what was spoken of through the prophet Joel."[16] Specifically, "all flesh," on whom the Spirit is poured,

---

11. In 2:23's last line the Heb. word for "former rain," "*mōré*, should be *yōré*, as 34 MSS. read; the *m*, is due to dittography," ICC, *Obad-Joel*, p. 120. But in the second line *mōré*, is thus a distinct word (shown also by the definite article, which is not used with *yōré*) and should have its normal rendering, *teacher:* "He giveth you the teacher for righteousness"—not the Messiah, or the leader of the sect at Qumran, who was claimed to be "the teacher of righteousness," but seemingly the prophet Joel, referring to himself and his own preaching (as in 2:12–17); for the context is contemporary, KD, *Minor Prophets*, I:205–207.

12. Though "since Israel's historic (Jer 13:20) and eschatological (Ezek 38:6, 15) enemies are from the north, some commentators consider this a term for invaders," IB, VI:749.

13. Ibid., 749–750.

14. Ibid., 759.

15. KD, I:209: see above, p. 65.

16. As opposed to Feinberg, *Premillennialism or Amillennialism?* pp. 76, 211, who designates Pentecost as a "partial fulfillment," or J. Dwight Pentecost, *Things to Come*, p. 470, who asserts, "Peter is not citing the experience before them as the fulfillment of Joel's prophecy," but only as an analogy to a yet future accomplishment, namely, "the Spirit in the millennial age."

is defined as "all whom God calls to Himself" (Acts 2:39); for this gift is no longer limited to the leaders of Israel, and it includes all classes, even *servants* (Joel 2:29).[17]

9. Joel 2:30–31; 3:15, *16b* (3 vv.): "The sun shall be turned into darkness, and the moon into blood [= color; see Rev 6:12, "like blood"]." This description is drawn from 2:2, 10, where it was used figuratively for the locusts darkening the sky. But here Joel's intent is literal; compare the narrative elements in Luke 21:25–27. Joel 3:15–16 indicates that the heavenly phenomena continue through the battle of the valley of Jehoshaphat (see 3:2), adding, "the heavens and the earth shall shake." Fulfillment (per. 15): the *wrath of God* that is to accompany Christ at His return,[18] as shown by parallel prophecies in the NT, e.g. Mt 24:29, Rev 6:12, 17.

10. Joel 2:32a; 3:16c (2 vv.): those who "call on the name of Yahweh shall be delivered"; see above, p. 79. This is elaborated as to its function in 3:16: when the earth shakes, "Yahweh will be a refuge unto His people." Fulfillment (per. 15): the rapture of the church, as in Hos. No. 27 (11:10), snatched up to meet Christ in the clouds as His wrath (vv. 30–31) is poured out.[19]

11. Joel *2:32b;* 3:1 (1 v.): those who escape will be "in mount Zion and in Jerusalem." The next verse, 3:1, explains this, saying, "In those days I shall bring back the sh'vūth, 'captivity,' of Judah and Jerusalem": not that those brought back were captives; for sh'vūth, signifies "the imprisonment of debt," and to *bring it back* for someone is to "turn one's [here Jerusalem's] fortune to the good."[20] Fulfillment (per. 15): the raptured church to "fall in" behind Christ in His triumphal descent to Jerusalem, for the city's good. Those included should not be limited to believers who just happened to be in Jerusalem at His appearing; for their very presence, now, in the city is proof that, v. 32a, "whosoever" called on Yahweh was saved (per No. 10, above).

12. Joel *2:32c:* "and among the remnant, those whom Yahweh doth call," ASV.[21] Fulfillment (per. 14): as in Gen. No. 19, the inclusion of Gentiles in the Israel that is the household of God (Eph 2:19). The *called* form a part of the larger group that makes up the total rapture. They correspond to those additional, non-Jewish elements indicated by the *all flesh* of v. 28; that is, "Not only citizens of Judah would be saved in

---

17. Prophecy, dreams, and visions should not be pressed as applying only to the respective classes listed.
18. These 2 vv. are quoted in Acts 2:19–20 as a part of the whole selection from Joel 2, not so as to apply them to Pentecost, but so as to lead the hearers down to Joel 2:32 with its proclamation of proffered salvation.
19. Rev 7:1–8 speaks of the saints as sealed from the wrath by angels, but Joel emphasizes their subsequent protection by being gathered to His Person.
20. KB, p. 940.
21. See KD, I:215, for the arguments in favor of this rendering.

the time of judgment, but all who called upon the Lord out of every nation."[22]

13. Joel 3:2, 9–11a, 12–14 (7 vv.): "I will gather all nations into the valley of Jehoshaphat [situated near Jerusalem[23]], and I will execute judgment upon them there." 3:13 depicts a battle: "putting in the sickle" and "treading the wine press." Fulfillment (per. 15): the initial engagement that climaxes in the battle of Armageddon; see Num 24:17c. It follows Christ's return and the rapture, 3:1, and develops from the advance of the saints upon Jerusalem (see No. 11, above). Zech 14:2 speaks also of the "gathering of all nations."

14. Joel 3:4a, 7b–8 (1 v.): against Tyre, "I will return your recompence upon your own head"; the slave-trading of captive Judeans, sold to Greeks by the Phoenicians and Philistines (II Chron 28:17–18), to be rewarded in kind, as the Jews sell them to Arabians. "In fulfillment [per. 10] of this warning . . . the Tyrians and the people of Gaza in Philistia were sold into slavery by Alexander the Great in 332. No doubt Jews were among the buyers."[24] The context of 3:1–2 might suggest conflicts that are yet future; but v. 4 seems simply to introduce these specified peoples, as similar afflicters of Jews in the past. The principle is that particular offenders are to receive appropriate punishments.

15. Joel 3:4b: Sidon to suffer the same way. But their selling into slavery was 13 years earlier, under Artaxerxes III (per. 9). The city had revolted in 351; it was finally reduced to ashes and many slain in 345.

16. Joel 3:4c (1 v.): Philistia to suffer the same way. Fulfillment (per. 10): as in No. 14, above. Isa 14:28–31 prophesies a punishment that fell on Philistia in 711 (see Hezekiah's victory, II K 18:8), but Joel's situation follows the Jewish restoration described next.[25]

17. Joel 3:7a (1 v.): "I will stir them up out of the place whither ye have sold them." Fulfillment (per. 9): Jewish slaves to return to Israel. "How this will be done we are not told";[26] perhaps at the general return from exile under the Persians; possibly earlier.[27]

18. Joel 3:11b: "Thither cause Thy mighty ones to come down, O Yahweh." Fulfillment (per. 15): Christ at His descent from glory, leading His "angelic hosts"[28] to the battle.

22. Ibid.
23. Laetsch, p. 131, may be overly specific, in locating it "in the wilderness of Tekoa, SE of Jerusalem, where the Lord annihilated the forces of Moab, Ammon, and Edom threatening Jerusalem [in the days of Jehoshaphat] (II Chron 20:1–30), also called Valley of Berachah (v. 26)." For the term *Jehoshaphat* may be merely descriptive, "Yahweh judges" (= the valley of decision, Joel 3:14), and the Kidron Valley, on the east side of Jerusalem toward Olivet, seems a more probable location; see Zech 14:3–4, KD, I:220, IB, VI:754–755.
24. IB, VI:756.
25. Keil, I:224, favors the Maccabean times, as the Jews progressively took over coastal territories; see I Macc 10:84–89, 11:59–60.
26. ICC, *Obad-Joel*, p. 132.
27. Keil, loc. cit., cites parallels in Greek times (per. 10).
28. IB, VI:757

19. Joel *3:16a* (fig.): "Yahweh will roar from Zion." Joel here quotes from Amos 1:2, which related to God's judgment on N. and S. Israel. Fulfillment (per. 15): an elaboration upon 3:2, 9 ff. (see No. 13, above), namely, that Yahweh, through his Messiah, would attack the pagans in the valley of Jehoshaphat from Jerusalem.[29] He must have occupied Zion, advancing from the Mount of Olives, Zech 14:2. Hos 11:10 would subsequently develop this figure one step further and associate God's *roaring* with the rapture, to which Joel does refer in 3:16, cf. 2:32 (No. 10, above).

20. Joel 3:*17a*: Yahweh's dwelling in Zion, His holy mountain. Fulfillment (per. 16), as in Isa. No. 16.

21. Joel 3:18a (1 v.): blessings of wine, milk, and rainfall. Fulfillment (per. 16): as in Ex. No. 49. For, "Linked with this judgment on the heathen is the restoration of Israel expressed in 3:18 in terms of those natural blessings which, after the locust and drought of the earlier chapters, would most readily conjure up a picture of happiness and prosperity."[30]

22. Joel *3:18b*: a fountain from the temple, to produce a stream watering the valley of Shittim (Heb., *acacias*), presumably the locality of Num 25:1, above the Dead Sea. Fulfillment (per. 16): the blessing later developed in Ezek 47:1–12, Zech 14:8, though Joel's could signify any desert area where acacias grow.[31]

23. Joel 3:*19a*, 21 (1 v.): Egypt to be desolate. Fulfillment (per. 16), corresponding to the curse that Zech 14:18–19 inflicts for nonobservance of the Feast of Tabernacles, which may thus be the immediate cause for Joel's condemnation. A more basic cause, however, is their having taken the lives of innocent Jews, whom God now vindicates: v. 21, "I will cleanse their blood that I have not cleansed." For "the desolation will wipe out all the wrong which they have done to the people of God, and which has hitherto remained unpunished,"[32] though the verse could, alternatively, refer to Israel made holy; see 3:17b, No. 7, above.

24. Joel 3:19b (1 v.): Edom also to be desolate. Fulfillment (per. 16): as above. But since God in Obad 15 (with Jer 12:17, 49:7; Ezek 25:12, 35:1) had already doomed Edom to permanent destruction in B.C. times, "Edom's judgment in the Day of the Lord refers more to the territory of Edom and its inhabitants than to the Edomite nation."[33] The desolate condition of the land to the south of the Dead Sea, at the very time of the miraculous fruitfulness of Israel to its north (v. 18, No. 23, above), will serve as a standing testimony to the reprehensibility of pride, violence, and unbrotherly malice (compare v. 19 with Obad 3, 10, 12).

25. Joel 3:20 (1 v.): "But Judah and Jesusalem shall abide for ever." Fulfillment (per. 18): the New Jerusalem, as in Ps. No. 30.

29. See Jer 25:26b, 30, on similar phraseology against the hosts of Gog.
30. NBC, p. 696.
31. See Cent., *Minor Prophets*, I:112, for discussion.
32. KD, I:232.
33. Bernard E. Northrup, "Joel's Concept of the Day of the Lord," unpublished Th.D. dissertation (Dallas Theological Seminary, May, 1961), p. 222.

AMOS

Although Amos was "a herdsman and a dresser of sycamore-fig trees" from Tekoa in SE Judah (Amos 1:1, 7:14), his recorded prophecies were directed to the northern kingdom of Israel. They consist of a brief series of messages that were delivered at the royal sanctuary of Beth-el (7:13), perhaps in but a single day. His times are those of Jeroboam II of Israel and of Uzziah in Judah, whose reigns overlapped from 790 to 753; but his prophecy comments on the fall of Gath (6:2) to Uzziah (II Chron 26:6), which occurred after the death of Amaziah in 767; and the prosperity and yet the corruption of the northern kingdom suggests a date of approximateiy 760 B.C., near the commencement, that is, of the more protracted ministry of Hosea.[1] The rugged morality and faith of Amos were appalled by the wanton luxuries and disregard for human values being displayed by the rulers of Ephraim; and his message consists of a cry for social justice, reinforced by predictive threats and promises of the intervention of God. His work is summarized by the plea in 5:15, "Hate the evil, and love the good, and establish justice in the gate: it may be that Yahweh . . . will be gracious unto the remnant of Joseph."

The Book of Amos falls into two basic parts: I. Messages of judgment, chs. 1–6; and II. Five visions of the wrath, and yet of the grace, of God, chs. 7–9—with a short biographical section (7:10–17) separating the third and fourth visions. Following his introduction, Amos' messages open with a series of oracles (1:3–2:5) that condemn the crimes of various nations that surrounded Samaria (predictions 2–11, below). His criticism even of the inhabitants of his own land (the sister kingdom of Judah to the south) for their disregard of the divine law on which they prided themselves (2:4–5) must have won Amos a responsive audience among the Ephraimites. But all this was but a prelude to his "zeroing in" on the transgressions of the northern kingdom. Similarly, his concluding visions —on the locusts, fire, wall and plumb line, summer fruit, and desolate sanctuary—proclaim destruction upon sinful Samaria. More than half the recorded predictions of Amos (47 out of 85 vv.) are devoted to foretelling this catastrophe. Yet 25 other topics for future fulfillment appear as well, so that prediction occupies 58% of the book's 146 verses.

Amos also has stern words for the leaders of the southern kingdom: "Woe to them that are at ease in Zion!" (6:1); but he terminates in 9:11–15 with a beautiful oracle of hope when "the tabernacle of David" will be restored in Jesus Christ, leading on both to the present-day church, with its converted Gentile members that are "called by Yahweh's name" (v. 12;

1. The prophet's own dating is "two years before the earthquake" (1:1; cf. Zech 14:5); but this event can no longer be pinpointed.

cf. Acts 15:15–19), and to that future-day kingdom, when "the plowman shall overtake the reaper" (v. 13).[2]

1. Amos 1:2; 2:6, 13–16; 3:2, 11–15; 4:1–3, 12; 5:1–3, 5b–6, 16–20; 6:7b–11, 14; 7:7–9a; 8:1–3, 7–10, 18; 9:1–3, 5, 8a (47 vv., fig.): "Yahweh will roar from Zion," a figure for punishment, so that "Carmel shall wither" (1:2). Because of their oppression and immorality, the men of Ephraim will be unable to save themselves (2:15). An enemy will plunder, and almost no one will escape (3:11–12). Among the troops, nine out of ten will fall (5:3). The pampered women of Samaria are to be led out through broken walls (4:1–3). The revelry of the nobility is to be brought to an end (6:7); and "the city" (presumably the capital, Samaria, v. 1) will be delivered up to death (vv. 8–9). In like manner, the major community of Beth-el, where Amos was preaching, is to come "to nought" (5:5), Heb. âwen, which is probably a play on words, involving Beth-el and its neighboring town, Beth-aven, Josh 7:2. Amos may speak literally of God's destruction of the sinful kingdom (9:8). He may employ a symbol: e.g., in his 4th vision (8:1–3), the basket of "summer fruit," Heb. qáyis, suggests the similar-sounding Heb. noun qēs, meaning "end," so that "the end is come upon My people Israel," with wailing and death; see above, p. 22. Or he may foretell Israel's doom through figures, as he speaks of the land's "trembling," "sinking" like a river, or being "darkened" (vv. 8–9); see above, p. 82. But the point is always the same: "Israel is fallen, she shall no more rise" (5:2, cf. 8:14), i.e. never again exist as a separate kingdom.[3]

The message of Amos is God-centered. The wailing of Ephraim occurs when God "passes through" (5:16–17); it is He who will "break out like fire in the house of Joseph" (v. 6); cf. His threat in 4:12, "Thus will I do unto thee, O Israel," which presumably constitutes a further reference to the "burning" of v. 11. Amos sums up the impending calamity in terms of "the day of Yahweh: it is darkness, and not light," 5:18, 20 (as in Isa 8:22).[4] In his 5th vision, Amos sees the Lord standing by the paganized altar of the golden calf at Beth-el, 9:1–3 (cf. 3:14), so that both it and its sanctuary fall and none can hide or escape; and in the 3rd vision, His standing by a wall "with a plumb line in His hand" reveals in symbol that "the sanctuaries of Israel shall be laid waste," 7:7–9. God is about to raise up "a nation" (unnamed, but clearly Assyria) to punish the whole northern kingdom, from Lebo-hamath southward, 6:14, i.e. the full territorial limits of Israel as attained under Jeroboam II (II K 14:25). Amos

2. For an analysis of liberalism's attempts to deny the authenticity, both of the Judean and of the more hopeful of the oracles of Amos, see G. L. Archer, *A Survey of OT Introduction*, p. 307.
3. Even for those who shared in Judah's decree of release, when it was issued by Cyrus in 538, there was no separate return from captivity.
4. See above, pp. 131–133.

warns his people, "Prepare to meet thy God," 4:12. Fulfillment (per. 7): as in I K. prophecy No. 25, the fall of Samaria to the Assyrians in 722 B.C.

2. Amos 1:3–5 (3 vv.): against Damascus, because of cruelties against the Israelites in Gilead, "Fire shall devour the palaces of Ben-hadad." The Syrians are to go captive, eastward, to Kir, the place from which they originally emigrated, 9:7. Fulfillment (per. 7): in 732 B.C. they suffered exile to this very locality, II K 16:9, when Rezin, the last king of Damascus, fell to Tiglath-pileser III of Assyria.

3. Amos 1:6–7 (2 vv.): the Philistine city of Gaza to be burned, in recompense for its ruthless slave-trading. Fulfillment (per. 7): it was captured and plundered by Tiglath-pileser in 734;[5] cf. Jer 25:20 and 47:5 on later destructions of Gaza.

4. Amos *1:8a:* the threat of God against another of the Philistine cities, "I will cut off the inhabitant from Ashdod"; c.f. Isa 14:28–31. Fulfillment (per. 7): this city became the primary object of the Assyrian attack directed by Sargon in 711 B.C.; and he boasted against its king, "I declared his images . . . as well as the inhabitants of his country as booty."[6] Cf. Jeremiah's later reference, 25:20, to "the remnant of Ashdod."

5. Amos *1:8b:* against Philistine Ashkelon, God says, "I will cut off him that holdeth the sceptre." Fulfillment (per. 7): at the time of Gath's opposition to Assyria (v. 6, No. 3, above) the ruler of Ashkelon, a certain Mitinti, revolted as well; and then, at Tiglath-pileser's successful advance in 734–733, he went insane and was succeeded by his son.[7] An actual *cutting off* of Ashkelon's ruler occurred when the king Sidqia joined Hezekiah's revolt of 701, only to be deported to Assyria.[8]

6. Amos 1:8c (1 v.): "I will turn My hand against Ekron, and the remnant of the Philistines shall perish." Fulfillment (per. 11): "After 165 B.C. the former Philistine cities regarded themselves as being Greek; the older elements in their population seem largely to have disappeared."[9] Then, specifically, in 148 Jonathan, brother of Judas Maccabeus, captured Ashdod and Ashkelon (I Macc 10:84–86); and Ekron was turned over to him by the Seleucid monarch Alexander Balas (v. 89). A final submission occurred in 146 when Jonathan burned and plundered Gaza (11:60–62).

7. Amos 1:9–10 (2 vv.): for its slave trade, "Fire shall devour the palaces of Tyre." Fulfillment (per. 7): Sennacherib claimed to have "overwhelmed Ushu, i.e. the mainland settlement of Tyre," in 701;[10] and Ashur-

---

5. ANET, p. 283; cf. IDB, II:357.
6. ANET, p. 286.
7. Ibid., p. 283.
8. Ibid., p. 287.
9. H. L. Ellison, *Ezekiel: The Man and His Message,* p. 101.
10. ANET, p. 287.

banipal reduced the entire city in 663: "I made scarce their food supply and forced them to submit to my yoke."[11] The island fortress was stormed by Alexander of Macedon in 332, but the nearer (Assyrian) accomplishment appears to be the more likely for this passage.

8. Amos 1:11–12 (2 vv.): divine condemnation upon Edom, for failing in brotherly pity, "I will send a fire upon [the district of] Teman and . . . [the city of] Bozrah." The nearest fulfillment (per. 7) is associated with the Assyrian invasions, owing to Edomite revolts in 711 and 701 B.C.;[12] see also Obad 1.

9. Amos 1:13–15 (3 vv.): Ammon to suffer for its aggressive acts against Israelites in Gilead; v. 14, its capital city of Rabbah to fall in the fire of battle, and v. 15, the Ammonite king (or perhaps the national god, "Milcom") and his leaders to go into captivity. These forecasts are then repeated in Jer 49:3 (see under 9:26d). Fulfillment (per. 8): Ammon appears to have escaped the wrath of 8th-century Assyria; and, like Moab, it was pro-Chaldean in 598, II K 24:2. Yet it thereafter plotted against Babylon, Jer 27:3; and while Ammon survived Judah's fall in 586 (40:14), "From this point on Ammon's revolt against Babylon was open and permanent." The once Israelite and then Moabite town of Heshbon is described as Ammonite in Jer 49:3; but since at the time of Moab's fall it is foreseen as already occupied by the Chaldean enemy (48:2, 45), Ammon's fall must have slightly preceded Moab's in Nebuchadrezzar's 582–581 campaign, namely, "in or about 582."[13]

10. Amos 2:1–3 (3 vv.): for foul acts against Edom, "Moab shall die with tumult, with shouting." Fulfillment (per. 7): in the 715 campaign of Sargon of Assyria, "To reach Arabia he swept through the length of Moab from the north, devastating and plundering as he advanced."[14]

11. Amos 2:4–5, 6:1a, 9:11b (2 vv.): Judah is to be punished for its rejection of the law of Yahweh, 2:4; and the palaces of Jerusalem are to be burned, v. 5, so the event concerned cannot be Sennacherib's mere siege of the city in 701. 9:11 then foresees the line of David as fallen and his "house" reduced to the status of a booth (ASV, tabernacle). Fulfillment (per. 7): as in Lev. No. 33, the final fall of Judah to the Babylonians in 586.

12. Amos 4:4–5, 5:22c (2 vv., typ.): peace offerings. Fulfillment (pers. 13 and 16): as in Lev. No. 5.

13. Amos 5:5a, 11, 27; 6:1b, 7a; 7:11b; 9:9a (6 vv.): 5:5 contains a play on words, *gilgāl gālō yigle,* "Gilgal shall surely go into captivity"; and v. 11, correspondingly, states that Israel is not to live in the houses

---

11. Ibid., p. 295.
12. IDB, II:26; cf. ANET, p. 287.
13. H. L. Ginsberg, "Judah and the Transjordan States from 734 to 582 B.C.E.," *Alexander Marx Jubilee Volume,* p. 368.
14. H. C. Leupold, *Exposition of Isaiah,* I:274.

they have built or to drink the wine of the vineyards they have planted. Instead, v. 27, Ephraim is to "go into captivity beyond Damascus"; cf. the secondhand citation of this prediction by Amaziah the priest in 7:11. Samaria's luxury-loving leaders will be among the first to go, 6:1, 7; and God "will sift the house of Israel among the nations," 9:9. Fulfillment (per. 7): as in Hos. No. 16 (4:19), the deportation of the Ephraimites in 722 B.C., to Assyria and beyond.

14. Amos 5:22a (1 v., typ.): burnt offering. Fulfillment (per. 13): as in Lev. No. 3.

15. Amos *5:22b, 25b* (typ.): meal offering. Fulfillment (per. 13): as in Lev. No. 4.

16. Amos 5:25a (1 v., typ.): sacrifice. Fulfillment (per. 13): as in Lev. No. 2.

17. Amos *7:9b, 11a*: that the house of Jeroboam II is to fall by the sword, 7:9. Amos' prediction was then misquoted—or, "suitably modified," so as to arouse governmental action (!)[15]—by Amaziah the high priest of Beth-el, as purportedly saying that Jeroboam himself would be murdered, v. 11.[16] Fulfillment (per. 7) was achieved, as in Hos. No. 1 (1:4a), by the slaying of Jeroboam's son Zechariah, the last of the dynasty of Jehu, in 752 B.C.

18. Amos 7:16–17a (2 vv.): the prophet's personal threat against the priest Amaziah (see No. 17, preceding), that his wife would be reduced to harlotry, his children destroyed by the sword, and his land confiscated. No record exists to document the fulfillment; but it would presumably have occurred at the fall of Israel to the Assyrians in 722 (see No. 1, above), or about 38 years after Amos' forecast (per. 7).

19. Amos *7:17b*: a further word, against the priest Amaziah himself, that he would die in an "unclean" land, i.e. on foreign soil; cf. Hos 9:3. Probable fulfillment (per. 7): his death in Assyria, as a part of the 722 deportation (see No. 13, above).

20. Amos 8:5 (1 v., typ.): sabbath. Fulfillment (per. 13): as in Ex. No. 41.

21. Amos 9:4, 10 (2 vv.): in their impending exile, "All the sinners of My people shall die by the sword," v. 10, as contrasted with the elect, who will experience divine protection, v. 9b (No. 22, following). Fulfillment (per. 8): as in Lev. No. 35, Israel's calamities in the exile.

22. Amos *9:8b, 9b:* a divine limitation, in connection with the threatened desolation of Samaria in v. 8a (No. 1, above), ". . . save that I will not utterly destroy the house of Jacob," v. 8b; cf. v. 9, that though He sift Israel among the nations, "yet shall not the least kernel fall upon

15. Ellison, *The Prophets of Israel*, p. 90.
16. Oxtoby quotes this verse as an example of the nonfulfillment of prophecy! *Prediction and Fulfillment in the Bible*, p. 83.

the earth." Fulfillment (per. 8): as in Lev. No. 37, God's protection for an elect remnant[17] during the exile, as opposed to the fate of the sinners, v. 10 (No. 21, preceding).

23. Amos 9:11 (1 v., fig.): "I will raise up the tabernacle [lit., "booth," stressing its humble estate; see under 2:4, No. 11, above] of David . . . I will build it as in the days of old." Fulfillment (per. 13): as in II Sam. No. 11, the revival of the line of David in the Person of Jesus Christ. The reference must be to His first coming; for Acts 15:16 emphasizes that it is this event which enables the Gentiles, from the apostolic period onward, to seek God.

24. Amos 9:12 (1 v.): the effect of the coming of Christ (v. 11, No. 23, preceding) in respect to "all the nations that are called by My name." The statement that God's name is, lit., *called upon* the Gentiles means that He possesses them; cf. Dt 28:10, II Sam 12:22. The prophecy, moreover, is quoted in Acts 15:17 to explain why Gentile Christians need not be circumcised, so it cannot refer to the times prior to the NT, when circumcision was still enforced. Yet "after these things" (Acts 15:16, i.e. the exile and the preservation of Amos 9:9–10, No. 21–22, above), and after Christ's incarnation (Amos 9:11, No. 23, above), came the engrafting of uncircumcised Gentiles into the church, to which Acts 15 applies the OT passage, so it cannot refer to times yet future. The first line of Amos 9:12 should probably be read, not as in the MT, *yīr'shū eth sh'ērīth edhōm*, "they may possess the remnant of Edom," but as indicated by the NT, *yidhr'shū ōthī sh'ērīth ādhām*, "they may seek Me, i.e. the remnant of mankind."[18] But even if not, the basic thought remains unaltered, of God's name being called upon a remnant of the Gentiles.[19] Fulfillment (per. 14): as in Gen. No. 19, the engrafting of Gentiles into the Israel that is the church.

25. Amos 9:13–14 (2 vv.): God's promise, v. 14, "I will bring back the captivity [= restore the fortunes[20]] of My people Israel, and they shall build the waste cities; they shall also make gardens and eat the fruit of them"—a concept the exact opposite of that in 5:11 (see under 5:5a, No. 13, above), in which others were foreseen as reaping the results of Israel's labors. But now, 9:13, will come unprecedented harvests and grape gatherings. Fulfillment (per. 16): as in Ex. No. 49, millennial prosperity.

17. C. H. Patterson, *The Philosophy of the OT*, p. 179, stresses that Amos' remnant concept is achieved in "a few individuals" who would "not be sufficient" to reestablish the northern nation (cf. 312), as contrasted, e.g., with Isaiah's broader hope for the remnant of southern Judah.

18. As argued by Allan A. MacRae, "The Scientific Approach to the OT," BS, 110 (1953), 315.

19. KD, I:334. The MT would then read that David's kingdom (Christ and His church) would possess the remnant, either of Edom or of mankind.

20. See above, p. 17.

26. Amos 9:15 (1 v.): Israel to be so established as never again to be plucked up. Fulfillment (per. 18): as in II Sam. No. 14, the permanence of the New Jerusalem.

OBADIAH

Though a dozen OT figures bear the name Obadiah, none of these can be equated with the fourth of the minor prophets, who thus remains unknown. His home, apparently, lay in the southern kingdom of Judah, in which his interest centers (Obad 12, 17). Obadiah's and Joel's dates are the least clear of the OT prophets. Obadiah belongs to a time of disaster for Judah, when "foreigners carried away his substance and cast lots upon Jerusalem" (v. 11), though Keil observes that "no carrying away of the nation *as such* had taken place at that time, as afterwards occurred at the destruction of the kingdoms of Israel and Judah."[1] Suggested placement for the book ranges from the days of Jehoram (848–841),[2] through the period of Jerusalem's fall in 586,[3] and on into postexilic times.[4] Yet Obad 1–6, 9, appears to be quoted in Jer 49:9–10, 14–16, 22,[5] which dates in turn to 604 B.C.; and Obadiah's expressions about Ephraim (Obad 19) imply a time before the fall of Samaria, in 722, when northern Israel was hostile toward the southern kingdom. Ephraim's attempt to "make a breach" in Judah (Isa 7:6) and the simultaneous attacks and taking of captives by Edom (II Chron 28:17) and the Philistines (v. 18, as related to Obad 19) favor a date near 735 B.C., as proposed by John Davis[6] and Raven.[7] If the book, however, be assigned to a later point, this affects only its first prophecy (vv. 1–4).

Obadiah has 21 verses, which makes it the shortest book in the OT. It stresses divine punishment that must come upon Edom for its violence and pride; yet it contains 10 distinct prophecies that extend progressively from contemporaneous, divided-kingdom times (per. 7), through the Persian (9) and Maccabean periods (11), and on into God's future

1. *Minor Prophets*, I:373: see A. F. Kirkpatrick, *The Doctrine of the Prophets*, pp. 38–39.
2. Gleason L. Archer, *A Survey of OT Introduction*, p. 288, per II Chron 21:16–17, which speaks of an attack that included Philistines and Arabians. He holds it "probable that the Edomites cooperated," though this is not stated.
3. G. Fohrer, *Introduction to the OT*, pp. 439–440, and other critical scholars.
4. R. H. Pfeiffer, *Introduction to the OT*, p. 586, assigns most of Obadiah to 460 B.C.
5. See E. J. Young, *An Introduction to the OT*, p. 277, and Kirkpatrick, op. cit., pp. 35–38.
6. *A Dictionary of the Bible*, p. 528.
7. *OT Introduction*, p. 222.

kingdom (16); cf. his conclusion as a key passage, "and the kingdom shall be Yahweh's," v. 21. Its predictions thus average one for almost every two verses, which is the highest frequency to be found in Scripture. The prophecies occur, moreover, in 17 out of the total of 21 verses, or in 81% of the whole, so that, second only to Zephaniah, Obadiah becomes the most highly predictive book in the entire Bible.

1. Obad 1–4 (4 vv.): Edom to be brought down—"I have made thee small among the nations" and despised. Fulfillment (per. 7): as in Amos No. 8 (1:11), Assyrian attacks in 711 and 701 B.C., after which Edomite power suffered a steady decline.[8] Proposals for later accomplishment include the campaign of 552, in which Nabunaid of Babylon "captured the city of Tema' in Adummu, the Biblical Edom, put the king to death, and built himself a palace"[9] (see Jer 9:26c, though Tema' is rather far removed from OT Edom), or the Arabian attacks of the following decades (see next).

2. Obad 5–10, 15–16 (8 vv.): Edom "cut off for ever," with no gleanings left, 5–6; treated cruelly and with mockery, just as they treated Judah, "for the day of Yahweh is near" (as it is, indeed, "upon all nations"), 15–16; driven out by her former allies, 7; and with the wise and the mighty dismayed, "that every one may be cut off from the mount of Esau," 8–9. Fulfillment (per. 9): by about 500 B.C. "the Arab tribes, formerly Edom's allies, completely expelled the Edomites from their original lands."[10] Thus Ezion-geber at the tip of the Gulf of Aqaba, which was under Edomite rule in 600, exhibits Arab names in the 5th century; and Albright speaks of the Edomite displacement to southern Judah by 500.[11] Keil maintains that "the threatened devastation of the land of Edom was brought about by the Chaldeans, as is clear from Mal 1:3";[12] but the latter verse, dating to about 430, shows simply that by that time Edom's land had been turned into its prophesied desolation, without reference to the human instrumentality. Jer 12:15, moreover (*q.v.*), requires a return of the Edomites, after a Babylonian captivity, and yet prior to the final desolation predicted by Obadiah.

3. Obad 17 (1 v.): "But in mount Zion there shall be those that escape . . . and the house of Jacob shall possess their possessions," i.e. their own land.[13] Fulfillment (per. 9): the return from Babylonian exile in 537 B.C., as in Dt. No. 43. The verse is quoted in reference to later times in Joel 2:32.

4. Obad *17b*: *w'hāyā qōdhesh*, "and it [Mount Zion] shall be a holy

8. *IDB*, II:26.
9. W. O. E. Oesterly, *A History of Israel*, II:15.
10. IB, VI:858.
11. In H. C. Alleman and E. E. Flack, *OT Commentary*, p. 167.
12. *Jer.*, II:250.
13. NBD, p. 712; Keil favors their taking the possessions of others, op. cit., I:368.

place = temple."[14] Fulfillment (per. 9): the temple, rededicated in 515 B.C., Ezra 6:15–16, its purpose being that of a "sanctuary,"[15] of protection. The ASV reading, "it shall be holy," has a similar import, of freedom from profanation (cf. Joel 3:17b, under Joel No. 7).

5. Obad *18a:* "The house of Jacob and the house of Joseph" are to return, a prophecy which involves ex-captives of both Judah and Israel. Fulfillment (per. 9): as in Hos. No. 9 (2:15); representatives of all 12 tribes, present in 515 and later, Ezra 6:17, 8:35.

6. Obad 18b, *19a,* 20, 21a (3 vv.): the Jews, to "devour" Edom; 20, "The captives[16] of this host of the children of Israel,[17] that are among the Canaanites, even unto Zarephath [ASVmg],[18] and the captives of Jerusalem, that are in Sepharad, shall possess the cities of the South," Heb., Negeb; "and saviors shall come up on mount Zion to judge the mount of Esau." The *captives* may be identified from II Chron 28:17–18 and Joel 3:2–6 (see under 3:4a, No. 14) as those taken by Edom, and also the Philistines and Phoenicians, in 735. Zarephath lay between Tyre and Sidon; it is seemingly styled the territory of *the Canaanites* because the latter had been driven from most of central Palestine by this time; see Mt 15:21–22. *Sepharad,* apparently Sardis, the capital of Lydia in Asia Minor, is known to have had a Jewish colony in 455 B.C.,[19] which accords with the statement by Obadiah's contemporary Joel (3:6) on "children of Jerusalem sold unto Grecians and removed far from their border." Fulfillment (per. 11): as in Gen. No. 50 after the Edomites had been driven from their land by the Arabs and had occupied the Negeb of Judah.[20] The *saviors* (plu.) are thus human (see Jd 2:16), Judas and his nephew John Hyrcanus, rather than the Messiah.

14. KB, p. 828b, for this passage.
15. KD, loc. cit.
16. See vv. 11, 14. The term "host" suggests a group who attempted to resist the attack by the Edomites and the others and were carried captive, II Chron 28:17.
17. *Israel* is equivalent to Jacob and seems therefore to represent the captives from Judah (see No. 5, above, where Judah is called *Jacob*) and not some group of prisoners from "Joseph" (N. Israel, as often claimed); see KD, I:372.
18. The reading of the ASV text (cf. also the 1st mg), "The captives of this host . . . shall possess even unto Zarephath, and the captives of Jerusalem shall possess the cities of the South," involves the problem that even under the farthest expansion of Aristobulus I (105–104) into Galilee and Iturea, in the far north, Israel seems never to have occupied Zarephath or the Phoenician coast. "The RV 2nd mg avoids the difficulty by regarding *the cities of the south* (at the end of the v.) as the destined possession of both groups of captives, defining the first as those *which are* among *the Canaanites even unto Zarephath,*" WC, *Micah,* etc., p. 84.
19. IB, VI:867.
20. The term "mount of Esau," as applied in vv. 19, 21, would therefore designate the Edomite people rather than their original trans-Arabah territory (though cf. vv. 8–9), even as the term "mount" Seir had itself become a name for all within the borders of Edom (Gen 36:9; cf. Dt 2:1, Josh 15:10, II Chron 23:20 where *Seir* is interchangeable with *Mount Seir,* and W. J. Farley, *The Progress of Prophecy,* p. 205). The *mount of Esau* thus identifies the Idumaeans, paralleling *mount Zion* for the Jews.

7. Obad *19b*: "They of the lowland [Heb., Shephelah, Judah's western piedmont] shall possess the Philistines," who collaborated with the Edomites, Amos 1:6, and had invaded this very territory in 735, II Chron 28:18. Fulfillment (per. 11): as in Amos No. 6; 164 and 148–146 B.C. (see No. 9, below).

8. Obad 19c (1 v.): the subject is indefinite, presumably Jews other than those already mentioned as being of the Negeb and the Shephelah,[21] to "possess the field of Ephraim and the field of Samaria." Fulfillment (per. 11, to accord with the three other parts of the v.): Jonathan received three districts of Samaria in 153 B.C., I Macc 10:38; and his nephew John Hyrcanus took the city in 128, destroyed the Samaritans' temple on Mount Gerizim, and later demolished the city.

9. Obad *19d*: Benjamin to occupy Gilead. Fulfillment (per. 11). Prophecies 6–9 are summarized in IB, VI:866, as follows: "These conquests were accomplished in the second century B.C., when northern Judah and Benjamin were the nucleus from which the Jews under the Maccabees pressed out into the areas indicated by the verse." Specifically, Judas conquered in Gilead, defending Jewish settlers there, I Macc 5:6, 24–54, 164 B.C.; and John Hyrcanus (d. 105) then gained control of most of Transjordan, except for a small section immediately surrounding Ammon-Philadelphia.[22]

10. Obad *21b:* "The kingdom shall be Yahweh's." Fulfillment (per. 16): the future Messianic kingdom, as in Gen. No. 68 (49:10b). This climax to the progressive prophecies of Obadiah appears, almost abruptly; as explained by Lancaster, "The prophet seems for a moment to be transported beyond the sphere of rivalry and cruelty and suffering, and to realize that all that has been happening, and all the future consequences of it, will in due time lead on to the establishment of the kingdom of the Lord."[23]

21. KD, I:371.
22. G. E. Wright and F. V. Filson, *The Westminster Historical Atlas to the Bible,* pp. 79–81; see plate XII:A, p. 80. So also Y. Aharoni and M. Avi-Yonah, *The Macmillan Bible Atlas*, map 208, p. 130.
23. Camb., *Obad-Jonah*, p. 35.

JONAH

Jonah the son of Amittai (Jonah 1:1) was a prophet of Gath-hepher, a small town located 3 miles NE of Nazareth, in the kingdom of northern Israel. His historical existence is validated by II Kings (14:25), which speaks of his nationalistic zeal in encouraging Jeroboam II (793–753) to "restore the border of Israel" after the Aramean and Assyrian depredations of the 9th century B.C. Yet the prophetic activities whose record is preserved in his book concern a brief, and seemingly subsequent, mission of Jonah, outside the border of Israel, to Assyrian Nineveh (Jonah 1:2, 3:2). It is, in fact, the prophet's very resistance against such a ministry to his nation's former enemy (cf. 1:3, 4:1–2), and the ridiculous straits, both physical (1:15, 17) and psychological (4:3–5, 9), to which his bigoted nationalism drove him, that most effectively sets forth the real teaching of the book: the contrasting love that moves God for those who are far from Himself. Yahweh's question, with which the book abruptly closes (4:11), thus serves as its key verse, "Should not I have regard for Nineveh, that great city?" Though this divine query stands without answer, and the prophet's reaction remains unrecorded, it is clear that "Jonah would not have written so frank and self-humiliating a confession of his sin if he had not been sincerely repentant and had not hoped to preserve and save others from similar bigotry."[1]

The four chapters of Jonah outline successive stages to the prophet's Assyrian ministry: ch. 1, Jonah and the storm, his disobedience to the "foreign missionary call" and its disastrous results; ch. 2, Jonah and the fish, his divine rescue from drowning[2] and his resultant prayer of thanksgiving while inside this creature; ch. 3, Jonah's preaching in Nineveh of repentance, or of destruction in 40 days; and ch. 4, Jonah's reaction to God's sparing of the Ninevites. The miraculous character of Jonah's deliverance by means of the fish and of the "un-Assyrian-like" repentance of the Ninevites (cf. Isa 10:7–15, 36:18–20) has provoked widespread criticism; and some would deny the historicity of the book altogether, treating it as mere parable or literary fiction. Yet the context in the OT lends no support to such theories; and Mt 12:39–41 in the NT cites both these incidents in such a way that H. S. Gehman concludes, "While it is conceivable that the words of Christ regarding Jonah in the belly of the fish and at Nineveh do not imply his belief in the events, it is highly probable that they do, especially since Jonah was a real person."[3] Further confirmation arises from Assyria's own contemporary chronicles, which record a national state of mind, at this very point, which was without equal before or after: "The total eclipse of the sun in the year 763 was regarded as a portent, a sign of celestial wrath. Assur, the home of Assyria's most ancient traditions, revolted and was joined by other cities. The king was probably murdered. For six years civil war raged, while pestilence devastated the

1. Th. Laetsch, *Bible Commentary: The Minor Prophets*, p. 243.
2. The figure of "the belly of *sheol* [= the *grave*]" in 2:3 describes Jonah's near-death in the depths of the ocean (vv. 5–6a) and must not be confused with "the fish's belly" (v. 1, a different word in Heb.), at which point Jonah was already looking back upon his escape (v. 3) with thanksgiving (v. 9); cf. v. 7. "The fish appears as a savior," C. Kuhl, *The Prophets of Israel*, p. 174.
3. *The Westminster Dictionary of the Bible*, p. 324.

land."[4] That Jonah's mission to Nineveh may have been providentially timed to about 760 B.C. appears quite reasonable. The Book of Jonah centers in the prophecy: "Yet forty days and Nineveh shall be destroyed," 3:3. But paradoxically, this oracle does not enter into the analysis of Jonah's predictive fulfillments, since it was conditional in nature and, with the repentance of the Ninevites (vv. 5–8), was not achieved at that time (v. 10; cf. v. 9).[5] The predictions of Jonah consist rather of two brief personal oracles and two allusions to matters that serve as regular types of Jesus Christ. The four of them are limited to the first two chapters of the book; and they involve only 5 out of the book's 48 verses, or some 10% of the whole. This is the lowest figure for any of the OT prophets and is due primarily to the literary character of the volume, that of preaching through a historical narrative rather than through directly prophetic messages. The Lord Jesus later utilized the period of Jonah's sojourn in the fish to *illustrate* His own three days in the grave (Mt 12:40); but He thereby neither constitutes the prophet as a type of Himself nor suggests that this had been God's original intent in decreeing Jonah's miraculous experience.[6]

1. Jonah 1:12 (1 v.): the prophet's instructions to the sailors, "Cast me into the sea; so shall the sea be calm unto you." Fulfillment (per. 7): they did, and the storm ceased raging, v. 15.

2. Jonah 1:16, 2:9 (2 vv., typ.): sacrifice. Fulfillment (per. 13): as in Lev. prophecy No. 2.

3. Jonah 2:4a (1 v.): Jonah had been in despair (v. 4) at the prospect of drowning (vv. 3, 5); but when it appeared that God was rescuing him through the means of his being swallowed by the fish,[7] he stated with confidence, "Yet I will look toward Thy holy temple." Fulfillment (per. 7): the prophet's subsequent worship at the temple is not confirmed in so many words; but that he did perform such worship may legitimately be inferred: on the basis of his promise to sacrifice and pay vows (2:9), on the basis of his known regaining of land (presumably Palestine), from which he only later set out for Nineveh (2:10, 3:1), and on the basis of his final

4. H. R. Hall, *The Ancient History of the Near East,* pp. 461–462.
5. See above, p. 63.
6. As John Davison notes in his *Discourses on Prophecy,* p. 267, "The book of Jonah contains no prediction of a direct Christian import." He then proceeds to explain, "The whole import of Jonah's mission partakes of the Christian character. For we see that he is sent to exemplify the grant of divine mercy to a great heathen city, and that the repentance of the Ninevites through his mission brings them to know 'a gracious God, and merciful.' . . . But in this the evangelical sense was clear. It needed not a future time to interpret it," pp. 275–276. Yet further afield is Feinberg's comment, *Premillennialism or Amillennialism?* pp. 54–55, "Jonah typifies the life history of the nation of Israel," e.g., cast out of Palestine and then regathered; and, he adds, "She will preach God's message to the nations in the [millennial] kingdom."
7. See above, introduction to Jonah, note 2.

return to Israel, and residence there, a probability that is vouchsafed by the very existence of his book.

4. Jonah 2:4*b*, 7 (1 v., typ.): the temple. Fulfillment (per. 13): as in Ex. No. 55.

MICAH

From his identification as a Morasthite (Mic 1:1), the prophet Micah would appear to have made his home in the country town of Moresheth-gath (v. 14) in SW Judah. His ministry touched upon the reigns of three Judean monarchs: Jothan (739–736), Ahaz (to 728), and Hezekiah (to 697). But while Mic 1:8 describes the prophet's reaction to the fall of Samaria in 722, the remainder of the chapter only predicts Assyria's devastation of Judah; and the accession of Sennacherib in 705 and his great Judean invasion of 701 do not appear to have fallen within Micah's recorded experiences. A suggested dating for the prophet is therefore 739–710 B.C. The Book of Micah includes divine revelations which this servant of God "saw concerning Samaria and Jerusalem" (1:1). Yet his interest centers in the latter; the termination of the former is recorded at 1:8; and by the time of 3:1, 9, "Jacob" and "Israel" seem to have become equivalent to Judah only; cf. 5:3, 7, 8. Micah's career thus presents correspondence, in both time and space, with the first half of Isaiah's ministry; and a number of verbal parallels between the writings of the two men[1] suggest some degree of personal contact. Yet in contrast to Isaiah's status as "the princely prophet," in the capital city of Jerusalem, Micah's viewpoint remains that of the countryman, and of the poor and lowly (cf. 6:12): he cries for social justice—like Amos (cf. Amos 5:24)—and pleads for steadfast love—like Hosea (cf. Hos 6:6). A key verse, therefore, that combines all these elements, and stands indeed as one of the greatest in all of Scripture, appears in Mi 6:8, "He hath showed thee, O man, what is good; and what doth Yahweh require of thee, but to do justly, and to love kindness, and to walk humbly with thy God?"

Micah's volume may be roughly divided between prophecies of condemnation, chs. 1–3 (though 2:12–13 forms a short redemptive interlude),[2] and prophecies of hope, chs. 4–7 (though 6–7:6 continues from 1:2–4 the theme of God's "lawsuit" against Judah).[3] Within the latter appear

1. Cent, *Minor Prophets*, I:220, exhibits a list of 15 such. Most striking are the prophecies of Mi 4:1–3 (No. 10–15, below), which reproduce Isa 2:2–4.
2. Ibid., I:238, "We may treat these two vv. as a ray of sunlight streaming for a moment through the cloudy and dark day of denunciation. . . ."
3. Liberal criticism often questions the authenticity of Micah's more hopeful oracles, or his miraculously long-ranged reference to Babylon in 4:10; but cf. their defense in G. L. Archer, *A Survey of OT Introduction*, p. 313.

two noteworthy examples of progressive prediction: the series of prophecies extending from 4:9 to 5:9, and that from 6:14 to 7:17.[4] Micah's separate forecasts total 40 and are found scattered throughout his 7 chapters. They involve 73 verses out of the 105 that make up the book, or some 70%. Yet more than a quarter of these (19 vv.) concentrate on the single threatening subject of Sennacherib's attack in 701 B.C. (No. 3, below).

1. Mi 1:3–7, 9a (5 vv., fig): "Yahweh will come down [from heaven] . . . and the mountains shall be melted," vv. 3–4. This figure is based on the phenomena that occurred at Mount Sinai in the Mosaic period (Ex 19:18, Jd 5:4),[5] and it thus portrays God's coming in power and action. Some would suggest an eschatological activity,[6] but this sort of terminology may be more generally "symbolic of disaster and devastation."[7] Cf. Amos 8:8–10, where convulsions in nature serve as figurative descriptions of the calamity of 722 B.C. Mi 1:5 explains that "for the transgression of Jacob is all this," and vv. 6–7 make it clear that the forecast concerns the total destruction of Samaria and its images. The offerings to these images, designated as "her hires [of spiritual prostitution]," v. 7, are to be plundered and used for idol worship elsewhere (i.e. in Assyria). "Her wounds are incurable," v. 9. Fulfillment (per. 7): as in I K. prophecy No. 25, the fall of the northern kingdom in 722.

2. Mi 1:8 (1 v., sym.): Micah states that he will go stripped, not simply in mourning, but probably also dramatically to portray Samaria's going into captivity;[8] cf. a similarly predictive object lesson performed by Isaiah in 711 (Isa 20:2–4), some 25 years later, to symbolize a deportation for Egypt. Fulfillment (per. 7): as in Hos. No. 16, the exile of N. Israel to Assyria in 722.

3. Mi 1:9b–15; 2:1, 3–5, 7; 3:4–7; 6:9, 14–15 (19 vv.): in 1:5 the prophet had spoken of the sins of Judah as well as of Samaria; so here the anticipation of punishment moves onward to the southern kingdom and foresees an attack "unto the gate of Jerusalem," vv. 9, 12. A series of threats follows, some involving plays on words in the Heb., against the towns neighboring upon Micah's native Moresheth-gath in the SW Shephelah (piedmont) region of Judah: v. 10, mourning in Beth-le-aphrah; v. 11, Shaphir taken captive, and Zaanan unable to march out, or Bethezel to give help; v. 12, grief in Maroth; v. 13, Lachish mustered to warfare; v. 14, Moresheth-gath itself taken captive, with no help to be had from Achzib; and v. 15, a possessor (the Assyrian invader, Sennacherib)

4. See above, pp. 129–130.
5. See above, pp. 20, 83.
6. IB, VI:902.
7. Th. Laetsch, *Bible Commentary: The Minor Prophets*, p. 246; cf. the inclusion in Amos 4:13 of His "treading upon the high places of the earth" as one in a series of generalized divine attributes.
8. KD, *Minor Prophets*, I:429–430.

coming to Mareshah, and refugees fleeing to Adullam. The prophet may even have completed such a geographical circuit in his preaching.[9] In ch. 2 he addresses the sinners among his people: "Woe to them," v. 1; "this family" (the nation, Judah) is to suffer humiliation, v. 3, and be "utterly ruined," v. 4. "The rebellious" (the Assyrians[10]) will seize their fields, v. 5; and it will be God's doings, v. 7. In 3:4 Micah says, "Then [at the time, presumably, of the calamities noted in 2:3 ff.[11]] shall they cry unto Yahweh" but receive no answer; it will be a black day, vv. 6–7, in which the optimistic messages of the false prophets will be discredited. 6:9 speaks of a "rod, appointed" by God; cf. Isaiah's similar prediction about Assyria (Isa 10:5), and vv. 14–15, of the accompanying losses of crops and property to the invaders; cf. Isaiah's reference to the interruption of Judah's agricultural cycle caused by the presence of Sennacherib (Isa 37:30). Fulfillment (per. 7): probably as in Isa. No. 18, the advance of Sennacherib against Judah in 701 B.C.,[12] though some prefer to think of the earlier campaign of Sargon against the Philistine Ashdod in 711, when the Assyrian did call himself the "subjugator of the land of Judah."[13]

4. Mi 1:16, 2:10 (2 vv. fig.): in 1:16 Micah addresses his desolated land (see No. 3, preceding), which he personifies, saying, "The children are gone into captivity from thee." 2:10 seems to be directed to the false prophets of v. 6 (cf. v. 11), who had claimed that Sennacherib's invasion of 701 could not come to pass, "Arise and depart for this [Judean land] is not [to be] your resting place." Fulfillment (per. 7): the Assyrian deportation, which Sennacherib claimed to have totaled more than 200,000 out of Judah's population; cf. II K 18:13 and the discussion under Isa 7:19.

5. Mi 2:12 (1 v.): the general gloom of Mi 1–3 is relieved by a ray of divine hope,[14] "I will surely assemble, O Jacob, all of thee; I will surely gather the remnant of Israel." This last phrase (though *the remnant* is still large enough to "make great noise by reason of the multitude," v. 12b) helps to define the *all of Jacob* of v. 12a. It is "not that every captive in Babylon will return. "All" means, rather, both Israel and Judah. God is saying that those desiring to return, whether originally from Israel or Judah, will be gathered together as one group."[15] Fulfillment (per. 9): as in Hos No. 9, the regathering of Israel, both N. and S. (cf. the use of "Jacob and Israel" in 1:5), to Palestine "under the edicts of Cyrus and

9. This circuit does not seem to refer to the actual course of one of Sennacherib's attacks (as does the listing of towns north of Jerusalem in Isa 10:28–32, a prediction that was uttered three or four years after this of Micah), but simply to the disasters that would come upon Micah's area in the course of the invasion.

10. ICC, p. 58.

11. Less likely is Cheyne's suggestion, Camb, p. 31, that this adverb refers back to a prophecy of doom not included in the present book of Micah.

12. Laetsch, op. cit., p. 252; BBC, V:196.

13. Cent, I:227; IB, VI:907.

14. See above, note 2.

15. BBC, V:206.

Artaxerxes" from 538 B.C. onward.[16] For 2:12 follows Micah's prediction of the exile in v. 10 (No. 4, preceding), and this link suggests the Persian period rather than that of the yet future rapture in v. 13 (No. 7, below): see above, p. 111.

6. Mi 2:13a (1 v., fig.): Micah continues his message of hope, "The Breaker [of restraints upon His people; see v. 13b, following] is gone up before them . . . their king is passed on before them, and Yahweh at the head of them." The Breaker seems to be equivalent to their king,[17] "a conqueror, who in the light of other prophecies can be no other than the Messiah."[18] Fulfillment (per. 15): as in Ps. prophecy No. 5, the second coming of Christ.[19]

7. Mi 2:13b (fig.): at the Messiah's coming (v. 13a, No. 6, preceding), He "goes up before them; they have broken forth and passed on to the gate and are gone out thereat." Like a flock, pictured in an enclosure, they will "rush (LXX) through the openings made for them . . . homeward to their own fold."[20] Fulfillment (per. 15): as in Hos. No. 27, the rapture of the church (cf. Joel No. 10) so as to follow Christ's progress on earth, and specifically to go in and go out at the gates of Jerusalem.[21]

8. Mi 3:12a; 4:9, 5:10–11, 14b; 6:16; 7:4, 8a (7 vv.): that Zion is to be plowed like a field, 3:12. This forecast by Micah is quoted in Jer 26:18–19, which adds that as a result King Hezekiah "entreated the favor of Yahweh, and Yahweh repented Him of the evil which He had pronounced against them." Yet the contrition of this pious monarch seems only to have postponed the accomplishment of the threat, and not annulled it. As Keil observes, "There is nothing in the addresses . . . to indicate that Micah uttered his threats conditionally."[22] Mi 4:9 foresees a day for Judah when her king will be no more, and her counselor[23] perished.[24] 5:10–11, 14, states that God will destroy the armed forces of Israel and the cities "in that day." This last expression may refer back to 4:9, or it may stand simply as a device for introducing a fresh trait into Micah's prophecies of the future.[25] Since he tells Judah, "all thy strongholds" are to fall, v. 11, the prediction cannot be limited to Sennacherib's depredations in 701. 6:16 states that Judah is to become an object of horror and that it will

16. Ibid.
17. Laetsch, op. cit., p. 258. Yet Keil, I:448, would equate their king with Yahweh (following) rather than with the Breaker (preceding).
18. Camb, p. 29. Liberalism may, however, treat the entire passage as non-Messianic and equate the Breaker and Yahweh, ICC, pp. 68–69.
19. See above, p. 115.
20. BBC, V:205–206.
21. See above, p. 138, and also 115.
22. I:469; see above, p. 68.
23. Perhaps a synonymous expression for her king.
24. I.e., she will be "deprived of them," Laetsch, op. cit., p. 268, though ICC, p. 91, suggests a tropical understanding, related to Hezekiah's helplessness in 701, but see v. 10 (No. 21–22, below).
25. See above, p. 133.

"bear their reproach," meaning, as in Joel 2:17, that they will be ruled over by others. The idea seems to go beyond Judah's past woes of Mi 6:13,[26] or the plundering of 701 B.C. as foreseen in vv. 14–15 (No. 3, above), after which the Hebrews did experience a wonderful rescue. Description of this same tragedy seems then to carry on into 7:4, which anticipates that "the day of thy watchmen [i.e. the day foretold by the prophets], even thy visitation [punishment] is come; now shall be their perplexity," namely, the same distress and *reproach* noted in 6:16. Finally in 7:8 Micah identifies himself with the plight of his people (cf. v. 9), saying, "I fall . . . I sit in darkness." Fulfillment (per. 7): as in Lev. No. 33, Judah's fall to Babylon in 586.

9. Mi *3:12b*: "the mountain of the house [shall become] as the high places of a forest." The fulfillment (per. 7) is stated in Jer 26:18 to have been postponed (see No. 8, preceding) but not necessarily abrogated: one thinks, indeed, as in I K 9:7b, of the destruction of the Jerusalem temple, burned in 586, II K 25:9.

Predictions 10–15 appear to have been incorporated by Micah from Isa 2:2–4;[27] for the latter seem to date from before the death of Uzziah (Isa 6:1) in 739 B.C. and therefore be prior to the period of Micah's own preaching ministry.

10. Mi 4:1a [see Isa 2:2a] (1 v.): an elevating of the temple hill.

11. Mi *4:1b, 2b* [see Isa 2:2b, 3b] (typ.): the millennial temple.

12. Mi *4:1c–2a* [see Isa 2:2c–3a] (1 v., fig.): the nations seeking God.

13. Mi *4:2c* [see Isa 2:3c]; 5:7 (1 v.): the teaching of God's truth in the Messiah's future kingdom. 5:7 states figuratively: "The remnant of Jacob shall be in the midst of many peoples as dew from Yahweh, as showers upon the grass." Fulfillment (per. 16): "Israel will be a teacher in the midst of the nations,"[28] as in Isa. No. 10.

14. Mi *4:3a* [see Isa 2:4a], *5:4b*, 7:15–17 (3 vv.): 5:4 states that the Messiah "shall be great unto the ends of the earth"; and among the "marvelous things" (supernatural acts, 7:15) that the Lord will show His people, 7:17 tells how "the nations . . . shall lick the dust . . . and come with fear unto Yahweh our God." Fulfillment (per. 16): as in Gen. No. 68, the universal rule of the Messiah.

15. Mi *4:3b–4* [see Isa 2:4b] (2 vv., fig.): Mi 4:4 adds to Isaiah's picture of international peace the concept of individual security, the sitting of "every man under his vine and fig tree." Fulfillment (per. 16): as in Lev. No. 29, millennial peace.

16. Mi 4:5 (1 v.): "For all the peoples will walk [KJV][29] every one

---

26. "Already" accomplished, Laetsch, op. cit., p. 282.
27. IB, V:180; and see above, note 1.
28. Cent, I:254.
29. Some would read the Heb. impf., with the ASV, as a present tense and contrast v. 5 with the preceding context, e.g. Cheyne, who argues: "The ideal time described in vv. 1–4 is still far distant," Camb, p. 36. Context, however, seems to favor a continuation of the future.

in the name of his god; and we will walk in the name of Yahweh our God." Keil observes, "Even at the time when many nations stream to the mountain of the Lord, there will still be nations that do not seek Jehovah and His word";[30] cf. 5:5–6, or Zech 14:17–19. Fulfillment (per. 16): the lack of total conversion during the millennial kingdom; cf. Rev 9:20.

17. Mi 4:6a, 7b (1 v.): "In that day [millennial; cf. No. 10–16, preceding], saith Yahweh, will I assemble . . . and I will gather that which is driven away [the Jews; see No. 18, following]; and I will make that which was . . . cast far off a remnant." Fulfillment (per. 16): as in Hos. No. 6, the regathering of converted Jews to Palestine, in the Messiah's future kingdom.[31]

18. Mi 4:6b–7a (fig.): God's people described in terms of a flock, as "lame . . . driven away, and that which I have afflicted." This condition precedes the millennial regathering (No. 17, preceding); and since phrases such as "that which was cast far off" are inappropriate for a characterizing of the Israel which is the present Christian church, their fulfillment (per. 14) must be sought in the scattered and divinely chastened condition of today's disbelieving Jews.[32]

19. Mi 4:7c, 8; 5:4a, 8–9 (4 vv.): the millennial people of God[33] in Palestine are to become "a strong nation," 4:7, described figuratively "as a young lion among the flocks of sheep, who . . . teareth in pieces," 5:8–9. 5:4 predicts how the Messiah "shall feed His flock [Israel; cf. 2:12, 7:14, in contrast with the other nations] in the strength and majesty of Yahweh; and they shall abide"; cf. 4:8, "And thou, O tower of the flock[34] . . . Zion, unto thee . . . the kingdom, the former dominion, shall come."[35] Fulfillment (per. 16): as in Dt. No. 37, the future status of privilege and of power among the nations for God's people.

20. Mi 4:7d (1 v.): "Yahweh will reign over them in mount Zion for ever." Fulfillment (per. 18): as in II Sam. No. 14, the eternity of the New Jerusalem; cf. Ps 48:9.

21. Mi 4:10a (1 v.): Zion is to go forth in sorrow, "and thou shalt come even unto Babylon."[36] Fulfillment (per. 8): as in Lev No. 34, Judah's Babylonian exile.

30. I:459.
31. See above, p. 104.
32. See above, p. 113.
33. See above, p. 104.
34. In the positive context of 4:7 the *tower of the flock* would hardly be indicative, per Cent, I:249, of the city's becoming desolate and a place for shepherds as in 3:12.
35. Some, as Pusey, would spiritualize this into a reference to Bethlehem, where Christ should be born, 5:2; but though the figure of God's "flock" may be given connotations of humility, or even humiliation, as in 4:6, the *kingdom* of this passage is one of *dominion*.
36. Many modern writers dismiss these words as non-authentic; e.g., Cent, I:248, "Micah could hardly have written 'unto Babylon,' which was not on his political horizon." But the horizon of the God who inspires Scripture is greater than that of man.

22. Mi *4:10b*: "There [Babylon, v. 10a, No. 21 preceding] shalt thou be rescued; there will Yahweh redeem thee from the hand of thine enemies." Fulfillment (per. 9): as in Dt. No. 43, Judah's return from exile (cf. No. 5, above, on the restoration of the northern tribes as well).

23. Mi 4:11 (1 v.): Following her return from exile (No. 22, preceding) Zion is warned, "Now many nations are assembled against thee." Fulfillment (per. 10): the oppression of Judah by the Seleucid Greek empire (cf. Dan 8:10) and "the small neighboring nations of the Jews"[37] (cf. I Macc 4:41): for note Mi 4:12–13 (No. 24–25 that follow) on the corresponding Maccabean deliverance of God's people.[38]

24. Mi *4:12–13a* (2 vv., fig.): a statement of the divine purpose behind the 2nd-century B.C. attacks on Judah (v. 11, No. 23, preceding), "But He hath gathered them as the sheaves to the threshing floor," v. 12, meaning, so that they may be decisively defeated; and further explanation follows from God's instructions to Israel in v. 13, "Arise and thresh: thou shalt beat in pieces many peoples." Fulfillment (per. 11): the spectacular victories of Judas Maccabeus; compare Dan 11:32c.

25. Mi *4:13b*: in connection with the Maccabean triumph of v. 13a (No. 24, preceding), Micah states, "I will devote their gain unto Yahweh." Fulfillment (per. 11): the consecration to God of the substance of those who were defeated by Judas, I Macc 4:18, 23–24, 57.

26. Mi *5:1* (1 v.): God's command: "Gather thyself in troops." Some have suggested that these words may refer to the enemy;[39] but the context seems to describe Jewish refugees crowding into Jerusalem. "Siege against us" is noted, and that "the judge of Israel" is "smitten upon the cheek," namely, defeated. In respect to its location in history, this tragedy is seen to follow the Maccabean victory of 4:13 (No. 24–25, above) but to precede the birth of Christ in 5:2 (No. 27, next). Fulfillment (per. 12): in light of prophecies No. 25 and 27,[40] Micah would appear to be speaking, centuries in advance, of the fall of Jerusalem to the Roman troops of Pompey in 63 B.C., when the Hasmonean monarchy was brought to an end by the captivity of Aristobulus II and his family.

27. Mi *5:2a* (1 v.): a revelation of the Lord addressed to the town of Bethlehem, "Thou . . . art little," yet "out of thee shall One come forth unto Me that is to be ruler in Israel," indicating the Messiah's "descent

---

37. KD, I:473.

38. Commentators from Calvin and Hengstenberg and onward—cf. the following quote from Keil—have suggested that these verses "point to a much greater event"; and Keil compares v. 11 with Joel 3:2 on the eschatological gathering of the nations to the Valley of Jehoshaphat, I:473–474. But that passage concerns *all* nations; and here in Micah it is better to maintain the chronological sequence between 4:10, on the return in 438 B.C., and 5:2 (No. 27, below), on the birth of Jesus; see above, p. 129.

39. Camb, p. 42.

40. See above, pp. 120–121.

from the ancient Davidic family."[41] But it also designates the place of His appearance and was so quoted to the wise men in Mt 2:6; cf. John 7:42. Fulfillment (per. 13): the birth of Jesus in Bethlehem, Mt 2:1, Lk 2:4–7, dated by Finegan to December or January, 5/4 B.C.[42]

28. Mi 5:2b: that the ruler born in Bethlehem (No. 27, preceding) will be One "whose goings forth are from of old, from everlasting." Attempts have been made to minimize either the uncreatedness or the eternity of the One whose coming forth is here anticipated: the RSV, for example, reads that from Bethlehem "shall come forth for me one whose origin [not, coming forth] is from of old, from ancient days [not, from everlasting]." Yet the nouns mōsā, and mōsā'ā, "coming/going forth," are never found at any other point in Scripture to signify "origin";[43] and their verbal root, in the line just preceding, clearly maintains the standard meaning of "come forth." In reference to the eternity, Horton has commented,

> From everlasting gives a deeper tone to the prophecy, which might come as easily to Micah as to any later prophet; it shows that Messiah will not be only David restored, but One who was in the beginning with God. We are not called on to explain away this solemn and wonderful forecast, especially when we have seen it fulfilled in the Babe of Bethlehem. . . . Micah could not understand his own deep saying; but how foolish of us to discredit it when history has made its meaning plain.[44]

Fulfillment (per. 13): the entrance into history of God the Son, who had been eternally with the Father; "this speaks to us of the Incarnation, for only God Himself is from eternity."[45]

29. Mi 5:3a: concerning the Israelites, that God "will give them up," referring to the defeat of v. 1 (No. 26, above),[46] until the birth of the Messiah in v. 2 (No. 27, above; cf. No. 30, following). It is Yahweh who decrees this humiliation, "Because the great divine Ruler of Israel, from whom alone its redemption can proceed, will spring from little Bethlehem, and therefore from the degraded family of David."[47] Fulfillment (per. 12): as stated by Laetsch, "We think of bloody persecutions under . . . Herod. At this time when the sceptre had departed from Judah, when an Idumean ruling by the grace of Rome, pompously calling himself Herod the Great, was king of the Jews, at this time of deepest humiliation and degradation, the Messiah came!"[48]

41. Camb, p. 44.
42. Handbook of Biblical Chronology, pp. 392, 409.
43. KB, p. 505.
44. Cent, I:251.
45. BBC, V:217.
46. Keil, I:476–477, relates the defeat backward to 586 B.C. in 4:9; but he allows for the Roman fulfillment as well.
47. Ibid., I:483, quoting Caspari.
48. Op. cit., p. 271.

30. Mi 5:3b: God's giving Israel up (v. 3a, No. 29, preceding), "until the time that she who travaileth hath brought forth." Fulfillment (per. 13): as in Gen. No. 7 (3:15b), the Messiah's birth from a woman. More specifically, this passage "is a commentary on the prophecy [of Mi 5:2, No. 27, above] which definitely refers to . . . Isaiah, the virgin bringing forth her son, 7:14."[49]

31. Mi 5:3c, 7:11b–12 (3 vv.): a forecast by the prophet that after the coming of the Messiah (Nos. 27, 28, 30, preceding), "Then the residue of His brethren shall return unto the children of Israel," 5:3. A number of interpreters would suggest reading, "He will give them up until the woman bears *and* until the remainder of His brethren return to Israel." But there appears to have been no major return just prior to Christ's coming forth from Bethlehem. A clue *is* provided by Cheyne, who observes: " 'Return' may be taken either in a physical or in a spiritual sense . . . the return of the long-lost tribes, and the thorough conversion of His own people."[50] But while there occurred no physical return after the ministry of Jesus, any more than before, and while a return at His second coming (as in 4:6a, No. 17, above) would not correspond to the time of this context in 5:3, His incarnation did result in the spiritual establishment of a Jewish remnant and of a far larger group of non-Jewish believers. Pusey concludes, "*My brethren are those who hear the word of God and do it. The residue* of these, the prophet says, shall *return to*, so as to be joined with, *the children of Israel*. . . . All, in the true Prince of Peace, shall be one . . . whether Jews or Gentiles."[51] 7:11b–12 goes on to speak of a time after the postexilic rebuilding of the walls of Jerusalem (v. 11a, No. 37, below), "In that day shall the decree be far removed. In that day shall they ["all nations"[52]] come unto thee from Assyria and the cities of Egypt . . . ," etc. Keil explains *the decree* as relating to "the ordinance or limit which God has appointed to separate Israel from the nations. This law will be far away, i.e. will be removed or set aside . . . inasmuch as numerous crowds . . . will then come to the people of God";[53] cf. Laetsch's references to Eph 2:11–22 and Col 1:18–29, 2:16–23, for further commentary.[54] Fulfillment (per. 14): as in Gen. No. 19, the joining of Gentiles into the Israel that is the church; see above, p. 100.

32. Mi 5:5a, 6 (2 vv.): after continuing his progressive sweep through history[55] up into millennial times (on v. 4, see No. 14 and 19, above), Micah adds, "When the Assyrian shall come into our land, within our border . . . and tread in our palaces . . . He [Christ, returned] shall deliver

49. Cent, I:251–252.
50. Camb, p. 45.
51. KD, II:72–73.
52. Laetsch, op. cit., p. 286.
53. I:510.
54. Loc. cit.
55. See above, p. 129.

us . . . and they [see No. 33, below] shall waste the land of Assyria with the sword"; see above, pp. 80–81. Such a Messianic deliverance has never been accomplished in the past;[56] yet Rev 16:12 predicts an attack in the future, coming from this very area across the Euphrates.[57] Fulfillment (per. 15): cf. Num. No. 36, an element in Christ's victory at Armageddon.

33. Mi *5:5b*: when confronted by the Assyrian forces of the Antichrist's invasion, "We shall raise up against him seven shepherds and eight principal men" to expedite the conflict. The progression, 7>8, seems to be a literary figure for augmented strength (cf. Amos 1:3, 6, Prov 30:15, 18, etc.); but the concept itself remains essentially literal.[58] Fulfillment (per. 15): the activity of Christian leaders at the Lord's return; cf. the more general forecast of Rev 20:4, 6, about those who "live and reign" with Christ.

34. Mi 5:12–14a (3 vv.): conditions that are to result from Judah's fall and destruction in 586 B.C. (vv. 10–11, No. 8, above). God says, "I will cut off witchcrafts . . . and thou shalt no more worship the work of thy hands," e.g. images, pillars, or Asherah poles. Fulfillment (per. 8): as in Dt. No. 16 or Hos. No. 7, Israel's purification through the exile.

35. Mi 5:15 (1 v.): "I will execute vengeance upon the nations which hearkened not," especially Assyria (6:9, under No. 3, above; cf. 5:5–6), though the various oppressors of Judah from 5:9 onward—Babylon, the Seleucids, Rome (No. 21–26, 29, above)—may also be included. Fulfillment (per. 7): as in Isa. No. 37, the destruction of Sennacherib.

36. Mi 6:7–8 (2 vv., typ.): burnt offering. Fulfillment (per. 13): as in Lev. No. 3.

37. Mi *7:8b*, 9, *11a* (1 v., fig.): although Micah identifies himself with his nation which is to be overthrown in 586 (v. 8a, No. 8, above), he yet adds, "I shall arise"; Yahweh "will bring me forth to the light"; and for Jerusalem there will be "a day for building thy walls." Though this last term is not the regular noun for a city's walls, but rather that for the wall of a vineyard,[59] still in v. 1 Micah had compared himself with gleanings from a vineyard; and "The language of the strophe as a whole shows that a literal rebuilding of the city's walls is meant, rather than any such general idea as the restoration of the fortunes of Israel."[60] Fulfillment (per. 9): the refortification of Jerusalem by Nehemiah in 444 B.C., Neh 6:15.

38. Mi 7:10 (1 v., fig.): in connection with Judah's restoration (No. 37,

56. E.g., at the time of Hezekiah in 701, as proposed by BBC, V:219.
57. Assyrian people, and in particular the Assyrian district, do exist to this day (see above, p. 81), though the making of such a correlation has been styled by its critics as "the insanity of literalism"; cf. Ramm, *Protestant Biblical Interpretation* (1956 ed.), p. 235.
58. See above, pp. 80–81.
59. *Gādhēr*, "wall of stones, without morter," KB, p. 173.
60. ICC, p. 149.

preceding), Micah predicts, "Mine enemy shall see it, and shame shall cover her; now shall she be trodden down as the mire of the streets." Fulfillment (per. 8): as in Dt. No. 46, the fall of Babylon in 539. Commentators thus speak of "the anticipated astonishment of Babylon (*my enemy*) in the day of God's redeeming his people from exile. . . . But it would be too late, because God had already marked Babylon for destruction."[61]

39. Mi 7:13 (1 v.): despite Judah's postexilic revival, vv. 8–10 (Nos. 37–38, preceding), and the Gentile engrafting into the church of Israel commencing midway in the Book of Acts, vv. 11–12 (No. 31, above), Micah says, "Yet shall the land be desolate because of . . . their doings." Some would seek to relate this phrase eschatologically to all "the earth";[62] but Cheyne, who inclines toward such a view himself, says of *land*, "i.e. the land of Canaan. Before the great promises of a golden future can be realized, judgment must have its perfect work."[63] The oracle thus poses, indeed, a problem that liberalism cannot handle: Horton, for example, asks, "What use is the return from exile if the land is still to be desolate?"[64] Yet the analogy of history provides a ready answer (per. 14), for those who take this as inspired, long-range prophecy: the desolation of Jerusalem in A.D. 70, because of their rejection of Christ; see below under Mt 10:23b.

40. Mi 7:19–20 (2 vv., fig.): God "will tread our iniquities under foot and cast all their sins into the depths of the sea"; cf. Jer 31:34. This prediction serves as an explanation of the generalized statement that precedes (Mi 7:18), namely, that Yahweh "is a God . . . that pardoneth iniquity." It is "fulfilled [per. 13] in the salvation provided by the Babe of Bethlehem of whom Micah had spoken earlier in 5:2,"[65] as in Job No. 4.

61. IB, VI:946.
62. KD, I:511–512.
63. Camb, p. 59.
64. Cent, I:269; his solution is that v. 13 may be a fragment from another collection."
65. BBC, V:233.

NAHUM

The latter six of the Minor Prophets are post-8th century in date and thus concern only the one surviving Hebrew state, the southern kingdom of Judah. Nahum is the first of the three 7th-century minor prophets— Nahum, Habakkuk, and Zephaniah—for while his writing must have occurred subsequent to the fall of Egyptian Thebes ("No-amon," Nah 3:8–10) to Assyria in 663 B.C., it still depicts the Assyrians as abiding "in full strength" (1:12). It would thus precede their withdrawal before the barbaric Scythian invasions of 628.[1] Walter Maier presents evidence for a dating of Nahum to the year 654.[2] The prophet's town of Elkosh (1:1) can no longer be identified but presumably lay somewhere within Judah (v. 15).[3]

The theme of Nahum is his anticipation of divine vengeance upon Judah's Assyrian oppressors (1:1, 2:1, 3:1); cf. Obadiah's similar sort of emphasis, in the 8th century, against the Edomites. Indeed, of the 47 verses in Nahum's three brief chapters, 35 of them (or 74%) are predictive in character; and 34 out of these 35 are devoted to the single subject of the future fall of Nineveh—the remaining verse, 2:2 (No. 2, below) concerns Judah's recovery from this same Assyrian oppression. Nahum's "burden" (1:1) may thus be summarized by his conclusion: "All that hear the report of thee [Nineveh, at its collapse] [will] clap their hands over thee; for upon whom hath not thy wickedness passed continually?" 3:19.

The Book of Nahum falls into two sections, both poetic in nature. Ch. 1 consists of a psalm on the majesty of God, derived from an earlier composition whose acrostic structure is still somewhat visible in the present Hebrew text, while chs. 2–3 make up a song which amounts almost to a taunt against proud Assyria. Some recent scholarship has hesitated to affirm either the authenticity of the former section[4] or the predictive character of the latter.[5] The result is to question the revelatory value of much of the book.[6] Pfeiffer concludes: "Nahum was not a prophet but a poet.

1. Some scholars, preferring not to allow a "prediction" of Nineveh's fall until this eventuation had become naturally foreseeable, fix a later date for the book; cf. R. H. Pfeiffer's argument, *Introduction to the OT*, p. 596, "The rapid decline of the Assyrian Empire began in 625 with the death of Ashurbanipal, and soon after the subject nations shook off the Assyrian yoke. . . . Nineveh was not directly threatened before 614, when Cyaxares king of the Medes attacked it without success but captured Ashur before the arrival of Nabopolassar king of Babylonia. The alliance between the two kings resulted in the final assault upon Nineveh in June, 612, and its fall in August of that year. The poem was undoubtedly written between 625 and 612, and probably between 614 and 612."

2. *The Book of Nahum, a Commentary*, pp. 34–37.

3. Traditions that associate it with Galilee, or even Mosul in Mesopotamia, seem unlikely.

4. Pfeiffer, op. cit., p. 494, "A redactor living about the year 300 B.C. prefaced Nahum's superb ode, dating from the years immediately preceding the fall of Nineveh in 612, with an alphabetic psalm of his own time."

5. *Ibid.*, p. 595, "We owe the preservation of Nahum's magnificent ode to a misunderstanding. As appears in the title, this martial song was considered a prophetic oracle or prognostication against Nineveh, and thus given a place in the Book of the Twelve. In reality, however, to judge from his one extant poem, Nahum was not a prophet . . ."

6. S. Sandmel, *The Hebrew Scriptures*, pp. 112–113, "The main poem is a blood-curdling song of rejoicing that Nineveh has fallen. . . . The paradox of the Book of Nahum is that the literature is as good as the religion is bad." Contrast the more moderate criticism of C. Kuhl, who recognizes the authenticity of the book's intial portion, but concludes in *The Prophets of Israel*, pp. 102–103: "The total impression given by the Book of Nahum is the apparently singular fact that all the oracles and poems are extremely secular in character and are seldom or never authenticated

Even though Jehovah himself occasionally threatens Nineveh (2:13, 3:5 ff., 'I am against thee'), there is nothing specifically religious in this exultant outbursts of joy over the inevitable downfall of the Assyrian Empire."[7] Concerning Nahum's personal feelings, that they *were* involved in his writing is hardly to be questioned; cf. the pervasive emotionalism of the Psalms. But that this emotional involvement of the prophet, just like that of David the king, is not without justification appears from C. H. Patterson's comment: "No wonder the poet rejoiced when he saw that a death blow was soon to be administered to this wicked power. . . . He was confident that the time had come when Yahweh was about to inflict on the enemy the punishment which they justly deserved."[8]

John Davison even linked the righteous zeal for retribution of the seventh Minor Prophet with the righteous love for the lost of the fifth:

The Book of Nahum is best understood as a continuation, or supplement, to the Book of Jonah. The prophecy of both is directed against Nineveh. But that of Jonah was followed by the preservation of that city; that of Nahum, which is more detailed in its circumstances, indicating the actual doom, was followed by its captivity and destruction. They form a connected account of one moral history: the remission of God's judgment being illustrated in the one, the execution of it in the other.[9]

1. Nah 1:8–10, 12–15; 2:1, 3–13; 3:1–3, 5–7, 11–19 (34 vv.): because Assyrian Nineveh has "devised evil against Yahweh," 1:11, and is filled with idolatry, 1:14, and witchcraft, 3:4, Yahweh proclaims, "I am against thee," 2:13, 3:5. "He will make a full end: affliction will not rise up the second time," 1:9. The point is not that Nineveh's punishment will be so thorough as to be unrepeatable, but that Assyrian affliction upon Judah will come to a complete end; see vv. 12–13, 15 (which is quoted from Isa 52:7), and 2:13.[10] "Her place" will end up in darkness, 1:8, and her name not be perpetuated, v. 14. 2:1–6 describes how Nineveh's

---

as being the word of Yahweh. Political and national considerations are so predominantly in the foreground of his prophecy that all others, even that of religion itself, are submerged in the shadow. Of this Nahum may himself have been aware, and so on his utterances being compiled he prefaced his book with a psalm (1:2–9) singing of Yahweh's goodness to the righteous and His annihilating anger against all His enemies."

7. Pfeiffer, op. cit., p. 594. Cf. the echoing of this position in C. H. Patterson, *The Philosophy of the OT*, p. 305, "Nahum was essentially a poet rather than a prophet. He wrote not for the purpose of reforming the people in the face of coming disaster but in order to express his personal delight and satisfaction over the destruction of Israel's enemies." Yet he adds, p. 306, "Yahweh is not only a just God but a powerful one as well. . . . The Assyrians no less than the Hebrews are subject to Yahweh's principles of justice."

8. Op. cit., p. 306.

9. *Discourses on Prophecy*, p. 277.

10. KD, *Minor Prophets*, II:12–13; Nah 1:9 thus elaborates the principle stated in v. 7.

attacker (Cyaxares the Mede) will advance against her, v. 1, wearing scarlet, v. 3, as Persians did,[11] and with his chariots charging through the parts of the city that lay outside the walls, v. 4 (= 3:2–3). The Assyrians may seek to defend the ramparts, v. 5 (= 3:14); but the fortifications will be breached, v. 6. The defenders will be stupefied, bereft of morale, 3:11; and the outer defenses will collapse, 3:12–13. 2:7–13 describes the city's capture and sack: the queen will be taken, v. 7; the inhabitants flee, v. 8 (= 3:16–18); the treasures will be plundered, vv. 9–10; and death and destruction become Nineveh's final lot, vv. 11–13 (= 3:15), along with public shame, 3:5–7, 19. Fulfillment (per. 7): the fall of Assyria to the combined forces of Media and Babylonia in 612 B.C.[12]

2. Nah 2:2 (1 v.): Yahweh restoreth[13] the excellency of Jacob, as the excellency of Israel," i.e. He is bringing back Judah's eminence in a way that will correspond to the national name of honor, *Israel.*[14] Fulfillment (per. 7): as Assyria withdrew from the west, Josiah was enabled to expand northward into Ephraim and even Galilee, II Chron 34:6.

11. Cent, *Minor Prophets,* II:30.
12. See above, note 1.
13. As opposed to the KJV reading, "hath turned away" the excellency.
14. KD, II:19.

HABAKKUK

The introduction to the book of Habakkuk (1:1) provides no information about the life and times of its author, except for stating that he was a prophet. Yet his circumstances may be deduced from what follows. Verse 6 describes the Chaldeans as "marching through the breadth of the earth," which became true only after their victory at Carchemish in the early summer of 605 B.C. (Jer 46:2); and v. 13 indicates that they were threatening to assume control over Palestine, if they had not in fact already done so, an event which occurred shortly thereafter, by August of that same year (II K 24:7; see v. 1). Such a date in 605 would place Habakkuk's oracle early in the reign of Jehoiakim (609–598 B.C.), a monarch whose depravity stood in marked contrast to the piety of his father, Josiah (see Jer 22:15–19).

Habakkuk's concern is with this problem of evil; like the OT book of Job before him, or the NT book of I Peter after him, his question is one of theodicy, of "the justice of God" in the light of earth's wrongs. His book, accordingly, assumes the form of a dialogue, in three stages: Habakkuk's question about injustice (1:2–4) and God's first answer, that He was sending the Chaldeans in reprisal (1:5–11); Habakkuk's next question, about these Babylonians being worse than the Jews they were punishing (1:12–2:1), and God's second answer, that the oppressors would receive their due, if one would but wait (2:2–20); and Habakkuk's final prayer-poem (ch. 3), which required no answer at all, for he concluded by affirming, "Although the fig tree shall not flourish . . . yet I will rejoice in the God of my salvation. Yahweh the Lord is my strength" (3:17–19). Habakkuk, in other words, had mastered the key verse of his own book— that while the soul of the Chaldeans might be puffed up, still the just shall live by faith (2:4).

The divine answers to Habakkuk are thus essentially predictive; and while the book contains only four distinct prophecies, primarily in chs. 1–2, these nevertheless occupy 23 out of the 56 verses, or 41% of the whole. Some of the verbs in ch. 3 occur in the Hebrew imperfect aspect,[1] which might suggest a future; but in view of the predominating perfects these former are best understood as examples of the old aorist form that is common to OT poetry. As Lancaster concludes, "Upon the whole it is easiest to read vv. 3–15 as a delineation of the historical 'work' of God at the Exodus."[2]

1. Hab 1:5–11 (7 vv.): answering the problem of injustice in Judah, God is to "raise up the Chaldeans" (v. 6), coming from afar (v. 8), "for violence . . . and captives" (v. 9), to take strongholds (v. 10) and sweep along, but to become guilty by making their might their god. Their coming was for the particular chastening of Judah, but the prophecy is not so limited at this point. Fulfillment (per. 7): Babylonian expansion, 605 B.C., II K 24:7.

2. Hab 1:12, 3:16b (1 v.): God's ordaining of Babylon for the corrective judgment (see 1:12, "we shall not die") not only of the earth in general, as in v. 6, but now specifically of Judah: "we." He swallows up the one who is more righteous than he: "the godly portion of Israel, who have to share in the expiation of the sins of the ungodly, and suffer when they are punished."[3] The ASV text of 3:16 reads, "I must wait for the day of trouble, for the coming up of the people that invadeth us."[4] A more accurate rendering (see the ASVmg) understands the *trouble* "to come up to a people that troopeth upon him"; but even so the *people* (Babylon) must first troop to the attack against *him* (Judah) before experiencing the trouble upon themselves. Fulfillment (per. 7): as in Lev. prophecy No. 33, Babylonian attack, climaxing in the fall of Judah in 586 B.C.

3. Hab 2:6–13, 15–19; 3:16a (14 vv.): ch. 2 contains Habakkuk's

---

1. See the ASV footnote to 3:3.
2. Camb, *Nah, Hab, and Zeph,* p. 85; see his further remarks, and also above, p. 30, note 13.
3. KD, *Minor Prophets,* II:65, though the verse here explained (1:13) is general, referring to what the Babylonians were already doing, so it is not counted among the predictions.
4. So Keil, ibid., II:114: and see above, p. 61.

five woes, vv. 6, 9, 12, 15, 19—the Chaldeans to be: plundered (vv. 7–8), guilty of bringing "shame to thy house" (v. 10), and consumed by fire (v. 13), with violence and "foul shame upon thy glory" (vv. 16–17). On the alternate renderings of 3:16, see No. 2, above. Its basic thrust is apparently that of trouble coming upon the Babylonian invaders of Judah;[5] its limitation to trouble (586 B.C.) coming upon the Judeans seems less likely, for the theme of the preceding context (3:3–15) is that of God's vindicating His own. Fulfillment (per. 8), as in Dt. No. 46, the fall of Babylon in 539.

4. Hab 2:14 (1 v.): after noting the punishment to come upon Babylon (2:6–13), Habakkuk then quotes Isa 11:9, "For the earth shall be filled with the knowledge of Yahweh, as the waters cover the sea." Laetsch identifies the connection: "Not only shall the destruction of Babylon manifest the glory of Jehovah . . . [but] there shall come a time when all the earth shall be filled with the glory of God."[6] Fulfillment (per. 15): the curseless world at Christ's return, as in Isa. No. 43 (11:6).

5. Camb, *Nah-Zeph*, p. 96.
6. *Minor Prophets*, p. 337: see above, p. 138, on such "telescoping."

ZEPHANIAH

The most thoroughly predictive book in the Bible is Zephaniah. It has three short chapters; but out of its total of 53 verses, 47 prophesy about matters that were yet future at the time of their writing, and they make up 89% of the whole. They are distributed among 20 separate predictions, though almost half of these verses concern the event of Jerusalem's fall to Babylon in 586 B.C.

Zephaniah 1:1 introduces the prophet through a genealogy that goes back four generations. This is the longest for any of the writing prophets, for it identifies Zephaniah's great-great grandfather as the famous King Hezekiah (KJV, misleadingly, "Hizkiah"), who reigned 726–697; and this may, in turn, help account for the prophet's insight into the royal family (1:9) and into the contemporaneous international situation (as in 2:8). Zephaniah's ministry is dated simply to "the days of Josiah, king of Judah"; and these extended from 640 to 609 B.C. His allusions, however, to the Chemarim (pagan priests) and to various idolatries (1:4–5) indicate a time prior to Josiah's great reformation of 622 (II Chron 34:8 ff.), while his reference to "the remnant of Baal" (Zeph 1:4) might suggest this young king's turning to God in 632 and beginning to purify Judah of its paganisms in 628 (II Chron 34:3). In fact, the coming in 628–626 of barbarian Scythian hordes, which swept down from the plains of central

Asia onto the whole Near Eastern "fertile crescent" and shook Judah from its former complacency (see Zeph 1:12, 16, and Jer 6:22–26), may have been the precise providential cause for Josiah's zeal at purification in 628, for Zephaniah's ministry—which can therefore be assigned to this same time—and for Jeremiah's call in the following year (Jer 1:2; see the discussion on 4:5, above, on his Scythian prophecies).

The Book of Zephaniah is organized into three parts. Like Isaiah before it and Ezekiel after it, Zephaniah, on its own smaller scale, contains a central section (2:4–15) directed against the pagan nations (cf. Isa 13–23 or Ezek 25–32). The first section (Zech 1:2–2:3) consists of prophecies about God's impending judgment on Judah, with a corresponding appeal to seek Yahweh, 2:3, while the last section (ch. 3) moves on to include the more distant future, with the judgments but also the blessings of the Messianic kingdom. The theme of Zephaniah appears in 1:7, "The day of Yahweh is at hand." Zephaniah furnishes, moreover, a succinct Biblical demonstration of the comprehensiveness of this phrase, to identify that wide range of points in history at which God lays bare His holy arm to achieve His redemptive, testamentary goals.[1] Zephaniah applies "the day of Yahweh"

	to his own period, or	to the future	
		for Gentiles	for Israel
in judgment, and	1:14–18	3:8	3:11
in restoration	2:3	3:9	3:13–17

1. Zeph 1:2–18; 2:1–3; 3:1, 7 (22 vv.): "I will utterly consume all things from off the face of the ground . . . man and beast, birds and fish." This might suggest per. 17, earth's final destruction. But the immediate context moves into the punishment of sinful Judah at the exile (v. 4) and concludes in v. 18 with the parallel words that therefore "the whole land shall be devoured . . . He will make an end of all them that dwell in the land."[2] The reason as stated in v. 3, to consume "the stumbling blocks of the wicked" (all wicked acts that cause offense), corresponds to the paganisms that are spelled out in v. 5; and the elevated discourse of prophecy in general[3] speaks repeatedly of the 586 disaster in terms of "the land utterly waste, without man" (Isa 6:11), when "the birds and the beasts are fled" (Jer 9:10[4]): see above, p. 112. Specifically, "The day of Yahweh is at hand" (1:7; also 1:14–16, 2:2), "the day of Yahweh's anger" (2:3). Judah is to become a sacrificial meal, to which "Yahweh hath consecrated His guests" (1:7), which depicts her fall to other nations,

---

1. See above, pp. 131–133.
2. The phrase could also be rendered "the whole earth"; and Keil, *Minor Prophets*, II:136, thus suggests that the prophecy "here returns to its starting point," meaning vv. 2–3, understood as the destruction of all the world.
3. See above, pp. 18–19.
4. Though contrast 4:23–26, on God's eschatological outpouring of wrath.

perhaps suggested by the Scythian raids though actually accomplished by the Babylonians. Judah's royalty and officialdom, carried away with foreign ideas and a corresponding corruption, will be punished (vv. 8–9); and Canaanite merchants in the Maktesh section of Jerusalem (?) will howl (v. 11), in the fact of the siege (v. 16), slaughter (3:7), plundering and desolation (1:13, 15), and crying and woe (1:10, 14; 3:1). Fulfillment (per. 7): as in Lev. prophecy No. 33., Judah's fall in 586 B.C.

2. Zeph 2:4a, Gaza to be forsaken. Fulfillment (per. 7): that "Pharaoh smote Gaza" is mentioned in Jer 47:1, and presumably by Herodotus, ii, 159, concerning Necho II, after his battle against Babylon at Carchemish in 605 B.C.; on the subsequent advance of Nebuchadrezzar against the Philistines, see Jer 25:20c, 47:2–7.

3. Zeph 2:4b, d, 5–6 (3 vv.): Ashkelon to be a desolation; Ekron, rooted up; and Philistia as a whole to be a desolation, leaving no inhabitant except poor shepherds. Fulfillment (per. 11): as in Amos No. 6.

4. Zeph 2:4c, Ashdod to be driven out at noonday. Fulfillment (per. 7): it was currently undergoing a 29-year siege by Psamatik I (663–609) of Egypt; cf. Jeremiah's reference to the remnant of Ashdod, 25:20.

5. Zeph 2:7a (1 v.): "the remnant of the house of Judah" to occupy Philistia, "for Yahweh will visit them."[5] Fulfillment (per. 11): see the discussion under Amos No. 6 for this also.

6. Zeph 2:7b, 9c: within these Maccabean (per. 11) prophecies, Zephaniah alludes to "the remnant, or residue, of Judah." So there is implied some recovery from the desolation predicted in 1:2 ff. This must, in turn, indicate the restoration from exile (per. 9), as in Dt. No. 43.

7. Zeph 2:9a: because of their insolence toward God and His people, "Moab shall be as Sodom."[6] Fulfillment (per. 9): from the 6th century onward, nomads wandered through the land,[7] especially after Moab's defeat in 582–581 by the Babylonians;[8] cf. Jer 9:26e. Some of the Moabite exiles may have attempted to return after the fall of Babylon in 539, Jer 12:15. But while Ammon (v. 9b) was able to repel the "Arab encroachments, constantly on the increase since the 7th century,"[9] until the 2nd century B.C., Moab collapsed at this earlier time.

8. Zeph 2:9b–11a (2 vv.): Ammon likewise to be a perpetual desolation, namely the people[10]—"the remnant of My nation shall inherit them" as a possession. Fulfillment (per. 11): as in Obad, No. 9.

---

5. The added phrase, "and bring back their captivity," need suggest no more than that He would "restore their fortunes" (see under Joel 3:1), without teaching a predicted return from exile; see IB, VI:1025. The case is different in Zeph 3:20, where context does specify the return (see 3:10c, No. 16, below).
6. With whose overthrow Lot, the ancestor of Moab, had been associated, Gen 19.
7. IDB, III:418.
8. A. H. Van Zyl, The Moabites, p. 157.
9. IDB, I:113.
10. Note the masc. plu. pronouns with the final verbs of 3:9; and cf. KD, II:143.

9. Zeph *2:11b*; 3:8, *19a* (1 v., fig.): "for Yahweh will famish [lit., *weaken, diminish*] the gods of the earth," that is, defeating their national armies and thus proving the invalidity of the gods. So 3:8 speaks of "the day [of Yahweh]," when He assembles the kingdoms of the earth, to pour out His anger upon them to devour them. Fulfillment (per. 15): the battle of Armageddon, as in Num. No. 36, here adduced to substantiate God's more immediate activity against the peoples of Transjordan (Zeph 2:9, No. 7–8, above).

10. Zeph 2:11c, 3:9 (2 vv.): all men, "even all the isles of the Gentiles,"[11] to worship God, "every one from his place." This last phrase means either coming from their own lands or worshiping from within their own lands, though in light of Mi 4:1, Zech 14:16, the former deserves the preference. 3:9, "Then will I turn to the peoples a pure language," lit., a "pure lip"; contrast the "unclean lips" of Isa 6:5, 7, caused by talk that involved the names of idols; cf. Hos 2:17. Fulfillment (per. 16): their calling on God and serving Him in the future Messianic kingdom, as in Gen. No. 47.

11. Zeph 2:12 (1 v.): Ethiopians, "Cushites," to fall by the sword. Fulfillment (per. 9): after 525 B.C. Cambyses II of Persia raided up the Nile into Nubia and forced the Cushite capital to move south from Napata to Meroe. If *Cushite* be but a scornful reference to Egypt, which had been under the Ethiopian XXVth Dynasty from 735 to 663, Zephaniah could be referring to Cambyses' conquest of Egypt proper in 525, as in Isa 19:1.

12. Zeph 2:13–15 (3 vv.): Assyria and Nineveh to become a desolation; "every one that passeth by will mock." Fulfillment (per. 7): 612 B.C., as in Nah. No 1. Cf. the report of the 10,000 Greeks of Xenophon's *Anabasis* in 401, who found Nineveh a mere mound.

13. Zeph 3:4 (1 v., typ.): the temple. Fulfillment (per. 13): as in Ex. No. 55.

14. Zeph *3:10a*, 11a, 12–13a (3 vv.): "In that day [of Yahweh]" (3:10; cf. v. 8, 2:3, and 1:14), the converted Jews (see 3:10, No. 16, below), "My suppliants," need have no more feelings of shame (v. 11);[12] for transgression will be replaced by trust in God (v. 12). They will no longer be haughty, iniquitous, or lying (v. 13). Fulfillment (per. 16): as in Dt 30:8's prediction (No. 45) of holiness for God's people in general.

15. Zeph *3:10b, 19d*: the Jewish people, "Israel after the flesh," to be scattered; for they are designated "My dispersed" (v. 10), afflicted, "lame," driven out, and put to shame (v. 19; cf. v. 20, in need of gathering). Fulfillment (per. 14): the present Jewish situation; as in Mi. No. 18, cf. Hos 3:3.

---

11. This phrase is "used primarily of the islands and jutting promontories of the Mediterranean Sea . . . [but here] these are taken as representative of the heathen world generally," Cent, *Minor Prophets*, II:128.

12. On the basis of context, KJV is here to be preferred to ASV, "be put to shame."

16. Zeph 3:10c, 18, 19b, 20a (4 vv.): with ASVmg, "My suppliants [the scattered Jews, as in v. 11 that follows; not the church, for these suppliants have *not* been raptured to be with Christ], the daughter of My dispersed, shall they [the Gentile peoples, v. 9, preceding] bring as Mine offering" (v. 10); they will be gathered, though once driven out (vv. 18–20). The ASV text, "My suppliants . . . shall bring Mine offering," represents a possible alternative. But context favors a continuation of the same subject for the verb as in the preceding verse, namely the Gentiles, as does also the analogy of Isa 14:2, 49:22, or 66:20 (see under Isa 11:11). Fulfillment (per. 16): Gentiles bringing converted Jews back to Palestine, as in Hos. No. 6.

17. Zeph *3:11b*: "I will take away out of thee thy proudly exulting ones." Fulfillment (per. 16): the removal of unrepentant Jews—in Zephaniah's day, the upper classes, vv. 3–4—from the Messianic kingdom.

18. Zeph 3:*13b*, 15–16, *19c, 20b* (2 vv.): "They shall feed and lie down as a flock, and none shall make them afraid"; there shall be no more judgments by enemies or fear of calamity (v. 15), but they shall be praised by all peoples (v. 20) in the lands where once despised (v. 19). Fulfillment (per. 16): the peace of the converted Jews, as in Lev. No. 29.

19. Zeph 3:14 (1 v.): joy and gladness; cf. Yahweh's own joy in v. 17. Fulfillment (per. 16): the joy of the millennial kingdom, as in Isa. No. 46.

20. Zeph 3:*15b*, 17 (1 v.): "Yahweh thy God is in the midst of thee, a mighty one who will save; He will rest in His love; He will joy over thee with singing." Fulfillment (per. 16): the presence of God in the future Messianic kingdom, as in Isa. No. 16.

HAGGAI

Next to Obadiah, with its single chapter, the two-chaptered prophecy of Haggai constitutes the shortest book in the Old Testament. Of Haggai's personal life nothing is known, except for his ministry of the year 520 B.C. in arousing the postexilic governor of Judah, Zerubbabel, and his associates to complete God's house in Jerusalem (Ezra 5:1, 6:14). For while the foundations of the temple had been relaid in 536 B.C., soon after the Jewish return from Babylon, Samaritan opposition had stopped the work during the rest of the reign of Cyrus, throughout that of Cambyses II (529–522), and on into the time of Darius I of Persia (4:5, 24). The great burden of Haggai is expressed in the key words of 1:8, "Build the house, and I will be glorified, saith Yahweh," a theme that was to be elaborated shortly thereafter by Haggai's younger contemporary Zechariah.

Yet the prophecy of Haggai holds the distinction of being the most closely dated book in the Bible. It consists of four messages delivered during the second year of Darius: ch. 1, on the need to rebuild, spoken on the 1st day of the 6th month (Aug./Sept., 520), which so stirred up the Jews that the work recommenced 23 days later (1:14–15); 2:1–9, to encourage them in the face of the new temple's comparative poverty, dated to the 7th month, 21st day; 2:10–19, in the 9th month, 24th day, on the relationship between the temple's reconstruction and Judah's prosperity— or lack of it; and 2:20–23, delivered on that same day, a private assurance to Zerubbabel. Except for references to the temple, which became in itself a type of Christ (No. 1, below), Haggai's 7 predictions are restricted to his second and fourth messages, to motivate his people to a more dedicated work. They occur in 15 of the book's 38 verses, or in 39% of the whole.

1. Hag 1:2, 4, 8–9, 14; 2:3, *7c, 9b,* 15, 18 (8 vv., typ.): the temple. Fulfillment (per. 13): as in Ex. prophecy No. 55.

2. Hag 2:5 (1 v., typ.): "according to the word that I covenanted with you . . . fear ye not." Although the noun *b'rīth* "testament," does not occur in the verse, the verb lit., "cut," is a standard one for "covenanting"; and context indicates the testamentary promise of Israel's divine adoption and favor.[1] Fulfillment (per. 13): as in Ex. No. 45 (19:5).

3. Hag 2:6, 21 (2 vv.): "Yet once, it is a little while, and I will shake the heavens and the earth." *Yet once* more: God shook them formerly at Sinai (Ex 19:16–18). *A little while:* "The future, as often in prophecy, is foreshortened."[2] The passage is quoted in Heb 12:26, and explained in 12:27 as meaning the removal of the things shaken, so that the saints may receive the kingdom which cannot be removed. Fulfillment (per. 17): as in Gen. 8:22 (Gen. No. 14) and Ps 102:26a (Ps. No. 47) the passing away of the present universe; cf. Rev 20:11. As Keil notes, "It is only fully accomplished at the breaking up of the present condition of the world in the destruction of this heaven and this earth."[3]

4. Hag 2:7a, 22 (1 v., fig.): "I will shake all nations" (v. 7a); elaborated in v. 22, "I will destroy the strength of the nations . . . every one by the sword of his brother." Driver suggests the overthrow of nations at Haggai's own time: the revolts faced by Darius I, 520 B.C.[4] But Keil cautions, "What is here predicted was . . . the overthrow of the might of all the kingdoms of the heathen, and therefore could not take place in Zerubbabel's lifetime."[5] In view of the preceding verse (above), the fulfillment would here too be in per. 17, as in Jer. No. 56, on the defeat of

---

1. KD, *Minor Prophets,* II:188–189.
2. Cent, *Minor Prophets,* II:161.
3. Op. cit., II:197.
4. Cent, loc. cit.
5. Op. cit., II:214.

Gog and Magog; cf. the references to Gog's *shaking* in Ezek 38:19–20, and his similar destruction by internal strife, v. 21.[6]

5. Hag 2:7b (1 v.): "The precious things of all nations shall come; and I will fill this house with glory" (= wealth).[7] The preceding context might suggest an eschatological fulfillment;[8] but it has been explained that "the prophet mentions at the very outset the utmost and the last that God will do . . . and then passes on to . . . the immediate future, just as Micah in ch. 4 comes back from the most remote future to the less remote."[9] Fulfillment (per. 9): the coming of silver and gold (v. 8) from various heathen lands for the completion and beautification of the second temple, then under construction (1:14); see Ezra 6:8–9 and Zech 6:11 for particular examples.[10] Such a prophecy was needed in the face of current discouragement (Hag 2:3–4). The plural verb prohibits the Messianic interpretation suggested by the KJV, "the Desire of all nations shall come."

6. Hag 2:9 (1 v.): "The latter glory of this house ["namely . . . the temple of Zerubbabel or the temple as altered by Herod"[11]] shall be greater than the former, and in this place will I give peace." Haggai thus moves on from the material glory of vv. 7–8 to "the spiritual glory, without which in the sight of God material splendor is worthless."[12] It is the *glory* of *peace*, that reconciled relationship to God which sums up the blessings of testamentary inheritance, specifically, "that the Messiah should come before the destruction of the second temple, and that his presence should fill it with a glory which the first temple had not, though it was far richer and more magnificent."[13] Fulfillment (per. 13): "In fact, it was in this temple that Christ taught";[14] hence, the glory of Jesus, as He ministered in the courts of the second sanctuary, John 1:14; 7:14, 37; 8:12, 32, 36, and especially Mt 21:5, 12, 23, etc.; see Zech 2:5b.

7. Hag 2:23 (1 v.): "In that day [after the final overthrow of the heathen, v. 22, and after the final judgment, v. 21], I will take thee, O Zerubbabel, and make thee as a signet." "He would give him a position in which he would be and remain inseparably connected with Him";[15] cf. the opposite statement in reference to Jehoiachin when he was deposed by God (Jer 22:24). Fulfillment (per. 18): Zerubbabel to receive high standing, close to God, in the New Jerusalem. Keil, however, proposes a

6. Also true at the battle of Armageddon, before the millennium, Zech 14:13.
7. ICC, p. 63.
8. Similar happenings do occur in Biblical eschatology, Isa 60:5, Rev 21:24, 26.
9. KD, II:197.
10. NBC, p. 746.
11. KD, II:195.
12. Camb, *Hag-Mal*, p. 39.
13. J. B. Payne, *Theology of the Older Testament*, p. 429; and quotation from T. H. Horne, *An Introduction to the Critical Study and Knowledge of the Holy Scriptures*, I:127.
14. JB, p. 1529.
15. KD, II:214.

Messianic interpretation: "The promise did not apply to his own particular person, but rather to the official post he held."[16] But in view of the Biblical doctrine of immortality, resurrection, and reward at the final judgment, Zerubbabel himself would appear to constitute the adequate subject for its fulfillment. So understood, the prophecy became an assurance to him, in his work for the temple, 2:4.

16. Ibid.; liberalism here sees an abortive attempt to crown Zerubbabel as the Messiah, IB, VI:1049.

ZECHARIAH

Zechariah, in the Old Testament, parallels Revelation in the New, not simply by its position as the last extensive book before the close of that half of Scripture, but more significantly by its character as apocalyptic writing.[1] Each of the two prophecies is unique to its respective testament, by being the only full book of apocalyptic to be found therein; and yet each constitutes a climax to a series of apocalyptic portions that were revealed through earlier Biblical writers. For even as the Revelation builds upon and brings into ultimate focus the apocalyptic discourse of Christ (Mt 24, Mk 13, Lk 21) and those blocks of apocalyptic matter that appear in Paul (as I Thess 4–5, II Thess 1–2), so Zechariah synthesizes the apocalyptic of the OT, from its beginnings in Joel (735 B.C.), on through Isaiah's "little apocalypse" (chs. 24–27, 711), and into the major exilic visions of Ezekiel (chs. 34–39, 47–48) and Daniel (chs. 2, 7–12). Furthermore, both Zechariah and Revelation exhibit an internal organization based on cycles of predictions, each generally chronological in pattern but marked by the repetition and development of themes from the earlier cycles.

Zechariah was a priest who belonged to the course of Iddo (Zech 1:1, 7), the 10th of the priestly courses that returned from exile with Zerubbabel in 537 B.C. (Neh 12:1, 4). By the year 500 Zechariah had apparently become its chief (vv. 12, 16). His ministry as a prophet began in 520, two months after Haggai's initial preaching (cf. Hag 1:1 and Zech 1:1). These two prophets exercised, in fact, a joint ministry, which resulted in the completion of the Jerusalem temple in 515 (Ezra 5:1, 6:14–15), after a lapse of more than 20 years because of Samaritan opposition (3:6, 8; 4:4–5, 24). Zechariah, however, seems to have been Haggai's junior contemporary; for while his last dated prophecy reaches only to 518 B.C. (7:1), this lies but midway in his book, and Zechariah's subsequent reference to Greece as one of the powers of the ancient world (9:13) suggests

1. See above, pp. 85–89, and especially p. 87 on the concept of predictive cycles.

the spectacular Greek victories over Persia in 480–479 and hence a career of at least 40 years for the prophet. Such a passage of time, moreover, would account for his changed emphases from ch. 9 on, with less on the temple and more on an apocalyptic anticipation of even further developments among the world powers. Modern criticism questions the Zecharian authenticity of chs. 9–14 altogether, assigning them to a "Deutero-Zechariah" after the time of Alexander's conquest of Palestine in 332.[2] This assignment, however, rests basically on the "rather circular arguments" of liberalism's placing of all true apocalyptic in post-OT times;[3] and it flies in the face of Scripture's own datings for these materials. Of Zechariah's later life nothing is known except that he met martyrdom in the very temple that had been so much on his heart as a priest and for which he had labored so effectively as a prophet (Mt 23:35).[4]

The general theme of Zechariah is stated in the book's introduction, with its appeal, "Return unto Me, saith Yahweh of hosts, and I will return unto you," 1:3; yet the body of the book falls into three distinct sections, the two longer being apocalyptic in both form and content. The former divides itself into two of the aforementioned cycles of visionary prediction, with an opening stress in each upon Zechariah's immediate burden for the reconstruction of the temple. The latter falls into four such cycles, when Zechariah, apparently following the pattern of his former colleague Haggai (see Hag 2:6, 22), lifted his eyes from Judah's local situation to God's overall purposes in human history.[5] Table 11 suggests something of the progress of the revelation within each of these cycles—a major aid in determining the periods of probable fulfillment for a number of the specific verses. It also identifies important points of correspondence between the respective cycles. Thus, for example, between the two cycles of the prophet's inaugural year: Zech 1:16, in the first, on rebuilding God's house, closely parallels 4:9, in the second; 1:21, on the casting down of the nations by four carpenters or smiths, corresponds to 4:8, on the overpowering work of the four chariots that go out through the earth; 2:7, on Zion's escaping from Babylon, is answered by 5:11, as Wickedness is sent back to Babylonian Shinar; and the redemptive career of the Messianic Branch (3:8, 6:12), typified by the high priest Joshua (3:1, 8, 6:11), strikingly climaxes both of these earliest cycles. The 4th cycle (9:11–ch. 10) is perhaps the least clear as to its limits; and some would interpret

2. E.g., JB, p. 1139.
3. See R. K. Harrison, *Introduction to the OT*, pp. 950–955.
4. Cf. the Targumic tradition in this regard, and the way Christ links Zechariah's death with that of Abel, the two of them marking the limits of the threefold canon of the OT (as in Josephus): from Abel's, at the beginning of Genesis in the Law, through the poetical Writings, down to Zechariah's as the last such death for one of the writing Prophets, J. B. Payne, "Zachariah Who Perished," *Grace Journal*, 8 (1967), 33–35.
5. See Payne, "The Church and Zionism in the Predictive Cycles of Zechariah 9–14," ETS P (1956), 55–63.

TABLE 11
The Prophecies of Zechariah

Introduction (1:1-6): Zechariah's call, 520 B.C.

I. EIGHT VISIONS AND AN OBJECT LESSON (1:7-ch.6), 519 B.C., in 2 parts (note break at 4:1)

1st cycle of predictions (1:7-ch. 3), from the contemporary building of the postexilic temple to Christ's 1st and 2nd comings:

Vision #1 (1:7-17), the Man and horses among the myrtle trees: all earth is still (v. 11), dominated by heathen (v. 15); but God will act (v. 14) and the temple be rebuilt (v. 15)

#2 (1:18-21), horns broken by carpenters: Gentiles who oppressed Judah, to fall (v. 21)

#3 (ch. 2), the Man and the measuring line: God's glory (Jesus) will dwell (v. 10) among the former Babylonian exiles (v. 7), and many nations be joined to His church (v. 11)

#4 (ch. 3) the Priest Joshua: a type of Messiah (v. 8), atonement (v. 9), and millennium (v. 10)

2nd cycle (4-6), in the same night (?)(see 4:1), visions showing similar progression:

Vision #5 (ch. 4), lamps and two olive trees: Zerubbabel and Joshua to build the temple (v. 9)

#6 (5:1-4), a flying scroll: sinners cut off from the whole "land" (v. 3 = Judah, see #7)

#7 (5:5-11), a woman in an ephah-measure: others drained off to Babylon (v. 11)

#8 (6:1-8), horses from mountains of brass: surrounding countries to be subdued (v. 8)

Object lesson (6:9-15), Joshua crowned: a type of the priest-king Messiah, making peace (v. 13)

II. QUESTION OF ANNUAL FASTS (7-8), 518 B. C., now that the mourned-for temple is being rebuilt (7:3) Zechariah predicts that fasts will become feasts, if Judah seeks the right (8:19)(fasts continue!)

III. FOUR CYCLES OF PREDICTIONS (9-14), APOCALYPSES: God's universal judgments and triumph. After the Greco-Persian War (?) (see 9:13) of 480 B.C.; Zechariah comforts, though kingdoms totter

B.C. fulfillments	NT fulfillments	Still future fulfillments
3rd cycle (9:1-10), stressing the rise of Greek power under Alexander the Great		
9:1, He takes Syria; Jews pray and are preserved	9:9, Jesus on Palm Sunday (Mt 21:5)	9:10c, Christ's universal (millennial) dominion (see Ps 72:8)
9:4, Alexander takes Tyre, 332 B.C.	9:10a, Jerusalem destroyed, A.D. 70	
9:7, Philistia accepts Judaism, 150 B.C.	9:10b, the church's gospel to the heathen	

4th cycle (9:11-ch. 10), stressing the Maccabean revolt against the Greek Antiochus

9:11-12, Jewish exiles return to Palestine	10:8a, redemption won	10:10, the church will be raptured and brought with Christ to Palestine
9:13, Judas Maccabeus defeats the Greeks, 165 B.C.	10:8b, others gathered, increase (church?)	10:11a, rivers dry up (Rev 16:12)
10:3, false leaders fall	10:9, believers live, though scattered	10:11b, world powers are brought down
		10:12, the saints rule (Rev 2:26)

5th cycle (11-13:6), stressing Christ's first, humble, and second, glorious, comings

11:6, the Jews suffer under rival Greek kings	11:11, the pious accept the Good Shepherd (John. 10:11)	12:2, Jerusalem besieged, for
11:8, Hellenizing high priests are driven out by Maccabeus	11:12, others betray Him (Mt 26:15)	12:7, "Judah" will be saved first
11:9, the Jews fall by civil strife to Rome, 63 B.C.	11:17, Rome destroys in A.D. 70 (John 19:15) but falls in 476 (Rev 17:16)	12:10, then Jerusalem accepts her pierced Messiah (John 19:34)
		13:1, and is cleansed (Rev 1:7)
		13:4, false religion ceases

6th cycle (13:7-ch. 14), stressing Christ's millennial kingdom (no B.C. predictions)

	13:7a, the Good Shepherd though God's equal is smitten (Mt 26:31)	14:2, all nations gather to Jerusalem and rifle it; for,
	13:7b, the little flock, the faithful, church, scattered (see Acts 8:4)	14:4, Messiah will stand on Olivet,
	13:8, the flock in the land, Jews, two-thirds destroyed, A.D. 70	14:5, with his raptured saints; then converted Jews of Jerusalem will flee to Him
	13:9a, the Jews ever since	14:7, light (victory) by evening
		14:8, the curse removed from nature
		14:9, the Lord rules the world
		14:16, and all remaining nations will worship Him in Jerusalem

it simply as a continuation of the 3rd and therefore wholly millennial in its application (see below, under prediction 40).

Concerning statistics, Zechariah's 78 predictive prophecies involve 144 out of the book's 211 verses, or a high 69%, as might be expected within an apocalypse.

1. Zech 1:16a, 3:9a, 4:1–14, *6:12c–13a* (16 vv.): "My house shall be built in it [Jerusalem]." 3:9 is symbolical, "Behold the stone, set before Joshua; upon one stone are seven eyes; I will engrave the gravings thereof"; but it is not explained.[6] Probably the reference is again to the temple:[7] the high priest Joshua was engaged in building it (Hag 1:14, 2:4; cf. Zech 3:7); Zech 4:6 refers to the top stone that would complete it; and God's eyes rest upon it (4:10; cf. 1:12–16 and Ezra 5:5). The words "I will engrave" suggest that "the inscription has not yet been cut: the building is not finished."[8] Then in the corresponding 2nd cycle comes Zechariah's vision of the golden lamp stand, supplied with oil from two olive trees. Explanation: v. 9, Zerubbabel is to "bring forth the top stone," by the power of the Holy Spirit (v. 6), as the people invoke God's grace (v. 7) and the Spirit rejoices (v. 10); v. 14, Joshua also seems to be included, as the second of the "two anointed ones." In the clauses of 6:12–13 that match with 3:9, "He shall build the temple of Yahweh; even he shall build," the stress that is placed upon the subject—which might have been accompanied by a gesture toward Joshua, before whom the message was being spoken (6:12a)—suggests a backward allusion in the midst of the prophecies concerning the Branch to the Branch's type, Joshua. For the contextual emphasis rests on the building of the literal, contemporaneous temple (vv. 14–15[9]), which was a task not of the Messiah but of Joshua (see above). Fulfillment (per. 9): the rebuilding of the temple, as in Obad. prophecy No. 4.

2. Zech 1:*16b*–17 (1 v., fig.): "A line shall be stretched forth over Jerusalem." Explanation, v. 17: God's cities (the cities of Judah, v. 12) are to "overflow with prosperity; and Yahweh shall yet . . . choose Jerusalem," meaning, "comfort Zion"; cf. a correspondingly measurable (by *line*) increase in people in 2:2. Fulfillment is conceivably millennial;[10] but nearer fulfillment when adequate, as here, is on principle to be preferred,[11] specifically (per. 9), as in Mi. No. 37 and Dan. No. 37, Jerusalem's rebuilding by Nehemiah in 444 and the recovery of Judah that followed.

6. KD, II:260–261, relates it to the land, preparing it for Christ, who is under discussion in the last line of 3:9.
7. NBC, p. 751.
8. JB, p. 1533.
9. See ICC, p. 187; and see above, on the interpretation of prophecy, p. 82.
10. Merrill F. Unger, *Unger's Bible Commentary, Zechariah*, p. 33.
11. See above, p. 118.

3. Zech 1:20–21, 2:8–9, 6:1–5, 7 (10 vv., sym.): "These [smiths] are come to cast down the horns of the nations, which lifted up their horn against the land of Judah to scatter it." Four *horns* had scattered Israel and Judah (1:18–19), presumably Assyria, Egypt, Babylonia, and Medo-Persia[12]—not the four empires of Dan 2 and 7, for the four of Zech 1 were no longer future to the prophet. Persia's *lifting up of their horn* would thus refer to its frustrating of the temple's rebuilding (Zechariah's theme at this point, v. 16), under Samaritan pressure (Ezra 4:4–5, 24; cf. 5:3). Especially would Cambyses II have opposed any operation that might seem to affect his great Egyptian campaign of 525; compare how the later Artaxerxes III crushed the Jews and carried off many as captives in 345. As summarized by C. H. H. Wright. "The Medo-Persian empire, though friendly at the outset, had no little share in the work of dispersion and in keeping Israel and Judah in a scattered condition."[13] Zech 2:8–9 adds, "After glory hath He [Yahweh] sent Me [Christ, the Angel of Yahweh[14]] unto the nations which plundered you . . . and they shall be a spoil unto those that served them." So in the 2nd cycle, 6:1–5, 7, Zechariah's vision of the four charioteers—"probably the most obscure of the series"[15]—"four spirits (KJV, ASVmg) go from before the Lord" (v. 5). Two of them gave God rest (cf. His displeasure, in 1:15)[16] against Assyria (?) in "the north country" and Babylon (vv. 6, 8), indicating divine punishment. The fourth, after going against Egypt in "the south country" (v. 6) walks to and fro "through the earth" (v. 7), presumably Persia with its empire that had become universal by this year of 519 B.C., and for similar rest-giving punishment.[17] Fulfillment (per. 10): Assyria, Egypt, and Babylon had already been broken; but Persia was yet to be, as in Dan. No. 4, in 331 B.C. by Alexander, who must therefore be the figure predicted by the fourth smith.

4. Zech 2:1–5a, *11a*, 10:8a (6 vv., sym.): "Behold, a Man with a line . . . to measure Jerusalem." Explained, 2:4, "Jerusalem shall be inhabited as villages without walls, by reason of the multitude therein"—a large number, yet protected, not by walls, but by God's being "a wall of fire" around her and "the glory in the midst of her" (v. 5). Further explanation appears in v. 11, "Many nations shall join themselves to Yahweh in that day, and shall be My people." Parallel expressions occur in Zechariah's 4th cycle, 10:8, "I will gather them . . . and they shall increase as they have increased," meaning, be as many as they ever have been.[18] Interpre-

---

12. Though note NBC's caution, p. 749, that "the horns may be of less particular application and symbolize the four points of the compass"; cf. ICC, p. 133, accepting Babylon, but: it is "impossible to identify the other three."
13. *Zechariah and his Prophecy*, p. 28.
14. Th. Laetsch, *Bible Commentary, Minor Prophets*, p. 419.
15. NBC, p. 753.
16. Cf. Ezek 5:13, 16:42, on the expression, God's "resting."
17. Laetsch, op. cit., p. 439.
18. ICC, p. 291.

tation of *them* might be retrospective: a generalization on the return of the dispersed Israelites to Palestine in 537 B.C., as in 9:11–12a.[19] 10:8–9 would then, according to S. R. Driver, explain "the means by which their return will be effected."[20] But Driver must then emend v. 9, on their being *sowed among the peoples.* Furthermore, v. 8 continues on from the Maccabean rejoicing in v. 7 (see No. 41, below). The *them* must therefore refer to the immediately preceding group in v. 7, *their children.* Yet the natural children of the Ephraimites would already be in Palestine by then, seeing the Lord's blessings of v. 7. The fulfillment (per. 14) results from the coming of the glory of Christ to Jerusalem (2:5b; see No. 5, below). But a Jerusalem without walls[21] and protected by God does not correspond to the known material city of NT Jerusalem and must rather be Zechariah's anticipation of that community to which the Gentiles are to join themselves so as to *be My people,* namely that Zion into which all the regenerate are born (see Ps 87:4). "Zechariah is speaking of the ideal Jerusalem—the church,"[22] as cared for by God (see Gal 4:26–30, quoting Isa 54:1). Compare Hos. No. 4 (1:10) on the engrafting of Gentiles into the testamental status of "My people"; and see Gen. No. 19 (9:27). Zech 10:8 should therefore also represent foreigners joining Israel as "sons and daughters" (Isa 60:4, discussed under 14:2b; and cf. Ezek 16:61, under 16:53a and b) and producing the predicted increase (Jews and Gentiles), beyond what had been in the past. Laetsch thus speaks of "the Gentiles gathered into one swarm. Through the preaching of the Gospel (Lk 10:16) the Lord calls them into His church on earth."[23] It is based on the fact that "I have redeemed them" (see below under 3:9b, No. 11): and, even though the fulfillment lay centuries ahead of Zechariah's contemporaries, their realization of the very existence of such promises could not help but stimulate them to the task at hand, of completing God's temple.

5. Zech 2:*5b*, 10, 11b–13, 9:9a (5 vv.): 2:13 states that God is "waked up out of His holy habitation" (heaven[24]). The object of His descent from heaven appears then in v. 5, "I will be the glory in the midst of her [Jerusalem]"; cf. v. 10, "Sing and rejoice, O daughter of Zion; for I will dwell in the midst of thee" (= v. 11b), and the parallel in 9:9, which specifies, "thy King cometh unto thee." Fulfillment (per. 13): as in Hag. No. 6 (2:9), Christ the glory of God, appearing in Jerusalem, with 9:9 specifically quoted in Mt 21:5 as accomplished in His triumphal entry

---

19. IB, VI:1100.
20. Cent, *Minor Prophets,* II:249.
21. A description elsewhere of millennial Zion, Ezek 38:11, and so KD, II:245, and Unger, op. cit., pp. 43–46; but see No. 5, following, on the preferability of earlier fulfillment here. The yet future Messianic kingdom comes as the *climax* to both of Zechariah's first cycles, see below, No. 12 and 15.
22. H. C. Leupold, *Exposition of Zechariah,* p. 56; cf. BBC, V:353.
23. Laetsch, op. cit., p. 465.
24. IB, VI:1067.

on Palm Sunday. This NT period is suggested, initially, by the context of ch. 2: lying between Zechariah's second vision (1:20, No. 3 above), on Alexander (per. 10) and his fourth (ch. 3, below), which moves on from Jesus (3:8, Nos. 9 and 10, per. 13) to the future kingdom (v. 10, No. 12, per. 16). Further, since this *dwelling* is presented as a reason for return from Babylon (Zech 2:7), it would not appear to refer to the Lord's presence in the yet future kingdom. The prophecy serves to confirm, then, both the validity of the revelation as truly from the Angel of Yahweh (v. 11, just as in v. 9, No. 3, above; and see v. 4 and p. 10 above) and the reality of Yahweh's "choice" of Jerusalem (v. 12), not simply by comforting it (as in 1:17), but by *inheriting* it, claiming it as *His own portion in the Holy Land.*

6. Zech 3:5 (1 v., typ.): Joshua's priestly garments; contrast vv. 3–4, in which the typical purity was *not* present. Fulfillment (per. 13), as in Ex. No. 60.

7. Zech 3:7, 6:14, 7:3, 8:9, *11:13b* (4 vv., typ.): the temple. Fulfillment (per. 13), as in Ex. No. 55.

8. Zech 3:8a (1 v., typ.): the priests under Joshua, a "sign." They were *anshē mōfēth,* "men of portent," of an "omen," of "the Messianic age."[25] Fulfillment (per. 13): as in Ex. No. 59.

9. Zech *3:8b*: "Behold, I will bring forth My Servant." Fulfillment (per. 13), Christ the Suffering Servant, as in Isa. No. 91.

10. Zech *3:8c*, 6:12a (1 v.): God to bring forth the One called *Branch, sémah,* lit., "shoot," as in Jer 23:5 and 33:15; cf. Isa 11:1 and 53:2. Fulfillment (per. 13); Christ, descended from David, as in II Sam. No. 11 (cf. II Sam 25:5b, where the verb is *sāmah,* "to shoot forth").

11. Zech *3:9b, 6:13d, 10:8b:* God will "remove the iniquity of that land in one day." 6:13d, "and the counsel of peace shall be between them both": an elaboration on the typical transaction that is defined in v. 13c, immediately preceding (see under v. 11, No. 13, below). Wardlaw comments on the character of the *peace* that results: "It is the priest that is to wear the regal, not the prince to wear the sacerdotal. This has the important meaning—that is was to be by the execution, to the divine satisfaction, of His priestly work, that He was to obtain, in reward, His kingly crown."[26] 10:8b, "for I have redeemed them": the basis upon which the gathering and increase (see the immediately preceding prediction in v. 8a, No. 4, above) are predicated. Fulfillment (per. 13): Christ's atonement, as in Job No. 4, and Prov. No. 4. On the phrase "in one day," cf. Heb 7:27, 9:12, 10:10, *efápax,* "once for all," the *day* being that of Calvary.[27] From a theological viewpoint, one understands that "in virtue of this fusion of offices in Christ, there is a counsel of *peace,* a lasting

25. JB, p. 1533.
26. NBC, p. 753.
27. KD, II:262.

reconciliation between God and His people";[28] as Laetsch comments on 10:8, "They are His redeemed people, purchased by the vicarious suffering of His Servant."[29]

12. Zech 3:10, 8:5–6 (3 vv.): "In that day," after Christ makes the atonement of 3:9, they will call their neighbors to come and sit "under the vine and fig tree" and in 8:5, "The city shall be full of boys and girls playing." Fulfillment (per. 16): the peace of the Messianic kingdom (see Mi 4:4), as in Lev. No. 29; and note the corresponding kingly rule in Zechariah's 2nd cycle, 6:13 (No. 15, below).[30]

13. Zech 6:11, 13c (2 vv., typ.): the Lord instructed Zechariah, "Make crowns [the two circlets combing to produce one crown, hence the sing. verb in v. 14[31]], and set them upon the head of Joshua the high priest." If this act were only one of contemporaneous symbolism it "would in effect make the high priest the king of Israel."[32] Its import, however, is that of a type, for the future, as explicated by v. 13: "He [Joshua's antitype, *Branch*, v. 12; see under 3:8c, No. 10, above] shall sit and rule upon His throne; and He shall be a priest upon His throne; and the counsel of peace [see Hag 2:9] shall be between them both," that is, "between the two offices united in Him."[33] Fulfillment (per. 13): Christ's possession of the crowns both of priesthood and of kingship, though they rest upon His head as priest; see v. 13d, No. 11, above.

14. Zech *6:12b*: "He [Branch] shall grow up out of His place"; see Ex 10:23 for the same expression, *mit-taḥtāw*, "where He is." Fulfillment (per. 13): the childhood growth of Christ, as in Isa. No. 26, and specifically, "from His soil, from His lowliness to eminence."[34]

28. NBC, p. 754.
29. Op. cit., p. 465.
30. Amillennialism would tend to limit the import, especially of 3:10, to the more psychological aspects of sin. So Keil, "By the wiping away of all guilt and iniquity . . . all the discontent and all the misery which flow from sin will be swept away, and a state of blessed peace will ensue for the purified church of God," *Minor Prophets*, II:262.
31. Cf. Camb, *Hag-Mal*, p. 57; KD, II:298.
32. BBC, V:371.
33. NBC, p. 754, and see above, pp. 52 and 90, though rather than such a neuter sense for *them both*, Keil would prefer a masc. of individuals, "the ruler and priest united in one person, in the Branch," op. cit., II:300. The RSV proposes a more far-reaching alternative translation and interpretation for the latter clauses of v. 13: ". . . and there shall be a priest [Joshua] by his throne [Zerubbabel's]; and peaceful understanding shall be between them both." But this rendering, while grammatically possible, is opposed to the total context of the passage. (1) Zerubbabel was not a king, though some would interpret this v. as Zechariah's misguided effort to proclaim him Israel's Messiah. (2) Joshua the priest wears the crown (v. 11), not a separate person who was enthroned by him (unless the unwarranted practice is followed of introducing emendations into the text; cf. Driver, Cent, *Minor Prophets*, II:212–214). (3) The phrase that occurs twice in v. 13, "upon his throne," is inconsistently rendered by the RSV: in the first instance the RSV translates it, for the king, "upon his throne," but in the next, for the priest, "by his [the king's] throne." Driver would thus emend the second to read, "on his right hand," ibid., p. 214.
34. KD, II:299.

15. Zech *6:13b, 14:9a:* "and He [reverting to the Branch, the antitype of which Joshua was the type] shall bear the glory and shall sit and rule upon His throne." 14:9, "Yahweh, King over all the earth." The *glory,* 6:12, is here not *kāvōdh,* "divine glory," as in 2:5b, but *hōdh,* "eminence, regal majesty."³⁵ So fulfillment (per. 16), the Messianic kingdom, as in Gen 49:10b, assurance over which would further motivate the Jews who were Zechariah's contemporaries to a greater dedication in rebuilding God's house in 519 B.C.

16. Zech 6:15 (1 v.): "They that are far off shall come and [help] build in the temple of Yahweh." Fulfillment (per. 9): as in Hag. No. 5. Darius' decree in Ezra 6:8–12 was of this very nature, and it was carried out (6:13).

17. Zech 7:13–14 (2 vv.): a quotation of God's message by the pre-exilic prophets, "They shall cry, and I will not hear, said Yahweh; but I will scatter them with a whirlwind among all the nations." On the hyperbole of this term, "all," see above, p. 81. Fulfillment (per. 8): the exile, as in Lev. No. 34 and specifically affirmed by Zechariah in 7:14, "Thus the land was desolate after them."

18. Zech *8:3a, 12:10c:* in the former v., God's return to Jerusalem; and in the latter, "They shall look unto Me [= upon Me³⁶]," a teaching later repeated in Rev 1:7. Fulfillment (per. 15): Christ's second coming, as in Ps. prophecy No. 45.—visible, especially to the Jews (see 12:10b). Context disfavors reference to His first coming, for Jerusalem is identified as a faithful city (8:3c, see No. 20, below), and a supernaturally extended life span is indicated for the people (v. 5, No. 21).

19. Zech *8:3b:* "I will dwell in the midst of Jerusalem." Fulfillment (per. 16): God's presence in the Messianic kingdom, as in Isa No. 16.

20. Zech 8:3c, 8b; 13:2–6; 14:20a, 21a (9 vv.): "Jerusalem shall be called The city of truth" (= Faithful City³⁷); and Zion, "the holy mountain." 8:8, "They shall be My people, and I will be their God, in truth and in righteousness": this last phrase refers both to God's character *and* to the people's at that time.³⁸ 13:2–6, idols to be forgotten: their names—meaning their authority and not just their use in nomenclature, e.g., in names compounded with Baal, as Kiriath-baal or Baalah, though note Hos 2:17—will be cut off from the land. "Also I will cause the prophets to pass out of the land," demonstrably, false prophets; for this is combined in v. 2 with "the unclean spirit," namely, the Jews' unclean attitude. Such false prophets are to be executed, even by parents (v. 3). They themselves will be ashamed and cease practicing (v. 4). There follows an example: "He shall say, 'I am no prophet, [rather] I

35. Ibid., II:300.
36. Ibid., II:387.
37. JB, p. 1535.
38. KD, II:314.

am a tiller of the ground . . . a bondman from my youth" (v. 5). V. 6, but if someone is suspicious and asks him, "What are these wounds between thine arms?" he will answer, "Those with which I was wounded in the house of my friends." "The *wounds* are presumably the scars of incisions made during prophetic ecstasy (I K 18:28). The one-time prophet attempts to explain them as caused by blows during a drunken revel."[39] 14:20–21, on even horse bells, and on pots in the temple, shall be written "Holiness to Yahweh," the same inscription formerly restricted to the high priests' miter. So, v. 21, "In that day there will be no more a 'trafficker'[40] [merchants, that is, providing the sacred bowls; and cf. John 2:14, Mk 11:15] in the house of Yahweh." Fulfillment (per. 16): Judah's millennial reformation, as in Dt. No. 45, with consecration and universal holiness, so that distinction ceases between the secular and the sacred.

21. Zech 8:4 (1 v.): many aged men and women in Jerusalem. Fulfillment (per. 16): life to old age, as in Ex. No. 52; cf. Isa 65:20.

22. Zech 8:7, *10:9b–10a,* 12:7 (2 vv.): "I will save My people from the east and the west." 10:9–10, "They shall return. I will bring them again also out of the land of Egypt and Assyria [places of subservience]." 12:7, "Yahweh shall save the tents of Judah first, that the glory of the house of David and the inhabitants of Jerusalem be not magnified above Judah." "The house of David" and "inhabitants of Jerusalem," thus kept humble, must be unregenerate Jews, who are converted in v. 10 (see No. 62, below): the tents of Judah, saved first, should therefore identify the church.[41] Others see "people out in the country of Judah, in lowly condition" as opposed to the Jerusalem city dwellers.[42] Fulfillment (per. 15): the rapture of the church, as in Hos No. 27 (11:10), which precedes the deliverance of Jews in Jerusalem (see No. 58, below).

23. Zech *8:8a,* 10:10b (1 v.): God's raptured people brought to dwell in Jerusalem; 10:10, "and I will bring them into the land of Gilead and Lebanon ["the area once occupied by the kingdom of David";[43] more specifically, some of its frontiers]; and place shall not be found for them," because of their being so numerous. Fulfillment (per. 15): as in Joel No. 11.

24. Zech 8:20–23; 14:9b, 16b (6 vv.): "There shall come many peoples and strong nations ["now hostile or indifferent to the Jews"[44]]. . . to seek Yahweh of hosts in Jerusalem." 8:23, "Ten men out of all the nations shall take hold of him that is a Jew, saying, We will go with you," converts, that is, outnumbering those who were God's people prior to

---

39. IB, VI:1109.
40. For *Canaanite,* as in Hos 12:7, Zeph 1:11 (listed under Zeph 1:2, above).
41. So held by Ebrard (*Offenb. Joh.*) and Kliefoth, cited by Keil, *Minor Prophets,* II:382; cf. Laetsch, op. cit., p. 480.
42. Leupold, op. cit., p. 233; cf. Unger, op. cit., pp. 210–212.
43. IB, VI:1101.
44. ICC, p. 216.

this point by figures of ten to one, or more (the idea is indefinite[45]).
14:16, the survivors of Armageddon (see under 12:9, No. 61, below)
"shall go up from year to year to worship the King, Yahweh of hosts,
and to keep the feast of tabernacles." 14:9b, "In that day shall Yahweh
be one and His name one": "the Jewish confession of faith—the [mono-
theistic] Shema (Dt 6:4)—will become the universal creed."[46] Fulfillment (per. 16): the universal seeking of God, as in Gen. No. 47, Isa.
No. 9, specifically, to attend feasts. The situation is millennial, because of
its localization to Jerusalem and the analogy of Isa 2:2–4.

25. Zech 9:1–2a (2 vv.): God's punitive word to have the lands of
Hadrach, Damascus, and Hamath for its "resting place." Hadrach was an
ancient Syrian city north of Hamath, which lay in turn to the north of
Damascus.[47] Fulfillment (per. 10): Damascus was treacherously surrendered to Alexander's general Parmenio, after the Greek victory over
the Persians at Issus in Asia Minor in the late fall of 333 B.C.

26. Zech 9:2b, 4 (1 v.): of Tyre, "The Lord will smite her power in
the sea; and she shall be devoured with fire." Fulfillment (per. 10): by
Alexander, as in Joel No. 8 (3:4a) and with greater detail in Ezek
26:4b ff.

27. Zech 9:2c: God's opposition to Sidon, so proud and "very wise."
Fulfillment (per. 9): 345 B.C., as in Joel No. 15. Sidon, having surrendered, was not attacked by Alexander in 332.

28. Zech 9:5a, 5c, 6 (2 vv.): "Ashkelon shall see it [the fall of Tyre,
No. 26, above] and fear"; Ekron too shall be ashamed of "her expectation." "A bastard [half-breed race, or king] shall dwell in Ashdod [repre-
renting all Philistia], and I will cut off the pride of the Philistines."
Fulfillment (per. 10): they surrendered to Alexander in 332, though after
the fall of Syria (No. 25, above) they must have expected Tyre to block
his progress. Thus broken, and subject to Greek colonization (see Ezek
25:15), they lost the distinctive features of their race: "The Philistines
appear first on the stage of history as conquerors and warriors; they are
last seen as traffickers like the Phoenicians."[48]

29. Zech 9:5b, d: Gaza to be "sore pained" and lose her king. Fulfillment (per. 10): this one Philistine city resisted Alexander and was
stormed in November, 332, after a two-month siege.

30. Zech 9:5e: "Ashkelon shall not be inhabited." The precise fulfillment is unknown, though, by context, it would seem to have occurred
(per. 10) at the time of Alexander's campaign against Gaza (No. 29)
in the fall of 332, when "some of the cities became depopulated."[49]

45. KD, II:318.
46. IB, VI:1112.
47. Ibid., VI:1093.
48. Camb, Hag-Mal, pp. 72–73.
49. Laetsch, op. cit., p. 452.

31. Zech 9:7 (1 v.): on Philistia, "I will take away his blood out of his mouth [no more nonkosher food, or pagan feasts] . . . he also shall be a remnant for our God," even to becoming "as a chieftain in Judah,"[50] assimilated into Israel just as the Jebusites had been. Fulfillment (per. 11): the conversion of the Philistine remnant, to become Jewish proselytes, especially Ekron (v. 7), the most inland city, at the time of its incorporation into Judah, and Judaism (?) 148–146 B.C.; see Amos No. 6.

32. Zech 9:8 (1 v.): "I will encamp about My house [possibly Zechariah's newly rebuilt temple, but more likely the Israelite nation, the subject in v. 7[51]] against the army, that none pass through . . . no oppressor shall pass through them any more." Fulfillment (per. 10): Alexander passed along the Palestinian coast in the summer of 332 and returned in 331; the *oppressor* would thus refer to Persia, as in 1:20–21, 6:7 (No. 3, above). Jewish legends about Alexander at least indicate peaceful relations; and "the Jews believed Alexander had been restrained from attacking them by Yahweh, and that He could always protect them."[52] Others would refer this verse to the times of the Diadochi who succeeded Alexander,[53] "probably later than Ptolemy I in 320."[54]

33. Zech *9:9b:* "Thy king [see 2:5b, No. 5, above, on His coming] is just." Fulfillment (per. 13): Christ's kingdom one of righteousness; so also in Isa. No. 40 (11:2), as God's Spirit rests upon Him.[55]

34. Zech *9:9c:* "Thy king is *nōshā,* saved" (ASVmg), victorious (cf. Dt 33:29, Ps 33:16), not "saving,"[56] for the niphal stem is not active, which would be hiphil, but "having salvation"; "endowed with salvation, help from God, or furnished with the assistance of God requisite for carrying on His government."[57] Fulfillment (per. 13): Christ "saved," under the Father's protection, John 8:29–30.

35. Zech *9:9d:* the King's entering Jerusalem "lowly, and riding upon an ass, even upon a colt the foal of an ass"; contrast the horse of v. 10. "Israel's ideal king will differ alike from the earlier kings of Israel and from ordinary worldly rulers; he will appear riding, not like a worldly conqueror on his war-horse, but upon the ass, the beast of peace. . . . See the fulfillment [per. 13] in Mt 21:5, John 12:15,"[58] Christ's triumphal

---

50. The group is thus personified as a clan prince, under whom all the Philistines would be included: not that he would rule over Jews; see KD, II:330.
51. Ibid., II:332; ICC, p. 269.
52. ICC, loc. cit.
53. Driver, Cent, II:240.
54. G. A. Smith, *The Book of the Twelve Prophets,* II:453.
55. Righteousness in the millennial kingdom is of course true as well, Jer 23:5–6, 33:15–16; but this is not the issue here.
56. Significantly, this phrase is not quoted in the NT, either in Mt 21:5 or in John 12:15: His saving activity is not the point.
57. KD, II:334.
58. Cent. II:241; and see above, p. 61. Yet Driver goes on to identify v. 10 with v. 9 and thus concludes, "But, as in other cases, the prophet's ideal as a whole,

entry, with the disciples placing their garments on both animals, to seat Jesus (Mt 21:7), though actually He rode only the colt (Lk 19:35; cf. v. 30).

36. Zech 9:10a; 11:1–3, 15–16; 13:7c (see below, under No. 66), 8a (7 vv.): in Zechariah's 3rd great predictive cycle,[59] 9:10 reads, "I will cut off the horse and battle bow from Jerusalem." Liberal writers tend to refer this to "peace over all the earth, with no further need of armaments,"[60] but the use of "cut off" in v. 6 favors the concept of overpowering defeat.[61] In the 5th cycle, 11:1–3 predicts, figuratively, fire devouring cedars in Lebanon (v. 1) and oaks in Bashan (v. 2) and shepherds grieving for the loss of pastures and lions for the Jordan jungle (v. 3). The point of reference is uncertain, but it appears to be a "prelude" to what follows.[62] In vv. 15–16 then, as a part of his symbolical object lesson (see No. 51–56, below) Zechariah now takes "the instruments of a foolish shepherd," which v. 16 explains by saying, "I will raise up a shepherd in the land" who will not help the flock, "but he will eat the flesh and tear apart even the hoofs." Finally the 6th cycle adds, 13:8, "In all the land [of Palestine]" two-thirds of the flock of Israel is to die, thus uniting the thought of 13:7 with that of 11:16. Fulfillment (per. 14): as in Mi No. 39 and Dan No. 38, the destruction of Jerusalem by Rome in A.D. 70. In ch. 11 (5th cycle), therefore, since v. 12 refers to Christ's betrayal (see No. 54, below) and v. 16 to the punishment on the land that results, the opening three-verse summary would likewise be descriptive of Rome's acts in 66–70, destroying the country.[63]

37. Zech *9:10b:* "He shall speak peace unto the nations." Fulfillment (per 14): Christ's peaceful gospel (cf. Rom 12:18–21), presented by the church to the Gentiles, as in Isa No. 69 (24:16a). Keil overly identifies the church with the defeated Jews of v. 10a, preceding, but seems to have grasped the basic thought: "Through the destruction of their military power will their nature be also changed; the covenant nation will be divested of of its political and worldly character, and made into a spiritual nation or kingdom."[64]

38. Zech *9:10c:* "His dominion shall be from sea to sea, and from the River [Euphrates] to the ends of the earth," repeating Ps 72:8. Fulfill-

---

in the form in which he projected it, has never been fulfilled: for the picture drawn by him is not that of a spiritual ruler, swaying the hearts of men by the influence of a great religion, but that of a conqueror, returning from the defeat of earthly foes, cutting off the implements of war, and securing peace for his subjects by righteous government."

59. See Table 11.
60. IB, VI:1096.
61. Though Leupold, op. cit., p. 177, takes issue with Hengstenberg here.
62. KD, II:355.
63. Ibid., II:357.
64. Ibid., II:335–336.

ment (per. 16): the worldwide Messianic rule of Christ, as in Ps. prophecy No. 35 (72:8).

Zechariah's 4th great predictive cycle commences as he turns back to portray the events which precede the coming of Judah's King, 9:9–10.

39. Zech 9:11 (1 v., typ.): he accounts for the release of the Babylonian exiles, "because of the blood of thy testament." Fulfillment (per. 13): the shed blood of Christ, as in Ex. No. 45 (19:5).

40. Zech 9:12–16, 10:3–5 (8 vv.): "I will render double unto thee," a double compensation of blessing, in place of the hardships of the exile and return described in vv. 11–12a. God is to use Israel, as strong weapons, against Greece (v. 13); "Yahweh shall be seen over them" with arrow, trumpet, and whirlwind [figurative; cf. Hab 3:10–11[65]] (v. 14), defending Israel (v. 15). They will trample down slingstones and will drink the Greek enemies' blood. "Yahweh will save them in that day" (v. 16). 10:3 (fig.), "Mine anger is kindled against the shepherds and the he-goats." Instead of these, v. 4, "From himself [Judah, v. 3[66]] shall come forth the corner-stone [the same word that is used in Jd 20:2, I Sam 14:38, Isa 19:13, for leading men, who uphold government], the nail [a leader, Isa 22:23], the battle bow, and every ruler," nōgēs, in 9:8 an exacter, but here in a good sense, one who enforces the military service, a marshal, as in Isa 3:12, 60:17. "And they shall fight" and win, because God "is with them" (v. 5). Fulfillment (per. 11), Judas Maccabeus' victories, as in Mi. No. 24 and Dan. No. 51: the shepherds (10:3) are those who took the place of the shepherd who was destroyed at Judah's time of exile (v. 2), her last king, and so must be foreign rulers of Palestine, at this time the Seleucid kings of Greek Syria; the he-goats, correspondingly, represent "subordinate leaders of the people; cf. Ezek 34:17,"[67] Hellenizers among the Jewish priests and aristocracy. But, as Zechariah mixed his metaphors, the flock will become like a goodly horse in the battle, "a prophecy which was remarkably fulfilled in the Maccabean age."[68]

41. Zech 9:17, 10:6–7 (3 vv.): "Grain and wine shall make the young men flourish." Even of the northern tribes, "I will cause them to dwell"

---

65. "The imagery is evidently suggested by a great storm," Cent, II:243; and see above, p. 82. Unger, however, representing dispensational interpreters, connects it with God's future deliverance of the Jewish nation and asserts that "this section of the prophecy doubtless refers to the time of Israel's trouble during the great tribulation just preceding the coming of the King" (op. cit., p. 166). He would thus join Zechariah's 4th cycle (9:11-ch. 10) to his 3rd, as a continuation of it (pp. 165-186). Yet he cannot avoid the Maccabean setting of Greece in 9:13 (p. 167) and can only conclude that "the struggles of the Maccabean period loom in the background . . . and portray prophetically Armageddon and the final windup of wars preceding the advent of the Prince of Peace" (p. 166).

66. Not God, as indicated especially by the last phrase of v. 4.

67. Camb, Hag-Mal, p. 80.

68. Cent, II:247.

(ASVmg)[69] as before the exile; "their heart shall rejoice; yea, their children shall see it[70] and rejoice" in the Lord too. Fulfillment (per. 11): the Jews to possess the products of their own land, after victory over the Seleucids. Their independence was officially recognized by the Greeks in 143 B.C., I Macc 13:36–43.

42. Zech 10:9a (1 v.): following Israel's redemption and augmentation (v. 8, No. 4 and 11, above), "I will sow them among the peoples; and they shall remember Me in far countries; and they shall teach [JB; ASV, "live with"][71] their children." The first verb is to "sow" (see Hos 2:23), not "scatter"; "consequently the reference cannot be to a dispersion of Israel inflicted as a punishment."[72] G. N. M. Collins speaks of "its good effects. . . . We learn from Acts how the dispersed Jews of those days became the means of helping forward the missionary effort of the infant church."[73] He thus indicates a proper period of accomplishment, though from the context it would appear that the worldwide church, rather than the synagogue, is the subject (see above, No. 4). Fulfillment (per. 14): the geographical spread of the church, as begun in Acts 8:4.

43. Zech *10:11a* (fig.): strict rendering of the text produces, "He [God] will pass through the sea [cf. No. 44, next], distress"[74] His coming, that is, will break in on a time of tribulation. The similarity to Ex 14, moreover, suggests that He comes to rapture His people (see v. 10, No. 22, above) even as they pass through their tribulation. Fulfillment (per. 14): the great final tribulation, as in Dan. No. 20.

44. Zech *10:11b*: "He shall smite the waves in the sea, and all the depths of the Nile shall dry up." Since v. 11c presents a parallelism of Assyria and Egypt (No. 45, next), even so at this point Barnes suggests, "No doubt the reference here, as in Jer 51:36–37, is to the Euphrates. *The waves in the sea*: heavy storms occur on the Euphrates."[75] Fulfillment (per. 15): Scripture's second suggestion of the drying up of the Euphrates (cf. Rev. 16:12), and also the Nile, in preparation for the battle of Armageddon (next), as first in Isa. No. 45 (11:15).

45. Zech 10:11c (1 v.): the pride and scepter of Assyria and of Egypt to depart. Fulfillment (per. 15): as in Num. No. 36, the battle of Armageddon.

46. Zech 10:12 (1 v.): God's people to "walk up and down in His

---

69. See KD, II:349.
70. An alternate rendering is, "They shall see their children"; but this seems less appropriate.
71. The alternative, "they shall live, with their children," assumes the qal. But it would appear better to read the piel, *w'hiyyū*, "preserve alive," and then, "rear their children" (ICC, pp. 292, 301) in the faith too.
72. KD, II:351.
73. NBC, p. 757.
74. See Laetsch, op. cit., p. 465.
75. Camb, *Hag-Mal*, p. 82.

name"; to live in His authority. Fulfillment (per. 16): the privileged status of Israel, as in Isa. No. 51.[76]

47. Zech 11:6 (1 v.): the predictions of Zechariah's 5th cycle open with Yahweh's words, "I will no more pity the inhabitants of the earth," not *the land*, of Palestine;[77] for it does not have *kings* (v. 6b), and God's flock is being protected up to this point (vv. 4, 7). These *inhabitants* God does not spare, but they are to be smitten by their neighbors and rulers.[78] Fulfillment (per. 10): this especially fits the contests of the Diadochi, the "world powers"[79] at the period predicted (see v. 8, No. 49, below), developing the process initiated by Zechariah's contemporary Persian and even native Jewish overlords (v. 5), as they fought and destroyed one another; see Dan 11:5–20.

48. Zech 11:7, 11 (2 vv., fig.): "Thus the poor of the flock, that gave heed unto me, knew. . . ." This is a group within the flock as a whole, "God's elect,"[80] who pay heed, when the Jewish nation as a whole is given up (vv. 9–10, No. 51–52, below). Fulfillment (per. 14): the believers as existing in Palestine, the church;[81] cf. 13:7d, No. 67, as well. So Acts 3:23 shows their anticipation of impending destruction, coming upon their unbelieving compatriots.

49. Zech 11:8a (1 v., fig.): "I cut off three shepherds in one month, for My soul was weary of them." These must belong to the general group of shepherds of v. 5, who sell Israel to foreign oppressors. Proposed identifications "number at least forty, ranging from the days of the Exodus . . . to Roman emperors."[82] It could, for example, refer to evil Israelitish kings of the past, whom God destroyed. Fulfillment (per. 10): Leupold himself, with most, favors the deaths of the corrupt pre-Maccabean leaders, Jason, Menelaus, and Lysimachus.[83]

50. Zech *11:8b*: God's soul was weary of them, "and their soul loathed Me." The *them* must describe the Israelite nation, not simply the three evil leaders cut off in v. 8a; for v. 9 develops progressively from this, on the flock as a whole. Fulfillment (per. 12): so the Jews rejected God; and the Hellenistic patterns of life that had marked the last pre-Maccabean high priests became the preference of the later Hasmoneans themselves and characterized the Herodian and the Sadducean (priestly) parties, as the NT period drew on. Against Christ, their rejection of God received explicit formulation in their stated desire for "no king but Caesar" (John 19:15), whom God had permitted to rise in domination over them (see next).

---

76. Cf. Unger, op. cit., p. 185.
77. As IB, VI:1103.
78. Cent, II:256, and Leupold, op. cit., p. 206.
79. KD, II.360.
80. Laetsch, op. cit., p. 472.
81. See Unger, op. cit., p. 194.
82. Leupold, op. cit., p. 212.
83. So Driver, Cent, II:254.

51. Zech 11:9a, 10 (2 vv., sym.): "Then said I, "I will not feed you: that which dieth, let it die'; . . . and I took my staff Beauty, and cut it asunder," suggestive of God's favor being broken off. V. 10 goes on to explain it as God's breaking the covenant He had made with all the peoples: He had, heretofore, been ordering world history in favor of Israel (Dt 32:8); but now the pagans are freed from such obligation.[84] Fulfillment (per. 12): as in Mi. No. 26 God's ending the independent Jewish kingdom by Pompey's occupation of Jerusalem by Rome in 63 B.C.

52. Zech 11:9b: following God's decision to break His covenantal staff and to let the Jewish kingdom die (above), He adds, "And let them that are left eat every one the flesh of another." This parallels what is suggested by the breaking of the internal Jewish brotherhood in v. 14 (see No. 55, below). But this latter *follows* the rejection of the Messiah (vv. 12–13) and was symbolized by the breaking of "mine other staff." Fulfillment (per. 12): this, which precedes the Messiah, may thus indicate the inner Jewish struggle between the high priest and ethnarch for the Romans, Hyrcanus II (63–40) and his nephew Antigonus II (40–37), who performed the equivalent of a literal accomplishment of the prophecy by disqualifying his uncle from the priesthood, trhough physical unfitness, by cutting off his ears.[85]

53. Zech 11:12 (1 v., sym.): "I [Zechariah] said unto them, 'Give me my hire,' " God's request of the Jews to see how they would respond to His lordship as the Good Shepherd. "So they weighed for my hire thirty pieces of silver," presumably shekels (though this is not stated), the price of a slave, Ex. 21:32. Fulfillment (per. 13): Zechariah thus enacted the evaluation of Christ by the Jews, at His betrayal, Mt 26:15;[86] cf. Hos. No. 14 (3:2).

54. Zech 11:13a (1 v., sym.): "And Yahweh said unto me, 'Cast it unto the potter, the goodly price [contemptuous irony] that I was prized at by them.' And I took the thirty pieces of silver and cast them unto the potter, in the house of Yahweh," for God is both the witness and the object of the insult. A potter must have been there in the temple, perhaps delivering vessels, or at least something of small value (see II Tim 2:20),

84. KD, II:366.
85. Jos, *Ant*, XIV:13, 10.
86. The difficulty in interpreting this prediction apart from the light of the NT may be illustrated by the following comments: "The prophecy is the most enigmatic in the OT. It is obviously an allegory. . . . The meaning of the allegory is, however, obscure: it is neither interpreted nor apparent, as in the case of the allegories in Ezek. If our information from Nehemiah to Antiochus, 432 to c. 175 B.C. were fuller, we might perhaps find that it described events which had actually happened," Cent, II:253. "Who is the shepherd? This is the crucial question. He is unfortunately a somewhat Protean figure [constantly changing] and the allegory is obviously confused, but the facts that only God can be speaking in v. 10 and in v. 14 lead to the belief that the shepherd represents primarily God's governance of his people. It is not impossible that the prophet who speaks these words may himself have once occupied for a brief period the position of governor under the Ptolemies," IB, VI:1103.

for this further depicts God's contempt for the money. Fulfillment (per. 13): in the actions of Judas, as quoted in Mt 27:5–10.[87]

55. Zech 11:14 (1 v., sym.): another object lesson, as Zechariah's second staff, Bands, is broken up (compare v. 10, No. 51, above). Explained (v. 14b): the brotherhood between Judah and Israel to be broken. Fulfilled (per. 14) in the internal strife among the Jewish factions, both leading up to and during the war with Rome.[88]

56. Zech 11:17 (1 v., sym.): "Woe to the worthless shepherd [see v. 16, under No. 36, above]! The sword shall be upon his arm; his arm shall be clean dried up." Fulfillment (per. 14): the fall of Rome, as in Num. No. 42 (24:24b), for mistreatment of the flock (Israel, in A.D. 70, for whom Roman government failed badly).

57. Zech *12:2b, 3b*; 14:1–2 (2 vv.): on "a day of Yahweh" (14:1), Jerusalem to be under siege by "all the peoples round about" (12:2), namely, v. 3, "all the nations of the earth[89] shall be gathered together against it" (in Zechariah's 5th cycle = 14:2 in his 6th), with Judah as a whole under siege too (13:2b). "Thy spoil shall be divided in the midst of thee, and the city shall be taken, and the houses rifled, and the women ravished; and half the city shall go forth into captivity" (14:1–2). Fulfillment (per. 15): as in Joel No. 13 (3:2), the eschatological attack upon Jerusalem, the world's response to the second coming of Jesus Christ (see 14:4a, No. 69, below).[90] The three vv. preceding 14:1–2 (13:7–9) had concerned A.D. 70 and the subsequent trials of the Jews (see No. 36 and 68); but 14:1–2 cannot be so taken,[91] for at this point "the residue of the people shall *not* be cut off from the city" (v. 2); it is here, rather, that God personally intervenes (v. 3, see next).

58. Zech 12:1–2, 3a, 4, 6a, 8; 14:3, 12–15 (11 vv., fig.): "I will make Jerusalem a cup, *saf* [*a bowl, basin*,[92] so that many may drink] of reeling,"

---

87. The reference to Jeremiah in Mt 27:9 may concern the purchase of the field (v. 10) from the potter, a feature which is not mentioned in Zech, but is in Jer 19:1; or it may simply designate Jer as the first book (?) in Mt's prophetic division of the OT canon.

88. Laetsch, op. cit., pp. 473–474.

89. Or, *all the nations of the land*; that is, of the Near Eastern nations in the immediate vicinity of Israel; cf. v. 2, "all the peoples round about," or v. 6, "the peoples round about, on the right hand and the left." Dr. B. E. Northrup of the Baptist Bible School of Theology has therefore proposed that the more local understanding might produce correspondence with the acts of Arab hostility against Israel from 1948 through the war of 1967, e.g. in v. 6, "they of Jerusalem [the Israeli new city] shall yet again dwell in their own place, even in Jerusalem [the Old City, after the June, 1967, reunification]." Yet the believing and faithful condition of "the inhabitants of Jerusalem" (v. 5; cf. vv. 10ff., No. 62, below) and the compensatory destruction of "all the nations" (v. 9; cf. the eschatological character of the parallel in Zechariah's 6th cycle, 14:2–4), militate against the local interpretation.

90. See above, p. 140. The potential rapidity of such hostile countermeasures can be more easily grasped now, in the light of modern military technology, than ever before; see Payne, *Theology of the Older Testament*, p. 482.

91. As in NBC, p. 761; contrast BBC, V:398.

92. KB, p. 663.

i.e., one that causes it. The defeat of the enemy is compared with staggering in intoxication (cf. Ps 60:3, Isa 5:22–23, Hab 2:15–16). 14:3, "Then shall Yahweh go forth and fight against these nations," as He had done in the past; v. 12, their flesh (especially feet, eyes, and tongues) is to consume away in a plague "while they stand upon their feet" in the siege. The plague will affect their animals too, v. 15. 12:3. "All the nations of the earth," who attack, are to be cut in pieces. 12:4, God will throw the enemy into blind confusion, so that (14:13) they fight each other, but will uphold Judah (the church, see 12:7 and No. 22, above), whose leaders will devour like a flame on every hand (12:6). 12:8, the Jerusalemites themselves will become as strong as David once was; and the princes of David's house, as strong as God—God defends them. 14:14b, the enemy will thus leave a great plunder, including gold, silver, and clothing. Fulfillment (per. 15): Jerusalem victorious against the siege, as implied in Joel 3:16a; cf. Ps 102:13.

59. Zech 12:5, *14:14a* (1 v.): "The chieftains of Judah shall say, 'The inhabitants of Jerusalem are my strength in Yahweh of hosts their God.' " So Judah, 14:13, fights *b-, along with,* not against,[93] the Jerusalem Jews. Fulfillment (per. 15): the church's leaders (see No. 22) will discover that the Jews (12:10) have become their allies and now contribute their assistance against the attacking nations (vv. 2–3, No. 57, above). This is because they have received Christ as their God (see No. 62, below).

60. Zech *12:6b,* 14:11 (1 v.): "They of Jerusalem shall yet again dwell in their own place, in Jerusalem," following the attacks of 12:2–3, 14:2–3, which had routed them. 14:11, "and there shall be no more curse" (ASVmg, "ban, devoting to destruction"): not yet the removal of God's curse from nature, as in Ps 96:12, but simply Jerusalem resettled and restored in the Messianic kingdom (per. 16), no longer subject to spoiling, as in 14:2.

61. Zech 12:9, *14:16a* (1 v.): "In that day I will seek to destroy all the [pagan] nations that come against Jerusalem": "the phrase suggests *effort* and so has a strange sound when attributed to the Almighty. The Hebrew may however bear the sense: 'I will make research as to destroying' . . . Zech 12–14 does not use indiscriminate denunciation of the Gentiles."[94] Cf. 14:16, "every one *that is left* of all the nations that came against Jerusalem." Fulfillment (per. 15): divine discrimination in the punishment of those attacking Jerusalem, so that some are left.

62. Zech 12:10–14; 13:1, 9b (7 vv.): "I will pour out upon . . . the inhabitants of Jerusalem the spirit of grace and of supplication." They will have a spirit or impulse of (i.e. seeking for) grace, by supplication, involving bitter lamentation, the sorrow of repentance. Two royal and two priestly families—one each that is important (David and Levi) and one inferior

---

93. So Driver favors *with* and renders *al* (14:12) as *against* Jerusalem, Cent, II:279.
94. Camb, *Hag-Mal,* p. 93.

(Nathan, II Sam 5:14, though cf. Lk 3: 31, and Shimei, a grandson of Levi, Num 3:18)—are mentioned as representative of the completeness of the conversion (12:12–13). 13:1, the result: "There shall be a fountain opened for [washing from] sin"; cf. v. 9, "They shall call on My name, and I will hear them." When they say, "Yahweh [and Christ] is my God," they again become God's people. Fulfillment (per. 15): the conversion of the Jews (see next); cf. Dt 30:8.

63. Zech *12–10b*: "The house of David and the inhabitants of Jerusalem . . ." shall look upon the divine Messiah whom they have pierced. The subject must be Jews, those who were primarily responsible for the death of Christ (Mt 27:35, John 19:12, Acts 4:13, 13:28; cf. Acts 5:28, Rev 1:7); and Zechariah predicts that some will be residing in Jesusalem at the Lord's return. Fulfillment (per. 14): the existence of an unconverted Jewish community (cf. No. 62, above) in Jerusalem, in the period immediately preceding Christ's second coming. It should be cautioned, however, that such a community does not necessarily entail the existence of an independent (Zionist) state. The *house of David* need not imply a Knesset (though it of course might): these are simply "people of high or royal status in distinction from the lowly or common inhabitants of the city."[95]

64. Zech *12:10d, 13:7a*: "Me" whom they pierced, God speaking; and 13:7, ". . . My Shepherd [fig.], the man that is My fellow," God's *āmīth*, "associate," in a fellowship of equality. Keil notes that this noun is "only used as a synonym for brother, cf. Lev 25:15, 'My nearest One,' by community of physical or spiritual descent"; cf. Edghill's conclusion, "Jehovah Himself was wounded in the person of the shepherd that was His fellow." Fulfillment (per. 13): the deity of the Person of Christ the Good Shepherd (see 11:12), who "participated in the divine nature,"[96] as in Ps. prophecy No. 53 (110:1a).

65. Zech *12:10e, 13:7b* (1 v.): Me "whom they have pierced." 13:7, "Smite the Shepherd," a commentary on how God the Good Shepherd (above) is pierced. Fulfillment (per. 13): Christ smitten (so quoted, Mt. 26:31, Mk 14:27) and pierced on the cross (so quoted, John 19:37).

66: Zech *13:7c* (fig.): smite the Shepherd "and the sheep shall be scattered." Fulfillment (per. 13): at Christ's death, His disciples scattered, just as He had anticipated, quoting this verse (Mt 26:31, Mk 14:27). But the disciples formed only a part, the preserved "little ones" (see 11:7, No. 48, above), of the flock as a whole, 11:8–9. Two elements, both the disciples and the unbelieving nation, are included in the one "flock";[97] so

95. Unger, op. cit., p. 215; cf. Payne, ETS P (1956), 62–65.
96. KD, *Minor Prophets*, II:397; cf. E A. Edghill, *An Inquiry into the Evidential Value of Prophecy*, pp. 234–235, who adds, "It seems most probable that Zechariah here definitely connects the good shepherd with the Servant of the Lord."
97. KD, II:398.

the fulfillment of 13:7c may also be noted as occurring (per. 14) at the fall of Jerusalem in A.D. 70 (9:10a, No. 36, above).

67. Zech *13:7d*: "I will turn My hand upon the little ones"; lit., "bring back My hand over": not in an evil sense, as in Amos 1:8, but in a good sense, as in Isa 1:25, "to make them the object of His active care once more."[98] Fulfillment (per. 13): in Mt 26:32, Mk 14:28, Jesus thus went on to speak of meeting His disciples in Galilee, after He had risen from the dead.

68. Zech *13:8b–9a*: "But the third part shall be left therein [in the land of Israel], and I will bring into the fire and refine them as silver." Fulfillment (per. 14): the survival of Israel after the flesh following A.D. 70, as in Mi. No. 18; cf. Hos 3:3, yet in the fires of persecution; see above, p. 100.

69. Zech *14:4a*: "His feet shall stand in that day upon the mount of Olives." Fulfillment (per. 15): the place of Christ's return, Olivet, as the climax to His initial appearing in the clouds. Driver's statement about v. 5 would thus appear applicable to v. 4 as well: "Yahweh . . . will now come, i.e. apparently come nearer . . . to complete the defeat of His foes, and establish His kingdom."[99]

70. Zech 14:4b–5a (2 vv.): the Mount of Olives to be divided by an east–west valley,[100] allowing escape from Jerusalem: "and ye shall flee by the valley . . . unto Azel," an unknown locality but presumably "at the foot of the Mount of Olives."[101] Fulfillment (per. 15): the rescue of converted Jews from Jerusalem, just having fallen to "all nations" (v. 2).

71. Zech *14:5b*: ". . . and all the holy ones with Thee." Fulfillment (per. 15): Christ's return with angels, as in Joel No. 18 (so Mt 25:31), although the precise *coming* in v. 5 is to battle (v. 3; see under 12:1, No. 58); cf. a similar angelic retinue at appearances of Yahweh, Dt 33:2. The presence also of the raptured church of God is not to be excluded, for "the NT reveals that Christ in His coming again to the earth will be accompanied by an innumerable company both of angels and glorified saints of the church period."[102]

72. Zech 14:6, 7b (2 vv.): "In that day there shall not be light; the bright ones [stars] shall withdraw themselves . . . not day and not night [half light]; but at evening time there shall be light," when Christ's victory

98. Ibid.
99. Cent, II:274.
100. "If the coming of Messiah is literal, so must this catastrophe be literal. . . . Even believeing scholars frequently balk at a literal interpretation of the earthquake and the other marvels of this passage and either mysticalize them altogether or apply them to past events with which they only inexactly agree. The only true interpretation is to relate the chapter wholly to the still future 'day of the Lord,'" Unger, op. cit., pp. 248–249.
101. Leupold, op. cit., p. 263.
102. Unger, op. cit., p. 249.

is won. Fulfillment (per. 15): heavenly phenomena, a part of the wrath of God, as in Joel 2:30.

73. Zech *14:7a*: "It shall be one day which is known unto Yahweh." Fulfillment (per. 15): Christ's second coming, the time of which is known only to God;[103] cf. Dt 29:29 and Mk 13:32.

74. Zech 14:8 (1 v.): living water to flow perennially from Jerusalem, descending to the Dead Sea on the east and the Mediterranean on the west. Fulfillment (per. 16): as in Joel No. 22.

75. Zech 14:10 (1 v.): "All the land from Geba [in Benjamin] to Rimmon south of Jerusalem [near Beersheba]," indicating, essentially, all the southern kingdom, is to be leveled. But Jerusalem is to maintain its high elevation and will fill out its urban boundaries (which are stated, in part). Fulfillment (per. 16): geographical changes, as in Isa. No. 7 (see note 99, above); cf. the flow of the water in v. 8.

76. Zech *14:16c*: "All nations shall go up from year to year [to Jerusalem] to worship the King, Yahweh of hosts, and to keep the feast of tabernacles." Fulfillment (per. 16), thus accomplishing the typology of ingathering that had characterized this OT observance; see Ex 23:16.

77. Zech 14:17-19 (3 vv.): the penalty for failure to worship God, v. 17, no rain; v. 18, Egypt, which has no rain, to have the same effects— perhaps by failure of the Nile's annual flood. Fulfillment (per. 16); see Joel 3:19a for further thought on Egypt.

78. Zech *14:20b, 21b* (typ.): there will be a "house of Yahweh" and an altar and sacrificers (on the Feast of Tabernacles [?], v. 16). Fulfillment (per. 16): as in Isa No. 8.

103. IB, VI:1111.

MALACHI

The last of the prophets, and indeed the only volume of prophecy to appear during the period that led up to the close of the OT canon in the latter 5th century B.C.,[1] was the Book of Malachi. Whether an individual man was actually named Malachi has sometimes been questioned, since the term *malākhī*, meaning "My messenger," does occur in Mal 3:1 as a common noun and not as a proper name.[2] But since the *messenger* of God who mediated the prophecy (1:1) could hardly be the same "Malachi" who is predicted in 3:1[3] (which refers to John the Baptist; see No. 9,

1. See above, pp. 249-250.
2. The Targum of Jonathan thus ascribes the Book of Malachi to Ezra.
3. Because of the similarity of the titles in Zech 9:1, 12:1, and Mal 1:1, liberal criticism generally connects Zech 9 through Mal 4 as a single, anonymous com-

below), and since the prophets seem elsewhere to have made occasional use of their own names to enliven their preaching,[4] the word Malachi is best understood in the prophecy's opening verse, just as in the case of the other eleven Minor Prophets, as the true name of the book's author. Though the life of Malachi remains unknown, his times are those of Jewish worship by means of altar and sacrifice in a temple (1:7–10) and of Jewish rule by a governor in Jerusalem (1:8). He must therefore have made his appearance after the postexilic, 6th-century prophets Haggai and Zechariah. This servant of God might possibly be located prior to the coming of Ezra and of the second major return of the Jews from Babylon in 458 (Ezra 7–8) or between this event and the arrival of Nehemiah in 444 (Neh 2:1). But Malachi's ministry seems most probably to have fallen between the termination of Nehemiah's first governorship in 432 (13:6) and the return of this leader some time later, for in his second governorship Nehemiah was concerned about reforming the very kinds of failures against which Malachi directs his preaching.[5] The prophet may thus be dated about 430 B.C.;[6] and his volume becomes the latest book in the OT, next to the final, historical writing of Nehemiah himself.

Malachi's four brief chapters fall into two general halves: chs. 1–2, on the need for divine intervention in the life of Judah, because of the people's sin; and chs. 3–4, on the nature of this intervention, as foreseen by the prophet (though 3:7–15 is once again taken up with various failures of Israel). Malachi's is a book of transition. He stands at the close of the OT period, as the last representative of divine prophecy before its reappearance in the preaching of John the Baptist.[7] For the prophetic movement's basic goal of preserving the principles of the Mosaic theocracy[8] had been finally

---

pilation (see above, introduction to Zechariah p. 447); cf. G. Fohrer, *Introduction to the OT*, pp. 465, 469. Yet Zech 9–14 is in fact bound closely with the rest of Zech as one authentic work of 520–480 B.C.; cf. its basic format of six apocalyptic cycles, Table 11, above; and Malachi preserves its own distinctive literary patterns throughout, e.g., that of rhetorical questions (cf. 1:2, 6; 2:10, 17; 3:7–8, 13). It is possible that Malachi may have designed his title after Zechariah's; cf. the common "postexilic" style of Hag 1:2, 4, 7; Zech 1:3–4; and Mal 1:5–9, ibid., p. 469.

4. Compare how Micah, whose name means, *Who*(is) *like Yah*(weh), concludes his book with the question, "Who is a God like unto Thee . . ." (Mi 7:18).

5. Eg. on temple tithes

and revenues:	Neh 12:44–47, 13:10–14	cf. Mal 3:7–10
on mixed marriages with pagans:	13:1–3, 23–27	2:10–16
on the presence of corrupt men in the priesthood:	13:4–9, 28–29	2:1–9
on profaned sabbaths and Levites needing cleansing:	13:15–22	1:6–14 (on polluted sacrifices)

6. Cf. E. J. Young, *An Introduction to the OT*, p. 301.

7. See I Macc 9:27, on Judah's intertestamental awareness of the cessation of this gift.

8. See above, p. 3.

achieved through the Book-centered revivals of Ezra the scribe (Ezra 7:10, Neh 8:1–9); and a key verse to the thought of Malachi is therefore his injunction, "Remember ye the law of Moses" (Mal 4:4). Yet he stands also, with his inspired eyes lifted across the "400 silent years," viewing God's next great events for the achievement of His redemptive purpose in human history: the coming of Elijah—the human messenger, John (3:1, 4:5–6)—to herald the incarnation of God's divine Messenger, the Angel of the testament, in the Person of Jesus Christ (3:1). And Malachi moves onward to speak also of Christ's second coming (v. 2), millennial kingdom (v. 3),[9] final judgment (vv. 5, 17–18; cf. 4:1), and ultimate rule in the New Jerusalem (4:2–3). A total of 19 different predictions appear throughout the book, which involve 31 of its 55 verses, or 56% of the whole. As Laetsch has summarized the witness of this messenger of the Lord, "To the last, the last prophet of the OT points out to all sinners the need of repentance and faith in the promised Redeemer, the Angel of the Covenant, the Sun of righteousness. This promise connects the OT, the time of prophecy and hopeful waiting, with the time of fulfillment and joyous realization, the era of the Gospel of Jesus Christ."[10]

1. Mal 1:4–5 (2 vv.): concerning the material that precedes this oracle, Keil states, "Verses 2 and 3 evidently contain the thought, that whereas Jacob had recovered, in consequence of the love of Jehovah, from the blow which had fallen upon it [through the Chaldeans], Esau's territory was lying in ruins, in consequence of Jehovah's hatred,"[11] the Nabatean Arabs having actually expelled the Edomites from their lands by 500 B.C. (see Obad, v. 5). So, as a countermove, "Edom saith, We will return and build the waste places," Mal 1:4 meaning: "They looked forward hopefully to reestablishing their life in the old environs."[12] But Yahweh replies, even in respect to their efforts in southern Judea (Idumaea), to which they had emigrated, "They shall build, but I will throw down; and men shall call them The border of wickedness [i.e. their punishment will be so severe that men will assume them to have been most wicked], and The people against whom Yahweh hath indignation for ever.

---

9. Versus C. Feinberg, *Premillennialism or Amillennialism?* p. 52, who thinks of Malachi as the one Minor Prophet "who does not directly or by type speak of the kingdom age, although he deals with . . . the visible coming of the Sun of righteousness with healing in His wings." Yet on the other hand, prophets such as Jonah (see above, p. 423, note 6, on his nontypical character), Nahum (who spoke only to his immediate period, though Feinberg seeks to introduce a second [millennial] sense within his prophecy, ibid., p. 56). Habakkuk (see above, p. 438, on Hab 3:3–15's reference to Sinai in the past, rather than to Christ's second coming), and Haggai appear to contain no identifiable predictions of the Messiah's future, earthly kingdom.

10. *Bible Commentary: The Minor Prophets*, p. 547.

11. *Minor Prophets*, II:432.

12. IB, VI:1124.

And your eyes shall see, and ye shall say, Yahweh is great [ASVmg] beyond the border of Israel," vv. 4–5, specifically, when His words against Edom should be vindicated. Fulfillment (per. 11): as in Gen 25:23b, 3rd stage, the ultimate overthrow of the Edomites in Judah's Negeb country by John Hyrcanus in 109 B.C.[13] The prophet's oracle could hardly refer to their recovery after the attacks of the Babylonians in the 6th century (see Jer 9:26c and 12:15), since Malachi is some 70 years later than their *subsequent* destruction by the Nabateans.

2. Mal 1:6 (1 v., typ.): priests, officiating at the altar.[14] Fulfillment (per. 13): as in Ex. prophecy No. 59.

3. Mal 1:*7a,* 8, *10b, 12b,* 13–14; 2:12, 13b (5 vv., typ.): sacrifice. 1:7 may indeed state, "Ye offer bread," ASV, but the thought is that of "the fat and the blood" of animals.[15] Fulfillment (per. 13): as in Lev. No. 2.

4. Mal 1:7b, 10a, 12a; *2:13a* (3 vv., typical): "Mine altar, the table of Yahweh," 1:7. Fulfillment (per. 13): as in Ex. No. 44.

5. Mal 1:11 (1 v.): "From the rising of the sun to the going down of the same My name shall be great among the Gentiles; and in every place incense shall be offered unto My name, and a pure offering." This verse could be taken nonpredictively as meaning that in all nations God's name *is* great: either in the sense of pagan sacrifices that God accepts, or in the sense of worship performed by the Jewish diaspora as being better than that conducted in Jerusalem.[16] Keil however says, rightly, of the former alternative, "The idea that the statement, that incense is burned and sacrifice offered to the name of Jehovah in every place, refers to the sacrifices which the heathen offered to their gods, is inadmissible"; and of the latter, "At the time of Malachi the name of Jehovah was not great from the rising to the setting of the sun. . . . [The verse is] saying too much. Consequently we must understand the words prophetically as relating to the spread of the kingdom of God among all nations."[17] Concerning then the subject that Mal 1:11 is predicting, Girdlestone insists that one is "to interpret in the light of the [NT] epistles; and we may fairly point to the offering of the Gentiles (Rom 15:16) as being foreshadowed in the prophetic word."[18] This means that, of the terms "incense" and "offering," at least the latter is to be understood figuratively, as in Rom 12:1, Heb 13:15, I Pet 2:5, Rev 5:8, 8:3–4, and not literally, as in Heb 7:27, etc.[19] Indeed, if the circumstances of accomplishment are taken to be those of the

13. ICC, p. 6.
14. Contrast 2:2, which concerns their (nonpredictive, or typical) blessings.
15. ICC, p. 26.
16. So E. A. Edghill, *An Enquiry into the Evidential Value of Prophecy,* pp. 333–335.
17. II:438.
18. *The Grammar of Prophecy,* p. 80.
19. See above, p. 84.

diaspora of Malachi's own time (or of the millennium, which is yet to come), in which overall historical context would require the sense of literal offerings,[20] then one is faced with the problem that according to Biblical law these simply could not have been acceptable in every place.[21] Fulfillment (per. 14): as in Gen. No. 19, the universal worship of the Lord by Gentiles, upon their incorporation into the church, the Israel of God.

6. Mal 2:2–3 (2 vv.): if the Jewish priests will not hear God's command, so as to glorify His name, Yahweh says, "I will send the curse upon you," 2:2, and specifically the destruction stated in v. 3, "Behold, I will rebuke your *zéra, seed*," i.e. your "posterity,"[22] though this last word may also be pointed *z'rō'a*: He will rebuke your "arm," which would suggest "the neutralizing of the official duties performed at the altar and in the sanctuary."[23] Yahweh goes on to warn them, "Ye shall be taken away with the dung of your feasts," that is, be "removed from the city along with the dung of the sacrifice (cf. Lev 4:12)."[24] The nature of these words could be simply that of a general threat, signifying that they will be "thoroughly discredited unless they learn to be worthy representatives of God"[25] (cf. 2:9, 12); but the violence of the retribution and its specific application to their posterity combine with the known pronouncements of Jesus against the priests of His day (Mt 21:23, 41, 44–45; see under 10:23b) to suggest a fulfillment (per. 14) in the destruction of the priesthood at the fall of Jerusalem in A.D. 70, as in Mi. No. 39 (7:13).

7. Mal 2:4–5, 8 (3 vv., typ.): the Levitical testament. Fulfillment (per. 13): as in Num. No. 43 (25:12).

8. Mal 2:10 (1 v., typ.): the Sinaitic testament. Fulfillment (per. 13): as in Ex. No. 45 (19:5).

9. Mal *3:1a* (taken from Isa 40:3),[26] 4:5 (1 v.): God says, "Behold, I send My messenger; and he shall prepare the way before Me," 3:1, that is, "prepare men to receive Him,"[27] to which 4:5 adds, "Behold, I send you Elijah the prophet before the day" of judgment. Fulfillment (per. 13): as in Isa. No. 90 (40:3), by the ministry of John the Baptist.

20. Cent, *Minor Prophets*, II:305.
21. Though liberalism would maintain, "It is by no means clear that the Deuteronomic legislation intended to condemn sanctuaries on foreign soil. . . . The further development of the ritual was along narrowly exclusive lines; but it was not carried through without a fierce struggle. Many devout Jews aligned themselves with the more liberal tendencies," ICC, p. 32, though cf. John 4:22.
22. NBC, p. 766.
23. KD, II:443.
24. BBC, V:420.
25. NBC, loc. cit.
26. And perhaps Isa 62:10?
27. Cent, II:318; cf. Keil, II:457, "Preparing the way, by clearing away the impediments lying in the road, denotes the removal of all that retards the coming of the Lord to His people, i.e. the taking away of enmity to God and of ungodliness by the preaching of repentance and the conversion of sinners."

While John was not literally a conscious reincarnation of Elijah,[28] and while his ministry has now proved to be a long period "before the day" of God's judgment, these passages were quoted in the NT both by the people in general and by Christ Himself, who said that "Elijah came" in John the Baptist, Mt. 17:12 (see below, under Mt 3:3 [especially notes 15–17] and Lk 1:17a).

10. Mal 3:1b (1 v.): "The Lord, even the Angel [ASVmg] of the testament, will suddenly come to His temple"; for this was the proper place for the great, future theophany to occur, Hag 2:9. Fulfillment (per. 13): as in Haggai No. 6, Christ's appearance in the Jerusalem temple; for He *is* divine, God Himself, as was the Angel of Yahweh, cf. Ex 3:2, 4–6,[29] and He embodies the testament, giving His life in redemptive sacrifice; see Isa 42:6a. As indicated by the "Angel's" association with John the Baptist (see Mal 3:1a, No. 9, preceding), this oracle must refer to the Messiah's first coming rather than to His second (No. 11, next).

11. Mal 3:2 (1 v.): moving directly from Christ's testamentary, first advent (No. 10, preceding; and see above, p. 138) Malachi exclaims, "But who can abide the day of His coming? and who can stand when He appeareth? For He is like a refiner's fire." Fulfillment (per. 15): as in Ps. prophecy No. 5, the Savior's reappearing, in power, so as to destroy or to purify (see v. 3a, No. 12, following).

12. Mal 3:3a (1 v.): at the Messiah's return (No. 11, preceding), "He will purify the sons of Levi and refine them." Fulfillment (per. 16): as in Dt. No. 45 (see under Zech 8:3c for details), the final purification of God's people; cf. Isa 66:21 on the predicted broadening out of the category of Levites, though Jews are also to be included,[30] as suggested by the castigation of this same Levitical group in Mal 2:8.

13. Mal 3:3b–4 (1 v.): the Levites "shall offer unto Yahweh offerings in righteousness," 3:3b. That is, purged at Christ's second coming (v. 3a, No. 12, preceding), they are to officiate at "the offerings of Judah," v. 4, which will have become acceptable to God, as in former times. Fulfillment (per. 16): millennial sacrifice, as in Isa. No. 8.

14. Mal 3:5, 4:1 (2 vv.): after the future purifying of 3:3, and the restored worship of 3:4 (No. 12–13, preceding), the Lord warns, "I will come near to you in judgment," 3:5; and punishment is specified as meted out against crimes of both a religious nature (e.g. sorcery, or a lack of fear for God) and a social nature (e.g. adultery, or oppression). He continues, 4:1, "The day cometh, it burneth as a furnace," against "all the proud and all that work wickedness"; contrast the hope of the righteous in 3:17–18 (No. 16, below). Fulfillment (per. 17): as in Ps. No. 1 (1:5), the final judgment, to burn up all the wicked.

28. See above, pp. 72, 83.
29. J. B. Payne, *Theology of the Older Testatament*, pp. 167–170.
30. See above, p. 104.

15. Mal 3:10 (1 v., typ.): the temple. Fulfillment (per .13): as in Ex. No. 55.

16. Mal 3:17–18 (2 vv.): because "a book of remembrance" had been written before Yahweh for them that feared Him, v. 16, the Lord promises, "They shall be Mine own possession ["My jewels," KJV], in the day that I make; and I will spare them," v. 17. He adds, "Then shall ye discern between him that serveth God and him that serveth Him not," v. 18, and so furnishes His own answer to the criticism of 2:17, that questioned the reality of a God of justice. Fulfillment (per. 17): as in Job No. 5, the sparing and the rewarding of those who are faithful to the Lord, at His final judgment.

17. Mal 4:2 (1 v., fig.): "Unto you that fear My name shall the sun of righteousness arise," that is, a day of righteous vindication. The figure is then explained as indicative of "healing" (cf. Rev 22:2); "and ye shall go forth and gambol as calves of the stall," comparing the joy of the redeemed to "the healthy exuberance of a calf when released from the confinement of its stall."[31] Fulfillment (per. 18): as in Rev. 2:7, the restored, or "healed," state of the righteous in God's New Jerusalem.

18. Mal 4:3 (1 v. fig.): the saved are to "tread down the wicked; for they shall be ashes under the soles of your feet." Laetsch explains that though the action of the saints in *treading down* the wicked may be a figure of speech, the remainder of the oracle possesses a more literal significance: "They have been reduced to ashes (v. 1); and you, believing My word, shall regard them as ashes."[32] Fulfillment (per. 18): as in II Sam, No. 20, the eternal fate of the lost in the fires of hell; cf. also Isa 66:24 on this awareness on the part of the saved in respect to the lost.

19. Mal 4:6 (1 v.): at the coming of Elijah, v. 5 (No. 9, above), "He shall turn the hearts of the fathers to the children, and the heart of the children to their fathers, lest I come and smite the land [ASVmg] with a curse." Fulfillment (per. 13): John the Baptist's preaching in the 1st-century land of Israel for general repentance and for the overcoming of social discord, Lk 3:12–18; and the oracle is so quoted in Lk 1:15, which adds the clarifying note that his ministry will be to turn "the disobedient to the attitude of the righteous." Keil thus indicates that the prophecy's scope extends beyond "merely directing the love of the fathers to the sons once more, but also restoring the heart of the fathers, and generally the pious forefathers, in the sons, the degenerate descendants." God's punishment would thus be averted, or at least postponed until A.D. 70.[33]

31. IB, VI:1143.
32. Op. cit., p. 543.
33. II:472.

THE
NEW TESTAMENT

MATTHEW

The Gospel of Matthew contains more predictions than any other book of the New Testament, namely 81. Within the whole of Scripture, indeed, this number is exceeded only by the major prophecies of Isaiah and Jeremiah in the OT. Interestingly enough, a similarly high figure (77) appears for the historical book of Genesis, which opens the older Testament. Matthew's total of 1,067 verses is almost a hundred fewer than Luke's; yet 278 of these involve prophetic material, which again is the greatest number for any NT writing—26% of the book, a truly high figure for historical narrative, but one which is exceeded in certain of the NT epistles and in John's apocalyptic visions of the Revelation.

Matthew's emphasis on prediction stems from the Gospel's basic purpose: to demonstrate to a primarily Jewish audience[1] that "Jesus, the son of David, the son of Abraham," is "Christ" (1:1), the Messiah, as foretold by the prophecies of the OT. A number of Matthew's citations from the older canon are of a merely illustrative nature, e.g. the allusions in its second chapter (vv. 15, 18) to Hos 11:1 and Jer 31:15. Neither passage was originally spoken in predictive terms; and both are introduced in Matthew by the verb *plērōthē*, which suggests an intent of "fulfilling" the earlier passages to the extent of *giving* their teaching *an additional illustration* (cf. James 2:23).[2] Yet the evangelist's references to authentic Messianic prophecies abound, a fact which corresponds to "the early Christians' absorbing interest in the OT predictions which were fulfilled in Jesus Christ."[3]

The Biblical text itself gives no direct information about the circumstances surrounding the origin of the first Gospel—or of the other Gospels either, for that matter. But there seems to be no compelling reason for questioning the unanimous and early tradition which assigns it to the

1. As indicated not simply by the writer's general stress upon the OT, but also by certain specific phenomena: e.g., his adaptation to the Judaistic practice of not using the divine name but referring, ordinarily, to the "kingdom of heaven" rather than "kingdom of God" as in the Gospels (see above, pp. 96, 134) or, his reference to Christ, as above, as "son of David"—nine times, as opposed to no more than three in any of the others.
2. See discussion in the Introduction, pp. 177–78.
3. Donald Guthrie, *The Gospels and Acts: NT Introduction*, p. 19.

apostle Matthew (or Levi), the tax collector, the son of Alpheus (Mk 2:14).[4] At the outset of the 2nd Christian century, the patristic writer Papias testified that "Matthew composed the Logia—i.e. the *sayings*, but perhaps also narratives, of Christ; cf. Rom 3:2—in the Hebrew [= Aramaic] dialect, and each one interpreted them as he was able."[5] Some interval of time must therefore have elapsed before God's Holy Spirit inspired him to the composition of his eventual Gospel in the Greek;[6] and yet this latter inscripturation could hardly have occurred subsequent to the fall of Jerusalem to Titus in A.D. 70 without the author's leaving in his work traces of an event that was so momentous to all Jewish Christians.[7] M. C. Tenney thus assigns a date to the Gospel "just before the destruction of Jerusalem,"[8] which designates Matthew as the latest of the Synoptics (see introductions to Mark and Luke, below), but still previous to John.

The problems of interrelationship between the four Gospels exceed the limits of the present discussion. Suffice it that a number of evangelical authorities on the NT have recognized as legitimate the so-called two-document hypothesis, under which the Gospel of Mark and an assumed Greek document styled Q—from the German, *Quelle*, "source": presumably a collection of logia, similar to Matthew's in Aramaic—are accepted as constituting major literary sources for the Gospels of Luke and Matthew.[9] The chief concern of evangelicals is that while "the authors may have used 'sources' for some of the materials in the Gospels, they used them under the guidance and direction of the Holy Spirit. . . . It is in this way that each one of the three produced in a most natural way . . . a verbally inspired account of the life of Christ."[10] All four remain equal in historical value.

In the study which follows, where one prophecy has been recorded in several of the Gospels, it is discussed under that book in which it appears

---

4. Ibid., pp. 31, 39–42.

5. Preserved in Eusebius, *Ecclesiastical History*, III:39, 16; cf. Irenaeus, *Against Heresies*, III:1, 1.

6. Though Thiessen dates the latter "shortly after he wrote the Aramaic . . . about A.D. 50," *Introduction to the NT*, p. 137.

7. Cf. Lenski's reference to the inclusion of Christ's word about His followers' not completing their evangelization of the cities of Israel before His "coming" in the judgment of A.D. 66–70, as suggestive of composition prior to this event, *The Interpretation of Matthew*, p. 406.

8. Further qualified: "or a bit earlier," *The Genius of the Gospels*, p. 20. Liberal writers do, however, usually date Matthew shortly *after* the events of A.D. 70, e.g., E. J. Goodspeed, *An Introduction to the NT*, p. 159, or John L. McKenzie, in *The Jerome Bible Commentary*, II:65; but this is based on Matthew's dependence on Mark and on an assumed date for Mark just before A.D. 70; see below, introduction to Mark, and Guthrie, op. cit., p. 43.

9. See A. T. Robertson, *Studies in Mark's Gospel*, pp. 29–31; Guthrie, op. cit., pp. 209–211; or W. Graham Scroggie, *A Guide to the Gospels*, pp. 140, 180–184. Yet Thiessen feels that a combination of the hypothesis with a belief in full Scriptural inspiration is only "theoretically possible, but not probable," op. cit., p. 127; cf. Tenney, op. cit., pp. 28–37.

10. Thiessen, op. cit., pp. 121–122.

first in the historical chronology of events, as indicated in A. T. Robertson's *Harmony of the Gospels*; Matthew 1:21a, for example, is analyzed under Luke 1:31b. If the contexts are the same, the preference in listing is given to Mark, Luke, or Matthew in that order, in accordance with their presumed order of composition. Exception occurs where a given prophecy receives subsequent elaboration in a certain one of the Gospels, under which all of the predictive material is then listed and treated. The existence of parallel passages in other books is indicated by parentheses, added to the listing in the Gospel which contains the basic discussion. If the other passages are not parallel in the sense of being a report of the same incident, but of a second incident—similar in content, but later in occasion—this is noted by inserting the abbreviation "sim(ilar)": e.g., "Lk 1:31b (sim, Mt 1:21a)." Passages that receive primary discussion under their listing in another of the Gospels, and to which reference should be made, are followed by brackets, within which the parallel passage is indicated: e.g. "Mk 1:7 [see John 1:15]"; or, "Mt 1:21a [see Lk 1:31b, sim]." If the parallel is itself listed under an earlier passage in the other Gospel, this too is indicated: e.g. "Mk 1:2–3 [see Lk 3:4–6, under 1:17a]." There are only six prophecies that appear in all four of the Gospels: (1) the rite of baptism, preached by John, as a type foreshadowing redemption in Christ; see under Lk 3:3; (2) the citation of Isa 40:3, as fulfilled by John the Baptist, Lk 3:4, under Lk 1:17a; (3) John's prediction of Christ's coming after him, John 1:15; (4) John's prediction of Pentecost, Lk 3:16c; (5) Christ's forecasting Judas' betrayal, John 13:21, under 6:70; and (6) His foretelling of Peter's denial, Mk 14:30.

Concerning the arrangement of the first Gospel in recording the life of Christ, Thiessen states: "The first 4 chapters of Matthew are chronological; chs. 5–13 are topical; and chs. 14–28 are again chronological."[11] Of the 14 major parts into which Robertson's *Harmony* divides the Gospel records, Matthew is represented in all but three: Part I, on the sources of the Gospels (Luke); II, on the preexistence of Christ (John); and IX, on the later Judean ministry (Lk 10–13:21, John 7–10:39). Prophecies appear throughout the first Gospel.

1. Mt *1:21a* [see Lk prophecy No. 11, 1:31b), sim]. Mary to bear a son.

2. Mt 1:21b; 20:28 (Mk 10:45); *26:28b* (Mk *14:24b*)[12] (2vv., sym.): the Lord's name to be Jesus,[13] meaning *Yahweh is salvation*, "for

---

11. With the exception of 21:18–19; ibid., p. 138.
12. Lk 22:19b–20 is not here included because of its omission from the best MSS.
13. The subsequent act of naming that was carried out by Joseph (1:25) is more a matter of obedience than of the fulfilling of a prediction; see above, p. 40. A short time earlier Mary had received a similar command (Lk 1:31b); and, significantly, the phrasing of the actual act of naming in Luke 2:21 leaves room for

it is He who will save His people from their sins." Jesus Himself later stated that He came "to give His life a ransom for many" (20:28); and Edghill proposes Isa 53:10–11 as "the original passage which suggested to Christ" this phrasing.[14] A further predictive symbol appears in our Lord's use of the cup of wine at the Last Supper, representing His blood, "which is to be shed on behalf of many for forgiveness of sins." Fulfillment (per. 13): Christ's redemption of men, as in Isa 52:15a; cf. Job No. 4 etc. See also under Lk 1:54 and John 1:29.

3. Mt 1:22–*23a* (1 v.): the citation of Isaiah's virgin prophecy, as having been fulfilled (per. 13) by Christ's birth through the Virgin Mary, as in Isa 7:13–14a.

4. Mt 1:23b, 22:43–*44a*, 45 [see Lk 20:41, under Lk. No. 15] (3 vv., sym.): 1:23 is a citation of Isaiah's prophecy of the symbolic act of naming the Messianic child (see No. 3, preceding) *Immanuel*—"which translated means, 'God with us.' " It has been fulfilled (per. 13) by the incarnation of Christ: deity assuming human nature, conceived by the Holy Spirit (v. 20), as in Isa 7:14b.

5. Mt 2:5–6 (2 vv.): the citation of Mic 5:2, on the place of Christ's birth, in Bethlehem. Fulfillment (per. 13): as in Mi. prophecy No. 27.

6. Mt 2:13 (1 v.): warning by the Lord's angel to Joseph, "Herod is going to search for the Child to destroy Him." Fulfillment (per. 13): Herod did, v. 16.

7. Mt 2:23 (1 v.): an allusion to "what was spoken through the prophets" about Jesus, that "He shall be called a Nazarene." This probably refers back to Isa 11:1, that the Messiah should be a *néser,* "branch," out of the family of Jesse. Fulfillment (per. 13): as in Isa 11:1, under which its correspondence with the town name Nazareth, which comes from this same root and means "branch town," is elaborated.

8. Mt 3:3, 11:10, 16:14 [see Lk 3:4 etc., under Lk. No. 8], but also 11:14, 17:10–13 (Mk 9:11–*12a*, 13) (8 vv.): Luke had recorded that John the Baptist should go before Christ "in the spirit and power" of Elijah (1:17), but Matthew's supplementary verses add the idea of a more direct equation of the two. In Mt 11:14 Christ speaks of "Elijah, who was to come," quoting Mal 4:5 and claiming its fulfillment (per. 13) in John the Baptist: "If you care to accept it, this is Elijah."[15] In 17:12

---

the joint activity of both Joseph and his wife: "His name was then called Jesus, the name given by the angel before He was conceived in the womb." As Lenski notes, "The passive, *was called,* hides the persons who called the child by this name, but they were Mary and Joseph, *The Interpretation of Luke,* p. 140.

14. *An Enquiry into the Evidential Value of Prophecy,* p. 441.

15. John himself denied his equation with Elijah (John 1:21a; see under Lk. No. 8, below), at least in the sense implied by the scribes and Pharisees (cf. J. P. Lange, *Commentary on the Holy Scriptures, John,* p. 27), literally, as a conscious reincarnation: "He says he is not Elijah returned to earth again," Camb, *John,* p. 73; so also Girdlestone, *The Grammar of Prophecy,* p. 70. This is not, however,

He affirms, "Elijah already came,[16] and they did to him whatever they wished,"[17] to which the evangelist adds, v. 13, "The disciples understood that He had spoken to them about John the Baptist." See under Mal 3:1a, and p. 83 above.

9. Mt 3:5–7a, *11a*, 13–16; 21:25 [see Lk. No. 27 (3:3)] (8 vv., typ.); baptism.

10. Mt 3:*7b*, 10, 12 (Lk 3:*7b*, 9, 17); 5:29–30 (sim, Lk 12:5); 10:28; 13:*30c*, 40, 42, *48b*, 50; 18:8–9 (Mk 9:43, 45, 47–49), 34–35; 23:23; 25:*41b*, 46a (14 vv., fig.): the prospect of condemnation to hell. John the Baptist preached of the need "to flee from the wrath to come" (3:7), as demonstrated by a figure from nature: "Every tree that does not bear fruit is cut down and thrown into the fire" (v. 10). 3:12 adds that Christ will "thoroughly clean His threshing-floor," meaning, "to remove all the straw and chaff and leave in the center grain only";[18] In 5:29 Jesus speaks of one's whole body being thrown into hell, *gé'ennā*, Gehenna, the lake of fire (Rev 20:15) or "the eternal fire" (Mt 18:8): not simply the state of the lost after death, but their final post-resurrection condition, where "both soul and body" suffer destruction (10:28) and "where their worm does not die" (Mk 9:48).[19] In the parable of the tares, 13:30, He uses the figure of harvesting, "Bind them in bundles and burn

---

equivalent to a denial of his identification with the sort of Elijah proposed by Mal 4:5, namely, a reappearance of the prophet—same reforming work, same rigorous personality—though in the person of John the Baptist rather than of the 9th-century Tishbite. The thesis of Jack K. Willsey, "The Coming of Elijah: An Interpretation of Malachi 4:5," concludes similarly: "The prophetic statement given by Malachi was a reference to John the Baptist. There can be no doubt that John qualifies as the forerunner of the Messiah," p. 64. But when he goes on to suggest that his "identity as Elijah was dependent upon his reception," p. 65 (cf. Mt 11:14), he seems to have confused a matter of inherent nature with men's appreciation of it. On his further suggestion of "more than one person predicted in the same prophetic announcement," p. 87, see above, pp. 121–126.

16. This past tense (Gk. aorist) is not contradicted by the dialogue of the preceding vv., in which the disciples asked, "Why do the scribes say that Elijah must come first?" (v. 10), to which He replied, "Elijah is coming [Gk. present] and will restore [Gk. future] all things" (v. 11). For Christ here simply quotes Malachi, from the prophet's own, future perspective. V. 12 demonstrates that by the time of Mt 17 this was no longer the case and that Elijah's coming had now become a matter of the past; cf. Lange, loc. cit.

17. Mk 9:13 elaborates, "Elijah has indeed come, and they did to him whatever they wished, just as it is written of him"; cf. the similar opposition faced by Elijah, I K 18:10, 17; 19:2, 10.

18. Lenski, *Luke*, p. 203.

19. Mk 9:49 goes on to say, "For everyone will be salted with fire," and carries on with this same figure of salt in v. 50. "This is confessedly one of the most difficult passages to interpret in the NT. . . . Salt will have to denote a purifying element to connect vv. 49 and 50, and fire will have to denote a destroying element, to connect 48 and 49. The statement is that the destructive element performs a purifying part. The object of all retributions, even of the penal retribution of Gehenna, is to purify. They serve to warn man against violations of the law of his being," ICC, pp. 180–181.

them up"; and in the parable of the net, v. 48, He states in another figure that "they threw away" the bad fish. His parable of the unmerciful servant terminates, saying, "And his lord handed him over to the torturers until he should repay all that was owed him. So shall My heavenly Father also do to you, if each of you does not forgive his brother from his heart," 18:34–35. Lenski cautions: "It is spiritualizing to regard these 'torturers' as the pangs of conscience and self-accusation. Hell [cf. vv. 8–9, preceding, on Gehenna] will be full of these, to be sure. But it will also be full of hideous devils whose one occupation it will be to plague and to torture the damned."[20] Jesus asserts that after the final judgment the condemned "will go away into eternal punishment," 25:46; cf. their actual sentencing, v. 41, in which they are commanded to "depart into the eternal fire which has been prepared for the devil and his angels." Fulfillment (per. 18): as in II Sam No. 20, for in the parables of ch. 13, v. 30 is explained in vv. 40–42, "Therefore just as the tares are gathered up and burned with fire, so shall it be at the end of the age. The Son of Man . . . will cast them into the furnace of fire"; and v. 48 is explained in vv. 49–50, "At the end of the age, the angels shall take out the wicked from among the righteous and will cast them into the furnace of fire."

11. Mt 3:11b [see John No. 1 (1:15)] (1 v.): Jesus coming after John.

12. Mt *3:11c* [see Lk No. 30 (3:16c)]: Pentecost.

13. Mt *3:12b* (Lk *3:17b*); 13:*30d*, 43, 47–48a; *25:34b, 46b* (3 vv., fig.): both in John the Baptist's preaching and in the conclusion of Christ's parable of the wheat and the tares appears the figure of "gathering the wheat into my barn" (13:30; cf. 3:12). Again, in the parable of the net, "They gathered the good fish into containers." 25:46 states that after the judgment the righteous will go away "into eternal life," which is described in the judge's decision as "the kingdom prepared for you from the foundation of the world" (see v. 34, under 7:21, No. 20, below). Fulfillment (per. 18): as in Isa. No. 73, the New Jerusalem, prepared for the righteous; for it contrasts with the final destruction of the wicked, 13:40 (No. 10, above).

14. Mt 4:15–16 (2 vv.): a citation of Isaiah's prophecy about light arising for those in Galilee, as fulfilled in Christ's Galilean ministry, v. 14 (per. 13): as in Isa 9:1–2.

15. Mt 4:19 [see Mk No. 5 (1:17)] (1 v.): Peter's becoming a fisher of men.

16. Mt 5:18, 24:35 (Mk 13:31, Lk 21:33) (2 vv.): two passing allusions made by Christ: "until heaven and earth shall pass away. . . ." This might have been but a figure of speech, except for the analogy of other passages, which speak of its literal fulfillment (per. 17): as in Ps. No. 47.

20. *Mt.*, p. 723.

17. Mt 5:23a, 24a; 8:4 [see Lk 5:14, under Lk. No. 20]; 9:13; 12:7; 23:*18b*–19a (6 vv., typ.): sacrifice. Fulfillment (per. 13): as in Lev No. 2.

18. Mt *5:23b, 24b*; 23:18a, *19b*–20, 35 (sim, Lk 11:51) (3 vv., typ.): the altar. Fulfillment (per. 13): as in Ex. No. 44.

19. Mt 7:19, 22–23 (sim, Lk 13:24–28); 12:32, 36–37; 16:27c (Mk 8:38a, Lk 9:26a); 22:11–13; 24:51 (sim, Lk *12:46b*); 25:24–*28a*, 29b–30 (sim, Lk 19:20–24a, 26b–27), 41–45 (22 vv., fig.): in ch. 7 Christ used the figure, "Every tree that does not bear good fruit is cut down and thrown into the fire. . . . Many will say to Me on that day, 'Lord, Lord' . . . and then I will declare to them, 'I never knew you; depart from Me, you who practice lawlessness.' " So in ch. 12 He said that blasphemy against the Holy Spirit "shall not be forgiven him, either in this age, or in the age to come" (v. 32); and the latter age is defined in this way: "They shall render account in the day of judgment" (v. 36). 16:27 states that Christ will come again "and will then recompense every man according to his deeds," to which the parallel passages in Mk 8:38 and Lk 9:26 add, "Whoever is ashamed of Me and My words . . . the Son of Man will also be ashamed of him." In the allegory of the marriage feast of the king's son appears the punishment of the man without the wedding clothes: "Bind him hand and foot, and cast him into the outer darkness," 22:13; and this has been explained, "Something more is needed than merely to accept the invitation; one must be clothed with righteousness."[21] In the parable of the faithful and the evil servant, 24:51 (sim, Lk 12:46b), He said of the latter that his master "shall cut him in pieces and assign him a place with the hypocrites [Lk, unbelievers]." In the parable of the talents, the master concludes, "And cast out the worthless slave into the outer darkness," 25:30; cf. the parallel allegory of the pounds, in which the nobleman says to the fruitless servant, "By your own words I will judge you" (Lk 19:22)—for, "From the one who does not have, even what he does have shall be taken away" (Mt 25:29, Lk 19:26) —and to the enemies who did not want him to reign over them, "Bring them here and slay them in my presence" (Lk 19:27).[22] Similarly, in the figures of Mt 25:41–45, the goats (the condemned) are judged, according to deeds of righteousness not performed, and sentenced to depart from God into eternal fire. Fulfillment (per. 17): final judgment of the wicked and of hypocrites, as in Ps. No. 1 and Job No. 7.

20. Mt 7:21; 25:20–23, 28b–*29a* (sim, Lk 19:16–19, *24b–26a*), 34–40 (13 vv.): in 7:21 the Lord promises, "He who does the will of My Father . . . will enter the kingdom of heaven." This is not simply life after death, as it may be elsewhere (cf. II Tim 4:18, God's "heavenly kingdom");[23] for the context is that of the final judgment (per. 17), con-

---

21. IB, VII:515.
22. The application (per. 17), is, however, here left to inference.
23. See above, p. 36.

trast vv. 19, 22–23 (No. 19, preceding), on the wicked. In the parable of the talents, Christ relates that to the faithful servants their lord said, "Well done; you were faithful with a few things, I will put you in charge of many things, enter into the joy of your master" (25:21, 23); and in the similar allegory of the pounds, "Well done, be in authority over ten (or five) cities" (Lk 19:17, 19). For "to everyone who has shall more be given" (Mt 25:29, Lk 19:26). Finally in 25:34 Jesus refers in figure to the sheep (the saved), who are identified by their deeds of righteousness to Christ's "brethren"—either the poor and needy in general (vv. 35–36; cf. v. 45 with v. 44), or those among His followers in particular; cf. 12:50, in which His "brothers" are stated to be such as "do the will of My Father." To the righteous will be said, "Inherit the kingdom prepared for you from the foundation of the world," 25:34. This inheritance seems to refer to eternal life in the New Jerusalem, v. 46b; contrast the eternal punishment of the goats, v. 46a (Nos. 10 and 13, above; cf. No. 68, below), though some interpreters would favor its identification with the millennial kingdom, at the outset of which would appear this judgment, v. 31.[24] Fulfillment (per. 17): as in Job No. 5; cf. Mal 3:17. For as Girdlestone notes, "As Christians we are justified by faith; but we are judged according to works, which are the fruit and test of our real faith."[25]

21. Mt 8:11 [see Lk. No. 51 (13:29–30a), sim] (1 v.): Gentiles in the Messianic feast.

22. Mt 8:12 [see Lk No. 52 (13:30b), sim] (1 v.): condemnation for the Jews.

23. Mt 8:17 (1 v.): Matthew's citation of Isa 53:4, on the Servant's bearing men's diseases, as fulfilled (per. 13) in Jesus' healing ministry; see Isa. No. 101.

24. Mt 8:29 (1 v.): the cry of the demons to Jesus, "Have you come here to torment us before the time?" Fulfillment (per. 17): a judging of demonic angels on "the day of judgment, when they will be punished."[26] Lenski associates God's act of condemnation upon the demons with that upon Satan himself, when cast into the lake of fire, Rev 20:10:[27] but it could as plausibly occur later, when sinful men are consigned to this same awful fate, v. 15.[28]

25. Mt 9:15; 16:21a, 22; 17:22–23; 20:18–19a, 22; 21:39; 26:*24a*, 26–28a [see Lk 5:35 etc., under No. 24]; and *17:12b* [see Mk 9:12b,

---

24. See above, pp. 109–110.
25. Op. cit., p. 161.
26. ICC, p. 85, citing the Jewish tradition in I Enoch 15–16.
27. *Mt*, p. 351.
28. Cf. the statement of Jesus in Lk 8:31 that He would not, at the time of the miracle there described, "command them to depart into the abyss." This may not, however, be directly relevant; for "the abyss" appears to be Scripture's term for a more immediate place of confinement for demons (cf. Rev 9:1, 20:1), as contrasted with the final lake of fire.

under Mk. No. 7] (12 vv., fig.): the bridegroom taken away (Christ's death).

26. Mt 10:15; 11:22, 24 [see Lk. No. 39 (10:12), sim] (3 vv.): degrees of punishment.

27. Mt 10:17–*23a*, 34–36; 23:34b; 24:9–10, 12–13 [see Lk. No. 44 (11:49b etc)., sim] (14 vv.): persecution of the apostles.

28. Mt 10:23b; 16:28 (Mk 9:1, Lk 9:27); 21:*41a*, 44–45 (Mk 12:9a, 12; Lk 20:16a, 18–19); 22:7–8; 23:36; 24:15–22 (Mk 13:14–20, Lk 21:20–24a), 32–34 (Mk 13:28–30, Lk 21:29–32) (18 vv., fig.): the promise of Jesus to His disciples, "You shall not finish going through the cities of Israel, until the Son of Man comes" (10:23). The Jerusalem Bible here proposes that the "coming" be understood as a figure for divine judgment,[29] in light of the immediately preceding stress (see No. 27, above) on the criminal treatment to be suffered by the apostles: "The coming which is here foretold is not concerned with the world at large[30] but with Israel: it took place at the moment when God 'visited' his now faithless people and brought the OT era to an end by the destruction of Jerusalem and its temple."[31] Later, preceding His transfiguration, He said in similar fashion, "There are some of those who are standing here who shall not taste death until they see the Son of Man coming in His kingdom" (16:28), although Mark reads more impersonally, " . . . until they see the kingdom of God after it has come with power" (9:1; cf. Lk 21:31). Four major explanations have been proposed: that His words refer to the transfiguration itself, to Christ's resurrection and ascension, to Pentecost and the beginning of the missionary enterprise, or to the destruction of Jerusalem in A.D. 70.[32] The first and the last would appear to have the stronger evidence. For the first it has been claimed, "The primary reference to these words was to the three apostles who, within a week of that time, were to witness the transfiguration. So it seems to be understood in II Peter 1:16,"[33] in a passage, that is, written some years later by one of the very three. Yet the time lapse appears to be too short to account for the opening words, unless it be assumed that Jesus was not sure when this experience would occur—a theory which is not impossible, in light of Mk 13:32. The choice of A.D. 70 would place the fulfillment at a suitable point, 40 years distant.[34] It has the advantage of the parallel in Mt 10:23, just noted, and is the explanation

29. On the broad Biblical usage of this phrase, see above, p. 127.
30. Contrast ICC, pp. 106–107, which does so understand it, as a prediction of Christ's second coming during that generation, and therefore spoken in error.
31. JB, NT, p. 31.
32. NBC, p. 823.
33. Camb, *Lk*, p. 188.
34. As Girdlestone pictures it "There were some young people standing round the Lord who would see both the treading down of Jerusalem and the spread of the Kingdom of Christ far and wide," op. cit., p. 100; cf. NIC, "This means that most of His hearers will already be dead before that special revelation," *Lk*, p. 277.

here tentatively adopted. As Lenski elaborates it, the kingdom of the Messiah includes

the rule of his power in the world, protecting his believers and bringing judgment upon the wicked. In the judgment on the Jews this royal rule of Jesus would become visible. In this calamity some of the hearers were actually to "see" the Son of man coming in his kingdom, i.e., clothed with the royal majesty as the King that he is. . . . Those who live to see the destruction of Jerusalem will have in this fulfillment of Jesus' prophecy the proof that his prophecy concerning the final judgment [Mt 16:27, the verse preceding; see under 7:19, No. 19 above] shall also be fulfilled.[35]

The assertion that Christ was speaking of His second advent[36] has been countered by Dean Alford's observation, "That the Lord in His humanity did not know the day and the hour, we have from His own lips: but that not knowing it He should have uttered a determinate and solemn prophecy of it is utterly impossible."[37]

In the allegory of the wicked husbandmen, Mt 21:41, Jesus states that the owner of the vineyard "will bring those wretches to a wretched end." Explanation appears in vv. 44–45, which comment that the chief priests and Pharisees understood that Jesus was speaking of them, to be "broken to pieces and scattered as dust." Of the same import is His story of the marriage feast of the king's son, which is similar to the earlier parable of the guests invited to the dinner in Lk 14:16–24 (see under Lk 13:29); but Jesus here turns the parable into an allegory,[38] and for those who refused the invitation to the feast He adds this detail, Mt 22:7–8, "The king was enraged and sent his armies, and destroyed those murderers, and set their city on fire. . . . They were not worthy." Then in 23:36 He warns, "All these things [the guilt of all Jewish crimes] shall come upon this generation."

Mt 24:15 (Mk 13:14) is a citation of Dan 9:26b, 27b (q.v.), on abominations that are to enter Jerusalem.[39] Vv. 14–16 advise flight without delay; and vv. 21–22 state that there will be great tribulation, "such as has not occurred since the beginning of the world until now, nor ever shall. And unless those days had been cut short, no life would have been saved [i.e. "the lives of everybody in the nation"[40]]; but for the sake of the elect [i.e. "for the sake of the Christians"[41]] those days shall be

---

35. *Mt*, p. 649.
36. IB, VII:457.
37. *The Greek Testament*, I:163.
38. IB, VII:515.
39. Daniel's preceding chapter also speaks of an abomination of desolation, in the profanation of the temple by Antiochus IV (8:13); but its fulfillment was now already past and does not fit the context of the Gospels.
40. Lenski, *Mt*, p. 940.
41. Camb, *Mk*, p. 146. The term "elect" is indeed left undefined; it could, by definition, relate to any whom Christ has chosen (cf. Mk 13:20), e.g. OT Israel.

cut short." Commentators have observed, "Anyone who reads Josephus' *Jewish War* can understand the evangelists' feeling that no tribulation ever had been, or could be worse than this";[42] it was, however, to be kept within limits. Lk 21 preserves at this point Christ's words in their greatest detail: v. 20, "See Jerusalem surrounded by armies"; v. 24, "and they will fall by the edge of the sword, and will be led captive into all nations, and Jerusalem will be trampled under foot by the Gentiles."

Mt 24:32–34 then concludes with a warning concerning the time factor: even as a budding fig tree heralds summer, so when the signs (especially vv. 5–13) come to pass, you are to "recognize that it [KJV, ASVmg; cf. Lk 21:31, "the kingdom of God," just as in Mk 9:1, above] is near, right at the door." Jesus assures them: "This generation will not pass away until all these things take place," Mt 24:34. Alford would refer *this generation* to "the Jewish people";[43] but his approach seems forced. One would do better, following the lead of 10:23 and 16:28 (above), "to take *these things* as referring to the siege of Jerusalem, in contrast to [the point of reference of Christ's phrase,] *that day and that hour* (24:36) [see under Mk 13:32], which refers to the end of the world."[44] Luke is clearer, where the phrase "all things" in 21:32 suggests the same connotation as do the identical words "all things" in v. 22, namely the fall of the city, as above. Fulfillment (per. 14): the destruction of Jerusalem in A.D. 70, as in Mi. No. 39; see also the discussion under Lk No. 23. One might note that when Titus besieged the city, its resident Christians fled to the Transjordanian town of Pella, on the specific grounds of Mt 24:16–22.

29. Mt 10:32–33, *22:44b*, 25:15 [see Lk. No. 46 (12:8), sim] (3 vv.): Christ's ascension.

30. Mt 12:4 [see Lk 6:4, under Lk. No. 1] (1 v., typ.): the temple.

31. Mt 12:17–18a (2 vv.): that Christ is to be the "Servant." This is the first of a series of prophecies quoted from Isa 42:1–4 which are stated to have been fulfilled (per. 13) in Christ; for this initial one, see Isa No. 91.

32. Mt *12:18b*: that God's Spirit is to rest upon Christ. Fulfillment (per. 13): as in Isa 42:1b, listed under Isa. No. 40.

33. Mt 12:19–20 (2 vv.): our Lord's unpretentious ministry. Fulfillment (per. 13): as in Isa 42:2–3, No. 92.

34. Mt 12:21; and also 22:44c [see Lk 20:43, under Lk. No. 13],

---

But it would hardly carry that meaning here. Mt 24 was Christ's private discourse to His disciples (v. 3), after He had publicly turned away from His ministry to Israel (23:38). Earlier that same day He had equated the "elect," Gk. *eklektoi*, with those who were faithful to Himself (22:14), and of any nation, in fact, except Israel (21:43); cf. J. B. Payne, *The Imminent Appearing of Christ*, p. 55.

42. IB, VII:547; cf. Payne, op. cit., p. 116, and see above, p. 103, note 190.

43. Op. cit., I:226.

44. NBC, p. 801.

2 vv.: His yet future rule of righteousness, when "in His name the Gentiles will hope." Fulfillment (per. 16): as in Isa 42:4, listed under Isa. No. 35.

35. Mt 12:40 (sim, Lk 11:29–30), 16:4 (2 vv.): "Just as Jonah was three days and three nights in the belly of the sea-monster, so shall the Son of Man be three days and three nights in the heart of the earth," 12:40. Fulfillment (per. 13): Christ's three-day burial. He rose, indeed, "on the third day" (16:21, 17:23, 20:19, etc.); and because of this more common expression some interpreters suggest that Matthew here "tried to increase the parallelism [with Jonah 1:17] by adding *three nights,* when at the most there were only two."[45] Yet Lenski adduces parallel passages from Tobit 3:12–13, cf. Est 4:16, 5:1, and proposes, "The matter of numbering nights with the days is idiomatic Jewish usage. Since the day begins with the night (or evening), it is the night that forms part of the first day, which seems to us to be overcounted."[46] The latter reference (16:4) simply alludes to "the sign of Jonah" as the only sign that would be granted to the Pharisees. But though it stands without elaboration, it must assume the same fulfillment expressed earlier in ch. 12, namely, Christ's resurrection.[47]

36. Mt *12:41a, 42a* [see Lk. No. 41 (11:31a), sim]: the general resurrection.

37. Mt 12:41b, 42b [see Lk. No. 42 (11:31b), sim] (2vv.): Jews condemned by Gentiles.

38. Mt 13:24–*30a,* 36–38; *22:10b* (9 vv., fig.): that in the parable of the wheat and the tares the landowner should order, "Allow both to grow together" (13:30). Then in the allegory of the marriage feast of the king's son (see under 10:23b, No. 28, above) the king's servants "gathered together both good and evil" (22:10b). Fulfillment (per. 14): the growth of both good and evil in the present age (cf. II Pet 2:1, Jude 12); for Jesus went on to explain in Mt 13:38, "The field is the world," and the wheat and tares are "the sons of the kingdom and the sons of the evil one [the devil, v. 39]," respectively.

39. Mt 13:30b, 39, 41, 49 (4 vv., fig.): a further prophecy arising out of the parable of the tares, ". . . and in the time of the harvest I will say to the reapers, 'First gather up the tares and bind them. . . .' " Fulfillment (per. 17): the ministerial function of angels at the final judgment. A detailed explanation for the figure appears in Jesus' words in vv. 39, 41: "The harvest is the end of the age, and the reapers are angels. . . . The Son of Man will send forth His angels, and they will gather out of His

45. ICC, p. 139.
46. *Mt,* p. 493; cf. T. H. Horne, *An Introduction to the Critical Study and Knowledge of the Holy Scriptures,* I:406.
47. Some interpreters would insist that "the sign," at least in the parallel in Lk 11:30, consisted originally in nothing other than the prophet's preaching of repentance and that this was then misunderstood by Matthew; but see Lenski, *Lk,* pp. 647–648.

kingdom all . . . who commit lawlessness"; and this teaching is repeated after the parable of the net, v. 49. Angels are also to be involved with the saved; for they "gather the wheat into My barn" (see v. 30d, under 3:12b, No. 13, above).

40. Mt 13:31–32 [see Mk 4:30–32, under Mk. No. 9], 33 (sim, Lk 13:20–21, under Lk. No. 50), *16:18b*; *22:10c* (3 vv., fig.): 13:33 is the parable of the leaven, hidden in meal but growing "until it was all leavened." Then in the allegory of the marriage feast of the king's son, 22:10 states that "the hall was filled with dinner guests"; cf. vv. 9–10a, on the presence of the Gentiles, under Lk 2:30. Fulfillment (per. 14): the growth of the church in the world (cf. 13:38); cf. 16:18a (No. 41, following), out of which v. 18b affirms that not even the power of death will be able to destroy it.

41. Mt 16:18a (1 v.): Christ's revelation, "You are Peter [Gk. *pétros*, rock], and upon this rock, *pétrā*,[48] I will build My church." Fulfillment (per. 14): despite the impending demonstration of Peter's instability, 26:69–75 (cf. 14:30), a fault over which he seemed unable to gain complete victory even later, Gal 2:11–14, he yet became the instrument through whom God did build the early church, Acts 1:15, 2:14, 10:44–48, 15:7.

42. Mt 16:19, 18:18 (sim, John 20:23) (2 vv.): Christ's word to Peter, "I will give you the keys of the kingdom of heaven, and whatever you bind and loose on earth shall have been bound and loosed in heaven" (16:19). In 18:18 this same power is then bestowed upon all the disciples; cf. John 20:23, "If you forgive the sins of any, their sins have been forgiven them; if you retain the sins of any, they have been retained." Fulfillment (per. 14): the ministerial activity, as it developed in the apostolic church, of declaring to men the results of their response to the gospel; for

Peter and the other disciples were to continue on earth the work of Christ in preaching the gospel and declaring God's will to men, and were armed with the same authority as He Himself possessed. [Specifically,] by preaching the gospel, Peter would be the means of opening the kingdom of heaven to all believers and shutting it against unbelievers. The book of Acts shows us this process at work. By his sermon on the day of Pentecost (Acts 2:14–40) Peter opened the door of the kingdom for the first time. See also Acts 8:14–17, 15:7.[49]

43. Mt *16:21b* (Mk *8:31b*, Lk *9:22b*); 17:9, *23b* (Mk 9:9–10, *31b*); *20:19b* (Mk *10:34b*, Lk *18:33b*); *26:32a* (Mk *14:28a*); 26:61 and 27:40 (Mk 14:58 and 15:29) [see John No. 8 (2:19), which these vv. quote]; 27:63; 28:6 (Lk 24:6, *7b–8*) (5 vv.): that Christ "must . . .

48. The fem. form may be used in the second instance simply to make a distinction between the name of the man Peter and the substance, rock, with which he is compared.
49. NBC, p. 793.

be raised up on the third day" (16:21); "after three days" He would rise again (27:63; cf. the notes on 12:40, No. 35, above). Our Lord's prediction was later cited by the Jews, 27:53, and then, when fulfilled (per. 13), by the two angels at the open tomb, Lk 24:6–7.

44. Mt *16:27a* (Mk *8:38b*, Lk *9:26b*); *23:39b* (sim, Lk 13:35b); 24:*3b*, 27 (sim, Lk 17:24), 28, 30 (Mk 13:26, Lk 21:27); 25:*19b* (sim, Lk *19:15a*), 31a; 26:64 (Mk 14:62, Lk 22:69) (5 vv.): "The Son of Man is going to come [in His own glory and (Lk)] in the glory of His Father" (16:27); and men will exclaim, "Blessed is He who comes in the name of the Lord" (23:39). "All the tribes of the earth . . . will see the Son of Man coming on the clouds with power and great glory," 24:30 (= 26:64). Matthew prefixes the following words: "The sign of the Son of Man will appear in the sky," possibly some special portent, but probably the coming itself, considered as OT prophecy: "the well known sign of the Son of Man predicted by Daniel [7:13]."[50] Reference to the *sign* occurs also in Matthew's more complete citation of the opening questions of disciples (see 24:2–3a, under 23:38) than appears in the other Synoptics, when it includes, ". . . and what will be the sign of Your coming and of the end of the age?" (24:3b)[51] In the context of vv. 6, 13–14, these terms seem to denote the completion of the present age and so again to be simply synonymous with the coming of Christ. V. 27 states that the event will be sudden and unmistakable: "For just as the lightning comes from the east, and flashes even to the west, so shall the coming of the Son of Man be." Matthew then records a repetition by Jesus of His earlier proverb (Lk 17:37; see under 17:26) on the vultures gathering where corpses were, namely, where people were ripe for judgment; but in the context of Mt 24:28 the Lord was using the expression only to emphasize the circumstances of His return—whether for judgment or for blessing—so that instead of His followers being misled by false announcements (v. 26; see under Lk 17:23) they would be on the watch for the manifestation of His appearing (v. 27), to "discern when the Lord comes and where."[52] The Messiah's Parousia is finally depicted in the allegory of the talents, Mt 25:19, under the phrase "the master came," and in that of the pounds, Lk 19:15, when the nobleman "returned." Fulfillment (per. 15): the second coming of Christ, as in Ps. No. 5.

45. Mt *16:27b* (Mk *8:38c*, Lk *9:26c*), *25:31b*: Christ's coming "with His angels." Fulfillment (per. 15): as in Joel No. 18.

46. Mt 17:27 (1 v.): Christ's directions to Peter, so that he might pay the temple tax: "Go to the sea, and throw in a hook, and take the first

---

50. ICC, *Mt*, p. 259.
51. Girdlestone, op. cit., pp. 62–63, cautions about the variety of connotations to the word "end," concluding simply, "It has to do with what we ordinarily call a dispensation."
52. Camb, *Mt*, p. 185.

fish that comes up; and when you open its mouth, you will find a stater [mg, shekel]." The fulfillment (per. 13) is not stated; but, "The finding is assured by Jesus' word."[53]

47. Mt 19:28 (sim, Lk 22:30); 20:21, 23b (Mk 10:37, 40) (3 vv.): Christ's promise to Peter and the other apostles, "In the regeneration when the Son of Man will sit on His glorious throne, you also shall sit upon twelve thrones, judging the twelve tribes of Israel" (19:28). In 20:21, correspondingly, the mother of James and John requested of Jesus, "Command that in Your kingdom [Mk, "in Your glory," asked also by the men themselves] these two sons of mine may sit, one on Your right and one on Your left." While Jesus then refused the request, He still confirmed the legitimacy of this prophetic anticipation, saying, "To sit on My right and on My left, this is not Mine to give; but it is for those for whom it has been prepared by My Father," v. 23. At the Last Supper Christ uttered similar words again to the disciples, "who have stood by Me in My trials" (Lk 22:28); but He now prefixed this further promise, "I grant you that you may eat and drink at My table in My kingdom" (v. 30). So Lenski comments, "As kings who have been appointed such by him they shall dine together with the king."[54] Fulfillment (per. 16): positions of rule by the apostles in the future Messianic kingdom; see Rev 20:4.

48. Mt *20:23a* [see Mk. No. 18 (10:39)] (fig.): the suffering of James and John.

49. Mt 21:1–2 [see Mk. No. 20 (11:1)] (2 vv.): finding the Palm Sunday colt.

50. Mt 21:3 [see Mk. No. 21 (11:3)] (1 v.): the colt sent.

51. Mt 21:4–5 (John 12:14–16) (2 vv.): citation of Zech 9:9, fulfilled (per. 13) in Christ's triumphal entry into Jerusalem, as in Zech. No. 35 (9:9d).

52. Mt 21:41b, 43; 22:9–10a [see Lk 20:16b, under Lk. No. 22] (4 vv.): Gentiles to replace Jews.

53. Mt 22:29–32 [see Lk 20:34–38, under No. 55] (4 vv.): the first resurrection.

54. Mt *23:34a* [see Lk. No. 43 (11:49a), sim]: the apostles sent.

55. Mt 23:38; 24:2–3a (Mk 13:2–4, Lk 21:5–7) (3 vv.): Christ's word to Jerusalem, "Behold, your house is being left to you desolate." Alford calls attention to the fact that it is "no more God's but *your house*—said primarily of the temple, then of Jerusalem, and then of the whole land."[55] Then, as His disciples were exclaiming over the holy building, He prophesied, "Not one stone here shall be left upon another, which shall not be torn down" (24:2). Fulfillment (per. 14): the destruction of the temple in August of A.D. 70. Josephus subsequently affirmed that the

53. Lenski, *Mt*, p. 676.
54. *Lk*, pp. 1060–1061.
55. Op. cit., I:234.

temple area was "so thoroughly leveled and dug up that no one visiting the city would believe it had ever been inhabited."[56]

56. Mt 23:39a [see Lk. No. 53 (13:35a), sim] (1 v.): final Jewish penitance toward Christ.

57. Mt 24:4–5, 11, 23–24a, 26 [see Lk 21:7 etc., under Lk. No. 56] (6 vv.): false christs.

58. Mt 24:6–8 [see Mk. No. 31 (13:7)] (3 vv.): calamities preceding A.D. 70.

59. Mt 24:14 [see Mk. No. 33 (13:10)] (1 v.): universal gospel preaching.

60. Mt *24:24b, 29a* [see Mk. No. 34 (13:22b, 23a)]: the great tribulation.

61. Mt 24:29b [see Mk. No. 35 (13:24b)] (1 v.): the wrath of God.

62. Mt 24:31, 40–41 [see Lk 21:28, under Lk. No. 58] (3 vv.): the rapture.

63. Mt *24:31b*: Christ's prediction that at His return He will send forth His angels "with a great trumpet" to gather His elect church. Fulfillment (per. 15): as in Isa. No. 79 (27:13a).

64. Mt 24:36 [see Mk. No. 38 (13:32)] (1 v.): the unknown date of His second coming.

65. Mt 24:37–39 [see Lk No. 57 (17:26), sim] (3 vv.): false security, at His coming.

66. Mt 24:42 [see Lk 21:36, under Lk. No. 47], 43–50; 25:1–13 (22 vv.): the presentation by Jesus of a series of narrative lessons teaching present-day faithfulness, but in light of the predicted suddenness of His second coming: the parable of the master of the house, "for the Son of Man is coming at an hour when you do not think He will" (24:44); that of the faithful servant or the evil servant, "the master will come on a day when he does not expect him" (24:50); and that of the ten virgins, "Be on the alert then, for you do not know the day nor the hour" (25:13). Fulfillment (per. 15): the imminent return of Christ, as in Lk 12:35.

67. Mt *25:19a* [see Lk 19:12b, sim, under Lk. No. 60]: the kingdom not immediate.

68. Mt 25:19c (sim, Lk 19:15b), *31c*–33 (3vv., fig.): in the allegory of the talents, Jesus described how "the master came and settled accounts" (Mt 25:19); and in that of the pounds, how the nobleman ordered that his servants "be called to him in order that he might know what business they had done" (Lk 19:15). Detailed explanation of the figure follows in the next paragraph of Mt 25—"The Son of Man will sit on His glorious throne. And all nations will be gathered before Him; and He will separate them one from another, as the shepherd separates the sheep from the goats" (see further under the specific judgments of the wicked and the

righteous in No. 19 and 20, above). This judicial separation determines the eternal destiny of both groups (vv. 34, 46); so it must be fulfilled in per. 17, the final judgment, as in Eccl. No. 1; cf. Job 19:25a, 29 and Ps 1:5.[57]

69. Mt *25:41c*: Jesus reveals that the eternal fire of the condemned is that which "has been prepared for the devil and his angels." Fulfillment (per. 18): the ultimate fate of Satan and of his demonic followers; cf. Rev 20:10.

70. Mt 26:2, 5, 17–19 [see Lk 22:1, under Lk. No. 26] (5 vv., typ.): Passover.

71. Mt 26:6–12 [see Mk. No. 41 (14:3)] (7 vv., sym.): Jesus' anointing for burial.

72. Mt 26:13 [see Mk. No. 42 (14:9)] (1 v.): Mary's act to be remembered.

73. Mt 26:21–23, 25 [see John 13:21, under No. 17] (4 vv.): the betrayal of Jesus.

74. Mt 26:24b [see Mk. No. 45 (14:21b)] (1 v.): woe to Judas.

75. Mt 26:29 [see Lk 22:18, under Lk. No. 48] (1 v.): the Messianic feast.

76. Mt 26:31 [see Mk. No. 47 (14:27)] (1 v.): the flight of the disciples.

77. Mt 26:32b, 28:10 [see Mk. No. 48 (14:28b)] (2 vv.): post-resurrection meeting in Galilee.

78. Mt 26:34, 75 [see Mk. No. 49 (14:30)] (2 vv.): Peter's denial of Christ.

79. Mt 26:46 [see Mk. No. 50 (14:42)] (1 v.): the arrival of Judas.

80. Mt 27:9–10 (2 vv.): citation of Zech 11:13,[58] as fulfilled (per. 13) in the purchase of the potter's field with the 30 pieces of silver for which Judas had betrayed Christ; as in Zech. No. 54.

81. Mt 27:51 (1 v., typ.): that at Christ's death (v. 50), the veil of the temple "was torn in two from top to bottom," signifying the end of approach to God via the ceremonial of the OT, but also fulfilling (per. 13) the typology of the veil, as in Ex No. 58 (26:31), of the true access to God through the torn flesh of Jesus, Heb 10:20 (see under 6:19).

57. See above, p. 109, and Payne, *Imminent Appearing*, pp. 137–139.
58. Matthew's introduction reads, "Then that which was spoken through Jeremiah [not Zechariah] the prophet was fulfilled." NBC, p. 804, however, notes the inclusion in Matthew's quotation of more material than is found in the verse from Zechariah and states, "The most important addition is the word 'field' . . . from Jer 32:6–9, a passage in which occurs the purchase of a field for so many pieces of silver. It is natural, therefore, that the evangelist should mention Jeremiah, who was the greater of the two and the earlier of the two, from whom also was derived the word that gave point to the quotation." See M. F. Unger, *Bible Commentary: Zechariah*, pp. 200–201, who analyzes various explanations that have been proposed, though favoring a use of "Jeremiah" as a title for the total roll of the prophets, which would thus include Zechariah.

MARK

Mark is the shortest of the Gospels, and it is probably the earliest. Near the beginning of the 2nd century, Papias stated that Mark had been the interpreter of Peter, writing down "accurately but not in order" what the apostle taught that Jesus had said and done, so that Mark "erred in nothing."[1] Later in the same century, Irenaeus explained that after the "departure" of the apostles, Mark "handed down to us in writing the things preached by Peter."[2] The term *éxodos*, "departure," is, however, an ambiguous one and may indicate either a physical journey (as in Heb 11:22, Israel's "exodus") or a departure of the spirit at death (as in Lk 9:51). The latter alternative would date Mark to approximately A.D. 67. This is, indeed, the prevailing view of modern criticism;[3] but it answers to liberalism's conviction that Mark 13 cannot be an authentic message of Jesus and that its predictions about the fall of Jerusalem could have arisen only after the outbreak of hostilities between the Jews and Rome in A.D. 66. Yet Irenaeus' contemporary Clement of Alexandria, along with other early writers, is explicit that Mark wrote *during* Peter's lifetime.[4] His "departure" might thus refer to some unknown movement by the apostle away from Rome, but one recalls more naturally Peter's flight from Judea shortly before the death of Herod Agrippa I in A.D. 44 (Acts 12:17, 23). Confirmation may perhaps be found in a papyrus fragment from Qumran Cave 7, plausibly identified as Markan and datable to the year 50.[5]

Concerning the writer, "John who was also called Mark" (v. 25) came from Jerusalem. His mother's house (v. 10) was a meeting place for the early church, and it is just possible that the young man whom Mark describes as fleeing from Gethsemane at the time of Jesus' arrest (Mk 14:51–52) may have been the author himself. His cousin was Barnabas (Col 4:10); he experienced a variety of contacts with Paul (Acts 13:5, 13; 15:37–39; Col 4:10; II Tim 4:11); and Scripture identifies his position as one of "sonship" in respect to Peter (I Pet 5:13). His Gospel seems to

1. As recorded in Eusebius, *Ecclesiastical History*, II:39,16.
2. *Against Heresies*, III:1, 2.
3. Note also evangelical interpreters who do not advocate a chronological priority of Mark to Luke or to Matthew, e.g. M. C. Tenney, *The Genius of the Gospels*, p. 20.
4. He comments, in fact, on the apostle's response when he learned later of Mark's composition; in Eusebius, op. cit., VI:14, 6. Cf. Guthrie's discussion of the conflicting tradition in this regard, *The Gospels and Acts: NT Introduction*, pp. 68–69.
5. J. O'Callaghan, "Paperos neotestamentarios en la cueva 7 de Qumran?" *Biblica*, 53 (1972), 91–100. Cf. Guthrie's caution that "in spite of the confidence of the majority of scholars that Mark must be dated A.D. 65–70, it is by no means impossible to hold an earlier date," op. cit., pp. 70–71.

have been addressed primarily to Gentile believers,[6] perhaps in Rome.[7] Though he records a number of OT quotations by Christ, he cites the OT but once on his own account (Mk 1:2-3). His purpose, moreover, concerned not so much a chronological biography as the good news, "the gospel of Jesus Christ, the Son of God" (1:1); his emphasis rests on the mighty work of the Savior, particularly as this climaxed in the events of Passion Week, which occupies more than a third of the book.

Many have observed that Mark's outline follows the same sequence that appears in Peter's preaching in Acts 10:37-43. The second Gospel thus remains silent over the early life of Jesus; in a way that corresponds to Peter in Acts (v. 37), it commences with the ministry of John the Baptist (Part V, in A. T. Robertson's organization). Mark also passes by the Lord's later Judean ministry (Part IX, Lk 10-13:21, John 7-10:39), which consists largely of discursive material. But this is in line with the writer's general stress on action rather than on discourse.[8] The book's conclusion, which stands in most English Bibles as Mark 16:9-20, is not to be found in the better ancient MSS; it is accordingly omitted from the following discussion, as being no part of the inspired autographs of Scripture. As one might therefore have anticipated from the above, Mark contains fewer matters of a predictive nature than do the other Gospels. Yet these still embrace 50 distinct predictions and involve 125 of the book's 662 verses, or some 19% of the whole.

1. Mk 1:2—3, 6:15, 8:26 [see Lk 3:4-6, under Lk. prophecy No. 8]; 9:11-12a, 13 [see Mt 17:10-13, under Mt. No 8] (6 vv.): John the forerunner.

2. Mk 1:4-5, 8a, 9; 11:30 [see Lk. No. 27 (3:3)] (4 vv., typ.): baptism.

3. Mk 1:7 [see John No. 1 (1:15)] (1 v.): Jesus coming after John.

4. Mk 1:8b [see Lk. No. 30 (3:16c)] (1 v.): Pentecost.

5. Mk 1:17 (Mt 4:19, Lk 5:10) (1 v.): Christ's words to Simon (Peter) and Andrew, "Follow Me, and I will make you become fishers of men."[9] Fulfillment (per. 14): when Peter in particular became God's in-

---

6. For cumulative evidence, cf. ibid., pp. 50–51, 55–59.

7. Patristic evidence strongly favors a Roman origin for Mark's writing; but Guthrie cautions that "the original destination of the Gospel is impossible to decide with any certainty," ibid., p. 55.

8. Discourse, on the other hand, is felt to characterize the Logia, or Q document, which, together with Mark's more narrative-type Gospel, is assumed to have been the chief source underlying the present Gospels of Matthew and Luke; see above, introduction to Matthew.

9. This promise might plausibly be construed as generalization, rather than as particularized prediction. Yet as stated above, p. 33, even a generalization may become predictive, if it describes a condition which would become true in the future but which did not characterize the situation at the time of its announcement, as here.

strument for building up the apostolic church (see Mt 16:18a) and won, for example, 3,000 souls through his single Pentecost sermon, Acts 2:41.

6. Mk 1:44 [see Lk 5:14, under Lk. No. 20] (1 v., typ.): sacrifice.

7. Mk 2:20; 8:31a, 32; 9:31a, 32; 10:32–34a, 38; 12:8; 14:*21a*, 22–24a [see Lk 5:35 etc., under No. 24], but also 9:12b (Mt *17–12b*) (14 vv., fig., 2:20): 9:12 predicts that "the Son of Man should suffer many things and be treated with contempt," while 14:21 contains Jesus' utterance in connection with the forecast of His betrayal (see 14:18, No. 44, below), "The Son of Man is to go, just as it is written of Him" (see under Isa 49:7a). Fulfillment (per. 13): the rejection and death of Christ, as in Lk. No. 24.

8. Mk 2:26 [see Lk 6:4, under No. 1] (1 v., typ.): the temple.

9. Mk 4:26–28, 30–32 (Mt 13:31–32; sim, Lk 13:18–19) (6 vv., fig.): the former concerns the first part of the parable of the seed growing of itself; the latter is the parable of the mustard seed, which is a small thing, "yet when it is sown, grows up and becomes larger than all the garden plants." Fulfillment (per. 14): as in Ezek. No. 24, the growth of the church;[10] cf. Acts 2:47, 21:20, Phil 1:18.

10. Mk 4:29 (1 v., fig.): the latter part of the parable of the seed growing of itself, "He puts in the sickle, because the harvest has come." Fulfillment (per. 17): the bringing of the saved into God's final judgment for vindication; cf. the parallel figure of the wheat in Christ's parable of the tares, where its meaning is so explained, Mt 13:39.

11. Mk *8:31b*; 9:9–10, *31b*; *10:34b*; *14:28a*; 15:29 [see Mt. No. 43 (16:21b)]; 14:58 [see John 2:19] (4 vv.): the resurrection of Jesus.

12. Mk 8:38a [see Mt 16:27c, under Mt. No. 19] (1 v.): the judgment of the lost.

13. Mk *8:38b*, 13:26, 14:62 [see Mt. No. 44 (16:27a)] (2 vv.): the second coming of Christ.

14. Mk *8:38c* [see Mt. No. 45 16:27b)]: His coming with angels.

15. Mk 9:1; 12:9a, 12; 13:14–20, 28–30 [see Mt 16:28 etc., under Mt. No. 28] (13 vv., fig.): the destruction of Jerusalem, A.D. 70.

16. Mk 9:43, 45, 47–49 [see Mt 18:8–9, under No. 10] (5 vv.): Gehenna.

17. Mk 10:37, 40 [see Mt 20:21, under No. 47] (2 vv.): the apostles' thrones.

18. Mk 10:39 (Mt *20:23a*) (1 v., fig.): forboding words of Jesus to James and John, "The cup that I drink, you shall drink; and you shall be baptized with the baptism with which I am baptized"; cf. v. 38 (discussed

---

10. Some dispensationalist interpreters seem to have violated context by converting the parable's subject into an evil thing: "an abnormal external growth; that which was to be an herb has become a tree—it has developed into a monstrosity," J. D. Pentecost, *Things to Come*, p. 147. See also p. 42, above.

in Lk 12:50, under 2:34c). Fulfillment (per. 14): the death of James, Acts 12:2; and even for John "it meant suffering, instead of honor, and that this would increase with the advanced position attained."[11]

19. Mk 10:45, *14:24b* [see Mt 20:28, 26:28, under Mt. No. 2] (1 v.): Christ's atoning ransom.

20. Mk 11:1-2 (Mt 21:1-2, Lk 19:29-30) (2 vv.): Jesus's instructions to two of His disciples, just prior to the triumphal entry, "As you enter the village, you will find a colt tied there [with the mother donkey too, Mt], on which no one yet has ever sat; untie it." Fulfillment (per. 13): it proved to be so. This utterance was apparently not the result of prior information gained in some normal manner on Jesus' part; for even critical writers concede, "It is evidently the intention of the writers of the Gospels here to imply a supernatural knowledge on the part of Jesus."[12]

21. Mk 11:3 (Mt 21:3) (1 v.): our Lord's further instructions to those getting the donkey, "Say, 'The Lord has need of it,' and immediately he will send it back here." Fulfillment (per. 13): he did; cf. No. 20, preceding.

22. Mk *12:9b* [see Lk 20:16b, under Lk. No. 22] (fig.): Gentiles to replace Jews.

23. Mk 12:24-27 [see Lk 20:34, under No. 55] (4 vv.): the first resurrection.

24. Mk 12:33a (1 v., typ.): burnt offering. Fulfillment (per. 13): as in Lev. No. 3.

25. Mk *12:33b* (typ.): peace offering.[13] Fulfillment (pers. 13 and 16): as in Lev. No. 5.

26. Mk 12:35-37 [see Lk 20:41, under Lk. No. 15] (3 vv.): the deity of Christ.

27. Mk *12:36b* [see Lk 20:42b, under No. 46]: His ascension.

28. Mk *12:36c* [see Lk 20:43, under No. 13]: the future Messianic kingdom.

29. Mk 13:2-4 [see Mt 24:2, under Mt. No. 55] (3 vv.): the destruction of the temple.

30. Mk 13:5-6, 21-22a [see Lk 21:7-8, under Lk. No. 56] (4 vv.): false christs.

31. Mk 13:7-8 (Mt 24:6-8, Lk 21:9-11) (2 vv.): "When you hear of wars and rumors of wars," and also of earthquakes and famines, "do not be frightened; that is not yet the end." Luke includes Christ's added warnings of "plagues, terrors, and great signs from heaven," 21:11, perhaps a forecast, among other matters, of the comet mentioned by Tacitus and Josephus.[14] Fulfillment (per. 14): various calamities, both natural

---

11. ICC, *Mk,* p. 200.
12. Ibid., p. 207.
13. So Lenski, *The Interpretation of Mark,* p. 541.
14. Camb, *Lk,* p. 316.

and cultural, occurring before A.D. 70 (Mk 13:14); cf. Acts 11:28, and also Tacitus,[15] on further disasters at this time.

32. Mk 13:9, 11–13 [see Lk 21:12, under Lk. No. 44], 4 vv. Early church persecution.

33. Mk 13:10 (Mt 24:14), 1 v.: "The gospel must be preached to all the nations." Matthew adds, "and then the end shall come." Fulfillment (per. 14): as in Isa. No. 69, the proclamation to all of salvation in Jesus Christ.

34. Mk *13:22b, 24a* (Mt *24:24b, 29a*): attempts by false leaders (Mk 13:22a; see under Lk. No. 56) "to mislead, if possible even the elect" (Mt 24:24), Christ's followers (see Mt 24:22, under Mt. No. 28, note 41). The latter oracle (Mk 13:24a) then locates Christ's coming as "immediately after the tribulation of those days" (Mt 24:29). The *days* cannot refer back to Mk 13:19 (Mt 24:21; see under Mt. No. 28), which seems to apply to A.D. 70, but would relate to the period of those events which follow the break between vv. 20 and 21 (Mt 24:22 and 23).[16] Fulfillment (per. 14): as in Dan. No. 20, the great tribulation.[17]

35. Mk 13:24b–25 (Mt 24:29b, Lk 21:25–26) (2 vv.): immediately after the tribulation (No. 34, preceding), "The sun will be darkened and the moon will not give its light"; and stars, "the powers that are in the heavens, will be shaken" and fall. Luke adds, as further aspects of the distress, "the roaring of the sea, and dismay among nations." Fulfillment (per. 15): as in Joel No. 9, the heavenly phenomena of the wrath of God.[18]

36. Mk 13:27 [see Lk 21:28, under Lk. No. 58] (1 v.): the rapture.

37. Mk 13:31 [see Mt 24:35, under Mt. No. 16] (1 v.): the passing away of heaven and earth.

38. Mk 13:32 (Mt 24:36) (1 v.): v. 31 (No. 37, preceding) had suggested a shift in viewpoint from the local A.D. 70 reference in v. 30 (Mt 24:34; see under 10:23b) to the universal future; and v. 32 now focuses on the time of the second advent: "Of that day or hour no one knows, not even the angels in heaven, nor the Son, but the Father alone." Fulfillment (per. 15): as in Zech. No. 73, the unknownness of the date for Christ's second coming.

---

15. *Annals*, XII:38, 43, 64; XV:22; XVI:13.

16. Cf. Camb, *Mk*, pp. 184–185, or A. T. Robertson, *A Harmony of the Gospels for Students of the Life of Christ*, p. 179. A comparison, in particular, of the Lukan material with that which appears in Matthew and Mark leads to the conclusion that the corresponding shift in the latter two Gospels occurs as noted. The prophecies up to this point, including those of the unique tribulation of Mk 13:13 (Mt 24:21), are therefore now of preterest import only (see above, p. 103, note 190, and 487, note 42), while v. 24 (Mt 24:29) describes the heavenly phenomena of the future wrath of God (No. 35, following), which is immediately preceded by the, at least potentially present, great tribulation, vv. 21–23 (Mt 24:23–28); cf. J. B. Payne, *The Imminent Appearing of Christ*, p. 153.

17. See above, pp. 102–103.

18. See above, p. 104.

39. Mk 13:33–37 [see Lk 21:34, under Lk. No. 47] (5 vv.): Christ's imminent return.

40. Mk 14:1–2, 12, 14, 16 [see Lk 22:1 etc., under No. 26] (5 vv., typ.): Passover.

41. Mk 14:3–8 (Mt 26:6–12; John 12:2–5, 7–8) (6 vv., sym.): at Simon's house in Bethany, when Mary poured ointment on Jesus' head and feet, He explained (v. 8), "She has anointed My body beforehand for the burial." Fulfillment (per. 13): the anointing of the corpse of Christ in preparation for its entombment, 15:46.

42. Mk 14:9 (Mt 26:13) (1 v.): Jesus' statement, after Mary had anointed Him, "Wherever the gospel is preached in the whole world, that also which this woman hath done shall be spoken of in memory of her." Fulfillment (per. 14): true today.

43. Mk 14:13, 15 (Lk 22:10, 12) (2 vv.): Christ's Passover instructions for Peter and John, "A man will meet you carrying a pitcher of water." The owner of the house that he should enter "will show you a large upper room, furnished and ready." Commentators observe, "Jesus could tell in advance that a man—not a woman!—would be carrying a jar of water to a certain house; cf. 11:4. The whole anecdote moves in the realm of supernatural perception."[19] Fulfillment (per. 13): it was so, v. 16.

44. Mk 14:18–20 [see John 13:21, under Jn. No. 17] (3 vv.): Christ's betrayal.

45. Mk 14:21b (Mt 26:24b, Lk *22:22b*; sim, John 17:11) (1 v.): Christ's word concerning Judas, "Woe to that man by whom the Son of Man is betrayed! It would have been good for that man if he had not been born." John 17:11, in the Lord's prayer for His disciples, adds, "Not one of them perished, but the son of perdition"—"It signifies one whose end will be perdition."[20] Fulfillment (per. 13): as in Ps. prophecy No. 51, the fate of Judas (Mt 27:3–10 and Acts 1:18–19).

46. Mk 14:25 [see Lk 22:18, under Lk. No. 48] (1 v.): the Messianic feast.

47. Mk 14:27 (Mt 26:31; sim, John 16:32) (1 v.): predictive expressions of Jesus to His disciples, at the Last Supper, "You will all fall away, because it is written . . . ," and He proceeded to cite Zech 13:7. John records His further forecast that they were "to be scattered, each to his own home, and to leave Me alone" (16:32). Fulfillment (per. 13): as in Zech. No. 36 and 66, the flight of the disciples, in Mk 14:50.

48. Mk 14:28b (Mt 26:32b), 16:7 (sim, Mt 28:10) (2 vv.): Christ's assurance to the disciples that after the resurrection, "I will go before you to Galilee." His word was later cited by the angels at the empty tomb, 16:7, who added, "There you will see Him"; and this was paralleled by Jesus' own statement to the women as they were fleeing, Mt. 28:10. Ful-

19. IB, VII:872; so also Lenski, *Mk*, p. 611.
20. ICC, *John*, II:571.

fillment (per. 13): as in Zech. No. 67. Mt 28:16 speaks further of the disciples going to "the mountain which Jesus had designated," but without additional identification or discussion.

49. Mk 14:30, 72 (Mt 26:34, 75; Lk 22:34, 61; John 13:38) (2 vv.): after Peter's protestation of loyalty, at the Last Supper, Jesus warned him, "You yourself this very night, before a cock crows twice, shall three times deny Me." Fulfillment (per. 13): it was so, vv. 66–72.

50. Mk 14:42 (Mt 26:46) (1 v.): an announcement by Christ in Gethsemane, "Behold, the one who betrays Me is at hand." It was "not that Jesus heard him coming, or saw the lights; the Marcan Jesus has direct intuition, as in 2:8 and elsewhere."[21] Such an understanding is borne out by the evangelist's statement that describes the fulfillment (per. 13): "While He was still speaking, Judas came up," 14:43: "for apparently at the time that the Lord had started His speaking, the betrayer's coming was not yet observable."[22]

21. IB, VII:884.
22. Elsewhere, however, IB does allow an alternative: "Jesus either sees Judas or foresees him," VII:581.

LUKE

The third Gospel is the longest book in the New Testament, and its author's style is the most literary. Historical testimony is of one voice in assigning this work, together with its sequel in Acts, to Luke "the beloved physician" (Col 4:14); and there appears to be no sufficient cause for doubt in this regard.[1] Their writer accompanied Paul the apostle on a number of his missionary journeys, starting midway in the second; compare his use of the plural pronoun "we," which commences at Acts 16:10. The late 2nd-century patristic writer Irenaeus reported that "Luke, the companion of Paul, recorded in a book the Gospel preached by him."[2] Thus, while Luke himself was not an apostle, his writing is still marked by apostolic authority; cf. Paul's linking of words from Luke 10:7 with others from Dt 25:4, so as to present the two as equally canonical "Scripture," I Tim 5:18.

1. Some recent scholars have questioned the Lukan authorship; cf. Guthrie's survey, *The Gospels and Acts: NT Introduction*, pp. 98–103. Cadbury has in particular depreciated W. K. Hobart's thesis on *The Medical Language of St. Luke.* Evidence, however, still remains to support the author's special interest in disease and the sick, Guthrie, op. cit., pp. 96–97; and the admitted connection between Luke and Acts renders a Lukan origin for both most probable; see below, introduction to Acts, on the latter's authorship.
2. *Against Heresies,* III:1, 1.

Luke was present with Paul during his imprisonment in Caesarea (cf. the "we" in Acts 27:1) and during both his first and second imprisonments in Rome (Philemon 24, II Tim 4:11). His physician thus possessed ample opportunity for contact with eyewitnesses to the life of Christ. He would also have met other significant Christians, such as the four prophetess-daughters of Philip the evangelist at Caesarea (Acts 21:9–10), from whom he might have acquired, for example, the data for his narratives on the childhood of Jesus. Thiessen concludes, "It is probable that he wrote the Gospel during this period, say about A.D. 58."[3]

Luke was apparently a Gentile; contrast Col 4:14 with v. 11 and its reference to those "who are from the circumcision." He is therefore the only non-Jewish Christian among the writers of the NT, and his Gospel does seem to have been pointed toward those Greek audiences with whom he would have worked while serving Paul.[4] His emphasis, for example, rests on Christ, not primarily as the son of David (cf. Mt 1:1), but as "the son of Adam" (Lk 3:38), and on His concern for humanity in general. Luke speaks forth "the good news of great joy which shall be for all people" (2:10).[5]

The Gospel's prologue (1:1–4) provides special insight into the Lukan method of writing.[6] Its author recognized the existence of previously composed sources to the life of Christ (v. 1); he seems to have been particularly indebted to the Gospel of Mark and to the assumed group of Logia labeled Q.[7] Luke had recourse to personal sources as well (v. 2). After careful investigation he proceeded to write his Gospel to "most excellent Theophilus" (v. 3), apparently a believer of some rank, though this should not exclude its further goal of public reading and edification. And, as a medium of apostolic inspiration, he laid claim to "exact truth" (v. 4).

The third Gospel covers "in consecutive order" (v. 3) every period of the life of Christ except that of His preexistence (John 1:1–18). It is unique in its reporting of much of what A. T. Robertson designates Christ's Later Judean Ministry (Part IX, Lk 10–13:21) and Later Perean Ministry (Part X, 13:22–19:28). Of the book's 1,146 verses, 250 include predictive material, which amount to 22% of the total—this is just slightly more than is found for the Gospel of John. Luke's material embraces 75

---

3. *Introduction to the NT*, p. 158, though Finegan would terminate Paul's Caesarean imprisonment "at the end of summer A.D. 57," *Handbook of Biblical Chronology*," p. 324. Others, as Tenney, suggest that it probably was written during the imprisonment of Paul at Rome about A.D. 60 to 62," *The Genius of the Gospels*, p. 20. Liberal criticism prefers dates 80–90; cf. note 8 to Matthew, above.
4. Guthrie, op. cit., p. 90. This must not, however, be taken as implying that Luke "slanted" Christ's words: he reports faithfully what Christ said; and, just as is true of the other Gospel writers, his special interests affect only the selection of the quotations that were to be incorporated.
5. Cf. Thiessen, op. cit., pp. 156–160, or Guthrie, op. cit., pp. 84–86.
6. Cf. N. B. Stonehouse, *The Witness of Luke to Christ*, pp. 24–45.
7. See above, introduction to Matthew.

distinct prophecies; but the distribution is uneven: 26 of them first appear in the opening two chapters of the book, the part which Robertson entitles: The Birth and Childhood of the Baptist and Jesus. Explanation may be sought in the sources of which the writer must have availed himself at this point. Guthrie observes a corresponding phenomenon in Luke's type of language:

> After writing 1:1-4, he drops the literary style for a type of Greek strongly flavored with Semitisms. . . . Particularly noticeable is the Septuagint Greek used for the infancy narratives which seems to have been influenced by the style of the canticles which he includes in his narratives. The strongly Hebraistic character of Luke's Greek in this section is admirably adapted to link the incarnation of Jesus with the OT history, and that may well be the effect that Luke wished to create.[8]

The remainder of the work, particularly in those portions that are unique to Luke, shows less prophetic interest than do the other Gospels, perhaps because of the beloved physician's more Gentile and more universal outlook as a whole.

1. Lk 1:9, 21; 2:37; 6:4 (Mt 12:4, Mk 2:26) (4 vv., typ.): the temple. The verses in Lk 1 are the last references in Scripture to the temple as a valid, contemporaneous type, prior to its fulfillment (per. 13) in the incarnation of God with men that it had so far been predicting; see Ex. prophecy No. 55. The remaining references are retrospective, to the typical temple of previous days.

2. Lk 1:13, 14a, *20b*, 36–37 (4 vv.): words of the angel Gabriel to Zacharias, "Your wife Elizabeth will bear you a son, and you will give him the name John. And you will have joy and gladness." In v. 20, "My words shall be fulfilled in their proper time." This prophecy was later repeated to Mary (v. 36), with the added revelation that Elizabeth was then six months pregnant (v. 37; cf. v. 26). Fulfillment (per. 13), later in this same chapter: v. 57, the birth; v. 58, local rejoicing; and vv. 60, 63, the naming.[9]

3. Lk *1:14b*, concerning John the Baptist: "Many will rejoice at his birth." Fulfillment (per. 13): Israel's general joy over John is indicated by their widespread response to him, and their gladness is specifically stated in John 5:35; for, "The joy at the appearance of a prophet after centuries of need was immense, although not universal (Mt 14:5, 21:26)."[10]

---

8. Op. cit., pp. 109–110; cf. pp. 163–167.
9. The future naming is not limited in sense to the category of a command; see above, p. 40. Lenski insists, "The future tenses in the angel's announcement are prophetic . . . none of them are volitive by stressing somebody's will in what shall be," *The Interpretation of Luke*, p. 46.
10. ICC, p. 13.

4. Lk *1:15a*: that John the Baptist would be "great in the sight of the Lord." Fulfillment (per. 13): Christ testified that there had been no one greater up until John's appearing, 7:28.

5. Lk *1:15b*: that John would drink no wine or strong drink. Fulfillment (per. 13): he was a life-long Nazirite, 7:33, like Samson and Samuel.[11]

6. Lk 1:15c (1 v.), of John: "He will be filled with the Holy Spirit, while yet in his mother's womb."[12] This passage is not to be limited to the Spirit-given power of John that characterized his Nazirite-like ministry (No. 4 and 5, above). Fulfillment (per. 13): v. 44 quotes the words of his mother Elizabeth to Mary, at the latter's arrival: "When the sound of your greeting reached my ears, the baby leaped in my womb for joy." Earlier, in v. 41, Luke had stated that "the baby leaped in her womb, and Elizabeth was filled with the Holy Spirit"; but on the basis of v. 44 one would conclude that the unborn John had been so filled as well."[13] His person, that is, came under the direct control of God.

7. Lk 1:16, 17b, 77 (3 vv.): that John "will turn back many of Israel to the Lord their God." There follows a quotation from Mal 4:6, with the angel's added thought of turning "the disobedient to the attitude of the righteous," so as to "make ready a people prepared for the Lord." John's purpose is further clarified in Lk 1:77, "to give to His people the knowledge of salvation by the forgiveness of their sins." Fulfillment (per. 13): as in Mal. No. 19, on Lk 1:77, cf. especially John's actual work in Mk 1:4.

8. Lk 1:*17a*, 76; 3:4–6 (Mt 3:3, Mk 1:2–3; sim, John 1:21a, 23); 7:27 (Mt 11:10); 9:8 (Mk 6:15), 19 (Mt 16:14, Mk 8:26), (7 vv.): as first spoken to Zacharias, about John, "It is he who will go as a forerunner before Him in the spirit and power of Elijah," quoting Mal 3:5. Later, as spoken by Zacharias after John's birth, "You, child, will be called the prophet of the Most High" (1:76); and his father went on to quote Mal 3:1, on God's messenger who would prepare the way before the divine Angel of the testament. In 3:4–6 the evangelist himself cites Isa 40:3–5 as fulfilled in the appearing of John. The parallels in Matthew and Mark cite only Isa 40:3, introduced in Matthew by the words, "This is the one referred to by Isaiah the prophet." Mark cites Mal 3:1 and then Isa 40:3, introducing both by the phrase, "As it is written in Isaiah the prophet," since the quotation from Isaiah is the longer and applied more directly to John's immediate situation in the wilderness (Mk 1:4). In the parallel in John, John the Baptist denied his equation with the Elijah of Mal 4:5 (John 1:21; see the discussion under Mt 3:3); but he did claim that he fulfilled Isa 40:3 (John 1:23). The anticipation of Elijah receives

11. Ibid., p. 14.
12. Though ICC, p. 14, indicates a possible alternate translation, of "even from birth," and thus not meaning the period before it.
13. Cf. Alford, *The Greek Testament*, I:400.

further allusion in the Luke 9 verses. Fulfillment (per. 13): as in Isa. No. 90 and Mal. No. 9.

9. Lk 1:20a (1 v.), spoken to Zacharias because of his disbelief over the birth of John the Baptist: "You shall be unable to speak until the day when these things take place." Fulfillment (per. 13): v. 22, his dumbness; and v. 64, his release, at John's birth; see above, p. 14.

10. Lk 1:31a, 35a (2 vv.): Mary to conceive. When she questioned how this could be, in her virginity, the angel Gabriel explained that it would come about through the power of God and His Holy Spirit, so that "the holy offspring shall be called the Son of God" (see 1:32a, No. 12, below). Fulfillment (per. 13): as in Isa. No. 24 (7:14). The Lukan context records only Mary's acquiescence; but her conception by the Holy Spirit is directly stated in Mt 1:18, 20, and Jesus *was* the Son of God; see No. 12, below. At a later point Elizabeth, in looking back at the event, stated that Mary "believed that there would be a fulfillment of what have been spoken to her by the Lord," Lk 1:45.

11. Lk *1:31b* (sim, Mt. 1:21a): Mary to bear a son. The same forecast was later conveyed to Joseph, Mt 1:21a. On the subsequent naming of Jesus, see Mt 1:21b. Fulfillment (per. 13): Jesus, her firstborn, Lk 2:7.

12. Lk *1:32a, 35b*: Gabriel's prediction of Christ, "He will be great, and will be called the Son of the Most High" (1:32),[14] "the Son of God" (v. 35).[15] Fulfillment (per. 13): the divine Sonship of Jesus, as in II Sam No. 12.

13. Lk 1:32b, 20:43 (Mt 22:44c, Mk *12:36c*), 22:29 (3 vv.): "The Lord God will give Him the throne of His father David." In 22:29 Jesus Himself affirmed, "My Father has granted Me a kingdom," the future kingdom of the Messiah, according to the following verse. 20:43 is a citation of Ps 110:1c (see under Ps 2:6), on Christ's enemies being put under His feet. Fulfillment (per. 16): as in Gen 49:10b.

14. Lk 1:33, *55b* (1 v.): the eternity of Christ's reign over Israel (cf. 1:54, No. 17, below). Fulfillment (per. 18): the eternal New Jerusalem, as in II Sam. No. 14.

15. Lk 1:42–43; 20:41–42a, 44 (Mt. 22:43–*44a*, 45; Mk 12:35–37) (5 vv.): on the deity of Jesus, Elizabeth was inspired to anticipate Him as "blessed" and designated Him "my Lord" (vv. 42–43). 20:41 cites Ps 110 on Christ's *Lord*ship, even over His patriarchal "superior," David. Fulfillment (per. 13): the deity of Christ, as in Ps 110:1a.

16. Lk 1:48 (1 v.): Mary's assurance, "From this time on all generations will count me blessed," echoing the blessing that her relative Elizabeth had just bestowed upon her, v. 42. Fulfi'lment began in that genera-

---

14. ICC, p. 23: "He not only shall be the Son of God, but shall be recognized as such."

15. "This title is given to our Lord by almost every one of the sacred writers of the NT and in a multitude of passages," Camb., p. 13—even by Satan, Mt 4:3.

tion (per. 13), see 11:27; and Canon Farrar adds: her "inspired anticipations have been so amply fulfilled."[16]

17. Lk 1:54–55a, 67–75, 78–79; 2:10, *32b*, *34b*, 38 (15 vv.): Mary's prophecy about God's impending work through Christ, "He has given help to Israel His servant, in remembrance of His mercy, as He spoke to our fathers." Correspondingly, the Christmas angels brought good news of "a great joy which shall be to all the people" (2:10), that is, "to all Israel."[17] Zacharias also "was filled with the Holy Spirit and prophesied [1:67]" of God's accomplishing their redemption by raising up "a horn of salvation for us in the house of David" (v. 69), "the Sunrise from on high" predicted in Isa 9:1 (Lk 1:78–79); cf. Lk 1:72–73, No. 18, below, on God's remembrance of His testament to Abraham. The concept of *enemies* from which Israel is now to be delivered (vv. 71, 74) would therefore seem best "applied also to spiritual enemies";[18] for Zacharias goes on to state the purpose of the divine program, "that we might serve Him without fear, in holiness and righteousness before Him all our days" (vv. 74–75) and that the Messiah might "guide our feet into the way of peace" (v. 79). In this same vein Simeon predicted that the child Jesus had been appointed "for the rise of many in Israel" and "the glory of Thy people" (2:32, 34), and Anna spoke of Him as the hope for "all those who were looking for the redemption of Jerusalem" (v. 38). Fulfillment (per. 13): Lenski comments, "What God had done for Mary was a plain intimation of His purpose to remember His promise to Abraham . . . to carry His mercy into effect,"[19] namely, redemption at the cross of Christ; cf. Gen 15:10.

18. Lk 1:59, 2:21 (2 vv., typ.): circumcision,[20] even for the Son of God, to fulfill all righteousness, Mt 3:15—"not for Himself, as is sometimes supposed, but to redeem us."[21] Fulfillment (per. 13): as in Gen. No. 42.

19. Lk 1:72–73 (2 vv., typ.): retrospective references to the Abrahamic testament. Fulfillment (per. 13): as in Gen. No. 30.

20. Lk 2:24, 5:14 (Mt 8:4, Mk 1:44), 13:1 (3 vv., typ.): sacrifice. Fulfillment (per. 13): as in Lev. No. 2.

21. Lk 2:26 (1 v.): it had been revealed to Simeon "by the Holy Spirit that he would not see death before he had seen the Lord's Christ." Simeon stated that his prediction was fulfilled (per. 13) in his seeing of Jesus, vv. 30–32.

22. Lk 2:30–32 (3 vv.): in Christ, Simeon had seen "Thy salvation, prepared in the presence of all peoples" and "a light of revelation to the

16. Ibid., p. 56.
17. Cf. Lenski, op. cit., p. 130.
18. Camb, p. 60.
19. Op. cit., p. 93.
20. Its prospective, typical significance continues in force up until the point (Calvary) of ultimate redemption in Christ.
21. Ibid., p. 140.

Gentiles," quoting Isa 42:6, 49:6. Fulfillment (per. 14): the worldwide proclamation of the gospel, as in Isa. No. 69.

23. Lk 2:34a; 9:27 [see Mt 16:28, under Mt. No. 28]; 19:43–44; 20:16a, 18–19 [see Mt 21:41a, under No. 28]; 21:20–24a, 29–32 [See Mt 24:15–22, all under No. 28]; 23:28–31 (18 vv.), commencing with Simeon's word to Mary: "This child is appointed for the fall . . . of many in Israel"; cf. Christ's later statements about His causing those Pharisees and the others who opposed Him to be *broken* and *scattered* (Mt 21:44). In Luke 19:43–44 He addresses Jerusalem somewhat figuratively, saying that her enemies will place her under siege "and will level you to the ground and your children within you; and they will not leave in you one stone upon another, because you did not recognize the time of your visitation." 23:28–31 then concern Jesus' words on the way to Calvary, "Daughters of Jerusalem, stop weeping for Me, but weep for yourselves and for your children. The days are coming when they will say, Blessed are the barren. . . . For if they do these things in the green tree, whot will happen in the dry?" In paraphrase, "If the Romans treat Me, whom they admit to be innocent, in this manner, how will they treat those who are rebellious and guilty?"[22] Fulfillment (per. 14): as in Dan. No. 38; for further features of the events of A.D. 70, see under the discussion of the other vv., under Mt. No. 28.

24. Lk *2:34c–35a*; 5:35 (Mt 9:15, Mk 2:20); 9:22a (Mt 16:21a, 22; Mk 8:31a, 32), 30–31, 43–45 (Mt 17:22–23; Mk 9:31a, 32); 12:50 (sim, Mt. 20:22 and Mk 10:38); 13:32–33; 17:25; 18:31–34 (Mt 20:18–19a, Mk 10:32–34a); 20:15 (Mt 21:39, Mk 12:8); 22:*15b*, 17, 19 (Mt 26:26–28a, Mk 14:22–24a), 22a (Mt *26:26a*, Mk *14:21a*), 37; 24:7a (21 vv.): Simeon's prophecy to Mary, over the baby Jesus, that He is appointed "for a sign to be opposed, and a sword will pierce even your own soul" (2:34–35); cf. how Mary later stood as a witness to His crucifixion, John 19:25–27. In 5:35 Christ spoke in a figure: "The days will come, when the bridegroom is taken away from them." The first direct prediction to His disciples of His passion to come[23] was in 9:22, "The Son of Man must suffer many things [= 22:15], and be rejected by the elders and chief priests and scribes [= 17:25], and be killed." 9:30–31 describes how "Moses and Elijah, appearing in glory, were speaking of His departure [ASV text, "decease"] which He was about to accomplish at Jerusalem." In 12:50 He foretold, "I have a baptism to undergo [and Mk 10:38, Mt 20:22, add, a "cup" to "drink"]," with the idea that "His passion is a flood in which He must be plunged."[24] In 13:32 Christ states, with a figurative usage of terms for time, that He is to perform His ministry "today and tomorrow, and the third day I reach My goal." This He interprets in the next verse: "for it cannot be that a prophet should perish outside of Jeru-

22. ICC, p. 529.
23. 2:34 had been to Mary; John 3:14, to Nicodemus; and Lk 5:35, to others.
24. ICC, *Luke*, p. 334.

salem." 18:32–33 and its parallels add more detail, with which may be compared the precise fulfillments that followed (per. 13): from Mark 10:33, He would be "delivered up to the chief priests [fulfilled, 14:43–44, 53]; and they will condemn Him to death [14:64]"; and from Luke 18 itself, "He will be delivered up to the Gentiles [Lk 23:1] and will be mocked and mistreated [22:63–64, 23:11] and spit upon [Mk 14:65, 15:19] and scourged [15:15]." He predicted in Lk 20:15, in the allegory of the wicked husbandmen, "They cast him [the divine owner's son] out of the vineyard and killed him"; cf. Christ's death outside Jerusalem, John 19:20. Luke 22:17 and 19 contain the predictive symbols of the Lord's Supper: the broken bread, "This is My body," and the cup, "My blood," to which Matthew and Mark add His clarification, "which is to be shed."[25] Finally in Luke 22:37 appears Christ's citation of Isa 53:12b, "He was numbered with the transgressors," as about to be fulfilled in Himself.

25. Lk 2:35b (1 v.): Simeon, foretelling the purpose of Christ's ministry, "to the end that the thoughts from many hearts [presumably the many, good and bad, in v. 34] may be revealed." Lenski suggests that contact with Jesus would "produce and reveal to men certain thoughts of a decisive nature, either those of unbelief (John 3:19) or those of faith (3:21)."[26] Fulfillment (per. 13): as indicated above, in John 3.

26. Lk 2:41; 22:1 (Mt 26:2, 5; Mk 14:1–2), 7–8, 11, 13 (Mt 26:17–19; Mk 14:12, 14, 16), 15a (7 vv., typ.): Passover. Fulfillment (per. 13): as in Ex. No. 31.

27. Lk 3:3, 7a (Mt 3:5–7a; Mk 1:4–5; sim, John 1:28, 3:23, 10:40), 12, *16a* (Mt *3:11a*; Mk *1:8a*; sim, John 1:25–26, 31, *33a*), 21 (Mt 3:13–16, Mk 1:9); 7:29–30; 20:4 (Mt 21:25, Mk 11:30) (7 vv., typ.): baptism. John appeared in the wilderness, "preaching a baptism of repentance for forgiveness of sins." Jesus Himself came to him for baptism, Mt 3:14; John, however, protested his own need to be baptized by Jesus. But Jesus explained His special need "to fulfill all righteousness," v. 15; see No. 18, above. At His baptism the Holy Spirit then descended "in bodily form like a dove," Lk 3:22, vindicating Jesus' position as Son of God and signifying that "as the God man He will redeem the world and will furnish a cleansing that is far beyond any cleansing that any mere man could provide. The Baptist is nothing but a man, and his work consists in applying a means of grace that rests on a far mightier act."[27] Fulfillment (per. 13): redemption in Christ, of which baptism was here still a type, just as was OT circumcision; see Gen 17:10.

28. Lk 3:*7b*, 9, 17; 12:5 [see Mt. No. 10 (3:7b)] (3 vv., fig.): ultimate condemnation in hell.

29. Lk 3:16b [see John No. 1 (1:15)] (1 v.): Jesus coming after John.

25. Lk 22:19b–20 is lacking in the best MSS.
26. Op. cit., p. 154.
27. Lenski, *The Interpretation of John*, p. 117.

30. Lk *3:16c* (Mt *3:11c*, Mk 1:8b; sim, John *1:33c*); 24:49 (1 v.): John's prediction that, in contrast with normal water baptism, the Christ "will baptize you in the Holy Spirit and fire" (cf. Acts 2:3). This last expression has led to numerous interpretations such as judgment (for unbelievers), trials (for believers), true cleansing (as opposed to John's baptism), etc.;[28] but in the light of 24:29—"I am sending forth the promise of My Father upon you; but you are to stay in the city until you are clothed with power from on high"[29]—and in light of the citation of these words by Jesus in Acts 1:4–5, the fulfillment can only be that of Pentecost (per. 14): as in Joel No. 8.

31. Lk *3:17b* [see Mt. No. 13 (3:12b)]: New Jerusalem.

32. Lk 4:18–19 (2 vv.): citation of Isa 61, on the anointing of God's Servant, as fulfilled in Christ's ministry, Lk 4:21 (per. 13): as in Isa 61:1–2a, under Isa. No. 40.

33. Lk 5:4 (1 v.): Jesus' words to Simon Peter, Let down your nets "for a catch," this after his work of a whole night without results, v. 5. Fulfillment (per. 13): upon his compliance, "they enclosed a great quantity of fish," v. 6.

34. Lk 5:10 [see Mk. No. 5 (1:17)] (1 v.): Peter to become a catcher of men.

35. Lk *9:22b*; *18:33b*; 24:6, *7b*–8 [see Mt. No. 43 (16:21b etc.)]; 24:46 (3 vv.): 24:46 is retrospective, spoken by Christ after His resurrection, "Thus it is written, that Christ should suffer and rise again from the dead the third day." He was presumably citing Hos 6:2, as having been fulfilled (per. 13) in His resurrection, Lk 24:6, 23, 34; and see under Hos 6:1.

36. Lk 9:26a; *12:46b*; 13:24–28; 19:20–24a, 26b–27 [see Mt. No. 19 (16:27c etc.), under 7:19] (13 vv.): final judgment of the wicked.

37. Lk *9:26b*, *13:35b*, 17:24, *19:15a*, 21:27, 22:69 [see Mt. No. 44 (16:27a etc.)]; also 17:22 (4 vv.). The last reference is unique to Luke, a word of Christ to His disciples, "You will long to see one of the days of the Son of Man [namely, of His triumphant return, 17:26], and you will not see it." Fulfillment (per. 15): His second coming, as in Ps. No. 5.

38. Lk *9:26c* [see Mt. No. 45 (16:27b)]: His coming with angels.

39. Lk 10:12–14 (sim, Mt 10:15, 11:22, 24), 12:47–48 (5 vv.): Christ's announcement, "It will be more tolerable for Sodom [10:12]" or "for Tyre and Sidon [10:14] in the judgment, than for . . ." the Galilean cities where Jesus and His disciples ministered. Then in 12:47–48 He spoke in a figure, "That slave who knew his master's will and did not get ready shall receive many lashes; and the one who did not know it, and committed deeds worthy of flogging, will receive but few"; but He went on to explain, "From everyone who has been given much shall much be

---

28. See ICC, *Mark*, pp. 9–10.
29. Cf. the obedience of the disciples in Acts 1:13.

required." Fulfillment (per. 17): degrees of punishment at the final judgment. Alford cautions: "This is one of those mysterious hints at the future dealings of God, into which we can penetrate no further than the actual words of our Lord reveal, nor say to what difference exactly they point in the relative state of those [in] . . . the last great day of judgment."[30]

40. Lk 11:29–30 [see Mt. No. 35 (12:40), sim] (2 vv): Christ's 3-day burial, like Jonah.

41. Lk *11:31a, 32a* (sim, Mt *12:41a, 42a*): famous exemplars of repentance "shall rise up, *egerthḗsetai*, lit., *be raised up* [11:31]" or "shall stand up, *ānāstḗsontai, arise* [11:32], with this generation at the judgment"—not just standing up in court, but resurrection.[31] Fulfillment (per. 17): the general resurrection, as in Job No. 2 and Dan. No. 56 (12:2b).

42. Lk 11:31b, 32b (sim, Mt 12:41b, 42b) (2 vv.): "The Queen of the South [Sheba, I K 10:1] and . . . the men of Nineveh shall stand up with this generation and condemn it." Fulfillment (per. 17): participation by those who turned to God, in repentance, in the condemnation of the Jews who failed to repent when they heard Jesus. Lenski pictures it in this way: "Jesus sees them at the final judgment, standing up side by side with this generation of the Jews. When both appear before God's judgment bar, and their cases are laid before the Judge, the case of the Ninevites will in the eyes of the Judge serve as a condemnation of the case of the Jews; and the Judge will so pronounce."[32]

43. Lk 11:49a (sim, Mt *23:34a*) (1 v.): words of Jesus in condemning the Jews, "The Wisdom of God said, 'I will send to them prophets and apostles.'" The thought is clarified in His later, similar statement in Mt 23:34, "I am sending you prophets and wise men and scribes"; and the verse concludes by describing the persecutions that these men are to receive from the Jews (see No. 44, following). Lenski interprets, that the *"Prophets and apostles* are especially the Twelve and those who were associated with them in the promulgation of the gospel. . . . God will urge the final work of grace upon the Jewish nation."[33] Fulfillment (per. 14): cf. Acts 1:8; and they did become His "witnesses in Jerusalem and all Judea. . . ."

44. Lk *11:49b* (sim, Mt 23:34b); 12:11–12 (sim, Mt 10:17–20), 49, 51–53 (sim, Mt 10:21–*23a*, 34–36); 21:12–19 (Mt 24:9–10, 12–13; Mk 13:9, 11–13) (14 vv.): Christ's revelation to the Jews about His apostles and other church leaders, "Some of them you will kill [cf. Acts 7:60, 12:2] and crucify, and some of them you will scourge in your synagogues, and persecute from city to city" (Mt 23:34; cf Lk 11:49). Correspondingly, He warned His disciples, "They will deliver you up to

---

30. Op. cit., I:111.
31. ICC, *Mt*, p. 140.
32. *The Interpretation of Matthew*, p. 495.
33. *Lk*, p. 666.

the courts . . . and you shall even be brought before governors and kings for My sake, as a testimony to them and to the Gentiles" (Mt 10:17–18; cf. Mk 13:9). But "the Holy Spirit will teach you in that very hour what you ought to say" (Lk 12:12; cf. Mk 13:11). They will be hated and persecuted by all (Mt 10:22–23), even by their immediate families (Mt 10:21, 34–36; Lk 12:51–53);[34] but salvation is in store for those who "endure to the end" (Mt 10:22): not to the end of the Jewish state in A.D. 70 (as in the following v.; see Mt 10:23), but to the ends of their respective lives (v. 21). Fulfillment (per. 14): as demonstrated by a number of exact accomplishments recorded in the Book of Acts, e.g. 5:40, 22:19, 26:11; cf. Paul's testimony before governors and kings in chs. 24, 26.

45. Lk 11:51 [see Mt 23:35, sim, under Mt. No. 18 (5:23)] (1 v. typ.): the altar.

46. Lk 12:8–9 (sim, Mt 10:32–33), 19:12a (sim, Mt 25:15), 20:42b (Mt 22:44b, Mk 12:36b) (3 vv.): the first passage declares that for the one who confesses Christ before men, "the Son of Man shall confess him also before the angels of God," and so correspondingly for those who deny Him. The expression concerning Christ's testimony in heaven may not be predictive of any specific event—it seems rather to refer to a continuous process[35]—yet the very fact of our Lord's future presence in heaven does imply His ascension, made clearer in the prophecies which follow. In the story of the pounds (Lk 19:12) He seemingly transforms an original parable into an allegory[36] and uses this figure: "A certain nobleman [Jesus] went to a distant country [heaven] to receive a kingdom for himself." Finally 20:42 contains a specific citation of Ps 110:1b on the session of the Messiah at the Father's right hand. Fulfillment (per. 13): the ascension of Christ to glory, as in Ps. No. 8 (8:3): "The gospel story teaches that Christ is to go to heaven to receive his appointment as messianic king."[37]

47. Lk 12:35–36, 38–40, 46a; 21:34–36 (Mt 24:42, Mk 13:33–37) (9 vv., fig.): a doctrine conveyed by an illustration, "Be dressed in readiness, like men waiting for their master when he returns, so that they may immediately open the door to him when he comes and knocks . . . whether he comes in the second watch or even in the third, and finds them so" (12:35–36). Again, "If the head of the house had known at what hour the thief was coming, he would not have allowed his house to be broken into" (v. 39). Christ's explanation follows, "You too, be ready; for the

---

34. Compare His words in Lk 12:49, "I have come to cast fire upon the earth." "The context seems to show that the fire of division and strife is meant; or, comparing 3:16, we may understand the fire of holiness, which excites hostility and controversy," ICC, *Lk*, p, 334, which amounts to about the same thing.

35. See above, p. 36.

36. IB, VII:328; and see above, p. 20.

37. Ibid.

Son of Man is coming at an hour that you do not expect" (v. 40). The thought of 21:34–36 is similar: "Be on guard that your hearts may not be weighted down with dissipation . . . and that day come on you suddenly like a trap. . . . Keep on the alert." The parallel in Mk 13:33–37 builds on the immediately preceding prophecy of the hiddenness of the date of the second coming (v. 32, *q.v.*) and warns, "Take heed, keep on the alert" (v. 33). It then includes the parable of the porter, who is to stay on the watch, no matter whether his master's coming be "in the evening, at midnight, at cockcrowing, or in the morning, lest he come suddenly and find you asleep" (vv. 35–36). Fulfillment (per. 15): the unexpected, imminent return of Christ.[38]

48. Lk 12:37, 14:15, 22:18 (Mt 26:29, Mk 14:25) (3 vv., fig.): Christ's illustration continues, "Blessed are those slaves whom the master shall find on the alert when he comes; he will have them recline at table, and will come up and wait on them" (14:15); cf. the exclamation by one of our Lord's listeners, "Blessed is everyone who shall eat bread in the kingdom of God!" (14:15). So at the Last Supper, Christ anticipated a future feast: He would not drink of the wine "from now on until the kingdom of God comes" (22:18), "when I drink it new with you in My Father's kingdom" (Mt 26:29). Fulfillment (per. 15): the figure used in the first passage might convey nothing more than the idea of reward at the Lord's second coming (see Lk 12:43–44, No. 49, following); but in light of the other passages, it would seem to be describing the actual Messianic marriage feast, as in Ps. prophecy No. 22.

49. Lk 12:43–44 (2 vv., fig.): Christ foresaw that for the slave who is faithfully serving "when his master comes, he will put him in charge of all his possessions." Fulfillment (per. 16): the rule of the saints along with the Messiah, as in Isa. No. 51.

50. Lk 13:18–19 [see Mk 4:30–32, sim, under Mk. No. 9], 20–21 [see Mt 13:33, sim, under Mt. No. 40] (4 vv., fig.): the growth of the church.

51. Lk 13:29–30a (sim, Mt 8:11), 14:21b–23 (5 vv.): "They [Mt, "many," i.e. Gentiles, contrasted with the Jews, 8:10; cf. Lk 13:28] will come from east and west and will recline at table [Mt, "with Abraham, and Isaac, and Jacob"] in the kingdom of God. . . . Some are last who will be first" (Lk 13:29–30). 14:21–23 uses a figure: the parable of the guests invited to the dinner; but after their refusal, "the poor and crippled" were brought in from the lanes of the city; indeed, said the master, "Go out into the highways and compel them to come in, that my house may be full." Fulfillment (per. 15): Gentile participation in the Messianic marriage feast, predicted in Ps 22:29a; cf. Isa 25:6, and the emphasis in the following verse upon "all peoples . . . all nations." It is true that the Lord's

38. Cf. J. B. Payne, *The Imminent Appearing of Christ*, ch. III, and esp. pp. 95–98.

words are not explained in Luke 13, though they stand among other references to the Messianic feast (12:37, 14:15); and preceding the parallel passage in Mt 8:11 is Christ's statement concerning the Gentile centurion, "I have not found such great faith with anyone in Israel."

52. Lk *13:30b* (sim, Mt 8:12), 14:16–*21a*, 24 (6 vv.): "Some are first who will be last" (13:30). Mt 8:12 explains, "But the sons of the kingdom [Israel, those in the Jewish nation, v. 10] shall be cast out into the outer darkness; in that place there shall be weeping." Fulfillment (per. 17): the situation is eschatological by context (see No. 51, preceding); so these statements must refer to the condemnation, within the final judgment, of those Jews who disbelieve.

53. Lk 13:35a (sim, Mt 23:39a, but later, after Palm Sunday) (1 v.): Christ's word to Jerusalem, "You shall not see Me until the time comes when you say, 'Blessed is He who comes in the name of the Lord.'" Fulfillment (per. 15): as in Isa. No. 30; cf. Zech 12:10, not "the Hosannas of Palm Sunday (19:38) as though they meant, 'I shall not visit Jerusalem till the day of my humble triumph.' They clearly refer to the future and final penitance of Israel, [when] once again he would return as 'the Coming One.'"[39]

54. Lk 14:13–14a; on 19:16–19 and *24b–26a* [see Mt 25:20 etc., sim, under Mt. No. 20] (7 vv.): Jesus' teaching on behalf of care for the poor, because "you will be blessed; for you will be repaid in[40] the resurrection of the righteous." Fulfillment (per. 17): the reward of the saved at the final judgment, as in Job No. 5; cf. Mal 3:17.

55. Lk *14:14b,* 20:34–38 (Mt 22:29–32, Mk 12:24–27) (5 vv.): the first reference is an allusion by Christ to "the resurrection of the righteous." In the second, Jesus criticized the Sadducees for denying the resurrection, affirmed its reality, and cited Ex 3:6 on the permanence of God's relationship with His own. He added that those rising "neither marry, nor are given in marriage; for neither can they die any more, for they are like angels, and are sons of God, being sons of the resurrection," Lk 20:35–36. Fulfillment: Alford stresses that this is the first resurrection (per. 15), *ek nekrōn,* "out of (the rest of) the dead" (Mk 12:25), to which only sons of God (the saved) are counted worthy to attain (Lk 20:35).[41]

56. Lk 17:23, 21:7–8 (Mt 24:4–5, 11, 23–24a, 26; Mk 13:4–5, 21–22a) (3 vv.): in regard to the second coming of Christ (Lk 17:24), "They will say to you, 'Look there! Look here!' do not go away, and do

---

39. Camb, p. 243; cf. NIC, p. 383, "At His second coming, they would acknowledge Him with pangs of conscience as the Christ of God."

40. It occurs, not *at* (KJV, NAS) the resurrection of the just (see No. 55, following), but *en, in* (ASV) it; for by the time of the judgment the saints will already be in their resurrection bodies.

41. Op. cit., I:631; cf. ICC, p. 359, "It is possible that there is here a reference to the doctrine of a double resurrection, first of the righteous, and then of all," though Plummer recognizes the alternative of single resurrection as well.

not run after them," v. 23. "Be not misled; for many will come in My name, saying, 'I am He,' and, 'The time is at hand'; do not go after them," 21:8. Mt 24:11 also records words of Christ about "false prophets," but 24:24 goes on to unite the two concepts: for after the section on the fall of Jerusalem (see under 10:23b) the first Gospel speaks of the great tribulation in terms of "false Christs and false prophets," who together "show great signs and wonders" (cf. II Thess 2:9–11). Fulfillment (per. 14): premature and therefore false Messianic hopes. Some would limit the application of these references to the following hundred years, "the perpetual Messianic excitements, which finally ceased in the days of Barcochba,"[42] who died in A.D. 135. Actually, however, they are to reach their height immediately before Christ's return; see Mt 24:23–24, 29. Fairbairn cautions against undue restriction of the fulfillment, for when any persons "assume to be, or to do what by exclusive right and appointment belongs to Him, they then become, if not in name, at least in reality, false Christs."[43]

57. Lk 17:26–33a, 37 (sim, Mt 24:37–39) (9 vv.): just as it was prior to Noah's flood and to Sodom's fall, when "they were eating, they were drinking, they were buying, they were selling," etc., up to the very time of destruction, so "It will be just the same on the day that the Son of Man is revealed," 17:30–31. Our Lord therefore cautions, "On that day, let not the one who is on the housetop and whose goods are in the house go down to take them away. . . . Remember Lot's wife," vv. 31–32, who perished when she "looked back to recover worldly possessions and enjoyments."[44] V. 33 continues, "Whoever seeks to keep his life shall lose it"; and in v. 37, when the disciples asked, " 'Where, Lord?' He said to them, 'Where the body is, there also will the vultures be gathered,' " meaning, "where men are ripe for judgment."[45] Fulfillment (per. 15): false security, at the time of Christ's return—"careless enjoyment suddenly overwhelmed."[46]

58. Lk 17:33b–35 (sim, Mt 24:40–41), 21:28 (Mt 24:31, Mk 13:27) (3 vv.): "Whoever loses his life shall preserve it:[47] on that night there will be two men in one bed; one will be taken, and the other will be left. There will be two women grinding at the same place; one will be taken, and the other will be left" (17:33–35). The preceding context (vv. 29, 31) suggests that the one who is gathered in is the saved party,[48] though

---

42. Camb, *Lk*, p. 277.
43. *The Interpretation of Prophecy*, p. 354.
44. ICC, *Lk*, p. 409.
45. *Lk*, p. 891.
46. ICC, p. 408.
47. With particular reference to preservation at Christ's return; for as Alford notes, "In connection here, it leads the way to vv. 34–35," op. cit., I:550.
48. So Lenski, *Lk*, p. 890, and IB, VII:305. Even in Christ's later statement in Mt 24:40–41, immediately following words of warning on the destruction of those living in false security (vv. 38–39, No. 57, preceding), the men and women who are "taken" may still be composed of the saved, rather than of those taken away

the "taking"[49] could be in judgment rather than in redemption (cf. Mt 24:39). But in Lk 21:28, when the sun is darkened and the earth is in dismay (v. 25), Christ encourages His disciples, "Lift up your heads, because your redemption is drawing near." Matthew and Mark then include His more elaborate oracle, "The Son of Man . . . will send forth the angels and will gather together His elect [Christians, see Mt 24:22, under 10:23b, note 41] from the four winds." Fulfillment (per. 15): the rapture of the church, as in Hos. No. 27; see especially I Thess 4:17.

59. Lk 18:8 (1 v.): after the Lord's promise of speedy divine justice, He cautioned His disciples, "However, when the Son of Man comes, will He find faith on the earth?" Fulfillment (per. 14): widespread apostasy prior to the Lord's return.

60. Lk 19:11, *12b* (sim, Mt 25:*19a*) (1 v.): Jesus' refutation of the idea "that the kingdom of God was going to appear immediately." According to v. 12, His return would occur only after His journey to a distant country, i.e., heaven (see under 12:8, No. 46, above); cf. Mt 25:19, "Now after a long time the master came. . . ." Fulfillment (per. 14): the time lapse has now reached almost two millennia.

61. Lk 19:15b [see Mt. No. 68 (25:19c)] (1 v.): the final judgment.

62. Lk 19:29–30 [see Mk. No. 20 (11:1)] (2 vv.): finding the Palm Sunday colt.

63. Lk *20:16b* (Mt 21:41b, 43; sim, 22:9–10a; Mk *12:9b*), *21:24b* (fig.): in Luke 20, in the allegory of the wicked husbandmen, Christ later explained that the divine owner "will give the vineyard to others," Matthew adding, "who will pay him the proceeds at the proper season" (cf. Lk 20:16a, Mt 21:41a, under Mt. No. 28), and interpreting, "The kingdom of God will be taken away from you and be given to a nation producing the fruit of it" (Mt 21:43). At 22:9–10 Matthew includes a second allegory of Jesus,[50] on the marriage feast of the king's son,[51] again foreshadowing His replacement of the Jews (v. 8, see under 10:23b) by the Gentiles: "Go to the main highways, and as many as you find there, invite." Later, in Lk 21:24 He foretold that Jerusalem would be trampled underfoot by the Gentiles "until the times of the Gentiles be fulfilled," i.e.,

---

in judgment: ICC, *Mt*, p. 260, suggests that it "refers back to v. 31 . . . the angels will surprise men at work, and summon the elect from their daily toil."

49. Alexander Reese's contention, *The Approaching Advent of Christ*, p. 215, that the verb that is employed, *Parálambánō*, "is a good word, a word used exclusively in the sense of 'take away with' or 'receive,' or 'take *home*,'" is invalidated by the evidence of Mt 27:27. Cf. E. Schuyler English, *Re-thinking the Rapture*, p. 49.

50. Mt 22 uses phrases similar to those in Christ's earlier parable of the guests invited to the dinner, at Lk 14:16–24, though this latter is directed specifically to the future Messianic feast rather than to God's more general call of the Gentiles as in Mt.

51. For further comment, see under Mt 10:23b.

"the period during which the pagans will take the place of the unfaithful Jewish nation."⁵² Fulfillment (per. 14): God's substitution of Gentiles for the Jews as His people, thus going beyond His previous predictions of worldwide evangelism (as in Isa. No. 69; cf. Lk. No. 22) and of Gentile ingrafting into Israel (as in Gen. No. 19).

64. Lk 21:5–7 [see Mt 24:2, under Mt. No. 55] (3 vv.): the destruction of the temple.

65. Lk 21:9–11 [see Mk. No. 31 (13:7)] (3 vv.): calamities preceding A.D. 70.

66. Lk 21:25–26 [see Mk. No. 35 (13:24b)] (2 vv.): the wrath of God.

67. Lk 21:33 [see Mt 24:35, under Mt. No. 16] (1 v.): the passing away of heaven and earth.

68. Lk 22:10, 12 [see Mk No. 43 (14:13)] (2 vv.): Peter and John's finding the upper room.

69. Lk 22:16 (1 v., typ.): Christ's action of eating at the meal of the Last Supper, about which He explained, "I shall never again eat it until it is fulfilled in the kingdom of God"; cf. His verbalized prediction in v. 18 (listed under 12:37, No. 48, above), "I will not drink of the fruit of the vine from now on until the kingdom of God comes." Fulfillment (per. 15): the Messianic marriage feast, cf. Ps No. 22 (22:29a), Rev No. 49 (19:7–9), as typified by the communion service.⁵³ Compare the words of its institution as recorded in I Cor 11:26, "As often as you eat this bread . . . you proclaim the Lord's death *until He comes.*"

70. Lk 22:21, 23 [see John 13:21, under Jn. No. 17] (2 vv.): Christ's betrayal.

71. Lk *22:22b* [see Mk. No. 45(14:21b)]: woe to Judas.

72. Lk 22:30 [see Mt No. 47 (19:28), sim] (1 v.): the apostles' thrones.

73. Lk 22:32 (1 v.): Christ's predictive injunction to Peter, "When once you have turned again [which assumes his forthcoming denial, elaborated in v. 34, No. 74, following], strengthen your brothers." Fulfillment (per. 13): Peter's repentance and recovery, John 21:15–17, conditioned by his Lord's resurrection.⁵⁴

74. Lk 22:34, 61 [see Mk. No. 49 (14:30)] (2 vv.): Peter's denial.

75. Lk 23:43 (1 v.): Christ's promise to the repentant thief on the cross, "Today you shall be with Me in Paradise." The fulfillment (per. 13) cannot be proved, except that at His own death shortly thereafter Jesus committed His spirit to the Father, v. 46; and He *had* promised that His going to heaven was that "where I am, there you may be also," John 14:3.

52. IB, VII:129; see above, p. 100.
53. So IB, VIII:379.
54. IB, VIII:384.

JOHN

John's biography of Christ is the latest as well as the most theological of the four Gospels. Yet its existence is apparently attested by patristic writers early in the 2nd century;[1] and Rylands Papyrus 457, the earliest known fragment of the NT, preserves a portion of its actual text which may be dated as early as A.D. 130. Fifty years later Irenaeus, who claimed to be the pupil of Polycarp, who seems in turn to have been a pupil of the beloved disciple, testified that "John, the disciple of the Lord, who also leaned upon His breast, did himself publish a Gospel during his residence in Ephesus";[2] and with this claim to apostolic authorship agrees the internal evidence of the book (21:20, 24; cf. the writer's position as an eyewitness to the events recorded, 1:14, 19:35, and his use of oblique phrases to identify himself at points where the other Gospels would simply have named John, 13:23, 19:26, 20:2, 21:7). As summarized recently, "No other figure in John or in the Synoptic tradition corresponds to what the evidence requires, whereas John does."[3] During his later life John appears to have resided in Asia Minor (cf. Rev 1:4, 9); and Irenaeus states that he lived on until the time of Trajan, whose reign commenced in A.D. 98.[4]

The fourth Gospel seems to assume the existence of the earlier three and so repeats relatively little of what is found in the others. It alludes to Christ's Galilean ministry (2:12, 4:43, 6:1) but concentrates on His visits to Judea and on the dialogue that these produced. The volume provides a supplement to the Synoptics. It may have been written about A.D. 90 in Ephesus.[5] John's purpose is explicit: "These are written that you may believe that Jesus is the Christ, the Son of God, and that believing you may have life in His name" (20:31). The Gospel's prologue teaches

---

1. Summarized in D. Guthrie, *The Gospels and Acts: NT Introduction*, pp. 243–245.

2. *Against Heresies*, III:1, 1; cf. Eusebius, *Ecclesiastical History*, V:20.

3. *The Jerome Bible Commentary*, II:415. This would invalidate the widely held critical theory of authorship by "John the Presbyter," at Ephesus in Papias' day; though cf. H. B. Thiessen, *Introduction to the NT*, pp. 165–167, or Guthrie, op. cit., pp. 241–243, on the whole matter of the existence of this John as an individual separate from the apostle.

4. Op. cit., II:22, 5; III:3, 4.

5. M. C. Tenney, *The Genius of the Gospels*, p. 20. The older critical view that John reflects a Greek (not Palestinian) and Gnostic thought pattern (cf. E. J. Goodspeed, *An Introduction to the NT*, p. 308, though cf. p. 312) of the mid-2nd century is now generally rejected, in light of the discovery in 1946 of the Gnostic library of Chenoboskion in Upper Egypt, which shows that Gnosticism could *not* have provided John's background, and the discovery in 1948 of the Qumran MSS. of Essene Judaism, which validate as truly 1st century and Palestinian such Johannine distinctives as "light," "truth," and "belief."

of Christ's deity and preexistence (1:1–18). The main body of the book falls into two parts: 1:19–ch. 12, historical evidence for belief in Christ, as drawn from a few selected events in His public ministry; and 13–21, the facts of His rejection and execution by the Jews, but of His triumphant resurrection, offering life to those who will entrust their lives to Him.

The opening verse of John parallels that of Genesis in the OT. True also to his Jewish background, John stresses Christ's commitment to the OT, as a book that was divinely prophetic of Himself (5:39, 45, 7:38; cf. 10:35b);[6] and the fourth Gospel is marked by a concern over a detailed fulfillment for OT predictions (19:24, 36–37).[7] The book's high proportion of conversational material from Jesus must have contributed further to the inclusion of statements about the future. Statistically, the prophetic element involves 180 of the book's 866 verses, or 20%, a little less than the figure that is found for Luke; and these contain 45 separate predictions.

1. John 1:15 and 27 (sim: Mt 3:11b, Mk 1:7, Lk 3:16b), 30; 3:28 (4 vv.): John the Baptist's words, "He who comes after me has a higher rank than I . . . the thong of whose sandal I am not worthy to untie"; cf. Mk 1:7, "After me comes One who is mightier than I." In this way John predicted the One of whom he was the forerunner; No. 2, following. As he later confirmed, in retrospect, "I said, 'I am not the Christ,' but 'I have been sent before Him,' " 3:28. Fulfillment (per. 13): by the inauguration of Christ's public ministry shortly thereafter; cf. Mk 1:9. John then specifically quoted his own forecast as having been fulfilled in Jesus, John 1:30.

2. John 1:21a, 23 [see Lk 3:4–6, sim; under Lk. No. 8] (2 vv.): John the forerunner.

3. John *1:21b*, 6:14, 7:40 (2 vv.): citation of Dt 18:15, on the Messianic Prophet. The prediction was not claimed by John the Baptist for himself, 1:21; but people recognized its fulfillment (per. 13) in Jesus, 6:14, 7:40, as in Dt. No. 35.

4. John 1:25–26, 28, 31, *33a*; 3:23; 10:40, baptism by John [see Lk. No. 27 (3:3)]; 3:22, 26; 4:1 (total, 9 vv., typ.): Jesus too was baptizing, through His disciples, 4:2. Fulfillment (per. 13): the rite was typical of the redemption that He was about to perform, just as was OT circumcision; see Gen. No. 42.

5. John 1:29, 37; 3:15–18; 6:51c; 12:*24b*, *32b*, 47; 15:13–14 (10 vv.): "Behold, the Lamb of God who takes away the sin of the world!"

---

6. Cf. Guthrie, op. cit., pp. 212–213, on the place of the OT in John.
7. Compare in this regard the correspondence between John and Matthew in citing illustrative "fulfillments" of OT matters that were not in themselves predictive, e.g. 13:18, 19:28; see above, p. 77.

3:15–16 foretells that Christ is to be lifted up on the cross in death (see v. 14, No. 10, below), that believers "should not perish, but have eternal life." In 6:51 Jesus spoke of "My flesh . . . which I shall give for the life of the world"; cf. 12:47, "to save the world." 12:24 employs a figure, comparing His death with a grain of wheat in the earth: "If it dies, it bears much fruit." So in v. 28, when He prayed that glory might accrue to the Father's name and the Father replied that He would glorify it, Westcott comments, "How this should be is not expressed, but the reference is clearly to the thought of v. 32";[8] and v. 32, in turn, speaks of Christ's drawing all men to Himself by His death. In 15:13–14 Jesus affirmed, "Greater love has no one than this, that one lay down his life for his friends. You are My friends." This last pronoun, furthermore, is emphatic: "and when I say 'friends' I mean you."[9] Fulfillment (per. 13): Christ's atoning sacrifice, bearing men's sins, as in Isa. No. 100; cf. similar expressions, though on different occasions, listed under Mt. No. 2 (1:21b) and Lk. No. 17 (1:54).

6. John 1:33b (1 v.): that John the Baptist would recognize the Messiah when he should "see the Spirit descending and remaining upon Him." Fulfillment (per. 13): as stated in v. 32, preceding. "God told the Baptist in advance what he was about to behold."[10]

7. John *1:33c* [see Lk. No. 30 (3:16c), sim], 7:38–39, 16:8–9 (4 vv.): Christ said, "He who believes in Me, from his innermost being shall flow rivers of living water," 7:38. In the following verse the evangelist then explains, "This He spoke of the Spirit, whom those who believed in Him were to receive; for the Spirit was not yet given." Westcott elaborates, "He who drinks of the Spiritual Rock becomes in turn himself a rock from within which the waters flow to slake the thirst of others,"[11] as became indeed the case at Pentecost. 16:8 adds that the Spirit, or Paraclete (NAS, "Helper"), "will convict the world concerning sin, and righteousness, and judgment." Fulfillment (per. 14): Pentecost, as in Joel No. 8 (2:28); cf. Acts 2:37, "They were pierced to the heart." For other of the Johannine predictions on the Spirit, see below under 13:7 and 20:22 (typ.), No. 30 and 42.

8. John 2:19 (quoted in Mt 26:61, 27:40; Mk 14:58, 15:29), 14:*19c*–20 (2 vv., fig.): Christ's promise, "Destroy this temple and in three days I will raise it up" (2:19). This is explained two vv. later as referring to "the temple of His body" (2:21). In 14:19, at the Last Supper, He encouraged the disciples, saying that the world as a whole would see Him no more, but "because I live, you shall live also"; that is to say, "Not yet do ye live (in the present), for He was not yet risen from the dead, and His quickening power was not yet set free in those who 'believed on

8. *The Gospel According to St. John*, p. 182.
9. Camb, p. 290.
10. Lenski, *The Interpretation of John*, p. 136.
11. Op. cit., p. 123.

Him.' "[12] Fulfillment (per. 13): His resurrection—so stated, 2:22—as in Ps. prophecy No. 11.

9. John 2:23,[13] 6:4[14] (2 vv., typ.): Passover. Fulfillment (per. 13): as in Ex. No. 31.

10. John 3:14a (1 v. typ.): an allusion to the brazen serpent of Moses. Fulfillment (per. 13): as in Num. No. 30 (21:8).

11. John *3:14b*; 8:28; 10:15, 17–18; 11:50–51; 12:23–24a, 27–28, 32a, 33, *34b*; 13:31; 14:19a, 30; *15:13b*; 16:16a, 17a, 18–19a, 20a; 18:14, 32 (22 v.): "As Moses lifted up the serpent in the wilderness, even so must the Son of Man be lifted up," 3:14 (= 12:32); cf. 12:33, which states that His purpose was "to indicate the kind of death by which He was to die," and cf. its citation in 18:32, as denoting the manner of His execution. In 10:15 (= 15:13) He said, "I lay down My life for the sheep," the believers. Even Caiaphas told his Jewish colleagues, 11:50, "It is expedient for you that one man should die for the people, and that the whole nation should not perish"; cf. 18:14. He probably meant only that sufferance for the Jews by the Romans depended on their removing potential revolutionaries; but there was a higher meaning, as John explains, 11:51, "Now this he did not say on his own initiative; but being high priest that year, he prophesied that Jesus was going to die for the nation." See above, pp. 4 (note 8) and 5. In 12:23 Christ predicted, "The hour has come for the Son of Man to be glorified"; and then, v. 24, He compares Himself with a grain of wheat that falls into the earth and dies. This troubles His soul, v. 27; but He is determined to perform His God-given purpose. As a result, v. 28, God the Father says of His own name, "I will glorify it again." The same thought reappears in 13:31, "Now the Son of Man is glorified, and God is glorified in Him." This refers not to Christ's ascension, His victory over the cross (which follows in v. 32, see No. 16, below), but to the cross itself. Westcott explains, "Perfect self-sacrifice even to death, is the truest glory (compare 12:23)";[15] and God did receive glory as a result (cf. 10:17). On the other hand, in 14:30 our Lord could warn His disciples, "The ruler of the world is coming." ICC comments, "See on 12:31. It means Satan himself, to meet whose last assault Jesus now prepared."[16] Finally, at the Last Supper He foresaw that "After a little while the world will behold Me no more,"

---

12. ICC, II:548.

13. John 5:1, "a feast of the Jews," is probably another reference to the Passover; cf. A. T. Robertson, *A Harmony of the Gospels*, pp. 42, 267–270; but since this fact is not certain the passage has not been included.

14. 11:55–56, 12:1, 13:1, are also dismissed, since the night before this Passover, on Friday of Passion Week, Jesus had already celebrated the feast with His disciples (cf. 18:28, 39, 19:14) and replaced the whole ceremony with the Lord's Supper. By the time, therefore, that the Jews held their celebration on Friday evening the true Passover Lamb (I Cor 5:7) had already been sacrificed and the rite had ceased to be typical.

15. Op. cit., p. 196.

16. II:556.

14:19a; "for Jesus will have been removed from the world's sight after His Passion,"[17] and, temporarily, from the disciples' sight as well, 16:16a, 20: "You will weep and lament, but the world will rejoice." Fulfillment (per. 13): Christ's death, as in Isa. No. 99; cf. the corresponding predictions, on other occasions, listed under Lk 2:34c or Mk 2:20.

12. John 5:28–29 (2 vv.): after having spoken of a contemporaneous spiritual "resurrection" of those who would believe Him (v. 25), Jesus went on to predict, "An hour is coming in which all who are in the tombs shall hear His [the Son of Man's] voice, and shall come forth," though for those who rise only at this time—that is, for the unrighteous (for they are contrasted with the righteous in 5:29b; see No. 13, next)—it can be solely "to a resurrection of judgment." Fulfillment (per. 17): the general resurrection, as in Job No. 2 and Dan No. 56.

13. John *5:29b*; 6:39–40, 44, *50b, 51b, 54b, 57b, 58b*; 11:24–25 (5 vv.): "a resurrection of life" (5:29), for the righteous.[18] Christ promises to whoever believes on the Son, "I will raise him up on the last day" (6:40); he will "not die" (v. 50), but "live" (v. 57), "live for ever" (vv. 51, 58). So Martha affirmed over her dead brother Lazarus, 11:24, "I know that he will rise again in the resurrection on the last day"; and Jesus strengthened her faith by stating, v. 25, "I am the resurrection and the life." His words describe "a person representing an event in the future. . . . He diverts the thought of Martha, as it were, from the resurrection at the last day, which she feels is very far distant, to the resurrection of which He is potentially the Source as well as the Agent."[19] Fulfillment (per. 15): the first resurrection, as in Isa. No. 76.

14. John 6:32–36, 41, 48–50a, *51a*, 58a (10 vv., typ.): a citation of Israel's receiving manna, "It is not Moses who has given [past] you bread out of heaven [a phrase drawn from Ex 16:4], but it is My Father who gives [present] you the true bread out of heaven," v. 32, namely, Himself. The fulfillment of the type lies in His incarnation (per. 13): "I am the bread that came down out of heaven," v. 41; cf. vv. 35, 48, 51, and Ex. No. 39. That is, when God gave the OT saints manna (past), He was at the same time giving them life in Christ, just as He was to those with whom Jesus was talking in NT days (present). Alford therefore comments: Moses' manna was not "the true bread from heaven. It

---

17. Ibid., II:547.

18. As Plummer, commenting on John 6, says, "This is 'the resurrection of life' (5:29), 'the first resurrection,' the resurrection of the just," Camb, p. 151.

19. ICC, II:387. Specifically, this includes "an assurance that the 'rising again' of believers in Him is not to be postponed until then. If a man believes in Him, although his body dies yet his true self shall live (v. 25b). Or, as it may be put into other words, no believer in Jesus shall ever die, so far as his spirit is concerned (v. 26)," ibid., II:387–388. This, however, is a blessed but timeless generalization; it is thus not in the same prophetic category as the prediction of 11:24–25; see above, p. 36–38.

was, in one sense, bread from heaven—but not in *this* sense. It was a type and shadow of the true bread from heaven."[20]

15. John 6:52–54a, 55–57a (6 vv.): Jesus had been speaking of giving His flesh (His life) for the world and of constituting the living manna from heaven, v. 51. The Jews combined these two assertions and asked, "How can this man give us His flesh to eat?" So He then took up their own words and predicted, "He who eats My flesh and drinks My blood has[21] eternal life," v. 54 (with similar concepts in vv. 53, 55–58). Fulfillment (per. 14): the Christian communion service, as in Ps. prophecy No. 20. As Plummer cautiously summarizes the predictions of the passage, "The primary reference is to Christ's propitiatory death [v. 51; see under 1:29, No. 5, above]; the secondary reference [vv. 52–57] is to all those means by which the death of Christ is appropriated, especially the Eucharist. Not that Christ is here promising the ordinance, but uttering deep truths which apply, and which He intended to apply, to that ordinance."[22]

16. John 6:62; 7:33–36; 8:14, 21–22; 13:32–33, 36a; 14:2, 4–5, 28; 16:5–7a, 10, *17c*, 28; 17:11, 13; 20:17 (22 vv.): a proposal of Jesus to His listeners, "What then if you should behold the Son of Man ascending where He was before?" (6:62). He continued, "I go to Him who sent Me [7:33 = 8:14; 14:28; 16:5, 28; 17:11] . . . where you cannot come [7:34 = 8:21]"; and even the disciples will "no longer behold Me" (16:10). After God the Father will have been glorified by Christ's death, 13:31 (see under 3:14, No. 11, above), our Lord continues, "God will also glorify Him in Himself, and will glorify Him immediately," 13:32.[23] This oracle Jesus then explained in the next verse, that they would seek Him but not be able to come where He was going, a repetition of His words from 7:34, 8:21; "God," in other words, "would glorify the Son of Man by taking up His glorified humanity to fellowship with Himself."[24] Yet Jesus said also, 14:2, "I go to prepare a place for you . . . in My Father's house." Fulfillment (per. 13): His ascension, as in Ps. No. 8.

17. John 6:70; 13:10–11, 18, 21 (Mt 26:21–23, 25; Mk 14:18–20; Lk 22:21, 23), 22, 24–28 (11 vv.): in 6:70 Jesus spoke the words, "One of you is a devil," which John explains in the next verse, "He meant Judas, for he was going to betray Him." At the Last Supper He indicated, "You are clean, but not all of you," 13:10; and the evangelist again elucidates, "for He knew the one who was betraying Him; for this reason He said . . . ," v. 11. In v. 18 Christ next employed the phraseology

20. *The Greek Testament*, I:688.
21. Present tense; future resurrection follows in 54b, 57b, 58b (see under 5:29b, No. 13, above).
22. Camb, p. 154.
23. "The sufferings and the glories henceforth followed one another in unbroken succession," Westcott, op. cit., p. 197.
24. Ibid.

of Ps 41:9, about one who would "lift up his heel" against Him; and there follows in v. 21 His specific declaration, "One of you will betray Me." Then came His statement that the culprit would be one who was dipping food with Him into the bowl (Mk 14:20) and to whom He would give a morsel that He Himself had dipped; and, symbolically, "He took and gave it to Judas," v. 26. In Matthew is added the direct question by Judas, "It is not I?" to which Jesus answered, "You have said it yourself" (26:25). Fulfillment (per. 13): just as indicated, John 18:2–3.

18. John 7:2, 8, 10–11, 14, 37 (6 vv., typ.): the Feast of Tabernacles. Fulfillment (per. 16): as in Ex. No. 46.

19. John 7:22–23 (2 vv., typ.): circumcision. Fulfillment (per. 13): as in Gen. No. 42.

20. John 7:42a (1 v.): a reference to OT prophecy, "Has not the Scripture [e.g. II Sam 7:13, *q.v.*] said that the Christ comes from the offspring of David?" Fulfillment (per. 13): as in II Sam. No. 11, and cf. Mt 1:1, 20.

21. John *7:42b*: a citation of Mi 5:2, on the Messiah's birth in Bethlehem. Fulfillment (per. 13): as in Mi. No. 27, and cf. Mt 2:5.

22. John 10:16, 11:52 (2 vv., fig.): in the former passage Jesus said, "I have other sheep, which are not of this fold; I must bring them also, and they shall hear My voice, and they shall become one flock with one Shepherd." An explanation for the figure is suggested by the evangelist in the latter passage (11:52), that Jesus' death was "not for the [Jewish] nation only, but that He might also gather together into one the children of God who are scattered abroad." Fulfillment (per. 14): the Gentile ingathering into the church,[25] as in Gen. No. 19.

23. John 11:4, 11, 23, 40 (4 vv.): anticipations by Jesus of the death and return to life of Lazarus. "This sickness is not unto death, but that the Son of God may be glorified by it" (11:4; cf. v. 40). The Lord had recourse to a figure in v. 11, "Our friend Lazarus has fallen asleep [= died, v. 14]; but I go that I may awaken him out of sleep." To Martha, v. 23, He predicted, indefinitely, "Your brother shall rise again"; and Martha took it as simply a reference to his final resurrection (see v. 24, under 5:29b, No. 13, above). But the previously cited verses indicate Jesus' intent to have been one of more immediate fulfillment (per. 13): the raising of Lazarus at that time, v. 44.

24. John 12:2–5, 7–8 [see Mk. No. 41 (14:3)] (6 vv., sym.): Christ's burial.

25. John 12:14–16 [see Mt. No. 51 (21:4–5)] (3 vv.): Zech 9:9 fulfilled on Palm Sunday.

26. John 12:31, 16:11 (2 vv.): Christ's forecast, "Now judgment is upon this world; now the ruler of this world [a well-known Jewish title

25. Cf. ibid., p. 155.

for Satan[26]] shall be cast out" (12:31). That the accomplishment is said to be *now* links it with His crucifixion (v. 32) and the events which were to follow it.[27] 16:11 then states what would already have become true by the time of the Spirit's coming at Pentecost (see No. 7, above), " . . . the ruler of this world has been judged." Fulfillment (per. 13): as in Gen. No. 8 (3:15c); "The accuser of our brethren has been thrown down," who accused them before our God night and day (Rev 12:10), specifically, at our Lord's ascension (v. 5).

27. John 12:34a (1 v.): a citation from "the law" (meaning the OT in general), made by the multitude on Monday of Passion Week, that "the Christ is to remain forever." Fulfillment (per. 18): as in Ps. prophecy No. 37, Christ's eternity.

28. John 12:37–38, 41 (3 vv.): a citation of Isa 53:1, on the rejection of the Servant of Yahweh, as fulfilled (per. 13) in Christ; see Isa. No. 91. John 12:41 reaffirms that "Isaiah spoke of Him."

29. John 12:48 (1 v.): of a man who might reject the gospel, Jesus said, "The word I spoke is what will judge him at the last day." Fulfillment (per. 17): the final judgment of the lost, as in Ps No. 1 (1:5).

30. John 13:7; 14:16–17, 21–23, 26, *28b*; 15:26; 16:*7b*, 13–15, 25; 17:26 (13 vv.): Christ's words to Peter, "What I do you do not realize now; but you shall understand hereafter" (13:7). About this increased knowledge Lenski says, "The resurrection and the glorification of Jesus will shed a great light on everything";[28] cf. 14:26, "the Holy Spirit will teach you all things" (= 16:13–14, 25; 17:26); 15:26, and "will bear witness of Me." Jesus becomes more explicit in 14:16, that the Father would send "another Helper" (= 14:26, 15:26, 16:7), "the Spirit of truth" (14:17), with the result that "I will disclose Myself" (v. 21), "I will come to you" (v. 28), not simply in His external, resurrected body (as in vv. 18–19, see No. 8 and 34), but "My Father and I will come to him [any believer] and make Our abode with him" (v. 23). Fulfillment (per. 13): Christ's breathing upon the disciples in 20:22 that they might receive the Holy Spirit; see No. 42, below. This was not "a mere promise. The expression plainly implies that some gift was offered and bestowed then and there."[29] Its nature is described by Westcott as

the power of the new life proceeding from the Person of the risen Christ . . . the necessary condition for the descent of the Holy Spirit at Pentecost [see

26. ICC, II:441; cf. II Cor 4:4, Eph 2:2.
27. ICC, ibid., refers this removal to Satan's final casting out of the world (per. 17); but the contextual time elements favor "the empire of evil in the supraterrestrial sphere," IB, VIII:668, forfeiting its heavenly status in A.D. 30, as in Rev 12:10.
28. *John*, p. 917; he adds, "Especially Pentecost will bring the fullest revelation to them," pp. 916–917, though it was the Paschal experience that actually accomplished the increase in their knowledge.
29. Camb., p. 362.

No. 7, above]. By this He first quickened them, and then sent, according to His promise, the Paraclete to be with them and to supply all power for the exercise of their different functions. The relation of the Paschal to the Pentecostal gift is therefore the relation of quickening to endowing. The characteristic effect of the Paschal gift was shown in the new faith by which the disciples were gathered together into a living society (compare Lk 24:45).[30]

In the same vein Lenski comments: "On Easter evening the Spirit came to implant what Jesus revealed in Luke 24:44, etc. [i.e., the meaning of His own words, and of the Scriptures as a whole], but at Pentecost he came to send the gospel into all the world,"[31] cf. 7:38–39, under 1:33c (No. 7, above).

31. John *13:36b*, 21:18 (1 v.): Christ's revelation to Peter that he could not follow Him in His ascension to heaven, "but you shall follow later." Clarification appears in 21:18, "When you grow old, you will stretch out your hands, and someone else will gird you and bring you where you do not wish to go," with the explanation given in v. 19, that these words related to the apostle's execution. Fulfillment (per. 14): Peter's death, a fact that was understood by Peter himself; cf. 13:37. That he died by crucifixion is first mentioned by Tertullian, about 211.[32]

32. John 13:38 [see Mk. No. 49 (14:30)] (1 v.): Peter's denial.

33. John 14:12 (1 v.): the Lord's prediction, "He who believes in Me, the works that I do shall he do also; and greater works than these shall he do, because I go to the Father." Fulfillment (per. 14): church growth, and particularly as "the results of Pentecost . . . Christ's work was confined to Palestine and had but small success; the apostles went everywhere and converted thousands."[33]

34. John 14:18, *19b*; 16:*16b, 17b, 19b, 20b*–22 (3 vv.): Christ's promise to the disciples, "I will not leave you as orphans [KJV, comfortless[34]]: I will come to you" (14:18). His thought is explained by the next verse, that the world as a whole is not to see Him again, "but you will behold Me"; and, 16:20, "Your sorrow will be turned to joy." Fulfillment (per. 13): "The immediate reference of this is to the forty days (see Acts 10:41),"[35] following His rise from the dead. "He gives the disciples the promise of an appearance which will be a seal of His essential union with the Father. He is referring to His resurrection appearances,"[36] though the context does go on to speak of the subsequent abode of Christ, through

30. Op. cit., p. 295.
31. Op. cit., p. 1374.
32. *Scorp.*, 15.
33. Camb, p. 278.
34. Ibid., p. 281, "The inaccurate rendering 'comfortless' gives unreal support to the inaccurate rendering 'Comforter' [for the Holy Spirit, in vv. 16, 26]. In Greek there is no connection between orphans and the Paraclete."
35. Alford, op. cit., I:772.
36. NBC, p. 891.

the Spirit, in the disciples, 14:21–23 (see No. 30, above). Yet after His ascension they would "no longer behold" Him, 16:10.

35. John 15:6 (1 v., fig.): just as in Christ's illustration of the vine, "If anyone does not abide in Me, he is thrown away as a branch, and dries up; and they gather them and cast them into the fire, and they are burned." Fulfillment (per. 18): see Mt 5:29, under Mt. No. 10; these statements "seem to look forward to the future judgment of mankind."[37]

36. John 15:20–21, 16:2–4 (5 vv.): Christ's warning to the disciples, "If they persecuted Me, they will also persecute you" (15:20); "They will make you outcasts from the synagogue . . . [and] kill you" (16:2). Fulfillment (per. 14): persecution of the church; see Lk 11:49b (No. 44).

37. John 16:32 [see Mk. No. 47 (14:27), sim] (1 v.): the disciples scattered.

38. John 17:12 [see Mk. No. 45 (14:21b), sim] (1 v.): the fate of Judas.

39. John 19:24 (1 v.): citation of Ps 22:18, on the gambling for Jesus' garments, as fulfilled (per. 13) at the cross; see Ps. prophecy No. 17.

40. John 19:36 (1 v.): citation of the typical law of the Passover lamb, that not a bone should be broken, as fulfilled (per. 13) in Christ's legs not being fractured; see Ex 12:46 (under Ex. No. 33) and Num 9:12.

41. John 19:37 (1 v.): citation of Zech 12:10 as fulfilled (per. 13) in Christ's body being pierced; see Zech. No. 65.

42. John 20:22 (1 v., typ.): Jesus "breathed on them [the disciples] and said to them, 'Receive the Holy Spirit.' " On the contemporaneous reality of this phenomenon, see No. 42, above; "There was therefore a Paschal as distinct from a Pentecostal gift of the Holy Spirit, the one preparatory to the other."[38] The former was thus, in effect, a type of the latter.[39] Fulfillment (per. 14): in its prospective reference, this action was "an anticipation and earnest of Pentecost."[40]

43. John 20:23 [see Mt 18:18, sim, under Mt. No. 42] (1 v.): The power of the "keys."

44. John 21:6 (1 v.): a predictive command of Jesus to the disciples on Galilee, after they had fished unsuccessfully all night, "Cast the net on the right-hand side of the boat, and you will find a catch." Fulfillment (per. 13): vv. 8, 11, a net filled with 153 large fish.

45. John 21:22 (1 v.): a post-resurrection allusion by Christ to the possibility of John's survival "until I come." Fulfillment (per. 15): unlike 14:3, with its reference to Christ's coming again and receiving His own

---

37. ICC, II:481.
38. Camb, p. 362.
39. See the definition above, pp. 21, 22–23.
40. Camb, loc. cit. Some interpreters see this act as a Johannine replacement for the Pentecost experience. But cf. the express statement of Christ in Lk 24:49.

into heaven at death,[41] concerning this latter verse, "That it is meant to be interpreted by the Second Coming of Christ is not doubtful"[42]; cf. Ps. prophecy No. 45.

41. See above, p. 36.
42. ICC, II:711.

ACTS

"No finding of modern NT study is more assured" than that the Acts of the Apostles was written as a sequel to Luke (Acts 1:1; cf. the suggestion of Lk 22:49 that there would be more narrative to follow) and that the two volumes together form a continuous history of the beginnings of the Christian church.[1] Both were addressed to the believer Theophilus (Lk 1:3, Acts 1:1) and possess the same unique literary style, owing to their common source. The writer of the latter work must have been present with the apostle Paul during parts of all but the first of his missionary journeys, as indicated by the use of the plural pronoun "we" in 16:10-17, 20:5-21:18, and 27:1-28:16. The consistent tradition of authorship for Acts by Luke the beloved physician[2] is then substantiated by the particular "we" that is used in 20:5, since v. 4 excludes most of Paul's other companions except Luke. The record of the Book of Acts comes to a halt with Paul's first imprisonment in Rome, 28:30-31. The absence of further word about the disposition of his case would indicate that the book was inscripturated before its settlement, though the reference to Paul's "two full years" of confinement (v. 30, the legal interval after which charges were dropped, if no evidence had been produced) might imply his immediately impending release,[3] and thus a date of about A.D. 61.[4]

The key to the content of Acts is to be found in Christ's own promise, as stated in 1:8, "You shall receive power when the Holy Spirit has come upon you; and you shall be My witnesses both in Jerusalem, and in all Judea and Samaria, and even to the remotest part of the earth." The book, correspondingly, falls into three major sections on the expansion of Christianity: chs. 1-7, on the history of the early church in Jerusalem, until its scattering after the death of Stephen late in A.D. 33; chs. 8-12, on the spread of the gospel into Samaria, coastal Judea (including the crucial experience of Peter in opening the door of faith to Cornelius and the Gentiles

1. E. J. Goodspeed, *An Introduction to the NT*, p. 180.
2. See above, introduction to Luke.
3. Or immediately thereafter, JB, NT p. 196.
4. According to Donald Guthrie, *The Pauline Epistles: NT Introduction*, p. 278. J. Finegan, *Handbook of Biblical Chronology*, p. 325, would prefer A.D. 60, and IDB, I:607, A.D. 62.

in chs. 10–11), and the surrounding areas as far as Syrian Antioch; and chs. 13–28, on the missionary journeys of Paul throughout much of the Roman world, from A.D. 48 to 61.

The 63 prophecies of the Book of Acts make their appearance primarily in Luke's excerpts from early apostolic preaching. They involve 125 out of the work's 1,003 verses, or about 13%; and almost half find their fulfillment in the period of the church itself. Many consist of the quotation of previous prophecies, e.g., in Peter's sermon in Acts 2, on accomplishments that occurred during the life of Christ, or in Stephen's, in Acts 7, on fulfillments that were achieved as far back as the time of Israel's sojourn in Egypt. At still other points the apostles may repeat Biblical predictions whose accomplishment lay yet in the future, thus providing inspired reaffirmations of the certainty of their eventual fulfillment.

1. Acts 1:4–5, 8a; 2:16–18, 33, 39; 11:16 (9 vv.): Jesus' citation of His own previous prediction (Lk 24:49), "the promise" (Acts 2:39), that the disciples would receive baptism by God's Holy Spirit, 1:4–5. 2:16–18 consists of Peter's citation of the original OT forecast of Joel 2:28–29 as fulfilled (per. 14) at Pentecost,[5] and 11:16 is his later repetition of Christ's words in Acts 1:5.

2. Acts 1:6 (1 v.): a question addressed by the disciples to Jesus, who, even though He did not directly answer their query (see No. 3, following), still seems to have recognized the legitimacy of the idea—"Lord, is it at this time You are restoring the kingdom to Israel?" Fulfillment (per. 16): the position of privilege for Israel in the Messianic kingdom, as in Dt. prophecy No. 37.

3. Acts 1:7 (1 v.): a declaration by Jesus, to His disciples, about the anticipated kingdom and its restoration to Israel (No. 2, preceding), "It is not for you to know times or epochs which the Father has fixed by His own authority." Fulfillment (per. 15): the hiddenness of the time of the Lord's second coming, as in Zech. No. 73; cf. Mk 13:32.

4. Acts *1:8b*, that after the coming of the Holy Spirit the disciples were to be Christ's witnesses "in Jerusalem." Fulfillment (per. 14): starting at Pentecost, with the function of witnessing being specifically asserted in 2:32; cf. 3:15, etc.

5. Acts *1:8c*, ". . . and in all Judea." Fulfillment (per. 14): as the believers and the apostles moved out from Jerusalem., ·4. "those who had been scattered abroad went about preaching the word." Concerning Judea in particular, 9:32 explains: "As Peter was traveling through all those parts, he came down to Lydda."

6. Acts *1:8d*, ". . . and Samaria." Fulfillment (per. 14) began with Philip's ministry to the Samaritans, 8:5, 14.

5. Cf. under Lk 3:16c, though these prophecies are applicable to later baptisms by the Spirit as well, Acts 11:16.

7. Acts *1:8e*, 13:47b (1 v.): ". . . and even to the remotest part of the earth," 1:8. 13:47 goes on to cite Isa 49:6, that the Servant of Yahweh should "bring salvation to the end of the earth," which is the same phrase in Greek as in 1:8. The apocryphal Psalms of Solomon, 8:16, applied this expression to Rome in particular, which would correspond to the plan of the Books of Acts, terminating there as it does in 28:31. But the scope of Christ's prophecy appears to be even greater. As Lenski observes, "We know, too, that Paul reached Spain and Thomas reached India."[6] Fulfillment (per. 14): as in Isa. No. 69, world evangelization, especially in the widespread witnessing work of Paul (cf. Acts 13:31), but with its accomplishment still going on in missions today.

8. Acts 1:11, 3:19–20 (3 vv.): the message of the angels, to the disciples, at the time of Christ's ascension, 1:11, "This Jesus will come in just the same way as you have watched Him go into heaven." Then, in 3:19, Christian conversion is urged, "in order that times of revival may come from the presence of the Lord," a concept, in turn, that is to be explained by the next verse, which speaks of God's sending His Son to the earth again.[7] Fulfillment (per. 15): Christ's second coming, as in Ps. prophecy No. 5.

9. Acts 1:16, 20a (2 vv.): citation of Ps 69:25 (see Ps. No. 32), as fulfilled (per. 13) in the desolation of Judas' property.

10. Acts *1:20b*–22 (2 vv.): citation of Ps 109:8 (see No. 52), as fulfilled (per. 14) in the election of Matthias to occupy the office of Judas, Acts 1:25–26.

11. Acts 2:19–20 (2 vv.): quotation of Joel 2:30–31, as a part out of a larger selection from this prophet's 2nd chapter.[8] Fulfillment (per. 15): the wrath of God, as in Joel No. 9.

12. Acts 2:21 (1 v.): quotation of Joel 2:32a, as a part of the longer passage that Peter cited in his Pentecost sermon. Fulfillment (Per. 15): as in Joel No. 10, where the actual reference is to the rapture of the church, though its phrasing, that "whosoever shall call on the name of Yahweh shall be delivered," made also a suitable introduction to Peter's appeal to his own contemporaries to accept, on that very Pentecost Sunday, the salvation offered in Christ, Acts 2:22 ff.

13. Acts 2:27, 31; 13:32–38; *26:23b* (9 vv.): 2:27 and 13:35 are citations of Ps 16:10, with the explanation that David "looked ahead and spoke of the resurrection of the Christ" (2:31), "for . . . He whom God raised up did not undergo decay" (13:35). In this latter (13th) chapter, moreover, throughout the whole series of verses from 32 to 38, "the apostle's argument is on the resurrection of Jesus as a proof that He was the Messiah";[9] and in v. 33 he thus supports the truth of Christ's resurrec-

---

6. *The Interpretation of Acts*, p. 32.
7. So F. F. Bruce, *The Acts of the Apostles*, p. 111.
8. See above, p. 409, note 18.
9. Camb, p. 165.

tion from another OT passage: "as it is also written in the second Psalm" (v. 7), which speaks of the Messiah as being the begotten Son of God. Bruce has then correctly stated, "In the psalm David says that this declaration was made long ago";[10] and actually Ps 2:7 is not a prediction at all. But still, from the fact of the divine Sonship of the Messiah there may now be inferred His resurrection, even as Jesus has been "declared with power to be [this] Son of God by the resurrection from the dead" (Rom 1:4), so that the idea which Acts 13:33 infers from Ps 2:7 *should* be included among the list of the Bible's predictive promises. In a more general way, 26:23b cites simply "the prophets" on Christ's resurrection from the dead, thinking perhaps of Isa 53:10b (cf. the immediately preceding allusion in Acts 26:23a to His suffering) or of Hos 6:1–2. With greater specification Acts 13:34 then quotes Isa 55:3 (see Isa. No. 105) on "the sure mercies of David"; for the redemption that is anticipated by this Davidic testament was rendered *sure* by our Lord's resurrection. This was "the promise made to the [OT] fathers . . . fulfilled to our children [per. 13] in that He hath raised up Jesus" (Acts 13:32–33), as in Ps. prophecy No. 11.

14. Acts 2:30, 13:23, 15:15–16, 28:20 (5 vv.): the apostles make reference to God's oath to David "to seat one of his descendants upon his throne" (2:30), "according to promise" (13:23). Paul's allusion in 28:20 to "the hope of Israel," for which he had been placed in chains, must likewise be to this same Messianic anticipation.[11] 15:15–16 adds, "With this [i.e. God's taking a people for His name from among the Gentiles, commencing with Cornelius, v. 14] the words of the prophets agree, just as it is written, 'After these things I will return, and I will rebuild the tabernacle of David. . . .' " The words are a citation of Amos 9:11 (*q.v.*), on the restoration of the Davidic kingship through the incarnation of Christ. The opening line of Acts 15:16 is not from Amos but is an adaptation of Jer. 12:15, on the postexilic restoration of Edom and other nations surrounding Israel. Its phrase, "After these things," does however serve as a suitable summary for the preceding context (see under Amos 9:12) in Amos 9:8–10, on the exilic punishment of the ten northern tribes, in its function of destroying the sinners that were in Israel but of preserving God's own people (see under 9:4 and 9:8b).[12] The next phrase, "I will return," is then a Hebrew idiom for repetition; cf. the basic passage in Jer 12:15—ASV, "I will return and have compassion on them, and I will bring them . . . ," which the Jerusalem Bible renders by saying, "I will take pity on them *again* and bring them. . . ." Fulfillment (per. 13): Christ's descent from David, as in II Sam 7:13b, though the reference to God's *oath* arises from Pss 89:35, 49, and 132:11; see under Ps. prophecy No. 40.

10. Op. cit., p. 537.
11. Paul utilized a similar terminology, of *hope*, in 23:6, 24:15, 26:6–7 (see under 4:2, No. 23, below); and Bruce therefore includes in the thought of 28:20 a further fulfillment, "The expectation of the Messiah, and the belief in resurrection which, for Paul, was so closely bound up with it," ibid., p. 477.
12. J. B. Payne, *Theology of the Older Testament*, p. 477.

15. Acts 2:34 (1 v.): citation of Ps 110:1b, fulfilled (per. 13) in Christ's ascension, as in Ps. prophecy No. 8.

16. Acts *2:34b*, the quotation of Ps 110:1a (see Ps. No. 53), which was fulfilled (per. 13) in the fact of the Messiah's deity. This, however, is no longer the stress in the Acts 2 context, which simply quotes the entire verse, in Peter's demonstration of Christ's ascension (see No. 15, preceding).

17. Acts 2:35, 3:21 (2 vv.): the former is a quotation of Ps 110:1c (see under Ps. prophecy No. 5), on the Messiah's overthrow of His enemies. 3:21 then states that Christ has been received into heaven "until the period of restoration of all things," a phrase which suggests not just the restricted idea of kingdom favoritism for Israel, as in 1:6, but more likely the entire concept of "regeneration, when the Son of Man will sit on His glorious throne," Mt 19:28.

18. Acts 2:42, 46; 20:7, 11 (4 vv., typ.): in 2:42 the members of the church "were devoting themselves . . . to the breaking of bread and to prayer." This emphasis upon the act—relatively minor in itself—of breaking the bread suggests its symbolical value, indicating the sacrament of communion (the Eucharist).[13] Similarly, by the passage in 20:11—when Paul "had broken the bread [as he had planned in v. 7] and eaten"—"We are probably to understand a meal, in the course of which the Eucharist was celebrated."][14] This then involves a prophetic fulfillment (per. 15), since the communion service included a typical anticipation of the Messianic marriage feast, as in Lk. No. 69 (22:16).

19. Acts 3:18, 26:22–23a (2 vv.): citations of "all the prophets . . . that Christ was to suffer" (cf. 17:3), most prominently Isaiah's oracles of the suffering Servant. Fulfillment (per. 13): as in Isa. No. 99.[15]

20. Acts 3:22–23, 7:37 (3 vv.): citation of Dt 18:15, 19 (see No. 35), on the Messianic prophet, as fulfilled (per. 13) in Christ; cf. Acts 3:24.

21. Acts 3:25a, *13:47a*, 15:17–18, *26:23d* (3 vv.): the 1st passage is a citation of Gen 22:18, but with a passive rendering of the verb, as suggested by 12:3, 18:18b, etc., that in Abraham's seed "all the families of the earth" will be blessed. The 3rd quotes Amos 9:12 on the Gentiles as called by God's name and seeking Him. 13:47 cites Isa 49:6 on Christ as "a light to the Gentiles"; cf. 26:23 as a more general allusion to "the Prophets and Moses" as predicting the Messiah's proclamation of light to

13. Bruce, op. cit., p. 100; cf. IB, IX:51, "It was only later that the Eucharist became differentiated from the *agape*," or (love) feast.

14. Bruce, op. cit., p. 372.

15. Some schools of interpretation object that "strictly speaking, the prophets neither in the original passages nor in Jewish interpretations of them foretold that His Christ should suffer," IB, IX:59; but, as the same commentator goes on to explain, this is because these interpreters do not accept the Suffering Servant passages, as well as others that speak to this point (e.g. Dan 9:26), as truly Messianic. See above, pp. 283–284.

the pagan nations. Fulfillment (per. 14): the universal church, as in Gen. No. 19, Isa. No. 69, and Amos No. 24.

22. Acts *3:25b, 7:8a* (typ.): allusions to the Abrahamic testament. Fulfillment (per. 13): as in Gen. No. 30.

23. Acts 4:2; 23:6; 24:15a, 21; 26:6–8 (7 vv.): 4:2 describes how the apostles "were proclaiming in Jesus the resurrection from the dead." These last words define but a partial group out of a total body: "Some from among the dead are raised, while others as yet are not."[16] 23:6 then contains Paul's statement, "I am on trial for the hope [= 26:6–7][17] and resurrection of the dead"; and the resurrection which embodies such hope is specifically that "of the righteous," 24:15. Fulfillment (per. 15): the first resurrection, as in Isa. No. 76.

24. Acts 4:25–28, 8:32–*33a* (5 vv.): citations of Ps 2:1–2, on the heathen raging, and Isa 53:7–8a, as fulfilled (per. 13) in the trial of Christ by Herod and Pontius Pilate; see under Ps. No. 2 and Isa. No. 30.

25. Acts 5:9 (1 v.): Peter's forecast to Sapphira, for her lying to the church (and to God), "Those who buried your husband shall carry you out as well." Fulfillment (per. 14): her death, immediately thereafter, v. 10..

26. Acts 5:39 (1 v.): prophetic words by Gamaliel, about the future of the apostolic church, "If it be of God, you will not be able to overthrow them." Fulfillment (per. 14): the success of the church, as in Ezek. 17:23c (No. 24) or Mt 16:18b (see under No. 40).

27. Acts 6:14a (1 v.): an accusation brought against Stephen, of saying that Jesus would destroy the Jerusalem temple (v. 13). Fulfillment (per. 14): the destruction of the temple in A.D. 70, as Jesus had predicted in Mt 23:38, etc. (see Mt. No. 55).

28. Acts *6:14b*, Stephen's being further accused of saying that Jesus would "alter the customs which Moses handed down." The typical function of the Pentateuchal rituals was in fact terminated by Christ's accomplishment of redemption through His death; note how the veil of the temple was rent in two on Good Friday, Mt. 27:51. But the official decision of the church (per. 14) to exempt (Gentile) believers from the Mosaic law came later, at the council of Jerusalem, in 15:19–21. Bruce thus speaks of "Stephen's far-sighted comprehension of what was involved in the Gospel."[18] which amounted in effect to a prediction.

29. Acts 7:5 (1 v.): citation of God's promise to Abraham that his descendants should have the possession of Canaan. Fulfillment (per. 4): as in Gen. No. 24.

16. ExGkT, II:123.
17. W. J. Beecher generalizes 26:6–7 into the broad promise that all nations should be blessed in Abraham, *The Prophets and the Promise*, pp. 179–181; but the context (v. 8) would limit its point of reference to God's specific raising of the dead.
18. Op. cit., p. 158.

30. Acts 7:6 (1 v.): citation of Gen 15:13, on Israel's time of enslavement in Egypt. Fulfillment (per. 2): as noted under Gen. No. 31.

31. Acts 7:7a (1 v.): citation of Gen 15:14, on God's corresponding judgments upon Egypt. Fulfillment (per. 2): as in Gen. No. 32.

32. Acts 7:7b, 17, 34 (2 vv.): citations of Gen 15:14 and Ex 3:8 (in Acts 7:34) on Israel's exodus from Egypt. Fulfillment (per. 2): as in Gen. No. 33, Ex. No. 2.

33. Acts 7:7c, a citation of Biblical prophecy on Israel's return, so as to worship God in Canaan. Fulfillment (per. 4): as in Gen. No. 36 (15:16), though the phraseology is adapted from Ex 3:12, which concerned Israel's coming to Mount Sinai. Lenski therefore speaks of Acts 7:7 as "possibly an allusion to Ex 3:12 but not a quotation."[19]

34. Acts 7:8b (1 v., typ.): a reference to Abrahamic circumcision. Fulfillment (per. 13): as in Gen. No. 42.

35. Acts 7:42 (1 v., typ.): citation of Amos 5:25 on OT sacrifice. Fulfillment (per. 13): as in Lev. No. 2.

36. Acts 7:43 (1 v.): citation of Amos 5:27 on the exile of the northern tribes of Israel. Fulfillment (per. 7): as in Hos. No. 16.

37. Acts 7:44–49 (6 vv., typ.): references to Israel's tabernacle and temple. Fulfillment (per. 13): as in Ex. No. 55.

38. Acts 8:33b–35 (3 vv.): citation of Isa 53:8b, on the death of the Servant for the transgressions of men; and it is stated to have been fulfilled (per. 13) in Christ, as in Isa No. 100.

39. Acts 9:6, 22:10 (2 vv.): Christ's instructions to Saul at his conversion on the road to Damascus, "Enter the city, and it shall be told you what you must do." Fulfillment (per. 14): he was so told by Ananias, vv. 17–18 (cf. vv. 15–16); cf. Paul's own later testimony to the words of this devout man, 22:15–16.

40. Acts 9:12 (1 v.): the Lord's revelation to Ananias of a prophetic vision had by Saul, of Ananias' restoring sight to him. Fulfillment (per. 14): Ananias was so used, vv. 17–18.

41. Acts 9:15a; 22:15, 21 (3 vv.): the fact that Paul had been chosen of Jesus to bear His name before the Gentiles, 9:15, to be "a witness for Him to all men," 22:15, as Paul later quoted the words of Jesus, "I will send you far away to the Gentiles," v. 21. Fulfillment (per. 14): it did so develop, 13:46; and Paul was later given a particular commission to the Gentile ministry by the leaders of the church in Jerusalem, Gal 2:9; cf. Rom 1:5, 11:13.

42. Acts 9:15b, that Paul would also witness before kings. Fulfillment (per. 14): to Herod Agrippa II, in Acts 26, and even to the imperial court of Nero at Rome, 27:24 (cf. Phil 4:22 on his measure of success).

43. Acts 9:15c, Paul to witness to Israel. Fulfillment (per. 14): this was not the apostle's primary field (see v. 15a, No. 41, above); but when

19. Op. cit., p. 265.

he entered a new community he did generally begin his preaching in the synagogues, as in 13:14, and subsequently he had striking opportunities of witness to the Jews, e.g. in chs. 22 and 24.

44. Acts *9:16a,* Jesus to show Paul how much he must suffer for Him. Fulfillment (per. 14): there is no record of immediate revelations by the Lord to Paul in this regard, though the occurrence of such later on (as in 20:23 or 21:11–13) makes probable their existence at this point as well.

45. Acts 9:16b (1 v.): Ananias was told of the Lord that Paul "must suffer for My name's sake." The fulfillment of this forcast began while Paul was still in Damascus, v. 23 (cf. v. 29); and when in the midst of his 3rd missionary journey the apostle could record an extensive tabulation of his sufferings for Christ, II Cor. 11:23–33.

46. Acts 10:22, 11:13–14 (3 vv.): in their appeal to Peter, the messengers of Cornelius told how an angel had directed this officer "to send for you to come to his house and hear a message from you," 10:22. In itself this statement would have been simply a command and not a prediction; but the nature of the *message* that Cornelius was to anticipate from Peter, as this was later more fully reported, is shown to have been predictive. For the apostle subsequently testified that the angel's statement had been that Peter "shall speak words to you by which you will be saved, and all your household," 11:14. Fulfillment (per. 14): on his arrival he did speak to them just such words, 10:44–48.

47. Acts 10:42, 16:31, 24:25 (3 vv.): as Peter told Cornelius, Jesus was "the One who had been appointed by God as Judge of the living and the dead," 10:42; and Paul told the Athenians, God "has fixed a day in which He will judge the world in righteousness through a Man whom He has appointed," 16:31, i.e. Jesus, cf. his reference in 24:25 to "the judgment to come." Fulfillment (per. 17): the final judgment, as in Eccl. No. 1.

48. Acts 11:28 (1 v.): the prophecy of Agabus "that there would certainly be a great famine all over the world." The fulfillment (per. 14) is stated in that same verse to have occurred in the reign of Claudius I, 41–54; cf. the relief mission which the church accordingly carried out, 11:30, 12:25.

49. Acts 13:11 (1 v.): Paul's oracle to Elymas the magician, for opposing the gospel, "You will be blind and not see the sun for a time." Its fulfillment came about "immediately," v. 11 (per. 14), though the length of the *time* of this stroke is not recorded.

50. Acts 13:24, 19:3–4a (2 vv., typ.): John's baptism, as pointing to the work of Jesus "before His coming," 13:24. Fulfillment (per. 13): as in Lk. No. 27 (3:3).

51. Acts 13:25, 19:4b (2 vv.): citation by Paul, of the Baptist's announcement of Christ as the greater One who should succeed him. Fulfillment (per. 13): as in John No. 1 (1:15).

52. Acts 18:10 (1 v.): Christ's assurance to Paul, after he had been

opposed in the synagogue at Corinth, "I am with you, and no man will attack you to harm you," Fulfillment (per. 14): as stated in the next verse, Paul was able to continue in Corinth for 1½ years of teaching, 50–51, after which even the charges brought against him by the Jews were dismissed from court by the proconsul Gallia, vv. 15–16.

53. Acts 20:22–23; 21:4, 11–14 (7 vv.): on his 3rd missionary journey, as he was on his way to Jerusalem, Paul told the Ephesian elders, "The Holy Spirit testifies to me, saying that bonds and afflictions await me," 20:23. Shortly thereafter, in 21:4, the Tyrian disciples "kept telling Paul through the Spirit not to set foot in Jerusalem," NASmg, "i.e., because of impressions made by the Spirit." Bruce explains: "Their inspired vision foresaw the difficulties and dangers that lay ahead of Paul (cf. v. 11); they drew the conclusion that he should not go up to Jerusalem (cf. v. 12). We must not infer that his continuing the journey was contrary to God's will; it was 'under the constraint of the Spirit' (20:22) that he was going to Jerusalem."[20] Then in 21:11, after the apostle's arrival in Caesarea, the prophet Agabus symbolically "took Paul's belt and bound his own feet and hands, and said, 'This is what the Holy Spirit says: "In this way the Jews at Jerusalem will bind the man who owns this belt and deliver him into the hands of the Gentiles' "—they were, in fact, compelled to deliver him up, by the Roman troops who came to his rescue. Fulfillment (per. 14): Paul thus suffered attack by a Jewish mob, 21:30–31; was bound, v. 33 (cf. 22:29), and almost "examined by scourging," 22:24; was threatened by murder plots, 23:14; and was left imprisoned for 2 years in Caesarea, 24:27.

54. Acts 20:29–30 (2 vv., fig.): to the Ephesian elders Paul predicted, "After my departure savage wolves will come in among you, not sparing the flock; and from among your own selves men will arise, speaking perverse things, to draw away disciples after them"; cf. his later warning to this same church in I Tim 4:1. Fulfillment (per. 14): Ephesus subsequently encountered (and rejected) certain "false apostles," Rev 2:2, and seems also to have suffered from those who apostatized from within, I Tim 1:3–7, 6:21, II Tim 3:6.

55. Acts 22:18 (1 v.): a retrospective account by Paul, of words revealed to him by Jesus in a vision, while he was in the temple at Jerusalem after his conversion: "Get out of Jerusalem quickly, because they will not accept your testimony about Me." Fulfillment (per. 14): the historical narrative of Acts describes in 9:29–30 an attempt of the Jews even to take Paul's life, so that the church sent him away to Tarsus.

56. Acts 23:3 (1 v.): while Paul was on trial before the Sanhedrin, after the high priest Ananias had ordered him to be struck on the mouth, Paul retorted, "God is going to strike you, you white-washed wall!" Fulfill-

20. Op. cit., p. 385.

ment (per. 14): in A.D. 66, at the beginning of the Jewish war, Ananias was assassinated by "thieves,"[21] possibly some group of Zealots.

57. Acts 23:11, *27:24b* (1 v.): Christ's assurance to Paul, while he was imprisoned in Jerusalem, that he must witness for his Lord at Rome, 23:11 (cf. 9:15b, No. 42, above). Similarly, during the storm of ch. 27, God's angel told him, "You must stand before Caesar," v. 24. Fulfillment (per. 14): Paul's witness to Christ in Rome, both in prison, 28:17–31, and at his trials, II Tim 4:17.

58. Acts *24:15b,* "the resurrection . . . of the wicked." Fulfillment (per. 17): as in Job No. 2.

59. Acts 26:16 (1 v.): in recounting his conversion, Paul spoke of his appointment by Jesus as a witness "to the things in which I will appear to you." This last statement constitutes a prediction of appearance(s) by Christ to Paul, subsequent to his initial experience on the road to Damascus; compare the Lord's more specific promise, about revelations of sufferings that he would be called upon to endure (9:16a, No. 44, above). Fulfillment (per. 14): e.g., the vision of Jesus to which Paul bore testimony in 22:17–21, or those recorded in 18:9–10 and 23:11.

60. Acts 26:17a (1 v.): Christ's promise to deliver Paul from the Jewish people; cf. His more specific word of divine protection in 18:10 (No. 52, above). Fulfillment (per. 14) commenced with Paul's initial escape from Jewish enemies over the wall of Damascus (9:23–25), and it continued down to his current deliverance from Jewish plots through the medium of protective custody as afforded by Rome (23:20, 25:11–12, 26:22).

61. Acts *26:17b,* a similar promise (cf. v. 17a, No. 60, preceding) for Paul's deliverance from the Gentiles. Fulfillment (per. 14): as in Philippi, 16:35–39, or in Ephesus, 20:1, though up until the Neronic persecutions, the Gentiles were less active in opposition to Paul and to the church than were the Jews. Compare Paul's final testimony, II Tim 4:17, when he anticipated that his impending "deliverance" would then be to heaven, v. 18.

62. Acts 26:23c (1 v.): Paul's citation of "the Prophets" that Christ, "by reason of His resurrection . . . should be the first to proclaim light to the Jewish people," meaning that "out of His resurrection assurance was given . . . that in Him all the OT prophecies of the blessings of light and life were to be fulfilled (Isa 9:1–2, 60:1). *Light* means more than the blessing of immortality in the future: it means the present realization of the light of life, cf. Lk 2:32."[22] Fulfillment (per. 13): Christ's redemption for Israel, as in the passages listed under Lk. No. 17.

63. Acts 27:22–26, 31, 34 (7 vv.): in speaking to his shipmates during the storm of ch. 27, Paul disclosed a revelation given him by an angel of God—"There shall be no loss of life among you [= v. 34], but only of

21. Jos, *Wars,* II:17, 6, 9.
22. ExGkT, II:510.

the ship. . . . We must run aground on a certain island," vv. 22, 26. Thereafter, when the sailors were attempting to desert the ship, Paul stated to the centurion and the guard, "Unless these men remain in the ship, you cannot be saved," v. 31. But this negative condition was not fulfilled: the sailors did remain, as the troops prevented their escape, v. 32; and thus presumably those who were addressed *would* be saved. Paul's words at this juncture may not be dismissed as mere advice (as in vv. 10, 21)[23] but are to be considered as a part of the total revelation of divine protection. Lenski comments, "Paul's frustration of the wicked scheme of the sailors was known to God when He gave him the prophecy."[24] Fulfillment (per. 14): the ship ran aground at Malta, and all on board were saved, 27:39, 41, 44; 28:1.

23. See above, p. 70.
24. Op. cit., p. 1088.

ROMANS

Thirteen of the remaining 23 books of the New Testament consist of epistles composed by the apostle Paul during his missionary career in Roman Asia and Europe. They fall into four generally recognized groups: (1) the Thessalonian letters (I–II Thess), which date from Paul's 2nd missionary journey, A.D. 49–50; (2) the "great epistles" (Rom, I–II Cor, Gal), written during his 3rd journey, 52–56; (3) the prison epistles (Eph, Phil, Col, and also Philemon, though this last has no treatment in the present study because of its lack of predictive content), composed during Paul's two years of confinement in Rome, 59–61;[1] and (4) the Pastorals (I–II Tim, Titus), written between the apostle's release and his final reimprisonment and execution by Nero, probably in mid-64. For most of these 13 letters there arises little serious question about their authentically Pauline origin—on Ephesians and the Pastorals, see below under their respective introductions. Romans can be assigned, on the basis of its own testimony in 15:22–32,[2] to the conclusion of Paul's 3-month stay in Corinth (Acts 20:3; cf. his commendation of various Corinthians in 16:1, 23a [cf. I Cor 1:14], or 23b [cf. II Tim 4:20]), just prior to his departure for Jerusalem at the end of his 3rd missionary journey. The date would therefore have been early in 56.[3]

1. See above, introduction to Acts, note 4.
2. Liberal critics not infrequently deny an integral place within Romans to parts of ch. 15 and to ch. 16's long list of names and greetings; but it would seem natural for the apostle, in writing to a church that he had not yet personally visited, to specify as many points of contact as he could. See the discussion in D. Guthrie, *The Pauline Epistles: NT Introduction*, pp. 28–41.
3. Ibid., p. 276. IDB, I:607, prefers the end of 56, but J. Finegan, *Handbook of Biblical Chronology*, p. 322, A.D. 55.

The theme of Romans may be described as an amplification of Paul's earlier deliverance to the Galatians, namely, the doctrine of justification by faith in Christ. The apostle summarizes his inspired teaching in Rom 1:16, "I am not ashamed of the gospel, for it is the power of God for salvation to every one who believes." This he then develops through five major sections: 1:18–3:20, sinful humanity's need of redemption; 3:21–ch. 5, the provision of righteousness in Christ; 6–8, the Christian's life of sanctification; 9–11, the problem of the Jews' rejection of God's plan of salvation; and 12–15:13, practical guidance for the conduct of believers. Items of personal concern to Paul occupy a conclusion to the epistle. Predictions, which cover 29 separate subjects, appear in each of the book's 16 chapters except chs. 1 and 7. These involve a total of 91 out of the epistle's 433 verses (= 21 %), with the highest concentrations appearing in ch. 2, on the final judgment, in ch. 8, on glorification at Christ's return, and in ch. 11, on the future of Israel. More than half of the 29 consist of the citation of previous OT prophecies.

1. Rom 2:2–3, 5, 8–9, 12; 11:20–22 (9 vv.): in Rom 2 the opening declaration, that "the judgment of God rightly falls" on those who do evil, might seem to refer to contemporaneous actions of divine providence, as in 1:18. But see v. 5 that follows, "You are storing up wrath for yourself in the day of . . . the righteous judgment of God," or v. 12, "all who have sinned will be judged," whether by the Law, or for those without the Law by their conscience (cf. v. 15). That is to say, "In the present passage Paul is thinking of judgment under its future aspect."[4] The specific causes for condemnation are listed in vv. 8–9: selfish ambition, disobedience to the truth, and general unrighteousness. Cf. the warning in 11:20–22, "Do not be conceited . . . for neither will He spare you. . . . Continue in His kindness; otherwise you will be cut off." Fulfillment (per. 17): the final judgment of the wicked, as in Ps. prophecy No. 1.

2. Rom 2:6, 13–16; 3:6; 14:10–12 (9 vv.): more comprehensively, "God will render to every man according to his deeds," 2:6, in which the apostle is quoting Ps 62:12 and applying it to the future (see v. 5, No. 1, preceeding. Rom 3:6 states that God will judge the world; and 14:10, 12, "We shall all stand before the judgment seat of God . . . each one of us shall give account of himself to God." In 2:13 Paul explains that "not the hearers but the doers of the Law will be justified": that judgment for those without the written Law of God will be based upon the extent to which they "show the work of the Law written in their hearts," v. 15 (cf. v. 26); but there will be a universal assize, v. 16, in which "God will judge the secrets of men through Christ Jesus," in accordance with the gospel preached by Paul. Fulfillment (per. 17): the fact of final judgment, as in Eccl. No. 1.

4. IB, IX:407.

3. Rom 2:7, 10; 5:9–10 (4 vv.): that eternal life, honor, and peace are to be awarded to those, whether Jews or Gentiles, who are marked by "perseverance in doing good," 2:7, 10. This promise might seem to be unreal, because of its conditional character—a condition that none fulfills, 3:10, 19–20. But 5:9 adds, "We shall be saved from the wrath of God through Him [Jesus]," meaning that Christ the Savior does fulfill the divine standard of goodness, and that the Christian then stands in Him by faith: "All are sinners, yet not one of the sins of these 'endurers' is brought to light in the final judgment. Their endurance by faith, in good work, characterizes these sinners and not the faults that were removed by God's remission."[5] Fulfillment (per. 17): the final judgment of the righteous, as in Job No. 5.

4. Rom 2:27 (1 v.): Paul warns the Jews that if a Gentile "keeps the Law, will he not judge you who though having the letter of the Law are a transgressor of the Law?" Fulfillment (per. 17): as in Lk. No. 42 (11:31b), the judgment of Jews by Gentiles.

5. Rom 4:9–12 (4 vv., typ.): a discussion of Abraham's receiving "the sign of circumcision, a seal of the righteousness of . . . faith," v. 11. Fulfillment (per. 13): as in Gen. No. 42.

6. Rom 4:13–14, 16; *5:17b*; 15:8 (4 vv.): a citation of God's promise to Abraham and his descendants, both ethnic and engrafted (4:16), that "he would be heir of the world" (v. 13). No single oracle that is recorded in Genesis is worded in this exact way.[6] The mere promise of Canaan, as in Gen 12:7, or of the united kingdom's possession of the gate of its enemies, as in 22:17c, seems inadequate for the scope of this forecast. Better would be the millennial accomplishment of all nations seeking Christ, as in 22:18b. Yet a situation of special inheritance for the true seed of Abraham seems requisite; cf. the word of Rom 15:8, that Christ became a servant particularly to circumcised Jews with the goal of "confirming the promises given to the fathers."[7] A suggested fulfillment is therefore that of Dt. No. 37 (26:19) and Isa. No. 51 (14:2b): the privileged status of all Christian descendants of Abraham, "reigning in life through the one, Jesus Christ" (5:17),[8] in the future kingdom of the Messiah (per. 16).

7. Rom 4:17, 9:23–26, 10:20 (6 vv.): the 1st reference is a citation of Gen 17:5, that nations would spring from Abraham; the 2nd, of Hos 1:10 and 2:23, about the Gentiles becoming adopted sons of God; and the 3rd, of Isa 65:1, on God's being found by those who had not sought Him up

---

5. R. C. H. Lenski, *The Interpretation of Romans*, p. 150.

6. For a listing of the ways in which this passage has been taken, see C. Hodge, *A Commentary on the Epistle to the Romans*, pp. 119–120.

7. W. J. Beecher, *The Prophets and the Promise*, p. 182, thus refers 15:8 to "the one promise" of all nations being blessed in Abraham.

8. ExGkT, II:630, "The consummation of redemption in the Messianic kingdom in the world to come."

to that point. Fulfillment (per. 14): the engrafting of Gentiles into the Israel that is the church, as listed, respectively, under Gen 17:46 (2nd stage), Hos 1:10, and Isa 44:5.

8. Rom 4:18–21, 9:7 (5 vv.): citations, respectively, of Gen 15:5 and 21:12, on the increase of Abraham's descendants, and specifically through his son Isaac. Fulfillment (per. 2): as listed under Gen. No. 21, on the patriarch's physical offspring, Rom 4:19, though Paul also here uses this promise to illustrate the even greater number of his spiritual children, v. 18 (cf. v. 17, No. 7, preceding), the "descendants . . . who are of the faith of Abraham," v. 16.

9. Rom 5:2; 6:5, 8:11, 17–19, *21b*, 23–25, 29–30 (11 v.): 5:2 introduces the concept of the "hope of the glory of God," which is then elaborated in 8:17–18, 21, 30, on Christ's heirs being "glorified with Him," as children of God. 8:23 explains that this means "the redemption of our body," a thought that is equivalent to v. 19's, on "the revealing of the sons of God." V. 11 specifically states that "He who raised Christ Jesus from the dead will also give life to your mortal bodies through His Spirit"; cf. v. 29, that we are "to be conformed to the image of His Son," and 6:5, that "we shall become united with Him in the likeness of His resurrection." Fulfillment (per. 15): the transformation of the believer, when raptured into the presence of God at Christ's glorious return—"changed," I Cor 15:51, to have bodies like that of Christ at His resurrection, "the body of His glory," Phil 3:21.

10. Rom 5:14–19 (6 vv., typ.): the apostle's discussion of Adam as "a type of Him who was to come," i.e. Christ, whose ministry opens a way for men into life, in contrast with "the transgression of the one [Adam]" (v. 15), through which "there resulted condemnation" (v. 18). Fulfillment (per. 13): as analyzed under Gen. No. 5.

11. Rom 8:20–21a (2 vv.): hope for the physical creation, to be "set free from the slavery of corruption." Fulfillment (per. 15): the joy of nature at Christ's return, as in Ps. prophecy No. 44; for "Nature will be restored to its primeval character when the new age dawns. . . . It is impossible to suppose that all the innumerable references, scattered through the prophets, to the renewal of nature express mere metaphor, e.g., Isa 55:12–13."[9]

12. Rom 9:4 (1 v., typ.): Paul's historical allusion to Israel's being granted the testaments (plu: the Sinaitic, Levitical, and Davidic) and the various promises. Fulfillment (per. 13): as in Ex. No. 45 (19:5), etc.

13. Rom 9:8–9 (2 vv.): citation of Gen 18:10, on "children of the promise," specifically on the promise of Sarah's having a son. Fulfillment (per. 1): see under Gen. No. 29.

14. Rom 9:12 (1 v., fig.): citation of Gen 25:23, on the idea of

9. IB, IX:519.

Edom's being subdued by Israel. Fulfillment (pers. 6, 7, and 11): as in Gen. No. 50 (25:23b).

15. Rom 9:27 (1 v.): citation of Isa 10:22, on but a remnant of Israel returning from exile. Fulfillment (per. 9): as in Isa. No. 20, though this forecast is used by Paul to illustrate the fact of the mere remnant of Judah that had accepted Christ as well.

16. Rom 9:28, 10:19, 12:19 (3 vv.): citations, respectively, of Isa 10:23, Dt 32:21, and 32:35, on the destruction of Judah at its fall in 586 B.C., at the hands of a "foolish," i.e. foreign-speaking, nation, Dt 32:21. Fulfillment (per 7): as listed under Isa. No. 5 and Dt. No. 13, though the OT oracles are used in the first two of these Pauline passages (just as in Isa 1:9 in Rom 9:29) to illustrate Israel's current failure to accept Christ, in contrast with the Gentiles' response, and in the third (Rom 12:19), to illustrate the general principle of divine vengeance.

17. Rom 10:13 (1 v.): citation of Joel 2:32, on divine deliverance for those who are to be raptured at Christ's return. Fulfillment (per. 15): as in Joel No. 10, though the verse is used in Rom, just as in Acts 2:21, to motivate a contemporaneous response to the gospel call.

18. Rom 10:16 (1 v.): citation of Isa 53:1, on the rejection of the report about God's righteous Servant. Fulfillment (per. 13): as in Isa. No. 91.

19. Rom 11:12a, 15a, 16 (3 vv.): in speaking of the Jews, Paul exclaims, "If their transgression be riches for the world [meaning that whenever Paul and the Christian gospel were rejected by the Jews, he then turned to the Gentiles, vv. 17–19, to share its treasures with them], how much more will their fulfillment be!" v. 12; and v. 15 adds, ". . . what will their acceptance be but life from the dead." Some would understand this last phrase as being but a figure of speech for an awakening of spiritual life. But against such an approach is the fact that "in all contemporary Jewish literature the resurrection is a sign of the inauguration of the new era,"[10] and so likewise elsewhere in Paul (I Thess 4:16, I Cor 15:42). A. B. Davidson argues, furthermore, "Life from the dead cannot mean spiritual quickening, any converting effect among the Gentiles, for their fulness is already ere now come in. The expression must be taken literally . . . [for an actual] resurrection."[11] Fulfillment (per. 15): the the bodily first resurrection, as in Isa. No. 76, occurring at the time of Christ's second coming, which is also when Israel will be restored to faith (see No. 20, next).

20. Rom 11:*12b, 15b*, 23–24, 26b, *27b*–32 (8 vv.): Israel's "fulfillment" in Messianic times (v. 12, No. 19, preceding), their "acceptance" (v. 15) and being "shown mercy" (vv. 31–32), is elaborated in the figurative statement in vv. 23–24, "They, if they do not continue in their un-

10. ICC, pp. 325–326, with examples.
11. *OT Prophecy*, p. 483.

belief, will be grafted in . . . [as] natural brances into their own olive tree [of the true Israel, the people of God, cf. their failure in respect to this same standing, in 9:6] . . . for God is able." Vv. 24, 26–27, then make it clear that they *will* so believe: "Israel[12] will be saved; just as it is written [and Paul cites Isa 59:20, see under Isa 8:17], The Deliverer . . . will remove ungodliness from Jacob . . . when I take away their sins." Fulfillment (per. 15): the conversion of the Jews at Christ's return, as in Isa. No. 31, see above, p. 100.

21. Rom 11:25 (1 v.): Paul explains that a partial hardening has happened to Israel, "until the fulness of the Gentiles has come in." Interpreters ask, "Does *fulness, plērōmā,* mean all the Gentiles, or all those Gentiles whom God has foreknown and predestined to salvation?"[13] The noun is the same as that which is rendered "fulfillment" (NAS; "fulness," ASV) in v. 12, to describe the final conversion of the Jews (No. 20, above). But since the "all Israel" of v. 26 is not totally inclusive (See No. 22, following), a number of differing options have been proposed for this group of Gentiles in v. 25: "until the 'great multitude' of Rev 7:9 [coming out of "the great tribulation," v. 14] is complete";[14] or, "the complement to make full the vacancy left by the rejection of the Jews";[15] or, "that which makes the Gentiles, as to number full."[16] In line with this last proposal, the fulfillment herein suggested is that of Mk 13:10: the large, but still definite number of Gentiles that are to be converted (in this present period, 14) before the second advent of Christ.[17]

22. Rom *11:26a,* ". . . and thus all Israel will be saved." Fulfillment (per. 15): a general conversion of the Jews—not simply, "all that part of the nation which constitute 'the remnant according to the election of grace [v. 5]'; but the whole nation, as a nation."[18] Yet even so, it is "Israel as a whole, Israel as a nation, and not as necessarily including every individual Israelite";[19] for Isa 59:20, which Paul goes on to quote in very next verse (No. 23, following), had specified that the Redeemer would come "unto them that turn from transgression in Jacob."

23. Rom *11:26c,* citation of Isa 59:20a, on the second coming of Christ. Fulfillment (per. 15): as listed under Isa. No. 77.

24. Rom 11:27a (1 v.): citation of Isa 59:21a on the testament of

12. "*Israel,* here, from the context, must mean the Jewish people . . . not all the true people of God, as Augustine, Calvin, and many others explain it," Hodge, op. cit., p. 374.
13. IB, IX:575.
14. NBC, p. 959.
15. Hodge, op. cit., p. 373; cf. the phrase in v. 32, of God's "showing mercy to all," meaning both Jews and the corresponding Gentiles.
16. Ibid.
17. Though ICC, p. 335, would suggest, "the full completed number, the complement of the Gentiles, i.e. the Gentile world as a whole."
18. Hodge, op. cit., p. 374.
19. ICC, loc. cit.

peace. Fulfillment (per. 16): as listed under Isa. No. 104; cf. Lev 26:9b, and especially Ezek 34:25.

25. Rom 13:11–12 (2 vv.): "... for now salvation is nearer to us than when we believed. The night is almost gone and the day is at hand." Fulfillment (per. 15): "The imminence [as in Lk. No. 47 (12:35)] of the Parousia is cited as one of the strongest motives for Christian living."[20]

26. Rom 14:11, 15:21 (2 vv.): citations, respectively, of Isa 45:23, that every knee shall some day bow to God, and of 52:15b, that kings shall come to an understanding of the work of the Servant of Yahweh and shall submit to Him. Fulfillment (per. 16, millennial): as listed under Isa. No. 11, though these materials are used by Paul in Rom 14:11 to illustrate mankind's universal submission to the Lord at the final judgment as well (cf. the preceding and following vv., under Rom 2:6, No. 2, above), and in 15:21 to illustrate men's receptivity to his own current ministry.

27. Rom 15:10 (1 v.): citation of Dt 32:43, on a rejoicing by Gentiles along with Israel. Fulfillment: this phrase was originally concerned with the fall of Babylon (per. 8), as in Dt. No. 46, though Paul uses it to illustrate the more general need for the Gentiles to rejoice, because of God's saving revelation in Jesus Christ (cf. No. 28, following).

28. Rom 15:12 (1 v.): citation of Isa 11:10, on the Gentiles seeking God. Fulfillment (per. 16, millennial): as listed under Isa. No. 9.

29. Rom 16:20 (1 v., fig.): Paul's assurance to the Romans that "the God of peace will soon crush Satan under your feet." The name "Satan" seems here to be used by metonymy for his servants (cf. II Cor 11:13–15), i.e. those heretics who were causing dissensions at Rome by opposing the apostolic doctrine (cf. Rom 16:17–19, preceding). Fulfillment (per. 14): as in Gen. No. 8, 3:15c, 2nd stage, Satan's overthrow in the present-day church, and not in reference to his final defeat in periods 16 and 17 (3:15c, 3rd and 4th stages); for the triumph of Rom 16:20 is to be effectuated *soon* and by means of the Roman Christians themselves. History relevant to such an activity in the early church at Rome is lacking, yet there is no reason to question but that it was "not long until peace was restored."[21]

20. NBC, p. 962.
21. ExGkT, II:723.

I CORINTHIANS

Like the other "great epistles" of Paul, I Corinthians was composed during his 3rd missionary journey.[1] Internal evidence demonstrates that Paul was still at Ephesus in Asia Minor (I Cor 16:8) but that he was anticipating travel to Corinth, by way of Macedonia, in the near future (4:19, 16:5; cf. Acts 19:21). The book's date of composition would therefore belong to the early part of 55,[2] before Pentecost (I Cor 16:8). At this point the apostle had received a delegation from the Corinthian church (v. 17),[3] had sent Timothy ahead of him through Macedonia (I Cor 4:17, Acts 19:22), and was now dispatching Titus directly by sea[4] to supervise a collection for the poor saints in Judea (I Cor 16:1; cf. II Cor 12:17–18). Titus would most likely have been the bearer of I Corinthians.

Following its introductory greetings, the epistle falls into three main sections: 1:19–ch. 6 consists of Paul's reproofs over certain major failures that had been reported to him (1:11) as having developed within the church since his departure 3½ years before, on his 2nd missionary journey; chs. 7–14 contain his answers to a series of inquiries (cf. 7:1) that had been communicated to him by the delegation of 16:17; and ch. 15 involves further reproof (cf. v. 12) but presents an extended discussion on the doctrine of the resurrection of the dead. A conclusion follows in ch. 16. Paul's emphasis on the authority of Christ in all such matters may be summed up from his words in 1:23–24, "But we preach Christ crucified . . . Christ the power of God and the wisdom of God."

The Book of I Corinthians contains 25 separate subjects of prophecy, but more than half appear in ch. 15, with its teaching on the resurrection and other related topics. Predictive matter is found in 85 of the epistle's 437 verses, or in 19% of the whole. The volume includes a higher amount of typical prophecy than do most of the NT books, owing in part to the apostle's treatment of the communion service in chs. 10–11.

1. I Cor 1:7–8; *4:5a*; *11:26b*; *15:23b*; 16:22 (3 vv.): Pauline expressions for the return of the Messiah, e.g. "the *apokálupsis, revelation,* of our Lord Jesus Christ," 1:7, or "the day of our Lord Jesus Christ," 1:8. Concerning the Aramaic phrase in 16:22, Marana-tha, "Our Lord, come!"[5]

1. See the introduction to Romans.
2. Donald Guthrie, *The Pauline Epistles: NT Introduction,* p. 64.
3. Plus word from the household of Chloe, 1:11, and probably also from Apollos, 16:12 (cf. Acts 18:27).
4. Cf. I Cor 16:10, with its indication that Paul anticipated Titus' arrival in Corinth before Timothy's.
5. This verse thus parallels the prayer, and almost salutation, of Rev. 22:20. The expression could, however, be divided, Maran-atha, and mean either "Our Lord is coming" or "has come."

the idea conveyed is: "Here lives and prays a church for which the imminent coming of the Lord is a vital hope";[6] cf. Rom 13:11. Fulfillment (per. 15): Christ's second advent, as in Ps. No. 5.

2. I Cor 1:19, 14:21 (2 vv.): the former verse is a citation of Isa 29:14, on the destruction of the apparently wise; the latter, of 28:11–12, on Judah's being punished by men of a foreign speech. Fulfillment (per. 7): in Sennacherib's attack of 701 B.C., as in Isa. No 18, though the passages are employed by Paul to illustrate, respectively, the superiority of God to all human wisdom, and the proper use of the phenomenon of "tongues."

3. I Cor 3:12–14, 4:5b, 11:32a (5 vv., fig.): a picture of what results from the way in which men "build upon the foundation" of Christ (3:11). Paul declares: "Each man's work will become evident; for the day will show it, because it is to be revealed with fire; and the fire [of judgment[7]] will test the quality of each man's work. If it remains, he shall receive a reward," 3:13–14. 4:5 adds, "The Lord will both bring to light the things hidden in the darkness and disclose the motives of men's hearts; and then each man's praise will come to him from God." Above all, there is the basic judgment in respect to salvation, 11:32, that "when we are judged [this part of the verse is nonpredictive, referring to contemporaneous judgments, vv. 29–31], we are disciplined by the Lord in order that we may not be condemned [predictive] along with the world." Fulfillment (per. 17): as in Job No. 5, the judgment of the righteous, here referring specifically to God's testing of the work of the teachers of the church; see I Cor 3:10.

4. I Cor 3:15, 17; 5:5 (3 vv., fig.): "If any man's work is burned up, he shall suffer loss; but he himself shall be saved, yet so as by fire," 3:15, meaning: "His salvation is reduced to a minimum: he rushes out through the flame, leaving behind the ruin of his work."[8] The apostle goes on, v. 17: "If any man destroys the temple of God [the church, vv. 16, 17b, tearing it down by improper teaching], God will destroy him"; cf. the case of the incestuous man in 5:5, who suffers "the destruction [= chastisement] of his flesh," but whose spirit is still to "be saved in the day of the Lord Jesus." Fulfillment (per. 17): the judgment—the loss of reward, but not of salvation as such—of unworthy Christians, especially of teachers (see No. 3, preceding).

5. I Cor 5:7–8 (2 vv., typ.): a retrospective reference to the Passover as a type of the death of Jesus, "For Christ our Passover also has been sacrificed." Fulfillment (per. 13): as in Ex. No. 31.

6. I Cor 6:2 (1 v.): "The saints will judge the world." Fulfillment (per. 16): as in Dt. No. 37, the status of the church in Christ's future

---

6. IB, X:262.
7. IB, X:48, citing the parallel in II Baruch 48:39.
8. ExGkT, II:792.

kingdom, for "participation in the Messianic rule is not confined to the twelve disciples (Mt 19:28). It will be the privilege of all who are baptized in Christ; and this rule will come during the time when He destroys 'every rule and every authority' (I Cor 15:24)";[9] see the discussion on 6:3 (No. 7, following), and compare Rev 2:26.

7. I Cor 6:3 (1 v.): "We shall judge angels." Hodge offers the following commentary:

> As kings were always judges . . . to rule and to judge are in Scripture often convertable terms. So the case before us may mean to be exalted above the angels, and preside over them. . . . This explanation avoids the difficulty of supposing that good angels are to be called into judgment and is consistent with what the Bible teaches of the subordination of angels to Christ and to the church in Him.[10]

Fulfillment would seem to belong in per. 16 (the millennium), as suggested by the parallelism of v. 2 (No. 6, preceding), though it might conceivably pertain to per. 17, as a part of the final judgment, or to per. 18, after it.

8. I Cor 6:14; 15:23a, 29, 32 (4 vv.): "God has not only raised the Lord, but will also raise us up through His power," 6:14; cf. a similar hope for the living, as expressed in 15:51 (No. 24, below) and Rom 8:11 (listed under 5:2). I Cor 15 then speaks of the order of resurrections: first, that of Christ; and next, of "those who are Christ's at His coming." It was in anticipation of such a resurrection that contemporary Christians were willing to risk persecution by being *baptized for the dead* (v. 29), filling up as it were the ranks of the believers who had already perished for the sake of Christ (cf. v. 32).[11] Fulfillment (per. 15): the first resurrection, as in Isa. No. 76.

9. I Cor 10:1a, 2a (2 vv., typ.): a reference to Israel's experience at the exodus, "Our fathers were all under the cloud . . . and all were baptized unto Moses in the cloud." Fulfillment of this type (per. 14): in Christian baptism, as in Ex. No. 36 (14:19).

10. I Cor *10:1b, 2b* (typ.): another such reference (see No. 9, preceding) to the fact that they "all passed through the sea," being "baptized . . . in the sea." Fulfillment (per. 14): in Christian baptism, as in Ex. No. 37 (14:22).

11. I Cor 10:3 (1 v., typ.): similarly (see No. 9–10, preceding), on Israel's eating manna. Fulfillment (per. 13): as in Ex. No. 39 (16:4), in which the manna appears as a type of Christ's incarnation.

12. I Cor 10:4 (1 v., typ.): similarly, on their drinking of the rock; "and the rock was Christ." Fulfillment (per. 13): as in Ex. No. 42 (17:6).

---

9. IB, X:70.
10. C. Hodge, *An Exposition on the First Epistle to the Corinthians*, pp. 95–96.
11. Cf. ibid., pp. 336–338, on alternative approaches to this confessedly uncertain idea.

13. I Cor 10:16–17, 21; 11:20–29, 33–34 (15 vv., typ.): "the cup of blessing . . . the bread which we break . . . the table of the Lord," 10:16, 17, 21. Ch. 11 then speaks of the Lord's Supper as commemorative and sacramental, but also as typical (v. 26), proclaiming the Lord's death "till He comes." Fulfillment (per. 15): as in Lk. No. 69, the communion service as typical of the yet future Messianic marriage feast.

14. I Cor *11:32b*, that the Christian is chastened now, so that he may not be "condemned along with the world," that is, in "the final judgment [per. 17] against the world (I Pet 4:17),"[12] as in Ps. prophecy No. 1.

15. I Cor 13:9–12; 15:35–45a, 48–50, *52c*, 53–57 (23 vv.): Paul's answer to the question, "How are the dead raised? With what kind of body do they come?" (15:35). It will not be like the present, "earthly, perishable body" of flesh and blood, but a "heavenly, imperishable" one (vv. 40, 42, 50), "a spiritual body" (v. 44). It will be marked by glory, power, and life (vv. 43, 45), having "put on immortality" (v. 53, followed by citations of Isa 25:8 and Hos 13:14), like that of the heavenly, resurrected Christ (v. 48; cf. that similar change in bodes which is predicted for the living saints in v. 51 and Rom 5:2). Man's present, partial knowledge is thus to be only until "the perfect comes" (13:9–12), which is a somewhat indefinite expression but which Lenski elaborates, by saying, "The aorist subjunctive, *élthē, come,* marks the great future moment when the goal shall be reached, [at] the Parousia of Christ. Then this entire state of imperfection will be abolished. An entirely new way of apprehending shall take its place."[13] So 13:12 reads, "Then I shall know fully," presumably in the resurrection, which 15:57 describes as "the victory through our Lord Jesus Christ." Fulfillment (per. 15): the glorified nature of the bodies of the saints in the first resurrection (see 6:14, No. 8, above).

16. I Cor 15:3 (1 v.): "Christ died for our sins according to the Scriptures." A major Scripture source for this declaration (as well as for v. 42, No. 17, following) would be Isaiah's oracles of the suffering Servant. Fulfillment (per. 13): as in the passages listed under Isa. No. 100; cf. Acts No. 19 with its note 15.

17. I Cor *15:4a*, ". . . and that He [Christ] was buried . . . according to the Scriptures." Fulfillment (per. 13): as in Isa. No. 102 (53:9b).

18. I Cor 15:4b (1 v.): another reference to former prophecies, that Christ "was raised on the third day according to the Scriptures." This could possibly be a further reference to Isaiah's Servant Songs, e.g. 53:10b (cf. the observations made on Acts 26:23, under 2:27), but more likely— because of Paul's specification of *the third day*—to Hosea 6:1. Fulfillment (per. 13): as in Hos. No. 18.

19. I Cor 15:12–22, *24a*, 26 (12 vv.): arguments by Paul supporting the doctrine of the resurrection of the dead, climaxing with his assertion in v. 22: "As in Adam all die, so also in Christ all shall be made alive."

---

12. IB, X:143.
13. *The Interpretation of I Corinthians*, p. 566.

Some would restrict the word *all* in v. 22 (as must indeed be the case in Rom 5:18), with the assertion that it should "be qualified by *in Christ* [i.e. applying it only to] those who have become part of his body through faith."[14] But this rather unusual reading of the clause is opposed by the fact that Paul introduces his restriction in the next verse, where he precisely singles out *those who are Christ's.* The proposal of a restricted group in v. 22 appears to have arisen out of a failure to appreciate that, as Alford has pointed out, only "the two great opposites, Death and Life, are under consideration. . . . Bliss eternal which would, truly, be for Christian believers alone is not so much as thought of" at this point: and he insists that one "keep to the *universal* reference."[15] So in vv. 23–24, in his listing of the order of resurrections, Paul speaks of Christ's rising as the first; next will be that of those who are Christ's at His coming; and "then comes the end." This last expression is left without further definition, and some would limit its meaning to simply "the end of the world";[16] but on the analogy of other Scriptures one may infer "the resurrection of the rest of the dead, here veiled over by the general term, *the end*—that resurrection not being in this argument especially treated but only that of Christians."[17] Hence in v. 26, after all the other enemies have been overcome by Christ (see No. 21, below), the apostle again speaks in universal terms, "The last enemy that will be abolished is death." Fulfillment (per. 17): the second, or general resurrection, as in Job No. 2 and Dan. No. 56.

20. I Cor 15:*24b*, 28b (1 v.): after the final overthrow of death at the general resurrection (vv. 24a, 26; No. 19, preceding), Christ "will deliver up the kingdom to the God and Father. . . . Then the Son Himself also will be subjected to . . . Him, that God may be all in all," meaning, that is, that He may be "everything to everyone" (RSV). Hodge cautions, "This is a very difficult passage. . . . The Scriptures constantly teach that of Christ's dominion there is no end." He therefore proposes: "This kingdom, which extends over all principalities and powers, He was invested with in His mediatorial character for the purpose of carrying on His work to its consummation. When that is done, i.e. when He has subdued all His enemies, then He will no longer reign over the universe as Mediator, but only as God; while His headship over His people is to continue for ever."[18] As G. G. Findlay puts it, "When our Lord is able to present to the Father a realm dominated by His will and filled with His obedient sons, this is no ceasing of Christ's rule but the inauguration of *God's* eternal kingdom."[19]

14. IB, X:235.
15. *The Greek Testament*, II:575–576.
16. ExGkT, II:927; cf. IB, X:239, "Paul believed in a Day of Judgment, but nowhere in his letters is it asserted that there would be a resurrection of the unjust.
17. Alford, op. cit., II:576.
18. Op. cit., pp. 326, 330.
19. ExGkT, II:927; cf. W. C. G. Proctor, "The 'subordination of the Son' does not conflict in any way with the full deity of Christ, who shares with the Father the 'substance' of the Godhead. The 'subordination' is of office, not of person. The reference is to His work as Redeemer and as King of God's kingdom," NBC, p. 988.

Fulfillment (per. 17): the concluding act of world history, following even the final judgment, when Christ's earthly purposes will have been completed and He offers up His mediatorial kingship to God the Father.

21. I Cor 15:24c–25, 27b–*28a* (3 vv.): Christ "must reign until He has put all His enemies under His feet . . . [and] when He says, 'All things are put in subjection,' " it is "the joyful announcement by the Son that the grand promise recorded in the 8th Psalm [see No. 22, following] is fulfilled."[20] Accomplishment (per. 16): the millennial rule of Christ, as in Gen 49:10b. One source thus feels free to go into detail, recognizing the following points:

> There is to be a period of the rule of Christ during which he will complete the subjugation of all the opposing forces which had been defeated on the cross. . . [After] the Parousia, then the visible rule of Christ and the saints would come. The length of this rule of Christ is not specified, but it corresponds to the thousand years in Revelation (cf. the Jewish apocalypses from the period between Paul and Revelation: II Baruch 30:1, II Esdras 7:26–29). . . . An intermediate kingdom cannot be explained away here.[21]

22. I Cor *15:27a, 28c*, citation of Ps 8:6, "He [God the Father] has put all things under His feet," i.e. of Christ, the last Adam. Fulfillment (per. 13): as in Ps. prophecy No. 8, our Lord's triumph at His ascension; see Heb 2:9. At this point He is already crowned,[22] even though Christ's own putting of all things under His feet (I Cor 15:25, No. 21, preceding) is yet to be achieved on earth.

23. I Cor *15:45b–47* (2 vv., typ.): a retrospective allusion to Adam as a prefiguring of Christ "the last Adam," regaining the life that His type had forfeited. Fulfillment (per. 13): as in Gen. No. 5.

24. I Cor 15:51–52a (2 vv.): the hope held out for those Christians who will not have died at the time of Christ's return, "We shall not all sleep, but we shall be changed . . . in the twinkling of an eye," into the resurrection bodies just discussed (see under 13:9, No. 15, above). Fulfillment (per. 15): as in Rom. No. 9.

25. I Cor *15:52b*, at the first resurrection (v. 23a; see under 6:14, No. 8, above), "the last trumpet . . . will sound." Fulfillment (per. 15): as in Isa. No. 79 (27:13a) and Mt. No. 63 (24:31b).

20. ExGkT, II:929, though Alford, op. cit., II:578, would think rather of God the Father as the subject, declaring that the cosmic subjugation has come to pass.
21. IB, X:236–238.
22. See Hodge, op. cit., p. 332, "The man Christ Jesus, into whose hands all power in heaven and earth has been committed."

II CORINTHIANS

In contrast to I Corinthians, Paul's second epistle to the church at Corinth is not a particularly prophetic writing. Its predictions total only 7 and involve but 12 of the book's 257 verses, or some 5%. Several months had passed since the apostle's earlier letter;[1] and during this time Paul seems to have paid a brief, painful visit to Corinth (II Cor 1:23–2:1).[2] After returning to Ephesus (cf. the events of Acts 19:23–41),[3] he moved northward to Troas; but here he achieved no peace of mind (II Cor 2:12–13) and felt constrained to travel again toward Corinth (as in Acts 20:1). In Macedonia, however, he was met by Titus with the encouraging information that the Corinthians had experienced a change in heart toward the apostle (II Cor 7:5–7). So despite the possibility of continued resistance against Paul's authority (cf. chs. 10–13), the bulk of II Corinthians is an expression of his relief; cf. as a key verse his words in 7:9, "I now rejoice . . . that you were made sorrowful to the point of repentance." The place of writing would most likely have been Philippi, and the date in the fall of 55.[4] Apart from its introduction and conclusion, the epistle consists of: an analysis by Paul of his recent difficulty with the Corinthian church, 1:12–ch. 7; instructions about the offering for the poor saints in Judea, chs. 8–9 (cf. I Cor 16:1); and Paul's vindication of his apostleship, 10–13:10—but the book's prophecies are limited to the first 6 of its chapters.

1. II Cor 1:14, 5:10 (2 vv.): Paul speaks of having confidence "in the day of our Lord Jesus," 1:14. This last phrase is "a general expression signifying the manifest triumph of Christ as Savior and judge."[5] But in the present context its reference is to "the last day, when Christ . . . lays bare all hidden secrets at the judgment (5:10, I Cor 4:5)."[6] So 5:10 declares, "We must all appear before the judgment seat of Christ, that each one may be recompensed for his deeds in the body, whether good or bad." Fulfillment (per. 17): the judgment of the righteous, as in Job prophecy No. 5.

2. II Cor 3:14 (1 v., typ.): Paul's referring to the reading of "the old testament," or covenant. Fulfillment (per. 13): as in Gen. Nos. 7, 12, etc.

3. II Cor 4:14, 5:1–4 (5 vv.): "He who raised the Lord Jesus will

---

1. See introduction to I Corinthians.
2. Cf. 12:14, 13:1–2, which suggest some such second trip, subsequent to his first period of ministry during the 2nd missionary journey. For other interpretations of Paul's "painful visit," see Donald Guthrie, *The Pauline Epistles: NT Introduction,* pp. 50–52.
3. Against the theory that a "sorrowful letter" composed at this time (2:4, 7:8) is now partially preserved in II Cor 10–13, see ibid., pp. 53–60.
4. Ibid., pp. 64–65.
5. NBC, p. 991; see above, pp. 131–133.
6. IB, X:286.

raise us also with Jesus and will present us with you";[7] cf. Paul's close association of the believers' hope with the resurrection of Christ in Rom 8:11 (listed under 5:2).[8] In 5:1–2 he states in a figure that though we die, "we have[9] a house not made with hands, eternal in the heavens"; and we long "to be clothed with our dwelling from heaven." Explanation is suggested by the following elaborations: v. 4, "While we are in this tent [present bodies], we do not want to be unclothed [as immortal spirits only, in heaven after death]"—even though, v. 8, in contrast with the present life, we "prefer to be absent from the body and to be at home with the Lord"[10]—"but to be clothed [with resurrection bodies], in order that what is mortal may be swallowed up by life." Fulfillment (per. 15): the first resurrection, as in Isa. No. 76.

4. II Cor 6:2 (1 v.): citation of Isa 49:8 on Christ as the testament. Fulfillment (per. 13): the embodiment of the testament in Jesus, as in Isa. No. 93.

5. II Cor 6:16 (1 v.): citation of Lev 26:11–12, on God's presence with His people under the testament of peace. Fulfillment (per. 16): as in Lev. No. 31, though used by Paul to illustrate the presence of God in the church now.

6. II Cor 6:17 (1 v.): citation of Isa 52:11 on Israel's departure from unclean Babylon. Fulfillment (per. 9): the return from exile, as in Isa. No. 20, though used by Paul to illustrate separation from uncleanness in his own day.

7. II Cor 6:18 (1 v.): a free rendering of the idea of Hos 1:10—using phraseology from II Sam 7:8 (LXX), 14—on the inclusion of Gentiles in the family of God. Fulfillment (per. 14): as in Hos. No. 4.

7. Since Paul here includes his own resurrection with that of the Corinthian Christians, "it would appear that the Apostle did not hope to be alive at the Second Advent of Christ (cf. 1:8, I Cor 15:52), although at an earlier period he seems to have cherished such an expectation (I Thess 4:15)," ExGkT, III:63.
8. On the transformation of those still living.
9. "Paul may mean by the present tense that the spiritual body is even now prepared and waiting for us; or more likely he simply expresses the complete certainty that we are to have it," IB, X:326.
10. Cf. NIC, p. 176.

GALATIANS

The NT book that is most closely related to Romans—the first of Paul's "great epistles" in the arrangement of the NT—is Galatians, which stands today in fourth place, as the last of this particular group. Both volumes are concerned with the doctrine of the Christian's justification by faith in

Jesus, and by faith alone, apart from the works of the Mosaic law (Gal 2:16, Rom 3:20–22). Not by circumcision, or by the OT system that it represents, does a man now come to God; but "If you belong to Christ, then you are Abraham's offspring, heirs according to promise" (Gal 3:29, a key verse for the book).

But while Romans represents Paul's later systematization of the way of salvation, Galatians is written in the heat of conflict, as the apostle reacts to information he had just received about a lapse on the part of his Galatian congregations into a form of Jewish justification by works. The exact circumstances of the book's composition are a subject of uncertainty. But it would appear that the churches to which he was writing (1:2) were those of southern Galatia (i.e. Antioch, Iconium, Lystra, and Derbe of the districts of Pisidia and Lycaonia) rather than of the central or more northern parts of the province (Ancyra, etc.),[1] for which there exists little record of Pauline missions (though cf. Acts 16:6, 18:23). Gal 4:13 suggests[2] that the apostle had already labored in the churches in question more than once; cf. his ministries in *southern* Galatia on both his 1st and his 2nd missionary journeys (Acts 13:14–14:23; 16:1–6).

The dating of the epistle depends in part upon the identification of the visit to Jerusalem by Paul, Barnabas, and Titus that is mentioned in Gal 2:1–2. These verses could refer to the trip made by Paul and Barnabas, with offerings for famine relief, that is recorded in Acts 11:30–12:25.[3] It would thus precede their 1st missionary journey in 47–48 and would allow for the writing of Galatians after Paul's two circuits (?) through southern Galatia (i.e. outbound and return) during the course of that journey, even before the council of Jerusalem in 49. But the question of the status of Gentiles within the church, with which Galatians is so bound up (e.g. in 2:9), came up at the visit of Paul and Barnabas that is recorded in Acts 15:2–30, to present their case to the above-mentioned council. Despite certain differences in emphasis,[4] the record in Gal 2 does seem to fit in better with the situation found in Acts 15.[5] The epistle might then conceivably have been written after Paul's passage through Galatia on his 2nd journey (Acts 16:1),[6] though the connection of Galatians with Romans would more probably indicate the time of the 3rd journey, per-

1. For detail, see Donald Guthrie, *The Pauline Epistles: NT Introduction*, pp. 72–79.
2. Though it does not actually require this; cf. NASmg, "I preached . . . to you the former time."
3. The "again" in Gal 2:1 would thus mean literally "the second time," after Paul's first trip to Jerusalem in Acts 9:26.
4. Cf. the stress in Gal 2:10 on their need for "remembering the poor" rather than for conforming to the four prohibitions that involved Jewish feelings, as stated in Acts 15:20, 29, 16:4.
5. Note the probability that behind the words of Gal 2:2, 7, lie the accomplishments of Paul's 1st missionary journey.
6. Cf. E. J. Goodspeed, *An Introduction to the NT*, pp. 23–27.

haps after his arrival in Ephesis in 52/53,[7] when he had just gone through the Galatian country (18:23, 19:1; cf. Gal 1:6).

The book consists of an introductory greeting (1:1–5) and a conclusion (6:11–18), with the body of the composition falling into three parts: 1:11–ch. 2, a defense of Paul's apostolic authority in opposing the Judaizers; chs. 3–4, the argument for justification by faith rather than by Mosaic works; and chs. 5–6:10, a series of ethical instructions. The prophetic content of Galatians is restricted to its more central chapters, 3–5, and focuses on the promises made to Abraham and on their application to Gentile believers, apart from Jewish ceremonies, such as circumcision. They involve 7 distinct predictions and 16 out of the epistle's 149 verses (= 11%).

1. Gal 3:8, 14a, 22, 29 (4 vv.): citations of Gen 12:3, on the nations being blessed in Abraham, as fulfilled (per. 14) in the Gentiles' receiving the Christian gospel of justification by faith, as in Gen. prophecy No. 19.

2. Gal *3:14b*, an allusion to the fact of Christians' receiving "the promise of the Spirit through faith." The Scriptural source of this promise is not indicated; "Whether the apostle has in mind the prophecy of Joel 2:28, Ezek 36:27, or the tradition underlying Acts 1:5 [which had not yet been written] cannot be stated with certainty."[8] But since the context is one that stresses the fulfillment of the OT, even of Abrahamic promises (Gal 3:8, 14a; No. 1, above),[9] the earliest reference, i.e. Joel's in the 8th century B.C., would seem to be preferable. Fulfillment (per. 14): as in Joel No. 8, the outpouring of God's Spirit at Pentecost.

3. Gal 3:15–19, 21 (6 vv., typ.): references to the Abrahamic testament, the ceremonies of which stood as a type of Christ's death; cf. the RSV rendering of 3:15, "a will," which "no one annuls."[10] V. 16 thus goes on to cite Gen 17:7–8, with its assurance that God's testamentary promise (cf. vv. 17–19, 21) would be to Abraham "and to thy seed," as fulfilled (per. 13) fundamentally in the one (sing.) seed "that is Christ"; see under Gen. No. 30.

4. Gal 4:23, 28 (2 vv.): references to Isaac's birth, as having come about by promise. Fulfillment (per. 1): as in Gen. No. 29.

5. Gal 4:24 (1 v., typ.): reference to the Sinaitic testament; cf. 3:15 (No. 3, above). Fulfillment (per. 13): as in Ex. No. 45 (19:5).

6. Gal 4:26–27 (2 vv., fig.): citation of Isa 54:1 as fulfilled (per. 14) in the joyful freedom and expansion of the Christian church; see under Isa. No. 69.

---

7. J. B. Lightfoot, *St. Paul's Epistle to the Galatians*, pp. 48–49, favors a later date, only shortly before his writing to Romans from Corinth, late in 55, owing to the relative absence of references to the Judaizing problem in the Corinthian epistles, written earlier that same year.

8. ICC, p. 177.

9. See NIC, p. 128.

10. Cf. John Murray, *The Covenant of Grace*, p. 30.

7. Gal 5:5 (1 v.): that Christians, "by faith, are waiting for the hope of righteousness." Fulfillment (per. 17): as in Job No. 5, final judgment for the righteous. "The apostle has his eye on the final verdict of acquittal in the divine judgment. Elsewhere, in Rom 5:1, for instance, he speaks of righteousness in the past time, that is, as a verdict of acquittal that the believer has already received. But here the reference is to the verdict which God will pronounce before every ear and eye."[11]

11. NIC, p. 189; cf. IB, X:549.

EPHESIANS

The second group of Pauline epistles to occur in the NT (Eph–Col, plus Philemon) is classified third chronologically, since all give evidence of having been written from prison (Eph 3:1, 4:1, 6:20; Phil 1:7, 13; Col 3:10, 4:18; Philemon 1, 9, 13, 23). Furthermore, while the apostle suffered from incarceration on more than one occasion (II Cor 11:23), all four of these "prison epistles" would seem to belong to the period of Paul's first confinement in Rome (cf. Phil 1:13, 4:22),[1] which is datable to A.D. 59–61.[2] They contain in general a smaller percentage of predictive material than any other single block of the NT writings.

Ephesians is the only book of the group—and, in fact, the only one of the entire corpus of the 13 Pauline epistles, except for the Pastorals—whose authenticity as a legitimate work of the apostle Paul is generally questioned by modern scholars.[3] Linguistic peculiarities have been cited, as well as an artificially redundant style.[4] Yet Ephesians stands close to Colossians in its literary form and theological content; and the practical identity of Eph 6:21–22 with Col 4:7–8, on Paul's sending both letters to Asia Minor by the hand of Tychicus (compare also Philemon 10–12 with Col 4:9, on his sending back of the slave Onesimus at this same time), ties the epistles to one and the same occasion. Unless, therefore, one is prepared to classify the former as a deliberate forgery based on the latter, then the widely recognized authenticity of Colossians should carry with it that of Ephesians as well. Since Paul was by this time anticipating his speedy release from prison (Philemon 22), the date of writing would seem to lie early in 61. It is true that the last two words of the introductory phrase, "to the saints who are *at Ephesus*" (Eph 1:1), do not appear in the better Greek MSS; and this, combined with the generalized nature of the

1. See below, introduction to Philippians, note 2, on the alternative suggestion now often made for Philippians.
2. See above, introduction to Acts, note 4.
3. E.g., E. J. Goodspeed, *An Introduction to the NT*, pp. 222–239.
4. Cf. the analysis and refutation of this criticism by Donald Guthrie, *The Pauline Epistles: NT Introduction*, pp. 102–128.

epistle as a whole, suggests its composition as a circular letter to be read among the various churches of Asia Minor. It may, indeed, be the very epistle to which Paul referred in Col 4:16 as "my letter that is coming from Laodicea."

Ephesians commences by assuming the teaching of Colossians about the subordination of angelic powers to Christ (Eph 1:20–21)[5] and goes on to speak of the status and function of the church in relation to its Lord. The key passage of 1:22–23 thus sums up how God the Father "put all things in subjection under His feet, and gave Him as head over all things to the church, which is His body, the fulness of Him who fills all." The writing falls into two basic parts: chs. 1–3, on the status of the believer, in Christ; and chs. 4–6, on his conduct toward his fellow man. Of the 155 verses that make up the epistle, only 8 are involved in prophecy, or some 5%. These are divided among 7 separate predictions, though 4 of these occur in the latter half of the first chapter.

1. Eph 1:13 (1 v.): a reference to "the Holy Spirit of promise," meaning, "which had been promised";[6] cf. Gal 3:14b. Fulfillment (per. 14): the outpouring of the Spirit at Pentecost, as in Joel prophecy No. 8.

2. Eph 1:14, 4:30 (2 vv.): that the Holy Spirit has been given (see v. 13, No. 1, preceding) as a pledge of the Christian's inheritance, "with a view to the redemption of God's own possession," 1:14; or this last phrase may perhaps be more simply rendered, ". . . to the redemption of preservation."[7] The *redemption* that is here described is not the past work of Christ on Calvary but a future activity. In Rom 8:23 Paul had spoken of "the redemption of our body," to be changed into the likeness of Christ's resurrected body at the time of His second coming; and "it is probable that the passage is in the writer's mind here."[8] Fulfillment (per. 15): the change of believers at the rapture of the church, "the day of redemption," Eph 4:30, just as in Rom. No. 9.

3. Eph 1:18 (1 v.): Paul prayed that his readers might "know what is the hope of His calling, what are the riches of the glory of His inheritance in the saints." The Christian's *inheritance* is a broad concept (cf. No. 2, preceding) but would appear in this context of Christ's hoped-for rule (v. 21, No. 4, below) to signify "the future kingdom of God,"[9] fulfilled (per. 16) especially in the bliss of the saints in that Messianic kingdom, as in Ex. No. 49; cf. Heb 10:36, I Pet 1:3.

4. Eph 1:21 (1 v.): a prediction of Christ's sovereign position "far above all rule and authority . . . not only in this age, but also in the one

---

5. See below, introduction to Colossians.
6. ICC, p. 22.
7. Ibid., p. 23.
8. IB, X:625; cf. ExGkT, III:269.
9. ICC, p. 30.

to come," that is, "in the period beginning with the Parousia."[10] Fulfillment (per. 16): as in Gen No. 68, His millennial reign.

5. Eph 2:12 (1 v., typ.): "the testaments of promise" for Israel, i.e. the Sinaitic, etc. Fulfillment (per. 13): as in Ex. No. 45 (19:5).

6. Eph 5:14 (1 v.): a free citation of previous Scripture, "Arise . . . and Christ will shine on you." These words are apparently based on Isa 60:1 and its forecast that "the glory of Yahweh is risen upon you," at Christ's return. The passage is here used by Paul, however, to illustrate a more immediate illumination and may perhaps have been taken from an early Christian hymn (cf. v. 19).[11] Fulfillment (per. 15): the Lord's second advent, as listed under Isa. No. 77.

7. Eph 5:27 (1 v., fig.); that Christ gave His life for His bride-to-be, "that He might present to Himself the church in all her glory . . . holy and blameless"; cf. the reference in John's vision of the Messianic marriage feast (Rev 19:8) to her "bright and clean linen . . . the righteous acts of the saints." The marriage metaphor in Eph 5 is, however, a mixed one; for "the duty of presenting the bride to the bridegroom would normally be that of the bridegroom's friend. Cf. II Cor 11:2, where Paul regards himself in this light. Here Christ is both the one who presents and the one who receives."[12] Fulfillment (per. 15): the Messianic marriage feast of the Lamb, as in Ps. No. 22 (22:29a).

10. ExGkT, III:279.
11. NBC, p. 1027.
12. Ibid., p. 1028.

PHILIPPIANS

Paul's epistle to the Macedonian church of Philippi is the most prophetic of his four "prison epistles,"[1] though its predictions still involve but 10 out of the book's 104 verses, a relatively low 10%. These center on the eras of Christ's second coming and His final judgment, are scattered through each of the composition's 4 chapters, and cover 5 individual topics. Philippians may be assigned to the midportion of the apostle's imprisonment in Rome (cf. 1:13, on the praetorian guard, and 4:22, his allusion to "Caesar's household"),[2] during A.D. 59–61: for the Philippian Christians

1. See above, introduction to Ephesians.
2. On the basis, however, of geographical closeness to Philippi, as seemingly implied by 4:10 or 18, many modern critics would assign the epistle to ca. 54 in Ephesus, during Paul's 3rd missionary journey; cf. G. S. Duncan, *St. Paul's Ephesian Ministry*, pp. 66 ff., and the analysis (and opposition) in C. H. Dodd, *NT Studies*, pp. 85–128. But this hypothesis must assume, upon the doubtful evidence of I Cor 15:30 and II Cor 1:8, an unrecorded Ephesian imprisonment for Paul at this time;

had had time to exchange word with Paul and those who were with him (2:26), and yet the apostle was still anticipating further communication back and forth (v. 19).[3] It is one of the most personal of all the letters of Paul that have been preserved; and it is marked by a corresponding lack in strict, overall organization. The church at Philippi had sent a gift to assist in the apostle's support (4:10, 14, 18); cf. their similar generosity on previous occasions (v. 16; and II Cor 11:9). So while Paul's purposes in writing included his desires to inform (1:12), to exhort (2:2, 4:2), and to teach (3:2–3), the theme of his epistle could be summed up in his note of grateful thanks as expressed in 4:10, "But I rejoiced in the Lord greatly, that now . . . you have revived your concern for me."

1. Phil 1:6, 10; 3:20 (3 vv.): anticipations of "the day of (Jesus) Christ," 1:6, 10; cf. the similar phrase in I Cor 1:7–8; "we eagerly wait for the Lord Jesus" from heaven, 3:20. Fulfillment (per. 15): His second coming, as in Ps. prophecy No. 5.

2. Phil 2:9–11 (3 vv.): God the Father has granted Jesus "the name which is above every name [i.e. *Lord*,[4] v. 11], that at the name of Jesus every knee should bow, of those who are in heaven, and on earth, and under the earth, and that every tongue should confess that Jesus Christ is Lord." This list of confessors seems to correspond to angels,[5] to living men on earth, and to the dead, either in their graves or in hell. The phrase that "every knee should bow" is drawn from Isa 45:23 (listed under 2:4a) on the Messiah's millennial rule (and so quoted in Rom 14:11). But since the group of the submissive ones appears now to include the lost of all ages,[6] its fulfillment (per. 17) must be at the final judgment, as in Eccl. No. 1.

3. Phil 3:5 (1 v., typ.): an allusion to circumcision, prior to Christ's ministry, and so still a valid type of regeneration and redemption in Him. Fulfillment (per. 13): as in Gen. No. 42.

4. Phil 3:11, 21 (2 vv.): Paul's goal of "attaining to the resurrection from among the dead," 3:11, when Christ "will transform the body of our humble state into conformity with the body of His glory," v. 21. Fulfillment (per. 15): the first resurrection (for note the phrasing of v. 11,

---

contrast the tenor of Acts 20:31. An alternative theory, concerning Paul's confinement in Caesarea, 56–58, has few modern advocates. See D. Guthrie, *The Pauline Epistles: NT Introduction*, pp. 92–98, 149–154, and 144–145, respectively.

3. Though cf. also 1:26, on his anticipation (?) of release.

4. NIC, p. 87; or, though with less likelihood, (*Jesus*) *Christ*, ICC, p. 62.

5. A parallel list appears in Rev 5:13, which cites "every created thing which is in heaven and on earth and under the earth [burrowing] and on the sea"; but while that list stands in contrast to the angels in heaven, 5:11, this in Phil 2:10 is comprehensive of rational creatures, and so would signify more than just the four areas of physical life outlined in Rev.

6. See Camb, p. 70.

indicative of its partial, noncomprehensive character), as in Isa. No. 76.
5. Phil 4:5 (1 v.): "The Lord is near," mg, "at hand." Fulfillment (per.
15): the imminent coming of the triumphant Messiah, as in Lk. No. 47
(12:35). "Quite evidently Paul expects a speedy return of Christ . . . the
Judge is at the door."[7]

7. ExGkT, III:466; cf. J. B. Payne, *The Imminent Appearing of Christ*, p. 99.

COLOSSIANS

Though Paul may not have founded the congregation at Colosse (cf.
2:1), some 60 miles inland from Ephesus in Asia Minor, as he had the
churches of the Ephesians and the Philippians, still when he received word
through his co-laborer Epaphras of a doctrinal crisis that had arisen among
the Colossians (1:7), he did not hesitate to dispatch an epistle to them.
Their problem was what has been called "incipient Gnosticism," i.e. philosophical speculation about cosmic, angelic powers (2:8; cf. 1:20), combined with the older Galatian danger of lapsing into Jewish ceremonialism
and legalism (2:16, 20–21). The apostle recalls them to the simple faith
in Christ, as summed up in 2:10, "In Him you have been made complete,
and He is the head over all rule and authority."

Like its sister epistles of Ephesians and Philemon,[1] Colossians seems
to have been written near the close of Paul's first Roman imprisonment
in 61 and to have been transmitted to Asia Minor by Epaphras and
Onesimus. Like Ephesians it consists of two main parts: chs. 1–2, doctrinal, on the lordship of Christ; and chs. 3–4, practical, on the conduct of
the Christian. The 4 prophecies that are found in the book occur primarily
in its first half, not extending beyond 3:4. They involve 9 out of the
epistle's 95 verses, or about 9%. The proportion of typical prediction is
quite high (6 out of the 9 vv.) but carries a reduced significance, owing
to the limited amount of material that is under analysis.

1. Col 1:27–28, 3:4b (3 vv.): Paul tells the Colossian believers that when
Christ is revealed at His second coming (see 3:4a, No. 4, below), "you also
will be revealed with Him in glory," 3:4b; cf. 1:27, "Christ in you [is] the
hope of glory." The thought is: "You will share in that fulness of glory
which is yet to be displayed, on the day of 'the revealing of the sons of
God.' "[2] The apostle explains that his admonishing of them is to the end that
he may "present every man complete in Christ," 1:28. F. F. Bruce adds,

1. See above, introduction to Ephesians.
2. NIC, *Eph and Col*, p. 219, quoting Rom 8:19; see under 5:2, on "the glory
of God."

"He probably has the parousia in mind; compare his assurance to the Christians of Thessalonica that they are his hope 'before our Lord Jesus at His parousia' (I Thess 2:19)."[3] Fulfillment (per. 15): the change in living believers at the rapture of the church, as in Rom. prophecy No. 9.

2. Col. 2:11–14 (4 vv., typ.): reference to the rite of circumcision as fulfilled (per. 13) in "the circumcision of Christ." Bruce elaborates:

This "circumcision of Christ" is not primarily His circumcision as a Jewish infant of eight days (Lk 2:21); it is rather His crucifixion, "the putting off of the body of flesh," of which His literal circumcision was at best a token-anticipation. . . . Even in the OT the symbolical character of circumcision was emphasized, the "circumcision of the heart"—an inward purification, which to Paul was the true circumcision. But now . . . no longer is there any place for a circumscision performed by hands; the death of Christ has effected the inward cleansing, and of this our baptism is the visible sign."[4]

See Gen. No. 42.

3. Col 2:16–17 (2 vv., typ.): a reference to the sabbath and to other aspects of the OT ceremonial calendar and purity legislation as "a shadow of what is to come; but the substance belongs to Christ" (per. 13), as in Ex. No. 41.

4. Col *3:4a*, that Christ is to be *revealed, fānerōthē.* Fulfillment (per. 15): His second coming, as in Ps. prophecy No. 5.

3. Ibid., p. 220.
4. Ibid., pp. 234–235.

I THESSALONIANS

The two Thessalonian epistles constitute a group that represents both the earliest and the most highly prophetic of the Pauline writings. Their forecasts, moreover, take the form of consistently straightforward oracles, without reference to figurative language, symbolic actions, or typical motifs. Both books were written to the Christian church at Thessalonica, at the NW corner of the Aegean Sea in the province of Macedonia. Paul had founded the church in the fall of 49, in the course of his 2nd missionary journey (Acts 17:1–9). Opposition and rioting by the Jews had forced Paul to flee southward from this city to Berea, and eventually into Greece, from which area he dispatched the Thessalonian epistles for the guidance of the congregation he had been compelled to leave behind.

Upon the occasion of the writing of I Thessalonians, Paul had been rejoined by his co-workers Silvanus (Silas) and Timothy (1:1), whom he had sent back from Athens to encourage the Thessalonians in their faith (3:1–2; cf. Acts 17:14, 16). By the time of their return the apostle had moved on to Corinth; so its date must be early in the year 50,[1] and its content seems to embody Paul's reactions to the news that his friends had brought. The book consists of four basic parts: ch. 1, the apostle's thankfulness for their progress in the gospel; chs. 2–3, a survey of his relationships with the Thessalonians; chs. 4:1–12 and 5:12–28, practical exhortations and a conclusion; and within this last part, a significant insertion, extending from 4:13 to 5:11, for their encouragement over believers who may have died, in the light of the anticipated Parousia, or second coming of Jesus. The writing is apocalyptic in nature[2] and closely parallels Christ's own apocalyptic discourse in Mt 24–25 (Mk 13, Lk 21). The thought of the epistle could be summed up in the key words of I Thess 1:9–10, "You turned to God from idols to serve a living and true God, and to wait for His Son from heaven."

I Thessalonians contains 9 separate prophecies, 6 of which are represented in Paul's eschatological passage in 4:13–18. These verses contain the Bible's most detailed discussion of the twofold gathering of the saints, both the living and the dead, at Christ's appearing. The epistle's most significant single prediction is that of the Lord's Parousia (No. 1, below), which finds mention in each of the 5 chapters of the book. All in all, prophecy occupies 16 of the letter's 89 verses, or 18% of the whole.

1. I Thess 1:10, 2:19, 3:13a, 4:15–16a, 5:23 (6 vv.): that the Thessalonians turned to God "to wait for His Son from heaven . . . Jesus, who delivers us from the wrath [of hell[3]] to come," 1:10. This victorious arrival upon the clouds is His *pārousía*, 2:19, 3:13, 5:23, when "the Lord Himself will descend from heaven," 4:16. Leon Morris comments about the series of accompanying features in this last verse: "It is not certain whether the 'shout,' the 'voice of the archangel,' and the 'trump of God' are three ways of speaking about the same triumphant noise . . . but the impression left by the present passage is that there are three distinct sounds."[4] The first, the *shout*, is then "a loud authoritative cry, uttered in the thick of a great excitement . . . by the Lord."[5] Fulfillment (per. 15): Christ's second coming, as in Ps. prophecy No. 5.

2. I Thess 2:16 (1 v.): Paul threatens the Jewish persecutors (v. 14) of the Lord's church, "But wrath has come upon them to the utmost." Agreement is general that the verbal tense at this point is not intended to

1. J. Finegan, *Hankbook of Biblical Chronology*, pp. 320–321, though by a less likely calculation of the commencement of Gallio's proconsulship (cf. Acts 18:12), some would make this one year later.
2. See above, pp. 85–89.
3. For the verb "delivers" is in the present tense, so that the thought of this verse is not to be confused with His future deliverance of saints from the wrath of God at His second coming; see No. 9, below, and p. 102, note 188, above.
4. NIC, p. 143.
5. Ibid.

be taken as past: "Such a proleptic use of the aorist is natural in a prophetic passage."[6] Fulfillment (per. 14): the destruction of the Judean state in A.D. 70, as in Mi. No. 39; for "In the year 70 Jerusalem fell, after the most dreadful and calamitous siege known in history, and the Jewish people ever since have wandered without a home and without an altar."[7]

3. I Thess *3:13b*; 4:13–14, *16d*, 18 (3 vv.): the first reference speaks of the coming of the Lord Jesus "with all His saints." This phrase might refer to His coming with the *holy* angels, as in Mk 8:38. But since the company with whom Christ appears is contrasted with the Thessalonian Christians, who continue in the world, living in love toward one another (it is hoped), up to the time of the Lord's revelation, it probably refers to those other, disembodied human spirits of the Christian dead, who are about to receive their resurrection forms.[8] The Thessalonian context, moreover, goes on to state that "those who have fallen asleep in Jesus, God will bring with Him," 4:14. "The dead in Christ shall rise first," v. 16— not preceded by the rapture of the living, v. 17 (No. 6, below)—with their bodies "caught up" into the clouds, just like those of the yet surviving believers. That is to say, the souls of all the saints who departed from this earth at death, and who have meanwhile been "at home with the Lord" (II Cor 5:8; cf. John 14:3, Phil 1:23), must be brought back again to the world in order for them to be reunited with their resurrected bodies.[9] This prophecy has then a most practical application, against sorrow at the death of loved ones who are believers, from whom we are not permanently to be separated; and Paul concludes, "Therefore comfort one another with these words," I Thess 4:18. Fulfillment (per. 15): the first resurrection, as in Isa. No. 76.

4. I Thess *4:16b*, that the Lord's coming is to be associated with "the voice of the archangel." This second audible feature of accompaniment to the Lord at His return (see No. 1, above) is linked by the conjunction *kai*, "and," to the third, the trumpet of God (see No. 5, next). Fulfillment (per. 15), though "precisely what Paul has in mind is uncertain. It is conceivable that . . . Christ commands the archangel Michael to arouse the dead; and that this command is executed at once by the voice of the archangel who speaks to the dead (cf. I Cor 15:52) through a divine trumpet."[10]

5. I Thess *4:16c*, the Lord's coming "with the trumpet of God" (see No. 4, preceding). Fulfillment (per. 15): as in Isa. No. 78 (27:12).

6. I Thess 4:17a (1 v.): Scripture's most explicit presentation of the rapture of the living saints (per. 15), as in Hos 11:10—"We who are

6. ICC, p. 114.
7. Camb, p. 77.
8. L. J. Wood, *Is the Rapture Next?* p. 45; J. B. Payne, *The Imminent Appearing of Christ*, p. 75.
9. Payne, op. cit., p. 134.
10. ICC, p. 174.

alive and remain shall be caught up together with them [the bodies of the dead saints, whose souls are returning to earth with Christ, v. 16, see No. 3, above] in the clouds to meet the Lord in the air." Specifically, the church is to go up *eis āpántēsin, to* the *meeting,* of the Lord. That is, the Lord descends from heaven, and the church ascends from earth to meet Him. But when they meet (since they do not stay in midair), one party must therefore turn about; and it would hardly be the Lord. For in the usage of *eis āpántēsin* elsewhere in Scripture, the contexts consistently describe how the ones who do the meeting then turn around and accompany the one who is met for the remainder of his journey. Examples are the virgins meeting the bridegroom (Mt 25:6) and the disciples from Rome meeting Paul (Acts 28:15–16). Fulfillment (per. 15): even so the church is to meet Christ in the air and thus join in His triumphant procession down to earth; cf. Hos No. 27 and Rev. 19:14.[11]

7. I Thess *4:17b*: the rapture occurs, v. 17a (No. 6, preceding); "and thus we shall always be with the Lord." Immediately, this entails a return with Him (see No. 6) to the Mount of Olives and Jerusalem; and subsequently, the church's participation in His millennial reign that is to follow, as in Rev 2:26. Fulfillment (per. 15): as in Joel 2:32b, our rapture *to Jerusalem.*

8. I Thess 5:1–3 (3 vv.): Paul's prediction of divine wrath that will fall upon a world that is unprepared, coming "just like a thief in the night. When they are saying, 'Peace and safety!' then destruction will come upon them suddenly; and they shall not escape," vv. 2–3. Its "times and epochs," v. 1, are those of the triumphal appearing of Christ (4:16–18, just preceding), namely, "the day of the Lord," 5:2.[12] Fulfillment (per. 15): as in Lk No. 57, the overwhelming of those deceived by a false sense of security.

9. I Thess 5:4, 9 (2 vv.): an assurance to believers that "God has not appointed us for wrath, but for obtaining salvation through our Lord Jesus Christ," v. 9. The phrase "wrath" might indeed relate, as in 1:10, to the judicial wrath of God at His final judgment; but in the present context it would seem to concern the catastrophic phenomena at the premillennial return of Christ, cf. 5:1–3 (No. 8, preceding). Pretribulationist interpreters are accustomed to assert that this "day of the Lord" (v. 2) cannot apply to the church at all;[13] but what v. 4 says is that it will not overtake Christians *like a thief.* The very injunction to watch (v. 6) demon-

11. Payne, op. cit., p. 68. E. S. English, *Re-thinking the Rapture*, p. 57, interestingly associates I Thess 4:14 with Christ's return to earth, though he then disassociates vv. 15–17, which he places 7 years earlier.

12. Morris, NIC, p. 149, thus entitles 5:1–3, "The time of the Parousia"; the chapter division is here an unhappy one. Cf. G. H. Lang's demonstration of the impossibility of separating ch. 5 from ch. 4, *The Revelation of Jesus Christ*, pp. 25–26. Yet pretribulationist interpreters are forced to conclude that Paul must in ch. 5 be speaking of a "day of the Lord" some 7 years later than that of His coming in ch. 4; see note 11, preceding.

13. E.g., J. F. Strombeck, *First the Rapture*, p. 81.

strates the relevance of the "day" for those of the church who are yet alive to witness it on earth.[14] Fulfillment (per. 15): they will, however, be protected by God, so as not to be injured by its initial plagues (cf. Rev 7:3, 9:4, 16:2),[15] and will then be caught up to be with Jesus (No. 6, preceding), so as not to be harmed by those phases of His wrath that will continue subsequent to Christ's appearing (cf. Lk 21:28, 36).[16]

14. Payne, op. cit., p. 69.
15. Hence the fallacy of H. A. Ironside's booklet *Not Wrath, But Rapture*, for what I Thess 5:9 maintains is "not wrath, but salvation."
16. Cf. Payne, op. cit., pp. 76, 143–144.

II THESSALONIANS

Though only half the length of I Thessalonians, Paul's second epistle to the church at Thessalonica contains even more predictive matter than does his earlier work: 19 out of its total of 47 verses (40% of the whole), on 12 different prophetic themes, even though the apostle's inspired forecasts are restricted to the first 2 out of the book's 3 chapters. Most extensively treated is the subject of the eschatological "man of lawlessness," presumably the Antichrist (No. 8, below), and the related topics that are discussed in ch. 2.

The setting of II Thessalonians is still that of Corinth, in Greece, during Paul's 2nd missionary journey (cf. 1:1, on the continuing presence of Silas and Timothy with Paul).[1] Several months had passed since the apostle had sent his earlier letter; and, though the year is probably still 50, enough time had passed for Paul to receive disturbing news about the reaction of some of the believers at Thessalonica to his writing (cf. 2:2) as well as to his original, oral teaching (v. 5). It would appear that Paul's vivid hope for the Parousia of Christ (I Thess 4:13–5:11) had caused some to desist from productive activity (II Thess 3:11). So he hastens to remind them that the Lord's coming must be preceded by the development of apostasy and the rise of the Antichrist (2:3) and to assure them of their need, in the meantime, for hard, honest work (3:10). The epistle consists essentially of a clarification of Paul's apocalyptic teaching, in chs. 1–2, and a renewed practical exhortation, in ch. 3. A key verse appears in 2:2, "Be not disturbed, either by a spirit . . . or a letter as if from us, to the effect that the day of the Lord has come."

1. See above, introduction to I Thessalonians. Though once widely questioned by critics, the authenticity of II Thess as a true writing of Paul, from Corinth at the period indicated, is now generally accepted; cf. Guthrie's discussion, *The Pauline Epistles: NT Introduction*, pp. 184–193.

1. II Thess 1:5-6, 7d-8 (3 vv.): Paul speaks of "God's righteous judgment . . . to repay with affliction those who afflict you . . . in flaming fire dealing out retribution to those who do not obey the gospel." The time when this occurs is stated to be "when the Lord Jesus shall be revealed from heaven" (see 1:7b, No. 3, below). Fulfillment (per. 15): the wrath of God, as in Isa. prophecy No. 48, and see I Thess 5:1 for its unexpectedness.

2. II Thess 1:7a, *2:1b* (1 v.): God's promise "to give relief to you who are afflicted and to us as well," 1:7, by means of "our gathering together to Him," 2:1. These oracles correspond to His word in I Thess 4:17 and are accomplished at the same time as the outpouring of the wrath of God (No. 1, preceding). Fulfillment (per. 15): the rapture of the church, as in Hos. No. 27.

3. II Thess *1:7b*; 2:1a, 2 (2 vv.): the *pārousīā*, 2:1; "the day of the Lord," 2:2, when "the Lord Jesus shall be revealed [*en tē āpokālúpsei*, lit., "in the revelation"] from heaven," 1:7 "The manner in which the revelation is pictured, *in flaming fire* [see 1:5, No. 1, above], is in keeping with the descriptions of theophanies in the OT, for example . . . Isa 66:15,"[2] which reads, "For, behold, Yahweh will come with fire" (see under Isa 9:4, on Armageddon). Fulfillment (per. 15): Christ's second coming, as in Ps. prophecy No. 5.

4. II Thess *1:7c*, Christ's coming "with His mighty angels"; cf. the reference to the archangel (Michael) in I Thess 4:16b. Fulfillment (per. 15): as in Joel No. 18.

5. II Thess 1:9 (1 v.): the lost "will pay the penalty of eternal destruction, away from the presence of the Lord." Morris explains that this is "not so much annihilation as the loss of all that is worthwhile, utter ruin. The adjective 'eternal' means literally 'age-long,' and . . . there is never a hint that the coming age has an end—it is the continuing life of the world to come."[3] Fulfillment (per. 18): the lake of fire, as in II Sam. No. 20.

6. II Thess 1:10 (1 v.): Christ "comes to be glorified in His saints on that day." Fulfillment (per. 16): the purpose of the Messianic kingdom, for Christ to be honored by His own; cf. v. 12, on His present glorification in the church.

7. II Thess *2:3a*, that Christ's coming is to be preceded by apostasy.[4]

2. ICC, p. 232.
3. NIC, p. 205.
4. English proposes a secondary meaning for *āpostāsīā*, namely, "departure": "The day of the Lord will not be, except the *departure* [i.e. the rapture of the church] come first," *Re-thinking the Rapture*, pp. 67–71. Yet the "falling away" of v. 3 seems to be contrasted with "our gathering together to Him" in v. 1 (the rapture; see under 1:7a, No. 2, above), and to be an evil event, similar to that of the rise of the man of lawlessness (v. 3b, No. 8), a situation that will have to develop first, before the day of the Lord and the rapture. See N. F. Douty, *Has Christ's Return Two Stages?* p. 80, and J. B. Payne, *The Imminent Appearing of Christ*, pp. 76–77.

Fulfillment (per. 14): doctrinal declension in the church prior to the Lord's appearing; as in Lk. No. 59, and cf. I Tim 4:1.

8. II Thess 2:3b–5, 9–11 (6 vv.): before Christ's coming, "The man of lawlessness is revealed [cf. v. 8], the son of destruction, who . . . opposes every object of worship, so that he takes his seat in the temple of God, displaying himself as being God," vv. 3–4, "whose coming is in accord with the activity of Satan, with . . . false wonders, and with all the deception of wickedness for those who perish," vv. 9–10. Morris thus speaks of "supernatural force which actuates the miracles [of the lawless one] . . . in a spirit of falsehood."[5] As to the identity of this Satan-empowered *man of lawlessness*, the apostle John in his first epistle speaks of various "antichrists" that were active opponents of the Christianity of his day (2:18, 4:3); but he also uses Antichrist as a proper noun, for one person who is to be the preeminent embodiment of evil (2:18). It seems therefore legitimate to follow tradition and to apply this term to the eschatological leader of sin here as well.[6] Alford makes reference to those who understand *the temple* as one that will be in Jerusalem, but II Thessalonians says nothing about such a location; and he goes on to note: "The temple of God is used metaphorically by St. Paul in I Cor 3:17; see also II Cor 6:16, Eph 2:21," concluding that it here signifies the Antichrist's "sitting as a judge or ruler" in the place of God,[7] seeking to supplant Him as the object of men's devotion.[8] His being *revealed* must remain ultimately dependent upon the appearing of Jesus Christ, who will "bring [his power] to an end."[9] Fulfillment (per. 14): as in Dan. No. 14, the rise of the Antichrist.

9. II Thess 2:6–7 (2 vv.): in respect to the "man of lawlessness," the Antichrist (see No. 8, preceding), Paul reminded the Thessalonians that they had been advised about "what restrains him from being revealed in his time. For the mystery of lawlessness is already at work; only he who

5. NIC, p. 231. Yet v. 11 states about the nonelect that "God will send upon them a deluding influence so that they might believe what is false"; for deity lies behind it all. He "is using the very evil that men and Satan produce for the working out of His purpose," p. 234.

6. Payne, op. cit., p. 119; see above, p. 103.

7. *The Greek Testament*, III:275; cf. NIC, pp. 223–224, and Payne, op. cit., pp. 146–147.

8. Morris refers to "the attempt by Caligula to set up an image of himself in the temple at Jerusalem, A.D. 40, which aroused widespread horror among the Jews. It may well be that Paul had this incident in mind in writing these words," NIC, p. 223.

9. A question that naturally arises is whether the Antichrist might be at least potentially present at this moment. The 20th century has been peculiarly marked by totalitarian movements, which by propaganda, by psychological brainwashing, by state substitutes for the Christian religion, and, as a last resort, by ruthless persecution have sought to supplant God in the hearts of believers. Hitler and Mussolini are now long dead, but there live on in Moscow and Peking systems and their individual leaders that are definitely anti-Christ and opposed to the true church. The classical view of Christ's imminent return asks only that some such contemporary situation *could* be the setting for the end, Payne, op. cit., p. 121.

now restrains will do so until he is taken out of the way." In this much-debated passage, a framework of predicted matters is still clear: lawlessness existed in Paul's day; but it was hindered by an impersonal "what" (v. 6) and a personal "he who" (v. 7). Most plausibly, the restraint should act as the counterpart to the political lawlessness that it restrains and should thus be identified with lawful government,[10] which in the apostle's time was represented by the Roman authority. Some have proposed that the restraint might be that which lies behind all law, namely, the power of God, through whatever channel displayed. In such a case the restraining person would then also be God, Himself.[11] As to what could then happen to the restraint, the answer would have to be: nothing;[12] and the latter part of v. 7 is then translated—in a way that seems less likely but that is still possible— ". . . until he [not the restrainer, but the lawless Antichrist] comes out of the midst"; cf. the parallel structure of v. 6. Retaining, however, the standard translation, one could identify the person who restrains with the leading representative of lawful government at any given moment.[13] Paul's veiled form of language then becomes explainable as a means for avoiding offense to the Roman power, should his epistle be brought to their attention,[14] though it ensures the adaptability of his oracle to the period immediately preceding Christ's second advent as well.

Fulfillment (per. 14): a repudiation in the days just prior to the Lord's return of that responsible sort of government in which the spirit of Roman law has lived on.[15] It is to be replaced by publicly acknowledged principles

10. In Rom 13:3–4 Paul states in so many words that the restraint of evil is a divinely ordained function of proper government; and he himself was, on more than one occasion, rescued from his supposedly God-fearing countrymen by the intervention of Roman representatives of law and order.

11. G. E. Ladd, *The Blessed Hope*, p. 95.

12. Dispensationalism generally affirms that the restraint must be the Holy Spirit of God, in the church, Scofield Reference Bible, p. 1272, and that its being "taken out of the way" refers to the rapture of the church, prior to the lawlessness of the great tribulation. The Thessalonian context, however, suggests nothing about the Holy Spirit, or why such veiled language should be used if He were the one meant. Though he may indeed do so, the Spirit is never mentioned in Scripture with the function of restraining lawlessness; and vv. such as John 16:8, Eph 6:18, or I John 4:4 cannot be adduced as strictly germane to such an activity, though cf. the effort of J. F. Strombeck. *First the Rapture*, p. 101. Scripture, moreover, gives no hint of the Holy Spirit's ever being removed from the world—Strombeck's citation of Gen 6:3, ibid., p. 102, misinterprets its reference to the termination of life by the flood; cf. G. Vos, *Biblical Theology*, pp. 61–62. Modern dispensationalists concede that the Holy Spirit continues in the world after the rapture, convicting men of sin and judgment, and opening their hearts to the message of salvation. Thus the only thing really removed would be His presence as indwelling the church; cf. J. D. Pentecost, *Things to Come*, pp. 262–263, which would appear to be an interpretation dictated by pretribulationist preconceptions.

13. Or it might be a mere literary personification of the principle of trustworthy government, which is Lightfoot's view; cf. its analysis by Douty, op. cit., p. 85.

14. Cf. John's symbolical language in Rev 17.

15. Dispensationalism's objection to this historical interpretation, on the grounds that the Antichrist represents an increase and not a decrease in governmental power,

of self-interest and expediency. 20th-century disregard of solemn treaties as mere "scraps of paper" and the ruthless suppression by communism of the very concepts of integrity leave little more to be sought in the way of accomplishment for this Pauline prophecy.[16]

10. II Thess 2:8 (1 v.): that the lawless one (see v. 3b, No. 6, above) is he "whom the Lord will slay with the breath of His mouth [i.e. by His word; cf. Rev 19:15] and bring to an end by the appearance of His coming." Fulfillment (per. 15): as in Ps. prophecy No. 56, the destruction of the Antichrist at the battle of Armageddon.

11. II Thess 2:12 (1 v.): the long-range function in God's permission for the deeds of the Antichrist, that "all may be judged who did not believe the truth but took pleasure in wickedness." Fulfillment (per. 15): as in Num. No. 36, the overthrow of his followers at Armageddon (v. 8, No. 10, preceding).[17]

12. II Thess 2:14 (1 v.): the purpose in God's calling of men through the gospel, "that ye may gain the glory of our Lord Jesus Christ." Fulfillment (per. 15): the believer's change (glorification) at Christ's coming, as in Rom. No. 9, cf. Col 1:27.

---

misses the mark, as in English, op. cit., p. 78; for it is the failure of *lawful* government, not government itself, that is here predicted. Pretribulationists such as C. F. Hogg and W. E. Vine, in *The Epistles of Paul the Apostle to the Thessalonians*, have conceded that the restraint must be divinely constituted government. But if this is once granted, then the removal of these verses to a futuristic tribulation loses its cogency.

16. Payne, op. cit., pp. 109–111.

17. "This is not yet the Last Judgment, and it is possible that some under this retribution may yet repent, seeing how shameful is the delusion into which they have fallen by rejecting Christ," Camb, p. 153.

I TIMOTHY

Chronologically, the Pastoral Epistles—I Timothy, Titus, and II Timothy, seemingly in that order—form the fourth and final group of the writings of the apostle Paul.[1] Topically, they consist of "pastoral" instructions for his younger co-workers, among the churches to which they had been sent. Prophetically, they exhibit considerable unevenness in content; for while the subject matter of I Timothy and Titus averages out to be less than 4% which is concerned with forecasts of the future, that of II Timothy amounts to over 20%. Yet all the predictions of the Pastorals assume a simple oracular form, without figures, symbols, or types. Moreover, the genuineness of their authorship by Paul has been more consistently questioned than has that of any others out of the 13 epistles that bear his name.

1. See above, introduction to Romans.

I Timothy / 567

Dates as late as 150 have been assigned to these three letters,[2] both because of their concern over ecclesiastical offices and administration and
because of their stress on "sound doctrine" and "keeping the faith" (I Tim
1:10, 19, ASV): cf. II Tim 3:16, on the inspiration of the Bible,[3] or Titus
2:13, on the deity of Jesus, "our great God and Savior."

Yet with the developing church, here entering its fourth decade, and
with the aging of the apostles, the possibility of recognizing just such a
need for greater organization should hardly be ruled out from the range
of Paul's thought;[4] and a stress on Scriptural orthodoxy had characterized
the mind of Jesus Himself (Lk 24:25, John 10:35) and all of God's
faithful followers both before and after Him (Isa 8:20, Acts 24:14). The
literary style and vocabulary of the Pastorals do differ to some degree from
that employed by Paul in his earlier writings; but it seems hazardous to
deny that changes in an author's topics and recipients may not elicit corresponding changes in his literary forms.[5] Each of these epistles lays unquestioned claim to Pauline composition, and the numerous personal allusions that they contain (e.g. I Tim 1:12–13; II Tim 3:10; 4:10–11,
19–20) leave as the alternative to authenticity the harsh proposition of
unabashed forgery.

The routes of travel of the apostle after the conclusion of his first Roman
imprisonment in 61[6] remain matters of conjecture. He may have attained
his earlier goal of a missionary journey westward to Spain (Rom 15:24,
28); or he may have carried out the intention expressed just before his
release, of moving directly to Asia Minor (Philemon 22). In any event,
it is in this latter area that the Pastorals, some two years later, take up
their geographical notations. Paul's first epistle to Timothy was composed
after he had left his young co-worker and "true child in the faith" (I Tim
1:2; cf. Acts 16:1–3) to supervise the church at Ephesus in Asia Minor,
while the apostle himself had gone on to Macedonia (I Tim 1:3), perhaps
early in 63. He hoped to rejoin Timothy soon (3:14) but meanwhile inscribed the letter that opens the group of the Pastorals. It consists essentially of three parts, each of which follows a pattern of charge, of poetic
praise to God (1:17, 3:16, 6:16), and then of further charge:[7] the introduction, ch. 1; the body of the epistle, 2–6:2; and a conclusion, 6:3–21.

2. E. J. Goodspeed, *An Introduction to the NT*, pp. 328, 331.
3. Significant for the concept of the NT canon is the way in which I Tim 5:18
connects the Gospel of Luke with Dt in the OT, as being equally inspired Scripture.
4. It appears noteworthy, moreover, that the titles "bishop" and "elder" are still
employed interchangeably (Titus 1:5–7), in contrast with the hierarchical bishoprics
that began to appear by the turn of the century.
5. James Moffatt, *Introduction to the Literature of the NT*, p. 414, develops the
hypothesis of joint authorship by Paul and Luke, though cf. the defense of true
Pauline composition by Donald Guthrie, *The Pauline Epistles: NT Introduction*,
pp. 221–224, 230–231, 235–236.
6. See above, introduction to Acts.
7. As worked out by Wilbur Wallis, in C. F. Pfeiffer and E. F. Harrison, eds.,
The Wycliffe Bible Commentary, pp. 1368–1369.

The thought of I Timothy may be summarized by the following key verse, 4:12, "Let no one look down on your youthfulness, but rather in speech, conduct, love, faith and purity, show yourself an example of those who believe." The epistle contains but 2 predictions: one in the body, 4:1–3, and one in the conclusion, 6:14–15. These involve 5 verses, or about 4% of the 115-verse total of the book.

1. I Tim 4:1–3 (3 vv.): Paul's citation of a previous prophecy, seemingly drawn from his own past teaching, "The Spirit explicitly says that in later times some will fall away from the faith, paying attention to . . . doctrines of demons, by means of the hypocrisy of liars . . . men who forbid marriage and advocate abstaining from certain foods. . . ." Fulfillment (per. 14): the rise of apostasy in the church prior to Christ's return, as in II Thess. No. 7, or more specifically in this very Ephesian congregation, as in Acts No. 54 (20:29).

2. I Tim 6:14–15 (2 vv.): "Keep the commandment . . . until the appearing, *epifáneiā,* of our Lord Jesus Christ, which He will bring about at the proper time," a prediction whose final phrase reflects Christ's own caution about the Father's control over the "times" involved, Acts 1:7. Fulfillment (per. 15): the Lord's second coming, as in Ps. prophecy No. 5.

II TIMOTHY

In contrast with the other Pastoral Epistles, II Timothy maintains a consistently prophetic emphasis. Forecasts of the future occur in each of its chapters, reaching a climax at the end, in ch. 4, which touches on 5 out of the 8 predictive topics revealed in the book. A total of 17 verses, or some 20% of the 83 that make up the volume, involve prophetic material.

At the time when he wrote II Timothy, Paul had passed through Troas and Miletus on the coast of Asia Minor (4:13, 20) and was again chained as a prisoner in Rome (1:8, 16–17; 2:9): but on this occasion, in contrast to the optimism displayed in the "prison epistles" of his first confinement from 59 to 61 (cf. Phil 2:24, Philemon 22), he can anticipate only condemnation and death (II Tim 4:6, 18). He is lonely (vv. 11, 16) and urges Timothy to come to him "before winter" (vv. 9, 21), presumably that of 64;[1] and, in the light of Nero's persecutions from mid-64 onward, it seems doubtful that Timothy ever did see him again. Paul's charge to his younger friend may be summed up in the words of II Tim 2:8, "Remember Jesus Christ, risen from the dead, according to my gospel." Like

---

1. See above, introduction to Romans.

the more involved structure of I Timothy,[2] the epistle as a whole consists of an introduction and conclusion (1:1–5 and 4:9–22) and of two major segments of charge and admonition, separated by a hymn of doctrinal truth (2:11–13).

1. II Tim 1:12, 18; 4:8a (3 vv.): Paul's confidence that Christ will grant him protection "until that day," 1:12, namely, "the day of judgment and award, I Cor 3:13,"[3] the point being that "the day is now so present to his mind that it needs no defining."[4] Similarly in 1:18, it is "on that day" that Paul prays that Onesiphorus may "find mercy from the Lord"; and Paul reveals in respect to himself, 4:8, that "in the future there is laid up for me the crown of righteousness [i.e. the one "which is won by righteousness"[5]], which the Lord, the righteous Judge, will award to me on that day; and not only to me, but also to all who have loved[6] His appearing." Fulfillment (per. 17): the judgment of the righteous, as in Job prophecy No. 5.

2. II Tim 2:12 (1 v.): "If we endure, we shall also reign with Him"; cf. Rom 4:13 or I Cor 6:2. Fulfillment (per. 16): the special position of the saints in the Messiah's future kingdom, as in Dt. No. 37.

3. II Tim 2:18 (1 v.): some were saying, "The resurrection has already taken place," which must have meant that they "spiritualized" this future event to refer to the believers' present relationship to God, a theory similar to that opposed by Paul in I Cor 15:12.[7] This latter verse must therefore relate to the same fulfillment (per. 17), the general resurrection, as in Job No. 2; cf. Paul's reference to the judgment that immediately follows it, in II Tim 4:1a (No. 5, below).

4. II Tim 3:1–9 (9 vv): "In the last days difficult times will come. For men will be lovers of self, lovers of money . . . lovers of pleasure, etc. . . . rejected as regards the faith. But they will not make further progress, for their folly will be obvious to all." Some have questioned the predictive character of this passage: "The prophetical form of the sentence is a rhetorical way of saying that things are going from bad to worse";[8] cf. v. 13. Yet these thoughts form an oracle that corresponds to the predicted doctrinal apostasy in 4:3–4 (No. 8, below) and in I Tim 4:1–3, *q.v.* A. M. Stibbs protests, "But the reference here is explicitly to the consummation

2. See above, introduction to I Timothy.
3. ExGkT, IV:158, though Alford, *The Greek Testament*, III:353, suggests His Parousia; cf. I Tim 6:14 or I Cor 1:7–8.
4. ICC, *Pastorals*, p. 88.
5. Ibid., p. 115.
6. The form of the verb may thus suggest the priority of the second coming to the judgment: ExGkT, IV:179, "The perfect tense is used because their love will have continued up to the moment of their receiving the crown, or because St. Paul is thinking of them from the standpoint of the day of crowning."
7. See ibid., IV:166.
8. Ibid., IV:169–170.

of the age. Note the future tense, *shall come*, though the present tenses in 3:5–6 indicate that the evil later to mature was already at work."[9] Fulfillment (per. 14): moral decline in the days immediately preceding the Parousia.

5. II Tim 4:1a (1 v.): that Jesus Christ "is to judge the living and the dead." Fulfillment (per. 17): the final judgment, as in Eccl. No. 1.

6. II Tim *4:1b, 8b,* Christ's appearing, or *epifâneiā.* Fulfillment (per. 15): His second coming, as in Ps. prophecy No. 5.

7. II Tim *4:1c,* a reference to Christ's coming kingdom. Fulfillment (per. 16): His millennial rule, as in Gen. No. 68; for it is associated with His appearing (v. 1b, No. 6, preceding) and eventuates in His universal judgment (v. 1a, No. 5).[10]

8. II Tim 4:3–4 (2 vv.): "The time will come when they will not endure sound doctrine, but . . . will turn aside to myths." Fulfillment (per. 14): as in Lk. No. 59, apostasy prior to Christ's return; cf. I Tim 4:1.

9. NBC, p. 1077.
10. Cf. Alford, op. cit., III:375.

TITUS

In regard to its prophetic content, Titus in the NT forms the counterpart of Esther in the OT; for each contains but a single verse that predicts the future. The Book of Titus, in other words, ranks lowest in the NT in its percentage of prophetic material, next to Philemon and III John, which, owing apparently to their brevity, possess no predictions at all. Out of the book's 46-verse total, this one verse amounts to some 2%. Yet its lone forecast is one of the best known in all of Scripture, on "that blessed hope" of Christ's return, 2:13.

Despite the uncertainty that exists over the sequence of Paul's movements following his release from the first Roman imprisonment in 61,[1] it would appear that after leaving Timothy at Ephesus, and then writing him from Macedonia (I Tim 1:3), the apostle continued his counterclockwise circuit around the Aegean, so that he was able to leave Titus, "his brother" and co-worker in the Lord (II Cor 2:13), to direct church affairs on the island of Crete (Titus 1:5). Paul had then sailed up the western coast of Greece to Nicopolis (3:12), where he planned to spend the winter. If his appeal for Zenas the lawyer (v. 13) foreshadows his arrest there in Epirus and his subsequent, second imprisonment in Rome, then the date for his composition of Titus would lie near the end of 63.[2] The epistle pre-

1. See above, introduction to I Timothy.
2. See above, introduction to Romans.

sents the following outline: introductory greetings to Titus (1:1–4); the body of the letter, setting forth the responsibilities of teaching elders and of the other groups in the church (1:5–3:11); and a conclusion, emphasizing their need for "good works" (3:12–15). Its message may be summarized by the apostle's definition of the true church officer, as "holding fast the faithful word which is in accordance with the teaching, that he may be able to exhort in sound doctrine and to refute those who contradict" (1:9, a key verse).

1. Titus 2:13 (1 v.): that we are to be "looking for the blessed hope and appearing, *epifáneiā* [as in I Tim 6:14, II Tim 4:1, 8] of the glory of our great God and Savior, Christ Jesus." Fulfillment (per. 15): His second coming, as in Ps. prophecy No. 5.

HEBREWS

Just before the climactic conclusion to the NT in John's Revelation come the eight general epistles: Hebrews (if not classed with the Pauline letters), James, the two letters of Peter, the three of John, and Jude. Less apt as a title is the designation "catholic epistles"; for though many of the eight are addressed to the Christian church as a whole, rather than to congregations in specified cities or to particular individuals,[1] exceptions still do appear in I Peter, which speaks to a believing diaspora in five districts of what is now Turkey, in III John, which is written to an individual believer, and in II John, which is probably addressed to an unidentified church, though possibly to an individual.[2]

In a similar manner the Epistle to the Hebrews does not particularize its recipients. They may have formed a church, or a segment in a church, or even a limited group of churches (cf. 10:32–34, 13:24). From the detailed knowledge of the OT that they must have possessed, they may be assumed to have been Jewish Christians, i.e. "Hebrews"; and some of them are in specific danger of lapsing back into the practices of Judaism (2:1, 4:1, 5:12, 10:19–39, 12:12). They may have been located in Rome, since 13:24 seems to suggest that those who were away from Italy are sending them greetings.[3] Because the Jerusalem temple appears to be still standing at the time of writing (8:4), the epistle should date before

1. As in the case of the Pauline Pastorals.
2. See below, introduction to II John.
3. But this verse might also mean that the author was writing from Italy; cf. D. Guthrie, *Hebrews to Revelation: NT Introduction*, pp. 37–41, on various destinations that have been proposed.

A.D. 70;[4] but it also shows the influence of Paul's letters[5] and, if the "expectation of judgment" mentioned in 10:27 indicates the outbreak of hostilities between the Jews and Rome, the year might well be 67.

The authorship of this anonymous epistle has been a matter of uncertainty since early in church history. The writer must have been a friend of Timothy (13:23); and though Hebrews has often been assigned to Paul[6] and is so listed in the KJV title, its theological[7] and literary style are not Pauline. Especially distinct is its approach to the OT law, which it normally treats in its function as a typical foreshadowing of Christ (8:5, 9:11–12, though cf. 10:28), rather than as an agent of moral condemnation, as in Paul (Gal 3:21–24, Rom 5:20, though cf. Rom 2:17–18, Col 2:17). Hebrews, in fact, answers closely to the OT book of Leviticus, in that it is the NT volume that is the most involved in the phenomenon of typical prediction: some 18 of its 52 prophetic topics, and almost half of its predictive verses, are concerned with the types of the OT.[8] Indeed, Hebrews is the most important book in the Bible on the relationship of the OT to the NT: it emphasizes how the former is fulfilled in Jesus Christ, and it views the goal of the Sinaitic law as achieved through its being written upon men's hearts under the newer testament of the church (Heb 8:7–15). Correspondingly, this letter contains proportionately more about Biblical prophecy than any other book in the NT, with the exception of Revelation: 45% of the verses (137 out of the 303) of the book have to do with prediction, and these are scattered through all 13 of its chapters. The overwhelming majority consist of either references to or direct citations of OT prophecies. Hebrews, as a result, cites predictions that have accomplishments in all 18 of the periods of prophetic fulfillment as used in this study—from the flood of Noah in per. 1 (11:7) to the New Jerusalem and the final lake of fire in per. 18 (10:27, 12:28)—with the exception of five periods (5, 8, and 10–12). This is a greater number than for any other book of the Bible. Of the various authors that have been proposed for Hebrews, e.g. Barnabas, Silas, or even Priscilla, the most likely candidate would seem to be the Alexandrian Jew Apollos, who was distinguished for being "an eloquent

4. Some critics would argue for a later date, nearer 90, after the fall of Jerusalem had ceased to be a matter of vital concern (?)—cf. IB, XI:593–594—but prior to 95, when the epistle is quoted in I Clement.

5. Cf. Guthrie, op. cit., pp. 48–49.

6. But not, for example, in the Western Church until about 400.

7. The term "sanctification," as an illustration, connotes salvation in Hebrews (2:10–11; 10:10, 14, 29) rather than a subsequent growth in grace as in Paul (Eph 5:26, I Thess 5:23).

8. While it is true that the actual proportion of types, out of its total number of predictive verses—which amounts to 46%—is less than the percentages recorded for Colossians (see the Statistical Appendix, below), this phenomenon appears to be coincidental, owing to the latter's relatively small amount of prophetic material of any sort.

man . . . fervent in spirit . . . and mighty in the Scriptures . . . for he powerfully refuted the Jews, demonstrating by the [OT] Scriptures that Jesus was the Christ," Acts 18:24, 25, 28. This, in turn, is precisely the approach of the epistle, which is based so completely upon the OT. The theme of Hebrews revolves about the preeminence of Jesus Christ; and it may be summed up in 3:1–6 as a key passage, "Consider Jesus, the High Priest of our confession . . . for He has been counted worthy of more glory than Moses . . . a Son, whose house we are, if we hold our hope firm unto the end." The book consists of a prologue and a personal epilogue (1:1–4 and 13:18–25) and of 2 major parts: I, 1:5–10:18, a demonstration of the superiority of Christ—to angels (chs. 1–2), to Moses (3), to Joshua (4:1–13), to the Levitical priests (4:14–ch. 7), and to the older testament (8–10:18)—and II, 10:19–13:17, an appeal for faith in Him—based on Christian assurance (ch. 10, v. 19 on), on the OT examples of faith (11), and on the supreme example of Christ (12:1–11), with various practical conclusions (12:12–13:17). Interspersed in this main outline, moreover, is a series of warnings directed to the readers: 2:1–4, 3:7–19, 6:4–12, 10:26–31, and 12:15–17, exhorting them to "hold fast their confidence" (3:6).

1. Heb 1:5 (1 v.): citation of II Sam 7 on Christ's divine Sonship. Fulfillment (per. 13): as in II Sam. prophecy No. 12.

2. Heb 1:6 (1 v.): citation of Dt 32:43 LXX on angels worshiping Christ, when God "brings the firstborn into the world." Fulfillment (per. 13): at His first advent,[9] as in Dt. No. 47.

3. Heb 1:8–9 (2 vv.): citation of Ps 45:6–7 on the anointing of Christ. Fulfillment (per. 13): as in Ps. prophecy No. 3.

4. Heb 1:11a, 12a; 12:26–27a (4 vv., fig.): citations of Ps 102:26 and Hag 2:6, respectively, on the passing away of heaven and earth, "the removing of those things which can be shaken, as of created things" (12:27). Fulfillment (per. 17): as in Ps. No. 47.

5. Heb *1:11b, 12b,* citation of Ps 102:26b–27 on the eternity of Christ. Fulfillment (per. 13): as listed under Ps. No. 37.

6. Heb *1:13a,* 2:6–9 (4 vv.): the former a citation of Ps 110:1b, the latter of Ps 8:4–6, on Christ's ascension. Fulfillment (per. 13): as in Ps. No. 8.

7. Heb 1:13b, 2:5, 10:13 (3 vv.): the first and last references cite Ps 110:1c, on Christ's Messianic kingdom; and 2:5 speaks of God's making "the world to come" subject to Christ. That is, "The new world-order . . . had been inaugurated by Christ's enthronement [at His ascen-

---

9. The reading of the ASV and NAS texts, "When He again brings the firstborn into the world," might suggest the second advent; but the *again* seems simply to be introducing a fresh quotation, as in v. 5, 2:13, 4:5; cf. KJV and the mg. of ASV and NAS, though it stands confessedly in a transposed position; cf. NIC, p. 15.

sion, 2:7, listed under 1:13a, No. 6, preceding], although it is not yet present in its fulness; its consummation awaits the time when Christ appears."[10] Fulfillment (per. 16): His millennial rule, as in Ps No. 5.

8. Heb 2:12 (1 v.): citation of Ps 22:22 on Christ's post-resurrection ministry to *the church*; cf. Heb 2:13b (next v.), which cites the nonpredictive passage of Isa 8:18, the Messiah's words on His possessing "children," even in Isaiah's day. Fulfillment (per. 14): as in Ps. No. 19.

9. Heb 2:13 (1 v.): citation of Isa 8:17 on Christ's words about *waiting for Yahweh*, during the time before Israel's final conversion. Fulfillment (per. 15): the repentance of the Jews at His second coming, Isa. No. 31, though the prophecy is used at this point in Hebrews as a further illustration of "His solidarity with His people . . . the faithful Israel within the empirical Israel, the group in whose survival the hope of the future was assured, one might almost say the *ekklēsīā* [church] of the Messiah."[11]

10. Heb 3:11, 18; 4:3, 5 (4 vv.): citation of Ps 95:11, on the wilderness generation of the Israelites not entering God's promised land of rest. Fulfillment (per. 3): as in Ps. prophecy No. 43 and, originally, in Num. No. 19 (14:22), from which the NT writer proceeds to draw a warning about the possibility of a similar failure now, to enter into heaven's rest, Heb 4:1, 6–11.

11. Heb 4:4 (1 v., typ.): citation of Gen 2:3 (see Gen. No. 2) on the sabbath, typical of its fulfillment (per. 13) in Christ.

12. Heb 5:1–2, 4–5; 7:5, 11–12, 14, 23, 28; 8:*3a*, 4–*5a*; 9:6a, 7b; 9:25a; 10:11a; *13:11c* (14 vv., typ.): discussion of the OT priests, and particularly of Aaron, as typical of Christ's ministry of divine reconciliation. Fulfillment (per. 13): as in Ex. No. 59.

13. Heb 5:*1b*, 3; 7:27; 8:3b; 9:7d, 9b–10, *23b*; 10:1–3, *11b*; 11:4 (10 vv., typ.): discussion of OT sacrifice, as typical of Christ's atonement. Fulfillment (per. 13): as in Lev. No. 2.

14. Heb 5:6a, 10; 6:20; 7:15, 17a, 20–21a (7 vv.): citation of Ps 110, that the Messiah's anticipated priesthood would be like that of Melchizedek's. Fulfillment (per. 13): as in Ps. prophecy No. 55.

15. Heb 5:*6b*; 7:3b, 8, 16, *17b*, *21b*, 24 (4 vv.): citation of Ps 110:4b on the perpetuity (and hence resurrection) of Christ, as a priest *forever*, like Melchizedek. Fulfillment (per. 13): as in Ps. No. 11.

16. Heb 6:2a (1 v.): an allusion to "the resurrection of the dead." Fulfillment (per. 17): the general resurrection, as in Job No. 2.

17. Heb 6:*2b*, 9:27, 12:23 (2 vv.): an allusion to "eternal judgment," 6:2, following the resurrection (No. 16, preceding). Thus also 12:23 speaks of "God the Judge of all." Fulfillment (per. 17): the final judgment, as in Eccl. No. 1.

18. Heb 6:12–*14a*, 15; 7:*6c* (3 vv.): citation of Gen 22:17a on the

10. Ibid., p. 33.
11. Ibid., pp. 45, 47.

divine blessing that would come upon Abraham. So 7:6 describes him as "the one who had the promises." Fulfillment (per. 1): as in Gen. No. 22; cf. the statement in Heb 6:15 that "he obtained the promise."

19. Heb 6:14b, 17; 11:12–13, 17–18 (6 vv.): citation of Gen 21:12 (in Heb 11:18) and 22:17b on Abraham's becoming multiplied. 6:17 thus speaks of "the heirs of the promise," though according to 11:13 (cf. v. 12) Abraham himself "died without receiving the promise." Fulfillment (per. 2): Israel's increase in Egypt, as in Gen. No. 21.

20. Heb 6:19, *9:3a*, 10:20 (2 vv., typ.): reference to the veil of the tabernacle, as a type of the flesh of Christ (10:20), the God-given way into heaven (6:19), "where Jesus has entered as a forerunner for us" (v. 20). Fulfillment (per. 13): in Christ, as in Ex. No. 58; cf. Mt 27:51 on the rending of the veil at the time when our Lord's body was torn in death.

21. Heb 7:1a, *3a*, *6a* (1 v., typ.): discussion of the Canaanite king Melchizedek, as a type of Christ's non-Levitical genealogy. Fulfillment (per. 13): as in Gen. No. 26 (14:18a).

22. Heb 7:*1b*, 2b, *11b* (1 v., typ.): discussion of Melchizedek as a priest, particularly as typical of Christ's achievements of righteousness and peace. Fulfillment (per. 13): as in Gen. No. 27 (14:18b).

23. Heb 7:*1c–2a*, 4, 6b–7, 9–10 (5 vv., typ.): discussion of Melchizedek as a type of Christ's greatness, bestowing blessings and receiving tithes. Fulfillment (per. 13): as in Gen. No. 28 (14:19).

24. Heb 7:13 (1 v., typ.): reference to the OT altar as typifying Christ's atonement. Fulfillment (per. 13): as in Ex. No. 44.

25. Heb 8:5b; 9:*1b–3*, *6b–7a*, 8–*9a*, *21b*, *25b*; 13:10, *11b* (5 vv., typ.[12]): discussion of the tabernacle as typical of Christ's incarnation (per. 13), God's tabernacling with men, as in Ex. No. 55.

26. Heb 8:6, 8–12; 10:16–17 (8 vv.): citation of Jer 31:31–34 as fulfilled in Christ's newer testament with the church (per. 14), as listed under Jer. No. 7.

27. Heb 8:7, 13; 9:1a, *4b*, 15–18, *20b* (7 vv., typ.): reference to the Sinaitic testament as involving a type of Christ's death (see esp. 9:16–17), "the blood of the testament" (v. 20). Fulfillment (per. 13): as in Ex. No. 45.

28. Heb 9:4a (1 v., typ.): reference to the ark of the testament. Fulfillment (per. 13): as in Ex No. 56.

29. Heb 9:5 (1 v., typ.): the mercy seat. Fulfillment (per. 13): as in Ex. No. 57.

30. Heb *9:7c*, 12–14, 19–23, *25c*; 10:4; 12:24; *13:11a* (10 vv., typ.): references to the use of blood in the OT ceremonial, as typical of Christ's

---

12. References to the tabernacle as symbolical of God's eternal presence in heaven, such as 6:20, 8:1–2, 9:11, 24, have not been included, since they are not predictive of events yet to be fulfilled in subsequent human history; see above, pp. 36–38.

atoning surrender of His life. Fulfillment (per. 13): as in Lev. No. 20.

31. Heb 9:28; 10:25, 37 (3 vv.): "Christ shall appear a second time, [but] not to bear sin," 9:28, as at His first advent. 10:25 states, "You see the day drawing near," i.e. of Christ's Parousia (v. 37); cf. a similar usage of the phrase "the day" in I Thess 5:4. Heb 10:37 predicts, "For yet in a very little while, He who is coming will come, and will not delay." The wording of this last verse is based on Hab 2:3, which is a general statement about the accomplishment of the prophet's vision, that "*it* will come." The writer of Hebrews, however, here adapts it to the career of Christ, introducing the specifically Messianic title "the Coming One" (Mt 11:3). Fulfillment (per. 15): the Lord's second advent, as in Ps. prophecy No. 5.

32. Heb *10:5a, 8a* (typ.): references to "sacrifice," meaning Israel's peace offerings; for in vv. 6 and 8 they are specifically contrasted with the other classes of offerings. Fulfillment (pers. 13 and 16): as in Lev. No. 5.

33. Heb *10:5b, 8b* (typ.): references to an "offering" which is known from the OT text that is being quoted (Ps 40:6) to have been the particular meal offering. Fulfillment (per. 13): as in Lev. No. 4.

34. Heb 10:5c, 7, 9 (3 vv.): citation of Ps 40:6–7, as fulfilled (per. 13) in Christ's obedience to the Father; see Ps. prophecy No. 27.

35. Heb 10:6a, 8c (2 vv., typ.): burnt offering. Fulfillment (per. 13): as in Lev. No. 3.

36. Heb *10:6b, 8d*; 13:11d (1 v., typ.): sin offering. Fulfillment (per. 13): as in Lev. No. 6.

37. Heb 10:26–29, 31 (5 vv.): for those who "go on sinning willfully" and thus "regard as unclean the blood of the testament," there is "a terrifying expectation of judgment . . . a much severer punishment" than even the death penalty as administered under the Mosaic law. Fulfillment (per. 18): the lake of fire, as in II Sam. No. 20.

38. Heb *10:27b* (fig.), citation of Isa 26:11 on "the fury of fire" against God's adversaries at the battle of Armageddon. Fulfillment (per. 15): as listed under Isa No. 34, though here used to illustrate their condemnation following the final judgment as well (see No. 37, preceding).

39. Heb 10:30a (1 v.): citation of Dt 32:35, on God's taking vengeance on Israel at its fall in 586 B.C. Fulfillment (per. 7): as in Dt. No. 13, but here used to illustrate the final punishment of those who reject the gospel (see Heb 10:26, No. 37, above); cf. Rom 12:19 (listed under Rom. No. 16).

40. Heb *10:30b*, citation of Dt 32:36, that "Yahweh will judge His people" in the sense of interceding for them. Fulfillment (per. 9), in Judah's return from exile, as in Dt. No. 43, but quoted at this point in the sense of His act of condemning, at the final judgment; see Heb 10:26 (No. 37, above), and cf. v. 30a (No. 39, preceding).

41. Heb 10:36 (1 v.): the recipients of the epistle are exhorted to maintain their endurance, "so that you may receive what was promised"; for Christ's second advent was drawing near, v. 37 (see under 9:28, No. 31, above). F. F. Bruce explains, "Sometimes the promised bliss seemed close at hand, as they saw 'the day drawing nigh' (v. 25); but at other times it looked as though it would never come."[13] Fulfillment (per. 16): the blessings of the future Messianic kingdom, as in Ex. No. 49; cf. the promises of "inheritance" in Eph 1:18 and I Pet 1:3.

42. Heb 11:7 (1 v.): reference to Noah's being warned of God "about things not yet seen." Fulfillment (per. 1): prediction of the flood, as in Gen. No. 11.

43. Heb 11:8–9 (2 vv.): reference to God's promise of Canaan for the descendants of Abraham, though he, together with Isaac and Jacob, "lived as an alien in the land of promise." Fulfillment (per. 4): as in Gen. No. 24.

44. Heb 11:11 (1 v.): reference to God's promise of conception for Sarah, Gen 18:10. Fulfillment (per. 1): Isaac's birth, as in Gen. No. 29.

45. Heb 11:20a (1 v.): reference to Isaac's predictive blessing on his son Jacob, presumably the prophecy of Gen 27:29, in parallel with his similar words of political blessing for Esau (No. 46, following), though see also Gen 27:28 (under No. 51, below). Fulfillment (per. 6): David's empire, as listed under Gen. No. 45 (and cf. No. 50).

46. Heb *11:20b* (fig.): his blessing on his son Esau. Fulfillment (per. 7): Edom's independence from Judah, as in Gen. No. 54 (27:40).

47. Heb 11:21a (1 v., sym.): reference to Jacob's predictive act of blessing for the two sons of Joseph, especially Ephraim. Fulfillment (per. 7): the latter's rule over the northern kingdom of Israel, as in Gen. No. 62 (48:16).

48. Heb *11:21b* (fig.): his blessing on Manasseh as well. Fulfillment (per. 4): its rich inheritance, as in Gen No. 62.

49. Heb 11:22 (1 v.): reference to Joseph's prediction of the return of Israel to Canaan, Gen 50:24–25. Fulfillment (per. 4): as in Gen. No. 36.

50. Heb 11:28 (1 v., typ.): Passover. Fulfillment (per. 13): as in Ex. No. 31.

51. Heb 12:17 (1 v., fig.): reference to "the blessing" that had been predicted for Jacob by Isaac but in which Esau wished to share. It therefore presumably concerned that of the fertile land that Jacob had been promised (though see also No. 45, above). Fulfillment (per. 4): as in Gen. No. 52 (27:28).

52. Heb 12:*27b*–28 (1 v.): "We receive a kingdom which cannot be shaken." The writer's thought is explained in context as referring to that

13. NIC, p. 271.

which follows upon the removal of heaven and earth at the final judgment (see under 1:11a, No. 4, above), "in order that those things which cannot be shaken may remain." Fulfillment (per. 18): the believers' inheritance in the New Jerusalem, as in Isa. No. 74.

JAMES

The general epistle of James, like that of his brother Jude, appears to be the work of one of the half-brothers of the Lord (Mt 13:55; cf. 12:46–47).[1] The James of this relationship took an active part in the work of the early church at Jerusalem (Gal 1:19), from Pentecost and onward (Acts 1:14, 12:17, 15:13, 21:18), though he had not been a believer in Christ before (John 7:5). According to Josephus, James suffered martyrdom at the hands of the Jews in about 62.[2] The date of his book could be set at any time from the Jewish persecutions that began with the murder of Stephen in 33 down to the year of James's death. The existence, however, of a measure of church order, with teachers and elders (3:1, 5:14), suggests a lapse of years, though the lack of reference to the controversy over Gentiles in the church would seem to locate it some time before the Jerusalem council of 49. A date at 45 would constitute James the second earliest work in the NT,[3] being composed shortly after the Gospel of Mark.[4]

The Epistle of James reads like a portion of OT wisdom literature that has been modified by the teachings of Jesus; and it seems to have been directed to the same sort of audience as was the Epistle to the Hebrews, which now precedes it: i.e. to Jewish Christians of "the twelve tribes who are dispersed abroad" (1:1), meeting in "synagogues" (2:2 lit., ASV). The communication that James sent consists of a series of short paragraphs on ethical themes, such as the enduring of trials (1:2–8), the peril of riches (vv. 9–11), and the control of the tongue (v. 26). A key verse thus appears in 1:22, "Prove yourselves doers of the word, and not mere hearers."

1. Guthrie, e.g., notes a number of parallels between the language of the epistle and the known speech and letter of James the brother of Jesus in Acts 15, *Hebrews to Revelation: NT Introduction*, pp. 66–67. There do appear other men by the name of James in the early church; but James the brother of John suffered martyrdom in Acts 12:2, and James the less (Mk 15:40), though one of the twelve, seems to have held no such position of leadership and authority as does the writer of the epistle. On critical arguments that have been advanced against this identification, cf. ibid., pp. 71–82.
2. *Ant*, XX, 9, 1.
3. Cf. Guthrie, op. cit., pp. 85–88.
4. See above, introduction to Mark.

Just as in the case of the OT wisdom writings, the proportion of prophetic matter is small.[5] The four predictions of the book are limited to two of its paragraphs: 2:10–26, on the need for faith *and* works,[6] and 5:1–11, which continues the above-mentioned sections on the danger of riches and on the need for the endurance of trials. These forecasts involve but 7 verses, or 6% of the 108 that make up the book.

1. James 2:12, *13b* (1 v.): that Christians are "to be judged by the law of liberty," v. 12; for "the law of Christ brings liberty, guiding the new life in Christ."[7] V. 13b then adds, "Mercy triumphs over judgment," as a comment on v. 13a (see No. 2, next); i.e., "This gives the converse of the previous sentence. As the unmerciful will meet with no mercy, so a record of mercy will prevent condemnation."[8] Fulfillment (per. 17): the judgment of the saved, as in Job prophecy No. 5.

2. James 2:13a, 5:2–3 (3 vv.): the former passage states in general: "Judgment will be merciless to one who has shown no mercy"; the latter then speaks in a figure directed particularly to the wealthy, "Your riches [gained by fraud, 5:4–6] have rotted . . . and their rust will be a witness against you and will consume your flesh like fire. It is in the Last Days that you have stored up your treasure," vv. 2–3. "The warning expresses apocalyptic certainty: at the Judgment, riches, gained only by crime, bring eternal condemnation to their owners."[9] Fulfillment (per. 17): the judgment of the lost, as in Ps. No. 1.

3. James 5:7 (1 v.): James's admonition, "Be patient until the coming of the Lord." Fulfillment (per. 15): Christ's second advent, as in Ps. No. 5.

4. James 5:8–9 (2 vv.): "The coming of the Lord is at hand . . . the Judge is standing right at the door"; i.e., "The doors may not open until tomorrow, or the next week, or the next millennium; but they might open at any time!"[10] Fulfillment (per. 15): the imminence of Christ's appearing, as in Lk. No. 47.

5. See above, introduction to Job.
6. James and Paul thus emphasize different aspects of the same plan of salvation, by faith, with works that follow (cf. Rom 4:5–6, but also 6:1–4, 18–19).
7. NBC, p. 1121.
8. ICC, p. 202.
9. IB, XII:64.
10. J. B. Payne, *The Imminent Appearing of Christ*, p. 101.

I PETER

Both of the epistles of Peter exhibit a relatively high involvement in predictive prophecy, though the Second does so more than the First. I Peter has been recognized from the earliest days as an authentic composition of this leading apostle,[1] though whether its origin in Babylon (5:13) refers to the literal Mesopotamian city of that name, to which Peter may have fled when he left Judea in A.D. 44 (Acts 12:17), or to John's figurative "Babylon the great, the mother of harlots," namely Rome (Rev 17:5, 18), is a matter that is more open to question. The eastern Babylon had become largely uninhabited by this time[2] and had been replaced by nearby Seleucia, though many of the Jews there had been massacred in 41. Some 8 passages from Paul's Epistle to the Romans (dated 56) do seem to be reflected in the content of I Peter.[3] A dating of the letter to about 60 is suggested by the fact that on the occasion of the writing of II Peter, just before the apostle's death in 64,[4] the readers' memory of his former epistle was still expected to be sharp (II Pet 3:1), though Peter's injunctions about "honoring the king" (I Pet 2:13–17) favor a time prior to Nero's active persecutions.

The recipients of I Peter are localized to five of the districts in what is today Turkey and are identified in the introduction as a diaspora (1:1), a group of God's people who have become scattered out through alien lands. But unlike the Jewish-Christian diaspora of James (1:1)[5]—the NT book that now precedes I Peter—this latter epistle is directed to a group made up primarily of Gentile Christians (I Pet 1:14, 18; 2:10; 4:3). The apostle's purpose in writing may be summed up by his words in 4:12–13, "Beloved, do not be surprised at the fiery ordeal among you, which comes upon you for your testing . . . but to the degree that you share the sufferings of Christ, keep on rejoicing, so that also at the revelation of His glory you may rejoice" (cf. 1:6, 2:20, 3:14, 4:1, 5:9).[6] The book as a whole falls into four parts: 1:3–2:10, on the nature of salvation in Christ; 2:11–3:12, on the believers' social relationships; 3:13–ch. 4, on the particular problem of suffering; and ch. 5, on discipline in the church. Matters of prophecy appear in each of the book's five chapters.

---

1. On recent criticism of its Petrine authenticity, see D. Guthrie, *Hebrew to Revelation: NT Introduction*, pp. 98–114; cf. 121–125.
2. See above, p. 301 and note 105, on Isa 13:19.
3. ICC, *Rom*, p. lxxiv.
4. See below, introduction to II Peter.
5. See above, introduction to James.
6. Since Peter died at the outset of the official Neronian persecution in 64, it is significant that the "suffering" on which the epistle centers appears to be due primarily to individual rather than to governmental opposition; cf. 2:12, 3:16, 4:4.

They divide into 11 separate predictions and involve 21 of the epistle's 105 verses, or some 20%.

1. I Pet 1:3–6, 5:1 (5 vv.): the believers' "living hope . . . to obtain an inheritance [cf. Eph 1:18] which is imperishable and undefiled, reserved in heaven for you . . . a salvation ready to be revealed in the last time," 1:3–5. The *salvation* of which Peter speaks is

another aspect of that patrimony . . . the kingdom . . . which is the object of hope, here regarded as future. . . . In the present passage it is used of the great final deliverance, not from the wrath of God (4:18), but from the siege of Satan, from persecution and sorrow [cf. vv. 9–10]. . . . The deliverance is ready to be revealed in the day when Jesus Christ Himself will be revealed (1:7, 13).[7]

So Peter too, 5:1, is "a partaker of the glory that is to be revealed." Fulfillment (per. 16): the bliss of the future Messianic kingdom, as in Ex. prophecy No. 49; cf. Heb 10:36.

2. I Pet 1:7, 13; 2:12; 4:13; *5:4a* (4 vv.): "the revelation, *āpokálupsis,* of Jesus Christ," 1:7, 13; "the revelation of His glory," 4:13; and 5:4 speaks of "the time when the Chief Shepherd appears." In 2:12 Peter hopes that the Gentiles may be able to glorify God "in the day of visitation," i.e. in "that *āpokálupsis,* which occupies so large a place in St. Peter's thought."[8] Fulfillment (per. 15): the Lord's second coming, as in Ps. prophecy No. 5.

3. I Pet 1:10–11a (2 vv.): a backward reference about how "the prophets prophesied of the grace that would come to you. . . . The Spirit of Christ within them predicted the sufferings of Christ." Most prominent would be Isaiah's oracles of the suffering Servant. Fulfillment (per. 13): as in Isa. No. 99, and compare note 15 under Acts No. 19 and note 8, pp. 4–5.

4. I Pet 1:*11b*–12 (1 v.): their further prophecy (see No. 3, preceding), as they foresaw that the suffering Christ would have "glories to follow." Fulfillment (per. 13): as in Isa No. 103 (53:10b), on His resurrection and beholding a spiritual "seed"; cf. I Pet 1:12.

5. I Pet 2:8 (1 v. fig.): citation of Isa 8:14, about the "stumbling" of Israel. Fulfillment (per. 7): Judah's fall in 586, under Isa. No. 5 (cf. its note 29), though the passage is used by Peter to illustrate the fate of those who reject Christ.

6. I Pet 2:10 (1 v.): citation of Hos. No. 4 (1:10, 2:23), on the engrafting of Peter's Gentile readers (per. 14) into the people of God.

7. ICC, pp. 100–102.
8. Ibid., p. 138, though this source takes note also of an alternative (and non-predictive) possibility: "in the day of their conversion." Cf. IB, XII:113, "any time of crisis when God visits men in judgment or in blessing; not necessarily the Judgment Day."

7. I Pet 2:22 (1 v.): citation of Isa. No. 102 (53:9b) on the sinlessness of the Servant of Yahweh, as fulfilled (per. 13) in Jesus, whose purity led to His honored burial.

8. I Pet 3:20–21 (2 vv., typ.): discussion of the ark, riding safely through the water of Noah's flood, as a type of salvation through baptism. Fulfillment (per. 13): as in Gen. No. 13.

9. I Pet 4:5, 18 (2 vv.): that sinners "shall give account to Him who is ready to judge the living and the dead," v. 5.[9] V. 18 then asks rhetorically,[10] that if judgment is already beginning with Christian believers, "What will become of the godless man and the sinner?" Fulfillment (per. 17): not simply God's continuous judging, as in 1:17, but the final judgment for the lost, as in Ps. prophecy No. 1.

10. I Pet 4:7 (1 v.): "But, *de* [ASV], the end of all things is at hand." The conjunction that Peter employs is a significant one: "The 'but' introduces a new train of thought, suggested by the mention of the judgment"[11] (v. 5, No. 9, preceding), but not identical with it. Note also the verb, "to be at hand"; for while the final judgment possesses extended antecedents, "the second coming of Christ [who would serve] as judge was regarded an imminent."[12] Fulfillment (per. 15): as in Lk. No. 47, the imminence of His appearing.

11. I Pet 5:4b (1 v.): church elders are encouraged to faithful service; for when Christ reigns, "you will receive the unfading crown of glory"; cf. II Tim 4:8 (listed under 1:12). Fufilllment (per. 17): the judgment of the saved, as in Job No. 5.

9. V. 6, which follows, speaks of the gospel's being preached to the dead, so that though "judged in the flesh" they might "live in the spirit." But the passage does not seem to be predictive or to be related to the final judgment. The event of their being *judged* lies antecedent to the time when they are to *live* (ICC, p. 170; cf. RSV) and may refer simply to death in the flesh, specifically to that of the sinners in Noah's day who, preceding the flood, were trapped in the "prison" of sin in the doomed world (3:19–20). Thus "the deluge is spoken of as a judgment," ibid., p. 171. Even so the Spirit of Christ would seem to have preached through Noah. (II Pet 2:5) to these, the potentially dead of I Pet 4:6, in the unfulfilled hope that they might at least *live in the spirit* "in preparation for the final judgment," WC, p. 105; this is according to the traditional view of Augustine and others. Yet most liberal writers prefer the view that Peter was teaching a "second chance" for those who had already died, ICC, p. 162.

10. Quoting the language of Prov 11:31, which, however, applies more to God's contemporaneous acts of providence.

11. ICC, p. 172.

12. Cent, *General Epistles*, p. 244.

II PETER

The Second Epistle of Peter ranks next to Revelation and Hebrews as being the NT book that is the most concerned, proportionately, with God's predictions of the future. Of its brief 61 verses, 25, or 41%, are involved in prophecy. These refer to 11 separate forecasts, commencing in the latter part of ch. 1 and continuing on throughout the remainder of the epistle.

The internal testimonies of this letter are clear about its Petrine authorship: by direct assertion (1:1), by statements that require the apostle as their writer (e.g. 1:14, 16), and by association with the indisputably genuine book of I Peter (3:1). Nevertheless, the authenticity of II Peter is today more denied than that of any other book in the NT. It cannot be proved to have been quoted by church fathers prior to A.D. 200. Origen and Jerome reported that there had been some hesitancy about its reception, though they both accepted its canonical validity. II Peter's literary quality and fluency of Greek are below the style of I Peter, though the latter may have been affected by the apostle's having written "through Silvanus [Silas] our faithful brother" (I Pet 5:12). Ch. 2 of II Peter seems to be indebted to the briefer Epistle of Jude,[1] though with a suggested date of 61 for Jude's work[2] this need not affect the genuinely Petrine origin of II Peter. Finally, the general tone of the epistle is one of debate and sternness, while that of I Peter is marked more by encouragement and comfort,[3] though this contrast may be accounted for by the differing content of the two writings; compare, e.g., Paul's stern Galatian epistle with his words of appreciation to the Philippians. Guthrie has concluded, "There is no evidence from any part of the early Church that this Epistle was ever rejected as spurious";[4] and his detailed defense of Petrine authorship that follows provides a solid ground for its acceptance.[5]

Peter's second letter is presumably directed to the same Christians of Asia Minor as was the first (II Pet 3:1).[6] Its purpose is to warn these readers against false teachers, and particularly against those who would question the reality of Christ's second coming. Its message is summarized by the key passage of 3:3–4, that they should "know this . . . that in the

---

1. Guthrie, however, raises the possibility of an opposite relationship: "If Peter . . . shares the contents of his letter with Jude, suggesting that the latter use the passages about the false teachers in a letter to be sent to his own constituency . . . all the phenomena would be accounted for," *Hebrews to Revelation: NT Introduction*, p. 247.
2. See below, introduction to Jude.
3. Contrast the reference to Noah in I Pet 3:20 with that in II Pet 3:6—yet note also II Pet 2:5.
4. Op. cit., p. 142.
5. Ibid., pp. 143–171.
6. Though cf. Guthrie's hesitancy in this matter, ibid., pp. 171–172.

last days mockers will come with their mocking, following after their own lusts, and saying, 'Where is the promise of His coming?' " The book falls then into 3 parts, corresponding to its 3 chapters: 1, a plea for godliness; 2, the warning against teachers of falsehood; and 3, an assurance about the Lord's return. Its date belongs at the close of Peter's life, just before his anticipated execution (1:14) by Nero in 64. This is confirmed by its allusions to the passing on of the apostles (3:2) and to a corpus of completed Pauline epistles (v. 15).

1. II Pet 1:14–15 (2 vv., fig.): in v. 14 Peter predicts "that the laying aside of my earthly dwelling—my departure [v. 15]—is imminent, as also our Lord Jesus Christ has made clear to me."[7] Lenski comments, "We know nothing about when, how, and where the Lord made this indication to Peter about his dying soon . . . [except that] this letter must be dated shortly before Peter's end."[8] Fulfillment (per. 14): Peter's death, as impending in 64, during the Neronian persecutions.

2. II Pet *1:19a*; 3:9, 15 (2 vv., fig.): that Christians are to follow the lamp of the prophetic word "until the day dawns," 1:19; cf. Peter's subsequent stress in 3:9, "The Lord is not slow about His promise [of coming again, v. 4; cf. No. 8, below] but is patient toward you, wishing . . . for all to come to repentance." As he states in v. 15, they are to "regard the patience of our Lord to be salvation." Fulfillment (per. 15): His second coming, as in Ps. prophecy No. 5.

3. II Pet 1:19b (1 v. fig.): the apostle enjoins faithfulness, until the daytime of Christ's coming arrives (v. 19a, see No. 2, preceding) "and the morning star arises in your hearts," meaning, "when the signs of the approaching Day are manifest to Christians,"[9] with an accompanying joy in believers' hearts.[10] Lenski adds: "The best commentary is Luke 21:28, 'Straighten up and lift up your heads, because your redemption is drawing near.' These hearts will apprehend what is happening."[11] That is, what had once been commanded in Luke as a response for believers is now actually predicted in II Peter. Fulfillment (per. 15): the joyful hope of Christians at the signs of Jesus' return.

4. II Pet 2:1–3a (3 vv.): "There will be false teachers among you, who will secretly introduce destructive heresies, even denying the Master who bought them . . . many will follow . . . and because of them the way of truth will be maligned." Fulfillment (per. 14): apostasy before Christ's return, as in Lk. No. 59.

---

7. NBC, p. 1145, considers this passage as a reference to the Lord's revelation to Peter in John 21:18. But on that occasion there was no indication about the apostle's death as imminent but rather its opposite: it was something that would occur only when he grew old.
8. *The Interpretation of I-II Peter*, p. 282.
9. ExGkT, V:132.
10. ICC, p. 269.
11. Op. cit., p. 295.

5. II Pet 2:*1b, 3b,* 9–10, 12–13; *3:7b* (4 vv.): an oracle against the leaders of this apostasy within the church (No. 4, preceding) and against ungodly men in general (3:7), "Their punishment is not idle, and their destruction (2:3) . . . [they are kept] under punishment for the day of judgment (v. 9) . . . suffering wrong as the wages of wrong doing" (v. 13). Compare similar ideas, though not in the same words, in Jude 4, 15. Fulfillment (per. 17): for though the unrighteous are *under punishment* (II Pet 2:9) both in life now and in hell after death, there yet remains the final judgment for the lost, as in Ps. prophecy No. 1.

6. II Pet 2:4 [see Jude No. 2 (v. 6)] (1 v.): final judgment of demons.

7. II Pet 2:17 [see Jude No. 4 (v. 13)] (1 v. fig.): the lake of fire.

8. II Pet 3:3–5, 16–17 (5 vv.): Peter predicts a particular aspect to the future apostasy (2:1, No. 4, above), "In the last days mockers will . . . say, 'Where is the promise of His coming? All continues just as it was from the beginning of creation," 3:4; cf. vv. 16–17 on the way in which they distort the teachings of the Pauline epistles (e.g. in II Thess 2:3, 13–14) concerning the patience of Christ regarding His return (cf. II Pet 3:9, under 1:19a, No. 2, above, and v. 12a, No. 10, below). Fulfillment (per 14): contemporaneous denials of the reality of Christ's second coming.

9. II Pet 3:7a, 10–12 (4 vv.): "The present heavens and earth by His word are being reserved for fire, kept for the day of judgment," v. 7. So v. 10 adds that on the day of the Lord,[12] which will come upon the unprepared as a thief,[13] "the heavens will pass away with a roar, and the elements will be destroyed with intense heat, and the earth and its works will be burned up." Fulfillment (per. 17): the passing away of the present order, as in Gen. No. 14.

10. II Pet *3:12a,* that believers may be "hastening the coming of the day of God." Fulfillment (per. 14): present Christian activity that influences the time of the Lord's return, e.g. prayer, Mt 6:10; cf. I Cor 16:22. Or again, "The universal proclamation of the gospel of the kingdom must precede the end, and will presumably hasten it (Mt 24:14; cf. Acts 3:19). Conversely, the sins of men delay the coming (II Pet 3:9)."[14]

11. II Pet 3:13–14 (2 vv.): "According to His promise we are looking for new heavens and a new earth, in which righteousness dwells." Fulfillment (per. 18): the New Jerusalem, as in Isa. No. 74.

12. Here used, as in the references listed under II Tim 1:12, not for Christ's return, but for its climax in the final judgment.

13. The description of the day's coming *as a thief,* i.e. unexpectedly, must be understood in its context of warning (cf. I Thess 5:3–5); "It will, by no means, be unexpected, except for those who have willfully made themselves ignorant of it, and for whom in their ungodliness it brings destruction," J. B. Payne, *The Imminent Appearing of Christ,* p. 94.

14. IB, XII:203.

I JOHN

In contrast with the surrounding epistles of Peter and Jude, the three letters of John are not deeply involved in the subjects of prophecy. II John does rise to a 15% proportion of predictive matter, but III John contains none at all. Despite its traditional title, I John is the only NT epistle, other than Hebrews, in which the text makes no direct claim about authorship; and the writer of II and III John introduces himself simply as "the elder." But all three are closely related in both literary style and doctrinal teaching to the fourth Gospel, whose existence they apparently assume (cf. I John 1:1 with John 1:1).[1] As a result, a conclusion of apostolic, Johannine authenticity for the larger volume, and of its composition at Ephesus in ca. A.D. 90[2] carries with it the corollary proposition of similar circumstances of origin for the smaller works.

I John seems to have been written as an encyclical letter to the aged apostle's "little children" (2:1 etc.), who were "beloved" in the Lord (3:2 etc.) and were probably the members of various congregations in the Roman province of Asia Minor, for which Ephesus served as the capital. In his First Epistle, John combats the rising heresy of Gnosticism,[3] with its denial of the true incarnation of God in the humanity of Jesus Christ (cf. 2:22, 4:1–3). The apostle's message is summed up in 5:13, "These things have I written to you who believe in the name of the Son of God, in order that you may know that you have eternal life"; cf. John 20:31 as a key verse for his Gospel. The epistle is not tightly organized; but it moves along through themes of fellowship (chs. 1–2), of adoption as God's children (ch. 3), of love (ch. 4), and of faith (ch. 5). Its prophetic content is limited to four subjects in chs. 2–4, which involve 6 vv. out of a total of 105 for the entire book, or 6%.

1. I John 2:18, 4:3 (2 vv.): "Just as you heard that antichrist is coming, even now many antichrists have arisen," 2:18. The term "Antichrist," which appears here for the first time in Scripture, "denotes one great enemy of and rival to Christ, probably to be identified with the 'man of sin' of II Thess 2:3, who has yet to be revealed but who has many forerunners."[4] These latter include the heretics of John's own day (vv. 19, 22; cf. 4:3), though their existence by no means denies the reality of the one supreme manifestation who was yet to come. Fulfillment (per. 14): the Antichrist, as in Dan. prophecy No. 14.

1. Cf. the evidence presented in D. Guthrie, *Hebrews to Revelation: NT Introduction*, pp. 198–205, 211–212.
2. See above, introduction to John.
3. See above, introduction to Colossians, on one of its earlier forms.
4. NIC, *James & John*, p. 170.

2. I John 2:28, 3:2 (2 vv.): "Abide in Him, so that if He should appear [= 3:2], we may have confidence and not shrink away from Him in shame at His coming, *pārousía*," 2:28. 3:2 adds that "We shall see Him, just as He is." Fulfillment (per. 15): Christ's return, as in Ps. prophecy No. 5.

3. I John 3:2b, 3 (1 v.): when believers see the resurrected Christ at His Parousia (v. 2a, No. 2 preceding), "we shall be like Him," v. 2b; cf. Phil 3:21. Since, moreover, the Christian "has this hope fixed on Him," v. 3, he purifies himself now as well. Fulfillment (per. 15): the believers' glorification when the Lord appears, as in Rom No. 9.

4. I John 4:17 (1 v.): "We may have confidence in the day of judgment." Fulfillment (per. 17): the final judgment, but of the saved, as in Job No. 5.

II JOHN

The Second Epistle of John parallels the First in its assignment to the city of Ephesus at about the year 90.[1] It is addressed without further clarification "to the chosen lady and her children" (v. 1); and some would seek to render the term "lady" as a (rare) proper noun, *Kyria.* Yet the apostle's subsequent references to this "lady's" being loved by all who know the truth (v. 1), to the fact that "some of her children" were walking in truth (v. 4), and to the greetings that are sent her by "the children of your chosen sister" (v. 13) suggest that he was using figurative language to describe communications from the church at Ephesus to some nearby "sister" congregation (cf. a somewhat similar figure in II Cor 11:2).[2] The purpose of the letter, like that of I John, is to combat those who were promoting heresy, and specifically to preserve separation by the Christian community from fellowship in their evil deeds (v. 11). The thought of the epistle's one main paragraph (vv. 4–11) may be summed up by the words of v. 6, "This is love, that we walk according to His commandments." The predictive content of II John limits itself to two prophetic allusions in vv. 7–8—2 verses out of the book's 13, or some 15%.

1. II John 7 (1 v.): of deceivers in his own day, John says, "This is . . . the antichrist." That is, "Each of these, in his place, [is] a representative and *'praecursor Antichristi'* ";[3] cf. I John 2:18. Fulfillment (per. 14): the Antichrist, as in Dan. prophecy No. 14.

---

1. See above, introduction to I John.
2. Though cf. Guthrie's hesitancy on this matter, *Hebrews to Revelation: NT Introduction,* pp. 213–215.
3. H. Alford, *The Greek Testament,* IV:B, 218.

2. II John 8 (1 v.): "Watch yourselves . . . that you may receive a full reward," meaning, ". . . all the fulness of glory and honor when the crown of righteousness (II Tim 4:8), the crown of glory (I Pet 5:4), shall at last rest on their brows."[4] Fulfillment (per. 17): the judgment of the saved, as in Job No. 5; and see the above-cited verses (II Tim, listed under No. 1).

4. NIC, *James & John*, p. 230.

JUDE

The last of the general epistles is that of "Jude . . . [the] brother of James" (v. 1). Since the writer distinguishes himself from the group of the apostles (v. 17), he would not appear to be identifiable with that "Judas [the son] of James" who was one of the original twelve (Lk 6:16, Acts 1:13). He is most likely to be equated with Jude, less prominent than James, but still one of the half-brothers of the Lord (Mt 13:55, Mk 6:3).[1] The very obscurity of the position of Jude within the early church is an argument, indeed, for the authenticity of this ascription. His epistle is addressed generally "to those who are the called . . . and kept for Christ Jesus" (Jude 1); and its date, while problematic, might approximate that of Paul's letter to the Colossians in 61,[2] since the same sort of false teachers seem to be opposed (cf. v. 4 with Col 2:8–10). Shortly thereafter, much of Jude's letter was incorporated by Peter into ch. 2 of his own second epistle.[3]

Jude's purpose is to warn his readers against false leaders within the church, men who were marked by a moral laxness and by a doctrinal denial of Jesus Christ as Lord (v. 4). His message may thus be summed up in the words that follow his introductory greeting of vv. 1–2, "Contend earnestly for the faith which was once for all delivered to the saints" (v. 3, as a key verse). Apart from its introduction and a conclusion in vv. 24–25, the book consists of but 2 paragraphs: vv. 5–16, in admonition against the teachers of falsehood; and vv. 17–23, in exhortation to the believers in Christ. For a book with but a single chapter, Jude contains a considerable amount of prophetic matter: no fewer than 8 distinct predictions,[4] which involve 10 of the book's 25 verses, or 40% of the whole.

1. See above, p. 578.
2. Because it assumes the body of orthodox doctrine, "the faith" (v. 3), some critics would remove its date of composition to the close of the 1st century; but this would be too late for one who was probably only slightly younger than Jesus Himself; cf. similar objections that have been raised against the Pastorals in the introduction to I Timothy.
3. See above, introduction to II Peter.
4. Cf. the 10 that are found in Obadiah's slightly briefer work.

1. Jude 4 (1 v.): that the leaders of the apostasy in the church are "marked out for this condemnation"; cf. the passages listed under II Pet 2:1b. "Jude is thinking of the condemnation pronounced against men who live as the false brethren lived."[5] Fulfillment (per. 17): the final judgment of the lost, as in Ps. prophecy No. 1.

2. Jude 6 (II Pet 2:4) (1 v.): that fallen angels, now committed to eternal bonds, are reserved "for the judgment of the great day." Fulfillment (per. 17):[6] as in Mt No. 24 (8:29), a final judgment for fallen angels.[7]

3. Jude 12 (1 v., typ.): reference to "your love feasts." These *āgápai,* or "evening meals partaken of by Christians, [were] either accompanied or followed by the Eucharist."[8] They would seem therefore to have been types, even as it was, of the future Messianic feast (per. 15), as in Lk. No. 69.

4. Jude 13 (II Pet 2:17) (1 v., fig.): for those who would become false teachers within the church (Jude 4), "black darkness has been reserved forever." Fulfillment (per. 18): as in II Sam. No. 20, the fate of the lost, pictured elsewhere as "the lake of fire" (Rev 20:15), though here viewed under a different figure.

5. Jude 14–15 (2 vv.): as a further illustration of judgment (cf. vv. 5–7, 11), Jude records how "Enoch, in the seventh generation from Adam, prophesied, saying, 'Behold, the Lord came[9] with His holy ones, to execute judgment upon all, and to convict all the ungodly of all their ungodly deeds ... and harsh things spoken against Him.' " While suggesting the congruity of this prophecy with the demonstrably righteous character of Enoch (Gen 5:22, 24), the OT contains no preserved words of this early patriarch. The above citation is taken rather from the pseudepigraphic work of I Enoch, 1:9, the authenticity of this one verse being assured by the authority of Jude, though the way by which a genuine oracle of such ancient origin found its way into the normally spurious work of I Enoch is unknown. Fulfillment (per. 1): as in Gen. No. 11, the punishment of the flood.[10]

5. NBC, p. 1162. Others see no eschatological prediction at this point, e.g. IB, XII:324, "*This condemnation* refers back to v. 3 to the determined opposition the errorists will meet from those who will *contend for the faith.*" But cf. Jude's subsequent predictions in vv. 6 and 13, No. 2 and 4, below.

6. The somewhat similar thought of I Cor 6:3 (*q.v.*) seems to apply more to the previous, millennial era, per. 16.

7. Pentecost suggests that this judgment might be associated with the final judgment of Satan (Rev 20:10) and so would occur just before the other elements of the great throne judgment, *Things to Come,* p. 422, though see above, introduction to Matthew, and note 28 of that section.

8. NBC, p. 1164.

9. "The past tense is that of prophetic vision," WC, *Peter & Jude,* p. 214.

10. "The prophecy, as appears from the application made of it by St. Jude [cf. v. 4, on the final judgment, No. 1, above] ... might be understood even of the final manifestation of the Lord to execute judgment. But from the time and circumstances in which it was spoken, there can be no doubt that it pointed more immediately to the clouds of wrath which were already gathering around antediluvian sinners, and that when these burst in the deluge there was the ... realization of the Lord's threatened coming to judgment," P. Fairbairn, *The Interpretation of Prophecy,* p. 445.

6. Jude *14b,* God's coming (cf. No. 5, preceding) "with many thousands of His holy ones." Fulfillment (per. 1): an otherwise unrevealed angelic participation with Yahweh in His overwhelming of the primeval earth by means of the flood.

7. Jude 17–19 (3 vv.): Jude's reference to "words that were spoken beforehand by the apostles, 'In the last time there shall be mockers, following after their own ungodly lusts . . . who cause divisions, worldly minded.'" The phraseology of "mockers" parallels that which is found in II Pet 3:3–4; but there the skepticism centers on Christ's second coming, while here it is more in matters of conduct, of the sort about which Paul uttered warnings. Fulfillment (per. 14): moral decline prior to the Lord's return, as in II Tim No. 4 (3:1).

8. Jude 24 (1 v.): Christ "is able to make you stand in the presence of His glory, blameless, with great joy"; moreover, "The *glory* spoken of is that which is to be manifested at the coming of Christ, 'in his own glory, and that of the Father, and of the holy angels' (Lk 9:26)."[11] Compare I Pet 1:3. Fulfillment (per. 16): millennial joy and praise, as in Isa. No. 46.

11. Camb, *Peter & Jude*, p. 215.

REVELATION

"Behold, He is coming with the clouds, and every eye will see Him . . . ," Rev 1:7. With this key verse at the heart of its opening chapter, the last book of the Bible takes up its "revelation" of events surrounding the return of Jesus Christ and of God's all-embracing conclusion to the course of world history. This writing stands in a class by itself among the books of the NT. It is the only volume in Scripture's newer portion that is primarily devoted to the subject of prophecy; and it corresponds, somewhat, to the major and minor prophets that form much of the OT. John's recorded visions constitute, moreover, the only full book of NT apocalyptic:[1] its very title in Greek is *āpokálupsis,* "The Apocalypse," or *unveiling,* a term which became rendered into English by the Latinized noun Revelation. Apocalyptic symbolism marks its every page, and it constitutes a major parallel to the OT's climactic Book of Zechariah.[2] Each maintains the function of bringing together at the close of its respective testament the various facets of apocalyptic that had appeared in earlier portions, e.g. in the NT, Christ's apocalyptic

1. On the nature of this category of Biblical literature, see above, pp. 85–89.
2. See above, introduction to Zechariah.

statements in Mt 24–25, or Paul's in I Thess 4–5 and II Thess 1–2. The book also parallels Zechariah's cyclic structure, which is so characteristic of Biblical apocalyptic (see below). The importance of "The Apocalypse" for establishing God's final word to the long course of His progressive revelation, and for providing the Lord's comprehensive solution to the evils, fears, and perplexities of today's uncertain world, cannot be overestimated. As the Spirit of inspiration affirmed in its salutation, "Blessed is he who reads and those who hear the words of the prophecy, and heed the things which are written in it; for the time is near," 1:3 (cf. 22:7).

The Revelation of Jesus Christ (1:1) stands without question as the most highly predictive book in the NT. Though less than two-fifths the size of Matthew, its 56 separate prophecies occupy 256 verses; and this is out of a book whose total amounts to but 404. The proportion is over 63%; compare Matthew's slightly larger sum of 278 predictive verses, which however, come out of a total of 1,067 and amount to 26%. Prophecies occur in all of Revelation's 22 chapters, with the exception of ch. 12; for here its second major chronological cycle commences, by reverting to events, then past, in the life of Jesus. As might be expected, its proportion of symbolic prediction ranks higher than for any other book of the NT; and its total of 24 symbolic prophecies, out of the 56, exceeds even the largest figure found in the OT, Daniel's 20 out of 58.

Though expressly stated to have been authored by Jesus Christ's "bondservant John," i.e. by "John, your brother and fellow-partaker in the tribulation and kingdom which are in Jesus" (1:1, 9; cf. 1:4, 22:8), the difference in style and content between Revelation and the other Johannine writings has raised questions over the identity of its writer. Many modern commentators state with assurance that this author could not have been John the apostle[3] and adduce the possibility of some other prophet in Asia Minor who may have borne the name of John.[4] Yet the influence of Johannine language upon the Apocalypse has been widely recognized;[5] the writer speaks forth with an authority difficult to imagine for one who was less than an apostle (cf. 1:11, 19; 22:18–19); the manner by which he designates himself simply as John, in that very geographical area where the apostle was then ministering, renders any other identification unlikely; and 2nd-century patristic testimony speaks clearly of the Revelation as composed by "John, a disciple of the Lord."[6] This concept of authorship neither needs to be, nor ought to be, surrendered. It is true that such well-established Johannine themes as God's love, truth, light, and life do not enter into the

---

3. Cf. JB, NT p. 428, "It is impossible to identify the author of Revelation as it stands with the author of the Johannine literature."

4. ICC, I:xliii. On the theory of "John the elder," cf. the discussion in the introduction to John's Gospel, note 3, above.

5. Cf. D. Guthrie, *Hebrews to Revelation: NT Introduction*, pp. 258–260.

6. Irenaeus, *Against Heresies*, IV, 14, 2, etc.; and many others, from Justin Martyr (cf. his *Dialogue with Trypho*, 81) onward.

primary content of the Apocalypse; but this is probably because of two considerations. One relates to the nature of the subject under discussion; for the Revelation is closely tied up with earlier apocalyptic writings, particularly those from the OT; and it is designed to emphasize God's sovereignty over the nations, with the accompanying elements of divine wrath, cataclysm, and judgment. Though John, moreover, became best remembered as the apostle of love, particularly in his later years, still his title of Boanerges, a "son of thunder" (Mk 3:17), must not be disregarded, particularly in his earlier periods; cf. the fiery spirit of John as indicated by Lk 9:54 or Mk 9:38. The other consideration is, indeed, this matter of date.

The Apocalypse was composed to inspire endurance against Roman persecution (Rev 17:6, 18) on the part of Christians from the churches of Asia Minor (cf. 1:9–11, 14:12). John himself had been banished to the island of Patmos, SW of Ephesus; and his rallying cry is for the Asian saints to "be faithful until death" and so receive the Lord's crown (2:10). Particularly must they resist Rome's demand for the worship of the emperor (13:4, 12, 15; 14:9, 11). History records two such periods of state persecution during the lifetime of John: one under Nero, during the years 64–68, and the other under Domitian, 90–96. Patristic tradition asserts the later date. The extent of Rome's persecution, particularly in Asia Minor, together with the developing (or declining) condition of the seven churches of Asia (chs. 2–3), seems also to favor it, though this could apply to the earlier time as well. Yet the internal evidence, which is drawn from the predictions contained within the book itself, is more suited to the days of Nero. Unless John's reference in 11:1 to the (Jerusalem) temple be taken figuratively, this structure's mere existence would require a date before 70; the writer's silence in respect to the course of the Jewish War, and his *predictions* of its devastation and 3½-year duration in 11:2, suggest a date prior to the winter of 66; and his symbolical specification in 17:10 of the currently reigning Roman emperor as the sixth of this line of rulers accords most easily with the historical position of Nero.[7] 17:10 is, in fact, almost impossible to connect with Domitian, unless the five emperors that arose between 68 and 81 be omitted from the count. Unless one is therefore willing to assume that the Revelation consists at least partly of compilations of earlier materials (including the above),[8] or simply to "spiritualize" their application to a reference point that is other than historical,[9] it would appear logical, even in the face of ancient tradition and of what constitutes the majority vote of modern scholars, to maintain a Neronic situation, in about

7. See above, p. 50, though if the count is begun with Augustus rather than Caesar, it would bring the period down to Nero's successor; and "if so, the date of the vision is fixed at a time between June A.D. 68, and the 15th of January 69, when Galba was murdered," Camb, p. 105.

8. As in Cent, pp. 52, 56.

9. As in Guthrie, op. cit., p. 281.

65. This would place the Apocalypse a full quarter of a century before the other Johannine writings.

More than for any other portion of Scripture, the Book of Revelation has become a subject for differing interpretations. Its expositors divide themselves, in general, between the two lines of approach that have been identified above as "normal" and as "allegorized";[10] and even among the advocates of the former there still appear three distinguishable schools of thought. Allegorizing commentators may treat the Apocalypse according to principles of mystical interpretation, such as dominated the medieval church and go back to the time of Tyconius in 400,[11] or according to theories of liturgical, poetic, or dramatic literary forms, such as have been proposed by modern critics;[12] but all writers of this type unite upon reducing the book's "real" teaching to certain matters of timeless truth, or at least to interpretations that are devoid of concrete, historical specification. The three more "normal" schools would agree on the need for applying the visions, with all their undeniable symbolism, to actual situations in time; but the question then arises: Which time? Preterists, including many liberal interpreters, would limit the range of the book's applicability to the 1st Christian century. But this is a position which, when held with consistency, denies all modern relevance to John's predictions.[13] Historicalists, including the majority of Protestant interpreters up into the 19th century, discovered within the Revelation a full sweep of church history, often with amazing details on Mohammed, the papacy, Napoleon, etc. Yet whether living in the Middle Ages or in our own contemporaneous times, advocates of the historical school of interpretation seem always to discover the climax of prophecy in their own day—a sure proof of the illegitimacy of this approach, if it is to be one's exclusive method of Scriptural understanding.[14] Futurists, on the other hand, including many modern premillennialists, would relate the predictions of John's volume to events which have not yet occurred. When consistently applied, futurism treats even the details that are suggested about the seven churches of Asia as unfulfilled prophecies.[15]

An example by which to illustrate all four of these approaches may be taken from the section in Revelation 6 on "the four horsemen of the Apocalypse," the third of whom (vv. 5–6; see prediction No. 17, below) carries a pair of scales in his hand. By this symbol the preterist would com-

---

10. See above, p. 43.
11. Cf. H. B. Swete, *The Apocalypse of St. John*, pp. ccviii-ccx.
12. See Guthrie, op. cit., pp. 290–294.
13. See above, pp. 10–12, 120.
14. Cf. J. B. Payne, *The Imminent Appearing of Christ*, pp. 41–42.
15. This approach is treated by Wilbur M. Smith, in C. F. Pfeiffer and E. F. Harrison, eds., *The Wycliffe Bible Commentary*, p. 1499: "The seven churches of Asia will be reorganized and re-established at the end of the age, at which time the predictions concerning them will be fulfilled—a view wholly unnecessary and unreasonable."

prehend a famine in the days of ancient Rome; the historicalist would envisage famines throughout subsequent history, the futurist would have recourse to a famine during a not yet arrived "great tribulation"; while the allegorizer might think of some spiritual famine, of hunger for the word of God—or for almost anything else. This last feature indicates, indeed, the essential subjectivity and hence illegitimacy of allegorized interpretations, as has already been discussed.[16] As for the three former, for the "normal" interpretations, it is apparent that a rigorously consistent application of any one of the approaches leads to absurdity and to assertions that seem contrary to the mind of God's inspiring Spirit. In practice, most evangelical interpreters make some use of all three methods. Dispensational writers, for example, usually approach Rev 1 from a preterist viewpoint; they seek to find in the letters to the seven churches in chs. 2–3 an outline of the entire course of church history, naturally in seven periods;[17] and they then assign the remaining 19 chapters of the book to the future, commencing with an assumed rapture of the church in 4:1. But while the rigidity of such a division seems somewhat suspect, the principle of refusing to be bound to any single school of interpretation is a sound one. It is documented by the work of H. B. Swete, both in theory[18] and in practice—cf. his commentary as an illustration. That is to say, one should allow conclusions to be formed by the evidences that arise from each passage in respect to its own meaning. The result will then, of necessity, be one of mixed interpretations: largely futuristic, but with no small addition of matters understood to be of preterist import, where the data concerned is found to be more applicable to the original circumstances of the apostle John.

The structure of the Book of Revelation is marked by the same sort of cycles of prediction that appear elsewhere in the Bible's apocalyptic literature.[19] The fact of intentional repetition seems to be anticipated in John's vision in ch. 10, in the course of which he eats the little book (a scroll) that comes from the hand of an angel. On the basis of this, he is then told that he "must prophesy again concerning many peoples," v. 11. In other words, "After the 7th trumpet (11:15) a second prophecy will begin (12:1), in which the destinies of nations and their rulers will be yet more fully revealed."[20] Confidence over such a view on the Apocalypse's structure is strengthened by two further phenomena. First, there is the evidence of a close parallelism that exists between the content of the earlier half of the prophecy, as it concludes in the latter part of ch. 11, and the subject matter of its latter half, as it draws to an end in chs. 19–22.

16. See above, pp. 44–47.
17. C. Feinberg, *Premillennialism or Amillennialism?* pp. 84–85; or J. D. Pentecost, *Things to Come*, pp. 149–153, with a concluding chart.
18. Op. cit., pp. ccxviii–ccxix.
19. See above, pp. 86–87, 130–131.
20. Swete, op. cit., p. 132.

Compare:	which states that:	with:
11:15	"The seventh angel sounded . . . saying, 'The kingdom of the world has become the kingdom of our Lord, and of His Christ, and He will reign . . .' "	19:11, 16, 20
11:17	"Thou hast taken thy great power and hast begun to reign"	20:4, 6
11:18	"And the nations were enraged,	20:8
	and Thy wrath came,	20:9
	and the time came for the dead to be judged,	20:12
	and the time to give their reward to Thy servants . . .	21:3–4
	and to destroy those who destroy the earth."	21:8
11:19	"And the ark of His testament [KJV] appeared"; cf. the fulfillment of the concept of God's testamentary presence in	22:3

Second, there is the evidence of chronological sequence and of various duplications of ideas in the two halves of the book. Terry, for example, compares the seven plagues in Rev 8–9 with those in ch. 16 and concludes, "The striking resemblances between the two are such as to force a conviction that the terrible woes denoted by the trumpets are substantially identical with the plagues denoted by the vials of wrath."[21] The major units of the book may then be tabulated, in sequence, as shown in Table 12.

This is not to minimize the real differences between the content of chs. 1–11 and of 12–22 (cf. the irregularities in the first two columns in Table 12) or to deny the appearance of those other references (cf. the last column) through which a given item of prophecy may be introduced not simply in two, but perhaps in three, or even more passages; compare the announcement of Christ's eschatological appearing (listed under C in Table 12) in 6:16, 8:1, and in 14:14, but then also in 1:7 and 19:11.

Analyzed in more detail, the book as a whole may be outlined as follows:[22]

Prologue (1:1–8)
Preface (1:1–3) This prophecy is revealed to John from Christ via an angel. It must be carried out soon. Blessings on those giving attention.
Summary (1:4–8) Greetings to the seven churches in Christ our Savior. He is the focus of history and is coming back to the earth.

Introduction (1:9–20) John's vision of Christ in heaven. By His death, Christ controls death. John is commissioned to write.

I. The First Cycle (chs. 2–11)
   A. Exhortation for John's time, about A.D. 65 (chs. 2–3).[23]
        The letters to the seven churches of western Asia Minor.

21. *Biblical Hermeneutics,* pp. 319–320; cf. Table 12, below.
22. Payne, op. cit., pp. 170–176; cf. *Theology of the Older Testament,* pp. 532–536.
23. 1:4, 9 sets chs. 1–3 as referring to John's time. The messages to the churches exhibit eternally valid principles, but they give no indication of being predictions of any other periods.

TABLE 12
A Chronological Outline of the Events in Revelation

Major References			
1st cycle *chs. 1-11*	*2nd cycle* *chs. 12-22*	*Events*[24]	*Other References (inserted in Rev)*
A. John's Own Time			
	12-13	Christ's birth and ascension; Satan is cast to earth but persecutes the church in Roman empire	14:8-13
1-3		John, imprisoned on Patmos, writes to the 7 churches	10-11:2; 22:6-21
		Fall of the Roman empire, A.D. 476	17-19:5
B. General Matters Continuing Today			
	12:17	Satan continues to persecute the church	
4-6:11		God in heaven; aggression, war, famine, death, and martyrs on earth (the part = "the great tribulation")	7:9-17 11:3-10
C. God's Wrath, Immediately Followed by Christ's Second Coming			
6:12-7:8	15-16:9	The saints are "sealed" so as not to be hurt; then comes a great earthquake and 4 universal disasters	8:2-13
6:16, 8:1	14:14	Christ's glorious second coming	1:7; 19:11
	14:1-7	The first resurrection (the saved dead) and the	20:4-6
	14:15-16	rapture of the living church to be with Him	11:11-12; 19:6-10
D. God's Wrath Against the Unrepentant After Christ's Coming			
9	16:10-21	The last 3 woes: Jerusalem suffers, but the	
11:13-15	19:11-21	Antichrist is destroyed by Jesus at Armageddon	14:17-20
E. Christ's Reign on Earth and the Final Events			
11:16-17	20:1-6	The Lord's millennial kingdom	
11:18	20:7-15	The final rebellion; the final resurrection (including the lost) and the final judgment	
11:19	21-22:5	The new heaven and the new earth	

24. The above position is that of historical *premillennialism* as held by the early church (Payne, op. cit., pp. 12-26), "premillennial" meaning that Christ's coming (Part C) precedes the millennial kingdom (Part E); see above, pp. 46, 105-107.

This contrasts with: *amillennialism*, held by the Reformation church (inherited from Roman Catholicism), which believes that the church (Part B), either as is found on earth or in heaven, is the kingdom referred to in 20:1-6 (Part E), so that there would be no future earthly kingdom; and with *postmillennialism*, held by most 18th- and 19th-century Protestants, which believed that the millennium came between B and C; Christ's coming (Part C) would be after the church had "brought in the kingdom" (two world wars killed this optimism).

This also contrasts with two modern forms of premillennialism: *pretribulationism*, introduced by J. N. Darby and Plymouth Brethrenism about 1830, places the tribulation as future (as if = God's wrath, Parts C-D) and not potentially present (B) and divides the first resurrection and Christ's coming into 2: one for the church before the tribulation (end of B), another for Jews after the tribulation; and with *post-tribulationism*, which places the tribulation future (between Parts B and C), so that the rapture is no longer an imminent hope. See above, pp. 58-59.

B. General matters continuing today (4–6:11).[25] God's glory in heaven (4). Christ, the sacrificed Lamb, receives the roll of the elect, *cf.* 13:8 (5). Successive scenes appear as Christ breaks the roll's seals, before its reading at the last judgment; cf. 20:12 (6:1–11).

Seals 1–5: aggression, war, famine, death, and martyrdom.

C. God's wrath immediately preceding Christ's coming (6:12– ch. 7).

Seal 6: physical phenomena as Christ is about to appear (6:12– 17).[26] Just previously, certain members of the Israel of God are placed under special protection (7:1–8).[27]

[Reversion to seal 5; cf. 6:11: the saints triumph, though killed in the great tribulation that immediately precedes God's wrath; cf. Mt 24:29 (7:9–11).]

D. God's wrath immediately following Christ's coming, the "three woes" (8–11:15) Seal 7, at Christ's appearing, suspends the wrath for ½ hour (8:1).

[Reversion to the events of seal 6: the physical phenomena are elaborated as 4 angels sound the first four trumpets (8:2–13); see Table 13.]

Woes 1–2, the 5th and 6th trumpet angels, terrible war, preparations and mobilization via the Euphrates River (9).[28]

[Back to A: John's ministry resumed (10–11:2).[29] John is forbidden to reveal certain things; the end comes as prophesied (10:1–7). He is commissioned for further speaking (10:8–11). Jerusalem shall fall after 3½ years of destruction, A.D. 66–70 (?) (11:1–2).]

---

25. 4:1 commences the section after John's time, but 5:10 shows that the kingdom on earth has not yet been set up (so the NAS and RSV; manuscript differences provide the less likely ASV reading). 6:11, on the saints' souls in heaven, still applies at present, the climax of persecution being called "the great tribulation," 7:14.

26. Cf. Mt 24:29–31. Seal 6 is just before Christ's return, the same day, 6:17.

27. 7:3–4; the 144,000 appear to be identical with the same number in 14:1–5, a chosen youth group of the church, the Israel of God, Gal 6:16. Their sealing, as first fruits, 14:4, is symbolical of the protection for believers from the coming wrath of God, Lk 21:36. It must precede the wrath of the 6th seal, which answers the prayers of the saints in the 5th seal, 6:10, hence the reversion to describe the saints killed in the great tribulation; see above, p. 182, note 188.

28. The 5th and 6th trumpets, with war and preparations for Armageddon, presuppose Christ's visible presence as the One opposed. 9:5, 10: they extend five months into the millennium. 10:6, no more "delay": the 7th trumpet will finish world history as it is now known.

29. These verses seem to return to John's time: take courage from what has so far been revealed! 10:11 shows John's immediate responsibility. 11:1 suggests that Rev was written before Jerusalem's fall in 70, with v. 2 referring to the impending Jewish War and sieges.

TABLE 13
The 6th and 7th Seals, as Elaborated in the Trumpets and Bowls of Revelation

Seal	Trumpet	Bowl	Nature	Reference	Time
1			Conquests	Rev 6:2	
2			War	6:4	The
3			Famine	6:6	present
4			Death	6:8	age
5			Souls in heaven	6:9	
A great earthquake				6:12, 8:5, 11:13, 16:18	
	1	1	Thunder and hail	6:14, 8:7	
			Sores on men (bowl)	16:2	5 minutes (?)[30]
	2	2	The sea to blood	8:8, 16:3	5 minutes
6	3	3	Waters poisoned	6:13, 8:10, 16:4	(with No. 2 ?)[30]
	4	4	The sun affected	6:12, 8:12, 16:8	5 minutes
			Total time of God's		
			wrath so far,		15 minutes (?)
The appearing of Christ				6:17, 14:14, 19:11	
7			Silence in heaven	8:1	½ hour
			Flying woe-angel	8:13	5 minutes (?)
	5	5	Pain and war	9:3, 16:10	5 months
			Euphrates dried up	9:14, 16:12	
	6	6	The initial battle of		
			Jerusalem	11:13, 14:20, 16:18	
	7	7			
The Battle of Armageddon				11:15, 16:17, 19:19	

30. With reactions continuing into the 5 months.

[Back to B: Matters continuing today resumed: the law and the prophets in the witnessing church are condemned by the world, with martyrdoms (11:3–10).][31]
The church will be resurrected and raptured (11:11–12).[32]
Jerusalem will be punished and repent at Christ's appearing (11:13–14).[33]

31. Present-day preaching: the two witnesses, described in terms of Moses and Zerubbabel (governing) and Elijah and Jeshua (religious; cf. Zech. 4), seem to signify the law and the prophets, as proclaimed by the church. 11:3, the 1,260 days are simply Elijah's 3½ years, I K 17:1, Lk. 4:25, Js. 5:17. 11:7, the martyrdoms seem to correspond to those of 6:9. 11:8–9, cf. Stephen's death at Jerusalem, Acts 7:58, and exposed body, 8:2, though the 3½ days may be merely to contrast short (days) defeat with long (years) ministry.
32. See below, on 19:7; and cf. the treatment of 11:11, 12 by such mid-tribulation rapturists as Norman B. Harrison, *The End,* though their association of the seventh trumpet of Rev 11:15 with "the last (rapturing) trumpet" of I Cor 15:52 seems unwarranted.
33. This earthquake, 11:13, may simply repeat the thought of 6:12a or 8:5 (see under 6:10, No. 19 below); but it may equal Zech 14:4, the means of delivering

Woe 3, the 7th trumpet angel, Christ's conquest of the world at Armageddon (11:15).[34]

E. Christ's reign on earth, the final judgment, and the New Jerusalem (11:16–19).[35]

II. The Second Cycle (chs. 12–22:7)

A. Events of John's period (12–13). Israel produces Christ, who conquers Satan and casts him to the earth (12).[36] Political power (here Rome) comes from across the sea, apparently unphased by Christ's triumph, with emperor worship and persecutions, aided by native religions of the land (13).[37]

B. The present is Satan's continued persecution of true Israel, the church (12:17).[38]

C. God's wrath immediately preceding Christ's coming (15–16:9).[39] Vials (bowls) 1–4 review and intensify the preappearing physical phenomena.

D. God's wrath immediately following Christ's coming (14, 16:10–ch. 19) The true Israel (cf. 7:1–8) will be raptured to be with Him on Mount Zion (14:1–7).

Jerusalem, under "blitzkrieg" attack by those opposing Christ, who has returned to the Mount of Olives. On the conversion of the Jews, cf. Zech 12:10 and Rom 11:25–27.

34. The millennium follows the conquest of earth's kingdoms at Armageddon.

35. 11:19 looks on God's testament as fulfilled, Rev 22:3; and the first cycle of the book is finished.

36. 12:5 dates this section to Christ's birth and ministry. The second cycle therefore starts even before the first. Rev 1:19 would indeed suggest that the Apocalypse contains matters that are past, as well as contemporary and future, in respect to John's experience; and in any event, it repeatedly bases its predictions on the historic events of the incarnation (1:4–6, 4:8, 11:17, 16:5). 12:6, 14, may be associated with Dan 9:27, the rest of the "70th week," that is, from the crucifixion to the stoning of Stephen, when Christians (the woman, the true Israel, God's people) prospered among the Jews (the desert). See above, p. 49, note 103.

37. 13:1, the beast, is explained in 17:9–16 as supporting and yet surviving the ancient Roman empire; so it seems to equal world political power in general. 13:5 refers to some aspect of Roman rule, probably the 3½-year Jewish Wars, as 11:2. 13:12–16, the beast may be equated with one head (a king, or kingdom, 17:10), or even an 8th head (17:11); so his mark may equal some specific Roman persecution. See above, pp. 49–50.

38. "The rest of her seed" (Christ is the first) must be the church, both Gentile and Jewish.

39. 14:14–ch. 16 describes Christ's appearing and what follows, though 15:1 backtracks with the 7 vials, the first 4 of which precede His coming (see Tables 13 and 14). 15:4 shows that some things leading to the world's submission have already taken place. Except for the 1st and 7th, the vials equal the trumpets, but more intense. 16:2, the "mark of the beast," submitting to power other than God's, continues to be a factor beyond the fall of Rome; so 19:20.

[A' Exhortations to John's time for patience, because of victory over Rome (14:8–13).][40]

Christ returns with the clouds to reap His harvest (the rapture); wrath is executed at Jerusalem (14:14–20).

Vials (bowls) 5–7: men gather at Armageddon to oppose Christ (16:10–21).[41]

[A' John's ministry resumed (17–19:5)[42]

He is to encourage Christians with Rome's overthrow by other nations (17). Christians escape, pagans mourn, and heaven rejoices (18–19:5).]

The whole church will be raptured (along with the "first fruits" of 14:1–7) to meet Christ in the air and then celebrate the "marriage supper" on earth (19:6–10).[43]

Christ destroys worldly political power at Armageddon (19:11–21)[44]

E. Christ's millennial reign, the final judgment, and the New Jerusalem (20–22:5)[45]

Satan is bound and the resurrected Christian dead reign with Christ on earth 1,000 years (20:1–6). The final judgment (20:10–15).[46] The new heaven and earth: New Jerusalem (21–22:5).[47]

40. 14:1–7 moves to immediately after the appearing of Christ, though 14:9–13 is a parenthetical application to John's time. V. 12 gives a general, timeless principle. 14:8, Babylon the Great (Rome), anticipates 17:5–6, 18.

41. 16:19a: on the Jerusalem attack, see above, 11:13. 16:19b: the fall of cities leads logically to a description of the now historic fall of Rome.

42. On the Roman empire, contemporary with John: note references assuming his own time, 17:8–11, and particularly v. 12, the 10 kings of the "balance of power," as Dan 2:42, which has been the world situation ever since the fall of ancient Rome. 17:3, the woman must be Rome: makes martyrs (v. 6), sits on the 7 hills (9), has universal rule (15), and is a great city (18). 17:3, the beast, having survived the blow by Christ's incarnation into history (v. 8), is separate and bears both the woman and the 10 (16); it is pagan political power, and particularly its 8th (11) and final (19:19, Antichrist) embodiment. 17:3, the 10 horns were not contemporary with John, v. 12, but succeeded the woman. Rev suggests no place for a revived Rome in prophecies still future.

43. 19:6 onward applies to the future, with Christ reigning on earth (19:19, 20:8). 19:7, the marriage supper of the Lamb (Lk 14:15, 22:16) is the immediate result of the rapture of the church (I Thess 4:17), the bride of Christ (II Cor 11:2, Eph 5:25–27). The rapture cannot take place before this point; for it is preceded by the resurrection of the dead saints (I Thess 4:15–16), which is at this time, 20:6, and which depends on Christ's descent from heaven to earth (19:11, 14, 15).

44. 19:20, the future false prophet is similar to the ancient beast from the earth, 13:10–16: false religion aiding false politics.

45. 20:4, all the saints are included in the millennial reign, not just martyrs; cf. I Cor 15:21, I Thess 4:14.

46. The second resurrection and the second death are for all who are not Christ's.

47. A new (the old, purified, Heb. 12:27) and wonderful existence for Christ's own.

Conclusion (22:6–19). This is factual and soon (rapid). Let the faithful rejoice and sinners die or come to Christ, who is the focus of history and of God's unchangeable Book.

Epilogue (22:20–21) Come, Lord Jesus!

The main events of both cycles are summarized in Table 14.

1. Rev 1:1, 3; *3:11a*; 16:15; 22:6–7, 10, *12a*, 20 (7 vv.): the opening verse of the Apocalypse speaks of "things which must shortly, *en tákhei,* take place," i.e. "before long";[48] "for the time is near," 1:3 (= 22:10). In 22:7 Christ Himself affirms, "Behold, I am coming quickly, *tákhú*" (= 3: 11; cf. 2:16), a phrase which could mean "swiftly, all at once"; but "when the advent of Jesus is hailed as a relief, it is no consolation to say that the relief will come suddenly; sudden or not, it must come soon."[49] 16:15 is a parenthetical statement (cf. ASV, RSV, NAS), inserted within John's description of the 6th bowl of God's wrath (see 9:13, No. 29, below), in which the Lord says, "Behold, I am coming like a thief."[50] Blessed is the one who stays awake and keeps his garments, lest he walk about naked and men see his shame." This declaration does not concern unbelievers, who might be caught as by a thief (that is, unprepared) whether the Lord's coming were actually imminent or not (cf. I Thess 5:3–5); but it concerns believers—"*Blessed* is the one who stays awake. . . ." His coming, in other words, will be unexpected by all.[51] Fulfillment (per. 15): the imminence of Christ's return, as in Lk. prophecy No. 47, though Swete cautions that these verses "must be interpreted relatively to Divine measurements of time."[52] So while "imminence does not mean that Christ's coming *must* be soon . . . by the same token His day *could* be soon, close at hand in its incidence."[53]

2. Rev 1:4, 7–8; 2:25; 4:8; *6:16b*; 14:14; 19:11–13 (9 vv.): in 1:4, 8; 4:8, God the Father (contrast Jesus, in 1:5) is identified as He who is and who was "and who is to come," "because it adumbrates at the outset the general purpose of the book. . . . Used elsewhere chiefly of the Son, the Father also may be said to *come* when He reveals Himself in His workings,"[54] and specifically in Christ, of whom John goes on to affirm,

48. H. Alford, *The Greek Testament,* IV:545.
49. ExGkT, V:335.
50. Contrast 3:3, which has an immediate rather than an eschatological reference; see 2:5, No. 3, below.
51. Payne, *Imminent Appearing,* pp. 101–102. It is George Ladd's presuppositions, combined, perhaps, with a lack of recognition of the parenthetical character of this verse, which forces him to conclude, "Whatever this means, it cannot involve . . . an any-moment, unexpected return of Christ," *The Blessed Hope,* p. 111.
52. Op. cit., p. 2.
53. Payne, *Imminent Appearing,* p. 86.
54. Swete, op. cit., p. 5.

TABLE 14
The Two Cycles of the Book of Revelation

Cycle 1: Rev 1-11	1-3	4-6:11	6:12-11:15	11:16-17	11:18	11:19
	Letters to 7 churches	Seals 1-5 Historical troubles	Seals 6-7 Christ's 2nd coming	Christ's reign		The testament fulfilled
						Dead judged
		Seal 5 6:9-11 martyr- doms	Seal 6 6:12-7:8 Trumpets 1-4 ch. 8	Seal 7, Christ has come, 8:1 The church is raptured, 11:12 3 woes, Trumpets 5-7 9, 11:13-15		

History						
Date	5 B.C.	A.D. 65	A.D. 476			
Time			Christ and Rome	The present	age	

GREAT Very brief: THE WRATH
Today? 15 min.?

TRIBU- OF GOD
LATION

The
millennium

New Jerusalem

Event

Cycle 2: Rev 12-22

Christ born	Revelation written?	Fall of Rome	Great earthquake	Christ's return	Battle of Armageddon	Final judgment	Great white throne

Woman (Israel) bears son (Jesus) 2 beasts from sea (empire) and land (religion)

Harlot (Rome)

The harlot burned, 17:16

10 horns (balance of power)

Vials 1-4 15-16:9

Christ has come, 14:1-7, 14-16

Marriage supper of the Lamb, 19:6-10

Vials 5-7 16:10-21, 19:11-21

1,000-year reign with Christ

New heaven and New earth

Great white throne

12-13   12:17 (also 17-19:5)   14-19   20:1-6   20:7-15   21-22:5

"Behold, He is coming[55] with the clouds, and every eye will see Him, even those who pierced him [the Jews; see Zech 12:10d]; and all the tribes of the earth shall mourn over Him," 1:7. So 6:16 speaks of men hiding "from the presence of Him who sits on the throne, and from the wrath of the Lamb." 14:14, in the book's second cycle,[56] specifies, "Behold, a white cloud, and sitting on the cloud was one like a son of man [Jesus; cf. 1:13], having a golden crown on His head, and a sharp sickle in His hand [cf. 14:15, No. 41, below]"; for "John is now anticipating the second advent of the conquering Christ, which is given in its proper place in greater detail in 19:11–21."[57] In this last passage he reveals, "I saw heaven opened; and behold, a white horse, and He who sat upon it is called Faithful and True . . . the Word of God[58] . . . and upon His head are many diadems." Fulfillment (per. 15): His second coming, as in Ps. prophecy No. 5.

3. Rev 2:5 (1 v., fig.): God's word to the church at Ephesus, "Repent and do the deeds you did at first; or else I am coming[59] to you, and will remove your lampstand [= the church itself, 1:20] out of its place." Fulfillment (per. 14): "Though deferred, the visitation came at last. After the 11th century the line of Ephesian bishops seems to have become extinct, and in 130§ the place was finally surrendered to the Turks";[60] and no church or even much of any town exists there today.

4. Rev 2:7; 21:4–6, 24–27; 22:1–*3a*, 14, 17, 19 (13 vv.): God's promise, 2:7, to Christian overcomers: "I will grant to eat of the tree of life [= 22:14, 19], which is in the Paradise of God," or to drink "from the spring [or river, 22:1] of the water of life," 21:6, 22:17. While the term "Paradise" ordinarily stands as equivalent to heaven (Lk 23:43, II Cor 12:2, 4), it is "here the final joy of the saints in the presence of God,"[61] namely, the New Jerusalem (per. 18), conveying life and specifically, as in Mal. No. 17 (4:2), "the healing of the nations" (Rev 22:2); and, as a result, "the nations shall walk by its light and . . . bring their glory into it" (21:24; cf. v. 26). "Nothing unclean shall ever come into it" (v. 27; cf. 22:3). "He shall wipe away every tear from their eyes, and there shall no longer be any death . . . or pain; the first things have passed away . . . and I am making all things new" (21:4–5).

5. Rev 2:10 (1 v.): to the church at Smyrna, "You are about to suffer

55. On His coming in 2:5, 11, 3:3, see under 2:5, No. 3, next.
56. See Table 12.
57. IB, XII:474.
58. The "name written upon Him, which no one knows except Himself," 19:12, is paralleled by a similarly unknowable song, sung by the 144,000 in 14:3 (see at 7:1, No. 22, below), and may thus also indicate unique attainments; i.e., "He is the sole possessor of that power," NBC, p. 1192.
59. "A special coming or visitation, affecting a church or an individual, as in v. 16 [a conditional prophecy; see above, p. 66]," Swete, op. cit., p. 27; similar is Alford's comment on 3:3, "I will come upon you": "These words do not refer to our Lord's final coming, but to some signal judgment [now too indefinite to catalog] in which he would overtake the Sardian church," op. cit., IV:579.
60. Swete, op. cit., pp. 27–28.
61. Ibid., p. 30.

. . . [with] some of you cast into prison, and you will have tribulation ten days," the idea being that "the round number here points to a short period";[62] cf. Gen 24:55. Fulfillment (per. 14): the church's 1st-century persecution by the Romans,[63] and by blasphemous Jews as well (Rev. 2:9).

6. Rev 2:11a, *20:6b* (1 v.): Christian overcomers "shall not be hurt by the second death," 2:11a (cf. v. 11b, No. 7, following); it "has no power" over them, 20:6. Fulfillment (per. 18): the destiny of the righteous, never to be harmed by the lake of fire.

7. Rev *2:11b*; *11:18d*; 14:9–11; *19:20c*; 20:*6c, 10b,* 14b–15; 21:8; 22:15 (7 vv.): references to "the second death." After a mention of the final judgment (11:18c), the conclusion to the book's first cycle[64] alludes briefly to God's decision "to destroy those who destroy the earth" (v. 18d); but the second cycle provides greater elucidation. 14:9–11 describes the fate of the one who shares in the false worship of the Roman emperors,[65] "He will drink of the wine of the wrath of God . . . tormented with fire and brimstone in the presence of the holy angels and in the presence of the Lamb. And the smoke of their torment goes up forever, and they have no rest day and night" (cf. 20:10a, No. 55, below). Then the later portions of the second cycle speak of "the lake of fire which burns with brimstone" (19:20; cf. 20:10b); "This is the second death, the lake of fire. And if anyone's name was not found written in the book of life [see 3:11b, No. 12, below]"—and particularly the faithless and the immoral, 21:8, 22:15—"he was thrown into the lake of fire" (20:14–15). It is "the equivalent of Gehenna [see Mt 3:7b], the same as 'the eternal fire' of Mt 25:41, the complete reversal of 'eternal life' (25:46) [and is "outside" the New Jerusalem, 22:15]. It may consequently be described as *the second death.*"[66] Fulfillment (per. 18): the lake of fire, as in II Sam No. 20.

8. Rev 2:22 (1 v.): against a false prophetess who is designated "Jezebel," at Thyatira, "I will cast her upon a bed of sickness"—perhaps in contrast with the couches of immorality and of pagan feasting which she had been promoting (v. 20). The fulfillment of this oracle, by means of some actual disease (per. 14), remains unknown but seems not improbable in light of the divine execution of similar threats elsewhere within the apostolic church (cf. I Cor 11:30).

9. Rev 2:26–27; 3:21; 5:10; *20:4a, 6e* (4 vv.): to the one who overcomes "I will give authority over the nations, and he shall rule them with a rod of iron," 2:26–27;[67] "I will grant to him to sit down with Me on My

62. ICC, II:58.
63. See above, p. 592.
64. See above, p. 594.
65. See above, p. 50, 592, 599.
66. NBC, p. 1196.
67. The phrase in v. 28, "and I will give him the morning star," might symbolize this same sort of "world dominion" (IB, XII:390); but more likely it should be understood as a generalized promise for the believers' possession of Christ, who is so designated in 22:16.

throne," 3:21. Christ's redeemed have been "made to be a kingdom, and they will reign[68] upon the earth," 5:10. Finally, near the conclusion of the second cycle of Revelation, John declares, "I saw thrones, and they sat upon them, and judgment was given to them," 20:4, "and [they] will reign with Him for a thousand years," v. 6. The identity of the *they* is suggested by the preceding context as referring to that same great host of saints who accompany Christ in His descent from the clouds (19:14); and it is subsequently defined as composed of "the first resurrection" (20:5), namely all the raptured people of God, OT and NT (see 11:11, No. 32, below). The *thousand years* is, in turn, a much disputed topic; but it does appear to be literal and to correspond to the earthly Messianic kingdom as anticipated in the OT (see 20:2b, No. 52, below). Fulfillment (per. 16): the ruling status of the saints, as in Isa. No. 51; see above, p. 108.

10. Rev 3:9 (1 v.): God's word to the church at Philadelphia, "I will cause those of the synagogue of Satan, who say they are Jews, and are not, but lie, to come and bow down at your feet [a quote from Isa 60:14], and to know that I have loved you." The reason is because the church constitutes the true Israel (Rom 2:29, Gal 3:29, Phil 3:3) and because present, unitarian Jews do not (Rom 3:28, 9:6).[69] Fulfillment (per. 16): the millennial status of the church, as in Isa. No. 51 (cf. 14:2b, 60:14) and Rev 2:26 (No. 9, above), but here made more specific, as the passage describes how particular honor for Christians is to come from those who are presently in Judaism. "The homage that the Jews had expected from others in the messianic period they now will have to pay to the Christians."[70]

11. Rev 3:10 (1 v.): because of the faithfulness of those in Philadelphia, "I also will keep you from the hour of testing which is about to come upon the whole world, to test those who dwell upon the earth." C. Anderson Scott explains, "Trials arising from persecution were among the severest temptations which beset the early Christians. . . . This necessarily limits the reference to those, among them that 'dwell upon the earth,' who were believers in Christ."[71] Fulfillment (per. 14): "Their devotion will carry them through the storm of Roman persecution."[72]

12. Rev 3:11b; 11:18c; *20:12b, 15b* (2 vv.): steadfastness is enjoined upon the Philadelphians, "in order that no one take your crown"; cf. II Tim 4:8b (listed under 4:1b). The conclusions, then, of both the 1st and

68. See note 25, above.
69. See above, pp. 100–101.
70. IB, XII:394.
71. Cent., p. 153. An alternative approach would be to refer this verse to the more universal trials of the great tribulation period preceding Christ's Parousia. But such an interpretation involves the difficulty that the church at Philadelphia has not survived to be so kept, unless one would assume inaccuracy on the part of John the revelator because of "this final sifting of mankind . . . not being yet clearly differentiated from the imperial persecution which had already begun," Swete, op. cit., p. 56. For further correctives on pretribulationism's use of this verse, see Payne, *Imminent Appearing*, pp. 77–79.
72. ExGkT, V:368.

the 2nd cycles of the book speak more fully, 11:18, of "the time to give their reward to the prophets, saints, and those who fear Thy name, the small and the great [cf. 20:12a, under 11:18b, No. 35, below]"; and, 20:12b, about the opening of "another book [again cf. v. 12a], which is the book of life."[73] Fulfillment (per. 17): the judgment of the saved, as in Job No. 5.

13. Rev 3:12a; 11:19; 21:3, 7, 12–17, 22–23; 22:3b–5 (15 vv., fig.): concerning the overcomer, Christ says, "I will make him a pillar in the temple of My God, and he will not go out from it any more; and I will write upon him the name of My God, and of the New Jerusalem, and My new name [see 19:12, note 58, under No. 2, above]," 3:12. Each of these figurative phrases carries significance and is interrelated with the others. *The New Jerusalem* (See v. 12b, No. 14, following): this fixes the prophecy's fulfillment to per. 18; and "to bear the name of the city of God is to be openly acknowledged as one of her citizens."[74] *A pillar . . . and not go out*: permanently fixed, he shall stay forever. *In the temple*: "21:22 makes it clear that there is to be no temple other than God and the Lamb in the heavenly Jerusalem; the promise is thus an assurance of inseparable unity with God."[75] *Upon him, the name of God and Christ*: like a pillar with a dedicatory inscription, he is to be devoted to God, as revealed in Christ, in His new and final glories. So the 1st cycle of Revelation (chs. 1–11) concludes with this symbolic statement: "And the temple of God which is in heaven was opened; and the ark of His testament [KJV] appeared in His temple, and there were flashes of lightning . . . and a great hailstorm," 11:19. That is, even as the ark in the former temple had symbolized and typified the presence of God with men (as in Ex. No. 56), so now in this similarly described situation, "at the moment when the time had come for the faithful to receive their reward, [it] indicates the restoration of perfect access to God."[76] as in Isa. No. 74.

This truth is then sublimely elaborated in the last 2 chapters of the 2nd cycle. 21:3 states, "God shall dwell among them [= 22:3], and they shall be His people." For the overcomer He promises, v. 7, "I will be his God and he will be My son." These are words which mark the accomplishment of God's purpose, as it had been planned from the very first; cf. Gen 17:7–8. Various features of the New Jerusalem then suggest the composition of this people of God: the 12 gates in its wall—following the pattern of Ezekiel's vision concerning millennial Jerusalem, 48:31–34—are inscribed with the names of the 12 tribes of Israel; and the 12 chief foundation stones, with those of Christ's apostles, Rev. 21:12–14. When an angel measures the city, v. 15, this signifies its divine protection (as in 11:1–2); and the cubic dimensions that his act reveals, v. 16, may be

73. See above, p. 48.
74. Swete, op. cit., p. 79.
75. NBC, p. 1175.
76. Swete, op. cit., p. 145.

meant as a fulfillment to the idea of the most holy place in the Solomonic temple (I K 6:20) and may thus indicate the fully reconciled presence of God with His own.[77] But there would be no temple building, or even a sun or moon, "for the Lord God and the Lamb are its temple . . . and its lamp," Rev 21:22–23; cf. 22:5. "And they shall see His face . . . and His servants shall serve Him . . . and they shall reign forever and ever," 22:3–5.

14. Rev *3:12b*; 21:*1a*, 2, 9–11, 18–21 (8 vv.): in 21:1–2 John records, "I saw a new heaven and a new earth . . . and I saw the holy city, new Jerusalem, coming down out of heaven from God [= 3:12], made ready as a bride adorned for her husband [= 21:9]." Certain of the city's features particularly suggest this heavenly origin: its "having the glory of God . . . [and its having a] brilliance, like a very costly stone [cf. vv. 19–20], as a stone of crystal-clear jasper," v. 11; or, as John states almost incomprehensibly, "The city was pure gold, like clear glass," v. 18; cf v. 21. Fulfillment (per. 18): the descent out of heaven of a new and glorious way of life, into a transformed world.

15. Rev 6:1–2 (2 vv. sym.): at Christ's breaking of the first of the 7 seals on the Lamb's book,[78] "I looked, and behold, a white horse, and he who sat on it had a bow; and a crown was given to him; and he went out conquering and to conquer." This description has certain points of contact with that of Christ's return, also on a white horse, in Rev 19:11. But since the horseman of ch. 6 appears in parallel with three others that follow (Nos. 16–18, below), who in turn represent calamities that are to ride across the earth between John's own time (chs. 1–3) and the yet future coming of Christ (6:16),[79] he is more plausibly assigned to per. 14 and labeled "aggression," a facet of international relations which remains true up to this present moment.[80]

16. Rev. 6:3–4 (2 vv., sym.): at the breaking of the 2nd seal, John saw "a red horse, and to him who sat on it . . . a great sword was given." Its purpose is then explained: "to take peace from the earth, that men should slay one another." Fulfillment (per. 14): warfare, up to the present, the result of militaristic aggression (see No. 15, preceding).

17. Rev 6:5–6 (2 vv., sym.): with the 3rd seal came "a black horse, and he who sat on it had a pair of scales in his hand." High prices for

---

77. Similarly in v. 17, that the human measurements of the city wall "are also angelic measurements," may be designed to show that men will now be on an equal standing with the holy angels, IB, XII:536.

78. See above, pp. 48, 597.

79. See above, pp. 594 (the historical approach) and 596.

80. The period that begins in 4:1, which is identified as coming "after these things" (of chs. 2–3), "could well begin with the years immediately following the first century and could continue until the coming of the Lord," M. C. Tenney, *Interpreting Revelation*, p. 72. Dispensational interpreters, having located the rapture at the beginning of ch. 4 (see above, pp. 00, 000), naturally assign the four horsemen to days yet future, as the commencement of the great day of God's wrath, John F. Walvoord, *The Revelation of Jesus Christ*, p. 122.

food are then depicted. Fulfillment (per. 14): famine, as resulting from war (see No. 16, preceding).

18. Rev 6:7–8 (2 vv., sym.): with the 4th seal came "an ashen horse," whose rider is identified as Death, followed by the grave (the point intended by the ASV, NAS transliteration "Hades," as opposed to the KJV rendering "hell"), the end result of the aggression, war, and famine that have preceded. All four of the horsemen are thus said to have "authority over a fourth of the earth, to kill . . . ," and John proceeds to quote Ezek 5:12, 14:21, 33:27. Fulfillment (per. 14): extraordinary death rates, in the present unstable world. In respect to the proportion slain, "The *fourth* shows that this is no mere commonplace of human mortality, but describes an unusual visitation, in which Death is busy in various forms."[81]

19. Rev 6:10, *12a*, *14b*–17; 8:2–6; 11:13a; 15:1, 5–8; 16:1, 18–*19a*, 20–21 (18 vv.): the prayer of the martyrs, 6:10, for God's "judging and avenging our blood on those who dwell on the earth." The divine answer becomes apparent from the predictions that commence 2 vv. later, with the events at the breaking of the 6th seal; compare the similar demonstrations of heavenly wrath, in answer to "the prayers of all the saints" in 8:3–5. These events include: 6:12a, a great earthquake; vv. 12b–14a, specific phenomena in the sky (see No. 21, below); and v. 14b, "every mountain and island were moved out of their places, so that in vv. 15–17 men seek to hide from "the great day of the wrath of the Lamb."

In this way the 6th seal introduces John's readers to the wrath subsequently displayed in the visions of the angels who sound the trumpets in ch. 8. As Tenney observes, "The judgements of the trumpets are more specific, more cataclysmic, and more concrete than those of the seals. They can be more easily compressed into a narrow interval of time than can the seals";[82] they seem, indeed, to be limited to a correspondence with the contents of the 6th seal alone.[83] The trumpets are thus inaugurated by the earthquake (8:5, just as was the seal in 6:12) and are accompanied by thunders and lightnings, as an angel symbolically casts a censer of fire from heaven's altar down upon the earth. So in 11:13, when the saints are raised and caught up to meet their returning Lord (v. 12, see No. 32, below), "in that hour there was a great earthquake, and a tenth of the city [Jerusalem,[84] vv. 2, 8] fell; and 7,000 people were killed in the earthquake." In a more positive light, however, this quake may also be associated with the cleaving of the Mount of Olives, Zech 14:4–5, which becomes, in turn, the means for delivering the Jerusalemites from those who are attacking the city out of opposition to Christ, as He returns to Olivet.[85]

The corresponding 2nd cycle, in the latter half of Revelation, then speaks

81. Swete, op. cit., p. 89.
82. Op. cit., p. 71.
83. See above, Table 13.
84. Cf. ICC, I:291.
85. Cf. note 33 above.

of "seven angels who had seven plagues, which are the last, because in them the wrath of God is finished," 15:1.[86] Specifically, the seven angels come from God's temple in heaven, v. 5, with "seven golden bowls full of the wrath of God," v. 7, to pour out on the earth, 16:1. In association, moreover, with the outpouring of the 7th bowl, v. 17 (No. 30, below), "there were flashes of lightning and peals of thunder and a great earthquake, such as there had not been since man came to be upon the earth," v. 18. This could, of course, constitute a second and greater earthquake, which would terminate the wrath of God and would thus be distinct from the one so far described in the 1st-cycle references, which inaugurated it. But even as v. 19b consists of a flashback to what is now the historic fall of Rome (see 14:8, No. 40, below), so to a lesser degree the earthquake in 16:18 may serve to trace out once again this spectacular initial aspect of God's wrath, one which otherwise would not appear in the 2nd cycle at all. The fact that the earthquake is introduced at an earlier point in the 1st cycle seems simply to illustrate the principle that holds good for the entire series of the bowls in relation to the trumpets, namely, that the two sets of sevens are "not actually to be considered as following one upon another. but probably to be regarded as differing versions of the same eschatological woes."[87] Note then these further points of correspondence, of the bowls with the trumpets. In 16:19a, at the time of the earthquake, not only do the cities of the nations fall, but once again John speaks of "the great city . . . split into three parts; and "probably *the great city* is Jerusalem [cf. 11:8 and 14:20]. She is distinguished from the Gentile cities, [while] Rome-Babylon is reserved for a special fate"[88] (v. 19b, No. 40), with which compare 11:13 (above) in the 1st cycle. In 16:20 John predicts, "And every island fled away, and the mountains were not found"; cf. 6:14 (above) in the former cycle. Both, moreover, exhibit similar responses on the part of humanity; for even after the descent of "huge hailstones, about 100 pounds each," 16:21, unregenerate men are still much in evidence, with their continuing blasphemy of God; cf. 6:15–16 in the 1st cycle.

Fulfillment (per. 15): as in Isa. No. 48, the wrath of God (Rev 6:17), initiated by an unprecedented earthquake, and immediately preceding the appearing of Christ.

20. Rev 6:11, 7:9–17 (10 vv.): in the course of the 5th seal, while describing the rest that God was then granting (nonpredictive) to His martyrs, John spoke further of "their brethren who were to be killed even

86. See above, p. 595 and note 21. Tenney states that ch. 16 "constitutes in itself another series of judgments somewhat parallel in character to the judgments of the seven trumpets. . . . But they are more intense . . . they are climactic," op. cit., pp. 71, 80.
87. IB, XII:488.
88. ExGkT, V:499; cf. Camb, p. 99. Others, on the contrary, such as IB, XII:488, or Alford, op. cit., IV:698, would tend to identify *the great city* with "Babylon the great "(v. 19b) that follows.

as they had been," 6:11. This is elaborated in the interlude that makes up ch. 7,[89] in which vv. 9–17 picture "a great multitude, from every nation, standing before the throne and before the Lamb, clothed in white robes [of saints in heaven, 3:5, 6:11]," praising God's salvation, and serving Him in that place where there is no more sorrow. In v. 14 they are specifically identified as those "who come out of the great tribulation." Fulfillment (per. 14): Christian martyrdom, but particularly that last portion, which was future to John, when "the number of their fellow-servants . . . should be completed also" (6:11), in the great tribulation, as in Dan. No. 20. The Bible, in short, promises Christian believers no peculiar protection from the Antichrist in "the tribulation"; but that the church will survive his persecution is then indicated by their protective sealing from the wrath of God, which is to follow (No. 22, below, cf. No. 19, preceding).[90]

21. Rev 6:12b–14a, 8:12, 16:8–9 (6 vv.): celestial phenomena, as a major element in the outpoured wrath of God (see 6:10, No. 19, above). 6:12 speaks of the sun turning black and the moon becoming like blood; v. 13, of stars falling; and v. 14, "the sky was split apart like a scroll," "i.e. the expanse of heaven was seen to crack and part, the divided portions curling up and forming a roll on either hand."[91] This last anticipation is derived from Isa 34:4, which, together with Rev 20:11b (No. 56, below), describes the final removal of the present earth. Here in ch. 6, however, the heavens are simply opening for the return of Christ (v. 16), as in 19:11. So the world's ultimate destruction is apparently not yet involved; note how men still pray for the mountains to fall on them (6:16), which would have been impossible had these actually been destroyed in 6:14.[92] Then in chs. 8 and 16, all four of the first trumpets and bowls seem to belong together as an elaboration of the 6th seal (6:12–17).[93] Trumpets 1–3 do introduce new areas of prediction (see No. 24–26, below); but the fourth trumpet reiterates the concepts of ch. 6, for "a third of the sun, moon, and stars were smitten, [meaning that they were] darkened," that the day and the night "might not shine for a third of it," 8:12. In the plagues of ch. 16 too, the 4th golden bowl relates to these celestial phenomena, v. 8, for "The fourth angel poured out his bowl upon the sun; and it was given to it to scorch men with fire." Yet, sadly, "they did not repent, so as to give Him glory," and rather blasphemed God in their pain, v. 9. Fulfillment (per. 15): the heavenly features of the wrath of God, as in Joel No. 9 (2:30; cf. the 9th plague in Egypt, Ex 10:22–23).

22. Rev. 7:1–8, 14:1b–5 (12 vv., sym.): "After this [the wrath of God in 6:10, 12–17, No. 19, above] I saw four angels . . . holding back the four

---

89. See above, pp. 102 and 597, note 27.
90. Payne, *Imminent Appearing*, p. 63.
91. Swete, op. cit., p .93.
92. Cf. NBC, p. 1179.
93. See above, pp. 598, 609, and 610, note 87.

winds, so that no wind should blow on the earth. And I saw another angel having the seal of the living God; and he cried out to the four angels to whom it was given to harm the earth, 'Do not harm the earth or the sea or the trees, until we have sealed the bondservants of God on their foreheads' . . . 144,000," 12,000 from each of the tribes of Israel,[94] 7:1–8. This passage has thus been inserted into the course of the main visions of Revelation to explain the position of God's people during the outpouring of His wrath. The nature of the *sealed* ones is illumined by John's words about the 144,000 of ch. 14 (in his 2nd cycle), which apparently describe the same group.[95] They are identified as "purchased from the earth" and as "having the name of Christ and the name of His Father written on their foreheads," vv. 1, 3. They are "ones who are celibates, who follow the Lamb wherever He goes" (cf. Ps 110:3), and who "have been purchased from among men as first fruits to God and to the Lamb . . . blameless," vv. 4–5. They would seem therefore to be a group of dedicated Christian youth, chosen out of,[96] and yet representative *first fruits* of, the larger body of God's Israel (7:4).[97] Fulfillment (per. 15): as in I Thess. No. 9 (5:4), the believing church, the Israel of God (Gal 6:16),[98] seen as protected during the accomplishment of that part of His wrath which precedes His appearing.[99] Subsequently, of course, both the 144,000 and the whole church that they represent become safe forever, having been caught up into the clouds to be with Him and then stationed with Him on Mount Zion (see 14:1a, No. 38, below).

23. Rev. 8:1 (1 v., sym.): "When He [Christ, the Lamb] broke the 7th seal, there was silence in heaven for about half an hour." John offers no explanation. But this phenomenon seems to represent a temporary suspension of the wrath of God (per. 15) following Christ's appearing in 6:16, "but portending ominous developments ahead,"[100] namely the intensified

94. These are named, and include both Manasseh and Joseph (out of which Manasseh came) but omit Dan, without further explanation. Walvoord proposes that "Dan was one of the first to go into idolatry, was small in number, and probably thereafter was classified with Naphtali, born of the same mother as Dan," op. cit., p. 141.

95. See IB, XII:468.

96. They therefore sing a song of redemption, 14:3, to which others do not attain.

97. The group cannot be national Israel, Israel after the flesh, because the Jews are converted only after the outpouring of the wrath of God, and specifically, at that time when they look directly upon the Messiah whom they have pierced (Zech 12:10), Payne, *Imminent Appearing*, pp. 62–63. Contrast Walvoord, op. cit., p. 139, who speaks of them as a godly remnant of Israel, converted after the (assumed pretribulational) rapture of the church.

98. See above, p. 100. Dispensational interpreters insist that though the church corresponds to the "children of Abraham" it cannot be called the "children of Israel," E. Schuyler English, *Re-thinking the Rapture*, p. 101. But this seems to be a trifling objection in the light of the freedom with which Scripture equates the three patriarchs, Abraham, Isaac, and Jacob (Israel); cf. Lev 26:42.

99. Cf. Table 14.

100. Walvoord, op. cit., p. 151.

wrath of "the three woes" that succeed the Lord's return (see v. 13, No. 27, below).

24. Rev 8:7 (1 v., sym.): at the sounding of the first of the 7 trumpets, "there came hail and fire [paralleling the 7th plague in Egypt, Ex 9:23–24], mixed with blood;[101] and a third of the earth was burnt up." Fullfillment (per. 15): an elaboration on "the wrath of God"; see under 6:10 (No. 19, above).

25. Rev 8:8–9, 16:3 (3 vv., sym.): at the 2nd trumpet, "something like a great mountain burning with fire was thrown into the sea, and a third part of the sea became blood; and a third of the creatures which were in the sea died, and a third of the ships was destroyed." The 2nd trumpet thus parallels the 1st plague in Egypt, Ex 7:20–21. In the corresponding and more complete outpourings of wrath from the golden bowls, found in the latter half of the book, "the 2nd angel poured out his bowl into the sea, and it became blood like that of a dead man; and every living thing in the sea died." Fulfillment (per. 15): another element in the wrath of God immediately preceding Christ's return.

26. Rev 8:10–11, 16:4–7 (6 vv., sym.): at the 3rd trumpet, "a great star called Wormwood fell from heaven, burning like a torch, and it fell on a third of the rivers and on the springs of waters; and a third of the waters became wormwood[102] [a reversal of the healing miracles of Ex 15:23, II K 2:21–22, and one which will deny to men that alternative water supply to which the Egyptians were able to have recourse during the 1st plague]; and many men died from the waters, because they were made bitter," 8:10–11. In the corresponding section of ch. 16, "the 3rd angel poured out his bowl into the rivers and the springs of waters; and they became blood," v. 4—a differing result from that symbolized by the 3rd trumpet blast, and yet a righteous kind of retribution for those who had "poured out the blood of saints," v. 6. Fulfillment (per. 15): a divine plague on the fresh water of the earth, as another element in the final wrath of God, and corresponding to the 2nd plague, on its salt water (see No. 25, preceding).

27. Rev 8:13, 9:12, 11:14 (3 vv., sym.): John looked and heard "an eagle flying in mid-heaven, saying with a loud voice, 'Woe, woe, woe, to those who dwell on the earth; because of the remaining blasts of the trumpet of the three angels who are about to sound." Fulfillment (per. 15): an intensified continuation of the wrath of God, as symbolized up to this point by the first four trumpet sounds (8:7–12) and by the outpouring of

101. Swete, op. cit., p. 110, cites a case in 1901 of "blood-red rain in Italy and southern Europe because of fine red sand blown across the Mediterranean from the Sahara," though the emphasis in Rev seems to fall more on the bloodshed involved. Cf. also Joel 2:30 and its subsequent Biblical quotation.

102. *Āpsinthos,* equivalent to Heb., *la'anā,* a Palestinian plant that produces a bitter taste (but not deadly) when mixed with water; but this "wormwood" was still used to symbolize divine judgment (Jer 9:15. 23:15), and in this case the judgment *was* to become fatal.

the first four golden bowls (16:2–9), which have corresponded in turn with the 6th seal (6:12–17). But the latter three trumpets (and cf. the parallel, 5th–7th bowls) make up "the three woes" (No. 28–30, following), which form a second unit of wrath, after Christ's appearing at the end of the 6th seal (6:16). They are apparently introduced by the 7th seal (8:1, No. 23, above).

28. Rev 9:1–11, 16:10–11 (13 vv., sym.): as a commencement to the latter part of the series of trumpet plagues, and as the first of the three woes (No. 27, preceding), "the 5th angel sounded, and I saw a star from heaven which had fallen to the earth; and the key of the bottomless pit [lit., *the well of the ǎbussos, abyss,* the underground abode of demons, Lk 8:31] was given to him," 9:1. The star must therefore have symbolized a personal being, and probably an angel, as in 1:20—perhaps the elect angel who is to have the key of the abyss in 20:1, but more likely the *fallen* angelic ruler of demons, "the angel of the abyss," who is Abaddon, or Apollyon, namely Satan *the destroyer,* 9:11; cf. 12:9.[103] When he opens the pit, smoke darkens the sky, "and out of the smoke came forth locusts upon the earth," 9:3 (paralleling the 8th plague in Egypt, Ex 10:14), who do not kill but who torment men for 5 months, v. 5. The significance of the demonic locusts is suggested by their description: "like horses prepared for battle," v. 7 (compare Joel 2:4); "like the sound of chariots," v. 9; "and they had hair like the hair of women," v. 8—either supernaturally long antennae, or long hair like that of the ancient Parthian invaders of the Roman empire.[104] So in the revelator's 2nd cycle, "the 5th angel poured out his bowl upon the throne of the beast [the Antichrist; see 17:8a, No. 45, below]; and his kingdom became darkened, and they gnawed their tongues because of pain and blasphemed God," 16:10–11. Fulfillment (per. 15): the world's Satanically inspired military preparations against the returned Christ, and yet with its accompanying griefs.

29. Rev 9:13–21; 16:12–14, 16 (13 vv., sym.); with the 6th trumpet come divine orders to "release the four angels who are bound at the river Euphrates," 9:14, perhaps the same angels, or angels similar to those who had been previously restrained from unleashing the plagues of the 6th seal (= the first four trumpets) until God's saints had been protectively sealed (7:1–3).[105] Under their control appear armies of horsemen, numbering 200 million (9:16), which seem other than human, both because of their numbers and because of the "fire, smoke, and brimstone" that proceed from the mounts (v. 17). Their correspondence on the one hand with the "locusts" (No. 28, preceding) and on the other hand with the "frogs" that follow in

---

103. Alford, op. cit., IV:637; Swete, op. cit., pp. 114, 119–120.
104. Swete, op. cit., p. 118.
105. R. C. H. Lenski, *The Interpretation of St. John's Revelation,* p. 302; yet Walvoord sees them as fallen angels, but still instruments of God's judgment, op. cit., p. 165.

John's 2nd cycle, 16:13–14 (below), suggest demonic legions. But while the locusts only tormented people, this infernal cavalry "kills a third of mankind," 9:15, 18.

The 2nd cycle speaks similarly of "three unclean spirits like frogs" (cf. the 2nd plague in Egypt, Ex 9:6), proceeding from Satan and his associates, 16:13. The purpose of these demons and of the signs that they perform is specifically "to gather the kings of the whole world for the war of the great day of God," v. 14. It was to this same end that the 6th angel had "poured out his bowl upon the great river Euphrates; and its water was dried up, that the way might be prepared for the kings from the east," v. 12. The demons thus "gather them together to the place which in Hebrew is called Har-Magedon," v. 16 (see 19:15–21, No. 49, below, for the actual battle). In reference to the one-third of humanity destroyed 9:15, 18 (above), Walvoord has suggested that "the number slain is the total number involved in the conflict."[106] Fulfillment (per. 15): the world's mustering against Christ, those from the east crossing the dried-up bed of the Euphrates, as in Joel No. 22 (3:18b).

30. Rev 10:5–7; 11:15–17; 12:5; 16:17; 19:6, *15b* (9 vv., sym.): the oath of an angel that at the symbolic sounding of the 7th trumpet "there shall be delay no longer,[107] but in the days of the voice of the 7th angel, then the mystery of God is finished," 10:6–7. The *mystery* here denotes "the whole purpose of God in regard to the world,"[108] specifically, 11:15, that the kingdom of the world will "become the kingdom of our Lord, and of His Christ; and He will reign forever and ever"; cf. v. 17, "Thou hast taken Thy great power and begun to reign." So in the 2nd cycle of Revelation, at the pouring out of the 7th golden bowl, a loud voice came from heaven saying, "It is done," 16:17. "It signifies the final blow against the forces of evil, both human and satanic";[109] for Christ's kingdom follows the great battle of Armageddon, v. 16, to which the 5th and 6th bowls (and trumpets) had been leading up (see under 9:1 and 13, No. 28–29, preceding). 19:6 then anticipates Christ's appearing and His actual victory at Armageddon in vv. 11–21 and exclaims, "Hallelujah! For the Lord our God, the Almighty, *ebasíleusen*," an aorist form of the verb "to reign," which indicates that from the speakers' viewpoint His kingdom *has been* set up as well. Simcox explains that "reigneth," ASV, is "the only translation that will give the sense without cumberousness, though 'hath taken the kingdom' might express the tense of the original more accurately."[110] Finally, at

---

106. Ibid., p. 167, though his hypothesis that Armageddon does not originate because of the coming of Christ but that "more probably it reflects a conflict among the nations themselves in the latter part of the great tribulation," p. 237, is not a generally accepted one; cf. IB, XII:486, or Alford, op. cit., IV:696.
107. Not KJV, "there should be time no longer"; see above, p. 28.
108. ICC, I:265.
109. NBC, p. 1188.
110. Camb, p. 116; cf. ICC, II:126, "The reign of God is established on earth."

Christ's advance to Armageddon, 19:15, John foresees that "He will rule the nations with a rod of iron" (= 12:5), not simply in His immediate victory on the field; but, for the millennium that follows, "it represents unyielding, absolute government under which men are required to conform to the righteous standards of God."[111] Fulfillment (per. 16): the Messianic rule of Christ, as in Gen. No. 68.

31. Rev 11:1–2, 13:5 (3 vv., sym.): John was told to "measure the temple of God, and the altar, and those who worship in it," but not "the court which is outside the temple," 11:1–2. The explanation given for his not doing the latter is because "it has been given to the nations; and they will tread under foot the holy city for forty-two months." This and the following section in ch. 11 (see No. 32, next) are among the most difficult prophecies to interpret in all of Scripture, though certain aspects do seem to be capable of a measure of clarification. *The holy city* is apparently defined in v. 8 as "the great city . . . where their Lord was crucified," and hence the literal Jerusalem,[112] to which would correspond its literal *temple.* Likewise, the temple's *measuring* must here symbolize protection (as in Zech 1:16, 2:1–2) and not destruction (as in II K 21:13, Lam 2:8), since the area *not* measured is what suffers the harm. The *treading down* then seems to be derived from the Lord's forecast in Lk 21:24, "Jerusalem will be trampled underfoot by the Gentiles," and C. A. Scott's conclusion, therefore, to be a justifiable one: "With this so closely parallel prediction of Jesus before us, it is hardly possible to escape the conclusion that here also is a prophecy of the siege and fall of Jerusalem, coupled with an assurance that . . . God's true worshippers shall escape destruction."[113] So the 2nd cycle too speaks of a 42–month period of particularly arrogant activity by the Roman beast, 13:5.[114] Fulfillment (per. 14): John's inspired words of comfort for his Christian colleagues in Jerusalem, looking forward to their divine protection through the 3½ years of the Jewish War, which should extend from the initial attempts by Herod Agrippa II and the Roman Cestius Gallus upon the temple, at the close of A.D. 66, down to its destruction in August, 70 (cf. Dan 9:26b, or Mt. 24:15 under 10:23b); for before the end, the Christian community was able to escape across the Jordan to Pella (cf. Mt 24:16).

32. Rev 11:11–12; 20:4b, 5c–6a (4 vv., sym.): 11:3 introduces God's "two witnesses," who "will prophesy for 1,260 days"; but they will be slain

111. Walvoord, op. cit., p. 278.

112. Camb, p. 67, ExGkT, V:414–415; so too Walvoord, op. cit., pp. 175–176, though he relates it to a temple yet to be built during the tribulation period. Contrast IB, XII:444, or NBC, p. 1182, which speaks of "the spiritual security of the Church," despite (Roman) persecution.

113. Cent, p. 218; cf. ICC, I:274. It would appear to be a critical conclusion, against Revelation's being written at this early date, that has led many into an otherwise unjustifiable allegorization of the passage; witness IB, loc. cit., and cf. Cent, p. 219 and see above, p. 592.

114. See above, note 37.

by "the beast" (pagan political power),[115] v. 7. The following is then said of them: "After three days and a half the breath of life from God came into them . . . and they heard a loud voice from heaven saying to them, 'Come up here.' And they went up into heaven in the cloud, and their enemies beheld them," vv. 11–12. In this difficult passage, the main question is the identity of the two witnesses. They are described, on the one hand, in terms of Moses and Elijah, v. 6 (cf. Ex 7:20 and I K 17:1); and these OT figures seem in turn to have represented the revealed will of God to Israel, i.e. the law and the prophets—cf., for example, their appearing with Christ upon the mount of transfiguration (Mt 17:3–4). The *1,260 days* may thus be simply that of Elijah's well-known 3½ year judgment of drought upon the land (I K 17:1, Lk 4:25, James 5:17). But the witnesses would not appear to be Moses and Elijah, literally reincarnated,[116] since they are described, on the other hand, in terms of "the two olive trees . . . that stand before the Lord," Rev 11:8 (cf. Zech 4:3, 6, 14), namely Zerubbabel and Joshua, the governing and religious leaders of postexilic Judah. Moreover, "The beast is said to *make war* on the two witnesses (v. 7), a curious phrase in reference to two individuals, but it is applied to the Church in 13:7."[117] Since the resurrection and heavenward ascension of the two witnesses corresponds to the actual experience of the dead in Christ, rising at His shout and at the sounding of the last trumpet, so as to meet Him in the air upon His return in the cloud (I Thess 4:16), it seems proper to identify the witnesses with all believers who have died, too often slain for their proclamation of God's word, the law and the prophets. Preceding vv. 11–12, Rev 11:3–10 should thus not be classed as predictive; the symbolism is more naturally descriptive of the continuing reality of martyrdom, e.g. Stephen's in the same city of Jerusalem, where his corpse was abandoned for later burial by the disciples (cf. Rev 11:8 with Acts 7:58, 8:2).[118]

In 20:4–6, of the 2nd cycle, John relates, "I saw the souls of those who had been beheaded because of the testimony of Jesus . . . and those who had not worshipped the beast or his image . . . and they came to life and reigned with Christ. . . . This is the first resurrection. Blessed and holy is the one who has a part in the first resurection." This experience is therefore clearly one of blessing; but strong differences of opinion exist, both as to its period and as to its scope. Amillennialists assign it, even as they do the prior binding of Satan (see v. 1, No. 51, below), to the present church era and think of it as denoting that figurative resurrection which is either the new birth (as in John 5:25; see under 5:28) or the entrance of the believing

115. See above, pp. 49–50 and 599.
116. Though Tenney, op. cit., p. 191, mentions, with favor, a possible actual reappearance of Moses and Elijah.
117. NBC, p. 1182.
118. The display of *their dead bodies for three days and a half,* Rev 11:9, may signify the short defeat (in terms of days) as contrasted with the long, effective proclamation (in terms of years); cf. Swete, op. cit., p. 138.

soul at death into a kingly role in heaven. In the present context, however, which goes on to speak of the later, general resurrection (Rev 20:13) in terms that correspond to those of the first, such approaches seem unlikely. To quote Alford's classic, if somewhat caustic, evaluation:

> If, in a passage where *two resurrections* are mentioned, where certain *souls came to life* at the first, and the rest of the *dead came to life* only at the end of a specified period after the first [v. 5a]—if in such a passage the first resurrection may be understood to mean *spiritual* rising with Christ, while the second means *literal* rising from the grave—then there is an end of all significance in language, and Scripture is wiped out as a definite testimony to any thing.[119]

Other commentators, on the other hand, suggest what appears to be an unduly limited scope to the first resurrection. Speaking as a representative of modern dispensationalism, Feinberg seeks to restrict it to those saints who are martyred during the tribulation period, claiming, "The other groups are not mentioned as being raised here because their resurrection has been spoken of elsewhere."[120] But that seems to be just the point. At the conclusion of the 1st cycle of Revelation, the raising and rapture of the two witnesses (11:11–12) occurs *in* the same *hour* as the great earthquake and the conversion of the Jews at Christ's triumphant return (v. 13, No. 33, following); and in ch. 19 in the 2nd cycle, the marriage supper of the Lamb (vv. 7–9), which follows the rapture of the living church (I Thess 4:17), which in turn follows the resurrection of the dead in Christ (vv. 15–16), occurs just after the Lord has taken up His reign on earth (Rev 19:6, see under 10:5, No. 30, above). Since therefore John never mentions a resurrection of believers at any point other than this in ch. 20, at the commencement of the millennial reign, and since he calls this *the first* resurrection, it would appear unwarranted to postulate an earlier resurrection for "the other groups" of the church.[121]

A liberal commentator allows the first resurrection to include believers prior to the tribulation period but restricts the type of participants, claiming, "It is explicitly stated that the millennium is for but one group of people, viz., the martyrs, those who had been beheaded because of their testimony, who had died because they had not worshiped the beast."[122] But this limitation too appears unwarranted. The words of v. 4 itself seem to suggest the possibility of others; for as Swete notes, "The triumph of Christ is

---

119. Lenski, op. cit., p. 583; Alford, op. cit., IV:726; also, see above, pp. 105–107.
120. Op. cit., p. 106.
121. Hence even pretribulationists have granted that "sane interpretation" requires the placing of the rapture at this point, after the tribulation, English, op. cit., p. 31. Cf. George Ladd's singling out of this one passage as explicitly relating the hope of the church to Christ's post-tribulational return in glory, *The Blessed Hope*, p. 165.
122. IB, XII:520.

shared not by the martyrs only but by all who under the sway of the Beast suffered reproach . . . though they did not win the martyr's crown."[123] Furthermore, if one accepts the analogy of other Scriptures as valid, or even of other parts of the Revelation, it seems clear that all believers are to share in the rapture and millennium (I Cor 15:23, I Thess 4:14, and cf. No. 9, above); i.e., "The kingdom is promised to every Christian that overcomes (see 2:26–28, 3:21), while 5:9–10 declares that the whole Church is to reign on earth. . . . It is curious exegesis that makes the wife of the Lamb in 19:5–9 the martyrs only but in 21:2f. the whole Church."[124] Fulfillment (per. 15): the first resurrection, as in Isa. No. 76.

33. Rev *11:13b*, after the great earthquake that heralds the Lord's return, and particularly after its devastating effect on Jerusalem, causing the loss of 7,000 lives (v. 13a; see under 6:10, No. 19, above), "the rest [of the inhabitants of the city[125]] were terrified and gave glory to the God of heaven." Fulfillment (per. 15): this terror on the part of Jerusalem's Jews becomes a factor, along with their actually beholding the divine Messiah whom they were pierced (Zech 12:10), in "the conversion of Israel to Christianity in the last days."[126]

34. Rev *11:18a*; 20:*3c*, 7–9 (3 vv.): "And the nations were enraged, and Thy wrath came," 11:18. Context determines the point of this raging reaction by men; for vv. 17–18 "first recognize the establishment of God's sovereignty in the Millennial Kingdom [v. 17, under 10:5, No. 30, above], and the outbreak of Gog and Magog at its close [v. 18a, here], and then proclaim that the time has come for the final judgment [v. 18b, No. 35, next]."[127] Their outbreak is then considerably elaborated in John's 2nd cycle, ch. 20[128]—first, as to the basis for their revolt: "When the thousand years are completed, Satan will be released from his prison [see v. 1, No. 51, below] . . . for a short time [v. 3] . . . and will come out to deceive the nations which are in the four corners of the earth [cf. Ezek 38:6], Gog and Magog [cf. 38:2]," vv. 7–8a; second, as to its procedure, that Satan will "gather them together for war; the number of them is like the sand of the seashore," v. 8b (cf. Ezek 38:4, 15); third, as to its goal: "They came up on the broad plain of the earth [perhaps meaning, "through the breadth of the earth," probably indicating Jerusalem, which is described in Ezek 38:12 as those "that dwell in the middle (lit., *navel*) of the earth"[129]] and surrounded the camp of the saints and the beloved city," v. 9a; and fourth, as to its result, "and fire came down from heaven and devoured them," v. 9b (Ezek 38:22, 39:6). Fulfillment (per. 17): the rage, the invasion, and

123. Op. cit., p. 262.
124. NBC, p. 1195.
125. Alford, op. cit., IV:661.
126. ICC, I:292.
127. Ibid., I:293–294.
128. See above, p. 595.
129. ICC, II:190.

the destruction of Gog, as in Jer. No. 96 (25:26b), and especially Ezek. No. 53 (38:1).

35. Rev *11:18b*; 20:*11a*, 12a, *13b*; 22:12b (2 vv.): after the defeat of the hosts of Gog (No. 34, preceding) comes "the time for the dead to be judged," 11:18. As this is elaborated in John's 2nd cycle, 20:11–13, "I saw a great white throne and Him who sat upon it. . . . And I saw the dead, the great and the small, standing before the throne, and books were opened . . . and the dead were judged from the things which were written in the books, according to their deeds." Fairbairn speaks therefore of "an absolute universality . . . comprising the entire race of humanity in the whole of its two grand divisions of the saved and the lost."[130] While the occupant of the throne is not identified, it would seem to be God the Father, as distinguished from Jesus the Son; see 5:7, 13, 6:16, 7:10, as based on Dan 7:9–13, in which the one who was "ancient of days" occupied the throne and to whom one "like a son of man" came. But as the apostle records elsewhere, the Father on His part "has given all judgment to the Son" (John 5:22; see Mt 16:27, Acts 17:31); and at the conclusion of Revelation Christ reveals, "Behold, My reward is with Me, to render to every man according to what he has done," 22:12. Paul thus shows "the accurate relation between the two sides of the truth"[131] when he speaks of "the day when God will judge the secrets of men through Christ Jesus" (Rom 2:16).[132] Fulfillment (per. 17): the final judgment, as in Eccl. No. 1.

36. Rev 13:1a; 17:*3b*, *7b*, 12–13, *16a*, 17 (4 vv., sym.): the beast which John saw coming up out of the sea (world political power in general, supporting Rome at that particular time, 17:3, 18)[133] is pictured as "having ten horns . . . and on his horns were ten diadems," 13:1. Explanation for this symbol appears in 17:12–13, "The ten horns which you saw are ten kings, who have not yet received a kingdom; but they receive authority as kings with the beast for one hour . . . and they give their power to the beast" (= v. 17); "i.e. the unanimity of the ten appears in their worldly policy and hostile attitude toward Christ. The Seer entertains no illusions on this point; he does not anticipate that the rise of new and unknown forces will bring any immediate improvement."[134] Context then brackets their period in time: they will, on the one hand, v. 16, hate the harlot Rome and participate in her fall (see under 14:8, No. 40, below); but they will also, on the other, v. 14, wage war against Christ the Lamb and be overcome by Him at His return. Fulfillment (per. 14): as in Dan. No. 10, the

---

130. *The Interpretation of Prophecy*, p. 491; see above, pp. 109–110.
131. Camb, p. 128.
132. So Walvoord synthesizes, "It is God and more specifically Christ Himself," op. cit., p. 305. An alternative solution, though less satisfactory in the light of the total evidence, is the suggestion that Jesus may judge the living, 22:11, but the Father the dead, 20:12, ICC, II:192.
133. See above, pp. 49–50, 600.
134. Swete, op. cit., p. 223.

balance of power among world states, a situation which is true from the time of the historic fall of Rome in 476 up to the Lord's second advent. The grouping is made up of "kingdoms related to the Roman empire as the kingdoms of the Diadochi [were] to that of Alexander. Such are the principal kingdoms of modern Europe."[135]

37. Rev *13:1b*; 17:3a, 7a, 10 (3 vv., sym.): the nature of the beast from the sea (cf. No. 36, preceding), as "having seven heads . . . and on his heads were blasphemous names," 13:1. This symbolism is explained in 17:10 as meaning seven kings, presumably the godless and sometimes persecuting emperors of Rome, since five had passed and one was currently reigning at the time of John's composition.[136] Yet "the other has not yet come; and when he comes, he must remain a little while." Fulfillment (per. 14): one of the more short-reigned emperors of 1st-century Rome,[137] probably Nero's immediate successor Galba (68–69), or Galba's even briefer successor, Otho (ruling for 3 months in 69).[138]

38. Rev 14:1a (1 v.): "Behold, the Lamb was standing on Mount Zion, and with Him 144,000"; cf. 7:1 (No. 22, above). Fulfillment (per. 15): the return of the raptured church with Christ to Jerusalem, as in Joel No. 11.

39. Rev 14:6–7 (2 vv.): "I saw another angel flying in midheaven, having an eternal gospel to preach to those who live on the earth. . . . 'Fear God and give Him glory, because the hour of His judgment [meaning, His wrath, as in 16:5] has come.' " Fulfillment (per. 15): the opportunity for salvation, still held out after Christ's return to the earth, 14:1 (No. 38, preceding).

40. Rev 14:8; 16:19b; 17:1, 16b; 18:1–2, 4–23; 19:1–4 (30 vv., fig.): "Another angel followed, saying, 'Fallen, fallen is Babylon the great, who made all the nations drink . . . of her immorality,' " 14:8. After the eschatological material of vv. 1–7, this verse appears to involve a reversion to the conditions of John's day, as in chs. 12–13; and yet it also marks a specific anticipation of ch. 17, with its subject of "Babylon the great, the mother of harlots . . . with whom the kings of the earth . . . were made drunk

135. Camb, p. 107, which goes on into undue (and dated) speculation as to an exact 10 nations, though this figure seems in truth to have arisen, originally, simply out of correspondence to the 10 toes of the image in Daniel 2; cf. 7:7b etc.
136. See above, pp. 50, 592.
137. Alford, however, takes the kings as "empires," op. cit., IV:705–706, the 5 past being Egypt, Assyria, Babylon, Persia, and Greece; the 6th, Rome; and the 7th, Christendom. Dispensational interpreters generally agree, though substituting "the revived Roman Empire which will be in sway immediately after the rapture of the church" for the 7th, Walvoord, op. cit., p. 254. Others speak of 7 different types of Roman government: kings, consuls, dictators, and so on, with the 6th as emperors, the 7th as the tenfold division, and an 8th as the revived Roman empire, J. D. Pentecost, *Things to Come*, pp. 322–323.
138. See note 7, above. Others, who hold to a later composition for Revelation, would by-pass the above and find the predicted monarch in Vespasian's son Titus (79–81), Camb, p. 106.

with the wine of her immorality" (vv. 2, 5).[139] Likewise in 16:19b comes another, and closer, prefatory revelation, "And Babylon the great was remembered before God, to give her the cup of His wrath," in contrasting retaliation for the cup she had presented to others (17:4, 18:3). As Moffatt states, "The allusion to her downfall is proleptic, as a climax to the foregoing catastrophe,"[140] namely the earthquake damage suffered by Jerusalem at Christ's return (v. 19a). But then inspired prophecy presents the full, detailed revelations of chs. 17–19, "the judgment of the great harlot" (17:1, 19:2), when God remembers her iniquities (18:4–5). Specifically the 10 horns that represent Rome's successors and the beast that stands for world power in general (see 13:1a, No. 36, above) "will hate the [Roman] harlot and will make her desolate and naked, and will eat her flesh and will burn her up with fire" (17:16), all of which is a graphic description of Rome's consumption by surrounding barbarian groups, beginning with the sacking of the city by Alaric and the Visigoths in 410. "In one day her plagues will come . . . in one hour, her judgment" (18:8, 10, 17), meaning "sudden and utter ruin."[141] Ch. 18 then laments the former metropolis as having become desolate, "a dwelling place of demons" (v. 2), with her tremendous ancient commerce at an end (vv. 11–19):[142] "and the great city will not be found any longer" (v. 21).[143] Fulfillment (per. 14): the fall of the Roman empire, A.D. 476, as in Num. No. 42.

41. Rev 14:15–16 (2 vv., sym.): at His return (v. 14, No. 2, above), the Son of man is divinely authorized, through an angel, to "put in [His] sickle and reap, because the hour to reap had come. And He who sat on the cloud swung His sickle over the earth, and the earth was reaped." Since the reaping of those who are subject to condemnation follows separately in vv. 17–20 (No. 42, next), the fulfillment of the present prophecy would appear to concern the ingathering of the righteous from the earth (per. 15), namely the rapture of the living, as in Hos. No. 27;[144] cf. 11:11–12 on the

139. See above, note 40.
140. ExGkT, V:449.
141. Swete, op. cit., p. 231.
142. The presence of such "dated" material makes it unlikely that chs. 13, 14:8–13, and 17–19:5 should refer to a yet future "revived Roman empire"; see Payne, *Imminent Appearing*, pp. 154–155.
143. Statements that the city will have no more craftsmen, weddings, or even lighted lamps, vv. 22–23, and that "her smoke rises up forever and ever," 19:3—which are incongruous with the reduced but still reconstructed existence of Rome as a place—should be understood (like Ezek 26:13, on Tyre, which Rev 18:22 quotes; see under Ezek 26:4b) in reference to Rome as a universally ruling city; i.e. John's words "symbolize the complete submergence, the final disappearance of pagan Imperial Rome," Swete, op. cit., p. 239. One must also reckon with a measure of prophetic hyperbole; see above, p. 18: "The employment of such phrases in Biblical literature is often very loose," NBC, p. 1192, or IB, XII:506, "This prediction that the *smoke* of burning Rome will rise *for ever and ever* should not be taken too literally, for . . . even the earth on which Rome is situated . . . is soon to disappear (cf. 20:11, 21:1)."
144. Others suggest a more negative interpretation, on judgments in general, as opposed to the final, climactic judgment in vv. 17–20.

raising of the dead (No. 32, above). The picture parallels that of the parables of Mt 13 on the discriminatory gathering by angels (cf. Rev 14:17) of the wheat as distinct from the tares, v. 30, and of the good fish separately from the bad, v. 48, except that there Christ seemed to be speaking of the final ingathering of His own into the New Jerusalem, following the final judgment of the wicked (see under Mt. No. 13).

42. Rev 14:17–20 (4 vv., sym.): an angel from heaven "swung his sickle to the earth, and gathered the clusters from the vine of the earth, and threw them into the great wine press of the wrath of God. And the wine press was trodden outside the city, and blood came out, up to the horses' bridles, for a distance of two hundred miles." Since the symbolism is here drawn from Joel 3:13, on the nations that gather in the valley of Jehoshaphat at Lord's return, *the city* that is intended is probably Jerusalem,[145] and the fulfillment (per. 15), Christ's victory in this first engagement out of the total campaign of Armageddon, as in Joel No. 13 (3:2).

43. Rev 15:4 (1 v.): in a contemporaneous interlude between vv. 1 and 5,[146] the saints who are martyrs to the Roman beast, but who now stand as victors in heaven (v. 2; cf. 12:11), quote Ps 86:9, predicting the time when "all nations will come and worship before Thee." Fulfillment (per. 16): the millennial seeking of God, as in Ps. prophecy No. 21.

44. Rev 16:2 (1 v., sym.): at the outset of the plagues of ch. 16, "the first angel went and poured out his bowl into the earth; and it became a loathsome and malignant sore upon the men who had the mark of the beast and who worshipped his image" (cf. 13:15–16),[147] paralleling the 6th plague in Egypt, Ex 9:10. Fulfillment (per. 15): another element in the wrath of God that immediately precedes Christ's appearing (see 6:10, No. 19, above), but the only instance in which the plagues from the bowls do not closely correspond to those from the trumpet blasts of ch. 8 (cf. 8:7, No. 24, above).

45. Rev 17:8a, 11a (2 vv., sym.): the "beast from the sea" not only represents world political power in general (see 13:1, No. 36–37, above) but also may be particularized into an equation with certain individual monarchs as well. In respect to its "fatal wound," for example (13:12, 14; cf. 17:8), the beast seems to be equated with its single head that was wounded (13:3)—one of the first seven emperors of Rome, who survived the inauguration of Christ's kingdom;[148] cf. 17:11, "and the beast is one of the seven." But the "specialized" beast becomes preeminently identified with political power's final evil embodiment: v. 11, "And the beast is himself also an eighth"; v. 8, "the beast . . . is about to come up out of the abyss" (of demons, see 9:1, No. 28), and the unsaved will wonder "when they see the beast that . . . will come." Fulfillment (per. 14): the Antichrist,

---

145. IB, XII:476.
146. Swete, op. cit., p. 193.
147. See above, note 37.
148. Perhaps Augustus or Tiberius; see above, p. 50 and note 106.

as in Dan. No. 14: for he will be destroyed by Christ Himself, at His return, Rev 19:20.

46. Rev *17:8b, 11b; 19:20a* (sym.): in the former references the beast who is the Antichrist (17:8a, No. 45, preceding) is said "to go into perdition," ASV. The thought is then elaborated in 19:20, "The beast was seized, and . . . thrown alive into the lake of fire which burns with brimstone" (see 2:11b, No. 7, above). Fulfillment (per. 15): as in Dan No. 17, the fate of the Antichrist—not simply military defeat (see 19:15–21, No. 47, following), but " 'utter destruction,' referring to eternal damnation."[149]

47. Rev 17:14a; 19:15–19, 21 (7 vv., sym.): the 10 horns that represent the modern balance of political power (13:1a, No. 36, above) "will wage war against the Lamb; and the Lamb will overcome them, because He is Lord of lords," 17:14 (cf. 19:16). In 19:19 John adds, "I saw the beast [the Antichrist, 17:8a, No. 45, above] and the kings of the earth and their armies, assembled to make war against Him [Christ], and against His army." But our Lord will smite the nations with a sharp sword that "comes from His mouth," 19:15, meaning that "the victory of the messiah is single-handed": the mere word of His mouth "is the sole weapon of His victory."[150] No further description is given of the actual battle, only a summons to the vultures to gorge themselves on the flesh of kings and mighty men, vv. 17–18, which they proceed to do, v. 21. Fulfillment (per. 15): as in Num. No. 36, the battle of Armageddon.

48. Rev *17:14b*, 19:14 (1 v.): those who are present with Christ at the battle of Armageddon (see No. 47, preceding) "are the called and chosen and faithful," 17:14. They do not appear to be angels (as this point, though see Joel 3:11b) but the faithful among mankind, according to the parallel phraseology in 2:10, 13; cf. v. 27. So also in 19:14, at Christ's triumphant return, "The armies which are in heaven, clothed in fine linen, were following Him on white horses," again, "probably not angels, but the martyrs in their heavenly garments (6:11; cf. 3:5); it is they who 'follow the Lamb wherever He goes' (14:4)."[151] Fulfillment (per. 15): participation by the church in the battle of Armageddon.

49. Rev 19:7–9 (3 vv., fig.): following the announcement that God has taken up His kingdom on earth[152] (v. 6; see under 10:5, No. 30,

---

149. Walvoord, op. cit., p. 249.

150. ExGkT, V:468. Some would interpret this last expression to mean: "His weapons are spiritual and not carnal . . . the whole course of the expansion of Christianity is here in a figure, the conversion of the Western nations . . . ," Swete, op. cit., p. 254: but such an approach seems hardly to do justice to the apocalyptic context: "He treads the wine press of the fierce wrath of God," v. 15, and all the Antichrist's army "were killed with the sword which came from the mouth" of Christ, v. 21.

151. IB. XII:514.

152. "The Church is in view . . . for whom a wedding feast is now planned on earth," Walvoord, *The Rapture Question*, p. 49; cf. *The Revelation of Jesus Christ*, p. 270.

above), a great multitude exclaims, "Let us rejoice, for the marriage of the Lamb has come and His bride has made herself ready," v. 7—her clean linen clothes are then defined as depicting "the righteous acts of the saints," v. 8. John adds, "Blessed are those who are invited to the marriage supper of the Lamb," v. 9. Fulfillment (per. 15): the Messianic feast, as in Ps. No. 22 (22:29a), the church's formal reunion with her returned, divine "bridegroom."

50. Rev 19:20b (1 v., sym.) brings up the figure of "the false prophet who performed the signs in his [the Antichrist's] presence, by which he deceived those who had received the mark of the beast." This deputy, together with his master the Antichrist-beast, is to be "thrown alive into the lake of fire" (see 17:8b, No. 46, above). The verse's description of the false prophet identifies him as a counterpart—though future to John—of the beast out of the earth, who had appeared in 13:11–17 as a contemporaneous (nonpredictive) figure, and who represented the native religions of Asia Minor that abetted the 1st-century worship of the Roman emperors. Fulfillment (per. 14): those more modern forms of religion that lend support to the political philosophy of the Antichrist and whose essential opposition to Jesus will be manifested by our Lord's Parousia.[153]

51. Rev 20:1–3a (3 vv.): "An angel . . . laid hold of the dragon, who is the Devil, and bound him for 1,000 years, and threw him into the abyss [the subterranean abode of demons; see 9:1, No. 28, above] and sealed it over him, so that he should not deceive the nations any longer, until the 1,000 years were completed." Amillennialist interpreters, following Augustine, generally associate this period of Satan's binding with the present church era. Yet as Beasley-Murray summarizes it, this is to

confuse the earth with the abyss. Satan's [present] expulsion from heaven to earth is followed by a more intense activity on his part among the nations (12:12f, 13:1f), but his imprisonment in the abyss renders him helpless with regard to them (20:3). . . . Furthermore, it appears to be overlooked that 20:1–3 is vitally linked with 19:20–21; the latter tells of the fate of the Antichrist and false prophet [at Christ's second coming, see No. 46 and 50, above], the former continues without a break to narrate what happens to the one who inspires them; it is coincidence, and an unfortunate one, that the chapter division occurs at 19:21.[154]

Fulfillment consists therefore of the temporary restraint of Satan during the future Messianic kingdom (per. 16), as in Gen 3:15c (3rd stage), Isa 24:21a.

52. Rev *20:2b, 3b, 4c, 5b, 6f, 7b*: the saints "reigned with Christ for a thousand years" (v. 4), while Satan was bound (v. 1, No. 51, preceding); i.e. "until the thousand years were completed" (v. 3; cf. v. 7). This period

153. See above, pp. 50, 600, note 44; cf. Payne, *Imminent Appearing*, pp. 121, 133, 175.
154. NBC, p. 1194.

has been called "the cosmic sabbath . . . at the close of creation,"[155] or simply, "a long period of time, a great epoch in human history."[156] But while the precise lapse of the years that are involved may be subject to modification—though in six consecutive vv. the figure 1,000 is repeated six corresponding times, and would appear to be essentially unobjectionable —the fact of an earthly Messianic kingdom, of limited extent, preceding the universal resurrection and final judgment, "is the generally accepted opinion of modern scholarship" about what the Scriptures here teach.[157] That it transpires, moreover, upon the earth and not in heaven (as suggested by some amillennialists[158]) seems to be required by the context both before (19:19, 20:3) and after (20:8–9); see 20:4b, under 11:11, No. 32, above. Fulfillment (per. 16): a 1,000-year duration for the Messianic kingdom prior to the final judgment.

53. Rev 20:5a, 13a, *14a* (2 vv.): v. 5 is anticipatory, for it qualifies the first resurrection, of Christ's own people (No. 32), by explaining that "the rest of the dead did not come to life until the thousand years were completed." But then in vv. 13–14 John developed the thought as follows: "The sea gave up the dead which were in it, and death and the grave [Gk., *hádēs*] gave up the dead which were in them . . . and death and the grave were thrown into the lake of fire," that is, into the eternal hell (see under 2:11b, No. 7, above). For the phrase "the grave," both the ASV rendering, "Hades," and the KJV rendering, "hell," are misleading: the former because of its mythological connotations, and the latter because John's thought is not here restricted to the abode of the lost dead. One might, indeed, ask what other dead there could be; and it is true that all of the saved dead, *at the time of Christ's second coming*, would have been resurrected at that point (I Cor 15:23). Yet during the course of the succeeding 1,000 years (the millennium) many would have died whose spirits would have departed not to hell but to heaven: e.g., of Jews converted at its outset, or of others converted during it, whether living at His return or born subsequently (see 14:6, No. 39, above). *Hádēs*, in 20:13–14, indicates simply the grave (as in Acts 2:27, 31), the place where the body is laid.[159] Accordingly, *death and the grave* "represent the fact of dying and the condition entered upon after death, i.e. the unresurrected life. Both phenomena are symbolically represented as having ceased by being cast into the lake of fire."[160] Thus, while "the second resurrection is taken for granted in

155. ExGkT, V:472.
156. Swete, op. cit., p. 260.
157. NBC, p. 1193; and cf. IB, XII:520, which recognizes this as John's actual teaching; also, see above, pp. 105–107.
158. See Lenski, op. cit., pp. 583–584.
159. Paralleling the OT term *sh'ōl*, as used, e.g., in Job 17:13–14, Ps 88:3–4; see Payne, *Theology*, pp. 445, 528, and R. L. Harris, "The Meaning of the Word Sheol as Shown by Parallels in Poetic Texts," ETS B, 4 (1961), 129–134.
160. NBC, p. 1196.

20:12 and only indirectly described in v. 13,"[161] the fulfillment (per. 17) *is* that of the general resurrection, as in Job No. 2.

54. Rev *20:6d*, those who participate in the first resurrection (v. 5; see 11:11, No. 32, above) are not only to reign with Jesus (see 2:26, No. 9, above), "but they will be priests of God and of Christ." This "hints that there is a ministry for them to perform in that age amongst earth's inhabitants, perhaps with especial reference to evangelism";[162] cf. this particular activity as designated for those who escape from Armageddon, Isa 66:19. Fulfillment (per. 16): as in Isa. No. 7 (2:2a), a preaching and teaching ministry for God's millennial church.

55. Rev 20:10a (1 v.): following the final defeat of Gog and Magog (see under 11:18a, No. 34, above), "the devil who deceived them was thrown into the lake of fire and brimstone, where the beast and the false prophet are also [see under 17:8b, No. 45, above]; and they will be tormented day and night forever and ever." Fulfillment (per. 17): the ultimate judgment upon Satan, as in Gen 3:15c (4th stage), Isa 24:22b.

56. Rev 20:11b, 21:1b (2 vv.): before the presence of God upon His throne for the final judgment (see under 11:18b, No. 35, above), "earth and heaven fled away, and no place was found for them," 20:11. To this 21:1 adds, "and there is no longer any sea." Swete explains, "St. John, an exile in sea-girt Patmos, regarded with no favor the element which mounted guard over his prison and parted him from the Churches of Asia. . . . For this element of unrest, this fruitful cause of destruction and death, this divider of nations and Churches, there could be no place in a world of social intercourse, deathless life, and unbroken peace."[163] Fulfillment (per. 17): as in Gen. No. 14, the passing away of the present order.

161. Ibid., p. 1195.
162. Ibid.
163. Swete, op. cit., pp. 275–276.

SUMMARIES

PREFATORY NOTE

The following chronological and topical syntheses are suggested, in some measure, by T. H. Horne's century-old classification of prophecies into four groups: (1) relating to the Jewish nation, (2) relating to the nations that were neighbors to the Jews, (3) directly announcing the Messiah, and (4) delivered by Jesus Christ and His apostles.[1] The first and last are repsented in the chronological summary, A, that immediately follows. The second and third correspond to summaries B and C, respectively.

---

1. *An Introduction to the Critical Study and Knowledge of the Holy Scriptures,* I:119.

The Biblical Predictions in the Order of Their Fulfillments

For the entries appearing in Summary A, the number at the left (Col. 1) indicates sequence, the order of actual fulfillment. Next comes a brief statement of the prediction (Col. 2), followed by the Biblical book or books in which it occurs, together with its assigned number (based on the order of appearance) as a prophecy in each book. If an asterisk (*) is added after a given book and number, it designates that reference as containing the primary discussion, to which cross reference is made in the listings that appear in the other, generally later books. Then come the total number of Biblical books in which the prophecy appears (Col. 3) and the total number of full verses devoted to it (Col. 4). As an example, the Bible's second prophesied event (2.) to attain fulfillment was Noah's deluge (the flood). The forecasts of it are described in the preceding pages at three points: in Genesis (Gen), as the eleventh prophecy (No. 11) of that book, in Hebrews as its forty-second prophecy (Heb 42), and in Jude as its fifth (Jude 5). In these three (3) books, it occupies eight (8) full verses.

1. Primeval-Patriarchal

	Books	Full verses[2]
1. Death will become the "normal" lot of man, Gen 4	1	1
2. After a twice-stated interval of time, the flood will destroy all life, Gen 11, Heb 42, Jude 5	3	8
3. It will be effectuated by God's coming with many holy angels, Jude 6	1	–
4. But Noah, even according to his name, will be a source of comforting preservation, Gen 10	1	1
5. The Lord will establish His testament with Noah, Gen 12	1	1
6. God will become particularly associated with the Semites, Gen 18	1	1
7. He will show Abram the land of Canaan, 2058 B.C.,[3] Gen 20	1	1

2. Since a few of these predictions (listed on p. 136, above) are marked by a developmental fulfillment and are therefore listed under more than one period, the total of *all* the predictive verses of Scripture is noted separately under the Statistical Appendix.

3. See above, p. xix.

	Books	Full verses
8. He will bless Abram, Gen 22, Heb 18	2	3
9. He will make Abram's name (= his fame) great, Gen 23	1	–
10. Hagar will bear a son, Gen 39	1	1
11. After a one-year interval, Abraham will have a son by Sarah, 2033, Gen 29, Rom 13, Gal 4, Heb 44	4	8
12. Ishmael will grow up to a nomadic life, Gen 40	1	1
13. God will provide the offering for a sacrifice on Mount Moriah, Gen 44	1	1
14. A bride will be obtained for Isaac, 1993, Gen 48	1	2
15. Abraham's death will come at a good old age, 1958, Gen 35	1	1
16. God will establish His testament with Isaac, Gen 43	1	1
17. Jacob will supplant his twin brother Esau, Gen 51	1	1
18. Esau will settle in Edom, away from the more fertile land of Canaan, Gen 53	1	1
19. God will bring Jacob back to Canaan in safety, 1876, Gen 55	1	4
20. Pharaoh's butler will be restored after a 3-day interval, 1852, Gen 57	1	3
21. But at the same time his baker will be hanged, Gen 58	1	2
22. Egypt will experience 7 years of plenty, followed by 7 years of famine, to 1838, Gen 59	1	17
23. Joseph will rise in status, and his family will bow down to him, Gen 56	1	4
24. Job will come out of his trials like gold, Job 9	1	1
25. Joseph will perform the last rites for his father Jacob, 1826, Gen 60	1	1
Total:		65 vv.

2. Egyptian

26. Israel will sojourn in Egypt for 400 years, serving and being afflicted, Gen 31, Acts 30	2	2
27. The Ishmaelites will multiply greatly, Gen 38	1	4
28. Israel will increase into a great nation, *Gen 21, Ex 68, Rom 8, Heb 19	4	25
29. Israel and Edom will develop as two separate nations, Gen 49	1	1
30. A multitude of nations will develop from Abraham, some with kings, Gen 41	1	5
31. Aaron will meet Moses on his return to Egypt, 1447, Ex 13	1	1
32. God will empower Moses and Aaron to speak and to lead Israel, Ex 5	1	4
33. The Israelites will obey Moses, Ex 7	1	2
34. Pharaoh will refuse Moses' request for Israel's release, Ex 9	1	5
35. He will go out to the water on a stated morning, Ex 19	1	1
36. God will judge Egypt with His plagues, Gen 32, Ex 10, Acts 31	3	4
37. In the 1st plague, God will turn the waters into blood, Ex 20	1	3
38. The 2nd plague will consist of frogs, Ex 21	1	3
39. Pharaoh will again go out to the water, Ex 22	1	1
40. The 4th plague will bring flies, but not on Goshen, Ex 23	1	3
41. The 5th plague will affect the cattle of Egypt (except for Israel's) with a murrain, Ex 24	1	3

	Books	Full verses
42. The 6th plague will bring boils on man and beast, Ex 25	1	1
43. The 7th plague will bring hail, but not on Goshen, Ex 26	1	2
44. The hail will cease, Ex 27	1	1
45. The 8th plague will consist of locusts, Ex 28	1	3
46. In the 10th plague, God will slay the firstborn of Egypt, Ex 14	1	8
47. Pharaoh will release Israel, Ex 11	1	2
48. In 1446, after the 400 years, Israel will come out of Egypt, *Gen 33, Ex 2, Acts 32	3	4
49. The Egyptians, accordingly, will acknowledge Yahweh, Ex 18	1	1
50. Israel will depart with great substance, *Gen 34, Ex 12	2	2
Total:		91 vv.

3. Wilderness

	Books	Full verses
51. Pharaoh will pursue Israel, and yet fail, Ex 34	1	6
52. Israel will pass through the Red Sea on dry ground, Ex 35	1	1
53. God's glory will appear, along with quail and manna, Ex 40	1	4
54. Yahweh will grant His testament to Israel, Ex 17	1	1
55. Israel will worship God on Mount Sinai, Ex 6	1	1
56. The Canaanites will "melt" upon learning of Israel's crossing the Red Sea, Ex 38, Dt 8	2	5
57. The Angel of Yahweh will guard Israel and guide them through the wilderness, Ex 47	1	7
58. God will provide Israel with flesh to eat, Num 18	1	6
59. In its disobedience, the nation will be beaten by the Canaanites at Hormah, 1445, Num 23	1	1
60. Korah and his followers will be punished for claiming God's ministry, Num 25	1	3
61. The earth will open, and Dathan and Abiram go down alive into hell, Num 26	1	1
62. For 40 years the Israelites will wander, and all those over 20 die in the wilderness, *Num 19, Dt 2, Ps 43, Heb 10	4	15
63. Aaron will die on Mount Hor, 1407, Num 29	1	1
64. God will deliver Sihon into the hand of Moses, Dt 7	1	2
65. He will also deliver up Og into his power, Num 31, Dt 9	2	2
66. Moses will die, 1406, after viewing the promised land, Num 44, Dt 12	2	5
Total:		61 vv.

4. Conquest

	Books	Full verses
67. In 1406 the peole of Israel will reenter Canaan, *Gen 36, Ex 3, Lev 21, Num 21, Dt 6, Acts 33, Heb 49	7	32
68. Joshua will be privileged to enter the land, *Num 22, Dt 4	2	2
69. The men of Gad will march at the head of their brethren, Dt 54	1	2
70. The waters of the Jordan will be cut off, for Israel to cross its channel, Josh 5	1	4
71. The Canaanites will be rendered subservient, *Gen 17, Dt 58, Josh 21	3	4

	Books	Full verses
72. They will be overthrown in battle and driven out, *Ex 48, Lev 22, Dt 10, Josh 3	4	42
73. Jericho will fall to Joshua, as its walls collapse, Josh 10	1	5
74. Ai and its king will be given up to him, Josh 14	1	3
75. The sun will delay its visible setting, to aid Joshua in the battle of Aijalon, Josh 20	1	1
76. The Jerusalem confederacy of southern Canaanites will be overcome, Josh 19	1	2
77. The Hazor confederacy of northern Canaan will be delivered up to Joshua, Josh 22	1	1
78. God will grant the land of Canaan to the descendants of Abraham, *Gen 24, Ex 16, Num 16, Dt 1, Josh 1, Ps 49 (I Chron 11), Jer 27, Acts 29, Heb 43	10	80
79. Israel will thus inherit a fertile land, *Gen 52, Ex 4, Num 33, Heb 51	4	4
80. Joshua will be the leader to execute this, 1400, Dt 5, Josh 4	2	8
81. W. Canaan, with specified borders, will be allocated to the 9½ tribes, Num 49	1	12
82. God will bring Caleb into Canaan and grant him a possession in the very land he spied out, *Num 20, Dt 3	2	2
83. Ephraim and Manasseh will constitute a multitude in the midst of the land, Gen 62, Heb 48	2	5
84. Though attacked, they will maintain their strength through God, Gen 76	1	2
85. Judah will prosper, with wine and milk, Gen 69	1	2
86. Simeon (in dishonor) and Levi (in honor) will be scattered among the other tribes, Gen 64	1	1
87. Reuben will be isolated and lose its preeminence, Gen 63	1	1
88. Zebulun will lie on the route toward Canaan's coastal harbors, Gen 70	1	1
89. Issachar will toil and serve, Gen 71	1	1
90. Both Zebulun and Issachar are to enjoy abundance, Dt 53	1	2
91. Asher will produce excellent food, *Gen 74, Dt 57	2	3
92. Naphtali will possess Galilee and somewhat to the south, Dt 56	1	1
93. The Israelites' lands will not be coveted while they observe their pilgrimage feasts, Ex 69	1	1
	Total:	224 vv.

5. Judges

94. The Canaanites will be rendered subservient, Gen 17 (2nd stage)	1	1
95. Judah will assume possession of its tribal lands, Jd 1	1	1
96. The tribe of Dan will be dangerous, like a snake, *Gen 72, Dt 55, Jd 16	3	5
97. Benjamin will devour like a wolf, Gen 77	1	1
98. But they will be delivered up to the other united tribes, Jd 20	1	1
99. Intermarriage with the Canaanites will lead Israel into apostasy, Dt 20	1	14
100. Eglon's Moabite forces will be delivered up to Israel, 1316, Jd 5	1	1
101. The Canaanites left in the land will bring suffering to Israel, especially under Jabin, 1236–1216, *Num 47, John 26, Jd 3	3	4

	Books	Full verses
102. The men of Naphtali will advance swiftly, like deer, under Barak, 1216, Gen 75	1	1
103. Jabin's army, under Sisera, will fall by the river Kishon, Jd 6	1	2
104. Sisera himself will be given into the hand of a woman, Jd 7	1	1
105. There will be a gradual driving out of the Canaanites, *Ex 53, Dt 23	2	3
106. The sword of Gideon will overturn Midian like a tent, 1169, Jd 11	1	2
107. Gideon will strike down the Midianites and capture their two kings, Jd 8	1	6
108. Abimelech and the Shechemites will devour each other, 1126, Jd 12	1	2
109. Manoah's wife will bear a son, Samson, Jd 13	1	3
110. Samson will begin to save Israel from the Philistines, judge ca. 1090–1070, Jd 14	1	1
111. Gad will strike back when attacked, i.e. through Jephthah, 1085, Gen 73	1	1
112. Eli's house will be punished, as his two sons are slain, 1080, I Sam 6	1	7
113. God's own temple at Shiloh will suffer destruction, I Sam 7	1	1
114. Samuel will deliver Israel from the Philistines, 1063, I Sam 13	1	1
115. God will send Saul to visit Samuel, 1043, on the following day, I Sam 14	1	1
116. The asses of Kish will be found, I Sam 16	1	2
117. Three described groups of men will meet Saul after he leaves Samuel, I Sam 17	1	6
118. Saul will be found at Mizpah, hiding among the baggage, I Sam 18	1	1
Total:		69 vv.

6. United Kingdom

	Books	Full verses
119. God will send an untimely thunder storm as a warning to the new kingdom, I Sam 19	1	1
120. Israel will find exaltation in its king, *Num 34, Dt 33	2	7
121. Jonathan will overcome a Philistine garrison in front of Michmash, I Sam 22	1	1
122. Saul will there save Israel from the Philistines, 1041, Sam 15	1	–
123. Jonathan will be revealed as the violator of Saul's interdict against eating during that day, I Sam 24	1	2
124. God will cause David to triumph over Goliath, I Sam 25	1	3
125. He will deliver up the Philistines to him at Keilah, I Sam 27	1	1
126. Nabal will come to a sad end, I Sam 29	1	1
127. David will be divinely protected against capture by Saul, I Sam 28	1	1
128. He will overtake the Amalekites who raided Ziklag and recover the spoil, I Sam 31	1	1
129. Saul and his people will be consumed at Mount Gilboa, 1010, I Sam 20	1	1
130. His dynasty will not continue over Israel, *I Sam 21, II Sam 1, I Chron 5	3	12

	Books	Full verses
131. In David, Judah will receive the sovereignty over the other tribes, 1003, Gen 65	1	1
132. David, the tribe's representative, will win victories, *Gen 66, Num 32, Dt 49	3	5
133. He will save Israel from the Philistines (especially in 1003) and from others, II Sam 2 (I Chron 6)	2	5
134. The Canaanites will be rendered subservient, Gen 17 (3rd stage), Josh 24	2	2
135. David will strike down the Moabites, Num 35	1	1
136. The Edomites will serve their brother-nation Israel, *Gen 50, Num 37, Rom 14	3	3
137. The child conceived through David's sin with Bath-sheba will die, II Sam 17	1	1
138. For David's sin over the census, the nation will suffer 3 days of pestilence, II Sam 21 (I Chron 21)	2	9
139. God will choose a mountain for His dwelling place, *Dt 26, Josh 18	1	18
140. The sword will not depart from David's house, and his wives will be humbled, II Sam 16	1	3
141. God will establish David's son as king after him, 970, II Sam 9 (I Chron 15), Ps 58	3	6
142. The priestly line of Eli (in Abiathar) will be replaced by Zadok, I Sam 9	1	2
143. Abraham's seed will possess their enemies on all sides, *Gen 45, Dt 19, Heb 45	3	10
144. Their borders will extend from the Nile to the Euphrates, *Gen 37, Ex 54, Dt 25, Josh 2	4	4
145. Joab and his house will suffer for his murder of Abner, II Sam 3	1	2
146. Solomon will be the wisest of men, I K 7 (II Chron 5)	2	1
147. His reign will be quiet and prosperous, I Chron 23	1	2
148. He will excel other kings in riches and honor, I K 8 (Chron 6)	2	2
149. Solomon will build the temple, *II Sam 10 (I Chron 16), I K 10 (II Chron 14)	4	5
150. David's seed will be chastened for its sin, commencing with Solomon, II Sam 13, Ps 42	2	4
Total:		117 vv.

7. Divided Kingdom

151. Except for one tribe, the kingdom will be taken away from Solomon's son, 930 B.C., I K 17	1	6
152. Ephraim will assume leadership in the N., particularly over Manasseh, Gen 61, Heb 47	2	5
153. Ten of the Hebrew tribes will be given to Jeroboam, I K 18	1	2
154. Jeroboam's altar will be rent and its ashes poured out, I K 20	1	1
155. The prophet who predicted this but then disobeyed God will not return alive to Judah to be buried there, I K 21	1	1
156. The wife of Jeroboam will come disguised to see Ahijah, I K 22	1	1
157. Upon her return to Tirzah, Jeroboam's son Abijah will die, I K 24	1	1

	Books	Full verses
158. The dynasty of Jeroboam will be destroyed, 909, I K 23	1	1
159. Asa will be rewarded for having sought God, II Chron 23	1	2
160. But his unworthy alliance with Damascus will cause wars, II Chron 24	1	1
161. The dynasty of Baasha will be swept away, I K 26	1	2
162. By the word of Elijah, Ahab's land will suffer a 3-year drought, I K 27	1	1
163. The ravens will feed Elijah until the brook Cherith dries up, I K 28	1	1
164. A widow in Zarephath will sustain him, I K 29	1	1
165. Her meal and oil will continue miraculously to be supplied during the drought, I K 30	1	1
166. There will then come an abundance of rain, I K 31	1	2
167. The man who rebuilds Jericho will do so at the cost of 2 sons, Josh 12	1	1
168. Ahab will win a victory over Ben-hadad II of Syria, 857, I K 35	1	2
169. Ben-hadad will attack again in the following year, I K 36	1	1
170. Ahab will win a second, decisive victory, 856, I K 37	1	1
171. After this battle, a lion will slay the man who disobeyed the prophet, I K 38	1	1
172. Ahab will fall and Israel suffer a major reverse at Ramoth-gilead, 853, I K 39 (II Chron 25)	2	9
173. The dogs will lick up Ahab's blood, at Samaria, I K 40	1	1
174. For falsely predicting victory, Zedekiah will go into hiding, I K 44 (II Chron 26)	2	2
175. Jehoshaphat will suffer setbacks because of his alliance with N. Israel, II Chron 27	1	2
176. But he will experience God's salvation against invaders, II Chron 28	1	4
177. Ahaziah of Israel will not recover from a fall but will die, 852, II K 1	1	3
178. Yahweh will take away Elijah from Elisha on the day of this revelation, II K 2	1	3
179. But Elisha will be given a double portion of Elijah's spirit, II K 3	1	1
180. Jehoram of Israel and Jehoshaphat of Judah will find needed water in Edom, II K 4	1	1
181. Moab will be delivered up to the coalition, II K 5	1	1
182. A Shunammite woman will have a son, the next year, II K 7	1	1
183. A small supply of food will feed 100 of Elisha's people, II K 9	1	1
184. A 7-year famine will come upon Israel, II K 19	1	1
185. After 848, Edom will shake off the yoke of Judah under Jehoram, Gen 54, Heb 46	2	1
186. Naaman the Syrian will be cleansed of his leprosy, II K 10	1	3
187. His disease will be transferred to Gehazi and his family, II K 12	1	1
188. The Syrians will come down to specified places seeking Jehoram, II K 14	1	1
189. In the steps of his own messenger, Jehoram will come to Elisha, II K 15	1	1
190. Samaria will be delivered from its desperate siege by the Syrians, II K 16	1	1
191. On the next day, food will be sold at reduced prices, II K 17	1	1

	Books	Full verses
192. The captain at the city gate will see it but not share in it, II K 18	1	1
193. Ben-hadad II of Syria will not recover from his illness but will die, II K 20	1	1
194. Hazael will become king of Syria, ca. 843, II K 22	1	1
195. He will then slay many in Israel, *I K 32, II K 21	2	3
196. Jehoram of Judah will have his household struck down, II Chron 29	1	1
197. He will suffer a serious disease of the bowels, 843–841, II Chron 30	1	1
198. The body of Ahab's son Jehoram will fall in the field of Naboth, whom his father murdered, *I K 43, II K 26	2	2
199. The dogs will eat the body of Jezebel by the ramparts of Jezreel, *I K 42, II K 25	2	2
200. Ahab's dynasty will be wiped out and their bodies left unburied, 841, *I K 41, II K 24	2	5
201. In taking Israel's throne, Jehu will slay many people I K 33	1	–
202. Elisha too will cause the deaths of many, I K 34	1	–
203. Reuben will diminish in numbers, Dt 48	1	1
204. Ephraim will enjoy military success, starting especially with Jehoash, 798, Dt 52	1	5
205. This monarch will win a great victory over Syria at Aphek, II K 33	1	3
206. He will smite the Syrians on 3 occasions, II K 34	1	2
207. The Edomites will serve the Hebrews, especially Amaziah, 796, Gen 50 (2nd stage)	1	1
208. Yet Amaziah will be destroyed for his idolatry: losing power in 790 and dying in 767, II Chron 31	1	1
209. Jeroboam II, 793–753, will restore the borders of Israel, from Lebo-hamath to the Dead Sea, II K 36	1	1
210. When Jonah is cast into the sea, it will become calm, Jonah 1	1	1
211. Though inside a fish, he will yet worship at God's temple, Jonah 3	1	1
212. Jehu's dynasty will continue over Israel for 4 more generations, until 752, II K 27	1	2
213. But his bloodshed will then be avenged upon his house, Hos 1, Amos 17	2	2
214. There will be a great locust plague in Judah, ca. 735, Joel 5	1	12
215. But God will then remove it, Joel 6	1	8
216. Gaza will be burned by Tiglath-pileser III of Assyria, 734, Amos 3	1	2
217. The ruler of Ashkelon will be cut off: either Mitinti in 733, or Sidqia in 701, Amos 5	1	–
218. The 3½ northern tribes of Galilee and Transjordan will form an initial deportation of Israel, 733, Hos 23	1	1
219. The Kenites will then also be carried captive by Assyria, Num 40	1	1
220. Civil strife will mark the last days of N. Israel, Isa 36	1	3
221. The Syro-Ephraimitic alliance will be broken by Assyria; and Damascus will fall, 732, Isa 21, *Amos 2	2	17
222. Yet Ahaz will suffer calamities, even from his Assyrian allies, Isa 23	1	1

	Books	Full verses
223. Because of Jeroboam's sins, N. Israel will be rooted up, 722, *I K 25, II K 39, Isa 27, Hos 2, Amos 1, Mi 1	6	132
224. The family of Amariah priest of Bethel will suffer disgrace, loss of property, and death, Amos 18	1	2
225. Ephraim will go captive into Assyria and beyond, *Hos 16, Amos 13, Mi 2, Acts 36	4	17
226. Amaziah himself will die on foreign soil, Amos 19	1	–
227. Some gleanings of N. Israel will join with Hezekiah in his reforms, Isa 55	1	4
228. Moab will be devastated by Sargon's sweep through that land in 715, Isa 53, *Amos 10	2	20
229. Also to suffer will be the Arabs of Kedar, Isa 61	1	5
230. God will finally blot out the Amalekites, *Ex 43, Num 39	2	3
231. A shadow in Jerusalem will move backwards to confirm the word of Isaiah, Isa 89 (II K 45)	2	4
232. In 712 Hezekiah will be healed and granted 15 additional years of life, Isa 88 (II K 44)	2	6
233. Ashdod will be struck down by Sargon, 711, Isa 52, *Amos 4	2	4
234. The remnant of Moab will suffer even further through this campaign, Isa 54	1	2
235. Edom will undergo Assyrian attack, 711 and 701, Isa 69, *Amos 8, Obad 1	3	8
236. Shebna will lose his office over Hezekiah's palace and later die in exile, Isa 62	1	3
237. Eliakim will receive the post and prosper, but later be cast down, Isa 63		
238. Sennacherib will advance to overthrow Judah, 701, *Isa 18, Mi 3	2	58
239. Sidon will suffer, with some fleeing to Cyprus, only to fall there, Isa 65	1	1
240. One Assyrian army will follow a route down Palestine's central ridge, Isa 38	1	5
241. Egypt too will advance into Palestine, Isa 28	1	–
242. But Pharaoh Shabaka will be routed at Eltekeh, 701, Isa 82	1	2
243. Sennacherib will accomplish widespread desolations in Judah, Isa 29	1	15
244. He will carry many into an Assyrian captivity, Mi 4	1	2
245. God will preserve Judah by destroying the invaders, *Isa 37 (II K 41, II Chron 36), Hos 3, Mi 35, I Cor 2	6	72
246. Sennacherib will return to Assyria, Isa 86 (II K 42)	2	6
247. Judah will enjoy peace, reformation, and recovery, Isa 81 (II K 47)	2	36
248. Sennacherib will fall by the sword in his own land, 681, Isa 87 (II K 43)	2	–
249. By 669 B.C., or 65 years after Ahaz, the Ephraimite people will have ceased, having become Samaritan, Isa 22	1	–
250. Tyre will be wasted and lose its (mainland) fortresses, to Ashurbanipal, 663, Isa 64, *Amos 7	2	13
251. At this same time Assyria will take Egypt captive, Isa 59	1	6
252. Barbaric Scythian horsemen will spread terror in Judah, 628–626, Jer 12	1	27

	Full
Books	**verses**

253. But as Assyria withdraws, Josiah will expand into Galilee,
Nah 2   1   1
254. Remnants of N. Israel will be restored to God's people,
II Chron 34   1   1
255. Josiah (cited by name, 308 years in advance) will defile
Jeroboam's altar at Bethel, 622, I K 19   1   2
256. Ashdod will fall to Psamatik I of Egypt (663–609) after a
29-year siege, Zeph 4   1   –
257. Nineveh will be destroyed, 612, Ezek 42, *Nah 1, Zeph 12   3   39
258. Judah and Josiah will be broken by Necho II of Egypt at
Megiddo, 609, Jer 3   1   5
259. Josiah will die in 609, prior to Babylon's advance into the
land, II K 49 (II Chron 37)   2   2
260. Jehoahaz (609) will never return to Judah but will die in
Egyptian captivity, Jer 41   1   3
261. The Egyptians will fall before Babylon at Carchemish,
605, Jer 83   1   5
262. Gaza will be struck down by Necho, 605, Jer 85, *Zeph 2   2   –
263. Babylon will expand, after Carchemish, Hab 1   1   7
264. Nebuchadrezzar will destroy Ashkelon and take other
Philistine cities, Jer 53   1   7
265. He will plunder and destroy among the Arab tribes, 598,
Jer 25   1   8
266. Jehoiakim's corpse will be left in unburied disgrace outside
Jerusalem, 598, Jer 42   1   2
267. Judah will be defeated, lose its leaders, and be left in the
hands of "children," 597, *Isa 13, Jer 34   2   33
268. Jehoiachin will be given into the hands of Nebuchadrezzar
and die in Babylon, Jer 33   1   6
269. He will be childless in respect to human descendants on the
throne, Jer 43   1   3
270. The priest Pashhur and his family will go captive to Babylon
and die there, Jer 39   1   1
271. The false prophet Hananiah will die during the year 593,
Jer 60   1   1
272. The idolatrous leader Peletiah will experience sudden death,
592, Ezek 10   1   1
273. Nebuchadrezzar will select Judah for attack, over Ammon,
Ezek 26   1   6
274. He will commence Jerusalem's siege on a given date: Jan 15,
588, Ezek 30   1   2
275. Despite their temporary withdrawal in 588, the Babylonians
will return to take the city, Jer 77   1   4
276. A year before the calamity, Jeremiah's cousin will offer to
sell him a field, Jer 71   1   2
277. God will guard Jeremiah and bring his enemies to him in
supplication, Jer 2   1   8
278. Judah's allies, especially Egypt, will desert her in her need,
*Jer 63, Ezek 21   2   2
279. Jeremiah's persecutors from Anathoth will fall by famine and
the sword, Jer 28   1   4

	Books	Full verses
280. Juda will fall to Babylon, 586, in corrective judgment, *Lev 33, Dt 13, Josh 27, I K 15, II K 48 (II Chron 19), Isa 5, Jer 1, Ezek 1, Hos 17, Amos 11, Mi 8, Hab 2, Zeph 1, Rom 16, Heb 39, I Pet 5	17	608
281. Zedekiah will seek to escape by breaking out of Jerusalem, Ezek 15	1	4
282. But he will be captured, blinded, and exiled by Nebuchadrezzar, *Jer 40, Ezek 16	2	20
283. As his household surrenders to the Chaldeans, they will blame the misguided king, Jer 79	1	2
284. Ebed-melech will escape with his life from those he fears, Jer 80	1	2
285. The godly as a whole will be protected from being slain, Ezek 8	1	2
286. For the others, Jerusalem will afford no protection, and they will be judged at Israel's border, Ezek 9	1	3
287. God will destroy the temple, putting it out of His sight, *I K 16 (II Chron 20), Jer 20, Ezek 31, Mi 9	5	9
288. The temple vessels will be carried to Babylon, Jer 58	1	–
289. At the close of 586, a refugee will bring word to Ezekiel in Babylon, who would then once again be able to speak unhindered, Ezek 32	1	3
Total:	1	1421 vv.

8. Exilic

	Books	Full verses
290. As a member of the first group of exiles (taken in 605), Daniel will tell Nebuchadrezzar the interpretation of his dream, Dan 2	1	5
291. The bulk of Judah will go into captivity in 586, *Lev 34, Num 48, Dt 14, Isa 17 (II K 46), Jer 15, Ezek 3, Mi 21, Zech 17	9	55
292. A group will flee to Egypt, only to sell themselves into bondage, Dt 42	1	1
293. The Jews will be fearful, suffer calamities, and pine away in their exile, *Lev 35, Dt 41, Ezek 4, Amos 21	4	14
294. Jeremiah's scribe Baruch will escape with his life,wherever he may flee. Jer 82	1	–
295. Judah's civil rulers will cease during this period, Ezek 44	1	10
296. The false prophets Ahab and Zedekiah will be executed by Nebuchadrezzar for adultery, Jer 61	1	2
297. Many of the exiled Jews will lapse into idolatry, *Dt 15, Jer 36	2	1
298. The remnant still in Judah will experience further deportation, down to 582, Jer 16	1	1
299. The land of Israel will come to be desolate and essentially vacant, Ezek 43	1	3
300. Damascus will suffer a military setback, Jer 89	1	1
301. Tyre will suffer siege by the Chaldeans and be eclipsed for 70 years, 585–515, *Isa 66, Jer 54, Ezek 36	3	27
302. The Ammonites will fall to Babylon and go into captivity, 582, Jer 23, Ezek 28, *Amos 9	3	11
303. Moab will be overpowered as well, 582–581, Jer 24	1	42

	Books	Full verses
304. Pharaoh Hophra will be given into the hands of those seeking his life, 569, Jer 81	1	1
305. Nebuchadrezzar will invade and pillage Egypt, 568–567, *Jer 21, Ezek 41	2	35
306. The Jews who sought to escape him in Egypt will face extermination, Jer 49	1	20
307. But the land will recover from the invasion and continue as before, Jer 84	1	–
308. Nebuchadrezzar will suffer madness, for a period of 7 "times," until he acknowledges God, Dan 12	1	17
309. In remembrance of His testament, God will preserve exiled Israel, *Lev 37, Jer 14, Ezek 11, Hos 26, Amos 22	5	7
310. Zedekiah will die in peace and receive honorable burial, Jer 76	1	2
311. A godly remnant will continue to exist, Isa 19	1	2
312. Others will seek to return to God and will find Him, *Dt 16, Jer 68, Ezek 6, Hos 7, Mi 34	5	29
313. The Edomites will be diminished by attack, probably from Nabunaid, 552, *Jer 22, Lam 4	2	9
314. The nations of the W. Fertile Crescent will serve Babylon for 70 years, or through 3 generations, starting from shortly before the oracle's utterance in 604, up to 539, *Jer 29, Ezek 48	2	25
315. The Jewish exile will extend through a similar 70-year period, *Jer 50, Dan 32	2	2
316. The family of the false prophet Shemaiah will not return from the captivity, Jer 62	1	1
317. The Hebrews' exile will terminate approximately 390 years after the division of the kingdom in 930, after lasting for some 40 years after the final collapse, Ezek 2	1	3
318. Babylon will fall to Cyrus, 539, *Dt 46, Isa 47, Jer 51, Dan 13, Mi 38, Hab 3, Rom 27	7	145
	Total:	471 vv.

9. Persian

	Books	Full verses
319. Within the joint Medo-Persian empire, the Persian element will arise later but prove stronger, Dan 3	1	22
320. There will come a ruler named Cyrus to authorize Judah's restoration, 538, Isa 98	1	9
321. Survivors of Judah will return from the Babylonian exile, 537, *Dt 43, Isa 20, Jer 37, Ezek 12, Hos 22, Obad 3, Mi 22, Nah 2, Zeph 6, Rom 15, II Cor 6, Heb 40	12	91
322. Zerubbabel will be present, as an offshoot of Jehoiachin, Ezek 22	1	1
323. Benjamin will be prominent, in God's favor, Dt 51	1	1
324. A remnant of N. Israel will join with the southern tribes, II Chron 35, Jer 4, Ezek 19, *Hos 9, Obad 5, Mi 5	6	30
325. The temple vessels will be restored to Jerusalem, Jer 59	1	1
326. Other nations, such as Edom, will return from their Babylonian exile too, Jer 30	1	1
327. The Moabites will experience a restoration, Jer 86,	1	1

	Books	Full verses
328. as will also the Ammonites, Jer 88,	1	1
329. and the Elamites, Jer 90	1	1
330. Jews that had been sold into slavery by Greek traders will return, Joel 17	1	1
331. Judah will progress because of faithful leaders, *Isa 6, Jer 5	2	3
332. It will abandon idolatry and dedicate itself afresh to God, Ezek 13	1	11
333. Regeneration will occur, and divine reconciliation, *Jer 48, Ezek 14	2	10
334. Elam will be assimilated into the empire of Cyrus, Jer 55	1	7
335. Proselytes will increasingly seek to join Judaism, Isa 50	1	–
336. Tyre will furnish materials for Judah's reconstruction, Isa 67	1	1
337. Moab will be destroyed like Sodom, Ezek 33, *Zeph 7	2	3
338. After Cyrus—Cambyses II, Smerdis, and Darius I will arise in Persia, 529–485, Dan 40	1	1
339. Egypt will suffer from civil disorder and in 525 will fall before a cruel lord, Cambyses, *Isa 56, Ezek 40	2	72
340. He will raid into Ethiopia (Cush), Zeph 11	1	1
341. The temple will be reconstructed in Jerusalem, 520–515, *Obad 4, Zech 1	2	16
342. Wealth from distant nations will assist the rebuilding, *Hag 5, Zech 16	2	2
343. God will bestow general blessings of prosperity and joy, *Jer 67, Ezek 39	2	33
344. The land of Edom will be taken over by the Nabatean Arabs, ca. 500, and the Edomites permanently driven out, Isa 83, Jer 32, Ezek 47, *Obad 2	4	46
345. Xerxes will stir up all the Persian empire against Greece, 480–479, Dan 41	1	1
346. Haman will fall before Mordecai, 473, Est 1	1	1
347. Ezra will begin to rebuild Jerusalem in troublous times, 458, aided by a Persian decree, though this process will extend over a full 49 years, Dan 37	1	2
348. Jerusalem's restoration will be assured through its refortification by Nehemiah in 444, Neh 3, Jer 64, *Mi 37, Zech 2	4	4
349. After Artaxerxes III's capture of Sidon in 345, some of its people will be sold by Jews into slavery in Arabia, Ezek 38, *Joel 15, Zech 27	3	5
Total:		379 vv.

10. Greek

	Books	Full verses
350. Damascus and other Syrian cities will fall to Alexander after the battle of Issus, 333, Zech 25	1	2
351. Tyre will be destroyed by Alexander, 332, *Ezek 37, Zech 26	2	24
352. Tyrians will be sold by Jews into slavery in Arabia, Joel 14	1	1
353. Philistia will submit to Alexander, and to Greek culture, Zech 28	1	2
354. The Greeks will storm Gaza, Nov., 332, Zech 29	1	–
355. Ashkelon will become depopulated, Zech 30	1	–
356. Accordingly, Philistines will be sold by Jews into slavery in Arabia, Joel 16	1	1

	Books	Full verses
357. Alexander will protect the Jews and end Persian oppression, Zech 32	1	1
358. He will conquer Persia, 331, *Dan 4, Zech 3	2	17
359. At his death in 323, his empire will be seized by leading generals and divided into 4 major areas, Dan 23	1	3
360. Ptolemy I will be strong in Egypt, but his general Seleucus will become greater in Syria, Dan 42	1	1
361. The marriage alliance of Ptolemy II's daughter to Antiochus II of Syria will fail, 247, Dan 43	1	1
362. Her brother Ptolemy III will invade northward, Dan 44	1	2
363. Seleucus II will be driven back from Egypt, ca. 240, Dan 45	1	1
364. Seleucus III and his brother Antiochus III will attack Egypt, Dan 46	1	1
365. Ptolemy IV will defeat Antiochus III at Raphia, 217, but fail to follow up his victory, Dan 47	1	1
366. Antiochus will reattack in 202; and though Scopas will recapture Palestine in 200, he will surrender to Antiochus in 198, and the land will be wasted by their conflicts, *Dan 48, Zech 47	2	6
367. Antiochus will be defeated by Rome in Asia Minor, 190, and afterwards die, Dan 49	1	2
368. Seleucus IV will attempt to rob the Jerusalem temple, Dan 50	1	1
369. Antiochus IV will usurp the Seleucid throne in Syria and attack surrounding lands, but he will be checked by Rome, Dan 24	1	11
370. Serious apostasy will arise among certain Hellenizing Jews, Dan 28	1	–
371. The sanctuary will be profaned for 2,300 days, beginning with the thefts by Lysimachus in 171, Dan 29	1	3
372. The corrupt, Hellenizing priests of Judah—Jason, Menelaus, and Lysimachus—will be cut off, Zech 49	1	1
373. Antiochus will attempt to stamp out Judaism and will defile the temple with his "abomination," 168, Dan 26	1	10
374. By oppression, captivity, and martyrdom he will destroy faithful Jews, Dan 25, *Mi 23	2	7
Total:		104 vv.

11. Maccabean

375. Judas Maccabeus will defeat the Greeks of Antiochus, Dan 51, *Mi 24, Zech 40	3	11
376. He will devote their spoils to the Lord, Mi 25	1	–
377. In Dec., 165, he will cleanse the temple of its idolatrous Greek defilement, Dan 30	1	–
378. Antiochus will be "broken without hand" (die of sickenss), 164, Dan 31	1	1
379. Judaism will prosper in Egypt, with even a temple (of Onias IV) in Heliopolis, 160, Isa 57	1	5
380. Philistia will be overcome by Simon, 148–146, *Amos 6, Obad 7, Zeph 3	3	4
381. The remnant of Judah will occupy it, Zeph 5	1	1
382. Philistia will then be incorporated into Israel, Zech 31	1	1

	Books	Full verses
383. Judah will achieve a recognized independence, 143, Zech 41	1	3
384. Samaria will be occupied by John Hyrcanus, 128, Obad 8	1	1
385. Idumaea will be conquered by John Hyrcanus and incorporated into Israel, *Gen 50 (3rd stage), Num 38, Jer 31, Ezek 34, Obad 6, Mal 1	6	11
386. Ammon will be eliminated by the Nabatean Arabs, "children of the East," Ezek 29	1	7
387. Parts of Transjordan will also be occupied by John Hyrcanus, Jer 87, *Obad 9, Zeph 8	3	2
388. The Jews will assume control of the territories around Sodom, S. of the Dead Sea, Ezek 18	1	2
Total:		49 vv.

12. Roman

	Books	Full verses
389. From the west, Rome will afflict the Semitic Near East, *Num 41, Dan 5	2	6
390. God will bring an end to Jewish independence by means of the Romans, 63 B.C., *Mi 26, Zech 51	2	3
391. The last descendants of the Canaanites will be rendered subservient to outsiders, Gen 17 (4th stage)	1	1
392. Jewish factions, e.g. those of Antigonus II vs. Hyrcanus II, will devour each other, Zech 52	1	–
393. The Jewish parties will depart from God, Zech 50	1	–
394. The city of Babylon will be deserted, *Isa 49, Jer 52	2	34
395. God will give up Israel to degradation under Herod, preceding Christ's birth, Mi 29	1	–
Total:		44 vv.

13. Life of Christ

	Books	Full verses
396. The virgin Mary will conceive a child through the Holy Spirit, *Isa 24, Mt 3, Lk 10	3	4
397. Elizabeth will bear a son, who will be called John (the Baptist), Lk 2	1	1
398. He will be filled with the Spirit, while yet unborn, Lk 6	1	1
399. Zachariah will be dumb until the birth of his son John, Lk 9	1	1
400. Mary will bear a son, Jesus, Mt 1, *Lk 11	2	–
401. He will be God, participating in the divine nature, *Ps 53, Isa 25, Zech 64, Mt 4, Lk 15 (Mk 26), Acts 16	7	12
402. Mary's child will be the Son of God, *II Sam 12 (I Chron 18), Ps 41, Lk 12, Heb 1	5	2
403. His incarnation will bring the presence of God to men (type: tabernacle-temple), *Ex 55, Lev 1, Num 1, Dt 36, Josh 11, Jd 17, I Sam 2, II Sam 6, I K 1, II K 28, I Chron 1, II Chron 1, Ezra 1, Neh 5, Ps 7, Eccl 2, Isa 3, Jer 19, Lam 1, Ezek 5, Dan 1, Hos 25, Joel 2, Jonah 4, Zeph 13, Hag 1, Zech 7, Lk 1 (Mt 30, Mk 8), Acts 37, Heb 25	32	936
404. Yet He will have been with the Father from all eternity, Mi 28	1	–
405. He will come from heaven, as the bread of life (type: manna), *Ex 39, Num 17, Josh 9, John 14, I Cor 11	5	33

	Books	Full verses

406. But He will be man, springing from the seed of woman, Gen 7, Mi 30 — 2, –

407. His deity will be veiled in flesh (type: veil of the tabernacle), *Ex 58, Lev 15, Num 5, II Chron 8, Mt 81, Heb 20 — 6, 14

408. He will come from the Semitic branch of humanity, Gen 18 (2nd stage) — 1, 1

409. Within this branch, His descent will be from the family of Abraham, Gen 46 — 1, –

410. His family will be non-Levitical (type: Melchizedek), Gen 26, Heb 21 — 2, 2

411. He will come rather from the royal tribe of Judah, Gen 67 — 1, 1

412. He will be a shoot springing from the household of David, establishing his house forever, I Sam 30, *II Sam 11, I K 3, II K 23, I Chron 17, II Chron 15, Ps 40, Isa 39, Jer 45, Ezek 51, Amos 23, Zech 10, John 20, Acts 14, Heb 5 — 15, 56

413. He will be a sprout from the specific Davidic offshoots of Jehoiachin and Zerubbabel, Ezek 23 — 1, 3

414. He will be born in Bethlehem, *Mi 27, Mt 5, John 21 — 3, 3

415. The angels of God will worship Him at His birth, *Dt 47, Heb 2 — 2, 1

416. Simeon will not die until he has seen the Christ, Lk 21 — 1, 1

417. Herod will seek the child to destroy Him, Mt 6 — 1, 1

418. Jesus will be a nḗser, "branch," from Nazareth, "branch town," Isa 39 (2nd stage), Mt 7 — 2, 2

419. He will grow up in lowly circumstances, *Isa 26, Zech 14 — 2, 1

420. But He will trust in God from the time of his birth onward, Ps 16 — 1, 1

421. Many will rejoice over John the Baptist, Lk 3 — 1, –

422. He will be great, Lk 4 — 1, –

423. As a Nazirite he will drink no alcohol, Lk 5 — 1, –

424. He will turn many to the Lord, *Mal 19, Lk 7 — 2, 4

425. He will be a forerunner to Christ, the Elijah sent of God, *Isa 90, Mal 19, Mt 8 (Mk 1), Lk 8 (John 2) — 6, 26

426. Jesus, coming after John, will be greater than he, John 1 (Mt 11, Mk 3, Lk 29), Acts 51 — 5, 9

427. He will be anointed by God's Spirit for His ministry, *Ps 3, Isa 40, Dan 36, Mt 32, Lk 32, Heb 3 — 6, 10

428. This will occur in A.D. 26, 483 years after the decree of Artaxerxes to Ezra, under which Jerusalem began to be rebuilt, Dan 34 — 1, –

429. John the Baptist will see the Spirit descending upon Christ, John 6 — 1, 1

430. Jesus will be a man of purity (type: priests' garments), *Ex 60, Lev 10, Num 28, I Sam 26, II Chron 13, Ezra 2, Neh 6, Ezek 59, Zech 6 — 9, 36

431. He will be a man of holiness (type: miter-plate), *Ex 61, Lev 11 — 2, 7

432. He will fulfill the righteous requirements of the law (type: meal offering), Ex 64, *Lev 4, Num 6, Josh 25, Jd 15, I K 14, II K 37, I Chron 22, II Chron 18, Ezra 9, Neh 10, Ps 12, Isa 95, Jer 35, Ezek 58, Joel 1, Amos 15, Heb 33 — 18, 113

433. His life will be wholly surrendered to God (type: burnt offering), Ex 30, *Lev 3, Num 10, Dt 27, Josh 16, Jd 10,

	Books	Full verses
I Sam 11, II Sam 7, I K 6, II K 11, I Chron 8, II Chron 4, Ezra 4, Neh 11, Ps 13, Isa 2, Jer 17, Ezek 54, Dan 27, Hos 20, Amos 14, Mi 36, Mk 24, Heb 35	24	166
434. He will delight to do the Father's will, Ps 27, Heb 34	2	6
435. He will be sinless (type: Paschal lamb), Ex 32	1	1
436. He will live under the Father's protection, Zech 34	1	–
437. He will fulfill the role of the "Servant," laboring in humility, *Isa 91, Zech 9, Mt 31, John 28, Rom 18	5	15
438. His ministry will be unpretentious, *Isa 92, Mt 33	2	4
439. He will be a prophet, like Moses, *Dt 35, John 3, Acts 20	3	8
440. He will proclaim deliverance to men held in their servitude (type: Year of Jubilee), *Lev 27, Num 50	2	28
441. He will bring light to those living in darkness in Galilee, *Isa 32, Mt 14	2	4
442. He will confront men with the decision of faith or disbelief in Himself, Lk 25	1	1
443. Under the Roman empire, God will set up His kingdom, which will be eternal, Dan 7	1	–
444. This kingdom will be one of justice, Zech 33	1	–
445. Christ's ministry will include the healing of diseases, *Isa 101, Mt 23	2	2
446. By His ministry He will give men rest (type: sabbath), Gen 2, *Ex 41, Lev 23, Num 24, Dt 18, II K 8, I Chron 4, II Chron 7, Neh 9, Isa 4, Jer 38, Lam 2, Ezek 25, Hos 8, Amos 20, Col 3, Heb 11	17	88
447. Men will call Mary blessed, Lk 16	1	1
448. Peter will take a great catch of fish, Lk 33	1	1
449. He will later find a fish with a coin in its mouth, to pay the temple tax, Mt 46	1	1
450. Jesus will raise Lazarus from the dead, John 23	1	4
451. On Palm Sunday two of His disciples will find a donkey and its colt for Him to ride, Mk 20 (Mt 49, Lk 62)	3	6
452. The man who questions the disciples will yet send the donkey back to Jesus, Mk 21 (Mt 50)	2	2
453. Jesus will thus enter Jerusalem in triumph, *Zech 35, Mt 51, John 25	3	5
454. By His coming, He will constitute the glory of God within the temple, *Hag 6, Zech 5, Mal 10	3	7
455. To find the room for the Last Supper, Peter and John will meet a man with a water jar, Mk 43 (Lk 68)	2	4
456. Judas will arrive at the Garden of Gethsemane at a time stated by Christ, Mk 50 (Mt 79)	2	2
457. Jesus the Good Shepherd will be betrayed for 30 pieces of silver, Zech 53	1	1
458. At such a ransom price, He will repurchase men to God (type: Gomer's redemption), Hos 14	1	1
459. The man who betrays Him will be one of the 12 disciples, Judas, John 17 (Mt 73, Mk 44, Lk 70)	4	20
460. The Lord's disciples will be scattered, *Zech 66, Mk 47 (Mt 76, John 37)	4	3
461. The fate of Judas will make it better for him not to have been born, *Ps 51, Mk 45 (Mt 74, Lk 71, John 38)	5	16

	Books	Full verses
462. His property will become desolate, *Ps 32, Acts 9	2	3
463. His money will go for the potter's field, *Zech 34, Mt 80	2	3
464. Peter will deny Jesus 3 times before the cock crows twice, Mk 49 (Mt 78, Lk 74, John 32)	4	7
465. Gentile rulers will unite with the Jewish king and people in the Lord's trial, *Ps 2, Isa 30, Acts 24	3	11
466. He will be lifted up in crucifixion that all who truly see may live (type: brazen serpent), *Num 30, II K 40	2	3
467. He will suffer from thirst and pierced limbs as men gamble for His clothes, *Ps 17, John 39	2	9
468. Men will wag their heads in mockery at His crucifixion, Ps 15	1	3
469. He will devote Himself to the work of priestly atonement (type: priests' consecration), *Ex 63, Lev 8	2	24
470. He will be forsaken by God, while bearing men's sins on the cross, Ps 14	1	2
471. His rejection by men will climax in His being slain, *Isa 99, Mk 7, *Lk 24 (Mt 25), John 11, Acts 19, I Pet 3	7	80
472. He will thus give up His life for men (type: blood), *Lev 20, Dt 29, I Sam 23, Heb 30	4	23
473. This will occur in A.D. 30, 3½ years after the commencement of His ministry, Dan 35	1	1
474. His life will be offered to God (type: altar), Gen 25, *Ex 44, Lev 12, Num 3, Dt 38, Josh 15, Jd 9, I Sam 8, II Sam 22, I K 2, II K 29, I Chron 3, II Chron 3, Ezra 3, Neh 13, Ps 25, Isa 85, Lam 3, Ezek 7, Joel 4, Mal 4, Mt 18 (Lk 45), Heb 24	24	117
475. He will execute the ultimately atoning sacrifice (type: priests), *Ex 59, Lev 24, Num 2, Dt 34, I Sam 5, II Chron 16, Ps 59, Ezek 60, Joel 3, Zech 8, Mal 2, Heb 12	12	105
476. He will do so like Melchizedek (type: Melchizedek's priesthood), *Gen 27, Heb 22	2	1
477. He will be a priest "after the order [= manner] of Melchizedek," *Ps 55, Heb 14	2	8
478. This will be a greater priesthood than the Levitical (type: Melchizedek's greatness), *Gen 28, Heb 23	2	7
479. Christ will unite the offices of priest and king, with the priest coming first (type: Joshua's crowns), Zech 13	1	2
480. He will bear the penalty of men's sins (type: sin offering), Ex 63, *Lev 6, Num 9, II Sam 15, II K 32, II Chron 32, Ezra 7, Neh 12, Ps 28, Ezek 55, Heb 36	11	157
481. He will actively redress the claims of God upon sinful men (type: trespass offering), *Lev 7, Num 7, II K 31, Ezra 10, Prov 2, Ezek 56	6	43
482. By performing His atoning ministry toward God, He will remove iniquity, *Job 4, Ps 9, Prov 4, Jer 66, Mi 40, Zech 11	6	20
483. He will thus fulfill the central concept of sacrifice (type: sacrifice), Gen 9, Ex 8, *Lev 2, Num 11, Dt 30, Josh 23, Jd 4, I Sam 1, II Sam 5, I K 5, II K 6, I Chron 7, II Chron 11, Ezra 6, Neh 4, Job 1, Ps 6, Prov 3, Eccl 3, Isa 1, Ezek 49, Hos 24, Amos 16, Jonah 2, Mal 3, Mt 17, Lk 20 (Mk 6), Acts 35	29	151

	Books	Full verses
484. He will serve as an "atoning cover" between God and sinful men (type: mercy seat), *Ex 57, Lev 16, Num 12, I Chron 24, Heb 29	5	13
485. He will atone for the soul of each member of His people (type: the atonement money), Ex 66	1	6
486. He will return sin to its author, Satan, and break his hold over men (type: scapegoat), Lev 18	1	5
487. His death will constitute an atoning sacrifice and ransom before God, *Isa 100, Mt 2 (Mk 19), John 5, Acts 38, I Cor 16	6	22
488. He will be a redemptive substitute for sinful men (type: Passover), *Ex 31, Lev 25, Num 14, Dt 31, II K 50, II Chron 33, Ezra 8, Ezek 61, I Cor 5, Heb 50	10	72
489. He will make reconciliation for men to God, Gen 6	1	1
490. His divine presence will achieve testamentary reconciliation (type: the ark of the covenant), *Ex 56, Lev 17, Num 4, Dt 24, Josh 6, Jd 19, I Sam 10, II Sam 4, I K 4, I Chron 2, II Chron 2, Ps 57, Prov 1, Heb 28	14	160
491. He will justify men (type: the contrasting fall of Adam), *Gen 5, Rom 10, I Cor 23	3	12
492. He will wash men of their sins (type: laver), *Ex 67, Lev 9, Num 13, I K 11, II K 38, I Chron 20, II Chron 9, Jer 57	8	44
493. He will replace human unfitness with new life (type: circumcision), *Gen 42, Ex 15, Lev 13, Josh 7, Lk 18, John 19, Acts 34, Rom 5, Phil 3, Col 2	10	45
494. He will provide a new, cleansed life (type: pre-Calvary baptism), *Lk 27 (Mt 9, Mk 2, John 4), Acts 50	5	30
495. He will remove the illness of sin (type: the freed bird at the cleansing of lepers), Lev 14	1	9
496. The blood of Christ will cleanse the conscience (type: ashes of the red heifer), Num 27	1	23
497. He will bequeath men a testamentary inheritance of reconciliation with God (type: Edenic testament), II Cor 2,[4]	1	1
498. through the preservation of the seed of the woman (type: Noachian testament), Gen 16,	1	10
499. and by forfeiting His own life (type: Abrahamic testament), *Gen 30, Ex 1, Lev 36, Dt 17, II K 35, Neh 8, Ps 48 (I Chron 10), Lk 19, Acts 22, Gal 3,	11	28
500. and through the elect nation of Israel (type: Sinaitic testament), *Ex 45, Lev 32, Dt 11, Josh 13, Jd 2, I K 13, II K 30, II Chron 12, Neh 1, Ps 24, Isa 68, Jer 26, Ezek 17, Dan 33, Hos 21, Hag 2, Zech 39, Mal 8, Rom 12, Gal 5, Eph 5, Heb 27,	22	98
501. and by priestly atonement (type: Levitical testament), *Num 43, Neh 14, Ps 50, Mal 7,	4	7

---

4. Cf. Gen 6 (No. 88, above), though at that point the revelation of the Edenic testament is not in typical form. There its structure is that of a simple, though figurative prophecy. One finds neither the term *b'rīth* (as in the Noachian testament) nor the typifying of Christ's death through the use of dismembered animals (as in the Abrahamic).

	Books	Full verses
502. and through the seed of David (type: Davidic testament), *II Sam 19, II Chron 22, Ps 39, Isa 105, Jer 74	5	7
503. Christ will embody in His Person the entire concept of the testament, *Isa 93, Dan 39, II Cor 4	3	4
504. He will bring His saving help to Israel, *Lk 17, Acts 62	2	16
505. He will restore men's communion with God (type: peace offering), Ex 29, *Lev 5, Num 8, Dt 28, Josh 17, Jd 18, I Sam 12, II Sam 8, I K 9, II K 12, I Chron 9, II Chron 17, Ps 26, Isa 94, Jer 18, Ezek 57, Hos 19, Amos 12, Mk 25, Heb 32	20	114
506. He will provide men the water of eternal life (type: water from the rock in Horeb), Ex 42, I Cor 12	2	2
507. Christ's body will suffer no broken bone (type: Paschal lamb), *Ex 33, Num 15, John 40	3	5
508. But it will be pierced on the cross, *Zech 65, John 41	2	2
509. God will answer Him and receive Him after His sufferings, Ps 18	1	3
510. He will present His work of full atonement to His Father in heaven (type: Day of Atonement), Ex 65, *Lev 19, Num 45	3	23
511. The repentant thief on the cross will be with Him in paradise, Lk 75	1	1
512. Christ's body will be anointed in preparation for burial, Mk 41 (Mt 71, John 24)	3	19
513. In honor of His sinlessness, it will be placed in the tomb of a rich man, Joseph of Arimathea, *Isa 102, I Cor 17, I Pet 7	3	2
514. He will be buried for 3 days, paralleling the experience of Jonah, Mt 35 (Lk 40)	2	4
515. On the third day He will rise again from the dead, Ps 11, *Isa 103, Hos 18, Mt 43 (Mk 11), Lk 35, John 8, Acts 13, I Cor 18, Heb 15, I Pet 4	11	33
516. He will breathe the Spirit upon His disciples, to quicken and to instruct them, John 30	1	13
517. He will regather them in Galilee, *Zech 67, Mk 48 (Mt 77), John 34	4	7
518. The disciples will make a miraculous catch of fish, John 44	1	1
519. Peter will repent of his denial of Christ and be restored, Lk 73	1	1
520. Jesus will ascend into heaven, *Ps 8, Lk 46 (Mt 29, Mk 27), John 16, Acts 15, I Cor 22, Heb 6	8	40
521. He will crush Satan by casting him down from his place of power, *Gen 8, Job 10, John 26	3	3
522. At His ascension, He will achieve mankind's lost dominion by being crowned with glory (type: Adam's status), Gen 1	1	2

Total   3348 vv.

(Nontypical, 574; typical, 2774)

14. Church

| 523. Beginning with the Last Supper, Christ will inaugurate the new testament in His blood, *Jer 7, Ezek 20, Hos 10, Heb 26 | 4 | 19 |

	Full
Books	verses

524. After His passion, He will honor the name of God in the midst of the church, *Ps 19, Heb 8   2   5

525. Through Christian baptism, God will wash away guilt and mediate salvation (type: the ark of Noah), Gen 13, I Pet 8   2   9

526. Its observance will mark release from the enemy and protection in a new life (type: the cloud at the Red Sea), *Ex 36, I Cor 9   2   4

527. It will symbolize death to former bondage and the way to God's heritage (type: crossing through the Sea), *Ex 37, I Cor 10   2   1

528. The Christian communion service will mediate life that comes from Christ's flesh and blood, *Ps 20, John 15   2   7

529. The apostolic office of Judas will be taken by another, *Ps 52, Acts 10   2   3

530. The fullness of God's Spirit will be poured out at Pentecost, Isa 96, *Joel 8, Lk 30 (Mt 12, Mk 4), John 7, Acts 1, Gal 2, Eph 1   9   20

531. Pentecost will fulfill Christ's earlier, symbolical act by which He bestowed power (type: His breathing on the disciples), John 42   1   1

532. Peter and Andrew will become fishers of men: e.g., 3,000 at Petecost, Mk 5 (Mt 15, Lk 34)   3   3

533. Christ will send His apostles to the Jewish people, Lk 43 (Mt 54)   2   1

534. His followers will be witnesses to Him in Jerusalem, Acts 4   1   −

535. Through Peter the church will be built, Mt 41   1   1

536. By their preaching, leaders of the Christian church will hold the keys to heaven, Mt 42 (John 43)   2   3

537. For her falsehood, Sapphira will meet the same fate as her husband, Acts 25   1   1

538. The Jews will persecute and kill some of the apostles and other church leaders, Lk 44 (Mt 27, Mk 32), John 36   4   39

539. Christ's followers will be witnesses for Him in all Judea, Acts 5,   1   −

540. and in Samaria, Acts 6   1   −

541. The church will be sown among the nations, Zech 42   1   1

542. A believing remnant will continue in Palestine, Zech 48   1   2

543. In Damascus Saul will be told God's plans for his life, Acts 39   1   2

544. Ananias will restore his sight, Acts 40   1   1

545. The Lord will show him how much he must suffer for Him, Acts 44   1   −

546. And he *will* thereafter suffer for the name of Jesus, Acts 45   1   1

547. But the Lord will deliver him from the Jewish people, Acts 60   1   1

548. Christ will continue to appear to Paul, with revelations about which he is to witness, Acts 59   1   1

549. In Jerusalem the Jews will not accept his testimony but force him to flee, Acts 55   1   1

550. Peter will preach words by which Cornelius and his household will be saved, Acts 46   1   3

551. Gentiles will be included in the church as part of the true Israel of God, *Gen 19 (and 41, 2nd stage), Dt 44, Ps 38,

	Books	Full verses
Isa 97, Jer 6, Hos 4, Joel 12, Amos 24, Mi 31, Zech 4, Mal 5, John 22, Acts 21, Rom 7, II Cor 7, Gal 1, I Pet 6	17	49
552. A great famine will occur under Claudius (A.D. 41–54), Acts 48	1	1
553. James and John will suffer death and sorrow, as did Jesus, Mk 18 (Mt 48)	2	1
554. Elymas the magician will suffer temporary blindness, Acts 49	1	1
555. Paul will be Christ's special apostle to the Gentiles, Acts 41	1	3
556. But he will also witness to the Jews, Acts 43	1	–
557. Gentiles will come to replace the Jews as God's people, Lk 63 (Mt 52, Mk 22)	3	4
558. In time, the gospel will cause the customs of Moses to be set aside, Acts 28	1	–
559. The church will proclaim Christ's message of peace to the nations before his return, *Isa 69, Zech 37, Mk 33 (Mt 59), Lk 22, Acts 7, Rom 21, Gal 6	8	17
560. The church will experience a remarkable growth, *Ezek 24, Mt 40, Mk 9 (Lk 50), John 33, Acts 26	6	17
561. Satan will be crushed under their feet, *Gen 8 (2nd stage), Rom 29	2	1
562. Christ will deliver Paul from Gentile persecution, Acts 61	1	–
563. He will shield him from harm in Corinth, A.D. 50–51, Acts 52	1	1
564. But bonds and imprisonment will await him in Judea, 56–58, Acts 53	1	7
565. Paul will witness to Christ before kings, Acts 42	1	–
566. In the storm on his way to Rome, the ship will be wrecked on an island but all on board will be saved, Acts 63	1	7
567. Paul will witness in Rome itself, Acts 57	1	1
568. After his departure, wolflike false teachers will draw away disciples in Ephesus, Acts 54 (cf. I John 1)	1	2
569. Peter will suffer execution in his old age, A.D. 64, John 31	1	1
570. Shortly before this he was told: It will come soon, II Pet 1	1	2
571. In the same period, the church at Smyrna will undergo a limited tribulation, Rev 5	1	1
572. God will keep the church at Philadelphia during this hour of trial, Rev 11	1	1
573. The false prophetess Jezebel will succumb to sickness at Thyatira, Rev 8	1	1
574. The Jews will suffer from factional strife up until A.D. 70, Zech 55	1	1
575. The high priest Ananias will be assassinated, Acts 56	1	1
576. False christs will arise, Lk 56 (Mt 57, Mk 30)	3	13
577. During the 3½ years of the Jewish war with Rome, 66–70, the church in Jerusalem will be protected, Rev 31	1	3
578. There will be wars, earthquakes, and famines, Mk 31 (Mt 58, Lk 65)	3	8
579. Nero's successor Galba will remain a little while, 68–69, Rev 37	1	3
580. Jerusalem will fall to the Romans, 70, Dan 38, *Mi 39, Zech 36 (and 66, 2nd stage), Mal 6, *Mt 28 (Mk 15), Lk 23, I Thess 2	8	62

	Books	Full verses
581. The temple will be destroyed, *Mt 55 (Mk 29, Lk 64), Acts 27	4	12
582. The Jewish people will be scattered and suffer affliction, *Mi 18, Zeph 15, Zech 68	3	–
583. They will long abide without king or sacrifice, or idolatry (type: Gomer's seclusion), Hos 15	1	2
584. The future Messianic kingdom will not appear immediately, Lk 60 (Mt 67)	2	1
585. The church will witness from generation to generation of Calvary love, Ps 23	1	3
586. In the 4th century Rome will suffer decay and be divided into the E. and W. empires, Dan 6	1	3
587. The city of Rome will fall, officially A.D. 476, *Num 42, Zech 56, Rev 40	3	31
588. It will be succeeded by a balance of power, *Dan 10, Rev 36	2	5
589. Egypt will be a leading Christian nation, 3rd–7th centuries, one with Israel and Assyria, Isa 58	1	3
590. The Ephesian church will come to an end, 1308, Rev 3	1	1
591. Good and bad together will grow up in this age, Mt 38	1	9
592. Its course will be marked by acts of aggression, Rev 15	1	2
593. Following upon such acts will come warfare, Rev 16	1	2
594. The result of war will be famine, Rev 17	1	2
595. The final result will be an extraordinary death rate, Rev 18	1	2
596. Mary's act of anointing Jesus will be remembered, Mk 42 (Mt 72)	2	2
597. Rechabites will survive to worship God, Jer 78	1	2
598. Apostasy will characterize the time preceding Christ's return, *Lk 59, II Thess 7, I Tim 1, II Tim 8, II Pet 4,	5	9
599. and a corresponding moral decline, *II Tim 4, Jude 7	2	12
600. Particularly, mockers will deny the promise of Christ's coming II Pet 8	1	5
601. Yet believers may "hasten the day" through acts of consecration, II Pet 10	1	–
602. Antichrist will arise to power, by overthrowing 3 states, *Dan 14, II Thess 8, I John 1, II John 1, Rev 45	5	14
603. He will speak blasphemies against the Most High, Dan 15	1	–
604. He will seek to change seasons and laws ordained by God, Dan 21	1	–
605. Yet he will have support from organized religion, the "false prophet," Rev 50	1	1
606. The restraint of lawlessness by responsible government will be set aside, II Thess 9	1	2
607. The great tribulation will occur preceding Christ's coming, Isa 70, *Dan 20, Zech 43, Mk 34 (Mt 60), Rev 20	6	13
608. It will last for an indefinite amount of "times," Dan 22	1	4
609. The archangel Michael will protect God's people during this tribulation by the Antichrist, Dan 53	1	–
610. There will be a community of unconverted Jews in Jerusalem at the time of Christ's return, Zech 63	1	–
Total:		481 vv.
(Nontypical, 464; typical, 17)		

15. Christ's Second Coming

	Books	Full verses
611. The return of Christ will occur at any time; it is imminent, Mt 66, *Lk 47 (Mk 39), Rom 25, Phil 5, James 4, I Pet 10, Rev 1	8	49
612. It will be announced by "the wrath of God," including a great earthquake and divine punishments upon the world, *Isa 48, Jer 13, II Thess 1, Rev 19	4	35
613. There will be particular, heavenly phenomena, *Joel 9, Zech 72, Mk 35 (Mt 61, Lk 66), Acts 11, Rev 21	7	18
614. Hail, fire, and a blood-red rain will destroy a third of the earth, Rev 24	1	1
615. A malignant sore will come upon those who serve the Antichrist-beast, Rev 44	1	3
616. The sea will become blood, so that all life in it will die, Rev 25	1	3
617. The world's fresh-water springs and rivers will become bitter; and the remainder, blood, causing death for a large number, Rev 26	1	6
618. Because of false security, many will be overwhelmed by this wrath of God, *Lk 57 (Mt 65), I Thess 8	3	15
619. Yet God will protect His church from harm, as they pass through its initial stages, *I Thess 9, Rev 22	2	14
620. They will rather experience joy in their hearts, II Pet 3	1	1
621. Christ will return, visibly, Job 6, *Ps 45 (I Chron 13), Isa 77, Dan 19, Mi 6, Zech 18, Mal 11, Mt 44 (Mk 13), Lk 37, John 45, Acts 8, Rom 23, I Cor 1, Eph 6, Phil 1, Col 4, I Thess 1, II Thess 3, I Tim 2, II Tim 6, Titus 1, Heb 31, James 3, I Pet 2, II Pet 2, I John 2, Rev 2	29	63
622. His appearing will cause a temporary suspension to the wrath of God, Rev 23	1	1
623. A mighty army of angels will accompany Him, *Joel 18, Zech 71, Mt 45 (Mk 14, Lk 38), II Thess 4	6	–
624. Creation will rejoice at His return and be released from its curse, *Ps 44 (I Chron 12), Isa 43, Hos 11, Hab 4, Rom 11	6	19
625. Christ will send angels with a great trumpet to assemble His own, *Isa 79, Mt 63, I Cor 25, I Thess 5	4	–
626. The archangel Michael will utter his voice, I Thess 4	1	–
627. The souls of the righteous dead, accompanying Christ on His return, will experience "the first resurrection" and be reunited with their bodies, Job 7, Ps 10, *Isa 76, Dan 55, Hos 28, Lk 55 (Mt 43, Mk 23), John 13, Acts 23, Rom 19, I Cor 8, II Cor 3, Phil 4, I Thess 3, Rev 32	16	54
628. Their resurrected bodies will be imperishable, marked by power and life, I Cor 15	1	23
629. The prophet Daniel will share in this resurrection, Dan 58	1	1
630. The living church will be caught up, "raptured" to meet Christ in the clouds, Isa 78, Dan 54, *Hos 27, Joel 10, Zech 22, Lk 58 (Mt 62, Mk 36), Acts 12, Rom 17, I Thess 6, II Thess 2, Rev 41	13	21

	Books	Full verses
631. In His presence our bodies will be changed, conformed to the body of His glory, *Rom 9, I Cor 24, Eph 2, Col 1, II Thess 12, I John 3	6	20
632. The time is known only to the Father, *Zech 73, Mk 38 (Mt 64), Acts 3	4	3
633. The Jews will repent, in mourning, and accept Christ, *Isa 31, Hos 5, Zech 62, Lk 53 (Mt 56), Rom 20, Heb 9, Rev 33	8	23
634. This includes the nation as a whole, though perhaps not every individual, Rom 22	1	–
635. The wrath of God will resume, with "the three woes," Rev 27	1	3
636. Misled by Satan, the world will take up military preparation against Christ, Rev 28	1	13
637. The first wave of forces opposing Him will gather to a valley designated "Jehoshaphat," near Jerusalem, Joel 13	1	7
638. The city will be ravaged and half the population captured, Zech 57	1	2
639. Jesus' feet will stand on the Mount of Olives, Zech 69	1	–
640. The raptured church will return with Him to the Holy Land, Isa 80, *Joel 11, Mi 7, Zech 23, I Thess 7, Rev 38	6	3
641. The converted Jews will be rescued from Jerusalem by a special valley leading to Olivet, Zech 70	1	2
642. God will strengthen Christ, His "anointed," the Messiah, I Sam 4	1	1
643. The Jews will become allies of the church against the foe, Zech 59	1	1
644. Christ will make Jerusalem victorious over the siege and disastrous to its attackers, Ps 46, *Zech 58	2	13
645. From Jerusalem He will attack and overpower the besieging pagans in the valley of Jehoshaphat, *Joel 19, Rev 42	2	4
646. But there will be discrimination, so that some are left, Zech 61	1	1
647. Jerusalem will be resettled and restored, Zech 60	1	1
648. The Messianic marriage feast of the Lamb will be observed on Mount Zion, *Ps 22, Isa 75, Lk 48 (Mt 75, Mk 46), Eph 7, Rev 49	7	10
649. Gentiles from all quarters will sit at the banquet with Abraham, Lk 51 (Mt 21)	2	6
650. The church's former act of eating around "the Lord's table" will be fulfilled in this feast (type: Lord's Supper), *Lk 69, Acts 18, I Cor 13	3	20
651. The ágápē, or love feast, will have a similar accomplishment (type: love feast), Jude 3	1	1
652. A flying angel will proclaim the eternal gospel, appealing to men on earth, Rev 39	1	2
653. The Euphrates and Nile will be dried up, *Isa 45, Zech 44	2	1
654. The world's armies will assemble against Christ, those from the east crossing the dry bed of the Euphrates, Rev 29	1	13
655. When opposed by Egypt, the Antichrist will attack there but will spare Transjordan before advancing to the area of Armageddon, Dan 52	1	5

	Books	Full verses
656. Young believers will willingly offer themselves to Christ for His Armageddon campaign, Ps 54	1	1
657. A group of "principal men" will serve as particular leaders, Mi 33	1	–
658. The church will follow her Lord into battle, Rev 48	1	1
659. The armies led by the Antichrist will be destroyed by Jesus at Armageddon, *Num 36, Dt 40, I Sam 3, Ps 4, Isa 34, Jer 65, Dan 8, Zeph 9, Zech 45, II Thess 11, Heb 38, Rev 47	12	46
660. In the process, the land of Assyria will be wasted by the sword, Mi 32	1	2
661. The Messiah will strike through the head of the Antichrist over a wide land, *Ps 56, Isa 42, II Thess 10	3	2
662. The Antichrist, or "beast," will be cast into the lake of fire, *Dan 17, Rev 46	2	1

Total: $\overline{535}$ vv.

(Nontypical, 514; typical 21)

16. Millennium

	Books	Full verses
663. Satan will be overcome by Christ and bound during the millennial period, *Gen 8 (3rd stage), Isa 71, Dan 18, Rev 51	4	6
664. Jesus will rule the earth as Messiah, *Gen 68, I Sam 4, Ps 5 (I Chron 14), Isa 11, Ezek 27, Dan 9, Obad 10, Mi 14, Zech 15, Mt 34, Lk 13 (Mk 28), Acts 17, Rom 26, I Cor 21, Eph 4, II Tim 7, Heb 7, Rev 30	20	63
665. His kingdom will be worldwide, *Ps 35, Zech 38	2	1
666. God's true Israel will permanently repossess the land of Canaan, Gen 24 (2nd stage)	1	12
667. Unrepentant Jews will be removed, Zeph 17	1	–
668. Repentant Jews will return to Palestine, assisted by Gentiles, Isa 44, Jer 10, *Hos 6, Mi 17, Zeph 16	5	19
669. God will establish His ultimate Testament of Peace, Lev 31, Isa 104, *Ezek 45, Rom 24, II Cor 5	5	15
670. There will be peace, as all violence is restrained by God's presence, *Lev 29, Isa 12, Jer 47, Hos 12, Joel 7, Mi 15, Zeph 18, Zech 12	8	21
671. His rule will be in righteousness and goodness, *II Sam 18, Ps 31, Isa 35, Jer 46	4	11
672. He will proclaim deliverance from servitude (type: Year of Jubilee, 2nd stage), *Lev 27, Num 50	2	28
673. Crops will be abundant and prosperity general, *Ex 49, Lev 28, Dt 39, Ps 34, Isa 14, Ezek 46, Hos 13, Joel 21, Amos 25, Eph 3, Heb 41, I Pet 1	12	31
674. Those not in resurrection bodies will attain to a full length of life, *Ex 52, Zech 21	2	1
675. They will enjoy supernatural life spans, Isa 107	1	4
676. There will be a healing of infirmities and a freedom from disease, *Ex 50, Dt 22, Isa 84	3	4
677. There will be an absence of barrenness or miscarriages, with a resulting multiplication, *Ex 51, Lev 30, Dt 21, Isa 33	4	6

	Books	Full verses
678. God's people will be characterized by a Spirit-given holiness and obedience, to do His commandments, *Dt 45, Isa 15 Jer 11, Zeph 14, Zech 20, Mal 12	6	25
679. There will be joy and praise, *Isa 46, Zeph 19, Jude 8	3	22
680. The overall purpose is that Christ may be glorified in His people, II Thess 6	1	1
681. The saints will enjoy communion with God (type: peace offerings, 2nd stage); see No. 505, above	20	114
682. Christ will have a particular concern for the poor, *Ps 36, Isa 41	2	3
683. The land of Israel will possess enlarged borders and be divided into E–W strips for the 12 tribes, Ezek 63	1	31
684. The territory of Judah will be leveled, but Jerusalem will be elevated, *Isa 7 (Mi 10), Zech 75	3	3
685. The city will have specified borders and surrounding lands, Ezek 65	1	11
686. There will be a temple and sacrifice in Jerusalem, *Isa 8 (Mi 11), Ezek 52, Jer 73, Zech 78, Mal 13	6	9
687. Levites will continue to serve in the sanctuary, *Dt 50, Jer 72	2	2
688. The kingdom will center in Jerusalem and its temple, where the Shekinah (glory cloud) of Yahweh will reside, *Isa 16, Jer 8, Ezek 66, Joel 20, Zeph 20, Zech 19	6	5
689. The presence of God's Holy Spirit will be assured, Isa 106	1	1
690. A stream will proceed from the temple to bring water to surrounding areas, Ezek 62, *Joel 22, Zech 74	3	12
691. God's people will be reestablished as a permanent political political entity, Jer 69	1	3
692. The apostles will sit on thrones to judge the 12 tribes of Israel, Mt 47 (Mk 17, Lk 72)	3	6
693. Certain undershepherds, from the church, will assist in the Messiah's rule, Jer 44	1	3
694. God's people will enjoy a privileged status of power, Dt 37, *Isa 51, Dan 16, Mi 19, Zech 46, Lk 49, Acts 2, Rom 6, I Cor 6, II Tim 2, Rev 9	11	62
695. Former Jews will come to worship at their feet, Rev 10	1	1
696. Christians will even preside over angels, I Cor 7	1	1
697. All nations will worship God and the Messiah, *Gen 47, Ps 21, Isa 9 (Mi 12), Jer 9, Zeph 10, Zech 24, Rom 28, Rev 43	9	30
698. This will constitute their true "ingathering" (type: Feast of Tabernacles), *Ex 46, Lev 26, Num 46, Dt 32, I K 12 (II Chron 10), Ezra 5, Neh 7, John 18	9	34
699. The Feast of Tabernacles will be observed annually, Zech 76	1	–
700. Yet the world will not see a total conversion, Mi 16	1	1
701. A national group that fails to go up to worship will have no rain, Zech 77	1	3
702. Egypt will be desolate because of its former acts of violence Joel 23,	1	1
703. as will also the land of Edom, Joel 24	1	1
704. Those who escape from Armageddon will evangelize the nations, Isa 108	1	1

	Books	Full verses
705. Nations will experience conversion and be incorporated into Israel, *Ps 29, Jer 75, Ezek 64	3	4
706. God's truth will be universally taught, *Isa 10 (Mi 13), Rev 54	3	1
707. God will take some of the Gentiles for priests and Levites, Isa 109	1	1
708. Christ's rule, while Satan is bound, will last 1,000 years, Rev 52	1	–

Total: 614 vv.

(Nontypical, 438; typical, 176)

17. Final Judgment

709. Satan will be released and deceive the nations, but Gog and his allied nations will be overthrown in their postmillennial revolt, *Jer 56, Ezek 53, Hag 4, Rev 34	4	60
710. Christ will finally destroy Satan, casting him into the lake of fire, *Gen 8 (4th stage), Isa 72, Rev 55	3	7
711. Heaven and earth will pass away, *Gen 14, Job 3, Ps 47, Isa 73, Hag 3, Mt 16 (Mk 37, Lk 67), Heb 4, II Pet 9, Rev 56	11	20
712. At the voice of Christ, all those who are yet dead will rise from their graves in a general resurrection, *Job 2, Dan 56, Lk 41 (Mt 36), John 12, Acts 58, I Cor 19, II Tim 3, Heb 16, Rev 53	10	22
713. There will be a final judgment to determine the eternal destiny of all men, *Eccl 1, Mt 68 (Lk 61), Acts 47, Rom 2, Phil 2, II Tim 5, Heb 17, Rev 35	9	28
714. The righteous will be justified (by faith) to eternal life in the New Jerusalem, though also judged for reward according to their works, *Job 5, Mal 16, Mt 20, Mk 10, Lk 54, Rom 3, I Cor 3, II Cor 1, Gal 7, II Tim 1, James 1, I Pet 11, I John 4, II John 2, Rev 12	15	46
715. A saved man may yet suffer loss of reward, if his works are found to be unworthy, I Cor 4	1	3
716. Demons will be condemned, *Mt 24, Jude 2 (II Pet 6)	3	3
717. The ungodly will be sentenced to the ultimate hell of the lake of fire, Job 8, *Ps 1, Mal 14, Mt 19 (Mk 12, Lk 36), John 29, Rom 1, I Cor 14, James 2, I Pet 9, II Pet 5, Jude 1	13	65
718. Jews, though once chosen people, will be among the condemned, Lk 52 (Mt 22)	2	7
719. Gentiles will serve to condemn them, *Lk 42 (Mt 37), Rom 4	3	5
720. There will be differences in the punishments measured out, depending upon degrees of enlightenment, Lk 39 (Mt 26)	2	8
721. Angels will be employed to execute the sentences, Mt 39	1	4
722. Christ will finally offer up His mediatorial kingship to God the Father, I Cor 20	1	1

Total: 279 vv.

18. New Jerusalem

	Books	Full verses
723. God will rule over Israel forever, *II Sam 14 (I Chron 19), II Chron 21, Ezek 50, Dan 11, Amos 26, Mi 20, Lk 14	8	8
724. The Messiah will be eternal, *Ps 37, John 27, Heb 5	3	3
725. There will be shining rewards for those who are faithful to the Lord, Dan 57	1	–
726. Zerubbabel will be particularly rewarded, with closeness to God, Hag 7	1	1
727. Jerusalem will abide forever, *Ps 30, Jer 70, Joel 25	3	2
728. Specifically, there will descend from heaven to a transformed world the New Jerusalem, characterized by the glory of God, Rev 14	1	8
729. The righteous will be gathered in to the blessedness of this New Jerusalem of God, *Isa 74, Mt 13 (Lk 31), Heb 52, II Pet 11, Rev 13	6	35
730. There they will experience final life, a "healing" of the nations, *Mal 17, Rev 4	2	14
731. All will appear to worship God on the new moons and sabbaths, Isa 110	1	1
732. The redeemed will enjoy unimpared fellowship with God (type: the millennial temple), as in No. 686 above—*Isa 8 (Mi 11), Ezek 52, Jer 73, Zech 78, Mal 13	6	9
733. They will share in a perfected life (type: tree of life), Gen 3	1	3
734. There will be a lake of fire, prepared for the devil and his angels, Mt 69	1	–
735. The wicked will suffer the torments of this hell fire, *II Sam 20, Isa 111, Mal 18, Mt 10 (Mk 16, Lk 28), John 35, II Thess 5, Heb 37, Jude 4 (II Pet 7), Rev 7	12	42
736. But the righteous will not be harmed by such "second death," Rev 6	1	1
737. Men will reverence God forever, Ps 33	1	1
Total:		128 vv.

(Nontypical, 116; typical, 12)

SUMMARY B

Prophecies Concerning the Foreign Nations
More Prominent in Scripture

(* = the reference of primary discussion for repeated prophecies)

Ammon

Period   Event and numbered listing in each book
8. To fall to Babylon, 582 B.C. and be led into captivity there, Jer 23, Ezek 28, *Amos 9
9. To experience restoration after Babylon's fall in 539, Jer 88
11. To be destroyed by Nabatean Arabs from the east, Ezek 29
11. Parts of Transjordan also to be occupied by John Hyrcanus, Jer 87, *Obad 9, Zeph 8
15. Its better portions to be spared from attack by the Antichrist prior to Armageddon, Dan 52
15. But to be overpowered by Israel, Isa 34

Assyria

7. Tiglath-pileser III to take 3½ Hebrew tribes captive, 733 B.C., Hos 23
7. To carry the Kenites away captive, Num 40
7. To bring about the fall of Damascus, 732, Isa 21, *Amos 2
7. To bring the kingdom of N. Israel to its end, 722 B.C., *I K 25, II K 39, Isa 27, Hos 2, Amos 1, Mi 1
7. To advance against Judah in 701, under Sennacherib, *Isa 18, Mi 3
7. One army to march down Palestine's central ridge, Isa 38
7. To accomplish widespread desolation in Judah, Isa 29
7. Sennacherib's host to be destroyed, as God protects Jerusalem, *Isa 37 (II K 41, II Chron 36), Hos 3, Mi 35, I Cor 2
7. Sennacherib to return to Assyria, Isa 86 (II K 42)
7. Sennacherib to fall by the sword in his own land, Isa 87 (II K 43)
7. Ashurbanipal to take Egypt captive, 663, Isa 59
7. Nineveh to be destroyed, 612, *Nah 1, Zeph 12
14. To become a Christian land, along with Egypt, Isa 58
15. As an element in the campaign of Armageddon, the land of Assyria to be wasted by the sword, Mi 32

Babylon

Period   Event and numbered listing in each book
7. To expand under Nebuchadrezzar, after the battle of Carchemish, 605 B.C., Hab 1
7. To overthrow Ashkelon and other Philistine cities, 604, Jer 53
7. To plunder and destroy among the Arab tribes, 598, Jer 25
7. To overpower Jehoiachin and permanently banish him from Judah 597, Jer 33
7. To choose to attack Judah rather than Ammon, in 588, Ezek 26
7. To commence Jerusalem's siege on a given date, Jan. 15, 588, Ezek 30
7. After diversion due to Egypt, to return to the siege, Jer 77
7. To capture, blind, and exile Zedekiah, *Jer 40, Ezek 16
7. To bring the kingdom of Judah to an end, 586, Lev 33, and 16 others (No. 280 in Summary A)
8. To carry Judah into exile, Lev 34 and 8 others (No. 291)
8. To besiege Tyre and gain its capitulation, so that it is eclipsed for 70 years after 585, *Isa 66, Jer 54, Ezek 36
8. To invade and pillage Egypt, 568–567, *Jer 21, Ezek 41
8. Nebuchadrezzar to suffer madness until he acknowledges God, Dan 12
8. Babylon to be served by the W. Fertile Crescent for 70 years, through 3 generations, from before 604 to 539, *Jer 29, Ezek 48
8. To maintain the Jewish exile for a similar total period, Jer 50
8. To fall to Cyrus of Persia, 539, with his Medes and Elamites, Dt 46 and 6 others (No. 318)
12. The city of Babylon to become deserted, before NT times, *Isa 49, Jer 52

Edom

1. To be settled by Isac's son Esau, Gen 53
2. To develop into a nation, Gen 49
6. To serve their brother-nation Israel, especially under David, *Gen 50, Num 37, Rom 14
7. To shake off the yoke of Judah under Jehoram, after 848, *Gen 54, Heb 46
7. To be reconquered by Amaziah, 796, Gen 50 (2nd stage)
7. To suffer under Assyrian attack, 711 and 701, Isa 60, *Amos 8, Obad 1
8. To be diminished by Babylonian aggression, 552, Jer 22
9. Like others, to be returned to their land after Babylon's fall in 539, Jer 30
9. The area to be taken by the Nabatean Arabs, ca. 500, and the Edomites to be permanently driven out, Isa 83, Jer 32, Ezek 47, *Obad 2
11. Idumaea to be conquered by John Hyrcanus and incorporated into Judah, *Gen 50 (3rd stage), Num 38, Jer 31, Ezek 34, Obad 6, Mal 1
15. To be spared from the Antichrist's pre-Armageddon attack, Dan 52
15. But to be despoiled by Israel, Isa 34
16. The land to be desolate during the Messianic kingdom, Joel 24

Egypt

1. To experience 7 years of plenty, then 7 of famine, 1852–1838 B.C., Gen 59
2. To host Israel for 400 years, 1843-1446, but also to afflict them, Gen 31, Acts 30
2. To be judged by 10 divine plagues, Gen 32, Ex 10 (see also 9, 11–12, 14, 18–28), Acts 31
3. To pursue Israel in their exodus, but to fall at the Red Sea, Ex 34
7. To march into Palestine, as do the Assyrians, 720 and 701, Isa 30

Period   Event and .numbered listing in each book

7. The XXVth Dynasty pharaoh Shabaka to be routed by Assyria at Eltekeh, 701, Isa 82

7. To send Judah congratulatory presents upon Sennacherib's defeat, Isa 37

7. The XXVth (Ethiopian) Dynasty to end with captivity to Assyria, 663, Isa 59

7. To break Judah and its king Josiah at Megiddo, 609, Jer 3

7. To stumble and fall before Babylon at Carchemish, 605, Jer 83

7. To retreat from Judah in 588, leaving it to fall to Babylon, *Jer 63, Ezek 21

8. Pharaoh Hophra to be given into the hands of those who seek his life, 569, Jer 81

8. To be invaded and pillaged by Nebuchadrezzar, 568–567, *Jer 21, Ezek 41

8. Afterwards, to recover, as before, Jer 84

9. To be plagued by civil disorder and to fall to a cruel lord, Cambyses II of Persia, 525, *Isa 56, Ezek 40

9. Cush (Nubia) to be raided by Cambyses, after 525, Zeph 11

10. Ptolemy I to be strong, but less so than his former general Seleucus, in Syria, Dan 42

10. Ptolemy II's marriage alliance with Syria to fail, 247, Dan 43

10. Ptolemy III to counter by invading the north, Dan 44

10. To repulse the invasion of Seleucus II, Dan 45

10. An Egyptian fortress, probably Gaza, to be attacked by Antiochus III, Dan 46

10. Ptolemy IV to defeat Antiochus at Raphia, 217, but fail to follow it up, Dan 47

10. Ptolemy V to be attacked by Antiochus in 202, to regain Palestine in 200, but to lose it in 198, Dan 48

10. Ptolemy VII to be threatened by Antiochus IV until Rome intervenes, 168, Dan 24

11. Judaism to prosper in Egypt, with a temple at Heliopolis, 160, Isa 57

14. To be a leading Christian nation, 3–7th centuries, one with Israel and Assyria, Isa 58

15. To suffer under the Antichrist prior to Armageddon, Dan 52

16. Threatened with punishment for failure to worship at the Feast of Tabernacles, Zech 77

16. To be desolate during the Messianic kingdom, Joel 23

Greece (and the Greek Seleucids)

9. Xerxes of Persia to stir up his whole empire against Greece, 480–479, Dan 41

10. Alexander to conquer Persia, 331, and establish a world empire, *Dan 4, Zech 3

10. His empire to be divided into 4 parts and seized by his leading generals, Dan 23

10. Ptolemy's general Seleucus I to become greater than he and to rule Syria and eastward, Dan 42

10. The marriage alliance of Antiochus II with Egypt to fail, 247, Dan 43

10. The Seleucid realm to suffer invasion from Ptolemy III, Dan 44

10. Seleucus II to be driven back from counterattacking Egypt, ca. 240, Dan 45

10. Seleucus III and his brother Antiochus III to attack toward Egypt, Dan 46

10. Antiochus to be defeated by Ptolemy IV at Raphia, 217, but to be allowed to recover, Dan 47

10. To reattack in 202, lose Palestine in 200, but win the victory in 198, though the land be wasted by these conflicts, *Dan 48, Zech 47

10. Antiochus III to be checked by Rome at Magnesia, 190, and later die, Dan 49

10. Seleucus IV to attempt to rob the Jerusalem temple, Dan 50

10. Antiochus IV to usurp the throne and attack surrounding lands, Dan 24

Period   Event and numbered listing in each book
10. To attempt to stamp out Judaism, defiling the temple and setting up his "abomination," Dan 26
10. To persecute and martyr many Jews, Dan 25, *Mi 23
11. God to arouse Maccabean resistance against the Greeks, Dan 51, *Mi 24, Zech 40
11. Antiochus IV to be "broken without hand" (die by disease), 164, Dan 31

Moab

5. To be defeated by Ehud, 1316 B.C., Jd 5
6. To be struck down by David, Num 35
7. To be delivered up to a coalition of Jehoram (N.) and Jehoshaphat (S.), II K 5
7. To be devastated by Sargon's sweep through the land in 715, Isa 53, *Amos 10
7. To suffer even more during his campaign against Ashdod in 711, Isa 54
8. To be overpowered and largely deported by Nebuchadrezzar, 582-581, Jer 24
9. To experience a restoration after Babylon's fall in 539, Jer 86
9. To be destroyed, as Sodom, Ezek 33, *Zeph 7
15. The land to be spared from the Antichrist's pre-Armageddon attack, Dan 52
15. But to be despoiled by Israel, Isa 34

Persia

9. Within the joint Medo-Persian empire, Persia to arise later but to be the stronger, Dan 3
9. A ruler to be named Cyrus and to authorize the Jewish restoration, 538, Isa 98
9. After him to come three: Cambyses, Smerdis, and Darius I, 529–485, Dan 40
9. Xerxes to stir up the Persian empire against Greece, 480–479, Dan 41
10. To fall to Alexander, 331, *Dan 4, Zech 3

Philistia

5. Samson to begin to save Israel from the Philistines, 1090–1070, Jd 14
5. Samuel to deliver Israel from the Philistines, 1063, I Sam 13
6. Jonathan to overcome a Philistine garrison before Michmash, I Sam 22
6. Saul, to deliver Israel, at the battle of Michmash, 1041, I Sam 15
6. The Philistines to be defeated at the fall of the champion Goliath to David, I Sam 25
6. Philistines to be delivered up to David at Keilah, I Sam 27
6. David finally to overcome the Philistine oppression of Israel, 1003, II Sam 2 (I Chron 6)
7. Gaza to be burned by Tiglath-pileser III of Assyria, 734, Amos 3
7. The ruler of Ashkelon to be cut off: Mitinti in 733, or Sidqia, 701, Amos 5
7. Ashdod to be struck down by Sargon, 711, Isa 52, *Amos 4
7. and to fall after a 29-year siege by Psamatik I of Egypt (663–609), Zeph 4
7. Gaza to be struck down by Necho II of Egypt, 605, Jer 85, *Zeph 2
7. Ashkelon and others of the remnant to be overthrown by Nebuchadrezzar, Jer 53
10. Philistia to submit to Alexander and to Greek culture, Zech 28
10. Gaza to be stormed by Alexander, Nov., 332, Zech 29
10. Ashkelon to become depopulated, Zech 30
10. Philistines to be sold into slavery, by Jews, after Gaza's fall to Alexander, Joel 16
11. To be overcome by Simon the Hasmonean, 148, *Amos 6, Obad 7, Zeph 3
11. To be occupied by the Jews, Zeph 5

Period Event and numbered listing in each book
11. To become incorporated into Judah, Zech 31
15. To be the object of Israelite attack at Armageddon, Isa 34

Phoenicia

7. Sidon to be oppressed by Sennacherib, after the flight of its leaders to Cyprus, 701 B.C., Isa 65
7. Tyre to be wasted and lose its mainland fortresses to Ashurbanipal, 663, Isa 64, *Amos 7
8. To suffer Chaldean siege and pass into eclipse, 585–515, *Isa 66, Jer 54, Ezek 36
9. To furnish materials for Judah's postexilic reconstruction, Isa 67
9. Sidonians to be sold into slavery to Arabs, by Jews, after Artaxerxes III's capture of the city in 345, *Joel 15, Zech 27
10. Tyre to be destroyed by Alexander, July, 332, *Ezek 37, Zech 26
10. Tyrians to be sold into slavery to Arabs by Jews, Joel 14

Rome

10. To defeat Antiochus III of Syria at Magnesia, Asia Minor, 190, Dan 49
10. To compel Antiochus IV to withdraw from attack upon Egypt, 168, Dan 24
12. To come from the west and afflict the Semitic Near East, *Num 41, Dan 5
14. To attack the holy city of Jerusalem over a period of 42 months, 66–70, Rev 31
14. Nero's successor Galba to remain "a little while," 68–69, Rev 37
14. To destroy Judah and Jerusalem, 70, Mi 39, and 7 others (No. 580 in Summary A)
14. In the 4th century to suffer decay and be divided into the E. and W. empires, Dan 6
14. To fall, officially in A.D., 476, *Num 42, Zech 56, Rev 40
14. Its empire to be broken up into a balance of power, *Dan 10, Rev 36

Syria (Damascus)

7. Ben-hadad II to be defeated by Ahab of Israel, 857, I K 35
7. but to attack again in the following year, I K 36
7. only to suffer a more decisive defeat, 856, I K 37
7. Ben-hadad's forces to slay Ahab and repel Israel at Ramoth-gilead, 853, I K 39 (II Chron 25)
7. To come down against Jehoram of Israel at places specified by Elisha, II K 14
7. To abandon a siege of Samaria when Israel was most desperate, II K 16
7. Ben-hadad not to recover from illness but to die, II K 20
7. Hazael to become king in Damascus, ca. 843, II K 22
7. Hazael seriously to oppress Israel, I K 32, II K 21
7. Syria to suffer an overwhelming defeat by Jehoash of Israel, after 798, at Aphek, II K 33
7. To be smitten by him on 3 occasions, II K 34
7. The Syro-Ephraimitic alliance to be broken by Assyria, and Damascus to fall, 732, Isa 21, *Amos 2
8. Damascus to become feeble, with its soldiers silenced, Jer 89
10. To fall to Alexander, after the battle of Issus, 333, Zech 25

Prophecies with Personal Reference to Christ[1]

Old Testament[2]

Verse listing		*Numbered listing in each book*
Gen 3:15a	Jesus will reconcile men to God, at painful cost	Gen 6
3:15b	He will be a man, springing from the seed of woman	7
3:15c	He will crush Satan, cast him down, and eventually destroy him	8
9:26a	He will come from the Semitic branch of humanity	17
22:18a	Within this branch, His descent will be through the family of Abraham	46
49:10a	He will spring from the royal tribe of Judah	67
*49:10b	He will receive the obedience of the peoples	68
Num *24:17c	As a star out of Jacob, He will strike down all defiance (Armageddon)	Num 36
Dt 18:15	He will be a prophet, like Moses, speaking the words of God	Dt 35
32:43a	The angels of God will worship at His birth	47
I Sam *2:10b	God will strengthen His anointed (the first use of the term *Messiah* for Jesus) for His rule	I Sam 4
II Sam 7:13b	He will descend from the line of David as an eternal king	II Sam 11
7:14a	God will be His Father, and He will be His Son	12
*23:3	His rule will be righteous and good, in reverence toward God	18
Job 17:3	As the divine Angel of Yahweh, He will ransom men and restore their righteousness	Job 4
*19:25b	He will come again and stand over the dust of the righteous, to resurrect them	6
Ps 2:1	Gentile rulers will unite with Jewish people against Him at His trial	Ps 2
2:2b	He will be anointed, in gladness above all others	3
*2:4	He will break the nations with a rod of iron at Armageddon	4
*2:6	God will install Him on Mount Zion as king over the nations	5
8:3	He will ascend to the Father's right hand, gloriously crowned	8
16:10	God will not allow His holy One to see corruption	11

---

1. All references are to His first coming, unless marked by asterisk.
2. Not including types (see Summary D, below) or prophecies in later books that incorporate earlier ones (see pp. 676–679).

Verse listing		*Numbered listing in each book*
22:1	He will be forsaken of the Father while bearing men's sins	14
22:6	Men will wag their heads in mockery at His crucifixion	15
22:10	He will trust in God the Father, from His birth onward	16
22:11	He will suffer from thirst and pierced limbs, as men gamble for His clothes beneath the cross	17
22:19	But God will answer Him after His sufferings and receive Him	18
22:22	Shortly thereafter He will honor God in the midst of the church	19
*22:27	Men will pray for Him continually and give worship to God	21
40:6c	He will delight to do the Father's will	27
*72:7	He will come down like showers upon the earth and cause abundance	34
*72:8	He will rule from the Euphrates to the ends of the earth	35
*72:12	He will have a particular concern for the poor	36
*72:17a	His years will have no end	37
89:4	He will be the everlasting seed of David	40
89:26	He will be God's Son, His firstborn	41
110:1a	He will be deity, "Lord" even to King David	53
*110:3	In the day of His battle (Armageddon), young people will offer themselves to Him	54
110:4a	He will be a priest, after the manner of Melchizedek	55
*110:6	He will strike down the Antichrist over a wide land	56
Isa *2:4a	Kings will arise before His exalted presence, and princes worship	Isa 11
7:13	He will be conceived by a virgin	24
7:14b	He will be Immanuel, *God with us*, the "Mighty God"	25
7:15	He will experience moral growth, though in an oppressed land	26
8:9	Opposed by the counsels of raging nations, He will not open His mouth	30
*8:17	He will wait for Yahweh to convert Israel again to Himself	31
9:1	He will bring the light of His ministry to those in Galilee	32
*9:4	He will proclaim the day of vengeance of our God	34
*9:7	He will sit on the throne of David and be swift to execute righteousness	35
11:1	He will be a *néser*: a "branch" from David, living in *Nazareth*	39
11:2	He will be anointed with God's Spirit, for preaching the gospel	40
11:4a	He will decide with equity for the poor and the meek of the earth	41
*11:4b	He will slay the wicked, the Antichrist	42
*12:1	He will furnish His people with joy and praise	46
24:16a	He will be a light to the Gentiles, with worldwide salvation	69
*26:21	The victorious Redeemer will come to Zion	77
40:3	John will be His forerunner: "Prepare ye the way of the Lord"	90
42:1a	He will come as the prophetic Servant of Yahweh	91
42:2	His ministry will be unpretentious	92
42:6a	He will embody God's redemptive testament	93

Verse listing		*Numbered listing in each book*
49:7a	He will suffer, be rejected and slain, and be assigned burial with the wicked	99
52:15a	His death will serve as an atoning sacrifice to justify many	100
53:4a	He will carry our diseases, in a healing ministry	101
53:9b	He will receive honorable burial in the tomb of a rich man, Joseph of Arimathea	102
53:10b	He will prolong His days, experiencing resurrection from the dead	103
Jer 23:5a	God will raise up out of Israel an eternal Branch of David	Jer 45
*23:5b	He will execute justice and righteousness in the land	46
*23:6	He will be called "Yahweh (is) our righteousness," as men live in safety	47
30:21c	He will pledge His life in priestly mediation for God's people	66
Ezek 17:23b	He will be an offshoot of David, through Jehoiachin and Zerubbabel	Ezek 23
*21:27	Yahweh will grant the Davidic throne to the One whose right it is	27
Dan *7:13	The son of man will come with the clouds of heaven	Dan 19
9:24a	His baptism will occur in A.D. 26, 483 years after Ezra will have received the decree by which he would begin to rebuild Jerusalem	34
9:24b	3½ years later He will be cut off, to make atonement for sin	35
9:24c	As God's "Most Holy" One, He will be anointed by the Spirit	36
9:27a	He will confirm the testament with Israel and terminate OT sacrifice	39
Hos *1:11a	The Jews will seek the Davidic King, whom they accept as their head	Hos 5
6:1	After two days, i.e. on the third day, He will be raised from the dead	18
Joel *3:16	Through Him, Yahweh will "roar" from Zion and judge the attacking nations	Joel 19
*3:17	Representing Yahweh, He will dwell on Zion the holy mountain	20
Amos 9:11	In Christ, God will raise up the booth (humbled house) of David	Amos 23
Mi *2:13a	As the "Breaker" of restraints, He will move before His people	Mi 6
*4:3a	He will be great unto the ends of the earth	14
5:2a	The future ruler will be born in the little town of Bethlehem	27
5:2b	Yet He will have been with the Father from all eternity	28
5:3b	He will be brought forth by a woman, through childbirth	30
*5:5a	He will deliver His people from the Antichrist's attack from Assyria	32
Zeph *3:15	The King of Israel, of the essence of Yahweh, will be in Jerusalem	Zeph 20
Hag 2:9	In the temple rebuilt by Zerubbabel, God will give peace, in Christ	Hag 6

Verse listing		*Numbered listing in each book*
Zech 2:5b	God will dwell in the midst of Jerusalem as its glory	Zech 5
3:8b	The Lord will bring forth His "Servant"	9
3:8c	He will be the One called the "Branch," out of David	10
3:9b	He will remove the iniquity of the land in one day by His counsel of peace	11
6:12b	The Branch will grow up, where He is, through a childhood	14
*6:13b	But He will bear glory and sit and rule upon His throne	15
*8:3a	The Jews will look upon Him at His return to Zion	18
*8:3b	He will reside in Jerusalem, as deity present	19
9:9b	His kingship will be one of justice	33
9:9c	He will be granted saving help from God	34
9:9d	He will enter Jerusalem humbly, riding on a donkey	35
*9:10c	His dominion shall be from sea to sea	38
11:12	The Jews will weigh out 30 pieces of silver for His hire	53
*12:1	He will go forth and fight against the nations gathered at Jerusalem	58
*12:10	At His return, the Jews will mourn for Him and accept Him	62
12:10d	God will identify the Savior with Himself as deity, "My fellow"	64
12:10e	The Good Shepherd will be smitten and "pierced"	65
13:7d	He will bring back His hand over "the little ones" of His flock (the disciples) and regather them to Galilee	67
*14:4a	His feet will stand in that future day upon the Mount of Olives	69
*14:5b	He will be accompanied by a host of holy ones, angels (or saints)	71
Mal 3:1a	His way will be prepared by a messenger, John the Baptist	Mal 9
3:1b	As deity and as redeemer, "the Angel of the Testament," He will come to His temple	10
*3:2	At His second coming none will be able to stand before His refining power	11
*3:3a	He will purify His people who serve as Levites	12

New Testament[3]

Mt 1:21b	His name will be Jesus, for He will save His people from their sins	Mt 2
2:13	Herod will search for the child to destroy Him	6
*7:19	At the final judgment He will order the ungodly to depart from Him	19
*7:21	But He will invite the righteous into their eternal inheritance	20
12:40	He will experience a 3-day burial	35
16:21	On the third day He will rise from the dead	43
*16:27a	He will come a second time, on the clouds, with glory	44
Mk *13:32	Except to the Father, the date of His return is unknown, even to Himself	Mk 38
14:3	His body will be anointed for burial	41

---

3. Not including prophecies quoted from the OT, or repeating prophecies that appear in several of the Gospels (see pp. 676–679).

Verse *listing*		*Numbered listing* *in each book*
14:28b	After His resurrection, He will go before His disciples to meet them in Galilee	47
Lk 1:17a	John the Baptist will go as a forerunner to Him, as Elijah	Lk 8
1:31a	The virgin Mary will conceive Him by the power of God's Spirit	10
1:32a	He will be great and will be called the Son of God	12
*1:32b	The Lord God will give Him the throne of His father David	13
*1:33	His kingdom over Israel will have no end	14
1:42	He will be men's "Lord," and the blessed one	15
1:54	In the house of David God will thus raise up a horn of salvation for Israel	17
2:30	He will be a light of revelation to the Gentiles	22
2:34a	This child is appointed for the fall of many in Israel	23
2:34c	He will be opposed and suffer, be rejected and killed (cf. John, No. 11)	24
2:35b	He will reveal the thoughts, good and bad, of many hearts	25
12:8	He will ascend into heaven (cf. John, No. 16)	46
*12:35	His return is imminent, at any time, and will be unexpected	47
*12:37	At that point He will feast with His people	48
John 1:15	The One who comes after John will have a rank higher than he	John 1
1:29	Behold the Lamb of God who will take away the sin of the world	5
1:33c	John the Baptist will see the Holy Spirit descending upon Him	6
2:19	Christ will raise up the temple of His own body	8
*5:28	At His voice, all who are in the tombs will come forth	12
*5:29b	Those who believe on the Son, He will raise up in the resurrection of life	13
6:70	He will be betrayed by one of the 12, Judas	17
11:14	He will raise Lazarus from the dead	23
14:18	His disciples will behold Him again after His passion	34
Acts *1:11	Jesus will return in the same way as He was seen to ascend	Acts 8
9:16a	He will show Paul how much he must suffer for His name	44
*10:42	God has appointed Him to judge the living and the dead	47
26:16	He will appear to Paul with revelations about which he is to witness	59
Rom *2:6[4]	God will judge the secrets of men through Christ Jesus	Rom 2
11:12b	The Messianic Redeemer will convert the Jews from ungodliness to faith in Himself	20
I Cor 1:7	He will come again; cf. the early church expression, *Maranatha*	I Cor 1
13:12	He will judge the saints, bringing hidden things to light	3
15:24b	He will finally offer up His mediatorial kingship to God the Father	20
15:24c	He must reign until He has put all His enemies under His feet	21
II Cor 1:14	All the saints must appear before Him at His judgment seat	II Cor 1

4. Beyond the Book of Acts, all references should be considered as marked *, i.e., forecasting His second advent and subsequent activities.

Verse *listing*		*Numbered listing* *in each book*
Eph 1:21	In the age to come, Christ will have supreme rule and authority	Eph 4
5:14	He "will shine on you" at His second advent	6
5:27	He will present the church to Himself, spotless, at the marriage feast	7
Phil 1:6	He will come from heaven as Savior and Lord	Phil 1
2:9	At His name every knee will bow	2
4:5	His coming is "near," or "at hand"	5
Col 3:4a	Christ, who is "our life," will be revealed	Col 4
I Thess 1:10	The Lord will descend from heaven with a shout	I Thess 1
4:17a	He will be met in the air by the raptured saints	6
5:17b	They will continue to be "with Him," on earth, and henceforward	7
II Thess 1:5	He will deal out retribution to those disobedient to the gospel	II Thess 1
1:7b	He will be revealed from heaven, with His angels, in flaming fire	3
1:10	The purpose is that He may be glorified in His saints	6
2:8	He will slay the Antichrist through the breath (word) of His mouth	10
I Tim 6:14	God will bring about His appearing "at the proper time"	I Tim 2
II Tim 4:1a	Jesus Christ will judge the living and the dead	II Tim 5
4:1b	He will appear again on earth	6
4:1c	and assume its kingship	7
Titus 2:13	The appearing of Christ in glory is the "blessed hope" of the church	Titus 1
Heb 1:13b	To Him, God will subject the world to come	Heb 7
9:28	He will appear a second time and will not delay	31
James 5:7	The Christian is to be patient "until the coming of the Lord"	James 3
5:8	His coming is at hand; the Judge is standing at the door	4
I Pet 1:7	The Chief Shepherd will appear, in a revelation of glory	I Pet 2
II Pet 1:19a	The Lord is not slow about His promise of coming; the day will dawn	II Pet 2
I John 2:28	He will appear, and we shall see Him just as He is	I John 2
Rev 1:1	The time is near; He will come quickly, as unexpectedly as a thief	Rev 1
1:4	He is coming with the clouds, on a white horse, as heaven opens	2
10:5	He will rule the world, with a rod of iron	30
11:18b	He will render to every man according to what he has done	35
14:1a	He will stand on Mount Zion with his 144,000 chosen young people	38
14:15	At His return He will gather in the "harvest" of His elect church	41
17:14a	At Armageddon He will destroy the enemy by a mere word	47
20:2b	He will reign for 1,000 years while Satan is bound	52

Biblical Types[1]

Subject	Meaning[2]	Numbered listing under which discussed
Adam's status	Christ's achieving Adam's lost dominion, at His ascension	Gen 1
Tree of life	Perfected life in the New Jerusalem (per. 18)	Gen 3
Adam's fall	The contrasting act of representative justification by Christ the "last Adam"	Gen 5
Edenic testament	Christ's suffering to reconcile men to God	Gen 6
Ark of Noah	Baptism, washing away what is wrong and mediating salvation (per. 14)	Gen 13
Noachian testament	The preservation of the redemptive seed	Gen 16
Melchizedek:		
as without genealogy	Christ's non-Levitical descent	Gen 26
as priest	His Melchizedek-like ministry	Gen 27
in his greatness	His superiority to Leviticalism	Gen 28
Abrahamic testament	God's own life made forfeit, to become "their God"	Gen 30
Circumcision	New life made available in Chirst	Gen 42
Passover	Christ's sacrifice as a redemptive substitute	Ex 31
Paschal lamb:		
without blemish	Christ's sinlessness	Ex 32
no bone broken	Christ's body, similarly preserved	Ex 33
Cloud at the Red Sea	Baptism as protection in the believer's new life (per. 14)	Ex 37
Crossing through the Sea	Baptism as the way to God's inheritance (per. 14)	Ex 38
Manna	Christ's incarnation, bringing men the bread of life from heaven	Ex 39
Sabbath	The "rest" achieved by Christ's ministry	Ex 41
Water from the rock	Eternal life provided by Christ	Ex 42
Altar	Christ's giving His life for men	Ex 44
Sinaitic testament	Salvation through the elect nation of Israel	Ex 45
Feast of Tabernacles	The ingathering of the nations to God (per. 16)	Ex 46

1. On the nature and interpretation of typology, see above, pp. 21–26, 51–56, 89–91.
2. All are fulfilled in period 13, in the life of Christ, unless indicated to the contrary.

Subject	Meaning[2]	Numbered listing under which discussed
Tabernacle-temple	God's presence with man in Christ's incarnation	Ex 55
Ark of Yahweh	Christ's divine presence achieving testamentary salvation	Ex 56
Mercy seat	His serving as an "atoning cover" between God and men	Ex 57
Veil	His bodily incarnation, veiling His deity, yet opening up the way to God	Ex 58
Priests	His execution of the ultimate, atoning sacrifice	Ex 59
Priests' garments	Christ's priestly purity	Ex 60
Miter plate	The holiness of Christ	Ex 61
Priests' consecration	His devotion to the work of priestly atonement	Ex 63
Atonement money	His atoning for the soul of each member of Israel	Ex 66
Laver	His washing of men from their sins	Ex 67
Sacrifice	Christ's atoning death	Lev 2
Burnt offering	His life as wholly surrendered to God	Lev 3
Meal offering	His consecrated, righteous fulfilling of the law	Lev 4
Peace offering	The restoration of man's communion with God (2nd stage in per. 16)	Lev 5
Sin offering	Christ's passive bearing of the penalty of men's sins	Lev 6
Trespass offering	His active redressing of the claims of God	Lev 7
A freed bird (at the cleansing for lepers)	His removal of men's sins	Lev 14
Scapegoat	His carrying of sins back to their Satanic author	Lev 18
Day of atonement	His full atonement for sins, presented to God in heaven	Lev 19
Blood, reverenced	His shed blood	Lev 20
Year of Jubilee	His proclamation of deliverance (2nd stage, per. 16)	Lev 27
Ashes of the red heifer	His cleansing of men's consciences	Num 27
Brazen serpent	His being lifted up in crucifixion, that all who see may live	Num 30
Levitical testament	Salvation through priestly atonement	Num 43
Davidic testament	Inheritance of salvation through the seed of David	II Sam 19
Millennial temple	Unimpared fellowship with God in the New Jerusalem (per. 18)	Isa 8
Gomer:		
her redemption	Christ's repurchase of men to God at a price of 30 pieces of silver	Hos 14
her seclusion	Judaism's present lack of redemption (per. 14)	Hos 15
Joshua's crowns	Christ's combined priesthood-kingship	Zech 13
Pre-Calvary baptism	New life to be made available in Christ	Lk 27
Lord's Supper	The Messianic marriage feast of the Lamb (per. 15)	Lk 69
Christ's breathing upon the apostles	Their receiving the Holy Spirit at Pentecost (per. 14)	John 42
The *āgắpē* (love feast)	The Messianic feast (per. 15), as similarly foreshadowed by the Lord's Supper, above	Jude 3

STATISTICAL APPENDIX

Statistics by Biblical Books

	Predictions		Total verses in book:1	% pre-dictive	By literary form (numbers in parentheses = verses)				
	Number	Verses			Oracles	Figurative	Symbolical	Types	% typical
Genesis	77	212	1533	14	32	26 (34 vv.)	6 (31)	13 (67)	32
Exodus	69	487	1213	40	39	1 (3)	–	29 (387)	80
Leviticus	37	506	859	59	10	–	–	27 (462)	91
Numbers	50	458	1288	36	22	4 (6)	–	24 (396)	86
Deuteronomy	58	344	959	36	37	8 (18)	–	13 (68)	20
Joshua	27	89	658	12	14	1 (1)	1 (2)	11 (51)	57
Judges	20	41	618	7	10	1 (2)	1 (2)	8 (17)	41
I Samuel	31	124	810	15	19	1 (1)	2 (3)	9 (81)	65
II Samuel	22	68	695	10	12	2 (4)	–	8 (34)	50
I Kings	44	189	816	23	33	–	1 (2)	10 (132)	70
II Kings	50	144	719	20	34	–	2 (5)	14 (75)	52
I Chron	24	132	942	14	12	1 (1)	–	12 (101)	77
II Chron	37	268	822	31	20	–	–	17 (232)	87
Ezra	10	63	280	23		–	–	10 (63)	100
Nehemiah	14	45	406	11	2	–	–	12 (43)	96
Esther	1	1	167	.6	1	–	–	–	–
Job	10	22	1070	2	8	1 (1)	–	1 (2)	9
Psalms	59	242	2526[2]	10	38	7 (27)	–	13 (101)	42
Proverbs	4	7	915	.8	1	–	–	3 (6)	86
Ecclesiastes	3	7	222	3	1	–	–	2 (3)	43
Isaiah	111	754	1292	59	71	27 (285)	3 (18)	10 (25)	3
Jeremiah	90	812	1364	60	73	7 (25)	2 (244)	8 (60)	7
Lamentations	4	8	154	5		1 (2)	–	3 (6)	75
Ezekiel	66	821	1273	65	39	5 (71)	8 (230)	14 (198)	24
Daniel	58	161	357	45	35	–	20 (109)	3 (6)	4
Hosea	28	111	197	56	15	3 (18)	2 (62)	8 (6)	5
Joel	25	50	73	68	19	2 (12)	–	4 (6)	12
Amos	26	85	146	58	19	2 (48)	–	5 (5)	6
Obadiah	10	17	21	81	10	–	–	–	–
Jonah	4	5	48	10	2	–	–	–	–
Micah	40	73	105	70	26	11 (17)	1 (1)	2 (3)	60
Nahum	2	35	47	74	2	–	–	2 (2)	3
Habakkuk	4	23	56	47	4	–	–	–	–

Zechariah	78	144	211	69	59	6 (15)	7 (22)	6 (9)	6
Malachi	19	31	55	56	11	2 (2)	–	6 (14)	45
Total OT	1239	6641	23,210[3]	28½%	752	121 (595)	56 (731)	310 (2671)	40%
Matthew	81	278	1067[4]	26	62	10 (88 vv.)	3 (12)	6 (24)	9
Mark	50	125	661	19	37	6 (35)	1 (6)	6 (12)	10
Luke	75	250	1146	22	61	6 (21)		8 (27)	11
John	45	180	866	20	34	3 (5)	1 (6)	7 (31)	17
Acts	63	125	1003	13	56	1 (2)		6 (14)	11
Romans	29	91	433	21	24	2 (2)		3 (11)	12
I Corinth	25	85	437	19	16	2 (8)		7 (23)	27
II Corinth	7	12	257	5	6			1 (1)	8
Galatians	7	16	149	11	4	1 (2)		2 (7)	44
Ephesians	5	8	155	5	5	1 (1)		1 (1)	13
Philippians	4	10	104	10	4			1 (1)	10
Colossians	9	9	95	9	2			2 (6)	67
I Thess	12	16	89	18	9			–	–
II Thess	2	19	47	40	12			–	–
I Timothy	8	5	113	4	2			–	–
II Timothy	1	17	83	20	8			–	–
Titus		1	46	2	1			–	–
Hebrews	52	137	303	45	28	5 (5)	1 (1)	18 (63)	46
James	4	7	108	6	4			–	–
I Peter	11	21	105	20	9	1 (1)	1 (2)	1 (2)	10
II Peter	11	25	61	41	7	4 (6)		–	–
I John	4	6	105	6	4			–	–
II John	2	2	13	15	2			–	–
Jude	8	10	25	40	6	1 (1)	1 (1)	1 (1)	10
Revelation	56	256	404	63	28	4 (49)	24 (100)	–	–
Total NT	578	1711	7914[5]	21½%	431	47 (226)	30 (125)	70 (224)	13%
Total	1817	8352	31,124	27%	1183	168 (821)	86 (856)	380 (2895)	34½%

1. On the procedure followed for the calculation of the full number of predictive verse, see above, p. 149.

2. Includes 65 vv. that constitute numbered verses in the Hebrew text, though printed as titles rather than as numbered verses in most English versions; see above, introduction to Psalms, note 3.

3. Including 85 vv. for Ruth and 117 for Song of Solomon.

4. On the basis of The Greek New Testament of Kurt Aland et al. (New York: American Bible Society, 1966), and excluding those verses that are printed in double brackets, meaning "later additions" to the text. Specifically omitted from the above study, as not forming an authentic part of the inspired NT, are the following passages: Mt 17:21, 18:11, 21:44, 23:14; Mk 7:16, 9:44, 46; 11:26, 15:28, 16:9–20; Lk 17:36, 22:43–44, 23:7; John 5:4, 7:53, 8:1–11; Acts 8:37, 15:34, 24:7, 28:29.

5. Including 25 vv. for Philemon and 14 for III John.

Major Groups of Prophecies Incorporated from One Biblical Book into Another

II KINGS	drawn from ISAIAH
18:22 (II Chron 32:12)	36:7
18:30 (II Chron 32:11); 19:10, 21, 29–32, 34; 20:6b	36:15; 37:10, 22, 30–33, 35; 38:6
19:1, 14; 20:5b, 8b	37:1, 14; 38:20, 22b
19:7a, 28, 33	37:7a, 29, 34
19:7b	37:7b
20:5a, 6a, 8a	38:5, 7, 21–22a
20:9–10	38:8
20:17–18	39:6–7
20:19	39:9

I CHRONICLES	drawn from II SAMUEL
11:2	5:2
13:6–14; 15:25–16:1a; 17:1	6:2–17a; 7:2
14:10, 14	5:19, 24
15:26b	6:13b
16:1b; 17:5–6	6:17b; 7:6–7
16:1c, 2a; 21:23a, 24, 26b	6:17c, 18a; 24:22, 24, 25b
16:1d, 2b; 21:26c	6:17d, 18b; 24:25c

	drawn from PSALMS
16:15–17	105:8–10
16:18	105:11
16:29	96:8
16:33a	96:12–13a
16:33b	96:13b
16:33c	96:13c

	drawn from II SAMUEL
17:10–11	7:11–12
17:12a; 22:10a; 28:6a	7:13a
17:12b (= 22:10c, 28:7) 13b–14, 17, 23–27	7:13b, 15–16, 19, 25–30
17:13a; 22:10b; 28:6b	7:14a
17:22	7:24
21:9–13	24:11–14
21:18, 22, 26a	24:18, 21, 25a
21:23a, 24, 26b	24:22, 24, 25b
21:26c	24:25c

II CHRONICLES   drawn from I KINGS

1:6a; 6:12, 22a; 77d; 8:12b; and 23:10b,   3:4b; 8:22, 31a,   and II KINGS
  32:12   64e; 9:25c   11:11b, 18:22
1:6c; 7:7b; 8:12a   3:4a; 8:64b;   (from Isa
                                                        9:25a   36:7)
1:12a   3:12
1:12b   3:13
2:4a; 3:1–4, 5–13, 17; 4:16, 19–20, 22; 5:1   5:5a; 6:1–10, 14–38; 7:21, 45,
  5:5b, 7b, 9b, 11, 13–14; 6:1–2, 5–8, 10,   48–51; 8:4b, 6b, 8, 10–13,
  6:18–21, 22b, 24, 26, 29, 32–34, 38;   16–18, 20, 8:27–30, 31b, 33,
  7:5b, 7a, 11, 16; 8:1, 16; 9:4, 11; 12:9, 11;   35, 38, 42–44, 48, 8:63b, 64a;
  15:18; 16:2 (cont. with 22:12, below)   9:1, 3, 10, 25d; 10:5, 12; 14:
                                                        26, 28; 15:15, 18
4:2–5, 6a, 14–15   7:23–26, 38–40, 43–44
5:2, 4–5a, 6a, 7a, 8, 10a, 11a   8:1, 3–4a, 5a, 6a, 7, 9a, 21a
5:3; 7:8   8:2, 65
5:6b; 7:4   8:5b, 62
5:10b; 6:11b, 14; and 23:16; 34:30b–31   8:9b, 21b, 23   II K 11:17;
6:9   8:19   23:2b–3
6:16; 7:18   8:25; 9:5
7:5a, 7c   8:63a, 64d
7:7e   8:64c
7:20a, 22;   and 34:24–27   9:7a, 9   II K 22:16–19
7:20b–21   9:7b–8
18:16, 19, 22, 27   22:17, 20, 23, 28
18:24   22:25

                                    drawn from II KINGS

22:12 (cont. from 2:4a, above); 23:3, 5,   11:3, 4, 7b,
  23:9–10a, 12, 14, 18a, 20; 24:4–8, 12–14a;   11:10a–11, 13, 15, 18–19;
  25:24; 27:3; 28:21; 33:4–5, 7; 34:8–11,   12:4–9, 11–15, 16c; 14:14;
  34:14–17, 30a; 36:10, 18–19   15:35; 16:8; 21:4–5, 7;
                                                        22:3–6, 22:8–9; 23:2a; 24:13;
                                                        25:13a, 9 (Jer 52:17a, 13)
23:4, 8   11:5, 9
32:11   18:30 (from Isa 36:15)
34:38   22:20
35:1, 6–9, 11, 13, 16a, 17–19   23:21–23

EZRA   drawn from II CHRONICLES
1:2   36:23

JEREMIAH   drawn from II KINGS
52:13, 17a, 20b   25:9, 13a (II Chron 36:19, 18),
                                                        16b
52:17b, 20a   25:13b, 16a

                    drawn from
MATTHEW   MARK   or LUKE   cf. JOHN   Discussed under:
s1:21a[1]   1:31a   Lk 1:31a
3:3   1:2–3   3:4–6   s1:21a,23[1]   Lk 1:17a
3:5–7a   1:4–5   3:3, 7a   s1:28, 3:23,   Lk 3:3
                                                      10:40
3:7b, 10   3:7b, 9   Mt. 3:7b
3:11a   1:8a   3:16a   s1:25–26, 31   Lk 3:3
3:11b   1:7   3:16b   s1:15, 27   John 1:15
3:11c   1:8b   3:16c   s1:33c   Lk 3:16c

1. s = similar in content but later in occasion; see above, p. 479.

MATTHEW (cont.)	MARK	LUKE	JOHN	Discussed under:
3:12		3:17		Mt 3:7b
3:12b		3:17b		Mt. 3:12b
3:13–16	1:9	3:21		Lk 3:3
26:21, 27:40	14:58, 15:29		2:19	John 2:19
4:19	1:17	5:10		Mk 1:17
5:29–30	s12:5			Mt 3:7b
7:22–23	s13:24–28			Mt 7:19
8:4	1:44	5:14		Lk 2:24
9:15	2:20	5:35		Lk 2:34c
12:4	2:26	6:4		Lk 1:9
11:10		7:27		Lk 1:17a
12:40		s11:29–30		Mt 12:40
13:31–32	4:30–32	s13:18–19		Mk 4:26
13:33		s13:20–21		Mt 13:31
	6:15	9:8		Lk1:17a
16:14	8:26	9:19		Lk 1:17a
16:21a, 22	8:31a, 32	9:22a		Lk 2:34c
16:21b	8:31b	9:22b		Mt 16:21b
16:27c	8:38a	9:26a		Mt 7:19
16:27a	8:38b	9:26b		Mt 16:27a
16:27b	8:38c	9:26c		Mt 16:27b
16:28	9:1	9:27		Mt 10:23b
17:9	9:8–10			Mt 16:21b
17:10–13	9:11–12a, 13			Mt 3:3
17:12b	9:12b			Mk 2:21
17:22–23	9:31a, 32	12:43–45		Lk 2:34c
17:23b	9:31b			Mt 16:21b
18:8–9	9:43, 45, 47–49			Mt 3:7b
18:18			s20:23	Mt 16:19
s10:15; 11:22, 24		10:12–14		Lk 10:12
s12:41a, 42a		11:31a, 32a		Lk 11:31a
s12:41b, 42b		11:31b, 32b		Lk 11:31b
s23:34a		11:49a		Lk 11:49a
s23:34b		11:49b		Lk 11:49b
s10:32–33		12:8–9		Lk 12:8
s10:17–20		12:11–12		Lk 11:49b
s10:21–23a, 34–36		12:51–53		Lk 11:49b
s8:11		13:29–30a		Lk 13:29
s8:12		13:30b		Lk 13:30b
s23:39a		13:35a		Lk 13:35a
s24:37–39		17:26–33a, 37		Lk 17:26
s24:40–41		17:33b–35		Lk 17:33b
19:28		s22:30		Mt 19:28
20:18–19a	10:32–34a	18:31–34		Lk 2:34c
20:19b	10:34b	18:33b		Mt 16:21b
20:21, 23b	10:37, 40			Mt 19:28
20:22	10:38	s12:50		Lk 2:34c
20:23a	10:39			Mk 10:39
20:28	10:45			Mt 1:21b
s25:15		19:12a		Lk 12:8
s25:19a		19:12b		Lk 19:11
21:1–2	11:1–2	19:29–30		Mk 11:1
21:3	11:3			Mk 11:3
21:4–5			12:14–16	Mt 21:4
21:25	11:30	20:4		Lk 3:3
21:39	12:8	20:15		Lk 2:34c
21:41a, 44–45	12:9a, 12	20:16a, 18–19		Mt 10:23b

MATTHEW (cont.)	MARK	LUKE	JOHN	Discussed under:
21:41b, 43;				
s22:9–10a	12:9b	20:16b		Lk 2:30
22:29–32	12:24–27	20:34–38		Lk 14:14b
22:43–44a, 45	12:35–37	20:41–42a, 44		Lk 1:32a
22:44b	12:36b	20:42b		Lk 12:8
22:44c	12:36c	20:43		Lk 1:32b
23:35		s11:51		Mt 5:23
23:39b		s13:35b		Mt 16:27a
24:4–5, 11,				
23–24a, 26	13:4–5, 21–22a	21:7–8		Lk 17:23
24:6–8	13:7–8	21:9–11		Mk 13:7
24:9–10, 12–13	13:9, 11–13	21:12–19		Lk 11:49b
24:14	13:10			Mk 13:10
24:15–22	13:14–20	21:20–24a		Mt 10:23b
24:24b, 29a	13:22b, 24a			Mk 13:22b
24:27		s17:24		Mt 16:27a
24:29b	13:24b–25	21:25–26		Mk 13:24b
24:30	13:26	21:27		Mt 16:27a
24:31	13:27	21:28		Lk 17:33b
24:32–34	13:28–30	21:29–32		Mt 10:23b
24:35	13:31	21:33		Mt 5:18
24:36	13:32			Mk 13:32
24:42	13:33–37	21:34–36		Lk 12:35
24:51		s12:46b		Mt 7:19
25:19b		s19:15a		Mt 16:27a
25:19c		s19:15b		Mt 25:19c
25:20–23,		s19:16–19,		
28b–29a		24b–26a		Mt 7:21
25:24–28a,		s19:20–24a,		
29b–30		26b–27		Mt 7:19
26:2, 5	14:1–2	22:1		Lk 2:41
26:6–12	14:3–8		12:2–5, 7–8	Mk 14:3
26:13	14:9			Mk 14:9
26:17–19	14:12, 14, 16	22:7–8, 11, 13		Lk 2:41
	14:13,15	22:10, 12		Mk 14:13
26:21–23	14:18–20	22:21, 23	13:21	John 6:70
26:24a	14:21a	22:22a		Lk 2:34c
26:24b	14:21b	22:22b	s17:11	Mk 14:21b
26:26–28a	14:22–24a	22:19		Lk 2:34c
26:28b	14:24b			Mt 1:21b
26:29	14:25	22:18		Lk 12:37
26:31	14:27		s16:32	Mk 14:27
26:32a	14:28a			Mt 16:21b
26:32b	14:28b			Mk 14:28b
26:34	14:30	22:34	13:38	Mk 14:30
26:46	14:42			Mk 14:42
26:64	14:62	22:69		Mt 16:27a
26:75	14:72	22:61		Mk 14:30
28:6		24:6, 7b–8		Mt 16:21b
28:10	16:7			Mk 14:28b

II PETER	taken from JUDE
2:4	6
2:17	13

Statistics by Periods of Fulfillment[1]

Period	Number of prophecies fulfilled	Number of verses involved	
1. Primeval-patriarchal	25	65	
2. Egyptian	25	91	
3. Wilderness	16	61	
4. Conquest	27	224	
5. Judges	25	69	
6. United Kingdom	32	117	
7. Divided Kingdom	139	1421	
8. Exilic	29	471	
9. Persian	31	379	
10. Greek	25	104	
11. Maccabean	14	49	
12. Roman	7	44	
13. Life of Christ	127	3348	(82 nontypical, 574 vv.; 45 typical, 2774 vv.)
14. Church	88	481	(83 nontypical, 464 vv.; 5 typical, 17 vv.)
15. Christ's Second Coming	52	535	(50 nontypical, 512 vv.; 2 typical, 23 vv.)
16. Millennium	46	614	(43 nontypical, 435 vv.; 3 typical, 176 vv.)
17. Final Judgment	14	279	
18. New Jerusalem	15[2]	128[2]	(13 nontypical, 116 vv.; 2 typical, 12 vv.)

1. See above, pp. xxi, 93–110.
2. Not to be totaled, since a few of the predictions (listed on pp. 134–136) are marked by a developmental fulfillment and are therefore listed under more than one period.

Statistics of Particular Interest

Amount of predictive matter in the Bible: 8,352 verses, out of its total of 31,124

Proportion that is predictive: 27%   Old Testament: 28½%
                                      New Testament: 21½%

Amount of predictive matter in the Bible, not including types: 5,457 verses, or 17½%

Number of separate matters predicted: 737 (see Summary A, above)

Total number of predictions, counting subjects that are repeated in different books of the Bible: 1,817 (see Statistics by Books, above)

Proportionate amounts of Scriptural prediction, according to literary form:[1]
Verbal:
  simple oracles (employing language in which customary meanings appear):
    1,183 predictions out of the 1,817, or 65% of the prophetic material as a whole
  figurative predictions (employing language in which one thing is said under the form of another):
    168, or 9½%
Nonverbal (acted):
  symbolical predictions (such as dreams, or object lessons):
    86, or 4½%
  types (prefigurations with a simultaneous historical reality, objects that symbolize contemporaneously the same truth that is being predicted for the future):
    380 predictions out of the 1,817, or 21%
    But by verses, 2,895 out of the total of 8,352, or 34½%

Number of typical subjects in Scripture: 55 (see Summary D, above)

Books with the most predictive matter: in the New Testament:
  Ezekiel   821 verses   Matthew   278 verses
  Jeremiah   812   Revelation   256
  Isaiah   754   Luke   250

Books with no predictive matter: Ruth, Song of Solomon, Philemon, III John

Books most highly predictive, according to the proportion of verses involving
  forecasts of the future: in the New Testament:
  Zephaniah   89% predictive   Revelation   63% predictive
  Obadiah   81%   Hebrews   45%
  Nahum   74%   II Peter   41%

---

1. Calculated on the basis of the initial revelation in each book; see above, p. 148.

681

Books least predictive (that have some prophecy):   In the New Testament:
Esther .6% predictive (= 1 verse)   Titus   2% (= 1 verse)
Proverbs .8%   I Timothy 4%

Books with the greatest number of separate predictions:
Isaiah, 111; Jeremiah, 90; Matthew, 81; Zechariah, 78; Genesis, 77

Books with the most predictions in symbolical form:
Revelation, 24; Daniel, 20

Books with the most predictions in typical form:
Leviticus, 27 predictions involving 462 verses (91% of its predictive vv.)
Exodus, 29 predictions involving 387 verses (80% of its predictive vv.)
In the New Testament: Hebrews, 18 predictions involving 63 verses (46%)

Books that have the highest proportion of their predictive content in typical form:
Ezra, 100%; Nehemiah, 96 %
In the New Testament: Colossians, 67%

Books with the most material directly anticipatory of Jesus Christ:
Psalms, 101 verses, in 13 Messianic psalms
Isaiah,   59 verses

Book with the greatest variety in the periods of fulfillment for the prophecies it mentions:
Hebrews, whose cited prophecies involve 13 out of the 18 periods employed in this study

Land (other than Israel) most consistently concerned in Biblical prophecy:
Egypt, which involves 10 out of the 18 periods employed in this study

Prophecies appearing most frequently in Scripture:	Number of books involved:	Number of verses:
Typical:		
Tabernacle-temple, as a type of Christ's incarnation	32	936
Sacrifice, as a type of His atoning death	29	151
Burnt offering, as a type of His wholly surrendered life	24	166
Nontypical:		
Christ's second coming	29	63
Christ's future rule over the earth	20	63
Judah's fall to Babylon	17	608

Periods of Biblical history involving the most prophetic fulfillments (see "Statistics by Periods of Fulfillment," preceding):
Divided kingdoms of Israel: 139 predictions involving 1,421 verses
Life of Christ: 127 predictions involving 3,348 verses (82 nontypical, with 574 vv.; 45 typical, with 2,774 vv.)

The most extensive prophecies in individual books:
The fall of Judah to Babylon in 586 B.C.   Jeremiah, prediction No. 1, 222 vv.
The fall of Judah to Babylon in 586 B.C.   Ezekiel, No. 1, 194 vv.
The temple, as a type of the incarnation   II Chronicles, No. 1, 143 vv.
The tabernacle, similarly   Exodus, No. 55, 136 vv.

The most extensive quotation of a single prophecy:
The coming of the new testament   Jeremiah 31:31–34, as quoted in Hebrews 8:8–12

BIBLIOGRAPHY

Bibliography[1]

BOOKS

Aharoni, Y., and M. Avi-Yonah, *The Macmillan Bible Atlas*. New York: Macmillan, 1968.

Aland, Kurt, et al., *The Greek New Testament*. New York: American Bible Society, 1966.

Albright, William F., *From the Stone Age to Christianity*. 2nd ed.; Baltimore: The Johns Hopkins Press, 1957.

Alexander, Joseph A., *Commentary on the Prophecies of Isaiah*. Grand Rapids: Zondervan, 1953.

Alford, Henry, *The Greek Testament*. 2nd ed.; London: Rivington's, 1854.

Alleman, H. C., and E. E. Flack, *Old Testament Commentary*. Philadelphia: Muhlenberg Press, 1948.

Allis, Oswald T., *Prophecy and the Church*. Philadelphia: Presbyterian and Reformed Pub. Co., 1945.

————, *The Unity of Isaiah*. Same, 1950.

Angus, Joseph, *The Bible Hand-Book, an Introduction to the Study of Sacred Scripture*. Rev. by Samuel G. Green. London: Religious Tract Society, 1908.

Archer, Gleason L., *A Survey of Old Testament Introduction*. Chicago: Moody Press, 1964.

Barrows, E. P., *Companion to the Bible*. New York: The American Tract Society, 1867.

Barton, George A., *Archaeology and the Bible*. 6th ed.; Philadelphia: American Sunday School Union, 1933.

Beecher, Willis L., *The Prophets and the Promise*. Grand Rapids: Baker, 1963.

Berkhof, Louis, *Principles of Biblical Interpretation*. Grand Rapids: Baker, 1950.

Berry, George R., *Premillennialism and Old Testament Prediction*. University of Chicago Press, 1929.

Boettner, Loraine, *The Millennium*. Philadelphia: Presbyterian and Reformed, 1957.

Briggs, Charles A., *Messianic Prophecy*. Edinburgh: T. and T. Clark, 1886.

Bright, John, *The Authority of the Old Testament*. Nashville: Abingdon, 1967.

————, *A History of Israel*. Philadelphia: Westminster, 1959.

————, *The Kingdom of God*. New York: Abingdon-Cokesbury, 1953.

Brown, Raymond E., J. A. Fitzmyer, and R. E. Murphy, eds., *The Jerome Bible Commentary*. Englewood Cliffs, N.J.: Prentice-Hall, 1968.

Bruce, F. F., *The Acts of the Apostles*. 2nd ed.; London: Tyndale Press, 1952.

————, *Biblical Exegesis in the Qumran Texts*. Grand Rapids: Eerdmans, 1959.

1. See also the basic works that are cited by abbreviation, p. xxv, above.

Bullinger, E. W., *Figures of Speech Used in the Bible, Explained and Illustrated.* Grand Rapids: Baker, 1968.
————, *How to Enjoy the Bible.* London: Eyre and Spottiswoode, 1907.
Calvin, John, *Commentary on the Twelve Minor Prophets.* Grand Rapids: Eerdmans, 1950.
Carnell, E. J., *The Case for Orthodox Theology.* Philadelphia: Westminster, 1959.
Chafer, Lewis Sperry, *Systematic Theology.* Dallas, Tex.: Dallas Seminary Press, 1947.
Chafer, Rollin T., *The Science of Biblical Hermeneutics.* Dallas, Tex.: Bibliotheca Sacra, 1939.
Charles, R. H., *A Critical and Exegetical Commentary on the Book of Daniel.* Oxford: Clarendon Press, 19229.
Cheyne, T. K., *The Origin and Religious Contents of the Psalter.* London: Kegan Paul, Trench, Trübner, and Co., 1891.
Clarke, Adam, *A Commentary and Critical Notes: The Old Testament.* New York: Abingdon-Cokesbury, n.d.
Cowles, Henry, *The Revelation of John.* New York: D. Appleton and Co., 1871.
Craven, E. R., *The Revelation of John,* vol. 12, NT, J. P. Lange's *Commentary on the Holy Scriptures: Critical Doctrinal, and Homiletical.* Grand Rapids: Zondervan, 1876.
Cross, F. M., *The Ancient Library of Qumran and Modern Biblical Studies.* Garden City, N.Y.: Doubleday, 1958.
Culver, Robert D., *Daniel and the Latter Days.* Westwood, N.J.: Revell, 1954.
Davidson, A. B., *Old Testament Prophecy.* Edinburgh: T. and T. Clark, 1903.
————, *The Theology of the Old Testament.* Edinburgh: T. and T. Clark, 1925.
Davison, John, *Discourses on Prophecy.* 4th ed.; London: Rivington's, 1839.
Dentan, Robert C., *Preface to Old Testament Theology.* New Haven, Conn.: Yale University Press, 1950.
Dodd, C. H., *New Testament Studies.* Manchester University Press, 1953.
Douty, Norman F., *Has Christ's Return Two Stages?* New York: Pageant Press, 1956.
Driver, S. R., *Introduction to the Literature of the Old Testament.* 12th ed.; New York: Scribner's, 1906.
————, *Notes on the Hebrew Text and the Topography of the Books of Samuel.* 2nd ed.; Oxford: Clarendon, 1913.
Dummelow, R. R., ed., *A Commentary on the Holy Bible.* New York: Macmillan, 1918.
Duncan, G. S., *St. Paul's Ephesian Ministry.* New York: Scribner's, 1930.
Edersheim, Alfred, *Prophecy and History in Relation to the Messiah.* Grand Rapids: Baker, 1955.
Edghill, E. A., *An Enquiry into the Evidential Value of Prophecy.* London: Macmillan, 1906.
Ellison, H. L., *Ezekiel: The Man and His Message.* Grand Rapids: Eerdmans, 1956.
————, *Men Spake From God.* Grand Rapids: Eerdmans, 1958.
————, *The Prophets of Israel.* Grand Rapids: Eerdmans, 1969.
English, E. Schuyler, *Re-thinking the Rapture.* Travelers Rest, S.C.: Southern Bible Book House, 1954.
Erdman, Charles R., *The Book of Isaiah, an Exposition.* Westwood, N.J.: Revell, 1954.
Fairbairn, Patrick, *Hermeneutical Manual.* Edinburgh: T. and T. Clark, 1858.
————, *The Interpretation of Prophecy.* London: Banner of Truth Trust, 1964.
Farley, W. J., *The Progress of Prophecy.* London: Religious Tract Society, 1925.
Farrar, F. W., *History of Interpretation.* New York: E. P. Dutton, 1886.

Feinberg, Charles, *Hosea: God's Love for Israel*. New York: American Board of Missions to the Jews, 1947.
————, *Premillennialism or Amillennialism?* 2nd ed.; Wheaton, Ill.: Van Kampen Press, 1954.
Finegan, Jack, *Handbook of Biblical Chronology*. 2nd ed.; Princeton University Press, 1964.
Fohrer, G., *Introduction to the Old Testament*. Nashville: Abingdon, 1968.
Francisco, Clyde T., *Introducing the Old Testament*. Nashville: Broadman, 1950.
Froom, LeRoy E., *The Prophetic Faith of Our Fathers*. Washington, D.C.: Review and Herald, 1945.
Gaebelein, Arno C., *The Prophet Daniel*. New York: Our Hope Pub. Co., 1911.
Garstang, John, *The Foundations of Bible History: Joshua–Judges*. New York: Richard R. Smith, 1931.
Gevirtz, Stanley, *Patterns in the Early Poetry of Israel*. University of Chicago Press, 1963.
Girdlestone, R. B., *The Grammar of Prophecy*. London: Eyre and Spottiswoode, 1901.
Goodspeed, Edgar J., *An Introduction to the New Testament*. University of Chicago Press, 1937.
Guillaume, Alfred, *Prophecy and Divination among the Hebrews and Other Semites*. London: Hodder and Stoughton, 1938.
Guthrie, Donald, *New Testament Introduction*. London: Tyndale Press, 1961–65.
Hahn, H. F., *The Old Testament in Modern Research*. Philadelphia: Muhlenberg Press, 1954.
Harris, R. Laird, *Inspiration and Canonicity of the Bible*. Grand Rapids: Zondervan, 1957.
Hebert, A. G., *The Old Testament from Within*. Oxford University Press, 1962.
Harrison, Norman B., *The End*. Minneapolis: Harrison Service, 1941.
Harrison, R. K., *The Dead Sea Scrolls, an Introduction*. New York: Harper, 1961.
————, *Introduction to the Old Testament*. Grand Rapids: Eerdmans, 1969.
Heinisch, Paul, *Theology of the Old Testament*. Collegeville, Minn.: The Order of St. Joseph, 1955.
Hengstenberg, E. W., *Christology of the Old Testament*. Grand Rapids: Kregel, 1956.
Henry, Carl F. H., ed., *The Biblical Expositor*. Philadelphia: Holman, 1960.
Hodge, Charles, *A Commentary on the Epistle to the Ephesians*. Grand Rapids: Eerdmans, 1963.
————, *A Commentary on the Epistle to the Romans*. Grand Rapids: Eerdmans, 1955.
————, *An Exposition on the First Epistle to the Corinthians*. New York: Hodder and Stoughton, 1857.
————, *An Exposition on the Second Epistle to the Corinthians*. Same, 1859.
Hogg, C. F., and W. E. Vine, *The Epistle of Paul the Apostle to the Thessalonians*. Grand Rapids: Kregel, 1929.
Horne, Thomas H., *An Introduction to the Critical Study and Knowledge of the Holy Scriptures*. 2nd ed.; New York: Robert Carter and Brothers, 1872.
Hudson, Rolund V., *Bible Survey Outlines*. Grand Rapids: Eerdmans, 1954.
Huffman, Jasper A., *The Messianic Hope in Both Testaments*. Butler, Ind.: The Higley Press, 1934.
Ironside, H. A., *Not Wrath But Rapture*. New York: Loizeaux, n.d.
————, *Notes on the Minor Prophets*. New York: Loizeaux, 1950.
Jacob, Edmond, *Theology of the Old Testament*. New York: Harper, 1958.
Kirkpatrick, A. F., *The Doctrine of the Prophets*. Grand Rapids: Zondervan, 1958.
Kitchen, Kenneth A., *Ancient Orient and Old Testament*. London: Inter-Varsity Press, 1968.

————, *Notes on Some Problems in the Book of Daniel.* London: Tyndale Press, 1965.

Kuhl, Curt, *The Prophets of Israel.* Edinburgh: Oliver and Boyd, 1960.

Ladd, George E., *The Blessed Hope.* Grand Rapids: Eerdmans, 1956.

————, *Crucial Questions About the Kingdom of God.* Grand Rapids: Eerdmans, 1952.

————, *The Gospel of the Kingdom.* Grand Rapids: Eerdmans, 1959.

————, *Jesus and the Kingdom: The Eschatology of Biblical Realism.* New York: Harper and Row, 1964.

Laetsch, Theodore, *Bible Commentary: Jeremiah.* St. Louis: Concordia, 1952.

————, *Bible Commentary: The Minor Prophets.* St. Louis: Concordia, 1956.

Lampe, G. W. H., and K. J. Woollcombe, *Essays on Typology.* London: SCM Press, 1957.

Lang, G. H., *The Revelation of Jesus Christ.* 2nd ed.; London: Paternoster Press, 1948.

Lange, John Peter, *A Commentary on the Holy Scriptures: Critical, Doctrinal, and Homiletical.* Rev. by Philip Schaff. Grand Rapids: Zondervan, 1876 reprint.

Lenski, Richard C. N., *The Interpretation of St. Matthew's Gospel* (and the other NT books). Columbus, Ohio: Wartburg Press, 1932–46.

Leslie, Elmer A., *Jeremiah, Chronologically Arranged, Translated, and Interpreted.* New York: Abingdon, 1954.

Leupold, H. C., *Exposition of Daniel.* Columbus, Ohio: Wartburg Press, 1949.

————, *Exposition of Genesis.* Columbus, Ohio: Wartburg Press, 1942.

————, *Exposition of Isaiah.* Grand Rapids: Baker, 1968.

————, *Exposition of the Psalms.* Minneapolis: Augsburg, 1961.

————, *Exposition of Zechariah.* Grand Rapids: Baker, 1965.

Lightfoot, J. B., *St. Paul's Epistle to the Galatians.* London: Macmillan, 1896.

Lockhart, Clinton, *The Messianic Message of the Old Testament.* Pub. by the author, c. 1905.

McCarthy, Dennis J., *Treaty and Covenant.* Rome: Pontifical Biblical Institute, 1963.

McClain, Alva J., *The Greatness of the Kingdom.* Grand Rapids: Zondervan, 1959.

Maier, Walter, *The Book of Nahum, a Commentary.* St. Louis: Concordia, 1959.

Marsh, F. E., *The Structural Principles of the Bible.* Grand Rapids: Kregel, 1959.

Mickelsen, A. Berkeley, *Interpreting the Bible.* Grand Rapids: Eerdmans, 1963.

Moffatt, James, *Introduction to the Literature of the New Testament.* 3rd ed.; New York: Scribner's, 1918.

Moorehead, William G., *Studies in the Mosaic Institutions.* New York: Revell, 1895.

Murray, John, *The Covenant of Grace.* London: Tyndale Press, 1953.

Napier, B. D., *Prophets in Perspective.* Nashville: Abingdon, 1963.

Oehler, Gustav F., *Theology of the Old Testament.* New York: Funk and Wagnalls, 1883.

Orelli, Conrad von, *The Old Testament Prophecy of the Consummation of God's Kingdom.* Edinburgh: T. and T. Clark, 1889.

Oxtoby, Gurdon C., *Prediction and Fulfillment in the Bible.* Philadelphia: Westminster, 1966.

Patterson, Charles H., *The Philosophy of the Old Testament.* New York: Ronald Press, 1953.

Payne, J. Barton, *The Imminent Appearing of Christ.* Grand Rapids: Eerdmans, 1962.

————, ed., *New Perspectives on the Old Testament.* Waco, Tex.: Word, 1970.

————, *An Outline of Hebrew History.* Grand Rapids: Baker, 1954.

————, *Theology of the Older Testament.* Grand Rapids: Zondervan, 1962.

Peake, A. S., *The Servant of Yahweh and Other Lectures.* Manchester University Press, 1931.

Pentecost, J. Dwight, *Things to Come.* Findlay, Ohio: Dunham Pub. Co., 1958.

Peters, George N. H., *The Theocratic Kingdom*. Grand Rapids: Kregel, 1952.
Pfeiffer, Robert H., *Introduction to the Old Testament*. Rev. ed.; New York: Harper, 1948.
Pieters, Albertus, *The Seed of Abraham*. Grand Rapids: Eerdmans, 1950.
Pusey, E. B., *Daniel the Prophet*. New York: Funk and Wagnalls, 1891.
————, *The Minor Prophets*. New York: Funk and Wagnalls, 1885.
Rad, Gerhard von, *Old Testament Theology*. New York: Harper, 1962–66.
Ramm, Bernard, *Protestant Biblical Interpretation*. Boston: W. A. Wilde, 1950. Rev. ed., 1956.
Raven, John H., *Old Testament Introduction*. New York: Revell, 1906.
Reese, Alexander, *The Approaching Advent of Christ*. London: Marshall, Morgan, and Scott, n.d.
Riehm, Edward, *Messianic Prophecy, Its Origin, Historical Growth, and Relation to the New Testament*. Edinburgh: T. and T. Clark, 1900.
Ringgren, Helmer, *The Messiah in the Old Testament*. Naperville, Ill.: Allenson, 1956.
Robertson, A. T., *A Harmony of the Gospels for Students of the Life of Christ, Based on the Broadus Harmony in the Revised Version*. New York: Harper and Brothers, 1922.
————, *Studies in Mark's Gospel*. New York: Macmillan, 1919.
Rowley, H. H., *Men of God: Studies in Old Testament History and Prophecy*. Camden, N.J.: Thomas Nelson and Sons, 1963.
————, *The Re-discovery of the Old Testament*. Philadelphia: Westminster, 1946.
————, *The Relevance of Apocalyptic*. London: Lutterworth, 1944.
————, *The Servant of the Lord and Other Essays*. London: Lutterworth, 1952.
Rutherford. J. F., *The Harp of God*. Brooklyn, N.Y.: Watch Tower Bible and Tract Society, 1921.
Ryrie, Charles C., *The Basis of the Premillennial Faith*. New York: Loizeaux, 1953.
————, *Dispensationalism Today*. Chicago: Moody Press, 1965.
Sandmel, Samuel, *The Hebrew Scriptures*. New York: Knopf, 1963.
Sauer, Erich, *The Dawn of World Redemption*. Grand Rapids: Eerdmans, 1952.
Scofield, C. I., ed., *Reference Bible*. New York: Oxford, 1917.
Scroggie, W. Graham, *A Guide to the Gospels*. London: Pickering and Inglis, 1948.
Seiss, Joseph A., *Voices from Babylon, or, The Records of Daniel the Prophet*. Philadelphia: Muhlenberg, 1879.
Simons, J., *Jerusalem in the Old Testament*. Leiden: Brill, 1952.
Smith, George A., *The Book of the Twelve Minor Prophets*. New York: Harper and Brothers, 1928.
Snaith, Norman H., *The Distinctive Ideas of the Old Testament*. Philadelphia: Westminster, 1946.
————, *Mercy and Sacrifice*. London: SCM Press, 1953.
Stearns, O. S., *A Syllabus of the Messianic Passages in the Old Testament*. Boston: Percival T. Bartless, 1884.
Stonehouse, Ned B., *The Witness of Luke to Christ*. Grand Rapids: Eerdmans, 1951.
Strombeck, J. F., *First the Rapture*. Moline, Ill.: Strombeck Agency, 1950.
Swete, H. B., *The Apocalypse of St. John*. Grand Rapids: Eerdmans, 1951.
Tenney, Merrill C., *The Genius of the Gospels*. Grand Rapids: Eerdmans, 1951.
————, *Interpreting Revelation*. Grand Rapids: Eerdmans, 1957.
Terry, Milton S., *Biblical Hermeneutics*. New York: Phillips and Hunt, 1883.
Thiele, E. R., *The Mysterious Numbers of the Hebrew Kings*. Rev. ed.; Grand Rapids; Eerdmans, 1964.
Thiessen, Henry C., *Introduction to the New Testament*. Grand Rapids: Eerdmans, 1943.

Tregelles, S. P., *Remarks on the Prophetic Visions in the Book of Daniel.* London: Samuel Bagster and Sons, 1883.

Unger, Merrill F., *Introductory Guide to the Old Testament.* Grand Rapids: Zondervan, 1956.

————, *Unger's Bible Commentary, Zechariah.* Grand Rapids: Zondervan, 1963.

Urquhart, John, *The Wonders of Prophecy.* New York: Gospel Publishing House, 1906.

Van Zyl, A. H., *The Moabites.* Leiden: Brill, 1960.

Vos, Geerhardus, *Biblical Theology.* Grand Rapids: Eerdmans, 1948.

Walvoord, John F., *The Rapture Question.* Findlay, Ohio: Dunham Publishing Co., 1957.

————, *The Revelation of Jesus Christ.* Chicago: Moody Press, 1966.

Weiser, Arthur, *The Old Testament: Its Formation and Development.* New York: Association Press, 1961.

Westcott, B. F., *The Gospel According to St. John.* Grand Rapids: Eerdmans, 1958.

Westermann, Claus, ed., *Essays on Old Testament Hermeneutics.* Richmond, Va.: John Knox, 1963.

Whitcomb, John C., *Darius the Mede.* Grand Rapids: Eerdmans, 1959.

Wilson, Robert Dick, *Studies in the Book of Daniel: Series I.* New York: Putnam, 1917.

Wiseman, Donald J., *Chronicles of Chaldean Kings.* London: British Museum, 1956.

Wiseman, Percy J., *New Discoveries in Babylonia about Genesis.* London: Marshall, Morgan, and Scott, 1958.

Wood, Leon J., *Is the Rapture Next?* Grand Rapids: Zondervan, 1956.

Wright, C. H. H., *Zechariah and His Prophecy.* London: Hodder and Stoughton, 1879.

Wright, G. Ernest, and F. V. Filson, *The Westminster Historical Atlas to the Bible.* Rev. ed.; Philadelphia: Westminster, 1956.

Wright, J. Stafford, *The Date of Ezra's Coming to Jerusalem.* London: Tyndale Press, 1946.

Wyngaarden, Martin J., *The Future of the Kingdom in Prophecy and Fulfillment.* Grand Rapids: Baker, 1955.

Young, Edward J., *An Introduction to the Old Testament.* Rev. ed.; Grand Rapids: Eerdmans, 1963.

————, *My Servants the Prophets.* Grand Rapids: Eerdmans, 1952.

————, *The Prophecy of Daniel.* Grand Rapids: Eerdmans, 1949.

————, *The Study of Old Testament Theology Today.* London: J. Clarke, 1958.

ARTICLES AND UNPUBLISHED MATERIAL

Albright, William F., "Abram the Hebrew: A New Archaeological Interpretation," BASOR, 163 (1961), 36–54.

————, "The Date and Personality of the Chronicler," JBL, 40 (1921), 104–124.

————, "King Jehoiachin in Exile," BA, 5(1942), 49–55.

Aldrich, Roy L., "An Apologetic for Dispensationalism," BS, 112 (1955), 46–54.

Alonso-Schökel, Luis, "Sapiential and Covenant Themes in Genesis 2–3," Dennis J. McCarthy and William Callen, eds., *Modern Biblical Themes.* Milwaukee: Bruce, 1967.

Anderson, B. W., "Exodus Typology in Second Isaiah," B. W. Anderson and Walter Harrelson, eds., *Israel's Prophetic Heritage.* New York: Harper and Brothers, 1962.

Archer, Gleason L., "The Linguistic Evidence for the Date of Ecclesiastes," ETS B, 12(1969), 167–181.

Beegle, Dewey M., "Virgin or Young Woman?" *The Asbury Seminarian*, 8 (1954), 34.
Brown, Raymond E., "Hermeneutics," Brown, et al., eds., *The Jerome Bible Commentary*. Englewood Cliffs, N.J.: Prentice-Hall, 1968, II:605–623.
Bultmann, Rudolf, "Prophecy and Fulfillment," Claus Westermann, ed., *Essays on Old Testament Hermeneutics*. Richmond, Va.: John Knox, 1963, pp. 50–75.
Davison, W. T., "Psalms, Book of," HDB, IV:145–162.
Eichrodt, Walther, "Is Typological Exegesis an Appropriate Method?" Claus Westermann, ed., *Essays on Old Testament Hermeneutics*. Richmond, Va.: John Knox, 1963, pp. 224–245.
Greenberg, M., "On Ezekiel's Dumbness," JBL, 77 (1958), 101–103.
Gundry, Stanley N., "Typology as a Means of Interpretation," ETS J, 12 (1969), 233–240.
Harris, R. Laird, "The Meaning of the Word Sheol as Shown by Parallels in Poetic Texts," ETS B, 4 (1961), 129–134.
———, "On a Possible Revision of the Biblical Text During the Monarchy," ETS P (1953), 18–24.
———, "Psalms," Carl F. H. Henry, ed., *The Biblical Expositor*. Philadelphia: Holman, 1960, II:34–70.
Kaiser, Walter C., Jr., "The Eschatological Hermeneutic of Epangelicalism (Promise Theology)," ETS J, 13 (1970), 91–99.
Kline, Meredith G., "Dynastic Covenant," WTJ, 23 (1960), 13–15.
Ladd, George E., "Why Not Prophetic-apocalyptic?" JBL, 76 (1957), 192–200.
Lang, G. H., "God's Covenants Are Conditional," *The Evangelical Quarterly*, 32 (1958), 86–97.
Lattey, Cuthbert, "The Emmanuel Prophecy: Isaias 7:14," CBQ, 8 (1946), 369–376; 9 (1947), 89–95, 147–154.
MacRae, Allan A., "The Scientific Approach to the Old Testament, Part IV," BS, 110 (1953), 315.
Meyrick, Frederick, "Prophet," H. B. Hackett, ed., rev. ed. of *Dr. William Smith's Dictionary of the Bible*. Boston: Houghton Mifflin, 1881, III:2590–2602.
Minear, Paul, "The Wounded Beast," JBL, 72 (1953), 93–101.
Nicole, Roger R., "The Old Testament Quotations in the New Testament with Reference to the Doctrine of Plenary Inspiration," ETS P (1954), 46–55.
Northrup, Bernard E., "Joel's Concept of the Day of the Lord," unpublished doctoral dissertation, Dallas Theological Seminary, 1961.
O'Callaghan, J., "Paperos neotestamentarios en la cueva 7 de Qumran?" *Biblica*, 53 (1972), 91–100.
Orelli, Conrad von, "Jeremiah," ISBE, III:1588–1591.
———, "Prophecy, Prophets," ibid., IV:2459–2466.
Payne, J. Barton, "*Apeitheo*: Current Resistance to Biblical Inerrancy," ETS B, 10 (1967), 3–14.
———, "The Arrangement of Jeremiah's Prophecies," ETS B, 7 (1964), 120–130.
———, "The *B'rith* of Yahweh," Payne, ed., *New Perspectives on the Old Testament*. Waco, Tex.: Word, 1970.
———, "Chronology of the Old Testament," Merrill C. Tenney, ed., *The Pictorial Encyclopedia of the Bible*. Grand Rapids: Zondervan, 1973.
———, "The Church and Zionism in the Predictive Cycles of Zechariah 9–14," ETS P (1956), 53–68.
———, "Daniel," M. C. Tenney, ed., *The Zondervan Pictorial Bible Dictionary*. Grand Rapids: Zondervan, 1963, pp. 196–198.
———, "Daniel, Book of," ibid., pp. 198–199.
———, "The Effect of Sennacherib's Anticipated Destruction in Isaianic Prophecy," WTJ, 34 (1971), 22–38.

———, "Eighth Century Israelitish Background of Isaiah 40–66," WTJ, 29–30 (1967–68).

———, "I–II Chronicles," C. F. Pfeiffer and E. F. Harrison, eds., *The Wycliffe Bible Commentary*. Chicago: Moody, 1962, pp. 367–421.

———, "Hermeneutics as a Cloak for the Denial of Scripture," ETS B, 4 (1960), 93–100.

———, "Hosea's Family Prophecies and the Kingdom," ETS P (1954), 11–21.

———, "Inspiration in the Words of Job," in John H. Skilton, ed., *The Law and the Prophets*. Philadelphia: Presbyterian and Reformed Pub. Co., 1973. Ch. XXVI.

———, "Israel, History of," M. C. Tenney, ed., *The Pictorial Encyclopedia of the Bible*. Grand Rapids: Zondervan, 1973.

———, "Leviticus," Carl F. H. Henry, ed., *The Biblical Expositor*. Philadelphia: Holman, 1960, I:118, 150.

———, "Psalms, the Book of," M. C. Tenney, ed., *The Zondervan Pictorial Dictionary of the Bible*. Grand Rapids: Zondervan, 1963, pp. 694–697.

———, "The Relationship of the Reign of Ahaz to the Accession of Hezekiah," BS, 126 (1969), 40–52.

———, "Saul and the Changing Will of God," BS, 129 (1972), 321–325.

———, "So-called Dual Fulfillment in Messianic Psalms," ETS P (1953), 62–72.

———, "The Unity of Isaiah: Evidence from Chapters 36–39," ETS B, 6 (1962), 50–56.

———, "Zachariah Who Perished," *Grace Journal*, 8:3 (Fall, 1967), 33–35.

Reeve, J. J., "Sacrifice in the Old Testament," ISBE, IV:2638–2651.

Ridderbos, N. H., "Reversals of Old Testament Criticism," Carl F. H. Henry, ed., *Revelation and the Bible*. Grand Rapids: Baker, 1958, pp. 333–350.

Sampey, J. R., "Psalms," ISBE, IV:2487–2494.

Skehan, Patrick W., "A Fragment of the 'Song of Moses' (Deut. 32) from Qumran," BASOR, 136 (1954), 12–15.

Smith, Wilbur M., "Revelation," C. F. Pfeiffer and E. F. Harrison, *The Wycliffe Bible Commentary*. Chicago: Moody Press, 1962, pp. 1491–1525.

Wallis, Wilbur B., "I–II Timothy, Titus," ibid., pp. 1361–96.

Walvoord, John F., "A Review of 'Crucial Questions About the Kingdom of God.'" BS, 110 (1953), 1–10.

Willsey, Jack K., "The Coming of Elijah: An Interpretation of Malachi 4:5," unpublished master's dissertation, San Francisco Conservative Baptist Theological Seminary, 1969.

Wilson, Robert Dick, "The Headings of the Psalms," PTR, 24 (1926), 1–37, 353–395.

———, "The Meaning of Alma (A. V. 'Virgin') in Isaiah 7:14," PTR, 24 (1926), 316.

Wolff, Hans Walter, "The Hermeneutics of the Old Testament," Claus Westermann, ed., *Essays on Old Testament Hermeneutics*. Richmond, Va.: John Knox, 1963, pp. 160–199.

Wright, J. Stafford, "The Book of Esther as History," J. B. Payne, ed., *New Perspectives on the Old Testament*. Waco, Tex.: Word, 1970.

Yamauchi, Edwin M., "The Greek Words of Daniel in the Light of 6th Century Greek Influence in the Near East," ibid.

Young, Edward J., "The Alleged Secondary Deuteronomic Passages in the Book of Joshua," *The Evangelical Quarterly*, 25 (1953), 142–157.

Young, G. Douglas, "Old Testament Theology—a Method and a Conclusion," ETS P (1955), 80.

Zimmerli, Walther, "Promise and Fulfillment," Claus Westermann, ed., *Essays on Old Testament Hermeneutics*. Richmond, Va.: John Knox, 1963, pp. 89–122.

INDEXES

1. The Biblical Predictions

(Numbers opposite references indicate the prophecy numbers within each book.)

GENESIS		GENESIS		GENESIS	
1:26	1	13:18	25	18:18a	21
1:28	1	14:18a	26	*18:18b*	19
2:3	2	*14:18b*	27	21:4	42
2:9	3	14:19–20	28	21:12	21
2:17	4	15:4	29	21:13, 18	38
3:6	5	15:5	21	22:2–3, 6–7, 10, 13	9
3:15a	6	15:7	24	22:8	44
3:15b	7	15:10–11	30	22:9	25
3:15c	8	15:13	31	*22:17a*	22
3:17–19	5	15:14a	32	22:17b	21
3:22, 24	3	*15:14b*	33	*22:17c*	45
4:4	9	*15:14c*	34	*22:18a*	46
5:29	10	15:15	35	22:18b	47
6:3, 7, 13, 17	11	15:16	36	*24:7a*	24
6:18	12	15:17–*18a*	30	24:7b	48
7:4	11	15:18b	37	24:40	48
7:23	13	15:19–20	24	24:60a	21
8:1, 4, 16–19	13	16:10	38	*24:60b*	45
8:20–21	9	16:11	39	25:23a	49
8:22	14	16:12	40	*25:23b*	50
9:4	15	17:2	30	25:26	51
9:8–17	16	*17:2b*	21	26:3	24
9:25	17	*17:4a*	30	*26:4a*	21
9:26a	18	17:4b–6	41	*26:4b*	24
9:26b	17	17:7	30	*26:4c*	46
9:27a	19	17:8a	24	26:4d	47
9:27b	17	17:*8b*–9	30	26:24	21
12:1	20	17:10–14	42	26:25	25
12:2a	21	17:15	41	27:28	52
12:2b	22	*17:16a*	29	27:29a	45
12:2c	23	17:16b	41	*27:29b*	50
12:3	19	17:19a	29	27:33	52
12:7a	24	*17:19b*	43	27:37a	50
12:*7b*–8	25	17:20	38	*27:37b*	52
13:4	25	17:21a	43	27:39	53
13:15	24	*17:21b*	29	27:40	54
13:16	21	17:23–27	42	*27:40b*	50
13:17	24	18:10, 14	29	28:3	21

* Italics indicate a minor portion of a verse, not counted in verse totals; see above, p. 149.

LEVITICUS		NUMBERS		NUMBERS	
26:45a	37	7:21	10	8:9	1
26:45b	32	7:22	9	8:12a	9
27:9, 11	2	7:23	8	8:12b	10
27:17–18	27	7:25	6	8:15	13
27:21–24	27	7:27	10	8:19	1
27:25	1	7:28	9	8:20–21a	13
		7:29	8	8:21b	11
NUMBERS		7:31	6	8:22–26	1
1:1	1	7:33	10	9:1–11	14
1:50–51, 53	1	7:34	9	9:12	15
2:2, 17	2	7:35	8	9:13–14	14
3:1–6, 10	2	7:37	6	9:15–23	1
3:7–8, 23, 25, 26a	1	7:39	10	10:3	1
3:26b	3	7:40	9	10:10a	10
3:28–29	1	7:41	8	10:10b	8
3:31a	4	7:43	6	10:11, 17, 21	1
3:31b	3	7:45	10	10:29	16
3:31c	5	7:46	9	10:33, 35–36	4
3:32, 35–38, 47–		7:47	8	11:6–9	17
50	1	7:49	6	11:12	16
4:1–4	1	7:51	10	11:16	1
4:5a	5	7:52	9	11:18–23	18
4:5b–6	4	7:53	8	11:24, 26	1
4:13–14	3	7:55	6	12:4–5, 10	1
4:15	1	7:57	10	14:10	1
4:16a	6	7:58	9	14:16	16
4:16b–49	1	7:59	8	14:22–23	19
5:8	7	7:61	6	14:24	20
5:9	8	7:63	10	14:28–30a	19
5:15	6	7:64	9	14:30b	21
5:16–17	2	7:65	8	14:30c	20
5:18, 25–26	6	7:67	6	14:30d	22
6:10–11a	9	7:69	10	14:31	21
6:11b	10	7:70	9	14:32–35	19
6:12	7	7:71	8	14:40	16
6:13	1	7:73	6	14:43	23
6:14a	10	7:75	10	14:44	4
6:14b	9	7:76	9	15:1–3	11
6:14c	8	7:77	8	15:2b	16
6:15	6	7:79	6	15:4–7	6
6:16a	9	7:81	10	15:8	11
6:16b	10	7:82	9	15:9–14	6
6:17a	8	7:83	8	15:18	21
6:17b	6	7:84	3	15:22–24	9
6:18–19a	8	7:85	1	15:24b	10
6:19b	6	7:87a	10	15:24c	6
6:20	8	7:87b	6	15:25–29	9
6:21	11	7:87c	9	15:32–36	24
7:1a	1	7:88a	8	16:5–7	25
7:1b	3	7:88b	3	16:9, 18–19	1
7:2–9	1	7:89a	1	16:30	26
7:10–11	3	7:89b	12	16:38–39	3
7:13	6	7:89c	4	16:42–43	1
7:15	10	8:5–7	13	16:46–47	3
7:16	9	8:8a	10	16:50	1
7:17	8	8:8b	6	17:4, 7–8, 13	1
7:19	6	8:8c	8	18:1	2

DEUTERONOMY		DEUTERONOMY		DEUTERONOMY	
9:9	11	16:11	26	28:42–63	13
9:11	11	16:13–15	32	28:52b	1
9:15	11	16:15b	26	28:64a	14
9:23	1	16:16a	26	28:64b	15
10:1–3	4	16:16b	32	28:65–67	41
10:5	24	16:20	1	28:68	42
10:8	24	17:1	30	29:1	1
10:11	1	17:2	11	29:9–15	1
11:8	6	17:8	26	29:21	1
11:9	1	17:10	26	29:22–24	13
11:10	6	17:14a	1	29:26	20
11:17	13	17:14b	33	29:27–28a	13
11:21	1	17:20	33	29:28b	14
11:23	10	18:1–5	34	30:1–2	16
11:24	25	18:6	26	30:3–5a	43
11:25	9	18:9	1	30:5b–6	40
11:29	6	18:12	10	30:7	44
11:31	1	18:14	10	30:8	45
12:1	1	18:15	35	30:9	39
12:2	10	18:18–19	35	30:16	19
12:5	26	19:1	10	30:18	13
12:6a	27	19:2	1	30:20	1
12:6b	28	19:8	1	31:3a	10
12:7	28	19:14	1	31:3b	5
12:9	1	20:16	1	31:4–6	10
12:10	10	21:1	1	31:7–8	5
12:11a	26	21:23	1	31:9	24
12:11b	27	23:18	36	31:10	32
12:11c	28	24:4	1	31:11	26
12:13	27	25:15	1	31:14a	12
12:14a	26	25:19	10	31:–14b–15	15
12:14b	27	26:1	1	31:16a	12
12:16	29	26:2	26	31:16b	20
12:17	28	26:3a	34	31:17–18	13
12:18	26	26:3b	1	31:20a	1
12:20	19	26:4	34	31:20b	20
12:21	26	26:9	1	31:21a	13
12:23–25	29	26:15	1	31:21b	1
12:26	26	26:19	37	31:23	5
12:27a	27	27:2–3	1	31:25–26	24
12:27b	28	27:5	38	31:29a	20
12:29–30	10	27:6a	38	31:29b	13
13:17	19	27:6b	27	32:13–14	6
14:23–26	26	27:7	28	32:15–21a	20
15:4	1	28:1–3	37	32:21b–26	13
15:6	19	28:4	21	32:30, 32–33, 35	13
15:7	1	28:5–6	39	32:36a	43
15:20	26	28:7	40	32:36b	13
15:21	30	28:8	39	32:37–38	20
15:23	29	28:9–10	37	32:40–43	46
16:1	31	28:11	21	32:43a	47
16:2a	31	28:12	39	32:49	1
16:2b	26	28:13	37	32:50	12
16:4	31	28:15–35	13	33:6	48
16:6a	26	28:36a	14	33:7	49
16:6b	31	28:36b	33	33:9	11
16:7a	31	28:36c	15	33:10–11	50
16:7b	26	28:38–40	13	33:11b	27
16:8	18	28:41	12	33:12	51

I SAMUEL		II SAMUEL		I KINGS	
7:17	8	6:13b	5	3:12	7
9:12–13	1	6:17b	6	3:13	8
9:16a	14	6:17c	7	3:15a	4
9:16b	15	6:17d	8	3:15b	6
9:20	16	6:18a	7	3:15c	9
10:2–7	17	6:18b	8	5:3	1
10:8a	11	7:2	4	5:5a	1
10:8b	12	7:5–7	6	5:5b	10
10:16	16	7:11–12	9	5:17–18	1
10:22	18	7:13a	10	6:1–10	1
11:15	12	7:13b	11	6:12	1
12:17	19	7:14a	12	6:14–38	1
12:25	20	7:14b	13	6:19b	4
13:9a, 10, 12	11	7:15–16	11	7:12	1
13:9b	12	7:19	11	7:21	1
13:14	21	7:24	14	7:23–26	11
14:10	22	7:25–30	11	7:30	11
14:18	10	11:4	15	7:38–40	11
14:32–34	23	11:11	4	7:43–44	11
14:35	8	12:10–12	16	7:45	1
14:41–42	24	12:14	17	7:48–51	1
15:15	1	12:20	6	8:1	4
15:21	1	15:12	5	8:2	12
15:22a	11	15:24, 25	4	8:3–4a	4
15:22b	12	15:29	4	8:4b	1
15:22c	1	22:51	11	8:5a	4
15:28	21	23:3–4	18	8:5b	5
16:2–3	1	23:5a	11	8:6a	4
17:5	1	23:5b	19	8:6b	1
17:36–37	25	23:5c	11	8:7	4
17:46	25	23:6–7	20	8:8	1
20:6	1	24:11–14	21	8:9a	4
20:29	1	24:18	22	8:9b	13
22:18	26	24:21	22	8:10–13	1
23:4	27	24:22	7	8:16–18	1
23:17a	28	24:24	7	8:19	10
23:17b	21	24:25a	22	8:20	1
24:20	21	24:25b	7	8:21a	4
25:26	29	24:25c	8	8:21b	13
25:28	30			8:22	2
25:29a	28			8:23	13
25:29b	20	I KINGS		8:25	3
25:30–31	21	1:39	1	8:27–30	1
26:19	1	1:50–51	2	8:31a	2
28:17	21	1:53	2	8:31b	1
28:19	29	2:4	3	8:33	1
30:8	31	2:26	4	8:35	1
		2:28a	1	8:38	1
		2:28b	2	8:42–44	1
II SAMUEL		2:29a	1	8:48	1
3:10	1	2:29b	2	8:54	2
3:18	2	2:30	1	8:62	5
3:29	3	3:1	1	8:63a	9
3:39	3	3:2a	5	8:63b	1
5:2	1	3:2b	1	8:64a	1
5:19	2	3:3	5	8:64b	6
5:24	2	3:4a	6	8:64c	14
6:2–17a	4	3:4b	2	8:64d	9

II CHRONICLES		NEHEMIAH		PSALMS	
36:14–15	1	1:5	1	1:5–6	1
36:17	1	1:9	2	2:1–3	2
36:18–19	1	2:20	3	2:2b	3
36:23	1	4:2	4	2:4–5	4
		6:10–11	5	2:6	5
EZRA		7:70	6	2:8–9	4
		7:72	6	2:12	4
1:2	1	8:14–18	7	4:5	6
1:3–5	1	8:16b	5	5:7	7
1:7	1	9:8	8	8:3–8	8
2:68	1	9:14	9	9:7–8	1
2:69	2	9:32	1	9:11	7
3:2–3a	3	10:31	9	9:19–20	1
3:3b	4	10:32	5	15:1	7
3:4a	5	10:33a	10	16 title	9
3:4b	4	10:33b	11	16:9	10
3:5a	4	10:33c	9	16:10	11
3:5b	6	10:33d	12	17:15	10
3:6a	4	10:34a	5	20:2	7
3:6b	1	10:34b	13	20:3a	12
3:8–12	1	10:36–39	5	20:3b	13
4:1	1	11:11–12	5	22:1–2	14
4:2	6	11:16	5	22:6–8	15
4:3	1	11:22	5	22:10	16
4:24	1	12:40	5	22:11–18	17
5:2	1	12:43	4	22:19–21	18
5:8	1	13:4	5	22:22–25	19
5:13–17	1	13:5	10	22:26	20
6:3–8	1	13:7	5	22:27	21
6:3b	6	13:9a	5	22:28	5
6:9	4	13:9b	10	22:29a	22
6:10	6	13:11	5	22:29b	10
6:12	1	13:14	5	22:30–31	23
6:16–17a	1	13:15–22	9	23:6	7
6:17b	6	13:29	14	24:3	7
6:17c	7			25:10, 14	24
6:19–20	8			26:6	25
6:22	1	ESTHER		26:8	7
7:15–16	1	6:13	1	27:4–6a	7
7:17a	6			27:6b	6
7:17b	9			30 title	7
7:17c	3	JOB		36:8	7
71:7d	1	1:5	1	40:6a	26
7:19–20	1	14:12a	2	40:6b	12
7:23–24	1	14:12b	3	40:6c	27
7:27	1	14:13–15	2	40:6d	13
8:25	1	17:3	4	40:6e	28
8:29–30	1	19:25a	5	40:7–8	27
8:33	1	19:25b	6	42:4	7
8:35a	4	19:26	7	43:3	7
8:35b	7	19:27	5	43:4	25
8:36	1	19:26	7	44:17	24
9:4–5	4	19:29	8	45:6–7	3
9:9	1	23:10	9	46:4	7
10:1	1	25:2	10	47:9	29
10:6	1	33:23–30, 32	4	48:8	30
10:9	1	42:8	1	48:9	24
10:19	10			50:8a	26

Isaiah		Isaiah		Isaiah	
5:5–6	5	11:5	35	24:21a	71
5:9–10	5	11:6–9	43	24:21b	34
5:13a	17	11:10	9	24:22a	71
5:13b–17	5	11:11–12	44	24:22b	72
5:24	5	11:13	12	24:23a	73
5:26–30	18	11:14	34	24:23b	74
6:1	3	11:15	45	25:1–2	34
6:11–13a	5	11:16	44	25:3	11
6:13b	19	12:1–6	46	25:4–5	34
7:3	20	13:1–9	47	25:6	75
7:4	21	13:10–13	48	25:7–8a	76
7:7–8a	21	13:14–18	47	25:8b–9	46
7:8b	22	13:19–22	49	25:10–12	34
7:9a	21	14:1a	20	26:1–4	46
7:9b	23	14:1b	50	26:5–6	34
7:13–14a	24	14:2a	44	26:11	34
7:14b	25	14:2b	51	26:12	12
7:15	26	14:3	12	26:19	76
7:16a	27	14:4–20	47	26:20	48
7:16b	5	14:21–23	49	26:21a	77
7:17–18	18	14:24–27	37	26:21b	34
7:18a	28	14:28–31	52	27:1	34
7:19–25	29	15:1–9a	53	27:2–3	46
8:1–4	21	15:9b	54	27:4	34
8:7–8	18	16:1–4a	53	27:5	11
8:9–10	30	16:4b	37	27:6	51
8:14a	27	16:5	35	27:10–11	5
8:14–15	5	16:7–12	53	27:12	78
8:17	31	16:14	54	27:13a	79
8:18	3	17:1–3	21	27:13b	78
8:21–22	21	17:3a	27	27:13c	80
9:1–2	32	17:4–6	27	28:1–4	27
9:3	33	17:7–8	55	28:5–6	55
9:4	34	17:9–11	27	28:11–13	18
9:5	12	17:12–14	37	28:17–22	18
9:6	25	18:3–7	37	29:1–3	18
9:7a	11	19:1–17	56	29:4	29
9:7b	12	19:18–22	57	29:5–8	37
9:7c	35	19:19a	1	29:14–15	18
9:11	21	19:21a	1	29:17	37
9:12	23	19:23–25	58	29:18–24	81
9:14–17	27	20:1–6	59	29:20a	37
9:19–21	36	21:1–10	47	30:1–5a	18
10:3	27	21:11–12	60	30:5b–7	82
10:5–6	18	21:13–17	61	30:13–14	18
10:12	37	22:17–19	62	30:16–17a	18
10:15	18	22:20–25	63	30:17b	29
10:16–19	37	23:1–11	64	30:18–26	81
10:20–22a	20	23:12	65	30:27–28	37
10:22b–23	5	23:13–17	66	30:29	81
10:24–27	37	23:18	67	30:30–33	37
10:28–32	38	24:1–12	5	31:1–3	18
10:33–34	37	24:5b	68	31:4–5	37
11:1	39	24:13	17	31:7	81
11:2	40	24:14–15	19	31:8–9	37
11:3	35	24:16a	69	32:1a	35
11:4a	41	24:16b	70	32:1b–5	15
11:4b	42	24:17–20	48	32:9–14	29

DANIEL		DANIEL		DANIEL	
2:34b–35a	8	8:13	29	12:2a	55
2:35b	9	8:13b	27	12:2b	56
2:39a	3	8:13c	1	12:3	57
2:39b	4	8:14a	29	12:5–7	22
2:40	5	8:14b	30	12:11a	27
2:41a, 43	6	8:15, 20	3	12:11b	26
2:41b, 42	10	8:21	4	12:11c–12	31
2:44a	7	8:22	23	12:13	58
2:44b	11	8:23a	28		
2:44c, 45	8	8:23b–24a	24	HOSEA	
4:10–17, 20–26	12	8:24b, 25a	25		
4:31–32	12	8:25b	31	1:4a	1
5:2–3	1	8:26	29	1:4b–6	2
5:5, 24–28	13	9:2	32	1:7	3
5:23	1	9:4	33	1:10	4
7:1–3, 5	3	9:17	1	1:11a	5
7:6	4	9:24a	34	1:11b	6
7:7a	5	9:24b	35	2:1	5
7:7b	10	9:24c	36	2:3–4	2
7:8a	14	9:25a	37	2:6–7	7
7:8b	15	9:25b	36	2:11–13	2
7:9a	16	9:25c	34	2:11b	8
7:9b–10	8	9:26a	35	2:14	7
7:11a	15	9:26b	38	2:15	9
7:11b	17	9:27a	39	2:16–17	7
7:12	18	9:27b	38	2:18a	10
7:13	19	10:14, 20b	25	2:18b	11
7:14a	9	10:20a	37	2:18c	12
7:14b	11	11:2a	40	2:19–20a	10
7:15–17	3	11:2b	41	2:20b	4
7:18a	9	11:3	4	2:21–22	13
7:18b	11	11:4	23	2:23a	6
7:19	5	11:5	42	2:23b	4
7:20a	10	11:6	43	3:2	14
7:20b	14	11:7–8	44	3:3–4	15
7:20c	15	11:9	45	3:5	5
7:21	20	11:10	46	4:3, 5–7, 14	2
7:22a	8	11:11–12	47	4:19	16
7:22b	9	11:13–17	48	5:5a	2
7:23	5	11:18–19	49	5:5b	17
7:24a	10	11:20	50	5:10	17
7:24b	14	11:21–30a	24	5:7–12a	2
7:25a	15	11:22b, 28b	33	5:12b	17
7:25b	20	11:30b–32a	26	5:14a	2
7:25c	21	11:30c	33	5:14b	17
7:25d	22	11:31b	1	5:15	7
7:26	8	11:31c	27	6:1–3	18
7:27a	9	11:32b	33	6:6a	19
7:27b	11	11:32c	51	6:6b	20
8:1–4	3	11:33a, 34	51	6:7	21
8:5–8a	4	11:33b, 35	25	6:11	22
8:8b	23	11:36–39	26	7:12–13, 16	2
8:9	24	11:40–44	52	8:1–7	8
8:10	25	11:45a	8	8:1b	21
8:11–12	26	11:45b	17	8:8	15
8:11b, 12b	27	12:1a	53	8:10	23
8:11c	1	12:1b	20	8:13a	24
8:12c	28	12:1c	54	8:13b	16

MATTHEW		MATTHEW		MARK	
17:27	46	24:31b	63	1:8a	2
18:8–9	10	24:32–34	28	1:8b	4
18:18	42	24:35	16	1:9	2
18:34–35	10	24:36	64	1:17	5
19:28	47	24:37–39	65	1:44	6
20:18–19a	25	24:40–41	62	2:20	7
20:19b	43	24:42, 43–50	66	2:26	8
20:21	47	24:51	19	4:26–28	9
20:22	25	25:1–13	66	4:29	10
20:23a	48	25:15	29	4:30–32	9
20:23b	47	25:19a	67	6:15	1
20:28	2	25:19b	44	8:26	1
21:1–2	49	25:19c	68	8:31a	7
21:3	50	25:20–23	20	8:31b	11
21:4–5	51	25:24–28a	19	8:32	7
21:25	9	25:28b–29a	20	8:38a	12
21:39	25	25:29b–30	19	8:38b	13
21:41a	28	25:31a	44	8:38c	14
21:41b, 43	52	25:31b	45	9:1	15
21:44–45	28	25:31c–33	68	9:9–10	11
22:7–8	28	25:34–40	20	9:11–12a	1
22:9–10a	52	25:34b	13	9:12b	7
22:10b	38	25:41–45	19	9:13	1
22:10c	40	25:41b	10	9:31a	7
22:11–13	19	25:41c	69	9:31b	11
22:29–32	53	25:46a	10	9:32	7
22:43–44a	4	25:46b	13	9:43, 45	16
22:44b	29	26:2, 5	70	9:47–49	16
22:44c	34	26:6–12	71	10:32–34a	7
22:45	4	26:13	72	10:34b	11
23:18a	18	26:17–19	70	10:37	17
23:18b–19a	17	26:21–23	73	10:38	7
23:19b–20	18	26:24a	25	10:39	18
23:23	10	26:24b	74	10:40	17
23:34a	54	26:25	73	10:45	19
23:34b	27	26:26–28a	25	11:1–2	20
23:35	18	26:28b	2	11:3	21
23:36	28	26:29	75	11:30	2
23:38	55	26:31	76	12:8	7
23:39a	56	26:32a	43	12:9a	15
23:39b	44	26:32b	77	12:9b	22
24:2–3a	55	26:34	78	12:12	15
24:3b	44	26:46	79	12:24–27	23
24:4–5	57	26:61	43	12:33a	24
24:6–8	58	26:64	44	12:33b	25
24:9–10	27	26:75	78	12:35–37	26
24:11	57	27:9–10	80	12:36b	27
24:12–13	27	27:40	43	12:36c	28
24:14	59	27:51	81	13:2–4	29
24:15–22	28	27:63	43	13:5–6	30
24:23–24a	57	28:6	43	13:7–8	31
24:24b	60	28:10	77	13:9	32
24:26	57			13:10	33
24:27, 28	44			13:11–13	32
24:29a	60	MARK		13:14–20	15
24:29b	61	1:2–3	1	13:21–22a	30
24:30	44	1:4–5	2	13:22b	34
24:31	62	1:7	3	13:24a	34

LUKE		JOHN		JOHN	
21:5–7	64	*3:14b*	11	12:31	26
21:7–8	56	3:15–18	5	12:32a	11
21:9–11	65	3:22, 26	4	*12:32b*	5
21:12–19	44	3:23	4	12:33	11
21:20–24a	23	3:28	1	12:34a	27
21:24b	63	4:1	4	*12:34b*	11
21:25–26	66	5:28–29	12	12:37–38	28
21:27	37	*5:29b*	13	12:41	28
21:28	58	6:4	9	12:47	5
21:29–32	23	6:14	3	12:48	29
21:33	67	6:32–36	14	13:7	30
21:34–36	47	6:39–40	13	13:10–11	17
22:1, 7–8	26	6:41	14	13:18	17
22:10	68	6:44	13	13:21, 22	17
22:11	26	6:48–50a	14	13:24–28	17
22:12	68	*6:50b*	13	13:31	11
22:13, 15a	26	*6:51a*	14	13:32–33	16
22:15b	24	*6:51b*	13	13:36a	16
22:16	69	6:51c	5	*13:36b*	31
22:17	24	6:52–54a	15	13:38	32
22:18	48	*6:54b*	13	14:2	16
22:19	24	6:55–57a	15	14:4–5	16
22:21, 23	70	*6:57b*	13	14:12	33
22:22a	24	6:58a	14	14:16–17	30
22:22b	71	*6:58b*	13	14:18	34
22:29	13	6:62	16	14:19a	11
22:30	72	6:70	17	*14:19b*	34
22:32	73	7:2	18	*14:19c*	8
22:34	74	7:8	18	14:20	8
22:37	24	7:10–11	18	14:21–23	30
22:61	74	7:14	18	14:26	30
22:69	37	7:22–23	19	14:28	16
23:28–31	23	7:33–36	16	*14:28b*	30
23:43	75	7:37	18	14:30	11
24:6	35	7:38–39	7	15:6	35
24:7a	24	7:40	3	15:13–14	5
24:7b–8	35	*7:42a*	20	*15:13b*	11
24:46	35	*7:42b*	21	15:20–21	36
24:49	30	8:14	16	15:26	30
		8:21–22	16	16:2–4	36
		8:28	11	16:5–7a	16
JOHN		10:15	11	*16:7b*	30
1:15	1	10:16	22	16:8–9	7
1:21a, 23	2	10:17–18	11	16:10	16
1:21b	3	10:40	4	16:11	26
1:25–26	4	11:4	23	16:13–15	30
1:27	1	11:11	23	16:16a	11
1:28	4	11:23	23	*16:16b*	34
1:29	5	11:24–25	13	16:17a	11
1:30	1	11:40	23	*16:17b*	34
1:31	4	11:50–51	11	*16:17c*	16
1:33a	4	11:52	22	16:18–19a	11
1:33b	6	12:2–5	24	*16:19b*	34
1:33c	7	12:7–8	24	16:20a	11
1:37	5	12:14–16	25	*16:20b*	34
2:19	8	12:23–24a	11	16:22	34
2:23	9	*12:24b*	5	16:25	30
3:14a	10	12:27–28	11	16:28	16

ROMANS

15:12	28
15:21	26
16:20	29

I CORINTHIANS

1:7–8	1
1:19	2
3:12–14	3
3:15, 17	4
4:5a	1
4:5b	3
5:5	4
5:7–8	5
6:2	6
6:3	7
6:14	8
10:1a, 2a	9
10:1b, 2b	10
10:3	11
10:4	12
10:16–17, 21	13
11:20–29	13
11:26b	1
11:32a	3
11:32b	14
11:33–34	13
13:9–12	15
14:21	2
15:3	16
15:4a	17
15:4b	18
15:12–22	19
15:23a	8
15:23b	1
15:24a	19
15:24b	20
15:24c–25	21
15:26	19
15:27a	22
15:27b–28a	21
15:28b	20
15:28c	22
15:29, 32	8
15:35–45a	15
15:45b–47	23
15:48–50	15
15:51–52a	24
15:52b	25
15:52c	15
15:53–57	15
16:22	1

II CORINTHIANS

1:14	1
3:14	2
4:14	3

II CORINTHIANS

5:1–4	3
5:10	1
6:2	4
6:16	5
6:17	6
6:18	7

GALATIANS

3:8, 14a	1
3:14b	2
3:15–19, 21	3
3:22, 29	1
4:23, 28	4
4:24	5
4:26–27	6
5:5	7

EPHESIANS

1:13	1
1:14	2
1:18	3
1:21	4
2:12	5
4:30	2
5:14	6
5:27	7

PHILIPPIANS

1:6, 10	1
2:9–11	2
3:5	3
3:11	4
3:20	1
3:21	4
4:5	5

COLOSSIANS

1:27–28	1
2:11–14	2
2:16–17	3
3:4a	4
3:4b	1

I THESSALONIANS

1:10	1
2:16	2
2:19	1
3:13a	1
3:13b	3
4:13–14	3
4:15–16a	1
4:16b	4
4:16c	5

I THESSALONIANS

4:16d	3
4:17a	6
4:17b	7
4:18	3
5:1–3	8
5:4, 9	9
5:23	1

II THESSALONIANS

1:5–6	1
1:7a	2
1:7b	3
1:7c	4
1:7d–8	1
1:9	5
1:10	6
2:1a, 2	3
2:1b	2
2:3a	7
2:3b–5	8
2:6–7	9
2:8	10
2:9–11	8
2:12	11
2:14	12

I TIMOTHY

4:1–3	1
6:14–15	2

II TIMOTHY

1:12, 18	1
2:12	2
2:18	3
3:1–9	4
4:1a	5
4:1b	6
4:1c	7
4:3–4	8
4:8a	1
4:8b	6

TITUS

2:13	1

HEBREWS

1:5	1
1:6	2
1:8–9	3
1:11a	4
1:11b	5
1:12a	4
1:12b	5

2. Selected Passages Not Properly Predictive, Though Sometimes Mistaken for Such

(Numbers opposite references indicate pages.)

GENESIS

1:1	50–51
1:3	39
2:8–14	51
2:24	33n
3:14	39
3:19	35–36n
3:21	54n
8:22b	41
12:3a	33n
22:13	53
47:30	163
49:29–30	163

EXODUS

3:6	77
3:10	40–41
8:9–10	39–40
9:15	62
12:15–20	177
13:3, 6–10	177
15:26	33
25:23–40	183–184
28:6–35	186n
28:31	91
30:1–9	184
32:30	41
33:7–11	183
34:33–35	54
40:9–11	184

LEVITICUS

10:8–10	186n
11	55
12:1–2	55
14	55
19:19	55
25:1–7	179n

NUMBERS

14:23, 29–35	47
20:8–11	54n
33:52	40

DEUTERONOMY

21:1–9	189n
34:10	47

JOSHUA

1:13	29

JUDGES

5:11	31n
5:24	32

RUTH

1–4	147
4:15	41

I SAMUEL

6:5	41
8:11–18	35n
23:11–12	66
23:17b	70
24:4	70
26:24	31n

II SAMUEL

5:6–10	55n
7:9–11a	29n
22:44	30–31

I KINGS

3:14	67

I KINGS (cont.)

6:31–32	41
12:16	47
22:6, 11–12, 15	69

II KINGS

20:1–3	62
20:11	38
21:8	29n

I CHRONICLES

11:4–9	55n
17:8–10	29n

II CHRONICLES

15:3–6	246n
25:8	66n

JOB

31:14	35n

PSALMS

2:7	263, 272, 529
7:8	109
8:2	77
18:43	30–31, 76
21:4	76n
24:7	76
25:13	112
31:5	76
34:20	76
37:9, 11	112
38:11	76n
41:9	78
42:5, 11	76n

3. Subjects

Bold-faced numbers (*e.g.*, **Pred 499**) indicate prediction numbers, according to the listing in Summary A, "The Biblical Predictions in the Order of Their Fulfillments," pp. 631–659. The predictions in Summary A often list more than one prophecy number, to any or all of which—especially those marked with an asterisk (see p. 631)—reference should then be made.

Italicized numbers (*e.g., Rev No. 28*) indicate prophecy numbers within the discussion, in the body of the *Encyclopedia*, of a given book of the Bible.

Numbers in roman type indicate pages.

Aaron, *Ex Nos. 5, 13; Num 29; Heb 12*
Abaddon, *Rev No. 28*
Abel, *Gen No. 9*
Abiathar, *I Sam No. 9*
Abigail, *I Sam Nos. 20, 28–30*
Abimelech, *Jd No. 12*
Abiram, *Num No. 26*
Abomination, *Dan Nos. 27, 38;* 95, 103n, 385, 486
Abraham, **Pred 7–15, 30, 78, 143, 409, 649;** *Lk No. 51; Rom 5–8; Gal 1;* 4–5, 77, 135–136, 155, 551
Abrahamic testament, **Pred 499;** 64, 75
Abyss, *Rev Nos. 28, 45, 51*
Achor, *Hos No. 9*
Acts, 98, 526–536
Adam, *Gen Nos. 1, 4–5; Ps 8; Ezek 36; Dan 19; Rom 10; I Cor 23;* 24, 50n, 53, 56
Agabus, *Acts Nos. 48, 53*
Agape, *Jude No. 3;* 530n
Aggression, *Rev No. 15;* 596–598
Agur, 252n, 276
Ahab, king, *I K Nos. 27, 35, 37, 39–41, 43; II K 24, 26; II Chron 25;* 69
prophet, *Jer No. 61;* 69–70
Ahaziah of Israel, *II K No. 1*
Ahijah, *I K Nos. 18, 22;* 117–118
Ahimaaz, 219–220, 223
Ai, *Josh No. 14*

Alaric, *Rev No. 40*
Alexander, *Dan Nos. 4, 23; Joel 14; Zech 3, 32;* 131, 448–449
Alford, H., 618, 621n
Allegorization, xvii, 4n, 5n, 42–47, 84, 106, 121–122, 147n, 354, 593–594
Allegory, xvii, 19, 42–44, 510
Allis, O. T., 45, 58
Altar, **Pred 154, 255, 379, 474;** *Zech No. 78; Rev 19, 31;* 13, 385
of incense, 184
Amalekites, **Pred 59, 128, 230**
Amasis, *Jer Nos. 21, 81, 84;* 364n
Amaziah, king, *Gen No. 50; II Chron 31;* 66n
priest, *Amos Nos. 18–19*
Ambiguity, 29, 32, 117–121, 140–142, 144
Amillennialism, *Dan No. 55; Rev 51–52;* vi, 46, 58, 106–108, 115, 354, 596n, 617–618
Ammon, 660
Amos, 132, 412–418
Analogy, xvii, 52, 72–80, 83–84, 90, 92, 106, 114, 121, 123, 143, 434
Ananias, of Damascus, *Acts Nos. 39–40, 45*
high priest, *Acts No. 56*
of Jerusalem, *Acts No. 25*
Anathoth, *Jer No. 28*
Andrew, **Pred 532**

731

Rome, 664; also *Acts No. 57; II Thess 9; Rev 31, 36;* 49–50, 139, 370–373, 449, 580, 596, 599–600, 602–603
Romulus Augustus, *Num No. 42*
Rosh, *Ezek No. 53*
Rowley, H. H., 60–62, 87, 139
Ruth, 147, 213, 217n
Ryrie, C. C., 59, 328n

Sabbath, **Pred 446, 731;** *Lev No. 34; Dan 26;* 48, 196, 469n
Sabbatic year, 196
Sacramentalism, future, *Isa Nos. 8, 16*
Sacrifice (*see also* Burnt, Meal, Peace, Sin, and Trespass offering), **Pred 13, 483, 487, 583, 686;** *Ps No. 24; Isa 8; Dan 26, 39; Hos 15;* 23, 25, 113n, 115, 139, 193, 371, 385, 469n, 682
Saints, *Dan Nos. 19–20, 22*
Salem, *Gen Nos. 26–27*
Salt, 481n
Salvation (*see also* Atonement, Justification, Redemption), *I Pet No. 1*
Samaria, *II K Nos. 16–18;* 148
Samaritans, *Obad No. 8; Acts 6;* 443, 446
Samson, *Jd Nos. 13–14*
Samuel, I, 219–223
    II, 223–227, 240
    man, *I Sam Nos. 13–14, 19–20;* 30, 217, 219–220
Sapphira, *Acts No. 25*
Sarah, **Pred 11;** 164n
Sardis, *Obad No. 6*
Sargon II, **Pred 228, 233;** *Mi No. 3;* 280
Satan, **Pred 486, 521, 561, 636, 663, 708–710;** *John No. 11; II Thess 8;* 36, 49n, 87, 89, 105, 109, 135–136, 252–253, 596, 599–600
Sauer, E., 121
Saul, *I Sam Nos. 14–15, 17–18, 20–21, 24, 28; II Sam 1; I Chron 5;* 14, 35n
Scapegoat, *Lev No. 18*
Scipio Asiaticus, *Dan No. 49*
Scofield Bible, 47, 51, 53, 59, 96, 122n, 565n
Scopas, **Pred 366**
Scott, C. A., *Rev Nos. 11, 31*
Scripture, *see* Inspiration
Scythians, *Jer No. 12, Zeph 1;* 118n, 325, 435, 439–440
Sea, *Joel No. 6; Jonah 1; Mi 40; Zech 43–44; Mk 35; Rev 25, 53, 56;* 39, 598

Sealing, *Ezek No. 8; Rev 20, 22;* 596, 597
Seals, seven, *Rev Nos. 15–21, 23, 27;* 597–598
Season, *Dan Nos. 18, 21;* 371
Second coming, *see* Christ
Second death, *Rev Nos. 6–7;* 600
Second resurrection, *Rev No. 33*
Seed, *Gen Nos. 7, 21, 24, 38, 41, 43, 45–47; Ps 23, 40; Mal 6; Mk 9; Gal 3;* 599n
Seer, 6
Seiss, J. A., 384–385
Seleucia, 580
Seleucids, *Mi No. 23; Zech 41;* 82, 120
Seleucus I, *Dan Nos. 23, 42*
    II, *Dan No. 45*
    III, *Dan No. 46*
    IV, *Dan Nos. 24, 50*
Semites, **Pred 3, 389, 408**
Sennacherib, **Pred 238, 243–246, 248;** 18, 31, 47, 110n, 119n, 132, 280–282
Sepharad, *Obad No. 6*
Septuagint, *Dt No. 47; II Cor 7;* 239, 240n, 241, 269n, 321, 353n, 502
Serpent, *Gen Nos. 7–8, 72; Isa 52;* 39
    Brazen, **Pred 466;** *John No. 11;* 25
Servant, Suffering, **Pred 437;** 267n, 283–284
Shabaka, *Isa Nos. 28, 82*
Shadow, **Pred 231;** 14, 38, 60
    as type, 23n, 25
Shalmaneser V, *Isa No. 52;* 280n
Shear-jashub, *Isa No. 20*
Shebna, *Isa No. 62*
Shechem, *Jd No. 12*
Sheep (*see also* Flock), *Isa Nos. 36, 66; John 11, 22;* 126
Shekinah, 48, 108
Shem, *Gen Nos. 18–19*
Shemaiah, *Jer No. 62;* 70
Shepherd, *Zech Nos. 40, 49*
    foolish, *Zech Nos. 36, 56*
    Good, *Zech Nos. 53, 64–66*
Sheshbazzar, *Isa No. 6*
Shiloh, *Gen No. 67; Jd 17; I Sam 2, 7, 9; Jer 20; Ezek 29*
Shimei, *Zech No. 62*
Shinar (*see also* Babylon), 35, 477
Shipwreck, *Acts No. 62*
Shout, *I Thess No. 1*
Showbread, 184
Shunamite, *II K No. 7*
Sickle, *Rev Nos. 2, 41–42*

4. Biblical Words and Phrases

747

GREEK

ἐγώ	egó	71
εἰς ἀπάντησιν	eis āpántēsin	561
ἐκ νεκρῶν	ek nekrōn	512
ἐκκλησία	ekklēsiā	267, 574
ἐκλεκτοί	eklektoí	487n
ἔλθῃ	élthē	546
ἐν	en	512n
ἐν τάχει	en tákhei	601
ἔξοδος	éxodos	494
ἐπληρώθη	eplērōthē	77
ἐπιφάνεια	epifáneia	568, 570, 571
ἔρχεται	érkhetai	32
ἐσκήνωσεν	eskēnōsen	183
ἐφάπαξ	efápax	453
ἤγγικεν	éngiken	30
θλίψις	thlípsis	102
ἱλαστήριον	hīlāstērion	185-186
ἵνα πληρωθῇ	hīnā plērōthē	77, 79, 477
καί	kai	100, 560
λόγος	lógos	276

μέλλω	méllo	66n
μυστήριον	mustērion	98
παραβολή	pārābolē	53n
παραλαμβάνω	pārālāmbánō	514
παρουσία	pārousiā	559, 563, 587
πέτρα	pétrā	489
πέτρος	pétros	489
πληρόω	plēróō	135n, 477
πλήρωμα	plērōmā	541
προφήτης	profētēs	4, 8
σκιά	skiā	23n
σῶμα	sōmā	269n
ταχύ	tākhú	601
τύπος	túpos	23
τύπτω	túptō	23
ὑπόδειγμα	hupódeigmā	23n
φανερωθῇ	fānerōthē	556
χρόνος	khrónos	28
ὠτία	ōtiā	269n

5. Passages Discussed in the Introduction, with Scattered References to Other Significant Discussions

(Numbers opposite references indicate pages.)

751

www.ingramcontent.com/pod-product-compliance
Lightning Source LLC
Chambersburg PA
CBHW071337280326
41949CB00038B/18